STRATEGIC
MANAGEMENT
AWARENESS & CHANGE

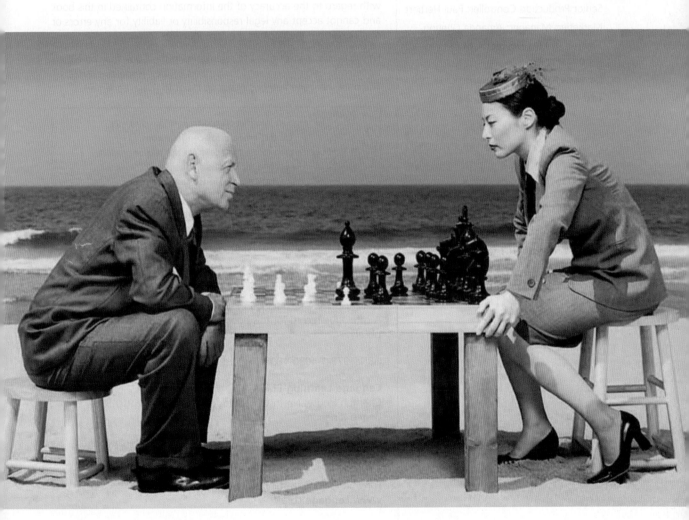

JOHN THOMPSON & FRANK MARTIN SIXTH EDITION

SOUTH-WESTERN
CENGAGE Learning™

Australia • Brazil • Japan • Korea • Mexico • Singapore • Spain • United Kingdom • United States

SOUTH-WESTERN
CENGAGE Learning

Strategic Management: Awareness and Change, 6th Edition
John Thompson and Frank Martin

Publishing Director: Linden Harris

Publisher: Thomas Rennie

Development Editor: Charlotte Loveridge and Jennifer Seth

Editorial Assistant: Charlotte Green

Content Project Editor: Oliver Jones and Adam Paddon

Manufacturing Manager: Jane Glendening

Senior Production Controller: Paul Herbert

Marketing Manager: Amanda Cheung

Typesetter: MPS Limited, A Macmillan Company

Cover design: Adam Renvoize

Text design: Design Deluxe, Bath, UK

For product information and technology assistance,
contact **emea.info@cengage.com**.
For permission to use material from this text or product,
and for permission queries,
email **clsuk.permissions@cengage.com**.

The Author has asserted the right under the Copyright, Designs and Patents Act 1988 to be identified as Author of this Work.

This work is adapted from *Strategic Management: Awareness and Change*, 5th Edition, published by South-Western a division of Cengage Learning, Inc. © 2005.

British Library Cataloguing-in-Publication Data
A catalogue record for this book is available from the British Library.

ISBN: 978-1-4080-1807-1

Cengage Learning EMEA
Cheriton House, North Way, Andover, Hampshire. SP10 5BE.
United Kingdom

Cengage Learning products are represented in Canada by Nelson Education Ltd.

For your lifelong learning solutions, visit
www.cengage.co.uk

Purchase your next print book, e-book or e-chapter at
www.CengageBrain.com

Printed by Seng Lee Press, Singapore
2 3 4 5 6 7 8 9 10 – 12 11 10

STRATEGIC
MANAGEMENT
AWARENESS & CHANGE

Brief contents

Contents

Part 1   Understanding strategy and strategic management 1

Part 2   Strategic positioning 65

Part 3   Strategic analysis and choice 263

Part 4   Issues in strategic growth   499

Part 5   Strategic management 627

17   Final thoughts: the purpose of strategy 777

List of cases

Online Cases

Lots more cases to enhance and strengthen your learning and understanding can be found online at www.cengage.co.uk/thompson6

Preface

This book is about strategic awareness, strategic analysis and the management of strategic change. It is designed for use by students who will become future managers and for managers in practice; after all, in some way or another, *all managers are strategy makers*. It looks at how managers become strategically aware of their company's position and potential opportunities for change, at how changes often happen in reality, and at how the process might be managed more effectively.

Strategic management is concerned with the actions that organizations take to deal with the changes, opportunities, threats, challenges and surprises in their external and internal environments. Put simply, strategies are means to ends. How, then, do organizations:

- determine desired outcomes?
- understand the circumstances and events affecting these outcomes and the means of attaining them?
- decide upon actions that they intend to take?
- implement these desired strategies through a series of tactical moves and changes?
- evaluate progress and relative success?

These are the broad themes addressed in this book.

Since the first edition was written some 20 years ago the subject of strategic management has been developed and our understanding of certain aspects has changed. In addition, the world of business has been transformed by the rapid growth of the Internet and the emergence of the new and entrepreneurial dot.com organizations. Indeed, entrepreneurship as a subject has also increased in popularity and significance and it is not realistic to treat it as completely divorced from strategy as the two are very clearly related. While some of these changes were reflected in the second, third, fourth and fifth editions, this sixth edition sees further revisions to both the structure and content to bring both the text and the case material fully up to date and to embrace the impact of the 2009 credit crunch and economic recession. The new sixth edition therefore has within it some significant changes in terms of bringing the text up to date across the whole book. Discernable changes have also been made to the structure of the book especially to the running order of chapters so as to make the book easier to navigate. In addition, the variety of short cases has been increased and in most cases the retained cases have been completely revised. For this edition John Thompson has continued his collaboration with Frank Martin from the University of Stirling.

Thinking strategically

Strategy is about how an organization sets about getting to where it wants to get. It is about setting, pursuing and achieving its mission and objectives. In the early stages of a company's development, this is usually straightforward. It is not difficult for everyone concerned to appreciate the desired end points and the routes forward. As the business grows and diversifies then it separates into different parts and these have to be co-ordinated. Strategy takes on a different complexity. The ideal outcome is synergistic – the sum of the achievements of the various parts exceeds what they might be expected to achieve individually and independently. At this stage issues of strategy and structure (including managing and controlling within the structure) have to be dealt with together. The ability to implement strategic ideas holds the key to prosperity.

If something goes wrong it could be that the organization has made a strategic misjudgement – it has attempted to do something for which it is inadequately or inappropriately resourced, for example – or it could be that it makes mistakes in implementation – it underestimates the reaction of its competitors, maybe.

Uncertainty (and therefore risk) is always prevalent in strategy. Organizations will plan to some extent, and they will vary in the extent to which they do plan. But managers can never plan for every eventuality and possibility. Strategies emerge as managers and organizations react to the world around them. They attempt to counter threats and seize opportunities. Flexibility is essential. How they do this comes down to the style and approach of the person in ultimate charge – the strategic leader. But in some way or other every manager is (potentially) a strategy maker.

Strategy may involve planning, plans and even formal documentation, but fundamentally it is a way of thinking and behaving.

In the end it is probably true that 'everything in strategy is simple, but nothing in strategy is very easy'. It is a mistake to over-complicate things. It is also a mistake to underestimate competition – in part because new competitors can enter an industry quickly and surprisingly – or to ignore change pressures and become complacent.

It has to be tempting, though, to sit back and enjoy the fruits of success once an organization has become an industry leader and maybe a global organization in the process. But size and success is no guarantee of permanency, especially in the uncertain and turbulent economic conditions we have witnessed all round the world in the recent past. Corporate history (like military history) contains numerous stories of once-great, once-dominant corporations that have fallen by the wayside. It is vital that stasis and inertia are avoided. Again, it is an attitude of mind.

Prolonged success, then, in part, depends upon how organizations deal with setbacks and crises when they occur. Astute companies will have made preparations for dealing with possible crises, but they will still have to be dealt with when they happen. Yet again, this comes down to an ability to think things through and to stay vigilant and flexible. As always happens, some organizations will emerge intact from the recession we are experiencing as we write these comments and be in a position to exploit the opportunities that are there. But other organizations will have fared less well. We need to understand why this is the case.

Of course, from time to time there will be changes of strategic leadership. When these changes happen, it is likely that newcomers will want to change strategies and/or structures. There is always the potential to improve things but it is equally possible to destroy something that works well.

From this short and cryptic explanation of strategy, you will see why we subtitle our book 'Awareness and Change'!

How to use this book

Structure and content

The content follows the established Analysis, Choice, Implementation model that is used in most strategy texts, and is structured in five parts, which systematically deal with a series of 12 key questions.

Part 1: *Understanding Strategy* looks at the strategy process as a whole and includes a comprehensive framework of the process around which the book is structured. An Appendix lists the various tools and techniques that can be used to carry out a strategic analysis of any organization. These are then developed throughout the book, but this appendix is particularly useful for assignments and case analyses. Part 1 includes a new Mindmap summary of the book as a whole and a short introduction – *Strategy in a Nutshell* – that outlines the key themes in strategy. The material on the business model in Chapter 2 of the Fifth Edition is absorbed into our new Chapter 1, which addresses the following question:

- Where is the organization going – and how might this have to be changed?

Content:

Chapter 1 Introducing Strategy

Part 2: *Strategic Positioning* looks at three distinct but clearly related approaches to strategy: market- or opportunity-driven; resource-based; and competitor-influenced strategic management. It is crafted around the Environment-Values-Resources (E-V-R) Model introduced in Chapter 1. Part 2 includes a number of tools and techniques which help us to understand the current competitive situation. This part also looks at strategic positioning and competitive advantage. This edition includes new material on scenarios and the concept of 'the long tail' that explains how and why e-commerce has affected demand for certain products. We ask:

- Where are the future opportunities and threats for the organization?
- How might it capitalize on its strengths, competencies and capabilities, and reduce any key weaknesses?
- How can its competitiveness be improved and strengthened?
- How good is the organization's information management?

Content:
Chapter 2 Environmental Analysis
Chapter 3 Resources and Capability
Chapter 4 Competition
Chapter 5 Introducing Culture

Part 3: *Strategic Analysis and Choice* describes and evaluates the different ways in which strategies are formulated and created. It also includes chapters on strategic purpose and strategic success. Culture is a vital element of our study as it determines how strategies and changes are determined and implemented.

Several valuable planning models and techniques are discussed. We also look at both entrepreneurship and intrapreneurship. For this edition we have strengthened the content on entrepreneurship and introduced material on 'blue ocean strategy'. It concludes with a study of the various strategic alternatives that a firm might consider and with the determinants of a good choice.

We therefore continue to ask:

- How is the organization doing? Where is it doing well and where is it doing less well?
- How might the organization be developed in the future?
- How can its competitiveness be improved and strengthened?

And look at

- What corporate strategic alternatives are available and worthy of serious consideration?
- What can, cannot, should and should not the organization do in the future?

Content:
Chapter 6 Strategic Purpose
Chapter 7 Strategic Success
Chapter 8 Strategy Creation and Strategic Planning
Chapter 9 Leadership, Entrepreneurship and Intrapreneurship
Chapter 10 Strategic Alternatives and Strategic Choice

Part Four: *Issues in Strategic Growth* deals with both growth and retrenchment issues. There is new material on private equity funding in Chapter 11, and, although new material on the 2009 credit crunch and economic recession can be found throughout the text there is specific coverage in this part. There is also a discussion of business failure and a chapter on international strategy. The relevant questions are (again):

- What corporate strategic alternatives are worthy of serious consideration and why?
- What can, cannot, should and should not the organization do in the future?

Content:
Chapter 11 Strategic Growth
Chapter 12 Internationalization
Chapter 13 Failure, Consolidation and Recovery

Part Five: *Strategic Management* evaluates the issues involved in strategy implementation. Organization structures, resource management and the complexities of managing change are included, as are issues of risk and crisis management. The following questions are therefore addressed:

● What criteria affect the proposed change decisions, how and why?
● How might the proposed changes be implemented and managed?

Content:
Chapter 14 Implementation and Structure
Chapter 15 Leading Change
Chapter 16 Managing Strategy and Implementation
Chapter 17 Final Thoughts: The Purpose of Strategy?

We have changed the order of content in Chapters 15 and 16 from earlier editions – where we concluded the main content of the book with a chapter on change.

Strategic management is a complex and dynamic subject and, as we said at the beginning of this Preface, since the first five editions of this book were published a number of new ideas and views have emerged. In addition, certain practices and priorities have changed to reflect developments around the world. Consequently, the whole text has been reviewed and where appropriate restructured. Every chapter has been edited and rewritten – although there are few radical changes – and some have been consolidated. Inevitably new material has been added and some taken out. Many of the short cases are new.

Key themes

Strategy in practice

This new book contains some 110 short cases within the various chapters. This increase is a result of the continued positive feedback we receive concerning the value of these cases. Clearly there is 'something here for everyone'. Lecturers who use the book will choose the ones that work best for their teaching and their students. Roughly half of the cases have a UK involvement but 62 of them have some further international dimension. Over 30 use well-known American companies, whose names are generally recognized around the world. The remainder are from Europe, the Far East, Australasia and South America. 10 cases on China and India are included. Additional full-length cases are available on the book's website. All the cases cover large and small businesses, both national and international in scope, manufacturing and service, and the private, public and non-profit sectors. The retail, leisure, financial and transport service industries are included, as are several non-profit and charity organizations. We have included a large number of retail examples for several reasons. First, they are mostly recognizable companies that students can readily visit and experience at first hand. Second, they sell products that many readers will buy regularly. Third, they are in an industry that is subject to fashion and innovation; strategies change frequently. We have also included several cases from industries that place a heavy reliance on the Internet. In part this is because they are typically very contemporary, but again it is because students can easily access them for follow-up material. Some of the cases have been included in earlier editions of this book, but where this is the case, they have been either updated or rewritten for this new edition.

Differing perspectives

It must be emphasized that no single approach, model or theory can explain the realities of strategic change in practice for all organizations; different organizations and managers will find certain approaches much more relevant to their circumstances and style. All approaches will have both supporters and critics. It is therefore important to study the various approaches within a sound intellectual framework so that they can be evaluated by students and other readers.

Students of business and management and practising managers must work out for themselves the intricacies and difficulties of managing organizations at the corporate level and of managing strategic change at all levels of the organization. It is no good being told how to be prescriptive when it is patently obvious that there is no universal model. Observations of practice in isolation are equally limited in their usefulness.

However, an attempt to find explanations that can be utilized does make sense. Testing and evaluating reality against a theoretical framework helps this process.

Key features

Cases and examples In addition to numerous references in the main text to organizations and events, as we mentioned above, 130 short Case examples are included. The cases are designed to illustrate points in the main text. They are also intended to supplement the reader's own experiences and investigation. Each chapter begins with a carefully written Case which represents the main themes of the chapter. There are specific questions at the end of every Case and relevant website addresses are provided to enable easy follow-up. Inevitably some of the cases will date during the life of the text, in the sense that the strategies and fortunes of the companies featured in the examples will change. Strategies have life cycles, and strategies that prove effective at certain times will not always remain so. Companies that fail to change their strategies at the right time are likely to experience declining fortunes. Questions are included at the ends of chapters to encourage the reader to research and analyse the subsequent fortunes of companies included as cases.

Additionally, full-length cases are also included on the accompanying website.

Learning objectives These appear at the start of every chapter to help you monitor your understanding and progress through the chapter.

Boxes These are used in the text and featured separately within the relevant chapter for special emphasis and easy reference. They cover three tasks:

1 Boxes define Key Concepts in strategy and also explain significant contributions which underpin an understanding of strategic management.

2 Critical reflections feature debates and discussions where there are differing opinions.

3 *Strategy in action* boxes provide annotated applications of particular ideas and concepts.

Finance in Action At the end of certain chapters, and in the form of appendices, there are Finance in Action supplements which expand upon points introduced in the text. They provide more detail than some readers will require; for others they enhance key aspects of strategic analysis.

Figures A comprehensive set of figures, which are either new or redrawn, illustrate and explain the issues covered in the text.

Quotations Short and pithy quotations from a variety of senior managers in the private and the public sectors are sprinkled throughout the text to illustrate a spectrum of opinions. These are useful for provoking class discussion and examination questions.

Chapter summaries An outline summary of the content and main points is given at the end of every chapter. This can help readers to check that they appreciate the main points and issues before reading on.

Questions and research assignments These are included at the end of each chapter. Some questions relate to the ideas contained in the text and the illustrative cases, and some are examples of the type that feature in non-case study examinations of this subject.

Several research projects, both library- and Internet-based, are included to encourage the reader to develop his or her knowledge and understanding further. The website provides a gateway of links to sites that are helpful in researching the Internet projects.

In addition we have included extra short cases at the ends of chapters to allow further exploration of strategy in action.

Further reading At the end of the chapters we include a short list of further reading references. It consists in part of 'classic' journal articles, some of which have been cited in the main text. These are spread over several years – as the subject has emerged – and we appreciate that some readers may find it difficult to access some of the older ones through their libraries. We therefore also include a number of more recent articles. It should be appreciated that although fresh articles are being published all the time, only a very small number add anything *really new* to our understanding of strategy and strategic management.

Glossary The book also includes a glossary, including definitions of well over 100 key terms. For ease of reference words that are included in the glossary are highlighted in purple in the text.

Website

An extensive accompanying website (at www.cengage.co.uk/thompson6) provides a comprehensive set of additional resources for both students and lecturers. It includes additional material and examples about strategic management, links to companies and further information sources, guidance for lecturers and interactive resources for students. For full details, see the 'About the website' page.

Advice for lecturers

Teaching aims

The main purpose of the book is to help students who aim to become managers, and managers in practice, to:

- develop their strategic awareness
- increase their understanding of how the functional areas of management (in which they are most likely to work) contribute to strategic management and to strategic changes within organizations
- appreciate how strategic change is managed in organizations.

The content is broad and the treatment is both academic and practical, in order to provide value for practising managers as well as full- and part-time students. The subject matter included is taught in a wide variety of courses, including undergraduate courses in business studies and related areas, MBA and other postgraduate Master's degrees, post-experience management courses and courses for a number of professional qualifications. The subject can be entitled strategic management, business policy, corporate strategy or business planning.

The material is relevant for all types of organization: large and small businesses, manufacturing and service organizations, and both the public and private sectors. The examples included relate to all of these. Although the topics discussed are broadly applicable, certain issues are sector specific, and these are discussed individually.

This edition has been written and structured into 16 main chapters to support courses that last up to a full academic year. Clearly, some lecturers will opt to spend longer than a single week or session on some topics or possibly switch the order of the chapters marginally. Neither of these should present any problems and suggested course outlines are provided on the website for different types of course. Some courses in strategy run for only a single semester, focusing more on the analytical aspects of the subject. A careful selection of chapters, in a logical sequence, can underpin such courses quite readily and a suggested outline is provided on the companion website.

Advice for students

Studying strategy

Strategic management is concerned with understanding, as well as choosing and implementing, the strategy or strategies that an organization follows. It is a complex process that can be considered from a number of different perspectives. For example, one can design prescriptive models based on a series of logical stages that look at how to choose and implement strategies aimed at achieving some form of long-term success for the organization. This is a systematic approach designed to bring about optimum results. An alternative paradigm, or conceptual framework, is a systemic approach that concerns understanding what is happening in reality and thinking about how things might be improved. The emphasis is on learning about how strategic management is practised by looking at what organizations actually do and by examining the decisions that they make and carry out.

In this book both perspectives are considered and linked together. While it is always useful to develop models that attempt to provide optimizing solutions, this approach is inadequate if it fails to explain reality. Strategic management and strategic change are dynamic, often the result of responses to environmental pressures, and frequently not the product of extensive deliberations involving all affected managers.

Managers should be aware of the issues and questions that must be addressed if changes in strategy are to be formulated and implemented effectively. At the same time, they should be aware of the managerial and behavioural processes taking place within organizations in order that they can understand how changes actually come about.

Prescriptive models are found quite frequently in business and management teaching. For example, there are models for rational decision-making built around the clear recognition and definition of a problem and the careful and objective analysis and evaluation of the alternative solutions. There are economic models of various market structures showing how an organization can maximize profit. However, decision-making invariably involves subjectivity and short cuts, and organizations do not always seek profit maximization as their top priority. Although organizations and individuals rarely follow these models slavishly – quite often they cannot, and sometimes they choose not to – this does not render them worthless. Far from it: they provide an excellent framework or yardstick for evaluating how people reach their decisions, what objectives are being pursued and how situations might be improved. The argument is that if managers observe what is happening and seek to explain it and evaluate it against some more ideal state then they will see ways of managing things more effectively. In this way managerial performance can be improved. Note the use of the expression 'more effectively'. For a whole variety of reasons situations cannot be managed *perfectly*.

The reader with personal experience of organizations, management and change (whether it is limited or extensive, broad or specialized) should use this experience to complement the examples and cases described in the book. Ideally the experience and the cases will be used jointly to evaluate the theories and concepts discussed. There is no universal approach to the management of strategy and strategic change. An individual must establish what approaches and decisions are likely to prove most effective in particular circumstances, and why. This learning experience can be enhanced by:

- evaluating the theoretical and conceptual contributions of various authors
- considering practical examples of what has proved successful and unsuccessful for organizations
- examining these two aspects in combination to see which theories and concepts best help an understanding of reality.

The manager's job is change. It is what we live with. It is what we are here to create. If we cannot do that, then we are not good at the job. It is our basic job to have the nerve to keep changing and changing and changing again.

SIR PETER PARKER

Pressures to change are always present in the form of opportunities and threats. At any point in time the significance of these pressures will vary markedly from industry to industry and from organization to organization. Managers may be aware of them and seek to respond positively; they may recognize opportunities and threats and choose to do little about them other than perhaps to avert crises; or they may be totally unaware of them. A lack of awareness can mean that potentially good opportunities are also lost; it may mean that businesses fail if they are not able to react and respond to the threats and problems when they arise. All businesses must react to pressures from the environment such as supply shortages, new products from competitors or new retailing opportunities, but some will be very proactive and thereby seek to manage their environment.

It is important to point out that students of strategic management may not be, or may not become, key strategic decision-makers in their organizations but instead may specialize in one particular function, such as marketing, production or finance. Similarly, their experience may be with only one product or one division if their employer is a multiproduct or multidivisional organization. Nevertheless, the decisions that they make or to which they contribute can affect the strategy for a particular product or service and in turn affect the organization. It is vital that they appreciate exactly how their function operates within an organizational context, and how decisions made in their area of interest can affect both other functions and the organization as a whole.

Finally, and to reinforce this last point, students occasionally ask whether 'strategic management' is about the management of strategy in organizations or about how people can manage strategically – an interesting point! The focus here is on the management of strategy in organizations but, by studying and applying the theory, and reflecting on its relevance in the context of personal observations and experience, readers should be able to improve their effectiveness as managers. In essence they will benefit – as will any organization in which they work – by being better placed to take a strategic perspective and to use it to inform decisions and actions. Remember, there are no finite answers to the decisions and actions that should be taken. Organizations, and many of the problem issues they have to deal with, are complex and ill-defined. After all, if strategy were straightforward, the relative success rate of organizations of every type and size would be much greater than it is.

Experience is a wonderful thing, but not a useful one. When you are young, you don't trust others' experience – for if you do, this can paralyse you. When you get old, it is too late to use it – and you cannot transmit it for the reasons outlined.

JACQUES CALVET, WHEN LE PRESIDENT DU DIRECTOIRE, PSA PEUGEOT CITROËN

Acknowledgements

The publisher would like to thank the following reviewers for their contribution:

Dermot Breslin,
University of Sheffield

Alison Dean,
University of Kent

Rodd Gunn,
University of Glamorgan

Louisa Jones,
University of Central Lancashire

David Pollard,
Henley Management College

Carsten Scheibye,
Copenhagen Business School

Conor Sheehan,
Brighton Business School

Kent Springdal,
Kingston University

Jan Stiles,
Henley Management College.

Walk-through tour

Learning objectives appear at the start of every chapter to help you monitor your understanding and progress through the chapter.

Quotes short quotes from senior managers in the private and public sectors are used throughout the text to illustrate a spectrum of opinions; these are ideal for provoking class discussion and examination questions

Cases these appear throughout the book to show how each chapter's main issues are applied in real-life business situations in different types of international and national companies. Each case is accompanied by questions to help test your understanding of the issues.

Glossary Terms key terms are highlighted in colour throughout and explained in full in a glossary at the end of the book, enabling you to find explanations of key terms quickly.

Summaries each chapter ends with a comprehensive summary that provides a thorough re-cap of the key issues in each chapter, helping you to assess your understanding and revise key content.

Questions and Research Assignments provided at the end of each chapter, these help reinforce and test your knowledge and understanding, and provide a basis for group discussions and activities.
Internet and Library Projects these more detailed questions and activities encourage you to further develop and build on your knowledge and understanding through online or library based research and project work.

Strategy Activity an activity appears at the end of each chapter to aid and promote strategic thinking and analysis.

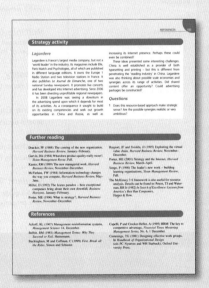

Further Reading and References comprehensive references and often annotated further reading at the end of each chapter allows you to explore the subject further, and acts as a starting point for projects and assignments.

About the website

Visit the *Strategic Management: Awareness and Change* website at **www.cengage.co.uk/thompson6** to find valuable teaching and learning material including:

For students

- Multiple Choice Questions
- Online Cases Bank
- Weblinks
- Glossary
- Student Cases Guide
- Student Referencing Guide

For lecturers

- An expanded secure teaching manual
- PowerPoint slides
- Online cases bank
- A guide to using cases in teaching
- A guide to using the web in teaching
- Test bank

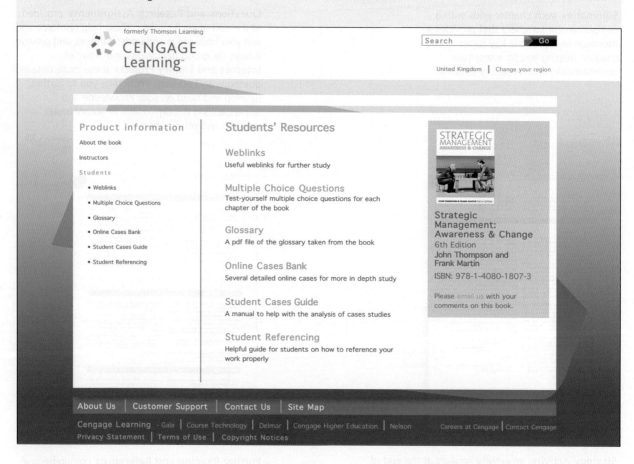

Part 1

Understanding strategy and strategic management

Organizations, their strategies, their structures and the management of them become ever more complex. Among the reasons for this are the increasing turbulence and propensity to change in the business environment, and the tendency for multiproduct multinational organizations to become commonplace. Organizations need to know where they are, where they are going and how to manage the changes. Managers in these organizations need to know where their roles fit in relation to the whole and how they can contribute to strategic developments and changes. These are the issues addressed by a study of strategic management.

This first part is designed to provide a broad appreciation of strategic management and to develop the framework used in the book in order to:

- outline the scope and complexity of the study area
- provide an initial overview of some major contributors to the subject in order to illustrate what is meant by, and included in, strategic management, and to demonstrate that there is no single universally accepted approach

- develop a framework which will provide a model for the structure and content of the book
- explain the significance of a robust business model
- examine what is meant by purpose, direction and objectives, and consider how these might be set and used
- help you think and act in a strategic way

Strategy in a nutshell

Strategy is about how organizations cope with the world, which is dynamic and emergent. Technologies, fashion and competitors all change all the time. Organizations have to harness all their strategic resources (including in particular their employees), deal with other stakeholders (such as funders and suppliers) and meet the expectations of their customers or clients. They sometimes have to deal with legislative and other constraints and often they have to out-manoeuvre competitors.

Strategies are means to ends; the process of strategic management involves:

- clarifying the desired ends
- mapping out a route for achieving them (creating strategies)
- putting those strategies into practice (implementation)
- changing what you are doing tactically in the face of competition and unexpected issues that arise
- evaluating progress and performance

To do this effectively, organizations need a clear, if broad, vision and a willingness to be flexible in its pursuit. Strategies are sometimes determinedly intentional but on occasions they emerge from the choices that organizations make in the face of dynamic uncertainty. Intention can come from the personal insight of individuals and from a more analytical process.

Organizations, then, need to be able to harness and deploy the necessary resources and to respond to both opportunities and competition. It is here that any distinctive competitive advantage (a real edge over rivals) is created.

To thrive and grow organizations must be able to meet the expectations of their customers or clients and to do what they do at least as well as, and ideally better than, any rivals. Competitiveness is based on many things, but being different (in both a distinctive and a meaningful way), cost management and speed are all critical.

We can, therefore, think of strategy from three distinct, but clearly linked, perspectives – opportunity, capability and competitiveness. These three themes, together with aspirations and values, are the four key strategy drivers. They affect the choices organizations make and they affect how well they perform.

Strategy involves creation and ideas and delivery – implementation. Implementation depends upon people who work together in organizations which can be cohesive and effective or more disjointed.

When organizations succeed it is highly likely that they are doing the right things well. But if things go wrong, was the real problem what they were doing (the strategies) or how they were doing it (implementation)? It can be either – or both!

Put another way, successful organizations have a clear business model, which they implement well. They are clear what their product (or service) is, for whom it is intended, and why these target customers (clients) have a compelling reason to do business with them. And they produce and deliver the right quality both on time and consistently. Their customers are satisfied.

A number of important themes emerge from this. It is people who produce and deliver the products and services and so their skills, capabilities and motivation are critical. In turn, people work in organizations – in which their roles need to be clear but where they have some freedom to influence what goes on. In a competitive and uncertain environment it will be necessary for organizations to change from time to time, and sometimes quite frequently. Organizations must react to what happens in the world and in their industry; and they should look to innovate proactively to get and stay one step ahead of their rivals.

The ability to match resources and opportunities effectively, to harness resources and satisfy customer expectations, meeting performance targets in the process, and to change things as and when necessary, are very dependent upon the strategic leadership of the organization and the culture and values prevalent within the organization. The congruency (or relative incongruence) of environment, resources and values is therefore a good test of strategic effectiveness.

Above all, strategy is about choices: choosing what to do and choosing what not to do. The secret is to keep things focused and straightforward and to 'deliver'.

Chapter 1

Introducing strategy and strategic management

Learning objectives

Having read to the end of this chapter you should be able to:

● define strategic management and strategic change

● distinguish between corporate, competitive and functional strategies

● summarize strategic management in terms of three interrelated aspects – awareness, choice and implementation

● appreciate that there are five complementary perspectives of strategy – vision, plan, tactics, position and pattern

● clarify the three broad approaches to strategy creation, namely visionary ideas, planning and emergence

● show how strategy has military origins

● trace the evolving views of strategy

● understand the place of strategy in small businesses, global companies, the public sector and non-profit organizations.

Strategies are means to ends. All organizations, large and small, profit-seeking and not-for-profit, private and public sector, have a purpose, which may or may not be articulated in the form of a mission and/or vision statement. Strategies relate to the pursuit of this purpose. Strategies must be created and implemented, and it is these issues which are addressed by our study of strategic management. This opening chapter begins by outlining how successful organizations manage their strategies, and what they achieve, before exploring the meaning of strategy in greater detail. It then continues with an explanation of the strategic management process in the context of the framework upon which this book is structured before explaining the different ways in which strategies are created. It then describes how the subject of strategic management has developed in the last 30 years, before concluding with a brief consideration of the similarities and differences in strategic management in various types of organization.

1.1 Strategy explained

The flame of competition has changed from smokey yellow to intense white heat. For companies to survive and prosper they will have to have a vision, a mission and strategy. They will pursue the action arising from that strategy with entrepreneurial skill and total dedication and commitment to win.

PETER B ELLWOOD, WHEN CHIEF EXECUTIVE, LLOYDS TSB GROUP

Far too many companies either have no goals at all, other than cost reduction, or their boss hides them in his head. There's no hope for companies in Britain unless more top managements accept the need for a widely communicated set of clear objectives.

PETER BECK, EX-CHAIRMAN, THE STRATEGIC PLANNING SOCIETY, 1987

Case 1.1

The Low-Price, No-Frills Airlines   US UK

This case features the three best known airlines in this sector of the industry. They have all been growing in recent years and their success has been earned at a time when the world's leading full-service carriers have all experienced problems. Their strategies may all be similar, but their stories, and the strategic leaders behind them, are quite different.

Herb Kelleher began **Southwest Air** in 1971 with a simple intention – 'fly people safely, cheaply and conveniently between Dallas, Houston and San Antonio', three key cities in Texas. Kelleher set out to compete against coach and car travel rather than the other airlines. He had been a champion college athlete and a successful Texas lawyer before he started the airline when he was 40 years old. The idea for Southwest, however, had come from a client (and co-founder of the business) who spotted the gap in the market.

Southwest has prospered and grown to become one of the largest carriers in the USA. After thirty successful years it served over 50 cities in 27 states and had some 2500 flights every day. Kelleher's strategy, competitive advantage and success has always been based on a number of factors:

- frequent and reliable departures
- relatively short journeys by American standards, now averaging 450 miles but with the average having increased as the airline has grown in size and destinations
- the choice of smaller airports nearer to city centres where relevant, in preference to international airports which are further away from the centre
- very low prices
- automated ticketing and direct bookings (without travel agents), and now using the Internet extensively
- limited *frills*, limited refreshments, no videos and just one class of seating – if airlines serve only soft drinks rather than coffee and tea (with the inevitable milk, sugar and stirrer) it is easier to collect passenger rubbish and thus speed up cabin cleaning between flights
- no seat assignments – which encourages passengers to turn up early so they can be towards the front of the boarding line, which in turn means planes are likely to take off on time. Now people who check-in on-line the day before they fly get boarding priority

- fast gate turnarounds, to maximize the time the planes are in the air
- a standardized fleet of Boeing 737s, to simplify maintenance.

Southwest is clearly America's leading short-distance, point-to-point carrier. Others have preceded it and others have joined the industry, but none of these has been able to make the equivalent impact. Southwest has won the US Department of Transport's coveted 'Triple Crown' award of best on-time record, best baggage handling and fewest customer complaints on several occasions. Every new route and destination is immediately popular and, as a result, Southwest has been consistently profitable for over 35 years, a unique record for an airline anywhere in the world.

Kelleher is a renowned 'people person'. Through profit-sharing schemes, employees own over 10 per cent of the company's stock, and he has made 'working in the airline industry an adventure'. Southwest is dynamic and responsive; employees accept empowerment and are motivated to work hard and deliver high levels of service consistently. Rules and regulations are minimized to allow staff the freedom to deal with issues as they arise. 'Ask employees what's important to them. Ask customers what's important to them. Then do it. It's that simple', says Kelleher. The frequent flyer programme, unusually, rewards passengers for the number of individual flights, not the miles flown.

But it is never that simple! Southwest is also renowned as 'one of the zaniest companies in history'. From the very beginning, Kelleher encouraged flight attendants to crack jokes during in-flight emergency briefings, but, at the same time, operate with very high safety standards. He was determined that passengers would enjoy their flights. Some of the planes are decorated externally to reinforce the fun image. Three of them, promoting major sponsor Sea World, are flying killer whales; one is painted with the Texas flag; another is christened Arizona One, a spoof of Air Force One. Flight attendants have been known to hide in the overhead lockers as passengers come on board, startling them as they open up the lockers. Kelleher often appears in fancy dress for certain flights and special occasions. A special prize for the passenger with the biggest hole in his sock is quite typical.

Consequently, a sense of humour has become a key element in the recruitment process. During their training, employees are given a book with sections on jokes, games and songs – but they are all encouraged to develop an individual style. 'At Southwest we don't want clones – everyone is expected to colour outside the lines'. Kelleher is dedicated and focused and in possession of a strong ego. He is creative and innovative and he understands the contribution that people can make. He has always had the courage to be different. When he was introduced to an idea he appreciated the opportunity and activated it. Truly profit orientated, he has been extremely successful in a dynamic and cruel industry, where many competing airlines have failed.

Southwest has become a hugely popular airline and an iconic brand in America. It has flown over 1 billion passengers wihout a single fatal accident, but in 2008 it was fined for security breaches and criticized by the Federal Aviation Authority. Staff had been skimping on-board inspections – which all take up time between flights. Higher security vigilance is not an easy issue for airlines which want their planes to be on the ground for as short a time as possible. Presidential hopeful, Hillary Clinton, even commented that 'Southwest had a lot to answer for'.

EasyJet, begun in 1995 by a 28-year-old Greek entrepreneur, Stelios Haji-Ioannou, the son of a wealthy shipping magnate, was a pioneer of no frills flying in Europe. Stelios intended to 'make flying in Europe affordable for more and more people'. Parodying British Airways' claim to be 'The World's Favourite Airline', EasyJet began to call itself 'The Web's Favourite Airline'. The majority of its bookings come via the Internet; the rest are direct over the telephone. There are no commissioned travel agency bookings, no tickets and no on-board meals. When passengers with a reservation check in at the airport, they are allocated a number, based on their time of check in, not when they prebooked, and this determines the order in which they board the aircraft. There are no seat reservations. EasyJet's first hub airports in the UK were the relatively uncongested and quick turnaround Luton and Liverpool; and destinations are concentrated in Scotland and continental Europe, including Athens, Barcelona, Geneva and Nice. All the aeroplanes were relatively new Boeing 737s, painted white and orange and featuring EasyJet's telephone number on the side. The airline became profitable for the first time in 1998. EasyJet acquired Go, the no frills competitor set up by British Airways. This meant a new hub at Stansted, the UK base of rival Ryanair, and rapid expansion. Early problems in co-ordinating the operations of the two carriers affected profitability.

Stelios had studied in the UK, at the London School of Economics and City University, and then worked for his father for a short while. He began his first business, Stelmar Tankers, in 1992. EasyJet's strategy was modelled on Southwest Air, but Stelios claimed he had been inspired by Richard Branson and Virgin Atlantic. His approach to customers and people mirrors that of Branson. Commuting from Nice – his main home is in Monte Carlo – he flew on his own planes several times a week and talked to the passengers. A television 'docusoap' on EasyJet which began in 1998 showed that Stelios was regularly present at Luton (his headquarters) and willing to help resolve passenger problems.

I lead by example. I believe that people will do things if they see their boss doing exactly the same things … the best way to motivate a team is to convince them they're always under attack … having an external enemy is the best way of focusing their mind on results, rather than fighting each other and becoming complacent … I'm keen that important information is available to everybody in the company … there are no secrets.

The EasyJet product is, in reality, a package of services, many subcontracted in. EasyJet provides the planes and their crews, and markets and sells the flights. As a company, it is focused. Check-in and information services, snacks (for passengers to buy before they board the aeroplane), baggage handling and fleet maintenance are all bought in from specialists.

Stelios recruited Ray Webster, a senior executive from Air New Zealand, to be the chief executive of EasyJet – and in 2002 he announced that he would relinquish the chairman's role so he could focus his energy and efforts on his other businesses. Sir Colin Chandler, who had been the strategic leader at defence giant, Vickers, replaced him. EasyJet had planes on order from both Boeing (more 737s) and Airbus Industrie; once its fleet comprised two different aircraft EasyJet had a different business model from that of Southwest Air and its main rival, Ryanair, the European market leader.

Stelios is a serial entrepreneur and he has begun a number of other businesses since the launch of EasyJet.

None of them has been consistently profitable though. They include:

> EasyInternet cafe
> EasyCar – low cost car rental, mainly at airports
> EasyInternetdotcom – providing free web access
> EasyValue – a price comparison site on the web
> EasyMoney – an Internet bank
> EasyCinema – a cut-price cinema seat business.

EasyJet's main rival is **Ryanair**, which was started by the Ryan family in Dublin in 1985 as a direct rival to Aer Lingus. A full-service carrier, it failed to grow into a profitable business. Michael O'Leary, a tax accountant, joined the business in 1991 and he soon became the strategic leader. O'Leary went to America to learn about Southwest Air and re-launched Ryanair as a no-frills, low-cost carrier. Again he has only used Boeing 737s; and Ryanair always looks for airports with relatively low charges even if they are several miles outside the city they serve. For example, the one serving Brussels (Charleroi) is 40 kms. to the south of the city; the commute to Stockholm is 100 kms.; and the one designated Copenhagen is actually over the border in Sweden. This provides a cost saving when compared with EasyJet. Ryanair acquired Buzz, a rival low-cost carrier started by the Dutch airline, KLM. Whereas Stelios retained most of the Go operations when he acquired that business, O'Leary has retained only certain Buzz routes and very few of the staff.

Michael O'Leary has been described as 'bullying, foul-mouthed, charming and humorous'. He is invariably the public face of Ryanair and keen to defend the airline against any criticism of its strategies. His very successful strategy is based on defining a rival-beating price for a route, undercutting EasyJet wherever they compete for a route, and then making sure costs are driven down to allow that route to be profitable. 'Everything we do is designed to pass on lower fares.' Like EasyJet most promotions feature low fares. Ryanair claim the first 70 per cent of seats on every flight are available at the two lowest fares – for later bookings the prices can rise substantially.

Ryanair is the cost leader in the European industry. O'Leary generally manages to keep the costs at two-thirds of EasyJet's, which means Ryanair's costs are 60 per cent of those incurred by UK holiday charter airlines and 50 per cent of those attributable to the leading full-service domestic carriers. O'Leary achieves savings in a number of ways, in particular:

- Buying aircraft when the manufacturers are experiencing trading problems, thus driving down the price
- Selling costs – there are only direct sales. Outlawing travel agents can mean a saving of up to 15 per cent
- Passenger services provided – there are no tickets in the normal sense and no air bridges – passengers have to walk out to the aircraft. There is a charge for any soft drinks served on board
- Crew costs – pay rates are lower than rivals, and there are just three cabin crew on every flight, low for an aircraft of this size, but they are not there to serve food and drinks but to look after passenger safety
- Ground handling – in part by not worrying how far away from cities airports are, and obtaining huge discounts by using airports which are chasing business
- Seat density – Ryanair packs 15 per cent more passengers in its Boeings
- Ryanair has begun charging for every case put into the hold and even experimented with flights where no hold bags are allowed – everything must be carried on, but with normal size restrictions applying. This helps speed up the check-in process and reduce the time planes are on the ground
- The airline charges people who need manual help to check in; instead customers are expected to use the self-service booths
- Ryanair designs its own advertisements, ignoring specialist agencies. One irreverent ad featured the Pope and the phrase *Psst ... want to know the 4th secret of Fatima* which upset the Catholic Church but earned a huge amount of free publicity. By allowing other brands to be advertised on the outside of its planes Ryanair earns additional revenue.

By striking alliances with local hotels and transport providers (such as car hire firms) Ryanair earns commissions, which constitute some 15 per cent of its net profits. The airline has also started allowing passengers to use mobile phones and BlackBerry's in the air – because it can earn a commission.

There are other less obvious reductions in the services provided by the no-frills airlines. Ryanair, for example, only have a relatively small customer services activity. The low cost model means they are likely to be less sympathetic than the full-service carriers if passengers miss their flight or the flight has to be cancelled.

Ryanair has had to face its critics. It has been fined for charging a passenger for the provision of a wheelchair, a practice it vigorously defended and it has been accused of low service and a lack of responsibility when cases are damaged. A television documentary suggested the cost cutting and time saving had gone too far because when things were tight passenger passports were not being inspected properly before they boarded the plane. In addition its pilots were flying the maximum number of hours allowed on a routine rather than an exceptional basis. On breakfast television in 2009 O'Leary joked about charging passengers to use the on-board toilets; when the newspapers proclaimed 'spend a pound to spend a penny' he quickly denied that he was being in any way serious.

In 2007 O'Leary gambled on oil prices falling, rather than rising, and he did not hedge. Ryanair profits were badly affected as fuel costs doubled to become 50 per cent of operating costs.

The no-frills carriers have certainly had a major impact upon the airline industry and their success has in part been at the expense of the full-service carriers, such as British Airways in the UK, who have had to respond. There are a proportion of passengers who will always opt for the lowest price; others will never compromise on service. In-between people have a choice to make and BA for one is working hard to trim its costs and reduce its fares in order to narrow the price gap.

There are some interesting paradoxes. Customers confirm they do not enjoy the low levels of service, but they accept it on short haul flights if the prices stay low. There is, therefore, potentially resistance against fare increases and so Ryanair has so far refused to increase prices even though its costs are escalating. To stay profitable it will need to persuade more people to fly, maybe with new routes, or to switch from other airlines – it committed to the delivery of 32 new aircraft in 2008 and there must be a real danger of seat capacity exceeding demand.

Its staff are partially exploited with long hours and relatively low wages for the industry, but there is no shortage of recruits. Enough people seem to like and want this type of work.

There are those who claim the low cost airline business model is broken and needs fixing, but this is denied by the airlines themselves.

Question/Task

This case introduces a number of important issues. Amongst them are:

- New competitors can dramatically change an industry
- Rivals compete to establish and maintain a competitive edge
- The role of a strategic leader is critical
- The Internet has offered new strategic opportunities.

Either think about or discuss with colleagues what you think the key messages are in relation to these issues.

The quotations from Stelios Haji-Ioannou are extracted from: Maitland, A (1998) No frills and lots of feedback, *Financial Times*, 17 September.

© ONNE VAN DER WAL/CORBIS

Introducing strategy

At their simplest, strategies help to explain the things that managers and organizations do. These actions or **activities** are designed and carried out in order to fulfil certain designated purposes, some of them short term in nature, others longer term. The organization has a direction and broad purpose, which should always be clear, articulated and understood, and which sometimes will be summarized in the form of a **mission statement**. More specific **milestones** and targets (objectives) can help to guide specific actions and measure progress.

Strategies, then, are means to ends

They are relevant for the organization as a whole, and for the individual businesses and/or functions that comprise the organization. They are created and changed in a variety of ways. They have, however, one common feature: they all have **life cycles** and need changing, either marginally or dramatically, at certain times.

To some extent all managers are strategy makers

While strategic management incorporates major changes of direction for the whole business, such as **diversification** and growth overseas, it also involves smaller changes in strategies for individual products and services and in particular functions such as marketing and operations. Decisions by managers in relation to their particular areas of product or functional responsibility have a strategic impact and contribute to **strategic change**.

Strategic management is a complex and fascinating subject with straightforward underlying principles but no 'right answers'. Strategy is about issues and perspectives on problems – there is no single, prescriptive doctrine which satisfies everyone's views.

Companies succeed if their strategies are appropriate for the circumstances they face, feasible in respect of their resources, skills and capabilities, and desirable to their important stakeholders – those individuals and groups, both internal and external, who have a stake in, and an influence over, the business. Simply, strategy is fundamentally about a fit between the organization's resources and the markets it targets – plus, of course, the ability to sustain fit over time and in changing circumstances.

Companies fail when their strategies fail to meet the expectations of these stakeholders or produce outcomes which are undesirable to them. To succeed long term, companies must compete effectively and outperform their rivals in a dynamic, and often turbulent, **environment**. To accomplish this they must find suitable ways for creating and **adding value** for their customers. A **culture** of internal co-operation and customer orientation, together with a willingness to learn, adapt and change, is ideal. **Alliances** and good working relationships with suppliers, distributors and customers are often critically important as well.

Some thirty years ago Morrison and Lee (1979) concluded that successful companies seem to be distinguished from their less successful competitors by a common pattern of management practices and these still hold:

- First, they identify more effectively than their competitors the key success factors inherent in the economics of each business. For example, in the airline industry, with its high fixed costs and relatively inflexible route allocations, a high load factor is critical to success. It is important, though, that high load factors are not at the expense of healthy sales of more expensive seats, and this requires skilful marketing.

- Secondly, they segment their markets so as to gain decisive competitive advantage, basing the segmentation on competitive analysis and often separating segments according to the strengths and weaknesses of different competitors. This enables them to concentrate on segments where they can both maximize their competitive advantage and avoid head-on competition with stronger competitors.

- Thirdly, they carefully measure and analyse any competitive advantage. This requires a sound basis for assessing a company's advantages relative to its competitors.

- Fourthly, they anticipate their competitors' responses. Good strategic thinking also implies an understanding of how situations will change over time. Business strategy, like **military strategy**, is a matter of manoeuvring for superior position and anticipating how competitors will respond, and with what measure of success.

- Fifthly, they exploit more, or different, degrees of freedom than their competitors. Specifically, they seek to stay ahead of their rivals by looking for new competitive opportunities. Whilst innovation and constant improvement are essential, there are also potentially huge rewards for organizations which are first to reach the new competitive high ground by changing the currently practised rules of competition.

● Finally, they give investment priority to businesses or areas that promise a competitive advantage.

Because there are many views on strategy and strategic management and no single, universally accepted, approach, a study of strategic changes in a variety of different organizations is valuable. An examination of outcomes, followed by an analysis of the decisions which led to these relative successes and failures, is rich in learning potential. Examples should not be confined to just one sector. Manufacturing and service businesses, the private and public sectors and **not-for-profit organizations** are all relevant.

Box 1.1

Key Terms in Strategic Management

Mission and Vision both relate to the essential purpose of the organization. The **Vision** concerns why it is in existence and what it aims to become; the **Mission** reflects what it needs to be if it is to pursue its purpose. It embraces the nature of the business(es) it is in, and the customers it seeks to serve and satisfy.

Values statements represent word pictures which reflect the future standing of the organisation and how it will behave and feel. They will typically comprise a set of behaviours and key values to which employees should subscribe. They are linked to the mission, but there is a subtle difference.

Objectives (or goals) are desired states or results linked to particular time-scales and concerning such things as size or type of organization, the nature and variety of the areas of interest and levels of success. Taken to a particular level of detail they can become targets and milestones.

Strategies are means to ends, and these ends concern the purpose and objectives of the organization. They are the things that businesses do, the paths they follow, and the decisions they take, in order to reach certain points and levels of success.

Tactics are the specific activities which deliver and implement the strategies in order to fulfil objectives and pursue the mission. Often short term, they can be changed frequently if necessary.

Strategic thinking is the ability of the organization (and its managers) to synthesize and share the learning from the organization's history, understand its present competencies and position and clarify ways forward.

Strategic awareness is the understanding of managers within the organization about: (a) the strategies being followed by the organization and its competitors, (b) how the effectiveness of these strategies might be improved, and (c) the need for, and suitability of, opportunities for change.

Strategic management is a process or processes which need to be understood more than it is a discipline which can be taught. It is the process by which organizations determine their purpose, objectives and desired levels of attainment; decide on actions for achieving these objectives in an appropriate time-scale, and frequently in a changing environment; implement the actions; and assess progress and results. Whenever and wherever necessary the actions may be changed or modified. The magnitude of these changes can be dramatic and revolutionary, or more gradual and evolutionary.

Strategic change concerns changes which take place over time to the strategies and objectives of the organization. Change can be gradual or evolutionary; or more dramatic, even revolutionary.

Synergy is the term used for the added value or additional benefits which ideally accrue from the linkage or fusion of two businesses, or from increased co-operation either between different parts of the same organization or between a company and its suppliers, distributors and customers. Internal co-operation may represent linkages between either different divisions or different functions.

Everyone who can make or influence decisions which impact on the strategic effectiveness of the business should have at least a basic understanding of the concepts and processes of strategy. The processes will often be informal, and the outcomes not documented clearly. But they still exist, and managing the processes effectively determines the organization's future. Without this understanding people often fail to appreciate the impact of their decisions and actions for other people within the business. They are less likely to be able to learn from observing and reflecting upon the actions of others. They are also more likely to miss or misjudge new opportunities and growing threats in the organization's environment.

As a starting point, key terms used in this book are defined in Box 1.1 and examples of strategic change in a number of different organizations are illustrated in Strategy in action 1.1.

Strategy in action 1.1

Examples of Historic Strategy Changes

Lex Service Group, sizeable distributor of Rover, Rolls Royce and Volvo cars in the main, felt too dependent on one area of business and sought to find suitable unrelated diversification opportunities. Lex chose four- and five-star hotels in the UK and USA but later chose to sell them when the results were below those desired. This took place in the 1970s and 1980s, since when Lex entered and exited the distribution of electronics parts. More recently Lex has acquired related businesses to become the UK's largest car distribution and leasing company. In 1995 Lex bought Multipart, a distributor of commercial vehicle parts; and more recently it has acquired the roadside assistance business, the RAC. Lex Service is now owned by the Bank of Scotland and the RAC by Aviva, the insurance company that was previously named Norwich Union.

WH Smith, desiring growth beyond the scope offered from its (then) current business lines (wholesaling and retailing newspapers and magazines, stationery, books and sounds), diversified into do-it-yourself with a chain of Do-It-All stores, introduced travel agencies into a number of its existing stores and acquired related interests in Canada and America. Travel was later divested, along with investments in cable television, to enable greater concentration on sounds, videos and consumer and office stationery. Important acquisitions included the Our Price and Virgin music stores and the Waterstone's chain of specialist booksellers. Do-It-All became a joint venture with Boots, but it struggled to be profitable with strong competition from B & Q and Texas, which was acquired by Sainsbury's in the mid-1990s. In 1996 WH Smith divested Do-It-All and its office stationery businesses.

Later in the 1990s both Waterstone's and Our Price were also divested, and the book publisher, Hodder Headline, was acquired. In the last few years the Group has split into two: WHSmith now incorporates the retail stores in town and city centres and at airports and railway stations, whilst WH Smith News is the newspaper and magazine wholesale and distribution business.

The Burton Group sold the last of its manufacturing interests in 1988. Once one of the leading men's clothing manufacturers in Europe the group, by a series of related acquisitions and divestments, became essentially a major retailer of fashion goods for both men and women, changing the group name to Arcadia. In recent years Burton acquired – and later divested – Debenham's. Arcadia is now owned by the entrepreneur and specialist in corporate turnarounds, Philip Green.

UK building societies, restrained by legislation until the mid-1980s, expanded their financial services to include current accounts with cheque books and cash-dispensing machines – to compete more aggressively with the high-street banks – and diversified into such linked activities as estate agencies and insurance. Mergers took place between, for example, the Halifax and Leeds Permanent societies and Abbey National and National & Provincial, to strengthen their positions as diversified financial institutions. Moreover, the largest ones (notably Abbey National and the Halifax) have given up their mutual status and become quoted companies. Halifax was later merged with the Bank of Scotland to form HBOS which was absorbed by Lloyds TSB during the financial difficulties of 2008.

During this time a number of the leading supermarket groups have opted to diversify into financial services, utilizing their customer databases and information for carefully targeted marketing. In a quite different (and more evolutionary way) the decision by high-street banks to open on Saturdays for a limited range of services was strategic change. Here the banks were copying the building societies and reacting to increased competition.

National Bus Company was privatized during the mid-1980s, mostly by splitting it up into small local or regional companies which were then bought out by their existing management teams. The sector has since become more concentrated as certain growth-orientated operators such as Stagecoach and First Bus (a name change from Badgerline) have bought out other smaller companies – following a mixed strategy of organic growth and acquisition. One major challenge for these aggressive companies has been to try and avoid intervention from the UK regulatory authorities, concerned with competition in the industry. Having acquired a number of local bus franchises in the UK, Stagecoach has also expanded overseas and bought a substantial minority shareholding (49 per cent) in Virgin Rail.

Oxfam is a UK based international charity that lobbies, campaigns, raises funds and carries out relief work related to famines and natural disasters such as the devastating tsunami in Indonesia a few years ago. One of its fund raising activities is Oxfam shops which are visible on high streets in most towns and cities and which rely extensively on volunteers and donated items. They have been described somewhat tongue-in-cheek as shops where middle class ladies sell their own mothers' cast-offs to their friends' daughters. In recent years Oxfam has opened specialist second-hand bookshops and in 2008 it announced a new venture in London. It was to open a fashion boutique in a deliberate attempt to move more up-market. The clothes would be new, remades or donations from designers. Oxfam is typical of many charities which have, on the one hand, to be aggressive fund raisers whilst, on the other hand, doing good and being seen to be doing good. In 2008 the shops were realizing that as the economy tightened many people were buying fewer new clothes and as a consequence discarding fewer clothes.

© MARIANKA / DREAMSTIME.COM

Introducing strategic management

There are a number of aspects to strategic management.

First, the *strategy* itself. This is concerned with the establishment of a clear direction for the organization and for every business, product and service, and a means for getting there which requires the creation of strong competitive positions.

Second requirement is excellence in the ***implementation*** of strategies in order to yield effective performance.

Third, *creativity and **innovation*** to ensure that the organization is responsive to pressures for change and that strategies are improved and renewed.

Fourth, the ability to manage *strategic change*, both continuous, gradual, incremental changes and more dramatic, discontinuous changes. Innovation and change concern the strategy process in an organization.

Sound implementation and innovation should enable an organization to thrive and prosper in a dynamic, global environment, but in turn they depend on competencies in strategic awareness and learning. Organizations must understand the strategic value of the resources that they employ and deploy, and how they can be used to satisfy the needs and expectations of customers and other stakeholders while outperforming competitors.

> *Strategy is about actions, not plans – specifically the commitment of resources to achieving strategic ends … concrete steps that immediately affect people's lives, not abstract intentions.*

ANDREW S GROVE, CEO, INTEL

Many of these points are evident in the story of the low-price, no-frills airlines, such as Ryanair and EasyJet (Case 1.1), which shows that:

- newcomers can change an industry – by being creative, innovative and different
- new competitors can, and will, find ways of breaking down apparent barriers to entry
- companies need to find some clear and distinct competitive advantage, something which is both attractive to customers and profitable
- this advantage will come from what organizations do, their distinctive competencies and capabilities
- charismatic and visible strategic leaders often have a major impact on the choice and implementation of key strategies
- people are critically important if strategies are to be implemented effectively
- the Internet is becoming increasingly important; and
- business can be fun!

It is, however, also important to realize that in many organizations certain parts may be 'world class' and highly profitable while other businesses are not. Good practices in the strong businesses can be discerned, transferred and learned, but this may not be enough. Some industries and competitive environments are simply less friendly and premium profits are unlikely. The real danger occurs if the weaker businesses threaten to bring down the strong ones that are forced to subsidize them. It is an irony that companies in real difficulty, possibly through strategic weaknesses, need to turn in an excellent performance if they are to survive.

Finally, it must be realized that past and current success is no guarantee of success in the future. Companies are not guaranteed, or entitled to, continued prosperity. They must adapt and change in a dynamic environment. Many fail to do this, for all sorts of reasons, and disappear. Some close down; others are acquired. The collapse of a number of airlines, especially low cost carriers such as Zoom, in the economic downturn of 2008, highlights that success when economies are booming, is no guarantee of long-term survival. Marks and Spencer (Case 1.2) is an excellent example of a previously outstanding company that has lost its way in recent years.

Case 1.2

Marks and Spencer plc   UK

Marks and Spencer (M&S) is a well-known and revered high-street retailer in the UK. The early growth of M&S was built around clothing, and its reputation owes much to the popularity of its underwear! M&S introduced us to lycra and Y-fronts. It built a second reputation for foods, pioneering chilled fresh varieties and bringing the avocado pear to the UK mass market. Always gradually, other ranges such as cosmetics, homewear, gifts and furniture have been added systematically. A home-delivery service for furniture has been expanded to include other items. Every shopping centre developer wants M&S to open a store, as they always attract customers.

The original foundations of the business lay with a young, Jewish immigrant and his Leeds market stall.

Michael Marks had a poor grasp of English, a clear disadvantage for a trader in a noisy street market! Opportunistically, he turned his disadvantage into a strength. He had a sign on his stall: *Don't Ask The Price – It's a Penny*, and for a penny he provided the widest range and best-quality items he could find. This philosophy of *value for money* has pervaded through the generations and been sustained with innovation and change – but the focus on value has never been lost. The market stall led to a store, and then to stores on most high streets in Britain. The Spencer in the name came from Marks' first business partner, an accountant. However the Marks family became related to the Sieff family through marriage, and it is these two families together who have controlled the business through most of its history. Indeed Simon Marks (strategic leader from 1916 to 1964 and the man who really established and cemented in place Marks and Spencer's high street dominance), and his successor Marcus Sieff, have both been described as 'retail genius'.

The strategy of M&S then, is concerned with diversification of their product ranges within these broad product groups, but at the same time seeking to specialize where their own St Michael label could be used effectively. All M&S products have traditionally carried the M&S name and quite often the St Michael brand. At the beginning of the new millennium a decision was made to reduce the emphasis on using the St Michael brand name and emphasize the company name more prominently. M&S seeks to innovate whilst upgrading and adding value to its existing ranges. Over the years, M&S has found that many of its long-established stores in town and city centres are simply too small. An expansion programme has therefore developed along several lines. Adjacent units have been acquired when practical and new larger stores created, especially in new out-of-town shopping centres; if land has been available, buildings have been extended; and new sales floors have been opened up by converting stockrooms and moving stock to outside warehouses. This brings its own logistics problems. Satellite stores – smaller branches some distance away from the main branch – have been opened in certain towns. These satellites typically carry complete ranges – it might be men's fashions, ladies' clothes or children's items. The choice depends on the square footage available and the local prospects for particular lines. In a similar vein, in towns considered too small to support a full branch, specialist stores, perhaps just for food, have been opened. M&S Simply Food stores at railway stations and motorway services are very popular. The selection of products within the whole M&S range varies between stores.

Other strategic changes are:

- Constant improvements in displays, partly to present products better, and also to get more items into the stores. 'Sales per square foot' is a vital measure of success.
- Electronic point-of-sale (EPOS). Information technology has been harnessed to improve productivity and to enable M&S to respond more quickly to market changes, particularly relevant for fashion items. Thanks in part to technology, M&S staff costs as a percentage of their turnover are less than those of many competitors, but the quality of service has remained high.

- The development of support financial services, such as unit trusts, building upon the success of the M&S Chargecard, the third most popular credit card in the UK. This business has now been divested.
- International growth in, for example, France, Belgium, Canada, the USA and Hong Kong. The development has been gradual, with one of the objectives being to introduce new types of competition. Some mistakes have been made as part of the learning process, and sales in some countries have been disappointing, but the risks have been contained in order not to threaten the UK interests. China has been added to the list in 2008. Recently there have been some withdrawals and attempted withdrawals.

In the 1930s M&S pioneered a new form of inventory control when it designed perforated tags in two identical halves. Half was torn off at the point-of-sale, dropped in a box and then sent to the Baker Street (London) head office, where it was used to direct store replenishment. Over time this enabled M&S to introduce sophisticated replenishment from out-of-town warehouses and reduce the in-store stockrooms in favour of more direct selling space.

M&S possesses a number of identifiable strategic resources which have been instrumental in meeting customer key success factors, and thereby providing long-term profitable returns for shareholders. They include:

Physical resources	The wide range of value-for-money, own-brand products
	The sites and store displays
Intangible resources	Image and reputation
	Staff knowledge, expertise and commitment to service
Capabilities/ processes	Supply-chain management.

While there have been, and continue to be, strategic changes, the fundamental principles or values upon which the business grew and prospered have remained constant until the last few years. These are:

- high-quality, dependable products, styled conservatively and offering good value for money
- good relations with employees, customers, suppliers and other stakeholders
- simple operations
- comfortable stores

- financial prudence (most properties, for example, are freehold – they have not been sold and leased back to fund the expansion).

The foundation for the unique (St Michael) products and competitive prices was the M&S system of supply-chain relationships, a considerable proportion of these being with UK manufacturers for much of its history. In recent years M&S has, somewhat controversially, included more and more goods sourced overseas, sometimes for particular quality issues, but mostly for lower costs. In general, where they have been successful, the arrangements with suppliers have been long term and non-contractual. They are based on mutual trust and common understanding. M&S is actively involved in product specification, input management (to their suppliers), quality control and production scheduling. M&S is frequently the supplier's most important customer. Why has it worked so effectively? The M&S reputation for fair dealing – with its suppliers, customers and employees – has for many years been seen as too valuable to put at risk.

But, at the end of the 1990s, this long-established business was suffering declines in sales and profits. Critics argued that too many product ranges were no longer the winners that people associated with the company, and its management needed strengthening at all levels. Interestingly, this setback occurred in the decade when the company had, for the first time in its history, a chief executive who was not a descendant of one of the Marks or Sieff families.

Simply, Marks and Spencer had:

- 'Taken its eye off' its customers and become over-reliant on its image and reputation
- Become too reliant on (typically UK based) suppliers whose costs were relatively uncompetitive in global terms and at the same time
- Allowed margins to increase gradually, tarnishing the longstanding value for money image
- Lost some of the fashion element in its key clothing ranges.

Peter Drucker (1985) had earlier summarized M&S as 'probably more entrepreneurial and innovative than any other company in Western Europe these last fifty years ... may have had a greater impact on the British economy, and even on British society, than any other change agent in Britain, and arguably more than government or laws'.

Was it conceivable that this visible and successful business was under real threat for the first time? Clara

Freeman (2000), at that time an M&S executive, admitted that M&S 'lost the pace, lost the focus ... no-one saw it coming. It was the classic management story – everything is going swimmingly and you don't tinker with a successful formula. After sales and profits declined, M&S put the magnifying lens on the business and asked what was wrong. Staff and customers told us that the quality was not as consistent as it used to be, and the service needs to be better than it is.'

In 1999 the current Chairman and Chief Executive, Richard Greenbury, announced he would retire early and, after a very visible and acrimonious internal wrangle, a new Chief Executive (Peter Salsbury) was appointed from inside the business. Later, a new Executive Chairman, Luc Van de Velde, previously the head of a major French supermarket chain, was recruited. Several ranges were quickly revamped and successful stock trials accelerated. M&S began to use more demographic and customer data to determine the product ranges for each store – previously stores of roughly the same size had carried similar ranges, regardless of their location. Sales did not pick up as rapidly as had been hoped, and rumours of possible takeover bids appeared in the press. Salsbury resigned as Chief Executive, to be replaced by Roger Holmes, recruited from Kingfisher.

Under Holmes, product ranges were changed again. Clothing was to be designed for people who prefer classic styles and for those who prefer the latest fashions. Leisure clothing has become more prominent. At the same time the branded Per Una range, designed and sourced by George Davies, the entrepreneur responsible for the growth of the Next chain and the introduction of the George clothing range to Asda, has been added. This was a joint venture deal with Davies, an unusual approach for M&S, but it secured the services of a leading designer and it has been very successful. David Beckham has endorsed a range of children's clothing. A number of stores have been sold and leased back to raise cash. A new format for furniture and furnishings, designed by Victor Radice, recruited from Selfridges, was trialled. More and more products are sourced overseas. Staffing levels are tighter than in the past. Sales and profits – and the share price – all improved but not dramatically. Holmes vowed that the company would never be complacent again.

In 2004 the entrepreneur Philip Green (owner of Arcadia and BhS) made a bid for the company, but the M&S Board rejected his offer. Some institutional shareholders were willing to accept it, though. The

Board was provoked, however, to make changes. Vandevelde left, along with Holmes and Radice. The new CEO is Stuart Rose, who had previously been responsible for the turnaround at Arcadia before its sale to Philip Green. Radice's new home store format was dropped and Rose negotiated to sell M&S' financial services business.

Stuart Rose described his approach in an article published in the *Harvard Business Review* in 2007.

- He had seen his immediate priority to be improved stock control – and in turn the supply chain – an increasing number of sub-brands had led to a growth in inventory
- The new store format pioneered by Radice was quickly abandoned but generally store layouts were improved up and down the country
- Financial services were divested and a new deal was struck with George Davies
- It was apparent that he needed to improve the product, improve the stores and improve the service – really the challenge for every retailer all the time! But first it was necessary to be clear just why M&S was as successful as it was – there was complacency about a number of things
- In the past M&S had come to rely on consultants, arguably an over-reliance, and there was now to be more emphasis on in-house solutions
- The senior management team was to be strengthened, although some would be leaving, and more decisions would be devolved to the store management teams, albeit within clear parameters
- Service quality would be pushed with stronger HR policies for staff in the stores
- The company needed to become more demand-led and less supply driven than it had traditionally been
- With clothing there would be three distinct price and quality bands – good, better and best – to give a different market position and appeal. In addition there are autograph designer brands, especially with male fashion. *This proved successful as clothing market shares improved*
- New brand advertising featured recognizable models such as Twiggy and Myleene Klass
- There was continuing innovation including, for example, machine washable men's suits and branded electronics products

- Energy efficiency and organic foods were targeted.

Had he succeeded? The decline was definitely halted and turn around begun. One prescient headline proclaimed 'out of intensive care but not yet fighting fit'. Profits and market shares, especially for clothing, were improved. In 2007/8 pre-tax profits exceeded the £1 billion threshold for the first time in ten years. The shares had performed well. Rose was something of a hero; Philip Green was almost forgotten.

But then the 2008 economic squeeze began to hit the high streets; many retailers were affected to varying degrees. M&S was robustly honest about anticipated profit fall-backs in the future and this became headline news. Food sales were most at risk as M&S was still seen by many as treat food rather than the main weekly shop. The Head of Food left. Rose himself did not escape without criticism – many shareholders were unhappy that he had been made Executive Chairman as well as CEO and would have preferred that the two roles remained split.

References

Drucker, PF (1985) *Innovation and Entrepreneurship*, Heinemann.

Freeman, C (2000) Interview, *Management Today*, January.

Rose, S (2007) Back in Fashion – How We're Reviving a Business Icon, *Harvard Business Review*, May.

Questions

1 Why do you think Marks and Spencer's fortunes changed as quickly as they did? How might such a decline have been avoided?
2 Is it realistic to claim they will 'never be complacent again'? If so, what is required to engineer this?
3 *(If you are an M&S customer …)* Did you notice many changes during recent years?

Task

Research the attempted bid by Philip Green for Marks and Spencer. Do you feel the outcome was 'the best all-round'?

SOURCE: THIS CASE STUDY WAS PREPARED USING PRIMARILY PUBLICLY AVAILABLE SOURCES OF INFORMATION FOR THE PURPOSES OF CLASSROOM DISCUSSION; IT DOES NOT INTEND TO ILLUSTRATE EITHER EFFECTIVE OR INEFFECTIVE HANDLING OF A MANAGERIAL SITUATION.

Case 1.3 then tells the story of how three new airlines failed to really take off as businesses. They all tried to develop a low frills all business class transatlantic service. This case provides an excellent contrast with our opening case, and with the Virgin case that comes later in the chapter – Richard Branson deliberately chose not to develop a business with this particular strategy and **business model** when he started his airline. We discuss business models below.

Case 1.3

Silverjet, Eos and Maxjet   Int

Before Richard Branson decided upon the business model for the hugely successful Virgin Atlantic he considered and rejected the idea of an all business class UK-US service. This was in 1984; maybe twenty years later the world had changed.

In 2002 Lufthansa started such a service between Dusseldorf and Newark, just outside New York City; and in 2005 KLM started a special service to Houston from Amsterdam especially for oil industry executives.

The first all business class service from the UK started in October 2005 when a new American airline, Eos, started flying daily from Stansted to JFK, New York's main international airport. Interestingly Stansted is mostly associated with Ryanair and EasyJet, who offer anything but an all business class service. Two flights per day were promised for 2006, and this did happen on schedule. Eos had been started by an entrepreneur who once worked for British Airways and who had been able to raise private equity funding.

Eos leased a Boeing 757, which with all economy seating would normally carry 228 passengers. With full flat bed seats the loading was 48 passengers. The service level was to be high and return flights were priced at £3500 or US$6500. This was slightly lower than BA but higher than American Airlines. But arguably the seats and service were better than normal business class; more like first class.

Almost immediately afterwards Maxjet, another US carrier, launched its daily all business class service on the same route. Maxjet offered fewer frills and 102 reclining business seats in a Boeing 767. The 767 is slightly bigger than a 757 and can seat 245 all economy. Early booking would secure a one way price of US$1000; later booking would see this double. In 2006 Maxjet started flights from Stansted to Washington Dulles and Las Vegas, but these were not daily flights.

The leading competitor airlines on the transatlantic routes hinted that they were unconcerned that Eos and Maxjet could pose a major threat as they did not have enough flights to offer corporate clients the flexibility they need. BA, for example, has 11 flights every day between London and New York, Virgin and American six each. The point was also made that the key perk of frequent flyer miles – which many executives build up for personal leisure use – was not available. But there was general agreement that break-even should be possible.

In 2006 a third competitor entered the fray. Silverjet was a new airline which would fly between Luton and Newark – one a day at first, rising to three a day. Silverjet's fares were a £1000 return, with a 30 minute checkin at Luton's business terminal – 45 minutes if someone had hold luggage – which seemed a real bonus in comparison to security delays at some airports. Silverjet also had 102 seats in a Boeing 767, but these were superior to those on Maxjet. They reclined further but they were not full flat beds. Optional extras included valet parking and helicopter transfers from the centre of London. The planes had ladies-only toilets and meals could be pre-ordered on line before the flight. Silverjet needed 20,000 passengers per year to break even, roughly 0.5 per cent of the market.

In 2007 both Eos and Maxjet stopped flying the route; they had failed to make money. Silverjet was also struggling financially. Investment from the Middle East might be on offer … but it never

© ANTHONY KAY/FLIGHT/ALAMY

happened, and in 2008 Silverjet also closed down. Its founder insisted the business model was not the real problem, nor was the rising cost of fuel. The problem had been hostile analysts' reports leading to a lack of confidence.

At roughly the same time as Silverjet crashed, Zoom started offering bargain basement prices to fly on a no-frills service between London Gatwick and JFK. Set up by two Scottish entrepreneurs, Zoom had been offering cheap flights between the UK and Canada for five years. However Zoom went into administration in August 2008. At the time it was flying from six airports in the UK to eight transatlantic destinations. Fuel prices had increased its costs and Zoom had unpaid bills. Once its planes were grounded, its passengers were left stranded.

In 2008 British Airways paid £54 million to buy L'Avion, a small all business class airline flying from Paris Orly to Newark. One reason for the purchase was access to take-off and landing slots at Orly.

Question

1 Why do you think these airlines failed to 'take off'?

SOURCE: THIS CASE STUDY WAS PREPARED USING PRIMARILY PUBLICLY AVAILABLE SOURCES OF INFORMATION FOR THE PURPOSES OF CLASSROOM DISCUSSION; IT DOES NOT INTEND TO ILLUSTRATE EITHER EFFECTIVE OR INEFFECTIVE HANDLING OF A MANAGERIAL SITUATION.

It is no longer adequate for organizations to have strong, professional management – if it ever was! – they also need good change management. What works effectively today may not be appropriate tomorrow. Organizations need new visions for the future and the capability to deliver them. They require open communications and a team approach, a willingness to listen and respond to customers, the delegation of real power, the ability to share learning across the organization and the ability to use culture to convey aims and values. Change is seen as an opportunity not a threat. This sometimes implies an entrepreneurial strategic leader. It invariably requires flexibility and innovation, which implies intrapreneurial managers who accept responsibility for driving the change initiatives. Typically such managers will exhibit the following skills and attributes:

- A tolerance of calculated risks
- A combination of **leadership**, general management and financial skills
- Planning, time and project management skills
- Receptiveness to innovation
- A commitment to continuous learning
- A willingness to delegate
- Motivated by factors other than financial gain
- Self-confident, resilient and persevering
- Good communication skills.

Five perspectives on strategy

More than anyone else, Henry Mintzberg has been responsible for drawing attention to alternative views and perspectives on strategy, all of them legitimate. Mintzberg *et al.* (1998) provide an excellent summary of his work on this topic.

The top oval in Figure 1.1 suggests that strategies can be seen in a *visionary* context. Here it is implied that strategy can be considered as a clear strategic purpose, intent and direction for the organization, but without the detail worked out. In a dynamic environment, managers would then determine more detailed and specific strategies in 'real time' rather than exclusively in advance. However, they would always have a framework of direction to guide their decision-making and help them to determine what is appropriate. In addition, some strategies come from a visionary input from an entrepreneurial manager, or strategic leader, who spots an opportunity and is minded to act on it.

This contrasts with some people's thinking that strategy and *planning* are synonymous. Certainly, as we shall see later in this chapter, strategic planning has a crucial role in strategy

Figure 1.1   Five views of strategy

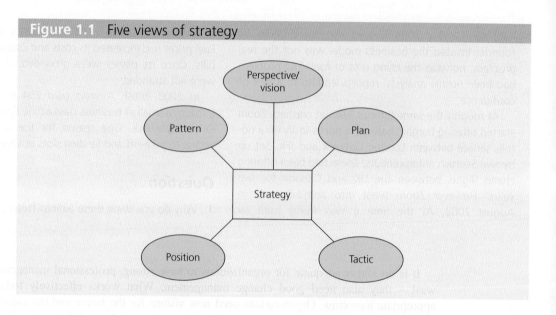

creation, but it does not fully explain how strategies are changed. Both the visionary and planning perspective are concerned with thinking ahead as far as it might be sensible to think and plan. While the *tactical* view is also about the future, it is really about the immediate future. The assumption being made here is that competitors in a dynamic market will constantly adopt new ploys in an attempt to steal a short-term gain or advantage. Their tactics may be easily copied, but there can be some temporary advantage when rivals are caught by surprise and need time to react.

Metaphorically, we can relate these ideas to a game of competitive football. There will be a broad purpose concerned with finishing at a certain level in a league or winning a cup competition, and this will influence the fundamental approach to every game. Sometimes a win would be seen as essential; on other occasions a 'clean sheet' would be more desirable or a draw could be perfectly satisfactory. From this, more detailed game plans will be devised for every match. But, inevitably, 'the best laid schemes o' mice and men gang aft a gley'. Early goals by the opposition can imply a setback and demand that plans are quickly revised and tactics changed. This is always possible at half-time, but during the match the team will have to rely on shouted instructions from the touchline and leadership from the team captain as play continues. Individual players will always be allowed some freedom of movement and the opportunity to show off their particular skills. New tactics will emerge as players regroup and adapt to the circumstances, but quite often games will be turned around by the individual vision, inspiration and brilliance of **key** players.

These three views all concern the future and imply change; the notion of *position* is akin to the idea of freezing time momentarily. It relates to strategic fit and the organization's competitive position at the present time. It is, in effect, a statement of what is happening; and it can be vital for 'taking stock', realizing and clarifying a situation so that future changes are based on clear knowledge rather than assumption.

Of course, organizations come to their present position as a result of decisions taken previously; plans have been implemented and tactics adjusted as events have unfolded. It is again crucial to analyse and understand this evolving *pattern*, appreciating just what has happened, why and how. This can be a valuable foundation for future decisions, plans and actions but, although history can be a guide to the future, rarely in strategy are events repeated without some amendment. The importance of clarifying the pattern from the various decisions and changes also explains why strategy has irreverently been described as a 'series of, mindless, random events, rationalized in retrospect'!

Our understanding of these alternative perspectives will be strengthened when we look at how strategies are created and changed.

In the following sections we look at the Business Model, which focuses on what a business is doing, for whom and how, and **E–V–R** congruence which addresses how well it is doing what it has chosen to do.

The Business Model

When we argue that an organization needs a sound, or a winning, business model we mean that there is a need for very clear picture concerning what the organization is – and what it isn't – and who will buy its products and services, and why. The business model thus embraces three key themes: the product (or service); the market; the 'compelling reason to buy'.

It is important to remember here that strategy always involves choices. Organizations have to make decisions about what they intend to do – at the same time ruling out things it is less appropriate or desirable for them to do. Maybe it is because competition is too intense. Or perhaps they do not possess the required competencies and capabilities. This picture then needs to be communicated and understood throughout the organization. Moreover, the model – and the strategies that underpin it – needs to be reviewed constantly. The picture should embrace the business as it is now, and how it will be in the future – where and how it will change and grow.

The Business Model provides an explanation of an organization's 'recipe for success', and it contains those factors that essentially define the business. It is, in many respects, the vehicle for delivering the purpose or mission. It encapsulates both 'big picture' and 'little picture' elements and it can be applied to both the present and the future. Over time the model, and the strategies it encapsulates, are likely to change, even if the basic purpose remains constant. Put simply, the Business Model should clearly show how the business is going to make money – this can be encapsulated or detailed separately as a **Revenue Model**. Many dot.com businesses essentially failed because they did not address the issue of how they were going to make money. They offered technology to deliver a product that customers simply were not prepared to pay for. They failed to blend business and technology innovation.

Every organization is practising a model, even though it may not have thought it through in any depth. Where this is the case, any success could well be short-lived as it implies there is a reliance on good fortune rather than analytical insight. One might argue that if the model can't be articulated or written down, then the organization's managers don't know what the model is.

It is, of course, important to recognize that good ideas and a plausible outline model are relatively easy to imagine and define … the secret lies in delivering the model and implementing the strategies. In military terms, tactics can be trickier than the grand strategy – even though we clearly need both.

The Business Model is outlined in Figure 1.2 and the elements of this diagram are discussed below.

The three fundamental elements of the model itself are shown at the top, metaphorically mounted on an important base.

Products and services constitute *what* the organization produces or markets. The range can be broad or narrow, focused or diversified. The choice, like the selection of target customers and competitive strategies, implies a decision concerning what to do and what not to do. There needs to be a clear strategic logic for what is in the range. Every one should be able to make a contribution to the business; none of them should be in a position where they bring harm to any of the others because, perhaps, they are under-performing and demanding cash subsidies.

Customers make up markets – they are the *who* in the model. Again the coverage can be narrow or broad. The scope of the business can be localized, national or international. And these can vary between the various products.

The link between products and customers represents the organization's strategic or competitive position. If it is a strong, or a winning, position, then there is a good reason for this.

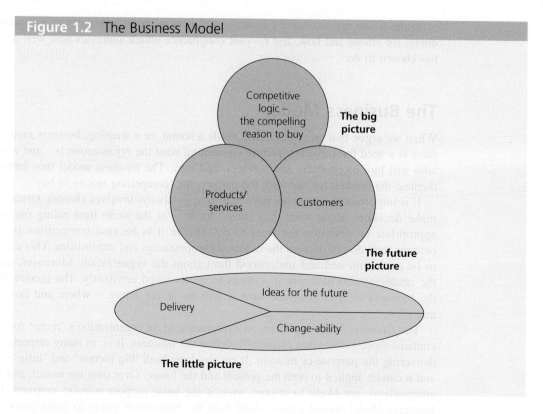

Figure 1.2   The Business Model

When we add the third element, **competitive logic**, we have our *why*, our compelling reason to buy. These three together constitute the organizational 'big picture'. The competitive logic can be based on price; equally it can be based on difference.

We shall see later in the book that there are four basic approaches to the positioning element of the model:

- A narrow product (or service) range for a broad range of customers – the basics of the business model for Starbucks and the low cost airlines
- A broad product range for a defined segment of the market – Harrods provides a vast choice of items for those people who are willing to pay premium prices and who enjoy being seen out with a Harrods bag
- A narrow range for a targeted niche – hand-made Morgan cars appeal to a limited number of people who want a sports car with an essentially pre-war style and who are willing to join a waiting list of some four years duration
- A broad range for a wide market – Amazon.com has added a diverse range of products to its original books and it sells to anyone who is interested in buying on-line.

The **delivery** section of the base is an essential adjunct, even though it may not strictly be part of the outline model. Without a clear strategy for implementing and delivering the model the organization will be compromising on **efficiency** and **effectiveness**. This, then, is the *how* element, and it includes the structure of the organization and the operations and activities carried out by people within the structure. Cost management and synergy are key themes. Unnecessary costs should be avoided; equally it can be a mistake to 'penny-pinch' on things that really matter to customers. At the same time it can be helpful if the activities complement and support each other. This is the 'little picture' behind the 'big picture'.

What works successfully today cannot be guaranteed to work for ever. Business models and strategies have life cycles and therefore organizations must address *when* they might need to make changes. They need an appreciation of a 'future picture', concerning changes to *what, how and for whom*. This is the **future model**.

Essentially the right model changes with circumstances. Therefore developing and adapting the business model is the key to business success. Getting it right is essentially the main test for the top management of any business. When they get the business model wrong profits suffer. The business model must, then, clearly show and prove how an organization is going to make money; and it must address and answer the following questions.

What is different about our value proposition?

Who are our customers?

What do customers value today?

What will customers value tomorrow?

The questions asked of customers should also be addressed of investors. The capital markets need to be convinced that a business understands the needs of investors. If not they will not buy into the business model.

Ensuring the future model can also be delivered when it is needed means that the organization needs *change-ability*, which in turn will be very dependent upon its strategic leadership.

Hamel (2000) argues that new business models are emerging all the time as fresh opportunities are found. Amongst the examples he cites are:

1   Consolidation in the SME sector as large organizations grow bigger by systematically absorbing a series of small (and sometimes local) businesses. Examples include funeral services in the UK; this industry now comprises national organizations which own several 'subsidiaries' which trade as local businesses and small independents which have often evolved as family businesses. We see the same with opticians practices

2   Throwaway varieties of such products as watches and cameras

3   Individual customizing. Collector's editions of the ubiquitous Barbie doll appeal to certain enthusiasts and command a premium price. Apple's iPod allows people to download music of their own choosing to compile a CD of their favourites.

The case illustration of Enterprise Cars (Case 1.4) shows a very successful business model and the following examples of some very different organizations provide further insight into the reality that there is any number of possible models – some of which imply clear choices and compromises. The Dell story (also Case 1.4) illustrates that their relative value may diminish over time.

Case 1.4

The Business Models for Dell Computers & Enterprise Cars   US

Dell

It has been said that Michael Dell, founder and CEO of Dell Computer, became the Henry Ford of the information age – as a mass producer of standardized products. Dell assembles and sells PCs and laptops and, more recently, servers and storage hardware. The company began when Dell was a university student in the 1980s. In the early days Dell sold only to the business market, and, although this remains important, home consumers have been a vital growth area. The business model was simple and powerful – and unusual for the industry.

Dell buys in standardized components in order to minimize the need for any expensive R&D. The company has relied extensively on Intel chips. Sales are direct to customers, typically over the Internet or telephone. Together with a telephone helpline, this alleviates the need for middlemen and the consequential distributor margins. Dell builds to order and carries very little inventory of finished products. This cannot happen effectively without strict attention to detail and constant process re-engineering. The assembly time for a PC was reduced to 4 minutes, with a further 30 seconds allowed to fix the holograms and logos for Microsoft and Intel.

Dell never set out to be a high-technology company, but instead relied on sales and logistics, driven by low costs.

As a result Dell had relatively low costs. It then adopts a very aggressive pricing policy in order to seize market share from any competitor who has 'taken its eye off the ball' and let its costs increase. The assumption was that this business model could be used for other consumer electrical products such as digital music players and flat screen televisions. Some critics always argued that the model has to be limited as a substantial proportion of consumers would be unwilling to buy without being able to inspect a model in a store. But the logic of this argument becomes thinner as more and more of us know people who have bought a Dell – we can inspect theirs.

However by 2005 it was apparent that the sales growth was slowing down. New products – servers and printers, which amounted to two-thirds of sales – were not as successful as PCs, where Dell was selling 1 in every 3 bought in the US.

It was less successful with notebooks, which were being supplied direct from manufacturers in Taiwan. Competitors, especially Hewlett Packard and Acer, had narrowed the price advantage. Between 2000 and 2005 Dell's cost advantage reduced from 20 per cent to 10 per cent and its price advantage more dramatically from 25 per cent to just 5 per cent. In addition it was developing a reputation for inadequate service when something was wrong with a product.

In 2006 the CEO resigned. Kevin Rollins had worked as an external management consultant for Dell prior to joining the business full-time in 1996. He was Number Two to Michael Dell and replaced him as CEO in 2004. He had been responsible for much of the manufacturing efficiency and cost saving. But Dell was accused of 'tunnel vision with its sales model' and Michael Dell felt it necessary to take over again.

Alongside job cuts, the company soon announced a renewed emphasis on product design, confirmed it would increase sales through third party vendors, including systems installers, and seek to acquire other businesses which had more of a customer services focus.

Enterprise Cars

Enterprise Cars was founded in St. Louis, Missouri, in 1957 as a car leasing business. Rentals began in 1963.

Today, with a turnover of multi-billion US dollars, it is the largest car rental business in the US and growing in Europe. It is still a private business controlled by the founding family. The company has over 500,000 vehicles, making it the largest buyer of cars in America. The real growth has occurred in and since the 1990s when the market began to realize the value of the Enterprise business model – which is different from the other majors like Alamo, Avis and Hertz.

The product and the demand

Whereas most car rental businesses specialize in the travelling public, Enterprise focuses on those car owners who have been parted from their own vehicles. This segment has generally been avoided by the other leading competitors. Enterprise customers' cars might be in a garage for service; more likely they have been subject to accident or breakdown. Enterprise staff collect customers from whichever garage they leave their car and drive them to their own compound. That said, Enterprise does also rent cars to people who just want to hire a vehicle.

The customers

Some customers can plan and book in advance, but most are making an inevitable late booking. Consequently they are often people experiencing some sort of distress and agitation because of the uncertainty. In addition, the actual customer might be an insurance company rather than the car owner himself.

Operational aspects

Enterprise is decentralised into over 5000 individual offices with an average of 10 employees each. They are all profit centres. There is extensive monitoring and tracking of cash and profit and customer satisfaction. The stated intention is to make every office feel like a local family business with staff who are 'passionate about service'. There is an extensive graduate recruitment programme to find able young people to work alongside mature, experienced front-line staff. Coffee and doughnuts are provided whilst customers fill in their paperwork.

Questions

1 How would you assess these two business models?
2 Is Dell becoming more robust again?
3 Does Enterprise have a defensible and sustainable model?

William Morrison

The Wm Morrison supermarket group, strongest in the North of England and still a family company in many respects, competes successfully with Tesco, Sainsbury and Asda. Fundamentally the large supermarket chains offer broadly the same product ranges, although there will be some clear differences. Across a wide range of goods there are the leading brands and own-label alternatives, which normally are cheaper.

Morrisons' customers are not going to be markedly different from those who pick Tesco or Asda. They all emphasize competitive prices. Location, of course, and convenience will influence customer choice. Sainsbury is somewhat different as their prices overall are slightly higher. Waitrose (owned by John Lewis) and Marks and Spencer, with a focus on premium products and higher prices, have a different market appeal. So where is the Morrisons 'compelling reason to buy'?

The Morrison strategy is not identical to those of its rivals. Morrison focuses on a composite package of 'everyday low prices' (which itself isn't unique – both Asda and Tesco claim the same), multi-buys and special offers. Unusually it also manufactures a substantial proportion of its own food products, even owning its own abattoirs. It packages most of its own fresh food and displays them in-store as they would feature in a traditional open street market. This is very deliberate and it reflects Morrisons' origins as market traders. In addition, every store looks the same. Bananas are hung up to keep them fresh, when normally they will be laid out in trays. Again unusually, it owns its own delivery fleet rather than relying on specialist logistics companies. In a Morrisons store you will see fishmongers and butchers in white hats and striped aprons – which is pretty ubiquitous – but they will be found in a section of the store which is designed to feel like an open street market. The focus is on food; Morrisons is less interested than its main rivals in clothing and other non-food products. There are no on-line sales and no loyalty cards.

In this respect we can see Morrisons' Northern roots being strongly reflected in its ambience and culture. Some would argue that these Northern roots are also reflected in Morrisons taking more trade credit days from its suppliers than any of its leading rivals. In recent years Morrisons has had to make certain changes and compromises in the details as it has absorbed the Safeway stores it acquired when it took over that business, but the basic fundamentals of the business model have been retained.

Avon

Like Dell, Avon's business model is also built around direct selling. Avon was 120 years old in 2006, having started life as the California Perfume Company. Most of us would recognize the brand from the 'army' of Avon ladies who deliver catalogues to their customers every few weeks, take their orders and later deliver their choices. Customers pay their local agent. The products themselves are manufactured in various countries around the world.

Although the direct selling remains constant, other elements of the model are constantly changing. Existing product ranges are likely to change at any time; and new products are added, often replacing poor-selling items. Packaging often changes to freshen the appearance of products. No two catalogues are identical, although some products do appear regularly; and there are always special offers. More recently 'well-ness' products for health- and fitness-conscious customers have been included. These range from vitamin supplements to yoga mats. Avon 'Cosmeceuticals', brands endorsed by dermatologists, fit somewhere between medications and cosmetics.

Avon has also diversified to widen its overall customer appeal. It became prominent as a convenient supplier to 'middle class mothers' who were short of time for personal shopping, but this is no longer adequate. Although the average age of Avon's customers is around 39, this average is falling slowly. In part this is affected by the wider product choices; it is also enhanced by the choice of younger role models to promote the products. Actress Reese Witherspoon, model

Yasmin le Bon and, in the past, tennis starts, Serena and Venus Williams, are included here. In addition, in the US, Avon has developed its new Mark range for 16–24-year-old customers.

Like Ikea, Avon has seen the benefit of moving into China and Russia, two huge consumer markets. However direct selling is illegal in China and so Avon trades through specialist boutiques.

London Zoo

In the case of London Zoo we can see evidence of difficult decisions concerning 'products' and customers. Without at least some retailing activities London Zoo would be out of business. A part of the Zoological Society of London, the zoo has a key scientific purpose related to conservation and the preservation of endangered species. However, those animals that are particularly attractive to most paying visitors are often not the most endangered. Moreover, there is a duty to educate as a large proportion of the visitors are children. Many national animal collections around the world are much more heavily subsidized, but in recent years London Zoo has not been allowed to become grant-dependent. It has had to establish a revenue-generating business model without losing sight of its origins and fundamental purpose – within the constraint of its location in a Royal Park which seriously affects any possibility of expansion. London Zoo has therefore had to build a model which balances conservation, education and entertainment.

The Opera

Globally, opera can only survive if it is subsidized, so again the business model must embrace this. The subsidy can be from government – in the UK the Arts Council, which, for example, accounts for 30 per cent of the budget at The Royal Opera House – or corporate and private donors.

Customers are willing to pay very high prices for the best seats as long as the quality performance merits it. And many opera-goers are discerning. In part opera is expensive because it demands a large number of singers and musicians. In the UK, prices for The Royal Opera House Covent Garden rise to over £160.00 – although the cheapest restricted view seats can sometimes be bought for £3.00. The Metropolitan in New York has top prices of around US$300.00. But opera houses have to be maintained through the year and orchestras retained. They are not going to be full of customers every night of the year. The market is too limited for that.

Opera has long enjoyed an elitist image; opera-goers are so-called aficionados. And yet the reality has changed in recent years. The opera 'product' now extends well beyond the world's leading opera houses. The change began when *Nessun Dorma* was used as the theme music for the 1990 football World Cup and, on the back of this, the concert by 'The Three Tenors' was broadcast to the world on television and the accompanying CD became the best-selling classical album of all time. More recently more populist singers like Lesley Garrett, Russell Watson and Katherine Jenkins, have brought operatic arias to an ever-wider audience. And who will ever forget Julia Roberts being introduced to the opera in the film *Pretty Woman* and being so moved she almost 'peed in her pants'!

In other words, the opera 'product' now encapsulates CD and popular television as well as actual performances for a growing and changing market. The leading singers have been very carefully 'packaged' and marketed to give them a wider appeal.

Manchester United

Manchester United is far more than a successful football club. It is a collection of diversified but related activities that can be associated with a distinctive brand – a brand which signifies success, such that association with it automatically implies being part of something that is successful. It reflects high **quality** – and consequently customers expect to have to pay premium prices to buy this association. The 'core market' might be the 70,000 plus fans who turn up at Old Trafford for Premier League matches, but there are many more people all round the world who are interested in having some part of this success story. In Porter terminology, Manchester United is very clearly differentiated – and very profitable.

Divine Chocolate

The main chocolate brands in the UK and elsewhere might be Cadbury's and Nestle, but there are clear niche opportunities as well. Divine Chocolate is marketed as 'heavenly chocolate with a heart'. It is, though, a Fairtrade social enterprise, one of a number in this industry. The business was set up in 1997 by a Farmer's Co-operative in Ghana, and the farmers retain a 45 per cent share. The lead owner is a Dutch fairtade enterprise, but the business is based in the UK where there are 16 employees. Manufacture is close to where the cocoa beans are grown. The European turnover is some £10 million per year, but the UK chocolate market alone is some £4.6 billion a year. But Divine is available in leading supermarkets, including Tesco, Waitrose and Asda, and it provides own-label products to Starbucks. The cocoa bean growers are guaranteed a fair price for their beans and they receive annual dividends; as a consequence customers will generally be asked to pay a premium price.

Drawing upon this introduction to the business model we can restate strategy as a set of four visions or articulated pictures for:

- The businesses and industries the organization should be in – its corporate strategy
- How it will compete in each one in its search for advantage – which takes in its targeted customers
- How every activity which supports these strategies can be linked effectively to create synergy and avoid fragmentation
- How and when to change strategies.

It will be appreciated that all of these support the essential purpose of the organization.

Functional, competitive and corporate strategies

Figure 1.3 reflects that there are three distinct perspectives of strategic analysis:

1 The strategic environment
2 The competing organization
3 The individual strategist.

The diagram summarizes three distinct, but interrelated and interdependent, levels of strategy: corporate (the whole organization), competitive (the distinct strategy for each constituent business, product or service in the organization) and functional (the activities which underpin the competitive strategies).

Simply, most organizations choose to produce one or more related or unrelated products or services for one or more markets or market segments. Consequently, the organization should be structured to encompass this range of product markets or service markets. As the number and diversity of products increases the structure is likely to be centred on divisions which are sometimes referred to as **strategic business units** (SBUs). Such SBUs are responsible individually for developing, manufacturing and marketing their own product or group of products. Each SBU will therefore have a strategy, which Porter (1980) calls a **competitive strategy**. Competitive strategy is concerned with 'creating and maintaining a competitive advantage in each and every area of business' (Porter, 1980). It can be achieved through any one function, although it is likely to be achieved through a unique and distinctive combination of functional activities. For each functional area of the business, such as production, marketing and human resources the company will have a functional strategy. It is important that **functional strategies** are designed and managed

Figure 1.3   Levels of strategy

in a co-ordinated way so that they interrelate with each other and at the same time collectively allow the competitive strategy to be implemented properly.

Successful competitive and functional strategies add value in ways which are perceived to be important by the company's stakeholders, especially its customers, and which help to distinguish the company from its competitors. Mathur and Kenyon (1998) reinforce these points and contend that competitive advantage is fundamentally about the positioning and fit of an organization in its industry or market, and that success is based on distinct differences and sound cost management.

Corporate strategy, essentially and simply, is deciding what businesses the organization should be in and how the overall group of activities should be structured and managed. It has been described by Porter as 'the overall plan for a diversified business', although it is perfectly acceptable for a business to elect to stay focused on only one product or service range. This does happen in many companies, especially small businesses. In this case the corporate and competitive strategies are synonymous. Corporate strategy for a multibusiness group is concerned with maintaining or improving overall growth and profit performance through **acquisition**, organic investment (internally funded growth), **divestment** and closure. The term strategic perspective is often used to describe the range and diversity of activities, in other words the corporate strategy. Each activity then has a competitive position or strategy. The management of corporate strategy concerns the creation and safeguarding of *synergies* from the portfolio of businesses and activities.

Synergy and change

Synergy (defined in Box 1.1) is a critical aspect of both corporate and competitive strategies. It is important that the functions and businesses within an organization work collectively and support each other to improve effectiveness and outcomes.

All the time, companies should carry out efficiently those activities which are essential for creating a distinctive or differentiated competitive position, and avoid incurring unnecessary costs by providing non-essential values. This implies that they clearly understand their markets, their customers and the key success factors that they must meet, i.e. their defined competitive

Figure 1.4 Strategic success through complementary activities

strategy. Moreover, they should constantly seek improvement by driving their operating efficiencies. These activities will be encapsulated in the organization's functional strategies, as illustrated in Figure 1.4.

Figure 1.4 highlights that these functional strategies must fit a defined, clear competitive strategic position and complement each other to achieve internal synergy. Where they fail to complement each other the company's competitive position will inevitably be weakened. The outcome will be a strong competitive position which can only be sustained by innovation and improvement, and sometimes by the move to a new competitive **paradigm**. Managing these changes effectively is very dependent upon the style and approach of the strategic leader and the culture and values of the organization. Michael Porter (1996) has argued along similar lines.

It is important to remember, though, that people are often naturally competitive and their competitive energy should be directed against external rivals rather than members of their own organization. Carefully managed, internal competition for scarce resources can, of course, sharpen managerial skills.

E–V–R congruence

If one wished to claim that an organization was being managed effectively from a strategic point of view, one would have to show, first, that its managers appreciated fully the dynamics, opportunities and threats present in their competitive environment, and that they were paying due regard to wider societal issues; and, secondly, that the organization's resources (inputs) were being managed strategically, taking into account its strengths and weaknesses, and that the organization was taking advantage of its opportunities. Key success factors and **core competencies** would be matched.

The factors behind these matching issues are ubiquitously listed in the form of a **SWOT analysis**, a simple framework that most readers will already be familiar with. SWOT stands for:

Strengths	)
Weaknesses	) the (internal) resource themes
Opportunities	)
Threats	) the (external) environmental themes.

Effective matching will not just happen, though. It needs to be managed. Moreover, potential new opportunities need to be sought and resources developed. It is also important, therefore, that the values of the organization match the needs of the environment and the key success factors. It is the values and culture that determine whether the environment and resources are currently matched, and whether they stay congruent in changing circumstances.

Values are traditionally subsumed as a resource in a SWOT (strengths, weaknesses, opportunities, threats) analysis, but it is useful to separate them out. The notion of E–V–R (environment–values–resources) congruence then is an integration of these issues. Basically, there is an overlap between the environment (key success factors) and resources (competencies and capabilities), and the organization is committed to sustaining this overlap with effective strategic change initiatives. This notion of E–V–R congruence is illustrated in the top left diagram in Figure 1.5 and the case story on The National Trust (Case 1.5).

The value of E–V–R analysis is that it provides a straightforward framework for assessing the organization's existing strategies and strategic needs. It is crystal clear at a conceptual level what organizations have to achieve and sustain strategically; the challenge then is to use the logic to explore and create opportunities and ways for achieving and sustaining congruence by dealing with the various, but different, risks that organizations have to manage if they are to avoid crises in the face of uncertainty.

If we conclude that an organization does enjoy E–V–R congruence it is important to test its robustness. Conceptually the three circles can merely overlay each other, and be easily pulled apart. Alternatively, like the old magician's trick, they can seem like inter-locking circles which seem difficult to separate.

The other four illustrations in Figure 1.5 illustrate alternative instances of incongruence. E–V–R analysis can be applied at more than one level; and consequently different managers should be in positions where they can address which of the alternatives in Figure 1.5 best represents their organization and their individual business. Having selected the one that they feel best sums up the present situation, they can immediately see the direction and thrust of the changes that are needed to create or restore congruency.

Managers at the individual business level might find it more expedient to recast the mnemonic E–V–R with three Cs – Customer expectations (for E); Competencies and capabilities (for R); and Culture (for V).

Working downwards from the top left in the figure, a 'lost organization' is seen next. Possibly there was congruency at some time, but now products, services and markets are out of alignment and the values inappropriate. Without major changes to strategy, structure and style, almost certainly involving a change of strategic leader, an organization in this situation has no future. This degree of incongruence would be relatively unusual, but the other three possibilities are not.

The 'consciously incompetent' organization is aware of the needs for success in its marketplace, and managers appreciate the importance of satisfying its customers, but it is simply not achieving the desired level of service and quality. Managers may well have some insight into what might be improved but not be in a position to achieve this improvement. Maybe there is a key resource shortage of some form or a lack of investment, or a person or people with key skills have left and not been replaced. Possibly too many managers are unwilling to grasp the changes that are needed and accept **empowerment** and responsibility. It is typical for a company in this situation to be constantly fighting crises and problems. Because of the customer orientation, there will be a commitment to resolving the problems and difficulties and, for this reason, some customers may be somewhat tolerant. However, the organization is likely to be highly reactive and, consequently, again the position cannot be sustained indefinitely. A more proactive and entrepreneurial approach will be required to strengthen the resource base and restore congruency with a fresh strategic position.

In contrast, the 'unconsciously competent' organization enjoys **strategic positioning** without any real commitment, especially to improvement and change. Things are working, at a surface level and possibly with some element of luck. Any success is taken for granted. The organization is unable to exploit its strengths and, if it fails to address this, then E and R will drift apart over

Figure 1.5 E–V–R congruence

E–V–R congruence

The lost organization

The consciously incompetent organization

The unconsciously competent organization

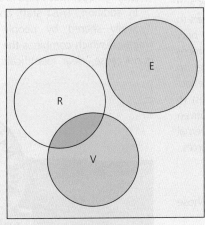

Strategic drift

Case 1.5

The National Trust   UK

The National Trust acquires and preserves countryside and historic places of interest in the UK 'for the benefit of us all', generally allowing access to members and fee-paying visitors. The National Trust is now responsible for over 900 square miles of land, 700 miles of coastline and over 250 houses and gardens. The Trust's estate comprises 28 castles, 66 nature reserves, 4000 ancient monuments, 37,000 buildings and 57 villages.

The Trust relies heavily on members' subscriptions to help to fund its various activities; and gifts and endowments, together with limited government funding, enable new acquisitions. There is additional revenue from non-member admission charges, holidays on its properties and the National Trust shops. Its income opportunities will always be constrained by its general purpose and mission. Any events held on Trust properties would have to be 'in keeping'. Foreign visitors with only limited time in the UK are perhaps likely to favour other attractions with a stronger tourist theme.

Maintenance standards are high and expensive, and conservation is seen as more important than commercial exploitation, and, where necessary, access. On occasions, but not very often, the numbers of visitors will be restricted either directly or indirectly by, for example, limiting the parking facilities. National Trust membership doubled from 1 million to 2 million during the 1980s and continued to grow, albeit at a slower rate, during the 1990s. It now exceeds 3.5 million in England, Wales and Northern Ireland. Generally The National Trust appears to display E-V-R congruence but a dilemma and a new challenge for the National Trust would arise if a more commercial orientation became necessary in order to fund desired activities. It is, therefore, interesting to reflect upon how difficult it might be for the National Trust to create and retain E-V-R congruence. It is a values-driven organization and there will be occasions when external (commercial) pressures threaten its values and resources.

Environment

The stakeholders and interested parties – those whose interests the Trust must serve – are:

- National Trust members and visitors
- donors of properties
- conservation agencies and ramblers' associations
- financial benefactors
- National Trust employees
- Government, and
- the nation as a whole.

Resources

The skills required are:

- property management – both upkeep of the buildings and the management of land resources; large areas of farmland are leased
- expertise in arts and furnishings
- public relations and marketing.

Values

The National Trust has proved successful in developing and deploying resources to meet the needs and expectations of its stakeholders. Staff are typically more 'property management' orientated than they are marketing orientated, but they are knowledgeable and expert. Preservation and the presentation of the properties to the standard maintained by their original owners are seen as important aspects of the service by both the Trust employees and its members. Theme parks and activities have never had a place in the National Trust; and there is a high moral tone to every activity, including the National Trust shops which tend to sell high-quality selected products at premium prices.

In addition, Trust staff appear to share an ethos (typically shared by people who work for other charities) which combines the feeling of working for a good cause, clear identification with its purpose and

© ICP / ALAMY

principles, and a certain readiness to accept lower rewards than those normally earned in manufacturing and service businesses.

However, in 2007, the National Trust declared it wished to become 'the largest green movement in the world'. It would seek to drive the conservation and quality of life agendas and combat climate change. In the past the Trust has generally been cautious about being vociferous.

Questions

1   How difficult will it have been for the National Trust to continue to grow during the current (2009) economic recession?
2   Should it seek to do this or consolidate?
3   Which strategy is more likely to help it maintain (or attain) E–V–R congruence?

time, possibly sooner rather than later, to create a lost organization. The required change in culture and values probably implies a change of leadership, certainly of leadership style, to increase **decentralization** and empowerment.

'Strategic drift' is commonplace. An organization which is internally cohesive simply loses touch with its environment. Demands may change, and fresh competition may make the company's products and services less attractive than in the past. The challenge then concerns realignment in a dynamic environment, which certainly requires a change in management style and, possibly again, leadership. This organization desperately needs new ideas, which may already be available inside the organization, but have not been captured.

An article by Peter Drucker (1994) complements both this model and these arguments when he states that all organizations have implicit or explicit 'theories' for their business, incorporating:

- assumptions about the environment, specifically markets, customers and important technologies
- assumptions about its mission or purpose, and
- assumptions about the core (content) competencies required to fulfil the mission.

These assumptions, at any time, must be realistic, congruent, communicated and understood; to achieve this they must be evaluated regularly and rigorously.

Pümpin (1987) uses the term strategic excellence positions (SEPs) to describe 'capabilities which enable an organization to produce better-than-average results over the longer term compared with its competitors'. SEPs imply that organizations appreciate the views of customers and develop the capabilities required to satisfy these needs. Moreover, they are perceived by their customers to be a superior competitor because of their skills and accomplishments.

It is important to deploy resources and to focus the drive for excellence (an aspect of the organization's culture) on issues which matter to customers. IBM, for example, have succeeded historically by concentrating on service, Rolls Royce motor cars on image and quality, and Procter & Gamble on advertising and **branding**.

Businesses should seek to develop competitive advantage and a strategic excellence position for each product and service. Overall E–V–R congruence then depends on these SEPs together with any corporate benefits from linkages and interrelationships.

The development of SEPs and E–V–R congruence takes time, and requires that all functional areas of the business appreciate which factors are most significant to customers. Once achieved, however, it cannot be assumed that long-term success is guaranteed. Situations change and new windows of opportunity open. The demand for guaranteed overnight parcel deliveries anywhere in the country, and immediate services within cities, opened up the opportunity for couriers; new technologies used in laptop computers, facsimile machines and the Internet have created demand and behaviour changes. Competitors may behave unexpectedly, and consequently there is a need for strategic awareness and for monitoring potential change situations.

Bettis and Prahalad (1995) argue that business decisions are affected by a 'dominant logic', championed by the strategic leader and communicated through the organization. This could be an articulated vision or a culturally integrated paradigm concerning 'what the business is about and how things get done'. It is shown next how strategic regeneration implies that this logic needs to be changed. IBM's growth and early industry dominance was built on a belief that mainframe computers were essential for organizations. Competitors such as Microsoft, which concentrated on software, highlighted that IBM's logic was outdated and it needed to be 'unlearned'. New products and new processes alone would prove inadequate. The new logic is one of decentralized personal computers in the hands of knowledgeable workers.

Organizations, therefore, should build on their past successes while always realizing that the past may not be the best guide to the future.

1.2 Strategic management

The strategic management process

All newly appointed chief executives should ask five key questions:

- *What are the basic goals of the company?*
- *What is the strategy for achieving these goals?*
- *What are the fundamental issues facing the company?*
- *What is its culture?*
- *And is the company organized in a way to support the goals, issues and culture?*

BOB BAUMAN, EX-CHIEF EXECUTIVE OF SMITHKLINE BEECHAM

When Sir Ian MacGregor took over the ailing British Steel Corporation he met each senior executive face-to-face and asked him to justify the existence of his part of the organization. Each one was given a maximum of ten minutes.

Traditionally, courses in strategic management have been built around three important elements:

- strategic *analysis*
- strategy *creation and choice*
- strategy *implementation.*

These three elements are shown in Figure 1.6, together with the key aspects of strategy that relate to them.

In this book, however, we typically use the term 'strategic awareness' to embrace the analysis of the current situation and an assessment of the routes forward that are available, and 'strategic change' to reflect the selection of the route to follow and its implementation all within the overall purpose of the organization.

Strategic management, then, involves awareness of how successful and strong the organization and its strategies are, and of how circumstances are changing. At any time, previously sound products, services and strategies are likely to be in decline, or threatened by competition. As this happens, new 'windows of opportunity' are opening for the vigilant and proactive companies.

New strategies must be created which may be changes to the corporate portfolio or changes at the competitive level. Sometimes these strategic ideas will emerge from formal planning processes; at other times, and particularly in the case of functional and competitive strategies, changes will emerge as managers throughout the organization try out new ideas.

Figure 1.6 Strategic management

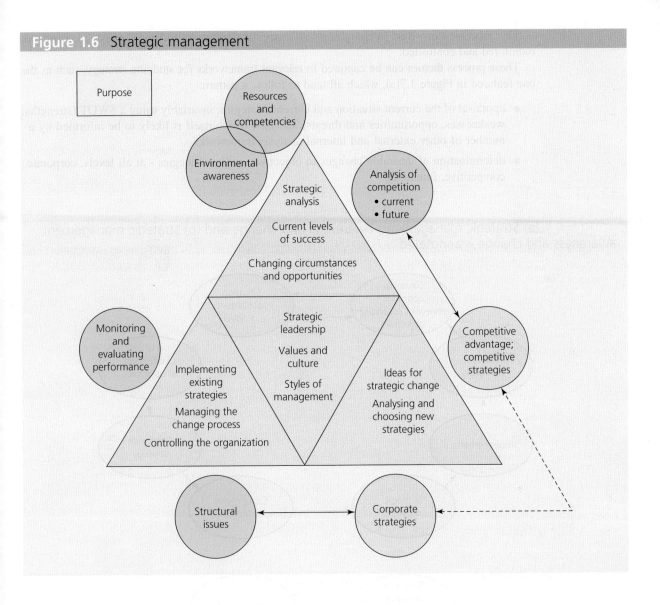

The actual strategies being pursued at any time reflect the organization's strategy content, and the important issues are:

- the ability of the organization to add value in meaningful ways, which exploit organizational resources to achieve synergy, and at the same time
- satisfy the needs of the organization's major stakeholders, particularly its shareholders and customers.

The selection of new strategies must take account of these criteria.

Existing and new strategies must be implemented. A strategy is only useful when it has been implemented, and hence the organization must have an appropriate structure, clear and contributory functional strategies and systems which ensure that the organization behaves in a cohesive rather than a fragmented way. The larger or more diverse the organization becomes, the more likely it is that this becomes a problem. In multiproduct, multinational organizations with considerable interdependence between the products or services and between subsidiaries, for example, divisions may become competitive with each other and not pull together.

The processes involved in designing and carrying through any changes must be managed, monitored and controlled.

These process themes can be captured in relevant frameworks for studying strategy, such as the one featured in Figure 1.7(a), which all tend to follow a pattern:

- appraisal of the current situation and current strategies, invariably using a SWOT (strengths, weaknesses, opportunities and threats) analysis, which itself is likely to be informed by a number of other external and internal analysis frameworks
- determination of desirable changes to objectives and/or strategies - at all levels, corporate, competitive, functional

Figure 1.7   (a) Strategic management: awareness and change and (b) strategic management: awareness and change – annotated

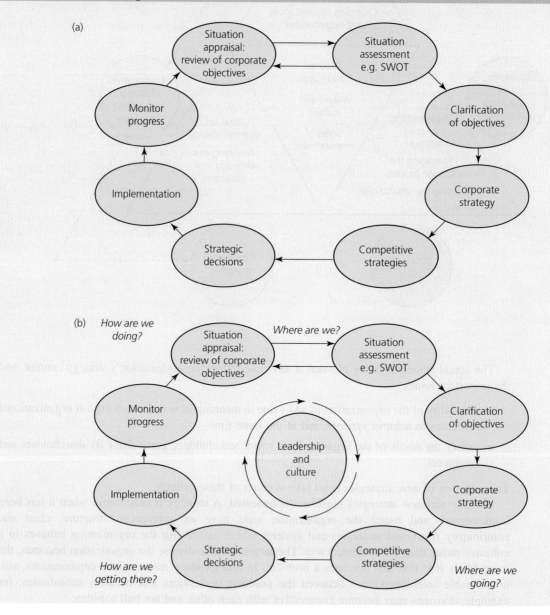

- a search for, and choice of, suitable courses of action
- implementation of the changes
- monitoring progress; ongoing appraisal.

Historically this process model has been seen as a deterministic framework for strategy creation and strategic management. However, whilst this framework certainly helps us to understand strategy, this is not the same as implying that effective strategies can always be created by systematically following the steps in a model such as this. Such an approach would imply that strategy is top-down and leader-driven, that creating routes forward is relatively straightforward and that the majority of problems are likely to be found at the implementation stage. This is not altogether realistic; and, in fact, many strategic leaders have confirmed it does not reflect the reality of strategic decision-making in practice.

Figure 1.7(a) therefore shows the process as an unbroken circle rather than a sequential analysis. Figure 1.7(b) goes a stage further and annotates this basic process model by, first, adding a number of key questions which, realistically, organizations, and managers at various levels in the hierarchy, not just the most senior layer, should be addressing *all the time*. These are not issues which only need to be considered once a year as part of a planning cycle; in dynamic environments circumstances are changing all the time and organizations must continuously search for new opportunities as well as appreciating the reactive changes to strategies and tactics that are required in order to remain effective. Leadership and culture have also been placed in the centre of the diagram, illustrating their critical impact on strategic decision making and strategic performance. Arguably, strategy and strategic change in organizations cannot be understood without some understanding of the contribution of the strategic leader and the way in which the culture acts either as stimulus or constraint on the necessary changes.

The way that an organization is structured into divisions and/or functions, and the amount of authority delegated to individual managers must inevitably influence day-to-day decision-making. These 'coal-face' decisions determine the actual strategies pursued and the levels of success. The objectives that an organization is pursuing in reality therefore stem from strategy implementation. In order to appreciate properly just how well an organization is doing relative to both its objectives and its competitors, to explore opportunities and threats, to appraise strengths and weaknesses, to evaluate alternative courses of action and so on, it is vital to have an effective information system. How an organization gathers and uses information is therefore another important aspect of strategic management.

A strategic management framework

> *To turn really interesting ideas and fledgling technologies into a company that can continue to innovate for years requires a lot of disciplines.*
>
> STEVE JOBS, CEO, APPLE COMPUTERS

> *The best way to predict the future is to invent it.*
>
> JOHN SCULLEY, WHEN CHAIRMAN, APPLE COMPUTERS

Figure 1.8 re-presents the constituent elements of strategy as a set of twelve questions concerning strategic awareness and strategic change.

Moving from left to right, the questions follow a logical sequence. If an organization needs to take stock of just where it is placed at the moment, evaluate emerging opportunities and threats before clarifying a set of objectives for which strategies, both corporate and competitive, can be evaluated, selected and implemented, then the model can be used in a sequential, and possibly iterative, way. It will be seen that information (the bottom box) implies monitoring and continuity.

However, these questions can also be thought of as a set of important issues that managers everywhere in the organization should be addressing all the time in a turbulent environment.

Figure 1.8 A strategy framework based on a series of questions

Nevertheless, they still need to be presented in a clear framework to ensure that any issues emerging can be placed in context, and any proposed changes assessed for their impact on other issues.

If managers seek answers to these questions continuously, and make and carry out appropriate strategic decisions, they will improve the performance and effectiveness of their organization by:

- generating increased strategic awareness
- ensuring that functional managers appreciate the strategic environment and the implications of decisions concerning individual products, services and markets; and
- making decisions about the need for, and appropriateness of, particular change opportunities.

1.3 Strategy creation

This section looks in greater detail at how strategies are changed and new strategies created. Points discussed in the earlier sections are now taken up.

Opportunities for change

A wise man will make more opportunities than he finds.

FRANCIS BACON

It is vital that managers are strategically aware both of potentially threatening developments and of opportunities for profitable change, and that they seek to match and improve the fit between the environment and the organization's resources.

There is, however, no single recommended approach for seeking out and pursuing new opportunities. There is a broad spectrum ranging from what might be termed entrepreneurial opportunism to what Quinn (1980) calls '**logical incrementalism**'.

Strategic change can be relatively evolutionary or gradual, or much more dramatic or revolutionary. The nature of the opportunities (and threats) is directly related to both the general and the specific industry environments; and the approach that particular organizations take in seeking to match resources to the environment is dependent on the basic values of the organization and the style of the strategic leader. However, as will be seen, it does not follow that the strategic leader is the sole manager of strategic change.

Effectively managed change requires a vision of the future – where the organization is heading or wants to go – together with the means for creating and reaching this future. Planning a way forward from where the organization is now may not be enough to create the future vision; at the same time, when there is a vision, it is illogical to set off in pursuit without the appropriate 'equipment'. There must be a clear vision of a route, and this requires planning; on the way, managers should stay alert for dangers and opportunity (see Figure 1.9). Well-tracked routes (strategies that have proved successful in the past) and experience can both be beneficial, but in a dynamic environment there will always be an element of the unknown.

Planning and strategy creation

All managers plan. They plan how they might achieve objectives. Planning is essential to provide direction and to ensure that the appropriate resources are available where and when they are needed for the pursuit of objectives. Sometimes the planning process is detailed and formal; on other occasions planning may be informal, unstructured and essentially 'in the mind'. In the context of strategy formulation a clear distinction needs to be made between the cerebral activity of informal planning ('planning strategy') and formalized planning systems ('**strategic planning**').

Formal strategic planning systems are most useful in stable conditions. Environmental opportunities and threats are forecast, and then, as we saw earlier, strategies are planned and implemented. Strategies which are appropriate, feasible and desirable are most likely to help the organization to achieve its mission and objectives.

Where the environment is more turbulent and less predictable, strategic success requires flexibility, and the ability to learn about new opportunities and introduce appropriate changes continuously. Planning systems can still make a valuable contribution but the plans must not be inflexible.

In addition, it is important not to discount the contribution of visionary strategic leaders who become aware of opportunities – and on occasions, create new opportunities – and take risks

Figure 1.9   Strategic change

based on their awareness and insight of markets and customers. Stelios Haji-Ioannou, founder of EasyJet and various other ventures using the 'Easy' brand, is an ideal example.

Formal strategic planning implies determined actions for achieving stated and desired objectives. For many organizations these objectives will focus on sales growth and **profitability**. A detailed analysis of the strategic situation will be used to create a number of strategic alternatives, and then certain options will be chosen and implemented.

Planning systems are useful, and arguably essential, for complex or diversified organizations with a large number of businesses that need integrating. There are several possible approaches. Head office can delegate the detailed planning to each division, offering advice and making sure that the plans can be co-ordinated into a sensible total package. Alternatively, the planning system can be controlled centrally in order to establish priorities for resource allocation.

While the discipline of planning and setting priorities is valuable, the plans must not be inflexible and incapable of being changed in a dynamic competitive environment. During implementation it is quite likely that some plans will be discarded and others modified.

Visionary and entrepreneurial leadership

Strategic planning systems imply that strategies are selected carefully and systematically from an analytical process. In other instances major strategic changes will be decided upon without lengthy formal analysis. Typically such changes will reflect strong, entrepreneurial leadership and be visionary and discontinuous: I have seen the future and this is it! A good example is provided by Richard Branson and Virgin (Case 1.6).

Case 1.6

Richard Branson and Virgin   UK

Sir Richard Branson is unquestionably a legend in his own lifetime. His name and presence are associated closely with all the Virgin activities and businesses, and he has demonstrated a unique ability to exploit a brand name and apply it to a range of diversified products and services. He *is* Virgin – so, will he leave a lasting business legacy like Ray Kroc (McDonald's) has done? Can this diverse business outlive its founder? Or would Virgin be split up into its many constituent businesses without Branson to lead it?

Branson is creative, opportunistic and dedicated to those activities in which he engages. Possessed of a strong ego, he is an excellent self-publicist. Popular with customers and employees, he has created a hugely successful people-driven business. His determination to succeed and his willingness to take risks are manifest in his trans-Atlantic power boating and round-the-world ballooning exploits. Although he has said that he 'wouldn't do this if I didn't think I'd survive', the *Financial Times* has commented that 'all those associated with Mr. Branson have to accept that he is an adventurer … he takes risks few of us would

contemplate'. He has chosen to enter and compete in industries dominated by large and powerful corporations. Having challenged British Airways very visibly, for example, Coca-Cola has also been a target. He is now offering pioneering short passenger flights into space. Significantly, and not unexpectedly, his name comes up frequently when other business people are asked to name the person they most admire.

Now around 60 years old, Branson has been running businesses for some 40 years; and from nothing he has built a personal fortune of £3 billion. He began *Student* magazine when he was a 16-year-old public schoolboy, selling advertising from a public phone booth. Ever opportunistic, he incorporated a mail-order record business, buying the records from wholesalers once he had a firm order and cash in advance. Thwarted by a 2-month postal strike, Branson decided to enter retailing. Realizing the importance of location, he started looking for something along Oxford Street in London. Spotting an unused first floor above a shoe shop, he persuaded the owner to let him use it rent free until a paying tenant came along, on the grounds that if he was successful he would generate extra business for the shoe shop! He had a queue stretching 100 yards when it opened and never looked back – characteristically, he had turned a threat into an opportunity. The London record shop was followed by record production: Branson signed and released Mike Oldfield's extremely successful *Tubular Bells* after Oldfield had been turned down by all of the leading record companies. Branson was always an astute and visionary businessman, carefully recruiting people with the necessary expertise to manage the detail of his various enterprises. His main skill has been in networking, finding opportunities and securing the resources necessary for their exploitation. In this he has had to show courage and flexibility.

He decided to begin a trans-Atlantic airline in 1984. The move had been prompted by an American who approached him with a proposal for an all-business-class trans-Atlantic service. Although Branson rejected this particular focus, he took just a few weeks to make his decision. In this short period Branson analysed why small airlines had previously failed with similar ventures. In particular he focused on Freddie Laker's Skytrain which had competed with a basic service and low prices. When the major airlines reduced their prices Skytrain was driven from the market as it had no other competitive advantage. Branson saw an opportunity: Virgin Atlantic Airways would offer added value and superior service at competitive prices, and concentrate on a limited number of the most lucrative routes. Branson had both a vision and many critics, who argued that he lacked the requisite skills.

He set about implementing his vision, initially leasing two Boeing 747 jumbo jets, and ensured that he generated publicity and notoriety for his initiative. More detailed planning came later after he began recruiting people with expertise in the industry. In this case the planning concentrated on the implementation of a visionary strategy. The airline has grown steadily since its creation and has won a number of awards for the quality of its service. Additional aircraft have been leased and bought, and new routes added. The growth has been in limited, incremental steps as Virgin Atlantic has learnt from experience in a very dynamic environment. The major carriers such as British Airways have clearly seen Virgin as a threat – but realistically only after Branson's early successes – and have been forced to respond. Simply, when Virgin broke into the trans-Atlantic market with its innovative new service, it took the existing carriers by surprise; this was competition from an unexpected source. A successful holiday business has also been developed alongside the airline.

Over many years Branson has successfully marketed a range of products and services by systematically applying the Virgin brand name. The products and services may have been diversified – holidays, consumer products such as Virgin Vodka and Virgin Cola, cinemas, a radio station, mobile phones, financial services and Virgin Railways are examples – but the customer-focused brand image has remained constant.

Virgin was floated in 1986 but later reprivatized; Branson had been uncomfortable with the accountability expectations of institutional shareholders. Since then he has used joint ventures, minority partners and divestments (such as the sales of his music business and record shops) to raise money for new ventures and changes of direction. In 1999 Branson sold a 49 per cent stake in the airline to Singapore Airlines, partly to strengthen its competitiveness, but also to raise money for investment in further new ventures. A similar percentage of Virgin Trains was sold to the bus and train operator, Stagecoach. When Virgin Music was sold to Thorn EMI the general belief was that the money was required to subsidize the growing airline. More recently profits from the successful airline have allegedly been used to shore up other Virgin businesses. His most recent major sale was Virgin Mobile to NTL/Telewest for £1 billion, plus £8.5 million a year for use of the name Virgin Media for the new group, of which he retains a 15 per cent shareholding.

Describing itself as a 'branded venture capital company', Virgin has created well over 200 businesses; and a few years ago Branson decided to increase his presence in electronic commerce and the Internet, believing that a vast range of products and services can be sold this way under the Virgin umbrella. A typical success story has been Virgin Wine. When BA and Air France decided, in 2003, to stop all Concorde flights, Branson was interested in continuing them with the Virgin brand. It is natural that there have been setbacks, one of the most notable being his failure to secure the National Lottery franchise from Camelot with his People's Lottery. When the Northern Rock Building Society was in real difficulties – and before it was eventually nationalized – Branson tried to piece together a rescue package.

Branson has moved into animation with Virgin Comics and healthcare with clinics that offer a package of conventional, homeopathic and complementary medicines together. He has also taken a lead with the 'green agenda'. Virgin Fuels is developing biofuels and he has dedicated some of the profits from Virgin Atlantic and Virgin trains for research. He is also funding the Virgin Earth Challenge, whereby a prize of US$25 million is available for anyone who can invent a safe and effective way of removing greenhouse gases from the atmosphere.

In 2004 Branson licensed the technology behind Spaceshipone – a private manned spacecraft. The technology was owned and developed by a business owned by Microsoft co-founder Paul Allen. Virgin Galactic was going to build five spacecraft to provide short trips into space for wealthy space tourists. Customers would be flown outside the earth's atmosphere and back – not to a spacestation. Each craft would have five seats. Those interested will not need to be young or especially fit, but they will have to be willing to commit three days to training ahead of their journey.

Branson's business philosophy is built around quality products and services, value for money, innovation and an element of fun. 'I never let accountants get in the way of business. You only live once and you might as well have a fun time while you're living.'

By focusing on customers and service he has frequently been able to add value where larger competitors have developed a degree of complacency. 'The challenge of learning and trying to do something better than in the past is irresistible.' Branson always realized that this would be impossible without the appropriate people and created an organization with a devolved and informal culture. Business ideas can, and do, come from anywhere in Virgin. And from people outside the organization. Branson has always made

sure he is approachable. Employees with ideas that Branson likes will be given encouragement and development capital. Once a venture reaches a certain size it is normally freed to operate as an independent business within the Virgin Group, and the intrapreneur retains an equity stake. Some, though, are sold and cease to be part of Virgin. Branson has always been willing to 'take punts' – and some do go wrong. Simply, on balance, he expects (and needs) to succeed more than he fails. 'Opportunities are like London buses. If you look at why you missed the last one, you will miss the next one as well.'

Branson runs Virgin from a large house in London's Holland Park, having outgrown the canal narrow boat that he used for many years. There has never been a traditional head office infrastructure.

Questions

1 What are Richard Branson's strengths and limitations as a strategic leader?
2 How have they been manifested as Virgin has developed?
3 Can this diverse business outlive its founder?
4 Or would Virgin be split up into its many constituent businesses without Branson to lead it?
5 What are the similarities and differences between the Branson/Virgin Atlantic strategy and those of the low-price, no-frills airlines such as Southwest and EasyJet? What routes has Branson added to his original transAtlantic services? What other airlines has he been instrumental in starting?

VIRGIN GROUP **http://www.virgin.com**

To an outsider it can often appear that the organization is pursuing growth with high-risk strategies, which are more reliant on luck than serious thought. This can under-estimate the thinking that is involved, because quite often these entrepreneurs and visionary leaders have an instinctive feel for the products, services and markets involved, and enjoy a clear awareness and insight of the opportunities and risks.

This mode of strategy creation is most viable when the strategic leader has the full confidence of the organization, and he or she can persuade others to follow his or her ideas and implement the strategies successfully. Implementation requires more detailed planning and incremental changes with learning: initially it is the broad strategic idea that is formulated entrepreneurially.

Formal planning and/or visionary leadership will invariably determine important changes to **corporate strategies**; competitive and functional level changes are more likely to involve **emergent strategy** in the form of adaptive and incremental changes. The actual implementation of corporate level decisions is also likely to be incremental.

It is, however, clear from the experiences of many organizations that planning and visionary leadership do not, in themselves, explain strategy creation as the following story illustrates.

Richard T. Pascale of Stanford University (1984) has described how a number of Honda executives arrived in Los Angeles from Japan in 1959 to establish an American subsidiary. Their original aim (intended strategy) was to focus on selling 250cc and 350cc machines, rather than 50cc Honda cubs, which were a big hit in Japan. Their instinct told them that the Honda 50s were not suitable for the US market, where everything was bigger and more luxurious than in Japan.

However, sales of the 250cc and 350cc bikes were sluggish, and the bikes themselves were plagued by mechanical failure. It looked as though Honda's strategy was going to fail. At the same time the Japanese executives were using the Honda 50s to run errands around Los Angeles, attracting a lot of attention.

One day they got a call from a Sears Roebuck buyer who wanted to sell them to a broad market of Americans who were not necessarily already motorcycle enthusiasts. The Honda executives were very hesitant to sell the 50cc bikes for fear of alienating serious bikers who might then associate Honda with 'wimp' machines. In the end they were pushed into doing so by the failure of the 250cc and 350cc machines. The rest is history. Honda had stumbled on a previously untouched market segment that was to prove huge. It had also found a previously untried channel of distribution: general retailers rather than speciality motorbike stores. By 1964 nearly one out of every two motorcycles sold in the US was a Honda.

Gladwell (2000) would refer to the call from Sears Roebuck as a 'tipping point', where some unexpected and unpredictable event has a major impact. A similar event happened to Hush Puppies in the mid-1990s. This brand of casual shoe had declined markedly in popularity and its owners were barely supporting it. However a number of young people in New York started wearing them as something of a fashion statement, and mainly because nobody else was wearing them. They were spotted and copied and suddenly there was a resurgence in the popularity of the brand. It had nothing to do with any marketing by the manufacturers.

The critical point that emerges from the Honda and Hush Puppies examples is that in contrast to the view that strategies are planned, successful strategies can emerge without prior planning.

Other classic business school examples of emergent or unintended strategies are Xerox, who set out to sell photocopiers when customers only really wanted the copies and not the machines, and Gillette, actively promoting shavers when the real desire of the customer is for a shave. The razor blade is what is wanted by the consumer. Arguably it is better to give the razor away if this ensures you sell the blades.

In more recent times we have seen the demise of many products relating to the delivery of music – including music cassette tapes, DAT, and of course vinyl. When the compact disk was introduced it was seen as being the 'nail in the coffin' of the old vinyl format. Yet vinyl has not died quite as anticipated. Vinyl is now sold in most music outlets as new types of music become popular, including dub step, reggae and techno, that are sold in the 12 inch vinyl size – previously the format for what was known as LPs. Driving this forward has been the fact that vinyl has also been put to new uses for the hand mixing of tracks by DJs in clubs all over the UK and beyond.

We can now argue that there are two distinct elements to emergent strategic change.

Incremental strategic change

In dynamic and turbulent competitive environments, detailed formal planning is seen to be problematic. The plans are only as good as any forecasts, which must be uncertain. It can make sense, therefore, not to rely on detailed plans, but instead to plan broad strategies within a clearly defined mission and purpose.

Having provided this direction the strategic leader will allow strategies to emerge in a decentralized organization structure. Managers will meet regularly, both formally and informally, to discuss progress and changing trends; they will plan new courses of action and then try them out: a form of 'real-time planning'.

When I was younger I always conceived of a room where all these [strategic] concepts were worked out for the whole company. Later I didn't find any such room... . The strategy [of the company] may not even exist in the mind of one man. I certainly don't know where it is written down. It is simply transmitted in the series of decisions made.

JAMES B QUINN, 1980

Quinn argues that organizations test out relatively small changes and develop with this approach rather than go for major changes. An example would be Marks and Spencer testing a proposed new line in a selected and limited number of stores before deciding to launch it nationally. Lex Group (see Strategy in action 1.1) followed an incremental approach when it diversified into hotels, building and buying properties one by one rather than acquiring a chain of hotels.

Adaptive strategic change

Some organizations will be characterized by extensive decentralization, empowerment and accountability. Here, managers throughout the organization are being encouraged to look for opportunities and threats and to innovate. The underlying argument is that managers 'at the coal face' are closest to the key changes in the organization's environment and should, therefore, be in a position where they can, on the one hand, react quickly and, on the other hand, be proactive or intrapreneurial in attempting to change or manage the external environment. Managers will be encouraged and empowered to make changes in their areas of responsibility and, ideally, rewarded for their initiatives. The implication is that functional changes will impact upon competitive strategies in a positive way as the organization adapts to its changing environment. Conceptually this is similar to incremental change.

Proponents of chaos theory such as Ralph Stacey (1993) argue that intentional strategies are, per se, 'too inflexible for unknown futures'. Relying on this approach is a 'recipe for stagnation and failure because of the extent of the complexity'. Companies must seek to 'achieve a state of creative tension on the edge of instability'. These theorists accept that organizational hierarchies and planning are needed to control day-to-day operations but, in the long-term, strategies must be allowed to emerge from the 'self-organizing activities of loose, informal, destabilizing networks'.

In summary, therefore, strategy can result from a stream of decisions and information fed upwards from the lower management levels of the organization. Quinn contends that this is sensible, logical and positive:

The most effective strategies of major enterprises tend to emerge step by step from an iterative process in which the organization probes the future, experiments and learns from a series of partial (incremental) commitments rather than through global formulations of total strategies. Good managers are aware of this process and they consciously intervene in it. They use it to improve the information available for decisions and to build the psychological identification essential to successful strategies. The process is both logical and incremental. Such logical incrementalism is not 'muddling' as most people understand that word. Properly managed it is a conscious, purposeful, proactive, executive practice.

Teamworking and learning are at the heart of the adaptive and incremental modes. Managers must learn about new opportunities and threats; they should also learn from the successes and mistakes of other managers. Managers must be willing to take measured risks; for this to happen understandable mistakes and errors of judgement should not be sanctioned harshly.

Change is gradual and comes from experimentation; new strategies involve an element of trial and error. Success is very dependent upon communications. Managers must know of the opportunities and threats facing them; the organization must be able to synthesize all changes into a meaningful pattern, and spread learning and best practice.

Figure 1.10   Strategic creation

Mintzberg (1989) argues that organizations should be structured and managed to ensure that formulators of strategies (managers whose decisions lead to strategic changes) have information, and that the implementers of strategies and changes have the appropriate degree of **power** to ensure that the desired changes are brought about.

Figure 1.10 pulls these ideas together and highlights that it is quite normal to find all of these modes in evidence simultaneously in an organization, although there is likely to be one dominant mode. Moreover different managers in the same organization will not necessarily agree on the relative significance of each mode; their perceptions of what is actually happening will vary.

The message for managers is that they need to recognize this process of emergence and to intervene where appropriate, killing off bad emergent strategies but nurturing potentially good ones. To make such decisions, however, managers must be able to judge the worth of emergent strategies. They must be able to think strategically. This viewpoint is probably the best argument for the continued use of the rationalist approach.

Strategy is necessarily incremental and adaptive, but that does not in any way imply that its evolution cannot be, or should not be, analyzed, managed, and controlled.

PASCALE, 1984.

Strategy at work

We conclude this section with Figure 1.11, which has its origins in Mintzberg's work cited earlier in. Here we can see it proposed that strategy comprises:

- Learning from the past
- Understanding (making sense of) the present
- Imagining the future and
- Competing and innovating to stay ahead of rivals and seize new opportunities.

Some authors would describe such different but linked perspectives as 'lenses'. Individually, but especially collectively, they can help us make sense of strategy. Simply, they are all legitimate ways of looking at strategy.

Individually we are all different and if we think about ourselves we would be able to explain which of these perspectives we find most natural and which we struggle with the most. Simply,

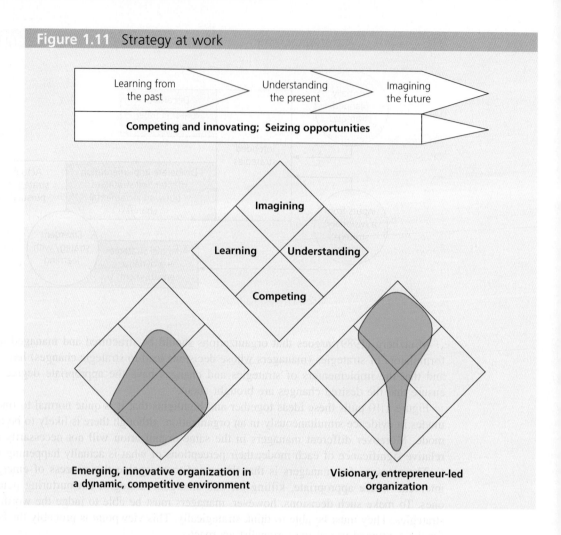

Figure 1.11   Strategy at work

some people are naturally analytical; others are naturally creative. Some of us see opportunities before others do because we form different mental patterns from what we see and observe. And, finally, some of us are very tactical and enjoy the buzz of competition; we are flexible in the face of adversity.

Metaphorically organizations are the same as individuals. And their behaviour will reflect the type of organization they are strategically. Moreover, the circumstances they face will influence they type of organization they ideally need to be or become, if they are to be strong and effective.

An emerging and innovative (entrepreneurial) business in a dynamic, competitive environment might be expected to be strong in the bottom diamond (competing) and less strong in the other three. One led by a visionary entrepreneur that is breaking new ground would be strong in the top diamond (imagining) and again less strong in the other three. That said, to some degree, it is important to have some degree of strength in every segment.

1.4 The emergence of strategic management

All men can see the tactics by which I conquer, but what none can see is the strategy out of which great victory is evolved.

SUN TZU, THE ART OF WAR, 400 BC

Strategy is the evolution of the original guiding idea according to continually changing circumstance.

HELMUTH MOLTKE, PRUSSIAN GENERAL CHIEF OF STAFF, 1858–1888

Origins in military strategy

Strategy has always had military roots and *Webster's New World Dictionary* defines strategy as 'the science of planning and directing military operations'.

Strategic manoeuvres use the principles of military strategy, a theme taken up by James (1984).

To survive you have to learn to fight by the rules of the game. The rules of the business game have changed in response to economic, technological and social dislocation and require new approaches to market combat. The companies that will survive and prosper [in the 1980s and beyond] will be those which recognise the new rules of the market-place and adopt end-game strategies which reflect the combative nature of the market-place. Those companies which continue to use game plans which are not conflict orientated will have a less-than-even chance of survival.

Thus, strategy would be seen as the set of policies used for the conduct of conflict and the securing of an advantage over the competition.

We do however need to be careful with the usefulness of the military analogy: a business cannot vanquish all its foes and go home. Business is there for the long haul. Modern warfare is based on the destruction of opposing forces and on the use of resources which are greater than that of the enemy so as to give an overwhelming advantage, presenting the victor with the opportunity to destroy the enemy. This seldom happens in business – although the use by British Airways of its resources to help destroy Freddie Laker, an issue explored later, is one worth considering in this light.

Success in business is usually about adding value of your own, not diminishing that of your competitors, and is based on distinctive capability, not destructive capacity. ... The second area in which the military analogy misleads is in inviting excessive emphasis on leadership, vision, and determination. ...

If General Custer or Lord Raglan had been businessmen, would we have been so keen to become their employees or to buy shares in their business. ... Fighting against overwhelming odds may sometimes be a necessary military strategy. It is almost always not a sensible business strategy.

KAY, 1993

Hinterhuber and Popp (1992) provide another example of the military analogy in the context of trying to identify the qualities needed to be a strategic manager. They contend that perhaps the greatest strategist of all time was not a business executive or an entrepreneur but a general ... Helmuth von Moltke, chief of the Prussian and German general staffs from 1855 to 1888, engineered the strategy behind the military victories that allowed Otto von Bismark to assemble a loose league of German states into a powerful empire. Moltke possessed two important characteristics that made him into a superior strategist:

1 The ability to understand the significance of events without being influenced by current opinion, changing attitudes, or his own prejudices.

2 The ability to make decisions quickly and to take the indicated action without being deterred by a perceived danger.

The two characteristics support each other and apply to managers and entrepreneurs as much as to generals and national leaders ...

Moltke issued directive guidelines for autonomous decision making. In the past, Prussian officers were discouraged from acting on their own. Moltke turned such tradition on its head by expecting the officers to show individual initiative. According to Moltke, strategy is applied common sense and cannot be taught. Moltke's general conception of strategy – viewing all obvious factors in the right perspective– cannot be learned in any school.

Of course, a fundamental difference between military and business strategy is that business strategy is formulated, implemented, and evaluated with an assumption of competition, whereas military strategy is based on the assumption of conflict. Nonetheless, military conflict and business competition are so similar that many techniques for the formulating, implementing, and evaluating of strategies apply to both.

Another important military metaphor relates strategy and tactics to guerrilla warfare, which is particularly relevant for understanding strategy and the small business. The small business owner usually lacks resources and is often competing with organizations much larger than himself.

This lack of resources usually takes the form of deficiencies in strategic management knowledge, lack of functional managerial skills, and insufficient capital to exploit external opportunities. The owner manager often is forced to adopt a day-to-day cognitive frame of reference. Fundamentally, this is the scenario of the guerrilla fighter. Resources need to be obtained and husbanded. Human and financial resources are often scarce and the 'enemy' is often much larger and well entrenched. The guerrilla, if he is to survive and prosper, must use resources wisely and pick the time and place of battle so as to make the best use of these scarce resources. The role of the 'military adviser' has always been important in such a campaign. Consider the success of the Viet Cong against the greatest military power on earth – acknowledged to be the only war the United States of America has ever lost. Arguably the Viet Cong would never be able to defeat, in a formal military sense, the United States. What the Viet Cong set out to do was to make the war one the Americans could never win conventionally. They therefore sought to 'sicken' the USA and to achieve success (that is to win the war) in the only way they could. In this case it was the winning of the public relations campaign. The USA was portrayed as the giant, the aggressor, and the poor Viet Cong as the victims fighting a titanic struggle against the odds. True or false it worked with the turning away, within America, of populist support for the war.

An earlier example of a successful guerrilla campaign is that of Robin Hood and the Sheriff of Nottingham. Robin and his so-called Merry Men had limited resources with which to take on a much bigger enemy. However, by winning popular support and not antagonizing too many key players in the external environment, the band were able to survive and prosper.

These points are expanded in Critical reflection 1.1.

Evolving views of strategy

In this section we refer to a number of approaches to strategic management, all of which are discussed in detail at different points in the book, where they are referenced more fully.

Since the 1960s, when we really began to study strategic management, the strategic planning framework has provided a valuable base for the understanding of the subject. Since then several other approaches have been added. They are all relevant and help to shed further light on this complex topic. If strategy were easy to understand and practise, then more organizations would be successful and sustain this success over time. However, although it is based in many ways on some simple points and common sense, strategy remains enigmatic.

Figure 1.12 shows that when Porter (1980, 1985) drew attention to the subject of competitive advantage, and the significance of strategic positioning, an important second layer was added to the planning foundation. The next important contribution was the clarification that many strategies emerge as decisions are taken all the time in dynamic circumstances, highlighting that while planning plays an important role, it is a partial one.

Critical reflection 1.1

Strategy – The Military Perspective

War is a means to an end – just as business strategy is. The end might be a desired one (either power or economic wealth) or it might be survival when under threat.

Like business strategy, it is characterized by uncertainty and threat. The downside, losing, can be very unpleasant.

The military strategist – just as a strategic leader – has control over the resources and s/he must deploy them. He must also make sure there is resource development and innovation, and mastermind the supply chain.

Visionary and motivational leadership at various levels is vital, as is individual enterprise (individual acts of heroism) within the boundaries of a framework of discipline.

We have all studied military history in school, even if only at a superficial level. We may have read books; we have almost certainly seen movies, ranging from Shakespeare's *Henry V* to John Wayne winning the war in the Pacific! If we can think of key aspects of conflict and warfare we can clarify a number of themes and concepts that are vital for our study of strategy in a business context. In warfare, as in business, there are lessons from defeat and lessons from success. Simply, military ideas can help us to be more effective strategic thinkers.

Important elements and themes

- Strategic intent – a broad plan
- Positioning and tactical ploys
- Detailed but flexible action plans – Napoleon, for example, seemed to plan by algorithm and always prepare for a variety of possibilities and contingencies
- Capability – resource adequacy and replenishment
- Competency – skills and weaponry represent technical and process competencies and capabilities
- Focus – so there are few diversions or distractions from the main thrust
- Thinking ahead – to develop new resources and technologies first

- 'The rules of the game' can always be changed with a new weapon or tactics – witness the potential of biological weapons
- Guerrilla fighters always imply a hidden, surprise threat – they are innovative and entrepreneurial
- Allies and alliances are likely to be essential – as with nations, it can sometimes be in a company's interests to form an alliance with a past or even an existing rival (enemy) to guard against an even greater enemy
- Fear is an important competitive weapon. Some actions are deterred or delayed because of the fear of competitive reaction. The 'Cold War' typified this. Image matters. It is possible to win without engaging in conflict if your reputation frightens people off. Image and reputation are thus a barrier to entry
- Self-belief is also vital. There has to be a will-to-win and a belief that winning is possible. This comes from envisioning and values-driven leadership
- In this context, people will die to help their colleagues – team belongingness is a key element
- This is particularly poignant in war when new team members have to be integrated quickly to replace those who have been lost
- Flexibility must be maintained. Anyone can be caught out by surprise
- All the time, gathering performance data and spotting new, emerging, developments and trends cannot be over-valued. This may be directly and indirectly related to the main focus of current activity
- With the military, of course, spying and hiding the competitor information you do have, is a legitimate tactic. Industrial espionage goes on, but it is not perceived as ethical.

Important rules of war

- Never engage a superior force without a clear plan of action that has a real chance of success. Until you have this plan, defend!
- Don't waste time and resources attacking a place that has no strategic or other value. Stay focused

- When you have made progress, reinforce to protect your back and flanks and prevent counter-attack as you continue onwards
- Whenever you can, stay on the move and keep reinforcing your advantage.

Reference

The material in this box has been sourced in part from: Davies, P, *Military Strategy* in Jenkins, M and Ambrosini, V (2002) *Strategic Management – A Multi-perspective Approach*, Palgrave.

Further reading

Clausewitz, C von (2003) *On War*, Penguin Classics.
Howard, M (2002) *Clausewitz: A Very Short Introduction*, Oxford University Press.
Sun Tzu (2008) *The Art of War*, Penguin Classics.

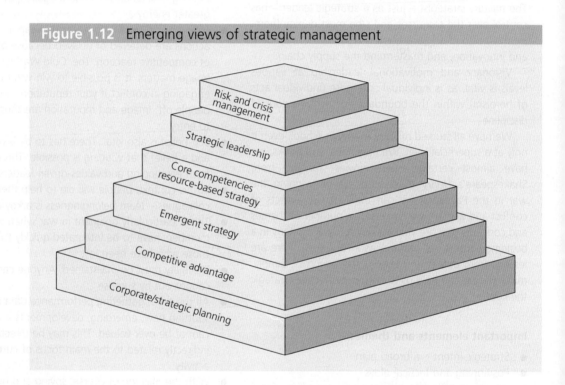

Figure 1.12 Emerging views of strategic management

Risk and crisis management

Strategic leadership

Core competencies resource-based strategy

Emergent strategy

Competitive advantage

Corporate/strategic planning

The general thrust of these approaches is market driven, based on the argument that organizations must react in a dynamic environment, seizing new opportunities and avoiding major potential threats. Responding to customers, suppliers and competitors will always be vital, but an alternative perspective is also relevant. This resource-based strategy argues that organizations must discern their critical strategic strengths and look for ways of building and exploiting them in order to mould the competitive environment. In the supplement to this chapter we look at the relevant issues of core competency and **strategic capability**. Successful organizations will blend both the market and resource perspectives so that they do not overlook potentially good opportunities.

In recent years the subject of strategic leadership has received greater prominence, stimulated in part by the media. Business success stories have been popular items for newspapers and magazines, especially where there is a high-profile figure who can be identified with the organization and the story. In addition, the 'falls from grace' of some very high-profile business people have proved newsworthy. The accompanying autobiographies of some of these people have added to this understanding.

Critical reflections 1.2 provides an alternative perspective on these important approaches.

Most recently, **risk management** and **crisis management** have joined the debate. Organizations have recognized that scenario building can help their understanding of uncertainty, where the future may depend in part on the past but will not replicate it. For some industries, such as pharmaceuticals (where huge investments in new drugs are required but carry no guarantee of success) and electronic commerce (which is changing by the day) serious risk assessment is vital. The environment is busy with information and triggers, never more so than now, thanks to the Internet, but discerning the real commercial opportunities is probably harder rather than easier than it was in the past. Organizational fortunes can, therefore, change rapidly, and crises can arise suddenly to catch out the unwary organization. The study of learning, and the involvement of people in an empowered and intrapreneurial culture, is a key element both of this topic and of emergent strategy.

The following discussion on strategic disturbances and groupthink support the significance of this sixth layer in Figure 1.12.

Strategic disturbance   Stacey (1993) advocates that strategy is about handling disturbance and this is related to changing both competitive advantage and competitive capability. We can see how disturbances constitute risk and, mishandled, crises.

To Stacey, strategy is not about a comprehensive and integrated set of actions or routes to objectives, instead it is about a comprehensive and integrated total control system, which will enable the strategic leader to deal with unforeseeable disturbances, changes in competitive advantage and capability as they occur. Handling disturbance effectively is, therefore, a question of control in its widest sense.

The starting point is not the mission, and certainly not detailed long term objectives, but the appropriate style of control.

This argument reinforces the significance of placing leadership and culture at the centre of Figure 1.7(b).

Disturbances can arise from anywhere and everywhere. The basic business flows, of orders/requisitions, inputs/outputs and money, all give rise to disturbances; machine breakdowns, material shortages, unpaid debts, rising stock levels, changes in the pattern of orders, also give rise to disturbances. The environment impacts on the flows, feeding disturbances into the organization – through, for example, the loss of a major customer, changing customer tastes and the appearance of a new competitor. The environment also feeds disturbances directly to the instruments of control – public opinion, changes in work culture, pressures to install training, reward pressures and so on. The environment could also directly contribute disturbance – changes in taxation, changes in health and safety requirements, trade union law, environmental legislation imposing uniform standards throughout the EU and so on. The instruments of control can directly contribute disturbance – new staff and managers may join the company with different cultural values. Roles can directly contribute disturbance through individual dissatisfaction with roles or a poor fit of people to their roles.

Disturbances are continuously bombarding the business from all directions and wherever they come from they have to be handled at the core of the control system by managers and workers who apply processes to control elements. The outcome is some form of action. This action is based on structured thinking, but not some analytical straitjacket.

Critical reflection 1.2

Directions of Strategic Thought

The classical approach – planning

Driven by the 'rational man' paradigm and based on the economists' profit-maximizing model.

Planning is the vehicle for rational strategy creation.

There are elements of creation and implementation, the classical strategy-structure framework.

Strategic positioning is at its heart. Appropriateness is therefore a key test.

Strong central leadership is required to drive the process.

The evolutionary approach – opportunity-driven emergent strategy

Driven by competition – and, in this respect, the work of Michael Porter – it is based around responding to identified opportunities and threats.

The idea is that only the best performers survive in a dynamic world, accepting there is always an element of luck and chance.

The approach questions whether organizations can create differences by a largely rational approach.

'Strategizing' – or thinking long-term – can be dangerous if it reduces organizational flexibility.

Rather strategy is about tactical moves (changes) in response to external events.

The appropriate resources are essential to put the organization in a position to 'engage the enemy'.

Appropriateness and feasibility are the key tests.

The processual approach – resource-based emergent planning

This is driven by internal stakeholders and assumes that adaptation to the outside world is through internal political bargaining, compromise and accommodation.

Along the lines of Mintzberg, strategies are crafted by trial, error and learning.

The organization needs to develop key strengths (core competencies and strategic capabilities) which become the foundation for resource-based strategies.

Feasibility and desirability for key internal stakeholders are important tests.

The systemic approach – visionary strategy driven by key players

Strategies emerge from the culture and values of key players, typically the strategic leader.

Very much affected by the 'wider picture' perspective, although this could embrace the needs of a local community as much as concerns for the global environment.

In some economies the systemic approach can correspond to the profit-seeking paradigm behind the classical approach.

Developed from:

Whittington, R (2001) *What Is Strategy-And Does It Matter? 2nd Edition* Cengage Learning

Commentary

Whittington sees the Classical and Processual approaches as internally-driven, on the grounds that the classical approach is driven by an internal desire to maximize profits. Evolutionary and Systemic are then external.

However we might argue that the Classical approach (like the Evolutionary) is external as they are both based on a search for economic opportunities in a competitive environment.

The Systemic (like the Processual) is internal because it is based on the values of powerful strategic leaders.

A serious drawback to the formal planning approach, then, is the problem of trying to foresee strategic disturbance over a period which extends much into the future. We all know that the early years of this century will see a rapid growth in the age group of over 60s in most industrialized countries. We know that this group will be healthier and wealthier than ever before in history. But just what does this mean for business? What will these rich, healthy pensioners be looking for – Club 65+ instead of Club 18-30? Moreover, when does it make sense for anyone to do anything about it? This major demographic change is a strategic disturbance, but should an entrepreneur start building holiday villas now?

Groupthink   Social psychologist Irving L. Janis (1972) argues 'groupthink' occurs when a group of decision makers embark on a course of action without questioning underlying assumptions. The group coalesces around a person or a policy. It ignores or filters out information which could be used to question that policy and develops after-the-fact rationalization for its decision.

Williams (1976) has analysed the problem of groupthink and crisis management in the nuclear age. Two main themes emerged from his work. Not only does a group strive for unanimity there also can be the additional problem of this striving for unanimity overriding the group's motivation to realistically appraise alternative courses of action. This might mean that the group is willing to take a level of risk that individually they would not take, and that members of the decision-making unit exude great self-confidence, firmly believing that the policy they adopt is almost bound to succeed.

Williams argues that The Bay of Pigs invasion and the escalation of the Vietnam War under President Johnson are both classic examples of over-confidence in one's own plans and under-estimation of the capabilities and resourcefulness of the enemy.

An excellent example of the difficulty of trying to remain objective during a crisis and make a rational decision based on the facts and not follow a narrow decision path, is the Cuban Missile Crisis in 1962. This is discussed by Williams (1976), but a valuable insight into what it might have been like at this time can be seen in the film made of the crisis, *Thirteen Days* (Hollywood Pictures), which features Kevin Costner as President Kennedy's principal adviser. The heavy pressure placed on Kennedy by the US military for a strike on Cuba is well depicted; however, the President resists this pressure and arrives at the blockade decision which ultimately proved successful. In this instance, groupthink was clearly resisted.

1.5 Mission, strategy, objectives and tactics

These four terms were all defined in Box 1.1 and they have either been introduced in brief or discussed in detail in this chapter. Figure 1.13 shows how they interrelate hierarchically, and looks at them in the context of intended and emergent strategy creation.

Strategies are means to ends. Where they are planned in some detail they will relate to specific objectives or targets. Both objectives and strategies set and pursued should help to achieve, or at least to pursue, the purpose or mission of the organization. Tactics and actions, carried out everywhere in the organization by various managers and other staff, represent on the one hand, the implementation of **intended strategies** and, on the other hand, new strategic ideas being tried out by empowered managers.

The left-hand section of Figure 1.13 highlights how, with intended strategies, the mission is used to establish objectives, which in turn lead to strategies and tactics. With emergent strategy – the right-hand section of the diagram – managers are expected to appreciate and support the broad purpose and direction of the organization, and it is a key role of the strategic leader to ensure that they actually do this. Within this context they are then empowered to decide upon, and try out, new strategic ideas. What they do determines the level of achievement and performance of the organization. Here we can see how tactical successes drive strategy and performance. In both cases environmental and resource considerations will guide decision-making, but the information will be used by different people at different levels in the hierarchy.

Figure 1.13 The strategy process

With intended strategies, performance evaluation straightforwardly concerns the achievement (or not) of stated objectives with the strategies and tactics used. In the case of emergent strategy, performance evaluation is really an assessment of what has been achieved in the context of the mission.

Finally, it is important to recognize that specific issues and events will be perceived differently at different levels of the organizational hierarchy, partly because individual businesses in a diverse organization can – and often will – have their own mission statements. While they may differ, they should be complementary.

We have already seen how strategy has its origins in warfare, and a recent military example provides a useful illustration of these points. In World War II the mission of the British government was, quite simply, to win the war. This required contributions from each of the armed services and from others. Winning the Battle of Britain was, consequently, one objective, supported by various strategies concerned with, for example, training pilots and building aircraft. The recruitment of women to work in the aeroplane factories was one of many tactics. An individual frontline squadron would, however, define its mission differently. It might, for example, have been concerned with shooting down enemy planes and minimizing losses. To the government, with a higher level purpose, this would be seen as an objective. Similarly, advancing against the enemy and capturing a hill might be the current mission for a group of soldiers; to them at the time nothing else would matter. In the context of the war as a whole, this, however, would be a very low-level and short-term tactic.

1.6 Strategy statements

Before we finish this chapter with a look at strategic management in different contexts, it is useful to draw together many of the points we have made by showing them in the form of a strategy statement, illustrated in Figure 1.14.

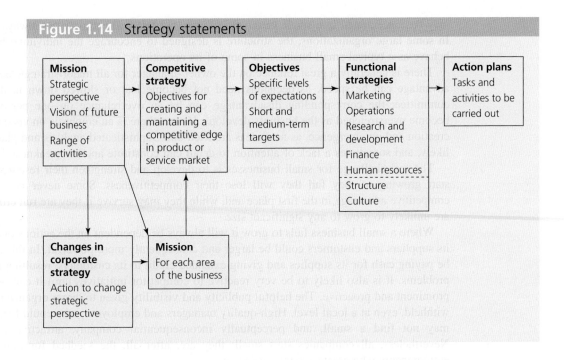

Figure 1.14   Strategy statements

The argument would be that all managers in an organization should be in a position to produce such a statement for their organization, and understand the inter-connections.

The overall mission or purpose may or may not change over time; a great deal depends upon the extent to which it allows the organization to develop and change its strategic perspective. Each business or division within the organization is likely to have its own mission, from which will be derived an appropriate competitive strategy. This leads on to the establishment of specific objectives and to firm levels of expectation in respect of sales, profits, production and so on. Functional strategies will be developed to ensure that these targets are achieved and that the appropriate action plans, or tasks to be carried out, are defined. Although not explicitly shown on the strategy statement, there should be monitoring and control systems to assess performance against targets.

1.7   Strategic management in specific contexts

Strategic ideas are relevant for all types of organization, and many of the key issues are the same, although they may differ in their relative significance. At the same time, there are some important differences, which are introduced in this section. Throughout the book an attempt is made to use examples and cases that reflect a range of different types and size of organization but, inevitably, large manufacturing and service businesses feature most prominently, largely because they are the organizations and brand names that most readers will recognize and relate to easily.

Small businesses

Typically, small businesses will focus on a single product or service, or at least a restricted range of related products and services, targeted at a defined market niche. Competitive and functional strategies are important, but many of the corporate strategy issues discussed herein will not be relevant until the organization grows larger, assuming that it does so. In addition, their customers may be concentrated in a single geographical area, but this will certainly not always be the case. In some large organizations, the structure is designed to encourage the individual businesses to behave as a typical small business in some of its operations.

There is generally a great reliance on the owner–manager for all major strategic decisions. The advantage can be speed, as decisions need not become lost or slowed down in discussion or committee; the corresponding disadvantage can be an overreliance on one person who may become overstretched as the business develops. Hence, there is an emphasis on visionary strategy creation and on emergence, as new ideas are tried out. Sophisticated analysis and planning is less likely, and sometimes a lack of attention to detail can constitute another weakness.

The real challenge for small businesses is to develop and strengthen their resources once they start growing: if they fail they will lose their competitiveness. Some never possess any real competitive advantage in the first place and, while they may survive if they are run efficiently, they are unlikely to grow to any significant size.

Where a small business fails to grow it will always be dependent on the actions of others. Both its suppliers and customers could be larger and consequently more powerful. In this case it could be paying cash for its supplies and giving extended credit to its customers, resulting in cash-flow problems. It is also likely to be very reactive to competitor initiatives until it can become more prominent and proactive. The helpful publicity and visibility given to larger organizations may be withheld, even at a local level. High-quality managers and employees, who could fuel the growth, may not find a small, and perceptually inconsequential company, attractive to work for. Nevertheless, all companies start small: they are, after all, the seedbed for those successful entrepreneurs who create growth businesses.

The success, or lack of it, then, will be hugely dependent on the strategic leader, and his or her culture and style. The future will be dictated by their skill and also by their ability to acquire resources, particularly in terms of finance. A lack of capital can often be a real restraint to growth. Banks often demand security and collateral and venture capitalists often only become interested once the business has reached a certain size and proved itself. We saw earlier how guerrilla warfare provides a useful metaphor for the strategic use of tactics by small businesses.

This traditional logic concerning small businesses, however, has to some degree been turned on its head in the case of many new Internet or '**dot.com**' companies who have been able to raise millions of pounds on the strength of a barely proven idea that appeared to offer a golden opportunity. Financiers have taken risks that they would previously have shunned because of the speed and growth of this sector and its inherent uncertainty.

Global companies

Here the emphasis is very much on corporate strategy: diversity, geographical scope and co-ordinating the countries where products are made with the countries where they are sold. Using low-cost labour factories in Eastern Europe and the Far East can prove controversial while still being an economic necessity. In addition, these are often very powerful companies whose annual turnover exceeds the gross national product (GNP) of many of the world's smaller countries. Nevertheless, issues of competitiveness and competitive advantage are as relevant as they are for a small business. One key complication can be currency fluctuations when component supplies and finished goods are moved around the world.

The major dilemma for many global companies concerns their need to achieve global scale economies from concentrating production in large plants whilst not sacrificing their local identity and relevance in the various markets. To accomplish this they must stay close to their customers and markets, whose specific tastes and preferences may differ markedly, even though they are buying essentially the same product.

The organizational structure can be, and often is, just as important as the strategy. This, in turn, raises a number of important people issues. People may be switched from business to business and from country to country as part of their personal progression. This movement also helps the whole organization to transfer skills and knowledge and to learn good practices from different parts of the business.

Global corporations also need to develop expertise in financial management. Attractive development grants and packages will be available in certain countries and influence strategic developments. Interest rates are not the same around the world and consequently loans can be more attractive in certain countries and not in others. Moreover, tax rates vary and it can be very beneficial to be seen to be earning profits in low-tax countries instead of high-tax ones.

Not-for-profit organizations

Organizations such as churches and charities clearly fit into this sector very well, but certain other profit-generating businesses, such as museums, zoos and local theatres, are relatively closely aligned. In the case of the latter examples, the profit objective is often designed to create a 'war chest' for future investment rather than to reward an owner or a group of investors. For this reason there are many common characteristics. Money may be perceived differently in not-for-profit organizations than in profit-seeking businesses, but there is still a need to create a positive cash flow. A charity, for example, can only spend on good causes if it can generate funds. For this reason, churches and charities can legitimately appear very commercial in their outlook, and this must be accepted alongside the cause that they are targeting.

These not-for-profit organizations need social entrepreneurs or strategic leaders who, in many ways, will be similar to those found in the profit-seeking sector. They will possess similar entrepreneurial and leadership qualities, but they will be driven by a cause, which attracts them to the particular organization and sector. This, in turn, guides the mission, purpose and culture. In addition, there is likely to be a greater reliance on voluntary helpers and possibly managers and others who readily accept salaries and wages below those that they might earn in the profit sector.

There are likely to be variations on the modes of strategy creation discussed herein. There is likely to be some committee structure, involving both salaried employees and unpaid volunteers, the latter often in senior roles. Decision-making can be slow and political in nature, although clearly it does not have to be this way. However, strong and dominant leaders (either paid or unpaid) quite often emerge and are at the heart of strategy-making. Because there is a need for accountability for the funds raised, planning systems are likely to be prominent.

Public-sector organizations

In many countries around the world the composition of this sector has changed over recent years. Typically, essential service industries, such as telecommunications, gas, electricity, water, and air, bus and rail transport, have been privatized, often resulting in the creation of a number of complementary or even competing businesses. The outcome in each industry has been one or more private company, some of which have since merged or been acquired, sometimes by overseas parents. In the case of the UK this privatization programme has also included individual companies such as British Airports Authority (BAA), which manages several airports but is largely a retail organization. Outside direct government control, BAA has expanded overseas and now manages a number of other airports around the world. Since privatization it has been sold to a Spanish parent and also required by the UK competition authorities to reduce the number of airports it controls, especially in London.

In every case there is some form of regulation and government influence, as distinct from the direct government control of the past. The trend towards privatization has gathered momentum for many reasons, one factor in Europe being the stronger stance on government subsidies to individual industries by the European Commission. The key appears to lie in the effectiveness of the regulation, which must attempt to balance the needs of all key stakeholders: customers, employees and investors.

As a result, we now tend to think of local authorities and public health and emergency services as the archetypal public sector organizations. Clearly these are service businesses, and ones which will always have to choose and prioritize between different needs and stakeholders. In general, they will always be able to achieve more outcomes if they can acquire more resources. However, they remain largely dependent on central government for their resources and are therefore influenced by the political agenda of the day. Increasingly, some have greater involvement with the private sector than was the case in the past. The British National Health Service works alongside the private health-care sector and, although their roles and remits differ, the same consultants operate in both sectors. Many services in local communities were subjected to compulsory competitive tendering (CCT) during the early and mid-1990s and, as a result, were outsourced to providers in the private, profit-seeking sector. CCT has now been replaced by the need to find and deliver 'best value'.

Another interesting and relevant development has been the Public-Private Partnerships that have emerged from the Private Finance Initiative. Here the public sector, say a local authority, is allowed to partner with a private sector provider who will contract to provide and deliver a particular service. If the provider fails to deliver or to meet quality targets, payments will be withheld. Any capital spending required can be obtained in the form of a central government loan paid back over an agreed period. The assumption is that this will result in greater efficiencies and effectiveness than would be the case if the public sector opted to provide itself all the services that it is responsible for.

Decision-making and style features some element of bureaucracy, in part because of the role of governing bodies, be they elected (local councillors) or appointed (e.g. NHS Trust Boards). As accountability has become increasingly public in recent years, analysis and planning will also be very prominent. Again, however, strong leaders can, and will, make an impact; and, as the public sector environment is no more stable than the one affecting commercial businesses, emergent strategy is also very important.

The closing case in this chapter, Case 1.7 on McDonald's, features many of the points we have discussed. McDonald's grew very rapidly around a winning business model and became a world leader in its industry. The brand was ubiquitous, visible and identifiable everywhere. However, in recent years, the company lost its way and the brand became tarnished. For McDonald's to survive and restore its previous high growth, it was necessary for it to change certain aspects of its strategy fundamentally. We see that this began when a previously successful strategic leader was tempted out of retirement to champion the necessary transformation.

Case 1.7

McDonald's   US

McDonald's, built by a visionary, the late Ray Kroc, has become a very successful international company, with outlets in some 120 countries. Its products are popular with large numbers of customers, and certainly not just children. In 1996, according to Interbrand consultants, McDonald's ousted Coca-Cola as the world's best-known brand. But later the company would record its first ever trading loss.

Ray Kroc has been described by *Time Magazine* as 'one of the most influential builders of the twentieth century'. Few children refuse a McDonald's burger – and its golden arches logo became a symbol of American enterprise. Kroc was a truly opportunistic and focused entrepreneur who built an organizational network of dedicated franchisees. Yet his entrepreneurial contribution began late in life and the McDonald's chain of hamburger restaurants was certainly not his own invention. Instead he saw – really he stumbled on – an opportunity where others missed the true potential for an idea. Once he had seen the opportunity he rigorously applied business acumen and techniques to focus on providing value for his customers. By standardizing his product and restaurants he was able to guarantee high and consistent quality at relatively low cost. Kroc was also wise enough to use the expertise that his franchisees were developing. The golden arches brand and the Ronald McDonald character became ubiquitous.

In 1955, at the age of 52, Ray Kroc completed 30 years as a salesman, mainly selling milkshake machines to various types of restaurant across America, including hamburger joints. His customers included the McDonald brothers who, having moved from New Hampshire to Hollywood, but failing to make any headway in the movie business, had opened a small drive-through restaurant in San Bernadino, California. They offered a limited menu, paper plates and plastic cups, and guaranteed the food in 60 seconds. When their success drove them to buy eight milkshake machines, instead of the two their small size would logically suggest, Ray Kroc's interest was alerted and he set off to see the restaurant. Kroc's vision was for a national chain which could benefit from organization and business techniques. He bought out the McDonald brothers and set about building a global empire. After he officially retired from running the business, and until his death in 1984, Ray Kroc stayed on as President and visited two or three different restaurants every week. He saw himself as the 'company's conscience', checking standards against his QSCV vision – quality food, fast and friendly service, clean restaurants and value for money.

The McDonald's empire grew to be 30,000 restaurants worldwide serving 40 million people everyday; America always remained the biggest market. At one stage up to 3000 new ones were being opened in a single year. The basic formula has worked as well in Moscow and Beijing as it has in the USA. Although the products available are broadly similar in the USA and Europe, menus are seen as flexible in other parts of the world. Japanese stores, for example, feature teriyaki burgers, sausage patties with teriyaki sauce. Many of the stores are franchises; the rest are mainly joint ventures. 8000 are company operated, and the recent trend has been for this proportion to decline in favour of more franchises. An 'ideal' franchise partner runs between 10 and 15 restaurants.

The growth and success in an industry where 'fast food is a by-word for low wages and an unskilled temporary workforce' is not accidental. It has been very carefully planned and managed, although McDonald's relies a lot on the people at the sharp end. Employees are often young; they work a closely prescribed system, operating internationally established rules and procedures for preparing, storing and selling food. Various incentive schemes are practised. Labour turnover is high, however, and consequently McDonald's has its critics as well as its supporters. Nevertheless, it is obvious that some competitors seek to emulate McDonald's in a number of ways: products, systems and employee attitudes.

Our competitors can copy many of our secrets, but they cannot duplicate our pride, our enthusiasm and our dedication for this business.

McDonald's has been profitable because it is efficient and productive; and it has stayed ahead of its competitors by being innovative and looking for new opportunities.

A lot of the developments are planned and imaginative. McDonald's does not move into new countries without thorough investigation of the potential; the same is true for new locations. There are now McDonald's branches in American hospitals, military bases and zoos; worldwide they can be found in airport terminals, motorway service stations, supermarkets (Tesco), and on board cruise ships and Swiss trains.

McDonald's relies heavily on its suppliers for fresh food; again, arrangements are carefully planned, monitored and controlled. The in-store systems for cooking and running branches are very tight, to ensure that products and service standards are the same worldwide. New product development has utilized all of the group's resources. The Big Mac, which was introduced nationally in the USA in 1968, was the idea of a Pittsburgh franchisee who had seen a similar product elsewhere. The aim was to broaden the customer base and make McDonald's more adult orientated. The company allowed the franchisee to try the product in his restaurant in 1967, although there was some initial resistance amongst executives who wished to retain a narrow product line, and it proved highly successful.

Egg McMuffins in the early 1970s were a response to a perceived opportunity – a breakfast menu and earlier opening times. Previously the restaurants opened at

11.00 am. Although the opportunity was appreciated the development of the product took place over 4 years, and the final launch version was created by a Santa Barbara franchisee who had to invent a new cooking utensil.

When Chicken McNuggets were launched in 1982 it was the first time that small boneless pieces of chicken had been mass produced. The difficult development of the product was carried out in conjunction with a supplier and there was immediate competitive advantage. The product was not readily copied. From being essentially a hamburger chain McDonald's quickly became number 2 to Kentucky Fried Chicken for fast-food chicken meals.

McDonald's continually tries out new menus, such as pizzas, in order to extend its share of the overall fast-food market, but for many years it avoided any diversification, nor did it offer any different 'food concept'. To enhance its image of good value, and to compete in a very dynamic industry, McDonald's offers 'extra-value meals', special combinations at low prices. However McDonald's has been criticized for increasing portion sizes as a marketing tool – which might seem like extra value but is, at the same time, encouraging greater consumption of fast food at any one time.

In addition, McDonald's is a 'penny profit' business. It takes hard work and attention to detail to be financially successful. Store managers must do two things well: control costs and increase sales. Increased sales come from the products, certainly, but also from service. Cost control is vital, but it must not be achieved by compromising product quality, customer service or restaurant appearance. Instead, it requires a focus on productivity and attention to detail. Success with these strategies has been achieved partly through serious attempts to share learning and best practice throughout the global network.

The company became an industry leader and contends there were six main reasons behind this:

- Visibility: to this end substantial resources are devoted to marketing. The golden arches symbol is instantly recognizable.
- Ownership or control of real-estate sites: McDonald's argues that this factor differentiates it from its competitors who lease more.
- Its commitment to franchising and supplier partnerships.
- It is worldwide, with restaurants in some 120 countries, and uses local managers and employees.
- The structure is very decentralized but lines of responsibility and accountability are clear.
- It is a growth company – or at least it has been for most of its existence.

Setbacks and renewal

By the mid 1990s, with the company still growing rapidly, the 'early warning signs' began to appear for the first time. The company held 40 per cent of the US market for its products, and yet its burgers were not coming out as superior to Wendy's and Burger King in taste tests. In addition, a special promotion in America, based around burgers for 55 cents each, did not prove successful because of the conditions attached to the offer. A new spicier – and premium price – burger for adults, the Arch Deluxe, had not taken off. New restaurants in the USA were beginning to take sales away from existing ones, rather than generating new business. Established franchisees were hardly delighted! One complained, sued and won $16 million in damages. A leading franchisee pressure group expressed the view that the entrepreneurial drive of founder Ray Kroc (who died in 1984) had been lost and replaced by a non-entrepreneurial bureaucracy. This change of culture was one reason why McDonald's recently pursued a libel action in the UK against two environmentalists: a case where McDonald's won the legal argument but lost the accompanying public-relations battle.

After a period of criticism and disappointing results McDonald's began to fight back. With franchisees paying half the costs, new computerized kitchen equipment has been systematically installed in its 30,000 restaurants, allowing fast cooking to order. Ready-to-serve meals no longer have to stand for a few minutes on heated trays. In addition, McDonald's began to experiment with new low-risk opportunities for its competencies in supply-chain management, franchising, promotion and merchandising by acquiring new restaurant chains. Included were a group of Mexican restaurants in Colorado, a chain of pizza outlets in Ohio, 23 Aroma coffee shops in London and the Boston Market chain of chicken restaurants. The US operations were split into five independent geographical regions.

But all of these initiatives failed to stop McDonald's starting to trade at a loss for the first time in 2002. Also for the first time, restaurants were closed down – some 700 in all, expecially where there was unnecessary duplication – as a response to falling sales. The share price tumbled. Jim Cantalupo, a retired strategic leader, was tempted back to try and restore the past glory. Was this possible – or was the brand at the beginning of the end of its life cycle? Interestingly McDonald's fastest growing competitior was Subway which markets fresh sandwiches and is perceived to be offering a far healthier alternative.

Cantalupo's strategy had a number of important elements:

- The focus was to be on new customers rather than new restaurants.
- In part this was to be achieved through healthier food options. Some of this would be achieved in the content and the preparation; at the same time people would be encouraged to eat more healthily.
- Existing customers would be encouraged to visit the restaurants more often – and to support this, service must get better. Fresh, hot food must be available within a three minute promise. The toilets must be spotless at all times, however busy the restaurant is. Underpinning this was to be a renewed emphasis on staff training.
- New products feature more imagination and innovation. There is now (rolled out from trials in America) a wider range of salads and new desserts, including bagged fresh fruit. Vegetables such as carrot sticks are available. For the adult taste, Mexican burgers are beginning to make inroads in America where there is a large Hispanic-speaking population.

Both sales and profitability rose again, but was McDonald's truly turned around?

A major setback was the sudden death (from a heart attack) of Jim Cantalupo in 2004 – he was 60 years old – and another strategic leader had to be found. Australian Charlie Bell, aged 43, who had worked closely with Cantalupo, seemed an ideal choice. Together they had introduced the slogan 'I'm Lovin' It' and adopted the mantra: 'attract more customers by being better rather than bigger'. But in 2005 Bell also died suddenly and unexpectedly, from cancer.

His replacement was Jim Skinner who opted to increase the company's presence in China ahead of the 2008 Olympic Games. The number of outlets was to double from 500 to 1000, with, for the first time, drive-throughs. The menus would feature both American and Chinese influences.

Range enhancements in the US included breakfast cereals and there was a deliberate drive to provide more nutrition information. But success around the world was uneven, with Europe showing a decline in sales.

Limited changes continued. The McCafe concept, pioneered successfully in Australia and New Zealand, was introduced to the US. McCafe's are situated alongside McDonald's restaurants and they mimic Starbucks. They sell light (cold) snacks and treats as well as a range of coffee products.

A major store revamp programme, already begun, intensified. There were 'too many tired stores'. New designs, new colours, new layouts, touch-activated self service screen ordering points, piped smells and sounds all featured. Sofa areas, much like those found in some Starbucks outlets, were trialled in selected locations. Opening hours were generally increased.

In 2007 McDonald's posted its 'best financial results for 30 years'. There had been four years of continuous monthly sales increases with 4 million more customers using basically the same number of restaurants.

Questions

1 How does McDonald's create value for its customers?
2 How might it create new values in the future?
3 What are its important competencies and capabilities?
4 To what extent do you think issues of strategic leadership and culture have influenced its growth and prosperity?

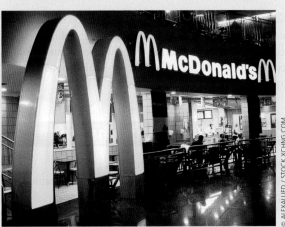

Summary

Strategies are means to ends – they are the means through which organizations seek to achieve objectives and fulfil their mission or purpose.

All managers can be strategy makers because of their influence in both strategy creation and strategy implementation.

Strategic management is a process which embraces the strategies together with the themes of excellence in their implementation, creativity and innovation when they are changed and the effective and timely management of these changes.

There is evidence that strategic thinking, and hence strategic management, could be improved in many companies by:

- *segmenting* and *targeting* markets more crisply and definitively
- appreciating clearly what the *key success factors* are in the targeted markets and segments
- creating real *competitive advantage*
- out-thinking rivals.

There are three levels of strategy:

- *corporate* – the overall portfolio of businesses within an organization
- *competitive* – the search for, and maintenance of, competitive advantage in each and every business, product and/or service
- *functional* – the activities that deliver the competitive advantage.

These activities, products, services and businesses should not be analysed exclusively at an individual 'ring-fenced' level, but also in terms of the whole organization. Links should be forged wherever possible to generate *synergies*.

Strategies should not be thought of as having one single definition or perspective. Five have been discussed: visionary strategies, planned strategies and tactics, all of which address the future; present strategic positions, and patterns that have emerged with past decisions and strategies.

Strategy comprises elements of learning, understanding, imagining and competing.

Organizations need a persuasive business model that deals with what product (or service), for whom it is intended and their compelling reason to buy.

E–V–R (Environment–Values–Resources) is a simple but very useful framework for examining the effectiveness of the current strategies and strategic position of an organization.

The strategic management process comprises three broad stages: analysis; creation and choice, and implementation. This three-stage approach can be linked to the popular and well-established concept of *strategic planning*.

Additional themes complement, but do not replace, strategic planning in the understanding of the realities of strategic management and strategic change, namely competitive advantage, emergent strategy creation, strategic competency, strategic leadership, and risk and crisis management.

There are three ways in which strategies are created: with visionary leadership, from a planning process, and adaptively and incrementally as new decisions are taken in real time.

Strategy and strategic management in different sectors, such as small and global businesses, the public sector and not-for-profit organizations, have many similarities, but there are clear differences, especially of emphasis.

Online cases for this chapter

The following case is relevant for this chapter:
Online Case 1.1: P&O: Peninsula & Oriental Steamship Company

Questions and research assignments

1 What exactly is a strategy? What have you learned about different perspectives, levels and ways in which they are changed?

2 What are the key elements in the strategic management process?

3 How has Marks and Spencer sought to attain and maintain competitive advantage? What do you think their objectives should now be?

4 From your background knowledge, what might be the key success factors required for success in the airline business? How do you feel Virgin and EasyJet have embraced these? How important a factor is 'risk taking'?

Internet and library projects

1 P&O – Peninsular & Oriental Steamship Company

Read this case on the website and then track down what has happened to the various parts of the P&O business under their new ownerships. Overall are the parts better off than they would have been had P&O not restructured in the way it has?

2 Sainsbury's first became UK market leader for 'packaged groceries' over twenty-five years ago (in 1983 in fact), with some 16 per cent market share. Tesco and the Co-op each had 14.5 per cent and Asda 8 per cent.

The company's shares continued to outperform the Financial Times Index of top shares throughout the 1980s, and an editorial in the *Financial Times* commented that Sainsbury's 'performance combines profitability, productivity and a sense of social purpose'.

However, there did not appear to be any 'grand strategy'.

We did not sit down in the early 70s and work out any corporate plan, or say that by a particular time we intended to be in a particular business, or to be of a particular size.

ROY GRIFFITHS, MANAGING DIRECTOR

Rather, Griffiths claimed, Sainsbury's had 'identified and obsessively pursued' opportunities that fitted the company's corporate values, the 'basics of the business'.

These were:

- selling quality-products at competitive (although not necessarily the cheapest) prices
- exacting quality-control standards
- extensive research into competitors and customers
- strict financial management
- tight control of suppliers
- planned staff involvement.

In recent years Tesco has overtaken Sainsbury (and everyone else) to become a very dominant UK market leader. Why and how do you think this might have happened? Do you feel Roy Griffiths' comments imply a strategic weakness in Sainsbury at that time?

Try to identify the successful strategies pursued by Tesco and the comparative shortcomings in the Sainsbury strategy – and also look into the fightback by Sainsbury.

Can you identify any influence from changes in strategic leadership?

Asda **http://www.asda.com**
J. Sainsbury plc **http://www.j-sainsbury.co.uk**
Sainsbury's **http://www.sainsbury.com**
Tesco **http://www.tesco.com**

And on the way up to add new pressures are:

Wm Morrison **http://www.morrisons.co.uk**
Aldi **http:www.aldi.co.uk**
Lidl **http:www.lidl.co.uk**

Strategy activity

Breakfast for one – the story of MyMuesli

MyMuesli was formed in 2007 by three university graduates from Passau in Germany. Within 5 months of setting up in business they have achieved rapid growth in both sales and numbers employed with their innovative business model which allows the customer to create on-line their own muesli recipe from 75 different ingredients and then have the product posted to them.

The three founders, Max Wittrock, Hubertus Bessau and Phillip Kraiss are all of the same age (being in their mid twenties) all educated at the University of Passau with Bessau and Kraiss also studying at the Budapest University of Economics. Each of the founders studied related business subjects in public relations, marketing and law. The M company web site is MyMuesli.com and it was developed by them. The ingredients they use for the muesli are all sourced from organic farmers and can be sold to customers as being their own personalized healthy high quality designs. In their first year of operation sales reached €125,000 with a labour force of 30 people who are a mixture of full-time and part-time workers. The three founders are looking ahead very optimistically as they believe they are riding the trend to individualization and to quality organic food.

Questions

1   Do you think this business will grow rapidly? Justify your response.
2   Is this a business model that truly reflects the new trends today in business start-up?

References

Beck, P, quoted in Lorenz, C (1987) Crusading for a clear strategy, *Financial Times*, 25 February.

Bettis, R and Prahalad, CK (1995) The dominant logic: retrospective and extension, *Strategic Management Journal*, Volume 16, January.

Drucker, PF (1994) The theory of business, *Harvard Business Review*, September–October.

Gladwell, M (2000) *The Tipping Point – How Little Things Can Make a Big Difference,* Little Brown.

Hamel, G (2000) *Leading the Revolution,* Harvard Business School Press.

Hamel, G and Prahalad, CK (1989) Strategic intent, *Harvard Business Review*, May–June.

Hinterhuber, H and Popp, W (1992) Are you a strategist or just a manager? *Harvard Business Review*, January-February.

James, B (1984) *Business Wargames,* Penguin.

Janis, IL (1972) *Victims of Groupthink,* 2nd edition, Houghton Mifflin.

Kay, JA (1993) *Foundations of Corporate Success: How Business Strategies Add Value*, Oxford University Press.

Mathur, SS and Kenyon, A (1998) *Creating Value: Shaping Tomorrow's Business*, Butterworth-Heinemann.

Mintzberg, H, Ahlstrand, B and Lampel, J (1998) *Strategy Safari*, Prentice Hall.

Mintzberg, H, quoted in Lorenz, C (1982) Strategic doctrine under fire, *Financial Times*, 15 October. The themes are developed extensively in Quinn, JB, Mintzberg, H and James, RM (1987) *The Strategy Process*, Prentice-Hall.

Mintzberg, H (1989) *Mintzberg on Management*, Free Press.

Morrison, R and Lee, J (1979) From planning to clearer strategic thinking, *Financial Times*, 27 July.

Pascale, RT (1984) Perspectives on strategy – the real story behind Honda's success, *California Management Review*, 26, 47–72.

Porter, ME (1980) *Competitive Strategy*, Free Press.

Porter, ME (1985) *Competitive Advantage*, Free Press.

Porter, ME (1996) What is strategy? *Harvard Business Review*, November–December.

Pümpin, C (1987) *The Essence of Corporate Strategy*, Gower.

Quinn, JB (1980) *Strategies for Change: Logical Incrementalism*, Irwin.

Stacey, RD (1993) *Strategic Management and Organizational Dynamics*, Pitman.

Williams, P (1976) *Crisis Management – Confrontations and Diplomacy in the Nuclear Age,* Martin Robertson.

Part 2

Strategic positioning

In Part 2 we see how the concept of environmental fit and a PEST (political, economic, social and technical) analysis illustrate the presence, absence or loss of strategic positioning, competitiveness and strategic effectiveness. We believe that culture and values hold the key to the existence and sustenance of positioning, competitiveness and effectiveness. This part looks in detail at positioning and competitiveness, and useful techniques for carrying out the appropriate analyses are explained. Chapter 2, which begins Part 2, introduces the important concepts of strategic thinking, environmental analysis and synergy, which are relevant for the whole book.

There are three distinct approaches to strategy and strategy creation. They should not be seen as opposing approaches, however, but as complementary approaches to opportunity finding. The entrepreneurial organization will certainly take account of all three, placing an appropriate emphasis on each one. They are:

- Market-driven. The market-based approach implies an active search for new product and marketing opportunities in the external environment. These might be found in industries in which the organization already competes or in new ones.

- Resource-based. Here the organization clarifies its distinctive core competencies and strategic capabilities – perhaps technologies and processes – which set it apart from its competitors in ways that customers value. It then seeks to build on these competencies and capabilities to build new values for both existing and new customers. This approach has the advantage of encouraging the organization to focus on what it can do well – as long as there is a market for it.

- Competitor-influenced. This is a more tactical approach which implies short-term vigilance. Whilst seeking to build the future, an organization must never lose sight of the present day. Its existing positions must be protected against active competition. This means an ability to react to competitor moves and proactive initiatives designed to surprise competitors. Of course, it is important not to become over-reliant on this tactical approach as this is likely to make the organization more reactive rather than proactive.

Organizations should be looking for ways of being different from their competitors. This is unlikely to come from imitation, from monitoring and copying what rivals do – although this approach can be seen in many organizations. In the end such mimicry will make all competing organizations look remarkably similar, making it difficult for customers to distinguish between them and placing too much emphasis on price competition. Instead organizations should be looking to innovate to achieve two purposes – one intention is to always be ahead of rivals with new ideas; the second intention is to draw apart from competitors with radical differences that they find hard to imitate in the short term. There are two important provisos. First, the differences should mean something positive to customers; it is not simply a question of being different for the sake of being different. Second, it should never be assumed that any gap or advantage is anything but temporary; all ideas can be copied eventually, and all good ones will be!

We look at these approaches in Part 2 before developing our understanding of culture and values.

Chapter 2

Strategic thinking, environmental analysis, synergy and strategic positioning

PART 1
Understanding strategy

1 Introducing strategy and strategic management

PART 5
Strategic management

14 Strategy implementation

15 Leading change

16 Managing strategy in the organization

17 Final thoughts – the purpose of strategy

PART 2
Strategic positioning

2 Strategic thinking, environmental analysis, synergy and strategic positioning

3 Resource-led strategy

4 The dynamics of competition

5 Introducing culture and values

STRATEGIC MANAGEMENT: AWARENESS AND CHANGE

PART 4
Issues in strategic growth

11 Strategic growth

12 International strategy

13 Failure, consolidation and recovery strategies

PART 3
Strategic analysis and choice

6 Strategic purpose

7 Strategic success

8 An introduction to strategy creation and planning

9 Strategic leadership, entrepreneurship and intrapreneurship

10 Strategic alternatives, strategy evaluation and strategy selection

Learning objectives

Having read to the end of this chapter you should be able to:

- explain the difference between the market- or opportunity-driven, resource-based and competitor-influenced views of strategy, appreciate the three views are frequently integrated in strategy creation and understand that some strategies are tactical responses to competition in a dynamic external environment

- explain why thinking is vital in strategy creation and implementation

- define synergy and explain its significance in both competitive and corporate strategy

- understand that opportunity-driven strategy depends upon an ability to manage, and to manage in, the business environment

- explain issues of complexity, dynamism and uncertainty in relation to the organiza-tion's environment

- identify how changes might be forecast

- summarize the important aspects of government policy on competition and its regulation

- discuss the organization as an open system and (using a PEST analysis) assess the impact of a number of environmental forces

- describe Porter's five forces model for analysing the attractiveness of an industry

- appreciate the significance of key success factors, effective strategic positioning and adding value

- conduct a SWOT analysis

- carry out scenario planning

- construct an experience curve and explain its significance.

Case 2.1

PartyGaming   UK

In recent years, and with growth of the Internet, on-line gambling has become a huge global industry. Poker is arguably the lead game, and international poker competitions are now televised on mainstream channels. This sector is monitored by PokerPlus and in the UK there is a dedicated gambling information website.

PartyGaming – which includes the sub-brand PartyPoker – is based in Gibraltar, and when it was floated in 2005 it was valued at £5 billion. Its leading rivals include 888.com, Empire Online and Sportingbet.

Shortly after the flotation PartyGaming upset some of its clients when it opted to reroute PartyPoker players to a new site where they could more easily be sold other gaming products. At this time there were talks of a merger with the smaller Empire Direct.

A new CEO, Mitch Garber, was recruited from Canada with a signing-on fee of US$6 million and an annual base salary of US$1 million. This was in March 2006, and two months later two of the founding Board Directors resigned. The lock-in arrangements which had prevented them selling their shares had now timed out, and they took advantage to realize their fortunes. The two were founding entrepreneur Ruth Parasol (she had previously established a very successful pornography business) and Anurag Dikshit, the IT expert behind much of the key software.

It was less than six months later, in October, that the US Congress passed a new Bill restricting on-line gambling. PartyGaming's share price began to tumble. At the same time bosses from Sportingbet were arrested on illegal gambling charges. William Hill suspended its US gaming businesses. Like others, William Hill relied on the US market. At one time 75 per cent of PartyGaming's revenue was coming from America. In the future there would need to be greater emphasis on Europe and other (newer) markets. To accomplish this PartyGaming knew it needed to offer games in more than the English language and set about implementing this.

In December 2006 one of the Las Vegas casino chains (Las Vegas Sands) decided it would open a new gaming website for the UK market.

© NETPICS/ALAMY

Questions

1   How might the opportunity for PartyGaming have been spotted and developed?
2   How easy or difficult to you think it might be to stay a leader in this emerging business?

SOURCE: THIS CASE STUDY WAS PREPARED USING PRIMARILY PUBLICLY AVAILABLE SOURCES OF INFORMATION FOR THE PURPOSES OF CLASSROOM DISCUSSION; IT DOES NOT INTEND TO ILLUSTRATE EITHER EFFECTIVE OR INEFFECTIVE HANDLING OF A MANAGERIAL SITUATION.

2.1 Introduction

Good ideas for the future can either start inside the organization or be obtained from external contacts, and the ability to synthesize and exploit the information that is available to develop new products, new services and new strategic positions is a reflection of the organization's *strategic thinking* capabilities. Think about how the idea for PartyGaming (Case 2.1) might have come about.

At one level, matching, exploiting and changing the linkages between resource competency and environmental opportunity is an expression of organizational competitiveness, and the presence (or absence) of competitive advantage. It was shown earlier (Chapter 1) how it is essential for organizations to seek competitive advantage for every product, service and business in their portfolios.

Figure 2.1 illustrates the organization in the context of its external environment. Its suppliers and customers, upon whom it depends, and its competitors – both existing and new-in-the-future – are shown as having an immediate impact. Wider environmental forces bear on all the 'players' in the industry, and these are shown in the outer circle as political, economic, social and technological (**PEST**) forces.

The forces and influences have been deliberately shown in concentric circles. It is quite typical for us to think of the organization as a group of activities (and/or functions) and then to place everything and everyone else, including suppliers and customers, in a so-called external **business environment**. Increasingly, it makes considerable sense for the organization to see itself working in partnership with its suppliers, distributors and customers. When this perspective is adopted, then only competitors from the middle ring would be placed in the external environment, together with the general forces which impact upon the whole industry.

Figure 2.2 extends this point, and shows the various concepts and techniques discussed in this part of the book in diagrammatic form.

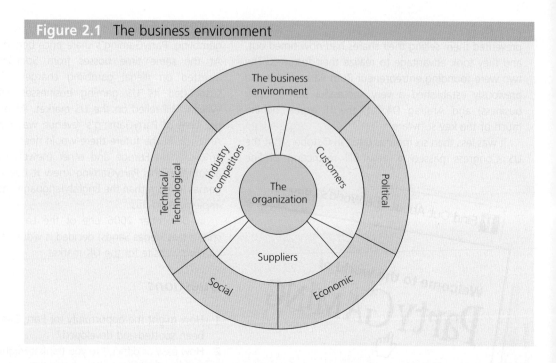

Figure 2.1   The business environment

2.2   Strategic thinking

Strategic thinking embraces the past, present and future. Understanding patterns and lessons from the past will certainly inform the future – but given the dynamic, turbulent and uncertain business environments that affect many industries and organizations, it would be dangerous to assume that the future will reflect the past and be a continuation of either past or existing trends.

Figure 2.2   Competitive strategy: A summary of techniques

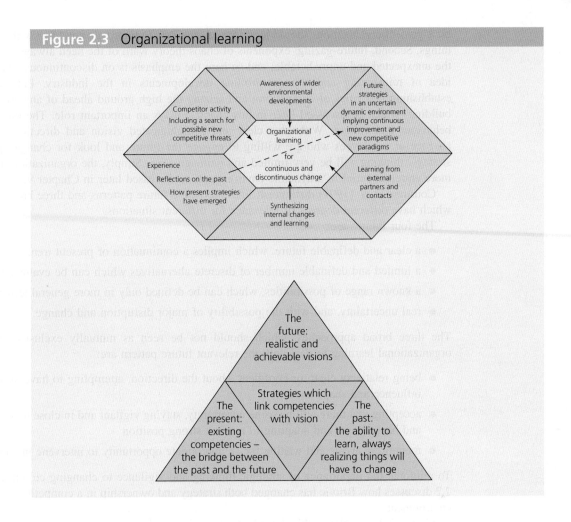

Figure 2.3   Organizational learning

Figure 2.3 shows (bottom triangle) how strategies which link competencies with a strategic vision for the future embrace learning from the past, an awareness of existing competencies and some insight into likely future trends. The top part of the figure highlights that *organizational learning* is required to build the future and that it encompasses:

- a reflection on how present strategies have emerged over time

- an understanding of current competencies and the strategic value of particular resources and the linkages between them

- knowledge of existing competitors and what they are doing at the moment – and preparing to do in the future

- an appreciation of possible new sources of competition

- an awareness of wider environmental opportunities and threats

- an ability to share information with, and thus learn from, external partners and contacts, including suppliers, distributors and customers.

The effective organization will synthesize this learning into insightful strategies for dealing with future uncertainties.

Campbell and Alexander (1997) offer a different, but clearly related, approach to strategic thinking. They delineate three elements. First, insight into operating issues: with **benchmarking** other organizations (searching for good practices), process re-engineering and total quality management organizations should look for opportunities to improve continuously the way they do things. Second, future-gazing: exponents of chaos theory warn of the need always to be ready for the unexpected and unpredictable; and so here the emphasis is on discontinuous change, and the idea of reinventing and thus controlling developments in the industry. Put another way, establishing new rules of competition and seizing the high ground ahead of any rivals. Scenario building (which is discussed later in this chapter) plays an important role. The third element is behaviour and culture. Without a clear and communicated vision and direction, and with an absence of employees who are willing to engage the future and look for change opportunities, strategic thinking will be very limited and unimaginative. Simply, the organization must become more entrepreneurial in a dynamic environment, as discussed later in Chapter 9.

Courtney *et al.* (1997) distinguish four alternative future patterns and three broad approaches, which have different degrees of relevance for different situations.

The four futures are:

- a clear and definable future, which implies a continuation of present trends
- a limited and definable number of discrete alternatives which can be evaluated and judged
- a known range of possibilities, which can be defined only in more general terms
- real uncertainty, and with the possibility of major disruption and change.

The three broad approaches, which should not be seen as mutually exclusive, for utilizing organizational learning to deal with the relevant future pattern are:

- being relatively clear, or confident, about the direction, attempting to have an important influence and shape events
- accepting that there will be some uncertainty, staying vigilant and in close touch with events and happenings, and adapting to retain a strong position
- monitoring events and waiting for an appropriate opportunity to intervene in some way.

To reinforce the importance of strategic thinking and vigilance to changing circumstances, Case 2.2 discusses how Britvic has changed both strategy and ownership in a competitive and changing environment.

Figure 2.4 completes this introductory section and summarizes the purposes and broad elements of strategic thinking.

Throughout this section on strategic thinking, the emphasis has been on the ability to take a holistic view and synthesize information. We need to synthesize information from the past and present and combine it with a view of the future. This embraces information which originates inside the organization and information that can be obtained from external partners and contacts. Synergy, which is discussed next, explains the importance of linkages and synthesis.

2.3 Synergy

Synergy is either a path to sustained growth or a 'bridge too far' for organizations. It is concerned with the returns that are obtained from resources. Ansoff (1968) argues that resources should be combined and managed in such a way that the benefits which accrue exceed those which would result if the parts were kept separate, describing synergy as the 2 + 2 = 5 effect. Simply, the combination of the parts produces results of greater magnitude than would be the case if the parts operated independently.

There are three basic synergy opportunities:

- *functional* – sharing facilities, competencies, ideas and best practice

Case 2.2

Britvic UK

Britvic was started some 70 years ago when the British Vitamin Product Company realized that bottled fruit juices were a good way for people to get extra Vitamin C. The company would become the second largest soft drinks business in the UK. It was quite normal for customers to ask for a 'Britvic orange' or 'Britvic pineapple' by name in pubs.

But other companies and brands were added to the business. Robinsons (best known for its fruit concentrates, often with added barley, and at one time very visible at the Wimbledon tennis championships) and Tango were important examples. Britvic had also developed the J2O range of bottled drinks – usually featuring more than one fruit in a blend – and these had more bite than the more traditional plain fruit juices. The company also had the UK distribution rights for Pepsi – which in turn held a 5 per cent shareholding in Britvic. In 2003 Britvic bought Ben Shaws, a smaller rival based in Huddersfield. Significantly Shaw's marketed Pennine Spring Water.

The company was sold as an IPO in 2005 when its three main shareholders – InterContinental Hotels,

Whitbread and Pernod Ricard – opted to sell their shares.

A year later sales and profits were declining. Sales of carbonated soft drinks were falling – although people were still consuming an average of one pint a day! One growth area was energy drinks – Lucozade was enjoying a revival and brands like Red Bull were also doing very well. Britvic was able to turn to Pepsi – still a shareholder – and gain access to its Gatorade brand. It also used its interest in Pennine Spring to make and market fruit-flavoured bottled water, another growth sector in the market.

Britvic was also interested to trial Pepsi Raw, where cane sugar and natural plant extracts are used to produce an all-natural version of Pepsi.

Question

1 To what extent can you see evidence of organizational learning and strategic thinking in the Britvic story?

SOURCE: THIS CASE STUDY WAS PREPARED USING PRIMARILY PUBLICLY AVAILABLE SOURCES OF INFORMATION FOR THE PURPOSES OF CLASSROOM DISCUSSION; IT DOES NOT INTEND TO ILLUSTRATE EITHER EFFECTIVE OR INEFFECTIVE HANDLING OF A MANAGERIAL SITUATION.

- *strategic* – complementary competitive strategies across a corporate portfolio: even in a diversified conglomerate some sharing is possible
- *managerial* – compatible styles of management and values in different functions and businesses.

Sometimes the synergy is obtained by transferring people between different parts of an organization, possibly for a period of secondment, in order to facilitate the sharing.

Figure 2.4 Strategic thinking – purposes and elements

(BASED ON: RHODES, J. AND THAME, S. (1988) COLOURS OF YOUR MIND, HARPER COLLINS)

In simple terms, if an organization manufactures and markets six different products, the organization should be structured to yield the benefits that might be possible from combining these different interests. For example, central purchasing for all products might yield **economies of scale**; factory rationalization might increase productivity or lower production costs; sales staff might be able to obtain more or larger orders if they are selling more than one product; each product might gain from name association with the others; and distributors might be more satisfied than if the company offered only a very limited range or a single product. Some of the benefits are clearly measurable, whereas others are more subjective; and the search for synergy clearly embraces structural as well as strategic decisions.

Similarly, if functions, products or business units were not co-ordinated, then efforts may well be duplicated, or delays might be built into the organization system because of a lack of understanding.

Corporate strategy decisions, such as acquisitions, alliances or divestments, should be made in the light of the overall synergistic implications of the change. Some – strategically sound – changes imply increased synergy opportunities, while others imply complexity, fragmentation and lost synergy. The synergy impact is seen in the competitive strategies and competitive success for each relevant activity. Simply, where an organization is considering increasing its range of products and services, or merging with or acquiring another company, synergy is an important consideration. In the case of an acquisition the combination of the companies should produce greater returns than the two on their own. Adding new products or services should not affect existing products or services in any adverse way, unless they are intended to be replacements. When such strategic changes take place the deployment of resources should be re-evaluated to ensure that they are being utilized both efficiently and effectively.

Obtaining synergy may well imply the sharing of knowledge and other resources between divisions or business units, possibly attempting to disseminate best practice. This is only feasible if resource efficiencies are measured and compared in order to identify which practices are best. Internal rivalries may prevent the attainment of the potential benefits from sharing. Synergy is more likely to occur if all the relevant activities are linked in such a way that the organization as a whole is managed effectively, which Drucker (1973) has defined as 'doing the right things'. Individual business units and functions must themselves be managed efficiently or, as Drucker would say, they must be 'doing things right'. It will be seen in Chapter 7 that resource efficiency considers how well resources are being utilized and the returns being obtained from them. Effectiveness incorporates an evaluation of whether the resources are being deployed in the most beneficial manner.

There are four key elements which must come together if potential synergy is to be achieved:

- *effective leadership* – which emphasizes the importance of co-operation, sharing, transfer and learning throughout the organization
- *facilitative structure* – which allows co-operation and inhibits internal conflict
- *supportive systems* – which encourage sharing and transfer. Examples include cross-functional and cross-business project teams and the provision of opportunities for managers to spend time in other parts of an organization
- *appropriate rewards* – such that parts of an organization can benefit from helping others.

Figure 2.5 pulls these themes together and shows how synergy potential must be examined inside a framework of strategic resources, strategic thinking and the relevant business environment. Potential exists from effectively combining the various functions and activities in each business, from sharing and learning between businesses and from the overall corporate strategic logic.

At the same time, though, it must be realized that the anticipated synergy from strategic changes is easily overestimated and quite frequently it does not accrue. Potential benefits from adding new activities may be misjudged. After all, there is always an element of subjective anticipation and promise – the synergy is justified with strategic logic but delivered through

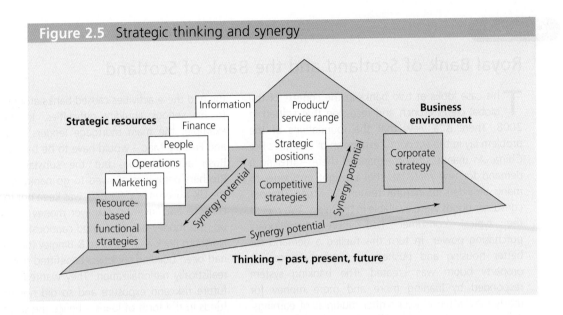

Figure 2.5 Strategic thinking and synergy

people and their behaviour – and this should not be an excuse for delusion. Admitting to strategic misjudgements rarely comes easy to strategic leaders (including bankers) and managers and, as a result, the appropriate exit or withdrawal when synergy is not obtained, may not happen when it should. Internal politics and conflicts, because businesses and divisions see themselves as rivals rather than partners, all too often inhibit synergy.

2.4   Analysing the business environment

The notion of strategic positioning helps us understand the fit between an organization and its external environment. Case 2.3 on the UK banking industry shows how company strategies have been influenced by external environmental forces. Opportunities begged and new strategies were developed – but how strong and realistic were they? Strategic positions are related to the organization's ability to create and add value and consequently added value can be examined in relation to a SWOT (strengths, weaknesses, opportunities and threats) analysis. This chapter continues by examining the nature of the business environment, followed by a consideration of the impact of competition regulations on industry and company strategies. Positions, also, have to be changed, as seen in the earlier discussion of E–V–R congruence. Sometimes the change is continuous and incremental; sometimes it is more dramatic or discontinuous. To help our understanding of the latter, the chapter concludes with a discussion of scenario building.

One thing is clear. Even if you're on the right track, you'll get run over if you just sit there!

SIR ALLEN SHEPPARD, WHEN CHAIRMAN, GRAND METROPOLITAN PLC

(NOW DIAGEO)

Managing in an increasingly turbulent world

We will now examine in detail the environment in which the organization operates and considers how the forces present in the environment pose both opportunities and threats. The topic of stakeholders is relevant here, as several of the environmental forces which affect the organization clearly have a stake in the business. Stakeholders are discussed further in Chapter 7. Freeman

Case 2.3

Royal Bank of Scotland and the Bank of Scotland   UK

This case looks at two banks in the context of the global credit crunch and recession that started in 2008. There is a view that the foundations of the problem lay in the economic expansion of countries like China. As manufacturing expanded there – fuelling a demand for raw materials that brought prosperity to many providers of natural resources – then cheaper consumer goods were available in the West. This meant the typical consumer had more discretionary purchasing power. In turn this fuelled a demand for better housing and pushed up property prices. A property boom was created. The banking system responded by loaning more and more money for mortgages, often in ever-higher multiples of earnings. As some building societies became banks they competed for this business and sub-prime (inadequate security or collateral) mortgage lending became more evident. Using sophisticated models to price them, the banks packaged these loans into bundles and sold them on to other financial institutions, thus raising more money for further lending. They also lent increasing amounts for buy-to-let mortgages to investors who wanted to benefit from property price increases. There was some adverse press regarding the scale of the bonuses that banks and hedge funds were awarding their high performing executives, but the practice continued. Everything would be fine until prices started to dip the other way – but in the euphoria many seemed to forget that history would repeat itself and what went up would come down again.

The banks were also diversifying more and more into other forms of investment and financing in a search to make money. One element of this was short selling. Here investors commit to sell stock, stock that they don't actually own, once a price hits a certain (low) point, believing that with prices falling they can quickly buy the shares they need on the open market before the point of settlement. They can thus make a very quick and often handsome profit. Supporters believe short selling reflects real fears about the performance and value of certain companies and helps their stock find a true valuation and price. But there are many opponents and critics.

The banks got hungry and greedy and arguably they took too many risks, leaving them much too exposed. In the end these activities caused banks around the world to hit serious liquidity difficulties. In the US, for example, the main mortgage lenders – Fannie Mae and Freddie Mac – would have to be bailed out by the Bush administration, but the substantial Lehmann Brothers bank was allowed to go bankrupt. Although the UK government, for one, was keen not to see banks collapse and invested taxpayer money to shore them up, this money was then used cautiously by the banks. Northern Rock and Bradford & Bingley (both banks that had been building societies) benefitted from what was realistically nationalization. They wanted to limit their future risk and exposure and so did not pass on the funds in the form of loans – hence the so-called credit crunch.

As the credit crunch took hold in 2008 it was clear that both HBOS (the merged Halifax and Bank of Scotland) and Royal Bank of Scotland (RBS) were in some difficulty – but for quite different reasons.

In 2007 Barclays had been negotiating a takeover bid for Dutch bank, ABN Amro, but it was outbid by an alliance of RBS, Santander (the Spanish bank that owned Abbey) and Fortis (the Dutch/Belgian bank). Their bid, at 72 billion Euros was ten per cent above Barclays' bid. The intention was to split up ABN Amro with RBS gaining the US retail interests and the London wholesale banking arm. Sir Fred Goodwin, CEO of RBS, was the mastermind behind the deal.

Goodwin was nicknamed 'Fred the Shred' because of his reputation as an aggressive cost cutter (with consequent job losses) after acquisitions – and there had been plenty of these. Since he took over as CEO in 2000, RBS had made 20 acquisitions in banking and insurance, including NatWest in 2002. He was also thought by some to be 'the most talented banker of his generation'.

Barclays had been planning to raise money in China and Singapore to fund the acquisition, and with hindsight they were probably fortunate to lose out! When the UK banks (along with many others throughout the world) got into serious financial difficulties and needed government investment, Barclays was able to avoid a UK government shareholding (in exchange for investment) and the consequent constraints on executive pay and dividend payments. It received funding from investors in the

Middle East instead. The banks were simply not lending to each other and thus there were cash shortages in the banking system – so loans and new mortgages were thin and expensive.

By spring 2008 RBS needed to raise £12 billion through a rights issue. It was writing down losses in the US linked to the sub-prime mortgage lending problems there – mortgages with inadequate security to potentially poor payers. In summer 2008 it was offering to sell its insurance businesses (including Direct Line and Churchill). By October 2008 it needed at least £20 billion to prevent collapse. Less than six months later, in February 2009, Sir Fred Goodwin (CEO of RBS) and Sir Tom McKillop (Chairman) were appearing before the Treasury Select Committee to say 'sorry' for the bank that had been taken over by the government.

In the end the government had provided the cash RBS needed, but at a cost. The bank was all but nationalized and Sir Fred Goodwin stepped down. The UK government was now the leading shareholder and a key influence on strategic decisions. This intervention followed the nationalization of Northern Rock and Bradford & Bingley, two mutual building societies that had become banks. A first tranche of funding had to be followed by a second as the real financial difficulties eventually became apparent and RBS announced a loss for 2008 of £28 billion, the biggest loss in British corporate history. When the press started to carry stories that Sir Fred Goodwin had departed with a pension of some £700,000 per year for life there was uproar and disgust at what appeared to be corporate excess and a reward for failure.

Meanwhile the Halifax part of HBOS had developed 'a sales culture that was so strong it had lost sight of certain key risks'. The bank was thus very exposed to falls in house prices, which were inevitable in the recession. The Halifax had long been the leading mortgage lender in the UK; it had diversified into the related insurance business before merging with Bank of Scotland.

Like RBS, HBOS was in need of a serious cash injection in 2008. The solution was also different. It became apparent the government favoured the acquisition of HBOS by Lloyds TSB. The newly merged businesses would become the UK's leading savings bank and leading mortgage lender. Its market share would be 33 per cent – when the normal competition threshold is set at 25 per cent. In the past one would have expected this merger not to have been allowed, but now it was positively encouraged.

The government would have a substantial equity stake in this bank as well, in return for cash. It was predicted that branches would be closed and jobs would be lost – but which region was most at risk? The activities were concentrated in London, Edinburgh and West Yorkshire. Yorkshire seemed the most likely casualty – but were the changes simply inevitable? The first executive casualty was Andy Hornby, CEO of HBOS who had also appeared in front of the same Treasury Select Committee.

The new company would own Birmingham Midshires Building Society, Cheltenham and Gloucester Building Society, Sainsbury's Finance and Scottish Widows Insurance. What might happen to them?

In early 2009 there was some speculation that the cash needs of the new Lloyds Group were greater than first realized and that this bank might also have to be nationalized. It was also clear that Lloyds was willing to sell some of its insurance interests to raise cash. These would be targeted disposals – Lloyds had also become the UK's leading provider of life insurance and did not want to lose this position. But it was willing to sell those activities which it remarketed through independent financial advisers rather than sold direct.

By March 2009, the Government stake in Lloyds had reached 63 per cent on the back of record losses in 2008 of £11bn by HBOS and the need to put another £11bn in liquidity into Lloyds. It was difficult to know whether the acquisition of HBOS by Lloyds TSB was rushed through without proper due diligence because the 'opportunity seemed too good to miss' or whether the government had been actively encouraging and engineering. In May Lloyds had a successful rights issue – existing shareholders bought new shares at prices below the prevailing market price – allowing the bank to pay money back to the government and thus reduce the state ownership to below 50 per cent. Shortly afterwards it was announced that all 164 Cheltenham and Gloucester branches would close although the brand would be retained. At least 1500 jobs would be shed – to add to the 3000 redundancies that had already been made. This decision would later be rescinded and a buyer sought for the business.

Questions

1 This case discusses how the banks sought ways to create new value in order to foster growth – but on what basis was it real value?

2 What does this story suggest are the real lessons to be learned from the collapse of the main UK banks?

3 What will have to change and how?

(1984) argued that stakeholders should be categorized in terms of their power and their interest. It is quite normal for organizations to draw up a two by two grid reflecting high and low power and interest on the two axes. Those with power must be satisfied, especially if they are also interested in the activities of the organization – these are key players as far as the organization is concerned. Some stakeholders may have power but little interest in what the organization does; they cannot be ignored though. Those with relatively low power but high interest should certainly be kept informed. Competitors inevitably constitute a major influence on corporate, competitive and functional strategies and they are the subject of Chapter 4. This type of analysis allows us to better understand the strategic situation and also to build relevant scenarios.

If a firm is to control its growth, change and development it must seek to control the forces that provide the opportunities for growth and change, and those that pose threats and demand responses. Not only must managers be aware of environmental forces and environmental change, they must manage the organization's resources to take advantage of opportunities and counter threats. In turn, the strategic leader should ensure that this happens and that the values and culture of the organization are appropriate for satisfying the key success factors. Quite simply, the environment delivers shocks to an organization, and the way in which resources are deployed and managed determines the ability to handle these shocks. This relates to E–V–R (environment–values–resources) congruence.

Over time, paradigms concerning 'what will work' to bring about success in a particular industry or competitive environment will be created and maintained. However, as environmental and competitive forces change, the current reality (at any time) of what is required for competitive success may be drifting away from the organization's paradigm; consequently, a new paradigm will be essential. In an age of discontinuity, paradigms will need changing more frequently and more dramatically; expediting these changes is a key managerial task.

Put another way, in a turbulent environment, the organization must change its strategies and possibly its beliefs if it is to maintain E–V–R congruence. A number of key themes underpin the issues discussed in this chapter:

- Traditional industries such as manufacturing and mining have given way to new, more technological – and frequently electronics-based – industries which demand new labour skills, and where 'knowledge workers' are of prime importance.

- New technologies can generate opportunities for substitutability, different forms of competition and the emergence of new competitors in an industry.

- In addition to changing skills demands, there have been other changes in the labour markets of developed countries. Many families have joint wage earners and more women are working. More and more people work from their homes, at least for part of their time.

- Many managers and employees are more time constrained and have less spare time than they would like. Not only does this imply less time for shopping (hence the potential for **e-commerce**), but demand has increased for convenient, time-saving products.

- People are living longer and, coupled with periods of lower birth rates, the average age of the population and the number of retired people are both increasing. These groups have more leisure time than working people.

- The Internet continues to change how we access information in a quite remarkable way.

- Multinational businesses have grown in strength and significance and they have become the norm for manufacturing industries.

- Manufacturers from the UK, US, Germany, Japan and other nations with a longstanding tradition in manufacturing have been willing to relocate factories in developing countries with lower wage costs. Technology which allows increasing levels of output from the same size factory has facilitated these changes. Hornby, which manufactures model railways and Scalextric racing car systems, switched their production to China to enable it to devote more than two labour hours for every one utilized in the UK. The outcome is visibly higher quality for the same market price. There has been a resurgence of sales and fortunes at the company.

- Consequently, the competitive arena has been changing with, recently, the highest economic growth being enjoyed by the US, although during the early and mid-1990s it was the Pacific Rim countries. In many industries, global supply potential exceeds demand, placing downward pressures on real prices.

- Product and service markets, supply chains, capital markets and communication systems have become global in nature.

- The speed of change in most industries and markets has increased and product life cycles have shortened. For some companies, success can be very transient: a classic example of this being the computer games industry for both hardware and software.

- Governments have masterminded increasing degrees of deregulation. Other countries have followed the UK's lead and privatized public-sector utilities; air travel and telecommunications markets have been opened up to more competition.

- Consumers are more aware and more knowledgeable; environmental groups have begun to wield increasing influence.

- Changes in politics and regimes in different parts of the world, such as Eastern Europe and the Far East, have introduced an element of chaos and greater unpredictability. Opportunities open up but carry a significant downside risk.

Simply, environments are more turbulent; managing them and managing *in* them demand more flexibility and more discontinuity than in the past.

> *There is no doubt that the world is becoming one marketplace. Capital markets, products and services, management and manufacturing techniques have all become global in nature. As a result, companies increasingly find that they must compete all over the world – in the global marketplace.*

MAURICE SAATCHI, WHEN CHAIRMAN, SAATCHI AND SAATCHI COMPANY PLC

> *In my experience, corporate life-threatening problems in large manufacturing companies have developed over a long period. These problems should never have been permitted to grow so large, but they were allowed to do so by top management who were lethargic and self-satisfied,*

who engaged in self-delusion and congratulated themselves on their exalted status. In short, the managements were the problem.

EUGENE ANDERSON, EX-CHAIRMAN AND CHIEF EXECUTIVE, FERRANTI INTERNATIONAL PLC

How can we expect to succeed when we are playing cricket and the rest of the world is practising karate?

SIR EDWIN NIXON, WHEN CHAIRMAN, AMERSHAM INTERNATIONAL

Figure 2.6 emphasizes that as industries and markets become increasingly global, quality is more important than origin. People in Britain might like to claim 'British is best' – as might other people in other countries – but a statement such as this is meaningless unless it can be demonstrate that British (or other) products and services really are world class. To achieve world-class quality and **reputation**, companies must use knowledge and ideas to be innovative, operate at the level of the best in the world and form international networks and partnerships to access the best resources from around the world.

In this dynamic environment, the US became the most competitive nation because it took a lead in technically advanced industries and transformed itself into a service economy. It found ways of generating the private-sector finances required for investment in new and relatively high-risk sectors, and it has ensured that regulations do not inhibit labour force flexibility. The US also has a compelling cultural will to win, the importance of which should never be underestimated.

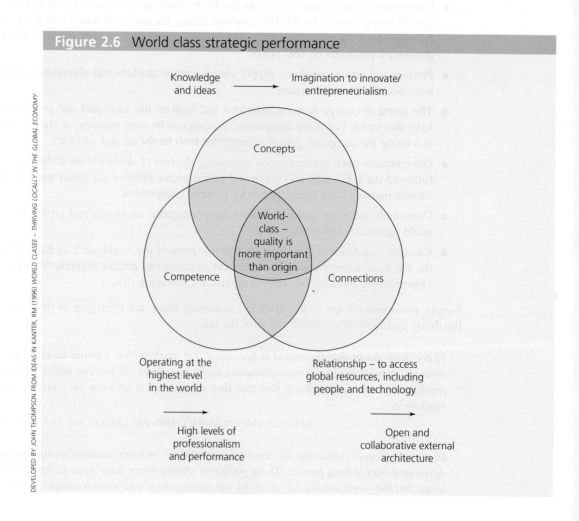

Figure 2.6   World class strategic performance

Knowledge and ideas → Imagination to innovate/ entrepreneurialism

Concepts

World-class – quality is more important than origin

Competence   Connections

Operating at the highest level in the world

Relationship – to access global resources, including people and technology

High levels of professionalism and performance

Open and collaborative external architecture

DEVELOPED BY JOHN THOMPSON FROM IDEAS IN KANTER, RM (1996) *WORLD CLASEE – THRIVING LOCALLY IN THE GLOBAL ECONOMY*

Europe is generally more restrictive, although practices do vary between countries, even within the European Union.

Although the following examples are British in origin and used to illustrate an important theme, similar stories can readily be told of other parts of the world. When the former British Prime Minister, Margaret Thatcher, came to power in 1979 she quickly identified a wide productivity gap between many British companies and those perceived to be the best in the world. She set about reducing the gap for both large and small companies – and she was successful, although in many industries a gap remains, albeit smaller than it would otherwise have been. In some industries Britain does have 'best in the world' companies, but relatively few industry-wide centres of excellence. In motor cars, really only one truly British owned – British designed company remains. This, Morgan Motors, is a very small niche player – and it still relies on other manufacturers for some parts, especially engines. Although it was owned by Ford for a period, Tata (India) now owns Jaguar and Land Rover; and Vauxhall is a subsidiary of General Motors. Peugeot, Honda, Nissan and Toyota all assemble vehicles in UK factories. Nissan's Sunderland factory has been their most productive plant in the world.

In a complex deal Volkswagen bought Rolls-Royce Vickers from Vickers without realizing the Rolls-Royce name belonged to BMW. Bentleys are now manufactured in Crewe, Rolls-Royce manufacture in Sussex. VW has rejuvenated Bentley, including reviving the company's sporting heritage. Yet, at the same time, British companies are dominant in the high-profile, advanced technology segment of Formula One racing. In recent years UK-based McLaren has been the main competitor for Ferrari – and Ferrari's technical development base is in the UK. Television assembly is similar in principle, with the last remaining British plants owned and operated by French and Japanese manufacturers.

Where there are individual world-class companies in an industry, there is also often a long tail of low performers. Most significantly, though, average productivity in Britain remains below the average for many of its leading competitors. Simply, while British companies have improved, so too have most others! Britain may have reduced the productivity gap, and may seem able and committed to it not widening again, but the gap has not been closed, and rivals have certainly not been overtaken.

The competitive future for the UK, however, or any other equivalent developed country, does not lie in reducing wages to compete with the Far East and Eastern Europe, and thus creating a downward spiral of expectation; rather it lies in finding new ways of innovating, adding value, differentiating and *leading* consumers.

Notwithstanding this, some cutting back to create and maintain trim and efficient organizations will always be essential. These points are explored further in Strategy in action 2.1.

There are several frameworks for studying the environment of an organization. In addition to considering the company's *stakeholders* in terms of their relative power, influence, needs and expectations, a PEST analysis (discussed in detail later in this chapter) can prove useful. This is an objective and straightforward consideration of changing political, economic, social and technological influences. This review should help to clarify changing opportunities and threats.

The nature of the stakeholders and the environmental forces is a useful indicator of the most appropriate strategic approach for the organization to take. Where the environment is complex, turbulent and uncertain it will be necessary for the organization to be vigilant and speedily reactive. A carefully planned approach is ideal in stable and predictable circumstances, and a positive and proactive approach should be adopted where the environment can be changed or influenced.

Uncertainty, complexity and dynamism

Duncan (1972) argued that the environment is more uncertain the more complex or the more dynamic it is. An example of an organization facing a generally stable, non-dynamic and hence

Strategy in action 2.1

Competitive Advantage and Strategy in the Late 1990s

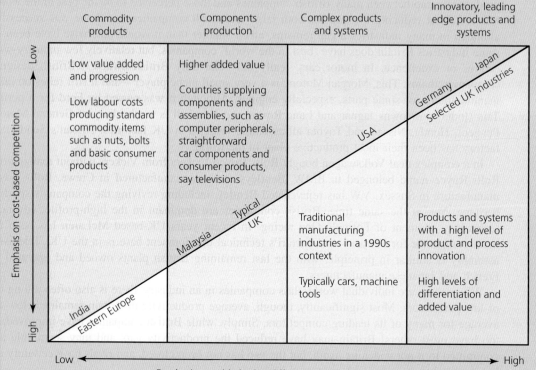

- Countries progress up and down the diagonal over time.
- Within each country different industries will be in different sectors. The position shown here on the diagonal is that with which the country is typically associated.
- The UK has drifted down to 'components' by offering incentives and relatively low labour costs to attract inward investments. However, with for example, aerospace and pharmaceuticals the UK is clearly in the innovatory sector.
- Arguably the UK should focus more intently on innovation to reverse the trend – otherwise the UK

will increasingly become a mere supplier to the industry leaders and drivers. However, innovation requires managerial and workforce strengths and skills which the UK may not have.

- Innovation relates to products and services (radical improvements in value, reconceiving form and function) and market boundaries (attracting new customers, providing new values by satisfying individual needs more effectively).

Based on ideas in Kruse, G and Berry, C (1997) A nation of shopkeepers, *Management Today*, April.

fairly certain environment is a small rural village post office. While most organizations face far more uncertainty, their managers also enjoy more challenges. In recent years the position of small village post offices has become more uncertain and many have closed. At the same time, however, the Post Office has looked at the possibility of offering a new range of banking services. The Post Office has realized that there is a window of opportunity as high-street banks consolidate and shut small branches. Moreover, they already have branches in every town and city that possess both spare capacity and a secure environment for handling cash. This development is not feasible without support and co-operation from the main clearing banks who, on the one hand, could benefit from the beneficial publicity, but, on the other hand, might see it constituting a new form of competition for some of their services. So far the banks have only co-operated reluctantly. The new position of state control over the main UK banks may or may not change this. However the government is presently trying to introduce change into the Post Office through an equity stake taken up by an outside organization – quite possibly TNT the Dutch transport business. This policy provoked vehement resistance by the unions and by many of the government's own MPs.

The **dynamic environment** Dynamism can be increased by a number of factors. Rapid technological change involving either products, processes or uses will mean that changes are likely to occur quickly and that organizations must stay aware of the activities of their suppliers and potential suppliers, customers and competitors. Where competition is on a global scale the pace of change may vary in different markets, and competition may be harder to monitor. In such cases the future is likely to be uncertain.

Risk-taking and creative entrepreneurial leadership may well be required as strategies pursued in the past, or modifications of them, may no longer be appropriate.

The **complex environment** An environment is complex where the forces and the changes involving them are difficult to understand. Quite often complexity and dynamism occur together. Technology-based industries and Internet-based businesses are excellent examples of this. The structure of the organization, the degree of decentralization and the responsibility and authority delegated to managers throughout the organization, and information systems can render complexity more manageable. Managers will need to be open and responsive to the need for change and flexible in their approach if they are to handle complexity successfully.

Managerial awareness and the approach to the management of change are therefore key issues in uncertain environments. If managers are strategically aware, and flexible and responsive concerning change, then they will perceive the complex and dynamic conditions as manageable. Other less aware managers may find the conditions so uncertain that they are always responding to pressures placed on the organization rather than appearing to be in control and managing the environment. Hence a crucial aspect of strategic management is understanding and negotiating with the environment in order to influence and ideally to control events.

Case 2.4 looks at issues of dynamism and complexity in the music industry.

The four myths of nature

John Adams (1995) in his book on risk cites a number of other authors in trying to explain why different organizations and managers adopt different approaches to the way they deal with the external environment. These approaches reflect underlying beliefs and values held by the organization and the apparent nature of the environment. In describing four basic states Adams uses the metaphor of a round ball.

When nature (the environment) is benign, the metaphor is of a ball coming to rest in the bottom of a bowl. If the bowl is moved the ball returns to its position. The environment here appears predictable, stable and forgiving – perhaps desirable, but a rare event for most organizations, it has to be said. Managers tend to be relaxed and non-interventionist. Opportunities to grow are naturally limited. Of course, change for the sake of change can be unnecessarily disruptive, and so this does not appear to be an opportunity for the entrepreneur.

When the environment is ephemeral, it is fragile, precarious and unforgiving. If managers make the wrong decisions it can be damaged or affected seriously by the organization. In this context, we can think of the catastrophes caused by combinations of human and technical error in train, airplane and space shuttle disasters. Here safety is sometimes compromised by the quest for speed and cost

Case 2.4

The Recorded Music Industry

UK

The recorded music industry has enjoyed a period of growth since the emergent popularity of Elvis Presley and The Beatles. From the mid 1980s to the mid 1990s the growth and prosperity was boosted by people's willingness to rebuild their collections by replacing their vinyl LPs and cassettes with compact discs. Since 1997, however, the popularity of singles has declined whilst sales of compilation albums and classical music has increased. Global revenues reached almost $40 billion dollars in 1999 but by 2003 these had declined by almost 20 per cent to $32 billion.

There are many forces at work driven by the public perception that they were paying too much for the product:

- People were downloading music from the Internet, sometimes legally, sometimes illegally. Eventually legal action would be taken to restrain the activities of Napster, a leading provider of on-line free downloads. The Internet also provided the opportunity to purchase CDs at significant discounts on high street prices.
- Pirate copies of CDs were increasingly available – some on the black market, some inadvertently through legitimate channels.
- The CD replacement market has matured as people have rebuilt their collections.
- More recently people have been able to make good home copies of their friends' CDs by purchasing a CD burner for the personal computer. To complete the task, CD labels can be downloaded from the Internet!
- The ways and means that people listen to music have changed to iPod and other MP3 players. Computer game playing and satellite television have competed for the same leisure time. In the past people would play CDs time and time again; now many people only play them infrequently. New cars typically provide a CD player and yet there are more radio stations as well to tune in to.
- In 2007, and for the first time, songwriters and publishers earned more from downloads than from the copyright payments resulting from the sales of their CDs.
- Young people – teenagers and others not in full-time employment – have often switched their discretionary purchasing away from music to their mobile phones.
- Retail competition has increased, stimulated in part by supermarkets increasing their sales of best sellers. As a result prices and margins have declined.
- Some analysts believe there is less creative talent being discovered than was the case in the past. Assuming this is true, there are potential causes. The industry is dominated by global conglomerates; the significance of small and entrepreneurial independent record labels has declined, although they are still around. The growth in popularity of television programmes designed to find new artistes and to form new boy and girl bands has also, for some, been a negative force. The real test is often whether sales of second and third albums exceed or fall below those of debut albums. In the past the successful groups and artistes saw sales grow; now it is less likely to happen.

By 2002 five companies controlled some 75 per cent of the global market, with the following market shares:

Universal (MCA and Polygram)	25.9 per cent
Sony Music	14.1 per cent
EMI (incl. Virgin)	12.0 per cent
Warner Music	11.9 per cent
Bertelsmann (BMG)	11.1 per cent

EMI was seriously interested in acquiring Warner Music from Time Warner Corporation, but the European competition regulators ruled against this in 2000. A year later a proposed merger between EMI and Bertelsmann received the same treatment. Meanwhile Bertelsmann and Sony started planning a joint alliance which subsequently became a merger – and which the European regulators approved in 2004. Ironically the European Court later concluded this was a poor decision. Together they were roughly the same size as Universal.

EMI was eventually bought by Guy Hands' private equity vehicle, Terra Firma, in 2007. Hands declared there would need to be annual savings of some £200 million and that between 1500 and 2000 jobs would need to be lost. Sir Paul McCartney and Sir Mick Jagger

SOURCE: THIS CASE STUDY WAS PREPARED USING PRIMARILY PUBLICLY AVAILABLE SOURCES OF INFORMATION FOR THE PURPOSES OF CLASSROOM DISCUSSION; IT DOES NOT INTEND TO ILLUSTRATE EITHER EFFECTIVE OR INEFFECTIVE HANDLING OF A MANAGERIAL SITUATION.

opted to leave EMI and Robbie Williams refused to deliver his latest album to them as a protest.

Interestingly, and also in 2007, Madonna parted company with Warner Music, with whom she had recorded for 25 years. In the future she would work with Live Nation, a concert promotion business, which would sell her albums as well as stage and promote her concerts. In 2009 a merger was proposed between Live Nation and leading distributor of tickets for shows, concerts and sporting events, Ticketmaster.

Questions

1 What future changes do you foresee – and will these have a predominantly positive or negative impact on (a) consumers and (b) the record companies?
2 How have your own musical tastes and listening habits been changing in recent years?
3 What are the implications of the proposed merger between Live Nation and Ticketmaster?

reduction. The appropriate style is one of caution and careful risk management, if not risk aversion. The metaphor is of a ball balanced precariously on an upturned arch.

If the environment is perverse or tolerant, it behaves with some degree of predictability but only within limits. Modest shocks can be tolerated. The ball is in a valley and can roll around. The organization knows the other inhabitants in the valley – metaphorically its customers and competitors. The issue is that the next valley might be more attractive, perhaps more fertile (potentially more profitable) or quieter (fewer competitors). There is perhaps some data which implies this, but from the current position the complete picture is not fully visible – to climb out and change valley requires courage and faith. With some strategic changes, some aspects will always remain uncertain. Organizations need to make sure they are 'fully kitted out and ready to go' when they embark on change. There is, though, generally a way back which reduces the risk and allows management of the downside. This is the measured way of some entrepreneurs and entrepreneurial managers.

A capricious environment is represented by a ball able to roll freely on a flat surface. Once there is any movement it is very difficult to predict where the ball might come to rest again. Any change of position or direction involves a degree of risk, but staying put is also high risk. If other balls are moving freely, the organization can get hit and moved out of position by competitors. Vigilance is essential but care must be taken with any change of direction.

Environmental influences

Figure 2.1 showed how the organization is typically one of a number of competitors in an industry; and to a greater or lesser degree these competitors will be affected by the decisions, competitive strategies and innovation of the others. These interdependencies are crucial, and consequently strategic decisions should always involve some assessment of their impact on other companies, and their likely reaction. Equally, a company should seek to be fully aware of what competitors are doing at any time.

Furthermore, this industry will be linked to, and dependent on, other industries: industries from which it buys supplies, and industries to which it markets products and services. Essentially this relates to Porter's model of the forces that determine industry profitability, the subject of the next section in this chapter.

The relationships between a firm and its buyers and suppliers are again crucial for a number of reasons. Suppliers might be performing badly and as a result future supplies might be threatened; equally they might be working on innovations that will impact on organizations to which they supply. Buyers might be under pressure from competitors to switch suppliers. It is important to be strategically aware, and to seek to exert influence over organizations where there are dependencies.

These industries and the firms that comprise them are additionally part of a wider environment. This environment is composed of forces that influence the organizations, and which in turn can be influenced by them. Particular forces will be more or less important for individual organizations and in certain circumstances. It is important that managers appreciate the existence of these forces, how they might influence the organization, and how they might be influenced.

Mintzberg (1987) has used the term 'crafting strategy' to explain how managers learn by experience and by doing and adapting strategies to environmental needs. He sees the process as being analogous to a potter moulding clay and creating a finished object. If an organization embarks upon a determined change of strategy, certain aspects of implementation will be changed as it becomes increasingly clear with experience how best to manage the environmental forces. Equally, managers adapt existing competitive and functional strategies as they see opportunities and threats and gradually change things. In each case the aim is to ensure that the organization's resources and values are matched with the changing environment.

External forces: a PEST analysis

A PEST analysis is merely a framework that categorizes environmental influences as political, economic, social and technological forces. Sometimes two additional factors, environmental and legal, will be added to make a PESTEL analysis, but these themes can easily be subsumed in the others.

Economic conditions affect how easy or how difficult it is to be successful and profitable at any time because they affect both capital availability and cost, and demand. If demand is buoyant, for example, and the **cost of capital** is low, it will be attractive for firms to invest and grow with expectations of being profitable. In opposite circumstances firms might find that profitability throughout the industry is low. The timing and relative success of particular strategies can be influenced by economic conditions. When the economy as a whole or certain sectors of the economy are growing, demand may exist for a product or service which would not be in demand in more depressed circumstances. Similarly, the opportunity to exploit a particular strategy successfully may depend on demand which exists in growth conditions and does not in recession. Although a depressed economy will generally be a threat which results in a number of organizations going out of business, it can provide opportunities for some.

Economic conditions are influenced by *politics and government policy*; equally, they are a major influence affecting government decisions. The issue of whether European countries join, or remain outside, the single European currency is a case in point. At any one time either exported or imported goods can seem expensive or inexpensive, dependent upon currency exchange rates. There are many other ways, however, in which government decisions will affect organizations both directly and indirectly as they provide both opportunities and threats.

While economic conditions and government policy are closely related, they both influence a number of other environmental forces that can affect organizations. Capital markets determine the conditions for alternative types of funding for organizations; they can be subject to government **controls**, and they will be guided by the prevailing economic conditions. The rate of interest charged for loans will be affected by inflation and by international economics and, although the determining rate may be fixed by a central bank (as it is, for example, by the Bank of England) it will always be influenced by stated government priorities. Government spending can increase the money supply and make capital markets more buoyant. The expectations of shareholders with regard to company performance, their willingness to provide more equity funding or their willingness to sell their shares will also be affected.

The labour market reflects the availability of particular skills at national and regional levels; this is affected by training, which is influenced by government and other regional agencies. Labour costs will be influenced by inflation and by general trends in other industries, and by the role and power of trade unions.

The *sociocultural environment* encapsulates demand and tastes, which vary with fashion and disposable income, and general changes can again provide both opportunities and threats for particular firms. Over time most products change from being a novelty to a situation of market saturation, and as this happens pricing and promotion strategies have to change. Similarly, some products and services will sell around the world with little variation, but these are relatively unusual. Figure 2.7 shows how washing-machine designs are different for different European countries to reflect consumer preferences. Organizations should be aware of demographic changes as the structure of the population by ages, affluence, regions, numbers working and so on can have an important bearing on demand as a whole and on demand for particular products and services. Threats to existing products might be increasing; opportunities for differentiation and **market segmentation** might be emerging.

Technology in one respect is part of the organization and the industry part of the model as it is used for the creation of competitive advantage. However, technology external to the industry can also be captured and used, and this again can be influenced by government support and encouragement. Technological breakthroughs can create new industries which might prove a threat to existing organizations whose products or services might be rendered redundant, and those firms which might be affected in this way should be alert to the possibility. Equally, new technology could provide a useful input, perhaps in both manufacturing and service industries, but in turn its purchase will require funding and possibly employee training before it can be used.

The examples referred to here are only a sample of many, and individual managers need to appreciate how these general forces affect their organization in particular ways. Table 2.1 provides a general list of environmental influences and forces. Strategy in action 2.2 provides a short and very selective PEST analysis of environmental forces affecting the credit-card industry and picks out a number of key influences. It will be realized how such an analysis can be useful for helping to identify emerging opportunities and threats.

For any organization certain environmental influences will constitute powerful forces which affect decision-making significantly. For some manufacturing and service businesses the most powerful force will be customers; for others it may be competition.

In some situations suppliers can be crucial. In the case of some small businesses external forces can dictate whether the business stays solvent or not. A major problem for many small businesses concerns the management of cash flow – being able to pay bills when they are due for payment and being strong enough mentally to persuade customers to pay their invoices on time. In the UK, the National Health Service (NHS) is similarly very dependent upon government policies which affect all decision areas. Consultants' salaries, nurses' pay, new hospitals and wards, and new equipment are substantially determined by government decisions, which they will seek to influence.

Figure 2.7 European preferences for washing machines

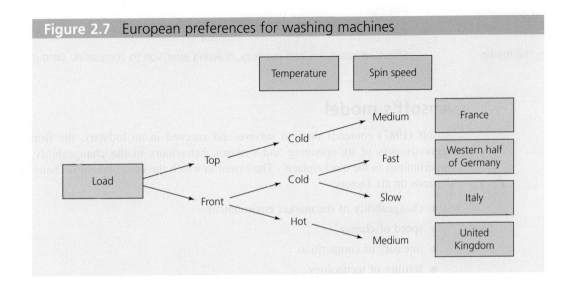

Table 2.1	Environmental influences
Influence	**Examples of threats and opportunities**
The economy	The strength of the economy influences the availability of credit and the willingness of people to borrow. This affects the level of demand. Interest rates and currency fluctuations affect both the cost and demand of imports and exports
Capital markets	This includes shareholders, and their satisfaction with company success. Are they willing to buy more shares if offered them to increase equity funding? Would they willingly sell if someone bid for the organization? Also included are the banking system, and the cost and availability of loan capital
Labour market	Changes in structure with an ageing population and more women seeking work Availability of skills, possibly in particular regions Influence of trade unions Contribution of government training schemes
Technology	Robotics in manufacturing in industries such as car assembly Computers for design and manufacturing Information technology such as electronic point of sale in retailing
Sociocultural environment	Pressure groups affecting demand or industry location. Changing population – by age groups Changing tastes and values Regional movements
Government	Regional aid policies Special industry initiatives, e.g. where high technology is involved The legal environment is part of this, including the regulation of competition Restraints on car exhaust emissions (pollution control) and labelling requirements would be other examples
Suppliers	Availability and cost of supplies, possibly involving vertical integration and decisions concerning whether to make or buy-in essential components
Customers	Changes in preferences and purchasing power Changes in the distribution system
Competitors	Changes in competitive strategies Innovation
The media	Effects of good and bad publicity, drawing attention to companies, products and services

Ansoff's model

Ansoff (1987) contends that 'to survive and succeed in an industry, the firm must match the aggressiveness of its operating and strategic behaviours to the changeability of demands and opportunities in the marketplace'. The extent to which the environment is changeable or turbulent depends on six factors:

- changeability of the market environment
- speed of change
- intensity of competition
- fertility of technology

Strategy in action 2.2

A PEST Analysis of the Credit-card Industry

Political	Legislation allowing young people to own credit cards. The threat of restrictions on Internet trading.
Economic	The future presence – or not – of the UK, Denmark and Sweden in the eurozone and the European single currency, and the impact of the single currency on interest rates generally.
	Future economic trends which will affect demand for consumption and credit. Freedom for, or restrictions on, new entrants to the industry.
Social	The willingness or reluctance to buy on credit – while credit is readily available for many people, there can be a rebellion against high interest charges. The increasing acceptance of Internet shopping, which depends on credit-card transactions – possibly affected by the age profile of the population.
Technical	Internet and e-business possibilities – and security.

© MOREPIXELS / ISTOCK

- discrimination by customers
- pressures from governments and influence groups.

Ansoff suggests that the more turbulent the environment is, the more aggressive the firm must be in terms of competitive strategies and entrepreneurialism or change orientation if it is to succeed. The firms in an industry will be distributed such that a small number is insufficiently aggressive for the requirements of the industry, and as a result they are unprofitable or go out of business. Another small number will be above average in terms of success because they are best able to match the demands of the environment. Many will achieve results above average; and some others may also fail because they are too aggressive and try to change things too quickly through lack of awareness.

Where an organization is multiproduct or multinational, the various parts of the business are likely to experience some common environmental influences and some which are distinctive, which reinforces the need for managers who are closest to the market and to competitors to be able to change things.

Ansoff suggests that the environment should be analysed in terms of competition and entrepreneurship or change. The degree of competitive and entrepreneurial turbulence can be calculated by attributing scores to various factors. The competitive environment is affected by market structure and profitability, the intensity of competitive rivalry and the degree of differentiation, market growth, the stage in the life of the products or services in question and the frequency of new product launches, capital intensity and economies of scale. Certain of these factors, namely market growth, the stage in the life of the product and profitability, also help to determine the extent to which the environment is entrepreneurial. Changes in structure and technology, social pressures and innovation are also influential.

The culture of the organization and managerial competencies should then be examined to see whether they match and be changed as appropriate if they do not. Again, scores are attributed to various factors. Culture encompasses factors such as values, reaction and response to change, and risk orientation. Problem-solving approaches, information systems, environmental forecasting and surveillance, and management systems are included in the competencies. Ansoff is really arguing that the resources of the organization and the values must be congruent with the needs of the environment.

2.5 Analysing an industry

Porter (1980) argues that five forces determine the profitability of an industry. They are featured in Figure 2.8 At the heart of the industry are rivals and their competitive strategies linked to, say, pricing or advertising; but, he contends, it is important to look beyond one's immediate competitors as there are other determinants of profitability. Specifically there might be competition from substitute products or services. These alternatives may be perceived as substitutes by buyers even though they are part of a different industry. An example would be plastic bottles, cans and glass bottles for packaging soft drinks. There may also be a potential threat of new entrants, although some competitors will see this as an opportunity to strengthen their position in the market by ensuring, as far as they can, customer loyalty. Finally it is important to appreciate that companies purchase from suppliers and sell to buyers. If they are powerful they are in a position to bargain profits away through reduced margins, by forcing either cost increases or price decreases. This relates to the strategic option of **vertical integration** which will be considered in detail later in the book. Vertical integration occurs where a company acquires, or merges with, a supplier or customer and thereby gains greater control over the chain of activities which leads from basic materials through to final consumption.

Any company must seek to understand the nature of its competitive environment if it is to be successful in achieving its objectives and in establishing appropriate strategies. If a company fully understands the nature of the five forces, and particularly appreciates which one is the most important, it will be in a stronger position to defend itself against any threats and to influence the forces with its strategy. The situation, of course, is fluid, and the nature and relative power of the forces will change. Consequently the need to monitor and stay aware is continuous.

Figure 2.8   Determining industry profitability – the five forces

(ADAPTED FROM PORTER, ME (1980) COMPETITIVE STRATEGY: TECHNIQUES FOR ANALYSING INDUSTRIES AND COMPETITORS, FREE PRESS.)

The threat of new entrants: barriers to entry

Where barriers to entry are high new entrants are likely to be deterred, and if they do attempt entry they are likely to provoke a quick reaction from existing competitors. Low barriers generally mean that responses will be slower, offering more opportunities. A number of factors can create barriers:

- **Economies of scale**: Some of the possible ways of achieving economies of scale have been considered earlier. In addition the **experience (or learning curve)** can be important. If there is a need for substantial investment to allow a new entrant to achieve cost parity with existing firms this may well be a deterrent. In such a case if a newcomer enters the market with only limited investment and is not able to achieve comparable economies of scale, he or she will be at a cost disadvantage from the start, in which case substantial differentiation will be required, but this introduces another issue.

- **Product differentiation**: If consumers perceive rival products or services to be clearly differentiated then newcomers must also seek to establish a distinct identity. Newcomers will therefore have to invest in advertising and promotion to establish their new brand, and this may be expensive. The major brewers and chocolate manufacturers, for example, spend millions of pounds each year promoting specific products and brands.

- **Capital requirements**: Any requirement for substantial investment capital in order to enter a market is a barrier to entry. The investment may be on capital equipment, research and development, or advertising to establish a market presence, and it may deter many aspiring competitors. However, large multiproduct companies that wish to break into a market may finance the necessary investment with profits from other areas of the business. Drugs is one industry we have already mentioned where huge investments are required to develop and test possible new products over several years. Whilst patent protection allows the costs to be recouped through prices, the investment is all 'up front'.

- **Switching costs:** These are not costs incurred by the company wishing to enter the market but by the existing customers. If a buyer were to change his supplier from an established manufacturer to a newcomer costs may be incurred in a number of ways. New handling equipment and employee training are examples. Buyers may not be willing to change their suppliers because of these costs, thereby making it very difficult for any newcomer to poach existing business.

- **Access to distribution channels:** Existing relationships and agreements between manufacturers and the key distributors in a market may also create barriers to entry. Some manufacturers may be vertically integrated and own or control their distributors. Other distributors may have established and successful working relationships with particular manufacturers and have little incentive to change. Companies aspiring to enter a market may look for unique distribution opportunities to provide both access and immediate differentiation.

- **Cost advantages independent of scale:** This represents factors which are valuable to existing companies in an industry and which newcomers may not be able to replicate. Essential technology may be protected by patent; the supply of necessary raw materials may be controlled; or favourable locations near to supplies or markets may not be accessible. Government restrictions on competition may apply in certain circumstances.

Case 2.5 illustrates the absence of significant barriers to entry in the DVD industry. The outcome is that an innovative business model can be copied by powerful rivals.

Potential entrants, attracted by high margins in an industry and not detracted by any of the above barriers, must try and gauge any likely retaliation by existing manufacturers; and Porter argues that this can be assessed by examining:

- past behaviour when newcomers have entered or tried to enter the market;

SOURCE: THIS CASE STUDY WAS PREPARED USING PRIMARILY PUBLICLY AVAILABLE SOURCES OF INFORMATION FOR THE PURPOSES OF CLASSROOM DISCUSSION; IT DOES NOT INTEND TO ILLUSTRATE EITHER EFFECTIVE OR INEFFECTIVE HANDLING OF A MANAGERIAL SITUATION.

Case 2.5

Barriers to Entry: Netflix and DVD Rentals   US

Netflix is an on-line DVD rental site begun by entrepreneur Reed Hastings in America in 1998. There is a monthly subscription which started out at $19.95 (£12.50) but which was soon reduced as customer numbers increased, and for this customers can borrow DVDs and keep them for as long as they like. It is a simple model. Once people join and subscribe they pick out a large number of titles they would like to borrow. Three are sent out with return envelopes, and when these are returned three more are dispatched from their list, based on prioritization and availability. Originally there were about 12,000 titles to choose from, but after three years this had grown to 50,000. Typically customers have to wait between 2 and 5 days after e-mailing their order, but turnaround is speeded up by Netflix having 36 distribution points across the US. Operatives basically unpack and repack – the systems are driven by IT at relatively low cost. By 2002, when 30 per cent of US households had a DVD player, Netflix had enrolled some 750,000 subscribers, and this number was growing at the rate of 100,000 every quarter. The target for 2012 was always 20 million subscribers. One can soon calculate this implies substantial revenues every year from a very simple business idea.

The leading competitor, although not offering the same service, was Blockbuster video, which rents videos to over 50 million customers through its ubiquitous retail outlets. Blockbuster will rent and even post out DVDs, but there is an individual item charge. It is a different business model. Netflix believes it has a competitive advantage because it can post summaries and reviews of all its DVDs on its website that all its customers have to use.

However, in 2002, a new and very powerful rival opted to enter the market and there was little Netflix could do in retaliation. Wal-Mart, which already sold DVDs, set up a rival service, undercutting Netflix's price by 10 per cent. Amazon, partnering with other organizations for which it provided a marketing vehicle, also entered the market with an almost identical business model to that of Netflix.

Project

Check out the performance of of Netflix and evaluate how this entrepreneurial business dealt with the threat from Wal-Mart and Amazon. Examine the progress made by LoveFilm in the UK.

- the resource capabilities of existing companies which will affect their ability to retaliate;
- the investment and commitment of existing companies which may make retaliation inevitable if they are to protect their investment and position;
- the rate of growth of the industry – the faster it is the more possibilities for a newcomer to be absorbed.

Existing firms may be prepared to reduce prices to deter entry and protect their market shares, especially if supply already exceeds demand. As a result, even in an oligopoly, profitability can be contained.

The bargaining power of suppliers

The behaviour of suppliers, and their relative power, can squeeze industry profits. Equally the ability of a firm to control its supplies by vertical integration (acquiring its suppliers) or long-term supply arrangements can be very beneficial. The relative power is affected by five major factors:

- Concentration amongst suppliers vis-à-vis the industry they sell to: if the supply industry is very concentrated then buyers have little opportunity for bargaining on prices and deliveries as suppliers recognize that their opportunities for switching suppliers are limited.

- The degree of substitutability between the products of various suppliers and the amount of product differentiation: a buyer could be tied to a particular supplier if his or her requirements cannot be met by other suppliers.

- The amount of, and potential for, vertical integration which might be initiated by either the supplier or the buyer: again government regulation on competition may prevent this.

- The extent to which the buyer is important to the supplier: if a buyer is regarded as a key customer he or she may well receive preferential treatment.

- Any switching costs that might be incurred by buyers will strengthen the position of suppliers.

The bargaining power of buyers

Any competitive action by buyers will act to depress industry profits, but specific arrangements with distributors or customers can be mutually beneficial. Vertical integration is again a possibility. The major supermarket grocery stores with their multiple outlets nationwide are in a very strong bargaining position with most of their suppliers.

This power has been strengthened by the success of private label brands, whose prices can be up to 60 per cent below those for the recognized major brands. Private labels have grown to over one-third of UK retail food sales. They have proved most successful with chilled meals, frozen vegetables, fruit juices and cheese; and least successful with pet foods, sugar, coffee and, for a long time, breakfast cereals. Barriers against private label products are provided by innovation and aggressive marketing and promotion.

As the market for overseas travel grew in the UK, the power of the leading travel agency groups also grew vis-à-vis the tour operators – it is, after all, the travel agency that actually sells the holiday and has direct contact with customers, who they are able to influence. As a consequence the leading tour operators (Thomson and Airtours, subsequently renamed My Travel) sought to acquire their own agencies and exercise greater control over the supply chain. At the same time, industry rationalization has meant that a small number of tour operators (all of whom also own their own airline) dominate the market. In recent years there has been a reaction from the airlines. The low-cost carriers chose to sell direct in order to avoid agency commissions; now the leading full-service airlines such as BA have reduced the commissions they are willing to pay for tickets issued by travel agents.

The bargaining power of buyers is determined by:

- the concentration and size of buyer
- the importance to the buyer of the purchase in terms of both cost and quality (the more important it is the more he or she must ensure good relations with the supplier)
- the degree of product standardization, which affects substitutability
- the costs, practicability and opportunity for buyers to switch supplier
- the possibility of vertical integration, initiated by either the supplier or the buyer.

The threat of product substitutes

The existence or non-existence of close substitutes helps to determine the elasticity of demand for a product or service. In simple terms this is price sensitivity. If there are close substitutes, demand for a particular brand will increase or decrease as its price moves downwards or upwards relative to competitors. Price changes can be initiated by any firm, but other competitors will be affected and forced to react. If products are not seen as close substitutes then they will be less price sensitive to competitor price changes.

For this reason firms will seek to establish clear product or service differentiation in order to create customer preference and loyalty and thereby make their product or service less price sensitive. Where this is accomplished industry profits are likely to rise, which of course may be attractive to prospective newcomers who will seek to create further differentiation in order to encourage customers to switch to them and enable them to establish a presence in the market.

Products and services can be substituted for something completely different, reflecting the ever-present possibility that new competitors can change the 'rules of competition' in a market or industry. The music industry is in flux today. The sales of album CDs are in decline due to downloading from Internet music sites. The price of CDs are expensive relative to the cost of production. Additionally the technology is now available to easily trawl for and capture music tracks on the Internet for a fraction of the cost of legally buying a CD. The music industry must come up with a solution to this problem which is more than just regulatory. It must suit the consumer!

Rivalry amongst existing competitors

Porter terms rivalry amongst existing competitors 'jockeying for position'. Competition may take the form of price competition, advertising and promotion, innovation, or service during and after sale. Where competitive firms are mutually interdependent, retaliation is a key issue. Before deciding upon aggressive competitive actions firms must attempt to predict how their competitors will react; when other firms are proactive an organization must at least be defensive in order to protect market share and profitability. The intensity of competition is affected by the market structure and depends on the following:

- the number of competitors and the degree of concentration
- the rate of growth of the industry – slow growth increases the pressure upon competitors to fight for market share
- the degree of differentiation – the less there is the more likely is price competition
- cost structures – where fixed costs are high relative to variable costs companies are very sensitive around the **break-even** point. Profits are very dependent upon volume.

As passenger aircraft become larger and more technologically sophisticated, the cost of buying (or leasing) and insuring them grows. The operating cost per seat mile – and break-even loadings – increases steadily, but with international overcapacity and competition, the revenue per seat mile has been falling. Some airlines have closed or been acquired; others have had to reduce salaries and numbers of employees.

An example of dedicated assets which have no obvious alternative use is multiplex cinema complexes. As the number of these has grown, cinema audiences have also grown, and an industry in decline has been given a new lease of life. In addition, it is quite normal for several fast food and retail outlets to open alongside the cinemas, helping to boost their traffic. But what would happen to the cinema buildings if audiences declined again? Additionally it could be argued that cinema going is now becoming expensive. The early alternative product offering in the market was easyCinema.com. This failed to make any real dent in the market against the power of the major cinema chains. History would suggest that sooner or later new competitive pressures will hit this industry. This may come from film downloads once the speed of broadband connections improves significantly.

Manufacturers of consumer electronics products have to invest continually to maintain the technology required for the necessary product improvements. To generate revenues to fund further investment they need volume sales; to create these they price with low, competitive margins. Profits are very slim, but the sunk costs are such that the cycle continues; it is too costly to come out of the industry. The cycle is reinforced by consumer purchasing behaviour. Consumers know which brands they are happy to consider, their shortlist depending upon the

Table 2.2 A checklist for industry analysis
How many firms are in the industry, and what size are they?
How concentrated is the industry?
To what degree are products substitutes?
Is the industry growing or contracting?
What are the relative powers of suppliers? Buyers? Competitors?
What are the prevailing competitive strategies?
What entry barriers exist?
What economies of scale are present?
What experience/learning curve effects are important?
What exit barriers exist (if any)?
What important external factors affect competition?

quality and differentiation they are seeking. They then buy on price, seeing certain brands as interchangeable. Inevitably, the retailers also earn only low margins.

Table 2.2 provides a summary checklist of factors for industry analysis, and Strategy in action 2.3 analyses the supermarket industry against Porter's model of five forces.

The rivalry factors discussed above, and the rivalry strategies, are both affected by any slowing down in the rate of industry growth, by acquisitions, and by changes in the marketing strategy of any one competitor resulting from the perception of new opportunities for differentiation or segmentation.

To be an effective competitor, a company must:

- appreciate which of the five forces is the most significant (it can be different for different industries) and concentrate strategic attention in this area
- position itself for the best possible defence against any threats from rivals
- influence the forces detailed above through its own corporate and competitive strategies
- anticipate changes or shifts in the forces – the factors that are generating success in the short term may not succeed long term.

Much will depend upon the strategic leader, the quality of management in the organization and the prevailing culture.

The role of government

Rather than incorporation as a separate sixth factor, Porter maintains the importance of government lies in an ability to affect the other five forces through changes in policy and new legislation. For example, the introduction of competition and an internal market in the National Health Service, a Conservative policy abandoned by the Labour government under Tony Blair and Gordon Brown.

Many industries in the UK, such as the main utilities of gas, electricity and water, were privatized – in order to prevent these (new) businesses becoming national or local monopolies in private ownership, with enormous potential to exploit their customers, industry regulators have been appointed in a number of cases. The regulators and the newly privatized businesses have at times disagreed over important **strategic issues**. Individual regulators are given freedom to establish specific guidelines within clear broad principles, and some would argue that this makes conflict between them and the regulated businesses inevitable. One of the reasons for the diversification strategies by privatized companies is that they create business activities which are outside the direct control of the regulator. Given a general trend away from diversification to a

Strategy in action 2.3

Industry Analysis – Supermarkets

Threat of new entrants

Barriers to entry are very high, because of the necessary supply network and distribution infrastructure. The continual investment in EPOS (electronic point-of-sale) and EDI (electronic data interchange) systems creates further barriers. In addition, it is very difficult and very expensive to acquire new sites in prime positions. It is possible, given financial reserves, to build a position in selected market niches.

Of course powerful companies, able to command huge financial resources, can break in with an acquisition, as we saw when Wal-Mart bought ASDA.

Relative strength of suppliers

Supply agreements with major retail chains, using EDI, make the leading suppliers and supermarkets more and more interdependent. Ownership of a leading brand yields power, but secondary and tertiary brands must be more vulnerable. Further interdependency with own-label supply agreements.

Relative strength of buyers

Invariably buyers will have more than one supermarket that they can access, especially if they are car owners. The power of the Internet to promote home deliveries also opens up choice. There will be some loyalty, but only if prices and service are competitive.

Threat of substitutes

Small independent stores have a niche and a role, but the supermarkets are dominant. However, they are vulnerable on price for those products/brands offered by smaller, discount stores, especially where customers are willing to multi-shop. Home shopping via IT continues to be a sector of the market the supermarkets must develop rather than relinquish.

Existing rivalries

The industry is very competitive, with four or five chains competing for the family shopping budget. Tesco, ASDA, Sainsbury and Morrisons (after their takeover of Safeway) have different competitive strategies (product ranges, pricing strategies, etc.) and have differing appeals, but they remain largely interchangeable. These companies must all invest to try and create differences as well as pricing competitively. The relatively speedy demise of the Co-op to a predominantly niche role illustrates how intense the rivalry is. The recent growth of the new price led supermarkets Lidl and Aldi show where things are now going as consumers cut their spending.

Summary

Barriers to entry	high
Power of suppliers	medium
Power of buyers	medium/high
Threat of substitutes	medium
Existing rivalries	intense

© VITALINA / ISTOCK

concentration on core businesses and competencies, this has sometimes proved to be risky. Maybe the impact of the regulators also needs regulating.

High and low profit industries

In 2008 Michael Porter (Porter, 2008) revisited his earlier work on industry analysis. He identified soft drinks, pre-packaged software, pharmaceuticals and spirits as attractive, relatively high **profit** potential, industries and air travel, wines and hotels as more naturally unattractive – and therefore very competitive. Scattered through this book you will find cases on most of these industries. Porter based his conclusions on return on investment data.

He emphasized that high growth does not guarantee high profits – and neither does the presence of innovation and the latest technology.

In terms of using Porter's ideas to evaluate any 'industry' it is important to be clear on what we are taking the word 'industry' to mean. It is possible to take a very broad definition – such as public transport – or a very narrow one. If the interpretation is too wide then it will obscure the identification of opportunities to be genuinely different; if it is too narrow it is possible to undervalue the potential to create synergy by linking different products and market niches.

We conclude this section with Case 2.6 on the English Premier League.

Case 2.6

The English Premier League   UK

It is debatable whether the English Premier League is the foremost football league in the world. Some would definitely argue it is. Matches are televised for a global audience. The leading teams have relied on overseas players for many years – there are matches when Arsenal may not even include one English player in their line-up. Chelsea is not far behind in this. There are several foreign managers in charge of the top clubs. A number of these clubs have become public companies, but at the same time a number of the leading clubs have been bought by wealthy foreign businessmen. Although it not this simple, two broad types are prominent: Russian (and other) oligarchs (such as the owner of Chelsea) and owners of US sports franchises (Manchester United and Liverpool). The owner of Fulham is Mohamed Al-Fayed (owner of Harrods) and until recently the owner of Manchester City was the ex-Prime Minister of Thailand. In September 2008 the ownership of City moved to that of the Abu Dhabi Investment Group for a reported £200m. In contrast many of the leading clubs in Europe still tend to be dominated by family dynasty ownership.

The big clubs are attractive because of their earnings potential. They are global brands which can be exploited in various ways and they are also a route to huge television earnings. But as businesses they carry risks. Success on the football field becomes something of a prerequisite, but only a few can succeed – and that success may not be sustainable season after season. In turn that success implies huge wage bills with some players earning well over £100,000 every week. It seems wage bills have been increasing at 12 per cent per year. Huge transfer fees are paid for top players, whose loyalty may change after just a few seasons and they choose to leave. New stadia, often linked to hotel and leisure complexes, are essential – but costs and planning restrictions are not always easily dealt with.

By 2008 the total indebtedness of English football was some £3 billion, with £2.6bn of this attributable to the Premier League. According to Deloitte (February 2009) Manchester United was £604 million in debt, Chelsea £620 million, Liverpool £350 million and Arsenal £268 million. However, this needs to be balanced by the value of the current Premier League TV deal for 2007–2010, which is £2.7bn. BSkyB attracted 171,000 new customers in the last six months of 2008, with fans apparently deciding it was cheaper to watch games at home rather than on large screens in their local pub. Attendances for the top clubs are also holding up, with only five clubs – Wigan, Blackburn, Bolton, Sunderland and Middlesbrough – using only 80 per cent of their seating capacity. Yet the average price of a ticket in the Premier League is £34, more than double the price of a similar ticket for the Bundesliga in Germany, where a similar pattern exists – namely the attendances of the top clubs remaining strong and only struggling clubs, performance wise, suffering any significant drop.

Early in 2009 the point was made that the credit crunch had yet to really hit English football. Contracts, sponsorship and season ticket sales for (at least) the

SOURCE: THIS CASE STUDY WAS PREPARED USING PRIMARILY PUBLICLY AVAILABLE SOURCES OF INFORMATION FOR THE PURPOSES OF

2008/9 season were in place. But what about further down the line? Is there a real risk a Premier League club could go into receivership?

Moreover, football governing bodies in Europe are suggesting this is unsustainable and clubs with huge debts should be banned from European competitions. Cynics would comment that this happened when England's top four clubs were particularly strong, if not dominant, in Europe. It is also an issue that these clubs are all able to service their debt. Chelsea is exceptional, of course. The money is owed to owner and benefactor Roman Abramovitch, so is it realistically any more than a paper figure?

A second problem that might have to be faced is the call from certain quarters to limit the number of overseas players in any one team. One other related and contentious issue is that as the Premier League has got stronger and stronger, the fortunes of the English team, which has won nothing since the 1966 World Cup, have waned.

Questions

1 Using Porter's Five Forces do you see the English Premier League as relatively attractive or unattractive?
2 Is it inevitable that the rich will only get richer?

2.6 Competition and the structure and regulation of industry

Readers who are familiar with the four economic models of pure or perfect competition, monopolistic competition, oligopoly and monopoly, will appreciate the links to Porter's industry analysis model. The opportunity for substantial profits is most likely to be found in oligopoly and **monopoly structures**. Competition in the other models, resulting mainly from lower barriers to entry, has the effect of reducing profit margins. It is now useful to consider which models are dominant in the UK, and most other developed nations, as this influences the ways in which firms compete. Specifically, it affects the opportunities for differentiation and for the achievement of cost advantages which, as will be seen in Chapter 4, are major determinants of competitive advantage.

Monopoly power

It is important to point out here that as far as the regulatory authorities are concerned, a 25 per cent market share offers opportunities for a company to exploit monopoly power. Hence, although the model of pure monopoly assumes only one producer with absolute power in the marketplace, a large producer with a substantial share will be regarded as having **monopoly power**. It does not follow that such power will be used against the consumer; on the contrary, it can be to the consumer's advantage. Large companies with market shares in excess of their rivals may be able to produce at lower cost (and sell at lower prices) for any one of several reasons, including the ability to invest in high output, low unit cost-technology; the ability to buy supplies in bulk and receive discounts; the ability to achieve distribution savings; and the opportunity to improve productivity as more and more units are produced. In fact, savings are possible in every area of the business. Economists call these savings economies of scale, and they are related to the notion of the experience or learning curve, which is explained in a Finance in Action supplement to Chapter 4.

It is quite normal to find an industry with a limited number (perhaps three, four or five) large mass market competitors with a broad product range and a number of much smaller niche producers. Interestingly if the largest companies control their costs well, then there will be a reduction in margin as market shares decline. The largest market shares will correspond to the highest margins. Conversely those competitors whose products are very specialist and with very limited market appeal to clearly defined niches or segments will enjoy higher margins than other niche producers whose products are less specialized. Here margin declines as market share increases.

A cost advantage, then, can be a major source of competitive advantage, and this point will be developed in greater detail later. The producer who is able to produce at a lower cost than his or her rivals may choose to price very competitively with a view to driving competitors out of the market and thereby increasing market share. Equally he or she may not; and by charging a higher price can make a greater profit per unit and thereby seek profit in preference to market share. In the first case the consumer benefits from lower prices and therefore monopoly power is not being used against the consumer. However, once a firm has built up a truly dominant market share it might seek to change its strategy and exploit its power more. This is when governments need to intervene in some way. This is the basis of the moves by both the EC and the US government to curb the power of Microsoft.

Concentration

Concentration is the measure of control exercised by organizations. There are two types.

Aggregate concentration, which will be mentioned only briefly, considers the power of the largest privately owned manufacturing firms in the economy as a whole.

Sectoral or market concentration traditionally considers the percentage of net output or employment (assets, sales or profits can also be measured) controlled by the largest firms in a particular industry, be it manufacturing or service. High **concentration ratio** figures tend to encourage monopoly or oligopoly behaviour, most probably the latter, which implies substantial emphasis on differentiation and non-price competition, with rivals seeing themselves as interdependent.

Many industries worldwide are essentially oligopolistic in structure, with a limited number of major competitors and barriers to entry in individual countries. In general, competition will be non-price rather than price, but price competition will be seen in situations where supply exceeds demand and there is aggressive competition for market share.

There may well be marketing and distribution advantages for companies which belong to conglomerates and this could increase their relative market power. Similarly, products which dominate particular market segments will yield advantages. Consequently, there is still opportunity for smaller companies to compete successfully in certain oligopoly markets, especially if they can differentiate their product so that it has appeal for particular segments of the market.

In the UK chocolate industry, Thornton's has been successful with a limited range of high-quality chocolate products distributed through the company's own specialist outlets. It is only recently, in 2009, with changing purchase habits of consumers that sales of high quality and therefore high price chocolates are under pressure. As we will see in Chapter 4 this trend is not confined to the chocolate industry, but is widespread. One must assume that once the recession is over and discretionary purchasing power grows back that this situation will also change back.

The dilemma for any government is to encourage firms to grow in size and become powerful competitive forces in world markets but at the same time to ensure that such size and power are not used to exploit their consumers. A recent example of this was the case of RBS, the Royal Bank of

Scotland, and its performance in the early part of the 21st century. The Royal Bank, in terms of its market capitalization, became the fifth largest bank in the world. In early 2004 the bank posted a pre-tax profit figure of £6.16 billion, up 29 per cent on 2003. The bank made £300 profit from every one of its private customers and it has been accused of both misleading and confusing its customers into taking on high interest-bearing credit cards. Five years later it was in very serious trouble – as we saw in Case 2.3. Now a new situation has emerged as many UK banks have had to be bailed out by the government as a consequence of their links to the US sub-prime catastrophe, but some would argue they still seemed to act as if they were private monopolies. Indeed the UK government may have created a new monster monopoly in the engineered **merger** of Lloyds TSB/HBOS that will created the largest mortgage lender, savings bank and life insurance business all in one. The new merged bank exceeded the 25 per cent market share monopoly power threshold, but the government was not minded to apply the brakes in this case.

The regulation of monopoly power

It is generally accepted in many countries that it is the state's role to monitor the forces of competition, to minimize any waste of resources due to economic inefficiency, to guard against any exploitation of relatively weak buyers or suppliers, and to ensure that powerful companies do not seek to eliminate their competitors purely to gain monopoly power.

Regulations are passed and implemented to police these issues. This section uses the situation in the UK to illustrate the point, but the principles and general approach are not unique to the UK. A new UK Competition Bill, passed in 1997 and operational in 1999, put the following structure in place.

In ultimate charge was the Department (or Minister) for Trade and Industry (DTI) now renamed as the Department for Business, Industry and Skills (BIS). The Office of Fair Trading (OFT), headed by a Director-General, has powers to carry out preliminary investigations of all proposed mergers or takeovers involving market shares of 25 per cent or more, or combined assets in excess of £75 million. If the OFT believes that major competition concerns are present, then it can refer the proposal to a second body, the Competition Commission, for further investigation. The Competition Commission is the delegated arbiter of referrals.

Each case is considered on merit, and the presumption is not automatically that monopoly power is against the public interest. High profitability is considered acceptable if it reflects efficiency, but not if it is sustained by artificial barriers to entry. The OFT also investigates cartels.

The delay involved in an investigation can be important strategically. The process is likely to take at least six months and in that time a company which opposes the takeover bid against it will work hard to improve its performance and prospects. If this results in a substantial increase in the share price, the acquisitive company may withdraw on the grounds that the cost has become too high. Companies may seek to prevent a reference by undertaking to sell off part of the businesses involved in an acquisition if competition concerns are raised. Recently the UK government has mused about legislation to make company executives personally liable for competitive misdemeanours, but it has not been passed.

Since September 1990 the European Commission has also been able to influence the growing number of corporate mergers and acquisitions in the European Union (EU). Mergers are exempted, though, if each company has more than two-thirds of its EU-wide turnover in any one EU country. The intervention of the European authorities has been controversial and some judgements have been criticized. There is a voice of opinion in the US that the EC is hostile to American mergers where the companies enjoy substantial sales in Europe. The EU in effect prevented General Electric acquiring another American business, Honeywell.

Examples of intervention

In February 2000 the Competition Commission in the UK ruled that Unilever should be banned from distributing its own Wall's ice cream direct to retailers. Wall's ice-cream products hold the largest market share in the UK, in excess of 50 per cent. The argument was that a newly formed subsidiary, Wall's Direct, was undermining independent wholesalers and, as a consequence, competitors such as Nestlé and Mars were being squeezed out of the supply chain. The DTI chose to water down the ban and recommended a capping of the scope and extent of the distribution operation. Unilever, however, concluded that a cap was not feasible and it began to wind down its distribution.

In parallel with this investigation the Competition Commission had also looked at Unilever's practice of providing retailers with free freezer cabinets but insisting that they were used only for Wall's products. Small retailers, with room for just one freezer cabinet, were effectively prevented from stocking other brands. The Commission recommended that retailers should be allowed to fill up to half of the cabinet with rival products.

In July 2003 Manchester United, JJB (the UK's leading sportswear retailer) and Umbro (sportswear manufacturer) were all fined for colluding to fix the retail prices of replica football kits. Those concerned all denied the allegations. In a case brought in 2003 and ruled on in 2004, Ryanair fell foul of the Commission for accepting unfair landing subsidies from municipal airports in Europe.

Highlighting the global nature of competition regulation, Microsoft, dominant in personal computer operating systems, has been judged by an American court to be exploiting its monopoly power. In early 2000 it was ruled that the basic operating systems (based on Windows) and the applications (Microsoft Office and Internet Explorer) should be separated into two separate businesses, and that Microsoft should also be required to give away to its competitors some of its operating systems code. The contention was that Microsoft had driven Netscape out of the Internet browser market by tying its own browser, Explorer, to Windows. Inevitably the company appealed against the ruling, and after a Democratic President was replaced by a more sympathetic to business Republican President in George W. Bush, this requirement was relaxed. Microsoft could stay intact. However, the European competition authority has also been taking a very firm line, convinced that Microsoft has exploited its monopoly power. The *Financial Times* commented at one stage: 'Surely, most seriously of all, is that at a time Microsoft should be focusing all its talent on keeping up with technological innovation, it is hamstrung by this case.'

Case 2.7 describes the impact of regulation on the structure of the UK brewing industry over a period of years. Sometimes regulation produces unexpected and unpredicted outcomes: it is a grey world.

Case 2.7

Regulation and Developments in the Brewing Industry   UK

When governments interfere in industries, there will be forced changes which often open up new opportunities. After all, detailed reports from the UK Competition Commission often contain significant information which becomes freely available to competitors and industry outsiders. This, then, is the story of the impact of regulation and changes of ownership in a dynamic, global industry.

An investigation by the Monopolies and Mergers Commission (the predecessor to the Competition Commission) into brewing resulted in the 1991 Beer Orders. The investigation was prompted by four brewers controlling 60 per cent of brewing and 80 per cent of the UK's 60,000 public houses. The Beer Orders required that brewers with over 2000 pubs had to divest half their estate. In addition, all pubs they retained had to offer 'guest beers', ones not produced by the owner–brewer. The intention was to break the tied link whereby particular beers could be forced on to tenants by the powerful brewers.

In response, the leading brewers set up independent companies to buy out their own pubs, typically with links back to the brewers who were loaning the money. Naturally, the brewers retained the most lucrative pubs in their estates. In reality, the tied link was never truly broken. At the same time, the brewers began to diversify into hotels and restaurants because they were unable to open any new pubs. Bass acquired Holiday Inn, for example. Bass also owned an interest in Harvester restaurants and Britvic soft drinks. Whitbread similarly built a portfolio which included Travel Inn, Marriott Hotels (in the UK), Beefeater, Brewers Fayre, the Bella Pasta, TGI Fridays (UK franchise) and Pizza Hut (another UK franchise) restaurants, and the wine and spirits retailers Wine Rack, Threshers and Victoria Wine.

The Beer Orders provided new opportunities for entrepreneurial outsiders. The guest beer requirement, for example, led to the growth of microbreweries, which produce only very limited quantities of generally very strong ales. Some pubs brew their own beer on-site. One manager with the Japanese bank, Nomura, came up with an idea to buy 2000 pubs from Bass for £2 billion. The bank had no interest in running pubs, but it was interested in property which could earn it some £300 million per year in rent. The bank raised the money for the deal by issuing bonds with a 10 per cent annual interest. Simply, the bank raised £2 billion for an annual interest payment of £200 million and earned £300 million in rents – a £100 million annual profit. Simple, really, if you have the idea and the resources to back the deal!

By 1999 the situation was:

	Percentage of UK beer sales	
	On-trade	*Take home*
Scottish and Newcastle	27	22
Bass	23	17
Whitbread	14	20
Carlsberg–Tetley	13	9
Other companies	23	32

The activity profile (percentages of total turnover) of the four leading brewers was as follows:

	Bass	Whitbread	Scottish and Newcastle	Carlsberg– Tetley
Brewing	33	22	61	77
Retail	30	30	27	0
Soft drinks	11	10	0	8
Other leisure activities	26	38	12	15

Shortly afterwards, both Bass and Whitbread announced that they were to withdraw from brewing in favour of

other leisure activities. In 1997 the then Monopolies and Mergers Commission had approved a proposed merger between Bass and Carlsberg Tetley, but Secretary of State at the time, Margaret Beckett, had intervened and stopped it. The Belgian brewer of Stella Artois, InBev, expressed interest in acquiring breweries from both companies – and thus become the UK market leader. This was also stopped, but allowed on appeal – as long as the Carling, Caffrey's and Worthington brands were sold on. The purchaser of these was American brewer Molson Coors. Meanwhile, Scottish and Newcastle (S&N) acquired Kronenbourg to become Europe's second largest brewer, second only to Heineken, although Carlsberg would subsequently overtake it. S&N also owned Lodge Inns, Chef and Brewer restaurants, and the Center Parcs and Pontin's holiday resorts. In 2000 S&N was looking to divest its least profitable pubs and Center Parcs.

Since then Whitbread has joined Bass in divesting brewing in favour of other leisure activities. In 2003 S&N opted to leave the pub trade and agreed to sell its interests to fast-growing pub chain, Spirit, one of a number of new operators. Other names were Enterprise Inns and Punch Taverns. All three had built up sizeable market shares through acquisition in recent years.

By 2006 S&N was the UK's leading brewer with a 25 per cent share. Molson Coors (American) with 21 per cent, InBev (Belgian) with 17 per cent and Carlsberg with 12 per cent made up the majority of the remainder. In 2007 Europe's two leading brewers, Heineken and Carlsberg, acquired S&N and split its breweries between them. In 2008 InBev acquired the leading American brewer Anheuser-Busch (whose brands include Budweiser) to establish the largest brewery group in the world. Shortly earlier two other American brewers, Miller and Molson Coors, had merged.

It is generally acknowledged that beer prices have risen more than the overall cost of living during this period – when supermarkets have also increased their presence in the industry. Of course, taxation policy cannot be ignored in considering this issue. It is clear that many UK motorists have discovered they can save money by crossing the Channel to France and buying beer and spirits in quantity there.

Question

1   On balance do you think regulation has had a positive or negative impact on this industry?

2.7   Key success factors, strategic positioning and adding value

Key success factors

A company will have to produce to high and consistent quality levels and meet delivery promises to customers. Delivery times have been reducing gradually in very competitive industries. Suppliers and subcontractors expect regular orders and accurate forecasting when very quick deliveries are demanded from them. Without such support **just-in-time** production systems are impractical. Just-in-time systems rely on regular and reliable deliveries from suppliers in order to maintain constant production without the need for high parts inventories.

Companies will try to minimize their stockholding because this helps both cash flow and costs. Conglomerate subsidiaries will have to generate a positive cash flow in order to meet the financial expectations of the parent company who, in effect, act as its bankers. Costs have to be controlled so that companies remain price competitive, although low prices are not always a marketing weapon.

These stakeholder requirements represent *key success factors*, those things that an organization must do well if it is to be an effective competitor and thrive. In addition, many companies have to be innovative and improve both their product range and their customer service if they are to remain a leading competitor in a changing industry.

Some key success factors will be industry and sector specific. For example, successful consumer goods manufacturers will need skills in brand management. Charities need skills in fund raising and public relations. There is intense competition between charities for donations, and consequently they must be run as businesses. They can only spend what they can raise. It is also essential that they use their money appropriately, are seen to be doing so and are recognized for their efforts. The differing demands of fund raising and aid provision lead to complex cultures and organizations.

BUPA, a private medical organization based in the UK, has a similar dilemma. Typical of such organizations around the world, the business comprises two parts: insurance, with a strong commercial culture and orientation, and care homes, which are naturally more of a caring community. When it owned hospitals, these were the same.

Resources must be managed with stakeholder needs in mind. Consequently, it is important that everyone in the organization recognizes and is committed to meeting key success factors, and is additionally responsive to change pressures in a dynamic and competitive environment. Without this commitment companies will be unable to sustain a match with the environment as it changes.

Figure 2.9 illustrates that if organizations are to satisfy their stakeholders, especially their customers, while outperforming their rivals, their competitive offering should comprise:

- the ability to meet the recognized key success factors for the relevant industry or market
- distinctive competencies and capabilities which yield some form of competitive advantage, and
- the ability and willingness to deploy these competencies and capabilities to satisfy the special requirements of individual customers, for which a premium price can often be charged. Hall (1992) suggests using the term 'customerizing' instead of marketing to reflect the importance of customers as individuals rather than as a generic group who constitute a market.

Strategic positioning

A straightforward, popular and well-known technique, a SWOT (strengths, weaknesses, opportunities, threats) analysis, implies that an organization's resources (which constitute its strengths and weaknesses) should match the demands and pressures from its external environment

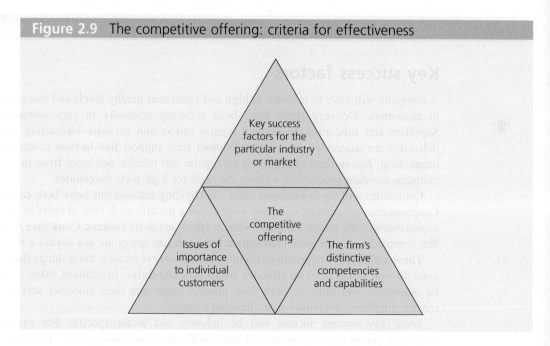

Figure 2.9   The competitive offering: criteria for effectiveness

(manifest as a set of opportunities and threats) as effectively as possible and, with change, stay matched in dynamic and turbulent times. The overlap of products and services (the outcome of the use of the organization's resources) with market needs is shown as strategic fit in Figure 2.10.

Here we can see illustrated two different, but complementary, approaches to strategy creation and strategic change.

Market-driven strategy (or opportunity-driven strategy) reflects the adoption of the marketing concept, and implies that strategies are designed – and resources developed and deployed – with customer and consumer needs in mind. Carefully and creatively defining the industry or industries in which an organization competes can influence its perspective on the products and

Figure 2.10   Strategic positioning

services it supplies. Marketing students will always remember that railway companies are in the transportation business! The approach is market-pull, and the value of a distinct competitive advantage is clearly synonymous with this approach. It should, however, never be forgotten that different sectors of the same industry require different competencies, and that the demands of creating new competencies may be readily underestimated.

Online Case 2.1 on Sainsbury's illustrates this approach.

Although it is convenient to see resources as organizational strengths and weaknesses (which they very clearly are) and the environment as the source of opportunities and threats, this is too simplistic. Resources can also constitute both opportunities and strengths – as we can see in Case 2.8 on Flying Brands.

See the online "Sainsbury's" case for an example of this section's theory in practice

Resource-based strategy implies that the organization clarifies its core strategic competencies and capabilities and seeks to exploit these by finding new market opportunities where they can be used to create new values and competitive advantage. The assumption is that the organization can mould and develop its market with innovatory new ideas, sometimes changing the rules of competition in an industry. This can imply the creation of new customer preferences and perspectives in the process.

Resources which are central to an organization's success can be a threat if they could be lost. Particular people can be a major asset, and a key reason for organizational success, and people can be lost. Although rare, one reality is that they could die, but more realistically they could leave and join a competitor. Obvious instances are professional footballers and restaurant chefs. Some football clubs lose star players to rivals, sometimes for a transfer fee, sometimes when they are out of contract. Although this can affect the playing fortunes of the club, it is unlikely that fans will follow them. Loyalty goes too deep. The same cannot be said of chefs, however. Top-quality chefs can be the reason customers frequent a particular restaurant, and if they move, customers may well go with them.

All the time competitors will be attempting to accomplish the same ends. Hence, while a company is trying to create a stronger fit between itself and its customers, its competitors will be attempting to force them apart by offering something superior which draws customers away and destroys fit. Hence, a third and more tactical approach to strategy is **competitor influenced** which implies short-term vigilance to deal with any threatening competitor initiatives. Whilst significant, it is important than an organization does not become over-reliant upon this tactical approach. We can also see this reflected in Online Case 2.1 on Sainsbury's.

Moreover, emerging opportunities can attract competitors with different backgrounds and motives. Developments in computer software and hardware (high-quality monitors, scanners and printers) have opened up an opportunity for digital cameras. Kodak were interested because of their dependency on the photographic industry and the potential long-term threat to film-based photography. Canon and Hewlett-Packard were both interested as they could see a new opportunity for exploiting technological competencies that they already possessed. The challenge for each rival was quite different.

Figure 2.11 emphasizes that effective strategic positions ensure that corporate strategic resources meet and satisfy **key (or critical) success factors** for customers and markets. Strategically valuable resources translate into core competencies and strategic capabilities (which are explained in more detail in Chapter 3), which are then manifest in a whole range of activities that the organization undertakes. Competencies and capabilities can be separated by thinking of core competencies being built around technologies and technological skills, and strategic capabilities referring to processes and ways of doing things. Capabilities thus exploit the competencies; technology must, however, be developed to a particular level for a company to be influential in an industry or market. Hence, while the real competitive strength of an organization can be built around either competencies or capabilities, both must be present for relative success. Over time, both competency and capability must be improved with innovation. In Chapter 9 it is shown that people, learning and information are critical elements of this innovation. In addition,

Case 2.8

Flying Brands   UK

Flying Brands began life as Flying Flowers, which, as the name suggests, sells flowers by post. The company was set up in Jersey in the Channel Islands in the early 1980s to save a struggling glasshouse business – a loss-making nursery needed and created a new opportunity. By 1996 turnover had grown to £35 million, with pre-tax profits of £4 million.

There are several key elements to the strategy and the success. First, the company holds only low stocks of the actual flowers, many of which it buys in cheaply from countries such as Colombia: flowers *from* Jersey does not have to mean flowers grown in Jersey!

Demand fluctuates markedly, peaking twice, at Christmas and Mother's Day, when the company typically receives 15,000 postal and 5000 telephone orders per day for a short period. Christmas sales amount to 5 million carnations in 330,000 boxed deliveries. Coping with this surge in demand is critical for success. The second key element therefore is staffing and staff management. As tourism is a leading source of employment in Jersey, and is strongest during the summer months, Flying Flowers was able to use casual hotel and restaurant staff. They are relatively plentiful on an island of scarce labour

© CPHOTO / STOCKXPERT

resources, and critically they are often laid off temporarily over Christmas and Mother's Day when tourism falls off.

Thirdly, the company uses a disused glasshouse to house a noisy, steam-breathing machine which produces polystyrene boxes every working day of the year. These are then piled high to ensure that any demand peak can be catered for.

Fourthly, and very critically, Flying Flowers has invested in IT to support both control and marketing. It soon built up a database of one million people and carefully targets its direct mail, analysing all responses and orders in detail. It has opened a telephone call centre in Essex.

Flying Flowers as a concept adds value for customers – high-quality, fresh flowers delivered directly to the door. Its operating costs are relatively low for the reasons described above and, of course, there are no returns to deal with.

The skills and competencies have been further exploited with the acquisition of other businesses – hence the change of name to Flying Brands. The company bought Gardening Direct (mail-order bedding plants), Listen2Books and Stanley Gibbons (publisher and stamp supplier) and another supplier of first-day covers. It operates as three divisions, which clearly can share resources and competencies.

In 2006 Scottish entrepreneur and venture capitalist, Sir Tom Hunter, bought a 29.9 per cent stake in the business. He was already a part owner of Wyevale Garden Centres and perhaps saw synergy opportunities.

Questions

1 How does Flying Brands add value?
2 What is the nature of its strategic position?
3 Did the acquisitions make sense in relation to its competencies and capabilities?

SOURCE: THIS CASE STUDY WAS PREPARED USING PRIMARILY PUBLICLY AVAILABLE SOURCES OF INFORMATION FOR THE PURPOSES OF

companies can benefit markedly from exploiting the linkages and relationships that they have with their suppliers and distributors.

It should be understood that strategic positioning, per se, is not a source of competitive advantage. Any relative advantage enjoyed by the organization comes from the resources and activities which establish and support the position. This can be tangible or intangible in nature. It

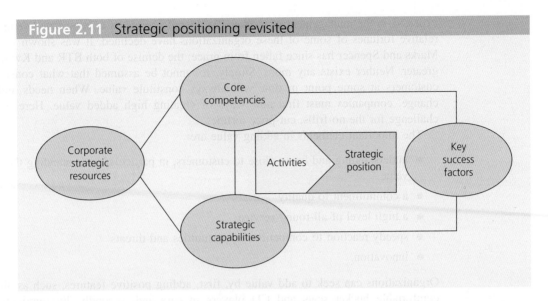

Figure 2.11   Strategic positioning revisited

could come from specific technological skills, from the reputation that an organization enjoys or from the way that its people deliver service. Simply, these are the ways through which it creates and adds value.

Added value

A business must add value if it is to be successful. As supply potential has grown to exceed global demand in the majority of industries, adding value has become increasingly important. In simple terms the extent of the value added is the difference between the value of the outputs from an organization and the cost of the inputs or resources used. Two fundamental questions are being addressed: what is the value created and what is the cost?

The traditional paradigm, based on the accountancy measure, is that prices reflect costs plus a profit margin. The lack of differentiation, for which a higher price can be charged, implies enormous downward pressures on costs. Performance measurement is then based upon economy of scale (low input costs) and efficiency (minimizing the actual and attributed costs of the resources used for adding further value).

While it is important to use all resources efficiently and properly, it is also critical to ensure that the potential value of the outputs is maximized by ensuring that they fully meet the needs of the customers for whom they are intended. An organization achieves this when it sees its customers' objectives as its own objectives and enables its customers to easily add more value or, in the case of final consumers, feel that they are gaining true value for money.

In the new paradigm, the key is value for the customer; if resources are used to provide real value for customers, they will pay a price which reflects its worth to them.

John Kay (1993) researched the most successful European companies during the 1980s, measured by their average costs per unit of net output. He found that each company had developed an individual strategy for adding value and creating competitive success. Glaxo (number 1 in the 10 at that time) successfully exploited the international potential for its patented antiulcer drug Zantac. LVMH (Louis Vuitton, Moët Hennessy), sixth in the list, generated synergy from the global distribution of a diverse range of high-quality, premium-brand products. It still does. Benetton, second, enjoyed beneficially close links with its suppliers and distributors, again worldwide. Marks and Spencer (tenth, and Case 1.2 in the previous chapter) was also expert at supply-chain management and further benefited from its value-for-money image and reputation. In contrast, low-price food retailer Kwik Save, fifth in the list, was selling its products with a low margin but enjoying a relatively very high turnover to capital employed. BTR (number nine) had expertise in the management of a diversified conglomerate. It is important to emphasize that the relative fortunes of some of these organizations have declined. It was shown in Chapter 1 that Marks and Spencer has since fallen from grace; the demise of both BTR and Kwik Save has been greater. Neither exists any more. Simply, it cannot be assumed that what constitutes value for customers at some point in time will always constitute value. When needs and requirements change, companies must find new ways of creating high added value. Here will lie a future challenge for the no-frills, cut-price airlines.

The important elements in adding value are:

- understanding and being close to customers, in particular understanding their perception of value

- a commitment to quality

- a high level of all-round service

- speedy reaction to competitive opportunities and threats

- innovation.

Organizations can seek to add value by, first, adding positive features, such as air conditioning, comfortable bucket seats and CD players in cars and, secondly, by removing any features perceived as negatives or drawbacks. Antilock braking systems and four-wheel drive gearboxes reduce the concerns that some people have about driving in bad weather, while extended warranty schemes remove the fear of unknown future repair costs. Each of these additions has a value for which some customers, not all, will pay a premium.

It is quite conceivable that organizations are pursuing strategies or **policies** which make life harder for their customers. Minimum order quantities and, possibly, volume discounts, may force or encourage customers to buy more than they need or can afford to stock. Obsolescence can then become an issue. Organizations could evaluate the merit of discounts based on annual sales rather than only on individual orders. Simply, organizations should be looking to ensure that they follow the top loop of Figure 2.12 and not the bottom one.

Organizations that truly understand their customers can create competitive advantage and thereby benefit from higher prices and loyalty. High-capacity utilization can then help to reduce costs.

Figure 2.12 Adding value for customers

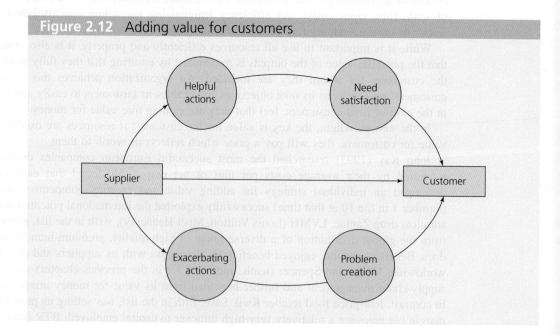

As an example, the prices of airline seats are related to the value that they have for customers and the benefits they offer, not simply the airline's cost for providing the seat and the associated service. With full-service airlines, the first-class cabin has traditionally offered space, comfortable seats which can be reclined almost to the horizontal, and high-quality food and service. Business class is based on similar principles but to a more limited degree. Now airlines have introduced sleeper seats, which can be converted into a horizontal bed, in these cabins for long-haul overnight flights. Both classes are quieter than the economy section, offering some opportunity for business travellers to work, and reservations can be changed. Premium economy, where it is available, provides some elements of business class service in a special section of economy. Economy seats at full fare allow for late bookings, open tickets to allow for flexible return schedules, upstairs seats on Boeing 747s with some airlines and special sections of the cabin on others, and, clearly, more chance of an upgrade. Reduced advanced purchase fares can be very good value for money, but they are inflexible. Travellers may have to stay for a prescribed period, flights and tickets cannot be altered and sometimes payment must be made early and in full.

One important key success factor for any airline is the ability to sell the right mix of tickets to maximize the revenue potential from every flight. Empty seats imply lost revenue; at the same time, if every ticket is sold at a discounted price, the flight is unlikely to be profitable. After flipping from profit to loss at the end of the 1990s, British Airways switched its emphasis and increased the size of its premium-price business class cabins at the expense of low-margin economy seating. Consequently, the airline performance measures include: load factors, passenger kilometres (the numbers of passengers multiplied by the distance flown), and the revenue per passenger kilometre.

It is quite typical of airlines, both full-service and the no-frills carriers, to increase the seat price as the flight fills. Only a certain proportion of seats are available at the lowest prices. Early bookers get prices that are denied to others. However, if a flight is not full it is sometimes, but certainly not always, possible to get distress prices at the last minute. But it can be a mistake for a customer to hold out for these – they may never become available.

Opportunities for adding value which attracts customers must be sought and exploited. Numerous possible opportunities exist at corporate, competitive and functional strategy levels. Resources must be deployed to exploit these opportunities. Pümpin (1991) argues that multiplication, i.e. strategic consistency and performance improvement by concentrating on certain important strategies and learning how to implement them more effectively, promotes growth. The matching process is led and championed by the strategic leader, who is responsible for establishing the key values. While striving to improve performance with existing strategies the organization must constantly search for new windows of opportunity. McDonald's (Case 1.7) provides an excellent example. Ray Kroc spotted an opportunity in the growing fast-food market and exploited it by concentrating on new product ideas and franchised outlets, supported by a culture that promoted 'quality, service, cleanliness and value'.

Figure 2.13 shows that organizations must add value, and continue to find new ways of adding fresh value, for their customers. They achieve this by developing, changing and exploiting core resource-based technological competencies. This exploitation involves organizational processes and capabilities, together with strong linkages with other companies in the supply chain (**strategic architecture**), in order to create differentiation and effective cost control and, thus, establish a superior competitive position. The situation is always fluid, though; organizations cannot assume that currently successful products, services and competitive strategies will be equally successful in the future. They must be changed at appropriate times. In turn, this requires competency in awareness, thinking and learning. Realizing which competencies are most important for long-term success, concentrating attention on them, developing them and measuring the desired improvements is a critically important task for the strategic leader.

All the time, companies should carry out efficiently those activities which are essential for creating a distinctive or differentiated competitive position, and avoid incurring unnecessary costs by providing non-essential values. This implies that they clearly understand their markets, their

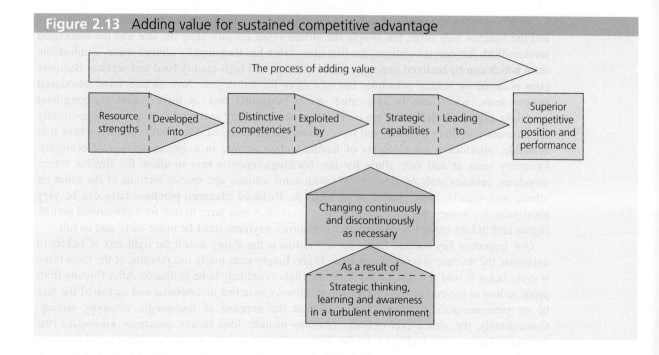

Figure 2.13   Adding value for sustained competitive advantage

customers and the key success factors that they must meet – their defined competitive strategy. Moreover, they should constantly seek improvement by driving their operating efficiencies.

An organization uses its various resources, both tangible and intangible, to create value. If customers recognize and appreciate that value and are happy with the price being asked they are likely to buy. The issue then is one of how profitable the business is. Figure 2.14 delineates two value-adding cycles, both of which can establish superior profits and allow for ongoing investment and innovation. They are not mutually exclusive because, whatever the competitive strategy, strong cost management is essential.

To be successful, products and services must fit into markets. Marketing and operations strategies are critical elements of competitive strategy but it is assumed that most readers will have already studied these topics elsewhere. These could be global or local markets, mass or niche markets. The products could be essentially commodities or substantially customized. The market

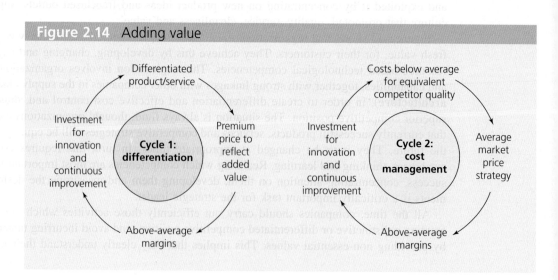

Figure 2.14   Adding value

(or the relevant niche) could be growing, static or declining. Each one can be profitable, but in different ways, with different strategies. Companies which target new markets, segments or niches may find that they are hard to penetrate, unless they have developed something radically new and different which is seen as a valuable alternative by customers. After all, most successful companies have realized that it is more expensive to win new business than it is to retain existing customers and, as a result, look after their customers. While patents can provide a barrier to new entrants and new rivals, so too can loyal customers!

However, some markets may equally be difficult to defend. This would be the case where the wider business environment is dynamic and turbulent, where the organization enjoys only a relatively weak strategic fit and where the service being provided is below the level expected. Hence, positioning and fit can be improved with customer care, product and service innovation and improvement, and by developing new products. All of this requires that companies take their competitors seriously, defend against any initiatives that they start and, on occasion, attack them. This can imply any or all of the following:

- finding and opening new windows of opportunity
- product and service development, improvement and enhancement
- direct attacks, such as price wars, either 'all-out' and sustained or short-term and guerrilla. Special discount promotions would be an example of the latter
- attempting to change the 'rules of engagement or competition' either openly (with genuinely new ideas) or more deviously (lobbying government for new regulations or buying out a key supplier or competitor)
- a 'war of words', seeking publicity for your activities and carefully disparaging your competitors. Sir Richard Branson was able to strengthen the image and position of Virgin Atlantic when he drew attention to British Airways' so-called 'dirty tricks' campaign to win over Virgin customers
- networking and collaboration with key partners in the supply chain.

Case 2.9 (Ann Summers) looks at opportunities for adding value and finding new windows of opportunity in a very interesting environment, and thus draws together many of these points.

To summarize this section, Markides (1999) provides a list of six factors for competitive and strategic success. These are:

1 Choose a potentially winning position. This requires understanding *who* your customers are, *what* they require and expect and *how* they can be reached. This corresponds with Porter's (1996) view that it is essential to focus on certain activities and ignore others, not attempting to be 'all things to all people'.

2 Make this choice by a proper exploration of options.

3 An active search for opportunities to be different in a meaningful way, not just adopting a strategy because it seems to work.

4 Ensure all the support activities work together effectively and synergistically.

5 Create a real strategic fit and position which links the organization with its customers.

6 Ensure there is flexibility in both the activities and the fit so that innovation and change can sustain competitiveness.

Appropriability

Kay (1993) uses the term **'appropriability'** to make the point that organizations must seek to ensure that they see the benefits of the value which they create and add. After all, few things cannot be copied and some positions of advantage will be transient without improvement.

Case 2.9

Ann Summers   UK

Jacqueline Gold joined her father's business empire in 1981. David Gold had been building a very lucrative business based on 'adult shops' – with darkened windows and located in back streets – and men's magazines. Many would describe it as soft porn; and these businesses have continued and thrived. His daughter, though, has successfully positioned Ann Summers as a high street retail chain, albeit one that still causes some controversy. Her clientele are mainly women. In the beginning she met resistance from inside the business; many of her father's colleagues believed 'women are not interested in sex'.

There are now over 100 shops, which display and sell fashion clothes as well as lingerie, and a very successful party-plan business. Women up and down the country invite other women to their homes, demonstrate and sell the products. Ann Summers is the UK's leading retailer of sex toys; its leading product is the Rampant Rabbit vibrator. The success of this is perhaps down to a 'recommendation' from the equally successful *Sex and the City* television series. Jacqueline Gold always believed 'sexy lingerie is to be worn as a fashion item and not just to turn on men'. She has clearly helped persuade many other women to this view.

In 2000 Gold bought out Knickerbox, a more conventional lingerie chain. It is rumoured that she can see opportunities in diversifying into other bedroom products such as bed linen and lampshades.

Two years later, in 2002, advertisements for staff in Ann Summers shops were banned in UK government Job Shops – a ruling later overturned in the High Court. Authorities in Dublin attempted to ban Ann Summers, but they were unsuccessful. When the first high street store opened in Dublin there were 10,000 customers at the launch. The publicity had helped enormously. Stores have been allowed to open in Spain but promotional advertising is restricted.

Questions

1 How has Jacqueline Gold added value for her target customers?
2 Do you believe her business model is sustainable and she can defend her strong market position?

Value can be provided for customers in a whole variety of ways, but unless they are willing to pay a premium price which at least offsets the cost of adding the value, then it is the customer and not the organization that benefits. Even if a premium price can be charged, if this is then used to reward suppliers and employees, additional profits may not accrue. Sometimes higher profits are used primarily to reward shareholders, or owner–managers in the case of small organizations. All of these possibilities imply that the organization is not creating and sustaining a position where it makes superior profits and uses these (at least in part) to reinvest and help to build new values through improvement and innovation. Quite simply, the ideal scenario is a virtuous one, where every stakeholder benefits.

Regulation of railways in the UK provides an excellent example of the inherent tensions. The network and infrastructure provider (originally Railtrack, but Network Rail since the government effectively reprivatized this part of the industry, and which essentially maintains the lines, signalling and stations) and the train operating companies (such as Virgin Rail, National Express and GNER who provide the actual train services) are independent businesses. The picture is complex. Bus and coach operator Stagecoach, for example, has substantial stakes in more than one franchise, including Virgin Rail. In addition, there is a Rail Regulator to oversee the whole industry – and he has removed franchises from underperforming businesses such as the French company, Connex, which ran commuter trains in the south-east.

Sometimes customers travel on services provided by just one train operator, but many journeys mean that customers are shared. Standards of reliability and service do vary. The government wants more people to use the railways (and other forms of public transport) to reduce traffic on the roads. This will only happen if services are good and prices acceptable. But attractive wages, required to recruit and retain a high calibre of employee, impact on costs and prices. So too do requirements for investment in new infrastructure (to improve services) and safety, particularly after a series of high-profile crashes. If investment demands, together with restraints on prices and profits imposed by the rail regulator, result in reduced profits and dividends, the individual train companies will find it increasingly difficult to generate and raise the funds they need for ongoing investment and improvement. Without the improvement, of course, they are likely to be fined by the regulator, making the profit situation even more precarious. There could very easily be a vicious rather than a virtuous circle.

2.8   SWOT (strengths, weaknesses, opportunities and threats) analysis

Environmental opportunities are only potential opportunities unless the organization can utilize resources to take advantage of them and until the strategic leader decides that it is appropriate to pursue the opportunity. It is therefore important to evaluate environmental opportunities in relation to the strengths and weaknesses of the organization's resources, and in relation to the organizational culture. Real opportunities exist when there is a close fit between environment, values and resources. Similarly, the resources and culture will determine the extent to which any potential threat becomes a real threat. This is E–V–R congruence, which was explained in Part 1.

All of the resources at the disposal of the organization can be deployed strategically, including strategic leadership. It is therefore useful to consider the resources in terms of where they are strong and where they are weak as this will provide an indication of their strategic value. However, this should not be seen as a list of absolute strengths and weaknesses seen from an internal perspective; rather, the evaluation should consider the strengths and weaknesses in relation to the needs of the environment and in relation to competition. The views of external stakeholders may differ from those of internal managers (who in turn may disagree among themselves) when evaluating the relative strength of a particular product, resource or skill. Resources should be evaluated for their relative strengths and weaknesses in the light of key success factors.

Even though an organization may be strong or weak in a particular function, the corresponding position of its major competitors must also be taken into account. For example, it might have sophisticated computer-controlled machine tools in its factory, but if its competitors have the same or even better equipment, the plant should not be seen as a relative strength. This issue refers to distinctive competencies – relative strengths which can be used to create competitive advantage. As any resource can be deployed strategically, competitive advantage can be gained from any area of the total business.

An evaluation of an organization's strengths and weaknesses in relation to environmental opportunities and threats is generally referred to as a SWOT analysis.

Figure 2.15 illustrates a popular and useful framework for a SWOT analysis applied to ASDA earlier in the 1990s, before the introduction of new strategies focusing on the product ranges, in-store layouts and a clear distinction between large ASDA superstores and smaller units with a limited range and discounted prices and finally its acquisition by Wal-Mart. The chart highlights how certain issues can be considered as either a strength or a weakness, an opportunity or a threat, depending on how they are managed in the future.

Once all of the important *strategic issues* have been teased out from a long list of strengths, weaknesses, opportunities and threats, the following questions should be asked.

- How can we either neutralize critical weaknesses or convert them into strengths?
- Similarly, can we neutralize critical threats or even build them into new opportunities?
- How can we best exploit our strengths in relation to our opportunities?

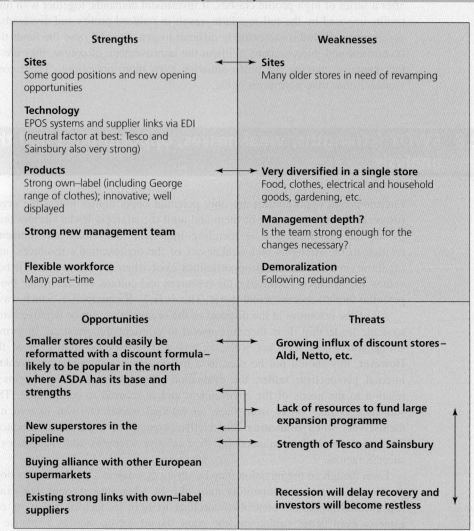

Figure 2.15   ASDA – SWOT analysis, early 1990s

- What new markets and market segments might be suitable for our existing strengths and capabilities?
- Given the (changing) demands of our existing markets, what changes do we need to make to our products, processes and services?

Finally, alongside a general SWOT analysis, it is essential to evaluate the relative strengths and weaknesses of the company's leading competitors.

2.9   Forecasting the environment

The extent of the credit crunch and subsequent economic recession that started in 2008 – which most forecasters underestimated – shows that a complex and dynamic modern environment is inevitably difficult to forecast; the inherent uncertainties can make it highly unpredictable and potentially chaotic. External events and competitor activities can trigger a chain reaction of responses and new **scenarios**; but Handy (1989) contends that 'those who know why changes come waste less effort in protecting themselves or in fighting the inevitable'. Consequently, however difficult it may be to forecast environmental change, organizations must attempt to stay strategically aware. They should reflect upon their experiences and look for emerging patterns or trends in the industry and business environment. They should be vigilant in tracking technological and other developments which may affect, possibly radically, their industries and markets. They should look for, and maybe even borrow or 'steal', appropriate ideas.

This issue has been manifested in the need for organizations to come to terms with the threats and opportunities posed by the Internet, both for information movement and for e-commerce. The Internet has expanded more rapidly than many people thought credible just a few years ago, and many organizations are a long way from exploiting its potential. However, there are inbuilt dilemmas. For example, relatively few German and Italian adults possesses a credit card, essential for buying online. Buying online for home delivery has varying degrees of relevance in different countries. Many Europeans live relatively close to the shops concerned and can easily fetch the goods themselves. In addition, relatively few Europeans have the larger, American-style, outside postboxes which can accept small parcel deliveries when people are out.

> *Don't try to eliminate uncertainty ... embrace it. Despite overwhelming evidence to the contrary many of us still view the future as an extension of the past.*
>
> CLEM SUNTER, ANGLO AMERICAN CORPORATION OF SOUTH AFRICA (THE WORLD'S LARGEST MINING GROUP)

> *The world's changing. People in the US and Europe aren't going to live the way they do 100 years from now unless they do a lot of things differently. Who says that because we have 240 million people on this big piece of land [USA] we should have two cars and second homes, while 800 million people in India and 1 billion in China should live the way they live? We've only been wealthy in this country for 70 years. Who said we ought to have all this? Is it ordained?*
>
> JOHN F. WELCH, CHAIRMAN AND FORMER CEO, GENERAL ELECTRIC

2.10 Scenario planning

Scenario planning was first properly used in a business context by Shell some 40 years ago, however it still remains a fringe activity for many organizations.

Scenarios are often used in strategic management to explore future possibilities. Possible happenings and events are considered by looking at potential outcomes from particular causes and seeking to explain why things might occur. The value is in increased awareness by exploring possibilities and asking and attempting to answer 'what if' questions. Although scenario planning can be predictive and can be used to plan strategic changes, it can also help decision-making by providing managers with insight so that they can react better when things happen or change. It can also be helpful for conceptualizing possible new competitive paradigms.

Environments for many organizations have become – and continue to become – increasingly dynamic, turbulent and uncertain. They feature an element of competitive chaos, where companies continually thrust and parry with new ploys and stratagems in an attempt to, at the very least, 'stay in the game' and, ideally, get ahead of their rivals. Scenarios and scenario planning concern the medium- or long-term future and they embrace the possibility of real and dramatic change. Anticipation and creativity can be invaluable in dealing with the turbulence and uncertainty. By considering and evaluating future possibilities, organizations can put themselves in positions where they might be better placed to deal with the unpredictable challenges of the future. Put another way: simply engaging in the process of acknowledging and anticipating change enables managers to be less shocked by whatever change does occur.

Three central themes underpin effective scenario planning:

● It is important to clarify just what a business can and cannot change. Small farmers, for example, cannot enjoy the scale economies of large farms, nor can they affect the climate. They can, within reason, improve their soil and they can change their crops.

● What seems trivial or a pipe-dream today could be crucial in the future. In 1874, Western Union in America turned down Alexander Graham Bell's prototype telephone!

● Multiple scenarios need to be explored and then *held* as real possibilities. Shell, which pioneered scenario planning, is arguably ready to respond quickly to shocks which affect supply or prevailing prices.

The scenarios considered may involve modified versions of current competitive paradigms (the future is not the past, but at least the two are related) or radically new paradigms (everything changes in the end). The implications of the scenarios will tend towards one of two themes: first, there will be environmental changes but organizations can learn to cope with, and influence or manage events, and thereby enjoy some degree of relative stability; second, the environmental turbulence will be so great that the competitive situation will become ever more chaotic in nature.

Readers might like to consider a number of emerging issues in the UK, evaluate their significance and implications and, where appropriate, consider how they might apply in their own countries.

● In recent years UK residents have increasingly become home owners. This trend has been in part caused by the long-term growth in property values, but in turn it has helped to fuel rises and falls in house prices. Negative equity (owning a mortgage that is greater than the price of the property) and repossessions have become a problem for some people at certain times. At the same time more and more people have been tempted to become owners of buy-to-let properties, many of them apartments. The availability of these properties and the inability of first-time buyers to afford the deposits required to secure a mortgage have worked together. There is an argument that one outcome is a housing stock that is inappropriate for the future. The credit crunch of 2008 brought many of these issues to a head with record numbers of repossessions and significant increases in negative equity.

● People are living longer; there is an ageing population. But will the more recent trend of people retiring earlier, many on good pensions, continue? As people are healthier, is it not logical for them to work longer, as long as employers do not discriminate on age grounds? Of course, for some jobs skills can become outdated and people do become less useful.
There is also the key dilemma of pensions. If people retire relatively early and live longer, there are two implications: one is that they will have to accept lower pensions; the other is that those people still in employment will have to pay far higher contributions to build up and sustain the pension funds. Many employers have had to reassess the pensions they provide – as they cannot afford them.

● In part thanks to television programmes such as *Dragons' Den* on BBC, an increasing number of people seem attracted to the idea of self-employment and starting their own businesses. It is debatable whether our education and business support networks are truly effective in terms of providing the support they need.

● According to most published statistics, unemployment had been consistently coming down, yet, at the same time, there are growing skills shortages in trades such as plumbing. Developing one point above, raising the retirement age could help here, but only for some jobs. In a knowledge-based society, does the need for skill retraining and updating become more critical through a person's working life?

● There are some who argue that there is 'grade deterioration' with school leaving qualifications and many young people are inadequately prepared. At the same time as this, and at the same time as there is a shortage of people in skilled trades, the numbers attending universities is increasing.

- The NHS is stretched and private medicine is expensive. This could become more problematical as people live longer and especially if pensions are reduced. Hence, economically, people might need to work longer.

- However, if the relative balance between salaried and 'permanent' career posts and self-employed people who contract themselves to various organizations continues to change, this issue of the length of working lives could be exacerbated.

- In addition, it is becoming increasingly difficult for many families to prepare for retirement because of the increasing costs of educating their children. In turn, this increases the number of two-income families and creates a larger number of childcare positions.

- The UK is a member of the enlarged European Union. This allows workers from other European countries to come to the UK and seek work without a visa. Although there are tighter rules for would-be immigrants from non-EU countries this has created some tensions in the recent economic recession.

In a wider context it might also be valuable to look at the implications of global climate change, the ever-increasing power of computing technology and the growth of new economies, such as China.

Developing useful scenarios

Organizations should really be looking to develop a number of scenarios that can be used to provoke debate among managers and possibly generate new creative ideas in the process – ideas that can be used as a basis for new strategies and action plans. As Schwartz (2003) points out, most future predictions will prove to be wrong – the real test of scenario planning is whether or not it changes how people manage their businesses, not whether the predictions are right.

The first step is to clarify the *key strategic issues*, mainly external, which will impact on the future that the company will face. Internally, many managers will already have formed views, which may not always accord, and which may be partial rather than comprehensive, but these preliminary views will have caused the development of current working assumptions about future trends. It is invariably invaluable to also consult outside experts.

There are three types of issue to consider:

- *predetermined elements* – for example, *social* changes to the size and structure of the population, lifestyles and values
- *key uncertainties* – *political* changes and the inevitable *economic* changes which accompany it; the entry of new competitors; possible changes of corporate ownership
- *driving forces* – developments in *technology* and education.

The link to a PEST analysis will be clearly seen.

The next step is to examine a number of *plausible outcomes* from the various key issues. It is particularly important to debate issues of positive and negative synergy, specifically the impact of interconnectedness. The discussions should generate some consensus, or possibly, and more realistically, accommodation on priorities, in the form of *viable scenarios* to test further.

These will often be presented as *stories*, illustrated creatively to generate interest and enthusiasm.

The *tests* against which they will be ultimately evaluated are:

- What has been left out? – in effect, the extent of the comprehensiveness and the absence of key omissions – and
- Do they lead to clearer understanding which informs future decisions and actions, while winning the commitment of everyone involved?

Yet in our rapidly changing world can even well-meaning scenario planning work?

The dream society

Jensen (1999) contends that we shall soon be living in a 'dream society' where the stories attributed to products and services – their image and reputation – will be an increasingly significant aspect of competitive advantage. Examples might relate to free-range eggs, organic vegetables and celebrity-endorsed training shoes. Simply, the story adds value. Jensen provides a number of themes for those organizations interested in creating 'dreams':

- *Adventure*. Involvement in the 'great outdoors' or leisure activities. Manchester United branded clothing appears to combine both

- *Networks*. BT (British Telecom) capitalized on this with its 'family and friends' name for its discounted call scheme as well as the television advertisements which feature a family of two children, a mother who has a new man in her life and various changes in their situation all based on telephone and Internet connections

- *Self-discovery* linked to products which allow people to say something about themselves. This theme has been exploited by VW (Volkswagen) with advertisements for the Golf which claim the only statement it needs to make is 'gone shopping'

Critical reflection 2.1

Scenario Planning

Task One

Outlined below are the skeletons for four quite different scenarios relevant for 2020. Expand each of these skeletons into a 150 word scenario and either individually or in groups assess or debate the implications of each one for you as an individual. Although there might be relevant elements in each one, which one of the four do you see as being the most realistic?

Scenario 1

Green thinking and climate warming concerns are dominant forces in consumer purchasing and consumption.

Sustainability is a 'mandatory' consideration for any new product.

Healthy living and an outdoor lifestyle are prominent in most people's lives.

Scenario 2

We live in a high tech society.

There is far more home working and on-line shopping than we have at the moment.

Living rooms are entertainment systems with all needs met through one central processor.

Our cars have technology that controls our speed and route.

Scenario 3

Society has become much more violent with high levels of education drop-out and unemployment.

There are more prisons and prisoners.

People live in more segregated areas. Those who can afford gated and secure communities live in this way.

More extreme political parties perform well at election time.

Scenario 4

There has been a rebellion against all these three trends and people have become more spiritual and creative.

People enjoy more leisure time and work less. They travel more and generally they are less materialistic as far as consumer goods are concerned.

A demand for better transport has forced improvements.

Task Two

Taking as your themes 'international politics', 'religious differences', 'the continued emergence of the East' and 'global terrorism' create four scenarios of your own and consider the implications.

- *Peace of mind*. Security, often linked to the perceived safety of the known past. Perhaps this explains why VW has been able to relaunch the Beetle model and BMW a new Mini (a model that it acquired when it owned Rover)
- *Caring* businesses that can exploit their community links and programmes
- *Convictions*. Ethical and environmental concerns are prominent. The Body Shop built a successful business around this, as shown in Chapter 5.

We conclude this chapter with an exercise on scenario planning (Critical Reflection 2.1) and a case on eBay – Case 2.10. EBay developed resources to seize a new opportunity that was being offered by the Internet. Typical of most of the truly successful Internet businesses to date, eBay provides a service rather than selling a specific product.

Case 2.10

eBay   Int

EBay has overtaken Amazon as the world's favourite e-commerce website. It is fundamentally an on-line auction house, dealing in almost anything. The most popular products are cars and motor cycles, computers, books, music and electronic goods – but eBay once sold a Gulfstream jet aircraft for $4.9 million. Altogether there are 16,000 categories and it is not unusual for 5 million items a day to be featured.

Described as an on-line flea market in the late 1990s, eBay had actually started life in 1995 when its founder, French-born computer programmer Pierre Omidyar, set up a site so that his wife, who collected Pez sweet distributors, could make contact with other collectors around the world. It was not the first on-line auction house – and, unlike a number of its rivals, it has always charged a commission rather than provided a free service. Omidyar was another Silicon Valley resident and he also went in search of venture capital to expand the business in 1997. He raised $6.7 million for a third of his business. Similar to Google, most of this has never been used. The company was and always has been profitable. In just over five years it was able to boast 40 million customers and deals amounting to almost $10 billion a year.

Head-hunters found Meg Whitman for Omidyar and she joined as CEO in 1998. Whitman had a corporate background – she had been working for Hasbro, the toy company, where she was running the Mr Potato Head franchise and masterminding the import into America of the Teletubbies. She recalls that she found a black and white website with a single typeface – courier. Despite the fact the company was successful and growing, she believed the website was 'confused'. She set about changing all this. She built up a fresh, strong management team and prepared the business for an IPO. When this happened late in 1998 it was the fifth most successful ever in US corporate history. Whitman has made the company international. Where sales have been disappointing – the case in Japan – she has simply closed the country site down. EBay arrived in the UK in December 1999. Its competitors now include Yahoo and Amazon, powerful names in Internet commerce.

On-line auctions have an interesting business model. There are no supply costs and there is no inventory. Goods are never handled – they simply move from seller to buyer and a percentage margin taken. Once established there is little need to advertise. Overall very little capital expenditure is required. Regular customers spend an average of ninety minutes when they are surfing the site – but they will make other quick visits to check progress when they are bidding for an item. Countless small businesses have increasingly found eBay a useful opportunity for selling their products. In 2007 eBay trade by UK based businesses exceeded £2 billion. Success has to depend on satisfied customers and eBay invests in customer feedback, which is collected for every transaction and made available as data for other customers to access. Whitman is strong on performance orientation. EBay maintains that it has always listened to its customers and responded whenever appropriate.

Interestingly there was little evidence of dishonest customer activity for quite a long time. Very few cheques ever seemed to bounce, for example. Moreover, customers have been very quick to respond if they notice any apparently rogue products being offered for sale – alleviating the need for eBay to invest heavily in security monitoring. However in 2008 eBay were faced with a bill for huge damages when it was shown they had inadvertently allowed fake designer goods, mainly Louis Vuitton brands, to be passed off as originals. There were also concerns that people were trading Marks and Spencer credit notes which some were convinced had been obtained by returning stolen goods to stores. Perhaps it was inevitable that certain 'rogue traders' would find opportunities to beat eBay's security.

An ever increasing proportion of the transactions are now handled on-line and eBay has had to develop the necessary competency. In July 2002 eBay bought PayPal, the world's largest on-line payment system. It is clearly possible to expand the scope of the business by offering the facility for customers to offer their products at a fixed price through the site – but this is different from the concept of an auction.

A further acquisition, in 2005, was Skype, the internet voice company that allows free conversation between people who are able to link their computers on-line. One can see how discussions between buyers and sellers could lift eBay to a new dimension.

Towards the end of 2008, as the economic recession bit in the UK, an interesting scenario evolved. It was reported that many people were no longer taking 'everything they no longer wanted' to charity shops but instead were looking to sell their 'best waste' through eBay. But at the same time, charity shops were taking trade away from the main high street retailers as customers looked to save money.

Another trend is the rising scale of BuyItNow price setting mainly by registered merchants who to some extent have turned eBay to an on-line department store where often whole categories are BuyItNow.

Project

Use the eBay website to track the bidding for a product that interests you. *You could, if you wish, sell something via eBay as an alternative.* Why do you think this simple business concept has been so successful? Examine eBay in terms of scenario planning. What could possibly happen to affect eBay in the future?

Summary

No organization deliberately plans to fail but many do fail to plan. Basically effectiveness is crucial if organizations are to succeed. Any organization, if it is to be successful, needs to 'do the right thing'. It can only do this through strategic thinking. This book provides the strategist with a range of strategic tools with which to guide their thinking. In the next sections we examine how strategy can be influenced by external environmental forces. Strategic thinking, then, relates to an organization's ability to gather, harness and utilize relevant information from inside the organization and from the (changing) external environment. The desired outcome is strong competitive strategies.

The external environment can usefully be seen as 'layered'. Suppliers, customers and competitors comprise the inner layer; the PEST (political, economic, social and technological) factors are the outer layer – because they affect the whole industry.

Strategic thinking demands an ability to learn from the past, to understand the present and to think ahead.

Effective thinking can be used to generate synergy, where the total achievements of the whole organization exceed what would be achieved if the various parts were working independently.

Synergy can be derived from sharing amongst the various functions of the organization, from complementary competitive strategies and from a cohesive management style.

Organizations operate with external environments that spring surprises on them from time to time. Indeed, many industries and markets are characterized by a form of 'competitive chaos' which arises from the natural dynamism, turbulence and uncertainty of both the industry and the environment.

It can make sense for the organization to see its boundary with the environment as relatively fluid. While suppliers, distributors and customers can be seen as outside the organizational boundary, they can also be identified as partners in a collaborative network which, more holistically, bounds with a number of external influences and forces.

Organizations must be able to react to the change pressures imposed by their environment (potential threats) and, at the same time, take advantage of opportunities which seem worthwhile. But this is arguably not enough. Leading organizations will create and sustain positions of strength by seeking to influence – and maybe even manage – their external environment.

A PEST (political, economic, social and technological forces) analysis provides a valuable framework for analysing relevant environmental forces.

All organizations should seek to understand the industries in which they compete. Industry attractiveness affects profitability and it can be assessed by considering five forces: barriers to entry; the relative power of suppliers; the relative power of buyers; the potential for substitutability; and inter-firm rivalry. Governments affect all five.

Over time, strong competitors create and seek to hold positions of power in markets and industries. For this reason governments everywhere will seek to exercise some degree of control. In the UK the relevant bodies are the Office of Fair Trading and the Competition Commission. However, in certain instances, UK companies will also be subject to regulation by the European Union.

Regulation is rarely clear-cut or black and white and sometimes the outcomes are not quite the ones desired.

To manage, and manage in, its environment an organization will need strong strategic positions. This implies finding and exploiting opportunities for adding value, in ways that consumers value and for which they will reward the organization with prices that imply superior margins.

Here we are talking about finding an effective blend between the opportunity-driven approach to strategy creation and the resource-based approach.

As organizations seek to exploit their *core competencies* and *strategic capabilities* to add value in this way, it is important that the value is appropriable. In other words, the benefits should not all go to shareholders (through high dividends), consumers (in, say, the form of relatively low prices) or employees (generous remuneration) such that the organization has inadequate resources for investment to build new ways of adding value for the future.

A SWOT (strengths, weaknesses, opportunities and threats) analysis is a second valuable framework for evaluating the position of an organization in relation to its environment. It is, however, important that the SWOT analysis is used to create ideas and is not just seen as a static statement of position.

It is important that organizations attempt to forecast their environment, however difficult this may prove. *Scenario planning* can make a very valuable contribution here if well done!

Online cases for this chapter

The following cases are relevant for this chapter:

Online Case 2.1: Sainsbury's
Online Case 2.2: Bidding for Safeway

Online Case 2.3: Deregulation and the International Airline Industry
Online Case 2.4: The European Drugs Industry
Online Case 2.5: Kellogg's

Questions and research assignments

1 Synergy has been summarized as the '2 + 2 = 5' effect. Can you think of instances from your own experiences (maybe in a sporting context) where it has been in evidence? Questions on the environmental influences discussed are to be found in later chapters.

2 Draw a diagram incorporating the environmental influences and stakeholders for any pub, discotheque or nightclub with which you are familiar. From this evaluation, develop a SWOT analysis and consider the strategic implications.

3 One of the growth sectors in the UK economy has been in the area of call centres. Many thousands of people are employed in UK call centres. Many of these jobs have been threatened with removal to India and other cheaper wage areas. How should the managers and workers of UK call centres respond?

4 Possibly in a group discussion, build a scenario relevant for the motor vehicle industry in ten years' time. How will people be using their cars? What will they expect in terms of size, performance, and external and interior design?

Internet and library projects

1 How have changes in competition from around the world affected the UK footwear industry? What are the strategies of the leading, remaining manufacturers? You may wish to use a leading manufacturer such as C&J Clark as a key reference point. You should also look at a specialist such as Jimmy Choo, Grenson or Church's. You might also investigate the source of your personal wardrobe of shoes, boots and trainers.
C&J Clark http://www.clarks.com
Church's http://www.churchsshoes.com
Grenson http://www.grensonshoes.co.uk

2 From your own experience, and from newspaper and other articles you have read or seen, list examples of where monopoly power and restrictive practices have been investigated, and where proposed mergers have been considered by the Competition Commission (or its predecessor the Monopolies and Mergers Commission). Evaluate the recommendations and outcomes. If you wish to follow up any of these investigations, all of the reports are published by HMSO.
Monopolies and Mergers Commission UK

http://www.coi.gov.uk/coi/depts/GMM/GMM.html
HMSO UK http://www.hmso.gov.uk

3 Take an industry of your choice, perhaps the one you work for, and assess it in terms of

a concentration
b Porter's model of five forces.

From this analyse one or more of the major competitors in terms of their chosen competitive strategies.

As well as the Internet the following library sources might prove useful sources of information:

- Business Monitors (PA and PQ series)
- Annual Report of the Director General of Fair Trading (as a source of ideas)
- Monopolies and Mergers Commission reports, and Competition Commission reports, which usually feature a comprehensive industry analysis
- McCarthy's (or similar) Index (press cutting service for firms and industries).

4 How could Porter's five forces model be applied to Camelot, the monopoly supplier of the UK's lottery? On the one hand, Camelot operates under licence for a fixed period of years without any direct competition; on the other hand, it provides only one gambling opportunity amongst many. Why has Camelot needed to introduce several new games during the period of its licence?

Strategy activity

Cream o' Galloway

The ice cream business that is Cream o' Galloway was started by David and Wilma Finlay in 1992 with the realization that if the family business Rainton Farm started in 1927 by the Finlay family was to survive it had to change. Although they had a relatively comfortable existence running the dairy farm, David and Wilma realized that if they wanted a sustainable business they had to move away from their dependence on small scale dairy farming. They investigated cheese, yoghurt and ice cream and decided to major in ice cream based on: the farm being located in a popular tourism area for families being based in the Dumfries and Galloway area of the South-West of Scotland; the luxury end of the ice cream market was growing; and the ice cream business did not seem an expensive business to enter.

The Finlay's identified the following key success factors that needed to be in place to start their new business. They needed: milk, land, office space, employees, product knowledge, equipment, and market knowledge. In depth product and market knowledge was missing alongside some equipment. The farming side of the business was kept going as they spent the next two years on research and development. In 1994 they felt that they were ready to launch their new business and they did so at the Royal Highland Show in Edinburgh in 1994 with ten flavours of ice cream. Customer feedback was so good they took the decision to move from small scale dairy farming to making ice cream to sell in the UK market. As a couple their skills were complementary. David provided the farming expertise whilst Wilma provided the friendly and driven personality and was the face of the business.

To support the development of their business they decided to take advantage of the family friendly image of ice cream and turn their farm into a tourist attraction creating an ice cream visitor centre out of their home. Initially the centre was little more than a shed where you could buy ice cream, with a few tables and a couple of swings for children. Over time the visitor centre has grown to accommodate a total of 70,000 visitors each year. The Finlays have created an adventure playground on the farm land with amongst other things a 50 foot viewing tower, Scotland's only 3D maze, nature trails and much more.

Since that time the business has developed and grown into one producing 30 different flavours of organic ice cream, smoothies and frozen yoghurts using only natural ingredients and organic milk. Their new 'Made Fair' product range is Fair Trade certified. They now produce 200,000 litres of ice cream a year with a turnover in 2007 of just over £1 million.

Their continued philosophy centres around being a sustainable business making a contribution to the local economy at the same time minimizing the impact on the environment:

'Bets are currently being taken on what is having the biggest negative environmental impact from our business whether it is the tourists travelling to our visitor centre; the distribution of our ice cream; the energy needed to make the ice cream; or the milk production'. (Wendy Finlay)

www.creamogalloway.co.uk

Question

1 What is the 'common' business model that Cream O'Galloway seems to fit?

Further reading

Campbell, A and Alexander, M (1997) What's wrong with strategy? *Harvard Business Review*, November–December.

Courtney, HG Kirkland, J and Viguerie, SP. (2001) Strategy under uncertainty, *Harvard Business Review*, March–April.

Emery, FE and Trist, EL (1965) The causal texture of organizational environments, *Human Relations*, 18.

Ginter, P and Duncan, J (1990) Macroenvironmental analysis, *Long Range Planning*, December.

Whipple, W (1989) Evaluating alternative strategies using scenarios, *Long Range Planning*, 22 (3).

References

Adams, J (1995) *Risk*, UCL Press.

Ansoff, HI (1968) *Corporate Strategy*, Penguin (originally published by McGraw Hill in 1965).

Ansoff, HI (1987) *Corporate Strategy*, Penguin.

Benoit, B (1999) Nearing 50, hale and hearty on home ground – a corporate profile of SAGA, *Financial Times*, 23 November.

Campbell, A and Alexander, M (1997) What's wrong with strategy? *Harvard Business Review*, November–December.

Courtney, H, Kirkland, J and Viguerie, P (1997) Strategy under uncertainty, *Harvard Business Review*, November–December.

Drucker, PF (1973) *Management*, Harper and Row.

Duncan, R (1972) Characteristics of organizational environments and perceived environmental uncertainty, *Administrative Science Quarterly*, 313–27.

Freeman, RE (1984) *Strategic Management: A Stakeholder Approach*, Pitman.

Hall, D (1992) *The Hallmarks for Successful Business*, Mercury Books.

Handy, C (1989) *The Age Of Unreason*, Hutchinson.

Jensen, R (1999) *The Dream Society*, McGraw Hill.

Kay, JA (1993) *Foundations of Corporate Success*, Oxford University Press.

Markides, C (1999) Six principles of breakthrough strategy, *Business Strategy Review*, 10(2).

Mintzberg, H (1987) Crafting strategy, *Harvard Business Review*, July–August.

Porter, ME (1980) *Competitive Strategy: Techniques for Analyzing Industries and Competitors*, Free Press.

Porter, ME (1996) What is strategy?, *Harvard Business Review*, November–December.

Porter, ME (2008) The Five Competitive Forces That Shape Strategy, *Harvard Business Review*, January.

Pümpin, C (1991) *Corporate Dynamism*, Gower.

Schwartz, P (2003) *Inevitable Surprises: Thinking Ahead in Times of Turbulence*, Gotham Books.

Chapter 3

Resource-led strategy

PART 1
Understanding strategy

1 Introducing strategy and strategic management

PART 5
Strategic management

14 Strategy implementation

15 Leading change

16 Managing strategy in the organization

17 Final thoughts – the purpose of strategy

STRATEGIC MANAGEMENT: AWARENESS AND CHANGE

PART 2
Strategic positioning

2 Strategic thinking, environmental analysis, synergy and strategic positioning

3 Resource-led strategy

4 The dynamics of competition

5 Introducing culture and values

PART 4
Issues in strategic growth

11 Strategic growth

12 International strategy

13 Failure, consolidation and recovery strategies

PART 3
Strategic analysis and choice

6 Strategic purpose

7 Strategic success

8 An introduction to strategy creation and planning

9 Strategic leadership, entrepreneurship and intrapreneurship

10 Strategic alternatives, strategy evaluation and strategy selection

Learning objectives

Having read to the end of this chapter you should be able to:

- explain the resource-based view of strategy

- conduct a strategic resource audit for an organization explain the key themes of core competency and strategic capability

- demonstrate how competitive advantage might be created through adding value in any functional area of the business

- define and discuss innovation and show how it is related to intrapreneurship in established organizations

- discuss the critical strategic contribution of people

- discuss the key aspects and implications of employee empowerment

- explain what is meant by the term learning organization

- appreciate the importance of information in strategic decision-making, the contribution information technology can make and the significance of personal perspectives

- realize the ways in which the Internet has affected company strategies – and continues to do so

- describe and produce an organizational value chain and explain how it might be used for evaluating competitive advantage

- discuss the significance of branding and corporate reputation as an organizational asset.

The resource-based view of strategy gradually emerged during the 1980s and 1990s with a series of important contributions, in particular work on core competency from Prahalad and Hamel (1990) and on added value by Kay (1993). This view helps to explain why some organizations succeed in creating competitive advantage and earning superior profits, while others do not. Consequently, it looks at strategies which can be identified with an individual company as distinct from those that are available to all competitors through an understanding of industries and markets. In other words, market opportunities have to be identified and then satisfied in an individual and distinctive way. Supporters of the resource-based view put forward a number of arguments. As long as there are opportunities which can be identified, it will normally be easier and less risky for organizations to exploit their existing resources in new ways than to seek to acquire and learn new skills and competencies. Innovation matters and new ways of exploiting resources must be found to sustain any competitive advantage. Relative differences which separate a company from its rivals are critical: just having a resource is not enough. For this reason, it can be useful if particular strengths are not easily learned and imitated by rivals. This is linked to the key themes of core competency and strategic capability. The opening case on Dyson shows how innovation and new ways of creating and adding value through design can markedly change an industry. In this particular case, innovation allowed a newcomer to establish a position of market dominance and force a reaction from established manufacturers.

This chapter looks first and briefly at the idea of a resource audit before considering resource linkages and synergy through **architecture** and the notion of the value chain. The chapter concludes with a section on reputation and branding, key intangible assets. Before reading this chapter you might usefully re-read the sections on core competencies and leveraging resources in the Part 1 supplement.

Case 3.1

James Dyson   UK

James Dyson is an entrepreneur who challenged the industry giants, in his case with a revolutionary vacuum cleaner. His dual cyclone cleaner now has a UK market share in excess of 50 per cent and international sales are blooming. A Hoover spokesman has said on the *BBC Money Programme*: 'I regret Hoover as a company did not take the product technology of Dyson … it would have been lain on a shelf and not been used'. Dyson has been compared by Professor Christopher Frayling, Rector of the Royal College of Art, with 'the great Victorian ironmasters … a one-man attempt to revive British manufacturing industry through design'. Dyson is creative, innovative, totally focused on customers and driven by a desire to improve everyday products. His dedication and ego drive is reflected in the following comment: 'the only way to make a genuine breakthrough is to pursue a vision with a single-minded determination in the face of criticism …' and this is exactly what he has done. Clearly a risk taker, he invested all of his resources in his venture. In the end his rise to fame and fortune came quickly, but the preceding years had been painful and protracted, and characterized by courage and persistence. They reflect the adage that 'instant success takes time'.

James Dyson's schoolmaster father died when he was just nine years old. The public school to which he was then sent 'made him a fighter'. At school he excelled in running, practising by running cross-countries on his own; and it was on these runs that he began to appreciate the magnificence of the railway bridges constructed by Brunel in the nineteenth century, an experience which helped to form his personal vision. An early leap in the dark came when he volunteered to play bassoon in the school orchestra, without ever having seen a bassoon! Naturally artistic, he won a painting competition sponsored by the *Eagle* comic when he was ten years old. Art became a passion and he later went on to complete a degree in interior

design. Dyson may be an inventor, but he has no formal engineering background.

Dyson's first successful product and business was a flat-bottomed boat, the Sea Truck. At this time he learnt how a spherical plastic ball could be moulded, an idea that he turned to good use in the wild garden of his new home. His wheelbarrow was inadequate as the wheels sunk into the ground, so he substituted the wheel with a light plastic ball and thus invented the Ballbarrow. Backed by his brother-in-law on a 50:50 basis, Dyson invested in his new idea. Made of colourful, light plastic the barrow was offered to garden centres and the building trade, both of whom were less than enthusiastic. With a switch to direct mail via newspaper advertisements, the business took off. A new sales manager was appointed but his renewed attempt to sell the barrow through more traditional retail channels was again a failure. The financial penalty was the need for external investors, who later persuaded Dyson's brother-in-law to sell the business. A second painful experience came when the sales manager took the idea and design to the USA, where Dyson later failed with a legal action against him.

Dyson's idea for a dual cyclone household cleaner came in 1979, when he was 31 years old. Again, it was a case of a need creating an opportunity. He was converting his old house and becoming frustrated that his vacuum cleaner would not clear all of the dust that he was creating. Particles were clogging the pores of the dust bags and reducing the suction capability of the cleaner. Needing something to collect paint particles from his plastic spraying operation for the ballbarrows, Dyson had developed a smaller version of the large industrial cyclone machines, which separate particles from air by using centrifugal forces in spinning cylinders. He believed that this technology could be adapted for home vacuum cleaners, removing the need for bags, but his partners in the Ballbarrow business failed to share his enthusiasm. Out of work when the business was sold, his previous employer, Jeremy Fry (for whom he had developed the Sea Truck), loaned him £25,000. Dyson matched this by selling his vegetable garden for £18,000 and taking out an additional £7000 overdraft on his house. Working from home, risking everything and drawing just £10,000 a year to keep himself, his wife and three children, he pursued his idea. Over the years he produced 5000 different prototypes.

When he ultimately approached the established manufacturers his idea was, perhaps predictably, rejected. Replacement dust bags are an important source of additional revenue. A series of discussions with potential partners who might license his idea brought mixed results. Fresh legal actions in the USA for patent infringement – 'with hindsight I didn't patent enough features' – were only partially offset by a deal with Apex of Japan. Dyson designed the G-Force upright cleaner which Apex manufactured and sold to a niche in the Japanese market for the equivalent of £1200 per machine, from which Dyson received just £20. At least there was now an income stream, but this had taken seven years to achieve. Finally, in 1991 Lloyds Bank provided finance for the design and manufacture of a machine in the UK. Several venture capitalists and the Welsh Development Agency had turned him down. Dyson was determined to give his latest version the looks of NASA technology, but further setbacks were still to occur. Dyson was let down by the plastic moulder and assembler with whom he contracted, and was eventually forced to set up his own plant. Early sales through mail-order catalogues were followed by deals with John Lewis and eventually (in 1995) with Comet and Curry's. In this year a cylinder version joined the upright. Dyson continues to improve the designs to extend his patent protection. By 1999 his personal wealth was estimated to be £500 million.

Dyson has always seen himself as more of an inventor than a businessman. He established two separate businesses, both in Malmesbury, Wiltshire, and he kept Dyson Manufacturing and Dyson Research (design and patenting) apart. The dress code for employees is perpetually informal and communications are predominantly face-to-face. Memos are banned and even e-mails discouraged. Every employee is encouraged to be creative and contribute ideas. Most new employees are young – 'not contaminated by other employers' – and they all begin by assembling their own vacuum cleaner, which they can then buy for £20. Designers work on improvements to the dual cyclone cleaners as well as new product ideas.

In early 2000 Dyson launched a robot version of the dual cyclone cleaner, which is battery-powered, self-propelled and able to manoeuvre itself around furniture. It retailed at some £2500, which limited it to a select segment of the market and it was slow to take off. He has since launched 'The Ball', a version which has a large ball instead of wheels to make it more versatile. Later in 2000 Dyson launched a revolutionary super-fast washing machine with short wash cycles and an ability to spin clothes almost dry, presenting a challenge to the manufacturers of both washing machines and tumble dryers. This time, however, Dyson had his own resources to launch the product. Another Dyson product is his own design of wall-mounted hand dryer – users don't hold their hands under a hot air outlet but place them between two flat plates. The machines are extremely powerful. He has also succeeded in penetrating the US and Japanese markets with his dual cyclone cleaners; he had to design a small version with a digital motor for Japan. Dyson controls 100 per cent of the shares in his

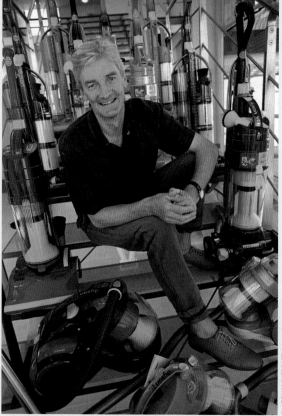

© ADRIAN SHERRATT / ALAMY

business. He has learnt some painful lessons but is now enjoying the rewards of his dogged determination.

However, in recent years Dyson has transferred the majority of his manufacturing to lower cost plants in Malaysia and Singapore. Perhaps inevitably this was opposed by the UK workforce and it has brought him adverse publicity. Before the transfer there were 1800 employees in the UK. This reduced to 1000, but has since been increased to between 1400 and 1500 none of them actually making any products. Several hundreds work in R&D and design.

Dyson himself has become a passionate spokesman for engineering and design and has funded the Dyson

School of Design Innovation in Bath. He believes the UK must focus on what it can do well and accept that the actual manufacture should take place in lower labour cost countries overseas.

Questions

1   Thinking about the issues of core competency and strategic capability, what is the 'secret' of James Dyson's competitive advantage?
2   Has he been able to appropriate the rewards of the value he has added?

DYSON: **http://www.dyson.com**

People feel the best about their work when they do a high-quality job! Getting a job done quickly is satisfying. Getting a job done at low cost is rewarding. But getting a job done quickly, at low cost and with high quality is exciting!

ROBERT C STEMPEL, WHEN CHAIRMAN, GENERAL MOTORS CORPORATION

3.1   Strategic resources

It is a fact of life for management that environments spring surprises on organizations from time to time. Sometimes the surprises constitute opportunities; at other times, threats. The most vigilant and aware organizations will be better placed to respond. Success lies in seeing opportunities 'ahead of the game' and responding in some individual way, ideally one that is genuinely different, appreciated by customers and not easily copied by rivals. The ability to do this comes down to individuals, specific to the organization competencies and capabilities, which in turn emanate from the organization's resources. Resources, therefore, make the difference. In this chapter this argument is explored in greater depth and frameworks are provided which can help us to audit and evaluate strategic resources.

There are many ways of studying strategic resources. We can, for example, look at key resource drivers – such as the following four:

Labour – Where a business or activity is labour intensive then it is highly likely that indirect costs (those that vary with levels of production) will be relatively high and imply a relatively low break-even level. Labour intensive businesses are attractive to countries with low labour costs. The extent to which labour needs to be skilled (or unskilled) will also affect the supply and the cost of labour.

The need for investment in technology – Up-front investment in technology is likely to imply high fixed (direct) costs and thus imply a relatively high break-even level. Such investment, though, can have a major impact on quality and uniqueness.

Supplies – It is sometimes important to evaluate their cost as a proportion of total costs and also consider their role in creating and adding value for customers. Some supplies are scarce or difficult to obtain and this can be strategically important.

Knowledge – What is the significance of intellectual property and research and development is the industry in question? In the so-called 'knowledge intensive industries' these can be drivers of competitiveness as well as cost drivers.

Similarly we might separate resources into those that are tangible and those that are intangible – whilst it will not always be the case, intangible resources can be the hardest to copy or replicate. All resources can lead to a relative cost advantage over competitors – and they can all be a source of important differences. For example, capital equipment and physical supplies are very obviously tangible; as is much technology. Organizational processes, networks and alliances are also tangible, but less so. Corporate reputation and strategic thinking and good examples of intangible resources.

Auditing strategic resources

It does not follow that every resource an organization possesses is strategically significant. Sometimes it is tempting to list every positive resource as a strength, but this may be illusory. When we evaluate the resources of an organization in terms of their strategic significance, five factors matter:

1 **Competitive superiority.** The relative value when compared to rival organizations. A resource is not really a competitive strength if it is possessed by every competitor.

2 **Barriers to replication.** It is useful if rivals can be stopped from imitating or replicating any valuable resources.

3 **Durability.** Basically a time advantage relating to 1 and 2.

4 **Substitutability.** Can competitors neutralize the value of a resource by substituting an alternative?

5 **Appropriability.** Kay (1993) contends that it is essential that the organization possessing the resource benefits from it, rather than the real benefit accruing to someone else, such as a supplier or distributor. We discussed appropriability in Chapter 2.

The relationship between environmental forces and internal resources is at the heart of Figure 3.1, which has been adapted from the Harvard Business School approach to strategy (Kelly and Kelly,

Figure 3.1   Matching the organization and the environment

ADAPTED FROM KELLY, FJ AND KELLY, HM (1987) *WHAT THEY REALLY TEACH YOU AT THE HARVARD BUSINESS SCHOOL.* PIATKUS

1987). Here, selected products, services and markets are seen as environment driven and the competitive environment and stakeholders are shown with resources and values as four key strategic elements linked to corporate objectives. These elements can be changed, but in many cases not readily and not quickly, and consequently at any point in time they are reasonably fixed.

Six operating elements are also incorporated. *Marketing* relates to how the various products and services are positioned in relation to competitors, and how they are priced, advertised and distributed. *Manufacturing* involves the types of production process, location issues and technology utilization. *Finance* incorporates both performance targets and sources of funding. *Research and development* considers how much to spend on research and development and whether the perspective is short or long term. *Human resources* relates to the types of people utilized and how they are rewarded. The *organization structure* encompasses how these functions are co-ordinated and controlled.

These operating elements determine whether or not the corporate objectives are achieved. The different functions in the organization are affected to varying degrees by different stakeholders, and certain stakeholders who have a significant impact on certain functions may have little direct importance for others. Equally, the specific stakeholders may influence individual functions in quite different ways. Their impact upon the whole organization is therefore affected by the organization structure and relative power and influence within the firm. The figure also highlights the strategic value of functional managers taking a more holistic view of the organization and their role and contribution.

How, then, might we audit and evaluate these operating elements or strategic resources?

An internal analysis should be a three-stage process:

1 an evaluation of the profile of the principal skills and resources of an organization

2 a comparison of this resource base with the requirements for competitive success in the industry

3 a comparison with competitors to determine the relative strengths and weaknesses and any significant comparative advantage.

Where internal managers carry out this analysis, it is inevitable that there will be some subjective judgement and it will be affected by their position in the organization.

In a SWOT (strengths, weaknesses, opportunities and threats) analysis, then, the strengths and weaknesses of resources must be considered in relative and not absolute terms. It is important to consider whether they are being managed effectively as well as efficiently. Resources, therefore, are not strong or weak purely because they exist or do not exist. Rather, their value depends on how they are being managed, controlled and used.

In auditing resources we consider the functional areas of the business, as this is where the human, financial and physical resources are deployed. These areas might include finance, production, marketing, research and development, procurement, personnel and administration. However, it is also important to consider how they are related together in the organization's structure and control systems. A brilliant and successful marketing manager, for example, might seem to represent a strength; however, if there is no adequate cover for him and he leaves or falls ill, it is arguable that the firm has a marketing weakness.

Control systems, such as production and **financial control**, and the ways in which managers co-operate within the organization influence how well resources are managed for efficiency and effectiveness. Table 3.1, which is not meant to be fully comprehensive, provides a sample of key resource considerations. In completing such an audit the various resources should be evaluated: their existence, the ways in which they are deployed and utilized, and the control systems that are used to manage them.

Efficiency measures of the salesforce might include sales per person or sales per region, but the effectiveness of the salesforce relates to their ability to sell the most profitable products or those products or services that the organization is keen to promote at a particular time, perhaps to

Table 3.1 Aspects of the resource audit

Resource/function	Key considerations
Marketing	Products and services: range, brand names and stage in life cycle
	Patents
	Strength of salesforce
	Distribution channels
	Market information
Operations	Location and plant
	Capital equipment
	Capacity
	Processes
	Planning and manufacturing systems
	Quality control
	Supplies
Research and development	Annual budget
	Technology support
	Quality of researchers
	Record of success and reputation
	Spending in relation to industry norm
Information	Organizational knowledge and extent of sharing
	Information systems
	Problem-solving capabilities and procedures
Finance	Capital structure
	Working capital
	Cash flow
	Costing systems and variances
	Nature of shareholders
	Relations with bankers
Human resources	Numbers and qualifications
	Skills and experience
	Age profile
	Labour turnover and absenteeism
	Flexibility
	Development and training record and policies
	Motivation and culture
	Managerial competencies and capacity

reduce a high level of stocks. The efficiency of individual distribution outlets can be measured by sales revenue in a similar way. However, the effectiveness of the distribution activity relates to exactly which products are being sold and to whom, whether they are available where customers expect them, and how much investment in stock is required to maintain the outlets. The efficiency of plant and equipment is linked to percentage utilization. The effectiveness involves an assessment of which products are being manufactured in relation to orders and delivery requirements, to what quality and with what rejection levels.

It is also important to assess the relative strengths and weaknesses in relation to competition.

Managers must be aware of and must address strategic issues if the resources are to be used for creating and sustaining competitive advantage. *Marketing* can be looked at from the point of view of managing the activities which comprise the marketing function. Product design and pricing, advertising, selling and distribution would be included here. However, if an organization is marketing orientated there is an implication that employees throughout the organization are aware of consumers and customers, their needs, and how they might be satisfied effectively while enabling the organization to achieve its objectives. Consumer concern becomes part of the culture and values. Consumers and customers are mentioned separately because for many organizations, particularly the manufacturers of products for consumer markets, their customers are distributors and their ultimate consumers are customers of the retailers that they supply.

Innovation and quality can be seen as aspects of production or *operations management*. Again, it is helpful if these factors become part of the culture. An innovatory organization is ready for change, and looking to make positive changes, in order to get ahead and stay ahead of competition. A concern for quality in all activities will affect both costs and consumer satisfaction.

In *human resources management* values are communicated and spread throughout the organization.

Financial management includes the control of costs so that profit is achieved and value is added to products and services primarily in areas that matter to consumers. This should provide differentiation and competitive advantage.

Lower costs and differentiation are important themes in competitive strategy. They relate to both an awareness of consumer needs and the management of resources to satisfy these needs effectively and, where relevant, profitably. Marketing orientation and the effective management of production and operations, people and finance are all essential aspects of the creation and maintenance of competitive strength and advantage.

Functional and competitive strategies are important for an understanding of strategic management in all types of organization, and they are especially important for a large proportion of small businesses and many not-for-profit organizations. Corporate strategic changes such as major diversification and acquisition, divestment of business units which are under-performing or international expansion may not be relevant for small firms with a limited range of products or services and a primarily local market, or for not-for-profit organizations with very specific missions. However, these organizations must compete effectively, operate efficiently and provide their customers and clients with products and services that satisfy their needs. Competitive and functional strategies are therefore the relevant issue.

As the Internet becomes more pervasive in our lives some organizations and industries are being presented with wonderful opportunities and, at the same time, real threats. Book retailing has changed with the growth of Amazon.com and the opening of online bookshops by the leading book retailers. Similarly, domestic banking has been changed with the growth of ATMs (automated teller machines or 'holes in the wall'), telephone call centres and Internet accounts. Competitors have had to develop new skills, competencies and capabilities in order to survive, let alone thrive. The challenge, though, did not stop here. It has also been necessary to clarify the key success factors for those customers who opted to avoid the Internet and stick with a personal service. What exactly are their needs and preferences? How can they be satisfied 'wonderfully well'? How can costs be trimmed in the process?

Success, then, depends upon understanding and linking with customers, and these points are explored further through the remainder of this chapter.

Core competencies

In order to meet their key success factors organizations must develop core competencies (Prahalad and Hamel, 1990). These are distinctive skills which yield competitive advantage, and ideally they:

- provide access to important market areas or segments
- make a significant contribution to the perceived customer benefits of the product or service
- prove difficult for competitors to imitate.

Once developed they should be exploited as, for example, Honda have exploited their skills at engine design and technology. Core competencies must, however, be flexible and responsive to changing customer demands and expectations. Canon have developed core competencies in precision mechanics, fibre optics and microelectronics, and these are spread across a range of products, including cameras, calculators, printers and photocopiers. There is constant product innovation.

Successful products and services, then, are the manifestation of important, underlying core competencies; and the true competition between organizations is at this competency level.

Prahalad and Hamel (1990) acknowledge that there are three strands to core competency:

- technologies
- processes (or capabilities) and
- strategic architecture.

Different competitors in the same industry may well build their success by emphasizing different key competencies. While the particular expertise may be different, they all need to be competent in a number of key activities, the key success factors. In the global oil industry, for example, Exxon has long been renowned for its financial expertise, crucial when huge speculative and high-risk investments are required for exploration and developing new fields. In contrast, British Petroleum (BP) has historically relied heavily on its exploration skills. It was BP who developed the huge Forties Field in the North Sea and the fields off the hostile North Coast of Alaska, aided by the imaginative trans-Alaska pipeline. Royal Dutch Shell, a joint Anglo-Dutch company with two head offices in the UK and The Netherlands, has developed a valuable competency in managing a decentralized and diversified global business. Mobil's outstanding competency was in the related field of lubricants produced from the oil. Later in the book we will look at how the oil industry has been consolidating in recent years as the industry environment has become more demanding.

Strategic capabilities

Stalk *et al.* (1992) argue that strategic success is based on capabilities – processes that enable the company to be an effective competitor. Distribution networks that achieve both high service levels (effectiveness) and low costs (efficiency) would be an example. Typically these processes will cut across whole organizations, rather than be product specific, and they will rely heavily on information systems and technology. In many respects Stalk's capabilities are the processes embedded in Hamel and Prahalad's core competencies. Whilst it is optional whether they are separated, or all seen as core competencies, we think that a valuable distinction can be made between competencies that are largely rooted in technologies and process-based capabilities. Although delivering similar outcomes, conceptually they are very different.

Retailers such as Boots in the UK (which has encompassed high-street department stores, specialist pharmacies, optical retailing, Halfords car products and service bays, Fads, Homestyle and Do-It-All DIY at various times) operate a number of different retail formats, capitalizing on their expertise in supply-chain, information and service management.

Hamel and Prahalad (1993) developed these ideas further when they argued that understanding processes should generate intelligence that can be used to create added or greater value from resources, in order to strengthen or enhance competitiveness. They refer to this as **stretching resources**. The ability to stretch resources is very dependent on strategic architecture, which is discussed later.

Kay (1993) further stresses that, to be beneficial, both core competencies and strategic capabilities must be capable of exploitation and be *appropriable*. In other words, the firm must be able to realize the benefits of the competencies and capabilities for the company itself, rather than the main beneficiaries being its suppliers, customers or competitors.

Leveraging resources

Hamel and Prahalad (1993) also emphasize the need to manage the organization's strategic resources to achieve ambitious, stretching objectives. Productivity can be improved by gaining the same output from fewer resources – this is **downsizing** (sometimes called rightsizing) – and by leveraging, achieving more output from given resources.

Clearly, internal and external architecture are both important for leveraging resources. In addition, organizations can benefit by ensuring that there is a clear and understood focus for the efforts. This could take the form of a properly communicated mission or purpose, which is acknowledged and understood. British Airways would claim that much of its success historically has been based around a commitment to the slogan 'The World's Favourite Airline'. This example again emphasizes the significance of corporate image.

Kay's framework

Kay (1993) proposed a three-strand framework for evaluating or auditing strategic resources. He proposed the following factors:

- Architecture – internal and external relationships and links
- Reputation – the value and power of the organization's reputation, including branding
- Innovation – continually improving everything the organization does – products, services and processes – partially in response to competition and partially to drive competitiveness in the industry.

3.2 Strategic architecture

Kay (1993) adopted the word 'architecture' to emphasize the importance of corporate networks and relationships. He argued that companies depend upon their people for their competitiveness and success, but strong and capable individuals, while important, are not enough. They must work together well and synergistically. Football clubs, and their need for skilled individuals to be moulded into a strong, winning team, provide a valuable metaphor. In addition, people's natural energies should not be focused on internal rivalries but on managing external demands. Success here can be enhanced through effective links between an organization, its suppliers, its distributors and its ultimate customers.

Strategic success requires:

- the organization to behave in a co-ordinated, synergy-creating manner, integrating functions and businesses
- the value-adding network (links between manufacturers, retailers, suppliers and intermediate distributors) to be managed as an effective, integrated, system.

Kay (1993) refers to the ability to achieve these demands as strategic architecture. The ability to build and control a successful architecture is facilitated by strong technological competency and effective functional process competencies.

Honda is renowned for its expertise in engine design and technology. However, its success as an international company has also been dependent on its ability to establish an effective distribution (dealer) network for all of its products. This has been enhanced by sound, information technology (IT)-supported, communications and control systems. As another example, Marks and Spencer's functional competencies and brand technology create both an image and a capability which enable it to trade in clothes, foods, cosmetics, household furnishings and credit. These competencies also bestow on the company the power to demand and obtain from its suppliers worldwide both a strict adherence to Marks' technological specifications and very keen prices.

The important themes in architecture are:

- internally: 'systemic thinking', which leads to synergy from the fostering of interdependencies between people, functions and divisions in organizations; and

- externally: the establishment of linkages or even alliances between organizations at different stages of the added **value chain**.

Successful internal architecture requires that managers think 'organizationally' rather than put themselves first or promote their particular part of the organization to the detriment of other parts. Synergy from internal architecture also depends on the ability of the divisions or businesses in a conglomerate to support each other, transferring skills, competencies and capabilities, and sometimes sharing common resources. This, in turn, is partially dependent on the ability of the organization to learn, and share learning. It is also affected by the actual portfolio of businesses managed by a corporation. Goold *et al.* (1994) use the term 'heartland' to describe that range of businesses to which a corporate head office can add value, rather than see value destroyed through too much complexity and diversity.

Alliances enable companies to focus on their core skills and competencies. Nike, for example, a leading company in sporting and leisure footwear, focuses on product design, marketing and personality endorsements; it avoids manufacturing, which it subcontracts to specialists world-wide. Partners have to support each other, however, and understand each other's various needs and expectations. The main benefits will come from sharing information, which in turn should enable companies to respond more quickly to new opportunities and threats. Alliance partners can also be an excellent means of overcoming relative weaknesses.

In summary, we should consider:

- The way managers and other employees co-operate within the organization. Communications and co-operation should work both horizontally and vertically. Transfer pricing arrangements and poorly crafted internal performance measures can all too easily set division against division and department against department, and create real internal competition for resources. Where managers find delight when another manager, department or division finds itself in trouble, something is wrong. But it still happens. Similarly, in some organizations, there is a reliance on top-down communications for issuing instructions coupled with an ability for managers lower down the organization to feed only good news upwards and suppress bad news. The valuable ideas that some junior and middle managers have are, consequently, neither sought nor listened to by their superiors.

- Suppliers, organizations, distributors and final customers and consumers working together supportively in a 'seamless' chain which builds and provides value for all the participants, or 'external architecture'. Members of this value chain can make life either relatively easy or problematical for the other members, depending on their philosophy. The ideal outcome is one where everyone feels they are gaining some benefit rather than they are being exploited by someone who is ruthless or selfish. It is a feeling of 'win–win' rather than 'I win, you lose' or 'you win at my expense', which happens in many negotiations and deals. Sometimes the members of such a value chain will establish formalized partnerships or alliances to seal the relationship more firmly.

The outcome should be shared knowledge, co-operation and the development of trust and trusted routines, as illustrated in Figure 3.2. All parties should feel that they could rely on each other.

The driving force in all the world's markets is competition. And the most aggressive drivers are the Japanese. Their competitive strength and ambitions are apparent around the world. Ultimately the only way to succeed is to be fully competitive in the marketplace.

Figure 3.2 Effective supply chain management

Fundamentally this means offering products with utility, style and value that the buyers want, making them with world-class productivity and quality, and serving the customers better than anyone else.

JOHN F SMITH JR, WHEN VICE CHAIRMAN (INTERNATIONAL OPERATIONS),
GENERAL MOTORS CORPORATION

A number of useful examples highlight the benefit of strong strategic architecture:

- For many years Japanese organizations have benefited from membership of corporate families or *keiretsu*. Businesses, typically those clustered together in a geographical area, will all own shares in each other. Their directors will hold part-time directorships in other organizations in the *keiretsu*. The whole philosophy will be one of helping each other with either preferred supplier arrangements or the provision of help and advice. It will be realized how a base like this can foster benchmarking and the exchange of ideas and good practice, and the ability to exploit just-in-time supply arrangement. Here, manufacturers can avoid inventory costs by relying on their suppliers to deliver the quantities they need exactly when they are required for production.

The process of the exchange of expertise, ideas and good practice has to a large extent shifted to the connection between famous US and Japanese manufacturers to include Chinese manufacturers both in terms of partnerships, alliances and strategic acquisitions. A good example of this in action is in the production of pianos both in volume and in quality terms. The competitive position in the piano industry is outlined in Case 3.2. To some extent the tactics of Pearl River mirror that of the tactics employed by Japanese motor-cycle manufacturers in breaking into the US market more than a decade ago.

- For many years Marks and Spencer was credited with having a valuable portfolio of key suppliers, many of them British, who were committed to it. Typically, M&S would take a substantial proportion of a supplier's annual output and would work with it on designs and quality. M&S knew that it was buying reliable, quality products; the suppliers knew they were working with one of the UK's strongest retailers. Customers were equally satisfied. M&S standards and expectations were exacting, but the mutual rewards were high and shared. Towards the end of the 1990s, as M&S was accused of having 'tired' ranges and manufacturing costs in Britain for many clothing and food products seemed relatively expensive, some of these arrangements broke down. One clothing supplier, William Baird, sued M&S for alleged breach of contract. They failed and many UK manufacturing jobs were lost.

- The legendary Silicon Valley, heart of the American, and arguably the global, computer and semiconductor industries, has long benefited from networks and alliances. Companies spin-off from each other, sometimes as rivals, but more often to develop new products or to supply each other. In the early days of the industry young entrepreneurs readily shared their ideas and knowledge. As a result, Silicon Valley as a whole became an opportunity which attracted people with ideas and ambition.

Case 3.2

Piano Manufacturing in China   Int US Cn

Pearl River Piano

Pearl River Piano is a piano company started in 1956 in Guangzhou, China and now lays claim to be the largest piano factory in the world with Pearl River pianos the fastest sellers in the United States and Canada with over 300 dealers selling their product. This success and the recent development of a new state of art woodworking facility has given Pearl River the ability to produce 100,000 pianos per year and they export to over 80 countries. This development is part of a strategy of heavy investment in technology and people development by Pearl River.

Pearl River pianos feature hardwood rims, sand-cast plates, and lower tension scales, features found in the world's best pianos such as that of Steinway and Bosendorfer. Pearl River Piano has been awarded the ISO 9001 certificate for its complete line of grand and vertical pianos. Pearl River Piano was the first piano company in China to receive this award along with the award of ISO14001 for the environmental standards practice by the company. Pearl River was the first Chinese piano manufacturer to both market pianos under its own name and to distribute them directly to dealers through opening in 2000 its own distribution business. Pearl River not only manufacture pianos, they are one of the world's largest guitar and violin manufacturers as well as selling drums, brass and woodwind instruments around the world.

One of the crucial elements of the success of Pearl River is its alliance with Yamaha and Steinway. In 1995 Yamaha formed a joint venture with Pearl River to establish a factory to build pianos for the Chinese market. This factory is located east of Guangzhou in an 'economic development zone' some 35 miles from the Pearl River factory. In turn, Pearl River produce a line of pianos for Steinway and benefit from the exchange of expertise between the two manufacturers.

Gibson Guitar and Dongbei Piano

In December 2006, Gibson Guitar Corp of the United States announced that it had acquired 100 per cent ownership of Dongbei Piano Co Ltd, one of the largest piano producers in China. Dongbei Piano Co is based in Yingkou, a city in Northeast China's Liaoning Province. Dave Berryman, President of Gibson Guitar Corp., said 'As a major producer in the Chinese mainland, Dongbei Piano boasts a great reputation the world over. Gibson will fully bolster Dongbei Piano's development by introducing advanced manufacturing and marketing concepts to upgrade its competitiveness in global markets'. The acquisition of Dongbei Piano is another important move for Gibson after it acquired the US piano maker Baldwin. Dongbei Piano will soon become the second-largest piano manufacturing facility in China and a major manufacturing base for Gibson, according to Henry Juszkiewicz, Chairman and CEO of Gibson

SOURCE: THIS CASE STUDY WAS PREPARED USING PRIMARILY PUBLICLY AVAILABLE SOURCES OF INFORMATION FOR THE PURPOSES OF CLASSROOM DISCUSSION; IT DOES NOT INTEND TO ILLUSTRATE EITHER EFFECTIVE OR INEFFECTIVE HANDLING OF A MANAGERIAL SITUATION.

Guitar Corp. The new company will be named Baldwin Dongbei Piano Instrument Co. Ltd.

Dongbei Piano was founded in 1952. It currently employs more than 2000 workers and produces 30,000 upright pianos and 10,000 grand pianos, a year, making it the third-largest piano producer in China. Dongbei Piano sells its products to more than 20 countries. 'There is no doubt that joining Gibson is the right choice for Dongbei Piano. Cooperation with an industry leader like Gibson greatly enhances our strengths, and we are expecting Dongbei Piano's continued and further success in both the domestic and overseas markets' – Zhang Daming, General Manager of Dongbei Piano.

www.chinaview.cn

Questions

1   Identify the main classic elements of the strategy of Pearl River. What should now be the tactics of Pearl River Piano?
2   What is the competitive strategy of Gibson?
3   How is Gibson trying to achieve competitive advantage?

Sometimes the value and constituency of these networks and partnerships can be hard to quantify or even explain. They owe a lot to people and to their history. They are relationships which emerge and strengthen over many years and are dependent upon personal relations and interactions. This often serves to make them even more powerful as they are automatically difficult to replicate. Consequently, architecture can be a vital element of competitive advantage.

As more and more organizations opt to focus on core strengths, activities and competencies, and divest those that are peripheral, the significance of architecture is reinforced and increased. When companies outsource important services such as information technology (IT) or payroll management, or choose to buy in key components they once made for themselves, they need to be able to rely upon, and trust, their new suppliers. Managing relationships, therefore, becomes an important new capability.

Some organizations, of course, have chosen to **outsource** their manufacturing. Dyson (Case 3.1) has switched its manufacturing to Malaysia to reduce costs. Hornby Hobbies (Case 3.3) manufacturer of model electric trains and Scalextrix car racing systems, also manufactures in China. However, this move was not directed at reducing costs, per se. Hornby found it could devote two labour hours for every one used in the UK and thus produce models with much higher quality and detail at the same total cost. Without changing its prices, Hornby has seen its sales grow rapidly because of the greater authenticity. At the same time the company has been innovatory with new products. For example, both Eurostar and the Hogwarts Express from the Harry Potter stories provided new sales opportunities. The Hornby brand names are important, as is the company's ability to ally with other well-known brands. This story is told in Case 3.3 Hornby Hobbies. Following this trend, Royal Doulton (China) now focuses on design and marketing and outsources production from Indonesia. Dr Martens boots and shoes are made in China.

Buckingham and Coffman (1999) also draw attention to the importance of architecture in their delineation of four levels of customer service. Level 1 is accuracy and level 2, availability. These, they argue, have to be seen as the relatively easy levels, and are generally taken for granted. In other words, without them, a company cannot hope to win repeated business. Levels 3 and 4 are working partnerships and the provision of advice and support. These relate to strategic architecture.

Porter also made a contribution to strategic architecture by providing a value chain framework for helping to identify valuable differences and manage cost drivers. This is looked at in the value chain section later in the chapter.

Before we look in depth at the value chain, however, we next consider two critically important strategic resources: people and information. We are concentrating on these as they are key drivers of change as well as being crucially important in the implementation of chosen strategies.

Case 3.3

Hornby Hobbies

UK Cn

Hornby is a rare survivor in the UK toy industry, which has a past characterized by (in their day) leading brands but which has been subject to intense competition from manufacturers in the Far East and by the growth and popularity of electronic and computer toys and games which has hit demand for more traditional toys.

Hornby began over 100 years ago in Liverpool; its founder, Frank Hornby, invented Meccano, a construction set based on the principle of 'mechanical engineering made easy'. Trevor Baylis, inventor of the clockwork radio, has always said he 'cut his teeth' with Meccano during and after the World War II. The company would follow this with model electric railway sets and Dinky Toys, scale model vehicles. The first Hornby trains were O gauge, but these were replaced by the Double O gauge that is most popular today. OO gauge is half the size of O gauge.

Meccano reached its heyday in the period between the 1930s and 1950s, but it is still available today. The company that manufactures it is joint French and Japanese, and sets are manufactured in both France and China. Modern Meccano is different, but the principle is the same. Pieces are bolted together to produce a whole variety of finished models. Like Lego bricks, which for many people were a substitute product, small engines can be added to provide power.

Dinky Toys competed with Corgi Toys – which were roughly the same size – and Matchbox Toys, which were much smaller. These were all die-cast and produced absolutely to scale and finished to look just like the original in respect of design and colour. Dinky eventually became part of Matchbox (started by Lesney) but are now most likely to be found as collector's items on eBay.

The Hornby company would eventually be merged with Triang, which, amongst other toys, also produced model railways, which it had started to do with encouragement from Marks and Spencer. Scalextric slot-car racing was later merged into the business. The combined business was first owned by Lines Brothers, but after this company went into liquidation, by Dunbee Combex Marx, from which there would be a management buy out. During the 1990s, and with new owners, Hornby diversified quite widely – one new product was Cassy dolls, which competed head-on with the more popular Barbie and Sindy dolls, although at 7" tall they were a good 5" shorter than their rivals. These changes were not a success; and after a few years of very mixed results a new Chief Executive took over in 2001. Frank Martin would succeed in rejuvenating the business with a number of important strategic changes.

- The company was located at Margate in Kent, where it manufactured everything. This was changed. Production was moved to China where there are now 3000 employees. The 130 staff in Kent control design and marketing and look after distribution. Although some organizations opt to manufacture in China to save as many costs as possible, Martin saw it as an opportunity to invest over twice the number of people hours into every product and thus increase its quality, whilst maintaining the existing market price and improving profitability. Quality improved markedly through this strategy and improved the 'model feel' (as distinct from a toy) with the railway equipment. In turn this opened up a new market opportunity for adult enthusiasts, who are now a main purchaser.
- New models of both railways and Scalextric have reflected licensing opportunities. One railway is based on the Hogwarts Express (from Harry Potter) and cars have been linked to cars from the James Bond movies. There are also deals with racing drivers such as Fernando Alonso, Lewis Hamilton and the McLaren Team.
- There has been product innovation, with engines that emit real steam and digital controls for Scalextric.
- Hornby has actively encouraged and supported Collectors' Societies.
- Distribution has been extended, with sets specifically for Marks and Spencer, for example. In addition sales across Europe have been targeted.
- To support this strategy Hornby has acquired rival (railway model) companies in Spain, Italy, France and Germany.
- In 2006 the company also bought another 'brand from the past' – Airfix, manufacturer of construction kits, mainly aircraft and warships. This business had started in Hull but, like Meccano, moved to French ownership. After this purchase,

one TV production company went into a school in South London to test whether the young teenagers (both boys and girls) could be persuaded to work on construction kits at the expense of playing computer games, and found that they could!

● In 2008 Corgi was added to the business portfolio. In recent years Corgi has focused on customized vehicles for the corporate gift market, a very lucrative niche.

Company profits – and its share price – have reflected a resurgent company and Hornby has been seen as a 'star performer'.

Questions

1 How would you define Hornby's business activities – is it, for example, a toy company or a model maker?

2 How will this affect its key success factors and the competencies and capabilities it needs?

3 Do you agree that the move to China probably saved the business?

© MALCOLM FAIRMAN / ALAMY

3.3 Human resource strategies

The 'people contribution'

Successful organizations meet the needs and expectations of their customers more effectively than their competitors; at the same time, they generate acceptable financial returns. Achieving these outcomes requires competent and committed people. People, then, are critically important strategic resources. Successful companies will be able to attract, motivate, develop, reward and keep skilled and competent managers and other employees. They will be able to create and implement strategic changes in a supportive culture. People need to be used and stretched to get the best out of them but, correspondingly, they need to be looked after and rewarded. However, even successful companies have lean periods, and when these occur, they will again be able to retain their most important people. There is no one best way of achieving this.

Everything that an organization does, in the end, depends on people. Although technology and IT can make a major strategic impact, it is people who exploit their potential. Managers and employees are needed to implement strategies and to this end they must understand and share the values of the organization. They must be committed to the organization and they must work together well. At the same time, where an organization is decentralized and operating in a turbulent environment, the strategic leader will rely on people to spot opportunities and threats, to adapt and create new strategies.

Consequently, it is people who ultimately determine whether or not competitive advantage is created and sustained. Adding new values with innovation, they can be an opportunity and a source of competitive advantage; equally, unenthusiastic, uncommitted, untrained employees can act as a constraint. People's capabilities are infinite and resourceful in the appropriate organizational climate. The basic test of their value concerns how much they – and their contribution – would be missed if they left or, possibly worse, left and joined a competitor. They could take customers with them and not be easily replaced.

Achieving the highest level of outcomes that people are capable of producing will therefore depend upon the human resource practices adopted by the organization. While the issues are clear and straightforward – they involve selection, training, rewards and work organization – there is no single best approach to the challenge. A relatively formal, 'hard' approach can prove very successful in certain circumstances; other organizations will derive significant benefits from a 'softer', more empowered style. One issue here is whether the business is being driven by a small number of identifiable, key decision-makers or by the employees collectively.

Case 3.4 tells the remarkable story of Ricardo Semler, who took over the family engineering business in Brazil and transformed its fortunes by releasing the abilities and energies of its people. It is worth considering whether either of the market-driven (the E in E–V–R congruence) and resource-based (R) views of strategy truly explain what has happened as Semco. Arguably the real driving force behind the changes has been values. Semler, in effect, deregulated Semco, allowing people the freedom to choose how they would work. Certain policies regarding competitiveness guided appropriate behaviour.

To bring out the best in people, they have to be managed well, and this requires leadership. A useful metaphor is that of an orchestra. Every member (manager/employee) is a specialist, with some making a unique contribution which, on occasions, can take the form of a solo performance. Nevertheless, all the contributions must be synthesized to create harmony (synergy), which is the role of the conductor (strategic leader). A single musician (weak link) can destroy a performance; a chain is only as strong as its weakest link.

A successful organization, therefore, needs people with appropriate skills and competencies who can work together effectively. People must be:

- committed (commitment can be improved)
- competent (competencies can be developed, and can bring improved product quality and productivity)
- cost-effective (ideally costs should be low and performance high, although this does not imply low rewards for success)
- in sympathy with the aims of the organization (are the values and expectations of all parties in agreement?)

Where people grow, profits grow.

DR ALEX KRAUER, WHEN CHAIRMAN AND MANAGING DIRECTOR, CIBA-GEIGY

Case 3.4

Ricardo Semler and Semco　　　　　　　　SA

Ricardo Semler was just 21 years old when he took over as chief executive of his family's business, Semco. This Brazilian company manufactured pumps, food mixers, meat-slicing equipment and dishwashers. Brazil is a country characterized by high inflation and a massive relative wealth gap between the rich and the poor. His father believed that if he handed over the reins when Ricardo was still young, 'he could make his mistakes while he was still around to fix them!' His father had run the business along traditional and autocratic lines; Ricardo was to change everything, and the company has thrived and prospered.

Although he has an MBA from Harvard, Ricardo Semler's stated business philosophy is: 'follow your intuition'. He inherited a company where 'people did

not want to come to work and managers watched everything and everybody constantly, trusting nobody', and transformed it into one which is 'ultimately democratic' and based on 'freedom, respect, trust and commitment'. Things did not happen instantaneously; many new approaches and experimental methods were tried and abandoned. However, in a ten-year period from the mid-1980s Semco achieved 900 per cent growth.

There is no reception area, no secretaries and no offices. Managers walk around constantly to provide help and assistance when it is requested; the workers organize their own flexible working time arrangements. Employees work in small clusters, and they can also rearrange their working space and environment as they wish. Semco has come to believe that clusters of no more than ten are required if this approach is to work effectively. Twelve layers of a management and supervisory hierarchy have been reduced to three. The appointment of any manager has to be approved by the workforce, and managers are subjected to regular assessment by their subordinates and shopfloor employees. People talk openly and 'when someone says they'll do something, they do it'. Consequently, managers also feel that they can spend time away from the plant, with customers and suppliers.

Profit sharing is by consultation and negotiation – 23 per cent of after-tax profits is available for the workforce – and all employees are trained to ensure that they can read the company accounts. There is no longer a formal chief executive post for Ricardo, who is now President. Instead, there is an informal board of six associates (the most senior managers) who elect a nominal chief executive for a six-month period. Ricardo sometimes attends their meetings as an adviser.

Ricardo has recently taken his ideas further, encouraging employees to consider starting up satellite supply companies and subcontracting for Semco. Those who have opted for this entrepreneurial route have been allowed to take Semco machines with them, leasing them on favourable terms. One advantage for Semco is the fact that it is no longer responsible for the maintenance and safety of the equipment. In addition, there is an opportunity for the machinery to be used more effectively as the satellite companies are free to work for other organizations; their efficiency gains can be passed through in the form of lower prices. If the venture fails, Semco takes back the equipment

and the people. It is a relatively low and managed risk for all concerned.

Ricardo Semler has not been a man who has hidden his achievements! He has written the story of his role at Semco with the title *Maverick*. Like Julian Richer of Richer Sounds in the UK, he helps other companies as a consultant and he has become a recognized member of the management guru circuit around the world. He has also campaigned against corruption in Brazil, and he has exposed government officials who have been demanding bribes for domestic planning permission. As a result, he has generated hostility from certain prominent people in his country.

'Successful companies will be the ones that put quality of life first. Do this and the rest – quality of product, productivity of workers, profits for all – will follow.'

Questions

1 Is Ricardo Semler really a 'maverick'?
2 Have these changes been sustainable?
3 Has Semco become even more 'maverick' or has it mellowed?

Sources

Semler, R (1993) *Maverick*, Century
Semler, R (2003) *The Seven Day Weekend*, Century

Also see: http://www.thunderbird.edu/pdf/about_us/case_series/a15980024.pdf

SOURCE: THIS CASE STUDY WAS PREPARED USING PRIMARILY PUBLICLY AVAILABLE SOURCES OF INFORMATION FOR THE PURPOSES OF CLASSROOM DISCUSSION; IT DOES NOT INTEND TO ILLUSTRATE EITHER EFFECTIVE OR INEFFECTIVE HANDLING OF A MANAGERIAL SITUATION.

Involving and empowering people

There are two recognized approaches to human resource management: the 'hard' approach and the 'soft' approach. The key tension or dilemma that is being addressed is the balance between centralization for control and decentralization for greater empowerment. The two approaches imply contrasting styles, but they can both be appropriate in certain circumstances. Moreover, companies can be hard on certain aspects and soft on others. In addition, the style may alter with the strategic demands placed on an organization. When times are difficult and a company must rationalize and downsize, a hard approach may prove to be appropriate for driving through the changes quickly. However, a softer, more empowered style may be required to rejuvenate the company and bring new sources of competitive advantage.

Hard human resource management assumes that:

- people are viewed as a resource and, like all resources, companies gain competitive advantage by using them efficiently and effectively
- the deployment and development of employees – who are essentially there to implement corporate and competitive strategies – is delegated to line managers who are responsible for groups of people
- scientific management principles and systems can be useful but should be used cautiously.

Soft human resource management assumes that:

- workers are most productive if they are committed to the company, informed about its mission, strategies and current levels of success, and
- involved in teams which collectively decide how things are to be done
- employees have to be trusted to take the right decisions rather than controlled at every stage by managers above them.

Soft human resource management argues that people are different from other resources (and often more costly) but they can create added value and **sustainable competitive advantage** from the other resources. Therefore, soft human resource management places greater emphasis on control through review and evaluation of outcomes, such that employees are led rather than managed.

Empowerment means freeing employees from instructions and controls and allowing them to take decisions themselves. Total quality management implies constant improvement; to achieve this employees should be contributing to the best of their ability. Proponents argue that rules stifle innovation and that future success relies not on past results but on the continuing ability to manage change pressures. Managers must be free to make appropriate changes in a decentralized structure.

There are three main objectives of empowerment:

- to make organizations more responsive to external pressures
- to 'de-layer' organizations in order to make them more cost effective. British Airways, for example, now has five layers of management between the chief executive and the front line who interface with customers. It used to be nine. Managers become responsible for more employees, who they are expected to coach and support rather than direct
- to create employee networks featuring teamworking, collaboration and horizontal communications. This implies changes in the ways in which decisions are made.

The important questions are why, how and when. The leading retailers, for example, benefited from increasing centralization throughout the 1980s. Information technology enabled cost savings and efficiencies from centrally controlled buying, store and shelf layouts, stocking policies and reordering. In the 1990s there was little support for changing this in any marked way and delegating these decisions to store level. In its early years, Waterstone's delegated book-buying responsibility to individual store managers, and this was regarded as exceptional. Once the company was acquired by WH Smith this decentralization was systematically removed. At the same time individual stores are judged in part on the quality of service provided to their customers; and it is in this area that there has always been considerable scope for empowering managers. However, in 2000, in an attempt to win back market share, Marks and Spencer begun with decentralized purchasing and stock decisions to give store managers more opportunity to ensure that they stock ranges which best match local needs.

As empowerment is increased it is important that employees are adequately informed and knowledgeable, that they are motivated to exercise power, and that they are rewarded for successful outcomes. In flatter organization structures there are fewer opportunities for promotion.

There are, then, three basic empowerment options:

- Employees can be encouraged to contribute ideas. As seen in Case 1.7, several new product ideas for McDonald's have come from individual franchisees. In reality, however, this may represent only token empowerment.
- Employees work in teams which share and manage their own work, but within clearly defined policies and limits. This should increase both efficiency and job satisfaction.

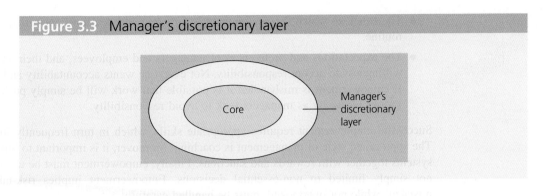

Figure 3.3 Manager's discretionary layer

Figure 3.4 Inverted pyramid structure

- More extensive decentralization means that individuals are much freer to change certain parameters and strategies. Evaluating outcomes is seen as the important control mechanism rather than rules and guidelines. An important distinction here is between making people accountable for their individual actions and making them accountable for the overall result. Constructive accountability gives people freedom to make decisions and demands so that they accept responsibility for the consequences. This requires strong leadership, a clear mission and effective communications, rewards and sanctions. Information must flow openly upwards and sideways as well as downwards. In many organizations there is a tendency for bad news to be selectively hidden, with perhaps two-thirds not flowing up to the next layer. Many potential threats are thereby not shared within the company. This would be unacceptable in an empowered organization.

For many organizations empowerment implies that the core organization strategies are decided centrally, with individual managers delegated a discretionary layer around the core (as shown below).

It is crucial first to find the right balance between the core and discretionary elements, and second to ensure that managers support and own the core strategy.

The deciding factors are:

- The competitive strategies and the relative importance of close linkages with customers in order to differentiate and provide high levels of service. When this becomes essential empowerment may imply an inverted pyramid structure. The structure exists to support front-line managers, as shown below.

- Successful empowerment means putting the 'right' people in place and ensuring that they are able to do their job, which they understand and own. In this way they feel important.

- The extent to which the environment is turbulent and decisions are varied rather than routine.

- The expectations and preferences of managers and employees, and their ability and willingness to accept responsibility. Not everyone wants accountability and high visibility. If empowerment is mishandled it is possible that work will be simply pushed down a shorter hierarchy as managers seek to avoid responsibility.

Successful empowerment requires appropriate skills, which in turn frequently implies training. The appropriate style of management is coaching. Moreover, it is important to link in monitoring systems together with rewards and sanctions. Finally, empowerment must be taken seriously and not simply limited to non-essential decisions. Empowerment implies risk-taking, and any mistakes, while not overlooked, must be handled carefully.

Finally, resources must be made available to support those who will embrace empowerment.

Empowerment is a powerful motivator as long as it does not suddenly stop when the really important and interesting decisions have to be taken.

JEREMY SOPER, EX RETAIL SALES DIRECTOR, WH SMITH

Turner (1999) argues that Wal-Mart's strategies for empowering people include:

- Every project has to have a clear end-date.

- Everybody must experience success. Success can be built on success and people must never become complacent. People are therefore moved from clearly successful to less successful activities, so they can experience elements of both success and relative failure. In this way, 'winners' help others improve their standards and confidence; and people who are experiencing disappointment are moved into positions where morale is much higher. Linked to this:

- There is a no-blame culture and no victims.

- By moving around, people also become more multi-skilled and thereby grow personally.

- People are encouraged to become involved in several, small, improvemental projects – many of them driven by ideas from customers.

- New ideas are tried out locally before being rolled-out more extensively.

- People are required to 'think, react and break down barriers'.

- There is a philosophy that: *Track record + Empathy = Credibility*. Empathy develops as people 'get out', network and meet people so they can better understand their needs. It is credibility that 'gets things done'.

- To get ahead and stay ahead, speed is 'everything'.

Manager competency

Simply, some companies will seek to develop their employees and managers, invariably promoting from within. A strong culture and vision should foster both commitment and continuous, emergent change. Necessary new competencies are *learned*. In such organizations, teamworking and networking are likely to be prominent. Other organizations prefer to search for the best people who might be available; they willingly recruit outsiders. They are seeking to *buy in* the new competencies that they require. People may feel less committed to such organizations in the long term, and consequently there will be a greater reliance on individualism and individual contributions.

The challenge for companies growing from within is that they need to become and stay very aware strategically if they are to remain ahead of their rivals; they will actively benchmark and look for new ideas that might be helpful. Companies securing new skills and competencies from outside face a different dilemma. If the competencies are available, and can be bought by any competitor, how can they ensure that they find the best ideas and people, and how can they generate some unique competency and competitive advantage?

Some companies will look to do both, finding, in the process, an appropriate balance. An analogy would be a leading football club which buys expensive, talented players in the transfer market while, at the same time, nurturing young players. There are many instances where highly skilled, experienced players do not fit in at a new club, certainly not at first; and when several arrive at once, it can be very disruptive until they are moulded into an effective team. Often this complex moulding process is signaled through frequent changes of manager or chief executive until the person with the right skills is found.

Capelli and Crocker-Hefter (1995) further distinguish between companies that seek to compete by moving quickly, perhaps by necessity, responding speedily to new opportunities, and those that have developed a more sustainable advantage in a long-standing market. They conclude that organizations competing on flexibility will typically find it more appropriate to recruit from outside. A reliance on developing new competencies internally may mean that they are too slow to gain early advantage from new opportunities. By contrast, organizations competing in established markets with long-standing relationships are more likely to rely on internally developed, organization-specific skills and strong internal and external architecture.

There are, inevitably, implications. In general, industries and markets are becoming more dynamic and turbulent, demanding that companies develop new product and market niche opportunities. This appears to imply an increasing reliance on recruiting strong, competent people from outside. In turn, this means that internal relationships and the culture may be under constant pressure to change. Companies are recruiting and rewarding individual experts; at the same time, synergistic opportunities demand strong internal architecture and co-operation. This is another organizational dilemma. Companies that succeed in establishing a strong, cohesive and motivating culture while developing new competencies flexibly and quickly are likely to be the future high performers.

Reinforcing points from earlier chapters, this demands effective strategic leadership and a shared, understood vision for the organization. The extent to which an organization can become a 'learning organization', discussed later in this chapter, is of great significance.

Figure 3.5 repackages the notion of manager competency in the form of five distinct mindsets. Managers, in different degrees, will and must possess all of these abilities. The issues concern the balance and the opportunity. Some managers will be extremely competent in certain areas, but their profile, approach and style may not be appropriate for the demands placed on them. In addition, and given the way in which managers work with constant interruptions, and performing a series of short, pragmatic tasks, it can be difficult for them to find time to think, reflect and challenge. Short-termism and 'more-of-the-same' can all too readily be the result.

Many books have been written, and continue to be written, describing the behaviour patterns and practices of successful organizations. While there is inevitably some element of idiosyncrasy and uniqueness, this approach is interesting and valuable. It can be a rich source of ideas. However, it is not the same as identifying those competencies which have been shown empirically to be associated with the creation of superior performance.

A real manager has to be a good leader in the sense that he has to embody an open-minded attitude of leadership in himself, in his fellow managers and even in the heads of each employee of his organization. Leadership, therefore, means to enable and help people to act as individual entrepreneurs within the frame of a commonly born vision of the business. A bad manager, on the other hand, is more an administrator who follows severe rules and customs within a stiff bureaucratic hierarchy.

DR HUGO M SEKYRA, CEO AND CHAIRMAN, AUSTRIAN INDUSTRIES

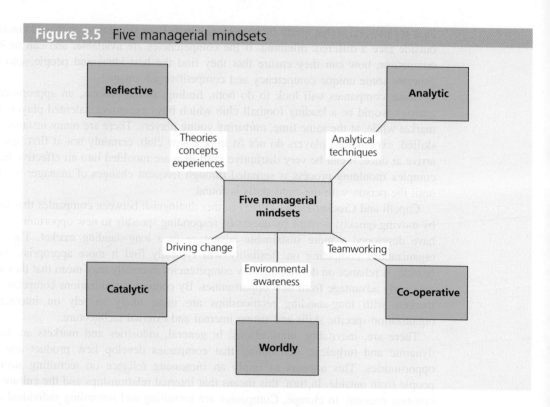

Figure 3.5 Five managerial mindsets

It is because these questions are complex that some organizations will adopt and build human resource practices that help to create and sustain competitive advantage. They are peculiar to that organization's environmental matching challenge. Such organizations enjoy strong E–V–R (environment–values–resources) congruence. The competitive value of their competencies lies in the fact that while the general approach may be transferable, the specifics are not.

3.4 Managing human resources

We need the right people if we are to foster effective emergent strategy. Appropriate people with the required and desired competencies, and/or the potential for growth and development, need to be recruited. They require clear objectives to give them both direction and performance yardsticks, backed by training and development opportunities. Outcomes should be measured, and performance reviewed and rewarded as appropriate. Underperformance or failure should be sanctioned in some way. This section looks briefly at a number of these issues, and also considers the importance of motivating employees, team building and succession planning.

Managers' objectives

Hersey and Blanchard (1982) contend that organizational success and performance are affected by the congruence between the objectives of managers and those of their subordinates. They argue that the organization can only accomplish its objectives if those of managers and subordinates are supportive of each other and of the organization. Moreover, McGregor (1960) has argued that people need objectives to direct their efforts, and that if objectives are not provided by the organization they will create their own. This may not necessarily be disadvantageous for the organization, as Schein (1983) has suggested that managers are generally orientated towards economic goals and see profit as being important. However, personal objectives are likely to be allowed more freedom if managers are not given clear objectives. Porter *et al.* (1975) contend that individual behaviour is affected by people's perceptions of what is expected of them; and hence it could be argued that objectives pursued by managers will be dependent on:

- personal motives
- their understanding and perception of what the strategic leader and their colleagues expect them to contribute (expectations, although still subject to some interpretation, may or may not be made clear to managers)
- the culture of the organization.

In this regard you can see the basis of investment traders and their managers taking on high levels of risk in order to generate the profit expected of them by the organization especially when the organization has previously rewarded them for ever more risky financial arrangements so as to generate revenue and profits. So when it goes wrong it causes financial meltdown through the wrong form of enlightened self-interest.

Various systems and policies for setting and agreeing managers' objectives are available, but they are outside the scope of this book. Ideally, the resultant objectives will be 'SMART': specific, measurable, achievable, realistic and with a timescale.

While objective setting is important for dealing with tasks and priorities, it should never be forgotten that managing people effectively also involves communicating and interacting, and making sure there is always time and opportunity available for dealing with unexpected events.

Rewards

Rewards are an important motivator, but it is important to appreciate that an individual may feel rewarded by things other than money or promotion (see Figure 3.6). However it is important to

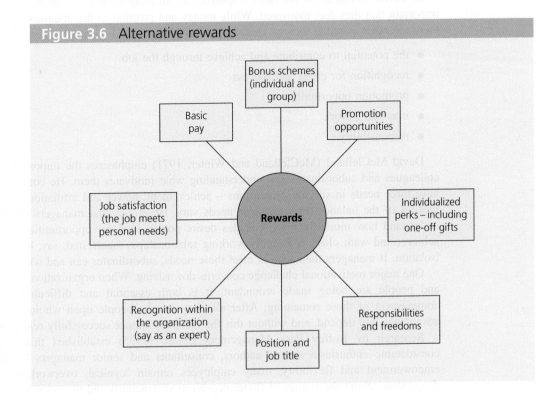

Figure 3.6 Alternative rewards

remember that some rewards can be controversial. At the beginning of 2009, for example, there was outrage in many quarters that bankers were being paid bonuses for what can be best described as 'failure' linked to the (largely self-inflicted) problems faced by the banks. The demands and responsibilities of a job, and the freedom that people are given to decide how to do things, can be rewarding. In addition, working with a particular group of people, especially if they are seen to be successful, can be rewarding. If people feel that their efforts are being rewarded and that future efforts will also be rewarded, their quality of work is likely to improve. In this way, total quality can be improved. Moreover, where **incremental strategic change** is dependent on individual managers seeing, and acting upon, opportunities and threats, the reward system must be appropriate and motivating.

A number of organizations, including BP, WH Smith and Federal Express, have at times experimented with formalized upward feedback as well as manager/subordinate appraisal. Although difficult to implement successfully, as these companies have all found, such systems can be very useful for increasing managers' awareness concerning their style and effectiveness. It is crucial that any performance evaluation systems which influence or determine rewards are open and fair, and perceived as such.

Rewards depend upon the success of the organization as a whole as well as individual contributions to that success. Hence, individual motivation and the issues involved in building successful management teams are looked at next.

Involving and motivating people

If people are to be committed to the organization, and to the achievement of key objectives, they must be involved. Employees at the so-called grass-roots level are likely to know the details of the business and what really happens better than their superiors and managers. If they are involved and encouraged to contribute their ideas for improvements, the result can be innovation or quality improvement.

Moreover, if managers and other employees are to make effective strategic contributions it is important that they feel motivated. While money and position in the organization can motivate, there are other essential factors. Hertzberg (1968) emphasized the importance of the following:

- the potential to contribute and achieve through the job
- recognition for effort and success
- promotion opportunities
- interesting work
- responsibility.

David McClelland (McClelland and Winter, 1971) emphasizes the importance of knowing colleagues and subordinates and understanding what motivates them. He contends that people have three needs in varying proportions – achievement, power and affiliation – and individual profiles of the balance between these needs vary. He argues that managers should attempt to understand how much their subordinates desire power, look for opportunities where they can achieve, and want close or friendly working relationships, manifested, say, by not working in isolation. If managers then seek to meet these needs, subordinates can and will be motivated.

One major motivational challenge concerns downsizing. When organizations are cutting back, and people are being made redundant, it is both essential and difficult to maintain the commitment of those remaining. After all, they are the people upon whom new competitive advantages will depend, and without this the company cannot successfully rejuvenate.

Research by Roffey Park Management Centre (1995) established that while there is considerable enthusiasm among authors, consultants and senior managers for teamworking, empowerment and flexibility, many employees remain 'cynical, overworked, insecure and despondent' about the impact of flatter organization structures and the consequent reduction in promotion prospects. Employees frequently perceive **delayering** to be a cost-cutting exercise which actually reduces morale. When such rationalization is essential, and often it is, the real challenge comes afterwards, in encouraging the remaining managers to look for innovative new ways of adding value and to take risks, albeit limited and measured risks. This reinforces the critical importance of finding the most appropriate reward systems, together with mechanisms for involving, managing and leading people to achieve superior levels of performance.

Succession issues

Succession problems can concern both strategic leadership and managerial positions throughout the organization. Small firms whose growth and success have been dependent upon one person, most probably the founder, often experience problems when he or she retires, especially where there has been a failure to develop a successor in readiness. Some very large organizations also experience problems when particularly charismatic and influential strategic leaders resign or retire. Although they may be replaced by other strong leaders there may be changes to either or both the strategy or culture which do not prove successful.

However, succession problems can be seen with key people in any specialism and at any level of the organization. Firms need management in depth in order to cope with growth and with people leaving or being promoted. This implies that people are being developed constantly in line with, and in readiness for, strategic change; and this relates back to appraisal and reward systems. Many global companies deliberately move managers between countries and product groups as part of their management planning. This, they claim, opens the company up to 'different ideas and outside perceptions'.

Team building

Both formal and informal teams exist within organizations. Formal teams comprise sections or departments of people who work directly together on a continuous basis and in pursuit of particular specified objectives, and teams of senior managers who meet on a regular basis with an agreed agenda. Informal teams can relate to managers from different departments, or even divisions, who agree informally to meet to discuss and deal with a particular issue, or who are charged with forming a temporary group to handle an organization-wide problem. In both cases relationships determine effectiveness. Ideally, all members will contribute and support each other, and synergy will result from their interactions. Simply putting a group of people together in a meeting, however, does not ensure that they will necessarily work well together and form an effective and successful team.

A successful team needs:

- shared and agreed objectives
- a working language, or effective communications
- the ability to manage both the tasks and the relationships.

Cummings (1981) contends that individual contributions to the overall team effort are determined by personal growth needs (for achievement and personal development) and social needs – perceived benefits from working with others to complete tasks, rather than working alone.

Within any team, therefore, there will be a variety of skills, abilities and commitments. Some people will be natural hard workers who need little supervision or external motivation; others, who may be diligent and committed, may need all aspects of their task spelt out clearly; the major contribution of particular members might be in terms of their creativity and ideas. Meredith Belbin (1981) argues that a good team of people will have compensating strengths and weaknesses, and that as a group they will be able to perform a series of necessary and related tasks. Belbin has identified a number of characteristics or contributions that individuals make to teams. They relate to the provision of ideas, leadership, the resolution of conflict, the gathering and analysing of data and information, carrying out certain detailed work which might be regarded as boring by certain members, organizing people to make their most useful contributions, and developing relationships within the group. Individuals will contribute in a number of areas, not just one or two, but they will often be particularly strong in some and weak in others. A balance is required if the team is to work well together and complete the task satisfactorily.

Whoever is responsible for leading the team – it might be the strategic leader and his or her team of senior managers, or department managers – should consider the various strengths and weaknesses of people and seek to develop them into an effective and cohesive team. If any essential areas of contribution are missing this should be dealt with, and any potential conflicts of strong personalities should be determined early.

The 'learning organization'

When we think of building strong, cohesive and integrated teams, we generally, and quite rightly, think of small groups of employees. However, the same themes can be extended to the scale of the whole organization. Where all the parts can be integrated effectively, share with each other and learn from each other we have what Senge (1991) has called a 'learning organization'. Simply, as shown in Figure 3.7, the whole organization is able to think strategically and create synergy by sharing its knowledge and ideas and generating actions which contribute to the interests of the whole. The process is self-reinforcing as managers objectively review their progress.

The basic arguments concerning **learning organizations** are as follows:

- When quality, technology and product/service variety are all becoming widely available at relatively low cost, speed of change is essential for sustained competitive advantage.

- If an organization, therefore, fails to keep up with, or ahead of, the rate of change in its environment it will either be destroyed by stronger competitors, or lapse into sudden death or slow decline. The ideal is to be marginally ahead of competitors – opening up too wide a gap might unsettle customers.

- An organization can only adapt if it is first able to learn, and this learning must be cross-functional as well as specialist.

Hence a learning organization encourages continuous learning and knowledge generation at all levels, has processes which can move knowledge around the organization easily to where it

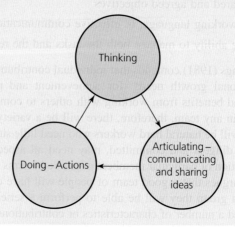

Figure 3.7 The learning organization – leadership and vision (based on the ideas of Charles Handy)

is needed, and can translate that knowledge quickly into changes in the way the organization acts, both internally and externally.

SENGE, 1991

Strategically important information, together with lessons and best practice, will thus be spread around; and ideally this learning will also be protected from competitors.

The essential requirements are

- Systemic thinking, such that decision-makers will be able to use the perspective of the whole organization; and there will be significant environmental awareness and internal co-operation. For many organizations the systemic perspective will be widened to incorporate collaboration and **strategic alliances** with other organizations in the added value chain.

- Management development and personal growth – to enable effective empowerment and leadership throughout the organization, and in turn allow managers to respond to perceived environmental changes and opportunities.

- A shared vision and clarity about both core competencies and key success factors. Changes should be consistent through strategic and operational levels.

- Appropriate values and corporate culture – to exploit core competencies fully and satisfy key success factors.

- A commitment to customer service, quality and continuous improvement.

- Kotter and Heskett (1992) argue that the appropriate culture is one which is capable of constant adaptation as the needs of customers, shareholders and employees change.

- Team learning within the organization through problem sharing and discussion.

Figure 3.8 Learning organizations

These points have been used to develop the following matrix (Figure 3.8) which draws together a number of issues discussed in this chapter and relates them to key issues of change management.

Case 3.5 looks at the attributes of a learning organization in the context of Team New Zealand, the sailors who took the America's Cup from the US. Clearly, the team was relatively small in size and it must be appreciated that creating a learning organization in a large company is no easy task. However, wherever it can be achieved to some creditable degree, there are likely to be substantial benefits.

Case 3.5

Team New Zealand   NZ

The America's Cup series of yacht races, between the current holder and a preselected challenger, lasts over several weeks and requires considerable preparation and dedication. When New Zealand won in 1995 it was only the second time a team from outside America had won in 144 years, the first being Australia in 1983. Moreover in the final races, New Zealand won 41 races and lost just one, an incredible margin of victory. The team had 'continually expanded its ability to create its destiny'. There had been a driving vision throughout the preparation and the race series: 'to build, modify and sail the fastest boat on any given day'. This vision had brought together the (technical) designers with the users, the sailors, and created synergy where often there is conflict. Their respective perspectives are, quite simply, different. Team New Zealand was successful in defending the trophy in 2000, but then events would take an unexpected turn.

There are seventeen sailors on board an America's Cup boat. The Skipper has overall responsibility and is the leader whilst the team are at sea. He relies on his Tactician (who keeps the boat on course) and Navigator (who looks after the sophisticated electronic tracking instrumentation). A Helmsman drives the boat and a Strategist monitors the slightest changes of wind speed and direction. Decisions to alter course or rigging are often made very quickly and they need implementing instantaneously. There are then 11 sailors with specific roles mainly related to the deployment of the huge sails. The seventeenth man is really something of a spectator and is often a team sponsor.

Several factors, all characteristic of a successful learning organization, have been put forward as important contributors to the success of Team New Zealand in 1995 and 2000:

There was an *inspirational leader* in the form of Sir Peter Blake, who was an experienced sailor, but not the skipper of the actual crew. Nor was he an experienced boat designer. Blake convinced everyone that winning was possible, and he then made sure that happened. The skipper was Russell Coutts. Blake had built his reputation as a round-the-world challenge sailor and he has been described as a 'meticulous planner and gifted leader who inspired loyalty'. Coutts, 33 years old in 1995, was an Olympic gold medallist for sailing (in 1984) and a previous winner of many leading races. He was 'obsessive about detail and technically very skilled'. Blake and Coutts became a formidable partnership who provided leadership on-shore and at sea.

There was a *strong sense of community* in the team. Blake was visible in driving this, leading from the front. He ensured that the designers were not allowed to drive the agenda without challenge from the sailors.

Open communications were sponsored, in the form of free-flowing ideas. No hidden or undeclared agendas were permitted. Resources had to be shared. Blake held meetings between the designers and sailors at regular intervals during the build-up period and ran them without ceremony or hierarchy. He encouraged people to be creative in their search for different and unusual answers to problems and issues. It was noted that the secretary at one meeting felt comfortable contributing an idea that turned out to be really valuable.

There was a *sustained record of improvement* in product design and racing skills right through to the end of the race series. Team New Zealand did not stop searching for improvements even when they were winning every race! They built on their successes to reinforce their advantage. There was a willingness by the sailors to accept design modifications if they made the boat go more quickly, even where it made their task of sailing it more difficult or uncomfortable. During the pre-race trials Team New Zealand sailed two identical boats, rather than two different designs in competition. Their choice of design had been made by simulation. Because the two boats began as identical, any successful modifications to the design of one could be copied by the team sailing the other. As a result, considerable emphasis was placed on improving sailing skills as well.

There was clear evidence of a very *strong commitment* by the individual team members, who were convinced that winning the America's Cup mattered immensely to the whole country, which was drawn behind the team in a positive and supportive way.

The *team* was *carefully selected* to ensure that they were people who would 'own' what they were taking on. They needed to have individual sailing skills and experience, but they had to be able to interact well with others. They also had to demonstrate they were able to handle disappointment and quickly put it behind them. Outstanding individuals who might be reluctant team players, however good they were personally, were rejected by Blake, who built his team around the tasks. (Interestingly, and in contrast, it sometimes appears that certain footballers are selected for the England football team because of their individual skills, and then asked to play out of position. Right-footed players play on the left of the field, for example, and then do not play to their potential.)

Could this successful combination defend the America's Cup for a second time in 2003 and make it three in a row? After the victory in 2000 both Russell Coutts and Tactician Brad Butterworth 'defected' to Alinghi, a team bankrolled by Swiss billionaire and yachting fanatic Ernesto Bertarelli, who would sail as the Navigator. The final Alinghi team for 2003 would include 7 New Zealanders and just 2 Swiss sailors. Its successful challenge was devastating for New Zealanders as really it was the core of the previous winning teams that won the America's Cup for a third time in a row – but this time not for New Zealand. Blake, unfortunately,

was unable to contribute to either team. In December 2001 he was shot on board his boat by people described as pirates whilst sailing up the Brazilian Amazon.

Alinghi would go on to defend the Cup successfully in Europe.

At the same time as this story New Zealand's film industry benefitted from the success of the *Lord of the Rings* trilogy. In addition the New Zealand marine industry has grown dramatically on the back of these successes. In value terms it is now on a par with wool and twice as significant as wine.

Questions

1   Do you agree that Team New Zealand was a learning organization?
2   How important do you think individuals are in building such a team?
3   How significant is it that their behaviour is transferable?

Source of basic material: Maani, K and Benton, C (1999) Rapid team learning – lessons from Team New Zealand's America's Cup campaign, *Organizational Dynamics*, Spring. Team New Zealand **http://www. teamnz.org**

© PJWORLDTOUR (PIERRE JEAN DURIEU) / DREAMSTIME

3.5   Information and information technology

The strategic value of information

People make decisions, but information is the fuel they use in decision-making; it can also be an important source of competitive advantage in certain circumstances. It must be stressed that IT, per se, is rarely a source of advantage, but information management can be. So, what exactly do we mean by 'information' and how might it be exploited?

Information has been defined as 'some tangible or intangible entity that reduces uncertainty about a state or event' (Lucas, 1976), which is a way of saying that information increases knowledge in a particular situation. When information is received, some degree of order can be imposed on a previously less well-ordered situation.

Information is needed for, and used in, decision-making. Information, information systems and information technology are all aids to decision-making. The more information managers and other employees have about what is happening in the organization, and in its environment, the more strategically aware they are likely to be. Information about other functional areas and business units can be particularly helpful in this respect.

Ackoff (1967), however, suggested that management information systems can easily be based on three erroneous assumptions:

- Managers are short of information. In many cases managers have too much irrelevant information.

- Managers know the information they require for a decision. However, when asked what information they might need, managers play safe and ask for everything which might be relevant, and thereby contribute to the overabundance of irrelevant information.

- If a manager is provided with the information required for a decision he or she will have no further problem in using it effectively. How information is used depends on perceptions of the issues involved. Moreover, if any additional quantitative analysis or interpretation is required, many managers are weak in these skills.

Nevertheless, decisions and decision-making do involve both facts and people. While the right information available at the right time can be extremely useful, the real value of information relates to how it is used by decision-makers, particularly for generating and evaluating alternative possible courses of action. In designing and introducing IT and management information systems into organizations it is necessary to consider the likely reaction of people as well as the potential benefits that can accrue from having more up to date and accurate information available. Information gathering should never become an end in itself, for the expertise and experience in people's heads can be more useful than facts on paper.

Moreover, it is important to evaluate who actually needs the information, rather than who might find it useful for increasing awareness, and to ensure that those people receive it. Although information technology and information systems can be expensive to introduce, those organizations that receive information, analyse and distribute it to the appropriate decision-makers more quickly than their competitors can achieve a competitive edge, particularly in a turbulent environment. Hence, the structure and culture of the organization should ensure that managers who need information receive it, and at the right time. However, while information can lead to more effective decision-making, it remains a manifestation of power within the organization, and this aspect needs monitoring. If information that could prove useful is withheld from decision-makers, negligently or deliberately by political managers pursuing personal objectives, the effectiveness of decision-making is reduced.

Information is used through a filter of experience and judgement in decision-making, and its relative value varies between one decision-maker and another. In certain instances the available information will be accurate, reliable and up to date. In other circumstances the information provided may already be biased because it is the result of the interpretation of a situation by someone who may have introduced subjectivity. Some managers, perhaps those who are less experienced, will rely more heavily on specific information than others, for whom experience, general awareness and insight into the situation are more important.

To complicate matters further, Day (1996) argues that organizations do not know what they know. In other words, they are awash with data that do not get translated into valuable information and hence real organizational knowledge. Linked to this, it is clear that quite frequently they also fail to realize the value of some of the information that some people in the organization possess. This can be taken even further. If organizations do not know what they know, it must follow they do not know what they do not know. They remain unaware of certain opportunities that others will seize and that they would have found valuable if they knew of their existence. Correspondingly, they do not find out about certain threats until it is too late to act.

The strategic information challenge

Why do some organizations, which are currently enjoying success and high profits, fail to realize when products, services or strategies are about to lose customer support? Why do they fail to anticipate competitor initiatives? Why are others able to be more proactive?

Being close to customers, and in touch with new developments in a dynamic and possibly chaotic marketplace, requires information, intelligence and learning. Successful organizations monitor the activities of their customers, suppliers and competitors; they ask questions and test out new ideas. They express a willingness to learn and to change both their perspective on competition – their mindset concerning which factors determine competitive success – and the things they actually do. Sophisticated analyses and models of past and current results and behaviour patterns make an important contribution but, as Day (1996) argues, it is also necessary to think through how a market might respond to actions designed to retain existing customers and win new business, while outflanking and outperforming competitors. One of the reasons for Canon's continued success has been its ability to spot new market opportunities for its advanced technologies and exploit them early. Canon has managed to remain a force in digital cameras and accessories.

In order to become and remain strategically successful, organizations must create and sustain competitive advantage. They must continue to enjoy E–V–R congruence, frequently in a dynamic and turbulent environment. To achieve this, information must be gathered and shared, but this is not merely a question of designing a new information system.

Day (1996) contends that many organizations 'do not know what they know' either because data and signals are misinterpreted or because the flows are inadequate. Decision-makers do not receive the information that they need, or they fail to learn about things that might prove useful. Organizations that prioritize vertical channels and ignore horizontal flows are the ones most likely to fail to learn. The important elements for strategic success are:

- tracking events in the market and the environment, choosing responses (both proactively and reactively) and monitoring the outcomes of the actions which follow. Competitor initiatives must be dealt with; benchmarking best practices and general awareness can suggest new ideas
- making sure that important information from the questioning and learning from these emergent changes is disseminated effectively
- reflecting upon outcomes in the context of E–V–R congruence to ensure that the organization can sustain an effective match with its environment
- where appropriate, adapting policies and procedures to better guide future decisions.

The implication is a constant willingness to be flexible and to change as necessary. Companies must work from the twin perspectives of opportunity and threat. First, a willingness to learn and grow and, second, a realization that without appropriate and timely change a company is likely to face a crisis. Gilbert (1995) further argues that strategically successful organizations **leverage** their innovative competitive ideas with speed and act quickly.

They obtain market feedback continuously and rapidly and adapt to the feedback ahead of their rivals. They exploit the potential of strategic as well as competitive and operating information systems.

Three levels of information

- *Operating information systems* – Cost accounting systems, sales analyses and production schedules are essential for efficiency and control. Used creatively as, for example, is the case with airline reservation systems, they can create competitive advantage, but they are not designed to drive strategic change.

- *Competitive information systems* – Important elements of the various operating systems need to be integrated and synthesized to ensure that the organization is using its resources both efficiently and effectively. Specifically, it is meeting the needs and expectations of important external stakeholders. Competitive information systems, therefore, relate to competitive advantage and E–V–R congruence. They require managers to think and work across functional boundaries and consider the total service package provided to customers, encapsulating all the ways in which an organization can add value in a co-ordinated way. However, Gilbert (1995) argues that managers will not always be aware of the information they have used in arriving at a competitively successful formula. Where organizations do not fully understand why they are successful, that success may be fragile.

- *Strategic information systems* – While competitive information systems will typically focus on existing competition, organizations must also be able to learn about the business environment in order that they can anticipate change and design future strategies. Marchand (1995a) stresses that strategic information management should not be confined to the level of the strategic leader, but rather it should be dispersed throughout the whole organization. This implies an innovative culture and an organization structure which facilitates the sharing of information – one essential element of a learning organization. A learning organization requires considerable decentralization and empowerment, which must not be at the expense of control. Centralized systems are often required for sound control and effective co-ordination, thus presenting organizations with the dilemma of how to obtain the speed and flexibility benefits of decentralization without sacrificing control. It is important to stress that appreciating the significance of particular events, and assessing the potential significance of opportunities and threats which have been spotted often requires judgement, which will be discussed at greater length in Chapter 10.

Hence, as one moves up these three levels of decision-making, the contribution of IT and information systems to decision-making changes. Once operating systems are established, they can be used to make a number of decisions and drive the operations. By measuring performance, the systems can again make a valuable contribution and highlight when things are going wrong. For strategic decisions, however, IT is primarily an aid to decision-making. Systems cannot realistically make the decisions, and consequently interpretation and meaning systems are particularly important. For such decisions the systems should be designed to provide information in a form that is useful to decision-makers.

Information uses   Expanding this point, Marchand (1995b) distinguishes among four important and distinct uses for information at the operating, competitive and strategic decision-making levels.

- *Command and control* – The formal gathering of information to allow centralized control and decentralized accountability. Budgeting and resource allocations will typically be included. Command and control is valuable for managing resources efficiently but, used in isolation, it does not drive rapid change. Many organizations use tight financial targeting and monitoring as an essential driver of their competitiveness. Command and control invariably requires an organization to be broken down into sub-units, such as independent businesses, divisions or functional departments.

- *Improvement* – Here the emphasis is on integrating the functions to improve both efficiency and effectiveness through better all-round service. Processes that link the functions are often the focus of attention, and initiatives such as total quality management and business process improvement will be integral.

- *Opportunities for organizational synergy* – If complex multibusiness organizations can find new opportunities for internal synergy, sharing and interdependency, they can clearly benefit. Teamworking and special project teams are one way of doing this. This can be particularly important if the organization acquires another business which needs to be integrated.

- *Environmental opportunities* – Market intelligence, competitor monitoring and benchmarking best practice can generate new ideas and opportunities, as we have seen. This requires that managers are vigilant and enquiring. Critically, ideas spotted by one part of an organization, and of no discernible use to that business, might be valuable for another business or division, and consequently the ability to share – based on an understanding of needs and a willingness to trust and co-operate – is essential.

Figure 3.9 illustrates that an organization must be able to manage all four information needs simultaneously and harmoniously if it is to benefit from improved efficiencies and manage change both continuously and discontinuously. Herein lies the real strategic information challenge. The deployment of organizational resources, the corresponding style of management and the cultural implications vary between the four information needs and the decision-making processes that they support. Command and control management requires the organization to be separated into functions, businesses and/or divisions for clarity; the others demand different forms of integration, both formal and informal, to share both information and learning.

Figure 3.10 illustrates how organizations need first, to develop a perspective on how they can add value and create competitive advantage. Through monitoring, measurement, continuous improvement and innovation they should seek to become increasingly efficient and effective. This continual process represents **single-loop learning** and it is essential if competitive advantage is to be sustained in a dynamic environment. This requires sound operating and competitive information systems. However, over time, on its own, this will not be enough. Organizations must always be looking for new competitive paradigms, really new ways of adding different values, ahead of competitors – both existing rivals and potential new entrants – looking for an opportunity to break into the market. Effective strategic information systems, relying on informality, networking and learning, are required for this **double-loop learning**.

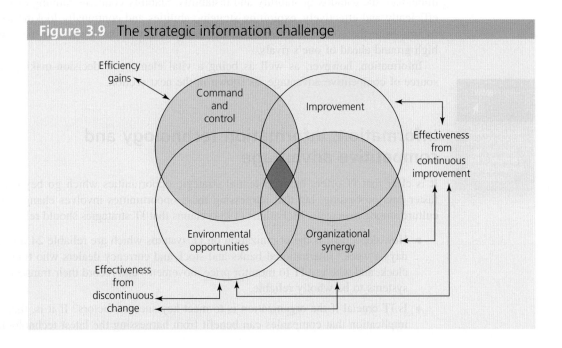

Figure 3.9 The strategic information challenge

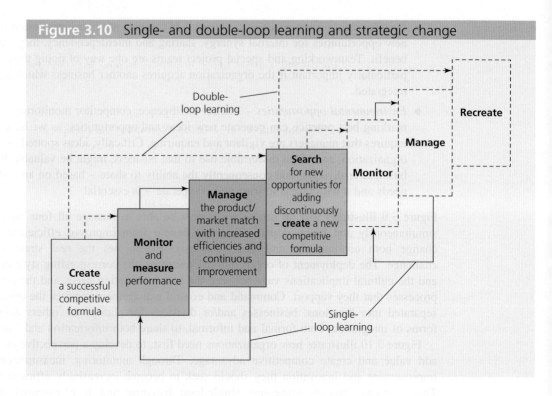

Figure 3.10   Single- and double-loop learning and strategic change

Fostering a culture of improvement and single-loop learning in an organization is more straightforward than the challenge of double-loop learning. Organizations that invest in strategic planning, research and development and new product/service programmes are locked into the process, but the real benefits cannot be gained if these activities and the requisite learning are confined to head office departments and specialist functions. They must permeate the whole organization and become embedded in the culture. This reflects a key organizational tension and dilemma – the paradox of stability and instability. Stability concerns running existing businesses efficiently and effectively, exploiting strategic abilities and continually looking to create higher returns from the committed resources. Instability refers to the search for the new competitive high ground ahead of one's rivals.

Information, however, as well as being a vital element in decision-making, can also be a source of competitive advantage, as shown in the next section.

See the online "British Airways" case for an example of this section's theory in practice

Information, information technology and competitive advantage

It is clear that IT offers many potential strategic opportunities which go beyond the notion of faster data processing, but that harnessing these opportunities involves changes in attitude and culture among managers. McFarlane (1984) claims that IT strategies should relate to two criteria:

● How dependent is the organization on IT systems which are reliable 24 hours a day, seven days a week? International banks and stock and currency dealers who trade around the clock, and who use IT to monitor price movements and record their transactions, need their systems to be wholly reliable.

● Is IT crucial if the organization is to meet key success factors? If it is, there is an implication that companies can benefit from harnessing the latest technological developments. An obvious example is the airline industry. Online Case 3.1 looks at IT in British Airways, but in fairness it reflects developments by all the leading airlines.

Rayport and Sviokla (1995) argue that competition is now based on two dimensions: the physical world of resources and a virtual world of information. Information clearly supports and enhances every activity in an organization, but it can itself be a source of added value and consequently competitive advantage as long as organizations are able to extract that value.

Michael Porter (1985) had earlier suggested that technological change, and in particular IT, is among the most prominent forces that can alter the rules of competition. This is because most activities in an organization create and use information. Porter and Millar (1985) contend that IT could affect competition in three ways:

- IT can change the structure of an industry, and in so doing alter the rules of competition
- IT can be used to create sustainable competitive advantage by providing companies with new competitive weapons
- as a result of IT new businesses can be developed from within a company's existing activities.

These three themes are examined in greater detail below.

Industry structure

As shown in Chapter 2, according to Porter (1980), the structure of an industry can be analysed in terms of five competitive forces: the threat of new entrants; the bargaining power of suppliers; the bargaining power of buyers; the threat of substitute products and services; and rivalry amongst existing competitors. Porter and Millar (1985) suggested that IT could influence the nature of these forces, and thereby change the attractiveness and profitability of an industry. This is particularly applicable where the industry has a high information content, such as airlines and financial and distribution services. Moreover, firms that were either slow or reluctant to introduce IT might well be driven out of the industry, because they would be unable to offer a competitive service. Where the cost of the necessary IT, both hardware and software systems, is high it can increase the barriers to entry for potential new firms.

Porter and Millar show that IT can both improve and reduce the attractiveness and profitability of an industry, and that as a consequence manufacturers should analyse the potential implications of change very carefully.

IT and the Internet – which is discussed below – have transformed such financial services as banking, enabling customers to carry out many of their financial transactions by telephone or personal computer without needing to queue for a cashier. However, there is the disadvantage that certain aspects of banking are being made more impersonal, and the personal service aspect is being reduced. Case 3.6 (Betfair) is an interesting example of a new business and business model that was made possible by the Internet.

The creation of competitive advantage

We will look in detail at cost management and difference as two critical themes in competition in Chapter 4, but in this section we link these important ideas to information technology.

Lower costs   If costs are reduced to a level below competitors' costs and this advantage is maintained, above-average profits and an increased market share can result. Porter and Millar (1985) suggest that while the impact of IT on lower costs has historically been confined to activities where repetitive information processing has been important, such restraints no longer

Case 3.6

Betfair   UK

Betfair has been described as the 'biggest British success story of the dotcom era'; it is the world's largest betting exchange. It is in effect 'eBay for gamblers'.

It was founded by Andrew Black in 2000. He had previously worked for the government and in the City but he was an expert in IT, especially databases, and he had a genuine passion for gambling. He understood horse racing – but Betfair also covers tennis, football and political elections – in fact, almost anything where people might want to place a bet on the outcome.

It is interesting that we often talk about entrepreneurs managing the risks in their business and not being gamblers. Black has worked out how to minimize his risk with his gambling customers. His business model is different but simple. He really resurrected how gambling was before bookmakers had come along – when people made bets with people they knew. With Betfair, punters place (and Betfair matches) bets against other punters, rather than with a bookmaker. Typically the odds will be some 20 per cent better than with high street bookmakers.

People can bet on individuals and a team losing as well as winning, and betting continues after competitions have started. This has raised some concerns about possible links with match fixing. In fact, champion jockey Kieren Fallon was one of a number charged with 'conspiring to defraud customers on Betfair'. The case was not proven.

Betfair easily processes 1 billion bets every year, with some 5 million a day from 80 countries being quite feasible. These countries do not include the US and Japan, where on-line gambling is illegal. There are no betting slips and no cash goes through the Betfair business per se. £1000 is bet every minute of the day. Betfair simply takes a commission of between 2 and 5 per cent; it is very lucrative. When he sold one quarter of Betfair to a Japanese technology company, in 2006, Black realized £355 million.

The business is run principally from offices in Hammersmith, London, but Black has cloned his operation and there is a replica business in Tasmania for Australasia.

Questions

1 Why do you think Betfair has been as successful as it has?
2 Will it be easy to defend its currently strong market position?

apply. IT can lead to lower labour costs by reducing the need for certain production and clerical staff. As a result, there should be both lower direct production costs and reduced overheads. IT applied to production systems can improve scheduling, thereby increasing the utilization of assets and reducing stocks, and in turn lowering production costs.

Enhancing differentiation Differentiation can be created in a number of ways, including quality, design features, availability and special services that offer added value to the end consumer. McFarlane *et al*. (1983) contend that IT offers scope for differentiation where:

- IT is a significant cost component in the provision of the product or service, as in banking, insurance and credit-card operations
- IT is able to affect substantially the lead time for developing, producing or delivering the product (CAD/CAM systems play an important role in this)
- IT allows products or services to be specially customized to appeal to customers individually
- IT enables a visibly higher level of service to customers, say through regular and accurate progress and delivery information, which might be charged for
- more and better product information can be provided to consumers.

Most insurance companies quote rates for insuring property and cars partially based on specified postcode districts. To achieve this they need accurate information on the risks involved in different areas and how these are changing. This in turn requires close liaison and information exchanges with brokers. The insurers, brokers and ultimately customers can all benefit as premiums more accurately reflect risks.

Supermarkets began to use hand-held computers several years ago, and these allowed staff to record the current stock levels each evening. Shelves could then be replenished overnight or the next day from regional warehouses. Sales representatives from, say, food manufacturers who sell extensively to small outlets were able to use similar hand-held computers for entering their orders. The computer could price the order immediately and a confirmation was then printed out. Further cost savings were possible where computer systems could be networked. As an example, Tesco has also sought to establish closer linkages with its suppliers. Orders for immediate delivery were transmitted electronically, although projections based on the latest sales analyses would have been provided some weeks earlier. If supplier delivery notes were sent ahead of the actual delivery these were then used to check the accuracy of the shipment and a confirmation was returned. This represents a promissory note to pay by an agreed date, and no further invoicing is required. These linkages made use of electronic data interchange systems to exchange information. More recently, using the Internet, **e-markets** have begun to appear. These developments clearly saved costs and allowed for lower prices, but they also streamlined the distribution network. Fast replenishment meant that customers should not find that stores have run out of an item; moreover, fresh produce could easily be replenished daily. Overall, the level of service was improved.

New competitive opportunities

IT has resulted in the creation of new businesses in three distinct ways.

- New businesses have been made technologically feasible. Telecommunications technology, for example, led to the development of facsimile services and organizations that provide fax services. In a similar way micro-electronics developments made personal computing possible.

- IT created demand for new products such as high-speed data communications networks that were unavailable before IT caused the demand.

- New businesses have been created within established ones. Several organizations have diversified into software provision stemming from the development of packages for their own use.

There are numerous examples of how competitive advantage has been derived specifically from IT. Debit cards, such as Barclay's Connect, have replaced cash and cheques for many customers; similar to credit cards in format, they allow money to be debited immediately from a bank account. Because computers can store and process information very quickly, they allow the banks and building societies to offer rates of interest which increase and decrease directly in line with the size of a customer's deposit.

The US company McKesson, which supplies over-the-counter pharmaceuticals to retail chemists, used its salesforce to record on a computer the counter and shelf layouts of their customers. This allowed McKesson to pack orders in such a way that customers could unpack them and display them quickly and sequentially.

Most newspapers now enjoy cost and differentiation benefits from computerized typesetting, whereby type is set directly by a journalist typing at a keyboard. The files can now be transmitted electronically via the Internet so the journalist need not be located in the newspaper building. In the case of UK national daily newspapers, and against some trade union resistance, computerized typesetting was pioneered by Eddie Shah, when he established the *Today* newspaper which, after changes of ownership has now been closed down. For the *Financial Times*, IT supports all the share prices, charts and other information included every day.

Most large hotel chains, including Sheraton and Marriott, operate clubs or programmes for their regular visitors. Participants receive such benefits as free upgrades and free meals as well as the programme points which they can exchange later for free stays or Air Miles. It is quite normal for travellers to prioritize a particular chain because of the perceived benefits of programme membership. These hotel chains typically cover much of the world, and often include independent hotels in franchise arrangements. Loyalty programmes would simply not be feasible without IT.

The US retailer Wal-Mart issues pagers to customers waiting for prescriptions so that they can continue shopping rather than either wait in line or come back speculatively to check whether their package is ready.

In summary, implementing IT for competitive advantage requires:

- an awareness of customer and consumer needs, changing needs, and how IT can improve the product's performance or create new services
- an awareness of operational opportunities to reduce costs and improve quality through IT
- an appreciation of how the organization could be more effective with improved information provision, and how any changes might be implemented. The impact upon people is very significant.

The argument is that competitive advantage can stem from any area of the organization.

3.6 The value chain

Supply-chain partnerships

In this section we develop the significance of internal and external architecture introduced earlier in the chapter and explain an important analytical framework. Developing his earlier work on industry structure (Porter 1980 – Chapter 2), where he highlights the significance of the relative power of buyers and suppliers, Porter (1985) argues that in the search for competitive advantage a firm must be considered as part of a wider system:

suppliers > firm > distributors > consumers.

As well as seeking improvements in its own activities, a firm should assess the opportunities and potential benefits from improving its links with other organizations. A firm is linked to the marketing and selling activities of its suppliers, and to the purchasing and materials handling activities of its distributors or customers. Prahalad and Krishnan (2008) go further, emphasizing the criticality of links between suppliers, manufacturers and customers. Instead of conceptualizing 'chains', they argue managers should seek to build 'constellations' of suppliers that can be reconfigured in different patterns to meet different needs. This can only work if people are flexible and IT is harnessed. Similarly, and reinforcing points from earlier in the chapter, Davenport and Harris (2007) argue that organizations have more information than ever before about their environment and their competitors, thanks to IT – but they must use it to become more effective strategic thinkers. They must understand what makes them different – and exploit it. 'Analytics', as they describe this information power, does not itself constitute a strategy, but using it does. 'The devil is in the detail' to generate greater insight. Davenport and Harris cite Wal-Mart as an organization that has exploited IT to better manage its supply network of over 17,000 suppliers in 80 countries. One example of detail is that Wal-Mart has analysed what products American consumers typically stock up on when a hurricane is forecast – and they make sure there are extra supplies available when an area is at risk. If you are wondering, the most popular item that people turn to is, apparently, Kellogg's strawberry Pop Tarts. UPS, FedEx and Amazon are other organizations that have harnessed IT to sharpen their supplier/customer networks.

The supply chain, then, is a process, and managing it is a key *strategic capability*. Cost savings and service differentiation can be achieved.

Organizations can create synergy, and enjoy the appropriate benefits, if they can successfully link their value chain with those of their suppliers and distributors. Just in time (JIT) deliveries integrate a supplier's outbound logistics with the organization's inbound logistics. Stock and costs can be reduced for the manufacturer, whose delivery lead time and reliability should also be improved. Set up properly, a JIT system can enable suppliers to plan their work more effectively and reduce their uncertainty. This requires an open exchange of reliable, up-to-date information and medium- to long-term supply arrangements. When Nissan was developing the supply chain for its UK manufacturing plant in Sunderland, it deliberately forged links with its suppliers' suppliers in its search to control costs without sacrificing quality and service. A retail bookseller, taking orders for non-stock items, needs to be sure of the delivery lead time from its publishers or wholesaler before quoting a date to the customer. This again demands accurate information, supported by reliable supply.

Carphone Warehouse, a leading retailer of mobile phones, has retailed telephones at prices ranging from 50p to over £300. Where the phone is sold as part of a package which involves a monthly line rental, the phone will typically have been provided free to the Carphone Warehouse by one of the major networks, such as BT, Orange or Vodafone, who in turn will have a supply arrangement with a manufacturer, perhaps Nokia or Motorola. The retailer will later receive a share of the future call revenues, normally between 3 per cent and 5 per cent. The ultimate value to Carphone Warehouse of the sale will average £300, regardless of the apparent selling price. In the case of phones used for prepaid calls without any monthly line rental, a typical sale will yield £200.

A new development here is the recent incentive of the giving of laptop computers for customers signing up to a specific mobile rental agreement. Many people now have a mobile that does not need to be replaced. The provision of laptop computers now offers companies the opportunity for new business streams.

Organizations looking to launch a new product need to ensure that their supply and distribution networks are properly in place; given this, all interested parties can benefit. Retailers will need to be convinced of a new product's viability and potential before they agree to stock it, normally at the expense of taking something else off their shelves. Manufacturers must be sure that stocks are available where customers expect to find them before they proceed with launch advertising.

The key lies in an integrated network, where all members of the supply chain see themselves as mutual beneficiaries from an effective total system; however, this does not always happen.

Preece *et al.* (1995) use the value chain to explain how Levi Strauss, producer of the internationally successful Levi's jeans, has created value and used its value-creating activities carefully to establish a distinctive corporate reputation, which is a form of competitive advantage. Key aspects include:

- established links with suppliers from around the world
- team manufacturing (underpinned by training and empowerment) and linked to high-technology equipment and sophisticated information support
- global advertising and branding
- alliances with retailers who concentrate on Levi's jeans and do not stock competitor products
- a programme of 'marketing revitalization' designed to reduce lead times and improve the availability of the products.

We look at other developments with Levi's in Case 3.8 at the end of this chapter.

Figure 3.11   The value chain

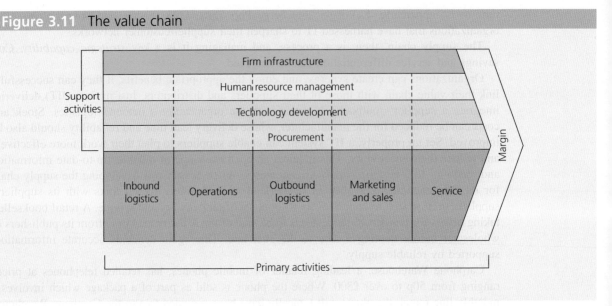

Strengthening the processes involved in managing the supply chain relates to the level of service that companies are able to offer their customers and to total quality management.

When ICI had an explosives division, which manufactured a range of explosive products, managers also developed expertise in detonating explosions. Quarry managers, who buy the products, really want stones and rocks on a quarry floor rather than the explosives. As a consequence ICI offered to produce a three-dimensional map of a quarry for their customers, indicating where the charges need to be placed, and then, when suitable holes have been drilled in the quarry face (by the quarry owners), carry out controlled explosions. In this way they add value for their customers and link the two value chains.

The organization's value chain

While strategic success depends upon the way in which the organization as a whole behaves, and the ways in which managers and functions are integrated, competitive advantage stems from the individual and discrete activities that a firm performs. A cost advantage can arise from low-cost distribution, efficient production or an excellent salesforce that succeeds in winning the most appropriate orders. Differentiation can be the result of having an excellent design team or being able to source high-quality materials or high-quality production. Value-chain analysis is a systematic way of studying the direct and support activities undertaken by a firm. From this analysis should arise greater awareness concerning costs and the potential for lower costs and for differentiation. Quite simply, argues Porter (1985), competitive advantage is created and sustained when a firm performs the most critical functions either more cheaply or better than its competitors. But what are the most critical factors? Why? How and where might costs be reduced? How and where might differentiation be created?

Activities in the value chain

The value chain developed by Michael Porter is illustrated in Figure 3.9. There are five primary activities, namely inbound logistics, operations, outbound logistics, marketing and sales, and service. In the diagram they are illustrated as a chain moving from left to right, and they represent activities of physically creating the product or service and transferring it to the buyer, together with any necessary after-sale service. They are linked to four support activities: procurement, technology development, human resource management, and the firm's infrastructure. The support activities are drawn laterally as they can affect any one or more of the primary activities, although the firm's infrastructure generally supports the whole value chain. Every one of the primary and support activities incurs costs and should add value to the product or service in excess of these costs. It is important always to look for ways of reducing costs sensibly; cost reductions should not be at the expense of lost quality in areas that matter to customers and consumers. Equally, costs can be added justifiably if they add qualities that the customer values and is willing to pay for. The difference between the total costs and the selling price is the margin. The margin is increased by widening the gap between costs and price. The activities are described in greater depth below.

Primary activities

- *Inbound logistics* are activities relating to receiving, storing and distributing internally the inputs to the product or service. They include warehousing, stock control and internal transportation systems.
- *Operations* are activities relating to the transformation of inputs into finished products and services. Operations includes machining, assembly and packaging.
- *Outbound logistics* are activities relating to the distribution of finished goods and services to customers.
- *Marketing and sales* includes such activities as advertising and promotion, pricing and salesforce activity.
- *Service* relates to the provision of any necessary service with a product, such as installation, repair, extended warranty or training in how to use the product.

Each of these might be crucial for competitive advantage. The nature of the industry will determine which factors are the most significant.

Support activities

- *Procurement* refers to the function or process of purchasing any inputs used in the value chain, as distinct from issues of their application. Procurement may take place within defined policies or procedures, and it might be evidenced within a number of functional areas. Production managers and engineers, for example, are very important in many purchasing decisions to ensure that the specification and quality are appropriate.
- *Technology development*: technology is defined here in its broadest sense to include know-how, research and development, product design and process improvement and information technology.
- *Human resource management* involves all activities relating to recruiting, training, developing and rewarding people throughout the organization.
- *The firm's infrastructure* includes the structure of the organization, planning, financial controls and quality management designed to support the whole of the value chain.

Again, each of these support activities can be very important in creating and sustaining competitive advantage.

Sub-activities   Porter argues that it can often be valuable to subdivide the primary and support activities into their component parts when analysing costs and opportunities for differentiation. For example, it is less meaningful to argue that an organization provides good service than to explain it in terms of installation, repair or training. The competitive advantage is likely to result from a specific sub-activity. Similarly, the marketing mix comprises a set of linked activities which should be managed to complement each other. However, competitive advantage can arise from just one activity in the mix, possibly the product design, its price or advertising, technical support literature, or from the skills and activities of the sales force.

Linkages within the value chain

Although competitive advantage arises from one or more sub-activities within the primary and support activities comprising the value chain, it is important not to think of the chain merely as a set of independent activities. Rather, it is a system of interdependent activities. Linkages in the value chain, which are relationships between the activities, are very important. Behaviour in one part of the organization can affect the costs and performance of other business units and functions, and this quite frequently involves trade-off decisions. For example, more expensive materials and more stringent inspection will increase costs in the inbound logistics and operations activities, but the savings in service costs resulting from these strategies may be greater. The choice of functional strategies and where to concentrate efforts will relate to the organization's competitive and corporate strategies concerning competitive advantage.

Similarly, several activities and sub-activities depend on each other. The extent to which operations, outbound logistics and installation are co-ordinated can be a source of competitive advantage through lower costs (reduced stockholding) or differentiation (high quality, customer-orientated service). This last example uses linkages between primary activities, but there are also clear linkages between primary and support activities. Product design affects manufacturing costs, purchasing policies affect operations and production costs, and so on.

Having introduced and discussed the concept of the value chain, it is now important to consider how it might be applied in the evaluation of costs and differentiation opportunities.

3.7 The value chain and competitive advantage

Cost leadership and differentiation strategies

In the next chapter we discuss how differentiation and cost management are two key themes in competition and also introduce Porter's generic strategies built around **cost leadership** and

Table 3.2 Indicative cost breakdown of a manufacturing and a service business

	Manufacturing firm (% of total)	Professional firm of accountants (% of total)	
Primary activities Inbound logistics	4	8	(data collection for audits)
Operations	64	26	(actual auditing)
Outbound logistics	1	5	(report writing and presentations)
Marketing and sales	7	21	(getting new business)
Service	1	3	(general client liaison)
	77	63	
Support activities Procurement	1	1	
Technology development	10	8	(IT development)
Human resources management	2	16	
Firm's infrastructure	10	12	
	100	100	

differentiation (Porter, 1985). Here, though, we look at how these themes relate to the value chain framework.

Cost leadership   Chapter 4 discusses the argument of Porter (1985) that the lowest cost producer in either a broad or narrow competitive scope (the broad market or specialist segments):

- delivers acceptable quality but produces the product or service with lower costs than competitors
- sustains this cost gap
- achieves above-average profits from industry-average prices.

This cost advantage will be achieved by the effective management of the key determinants of costs.

The differentiation strategy   Similarly, Porter argues that the successful application of a differentiation strategy involves:

- the selection of one or more key characteristics which are widely valued by buyers (there are any number of opportunities relating to different needs and market segments)
- adding costs selectively in the areas perceived to be important to buyers, and charging a premium price in excess of the added costs.

These figures are only indicative, and should not be seen as targets for any particular firm.

The success of this strategy lies in finding opportunities for differentiation which cannot be matched easily by competitors, and being clear about the costs involved and the price potential. Costs in areas not perceived to be significant to buyers must be controlled, and in line with competitor costs, for otherwise above-average profits will not be achieved.

The successful implementation of both of these strategies therefore requires an understanding of where costs are incurred throughout the organization. Understanding costs and the search for appropriate cost reductions involves an appreciation of how costs should be attributed to the various discrete activities which comprise the value chain. Table 3.2 compares a possible cost breakdown for a manufacturing firm with that for a firm of professional accountants. If an analysis of the value chain is to be meaningful, it is important that the costs are genuinely attributed to the activities that generate them, and not simply apportioned in some convenient way, however difficult this might prove in practice. Given the figures in Table 3.2 one might question whether the manufacturing firm is spending enough on human resources management and marketing, and on the accountancy practice, too much.

Cost drivers

It is important to appreciate which cost drivers are the most significant. The following cost drivers can all influence the value chain:

- Economies of scale and potential experience and learning curve benefits.
- Capacity utilization, linked to production control and the existence of bottlenecks.
- Linkages – Time spent liaising with other departments can incur costs, but at the same time create savings and differentiation through interrelationships and shared activities.
- Interrelationships and shared activities – Shared activities, possibly a shared salesforce, shared advertising or shared plant, can generate savings. Close links between activities or departments can increase quality and ensure that the needs of customers are matched more effectively.

Strategy in action 3.1

Cost Drivers – an Application

A key challenge for motor car manufacturers is one of reducing new product development times and costs while increasing the number of models that they offer their customers. To succeed, a car must look and feel different from its rivals, but the manufacturers have found that they can save both time and cost if they share components *which are hidden from view*. Examples would include floor pans (or platforms), engines and chassis. As a consequence, in recent years, there has been a tendency for new partnerships to emerge, as well as a number of important mergers.

Fiat, for example, owns the Alfa Romeo and Lancia marques and uses the same platforms for similar-sized models with the Fiat, Alfa Romeo and Lancia names.

Similarly, Volkswagen has acquired Audi, Seat and Skoda and adopts similar strategies. The platforms account for one-third of the costs incurred in designing a new car.

Manufacturers trade engines. Ford, for example, sells engines to other companies, as well as sharing components across the businesses it owns or has owned, which include Jaguar, Land Rover, Volvo and Mazda. In the same way, Peugeot diesel engines are common to Citroën and Peugeot cars.

- Integration – This incorporates the extent to which the organization is vertically integrated, say manufacturing its own component parts instead of assembling bought-in components, or even designing and manufacturing its own machinery. This again can influence costs and differentiation, and is an important element of the strategy of YKK, which is featured as an example later in this chapter.
- Timing – Buying and selling at the appropriate time. It is important to invest in stocks to ensure deliveries when customers want them, but at the same time stockholding costs must be monitored and controlled.
- Policies – Policy standards for procurement or production may be wrong. If they are set too low, quality may be lost and prove detrimental. If they are too high in relation to the actual needs of the market, costs are incurred unnecessarily.
- Location issues – This includes wage costs, which can vary between different regions, and the costs of supporting a particular organization structure.
- Institutional factors – Specific regulations concerning materials content or usage would be an example.

Porter argues that sustained competitive advantage requires effective control of the cost drivers, and that scale economies, learning, linkages, interrelationships and timing provide the key opportunities for creating advantage. In the case of a cost leadership strategy, the cost advantage is relative to the costs of competitors, and over time these could change if competitors concentrate on their cost drivers. Consequently, it is useful to attempt to monitor and predict how competitor costs might change in the future linked to any changes in their competitive and functional strategies.

Strategy in action 3.1 provides details of some cost drivers in the car industry.

Common problems in cost control through the value chain

It was mentioned above that it can prove difficult to assign costs to activities properly, and this is one of the difficulties likely to be encountered in using value-chain analysis as a basis for more effective cost management. Porter contends that there are several common pitfalls in managing costs for competitive advantage:

- misunderstanding of actual costs and misperceptions of the key cost drivers
- concentrating on manufacturing when cost savings are required. Often it is not the area to cut if quality is to be maintained, especially once a certain level of manufacturing efficiency has been achieved
- failing to take advantage of the potential gains from linkages
- ignoring competitor behaviour
- relying on small incremental cost savings when needs arise rather than introducing a long-term, permanently installed cost-management programme.

Differentiation opportunities

It has been mentioned on a number of occasions that competitive advantage through differentiation can arise from any and every area of the business. In relation to the component parts of the value chain, the following are examples of where differentiation might originate.

Primary activities

- *Inbound logistics* – careful and thoughtful handling to ensure that incoming materials are not damaged and are easily accessed when necessary, and the linking of purchases to production requirements, especially important in the case of JIT manufacturing systems.
- *Operations* – high quality; high-output levels and few rejections; delivery on time.
- *Outbound logistics* – rapid delivery when and where customers need the product or service.
- *Marketing and sales* – advertising closely tied to defined market segments; a well-trained, knowledgeable and motivated salesforce; and good technical literature, especially for industrial products.
- *Service* – rapid installation; speedy after-sales service and repair; and immediate availability of spare parts.

Support activities

- *Procurement* – purchasing high-quality materials (to assist operations); regional warehousing of finished products (to enable speedy delivery to customers).
- *Technology development* – the development of unique features, and new products and services; the use of IT to manage inbound and outbound logistics most effectively; and sophisticated market analyses to enable segmentation, targeting and positioning for differentiation.
- *Human resources management* – high-quality training and development; recruitment of the right people; and appropriate reward systems which help to motivate people.
- *Firm's infrastructure* – support from senior executives in customer relations; investment in suitable physical facilities to improve working conditions; and investment in carefully designed IT systems.

In searching for the most appropriate means of differentiating for competitive advantage it is important to look at which activities are the most essential as far as consumers and customers are concerned, and to isolate the key success factors. It is a search for opportunities to be different from competitors in ways which matter, and through this the creation of a superior competitive position. The Japanese zip manufacturer YKK, the world market leader, grew to enjoy a superior competitive position, and the company's strategy is analysed against the value chain in the next section. The underlying philosophy of YKK, the 'Cycle of Goodness', is a cultural issue and described in Chapter 5.

An application of the value chain

YKK succeeded in creating both cost leadership and substantial differentiation with its corporate, competitive and functional strategies, and these have resulted in effective barriers to entry into the industry and close relationships with customers. The idea might be illustrated in Figure 3.10.

The essential components of the strategy, summarized below, are illustrated in Figure 3.11, which places them in the context of the value chain and highlights the linkages.

YKK was structured as a multiplant **multinational** company with both wholly owned subsidiary companies and **joint ventures** throughout the world. The latter organizations were primarily the result of local politics, particularly in low labour cost countries in the Far East. While the subsidiaries were decentralized and enjoyed some local autonomy, they were often managed at the top by Japanese executives on a period of secondment. Consequently, there was substantial influence from the Japanese parent.

YKK invested a significant percentage of after-tax profits back in the business, and as a result became heavily automated and able to enjoy the benefits of the experience/learning curve. Moreover, YKK priced its finished products very competitively both to generate customer satisfaction and to create barriers to entry. The company was vertically integrated, designing and manufacturing its own production machinery, and this gave it a unique competitive edge. It was also particularly innovative as far as both machinery and finished products were concerned. This is shown by their introduction of environmentally friendly zippers.

Coils of semi-finished zips were produced in the Far East, particularly Japan, and exported to such countries as the UK, where they were cut to size and finished in response to customer orders. This resulted in both cost advantages and speedy deliveries from semi-finished stocks. A wide range of colours and sizes was kept ready for finishing. In the UK the key garment manufacturers and the retail outlets that they serve were targeted by YKK and given special service.

The 'Cycle of Goodness' philosophy (one prospers when the person renders benefit to others) was not exported in its complete form, but employee relations were an important aspect of the human resources strategy. Participation and involvement were essential features, and total quality management was a key feature.

Conceptually, the value chain is a useful way of analysing resources and functions within the organization in the context of how they might individually contribute to competitive advantage. At the same time the linkages between them should be assessed, because it is from these interrelationships and linkages that synergy in the form of additional cost savings or differentiation is created.

To apply the value chain properly it is important also to allocate costs to activities, and to evaluate whether costs could be saved in various areas or whether additional spending on certain activities might yield additional benefits by adding value in ways which are important to consumers. In practice it can be difficult to assign costs accurately. In this respect the actual application, rather than the concept, of the value chain is more applicable for managers than for students of this subject. In the authors' experience, applications of the value chain pose difficulties for managers, primarily because the management accounting systems in many organizations do not readily provide the data in the form required. Developing this theme,

Figure 3.12   YKK's competitive advantage

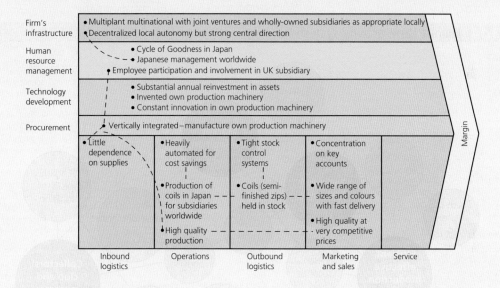

Figure 3.13   YKK's competitive advantage and the value chain

(DEVELOPED FROM MATERIAL IN CHANNON, DF AND MAYEDA, K (1979) YOSHIDA KOGYO KK 'A' AND 'B' CASE STUDIES. AVAILABLE FROM THE EUROPEAN CASE CLEARING HOUSE.)

Johnson and Kaplan (1987) contend that certain costs are extremely difficult to allocate to certain individual products, but they are the costs of activities which are very significant in relation to total quality and in turn competitive advantage. Machine failures are one example, and they affect a number of products and can mean that deliveries are late and possibly priorities are changed. But how should the costs be allocated? As production systems become increasingly sophisticated, overheads, as a proportion of total costs, increase relative to the direct costs of labour and materials. Genuinely allocating these production overheads is difficult.

Nevertheless, the value chain can provide an extremely useful framework for considering the activities involved in producing products and services and considering their significance for customers.

We continue this chapter by returning to Kay's (1993) framework and looking at reputation, but before we do this it is important to cross-reference activity mapping. In a 1996 *Harvard Business Review* article, Michael Porter developed activity maps as an adjunct to the value chain. The challenge is to produce a framework of the critically important activities, together with those that support them, and show how they all link together.

3.8 Activity mapping and strategy mapping

Activity mapping

Activity mapping, described here in outline only, provides a useful framework for explaining how resources work together to create and add value. Ideally all the selected activities will fit together and complement the corporate and competitive strategies in order to yield uniqueness and synergy. Porter (1996) uses the metaphor of a comparison of two people to make his point. They each have hands, feet, eyes, ears and so on, which, by-and-large, perform similar functions. Whilst there will be differences between two people's hands or feet, the real difference is in the way all the parts combine into a whole. Individual differences in parts – such as colour blindness or arthritis in a hand – do not in themselves explain different behaviours and outcomes. To understand this we need to understand more about the workings of the brain. In a similar way, if we are to understand organizations and organizational differences, we must understand how

Figure 3.14 Lilliput Lane activity system

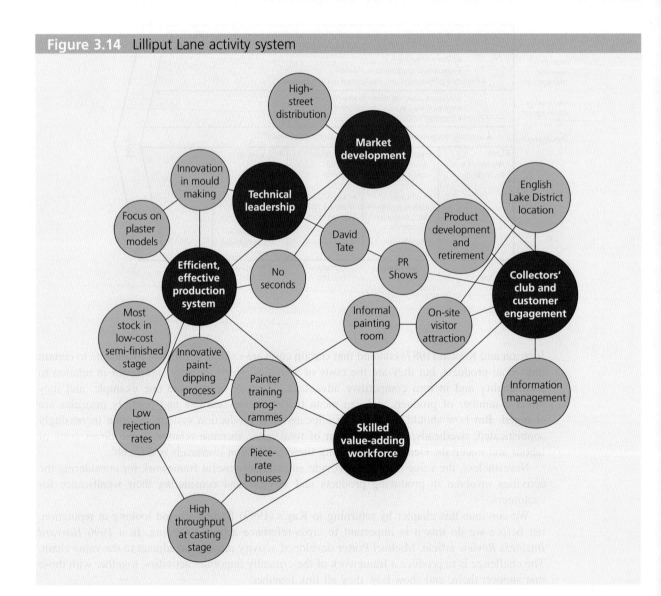

different organizations acquire and use knowledge – which is frequently related to the synergy created by the interactions of the functions and activities.

Figure 3.14 is an example of Porter's activity mapping idea. The organization selected is Lilliput Lane, manufacturer of plaster cottages and other collectable items. Lilliput Lane, along with nearby business, Border Fine Arts (best known for resin models of wildlife) are both owned by the American collectables business, Enesco, which derives synergy from distributing different collectable products from suppliers around the world through common retail channels. Using innovatory moulding technology, much of it invented by founder, David Tate, Lilliput Lane casts intricate figures and models out of plaster, a cheap and readily-obtainable commodity. Individual painters then transform a relatively bland model into a unique finished article.

Simply, the five larger circles in Figure 3.14 represent what we believe are the key activities in terms of difference and competitive strength; the smaller circles are important support activities. It will be realized that the key activities are all linked and complementary and that the other activities support often more than one key activity.

Over-time activities will be abandoned, added or changed to affect the competitive position. To a large extent the way that activities are carried out by people is crucially important and, consequently, the culture and style of management in the organization is a major determinant of the organization's ability to change and find new opportunities for creating different values for customers.

Strategy mapping

Kaplan and Norton (2000) developed the notion of strategy mapping from their earlier work on the Balanced Scorecard, which is explained in Chapter 7 (Kaplan and Norton, 1992). Irwin (2002) has usefully applied the idea to the public sector.

The Balanced Scorecard is basically about performance measurement – the argument being that financial measures alone are inadequate to evaluate performance. Measures relating to customers, internal processes and improvement are also essential, to give an all-round view. This all-round view concerns the extent to which the organization is progressing towards its vision and long-term purpose. Strategy mapping works the other way round. It demands that managers question what is going to be required (in terms of activities) to systematically and synergistically progress towards the vision and to then set targets for performance against these activities. In other words, one starts with the vision and then questions what needs to be done, how and when. Whilst the Balanced Scorecard measures activities and reviews outcomes, strategy mapping starts with desired outcomes and then seeks to make sure the necessary activities are in place – with performance targets attached. Again it embraces how activities can be used to create competitive advantage.

3.9 Reputation and branding

Reputation and branding are clearly linked but they are not one and the same. In a sense, a brand is a label that is attached to an organization's reputation. Kay (1993) contends that reputation is a key element of differentiation and that both reputation and branding are key **intangible resources**. What matters with differentiation is the customers' perception of the difference and what it means or conveys. It is, therefore, a qualitative indicator of quality; where quantitative measurement is difficult it can be a significant variable in decision-making and choice.

The reputation of Sir Richard Branson's Virgin brand has allowed him to diversify into a wide range of activities – customer confidence in the brand provides reassurance and allows him entry into areas where he has little if any previous experience or expertise. It is critically important, therefore, never to disappoint customers in ways which tarnish a reputation; somewhat paradoxically, this means that there can be a huge downside risk for companies with the strongest reputations if they make strategic errors of judgement.

In similar vein, a strong reputation provides a safe choice for customers who are new entrants to a market. A strong reputation therefore can help to sustain and build a strong position in a market. Moreover, it can sometimes be used to justify a premium price.

Famous-name endorsements provide an ideal opportunity for enhancing a company's reputation. Ownership of an endorsed product makes a statement about a person. People hold certain personalities in very high regard and would find it hard to imagine that they would endorse anything that was not good, even the best in the market. Whether such people actually use the products and services that they endorse is an entirely different matter!

Branding

Brand is only important when two products are identical. It is not important if one of the products has better technology or a better design than the other.

JAMES DYSON

Many differentiated products, and some services, are identified by brand names. These brand names, and/or the identity of the companies that own them, convey an image to customers. Simply, brands reflect reputations; and advertising is often used to create and reinforce this image and reputation. As competition intensifies, more and more products are perceived as commodities, sold essentially on price. When this happens, differentiation and branding become increasingly significant. The product needs a clear brand identity; a supportive corporate image, a company brand, is also valuable.

Case 3.7 explores the challenge faced by Burberry in supporting its brand, protecting its reputation and managing costs.

Brands add value, possibly the promise of some particular satisfaction or experience, a 'guarantee' of a specific level of quality, or reliability. Consequently, a brand can be seen as an actual product or service augmented by some additional added value. Branding is important and valuable; the drive to establish and maintain a recognized brand image can bring about differentiation and innovation. Nescafé, for example, has had several variants and improvements over the years. However, the value added must be real, as informed customers today will quickly see through any marketing hype. Moreover, the distinctiveness will not be achieved without investment, in both research and development and advertising, an issue which is taken up later.

Ideally, successful branding will generate customer loyalty and repeat purchases, enable higher prices and margins, and provide a springboard for additional products and services. Customers expect to find the leading brand names widely available in distribution outlets but, in the case of, say, grocery products, the supermarkets will typically only offer the number one and number two brands alongside their own-label competitor. In the case of groceries, strong branding has been essential for enabling the leading manufacturers to contain the growing power of the leading supermarket chains. Nevertheless, branding has not exempted them from tight pricing strategies. Edwin Artzt, until the mid-1990s a powerful and renowned Chief Executive of Procter & Gamble, has stated that 'winning companies offer lower prices, better quality, continuous improvement and/or high profits to retailers'.

The quality of own-label products has increased, and consequently the magnitude of the premium that customers will pay for the leading manufacturer brand has declined in recent years. Procter & Gamble, which is not alone in this strategy, has adopted perpetual 'everyday low prices' for all of its products. Marlboro cigarettes, the world's leading cigarette brand, were reduced in price dramatically in the mid-1990s. In the competitive food sector, product innovation, quality, specific features and, to a lesser extent, packaging are seen as the most effective means of distinguishing brands from own-label alternatives.

Case 3.7

Burberry   UK

Burberry was divested from Great Universal Stores in 2005 – GUS had owned the company for some 50 years. At this point its successful CEO, Rose Marie Bravo, opted to move on. In the previous eight years she had been credited with transforming the business – although she herself always attributed much of the credit to Creative Director Christopher Bailey, who has remained with the business.

The company had been changed from a 'staid mac maker' to a world class luxury goods company; its bags and scarves are particularly popular. The popularity of the brand helps explain why 'chavs' are regularly seen with fake Burberry bags. The products are recognizable for the distinctive check patterns in various colours. Kate Moss had been recruited to be the 'face of Burberry' to coincide with a widening range of fashionable clothing. Bravo had bought back some Asian licences to regain greater control of the brand.

Her replacement was Angela Ahrends, recruited from Liz Claiborne in America. She began to trial small boutiques that specialized in accessories only. She was also keen to focus on the balance between wholsesale (40 per cent of revenues) and retail (60 per cent) activities. As well as its own outlets Burberry distributes to the major name department stores, such as Saks and Nordstrom in the US.

In 2008 it seemed as if Burberry, along with certain other luxury brands, was holding up well in the credit crunch – it recorded its thirteenth consecutive quarter of double digit growth. But when sales in America dipped, revenues began to fall. Ahrends decided she must focus on cost cutting opportunities wherever it made sense to make sure Burberry was a really strong and robust business when customers came back. In the UK there were consequential job losses at Burberry factories in Yorkshire – although sales in the UK remained strong.

Questions

1 What do you see as the challenges in supporting a world class brand whilst looking for opportunities to reduce the cost base?

© CHRIS INCH / ISTOCK

Examples of leading brands

- *Persil* and *Pampers*: brand names not used in conjunction with the manufacturer's name – they are produced by Unilever and Procter & Gamble, respectively.

- *Coca-Cola*: manufacturer's name attributed to a product. *Levi's* is derived from Levi Strauss. Case 3.8 on Levi's looks at how a company with a significant brand and image has changed tactics in a dynamic and competitive environment.

- *Cadbury's Dairy Milk* and *Barclaycard Visa*: the first is a combination of a company and a product name, the second a combination of an organization (Barclays) and a service provided by a separate business.

- *St Michael*: the personalized brand name used historically on all products sold by Marks and Spencer to signify UK manufactured. Now no longer a viable cost concept and replaced with clothing related band names such as Per Una.

- Apple through new **product development** has created the iPod, iPhone, iTunes, MacBook and the ultra thin MacBook Air have all regenerated a struggling business to be a major player in the multi-media arena.

Case 3.8

Levi's   US

SOURCE: THIS CASE STUDY WAS PREPARED USING PRIMARILY PUBLICLY AVAILABLE SOURCES OF INFORMATION FOR THE PURPOSES OF CLASSROOM DISCUSSION; IT DOES NOT INTEND TO ILLUSTRATE EITHER EFFECTIVE OR INEFFECTIVE HANDLING OF A MANAGERIAL SITUATION.

Levi's, a global business with a base in San Francisco, has built an established brand and image which allows it to sell at premium prices and still command a sizeable market share for its jeans. During the 1990s two significant events took place. To protect its image Levi's took out a legal action against Tesco in the UK to stop the supermarket group selling imported Levi's 501s at reduced prices. In a sense Tesco was offering the same service as the outlet stores which sell branded products (often last year's ranges) at substantial discounts. In addition, the market for denim fashions began to fall away. As an initial response to this Levi's moved further upmarket and launched a new range in the £175 per pair price bracket.

Meanwhile competitor brands such as Lee and Wrangler, which sold at lower prices, were doing well. Levi's concluded it had to respond and decided it would switch its emphasis and target the mass market through supermarkets. In 2003 the company launched a new range in Europe, priced at around 60 per cent of the price for its traditional branded jeans. Its Signature Range had already been made available in the US through Wal-Mart. The target customers were people in their thirties with mortgages and families, people who had earlier been fashion-conscious but were now less so for economic reasons. The implied price was around £25 per pair, compared with a typical Levi's price between £40 and £45. At this time some 25 per cent of jeans customers were willing to pay £30 and above; just 8 per cent were in the £45 plus sector of the market. The lowest priced jeans available from Tesco in 2003 were £6.

Questions

1 In the circumstances do you think this was a sound or a risky tactic for Levi's to adopt?

2 To what extent do you believe the quality difference between various brands of jeans is based on design and fashion as distinct from workmanship and higher quality materials?

LEVI'S **http://www.levis.com**

Several large organizations have, through strategic acquisitions and investments in brands, established themselves as global corporations. Examples include:

- *Unilever*: now owns a variety of food (Birds Eye, Batchelors, Walls, John West, Boursin, Blue Band, Flora), household goods (Shield soap, Persil, Lux and Surf detergents) and cosmetics (Brut, Fabergé and Calvin Klein) brands.

- *Philip Morris*: US tobacco company which has acquired General Foods (US; Maxwell House coffee) and Jacobs Suchard (Switzerland; confectionery and coffee).

- *Nestlé*: including Chambourcy (France), Rowntree (UK) and Buitoni (Italy).

These companies can afford substantial investments in research and development to innovate and:

- strengthen the brand, say by extending the range of products carrying the name

- develop new opportunities, for example, Mars Bars ice cream, which was launched simultaneously in 15 European countries and priced at a premium over normal ice cream bars

- transform competition in the market. Pampers disposable nappies have been developed into a very successful range of segmented products selling throughout the USA and Europe.

Strong brand names are clearly an asset for an organization. The value of the brand, the so-called brand equity, relates to the totality of all the stored beliefs, likes/dislikes and behaviours associated with it. Customer attitudes are critical; so too are those of distributors. The fact that a brand can command a certain amount of shelf space in all leading stores carries a value. However, creating and maintaining the image is expensive. It has been estimated that manufacturers spend on average 7 per cent of sales revenue to support the top ten leading brands, covering all product groups; this percentage increases as the brand recognition factor decreases. Because of this, manufacturers need to control the number of brands that they market at any time; Procter & Gamble withdrew over 25 per cent of their brands in the 1990s. Similarly, new product launches need to be managed effectively.

There is a so-far unresolved debate concerning how these assets might be properly valued in a company balance sheet. In the mid-1990s the US magazine *Financial Week* postulated that the world's most valuable brand name was Marlboro (owned by Philip Morris) and that it was then worth in excess of $30 million. In terms of monetary value, Coca-Cola was perceived to be second, although it is generally accepted that it is better known. The most valuable European brand at that time was Nestlé's Nescafé; the three leading British brands (worldwide) were Johnnie Walker Red Label whisky, Guinness and Smirnoff Vodka (Diageo). By 2007 Coca-Cola was judged to be the world's most valuable brand; Marlboro did not even feature in the top ten, indicating the changing attitude to smoking. Microsoft, Nokia, Toyota, Intel, McDonald's and Disney were, though, in the top ten. Outside this leading group, but rising, were Google, Zara, Apple and Nintendo. The value of the iPod and the Wii can be seen in the last two. Where the most recognized brand names are tied to high market shares and above-average margins, they are typically valued at over twice their annual revenues.

However, not all brand names are strong and effective. Prudential, best known as an insurance business, launched its Internet bank in 1999. The company opted to call it 'Egg' partly to provide a distinctive and unusual launch platform. The business developed successfully and in 2004 Egg had between three and four million customers. Recognizing that Egg needed investment at a level that would stretch its own resources, Prudential attempted to find a buyer for the business, but none was forthcoming at the right price. This provided wonderful ammunition for some to criticize the name 'Egg', which had never been universally popular. Phrases such as 'egg on its face', 'half-baked' and 'gone off the boil' all appeared in the press.

Sometimes companies change their brand names – and not always for the better. In recent years The Post Office changed its corporate identity to Consignia. Unquestionably some design team created a clever play on the word 'consignment' but the public reaction was hardly supportive and the name was changed back!

Celebrity brands

High profile media figures have always been able to exploit their name and image by endorsing products. Actresses, football players, celebrity chefs and rap stars are well-known examples. And, as the shown by the recent success of Jamie Oliver with Sainsbury's and Alan Hansen with Morrisons, it does work. But celebrities have finite life cycles. Sports stars are not necessarily high profile once they stop playing; supermodels 'get old' and are replaced by younger models. The more astute celebrities have found new ways to exploit their name and reputation. Elle McPherson, supermodel and actress, for example, launched her own range of lingerie from a base in her native Australia. Some five years ago Claudia Schiffer opted to go down a similar route. The 33-year-old (in 2004) supermodel has now promoted brands and products such as Revlon, Chanel and L'Oréal cosmetics, Citroën cars, Ebel watches and Ferrero Rocher chocolates over several years. She then set out to find a business partner to help her develop her own products – 'perhaps in beauty, fragrance or children's clothing'.

Relationship marketing

Branding helps to establish, build and cement relationships among manufacturers, their customers and their distributors. The term 'relationship marketing' is used to reinforce the argument that marketing should be perceived as the management of a network of relationships between the brand and its various customers. Marketing, therefore, aims to enhance brand equity and thus ensure continued satisfaction for customers and increased profits for the brand owner. Implicit in this is the realization that new customers are harder, and more expensive, to find than existing ones are to retain. This potent mix of brand identity and customer care is clearly related to the whole service package offered by manufacturers to their customers, and to total quality management.

3.10 The impact of the Internet

The emergence and rapid growth of the Internet and the World Wide Web during the 1990s spawned a number of new and very entrepreneurial businesses. It is easy to be seduced by Internet possibilities and, supported by venture capital, many new Internet companies have grown rapidly. Few, however, have turned growing revenues into profits. At the same time, it has also demanded that every organization develop a strategy for harnessing its potential: it will not go away and, for some, will completely transform their ways of operating and doing business. This section briefly explores some of these issues.

The Internet:

- provides information – which can make decision-making much easier, but is potentially in quantities so great that it is hard to assimilate
- allows a company to advertise and promote itself and its products and services
- speeds up communication by replacing printed memos and telephone calls
- enables electronic trading. This again can take several forms. For consumer sales, information on a product (such as a book) can very readily be provided, along with reviews; moreover, in the case of a compact disc, sample tracks can be played. Virtual reality can be employed to move people around either a shopping mall or a supermarket.

In the so-called dot.com era certain organizations were able to secure very large amounts of capital to pursue any apparently good idea for an e-commerce business. However, it was also apparent how volatile the traded shares of these businesses could be as they grew in size but failed to post any profits.

The fundamental principle behind many new *e-commerce businesses* is trading without either manufacture or a long-term inventory. E-commerce cuts out the retail store element. New organizations dedicated to e-commerce are similar in principle yet distinctly different from the situation where established organizations (for example, Tesco and Waterstone's) sell via the web as well as through their own high-street outlets. The large retailers are increasingly moving in this direction because of the impact of the specialist e-commerce companies on customer buying habits. While the new businesses may own warehouses for collecting stock for onward transmission and holding limited numbers of fast-moving items, there will rarely be any need for them to employ either sales or production staff, and this element can be outsourced to specialists in logistics, leaving the e-commerce company to focus on creating and maintaining a successful website once the supply chain is set up. Simply, they are a virtual company.

The transaction begins when a potential customer uses a home computer to check out the website of the e-commerce business, selects an item and places an order electronically. Typically, credit-card information will be requested, and an instant credit check will be carried out by contacting the computer system of the relevant credit-card company. Once the payment details have been confirmed, an order is transmitted to the manufacturer of the product in question. If the e-commerce company is holding the product in stock, this would be replaced by an order to the company's own warehouse, who will later reorder from the manufacturer. Delivery to the customer can be direct from the manufacturer or via the e-commerce business who will receive bulk supplies and post out individual parcels.

Their fundamental advantage is their ability to reach a wide customer audience at low cost, as long as they can be attracted in the first place and then retained as a regular customer. Relatively specialist items can thus be made available to people who find it difficult to visit the shops that sell them directly. One key disadvantage is that the goods cannot be touched and inspected, which matters more for some customers and products than it does for others. The main infrastructure requirements for a successful e-commerce business are appropriate managerial and technical skills, venture capital to set up a sophisticated supply chain and secure payment systems. They also need customers who can and do access their site, recognize the convenience and benefits being offered, and believe that the payment systems are private and secure.

Every business needs an Internet strategy; it has to decide upon the extent to which it intends to use the Internet for promotion and for commercial transactions. For many organizations, it is far more important for business-to-business transactions than it is for direct sales to customers.

The ultimate popularity of Internet trading for consumer products remains difficult to predict for a number of reasons. More and more households are on-line but the penetration is uneven. While all age groups are involved, younger people are more likely to use the Internet than older generations. Men seem more comfortable with the technology than women in many cases, and there is a greater incidence when people have enjoyed higher education and have above-average earnings. The geographical coverage in the UK is biased to the southern counties. But this is now. Various predictions for future take-up have been offered and they are not all in accord. Some customers are keen to use the Internet for information gathering but stop short of buying electronically. This is partly linked to a reluctance to input credit-card details into a personal computer.

However, the potential of the Internet to link business with business is enormous and it offers both cost savings and service improvements. The term *e-markets* is normally used for this linkage. E-markets:

- link computers and databases
- constitute virtual and private networks where companies and their suppliers can share vital information
- allow easy and fast transfer of up-to-date information on current orders, contracts, prices, inventory, deliveries and so on – access can be controlled through passwords
- monitor and analyse activities
- have a facility for transactions
- enable cost reductions together with better information and a faster response time
- allow suppliers to auction any surplus stock, and
- allow buyers to ask for bidders against a special or an emergency need.

3.11 Conclusion: Information, knowledge and corporate capital

Information, then, is required to support the decision-making processes related to strategic change – both formally planned changes and emergent, adaptive, incremental change – at all levels of the organization. Figure 3.15 summarizes the key points. Information, itself supported by IT, is used by people to help them to make decisions. History and experience qualify the information and analysis. The information, and the way in which people use it, comprises the organization's knowledge.

Figure 3.16 attempts to draw together those elements and resources which comprise the organization's corporate capital. It is a summary of many of the points and issues raised and discussed in Parts 1 and 2 so far. Part 2 opened by distinguishing between opportunity-driven and resource-based strategy. Figure 3.16 is a comprehensive summary of all the resources that an organization possesses and which it should lever and exploit to create and sustain competitive advantage and strategic success.

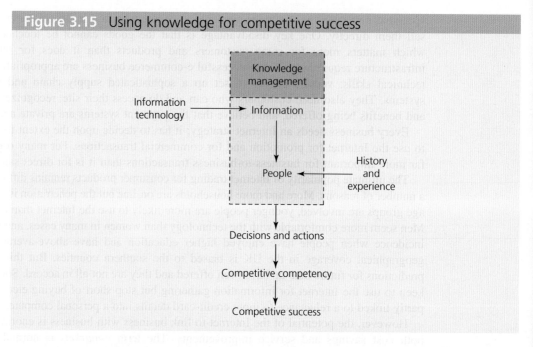

Figure 3.15   Using knowledge for competitive success

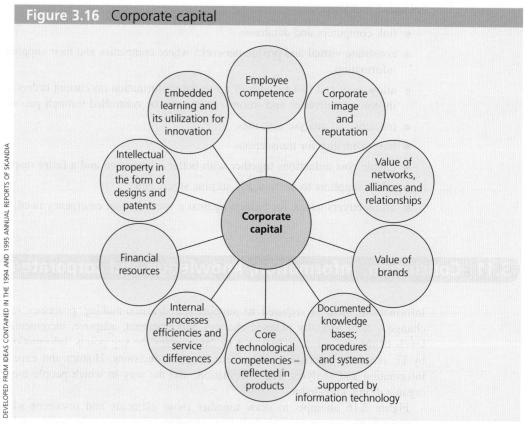

Figure 3.16   Corporate capital

DEVELOPED FROM IDEAS CONTAINED IN THE 1994 AND 1995 ANNUAL REPORTS OF SKANDIA

Logically, it can be argued that a company which aims to build and sustain competitiveness and success will audit these elements and use this analysis as a source of ideas for attention and improvement.

Summary

Acquiring, deploying and exploiting key resources in an individual and effective way is the source of important differences and, in turn, competitive advantage. The resource-based view of strategy looks at how organizations *individually* respond, and at how their core competencies and strategic capabilities determine their success as a competitor.

A simple *resource audit* is an attempt to assess the strengths and weaknesses of an organization; typically it will be carried out in conjunction with an assessment of opportunities and threats. However, any evaluation should be relative. The assessment should be in the context of, first, the key success factors for the markets and industries in question and, second, the comparable strengths and weaknesses of competitors for the same customers.

Strategic architecture refers to the linkages inside the organization (between different divisions, departments and managers) and the relationships, possibly partnerships, that an organization has with other members of the relevant value chain, such as suppliers and distributors. Synergy, mutual dependency and trust are key issues in the relationships.

People who contribute as innovators and intrapreneurs must be in a position where they feel stretched and rewarded. For some organizations, *empowerment* is a wonderful idea but no more than that. They find it difficult to create the appropriate climate and culture; their employees may not wish to be empowered to some considerable degree.

Emergent strategy possibilities are enhanced where people work well together and collectively. There is a team spirit, sharing and learning. *Synergy* is the outcome. Extended to the level of the organization, this constitutes a learning organization. Like empowerment, this can seem attractive as a theoretical idea and ideal but be difficult to implement effectively.

The information that feeds the whole process of decision-making comes from a variety of internal and external sources, both formal and informal. Formal information systems and *information technology* can both make a valuable input, but information is more than information technology.

However much information they have, managers are still not 'seeing reality', rather they are put in position where their perception of events can be more informed and hopefully more insightful. Because issues of meaning are crucial, it is possible that decisions lead to counterintuitive behaviour with unanticipated outcomes.

Nevertheless, as well as informing decision-making, information and information technology can be a source of competitive advantage in its own right.

The emergence of the *Internet* has spawned a host of new businesses. It has also required every company to formulate a strategy for harnessing its potential effectively.

Michael Porter has provided a useful value-chain framework for helping to understand where differences are created, where costs are incurred and how synergy might be generated through linkages. His value chain comprises:

Five primary activities	inbound logistics;
	operations;
	outbound logistics;
	marketing and sales
	service; and
Four support activities	procurement;
	technology development;
	human resource management;
	the firm's infrastructure.

Organizations must understand and manage their cost drivers. They should not attempt to cut corners with things that really matter for customers; at the same time, they should not incur unnecessary costs with things that do not add value in ways that customers believe are important.

The value of a strong reputation must not be underestimated. A sound corporate reputation reassures customers. It generates sales and, very significantly, repeat sales. It can enable price premiums. It is a crucially important intangible resource. It is frequently manifested in a strong, visible and readily identified brand name.

Online cases for this chapter

Online Case 3.1: British Airways
Online Case 3.2: Benetton
Online Case 3.3: Britt Allcroft

Online Case 3.4: The UK Holiday Travel Industry
Online Case 3.5: Tesco (IT case)

Questions and research assignments

1 What are the opportunity-driven and resource-based views of strategy? Where and why are they different? Why is it important for organizations to embrace both views simultaneously?

2 Think about your own buying habits and choices. Where do you specifically choose high-profile branded items, and where are you less concerned? Why? What do you think this behaviour is saying about you?

3 Consider how strategic changes in one retail sector, from an emphasis on hardware stores that specialize in personal service and expert advice to customers from all employees, to a predominance of do-it-yourself supermarkets and warehouses, might have affected issues of staff motivation, personal development needs and appropriate reward systems.

4 Albeit by rule of thumb, take a team of people with whom you associate closely and evaluate their behaviour characteristics Where is the team strong? Where is the team weak? Do you believe it is balanced? If not, what might be done to change things?

5 Consider how the increasing utilization of information technology in retailing has affected you as a customer. Do you feel that the major retail organizations who have introduced and benefited from the greater utilization of IT have attempted to ensure that the customer has also benefited and not suffered?

6 Consider why it is argued that the increasing utilization of IT by organizations is a cultural issue. How might managers be encouraged to make greater use of the technology which is available?

7 How do you personally use the Internet? Do you feel you are exploiting its potential?

Internet and library projects

1 Using the Internet to look at the current status of Dyson and the other main manufacturers of vacuum cleaners, to what extent has James Dyson transformed an industry? How has he now extended the product range of the business?
Dyson **http://www.dyson.com**

2 Selecting an organization of your choice, and ideally one with which you are familiar, carry out a resource audit. Make sure that you take account of industry key success factors and competitors' relative strengths in your evaluation.

3 Using the same organization, apply Porter's value chain. As far as you are able, and accepting that there may be elements of subjectivity, allocate the costs and consider whether your breakdown matches your initial expectations. Where are the all-important linkages?

4 For an organization of your choice ascertain the range of products and services offered and answer the following questions:

- What are essential information needs from outside the organization (the environment) for managing these products and services both now and in the future?
- Where are the limitations in availability?
- What role might IT play in improving availability?

5 By visiting and talking to staff at an appropriate level and with several years' work experience in that environment, in both a travel agency and a retail store which makes extensive use of an EPOS (electronic point of sale) system, ascertain the effect that IT has had on their decision-making. Do the staff feel they are more aware strategically? If so, has this proved valuable?

Strategy activity

Lagardere

Lagardere is France's largest media company, but not a 'world leader' in the industry. Its magazines include Elle, Paris Match and Psychologies, all of which are published in different language editions. It owns the Europe 1 Radio Station and two television stations in France. It also publishes *Le Journal de Dimanche*, one of two national Sunday newspapers. It promotes live concerts and has developed into Internet advertising. Since 2006 it has been divesting unprofitable regional newspapers.

In 2008 Lagardere was seeing a downturn in the advertising spend upon which it depends for most of its activities. As a consequence it sought to build on its existing competencies and seek out growth opportunities in China and Russia, as well as increasing its Internet presence. Perhaps these could even be combined?

These ideas presented some interesting challenges. China is well established as a provider of both typesetting and printing – but this is different from penetrating the 'reading industry' in China. Lagardere was also thinking about possible scale economies and synergies across its range of activities. Did shared content offer an opportunity? Could advertising packages be constructed?

Questions

1 Does this resource-based approach make strategic sense? Are the possible synergies realistic or very ambitious?

Further reading

Drucker, PF (1988) The coming of the new organization, *Harvard Business Review*, January–February.

Garvin, DA (1984) What does product quality really mean?, *Sloan Management Revue*, Fall.

Kanter, RM (1989) The new managerial work, *Harvard Business Review*, November–December.

McFarlane, FW (1984) Information technology changes the way you compete, *Harvard Business Review*, May–June.

Miller, D (1992) The Icarus paradox – how exceptional companies bring about their own downfall, *Business Horizons*, January–February.

Porter, ME (1996) What is strategy?, *Harvard Business Review*, November–December.

Rayport, JF and Sviokla, JJ (1995) Exploiting the virtual value chain, *Harvard Business Review*, November–December.

Porter, ME (2001) Strategy and the Internet, *Harvard Business Review*, March–April.

Senge, P (1990) The leader's new work – building learning organizations, *Sloan Management Review*, Fall.

The McKinsey 7-S framework is also useful for resource analysis. Details can be found in: Peters, TJ and Waterman, RH Jr (1982) *In Search of Excellence: Lessons from America's Best Run Companies*, Harper & Row.

References

Ackoff, RL (1967) Management misinformation systems, *Management Science* 14, December.

Belbin, RM (1981) *Management Terms: Why They Succeed or Fail*. Heinemann.

Buckingham, M and Coffman, C (1999) *First, Break all the Rules*, Simon and Schuster.

Capelli, P and Crocker-Hefter, A (1995) HRM: The key to competitive advantage, *Financial Times Mastering Management Series*, No. 6, 1 December.

Cummings, TG (1981) Designing effective work groups. In *Handbook of Organizational Design* (eds PC Nystrom and WH Starbuck), Oxford University Press.

Davenport, T and Harris, J (2007) Competing on Analytics – The New Science of Winning, *Harvard Business School Press*.

Day, G (1996) How to learn about markets, *Financial Times Mastering Management Series*, No. 12, 26 January.

Gilbert, X (1995) It's strategy that counts, *Financial Times Mastering Management Series*, No. 7, 8 December.

Goold, M, Campbell, A and Alexander, M (1994) *Corporate Level Strategy*, John Wiley.

Hamel, G and Prahalad, CK (1993) Strategy as stretch and leverage, *Harvard Business Review*, March–April.

Hersey, P and Blanchard, K (1982) *The Management of Organisational Behaviour*, 4th edn, Prentice-Hall.

Hertzberg, F (1968) One more time how do you motivate employees? *Harvard Business Review*, January–February.

Irwin, D (2002) *Strategy Mapping in the Public Sector*, Long Range Planning, Vol 35, Pp 637-647.

Johnson, HT and Kaplan, RS (1987) *Relevance Lost: The Rise and Fall of Management Accounting*, Harvard Business School Press.

Kaplan, R and Norton, D (1992) The Balanced Scorecard – Measures that Drive Performance, *Harvard Business Review*, January-February.

Kaplan, R and Norton, D (2000) *The Strategy Focused Organization*, Harvard Business School Press.

Kay, JA (1993) *Foundations of Corporate Success*, Oxford University Press.

Kelly, FJ and Kelly, HM (1987) *What they Really Teach you at the Harvard Business School*, Piatkus.

Kotter, JP and Heskett, JL (1992) *Corporate Culture and Performance*, Free Press.

Lucas, H (1976) *The Analysis, Design and Implementation of Information Systems*, McGraw-Hill.

Maitland, A (1999) Strategy for creativity, *Financial Times*, 11 November.

Marchand, DA (1995a) Managing strategic intelligence, *Financial Times Mastering Management Series*, No. 4, 17 November.

Marchand, DA (1995b) What is your company's information culture? *Financial Times Mastering Management Series*, No. 7, 8 December.

McClelland, D and Winter, D (1971) *Motivating Economic Achievement*, Free Press.

McFarlane, FW (1984) Information technology changes the way you compete, *Harvard Business Review*, May–June.

McFarlane, FW, McKenney, JL and Pyburn, P (1983) The information archipelago – plotting a course, *Harvard Business Review*, January–February.

McGregor, DM (1960) The Human Side of Enterprise, McGraw-Hill.

Peters, TJ and Waterman, RH Jr (1982) *In Search of Excellence: Lessons from America's Best Run Companies*, Harper & Row.

Porter, LW, Lawler, EE and Hackman, JR (1975) *Behaviour in Organisations*., McGraw-Hill.

Porter, ME (1980) *Competitive Strategy: Techniques for Analysing Industries and Competition*, Free Press.

Porter, ME (1985) *Competitive Advantage: Creating and Sustaining Superior Performance*, Free Press.

Porter, ME (1996) What is strategy? *Harvard Business Review*, November–December.

Porter, ME and Millar, VE (1985) How information gives you a competitive advantage, *Harvard Business Review*, July–August.

Prahalad, CK and Hamel, G (1990) The core competency of the corporation, *Harvard Business Review*, May–June.

Prahalad, CK and Krishnan, MS (2008) *The New Age of Innovation – Driving Co-created Value through Networks*, McGraw Hill.

Preece, S, Fleisher, C and Toccacelli, J (1995) Building a reputation along the value chain at Levi Strauss, *Long Range Planning*, 28, 6.

Rayport, JF and Sviokla, JJ (1995) Exploiting the virtual value chain, *Harvard Business Review*, November–December.

Roffey Park Management Centre (1995) *Career Development in Flatter Structures*. Research report.

Schein, EH (1983) The role of the founder in creating organizational culture, *Organisational Dynamics*, Summer.

Senge, P (1991) *The Fifth Discipline – The Art and Practice of the Learning Organization*, Doubleday. Skandia (1994, 1995) Annual Reports and Accounts.

Stalk, G, Evans, P and Shulman, LE (1992) Competing on capabilities: the new rules of corporate strategy, *Harvard Business Review*, March–April.

Turner, K (1999) *The Wal-Mart Experience*, Presentation to a Retail Solutions International Conference, May.

Chapter 4
The dynamics of competition

PART 1
Understanding strategy

1 Introducing strategy and strategic management

PART 5
Strategic management

14 Strategy implementation

15 Leading change

16 Managing strategy in the organization

17 Final thoughts – the purpose of strategy

PART 2
Strategic positioning

2 Strategic thinking, environmental analysis, synergy and strategic positioning

3 Resource-led strategy

4 The dynamics of competition

5 Introducing culture and values

STRATEGIC MANAGEMENT: AWARENESS AND CHANGE

PART 4
Issues in strategic growth

11 Strategic growth

12 International strategy

13 Failure, consolidation and recovery strategies

PART 3
Strategic analysis and choice

6 Strategic purpose

7 Strategic success

8 An introduction to strategy creation and planning

9 Strategic leadership, entrepreneurship and intrapreneurship

10 Strategic alternatives, strategy evaluation and strategy selection

Learning objectives

Having read to the end of this chapter you should be able to:

- explain the notion of dynamic, tactical change in a competitive environment

- define product (service) differentiation and cost leadership and explain their role in the creation and maintenance of competitive advantage

- show how Michael Porter used these themes to create four important generic strategies

- appreciate why competitive strategies must be changed in a dynamic environment if any advantage is to be sustained

- describe a number of key competitive platforms

- show how an organization can evaluate its competitive strategies against those of its competitors

- explain the notion of 'blue ocean' strategy.

One advantage when you're No. 1 or 2 in an industry is that you can really have a hell of a lot of say in what the future's going to be like by what you do. I'm not a believer in always forecasting the future. But if you take actions that can create that future, at least shape it, then you can benefit from it.

They say: 'Do you sleep well at night with all the competition?' I say: 'I sleep like a baby'. They say: 'That's wonderful'. I say: 'No, no. I wake up every two hours and cry!' Because it's true, you know. You have to feel that restlessness.

ROBERTO GOIZUETA, LATE CHIEF EXECUTIVE, COCA-COLA CORPORATION

Few companies enjoy the luxury of having no serious competitors or little likelihood of any need to change their competitive strategy. It is essential for companies to look for opportunities to create – and sustain – a competitive edge over their rivals and build customer loyalty that provides something of a comfort zone. Logically this should lead to superior profits.

However, competitive advantage, as a term, is easily misunderstood. Some organizations clearly believe, and thus delude themselves, that a clear competitive strategy constitutes advantage. It does not. Advantage comes from being better or different in some meaningful way.

See the online "Nintendo's Rise From The Ashes" case for an example of this section's theory in practice

Even the strongest companies cannot afford to stand still, as shown in Online Case 4.1 – where we can see how Nintendo has been successful because (a) it understands its industry, (b) it found a winning opportunity and (c) it surprised both Sony and Microsoft. A cynic, of course, would argue that a company must change more rapidly than its rivals can steal its ideas!

This chapter then begins by looking at the nature of competition in general, before discussing models and frameworks which help us to understand competitive strategy, competitive advantage and competitive dynamics.

4.1 Competition: an introduction

Causes generate effects. Actions lead to outcomes. On occasions companies may attempt to seize the competitive initiative and introduce an innovatory change. An action by one competitor which affects the relative success of rivals provokes responses. One action can therefore provoke several reactions, depending on the extent of the impact and the general nature of competition. Each reaction in turn further affects the other rival competitors in the industry. New responses will again follow. What we have in many markets and industries is a form of *competitive chaos*. Figure 4.1 shows a competitive business environment which is permanently fluid and unpredictable. For example, British Telecom (BT) continues to face competition from cheap phone call and Internet service providers as well as demands that it provides free access to its network. The impact of this is that telephony revenues are falling at around £500 million per year as business drifts to both fixed line rivals and mobile companies. In the UK with its broadband services BT must adapt and respond to defend its place in the market, or eventually the government will force regulatory change on them on a weakened business. The BT plan is to introduce to 40 per cent of UK homes by 2012, a broadband speed of 100Mbps a ten-fold increase on its current best offering. Case 4.1 shows how one competitor, Mattel, reacted to a serious competitive threat.

It is important to differentiate between two sets of similar, but nevertheless different, decisions. First, some actions are innovatory and represent one competitor acting upon a perceived opportunity ahead of its rivals; other actions constitute reactions to these competitive initiatives. Second, some decisions imply incremental strategic change to existing, intended strategies; on different occasions companies are adapting their strategies (**adaptive strategic change**) as they see new opportunities which they can seize early, or possible future threats which they are seeking to avoid. The process is about *learning and flexibility*. Often, as shown in Chapter 9, they involve an *intrapreneur*, an internal entrepreneur.

The skills required by organizations are:

- the ability to discern patterns in this dynamic environment and competitive chaos, and spot opportunities ahead of their rivals

- the ability to anticipate competitor actions and reactions

- the ability to use this intelligence and insight to lead customer opinion and outperform competitors.

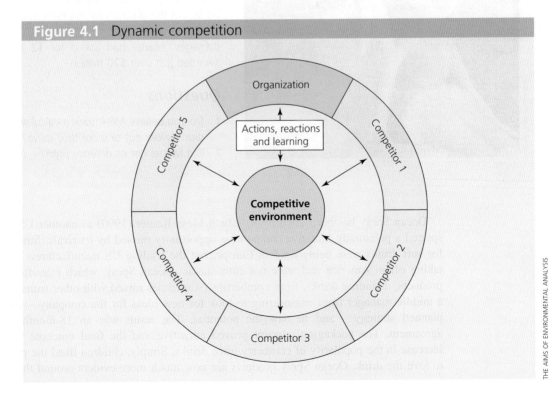

Figure 4.1 Dynamic competition

Case 4.1

Barbie and Mattel

US Int

Barbie dolls were launched in 1959 and they have enjoyed constant popularity with young girls. People can buy multiple outfits for the same doll but there are also special collector's editions with distinctive outfits. They are manufactured by leading toy maker, Mattel, which is based in California. The dolls are 11.5 inches tall and the idea came to designer Ruth Handler when she saw her daughter imagining paper dolls in grown up roles.

In 2001 MGA Entertainment, also based in Los Angeles, launched a rival product, Bratz. The 10 inch tall Bratz doll features racier outfits – it is more 'urban fashion' than Barbie – and facially she is different. She has accentuated lips and, with a relatively large head, has more of a cartoon appearance. The inspiration came from 'children walking home from school and the cover of a Dixie Chicks album'. But MGA sold 150 million dolls in six years and was becoming a real threat to Barbie's market leadership.

Mattel then sued MGA and claimed the designer, Carter Bryant, had come up with the designs whilst he was employed by Mattel, who were entitled to his designs through the terms of his contract. MGA countered that Bryant had come up with the idea in the time between two contracts with Mattel. One might speculate Mattel would not be interested in launching a new doll that might threaten sales of Barbie and so any real interest in developing the designs was always likely to be with a competitor. Mattel had in fact launched a new doll to try and affect the popularity of Bratz, but the doll had by this time established herself.

Mattel won the case and multi-million dollar damages. Mattel had asked for $2 billion but was awarded just over $20 million.

© HUGH THRELFALL/ALAMY

Questions

1 Do you believe MGA took a calculated risk that didn't work out or were they naïve?
2 Did Mattel get its defence right?

Ocean Spray has been cited by Rosabeth Moss Kanter (1990) as another US company which spotted a potentially lucrative competitive opportunity missed by its rivals. Small 'paper bottles' for soft drinks were being used in Europe, but the leading US manufacturers did not see them taking off in America and were not enthusiastic. Ocean Spray, which manufactures a range of products, including drinks, from cranberries (sometimes mixed with other fruits) had empowered a middle manager from engineering to look for new ideas for the company – an aspect of their planned strategy – and he saw the potential. The result was an 18-month exclusive rights agreement. The packaging concept proved attractive and the final outcome was a substantial increase in the popularity of cranberry juice drinks. Simply, children liked the package and came to love the drink. Ocean Spray products are now much more evident around the world.

The Ocean Spray example illustrates how competition can come from unexpected sources. It is dangerous for any organization to assume that future competitive threats will only come from rivals, products and services that they already know and understand; in reality, it can be the unrecognized, unexpected newcomers which pose the real threat because, in an attempt to break into an established market, they may introduce some new way of adding value and 'rewrite the rules of competition'.

Bill Gates' view of the future, based on personal computers on every desk, was radically different from that of long-time industry leader, IBM, and it enabled Microsoft to enter and dominate the computer industry. British Airways was surprised by the entry and success of Virgin Atlantic Airways on profitable transatlantic routes, as it perceived its main competition to come from the leading US carriers. Virgin was adding new values, offering high and differentiated levels of service at very competitive prices. The success of Direct Line, with telephone insurance services at very competitive prices, has provoked a response from existing companies and has seen the creation of a whole new phenomenon, that of price comparison websites, forcing Direct Line to change its pricing offer. In both cases the nature of the service has been changed dramatically, and improved for many customers.

Figure 4.2 shows how organizational resources need to be used to drive the competitive cycle. Constant, or ideally growing, sales and market share can lead to economies of scale and learning and, in turn, cost reductions and improved profits. The profits could, in a particularly competitive situation, be passed back to customers in the form of lower prices, but more normally they will be

Figure 4.2 The competitive cycle

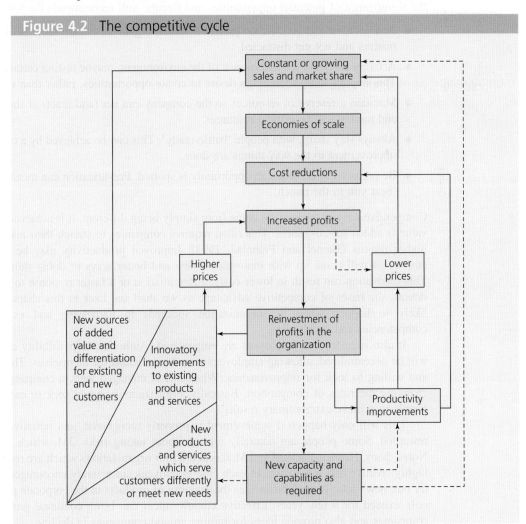

reinvested in the organization. This can generate productivity improvements, sometimes with new capacity and, then, lower prices and/or further cost reductions.

The investment can also bring about new sources of added value and differentiation, possibly allowing higher prices and further profit growth. The improved competitiveness should also increase sales and market share and drive the cycle round again. These changes might take the form of gradual, continuous improvements or radical changes to establish new rules of competition.

In this regard the market for DVD players has shown both dramatic growth and massive price reductions. When first introduced, a DVD player was a premium item. Now they are being sold in supermarkets for a fraction of the initial entry price.

The future, of course, is uncertain. What is popular today may not be popular tomorrow. Tomorrow's competitors may be different from today's. Sull (2006) points out that all organizations competing in an industry, as well as those thinking of entering the industry, have the opportunity to look for trends and signals and search for competitive opportunities. Why do some spot genuine opportunities whilst others fail to appreciate the significance of emerging threats? Part of the answer lies in the ability to make sense of events and to interpret the data and information available.

Sull contends the winners are 'actively waiting'. They (a) *anticipate* – maybe using scenarios – and (b) *prepare* for opportunities and threats that they can neither fully predict nor control. They remain vigilant and prepared. But, of course, they still need to be able to (c) *screen and evaluate* the significance of potential opportunities and threats. Sull recommends the following:

- Stay focused and be clear on priorities – then organizations are more likely to spot what matters and not get distracted

- Actively carry out reconnaissance of the environment, maybe testing certain projected ideas. This implies innovation and a desire to create opportunities, rather than rely on reaction.

- Maintain a reserve of resources so the company can act (and react) at short notice. People and money will be critical resources.

- Always stay sharp, with people 'battle-ready'. This can be achieved by a constant search for improvement in the way things are done.

- Be prepared to act when an opportunity is spotted. Prevarication can mean a competitor can 'beat you to the punch'.

Competitive advantage does not come from simply being different. It is achieved if and when real value is added for customers. This often requires companies to stretch their resources to achieve higher returns (Hamel and Prahalad, 1993). Improved productivity may be involved; ideally employees will come up with innovations, new and better ways of doing things for customers. This innovation can result in lower costs, differentiation or a faster response to opportunities and threats, the bases of competitive advantage as we shall see later in this chapter; and it is most likely to happen when the organization succeeds in harnessing and exploiting its core competencies and capabilities.

It also requires that employees are empowered. Authority, responsibility and accountability will be decentralized, allowing employees to make decisions for themselves. They should be able and willing to look for improvements. When this is managed well, a company may succeed in changing the rules of competition. Basically, organizations should seek to encourage 'ordinary people to achieve extraordinary results'.

This will only happen if achievement is properly recognized, and initiative and success are rewarded. Some people are naturally reticent about taking risks. 3M, which developed Post-it Notes, Sony, Hewlett-Packard and Motorola are four organizations which are recognized as being highly creative and innovative. In each case employees are actively encouraged to look for, and try out, new ideas. In such businesses the majority of products in the corporate portfolio will have only existed for a few years. Effective empowerment can bring continual growth to successful companies and also provide ideas for turning around companies in decline.

Competitive advantage is also facilitated by good internal and external communications, achieving one of the potential benefits of linkages. Without this businesses cannot share and *learn* best practice. Moreover, information is a fundamental aspect of organizational control. Companies can learn from suppliers, from distributors, from customers, from other members of a large organization, and from competitors.

Companies should never overlook opportunities for communicating their achievements, strengths and successes. Image and reputation are vitally important, as they help to retain business.

Competitive themes and frameworks

Ohmae (1982) contends that business strategy is all about competitive advantage. He argues that without competitors there would be no need for strategy, for the sole purpose of strategic management is to enable the company to gain, as effectively as possible, a sustainable edge over its competitors – to alter a company's strength relative to that of its competitors in the most efficient way. Actions affecting the health of a business (value engineering or improved cash flow which improve profitability) widen the range of alternative strategies that the company may choose to adopt *vis-à-vis* its competitors.

A good strategy is one by which a company can gain significant ground on its competitors at an acceptable cost to itself. There are basically four ways:

- Identify the key success factors in an industry and concentrate resources in a particular area where the company sees an opportunity to gain the most significant strategic advantage over its competitors.
- Exploit any area where a company enjoys relative superiority. This could include using technology or the sales network developed elsewhere in the organization for other products or services.
- Aggressively attempt to change the key success factors by challenging the accepted assumptions concerning the ways in which business is conducted in the industry or market.
- Innovate: open up new markets or develop new products.

The principal concern is to avoid doing the same thing, on the same battleground, as the competition. The aim is to attain a competitive situation in which a company can

- gain a relative advantage through measures that its competitors will find hard to follow, and
- extend that advantage further.

Ohmae offers a framework for studying competitive advantage; he focuses on three Cs: customers, competitors and the corporation.

- *Customers* will ultimately decide whether or not the business is successful by buying or not buying the product or service. However, customers cannot be treated *en masse*. Specific preferences should be sought and targeted. Products should be differentiated to appeal to defined market segments.
- *Competitors* will similarly differentiate their products, goods and services, and again incur costs in doing so. Competition can be based on price, image, reputation, proven quality, particular performance characteristics, distribution or after-sales service, for example.
- *Corporations* are organized around particular functions (production, marketing, etc.). The way that they are structured and managed determines the cost of the product or service.

There are opportunities to create competitive advantage in several areas of business, such as product design, packaging, delivery, service and customizing. Such opportunities achieve differentiation, but they can increase costs. Costs must be related to the price that customers are willing to pay for the particular product, based to some extent upon how they perceive its qualities, again in relation to competitors.

Strategic success, in the end, requires a clear understanding of the needs of the market, especially its segments, and the satisfaction of targeting customers more effectively and more profitably than by competitors.

According to Michael Porter (1980), the author most associated with competitive advantage, effective strategic management is the positioning of an organization, relative to its competitors, in such a way that it outperforms them. Marketing, operations and personnel, in fact all aspects of the business, are capable of providing a competitive edge – an advantage which leads to superior performance and superior profits for profit-orientated firms.

Two aspects of the current position of an organization are important:

- the nature and structure of the industry and

- the position of the organization within the industry.

1 The number of firms, their sizes and relative power, the ways they compete, and the rate of growth must be considered. An industry may be attractive or unattractive for an organization. This will depend on the prospects for the industry and what it can offer in terms of profit potential and growth potential. Different organizations have different objectives, and therefore where it is able an organization should be looking to compete in industries where it is able to achieve its objectives. In turn, its objectives and strategies are influenced by the nature of the industries in which it does compete. Porter (1980) has developed a model for analysing the structure of an industry, which we discussed in Chapter 2. The flow chart illustrated in Figure 4.3 reinforces the basic principles.

2 The position of a firm involves its size and market share, how it competes, whether it enjoys specific and recognized competitive advantage, and whether it has particular appeal to selected segments of the market. The extent of any differentiation, which is discussed below, is crucial here.

An effective and superior organization will be in the right industry and in the right position within that industry. Size can matter, as we see in Figure 4.4. The largest of the mainstream competitors, as long as it is run effectively and efficiently, will be able to enjoy superior margins in comparison to its nearest rivals because it can generate scale economies. However, at the other end of the scale, the small competitor with a very carefully defended niche can also enjoy superior margins.

An organization is unlikely to be successful if it chooses to compete in a particular industry because it is an attractive industry which offers both profit and growth potential but is one for which the organization has no means of obtaining competitive advantage. Equally, a company should not concentrate only on creating competitive advantage without assessing the prospects for the industry. With competitive advantage a company can be profitable in an unattractive industry, but there may be very few growth opportunities if the industry is growing at a slower rate than the economy generally. Much depends on objectives and expectations.

- Markets, except truly global ones, almost always have three full-line suppliers

- Competition between no. 1 and no. 2 always impacts negatively on no. 3

- Size matters …!

In the economy profit is the reward for creating value for consumers; and in individual businesses profits are earned by being more successful than competitors in creating and delivering that value. Profit may or may not be an end in itself, but profits are important for achieving other objectives and for helping to finance growth. The profit remaining after interest and tax can be paid in dividends or reinvested in the firm (an issue explained later in Chapter 7). A firm will be healthier in the long run if it can invest as it wishes and finance the investments without building up too substantial a debt. In the same way, a not-for-profit organization may not have a profit-orientated mission, but it must generate revenue to stay viable and a surplus over expenditure to develop the organization.

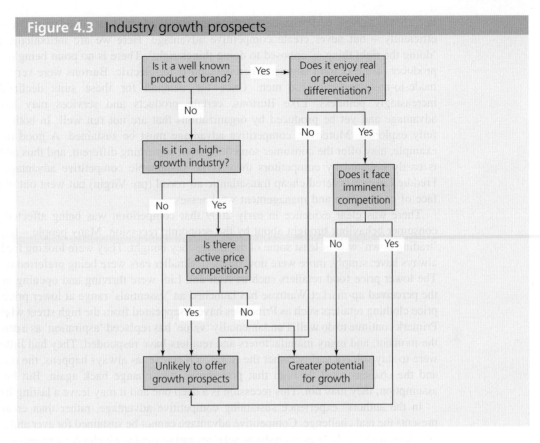

Figure 4.3 Industry growth prospects

The most successful competitors will:

- create value
- create competitive advantage in delivering that value and
- operate the business effectively and efficiently.

Figure 4.4 Market share and profit margin

(DEVELOPED FROM IDEAS PROVIDED BY GEORGE BUCKLEY, WHEN CEO, BRUNSWICK CORPORATION)

For above-average performance all three are required. It is possible to run a business well – efficiently – but never create competitive advantage. Here we are introducing the concept of 'doing the right thing as opposed to doing things right'. There is no point being the most efficient producer of diesel train engines when demand is for electric. Burtons were very good at making made-to-measure suits for men. Once the demand for these suits declined this became increasingly pointless. Like Burtons, certain products and services may have competitive advantage and yet be produced by organizations that are not run well. In both, potential is not fully exploited. Moreover, competitive advantage must be sustained. A good new product, for example, may offer the consumer something new, something different, and thus add value; but if it is easily imitated by competitors there is no sustainable competitive advantage. For example, Freddie Laker pioneered cheap transatlantic air travel (pre Virgin) but went out of business in the face of competition and management weaknesses.

There was clear evidence in early 2009 that competition was being affected by changes in consumer behaviour brought about by the economic recession. Many people – but not all – were 'trading down' with at least some of the things they bought. They were looking for bargains. Some always have; simply, more were now doing it. Smaller cars were being preferred to 'gas guzzlers'. The lower price food retailers such as Aldi and Lidl were thriving and opening new stores; even the perceived up-market Waitrose has launched an 'essentials' range at lower price points. Higher price clothing retailers such as Principles have disappeared from the high street whilst Matalan and Primark continue to do well. Fundamentally 'value' has replaced 'aspiration' as a driver – at least for the moment, and many manufacturers and retailers have responded. They had little choice if they were to stay solvent and 'weather the storm'. Of course, as always happens, the recession will end and the chances must be high that preferences will change back again. But herein lies a key assumption; they may not. This recession is a deep one and it may leave a lasting legacy.

In the authors' experience sustaining competitive advantage, rather than creating it initially, presents the real challenge. Competitive advantage cannot be sustained for ever and probably not for very long without changes in products, services and strategies which take account of market demand, market saturation and competitor activity. People's tastes change, the size of markets is limited not infinite, and competitors will seek to imitate successful products, services and strategies. Competitive advantage can be sustained by constant innovation. Companies that are change orientated and seek to stay ahead of their competitors through innovatory ideas develop new forms of advantage. Case 4.3 later considers how Coca-Cola retains global leadership of the soft drinks market.

Heller (1998) has suggested that organizations which sustain competitive advantage over time will be addressing seven questions effectively:

1 Are we supplying the 'right' things?

2 Are we doing it in the most effective way?

3 And at the lowest possible economic cost?

4 Are we as good as – and ideally better than – our strongest competitor?

5 Are we targeting and serving the widest possible market?

6 Do we have a unique selling proposition – something which will persuade customers to buy from us rather than anyone else?

7 Are we innovating to make sure the answer to all these questions will remain 'yes'?

Differentiation and market segmentation

A product or service is said to be differentiated if consumers perceive it to have properties which make it distinct from rival products or services, and ideally unique in some particular way. Differentiation is most beneficial when consumers value the cause of the difference and will pay a premium price to obtain it, and where competitors are unable to emulate it.

Differentiation recognizes that customers are too numerous and widely scattered, and with heterogeneous needs and adequate spending power, for them all to prefer exactly the same product or service. Hence competitors will distinguish their brand, product or service in some way, perhaps size, quality or style, to give it greater appeal for certain customers. Those customers who value the difference will be willing to pay a premium price for it and ideally buy it consistently in preference to the alternatives.

Consequently, effective organizations will be both customer-driven (responsive) and customer-driving (innovative).

Sources of differentiation

- *Speed* – Companies such as Amazon compete on their speed of service using courier businesses who are successful because of the speed at which they can move items.

- *Reliability* – Consistent quality and the ability to keep promises: providing what customers want, where, when and how. One example is McDonald's.

- *Service* – Adding extra values to augment the service and thereby satisfy customers. Staff in certain hotels illustrate this point; some years ago Xerox provided a new level of service by incorporating a self-diagnostic computer chip in its copying machines.

- *Design* – both in the product itself (Bang and Olufsen hi-fi equipment, for instance) and in its reparability. This also relates to:

- *Features* – such as cordless irons, kettles and drills. The balance, though, is critical; some products such as DVD recorders now have too many features for most customers.

- *Technology* – which, say, led to the development of laser printers.

- *Corporate personality.* There is a value in certain corporate names and images, such as the Body Shop and Apple.

- *Relationships with customers* – through effective supply-chain management.

The differentiation need not be clearly tangible as long as customers believe that it exists.

Where specific groups of customers with broadly similar needs can be identified and targeted they are known as market segments, and often products and services are differentiated to appeal to specific segments. The segmentation might be based on ages, socio-economic groups, lifestyle, income, benefits sought or usage rate for consumer markets, and size of buyer and reasons for buying in the case of industrial markets. To be viable the segment must be clearly identifiable, separated from other segments, easily reached with advertising and large enough to be profitable. Given these factors and a differentiated product, prices, distribution and advertising can all be targeted specifically at the segment.

Successful differentiation and segmentation require that products and services are clearly positioned. Toyota, for example, wanted to appeal to the lucrative executive market with a car that offered the 'ultimate in quality' and succeeded against BMW, Mercedes and Volvo. The car needed to be differentiated from the main Toyota brand and consequently it was named Lexus. It now has a brand niche status all of its own.

4.2 Competitive strategy

As far as customers are concerned, the link between price and perceived quality must make sense. Products and services should be neither overpriced (resulting in a loss of goodwill and often lost business) nor underpriced. In this latter case, potential profits must be lost and, perversely, orders may be lost as well – people may become suspicious of the unexpectedly low price and begin to question their perception of the relative quality. Companies must, therefore, also be realistic about customer perception of the relative quality of their products and services and neither overestimate nor underestimate the situation. Companies may think, or wish to believe, that they are 'the best'; customers may disagree.

Figure 4.5 offers a simple matrix of competitive strategies developed from this reasoning.

Porter (1985) developed his earlier work on industry analysis to examine how a company might compete in the industry in order to create and sustain a position of strength. In simple terms, he argued, there are two basic parameters:

- Parameter 1. A company can seek to compete:
  by achieving lower costs than its rivals and, by charging comparable prices for its products or services, creating a superior position through superior profitability, or through differentiation, adding value in an area that the customer regards as important, charging a premium price, and again creating a superior position through superior profitability.

- Parameter 2. The arena in which the company seeks to compete can be a broad range of segments or a narrow range, perhaps just one.

These arguments led to Porter's valuable model of generic strategies, which is discussed below. It also focused attention on the relevance of differentiation, adding value and cost management for helping to create – and sustain – competitive advantage. It is important, first, to appreciate that the generic strategy framework is a reflection of current (or targeted) positioning, and that competitive advantage is by nature a relative (to other competitors) and dynamic notion. Second, as mentioned briefly before, it is essential to realize that competitive strategy and competitive advantage, although clearly linked, are not one and the same. Competitive strategy concerns the way in which organizations choose to compete and position themselves – competitive advantage may or may not be an outcome of this. To achieve true advantage an organization must find opportunities to be different in ways which are meaningful for customers. The activities which create the position are the key to advantage. Witness the success of Apple with what are expensive laptop and notebook computers but considered highly desirable at the same time.

Generic competitive strategies

Porter's two parameters, then, lead to the three generic strategies illustrated in Figure 4.6a. **Cost leadership** is where the company achieves lower costs than its rivals and competes across a broad range of segments. **Differentiation** occurs when the company has a range of clearly differentiated products which appeal to different segments of the market. Focus strategies are where a company

Figure 4.5 Simple competitive strategy matrix

(BASED ON AN IDEA FOUND ON THE ABRAM HAWKES PLC WEBSITE)

Figure 4.6a Porter's model of generic strategies

Figure 4.6a Porter's model of generic strategies

(ADAPTED WITH THE PERMISSION OF SIMON AND SCHUSTER FROM PORTER, ME (1985) COMPETITIVE ADVANTAGE: CREATING AND SUSTAINING SUPERIOR PERFORMANCE, FREE PRESS)

chooses to concentrate on only one segment or a limited range of segments. With this approach it can again seek either lower costs or differentiation.

Before considering these generic strategies in greater detail it is useful to apply them to particular industries. Porter argues that in the motor vehicle industry (Figure 4.6b) Toyota became the overall cost leader. The company remains successful in a number of segments with a full range of cars, and its mission is to be a low-cost producer. Case 4.2 outlines Toyota's competitive strategy. In contrast, General Motors (GM) also competes in most segments of the market but seeks to differentiate each of its products with superior styling and features. GM also offers a wider choice of models for each car in its range. The problem for GM is that its cost of production is not in line with its overseas rivals.

Hyundai became successful around the world with a restricted range of small- and medium-size cars which it produced at relatively low cost and priced competitively. It should be noted that neither Toyota nor Hyundai markets the *cheapest* cars available. BMW and Mercedes have both succeeded historically by producing a narrow line of more exclusive cars for the price-insensitive, quality-conscious customer. Both companies have widened their ranges in recent years without fundamentally changing their basic strategy. There are several cars available from both companies but they are clearly targeted at people who are willing to pay premium prices for perceived higher quality. Mazda was similarly successful with a narrow and sporty range.

It is never going to be easy to identify who the true cost leader is in any industry or segment. To ascertain this we need accurate information on gross margins and profitability

Figure 4.6b Porter's model of generic strategies applied to the world motor industry

Figure 4.6b Porter's model of generic strategies applied to the world motor industry

(ADAPTED WITH THE PERMISSION OF SIMON AND SCHUSTER FROM PORTER, ME (1985) COMPETITIVE ADVANTAGE: CREATING AND SUSTAINING SUPERIOR PERFORMANCE, FREE PRESS)

Case 4.2

Toyota's Cost Leadership Strategy   Int

SOURCE: THIS CASE STUDY WAS PREPARED USING PRIMARILY PUBLICLY AVAILABLE SOURCES OF INFORMATION FOR THE PURPOSES OF CLASSROOM DISCUSSION; IT DOES NOT INTEND TO ILLUSTRATE EITHER EFFECTIVE OR INEFFECTIVE HANDLING OF A MANAGERIAL SITUATION.

- Toyota historically has enjoyed a 40 per cent plus market share in Japan, supplemented by a growing percentage of the US and European markets (where it also manufactures) – Toyota followed Nissan in manufacturing in the UK. This strategy is clearly long-term as it took Toyota seventeen years (1989 – 2006) to become profitable in the UK.
- Toyota has focused on organic growth and avoided the acquisition and alliance strategies of its major rivals. It has invested in local plants in key countries around the world. Its European plants, however, are less profitable than those in the US and Japan.
- Toyota has sought to sell a range of cars at prices marginally below those of comparable Ford and General Motors cars. Historically Ford and GM have both sold more cars than Toyota worldwide. Toyota overtook Ford in 2006 and was 'neck-and-neck' with GM. However, Toyota's operating profits have exceeded those of its rivals because it has ruthlessly controlled its costs.
- Production systems, based on JIT (just-in-time supply of components), are very efficient. Toyota claims fewer defects than any other manufacturer, resulting from the vigilance of each worker on the assembly lines. The Lexus range of top-quality cars requires one-sixth of the labour hours used to build a Mercedes. During the mid-1990s the best Toyota plant was assembling a car in 13 person-hours, whereas Ford, Honda and Nissan all required 20. Its sophisticated assembly techniques eliminate waste at every stage and are driven by strong just-in-time delivery systems.
- 'Toyota does not indulge in expensive executive facilities'.
- Toyota also spends 5 per cent of sales revenue on research and development (as high as any major competitor), concentrating on a search for continuous improvements 'to inch apart from competitors', rather than major breakthroughs.
- Continuous improvement is a 'way-of-life' as Toyota strives to ensure its costs are always below the prices customers are willing to pay.
- There is a policy of fast new model development. In the 1990s Toyota models had an average age of

two years; Ford and GM cars averaged five years. Many cars tend to be a refinement of previous models rather than revolutionary designs. Some would argue this implies many Toyota cars lack passion, of course.

Revenues began to fall back in 1995. Sales of Toyota's new, revamped version of its best-selling Corolla saloon were disappointing. 'In its hot pursuit of cost savings, Toyota had produced a car that lacks character'. Overall cost leaders, slicing through the competitive middle market, must still produce distinctive, differentiated products to justify their near-market-average pricing policy. More recently Toyota has launched the Yaris, which has received wide acclaim. In addition, the growing popularity of four-wheel drive recreational vehicles affected saloon car sales, but Toyota responded with its own models, especially the popular Rav 4. Toyota is an established world-leader in hybrid cars with its successful Prius car; and it has started to manufacture and sell pick-up trucks in America. Its Tundra brand has begun to take market share in this critically important segment.

Chairman Hiroshi Okuda describes Toyota as a 'clever engineer that is quick to spot consumer trends and which captures customers with high quality products'.

But is there a danger in growing quickly? In 2007 some commentators questioned this when Toyota was involved in a series of product recalls. It was experiencing quality problems – whilst the number of incidences was not excessive in industry terms it was still unusual for Toyota. The Japanese plants remained the quality leaders but Honda and Subaru were beating Toyota in quality surveys.

Question

1 What do you believe the competitive position of Toyota to be now?
   (To answer this it would be useful to look at the margin and profitability figures for the leading manufacturers.)

TOYOTA **http://www.toyota.com**

together with an acceptance of the relevant segment boundaries. We can, nevertheless, make educated guesses.

Applying the same ideas to credit cards, it is quickly and readily appreciated that Barclaycard, by offering both Visa and Mastercard credit cards, together with platinum, gold and special business versions, is differentiated and covers most segments of the market. American Express, and the increasingly popular affinity cards, such as those linked to football clubs, are focused differentiators because they concentrate on identifiable interest groups. Some would argue that MBNA, because of its international coverage and strategy of persuading other cardholders to transfer, has become the overall cost leader. Egg, linked to Prudential's competitive but niched banking activity, is following a strategy of focused cost leadership. It may well end up part of the MBNA stable.

In retailing Wal-Mart is clearly the global cost leader. Tesco and Marks and Spencer both follow differentiation strategies, albeit with a different underlying promise. Toys R Us and Aldi adopt quite different cost focus strategies whereas Matalan and Harvey Nicholls pursue radically different differentiation focus strategies.

The cost leadership strategy

To achieve substantial rewards from this strategy Porter argues that the organization must be *the* cost leader, and unchallenged in this position. There is room for only one; and if there is competition for market leadership based on this strategy there will be price competition.

Cost leadership as a generic strategy does not imply that the company will market the lowest price product or service in the industry. Quite often the lowest price products are perceived as inferior, and as such appeal to only a proportion of the market. Consequently, low price related to lower quality is a differentiation strategy. Low cost therefore does not necessarily mean 'cheap' and low-cost companies can have up-market rather than down-market appeal. Equally, low cost does not imply lower rewards for employees or other stakeholders, as successful cost leaders can be very profitable. Their aim is to secure a cost advantage over their rivals, price competitively and relative to how their product is perceived by customers, and achieve a high profit margin. Where this applies across a broad range of segments turnover and market share should also be high for the industry. They are seeking above-average profits with industry-average prices.

Cost focus strategies can be based on finding a distinct group of customers whose needs are slightly below average. Costs are saved by meeting their needs specifically and avoiding unnecessary additional costs.

Figure 4.7 illustrates the above points and relates the generic strategies to efficiency and effectiveness.

There is little advantage in being only one of a number of low-cost producers. The advantage is gained by superior management, concentrating on cost-saving opportunities, minimizing waste, and not adding values which customers regard as unimportant to the product or service – many products do have values added which are not regarded as necessary by the market. Cost savings can generally be achieved in any and every area of the business, and quite often they begin with the strategic leader. Senior executives who enjoy substantial perks are unlikely to pursue a cost leadership strategy. Porter suggests that it is a mistake to believe that cost savings are only possible in the manufacturing function and that this strategy is only applicable to the largest producers in an industry. However, where cost leadership generates market share and volume production opportunities, economies of scale in manufacturing do apply. Organizations which are able to exploit the potential benefits of the learning or experience curve can use this to help create a cost advantage. This is explored in greater detail in an appendix to this chapter.

The differentiation strategy

Cost leadership is usually traded off against differentiation, with the two regarded as pulling in opposite directions. Differentiation adds costs in order to add value for which customers are

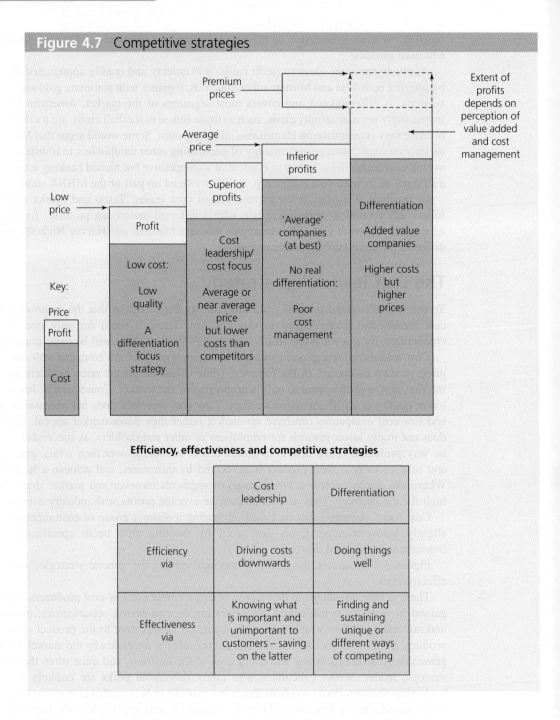

Figure 4.7   Competitive strategies

willing to pay premium prices. For a differentiation **focus strategy** to be successful the market must be capable of clear segmentation, and the requirements for this were highlighted earlier.

With differentiation superior performance is achieved by serving customer needs differently, ideally uniquely. The more unique the difference, the more sustainable is any advantage which accrues. Differentiation must inevitably add costs, which can only be recouped if the market is willing to pay the necessary premium prices. It is crucial that costs are only added in areas that customers perceive as important, and again this can relate to any area of the operation. A solicitors' practice, for example, might find competitive advantage in the manner and promptness with which customer queries are dealt, both over the telephone and in person. A fuller list might include the following possibilities:

- quality of materials used (related to purchasing)
- superior performance (design)
- high quality (production; inspection)
- superior packaging (distribution)
- delivery (sales; production)
- prompt answer of queries (customer relations; sales)
- efficient paperwork (administration).

Furthermore, it is insufficient merely to add value; customers must recognize and appreciate the difference.

The differentiation strategy can be easily misjudged, however, for a number of reasons, including:

- by choosing something that buyers fail to recognize, appreciate or value
- by over-fulfilling needs and as a consequence failing to achieve cost-effectiveness
- by selecting something that competitors can either improve on or undercut
- by attempting to overcharge for the differentiation
- by thinking too narrowly, missing opportunities and being outflanked by competitors.

Case 4.3 illustrates four distinct differentiation strategies.

Case 4.3

Four Differentiation Strategies   Int

BMW, Miele, Bang & Olufsen and James Purdey

BMW

BMW follows a number of strategies designed to protect its market niche, especially from Japanese competition. Notably, these cover both the cars and the overall service package provided by BMW for its customers.

- Cars can be tailored and customized substantially. Customers can choose any colour they want, a benefit normally restricted to Rolls Royce and Aston Martin; and there is a wide range of interior options and 'performance extras'.
- Safety, environment, economy and comfort are featured and stressed in every model.
- National BMW sales companies are wholly owned, together with strategically located parts warehouses. The independent distributors place their orders directly into BMW's central computer.

- There are fleets of specially equipped cars to assist BMW motorists who break down.
- In 1994 BMW became the first European car manufacturer to produce in the USA.
- Historically, BMW chose to ignore sports cars and hatchbacks, which it saw as downmarket from luxury saloon cars. However, market trends and preferences brought a change of heart. The 1994 BMW Compact was launched as a hatchback version of the successful 3-series; a BMW sports model was used for the James Bond film *Goldeneye*.

The acquisition of Rover gave BMW a range of successful, smaller hatchbacks, along with Land Rover recreational and multipurpose vehicles. But the two companies, with their very different histories and cultures, were not easily integrated. In 2000 Rover was bought back by a financial consortium and Land Rover was sold to Ford.

When BMW divested Rover it retained the rights to the Mini, which it has redeisgned and successfully relaunched. It is quite normal for demand to exceed supply, such that there is a waiting list for new models. It is significant that, although they may be adjacent on the same site, mainstream BMW and Mini models are typically sold from separate showrooms.

BMW **http://www.bmw.com**

Miele

The German company Miele is a global leader in high quality domestic appliances – washing machines, vacuum cleaners and dishwashers. The business was formed in 1900 and it is still run by two great-grandsons of the founding partners. Around 90 per cent of the sales are in Europe, where the company has a 6 per cent market share. The other 10 per cent come from America. It does not look to compete on price – indeed the prices of a Miele can be up to 70 per cent higher than some rival branded products. The brand stands for quality. The typical life of a Miele machine is 20 years, and the company enjoys a tradition of loyal customers and repeat purchases.

Most of the products are manufactured in Germany, regarded as a relatively high wage country. Miele even manufactures its own motors at a plant near Cologne. However, as a result of the German recession at the end of the 1990s/early 2000s, Miele has established a small production plant in the Czech Republic – where wages are one quarter of those it is paying in Germany. It already had one plant in Austria and a joint venture in China. Some 12 per cent of revenues are re-invested in product development, a figure much higher than the industry average. The company has around 700 different patents to protect its designs. There is a strategy of rigorous and lengthy product testing.

Innovation is simply seen as routine and significant. The drums in large front-loading washing machines, for example, have some 4000 holes for letting the water in and out. Miele reduced this to 700 without reducing performance, thus making the drums both stronger and easier to manufacture at the same time. Interesting Miele has not copied the principle of the Dyson vacuum cleaner – it continues to believe bags are superior.

Bang & Olufsen

Now 80 years old, Bang & Olufsen is a Danish manufacturer of hi-fi equipment and televisions, which enjoys an elite reputation and status worldwide for the quality of its products. Its customers tend to be very loyal.

The company has adopted sleek, tasteful designs, clever technologies and high standards of manufacture for many years. During the 1980s its performance deteriorated because it was seen as too much of a niche competitor. As a response, ranges of slightly less expensive – but still exceptionally high-quality – products were launched. From this a new philosophy has emerged – that the products are about lifestyle and technical excellence is more of a 'given'.

Company advertising uses the slogan 'a life less ordinary' to suggest that 'distinctiveness is a value in itself'.

Bang & Olufsen never asks its customers about future designs and products. Instead, its 'free thinking designers plant their ideas in the marketplace'. The company sees itself as a fashion leader. In addition, the company is very concerned to maintain control over who retails its products and how they are displayed in stores.

The company's niche must be potentially under threat if its rivals are able to improve the quality and reliability of their designs and exploit the manufacturing competencies of lower-cost labour countries. However, it is probably the case that only poor decision making by Bang & Olufsen can threaten their niche.

BANG AND OLUFSEN
http://www.bang-olufsen.com

James Purdey

Purdey firearms would be classified as a super-luxury product; they retail at 'prices more normally associated with small houses'. The company manufactures something in the order of 60 guns per year, over 85 per cent of which are sold abroad. America and, in recent years, Russia are the main markets. Purdey is an iconic up-market British brand but the company is now Swiss-owned.

There is close attention to detail, and quality control is incredibly tight. Every order is perceived as a special; nothing is seen as standard. The Turkish walnut stocks are polished several times in linseed oil and beeswax rather than varnished in what is a lengthy, labour-intensive process; and buyers can choose almost any special, idiosyncratic feature as long as they are happy to pay the appropriate premium. It takes some 650 hours to make a basic side-by-side 12 bore rifle and 750 hours to make the more complicated 'up and under' where the barrels are one above the other. The basic prices of these hover below and above £50,000 respectively for each rifle. Once refinements and customizing are factored in the bill for a pair (they are always sold in pairs) will be in the region of £250,000. Typically, orders are placed two years in advance of delivery.

Because they appeal to a very limited market segment, and because they literally last a lifetime (and frequently longer!), growth potential for James Purdey, without diversification, is clearly limited. Despite the special market position it holds Purdey struggles to make a profit from rifles and in recent years has divested into related outdoor clothing and accessories.

JAMES PURDEY **http://www.purdey.com**

Question

1   To what extent are these companies successfully defending their differentiation focus strategies?

A critique of Porter's generic strategies

Care must be taken not to misunderstand the implications of delineation. Porter has stated that successful organizations will select and concentrate their efforts on effectively implementing one of the generic strategies that he identified; they will avoid being 'stuck in the middle'. However, it does appear that while cost leadership and differentiation may be seen as mutually exclusive, successful strategies can be based on a mix of the two. YKK, the Japanese zip manufacturer and world market leader, achieves both cost leadership and significant differentiation, as we saw in Chapter 3.

Hendry (1990) has suggested that as there can be only one cost leader, cost leadership is not so much a strategy as a position that one company – which is almost certainly differentiated – enjoys. Toyota may be overall cost leader, but it still differentiates all of its cars. There are different models for different market segments, as well as the associated Lexus range. Because it is a position, and because competitors are always likely to be following cost reduction strategies, it can be a very risky and precarious position if other opportunities for adding value are ignored. Simply, cost leadership is based on efficiencies and sound cost management, but being different still matters.

Similarly, differentiation may be concerned with adding value, and therefore costs, but costs must still be managed. We must understand the cost drivers for any business. It is important to incur and add costs only where they can be recouped in the form of premium prices. Yet, where a company is particularly concerned with issues of size and market share it may deliberately choose to charge relatively low prices and not attempt to recover the extra costs it has added in its search to be different. It sacrifices superior profits, at least in the short term while it builds a power base.

Hendry also questions the value of broad and narrow focus, arguing that internal industry boundaries are always changing, enhanced by the speed of technological change. New niches are emerging all the time, such that what appears to be a solid niche can quickly become a tomb.

To summarize, while the ideas of Michael Porter can be questioned and debated, they nevertheless provide an extremely useful framework for analysing industries and competitive strategy. It is important not to take them simply at face value and assume that the idea of generic strategies is the key which unlocks the secret of competitive advantage. They are not prescriptive.

4.3 Competitive advantage and competitive success

So far it has been argued that competitive strategies are *built around* differentiation and cost leadership. Competitive advantage is *reflected in* and accrues from perceived differences and real cost advantages, both of these relative to competitors. Hence, competitive advantage is *dependent upon* strategic positioning, but the two are not the same.

Competitive advantage will normally, at least in the long term, result in superior margins. Table 4.1 shows that any individual functional area, or a combination of several functions, can be the actual source of the advantage.

Porter (1996) later reinforced these points, and attempted to answer some of the criticisms of his generic strategy approach, when he restated that competitive success is based on one of two alternatives. First, an organization can aim to be better than its rivals and focus on operating efficiencies to achieve this. Second, it can seek either to do different things, or to do things differently. This concerns effectiveness, and it relates to strategic positioning. He identified three broad approaches to positioning:

- An organization can focus on a particular product or service – or an identifiable and limited range – and sell it to every customer who is interested. This is the approach favoured by BMW and EasyJet.

- It can, alternatively, target a segmented group and provide a wider range of products which can serve a variety of their needs. This is the IKEA approach.

- Third, it can identify and focus on a carefully defined niche with a single product or service. James Purdey in (Case 4.3) provides an ideal example.

As we saw in the previous chapter, Porter pointed out that it is activities – what the organization actually does both directly and indirectly for its customers, its functional strategies – that create and build value and, in turn, advantage. Together these activities determine the strategic position that an organization enjoys, and competitive advantage comes from the strength of the position. While being able to do something better or differently is essential, the way in which the activities are

Table 4.1 Functional strategies and competitive advantage

Functional strategy	Competitive strategy	
	Low Cost	Differentiation
Marketing	Large companies can obtain media discounts	Image – reinforced by well-known strategic leader
Operations	Efficient plant management and utilization (productivity) Re-engineered processes which reduce costs	Low defect rate and high quality Re-engineered processes which add extra value
Human resources	Training to achieve low rejections and high-quality policies which keep turnover low	Incentives to encourage innovation
Research and development	Reformulated processes which reduce costs	New, patented breakthroughs
Finance	Low-cost loans (improves profit after interest and before tax)	Ability to finance corporate strategic change, investments and acquisitions
Information technology	Faster decision-making in flatter organization structure	Creative use of information to understand customer needs, meet them and outperform competitors
Distribution logistics	Lower stock-holding costs	Alliances with suppliers and/or distributors which are long-term and mutually supportive

This list of examples is indicative only, and not an exhaustive set of possibilities.

combined to generate synergy is also critical. Most individual activities can be copied, but it is much more difficult to replicate what might be a unique combination of activities. Porter (1996) developed activity maps as a way of capturing this.

Consequently, organizations must choose what to do and what not to do, which activities to undertake and which to ignore, and how they might be fused into a powerful mix. Activities that affect the value proposition must not be neglected, but those that have little impact should not consume resources. Critical trade-offs must be made in an attempt to find a unique position. It can be expensive, even self-destructive, to try and do too much and not focus on what does make a difference.

IKEA has chosen to trade-off in a number of ways, for example, it sacrifices being able to offer a wide range of bought-in products by designing and manufacturing its own. By choosing to hold stock in all of its stores and warehouses IKEA sacrifices the low inventory costs some of its competitors enjoy by only delivering against orders. It sacrifices the use of the highest quality materials in favour of function and affordable prices. IKEA also sacrifices sales assistance in favour of self-service; and it opts for only out-of-town locations.

> *Many companies spend a lot of time and money researching customers' views, but most spend nothing like enough on observing competitors. The main reason for change is to keep ahead of competitors or to catch up on the complacent market leaders. Companies must invest in development – it's a case of 'duck or no dinner'.*
>
> SIR SIMON HORNBY, EX-CHAIRMAN, WH SMITH PLC

> *When I'm on a plane, I prowl around and talk to passengers and ask the staff about everything. I normally come back with a hundred notes in my pocket scribbled on little pieces of paper. Direct feedback is far better than market research.*
>
> SIR RICHARD BRANSON, CHAIRMAN, VIRGIN GROUP, QUOTED IN FERRY (1989)

The strategy of Virgin Atlantic Airways is built around quality service and differentiation. Virgin's 'Upper Class' aims to offer a first-class-equivalent service at business-class prices and has provided for a number of years, for example, electrostatic headphones that customers can keep afterwards, a large selection of films to watch on in flight personal players, and chauffeur-driven rides to and from airports.

Sustaining competitive advantage

Few positions are defensible long term against rivals. Competitors will copy good ideas and maybe even improve on them. Change is the key. Competitors, having created a competitive advantage, will stay ahead if they innovate and look for improvements on a continuous basis and, at the same time, look for discontinuous opportunities to effect change on industries and markets. Case 4.4 explores how Coca-Cola has managed to sustain competitive advantage and market leadership.

Figure 4.8 combines a number of the points made here, emphasizing that successful companies create advantage and success by being committed to their customers through careful positioning and managed change. The differences and cost advantages which create a position must be supported by high levels of service in strategy implementation and ideally by a strong reputation and brand, as discussed earlier in Chapter 5.

Figure 4.9 shows that competitive advantage can be rooted in technology, organization and people, but that it is people and people-driven processes that are the real source of *sustained* advantage, because it is these that are most difficult for rivals to copy. People must be convinced that they are important, and that their contribution is valued – logically through an appropriate reward system – as otherwise they may not deliver and improve the all-important service.

Case 4.4

Coca-Cola   Int

Although it is typically priced higher than many competing products, Coca-Cola (Coke) remains the world's best-selling soft drink and the world's best-known (and most valuable) brand name. Coca-Cola is reputed to see its only serious competitor as water! Ideally an adult requires a daily liquid intake of 64 ounces, and overall Coke provides just two of these. The soft drinks industry has been categorized in the following way:

- Refreshment – typical carbonated drinks, such as Coke
- Rejuvenation – ready-to-drink teas and coffees, for example
- Health and nutrition – juices and milk drinks
- Replenishment – bottled water and sports drinks

The Coca-Cola company was founded over 100 years ago, and today it remains largely focused; Columbia Pictures was acquired some years ago, but later sold to Sony. Seventy per cent of Coke's sales and 80 per cent of its operating profits are now earned outside the USA. The company has enjoyed a 50 per cent share of the world market for carbonated drinks, including 44 per cent of the US market. A typical American adult who drinks Coke will consume 400 eight-ounce servings in a year, just over one a day. Because Americans own very large refrigerators which can store the largest bottles available, this can work out relatively inexpensive. By contrast, a regular British Coke drinker consumes 120 eight-ounce servings in a year, often from smaller and more expensive bottles and cans. The UK is still perceived to be a developing market for the product. Other 'established' territories, which include Switzerland, Chile and Mexico, have a consumption of 300 eight-ounce servings per year.

Over the years critics have predicted that something would happen to stem the continual and successful growth of the business, possibly changing tastes, stronger competition or market saturation. This really has not happened; Coca-Cola has continued to increase worldwide sales through clever marketing and occasional new products. In 1996 Coca-Cola was America's most admired company in the Fortune rankings but it has not sustained this position in the late-1990s and early 2000s, although it continues to enjoy high global admiration. In terms of increases in shareholder wealth, Coca-Cola was unrivalled in the USA throughout the leadership of its charismatic chief executive, Roberto Goizueta. Goizueta was the strategic leader from 1981 until his death in post in 1997. Coca-Cola made a number of strategic misjudgements during his time in charge, but overall he was perceived to be a hero in the company's folklore. He kept Coca-Cola strongly focused on Coke when, with hindsight, he should have introduced other drinks – as his competitors were doing.

Competitive strategies

Coke had successfully established Fanta (the fizzy orange drink launched in 1960) and Tab (sugar-free Coca-Cola, 1963) when Goizueta took over. In 1982 Diet Coke was launched. Diet products are particularly important for the American market, but generally less significant elsewhere.

However, in 1985, New Coke was launched to replace the original blending, but subsequently withdrawn after a consumer outcry. It was sweeter and some critics suggested it had been developed because of the increasing popularity of the sweeter Pepsi Cola. One lady Coke fan who lived on the East coast went round all the local stores in her district buying up all their remaining stock of the original blend. Two middle-aged men on the West coast started a society pledged to restore the original taste. Members from across the nation paid to join and the group organized demonstrations. Inevitably there was huge publicity. The company eventually backed down and re-launched the original blend as Coca-Cola Classic. Some time later New Coke was withdrawn. Whilst one might have imagined the company would be damaged, it actually benefited from the enormous publicity it generated. The debacle cost money, but sales increased.

The Fresca range had also been launched. Sprite is another famous Coca-Cola brand, as are Minute Maid fruit juices. Under Goizueta's successor, in 1998, an agreement to buy the Schweppes soft drinks businesses outside the USA from Cadbury's was thwarted by the European regulatory authorities. Coca-Cola has also been affected by economic crises and recessions in countries where it is particularly popular, especially Russia and Asia. In 1999 it was forced to withdraw the product in Belgium after a health scare resulting from minor contamination. Arguably, the company's public relations could have been better. Five years later it had to deal with an even more significant self-imposed crisis. Dasani Water in Europe was exposed as treated tap water and not natural spring water. The company never claimed anything else, but consumer expectations were that it was. It was withdrawn. In the US the product is different; simply the same brand name is used.

In 2001 Coca-Cola formed a joint venture with Procter & Gamble to link its soft drinks with P&G's snacks, such as Pringles. This was really following a strategy developed by PepsiCo. Also in 2001 Coca-Cola allied with Disney to allow it to use Disney characters for promotional purposes. The company has also extended its product ranges into Fruitopia, a 'new age' fruit drink, bottled water (the Dasani brand mentioned) and Lemon and Vanilla Coke.

Coke had really became popular overseas when it was shipped out to GIs during World War II, and systematically it has been introduced to more and more countries. For many years its stated goal was to 'always have Coca-Cola within an arm's reach of desire' and preferably in chilled storage, whether this was on retail shelves or through vending machines. It has benefited from being associated with the image and persona of America. When GIs drank it during World War II – and subsequent wars in Korea and Vietnam – it was seen as a reminder of exactly what they were fighting for. Early in 1999 Coca-Cola's name was linked to a line of fashion and sports clothing, the first significant extension of the brand.

Coca-Cola controls production of the concentrated syrup from Atlanta; mixing, bottling/canning and distribution is franchised to independent businesses worldwide. In truth, the issue of the 'secret formula' is more mystique than necessity, but it provides another valuable story to reinforce the brand and its image. Goizueta inherited a distribution network which was underperforming and he set about strengthening it with proper joint venture agreements and tight controls. Effective supply management is absolutely vital for the business.

Goizueta chose to acquire its smaller, underperforming bottlers, invested in them and, when they were turned around, sold them to stronger anchor bottlers – specifically those with the financial resources to invest in developing the business. 'Coca-Cola's distribution machine is [now] the most powerful and pervasive on the planet.'

Coca-Cola has always advertised heavily and prominently; and Goizueta has also negotiated a number of important promotional agreements. Coca-Cola has special aisles in Wal-Mart stores; Coke's Hi-C orange juice is supplied to McDonald's, for example. In recent years there has been increased emphasis on branding and packaging at the expense of pure advertising. 'We had really lost focus on who our customer was. We felt our customer was the bottler, as opposed to the McDonald's and the Wal-Marts' (Goizueta).

Faced with increased competition from retail own-label brands sold mainly through supermarket chains, Coca-Cola has carefully defended and strengthened its other distribution outlets such as convenience stores, fast-food restaurants and vending machines.

Competitors

Coca-Cola's main rival is Pepsi Cola, which has a 30 per cent share of the US market and 20 per cent of the world market. Its share has been growing since the 1993 introduction of Pepsi Max, a sugar-free product with the taste of the original Pepsi. Pepsi diversified into snack foods (Frito-Lay in the USA, Walkers and Smiths crisps in the UK) and restaurants (Pizza Hut, Taco Bell and Kentucky Fried Chicken in the USA); just one-third of global profits came from soft drinks in the mid-1990s. Pepsi also owns much of its bottling network. In 1996 the Pepsi brand was relaunched with a massive international promotional campaign. The new Pepsi colours, predominantly blue, were chosen to appeal to the younger buyer. In 1997 PepsiCo divested its restaurants into a separate business, and followed this up with the acquisition of the French company, Orangina – after the European competition regulators had prevented Coca-Cola from buying the business. A year later Pepsi acquired Tropicana, the world's largest marketer of branded juices, which it bought from the Canadian company Seagram. With this purchase, Pepsi controlled 40 per cent of the US chilled orange juice market, twice the share of Coca-Cola.

Another significant competitor is Cott of Canada, which produces discounted colas with acceptable alternative tastes. Cott produces concentrate for Wal-Mart in the USA and for Sainsbury and Virgin in the UK.

Renewal

In 2004 Douglas Daft, the second CEO since Goizueta, announced he would retire at the end of the year. He would be 61 and have completed five years in charge. The company had a succession problem all over again and moreover it was not performing particularly well. It was rumoured Coca-Cola might seek to split the Chairman and CEO posts but that did not happen. Instead retired executive Neville Isdell (an Irishman) was persuaded to return and he would stay firmly in charge until 2008, by which time Coca-Cola was much stronger.

Isdell immediately declared there would be investment in marketing, brand building and brand protection. Where there were gaps in the product line they would be filled. In 2005 Vault was launched to compete with Pepsi's citrus flavoured Mountain Dew. Rockstar was acquired to add to Full Throttle – both would compete with Red Bull. Powerade, launched to compete with Pepsi's Gatorade was doing well but it had a lot of ground to catch up. Coca-Cola bought a minority share in Honest Tea (organic teas and juices) in 2007 and also acquired the French company, Glaceau, which produces and markets a range of different enhanced water drinks. They all have added vitamins and distinct fruit flavours.

When Isdell stepped down Coca-Cola was showing healthy sales in four key emerging markets: China, India, Russia and Brazil.

Questions

1 Why is Coca-Cola 'number one' in its industry?
2 Where is its competitive advantage?
3 If it avoids serious mistakes, does it need to do anything radically different to retain its position?
4 Can you think of anything its leading rivals might do to 'upset the applecart'?

COCA COLA **http://www.coca-cola.com**

This will always prove difficult in a culture where cost management and resource savings have become dominant.

There are many examples where once-powerful and prominent companies have lost their edge and failed to sustain their competitive advantage:

- Case 1.2 showed how Marks and Spencer took its eye off the ball and allowed some of its ranges, particularly clothing, to become tired. Large retailers such as M&S normally control

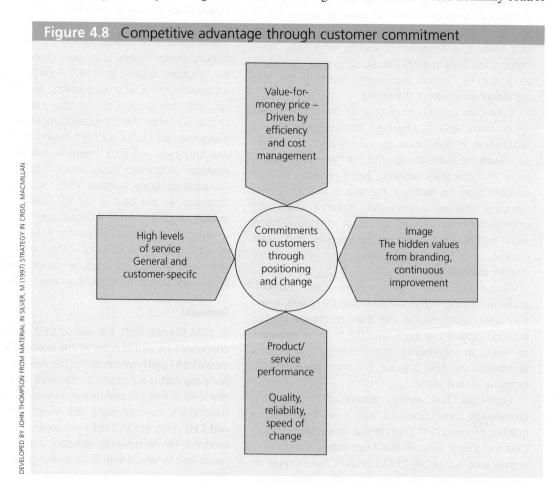

Figure 4.8   Competitive advantage through customer commitment

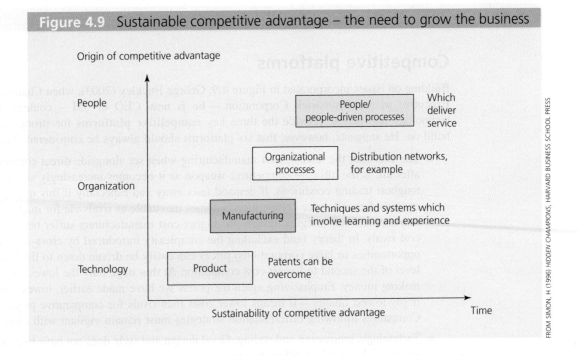

Figure 4.9 Sustainable competitive advantage – the need to grow the business

buying, product and range selection for every store centrally, because this can save costs. In an attempt to re-establish its position, M&S is allowing individual store managers to have more of an input than in the past. After all, they are closest to local customers.

- With Next, George Davies opened a niche for stylish clothing for slightly older age groups. However, once such a niche has been opened it is relatively easy for rivals to copy the broad strategy, and they did. When Next failed to defend its position by improvements, and instead committed resources to the acquisition of other retail brands and formats, its early advantage was lost. Davies was a corporate casualty. However, as a designer, George Davies has proved much more resilient than many retailers with successful retail clothing developments within both ASDA and Marks and Spencer. His Per Una range of fashionable clothing designed exclusively for M&S provided one of the few welcome highlights for the embattled retailer in 2003. In October 2004 M&S bought Per Una from George Davies for £125m. However in 2005 Davies walked out after a row with Sir Stuart Rose the then Chief Executive only to return. From this Per Una surged ahead and in 2007 Per Una accounted for 25 per cent of M&S womenswear sales of £500m. In December 2008, Davies stepped down as Chairman of Per Una at a time when M&S had suffered a 34 per cent decline in pre-tax profits. Per Una is seen by some business analysts as having lost its edge especially in failing to cater for the younger element amongst M&S customers.

- Toys Я Us are the American toy superstores who grew at the expense of independent retailers. More recently, Toys Я Us has suffered at the hands of Wal-Mart, which has used its purchasing power to compete on price and gain a significant market share. Wal-Mart simply focuses on the best-selling toys which it offers at rock-bottom prices. Toys Я Us has a wider choice but that clearly is not what every customer wants. According to Tomkins (1998), 'the company's big mistake was complacency ... they stopped renewing and refreshing their stores', and thus provided a way in for Wal-Mart. Toys Я Us became 'stuck in the middle'. The remaining high-street independents are often more convenient and the discounters are cheaper. Their demise was exacerbated by a reputation for relatively poor in-store service.

4.4 The dynamics of competition

Competitive platforms

Building on issues incorporated in Figure 4.9, George Buckley (2003), when Chairman and Chief Executive of the Brunswick Corporation – he is now CEO of 3M – contended that costs, technology and people provide the three key **competitive platforms** for strong competitors to build on. He suggests, however, that six platforms should always be considered. These are:

- The best (not the lowest) cost manufacturing when set alongside direct competitors. Cost, after all, is the ultimate competitive weapon as it becomes increasingly significant in the toughest trading conditions. If demand falls away and especially if this means supply exceeds demand, price competition becomes inevitable as rivals vie for market share. When this happens and margins tighten, the higher-cost manufacturers suffer before their lower-cost rivals. In theory (and excluding the complexity introduced by cross-subsidy opportunities in large corporations) prices can easily be driven down to the break-even cost level of the second to lowest-cost competitor. At this stage only the lowest cost company is making money. Emphasizing again the points we have made earlier, lowest cost does not imply lowest quality – it means lower costs than rivals for comparative perceived quality. Companies following differentiation strategies must remain vigilant with costs.

- Technology, innovation and styling. Good design and style does not have to cost a great deal but it can be an ideal differentiator.

- Customer service.

- Brands, marketing and reputation.

- Distribution. The best products in a design sense will be wasted opportunities if their manufacturers cannot put them in front of potential customers where and when they expect them. Entrepreneurs developing new ideas must always address this key issue of how to reach the market. It is clear that there are better alternatives to many of the products and services we consume on a regular basis, but our choice is affected by availability.

- People. Competitors can acquire equivalent technology and tooling and copy processes, but it is much harder to replicate the contribution made by people.

Competitor benchmarking

Again recapping key points from earlier in the chapter, a true cost leader will also enjoy some form of differentiation, and successful differentiators will be effective cost managers. Differentiation and cost control are compatible. All companies should continually search for innovatory differentiation opportunities and for ways of improving their cost efficiencies. As seen in earlier chapters, leveraging resources and setting stretching targets for employees can help to bring about innovation and savings; benchmarking good or best practice in other organizations (a process of measurement and comparison) can also provide new ideas and suggestions for reducing costs and improving efficiency. Organizations from different sectors and industries can be a useful source of ideas if they have developed a high level of expertise. It should be stressed that this process is a search for ideas that can be customized for a different organization rather than an exercise in simply copying. Managers should be open-minded and inquisitive and look *everywhere* for ideas.

At the same time, it is vital for an organization to understand clearly its position relative to its competitors. Table 4.2 provides a general framework for considering competitive strategies and Figure 4.10 shows how we might benchmark competitors for comparison with an organization and with customer preferences. The key order criteria – key success factors – are listed down the

Table 4.2 A framework for evaluating competitive strategies

Scope	Global; industry-wide; niche
	Single or multiproduct/service
	Focused or diversified
	Vertical linkages with suppliers/distributors
Objectives	Ambitious for market or segment leadership
	Market presence just to support other (more important) activities
Success	Market share
	Image and reputation
	Profitability
Commitment	Aggressive – willing to acquire to grow
	Passive survivor
	Willing to divest if opportunity arises
Approach	Offensive – attacking other competitors
	Defending a strong position. Note that the same strategy (new products, price cuts) can be used both offensively and defensively
	Risk-taking or risk averse
	Teasing out new segments or niches
Strategy	High quality – perhaps with technological support
	High service
	Low price
Position	Cost advantage or even cost leadership enjoyed
	Clearly differentiated
Competitive resources	High-technology base; modern plant
	Location relative to markets
	Quality of people (ability to add value)
	Reputation

The examples provided for each of the eight criteria are not offered as an exhaustive list.

left-hand side and ranked in order of their importance to customers. Their relative significance is plotted against the horizontal axis. The ability of different competitors to meet these key success factors is illustrated by the dotted lines. Competitor A is clearly relying on its quality and technical back-up, for which it has a good reputation, but is it truly satisfying customer needs? Competitor B seems to offer an all-round better service, and in a number of areas is providing a service beyond that demanded. Given the areas, this may be good as it will indicate a reliable supplier.

How would our customers rank our products/services in relation to those of our competitors?

- *Not as good as. We must improve!*

- *No worse than. This implies a general dissatisfaction, so there must be real opportunities to benefit from improvement and differentiation.*

- *As good as the others, no better, no worse. Again opportunity to benefit if new values can be added and real differentiation perceived.*

- *Better than. We must still work hard to retain our lead.*

I subscribe absolutely to the concept of stealing shamelessly! Wherever you come across a good idea, if it's likely to work, pinch it. There's nothing wrong with that. There is a quite respectable word – benchmarking – which is the same thing if you think about it.

BILL COCKBURN, WHEN GROUP CHIEF EXECUTIVE, WH SMITH PLC

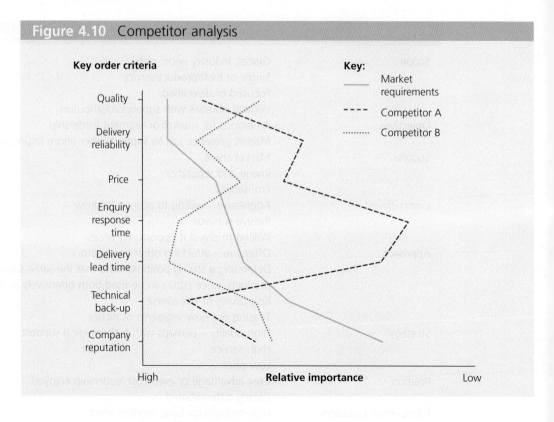

Figure 4.10 Competitor analysis

Changing competitive positions

A successful competitive position implies a match between customers' perceptions of the relative quality or value of a product or service – in comparison to rival offerings – and its price, again in relation to the prices of competing products or services. The relevant area of **competitor gap analysis** is the segment or segments in which an organization chooses to compete; and, in addition, the total price should be used for comparison purposes. Customers, for example, may willingly pay a premium purchase price initially for a particular brand of, say, an electrical good or car if they believe that over its life it will incur lower maintenance and service costs than competing brands. Products offered at initially lower prices may be perceived to be more expensive overall.

Figure 4.11 (which develops Figure 4.5) features a competitive positioning grid. Three basic positions are shown by sectors 1, 2 and 3. Sector 6, high perceived prices but only average (at best) quality, is an untenable position in the long run. Sector 4 illustrates a company competing on price, which can be a successful strategy, but it can provoke competitive responses; in which case, it may only serve in driving down all prices and making all competitors less profitable. Do-it-yourself chains, such as B&Q, have come to believe that the key to survival in a crowded market is to offer permanently competitive prices as well as developing a unique identity. Sporadic high discounts are being replaced by 'everyday low prices' success is more dependent on volume sales than the actual margins on individual products.

Effective differentiators, commanding premium prices and earning superior profits with high margins, are shown as Sector 5. Their success is partially dependent upon sound cost management.

Figure 4.12 illustrates a number of possible competitive strategy changes for companies in selected positions in the matrix.

Figure 4.11 A competitive position matrix

		Low	Average	High
High		**Low price/discount strategies** • can be attractive for new customers and those willing to switch brands	**Differentiation and product improvement** – coupled with greater efficiencies	**High price/high quality position**
Average		**but** • price cuts can be followed readily • customers may become suspicious of quality if prices seem 'too low'	**Market average position**	**Uncompetitive positions:**
Low		**Low price/quality position**	• Prices not justified through lower quality perceptions • Possibly a company has failed to innovate and slipped back in comparison to competitors • Possibly it is relatively less efficient with a high cost base	

Perception of relative quality and added value (vertical axis)

Perception of relative price (horizontal axis)

4	5	3
	1	
2		6

1,2,3   Acceptable strategies and positions
4   Competition on price – successful if not copied and costs controlled - potentially lucrative
5   Effective differentiation
6   Uncompetitive, unsustainable positions

Blue Ocean Strategy

The basic presumption of Kim and Mauborgne's 'Blue Ocean Strategy' (2005) is that some dynamic and leading organizations are successful because they discover radical new opportunities for competitive advantage. They move outside the metaphorical box and do things differently. They move on and away from what has gone before. They do not set out to compete directly with their rivals by offering 'similar' products and services – this might well result in a 'red ocean' where there is blood from cut-throat price competition. Rather they look to offer their customers something really new and different. They create fresh opportunities. They are, therefore, entrepreneurial. Case 4.5 on Cirque du Soleil shows how this Canadian organization has changed the rules in the circus industry.

Sometimes with entrepreneurs we accept they spot new opportunities before others realize there is an opportunity and put this down to some form of 'second sight'. They find the opportunity by insight and inspiration. They have a 'gut-feel' for something new that will find favour with customers. They spend their lives looking at what is, questioning why it is as it is, and believing there is always going to be a better way – and that you will find that way if you ask yourself the right questions – based around 'how can I improve on this?'

But are such new opportunities naturally and automatically subjective and not the outcome of something more logical and analytical?

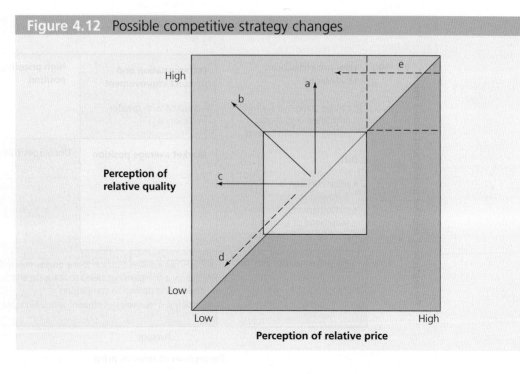

Figure 4.12   Possible competitive strategy changes

Case 4.5

Cirque du Soleil

Int

The big top travelling circuses of the type pioneered by showmen such as the legendary PT Barnum – and which featured animals, typically lions, tigers and elephants, alongside acrobats and the ubiquitous clowns – still exist, but they cannot command the audiences they once did. And there are fewer of them. The main ones include the Ringling Brothers and the Russian and Chinese State circuses. Competition for the 'entertainment spend' has increased.

Spectacular specialist acts featuring animals became popular in Las Vegas many years ago, although when a white tiger mauled one of the partners in the Siegfried and Roy Show in 2003, serious questions were raised about them. There were, of course, already many animal lovers who were critics of shows such as this. Meanwhile the circus industry had been reinvented without needing animals.

Dubbed 'the New American Circus', Cirque du Soleil was started in Montreal, Quebec, Canada, in 1984, the invention of a small group of street performers led by partners Guy LaLiberte and Daniel Gauthier. By the end

of the century they had entertained some 30 million people with a range of innovative and daring production shows. The shows combine circus acts with performing arts and they typically feature jugglers, trampolinists, trapeze artists and clowns – who work together rather than have individual feature spots. The shows are operatic as well as acrobatic, they are choreographed, they stretch the talents of the performers, they are visually impressive and they all have a clear theme or story.

The shows are different and innovative and so Cirque du Soleil enthusiasts are likely to attend regularly, if they can get to where the shows are. Originally the focus was on a traditional moveable 'big top' but quite soon Cirque du Soleil moved into dedicated resident theatres and also introduced some shows that worked in existing venues such as the Royal Albert Hall in London, which they visit regularly.

Las Vegas was an obvious early target, with the first venue being the Treasure Island hotel and casino. The specialist show 'O', which needs a tank filled with 1.5

million gallons of water, was put on in a dedicated 1800 seat theatre at the Bellagio. Walt Disney World Resort is another home.

Fundamentally Cirque du Soleil has eliminated animals and markedly cut down on the sales of food and other

© FRIDAY | DREAMSTIME.COM

merchandise whilst the show itself is live – something quite different from the traditional circus and most American sporting events. There is less emphasis on thrills and danger – something circuses used to try and create competitive advantage – and a more creative use of different venues. What really sets it apart from the original circus model is the 'seamless' element of the show where music, opera, dance and acrobatics are combined into a holistic show.

In 2008 there were 18 different shows still operational; some have been retired. Cirque du Soleil will typically trial a new travelling show for approximately a year in Montreal before sending it out to America for some 3 years. Europe and then Asia follow. There are few concessions for children and so it is clear the target audience is not the families for whom the traditional circus was appealing. In addition seat prices are relatively expensive.

It has been reported that Cirque du Soleil has received several takeover offers, but so far it remains independent. Guy LaLiberte is still the controlling shareholder. In summer 2008 a proportion of the equity was sold for US$2 billion to one fund controlled by the government of Dubai.

Questions

1 Is it a fair comment to make that Cirque du Soleil has 'reinvented the circus industry'?
2 Apply the questions from the text concerning adding and reducing value to explain the choices Cirque du Soleil made. What are the challenges of sustaining the position is has built up?

SOURCE: THIS CASE STUDY WAS PREPARED USING PRIMARILY PUBLICLY AVAILABLE SOURCES OF INFORMATION FOR THE PURPOSES OF CLASSROOM DISCUSSION. IT DOES NOT INTEND TO ILLUSTRATE EITHER EFFECTIVE OR INEFFECTIVE HANDLING OF A MANAGERIAL SITUATION.

Kim and Mauborgne suggest that entrepreneurs and organizations can analyse and list those factors that make up the competitive offering for any product or service. These factors can then be examined individually and a new business model/product offering sought by looking at:

1 Which factors might usefully be raised above current expectation levels because they really matter to (certain) customers?
2 Which factors can easily be reduced because they are relatively unimportant?
3 Which elements are of no importance but are there 'because they always have been there' but could easily be eliminated
4 What new elements could be created and added that would make a new and real difference and set this new product apart in a meaningful way?

Questions 1 and 4 set alongside Questions 2 and 3 help to identify those factors the organization should focus on to create a compelling business model and which ones can be safely played down. Strategy, remember, is about choices – choosing what to do and choosing what not to do, with the latter sometimes being the more important decision. Question 4 and to a lesser extent Question 1 also flag where the organization should seek to diverge from competitors. The example of a leading Australian wine brand, Yellow Tail, provides an ideal example. Yellow Tail offers a limited range of single grape branded wines and has capitalized on the surging demand for wine in recent years. Against the above four criteria, the following answers were generated:

1   There is no requirement to be the cheapest wine available as this affects perceptions of quality. So the price should be affordable and the wine readily available through the leading supermarkets and other relevant outlets. Company staff must be enthusiastic and champion the product.

2   Customers do not expect a huge range of different grapes and so a limited range of 'favourites' will suffice. Similarly many customers are not really interested in the prestige of the vineyard (but they are interested in the taste).

3   Wine aficionado technology is important to only a minority of people and not the mainstream buyer, and relatively few concern themselves with ageing properties. Availability and word-of-mouth are more important that above-the-line advertising.

4   Easy drinking, easy selection and a sense of fun and adventure can be utilized to marked effect to promote a new brand.

It is relatively straightforward to apply the same criteria to the no-frills airlines (Case 1.1) which also created a whole new market opportunity.

Kim and Mauborgne also suggest organizations can make use of what they call a 'buyer utility map' – see Table 4.3 – drawn up to try and identify just which messages are most compelling for their customers. Again it is based on focus and divergence. The grid for the map illustrated in Table 4.3 would be relevant for a new model of a car.

Kim and Mauborgne argued that the Model T Ford was able to make a huge impression when it was launched early in the last century because it focused on two things that set it apart from rival models at the time. These are marked in the grid with an x. First the car was small, strong and rugged and could be used on the roads and lanes available at the time with little risk to the driver or the vehicle – it was convenient. Second the engineering was simple and straightforward and the maintenance would be easy – there were few consequential risks to ownership for the unsophisticated motorist. Also significant was the fact the car was readily available (because of the new production line manufacturing systems) and, in part because of this, relatively affordable.

In this context it is interesting to evaluate the new Tata Nano car, launched in 2008 for the Indian subcontinent at a very affordable price. Huge numbers of people who could not previously afford a car now can – but this will add to the world's carbon emission problems in a big way! The story is outlined in Case 4.6.

Table 4.3   Buyer utility map applied to the Model T Ford

	Showroom experience	Availability and delivery	Model capability	Extras available	Service costs	Residual Value or Scrapping Issues
Perceived price relative to quality		(X)				
Easy of handling						
Size and convenience			X			
Image						
Safety issues and risks					X	
Environmental issues						

Case 4.6

The Tata Nano – a Low Cost, No Frills Car Int

We typically associate 'low cost and no frills' with the airline industry but it clearly has a relevance as a competitive strategy elsewhere. Historically certain cars have been seen as relatively low quality and low price – Eastern European brands such as Lada, Trabant and Skoda before its acquisition by Volkswagen – might be included.

But low price and lower quality is not necessarily quite the same as low cost, no frills. Passengers on airlines such as EasyJet and Ryanair sacrifice certain services in order to get low prices, but the seats are comfortable enough, the safety records stand scrutiny and the planes generally fly on time. This is different from low quality leading to unreliability.

In this context two recent strategies by two quite different competitors are worthy of evaluation.

Renault is a long-established French car manufacturer with a defendable reputation. In 2007 it chose to enter the 'global emerging markets' sector with a new car, the 4-door Renault Logan saloon. The car was launched in India, where it was manufactured in a joint venture with Mumbai based car manufacturer, Malindra & Malindra.

Priced at around £5000, the car was certainly not ultra-cheap, but it was certainly competitive. It was not described as 'stylish' and it dispensed with frills. Costs were contained by certain design features: almost flat windscreens which are cheaper to make; identical right and left wing mirrors, for example. It uses interior parts designed for other Renault cars and it has the Clio engine. Development costs were shaved by relying on computer modelling rather than actual mock-ups.

The Tata Nano is different. The diversified Indian conglomerate Tata is best known as the world's leading tea company, but it has bought Jaguar and Land Rover from Ford in the recent past.

The Nano is marketed as the world's cheapest car. It is again manufactured in India and priced at just £1275. The Nano is a 5- door 4-seat car with a rear mounted 624cc engine. It offers 50 miles to a gallon of fuel. Air conditioning, electric windows and power steering are all features that simply are not available. It is designed to be affordable to less affluent buyers and thus make cars more widely available. It is basically 'safe, affordable and all-weather transport'. In this respect it is the Model T Ford story all over again, which, on the face of it, seems a positive development.

However, whilst it does meet minimum standards, its emissions are higher than other small cars. One question, therefore, is whether increasing the number of cars on the planet that add to the carbon footprint in a relatively inefficient way is genuine progress or a mixed blessing.

Questions

Is the Tata Nano 'blue ocean' or has Tata more realistically discovered a new niche which could be potentially very valuable?

© ULI DECK/EPA/CORBIS

4.5 Concluding comments

This chapter has concentrated on how an organization can gain a deeper understanding of its competitive environment with a view to becoming a stronger, more effective competitor through creating and sustaining competitive advantage. The closer a business is to its customers, the more it will understand the market and the industry. Competitive strategy, essential for every product and service that the organization makes and markets, involves a vision about how best to compete.

There are a number of ways to generate competitive advantage, and the process is both logical and creative. The choice will also be influenced by the strategic leader and by the organization's culture. However, every employee contributes in some way to both lower costs and uniqueness, and therefore it is important that the competitive strategy is communicated and understood throughout the organization.

In the end, the most successful companies will be those with:

- differentiated products and services which are recognized for their ability to add value, and are:
- produced efficiently
- upgraded over time through innovation and improvement, and which
- prove relevant for international markets.

Porter contends that competitors can be viewed as good or bad. Good ones differentiate, innovate and help to develop an industry; bad ones just cut prices in an attempt to drive others out of business. We could perhaps debate whether EasyJet is a good competitor and Ryanair is a bad competitor!

New windows of competitive opportunity are always opening:

- Products and services can be improved to open up new markets and segments, as was the case with PDA organizers which compete for the market pioneered by Filofax.
- New technologies change behaviour and demand, e.g. mobile phones, personal computers, and MP3 players such as the iPod.
- Changes in attitude – concern for the environment created the opportunity for unleaded petrol – and in the recent acceptance of organic food and the wind power turbines now being accepted when previously they may have been considered as a blot on the landscape.

Summary

Many industries and markets are characterized by competitive 'chaos' – they are dynamic and uncertain. All the time rivals may be trying out new initiatives which cannot be ignored. To succeed long term, organizations must be able to manage both continuous and discontinuous change pressures. This is achieved with a mix of incremental and more dramatic changes to competitive and corporate strategies.

In an endeavour to manage, their competitive environment, organizations must understand the nature and attractiveness of their industry, and their relative position in it.

Positioning can be examined against a framework of generic strategies, which are based on differentiation and cost leadership. The issue of a broad or narrow market focus is another important consideration.

Michael Porter has provided two useful frameworks to help with these assessments.

However, competitive positions, per se, do not yield competitive advantage. Advantage is a reflection of a strong position, but it is the result of the activities which create the position and, in particular, the synergistic links between them. Successful organizations achieve a unique mix which is hard to replicate, although the individual activities, at a basic level, can be copied.

While competitive advantage comes from technologies, organization and people, it is the people-driven processes that enable advantage to be sustained and extended.

All the time the pace of change and competition is speeding up in many markets and industries. To deal with this it is essential for organizations to benchmark both their competitors and other high-performing organizations in a search for good ideas and best practice. Specifically, they are looking for new opportunities to add or build value in ways that are meaningful for customers.

Kim and Mauborgne have introduced the term 'Blue Ocean Strategy' to explain those entrepreneurial organizations that innovate in a distinctive way and impact upon the rules of competition in an industry.

Online cases for this chapter

Online Case 4.1: Nintendo's Rise from the Ashes

Online Case 4.2: Schick versus Gillette

Questions and research assignments

1 Study Figures 4.6 (a) and (b) and consider where you would place British Airways and other major carriers such as Air France as opposed to EasyJet and Ryanair.

2 Apply Figures 4.11 and 4.12 to this industry.

Internet and library projects

1 Take an industry of your choice and analyse one or more of the major competitors in terms of their chosen competitive strategies. As well as the Internet the following library sources might prove useful sources of information:

- *Business Monitors* (PA and PQ series)
- *Annual Report of The Office of Fair Trading* (as a source of ideas)

Strategy activity

The Fiat Cinquecento

The Fiat Cinquecento is similar to two other iconic cars – the BMW Mini and the Vokswagen Beetle. It is a relatively old brand, but one with enduring qualities. Although it would be categorized as a supermini, it also competes in the same sector of the market as the Mini and the Beetle.

The Italian family-dominated Fiat organization (owner of the Alfa Romeo brand and allied to Ferrari) lost some of its shine and popularity, but with a series of new models, including the Panda and the Punto, it was able to restore some of its past glory. In 2007 the Fiat 500, the Cinquecento, was proclaimed European Car of the Year. Made in Poland, demand exceeded supply.

The original Cinquecento was launched in 1957 (exactly 50 years earlier) and it was soon popular, especially in certain Hollywood movies. It predated the original Mini by a few years. It lasted almost twenty years before it was seen as unfashionable and withdrawn.

With a completely fresh design and improved technology this car carries a premium price, and in this respect the strategy is the same as BMW has for the Mini. The car can be customized in various ways and Fiat claim that 500,000 permutations are possible. It has a high crash rating and is a relatively safe car; it offers high fuel consumption and is energy efficient. In a world of high fuel prices and carbon emission concerns, one can see logic in Fiat's strategy.

Fiat has been reported to be developing a sports version for the American market, which it would promote alongside Alfa Romeo models when these are relaunched in 2009.

Questions

1 Do you see this as effective differentiation by Fiat?
2 Do you think the 2008 link between Fiat and Chrysler will improve the prospects for the American market?

- Monopolies and Mergers Commission reports, and Competition Commission reports, which usually feature a comprehensive industry analysis
- McCarthy's (or similar) Index (press-cutting service for firms and industries).

2 How successful has Porsche been since the introduction of its new models? Do you believe that the size of its niche is viable, or might the company have to extend its range? Porsche at http://www.porsche.com

Further reading

Clarke, CJ (1988) Using finance for competitive advantage, *Long Range Planning*, 21 (2).

Hamel, G and Prahalad, CK (1994) Seeing the future first, *Fortune*, September 5.

Porter, ME (1979) How competitive forces shape strategy, *Harvard Business Review*, March–April.

Stalk, G (1988) Time – the next source of competitive advantage, *Harvard Business Review*, July–August.

References

Buckley, G (2003) Presentation at the University of Huddersfield, November.

Ferry, I (1989) Branson's misunderstood Midas touch, *Business*, November.

Hamel, G and Prahalad, CK (1993) Strategy as stretch and leverage, *Harvard Business Review*, March–April.

Heller, R (1998) *Goldfinger – How Entrepreneurs Grow Rich by Starting Small*, HarperCollins.

Hendry, J (1990) The problem with Porter's generic strategies, *European Management Journal*, December.

Kanter, RM (1990) Strategic alliances and new ventures, Harvard Business School Video Series.

Kim WC and Mauborgne R (2005) *Blue Ocean Strategy,* Harvard Business School Press.

Ohmae, K (1982) *The Mind of the Strategist*, McGraw-Hill.

Porter, ME (1980) *Competitive Strategy: Techniques for Analysing Industries and Competitors*, Free Press.

Porter, ME (1985) *Competitive Advantage: Creating and Sustaining Superior Performance*, Free Press.

Porter, ME (1996) What is strategy? *Harvard Business Review*, November–December.

Sull, D (2006) Good things come to those who actively wait, *Financial Times,* 6 February.

Tomkins, R (1998) Trouble in toyland pushes Toys R Us on the defensive, *Financial Times*, 29 May.

Chapter 4 appendix

Finance in action: The experience curve

A large size, relative to competitors, can bring benefits. In particular, if a company has a market share substantially greater than its competitors it has opportunities to achieve greater profitability. Lower costs can be achieved if the company is managed well and takes advantage of the opportunities offered by being larger. These lower costs can be passed on to the consumer in the form of lower prices, which in turn puts pressure on competitors' profit margins and strengthens the position of the market leader.

Lower costs are achieved through economies of scale and the experience or learning effect. In the 1960s the Boston Consulting Group in the US estimated that the cost of production decreases by between 10 per cent and 30 per cent each time that a company's experience in producing the product or service doubles, as long as the company is managed well. In other words, as cumulative production increases over time there is a potential cost reduction at a predictable rate. The company learns how to do things better. The savings are spread across all value-added costs: manufacturing, administration, sales, marketing and distribution. In addition, the cost of supplies decreases as suppliers experience the same learning benefits.

The experience effect has been observed in high- and low-technology industries, in new and mature industries, in both manufacturing and service businesses, and in relation to consumer and industrial markets. Specific examples are cars, semiconductors, petrochemicals, long-distance telephone calls, synthetic fibres, airline transportation, crushed limestone and the cost of administering life insurance.

The experience curve is illustrated by plotting on a graph the cumulative number of units produced over time (the horizontal axis) and the cost per unit (the vertical axis), as shown in Exhibit 4.1. This particular curve is called an '85 per cent experience curve' as every time output is doubled the cost per unit falls to 85 per cent of what it was. In reality, the plot will be of a least-squares line but the trend will be clear. However, it is more common to plot the data on logarithmic scales on both axes, and this shows the straight-line effect illustrated in Exhibit 4.2.

Sources of the experience effect:

- increased labour efficiency through learning and consequent skills improvement
- the opportunity for greater specialization in production methods

Exhibit 4.1 An 85 per cent experience curve plotted on a normal scale

Exhibit 4.2 The same 85 per cent experience curve plotted in log form

Exhibit 4.3 Pricing in relation to costs and the experience effect

Cumulative industry production

- innovations in the production process
- greater productivity from equipment as people learn how to use it more efficiently
- improved resource mix as products are redesigned with cost savings in mind.

This is not an exhaustive list and the savings will not occur naturally. They result from good management.

Pricing decisions and the experience effect

A market leader or other large producer who enjoys a cost advantage as a result of accumulated experience will use this as the basis for a pricing strategy linked to his or her objectives, which might be profit or growth and market share orientated. Exhibit 4.3 illustrates one way in which industry prices might be forced down (in real terms, after accounting for inflation) as the market leader benefits from lower costs. Initially, prices are below costs incurred because of the cost of development. As demand, sales and production increase prices fall, but at a slower rate than costs; the producer is enjoying a higher profit margin. This will be attractive to any competitors or potential competitors who feel

that they can compete at this price even if their costs are higher. If competition becomes intensive and the major producer(s) wish to assert authority over the market they will decrease prices quickly and force out manufacturers whose costs are substantially above theirs. Stability might then be restored.

Companies with large market shares can therefore dictate what happens in a market, but there is a need for caution. If a company ruthlessly chases a cost advantage via the experience effect the implication could be ever-increasing efficiency as a result of less flexibility. The whole operating system is geared towards efficiency and cost savings. If demand changes or competitors innovate unexpectedly the strategy will have run out of time, as we have already seen. Companies should ensure that they are flexible enough to respond.

This material has mainly been summarized from:

Abell, DF and Hammond, JS (1979) *Strategic Market Planning: Problems, and Analytical Approaches*, Prentice-Hall.

Exhibit 4.3 is adapted from The Boston Consulting Group (1972) *Perspectives on Experience. Environmental Analysis and Strategic Positioning.*

Chapter 5

Introducing culture and values

PART 1
Understanding strategy

1 Introducing strategy and strategic management

PART 5
Strategic management

14 Strategy implementation

15 Leading change

16 Managing strategy in the organization

17 Final thoughts – the purpose of strategy

STRATEGIC MANAGEMENT: AWARENESS AND CHANGE

PART 2
Strategic positioning

2 Strategic thinking, environmental analysis, synergy and strategic positioning

3 Resource-led strategy

4 The dynamics of competition

5 Introducing culture and values

PART 4
Issues in strategic growth

11 Strategic growth

12 International strategy

13 Failure, consolidation and recovery strategies

PART 3
Strategic analysis and choice

6 Strategic purpose

7 Strategic success

8 An introduction to strategy creation and planning

9 Strategic leadership, entrepreneurship and intrapreneurship

10 Strategic alternatives, strategy evaluation and strategy selection

Learning objectives

Having read to the end of this chapter you should be able to:

● explain the impact of corporate culture on the management of an organization, and on managers and other employees

● discuss the manifestations of culture in an organization

● define Handy's four organizational cultures

● list and define different sources of power

● show how broad cultures differ throughout the world and appreciate the important aspects of Japanese business culture.

See the online "The Body Shop" case for an example of this section's theory in practice

Because culture and values influence strategic positioning, the strategic choices that are made and the feasibility of change – which in turn help determine success – this chapter looks into these implications and into the determinants of culture and cultural differences. The culture varies between organizations, although some elements will be common and transferable. It also varies between countries, influencing the relative competitiveness of industries and organizations in different countries.

5.1 Culture – an introduction

When any group of people live and work together for any length of time, they form and share certain beliefs about what is right and proper. They establish behaviour patterns based on their beliefs, and their actions often become matters of habit which they follow routinely. These beliefs and ways of behaving constitute the organization's *culture*.

Culture is reflected in the way in which people in an organization perform tasks, set objectives and administer resources to achieve them. It affects the way that they make decisions, think, feel and act in response to opportunities and threats. Culture also influences the selection of people for particular jobs, which in turn affects the way in which tasks are carried out and decisions are made. Culture is so fundamental that it affects behaviour unconsciously. Managers do things in particular ways because it is implicitly expected behaviour.

The culture of an organization is therefore related to the people, their behaviour and the operation of the structure. It is encapsulated in beliefs, customs and values, and manifested in a number of symbolic ways.

In a nutshell, attitudes and assumptions form the core of the organization's culture. Values represent implicit aspects of the culture; and behaviours are the explicit elements.

The formation of, and any changes to, the culture of an organization is dependent on the leadership and example of particular individuals, and their ability to control or influence situations. This is itself dependent on a person's ability to obtain and use power.

Online Case 5.1, The Body Shop, shows how the values of the founder, Anita Roddick, inspired employees and attracted customers. The distinctive culture enabled The Body Shop to grow and prosper, but it was not totally appropriate for the large, international business that The Body Shop became. Eventually, in 2006, The Body Shop was sold to L'Oreal as a way of making sure that the business (which is The Body Shop) could survive and prosper as part of a large multinational. Unfortunately Anita Roddick died in September 2007. She, however, left behind a legacy of campaigning for ethical issues and for philanthropy throughout her life.

Culture and power, then, affect the choice, incidence and application of the modes of strategy creation, which will also reflect the values and preferences of the strategic leader. The preferred mode must, however, be appropriate for the organization's strategic needs, which are affected by competition. Moreover, culture and power are such strong forces that, if the prevailing culture is overlooked, implementation may not happen. Strong cultures can obstruct strategic change, particularly if companies are in decline and people feel vulnerable.

Quite simply, culture is at the heart of all strategy creation and implementation. Organizations are seeking to respond to perceived strategic issues. Resources must be deployed and committed, but successful change also requires the 'right' attitude, approach and commitment from people. This mindset, which might, for example, reflect a strong customer and service focus, could imply further empowerment and consequently cultural change.

In the early 1980s, Berry (1983) claimed that after some 20 years of emphasis on analytical techniques in strategic management, the concentration switched to the softer aspect of culture. The emphasis was no longer on the marketplace, but on what managers could do to resolve internal problems; by using culture, companies could become more strategically effective. The perspective of this book is that both the hard and soft aspects of strategy have important roles to play in strategic management.

Strong cultures, then, are an important strategic asset. Internalized beliefs can motivate people to exceptional levels of performance. An effective strategic leader will understand and mould the culture in order that a vision can be pursued and intended strategies implemented. Most successful companies develop strong cultures; the major doubt concerns an organization's ability to change the culture.

Moreover, large organizations formed by a series of acquisitions will frequently exhibit different cultures in the various divisions or businesses; in many international businesses this is inevitable. The challenge for corporate headquarters is to ensure that certain critically important values are reflected in all branches of the corporation and cultural differences do not inhibit internal architecture and synergy. The acquisition of Compaq by Hewlett-Packard in 2002 (Case 5.1) provided exactly this challenge – and it would ultimately lead to the downfall of the strategic leader behind it.

Case 5.1

Hewlett-Packard   US

Hewlett-Packard (HP) began life in a garage in Palo Alto, California, in 1939. It happened because Stanford Professor Fred Terman brought together two of his PhD students, Bill Hewlett and Dave Packard, and encouraged them to start a business based on their research. Not long after the business started Bill Hewlett was called up for military service and in his absence Dave Packard held everything together. When Hewlett returned after the war he was able to introduce fresh ideas. The two partners were different in character but they complemented each other well. HP not only became a leading computer company, it was also the foundation upon which Silicon Valley was built. Some 60 years later HP was probably best known for its computer printers – it had some 40 per cent of

the world market and also earned substantial revenues from sales of replacement ink and toner cartridges. But HP was a diversified business and also supplied PCs, laptops, servers, scanners and digital cameras as well as providing IT consultancy services. In 1999 Carly Fiorina became the new CEO and she was determined to strengthen HP's position in the market and make it the number two company behind IBM. Fiorina had been CEO of the newer and 'fashionable' Lucent Technologies.

Fiorina soon launched an agreed $19 billion bid for Compaq. The opposition to this strategy was led by Walter Hewlett, the son of Bill Hewlett, who believed that instead of moving further into computers, HP should become more focused on printers and associated digital businesses. Fiorina's logic was that sales of computers, scanners and digital cameras drive printer sales. HP had a special range of photo printers.

In contrast Compaq was a much younger company which had been founded in 1982 by three senior mangers from Texas Instruments. They set out to make affordable and portable PCs to run the software being developed for the IBM PC. These were commonly known as IBM clones, and the design for the first model was sketched out on a restaurant placemat.

The emphasis was on volume production and managed costs to fuel competitive prices.

The company became one of America's fastest growth businesses. Over 50,000 were sold in the first year of operations. By 1994 Compaq was the world's leading PC supplier. However, in 1998 Compaq acquired Digital Equipment for $9.6 billion in cash. Digital provided high-end servers, operating systems and chip technology. It might have been complementary, but it was certainly not a direct competitor. At the same time Compaq was experiencing more intense competition from the aggressive and fast-expanding Dell, started in Texas by the entrepreneurial Michael Dell, whose business model relies on sourced-in components and direct sales. There were post-acquisition problems and soon Compaq was carrying expensive excess inventory. The product lines and distribution had to be rationalized. Jobs, including senior executives, were lost. Fast, aggressive and competitive, for some analysts the company had lost its way strategically. Under a new CEO, however, the decline was staunched and the situation was stabilized with a stronger focus on services – but not sufficiently to withstand a market slump in 2001, when more jobs were lost.

Compaq Computer lived the Hank Williams life – it ran hard, got famous and died before its time.

CNET News.com.

HP's values, known widely as 'The HP Way' were based on trust, respect, passion for customers, speed and agility of service. HP believed in involving managers in decision making. These had all evolved over 60 years. The company saw itself as process-intensive and very much technology-based. One strap line used by the company is 'HP Invent' and this really tells its own story.

At HP we believe ideas thrive on teamwork. Everyone at every level in every function is encouraged to have original ideas and to share them. We believe

anything can be achieved if you really believe in it and will invest in your ideas to change lives and working practices. That's because we work across borders and without limits. Global virtual teams share resources and pool their brainpower to solve business issues and meet personal goals. You will be valued for your unique skills, experiences and perspective. You will add value with every idea you have.

Statement to employees

One analyst, John Madden (Summit Strategies, Boston) mused that it was unclear whether a combined HP-Compaq would have a cohesive strategy but acknowledged that 'culture issues aside, services for both companies are at the heart of the bulls-eye'.

One interesting and maybe significant development in 2004 was HP's decision to launch a range of notebook computers with the Linux open-source operating system installed. Started by Finnish entrepreneur, Linus Torvalds, Linux has been made available either free of charge or for a small licence fee from certain organizations who will provide technical support. It is a growing competitor to the ubiquitous Microsoft Windows, but, as yet, had only had a limited impact on the market. Leading rival, Dell, sells 'naked' machines – with no operating system installed – but it has yet to offer Linux pre-installed, possibly concerned about its long-term relationship with Microsoft. HP was the first to do so. The price saving was not huge – some $60 in a $1000 plus notebook; the real issue is one of consumer choice.

In 2005 Carly Fiorina resigned over 'differences of opinion over strategy' with the Hewlett-Packard Board. The company had been missing earnings targets. Given the opposition to her acquisition of Compaq by some members of the Board, it was always going to be necessary to deliver on earnings promises. HP shares had lost two-thirds of their value since she had been appointed.

Some new strategies were being developed in-house.

In March 2006 HP entered retail photo printing in competition with Kodak and Fuji, another strategy some questioned. The company had developed a number of machines that it would sell to stores and others which were integral in a stand-alone kiosk. Wal-Mart became an early customer for the kiosks. Store machines were available which would digitally print posters and promotional material to a very high quality. HP was 'moving from being a printer company to being a printing company'. But did this make sense?

Later in 2006 HP launched new high-end video conferencing equipment.

Also later in the same year HP acquired Mercury Interactive for $4.5 billion. This was a business software company, and the latest in a line of recent software acquisitions. HP wanted to be able to help its customers with a range of packages and systems that would help with their more complex needs, and thus provide a 'complete package' of products and services.

In January 2007 the Chairman, Patricia Dunn, resigned. She had apparently employed private detectives to tap directors' phone calls in an attempt to plug an information leak. There were clearly still problems at Hewlett-Packard.

Questions

1 How different do you imagine the HP and Compaq cultures were when Compaq was thriving as a manufacturer of PCs and laptops? How difficult might it be to reconcile the differences and create a cohesive culture? In a company like Hewlett-Packard would it have been inevitable that the CEO would have to go if results did not follow a controversial strategic decision?

2 What do you think the decision to launch a Notebook with Linux installed is saying about the HP culture?

3 Is there a defensible strategic logic in the moves into imaging and printing (favoured by Walter Hewlett) and software?

Another example of culture at the strategic level are the thoughts of Dieter Zetsche the Chairman of Daimler AG and head of Mercedes-Benz Cars. After the problems of the merger of Chrysler and Daimler in 1998 and the break-up of the group in 2007 with the sale of Daimler's equity stake in Chrysler to Cerebus Capital Group – discussed in Case 11.1 – Zetsche commented on leading across cultures. 'Some stereotypes seem based in individual cultures such as the notion that American businesses have a relaxed style and German managers hold long meetings. At the end of the day, my experience is that those differences are minor. For me the same issues are important everywhere. People want to see that you mean what you say. If they feel you are not straightforward, you are lost. This is important whether you work in Asia or Africa or whatever.'

5.2 Aspects of culture

The points discussed in this section are summarized in Figure 5.1.

Manifestations of culture

Edgar Schein (1985) contends that it is important to consider culture as having a number of levels, some of which are essentially manifestations of underlying beliefs.

The first and most visible level Schein terms '*artefacts*'. These include the physical and social environment and the outputs of the organization. Written communications, advertisements and the reception that visitors receive are all included.

Values are the second level, and they represent a sense of 'what ought to be' based on convictions held by certain key people. For example if an organization has a problem such as low sales or a high level of rejections in production, decisions might be made to advertise more aggressively or to use high-quality but more expensive raw materials. These are seen initially as the decision-maker's values, which can be debated or questioned. Many of the strategies followed by organizations start in this way, and many will reflect values held by the strategic leader.

If the alternative is successful it may well be tried again and again until it becomes common practice. In this way the value becomes a belief and ultimately an assumption about behaviour

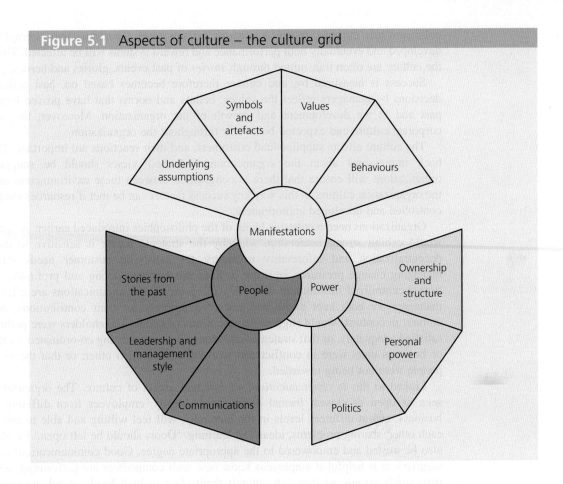

Figure 5.1   Aspects of culture – the culture grid

practised by the organization. These basic *underlying assumptions* are Schein's third level, and they represent the taken-for-granted ways of doing things or solutions to problems.

One belief accepted by employees within a bank might be that all lending must be secure. A football team could be committed to always playing attractive, open football. A university might be expected to have clear beliefs about the relative importance of research and teaching, but this is likely to be an issue where employees 'agree to disagree', leading to a fragmented culture. Examples of *behaviours* are speedy new product development, long working hours, formal management meetings and regular informal meetings or contacts with colleagues, suppliers and customers.

It is also important to appreciate that certain organizations may state that they have particular values, but in reality these will be little more than verbal or written statements or aspirations for the future.

Schein argues that cultural paradigms are formed which determine how 'organization members perceive, think about, feel about, and judge situations and relationships' and these are based on a number of underlying assumptions.

People and culture

For Schwartz and Davis (1981) culture is 'a pattern of beliefs and expectations shared by the organization's members, and which produce norms that powerfully shape the behaviour of individuals and groups in the organization'. They argue that the beliefs held by the company are seen as major aspects of corporate policy as they evolve from interactions with, and in turn form policy towards, the marketplace. As a result, rules or norms for internal and external behaviour are developed and eventually both performance and reward systems will be affected. These aspects of the culture are often transmitted through *stories* of past events, glories and heroes.

Success is measured by, and culture therefore becomes based on, past activities. Current decisions by managers reflect the values, beliefs and norms that have proved beneficial in the past and in the development and growth of the organization. Moreover, they reinforce the corporate culture and expected behaviour throughout the organization.

The culture affects suppliers and customers, and their reactions are important. They will feed back impressions about the organization, and their views should be sought. Successful organizations will ensure that there is congruence between these environmental influences and the organization culture. In this way key success factors can be met if resources are administered, controlled and developed appropriately.

Organizations need a cohesive blend of the philosophies introduced earlier. A cohesive culture would exhibit strong *leadership*, whereby the strategic leader is sensitive to the degrees of decentralization and informality necessary for satisfying customer needs efficiently, and managing change pressures, in order to keep the business strong and profitable. At the same time a centralized information network will ensure that communications are effective and that managers are both kept aware and rewarded properly for their contributions. A fragmented culture, in contrast, would suggest that the needs of certain stakeholders were perhaps not being satisfied adequately, or that strategies and changes were not being co-ordinated, or that managers or business units were in conflict and working against each other, or that the most deserving people were not being rewarded.

Linked to this is *communication*, an essential aspect of culture. The organization might be seen as open or closed, formal or informal. Ideally, employees from different parts of the business, and at different levels in the hierarchy, will feel willing and able to talk openly with each other, sharing problems, ideas and learning. 'Doors should be left open.' Employees should also be trusted and empowered to the appropriate degree. Good communications can stop nasty surprises. It is helpful if employees know how well competitors are performing, where they are particularly strong, so they can commit themselves to high levels of achievement in order to outperform their rivals.

Communication is clearly essential for creating effective internal and external architecture.

Hampden-Turner (1990) argues that culture is based on communication and learning. The strategic leader's vision for the organization must be communicated and understood; events and changes affecting the organization also need to be communicated widely. Managers should be encouraged to seek out new opportunities by learning about new technology and customer expectations, and to innovate. The organization should help them to share their experiences and their learning.

Power and culture

Power is reflected in the *ownership* of the business. It may be a family company with strong, concentrated power. A small group of institutional shareholders could control the business, in which case it is conceivable that short-term financial targets will dictate strategies. *Structural issues* include the extent to which the organization is centralized or decentralized, the role and contribution of corporate headquarters, and control and reward systems. *Personal power* is discussed later in this chapter; *politics* refers to the ways in which managers use power and influence to affect decisions and actions.

Case 5.2 analyses IKEA against this model. IKEA focuses on being a low-cost competitor and achieves this while maintaining a complex supply-chain network. IKEA also has an ability to be flexible in response to local opportunities, which could easily add costs as well as value. The company is product and production driven, but able to capture and use ideas from customers and employees.

Case 5.2

IKEA

Eur

IKEA was started in Sweden by Ingvar Kamprad, who pioneered the idea of self-assembly furniture in handy packs. His vision of 'a better, more beautiful, everyday life for the many' led to 'a wide range of home furnishings, of good function and style, at low prices, for mass consumer markets'. Kamprad began with a mail-order business in 1943; the first IKEA store was opened in 1958. Every year IKEA prints over 110 million catalogues – this is by far the single largest print run of any comparable item anywhere in the world.

Growth has been carefully regulated. IKEA waited for seven years before opening a second branch; the first branch outside Sweden was in the early 1970s; the first US store opened in 1985, with typically one new store being added every year. This approach allows IKEA to establish local supply networks and ensures that it does not become stretched financially. The expansion programme has always been funded from cash generated by the retail activities. IKEA does not have a large market share in any single country; instead, it has a global brand and an intriguing reputation which draws customers from substantial distances away.

By 2006, IKEA had some 207 shops in 24 countries. By 2009 there will be 18 stores in the UK and one in Ireland. IKEA's strategy has always involved high-quality merchandise at prices which undercut the competition. In the mid-1990s IKEA's annual turnover passed the $5 billion mark; after-tax profits were estimated to be 8 per cent of revenue. Sales have risen in every year of its existence, and by 2001 revenues had doubled to $10 billion. They are currently growing at 15 per cent per year. Reputedly worth at least $25 billion, IKEA has always been reticent about the financial data it releases. Moreover, as IKEA has only recently started to target Russia and China, growth prospects appear to remain healthy. In 2006 IKEA returned to Japan, a country it had abandoned in 1994 after being there for twenty years.

IKEA stores focus on sales of self-assembly packs which customers take away themselves. IKEA will, however, deliver fully assembled pieces for a premium price. The stores have a wide range of facilities, typically including restaurants and games and video rooms for children; these are normally on the top floor, which is where customers come in. People are then routed carefully through a series of display areas to the downstairs purchase points which resemble a typical discount warehouse.

The furniture packs are commissioned from over 2300 suppliers in some 70 countries, many of them low labour cost countries in the Far East and Eastern Europe. IKEA has an equity stake in several of its suppliers and insists on tight stock control programmes to reduce costs through the whole supply chain. IKEA designs all its own products and aims to lead customer taste. There is just one range of products for the global market, but not every country and store stocks the full range. IKEA chooses not to have mini-ranges for specific countries and prides itself on an ability to respond to local fashion and opportunities by quickly adjusting the range in any one store. Sales per square foot invariably exceed industry averages.

Manifestations of IKEA's Distinctive Culture

The artefacts clearly include the stores, the products and the prices. There are no brands other than IKEA's own. There are no annual or seasonal sales; prices stay valid for a whole year. There is a plethora of in-store information and communications, but no commissioned sales people.

Values – IKEA's mission statement emphasizes 'functionality, good design, low price and good quality'. The company uses the word 'prosumers' to imply that value is added by both IKEA and their customers in partnership. Employees are empowered to be innovative and helpful and challenged to 'dare to be different'. IKEA recognizes that always offering prices substantially below those of its competitors places considerable pressure on its staff. IKEA also expect, and get, some complaints about busy stores and slow check-out service – a price they claim that has to be paid for low prices. Even though IKEA prices could easily have been increased, Kamprad has stuck with his original approach and mission.

Underlying assumptions   can be summarized in the following quotes:

We do not need to do things in traditional ways (window manufacturers have been approached to make table frames; shirt manufacturers for seat cushions).

Break your chains and you are free; cut your roots and you die. IKEA should look for constant renewal.

Experiments matter; mistakes (within reason) will be tolerated.

IKEA also emphasizes the shared experience – *if we contribute 50 per cent and you [the customer] contributes 50 per cent, we both save.*

Behaviours – Every IKEA manager flies economy class and uses taxis only if there is no suitable alternative. In The Netherlands, managers have been encouraged to stay with typical IKEA customer families to learn more about their needs. Kamprad himself, despite his enormous wealth (estimated at £9 billion), drives a ten year old Volvo car. In this respect he can be likened to the late Sam Walton of Wal-Mart who opted for a pick-up truck.

People

A variety of **stories** permeates the IKEA culture. Initially customers in the US stores were simply not buying any beds – there had been no market research into US tastes; it was IKEA's global product. Eventually, it was realized that Americans sleep in bigger beds than Swedes. Similarly, kitchen units had to be adjusted to handle extra-large pizza plates.

Kamprad denies that there is any truth in the story that his parsimony stretches to him buying cans of Coca-Cola from local supermarkets to replenish hotel room mini-bars because he is reluctant to pay hotel prices for soft drinks.

One less desirable but well-publicized story concerns a stabbing during crowd trouble at the midnight opening of a new store in North London in 2005. IKEA openings are always popular!

Leadership and management style – Kamprad rarely shows his face to the public. At one stage there was some adverse publicity concerning alleged wartime allegiances, but no lasting damage. The lack of published financial information reinforces this hidden aspect of IKEA. Now well into his 70s, Kamprad has declared his three sons will take over the business from him.

Communications – Both customers and employees are encouraged to provide ideas and suggestions, which may be translated into new products. Information enters the system from several points. When Kamprad visits stores he encourages staff to use his Christian name and he spends time with them and IKEA customers receiving feedback.

Power

Ownership and structural issues – IKEA remains a private company which owns all of its sites. It pays for new sites in cash. 'We don't like to be in the hands of the banks.' There are no plans to become a limited company either; Kamprad has criticized the short-term interests of many investors.

The company operates as three distinct activities. The core retailing business is now a Dutch-registered charitable foundation. The profits of the operations are subjected to a top-slice of 3 per cent to fund a separate business which has responsibility for managing the brand and IKEA's franchisees. The third arm is a banking and finance business; IKEA, for example, owns a majority shareholding in Habitat in the UK.

Power – The organization is structured as an inverted pyramid and based on managers and co-workers. 'Employees are there to serve customers'. Kamprad was always concerned that IKEA should not become inflexible as it grew in size. There are no directors, no formal titles and no dining rooms or reserved parking spaces for executives. Managers are quite likely to switch between functions and countries. The organization is fundamentally informal with 'few instructions'. Every year there is an 'anti-bureaucracy' week when everyone dresses casually.

Questions

1 IKEA believes that fashionable and modern furniture and furnishings can be affordable for most families. It need not be prohibitively expensive. How does it achieve this?
2 Do you believe IKEA enjoys E-V-R congruence? If so, what are the key congruency themes? If not, in what way is it incongruent?

IKEA **http://www.ikea.com**

5.3 Determinants of culture

Deal and Kennedy (1982) argue that employees must be rewarded for compliance with the essential cultural aspects if these values are to be developed and retained over time; and they conclude that people who build, develop and run successful companies invariably work hard to create strong cultures within their organizations.

From their research Deal and Kennedy isolated five key elements or determinants of culture.

- The environment and key success factors: what the organization must do well if it is to be an effective competitor. Innovation and fast delivery are examples quoted.

- The values that the strategic leader considers important and wishes to see adopted and followed in the organization. These should relate to the key success factors, and to employee reward systems.

- Heroes: the visionaries who create the culture. They can come from any background and could be, for example, product or service innovators, engineers who build the appropriate quality into the product, or creative marketing people who provide the slogans which make the product or brand name a household word.

- Rites and rituals: the behaviour patterns in which the culture is manifest. Again there are any number of ways in which this can happen, including employees helping each other out when there are difficulties, the way in which sales people deal with customers, and the care and attention that go into production.

- The cultural network: the communications system around which the culture revolves and which determines just how aware employees are about the essential issues.

When the culture is strong, people know what is expected of them and they understand how to act and decide in particular circumstances. They appreciate the issues that are important. When it is weak, time can be wasted in trying to decide what should be done and how. Moreover, it is argued that employees feel better about their companies if they are recognized, known about and regarded as successful, and these aspects will be reflected in the culture.

There can be a number of separate strands to the culture in any organization, which should complement each other. For example, there can be aspects relating to the strategic leader, the environment and the employees. There could be a strong power culture related to an influential strategic leader who is firmly in charge of the organization and whose values are widely understood and followed. This could be linked to a culture of market orientation, which ensures that customer needs are considered and satisfied, and to a work culture if employees feel committed to the organization and wish to help in achieving success.

5.4 Implications of culture

Pümpin (1987) suggests that seven aspects comprise the culture of an organization, and that the relative significance of each of these will vary from industry to industry. The seven aspects are:

1 The extent to which the organization is marketing orientated, giving customers high priority.

2 The relationships between management and staff, manifested through communication and participation systems, for example.

3 The extent to which people are target orientated and committed to achieving agreed levels of performance.

4 Attitudes towards innovation. It is particularly important that the risks associated with failure are perceived as acceptable by all levels of management if innovation and entrepreneurship are to be fostered.

5 Attitudes towards costs and cost reduction.

6 The commitment and loyalty to the organization felt, and shown, by staff.

7 The impact of, and reaction to, technology and technological change and development. One major issue concerns whether or not the opportunities offered by information technology are being harnessed by the firm.

Many of these aspects are developed further in later chapters of the book.

Hampden-Turner (1990) believes that the culture is a manifestation of how the organization has chosen to deal with specific dilemmas and conflicts. Each of these can be viewed as a continuum, and the organization needs a clear position on each one. As shown earlier, one dilemma might be the conflict between, on the one hand, the need to develop new products and services quickly and ahead of competitors and, on the other hand, the need for thorough development and planning to ensure adequate quality and safety. Another dilemma is the need for managers to be adaptive and responsive in a changing environment, but not at the expense of organization-wide communication and awareness. Such change orientation may also conflict with a desire for continuity and consistency of strategy and policy.

Tables 5.1 and 5.2 take this idea further. Table 5.1 highlights how every apparent virtue also has a 'flip side', and consequently something which is positive at one point may suddenly prove

Table 5.1   Every coin, every virtue, has a flip side!

Team players	May be indecisive and avoid risks
Customer focus	Can lead to reactivity and lack of innovation
Action orientation	Can become reckless and dictatorial
Analytical thinking	Can result in paralysis
Innovation	Which is impractical, unrealistic, ill thought-through, wastes time and money
A global vision	May mean valuable local opportunities are missed
Being a good 'people manager'	May allow someone to become soft and walk away from tough decisions

(DEVELOPED FROM IDEAS IN MCCALL, MW (1998) HIGH FLYERS, HARVARD BUSINESS SCHOOL PRESS.)

Table 5.2   The imperfect world of organizations

A market-driven business is likely to be:	An efficient operations-driven business is likely to be:	A growth-orientated business is likely to be:
Resourceful	Efficient	Competitive
Entrepreneurial	Strong on teamworking	Strong on targets and achieving results
Risk oriented	Good at executing plans	Full of hard-working people
Pragmatic in terms of getting things done	Sophisticated with its systems and procedures	Flexible
		Changing quickly
But it may not be:	*But it may not be:*	*But it may not be:*
Consistent	Responsive to customers	Taking a long-term perspective
Disciplined in what it does	Good at managing change	Offering a balanced lifestyle for its employees
Adhering to systems and procedures	Able to see 'the big picture'	Sensitive to people's needs
Strong on teamworking		

(DEVELOPED FROM IDEAS IN MCCALL, MW (1998) HIGH FLYERS, HARVARD BUSINESS SCHOOL PRESS.)

disadvantageous. Table 5.2 looks at the advantages and drawbacks of three business paradigms: a market-orientated business, an organization focused on resource efficiency, and a growth-driven business. Taken together, these confirm that there can never be one best or ideal culture. The culture needs to be flexible and adaptive as circumstances change. The cultural factors that bring initial success may need to be changed if success is to be sustained. Similarly, it is not enough simply to look at what other successful organizations are doing and copy them. Benchmarking and teasing out good practices is both important and beneficial, but these practices again need customizing and adapting to the unique circumstances facing an individual organization.

5.5 Culture and strategy creation

We have already seen that the essential cultural characteristics will dictate the preferred mode of strategy creation in an organization; all the modes are likely to be present to some degree.

The culture will influence the ability of a strategic visionary to 'sell' his or her ideas to other members of the organization and gain their support and commitment to change. The planning mode is most suitable in a reasonably stable and predictable environment, but a reliance on it in a more unstable situation can lead to missed opportunities. It is an ideal mode for a conservative, risk-averse, slow-to-change organization. Where environmental opportunities and threats arise continuously in a situation of competitive chaos an organization must be able to deal with them if it is to survive. It is the culture, with its amalgam of attitudes, values, perceptions and experiences, which determines the outcomes and relative success. The structure must facilitate awareness, sharing and learning, and people must be willing and able to act. People 'learn by doing' and they must be able to learn from mistakes. Peters (1988) states that 'managers have to learn how to make mistakes faster'. The reward system is critical here. Managers and employees should be praised and rewarded for exercising initiative and taking risks which prove successful; failures should not be sanctioned too harshly, as long as they are not repeated!

Berry (1983) argues that if a strategic leader really understands the company culture they must, by definition, be better equipped to make wise decisions. They might conclude that 'cultural change will be so difficult we had better be sure to select a business or strategy that our kind of company can handle well'. This is just as valid as, and perhaps more useful than, believing that one can accomplish cultural change in order to shift the firm towards a new strategy.

Moreover, if business strategies and culture are intertwined, the ability to analyse and construct strategies and the ability to manage and inspire people are also intertwined. Hence, a good strategy acknowledges, 'where we are, what we have got, and what therefore managerially helps us to get where we want to be' and this is substantially different from selecting business options exclusively on their product/market dynamics. In other words, developing and implementing strategy is a human and political process that starts as much with the visions, hopes and aspirations of a company's leaders as it does with market or business analysis. Ideas drive organizations.

With ever-shortening product life cycles, intense global competition and unstable economies and currencies the future is going to require organizations that are ready to commit themselves to change. Strategy is going to be about intertwining analysis and adaptation. The challenge is to develop more effective organizations.

Miles and Snow (1978), whose research has been used to develop Table 5.3, have suggested a typology of organizations which can be looked at in relation to culture and strategy formation. The typology distinguishes organizations in terms of their values and objectives, and different types will typically prefer particular approaches to strategy creation. Defenders, prospectors and analysers are all regarded by Miles and Snow as positive organizations; reactors must ultimately adopt one of the other three approaches or suffer long-term decline. Suggested examples of each

Table 5.3   Organizational values and strategies

Type	Characteristics	Strategy formation
Defenders	Conservative beliefs Low-risk strategies Secure markets Concentration on narrow segments Considerable expertise in narrow areas of specialism Preference for well-tried resolutions to problems Little search for anything really 'new' Attention given to improving efficiency of present operations	Emphasis on planning
Prospectors	Innovative Looking to break new ground High-risk strategies Search for new opportunities Can create change and uncertainty, forcing a response from competitors More attention given to market changes than to improving internal efficiency	Visionary mode
Analysers	*Two aspects: stable and changing* Stable: formal structures and search for efficiencies Changing: competitors monitored and strategies amended as promising ideas seen (followers)	 Planning mode Adaptive/Incremental mode
Reactors	Characterized by an inability to respond effectively to change pressures Adjustments are therefore forced on the firm in order to avert crises	Adaptive mode

type are as follows. GEC, despite being in high-technology industries, was for most of its life relatively conservative and a defender. It built up cash reserves that protected it during cyclical downturns – but was accused of not taking risks! The risk-oriented, innovative Amstrad has always been a prospector. Sometimes Amstrad struggled to implement its innovative ideas. The respective strategic leaders of these organizations, the late Lord Weinstock (until his retirement in 1996) and entrepreneur Sir Alan Sugar adopted different styles of management and leadership and exhibited different corporate values. Weinstock's successor, Lord Simpson, changed to a far higher risk 'prospector' strategy, divesting defence businesses and acquiring telecommunications companies. The outcomes were disappointing and led to the collapse of the company, which had been renamed Marconi. Arguably, as we shall see, cultural change can be disturbing.

Historically, many public-sector bureaucracies have been stable analysers, while Marks and Spencer has long been a changing analyser. Prior to its decline and acquisition by BTR, Dunlop, in the 1970s, exhibited many of the characteristics of a reactor organization, and failed to change sufficiently in line with environmental changes. BTR turned the company around and it was then sold on; the Dunlop and Slazenger branded sporting goods are still popular today. Acquisition saved the business – and was arguably required to save the business.

Miles and Snow argue that, as well as being a classification, their typology can be used to predict behaviour. For example, a defender organization, in a search for greater operating efficiency, might consider investing in the latest technology, but reject the strategy if it has high risk attached.

The power of 'corporate culture' should not be underestimated, both for a company's success and, if it is inappropriate, in frustrating change. Values, strategies, systems, organization and accountabilities – the components of culture – are a very strong mix which can either make a company successful or, alternatively, lead to its decline. The task of corporate leadership is to apply energy and judgement to the corporate culture to ensure its relevance.

SIR ALLEN SHEPPARD, WHEN CHAIRMAN, GRAND METROPOLITAN PLC

5.6   Culture, structure and styles of management

Charles Handy (1976), building on earlier work by Harrison (1972) has developed an alternative classification of organizations based on cultural differences, and this is illustrated in Figure 5.2.

The club culture or power culture

In the club culture type of organization, work is divided by function or product and a diagram of the organization structure would be quite traditional. There would be departments for sales, production, finance and so on, and possibly product-based divisions or strategic business units if the organization was larger. However, this structure is mostly found in smaller firms.

Figure 5.2   Handy's four cultures

Culture	Diagrammatic representation	Structure
Power or club		Web
Role		Greek Temple
Task		Net
Person or existential		Cluster

(ADAPTED FROM HANDY, CB (1976) *UNDERSTANDING ORGANIZATIONS*, PENGUIN)

These functions or departments are represented in Handy's figure by the lines radiating out from the centre; but the essential point is that there are also concentric lines representing communications and power. The further away from the centre, the weaker is the power and influence. This structure is dominated from the centre and therefore is typical for small entrepreneurial organizations. Decisions can be taken quickly, but the quality of the decisions is very dependent on the abilities of managers in the inner circle.

In its heyday Hanson was described by a former director as a 'solar system, with everyone circling around the sun in the middle, Lord Hanson' (see Leadbeater and Rudd 1991). This analogy suggests both movement and dependency. The Hanson story is discussed in detail in Chapter 16 and in a full-length case on the accompanying website.

Decisions depend a great deal on empathy, affinity and trust, both within the organization and with suppliers, customers and other key influences.

People learn to do instinctively what their boss and the organization expect and require. Consequently, they will prove reliable even if they are allowed to exercise a degree of initiative. Foreign-exchange dealers provide an illustration of this point.

For this reason the culture can be designated either 'club' or 'power'. Employees are rewarded for effort, success and compliance with essential values; and change is very much led from the centre in an entrepreneurial style. A culture such as this may prevent individual managers from speaking their minds, but decisions are unlikely to get lost in committees.

The role culture

The role culture is the more typical organization as the culture is built around defined jobs, rules and procedures and not personalities. People fit into jobs, and are recruited for this purpose. Hence, rationality and logic are at the heart of the culture, which is designed to be stable and predictable.

The design is the Greek temple because the strengths of the organization are deemed to lie in the pillars, which are joined managerially at the top. One essential role of top management is to co-ordinate activity, and consequently it will be seen that both planning systems and incremental changes can be a feature of this culture. Although the strength of the organization is in the pillars, power lies at the top. As well as being designed for stability the structure is designed to allow for continuity and changes of personnel, and for this reason dramatic changes are less likely than more gradual ones.

High efficiency is possible in stable environments, but the structure can be slow to change and is therefore less suitable for dynamic situations.

Aspects of this culture can prove beneficial for transport businesses such as railways and airlines, where reliability and timekeeping are essential. Unfortunately, it is not by nature a flexible, service-orientated culture. Intrapreneurship or elements of the task culture are also required for effectiveness.

The task culture

Management in the task culture is concerned with the continuous and successful solution of problems, and performance is judged by the success of the outcomes.

The challenge is more important than the routine.

The culture is shown as a net, because for particular problem situations people and other resources can be drawn from various parts of the organization on a temporary basis. Once the problem is dealt with people will move on to other tasks, and consequently discontinuity is a key element. Expertise is the major source of individual power and it will determine a person's relative power in a given situation. Power basically lies in the interstices of the net, because of the reliance on task forces.

The culture is ideal for consultancies, advertising agencies and research and development departments. It can also be useful within the role culture for tackling particularly difficult or unusual problem situations.

In dynamic environments a major challenge for large organizations is the design of a structure and systems which allow for proper management and integration without losing the spirit and excitement typical of small, entrepreneurial businesses. Elements of the task culture super-imposed over formal roles can help by widening communications and engendering greater commitment within the organization. One feature is cost. This culture is expensive as there is a reliance on talking and discussion, experimentation and learning by trial. Although Handy uses the expression problem solving, there can be problem resolutions or moves towards a solution along more incremental lines, as well as decisions concerning major changes. If successful changes are implemented the expense can often be justified.

The person culture or existential culture

The person culture is completely different from the other three, for here the organization exists to help the individual rather than the other way round. Groups of professional people, such as doctors, architects, dentists and solicitors, provide excellent examples. The organization with secretarial help, printing and telephone facilities and so on provides a service for individual specialists and reduces the need for costly duplication. If a member of the circle leaves or retires, he or she is replaced by another who may have to buy in.

Some professional groups exhibit interdependencies and collaboration, allocating work among the members, although management of such an organization is difficult because of individual expertise and because the rewards and sanctions are different from those found in most other situations.

However, in an environment where government is attempting to increase competition between professional organizations, and in some cases to reduce barriers to entering the profession, it is arguable that effective management, particularly at the strategic level, will become increasingly necessary. Efforts will need co-ordinating and harnessing if organizations are to become strong competitors.

5.7 Management philosophies

Press (1990) suggests that the culture of an organization is based upon one or more philosophies. His ideas are developed in Figure 5.3. The specific philosophies are related to the various stakeholders in the business, and are determined by two intersecting axes. One relates to whether the business is focused more internally or externally; the other is based on performance measures. Do they concentrate more on resource management and efficiency, or outcomes and effectiveness? This creates four discrete philosophies:

- the resource focus, which concentrates on internal efficiencies and cost management
- the shareholder focus, which sees the business as a portfolio of activities which should be managed to maximize the value of the business for its shareholders
- the people focus, which emphasizes the skills and contribution of employees, and their needs and expectations
- the market focus, which stresses the importance of satisfying customers by adding value and differentiating products and services.

All of these are important; none of them can be ignored. The culture can be analysed in terms of how these four philosophies are perceived and prioritized. As pointed out earlier, the philosophy may have to change if success is to be sustained.

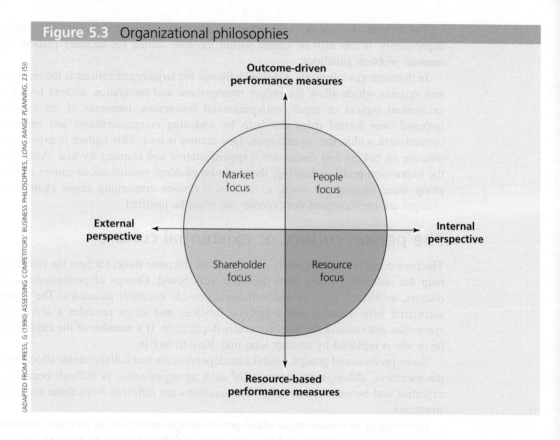

Figure 5.3   Organizational philosophies

(ADAPTED FROM PRESS, G (1990) ASSESSING COMPETITORS' BUSINESS PHILOSOPHIES, *LONG RANGE PLANNING*, 23 (5))

A company which relies heavily upon formal strategic planning, for example, is likely to appear to concentrate more upon shareholders and resources. It used to be argued that at a corporate level the diversified conglomerate, Hanson, was similarly inclined; its individual subsidiary businesses typically had a resource focus, supported by people and market philosophies. Hanson was ultimately split into five separate businesses; the outcomes are discussed in a case in Chapter 16. General Electric (GE) of the US, on the other hand (see Chapters 15 and 16 for further discussion) is another diversified conglomerate but one with a different policy and style from Hanson; GE is perceived to focus more on empowerment and decentralization. GE places most emphasis upon people and its style and culture has proved more enduring. That said, this did not prevent GE being accused of being bottom-line oriented. Japanese companies, discussed later in this chapter, exhibit a particular and distinctive blend of people, markets and resources.

5.8 Styles of management

The style adopted by the strategic leader can have a strong influence on the culture of the organization. Individual leaders can, for example, be relatively autocratic or democratic, visionary or essentially champions of the past, orientated more towards markets or more towards financial controls.

Styles which differ from the 'normal and traditional' can prove to be very effective in particular circumstances. The John Lewis Partnership, Britain's third largest department store chain after Debenhams and House of Fraser, practises worker participation and democracy. John Lewis is also diversified into supermarkets with its Waitrose chain. The company has a chairman, a board of directors and a management structure, as do most companies, but parallel to this commercial structure stands a second structure which represents the interests of the ordinary worker who is also a partner in John Lewis. While a partner working in a department in a store cannot directly influence management decisions, as a result of the partnership and its constitution the ordinary workers are again in ultimate control of the company for which they work. This is supplemented by a profit-sharing scheme. Decision-making and communications within the organization must be affected by high levels of participation. John Lewis's motto of 'never knowingly undersold' is based on value for money which is helped by employee involvement. Through its workforce the company can relate well to its customers.

> *Everyone in the business feels (and is) involved. Everyone also feels (and is) accountable, especially those at the top. Top management are given lots of freedom to determine and change strategy, but they can be questioned on anything by the rank-and-file partners ... this ... makes people think ahead and consider the consequences of their actions.*

STUART HAMPSON, CHAIRMAN, JOHN LEWIS PARTNERSHIP SPEAKING IN 1993. HAMPSON WAS ONLY THE FOURTH CHAIRMAN SINCE THE PARTNERSHIP WAS FORMED IN 1929

5.9 Culture and power

In Charles Handy's classification of organizations in terms of their culture, power is an important element which needs further consideration. While an introduction to the topic is included here, the subject of power is explored more fully in Chapter 15 when its impact on strategy implementation and strategic change is considered.

Power is related to the potential or ability to do something. Consequently strategic change will be strongly influenced by the bases of power within an organization and by the power of the organization in relation to its environment.

Internal power

Change is brought about if the necessary resources can be harnessed and if people can be persuaded to behave in a particular way. Both of these require power. Power results in part from the structure of the organization, and it needs exercising in different ways in different cultures if it is to be used effectively. At the same time power can be a feature of an individual manager's personality, and managers who are personally powerful will be in a position to influence change.

The ways in which managers apply power are known as 'power levers'; Critical reflections 5.1 describes seven major sources of power. The classifications of power bases produced by a number of authors differ only slightly. Critical reflections 5.1 has been developed from a classification by Andrew Kakabadse (1982), who has built on the earlier work of French and Raven (1959).

In order to understand the reality of change in an organization and to examine how change might be managed, it is important to consider where power lies, which managers are powerful, and where their sources of power are. While a visible, powerful and influential strategic leader is often a feature of an entrepreneurial organization, the nature and direction of incremental change will be influenced significantly by which managers are powerful and how they choose to exercise their power.

A power culture has strong central leadership as a key feature and power lies with the individual or small group at the centre who controls most of the activity in the organization. In contrast, role cultures are based on the legitimacy of rules and procedures and individual managers are expected to work within these. Task cultures are dependent on the expertise of individuals, and their success, in some part, depends on the ability of the individuals to share their power and work as a team. Managers are expected to apply power levers in ways that are

Critical reflection 5.1

Power Levers

1 Reward power is the ability to influence the rewards given to others. These can be tangible (money) or intangible (status). Owner managers enjoy considerable reward power, managers in larger public sector organizations very little. For reward power to be useful, the rewards being offered must be important to the potential recipients.

2 Coercive power is power based on the threat of punishment for non-compliance, and the ability to impose the punishment. The source can be the person's role or position in the organization, or physical attributes and personality.

3 Legitimate power is synonymous with authority, and relates to an individual manager's position within the structure of the organization. It is an entitlement from the role a person occupies. The effective use of legitimate power is dependent on three things: access to relevant information; access to other people and communication networks inside the organization; and approaches to setting priorities – this determines what is asked of others.

4 Personal power depends on individual characteristics (personality) and physical characteristics. Charm, charisma and flair are terms used to describe people with personality-based power. Physical attributes such as height, size, weight and strength also affect personal power.

5 Expert power is held by a person with specialist knowledge or skills in a particular field. It is particularly useful for tackling complex problem areas. It is possible for people to be attributed expert power through reputation rather than proven ability.

6 Information power is the ability to access and use information to defend a stance or viewpoint – or to question an alternative view held by someone else – and is important as it can affect strategic choices.

7 Connection power results from personal and professional access to key people inside and outside the organization, who themselves can influence what happens. This relates particularly to information power.

acceptable to the predominant culture of the organization, and at the same time the manner in which power levers are actually used affects what happens in the organization. Power is required for change; change results from the application of power. Hence the implementation of desired changes to strategies requires the effective use of power bases; but other strategic changes will result from the exercise of power by individual managers. It is important for the organization to monitor such activity and ensure that such emergent changes and strategies are desirable or acceptable.

The relative power of the organization

The ability of an organization to effect change within its environment will similarly depend on the exercise of power. A strong competitor with, say, a very distinctive product or service, or with substantial market share, may be more powerful than its rivals. A manufacturer who is able to influence distributors or suppliers will be similarly powerful. The issue is the relative power in relation to those other individuals, organizations and institutions – its stakeholders – on whom it relies, with whom it trades, or which influence it in some way.

5.10 Culture and competitive advantage

Barney (1986) has examined the relationship between culture and 'superior financial performance'. He has used micro-economics for his definition of superior financial performance, arguing that firms record either below-normal returns (insufficient for long-term survival in the industry), normal returns (enough for survival, but no more) or superior results, which are more than those required for long-term survival. Superior results, which result from some form of competitive advantage, attract competitors who seek to copy whatever is thought to be the source of competitive advantage and generating the success. This in turn affects supply and margins and can reduce profitability to only normal returns and, in some cases, below normal. Therefore, sustained superior financial performance requires sustained competitive advantage. Barney concluded that culture can, and does, generate sustained competitive advantage, and hence long-term superior financial performance, when three conditions are met.

- The culture is valuable. The culture must enable things to happen which themselves result in high sales, low costs or high margins.
- The culture is rare.
- The culture is imperfectly imitable, i.e. it cannot be copied easily by competitors.

Peters and Waterman's (1982) research-based book *In Search of Excellence* identified a number of factors which appeared to explain the success of a number of large American businesses. Although this work was in part discredited, as some successful companies experienced declining fortunes, the book focused on aspects of corporate culture and emphasized its impact on corporate performance. At the time the question raised was: if the cultural factors identified by Peters and Waterman were in fact transferable easily to other organizations, could they be the source of superior financial performance? Barney contends that valuable and rare cultures may be difficult, if not impossible, to imitate. For one thing, it is very difficult to define culture clearly, particularly in respect of how it adds value to the product or service. For another, culture is often tied to historical aspects of company development and to the beliefs, personality and charisma of a particular strategic leader.

Case 5.3, Club Méditerranée and Online Case 5.1 earlier (The Body Shop) both provide examples of companies which have gained success and renown with a culture-based competitive advantage. While maintaining the underlying principles and values, both companies have had to rethink their strategies to remain competitive. Club Méditerranée highlights how difficult it can

Case 5.3

Club Méditerranée   Eur

Club Med, founded in 1950 in France, became Europe's largest tour operator with a clearly distinguished product.

The original Club Med represented 'beautiful people playing all sorts of sports, white sand beaches, azure sky and sea, Polynesian thatched huts, free and flowing wine at meals, simple yet superb food' (*Economist*, 12 July 1986). It was an 'organized melange of hedonism and back to nature'.

The organization systematically spread around the world, opening over 100 holiday villages and over 60 holiday residences (hotel/sports complexes) for both summer and winter vacations. Organizers were present in a ratio of 1:5 with guests, for whom they provided sports tuition and organized evening entertainment. Traditionally all tuition, food and drinks with meals

were paid for in advance in the holiday cost, and guests were provided with beads which they used as they chose to buy extra drinks and so on. Clothing was permanently casual.

Club Med has traditionally charged prices above the average for package holidays, its clientele have been mainly above-average income earners, and the organization has enjoyed a reputation for delivering customer service and satisfaction. The strategy was developed and maintained by one of the two founders of the business, Gilbert Trigano. Although Trigano was always an influential strategic leader, Club Med is a public company, with most of its equity held by institutional shareholders.

In the early days a culture of creativity and teamworking was encouraged at all levels in Club

Med. Gilbert Trigano always saw the organization as 'one big, happy family'. No employee should feel as if they are simply a pawn; promotions are typically from within. The loyalty of Club Med staff has typically been very high, making it difficult for outsiders to come in as managers. Trigano and his partner, Gerald Blitz, set up Club Med as an organization 'without rules – in a world where most companies operate with fixed rules and structures. Everyone is under an obligation to create, but, of course, not every idea is a success'.

The company grew successfully for over 30 years with little change to the basic strategy. By the mid-1980s, however, occupancy rates had fallen, and profits declined and then stagnated. While the underlying concept was still sound, people's tastes were changing. Holidaymakers increasingly sought higher quality facilities than the straw huts provided. Many Americans wanted televisions and telephones – yet it was the absence of these which helped make Club Med unique.

Building on the original concept and strategy, Club Med developed new products in order to better satisfy selected audiences around the world. In addition to the traditional villages, where in some cases straw huts were replaced by bungalows, Club Med introduced cheaper, half-board holidays in newly acquired hotels and villages, at the same time as it opened more expensive properties. This latter development was pioneered at Opio, near Cannes, which opened in 1989. Opio has expensive rooms with facilities, and, unusually, is open 12 months of the year. The international conference trade was being targeted. A limited number of villages experimented with a multilingual staffing policy to ensure that visitors from different European countries could all be greeted in their own language. Attempts have been made to attract more American visitors, but there has always been some scepticism. Americans are more puritanical in their tastes and expectations, and Club Med's sexy image has not proved as successful in the USA.

There have also been problems with certain other strategic developments:

- Profitability at the Vienna City Hotel and from two cruise ships was never adequate.
- New developments in Japan were delayed.
- In 1991 Club Med bought a controlling stake in a second charter airline – its first airline came when Club Med acquired a competitor in the 1980s. Combined the two could fly to 100 destinations spread over 20 countries on four continents. In reality, Club Med had too much capacity and ended up selling 80 per cent stakes in both airlines.

In 1993, with European occupancy rates depressed, Club Med recorded its worst ever results to date. Gilbert Trigano (then aged 72) partially retired and was succeeded by his son, Serge, who was determined to:

- accelerate developments in new territories such as Asia and
- reduce costs to allow for more competitive prices, still with quality and innovation – it was 'time to realize people would not always come just because it is Club Med'.

'It is by focusing on our core business that we will return to profit.'

Nevertheless, Rosemary Astles, Marketing Director at Thomson Holidays, was quoted as saying 'Club Med has a reasonably unique formula that has worked well in a number of markets … but there will be [only] limited growth for the club concept in the future. It's a fairly mature market.'

Serge Trigano resigned after losses in 1995. Interestingly – and unusually – Serge Trigano had no personal shareholding; and his father owned just 0.8 per cent of the business. He reflected: 'Perhaps I was not quick enough to take the necessary measures … perhaps we should have closed loss-making villages more quickly.'

Club Med appointed a new Chief Executive in February 1997; Philippe Bourguignon had previously been Chairman of Euro Disney.

Club Med reportedly 'began preparing for a future of tougher professional management' while conscious of the need to retain the important aspects of its culture, image and strategy. After all, the company was still successful. There had been 20 million customers in its 47 years and 1.4 million of those holidayed at Club Med villages and hotels in 1995–96. New imitations were happening all the time as the idea of the 'all-inclusive' holiday has grown in popularity. Nevertheless, the emphasis has been changing. Telephones in rooms and tables for two instead of eight, for example, were becoming increasingly normal as the average age of customers increased.

The first main change announced by Bourguignon implied the abandonment of the ubiquitous beads (for purchasing extra drinks) in favour of smart cards, which would enable tighter management controls. The fully inclusive package concept was retained; earlier trials with à la carte alternatives had not proved successful. It is relevant to mention the increasing popularity of all-inclusive resort holidays in general in recent years. Bourguignon commented: 'Club Med is a well known product but with a fuzzy identity. It is far too French in an international context. We need a complete recreation of the group. The concept is not outdated but the image is stuck in the 1970s.'

After a period of review it was decided to abandon the Club Aquarius budget format, re-creating most of these villages in the traditional Club Med style. At the other end of the scale, the most luxurious five-star villages were phased out in favour of the typical mid-range three-star village. Between 1998 and 2000 some 74 out of a remaining 120 villages were renovated. Some now had a more limited range of activities. Linked to this was a major price restructuring – low-season holidays in particular were discounted by up to 30 per cent – and new advertising was targeted directly at younger people.

In 2000 turnover touched 2 billion Euros from 1.6 million guests in 130 locations across 40 countries. There were 21,500 employees of many nationalities. Many Club Med employees – especially those who work directly with guests – are expected to speak more than one language. They are typically young, on fixed term contracts and paid only modestly. Over half stay for just one season. They are charged with keeping guests happy whilst operating profitable resorts for the company's shareholders.

In 2001 Bourguignon announced a new diversification – into entertainment centres in or near the world's largest cities, beginning with Paris. Bookshops, travel agencies, restaurants, gymnasiums, restaurants, concert halls and nightclubs would all fit the concept.

A year later Club Med saw jobs being axed as profits fell back again – the first recorded loss since 1997. Bourguignon left just before the end of the year. Yet again, the powerful Agnelli family – the Italian family behind the Fiat and Ferrari empire – had exercised their power as leading shareholders. Together with others they had not been sold on the entertainment centre strategy. The new Chief Executive was Henri Giscard d'Estang, son of the former French President, who opted to focus more on the core product. The fundamental business model 'was not broken'. In 2004, after experiencing financial difficulties with their mainstream

businesses, the Agnelli family sold its stake to Accor, the French hotel chain, perhaps best known for its Sofitel brand.

After a period of consolidation, leaving 95 villages, Giscard announced a new line of super de-luxe boutique hotels, beginning with a 60-bed property in Marrakesh, The Riad. Some 40 poorer-grade properties had been closed down and the remaining 95 had been or were being refurbished. The idea behind the boutique properties is to locate them close to the traditional villages. That way, residents can enjoy luxury and privacy but still use the sports and other leisure facilities at the villages whenever they want.

After four years of trading losses there was a return to profitability in 2005. In 2006 Accor sold the bulk of its investment to focus on its core hotels business. Club Med is left with a variety of international shareholders with small stakes, including Air France-KLM. During this year some 500 million Euros was invested in refurbishments. In 2008 there are 80 villages operating and Club Med has a new global advertising campaign on the theme: 'Where Happiness Means The World'.

Questions

1 Is Club Med now realistically a limited-appeal niche product? If so, what are the implications of this fact? If not, how might the business be expanded?
2 Is there actually a real future for the Club Med business model?
3 Is there a risk in having a dispersed shareholder portfolio if a business has valuable property assets?

© BRITISH RETAIL PHOTOGRAPHY/ALAMY

be to sustain competitive success when values are core but the competitive environment changes. This case also brings out the use of power by external shareholders to change the strategic leader when the strategy is proving unsuccessful.

The limits to excellence To summarize, some firms do appear to obtain superior financial performance from their cultures, but it does not follow that firms who succeed in copying these cultural attributes will necessarily also achieve superior financial results. Organizations which pursue the excellence factors must surely improve their chances of success, but clearly there can be no guarantees. Ignoring these issues will, however, increase the chances of failure.

The need to maintain E–V–R congruence in a dynamic, competitive environment must never be forgotten. During the early 1980s Jan Carlzon turned around the struggling SAS (Scandinavian Airlines System) by focusing on improvements in service and communications. Profits were restored with improved revenues, but costs later increased as well. As a driving philosophy, the service culture had to give way to a focus strategy and rationalization.

Changing culture

The culture of an organization may appear to be in need of change for any one of a number of reasons. It could be that the culture does not fit well with the needs of the environment or with the organization's resources, or that the company is not performing well and needs major strategic changes, or even that the company is growing rapidly in a changing environment and needs to adapt.

Ideally, the culture and strategies being pursued will complement each other and, again ideally, the organization will be flexible and adaptable to change when it is appropriate. But these ideals will not always be achieved.

The culture of an organization can be changed, but it may not be easy. Strong leadership and vision is always required to champion the change process. If an organization is in real difficulty, and the threat to its survival is clearly recognized, behaviour can be changed through fear and necessity. However, people may not feel comfortable and committed to the changes they accept or are coerced into accepting. Behaviour may change, but not attitudes and beliefs. When an organization is basically successful the process of change again needs careful management – changing attitudes and beliefs does not itself guarantee a change in behaviour. It is not unusual for a team of senior managers to spend time, frequently at a location away from the organization itself, discussing these issues and becoming excited about a set of new values that they proclaim are the way forward. After the workshop any commitment to the new values and to change can be easily lost once managers return to the daily grind and they become caught up again in immediate problems and difficulties. Their behaviour does not change and so the culture remains largely untouched.

The potential for changing the culture is affected by:

- the strength and history of the existing culture
- how well the culture is understood
- the personality and beliefs of the strategic leader and
- the extent of the strategic need.

Lewin (1947) contends that there are three important stages in the process of change: unfreezing existing behaviour, changing attitudes and behaviour, and refreezing the new behaviour as accepted common practice.

The first steps in changing culture are recognizing and diagnosing the existing culture, highlighting any weaknesses and stressing the magnitude of the need to change.

One way of changing behaviour would be the establishment of internal groups to study and benchmark competitors and set new performance standards. This would lead to wider discussion throughout the organization, supported by skills training – possibly including communication, motivation and financial awareness skills. People must become committed to the changes, which requires persistence by those who are championing the change and an emphasis on the significance and the desired outcomes.

Unless the changes become established and part of the culture, there will be a steady drift back to the previous pattern. While critical aspects of the culture should remain rock solid and generate strategic consistency, this must not mean that the organization becomes resistant to change without some major upheaval. Competitive pressures require organizations to be vigilant, aware and constantly change-orientated, not change-resistant.

Resistance to change should always be expected. People may simply be afraid because they do not understand the reasons behind the proposed changes; they may mistrust colleagues or management because of previous experiences; communications may be poor; motivation and commitment may be missing; internal architecture may be weak, causing internal conflict and hostility; and the organization may simply not be good at sharing best practice and learning. This topic is revisited in Chapter 15, Leading change.

Culture – an international dimension

(In my mind) the England (football) team plays with passion; Germany is about determination; the French have subtlety and Spain demonstrate pride.

ARSENE WENGER, MANAGER, ARSENAL FC

There are cultural differences between nations and ethnic groups. What constitutes acceptable behaviour in one country (for example, bribes) would be totally unacceptable in others. Ways of conducting discussions and deals vary – Indians always like and expect to negotiate, for instance. Some countries, such as France, have a high respect for tradition and the past, while others, such as the US, are more interested in future prospects. This influences the extent to which both individuals and organizations are judged on their track record and on their promise. These differences are important because business is conducted across frontiers and because many organizations have bases in several countries. Organizations, therefore, have to adjust their style for different customers and markets and accept that there will be cultural differences between the various parts of the organization. This reality affects the ability of the strategic leader to synthesize the various parts of the organization and achieve the potential synergies.

Related to these issues, research by Kanter (1991) drew out different perspectives on competitive success between the leading nations, where she argued that these stemmed from national cultures and cultural differences. Her findings indicated the following priorities:

- Japan   Product development

  Management

  Product quality

- USA   Customer service

  Product quality

  Technology

- Germany   Workforce skills

  Problem-solving

  Management

These conclusions may be summarized by arguing that Japan is driven by a commitment to innovation, America by customers and Germany by engineering.

Interestingly, the report highlighted how UK competitiveness had been enhanced by its drive to privatize public services and other state-owned organizations, the opening up of its capital markets and its encouragement of inward investment. At the same time it is arguably inhibited by an education system which discourages rather than encourages creativity, individualism and entrepreneurship, by a general lack of language skills and, for many, a preference for leisure over work. While a case can be made that these issues are being addressed in various ways, they remain relative weaknesses.

Differences in international cultures have been examined by various authors, including Hofstede (1991), Kluckhohn and Strodtbeck (1961) and Trompenaars and Hampden-Turner (1997). The following points have been distilled from their findings. From these points general conclusions may be drawn about cultural differences between nations; but it must also be recognized that certain organizations in the same country do not automatically fit the national picture in every respect. In some respects, for example, Sony is typically Japanese. In other respects it behaves more like an American company, such that research has confirmed that many US citizens think that Sony is American!

- Some countries and cultures prefer a watertight contractual approach while others are more comfortable with trust and a handshake. The appropriate way of conducting business therefore varies accordingly.

- In some countries managers operate with individual freedom and responsibility, and negotiations are on a one-to-one basis. In others there will invariably be a team of people involved. Where there are multiple decision-makers like this, there will sometimes be a clear hierarchy and recognition of the relative power of various individuals. On other occasions such demarcations will be less obvious or visible.

- In addition, individual managers can be relatively selfish in their outlook, or far more corporate. This can have a particular bearing on where managers' natural competitive energy is channelled. Is it directed at outside competitors, as realistically it should be, or at perceived internal rivals? Simply, would a culture of internal rivalry inside an organization be typical or rare?

- There is also an issue of women managers. In some countries they will not be found, either at all, or at least in positions of real authority.

- Leisure activities can play a relatively minor or more prominent role in business. The image of the British bank manager who enjoys long lunches and regular golf matches with clients has been largely confined to history, but negotiations and networking away from the place of business can still be important. Corporate hospitality at major sporting events would be one example, but it is not practised universally.

- Senses of humour also vary, which begs the question: is creativity more likely to be found in some countries than others? Creativity implies elements of fun and irreverence, challenging existing ways and looking for new and different alternatives. Certainly humour, together with other issues, such as the symbolism of certain objects and colours, affects advertising and promotion. The same campaigns cannot necessarily be used on a global scale.

- This leads on to a final point: do managers in different countries have similar or different perspectives on uncertainty? Some countries, organizations and managers are relatively risk orientated and view environmental turbulence as a source of opportunity. They look to be proactive. Others seek to be more reactive and adaptive, attempting to find positions of stability amongst the perceived chaos.

Since the end of the World War II Japan has risen to become a major economic force around the world, with some Japanese companies extremely prominent in certain industries. The Japanese style of management is very different in some respects from that found in most Western countries and, while it cannot simply be copied – largely because of cultural differences – it offers a number of important and valuable lessons. Consequently, this chapter finishes with a section on Japanese culture and management style. At the end we present a brief and contrasting summary of China. In recent years China's economy has grown rapidly as China has emerged as a leading manufacturer for the world. One key difference is that the Chinese have not – as yet – provided the technological inspiration that has come from Japan. Despite the great success of the Far East it is significant that neither China nor Japan is immune from the global recession of 2009. Inevitably they are affected by the problems of the West as located here are some of their main markets. Globalization really does mean sharing the pain as well as the profits.

The Japanese culture and style of management

Without question, Japanese companies have become formidable competitors in several industries. We saw earlier that Toyota and Sony were the only two non-American businesses to appear in the world's top ten most respected companies. For many years they have been the principal challengers of Western firms serious about world markets. More recently domestic recession, a high yen and intensifying competition from other Pacific Rim countries (many with lower wages) have restrained Japan's global expansion. However, a study of the philosophies, strategies and tactics adopted by Japanese companies will yield a number of valuable insights into competitive strategy, even though it is impractical to suggest that Western businesses could simply learn to copy their Japanese rivals. This section looks at some of the reasons for Japan's economic rise and success; it has to be acknowledged that in the 1990s some of the practices have changed. 'In the long-run the only feasible response is to do better what the Japanese are doing well already – developing management systems that motivate employees from top to bottom to pursue growth-oriented, innovation-focused competitive strategies' (Pucik and Hatvany, 1983).

Deal and Kennedy (1982) have argued that 'Japan Inc.' is a culture, with considerable co-operation between industry, the banking systems and government. For this reason certain aspects of the Japanese culture are difficult to imitate. For example, banks in the UK are public companies with their own shareholders and they borrow and lend money in order to make profit; this is their basic 'mission'.

Another key structural feature historically has been the *keiretsu*, or corporate families, whereby a unique mix of ownerships and alliances makes hostile takeovers very unlikely. At its height, for example, the powerful Mitsubishi *keiretsu* represented 216,000 employees in 29 organizations as diverse as banking, brewing, shipping, shipbuilding, property, oil, aerospace and textiles. The companies held, on average, 38 per cent of each other's shares; directors were exchanged; and the fact that 15 of the companies were located together in one district of Tokyo facilitated linkages of various forms, including intertrading wherever this was practical. The *keiretsu* influence is fading as Japanese companies are locating more and more production overseas in their search for lower manufacturing costs. Mitsubishi's shipping company, for instance, has begun to buy vessels manufactured in Korean yards; Japanese shipbuilders are no longer an automatic low-price competitor.

Culture plays a significant role at the heart of the Japanese strategy process.

In Japan the historic focus has been on human resources (Pucik and Hatvany, 1983) and this became the basis for three key strategic thrusts which are expressed as a number of management techniques. These have acted as key determinants of the actual strategies pursued (Figure 5.4). The three strategic thrusts are the notion of an internal labour market within the organization, a unique company philosophy, and intensive socialization throughout the working life.

The internal labour market is based on the tradition of lifetime employment whereby young men (not women) who joined large companies after school or university were expected to remain with them for life and in return were offered job security. Commitment and loyalty to the

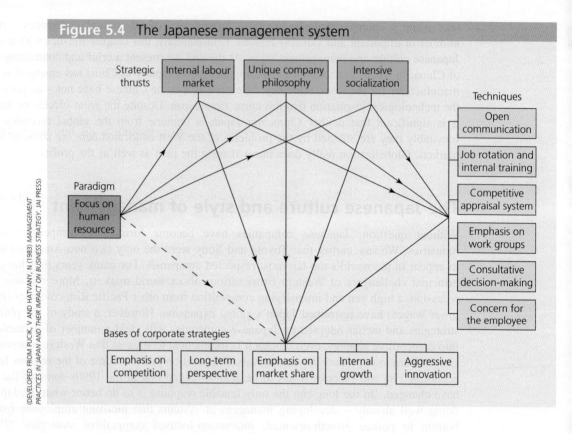

Figure 5.4 The Japanese management system

(DEVELOPED FROM PUCIK, V AND HATVANY, N (1983) MANAGEMENT PRACTICES IN JAPAN AND THEIR IMPACT ON BUSINESS STRATEGY, JAI PRESS)

employer result. With recession in recent years and the growing use of sub-contractors this practice has been less widespread.

The articulated and enacted unique philosophy is again designed to generate commitment and loyalty with the argument that familiarity with the goals of a company helps to establish values and provides direction for effort and behaviour. YKK's 'Cycle of Goodness' (Strategy in action 5.1) is an excellent example. We introduced YKK when we discussed the value chain in Chapter 3.

The potential benefits of a company philosophy will only be gained if the philosophy is communicated to employees and demonstrated by managers. Hence this is a key aspect of company socialization in Japan, which starts with initial training and continues with further training throughout the working life.

These three strategic thrusts are closely linked to six management techniques used extensively in Japanese firms.

Open communication and sharing information across departmental boundaries aims to develop a climate of trust and a team spirit within the organization. This is enhanced by close integration between managers and employees. Job rotation and the internal training programmes supplement this communication system because through them employees become more aware of what happens throughout the organization. Because of relatively low labour turnover, promotion opportunities are very limited and advancement is slow and often based on seniority. However, performance is essential, and employees are carefully and regularly appraised in their abilities to get things done and to co-operate with others. This is particularly important as Japanese companies revolve around groups rather than individuals, with work being assigned to teams of employees. This, together with the use of quality circles (whereby groups of employees are encouraged to discuss issues and problems and suggest improvements), is seen as a key motivator. There is considerable emphasis on consultative decision-making, involving these

Strategy in action 5.1

The Cycle of Goodness

The Cycle of Goodness was created by Tadeo Yoshida, President, YKK

YKK is the world's leading manufacturer of zip fasteners. YKK produces and markets zips throughout the world, and is vertically integrated, designing and manufacturing much of its own machinery.

I firmly believe in the spirit of social service.

Wages alone are not sufficient to assure our employees of a stable life and a rising standard of living. For this reason we return to them a large share of the fruits of their labour, so that they may also participate in capital accumulation and share in the profits of the firm. Each employee, depending on his means, deposits with the company at least ten per cent of his wages and monthly allowances, and 50 per cent of his bonus; the company, in turn, pays interest on these savings. Moreover, as this increases capital, the employees benefit further as stockholders of the firm. It is said that the accumulation of savings distinguishes man from animals. Yet, if the receipts of a day are spent within that day, there can be no such cycle of saving.

The savings of all YKK employees are used to improve production facilities, and contribute directly to the prosperity of the firm. Superior production facilities improve the quality of the goods produced. Lower prices increase demand. And both factors contribute to the prosperity of other industries that use our products.

As society prospers, the need for raw materials and machinery of all sorts increases, and the benefits of this cycle spread out not just to this firm, but to all related industries. Thus the savings of our employees, by enhancing the prosperity of the firm, are returned to them as dividends that enrich their lives. This results in increased savings which further advance the firm. Higher incomes mean higher tax payments, and higher tax payments enrich the lives of every citizen. In this manner, business income directly affects the prosperity of society; for businesses are not mere seekers after profit, but vital instruments for the improvement of society.

This cycle enriches our free society and contributes to the happiness of those who work within it. The perpetual working of this cycle produces perpetual prosperity for all. This is the cycle of goodness.

YKK **http://www.ykk.com**

© RETINA 2020/DREAMSTIME.COM

working groups, and a desire for consensus decisions. This generates greater loyalty to the decisions and to implementation. Finally, managers are encouraged to spend time with employees discussing both performance and personal problems. Companies have also frequently provided housing and various other services for employees.

Several Japanese companies have invested in manufacturing plants in the US and Europe in recent years. In a number of cases they have selected industries where the country had already ceased to manufacture products because of an inability to compete (e.g. television sets and video recorders) or where the competitive edge had declined. Motor vehicles is an example of the latter. The British car industry fell behind the Japanese and German producers in terms of quality and productivity and has struggled to catch up. The first Japanese car plant in the UK was built by Nissan near Sunderland and, using a Japanese approach – rather than adopting all the techniques described in this section – it has become the most productive car plant in the UK, and one of Nissan's most efficient anywhere in the world. Yet again, Nissan's most productive plant has had to reduce output in 2009 – the market for its cars had declined.

Hill (1990) explains that the key human resources aspects of the Nissan UK strategy are as follows:

- There is a single union agreement, with the AEU.
- All employees (including managers) have the same conditions of employment, and wear similar blue overalls at work.
- There are no (inflexible) written job descriptions.
- There is no clocking on and no privileged parking.
- Absenteeism has remained very low.
- There are daily communications meetings – searching for continuous improvement.
- Employees often go to Japan for training – skilled workers learn both operational and maintenance skills.
- The training budget, equivalent to 14 per cent of sales revenue, is exceptionally high for a British company. A typical employee will receive 9 days on-the-job and 12 days off-the-job training each year.
- Supervisors are empowered managers. They recruit and select their own staff (individually they are responsible for about 20 employees), and they control the layout and operation of their own part of the production line.

The core of management is the art of mobilizing every ounce of intelligence in the organization and pulling together the intellectual resources of all employees in the service of the firm. We know that the intelligence of a handful of technocrats, however brilliant and smart they may be, is no longer enough. Only by drawing on the combined brain power of all its employees can a firm face up to the turbulence and constraints of today's environment.

MR. KONOSUKE MATSUSHITA, MATSUSHITA ELECTRICAL INDUSTRIAL COMPANY LTD

Quality and competition Prahalad and Hamel (1985) have suggested that the Japanese 'rewrite the rules of the game to take their competitors by surprise'. Through technology, design, production costs, distribution and selling arrangements, pricing and service they seek to build 'layers of competitive advantage' rather than concentrate on just one aspect. Many competitors in the West think more narrowly. Prahalad and Hamel suggest that Japanese companies are successful in part because they have a clear mission and statement of strategic intent, and a culture which provides both opportunity and encouragement to change things incrementally. Getting things right first time and every time – total quality management – is endemic in the culture.

Internationally, Japanese companies may not be consistent with their strategies; instead they will seek the best competitive opportunities in different places and they will change continually as new opportunities arise and are created.

Japanese companies benchmark against the best in the world and willingly customize their products to meet local market demand.

Long-term perspective While many Western companies concentrate on short-term strategies, influenced often by financial pressures, the Japanese take a long-term perspective.

Emphasis on market share Japanese companies are competitive, growth orientated and anxious to build and sustain high market shares in world markets. This will enable them to provide the job security that is a fundamental aspect of the culture. They often use their experience curve (which is examined in detail in the supplement to Chapter 4) to develop strategies aimed at market dominance with a long-term view of costs and prices.

Internal growth Mergers, acquisitions and divestitures are relatively uncommon in Japan – the Japanese favour the internal production system and innovation.

In a book on Japanese manufacturing techniques, Schonberger (1984) argued that a major reason for Japan's success has been its ability to use its resources well, better than many Western competitors. In many factories, he contends, the equipment is no better than that used elsewhere in the world, but wherever they can Japanese companies invest in the best equipment available. Managerial skills are used in improvement drives, a search for simple solutions and, in particular, a meticulous attention to detail. Simplicity is important since management and shop floor can relate better to each other; and flexible techniques and workforces result in low stock production systems, efficiency and lower costs.

The ability to trust and establish close links with other companies in the supply chain allows focused specialization and just in time manufacturing with low inventories. However, this type of dependency can act as a hindrance to global expansion until comparative supplier links can be established.

Innovation Research and development is deemed important and funded appropriately. As a result much of Japan's technology has advanced quickly, and firms who fail to innovate go out of business. Ohmae (1985) has described Japan as a 'very unforgiving economy', with thousands of corporations destroyed every year through bankruptcy. He points out that Japan is selective about the industries in which research and development will be concentrated. Japan has, for example, spent a relatively high proportion of its research and development money in ceramics and steel, and as a result has become a world leader in fibre optics, ceramics and mass-produced large-scale integrated circuits. For similar reasons the US is world leader in biotechnology and specialized semiconductors, and Europe in chemicals and pharmaceuticals.

Product innovation in Japan is fast and competitive. For example, Sony launched the first miniaturized camcorder (hand-held video camera and recorder) in June 1989. Weighing less than 700 g (1.5 lb) it was one-quarter of the size of existing camcorders. Within six months Matsushita and JVC had introduced lighter models. Within a further six months there was additional competition from Canon, Sanyo, Ricoh and Hitachi. Sony introduced two new models in summer 1990. One was the lightest then available; the other had superior technical features. More recent models feature larger viewfinders and allow the user to hold the camcorder at arm's length instead of up to the eye. In recent years we have seen exactly the same trend with laptop computers.

This faster model replacement is linked to an ability to break even financially with fewer sales of each model. Japan has achieved this with efficient and flexible manufacturing systems and a greater willingness to use common, rather than model-specific, components.

Individual Western companies have proved that it is possible, with determination and distinctive products, to penetrate Japanese markets successfully, but contenders can expect fierce resistance and defensive competition.

Although they are relatively close neighbours in the Far East, China and Japan are very different in their approach and culture. Table 5.4 provides an overview of the contrasting and

Table 5.4 The Chinese culture and style of management

Positive features	Negative features
Will work even harder to solve a crisis	Poor on punctuality
Takes direction well	Not natural team workers
Very committed to the organization	Do not share knowledge easily
Desire to learn	Lack of questioning on strategic options
More risk taking than Japanese managers	Dislike of change

DEVELOPED BY FRANK MARTIN FROM A NUMBER OF CHINESE STUDENT MANAGEMENT DISSERTATIONS.

often contradictory Chinese business culture. Our final case, Case 5.4 on Aiptek, a Taiwanese business, allows you to consider the cultural features of both Japan and China in a particular context.

Case 5.4

Aiptek   Taiwan

Aiptek was founded in 1997 by Peter Chen in Taiwan and was located in the HsinChu Industrial Park. This location is commonly known as Taiwan's 'Silicon Valley'. The company set out to develop a range of innovative products based on electronic hand writing, digital video, wireless communication and opto-electronic technologies. In 2000 the company launched its first generation PenCam and the product soon became available in retail stores in Japan and in the US. In 2001 its PenCam II was a big success in the CeBit Computer Exhibition in Germany. From this point Aiptek sales and profits increased rapidly.

The company continued to launch new innovative products. In 2003 it launched the world's first MP3 digital video player called Pocket DV. Peter Chen the founder of Aiptek hoped to take advantage of the surging demand for high-tech products brought about in part by the rapid decrease in the cost of crucial hi-tech components brought about by standardization in the manufacturing processes involved. In Taiwan the government sought to assist companies such as Aiptek with tax incentives for investing in technology based research and development.

The initial success of Aiptek was based on the adoption of a simple management structure with all employees directly involved in projects with the company actively promoting its share plan for all employees. As Aiptek became an international business it became involved in product diversification, joint ventures and alliances. Issues began to arise with poor product quality and rushed new product development whereas initially the success of the business had been based on the swift development and launch of new products. The resources of Aiptek became stretched between conflicting demands for capital to fund research as opposed to marketing. The company found itself unable to quickly expand production capacity as it took too long to install manufacturing equipment and recruit and train new skilled employees. Because of these conflicting pressures Aiptek formed a strategic alliance with an OEM called YHi Company who could provide the high

volume manufacturing capacity Aiptek needed to meet the demand for its products.

To raise further funds Aiptek had successfully offered an IPO in Taiwan in May 2001. However major concerns over increasing competition led Aiptek to both relocate and expand its production capacity by moving its production facility to China. This meant that Aiptek could consolidate back in Taiwan its research and product development, marketing and brand development functions away from its manufacturing division. On the opposite side the termination of the OEM alliance with YHi due to poor quality issues meant that Aiptek had to shoulder all the risks relating to product quality. At this time Aiptek formed another strategic alliance with AVAC Co. Ltd to coordinate the development of crucial components inside digital cameras thus sharing R&D risks.

By 2003 Aiptek had become an international based company with a manufacturing subsidiary in China employing 1000 people, three marketing subsidiaries in the US, Europe and China respectively with its head quarters in HsinChu in Taiwan. However Aiptek had problems. As indicated, its move to China had presented quality problems. The previous alliance with YHi saw losses due to bad quality at 3 per cent of inventory value. By 2007 losses from bad quality had surged to 30 per cent of inventory value. The initial strategy of having production in China but R&D and marketing in Taiwan had not worked as well as the company intended. Research groups had to support product manufacturing in China to such an extent that the research crews were complaining of exhaustion. The pressures on them led to delays in new product development. In addition, marketing subsidiaries were feeling the pressures on them from bad product quality. As a result the company was facing a worsening cash flow problem.

The solution that they arrived at in 2007 was to sell the manufacturing subsidiary in China to Gemtek Co. Ltd and to sign a long term deal with Gemtek as the OEM supplier to Aiptek.

SOURCE: THIS CASE STUDY WAS PREPARED USING PRIMARILY PUBLICLY AVAILABLE SOURCES OF INFORMATION FOR THE PURPOSES OF CLASSROOM DISCUSSION; IT DOES NOT INTEND TO ILLUSTRATE EITHER EFFECTIVE OR INEFFECTIVE HANDLING OF A MANAGERIAL SITUATION.

Questions

1   What are the main lessons of the Aiptek change of strategy in 2007? Is being a manufacturer incompatible with a major R&D function in such a fast moving industry as digital cameras and camcorders?

2   Can you see evidence of the Chinese culture (Table 5.4) in this case? Is Aiptek more Japanese than Chinese in its culture?

AIPTEK **www.aiptek.com.tw**

© IAIN MASTERTON/ALAMY

Summary

Culture is the way in which an organization performs its tasks, the way its people think, feel and act in response to opportunities and threats, the ways in which objectives and strategies are set and decisions made. It reflects emotional issues and it is not easily analysed, quantified or changed. Nevertheless, it is a key influence on strategic choice, strategy implementation and strategic change – until we understand the culture of an organization we cannot understand strategic management in that organization.

A large organization is unlikely to be just one single, definable culture. It is more likely to be a loose or tight amalgam of different cultures.

It is quite normal for the culture to be influenced by a strong strategic leader and his or her beliefs and values.

In a very broad sense we can think of culture as a mixture of behaviours (manifestations) and underlying attitudes and values. It is easier to change one of these rather than both simultaneously.

There is no 'ideal culture' as such. Key elements typically have a flip side and, therefore, a style and approach that is appropriate at a particular time can quickly become out of date and in need of change.

A useful grid for analysing the culture of any organization would comprise:

- Manifestations – artefacts; values; underlying assumptions; behaviours
- People – stories; leadership; communications

- Power – ownership and structure; personal power; organizational politics.

Charles Handy proposes four cultural types which help to explain the culture, style and approach of different organizations. These are the power culture (typical of small, entrepreneurial organizations), the role culture (larger and more formal organizations), the task culture (the complex organization seeking to achieve internal synergies through effective linkages) and the person culture (built around the individual managers' needs).

In an alternative and equally significant contribution Miles and Snow differentiate among *defenders* (conservative and low-risk organizations), *prospectors* (innovative and entrepreneurial), *analysers* (limited change with measured steps) and *reactors* (followers). These can be readily linked to styles of strategy creation.

We can only understand culture when we understand power inside an organization. Who has power, how do they acquire it and how do they use it?

A number of books on the general theme of 'organizational excellence' have highlighted how it is culture that is at the heart of success. Although general themes and lessons can be teased out, an organization cannot simply replicate the culture of another successful organization and become successful itself.

There are important cultural differences between nations. This has implications for businesses which operate or trade globally.

Online cases for this chapter

Online Case 5.1: The Body Shop

Questions and research assignments

1 Use the text in Case 5.2 (IKEA) to complete a culture grid (Figure 1) for IKEA.
2 Take an organization with which you are familiar and evaluate it in terms of Handy's and Miles and Snow's typologies.
3 List other organizations that you know which would fit into the categories not covered in your answer to Question 2.
For both Questions 2 and 3 you should comment on whether or not you feel your categorization is appropriate.

4 Considering the organization that you used for Question 2, assess the power levers of the strategic leader and other identifiable managers.
5 Thinking of the identified cultural priorities for Japan, Germany and the US, listed in the text, what do you think the cultural priorities of your own national businesses are?

Internet and library projects

1 **The National Health Service**
British Prime Minister John Major announced a new Citizen's Charter in July 1991. This implied a change of attitude for the NHS: patients should be seen as customers with rights, rather than people who should be grateful for treatment, however long the wait. From April 1992 hospitals would have to set standards for maximum waiting times.
This followed on from the 1989 NHS White Paper, Working for Patients, which was designed to achieve:

- raising the performance of all hospitals and general practitioners (GPs) to the level of the best (significant differences existed in measured performances)
- patients receiving better health care and a greater choice of services through improved efficiencies and effectiveness in the use of NHS resources
- greater satisfaction and rewards for NHS staff.

In subsequent years, how did this impact on NHS strategies?

2 In 1997 a Labour government was elected and it set about changing the Conservative philosophy, dismantling and replacing a number of strategies.

What was the Labour approach? Has it changed the culture in any way? Indeed did the culture need changing?

3 Can the relative success of the NHS ever be evaluated effectively without imputing political and cultural concerns?
Citizen's Charter **http://www.cabinet-office.gov.uk/servicefirst**
NHS **http://www.nhs50.nhs.uk**

4 Research how profitable John Lewis and Waitrose have been in comparison with their major competitors in the last five years. What conclusions can you draw?
John Lewis Partnership **http://www.johnlewis.co.uk**
Waitrose **http://www.waitrose.com**

5 Find out where your nearest John Lewis or Waitrose store is and if possible visit it. Can you detect any differences in attitude between the John Lewis staff and those who work in similar mainstream department stores?
John Lewis Partnership **http://www.johnlewis.co.uk**
Waitrose **http://www.waitrose.com**

Strategy activity

BP and Shell: cultural roots

British Petroleum (BP) and the Anglo-Dutch Shell are two of the leading four oil companies in the world. American Exxon-Mobil and the amalgamation of Total and Elf (both French) and Petrofina (Belgian) are the others. They are all involved in exploration, drilling, refining and transporting oil and its derived products.

The industry has been characterized by mergers and consolidation in a search for scale and critical mass. The oil companies are pressurized by the countries where oil is located (who, not unexpectedly, want to control both access and prices) and governments in consumer countries who are worried about escalating oil prices. The powerful OPEC (Organization of Petroleum Exporting Countries) acts as a cartel to regulate commodity prices.

In recent years both BP and Shell have had to deal with crises, some of them self-created. Shell was found to have misreported its assets by over-estimating reserves. BP had to deal with the fall-out when its highly acclaimed Chairman, Lord Browne, resigned following published details about his personal life. The company was also in trouble after a fatal explosion at one of its refineries in Texas.

In the context of the supply chain BP is seen as primarily a downstream business. Started over 100 years ago in what is now Iran, BP began in exploration. Year-on-year it replaces in reserves at least as much as it takes out. It is currently developing fields in Azerbaijan, Egypt, Angola, Libya and Oman. But in recent years its upstream refineries have not been operating at full capacity.

By contrast Shell is more upstream, having started as a shipping company. Shell pioneered bulk oil tankers. Having been caught out for over-estimating its reserves it is seen to be weaker than BP in terms of future supply potential. But its refineries deliver three times the profits of those owned by BP. Shell is investing heavily in different sources of energy, such as liquefied natural gas.

One analyst has commented that BP looks strong in the short term but Shell might be a better long-term prospect.

Questions

1   How much do you think cultural roots will affect strategy and culture?

Further reading

Barney, JB (1986) Organizational culture – can it be a source of sustainable competitive advantage?, *Academy of Management Review*, 11 (3).

Harrison, R (1972) Understanding your organization's character, *Harvard Business Review*, May–June. Miles, R, Snow, C, Meyer, A and Coleman, H (1978) Organizational strategy structure and process, *Academy of Management Review*, July.

Peters, TJ (1980) Putting excellence into management, *Business Week*, July 21.

Schein, EH (1984) Coming to a new awareness of culture, *Sloan Management Review*, 25 (2).

Waterman, R, Peters, T and Phillips, J (1980) Structure is not organization, *Business Horizons*, June.

References

Barney, JB (1986) Organization culture: can it be a source of sustained competitive advantage? *Academy of Management Review*, 11 (3).

Berry, D (1983) The perils of trying to change corporate culture, *Financial Times*, 14 December.

Deal, T and Kennedy, A (1982) *Corporate Cultures. The Rites and Rituals of Corporate Life*, Addison-Wesley.

Drucker, PF (1989) What businesses can learn from nonprofits, *Harvard Business Review*, July–August.

French, JRP and Raven, B (1959) The bases of social power. *In Studies in Social Power* (ed. D Cartwright), University of Michigan Press.

Hampden-Turner, C (1990) Corporate culture – from vicious to virtuous circles, *The Economist*.

Handy, CB (1976) *Understanding Organizations*, Penguin. The ideas are elaborated in Handy, CB (1978) *Gods of Management*, Souvenir Press.

Harrison, R (1972) Understanding your organization's character, *Harvard Business Review*, May–June.

Hill, R (1990) Nissan and the art of people management, *Director*, March.

Hofstede, G (1991) *Cultures and Organization: Software of the Mind*, McGraw Hill.

Kakabadse, A (1982) *Culture of the Social Services*, Gower.

Kanter, RM (1991) Transcending business boundaries: 12000 world managers view change, *Harvard Business Review*, May–June.

Kluckhohn, C and Strodtbeck, F (1961) *Variations in Value Orientations*, Peterson.

Leadbetter, C and Rudd, R (1991) What drives the lords of the deal? *Financial Times*, 20 July.

Lewin, K (1947) Frontiers in group dynamics: concept, method and reality in social science, *Human Relations*, 1.

Miles, RE and Snow, CC (1978) *Organization Strategy, Structure and Process*, McGraw-Hill.

Ohmae, K (1985) *Triad Power*, Free Press.

Peters, TJ (1988) *Thriving on Chaos*, Knopf.

Peters, TJ and Waterman, RH Jr (1982) *In Search of Excellence: Lessons from America's Best Run Companies*, Harper and Row. Original article: Peters, TJ (1980) Putting excellence into management, *Business Week*, 21 July.

Pramalhad, CK and Hamel, G (1985) Address to the Annual Conference of the Strategic Management Society, Barcelona, October.

Press, G (1990) Assessing competitors' business philosophies, *Long Range Planning*, 23 (5).

Pucik, V and Hatvany, N (1983) Management practices in Japan and their impact on business strategy, *Advances in Strategic Management*, vol. 1, JAI Press.

Pümpin, C (1987) *The Essence of Corporate Strategy*, Gower.

Schein, EH (1985) *Organizational Culture and Leadership*, Jossey Bass.

Schonberger, RJ (1984) *Japanese Manufacturing Techniques*, Free Press.

Schwartz, H and Davis, SM (1981) Matching corporate culture and business strategy, *Organizational Dynamics*, Summer.

Trompenaars, F and Hampden-Turner, C (1997) *Riding the Waves of Culture: Understanding Cultural Diversity in Business*, Nicholas Brealey Publishing.

Part 3

3

Strategic analysis and choice

In Part 2 we examined in much greater detail the techniques for conducting an analysis based on positioning and competitiveness. We examined the following approaches; market-driven, resource-based and competitor-influenced. Part 3 looks at how organizations might, and in reality do, generate new ideas for future strategies.

The following chapters will cover:

- Purpose. We will argue that organizations (as a whole) have a purpose and individual managers have objectives. Mission, vision and objectives all relate to the *direction* that the organization is taking – the ends from which strategies are derived. It is not, however, feasible to assume that the organization will always be free to set these objectives for its managers: there may be constraints from key stakeholders. A number of theories and models, mainly from a study of economics, can help us to understand why organizations do the things they do.

- Success. At a most basic level of argument, an organization is successful if it is meeting the needs and expectations of its stakeholders, such that their support and commitment are maintained. Strategically, this will imply a clear direction, from which are derived corporate, competitive and functional strategies, the implementation of which brings about the desired results. This needs both common sense and strategic competency.

- Creation and planning. Strategic planning using techniques and formalized procedures is just one of the ways in which strategies are created. Strategies can also be provided by the strategic leader and be decided by managers in real time. Intended strategies, say those selected by the leader or a formal planning system, have to be implemented, and during this implementation they may well be changed incrementally. In addition, flexible organizations will adapt all the time by responding to new opportunities and threats. Our contemporary approach to strategic planning is based on a mixture of planning techniques, intellectual input and action plans for implementing strategies; and central to the whole process are current strategic issues.

- Leadership. As well as leading from the front it is also important for a leader to create a climate that facilitates emergent change – appropriate employees should be empowered, encouraged and energized. Intrapreneurs then lead the emergent change initiatives. Leadership is both a job and a process – a process concerned with influence and change. It requires both personal characteristics and leadership skills. The skills can be learned, but effective leaders need to possess certain characteristics in the first place. Successful leaders also tend to build effective teams to support them. In exploring these issues, this chapter also looks at how some leaders are perceived to fail and fall from grace, and at the vital issue of leadership succession.

- Alternatives and choice. Organizations will change their directions and strategies and they do not always pursue the same strategy in the same way. We cannot finally judge the worthiness of a particular choice until we take account of the organization's ability to implement the strategy that it has chosen. This chapter outlines the various strategic alternatives that might be available to an organization in thinking and deciding where it wants to go, and for helping to close the planning gap.

Chapter 6

· ·

Strategic purpose

PART 1
Understanding strategy

1 Introducing strategy and strategic management

PART 5
Strategic management

14 Strategy implementation

15 Leading change

16 Managing strategy in the organization

17 Final thoughts – the purpose of strategy

STRATEGIC MANAGEMENT: AWARENESS AND CHANGE

PART 2
Strategic positioning

2 Strategic thinking, environmental analysis, synergy and strategic positioning

3 Resource-led strategy

4 The dynamics of competition

5 Introducing culture and values

PART 4
Issues in strategic growth

11 Strategic growth

12 International strategy

13 Failure, consolidation and recovery strategies

PART 3
Strategic analysis and choice

6 Strategic purpose

7 Strategic success

8 An introduction to strategy creation and planning

9 Strategic leadership, entrepreneurship and intrapreneurship

10 Strategic alternatives, strategy evaluation and strategy selection

Learning objectives

Having read to the end of this chapter you should be able to:

● explain the terms vision, mission and objectives

● identify the various stakeholders of the organization and assess their impact on objectives

● summarize a number of economic theories of the firm which help explain objectives and decisions

● discuss the significance of profits

● explain the possible objectives of certain not-for-profit organizations

● differentiate between official and operative objectives, and assess the impact of personal objectives

● define policies and explain how they are used to help achieve objectives

● identify the key issues involved in social responsibility and business ethics.

Strategies are means to ends – this chapter is about these ends. Organizations undertake purposeful activity; what they do is not without purpose. Ideally, that purpose will be understood, shared and supported by everyone in the organization such that there is a clear, if broad, direction for the activities and strategies. Establishing the purpose and direction is a key role of the strategic leader; and it will provide a basis for the more detailed objectives and performance targets for individual managers and employees. This does not imply that everyone always shares the more detailed objectives; indeed, there can often be internal conflicts over these. Moreover, what individual people actually do and achieve affects organizational performance. Hence, this chapter looks at the idea of purposeful activity by considering the organizational mission and objectives. To achieve the purpose, of course, we need a clear business model.

A number of economic and behavioural theories contributes to our understanding of this subject. Considered here are the potentially conflicting expectations of different stakeholders, the role of institutional shareholders, and whether the profit motive should be the key driving force. A separate section looks at inherent conflicts of interest in certain not-for-profit organizations and later at issues of social responsibility and **business ethics** which also affect behaviour, performance and outcomes in a variety of ways. The chapter opens with a case on Ben and Jerry's ice cream, a company which has always been proud of its commitment to social and environmental causes and which has recently been acquired by the Anglo-Dutch multinational corporation Unilever.

If you don't know where you are going, any road will take you there.

RAYMOND G VIAULT, WHEN CHIEF EXECUTIVE OFFICER, JACOBS SUCHARD, SWITZERLAND

A voyage of a thousand miles begins with a single step. It is important that that step is in the right direction.

OLD CHINESE SAYING, UPDATED

How can we go forward when we don't know which way we are facing?

JOHN LENNON, 1972

Life can only be understood backward, but it must be lived forward.

S KIERKEGAARD

Case 6.1

Ben and Jerry's Ice Cream

US

This idiosyncratic business was founded and developed by two partners, both entrepreneurs but, at face value, unlikely businessmen. Ben Cohen was a college dropout who had become a potter. His friend from his schooldays was Jerry Greenfield, a laboratory assistant who had failed to make it into medical school. They had become 'seventies hippies with few real job prospects'. They decided they wanted to do something themselves and 'looked for something they might succeed at'. They 'liked food, so food it was!' They could not afford the machinery for making bagels, their first choice, but ice cream was affordable. In 1977 they opened an ice-cream parlour in Burlington, Vermont, where there were 'lots of students and no real competition'. They fostered a relaxed, hippy atmosphere and employed a blues pianist. Their ice cream was different, with large and unusual chunks.

They were instantly successful in their first summer, but sales fell off in the fall and winter when the snow arrived. They realized they would have to find outlets outside Vermont if they were to survive. Ben went on the road. Always dressed casually, he would arrive somewhere around 4.00 a.m. and then sleep in his car until a potential distributor opened. He was able to 'charm the distributors' and the business began to grow. Ben and Jerry's success provoked a response from the dominant market leader, Häagen Dazs, owned by Pillsbury. Their market share was 70 per cent of the luxury ice-cream market. Häagen Dazs threatened to withdraw their product from any distributors who also handled Ben and Jerry's. The two partners employed a lawyer and threatened legal action, but their real weapon was a publicity campaign targeted at Pillsbury itself, and its famous 'dough boy' logo. 'What's the Dough Boy afraid of?' they asked. Their gimmicks generated massive publicity and they received an out-of-court settlement. More significantly, the publicity created new demand for luxury ice cream, and the company began to grow more rapidly than had ever been envisaged. A threat had been turned into a massive opportunity. Soon Ben and Jerry's had a segment market share of 39 per cent, just 4 per cent behind Häagen Dazs. The company has expanded internationally with mixed success. They have enjoyed only limited success in the UK 'because there was only limited marketing support'.

Perhaps not unexpectedly, given their background, Ben and Jerry have created a values-driven business; some of their ice creams have been linked to causes and interests they support and promote. Rainforest Crunch ice cream features nuts from Brazil; the key ingredients for Chocolate Fudge Brownie are produced by an inner-city bakery in Yonkers, New York; and they favour Vermont's dairy-farming industry. When the business needed equity capital to support its growth, local Vermont residents were given priority treatment. Ben and Jerry argue they are committed to their employees who 'bring their hearts and souls as well as their bodies and minds to work' but acknowledge that their internal opinion surveys show a degree of dissatisfaction with the amount of profits (7.5 per cent) given away every year to good causes. The company aims to donate at least $1 million every year.

The two realists with an unusual but definite ego drive later dropped out of day-to-day management '… the company needed a greater breadth of management than we had …' and were content to be 'two casual, portly, middle-aged hippies'.

In early Spring 2000 the business was acquired by Unilever, the multinational foods, detergents and cosmetics business. Unilever already owned the UK market leader, Walls ice cream, with its Magnum and Cornetto brands. Unilever and Walls had recently been investigated by the UK competition authorities because of their strategy of insisting that retailers only stock Walls ice cream if Unilever provide them with a freezer cabinet on loan.

This was an interesting acquisition for Unilever. Its main US ice cream brand is Breyer's and in the UK it has its own premium Carte D'Or brand, again with a (limited) range of distinctive flavours. Would it seek to absorb Ben and Jerry's into the Unilever culture and style? In the end Ben and Jerry's has continued to operate as a separate unit from the mainstream brands; and Ben and Jerry continue to enjoy their ambassadorial roles. The company has continued to launch new flavours and develop ever-more environmentally friendly packaging. Somewhat controversially they renamed one flavour, Yes Pecan, after Barack Obama was elected President. This move appears to have both gained and lost customers.

For some years Ben and Jerry's has published a mission statement with three inter-related parts. The first section concerns making, selling and distributing the finest quality, natural ice cream that contains wholesome ingredients – and to do this in an ethical way. The second part emphasizes sound finances and a profitable operation for the benefit of all stakeholders, including employees; and the third part commits the business to having a key role in society.

Question

1 Do you think it is unusual that the objectives of Ben and Jerry's have not had to change after the acquisition by Unilever?

Task

Access the company website and mission statement at: **http://www.benjerry.com/our_company/our_mission** and evaluate it.

© STUART KELLY / ALAMY

6.1 Introduction, definitions, terminology and examples

This chapter is about the idea of strategic direction and objectives – what is meant by the terminology used and the implications.

Figure 6.1 defines the terms *vision*, *mission* and *objectives* and provides a range of examples from the private and public sectors. Figure 6.1 shows the relationships between these terms. The examples in Strategy in action 6.1 were selected to illustrate the relevant points, not because they are superior or inferior to those of other organizations; they should be evaluated in this light. The

Figure 6.1 Vision, mission and objectives: a hierarchy of terminology

VISION
to become

MISSION
to be in order to become
how the organization will make a difference

VALUES
behaviours to support the vision and mission

BROAD AIMS & OBJECTIVES
to deliver the mission and vision

ENABLING FACTORS
things that need to be in place to support this process and achievement

KEY PERFORMANCE INDICATORS (KPIs)
specific targets and milestones for a defined time period linked to each and every aim, objective and enabler

(BASED IN PART ON THEMES FROM KAPLAN, R AND NORTON, D (2000), *THE STRATEGY FOCUSED*

Strategy in action 6.1

Examples of Vision, Mission and Objectives Statements

Vision statements

A vision statement describes what the company is to become in the (long-term) future.

The Sony spirit

'Sony doesn't serve markets; Sony makes markets.' Sony is a trail blazer, always a seeker of the unknown. Sony will never follow old trails. Through this progress Sony wants to serve mankind'

SONY **http://www.sony.com**

British Airways

'The world's favourite airline'.

This vision, first adopted in the 1990s, focuses on employees and customers. The related mission emphasized BA's desire to be the world's first truly global airline, which in turn generated a corporate strategy of carefully selected alliances. To be feasible, however, it has always been essential that BA staff believe in the vision and act accordingly. In recent years staff trust and morale has declined as costs have been cut dramatically and the airline's profitability has declined. The strapline has effectively been abandoned.

BRITISH AIRWAYS **http://www.britishairways.com**

The Girl Guides Association

'To help a girl reach her highest potential.'

These eight words cut straight to the heart of the movement; there is a clear and direct statement of purpose.

GIRL GUIDES ASSOCIATION **http://www .wagggsworld.org**

Mission statements

The mission statement *reflects* the essential purpose of the organization, and ideally captures why it is in existence, the nature of the business(es) it is in, the customers it seeks to serve and satisfy and how it will do this.

Financial Times conferences

'The mission of the FTC is to organize conferences on subjects of interest to the international business community, using the highest calibre speakers and providing attending delegates with the finest service, thereby providing a low-cost and time-efficient means of both obtaining impartial quality information and making senior-level industry contacts.'

We can see a clear definition of the business, a formulation of objectives, delivery strategies, means of differentiating the service and stakeholder relevance.

FINANCIAL TIMES **http://www.news.ft.com**

Virgin Atlantic Airways

'As the UK's second long-haul carrier, to build an intercontinental network concentrating on those routes with a substantial established market and clear indication of growth potential, by offering the highest possible service and lowest possible cost.'

Not particularly elegant in style, but it does clarify both the target markets and the source of competitive advantage.

VIRGIN ATLANTIC **http://www.virgin-atlantic.com**

Values statements

A set of values and the related behaviours that employees will demonstrate. To a real extent this is a statement of key elements of the desired culture.

Camelot's 'FITTER' list of corporate values

Camelot is the current organizer of the UK's national lottery.
Fair play
Integrity – honesty and transparency
Team work
Trusted to deliver
Excellence – something to be strived for
Responsible – to all the company's stakeholders

Long-term objectives

Objectives are desired (and measurable) states or results linked to particular timescales and concerning such things as size or type of organization, the nature and variety of the areas of interest and levels of success. Measurement can be straightforward for an objective such as 'the achievement of a minimum return of 20 per cent of net capital employed in the business, but with a target of 25 per cent, in the next 12 months'. If the objective is less specific, for example, 'continued customer satisfaction, a competitive return on capital employed and real growth in earnings per share next year', measurement is still possible but requires a comparison of competitor returns and the monitoring of customer satisfaction through, say, the number of complaints received. Richards (1978) uses the terms 'open' and 'closed' to distinguish between objectives that are clearly measurable and typically finance based (closed) and those that are less specific and essentially continuing.

British Airports Authority (BAA): Open objectives

'BAA aims to enhance the value of the shareholders' investments by achieving steady and remunerative long-term growth. Its strategy for developing and operating world-class international airports that are safe, secure, efficient and profitable is based on a commitment to continuously enhancing the quality of service to passengers and business partners alike. This process of constant improvement includes cost-effective investment in new airport facilities closely matched to customer demand.'

These are in the context of a declared mission to 'make BAA the most successful airport company in the world'.

BRITISH AIRPORTS AUTHORITY **http://www.baa.co.uk**

© GVISION / DREAMSTIME.COM

figure shows how the overall vision ultimately drives measurable key performance indicators which relate to specific objectives that have been derived from the high-order vision. Kaplan and Norton (2000) emphasize the significance of enabling factors – the resources and support that need to be in place to make sure targets are attainable.

The word '**values**' is important in this context, but is has a particular emphasis. It is important that a mission statement captures how an organization will create and add value for its customers; 'values' relates to the corporate values that should be held by employees, be visible to the outside world and support the organization in pursuing its mission. This is not the same as the value we talked about earlier in the context of creating and adding value for customers. In this latter case the value lies in what a product or service is and provides for others.

The expression *aims* is sometimes used as an alternative to mission. The term *goals* is seen as synonymous with objectives, and in this book the terms are used interchangeably. Specifically, where other works are being referred to and those authors have used the term goal as opposed to objective, their terminology is retained. It is also important to distinguish between long-term and short-term objectives or goals. Thompson and Strickland (1980) provide a useful distinction. They argue that objectives overall define the specific kinds of performance and results that the organization seeks to produce through its activities. The *long-term objectives* relate to the desired performance and results on an ongoing basis; *short-term objectives* are concerned with the near-term performance targets that the organization desires to reach in progressing towards its long-term objectives. Making use of such techniques as management by objectives, these performance targets can be agreed with individual managers, who are then given responsibility for their attainment and held accountable.

Taking the perspective of the entrepreneur looking to create a new business with growth potential, Gerber (2008) offers a similar but different approach. He argues that the highest-order theme is the **dream**, which he sees as a mental conceptualization of what will be the ultimate outcome for the customers being targeted. The **vision** follows and is a statement of what the business will be seeking to achieve. The third element is ***purpose***, a clarification of why you are doing what you are planning to do. The ***mission*** is then an explanation of what you (and the business) are going to create.

Vision statements

While mission statements have become increasingly popular for organizations, *vision statements* are less prevalent. The lack of a published statement, of course, is not necessarily an indication of a lack of vision. Where they exist they reflect the company's vision of some future state, which ideally the organization will achieve. Terminology and themes such as a world-class manufacturer, a quality organization, a provider of legendary service and a stimulating, rewarding place to work might well appear. The essential elements focus on those values to which the organization is committed and appropriate standards of behaviour for all employees. Possible improvement paths, employee development programmes and measures or indicators of progress should be established for each element of the vision.

> *Strategy development is like driving around a roundabout. The signposts are only useful if you know where you want to go. Some exits lead uphill, some downhill – most are one-way streets and some have very heavy traffic indeed. The trick is in picking the journey's end before you set out – otherwise you go around in circles or pick the wrong road.*
>
> GERRY M MURPHY, WHEN CHIEF EXECUTIVE OFFICER, GREENCORE PLC, IRELAND

> *Arne Ness said, when he climbed Everest: I had a dream. I reached it. I lost the dream and I miss it. When we reached our dream we didn't have another long-term objective. So people started to produce their own new objectives, not a common objective, but different objectives depending on where they were in the organization. I learned that before you reach an objective you must be ready with a new one, and you must start to communicate it to the organization. But it is not the goal itself that is important ... it is the fight to get there.*
>
> JAN CARLZON, WHEN CHAIRMAN AND CHIEF EXECUTIVE OFFICER, SCANDINAVIAN AIRLINES SYSTEM

Mission statements

The corporate mission is often seen as the overriding *raison d'être* for the business. Ackoff (1986), however, claimed that many corporate mission statements prove worthless, one reason being that they consist of loose expressions such as 'maximize growth potential' or 'provide products of the highest quality'. How, he queries, can a company determine whether it has attained its maximum growth potential or highest quality? His points are still valid today. Primarily, the mission statement should not address what an organization must do in order to survive, but what it has chosen to do in order to thrive. It should be positive, visionary and motivating.

Ackoff suggests that a good mission statement has five characteristics:

- It will contain a formulation of objectives that enables progress towards them to be measured.
- It differentiates the company from its competitors.
- It defines the business(es) that the company wants to be in, not necessarily is in.
- It is relevant to all stakeholders in the firm, not just shareholders and managers.
- It is exciting and inspiring.

Campbell (1989) argues that to be valuable mission statements must reflect corporate values, and the strategic leader and the organization as a whole should be visibly pursuing the mission. He takes a wider perspective than Ackoff by including aspects of the corporate vision and arguing that there are four key issues involved in developing a useful mission.

First, it is important to clarify the purpose of the organization – why it exists. Hanson plc, for example, which is referred to at various stages in this book, was led by Lord James Hanson for some 25 years and he stated:

> It is the central tenet of my faith that the shareholder is king. My aim is to advance the shareholder's interest by increasing earnings per share.

By contrast, and at the same time, Lex Service Group published an alternative view:

> We will exercise responsibility in our dealings with all our stakeholders and, in the case of conflict, balance the interest of the employees and shareholders on an equal basis over time.

The implications of these contrasting perspectives are discussed in the next section of this chapter.

Second, the mission statement should describe the business and its activities, and the position that it wants to achieve in its field. Third, the organization's values should be stated. How does the company intend to treat its employees, customers and suppliers, for example? Finally, it is important to ensure that the organization behaves in the way that it promises it will. This is important because it can inspire trust in employees and others who significantly influence the organization.

It is generally accepted that in successful companies middle and junior managers know where the strategic leaders are taking the company and why. In less successful organizations there is often confusion about this.

Mission statements, like vision statements, can all too easily just 'state the obvious' and as a result have little real value. The secret lies in clarifying what makes a company different and a more effective competitor, rather than simply restating those requirements that are essential for meeting key success factors. A mission (or vision) statement which could easily be used by another business, whether in the same industry or not – as many can be – is, simply, of no great value. Companies that succeed long term are those which create competitive advantages and sustain their strong positions with flexibility and improvement. The vision and mission should support this.

The principal purpose of these statements is communication, both externally and internally and, arguably, a major benefit for organizations is the thinking they are forced to do in order to establish sound statements. Nevertheless, many are still worded poorly. In addition, it is essential that the mission (or vision) is more than a plaque in a foyer; employees have to make the words mean something through their actions. For this to happen, employees must feel that the organization actually means what it is saying in the mission and vision statements. There must be an element of trust, for without it the desired outcomes will not be achieved.

The mission clearly corresponds closely to the basic philosophy or vision underlying the business, and if there is a sound philosophy, strategies that generate success will be derived from it.

The points we have covered so far are illustrated in Case 6.2 on The Republic of Tea.

Case 6.2

The Republic of Tea   US

The Republic of Tea is a relatively new business derived from the old regime of tea drinking, given tea has allegedly been drunk in China since 2737 BC. It was founded in California in 1992 to market organic and exotic teas from all round the world. There were three founders: Mel and Patricia Ziegler, who had earlier started the Banana Republic fashion store chain which they had sold to Gap, and Bill Rosenzweig, an academic at the Haas Business School, University of California Berkeley. They wrote a book on how the business started after an exchange of letters discussing their perception of a need and a possible business model. It is clear that, in their own words, the founders 'delight in drinking tea'.

The business was sold after just two years to an entrepreneur, Ron Rubin, who has grown it from essentially a 'fun idea' into a sizeable and profitable venture – but retained many of the founders' idiosyncrasies. The emergence and growth of the company has happened roughly parallel to the very rapid growth of the modern coffee bar, led by Starbucks. The persuasive argument would be that both tea and coffee benefit from using the best quality raw materials and preparing the drinks carefully and properly. In the UK the number of cups of tea drunk every day continues to exceed the number of cups of coffee, although the gap has been closed in the last twenty years.

The Zieglers and Rosenzweig had set out to 'create a tea revolution' and their early letters to each other postulated a mythical country – hence the business name. Employees are still described as ministers; customers are citizens; and retail outlets are embassies. There is, however, a strong focus on mail order sales and tea can be couriered to anywhere in the

US in two working days and anywhere in the world in 10–14 days.

The Republic of Tea sells only full leaf tea, not the ground tea leaves that most of us buy as loose tea or tea bags. The argument is that full leaf tea provides a better taste and aroma as well as being healthier. The company works closely with its growers and uses only young leaves. Its supply chain provides red, black, green and white varieties, as well as certain specialty teas, such as Moroccan Mint. Most branded tea consumed is black tea. Some varieties are very scarce and limited edition; and there is also a wide range of herbal infusions. Generally different tea leaves are not blended.

Company documentation proclaims the following:

The **purpose** is 'to enrich people's lives through the experience of fine tea' – there is a key balance between health and well-being.

The **mission** is to become 'the leading purveyor of fine teas and herbs in the world' and 'to be respected for unsurpassed quality'.

These will be achieved by providing 'outstanding products delivered in innovative ways'.

Questions

1 Do you believe these statements of purpose and mission capture the spirit of the business effectively?
2 Do you believe this is a sustainable business model?

6.2 Objectives: issues and perspectives

A full consideration of objectives incorporates three aspects:

- an appreciation of the objectives that the organization is actually pursuing and achieving – where it is going and why
- the objectives that it might pursue, and the freedom and opportunity it has to make changes
- specific objectives for the future.

This chapter looks at the issues that affect and determine the first two of these. Decisions about specific future objectives are considered later in the book (Chapter 9). We begin, though, by looking briefly at a number of theories of business organizations and considering the role and importance of stakeholders.

Market models

Basic micro-economic theory states that firms should seek to maximize profits and that this is achieved where marginal revenue is equal to marginal cost. A number of assumptions underpin this theory, including the assumptions that firms clearly understand the nature of the demand for their products, and why people buy, and that they are willing and able to control production and sales as the model demands. In reality, decision makers do not have perfect knowledge and production and sales are affected by suppliers and distributors.

However, this basic theory has resulted in the development of four market models (Table 6.1), and the characteristics of these in respect of barriers to entry into the industry and the marketing opportunities (differentiation potential; price and non-price competition) determine whether or not there is a real opportunity to achieve significant profits.

In markets which approach pure competition (pure competition as such is theoretical), firms will only make 'normal' profits, the amount required for them to stay in the industry. Products are 'commodities', not differentiated, and so premium prices for certain brands are not possible. There are no major barriers to entry into the industry and so new suppliers are attracted if there are profits to be made. Competition results, and if supply exceeds demand the ruling market price is forced down and only the efficient firms survive.

In monopolistic competition there are again several suppliers, some large, many small, but products are differentiated. However, as there are once more no major barriers to entry the above situation concerning profits applies. Newcomers increase supply and although those firms with distinctive products can charge some premium they will still have to move in line with market prices generally, and this will have a dampening effect on profits.

Only in **oligopoly** and monopoly markets, where a small number of large firms is dominant, is there real opportunity for 'supernormal' profits, in excess of what is required to stay in business. However, in oligopoly the small number of large firms tend to be wary of each other and prices are held back to some extent for fear of losing market share. Suppliers are interdependent and fear that a price decrease will be met by competitors (thus reducing profits) and price increases will not (hence market share will be threatened). There are two types of oligopoly, depending on whether opportunities exist for significant differentiation. In all of these models competition is a major determinant of profit potential and therefore objectives must be set with competitors in mind. In a monopoly (again somewhat theoretical in a pure sense) excess profits could be made if government did not act as a restraint. In the UK, although such **public sector organizations** as British Gas and British Telecom have been privatized, their actions in terms of supply and pricing are monitored and regulated.

Stakeholder theory

The influence of external stakeholders was first mentioned in Chapter 2, when we considered their relative power and their relative interest. A further assumption of profit-maximizing theory is that shareholders in the business should be given first priority and be the major consideration in decision-making, and this arose because early economic theorists saw owners and managers as being synonymous. This assumption no longer holds, however. A study of market models demonstrates the important role played by competitors and by government as a restraining force, and it was also suggested that organizations must pay some regard to their suppliers and distributors. In addition, managers and employees must be considered. The decisions taken by managers which create incremental change will be influenced by the objectives and values that they believe are important. Managers are paid employees, and whilst concerned about profits, they will also regard growth and security as important.

These are all *stakeholders*. Freeman (1984) defines stakeholders as any group or individual who can affect, or is affected by, the performance of the organization. Newbould and Luffman (1979) argue that current and future strategies are affected by:

- external pressures from the marketplace, including competitors, buyers and suppliers; shareholders; pressure groups; and government
- internal pressures from existing commitments, managers, employees and their trade unions
- the personal ethical and moral perspectives of senior managers.

Table 6.1 Structural characteristics of four market models

Market	Number of firms	Type of product	Control over price by supplier	Entry conditions	Non-price competition*	Examples[†]
Pure competition	Large	Standardized Identical or almost identical	None	Free	None	Agricultural products; some chemicals; printing; laundry services
Monopolistic competition	Large	Differentiated	Some	Relatively easy	Yes	Clothing; furniture; soft drinks; plumbers; restaurants
Oligopoly**	Few or a few dominant	Standardized or differentiated	Limited by mutual interdependence; Considerable if collusion takes place	Difficult	Yes	Standardized: cement; sugar; fertilizers Differentiated: margarine; soaps; detergents
Pure monopoly	One	Unique	Considerable	Blocked	Yes	Water companies in their regions (at the moment); local bus companies in certain towns

* Non-price competition occurs in many ways, e.g. by attempts to increase the extent of product differentiation and buyer preference through advertising, brand names, trade marks, promotions, distribution outlets; by new product launches and innovation, etc.

** There are many oligopoly models of a collusive and non-collusive type. They make varying behavioural and structural assumptions.

[†] Useful further reading: Doyle, P and Gidengil, ZB (1977) An empirical study of market structures. *Journal of Management Studies*, 14(3), October, 316–28. Some of the examples are taken from this.

Stakeholder theory, then, postulates that the objectives of an organization will take account of the various needs of these different interested parties who will represent some type of informal coalition. Their relative power will be a key variable, and the organization will on occasions 'trade off' one against the other, establishing a hierarchy of relative importance. Stakeholders see different things as being important and receive benefits or rewards in a variety of ways, as featured in Table 6.2.

Stakeholder interests are not always consistent. For example, investment in new technology might improve product quality and as a result lead to increased profits. While customers who are shareholders might perceptively benefit, if the investment implies lost jobs then employees, possibly managers, and their trade unions may be dissatisfied. If the scale of redundancy is large and results in militant resistance, the government may become involved.

The various stakeholders are not affected in the same way by every strategic decision and, consequently, their relative influence will vary from decision to decision. In 1995 Shell, one of Europe's most successful and respected companies, was forced to change an important strategic decision following a high-profile campaign by a leading pressure group. Shell wanted to sink its redundant Brent Spar oil platform in deep seas some 150 miles west of Scotland. It had reached an agreement with the UK government that, scientifically, this was the most appropriate means of disposal for the platform. Greenpeace objected and protesters boarded the platform, claiming that it still contained 5 000 tonnes of oil which would eventually be released to pollute the sea. The ensuing and professionally orchestrated publicity fuelled public opinion, and there were protests in a number of European countries, including attacks on petrol stations in Germany. Shell backed down and agreed to investigate other possibilities for disposal. The UK government expressed both anger and disappointment with this decision. Independent inspectors later proved that Greenpeace's claims were gross exaggerations – the residual oil was much, much less than 5 000 tonnes. The press concluded: 'Shell went wrong in spending too much time convincing government of the case for sea-bed dumping, but not attaching enough importance to consulting other stakeholder groups.'

Shell had been made to appear socially irresponsible, yet the ethics of the Greenpeace campaign are questionable; these issues are explored further at the end of this chapter.

Waterman (1994) contends that successful companies do not automatically make shareholders their first priority. Instead, they pay primary attention to employees and customers and, as a result, they perform more effectively than their rivals. The outcome is superior profits and wealth

Table 6.2 Examples of stakeholder interests

Shareholders	Annual dividends; increasing the value of their investment in the company as the share price increases. Both are affected by growth and profits
	Institutional shareholders may balance high-risk investments and their anticipated high returns with more stable investments in their portfolio
Managers	Salaries and bonuses; perks; status from working for a well-known and successful organization; responsibility; challenge; security
Employees	Wages; holidays; conditions and job satisfaction; security – influenced by trade union involvement
Consumers	Desirable and quality products; competitive prices – very much in relation to competition; new products at appropriate times
Distributors	On time and reliable deliveries
Suppliers	Consistent orders; payment on time
Financiers	Interest payments and loan repayments; like payment for supplies, affected by cash flow
Government	Payment of taxes and provision of employment; contribution to the nation's exports
Society in general	Socially responsible actions – sometimes reflected in pressure groups

creation for the shareholders. Simon (1964) argues that one of the main reasons for an organization's collapse is a failure to incorporate the important motivational concerns of key stakeholders. Small businesses, for example, are generally weak in relation to their suppliers, especially if these are larger well-established concerns; and if they neglect managing their cash flow and fail to pay their accounts on time they will find their deliveries stopped. For any organization, if new products or services fail to provide consumers with what they are looking for, however well produced or low priced they might be, they will not sell.

A 1999 survey by Deloitte Consulting confirmed that 'customer-centric' manufacturing companies worldwide are 60 per cent more profitable than those that are less committed to customers. In addition, they enjoy lower operating costs. Customer-centricity is seen as a 'systematic process which sets objectives for customer loyalty and retention and then tracks performance towards those goals'. It should facilitate the development of higher added value, premium-price products.

Figure 6.2 shows that shareholders, employees and customers are the three key stakeholders that the organization must satisfy, but invariably in a competitive environment: if they fail with any group long term they will place the organization in jeopardy through a spiral of decline. Figure 6.3 is an alternative presentation of the same points. On the left is a virtuous circle of growth and prosperity. Satisfied, perhaps even delighted, customers enable high financial returns,

Figure 6.2 Satisfying stakeholders

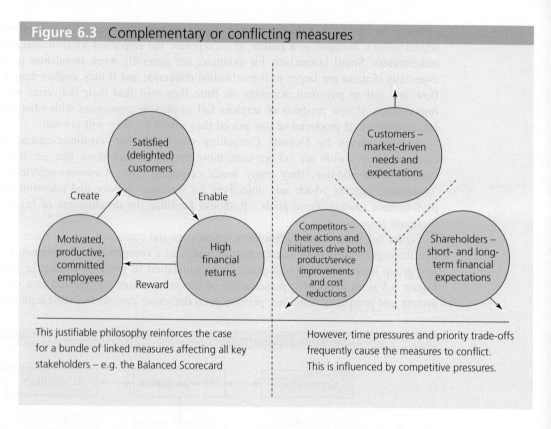

Figure 6.3 Complementary or conflicting measures

This justifiable philosophy reinforces the case for a bundle of linked measures affecting all key stakeholders – e.g. the Balanced Scorecard

However, time pressures and priority trade-offs frequently cause the measures to conflict. This is influenced by competitive pressures.

which can be used in part to reward employees. A perception of fairness here can be instrumental for motivating employees to keep customers satisfied and thus sustain the circle. The issues of measuring performance in relation to all of the stakeholders will be taken up in Chapter 7. The right-hand side clarifies that the needs of customers can sometimes conflict with the demands of some shareholders, especially those who are willing to trade off long-term achievement for short-term financial returns. Competitors are always trying to persuade customers to switch allegiance and thus impact on an organization's success.

While these arguments are, in themselves, convincing, many organizations still fail to satisfy their stakeholders long term. In the UK the demutualization of building societies such as Bradford and Bingley was pushed through by their management (in this case in July 2000) who typically indicated the need for greater commercial freedom and access to the funding the status of a bank would provide. To some extent they 'bribed' their depositers and customers with cash, an average of £620, plus 250 free shares, whose launch price was £2.47, to agree to demutualize. The same applied to Northern Rock and to the Halifax. Now what are they worth? Was the long-term interest of the mutual society stakeholders sacrificed for short-term management thinking?

The investor and the employee are in the same position, but sometimes the employee is more important, because he will be there a long time, whereas an investor will often get in and out on a whim in order to make a profit. The worker's mission is to contribute to the company's welfare, and his own, every day. All of his working life he is really needed.

AKIO MORITA, JOINT FOUNDER, SONY

Cyert and March's behavioural theory

Stakeholder theory is closely related to the ideas in Cyert and March's *A Behavioural Theory of the Firm* (1963). Cyert and March argue that the goals of an organization are a *compromise* between members of a coalition comprising the parties affecting an organization. The word compromise is used as the actual choice is linked to relative power and there are inevitably conflicts of interest. Cyert and March argue that there are essentially five directional pulls to consider:

- production-related, and encapsulating stable employment, ease of control and scheduling
- inventory-related – customers and sales staff push for high stocks and wide choice, management accountants complain about the cost of too much stock
- sales-related – obtaining and satisfying orders
- market share, which yields power relative to competitors
- profit, which concerns shareholders, senior management and the providers of loan capital.

This theory stresses the perceived importance of the short term, as opposed to the long term, because issues are more tangible and because decisions have to be taken as situations change. Organizations adapt over time and it is likely that changes will be limited unless it is necessary to change things more radically. In other words, once a compromise situation is reached there is a tendency to seek to retain it rather than change it, and the goals will change as the values and relative importance of coalition members change. As a result, organizational slack develops. This is 'payments to members of the coalition in excess of what is required to keep them in the coalition'. It is difficult, for example, to determine the minimum acceptable reward for employees; assets are generally under-exploited since it is difficult to know the maximum productivity of a person or machine; and uncertainties mean that less than optimal price, product and promotional policies will be pursued. The existence of slack does allow for extra effort in times of emergency.

This theory can be usefully considered alongside Herbert Simon's (1964) theory of satisficing. Here he contends that managers seek courses of action which are acceptable in the light of known objectives. These actions may not be optimal but they are chosen because of internal and external constraints such as time pressure, a lack of information and the vested interests of certain powerful stakeholders. The situation regarding the demutualization of UK building societies is a case in point here.

Objectives and constraints

Simon (1964) also makes an important distinction between objectives and constraints. Some of the ends that strategies are designed to achieve are not freely set objectives but constraints imposed on the organization by powerful stakeholders or agencies. Simply, organizational freedom – to set objectives – is constrained. For example, an animal food company might wish to offer low priced feeds for livestock but be constrained by dietary requirements which, by determining ingredients, influence costs and hence prices.

In recent years, many of the world's leading drug companies have changed their strategies as a result of external constraints. Governments have been increasingly reluctant to fund expensive drugs and treatments. Some companies have closed plants, while others have relocated for lower costs. There has been an increased research focus on treatments that are most likely to receive funding, arguably at the expense of potential breakthroughs in other areas. Priorities and strategies in the UK National Health Service (NHS) are affected by the government's waiting-list targets. Network Rail (which manages and maintains the UK railway infrastructure for the government) has an independent regulator who imposes specific requirements and targets for safety which inevitably affect costs and borrowing needs. This contributes to the wording of the mission statement of Network Rail which is: 'We strive to provide Britain with a safe, reliable and efficient railway fit for the 21st century'.

A number of other authors have offered theories in an attempt to explain the behaviour of organizations and the objectives they seek.

Baumol's theory of sales maximization

Baumol (1959) argues that firms seek to maximize sales rather than profits, but within the constraint of a minimum acceptable profit level. It can be demonstrated that profit maximizing is achieved at a level of output below that which would maximize sales revenue and that, as sales and revenue increase beyond profit maximizing, profits are sacrificed. Firms will increase sales and revenue as long as they are making profits in excess of what they regard as an acceptable minimum. Businessmen, Baumol argues, attach great importance to sales as salaries are often linked to the scale of operations. 'Whenever executives are asked "How's business?" the typical reply is that sales have been increasing or decreasing.'

Williamson's model of managerial discretion

Williamson (1964) argues that managers can set their own objectives, that these will be different from those of shareholders and that managerial satisfaction is the key. Satisfaction increases if a manager has a large staff reporting to him or her, if there are lavish perks and if profits exceed the level required for the essential development of the business and the necessary replacement of equipment. This extra profit can be used for pet projects or the pursuit of non-profit objectives. The manner in which managers reward themselves for success is discretionary.

Marris's theory of managerial capitalism

Marris (1964) again postulates growth as a key concern, as managers derive utility from growth in the form of enhanced salaries, power and status. The constraint is one of security. If, as a result of growth strategies pursued by the firm, profits are held down, say because of interest charges, the market value of the firm's shares may fall relative to the book value of the assets. In such a case the firm may become increasingly vulnerable to takeover, and managers wish to avoid this situation.

Penrose's theory of growth

Penrose (1959) has offered another growth theory, arguing that an organization will seek to achieve the full potential from all its resources. Firms grow as long as there are unused resources, diversifying when they can no longer grow with existing products, services and markets. Growth continues until it is halted. A major limit, for example, could be production facilities either in terms of total output or because of a bottleneck in one part of the operation. Changes can free the limit, and growth continues until the next limiting factor appears. Another limit is the capacity of managers to plan and implement growth strategies. If managers are stretched, extra people can be employed, but the remedy is not immediate. New people have to be trained and integrated, and this takes up some of the time of existing managers. Penrose refers to this issue as the 'receding managerial limit' because again the limiting factor decreases over a period of time. In a climate of reasonably constant growth and change managers learn how to cope with the dynamics of change; and properly managed, given that overambition is constrained and that market opportunities exist, firms can enjoy steady and continuous growth.

Galbraith's views on technocracy

Finally, Galbraith (1969) highlighted the particular role of large corporations, whose pursuit of size requires very large investments associated with long-term commitments. Because of these financial commitments the corporations seek to control their environment as far as they possibly can, influencing both government and consumer, and they in turn are controlled by what Galbraith calls 'technocrats' – teams of powerful experts and specialists. Their purposes are, first, to protect as well as control the organization, and hence they seek financial security and profit, and, second, to 'affirm' the organization through growth, expansion and market share. As is typical of oligopolists, price competition is not seen to be in their interests, and hence aggressive marketing and non-price competition are stressed. In addition, such firms will seek to influence or even control (by acquisition) suppliers and distributors, and they may well see the world, rather than just the UK, as their market. These issues are all explored later in the book.

Galbraith (1963) also identified the growth of 'countervailing power' to limit this technocracy. The growth of trade unions in the past is an example of this, but, as seen in recent years, the technocrats have fought back successfully. The increasing size and power of grocery retailers such as Sainsbury and Tesco, and their success with own-label brands, has put pressure on all product manufacturers, especially those whose products are not the brand leader. As a consequence the owners of the strongest brands have invested heavily to promote their brands and ensure that they are selected, even though there may be cheaper alternatives. Moreover, there have been mergers within retailing in an attempt to strengthen power bases. Tesco has expanded from the UK into Europe and even into the US, while Wal-Mart has, through ASDA, become a major force in the UK. Simply, over time there are swings in relative power and, as a result, the potential for consumer exploitation is checked and available profits are shared more widely.

Profit as an objective

Critical reflection 6.1 discusses whether profit is the ultimate objective of profit-seeking business organizations or whether it is merely a means to other ends, which themselves constitute the real objectives. Not-for-profit organizations are considered separately later in this chapter.

Ackoff (1986) argues that both profit and growth are means to other ends rather than objectives in themselves. He argues that profit is necessary for the survival of a business enterprise, but is neither the reason for which the business is formed nor the reason why it stays in existence. Instead, Ackoff contends,

> Those who manage organizations do so primarily to provide themselves with the quality of work life and standard of living they desire ... their behaviour can be better understood by assuming this than by assuming that their objective is to maximize profit or growth.

Critical reflection 6.1

Profit

A business school is likely to teach that an organization must be good to people because then they will work harder; and if they work harder the business will make a profit.

They will also teach that a firm should strive to produce better products and services, because with better products the firm will make greater profits.

What if they told the story the other way round?

What if they taught managers: you have got to make a profit, because if you do not make a profit you cannot build offices that are pleasant to be in. Without profit you cannot pay decent wages. Without profit you cannot satisfy a lot of the needs of your employees.

You have got to make a profit because without a profit you will never be able to develop a better product.

The profit would still be made. People would still get decent wages. Most employers would still make an effort to improve their products as they do now.

'But you would have a whole new ball game.'

It is clear that these approaches will lead to organizations that 'feel' different, that manifest different cultures.

Adapted from Cohen, P (1974) *The Gospel According to the Harvard Business School*, Penguin. Originally published by Doubleday, New York, 1973.

HARVARD BUSINESS SCHOOL **http://www.hbs.edu**

However, it is also important to consider the quality of life of investors (shareholders), customers, suppliers and distributors, as well as other employees of the firm who are not involved in decision-making. Developing earlier points, it can be argued that employees are the major stakeholders, because if the firm goes out of business they incur the greatest losses.

In many respects it does not matter whether profit is seen as an objective or as a means of providing service and satisfaction to stakeholders, as long as both are considered and not seen as mutually exclusive. However, the 'feel' and culture of an organization will be affected. In simple terms an organization will succeed if it survives and meets the expectations of its stakeholders. If its objectives relate to the stakeholders, it is successful if it attains its objectives.

We can, though, see evidence of the pursuit of profit becoming a real problem in the case of the banks in the years leading up to 2008. Banks have always borrowed from individual savers (in return for interest payments) and used a proportion of this money for lending to businesses and individuals (at a higher rate of interest). Building societies followed the same logic but provided mortgages. As these historically mutual societies became banks (with shareholders looking for dividends and capital growth) some of them started pursuing ever riskier loans. They lent to a higher mortgage to earnings multiple and they risked sub-prime lending to people with little collateral. They were comfortable doing this because they passed these sub-prime loans on to the wholesale market, where other financiers were willing to buy packages of these loans. The money was then re-lent. A culture of innovation and risk took over from an ability to manage the implications of the decisions being made. At the same time the high street banks merged with investment banks, whose role is different. As a consequence the savings of the 'general public' were now at risk of being gambled by professional bankers whose life is spent taking short-term risks on future commodity and stocks prices and whether they will go up or down. When huge amounts are traded for a few hours or days, then handsome profits can be made on very, very tight margins. But losses can be made just as easily. And this is what happened when these (so-called with hindsight) greedy bankers got carried away with the promise of very generous performance bonuses. The outcome was an eventual reluctance of the banks to lend very much if at all, even after the government supported them with taxpayers' money.

The purpose of industry is to serve the public by creating services to meet their needs. It is not to make profits for shareholders, nor to create salaries and wages for the industrial community. These are necessary conditions for success, but not its purpose.

DR GEORGE CAREY, RETIRED ARCHBISHOP OF CANTERBURY

The responsibility of business is not to create profits but to create live, vibrant, honourable organizations with a real commitment to the community.

ANITA RODDICK, FOUNDER, THE BODY SHOP

The influence of shareholders

Some commentators hold the view that too many companies are still encouraged to seek short-term profits in order to please their major institutional shareholders, and that it is only by considering the long term and the interests of all stakeholders that companies will become more effective competitors in world markets. In the UK, for example, Constable (1980) stated: 'Britain's steady relative industrial decline over the past 30 years is related to an insistence on setting purely financial objectives which have been operated in relatively short time scales'. Institutions such as pension funds effectively control the UK's largest companies through the sizeable blocks of shares that they own; in contested takeovers, for example, individual pension fund managers will be instrumental in determining the outcome. These managers have a remit to earn the best returns that they can obtain for their members. Since the mid-1990s there has been a drive to increase the transparency of these large shareholder blocks, and companies have been required to publish more information.

The issue of short-termism is complex, however, and Critical reflection 6.2 investigates the debate. Companies, obviously, cannot disregard powerful institutional shareholders. What is crucial is to ensure that there is dialogue and mutual understanding and agreement concerning the best interests of the company, its shareholders and other stakeholders.

Critical reflection 6.2

Long- and Short-termism: The Debate

Laing (1987) has argued that where owners and managers are the same people, the goals and means of achieving them are not in conflict; but institutional fund managers, themselves under pressure to perform in the short term, have often put pressure on public companies to pursue strategies that may be incompatible with sound long-term management. It is, however, generally acknowledged that companies must pursue strategies that increase the long-term value of the business for its shareholders, or eventually they are likely to be under threat of acquisition. It is also often argued that many companies believe that they are likely to be under threat from powerful institutional shareholders if short-term performance is poor, i.e. if sales and profits fail to grow. The result can be a reluctance to undertake costly and risky investments, say, in research and development (R&D), if the payback is uncertain.

Thus, it would follow that if a manufacturing business were seeking to boost short-term profits and earnings per share for reasons of expedience, it might well reduce quality and service and fail to invest adequately for the future. The price for this would be inevitable decline. This tendency could be worsened if the company were under threat of takeover and thus anxious to improve its immediate performance. For businesses in countries such as Germany and Japan, where historically 'the Damoclean sword of hostile takeovers was virtually unknown' (Laing, 1987) this has been less likely than in the UK.

Institutional shareholders must clearly want to be able to exercise some control or influence over large companies where they have substantial equity interests. One dilemma is that while they want to rein in powerful and risk-orientated strategic leaders, they do not want to forsake the potential benefits of strong, entrepreneurial leadership. They can exert influence by:

- pushing for the roles of chairman and chief executive to be separated, and arguing for a high

proportion of carefully selected non-executive (external part-time) directors
- attempting to replace senior managers whose performance is poor or lacklustre, but this can be difficult (it is often argued that shareholders are too passive about this option)
- selling their shares to predatory bidders.

While this final option is a perpetual threat, and the biggest fear of many strategic leaders, not all companies are prevented from investing in R&D. Logically, those which are well managed are in command of where they are going to invest. In addition, institutions argue that they are objective about their investments and turn down more offers for their shares than they accept.

In essence, 'managers should not be discouraged by their owners, their shareholders, from taking risks, from undertaking research and from investing in innovation' (Laing, 1987).

An analysis by the *Financial Times* (Martinson, 1998) suggests that large institutional shareholders do take a long-term view but rarely make helpful comments on strategy. When they exercise their voting power it is generally clear and visible, rather than covert. Many fund managers were seen as professional but, at the same time, 'ill-informed fund managers are making increasing demands on executive time'.

Undoubtedly more communication between directors and their shareholders concerning results, plans and philosophies would be desirable in many cases. Would this resolve the difficulties, or is something more drastic still required?

Lipton (1990) has controversially suggested that Boards should be subject to quinquennial reviews of their performance (partially conducted by independent outsiders) and their plans for the next five years. Hostile bids could be considered at the same time, but not between reviews. Boards may or may not be re-elected, depending on their relative performance. The idea is to generate more stability and to 'unite directors and shareholders behind the goal of maximizing long-term profits'.

The late Lord White of Hanson plc (1990) stated his disagreement, arguing that if institutional shareholders are willing to sell their shares it is usually the result of poor management generally, and not merely a reluctance to invest in R&D. 'Under-performing companies are frequently typified by high top salaries, share options confined to a handful of apparatchiks and generous golden parachutes.' Such companies are often legitimate takeover targets, and inevitably the bids are likely to be perceived as hostile.

In summary, long-term success requires that companies and their strategic leaders are properly accountable for their performance and, for many businesses, this really has to be to their shareholders. At the same time, shareholders must be objective and take a long-term perspective, and they must be active, not passive, about replacing poor managers and about intervening when they feel that the corporate strategy is wrong.

The dilemmas relate to the implementation of these ideas and to the issue of whether institutions have advisers with enough detailed, industry-specific, knowledge to make an objective judgement.

Footnote

The references used in this box may be dated but the arguments still remain. The issue has never been truly resolved. However, more recently, shareholder power has also been exercised in other ways. Institutional shareholders – partly as a reaction to media and public opinion – have joined the debate about director rewards especially in crisis business situations. It is not unusual for CEOs to have two or three year rolling contracts, such that if they resign or are fired, they receive handsome 'golden handshakes'. WH Smith is a case in point. In 2003 Kate Swann became the new CEO, joining them from a similar role at Argos. She was given a 'golden hello' as compensation for lost share options at her previous employer. At the same time, Retail Director Beverley Hodson was also paid compensation for being overlooked for the job. Soon afterwards she resigned and received a generous payoff. Some shareholders were unhappy as they blamed her for the company's deteriorating performance in 2003. The controversy over bankers' bonuses in 2009 is testimony to concern over what some describe as a 'reward for failure'.

Later in the chapter we also see how shareholders are increasingly concerned that companies come clean on any ethical risks involved in the business.

Sources

Laing, H (1987) quoted in *First*, 1 (2).

Lipton, M (1990) An end to hostile takeovers and short-termism, *Financial Times*, 27 June.

Martinson, J (1998) Companies say big shareholders take long view, *Financial Times*, 27 April.

White, G (1990) Why management must be accountable, *Financial Times*, 12 July.

In his debate on the short- and long-term perspective, Constable (Table 6.3) contrasts two sets of objectives, ranked in order of priority. He contends that company B is likely to grow at the expense of company A, and that these objective sets, A and B, are essentially those adopted by large UK and Japanese companies, respectively, for much of the period since the World War II. To suggest that Japanese success rests solely on a particular set of objectives is oversimplifying reality, but it has certainly contributed.

In Japan and Germany, however, shareholders do not exert pressure in the same way as they do in the UK. Cross-shareholding between companies in Japan means that only 25 per cent of

Table 6.3   Contrasting company objectives

Company A	Company B
1 Return on net assets, 1–3 year time horizon	1 Maintenance and growth of market share
2 Cash flow	2 Maintenance and growth of employment
3 Maintenance and growth of market share	3 Cash flow
4 Maintenance and growth of employment	4 Return on net assets

shares in Japanese businesses are for trading and speculation, and this generates greater stability. In Germany the companies hold a higher proportion of their own shares, and banks act as proxy voters for private investors. Banks thereby control some 60 per cent of the tradeable shares, again generating stability. German companies also adopt a two-tier board structure. A supervisory board has overall control and reports to shareholders and employee unions; reporting to this board is a management board, elected for up to five years.

Table 6.4 pulls together a number of the points discussed here by showing how organizational strategic leaders and institutional investors do not share completely the same perspective on stakeholder priorities, although there are clear similarities with the most important stakeholders. Interestingly, suppliers, key partners in the **supply chain**, receive a higher priority from strategic leaders, while the institutions rate politicians more highly than do organizational leaders. It is both significant and realistic, that small, individual shareholders are not particularly powerful, because they are generally too disparate to become organized. Individually, they may be able to embarrass an organization with difficult questions at its Annual General Meeting, but this is far from an expression of ongoing power.

A note on objectives, strategies and tactics

We can think in simple terms of 'objectives' relating to desired ends and so a 'why?' theme. Strategies then concern 'what' to do (the means) to achieve the desired end. Tactics break strategies down further and address 'how'. But we have said before that organizations carry out activities, activities are what they do. So, take the following list of activities:

1 Achieve a higher value (and hence price) for my property
2 Improve the appearance of my house
3 Paint my house
4 Do the painting myself
5 Buy some paint.

These are deliberately listed as a hierarchy. Our question to you is: which of these is an objective, a strategy, a tactic? Number 1 easily makes sense as an objective, making 2 a strategy and 3, 4 and 5 are tactics. But 2 could be seen as an objective – and maybe so too could 3 – at a

Table 6.4 Perceptions of stakeholder importance

Stakeholder	Prioritization by industry strategic leaders	Prioritization by analysts with institutional investors
Existing customers	1	1
Existing employees	2	3
Potential customers	3	2
Institutional investors	4	4
Suppliers	5	7
Potential employees	6	6
City analysts	7	5
Private (individual) shareholders	8	10
Business media	9	9
General media	10	11
Local communities	11	12
Members of Parliament/Local authorities	12	8

MORI http://www.mori.com

lower order. If the key influencer (perhaps one of our wives!) decides 1 is important she might delegate the required tasks to one of us. That is her strategy for making sure something happens; it is now our objective!

The simple point here is that different people in the same organization will be able to relate to activities that are happening, activities that sometimes they are responsible and accountable for. A particular activity can be one person's objective but a strategy carried out by someone else.

The importance of the strategic leader

To conclude this section it is useful to emphasize the key role of the strategic leader, and his or her values, in establishing the main objectives and the direction in which they take the organization. Personal ambitions to build a large conglomerate or a multinational company may fuel growth; a determination to be socially responsible may restrain certain activities that other organizations would undertake; a commitment to high quality will influence the design, cost and marketing approach for products. These points are illustrated in Case 6.3, Trade Plus Aid.

Case 6.3

Trade Plus Aid   UK

Trade Plus Aid began more by chance than design in 1992. Charlotte Di Vita, then aged 25, was in Ghana when drought ruined thousands of farms – something she realized when she was waiting to see a doctor for treatment for the severe dysentery she had contracted and witnessed the death of a baby in its mother's arms. Wanting to help in some way, she had an idea when the local elders refused her offer of money to buy seed. She suggested to local tribal chiefs that she would spend her £800 savings on seed for them if they would make her 800 pendant-size carvings. The deal was struck. Back in London, and calling on her friends to help her out, she began selling the pendants at Camden and Portobello Markets, plucking a price of £6.99 each out of thin air. Somewhat to her surprise, the carvings sold quickly and easily. The risk she took had paid off, and she was encouraged to want to do more. She envisioned a seed bank from which local farmers could borrow seed without any payment until they harvest their crops. To progress her idea, she negotiated an alliance with an established mail order business in Japan – and pendant sales were strong once the infrastructure and supply chain was in place. Her seed bank was started in 1995. The venture grew rapidly with a comprehensive Japanese mail order catalogue, which included jewellery, clothing and toiletries from various countries in Africa and South America. Unfortunately the 1995 earthquake at Kobe, in Japan, destroyed the warehouse that Di Vita's partner owned; the mail

order company was in trouble and the Japanese market disappeared overnight. Exhibiting courage in the face of setbacks, she managed to survive and rescue the business by spending hours and days searching out new mail order buyers in America and Germany – but they would only buy her supplies at cost.

Many of the Third World village supply groups she helped establish are now trading independently; they no longer need her help. 'A good year is seeing my groups become self-sufficient, not increasing my turnover'. The ever creative Trade Plus Aid, however, continues to experiment with new initiatives. Di Vita was able to raise money from business people around the world – who believe in what she does – to establish a 140-employee factory in China for producing hand-enamelled teapots. She started selling these at the Victoria and Albert Museum and various up-market department stores. Underestimating demand forced her to resort to airfreighting. A similar venture was started to produce wind chimes in South Africa. Altogether some 500 employees now work in her factories in China and South Africa. In the UK, Trade Plus Aid relies more on volunteer helpers than it does on paid employees and Di Vita herself takes only a limited salary from the operation. In 2003 Charlotte Di Vita agreed a world-wide licensing deal for her Collection (as it is now called) of gifts with leading giftware company Goebel – this guarantees a minimum revenue of US$1.3 million over four years.

In thirteen years Di Vita's efforts had enabled over $5 million to be returned to producer communities around the world – Africa, South America and the Far East – in payment for their handicrafts. Her charitable trust (founded in 1997) has also funded special projects in various countries.

Charlotte Di Vita's most recent new project was developed with the encouragement of Nelson Mandela. Entitled 'Twenty First Century Leaders' her project invites famous people – leaders, sports stars, musicians, and actors – to provide a simple design that reflects their message of hope for the world, together with a stick diagram self-portrait. These are then used as designs for plates, mugs, t-shirts and any other relevant product where she can secure a licence agreement with a suitable manufacturer. In the case of the plates, the illustrated message is on the front, the stick diagram on the back, and they are being sold as limited edition collectibles. In the case of wrist-bands and other smaller items, the production runs are unlimited. The surpluses from all sales of every item will be 'handed back' to their designers, who will choose which charity will receive them. The intention is to raise money to help tackle key global issues: poverty, child abuse and environmental conservation.

Questions

1 How would you apply the Gerber themes of dream, vision, mission and purpose (Section 6.1 Introduction) to this case?
2 To what extent is this organization dependent upon Charlotte di Vita?
3 Is a high level of dependency on a driven leader by nature good or bad?

© PENNY TWEEDIE / ALAMY

The objectives and values of the strategic leader can be a particularly important consideration in the case of small firms. While it is possible for small firms to enjoy competitive advantage, say by providing products or services with values added to appeal to local customers in a limited geographical area, many are not distinctive in any marked way. Where this is the case, and where competition is strong, small firms will be price takers, and their profits and growth will be influenced substantially by external forces. Some small firm owners will be entrepreneurial, willing to take risks and determined to build a bigger business, whereas others will be content to stay small. Some small businesses are started by people who essentially want to work for themselves rather than for a larger corporation, and their objectives could well be concerned with survival and the establishment of a sound business which can be passed on to the next generation of their family.

Each of the ideas and theories discussed in this section provides food for thought, but individually none of them explains fully what happens, or what should happen, in organizations. In the authors' experience certain organizations are highly growth orientated, willing to diversify and take risks, while others, constrained by the difficulties of coping with rapid growth and implementing diversification strategies, are less ambitious in this respect. Each can be appropriate in certain circumstances and lead to high performance, but in different circumstances they may be the wrong strategy.

Stakeholder theory is extremely relevant conceptually, but organizations are affected by the stakeholders in a variety of ways. Priorities must be decided for companies on an individual basis. Moreover, the strategic leader, and in turn the organization, will seek to satisfy particular stakeholders rather than others because of their personal backgrounds and values. There is no right or wrong list of priorities. However, while priorities can and will be established, all stakeholders must be satisfied to some minimum level. In the final analysis the essential requirement is congruence among environment, values and resources.

So far this chapter has concentrated on profit-seeking organizations and considered just how important the profit motive might be. Not-for-profit organizations may be growth conscious, quality conscious or committed to employee welfare in the same way as profit seekers, but there are certain differences which require that they are considered separately.

6.3 Objectives of public sector and not-for-profit organizations

In order to understand the objectives of not-for-profit organizations and appreciate where they are aiming to go, a number of points need to be considered.

- Stakeholders are important, particularly those who are providers of financial support.
- There will be a number of potentially conflicting objectives, and quite typically the financial ones will not be seen as the most essential in terms of the mission.
- While there will be a mix of quantitative (financial) and qualitative objectives, the former will be easier to measure, although the latter relate more closely to the mission of the organization.
- For this reason the efficient use of resources becomes an important objective.

These points will now be examined in greater depth, making reference to Case 6.4 on London Zoo together with a number of other examples, as public sector and not-for-profit organizations are many and varied.

Historically, and at one extreme, certainly in terms of size, *nationalized industries* with essentially monopoly markets have been seen as both public sector and non-profit. Throughout their existence different governments have strived to establish acceptable and effective measures of performance for them. At various times both **break-even** and return on capital employed have been stressed. There has always been an inbuilt objectives conflict between social needs (many of them provided essential services) and a requirement that the very substantial resources involved were managed commercially in order to avoid waste. The Conservative government of the 1980s followed a policy of privatizing certain nationalized industries partly on the grounds that in some cases more competition will be stimulating and create greater efficiency.

In Britain, the NHS can be viewed similarly. Fundamentally, its purpose relates to the health and well-being of the nation, and attention can be focused on both prevention and cure. The role of the police in terms of crime prevention and the solution of crimes that have taken place can be seen as synonymous. The health service can spend any money it is offered, as science continually improves what can be done for people. In a sense it is a chicken and egg situation. Resources improve treatments and open up new opportunities for prevention; and these in turn stimulate demand, particularly where they concern illnesses or diseases which historically have not been easily treated. However, these developments are often very expensive, and decisions have then to be made about where funds should be allocated. Quite simply, the decisions relate to priorities. To some employees in the NHS it will feel as if they are working for an organization whose purpose is to ration scarce resources, resources they are given by the State.

Customers of the health service are concerned with such things as the waiting time for admission to hospital and for operations, the quality of care as affected by staff attitudes and numbers, and arguably privacy in small wards, cleanliness and food. Doctors generally are concerned with the amount of resources and their ability to cope with demand; some consultants are anxious to work at the leading edge of their specialism; while administrators must ensure that resources are used efficiently.

The government funds the NHS, and as the major source of funds it is a key influence. It is very concerned with the political fallout from perceived weaknesses in the service, and inevitably its priorities are affected by this. It has been reported that the Labour government's emphasis on

Case 6.4

London Zoo

UK

London Zoo, in Regent's Park, is one of two zoological gardens which are controlled and administered by the Zoological Society of London (ZSL). The other is Whipsnade Park, in Bedfordshire, and this covers 600 acres compared with just 36 acres in London.

The Society's original charter laid down its primary purpose as 'the advancement of zoology and animal physiology, and the introduction of new and curious subjects of the animal kingdom', but this has been modified in the current mission. ZSL now exists to 'achieve and promote the worldwide conservation of animals and their habitats'. This is pursued by:

- Keeping and presenting animals at the two zoos
- Prioritizing threatened species
- Helping people become more aware of animal welfare and conservation issues
- Maintaining an education programme
- Undertaking both conservation work and serious zoological research
- Publishing activities.

However, ZSL has to generate an income from visitors to supplement its other sources of revenue. Therefore from the mission must stem a fundamental dilemma: how much is a zoo a place of entertainment and relaxation, with customers paramount, and how much is it an organization with primarily educational and scientific purposes? One commercial constraint for London Zoo is the fact that Regent's Park is a Royal Park, and that bylaws restrict certain activities such as on-site advertising.

There are basically five main activities: London Zoo, Whipsnade Park, The Institute of Zoology (conferencing and publishing), conservation programmes and the world-renowned library.

At times in the past the zoo has received a series of annual grants from the Department of the Environment, and in 1988 it was given £10 million as a designated one-off payment 'to put it on a firm financial footing'. It remains 'the only national collection in the world not publically funded on a regular basis'.

Income is essentially from visitors, the majority of whom live within comfortable travelling distance of London, through membership and admission fees and merchandising, but there are some research grants. Many of the visitors are on organized school trips, and weather conditions are very important in attracting or deterring people.

Many visitors are attracted by big animals, as evidenced by the commercial success of safari parks, but these are costly and dangerous, and well researched and relatively safe as far as endangered species go. Quite often the most endangered species are relatively unattractive to visitors. Whipsnade is regarded as more ideal for big animals. London Zoo for many years has had no hippos (since the 1960s – although there are pygmy hippos in the collection) and no bears (since 1986), but more recently some large animals have been brought back to counter visitor criticism. There are, for example, giraffes, lions, tigers and leopards. However, in 2001, and following an incident with a visitor, London Zoo's elephants were moved to Whipsnade. Visitors can drive around Whipsnade, parking in various places en route, but it is not a safari park. There are some 650 species at London Zoo, of which 112 can be classified as 'threatened'. There are breeding programmes for 130 species.

Critics have sometimes argued that London Zoo's management has failed to fully exploit the zoo's conservation work by featuring it in informative displays and that much of the zoo's important and scientifically renowned research is not recognized by the general public. This may be correct, but the fact remains that much of the important conservation work involves species which are relatively uninteresting for many public visitors, for example the rare Rodriguez fruit bat.

The Department of the Environment paid for a report by independent consultants (1987–8) and concluded that 'management at London Zoo did not reflect the commercial emphasis which was essential for survival and prosperity without a permanent subsidy'. They recommended the establishment of a new company to manage London and Whipsnade Zoos, separate from the scientific research of the Zoological Society. This company was established in October 1988, with the aim of reversing the falling trend in admissions and returning the zoo to profit in three years.

The numbers of visitors did increase in 1989 and 1990, but below the level required to break even. In April 1991 newspapers first reported that London Zoo might have to close, with some animals destroyed and others moved to Whipsnade. The government refused further financial assistance, not wholly convinced of the need for urban zoos. Cost reduction per se was ruled out as this was likely to provoke a new fall in admissions. Instead, rescue plans concentrated on a smaller zoo with a new concept: natural habitats such as an African rainforest complete with gorillas, and a Chinese mountain featuring the pandas. There would be less emphasis on caged animals. These developments have taken place but there have still been criticisms from some groups that the space for gorillas is inadequate when compared with the facilities they enjoy in some other zoos. The reality is, of course, that only so much can be done in 36 acres whilst still retaining a collection that is attractive to visitors.

Although changes were made, attendances continued to fall. The zoo's closure was announced formally in June 1992. New external funding has since provided a reprieve.

Since 1992 the zoo has secured its survival by emphasizing its role as a conservation centre, breeding endangered species and returning them to the wild. During the 1990s ZSL managed to break even by using publicity more effectively to attract some one million visitors a year.

More recently the zoo has stopped providing pony rides for children, declaring that this is not an appropriate form of entertainment. The Mappin Café was renovated in 2002. There is an ongoing renovation project in London to replace cages with enclosures which recreate the animals' natural environments, thus providing a better lifestyle for the animals and a more realistic visitor experience. In 2005 two walkthroughs for African birds and monkeys were opened, followed by a new Gorilla Kingdom and Rainforest Lookout in 2007. In 2008 the Bird House was reopened as a tropical rainforest. Whilst some changes in the last 20 years have been forced on the zoo by external pressures, others have been voluntary. In the end London Zoo has to find a business model that attracts sufficient visitors and revenue in the face of competition from a wide range of other tourist attractions. New rhino and cheetah exhibits were opened at Whipsnade in 2008.

In 2002/3 ZSL had incoming resources of £34 million. £13.1 million came from members' subscriptions and admission charges; £4.2 million from merchandising and catering and £3.7 million from grants. These grants did not amount to public subsidies. Half of the total was HEFCE (Higher Education Funding Council) research funding chanelled through the University of Cambridge; most of the other half came from individual grants related to specific projects. £7.5 million was recovered VAT payments – which partly explains why income had increased from £21 million in 2001/2. Profit after tax was £1.4 million, up from £1.2 million. In this year there were 815,000 paying visitors at London Zoo, with a further 445,000 at Whipsnade.

Five years later, in 2007 the corresponding figures were as follows. London Zoo attracted 1.1 million visitors and Whipsnade 475,000. The increase in numbers during the year was the highest for fifteen years. ZSL had incoming resources of £40.1 million and it spent £36.6 million, yielding a surplus of £3.5 million. There had been some grants for specific projects and a capital spend of nearly £8 million.

Questions

1   What should the objectives of London Zoo be?
2   Who are the major stakeholders, and how important are they?
3   If you were in charge (and remembering the constraints) what strategies would you recommend?

waiting lists, a key pledge in its 1997 election manifesto, has distorted clinical priorities, such that many minor ailments have been given priority for treatment over more major ones. Pfeffer (1981) has argued that the relative power of influencers is related to the funds that they provide. The less funding that is provided by customers, the weaker is their influence over decisions. Hence, a not-for-profit organization such as the NHS may be less customer orientated than a private competitive firm. Some would argue that the private medical sector is more marketing conscious. Without question, and in simple terms, the NHS is about patient care within imposed budgetary constraints. The issue really concerns whether patients perceive that it feels like a service driven by a culture of care or by a culture of resource-management efficiency.

All organizations will seek to measure performance in some way. It was stated earlier in the chapter that performance against quantitative objectives can be measured directly, whereas performance against qualitative objectives is typically indirect and more difficult. If attention is focused on the aspects that are most easily measured there is a danger that these come to be perceived as the most important objectives. Hospital administrators can easily measure the number of admissions, the utilization of beds and theatres, the cost of laundry and food and so on. Fundamentally more important is who is being treated relative to the real needs of the community. Are the most urgent and needy cases receiving the priorities they deserve? How is this measured? Performance measures therefore tend to concentrate on the efficient use of resources rather than the effectiveness of the organization. Although profit may not be an important consideration, costs are. In addition, these measures may well be a source of conflict between medical and administrative staff, and this is a reflection of the fact that there is likely to be disagreement and confusion about what the key objectives are.

Given this, the objectives that are perceived as important and are pursued at any time are very dependent on the relative power of the influencers and their ability to exercise power. Linked to this point is the relationship between hospitals and whatever area and regional health authorities are in existence at any time. Similarly, where not-for-profit organizations have advisory bodies, or boards of trustees, the relationship and relative power are important.

Tourist attractions such as London Zoo and leading museums (including the British Museum, the Natural History Museum and the Victoria and Albert, which is the National Museum of Art and Design) have a potential conflict of objectives concerning their inevitable educational and scientific orientations and the requirement that they address commercial issues. Museums can earn money from shops and cafeterias and they receive some private funding, but to a great extent they are reliant on government grants. In the 1980s these grants did not keep pace with their monetary demands and hence it became necessary for them to seek additional revenue as well as manage resources and costs more efficiently. Admission charges were introduced by some museums and, perhaps inevitably, they became a controversial issue in the UK. In November 1985 the Victoria and Albert Museum introduced voluntary admission charges, and in April 1987 the Natural History Museum started charging for entry. Some potential visitors are always going to be lost as they refuse to pay, and this has implications for the educational objective. It was reported that by 1987 admissions to the Victoria and Albert had fallen to one million a year from a peak of 1.75 million in 1983, but they began to increase again after 1988 as people became more accustomed to charging. However, the museum was criticized by some arts lovers for a poster campaign describing it as 'an ace cafe with quite a nice museum attached', although museum staff claimed that this was a major reason for the increase in attendances. Some museums, including the British Museum, adamantly opposed charging. The new Tate Modern, opened in 2000, did not charge for admission. In the last few years admission charges to London's main museums have largely been dropped as new grants and subsidies have been provided. That said, although admission to the main halls is free, visitors pay for the special exhibitions, which is what attracts many of them in the first place! However, it is still arguable that with either admission charges or larger grants the museums could employ more curators and provide an enhanced service. More exhibits could be put on show; exhibitions could be changed more often, for example. In the end a balance has to be found between level of service and the number of visitors. Is quality or quantity more important?

At the National Theatre the issue addresses art and finance. Subsidized theatres perceive their role to be different from that of commercial theatres and a number of them, including the Royal Shakespeare Company, English National Opera and the Royal Opera House, Covent Garden, compete for a percentage of Arts Council funding. When the Arts Council, as a major stakeholder and provider of funds, attempts to influence the strategies of the theatres they are often accused of meddling. Again there is a potential chicken and egg situation. If the theatres, under pressure from reduced subsidies (in real terms), raise more revenue and reduce their costs, they may find that this results in permanently reduced subsidies. Hence, as an alternative, they may choose to restrain their commercial orientation.

Cathedrals face a similar dilemma. The costs of repairs and maintenance are forcing some to charge visitors fixed amounts rather than rely on voluntary donations. Their mission is concerned with religion and charity but they are not immune from commercial realities.

Charities frequently have sets of interdependent commercial and non-commercial objectives. Oxfam's mission concerns the provision of relief and the provision of aid where it is most needed throughout the world. Additional objectives relate to teaching people how to look after themselves better through, say, irrigation and better farming techniques and to obtaining publicity to draw public attention to the plight of the needy. Their ability to pursue these objectives is constrained by resource availability. Consequently, Oxfam have fund-raising objectives, and strategies (including retailing through Oxfam shops) to achieve them. It is difficult to say which receives most priority as they are so interdependent.

While the coverage of not-for-profit organizations in this section has been partial, as many other organizations such as schools and universities are fundamentally non-profitable, the points are representative of the sector.

The issue of the displacement of objectives has been discussed in some not-for-profit organizations. Attention is centred on quantitative measures as they are relatively easily carried out. The efficient use of resources replaces profit as the commercial objective, and while this may not be an essential aspect of the mission, it will be seen as important by certain stakeholders. In reality attention has switched from evaluating outputs and outcomes (the real objectives) to measuring inputs (resources) because it is easier to do. Where the stakeholders are major sponsors, and particularly in the case of government departments, there will be an insistence upon cost-effectiveness. Many of the organizations mentioned in this section are managed by people whose training and natural orientation is towards arts or science, and this can result in feelings of conflict with regard to objectives. Quite typically the organization will pursue certain objectives for a period of time, satisfying the most influential stakeholders in the coalition, and then change as the preferences of stakeholders, or their relative power and influence, change.

While profit-seeking and not-for-profit organizations have essentially different missions, the issue of profit-making is complex. Some not-for-profit organizations rely on subsidies and these enable prices to be kept below what they would otherwise be. In nationalized industries the element of customer service has been seen to be important, with prices controlled or at least influenced by government. An independent regulator has been appointed when nationalized businesses have been privatized. However, unless the providers of grants and subsidies are willing to bear commercial trading losses and at the same time finance any necessary investment, there is a necessity for the organizations to generate revenue at least equal to the costs incurred. Where investment finance also needs to be generated a surplus of income over expenditure is important. This basically is profit. While profit may not therefore be an essential part of the mission, it is still required.

> *The objectives pursued by organizations frequently differ from those proclaimed. Some years ago I assumed that the principal objective of universities was the education of students. Armed with this assumption I could make no sense of their behaviour. I learned that education, like profit, is a requirement not an objective and that the principal objective is to provide their faculties with the quality of work life and the standard of living they desire. That's why professors do so little teaching, give the same courses over and over again, arrange classes at*

their convenience, not that of their students, teach subjects they want to teach rather than
students want to learn and skip classes to give lectures [elsewhere] for a fee.

RUSSELL ACKOFF, 1986

6.4 The impact of personal objectives

It has already been established that organizations are generally too large and complex to have
only one objective. As a result, and influenced by stakeholders, there are typically several
objectives with varying degrees of relative importance. It is now appropriate to consider why
organizations cannot be treated separately from the people who work in them.

Objectives can be set (and changed) in any one of three ways:

- The strategic leader decides.

- Managers throughout the organization are either consulted or influence the objectives by
  their decisions and actions.

- All or some of the external stakeholders influence or constrain the organization in some
  way.

The second of these is addressed in this section. With emergent strategy the decisions made by
managers determine the actual strategies pursued, and in turn revised, implicit, objectives replace
those that were previously declared as intended objectives. The incidence or likelihood of this is
affected by the culture of the organization, the relative power bases of managers, communication
systems, and whether or not there are rigid policies and procedures or more informal
management processes that allow managers considerable freedom. Box 6.1 defines policies and
discusses their role in strategy implementation. The following brief example illustrates the
impact of policies. Consider a multiple store that sells DVDs as one of its products and has
nearby a smaller independent competitor that appeals to different customers. This could easily be
WHSmith and an independent neighbour. If the small store closed down there could be new
opportunities for the manager of the multiple store if he changed his competitive strategy for
DVDs by changing his displays, improved his stock levels and supported these moves with
window displays promoting the changes. Head-office merchandizing policies concerning stocks
and displays may or may not allow him this freedom.

In the case of intended strategy, the strategic leader determines and states the objectives,
strategies and proposed changes for the organization. In arriving at decisions he or she may be
influenced in a minor or major way by stakeholders outside the organization and the managers
consulted. In order to ensure that the strategies are implemented (and the objectives achieved) the
strategic leader will design and build an organization structure – which may restrict managers or
allow them considerable freedom – and will determine policies which may be mandatory or
advisory. This will tie in to the culture of the organization and will be influenced by the style and
values of the strategic leader.

However, the types of policy and the authority and freedom delegated to managers guide,
influence and constrain decision-making. The motives, values and relative power of individual
managers, the relative importance of particular functions, divisions or strategic business units in
the organization, and the system of communications are also influential. The stated or *official*
objectives may or may not be achieved; there may be appropriate incremental decisions which
reflect changes in the environment; or managers may be pursuing personal objectives, which
Perrow (1961) has termed *operative goals*. This is happening when the behaviour taking place
cannot be accounted for by official company objectives and policies. The aggregation of these
various decisions determines the emergent strategic changes, the actual objectives followed and
the results achieved.

Box 6.1

Policies

You must provide a framework in which people can act. For example, we have said that our first priority is safety, second is punctuality, and third is other services. So if you risk flight safety by leaving on time, you have acted outside the framework of your authority. The same is true if you don't leave on time because you are missing two catering boxes of meat. That's what I mean by a framework. You give people a framework, and within the framework you let people act.

JAN CARLZON, WHEN PRESIDENT AND CHIEF EXECUTIVE OFFICER, SAS (SCANDINAVIAN AIRLINES SYSTEM)

- *Policies* are guidelines relating to decisions and approaches which support organizational efforts to achieve stated and intended objectives.
- They are basically *guides to thoughts* (about how things might or should be done) and *actions*.
- They are therefore *guides to decision-making*. For example, a policy which states that for supplies of a particular item three quotations should be sought and the cheapest selected, or a policy not to advertise in certain newspapers, or a policy not to trade with particular countries – all influence decisions. Policies are particularly useful for routine repetitive decisions.
- Policies can be at corporate, divisional (or strategic business unit [SBU]) or functional level, and they are normally stated in terms of management (of people), marketing, production, finance and research and development.
- If stated objectives are to be achieved, and the strategies designed to accomplish this implemented, the appropriate policies must be there in support. In other words, the behaviour of managers and the decisions that they make should be supportive of what the organization is seeking to achieve. Policies guide and constrain their actions.
- Policies can be mandatory (rules which allow little freedom for original thought or action) or advisory. The more rigid they are the less freedom managers have to change things with delegated authority, and this can be good or bad depending on change pressures from the environment.
- *It is vital to balance consistency and coordination* (between the various divisions, SBUs and departments in the organization) *with flexibility.*
- Policies need not be written down. They can be passed on verbally as part of the culture.
- Policies *must* be widely understood if they are to be useful.

Footnote

For governments, *policies* has a slightly different meaning. Government policy relates to what government 'intends to do' regarding specific issues and priorities.

Operative goals may complement official goals or they may conflict. A complementary situation would exist if the stated objective was in terms of a target return on capital employed, and if this was achieved through operative goals of managers and decisions taken by them regarding delivery times, quality and so on. If, however, a sales manager was favouring particular customers with discounts or priority deliveries on low-profit orders, or a production manager was setting unnecessarily high quality standards (as far as customers are concerned) which resulted in substantial rejections and high operating costs, profits would be threatened. In such cases operative goals would conflict with official goals.

In this context, a report from the Public Management Foundation (1999) highlights a dilemma. Arguing that the UK government was feeling frustrated by the slow speed at which the public sector was embracing certain objectives and strategies from the profit-seeking private sector, the Foundation discovered a 'public sector ethos' amongst its managers. They are driven to 'make a difference for the community'. Improving local services and increasing user satisfaction are their personal priorities. There are occasions when this conflicts with the prioritization, rather than the actual existence, of stated, intended objectives for cutting costs and improving efficiencies. There is also a perception among many public-sector managers that their funders prefer centralized management **controls**, while they would like more autonomy and delegated authority. The situation is confused further when changing political pressures and necessities impact upon objectives and priorities.

6.5 Social responsibility and business ethics

See the online "New York's Yellow Cabs" case for an example of this section's theory in practice

Having looked at some of the theories which are relevant for a study of objectives, and at typical objectives that organizations pursue and why, it is appropriate to conclude this chapter with a consideration of wider societal aspects. Objectives that relate to **social responsibility** may be affected by stakeholders; in some cases they result from legislation, but often they are voluntary actions. The issue is one of how responsible a firm might choose to be, and why – simply, firms can be socially responsible (proactive) or socially responsive (reactive to pressure). Again, the particular values of the strategic leader will be very influential. The impact of the Mayor of New York is seen in Online Case 6.1 on Yellow Cabs. There is, though, often an interesting 'Catch-22' at work. Starbucks promotes itself as a socially responsible business, citing its dealings with coffee growers and pickers in developing countries. That it makes a serious effort is not in doubt. And yet Starbucks gets singled out by environmental and other campaigners – because they believe that a company which promotes itself as responsible is a softer target and more easily influenced than one that is either hostile or ambivalent.

There are numerous ways in which a firm can behave responsibly in the interests of society, and examples are given below. It should not be thought, however, that social responsibility is a one-way process; organizations can benefit considerably from it. Social responsibility and profitability can be improved simultaneously (The Performance Group, 1999).

● Product safety: This can be the result of design or production and includes aspects of supply and supplier selection to obtain safe materials or components. Product safety will be influenced to an extent by legislation, but an organization can build in more safety features than the law requires. Some cars are an example of this, such as Volvo which is promoted and perceived as a relatively safe car. Product safety will have cost implications. Sometimes the safety is reflected in perceived higher quality, which adds value that the customer is willing to pay a premium for, but at other times it will be the result of the organization's choosing to sacrifice some potential profit.

● Working conditions: Linked to the previous point, these can include safety at work, which again is affected by legislation which sets minimum standards. Aspects of job design to improve working conditions and training to improve employees' prospects are further examples.

● Honesty, including not offering or accepting bribes.

● Avoiding pollution.

● Avoiding discrimination.

The above points are all subject to some legislation.

● Community action: This is a very broad category with numerous opportunities, ranging from charitable activities to concerted action to promote industry and jobs in areas which have suffered from economic recession. Many large organizations release executives on a temporary basis to help with specific community projects.

● Industry location: Organizations may locate new plants in areas of high unemployment for a variety of reasons. While aspects of social responsibility may be involved, the decision may well be more economic. Grants and rate concessions may be important.

- Other environmental concerns: These include recycling, waste disposal, protecting the ozone layer and energy efficiency. Strategy in action 6.2 illustrates a number of specific examples.

Porter (1995) contends that many companies mistakenly see environmental legislation as a threat, something to be resisted. Instead, he argues, they should see regulation as an indication the company is not using its resources efficiently. Toxic materials and discarded packaging are waste. The costs incurred in eliminating a number of environmental problems can be more than offset by other savings and improvements in product quality. Companies should be innovative and not reluctantly just complying with their legal requirements. However, the European chemical industry has argued that bulk chemical manufacture has been largely driven out of EU countries by the costs of complying with environmental regulation. Standards in many Far Eastern countries are less restrictive.

- Attitude of food retailers: For example, accurate labelling (country of origin), free-range eggs, organic vegetables, biodegradable packaging, CFC-free aerosols and products containing certain dubious E-number additives. It is a moot point whether retailers or consumers should decide on these issues.

Objectives of this nature become part of the organization culture. Social responsibility is at the heart of activities and objectives because it is felt that the organization has an obligation both to the community and to society in general. However, it must not be assumed that the approach receives universal support. Milton Friedman (1979), the economist, argues that 'the business of business is business … the organization's only social responsibility is to increase its profit'. Friedman also comments that donations to charity and sponsorship of the arts are 'fundamentally subversive' and not in the best interests of the shareholders. Social responsibility would then be the result of legislation. Drucker (1974) argues businesses have a role in society which is 'to supply goods and services to customers and an economic surplus to society … rather than to supply jobs to workers and managers, or even dividends to shareholders'. The latter, he argues, are means not ends. Drucker contends that it is mismanagement to forget that a hospital exists for its patients and a university for its students.

This contrasts with the comments by Russell Ackoff about university academics quoted earlier.

The topic is complex, and although the outcome of certain decisions can be seen to be bringing benefit to the community or employees the decision may have been influenced by legislation or perceived organizational benefit (enlightened self-interest) rather than a social conscience. One could argue that the organization will benefit if it looks after its employees; equally one could argue that it will suffer if it fails to consider employee welfare. The two approaches are philosophically different, but they may generate similar results. Some organizations feature their community role extensively in corporate advertising campaigns designed to bring them recognition and develop a caring, responsible image.

Business ethics

Disasters such as the explosion at the chemical plant in Bhopal, India, in 1984 have long raised the question of how far companies should go in pursuit of profits. More recent cases, such as Tyco and Enron, have raised different but related issues of ethical behaviour. The CEO of Tyco has been prosecuted for using corporate funds to provide a lavish personal lifestyle – at the same time as sponsoring a number of creative accounting practices to hide the company's true financial performance. Enron lost huge sums of shareholder money as it developed futures trading for energy including trying to hold the state of California to ransom for power supplied through Enron.

Ethics is defined as 'the discipline dealing with what is good and bad and right and wrong or with moral duty and obligation' (*Webster's Third New International Dictionary*). Houlden (1988)

Strategy in action 6.2

Examples of Environmental Strategies

1 McDonald's took an equity stake in a new venture for recycling the waste collected at their restaurants. Some plastic containers which could not be recycled have been withdrawn; food scraps are used for making compost. Sainsbury's started giving a one-penny refund for every plastic carrier that customers reuse. This saves the retailer the cost of providing a new bag; it also reduces the amount of waste plastic. Later Marks and Spencer started charging for plastic bags to encourage customers to recycle.

2 Marks and Spencer has worked with campaign groups to identify damaging pesticides and stopped its suppliers from using them.

3 Electricity generating has gradually switched to gas and cleaner coal (with a low sulphur content) because coal has been shown to cause acid rain.

4 Packaging. Smaller, lighter packages use fewer raw materials and they are cheaper to transport. Procter & Gamble and Unilever have both introduced more concentrated versions of their detergent brands which, ironically, many consumers have seen as poor value for money because they have been unconvinced by the instructions to use less of the product! Soft drinks manufacturers have switched to fully recyclable aluminium cans and plastic bottles. In 2003 the Co-op and Somerfield pioneered degradable plastic carrier bags which self-destruct to gas, water and a little mineral matter after a period of months. Tesco followed their lead in 2004.

5 ICI invested in the challenge to find a replacement for chlorofluorocarbons (CFCs), gases which are used extensively in aerosols and refrigeration equipment, and which are widely blamed for depleting the ozone layer.

6 The Body Shop produces a comprehensive, externally audited, environmental report, its Green Book. The emphasis on such factors as energy waste and product stewardship drives improvements. Among other initiatives, The Body Shop has sought to eliminate its use of polyvinylchloride (PVC) because of the environmental impact of such packaging.

7 The motor vehicle industry. Historically, car manufacturers exploited an opportunity very successfully: increased affluence and the desire for individual freedom had generated a demand for private cars. Their success in increasing levels of ownership created a number of threats: traffic density, pollution from exhaust emissions, material waste through obsolescence, the 'waste' of scarce resources in high-consumption, inefficient, engines, and safety problems arising from the sheer volume of traffic, congestion and hurry.

A response was needed, and this has involved both manufacturers and government:

- Legislation made catalytic converters compulsory on all new cars after January 1993.
- New models invariably feature improvements in design and technology which reduce waste and increase fuel efficiency.
- Some new plants feature strategies for reducing energy consumption, water consumption and solvent emissions.
- New concept vehicles are being developed, including electric cars and others which mix the

© BOGDAN / DREAMSTIME.COM

traditionally contradictory high performance with environmental friendliness. These have a long-term timescale.

- Links between different forms of transport (road, rail, air and water) are being strengthened. BMW, for example, has pioneered co-operative ventures in Munich, where research has shown that in one square kilometre of the city centre, during busy periods, drivers of 50 per cent of the cars on the move are driving round looking for parking spaces.
- Old parts are being recycled. In France both Peugeot and Renault opened plants for this, followed by other

European manufacturers, but these initiatives remain small ventures in relation to the total numbers of cars being scrapped.

- In 1998 Mazda promised to plant five trees for every Demio model it sold: more than enough to compensate for the carbon emissions from the cars, as trees absorb carbon dioxide.
- Recently the UK government introduced variable road tax charges based on the level of vehicle emissions. Some motorists saved money; others have to pay more.

suggests that **business ethics** encompasses the views of people throughout society concerning the morality of business, and not just the views of the particular business and the people who work in it.

Issues such as golden handshakes, pensions, insider dealing and very substantial salary increases for company chairmen and chief executives are topical and controversial. But is it ethical for large companies to pursue high-risk strategies which might leave several small company suppliers financially exposed? Again, when some large (and smaller) companies come to grief (often through ill-advised or ill-judged strategic choices) many employees may find their pension funds have disappeared. Is this also an ethical issue?

The high-profile (at the time) case of British Airways and Virgin Atlantic, where BA was accused of using privileged information to evaluate Virgin's route profitability and to persuade Virgin customers to switch airlines, suggested that BA acted unethically. Much more recently BA and Virgin colluded (illegally) to fix fuel surcharges when oil prices rose. Virgin decided after-the-event to confess to its role and was thus exempted from prosecution when the issue was investigated. BA was fined and a number of senior executives individually charged for a criminal act. If they end up in prison, would Virgin's role be seen as ethical or unethical? In contrast, Hewlett-Packard, the US electronics multinational is widely regarded as being highly ethical, although not always. In September 2006 Newsweek published a story revealing that the chairwoman of HP, Patricia Dunn, had hired a team of independent electronic-security experts who had spied on HP board members and several journalists to determine the source of a leak of confidential details regarding HP's long-term strategy that had been published as part of a CNET article in January 2006. HP operates an internal ban on the use of improper means for obtaining competitor information. The company also insists that any statements about its competitors must be fair, factual and complete.

Public attention is drawn to these issues, and people's perceptions of businesses generally and individually are affected. However, their responses differ markedly. Some people feel disgruntled but do nothing, whereas others take more positive actions. Managers, however, should not ignore the potential for resistance or opposition by their customers, who may refuse to buy their products or use their services.

Another ethical concern is individual managers or employees who adopt practices which senior managers or the strategic leader would consider unethical. These need to be identified and stopped. If they remain unchecked they are likely to spread, with the argument that 'everyone does it'. Sales staff using questionable methods of persuasion, even lying, would be an example. However, it does not follow that such practices would always be seen as unethical by senior managers – in some organizations they will be at least condoned, and possibly even encouraged.

Case 6.5 on the Co-operative Bank highlights how one organization decided to use an ethical stance to create a competitive advantage – and thus provides an interesting contrast to some of the other comments we have made on UK banks and their role in the credit crunch.

Ethical dilemmas

One classic ethical dilemma concerns the employee who works for a competitor, is interviewed for a job, and who promises to bring confidential information if he is offered the post. Should the proposition be accepted or not? The issue, featured at the beginning of this section, is how far companies should go in pursuit of profits. In such a case as this, long-term considerations are important as well as potential short-term benefits. If the competitor who loses the confidential information realizes what has happened it may seek to retaliate in some way. Arguably, the best interests of the industry as a whole should be considered. Critical reflection 6.3 presents three more ethical dilemmas.

Another example is the company with a plant that is surplus to requirements and which it would like to sell. The company knows the land beneath the plant contains radioactive waste. Legally it need not disclose this fact to prospective buyers, but is it ethical to keep quiet? Research commissioned by the Rowntree Foundation (see Taylor, 1997) concluded that housebuilders and estate agents generally do not warn buyers when new homes are built on previously contaminated industrial land. Pet food manufacturers, looking to expand their sales, would logically seek to differentiate their products by featuring particular benefits and satisfied, friendly pets, but they will also hope to persuade more people to become owners. Given the publicity on potentially dangerous breeds of dog, and the numbers of abandoned pets,

Case 6.5

The Co-operative Bank   UK

R etail banking in the UK has become extremely competitive as traditional building societies and foreign banks have entered the sector. To compete, charges have been kept relatively low, leaving the banks with too many unprofitable accounts. Their challenge: attracting the 'right customers', those who will retain a sizeable current account balance and also purchase other products such as insurance policies. A typical 'good customer' would be 25–40 years old and a member of the ABC1 social groupings.

The Co-op Bank, owned by the Co-operative Wholesale Society, began an advertising campaign in the early 1990s which concentrated on the bank's ethical stance towards business. The bank stated it would not deal with tobacco companies, cosmetics companies which used animals for testing, companies involved in blood sports, factory farming and animal fur products, and any business which caused pollution. Some corporate accounts were closed.

Almost immediately, the volume of retail deposits increased by over 10 per cent, with new customers actively citing the advertising campaign. Profits accrued after two years of losses. Many customers also took out the bank's new gold credit card.

The bank began to develop a customer profile which featured a disproportionate percentage of ABC1s. The

Managing Director at the time, Terry Thomas, commented: 'After all, what bank would want to attract low income, badly-educated, ignorant people?'

Questions

1   Did it make sense for the Co-operative Bank to trade off corporate clients for new personal accounts in this way?
2   Do you know whether the strategy is still in place?

CO-OPERATIVE BANK
http://www.co-operativebank.co.uk

particularly after Christmas, what would constitute an ethical approach to promotion? In 1991 a small number of ministers in the Church of England questioned whether the Church Commissioners, with £3 billion to invest to cover the future salaries and pensions of clergy, should be free to invest the money anywhere (in an attempt to maximize earnings) or whether they should be restricted to organizations which were known to be ethical in their business dealings. Interestingly, Martinson (1998) reported that the shares of companies widely perceived to be ethical in their strategies, policies and behaviour do not underperform when measured against the equity markets overall. In this context community involvement is seen as positive; any involvement with tobacco, alcohol or military equipment is negative.

Badaracco and Webb (1995) also highlight how internal decisions can be influenced by unethical practices. They quote instances of invented market-research findings, and altered investment returns which imply, erroneously, that the organization is meeting its published targets. They distinguish between 'expedient actions' and 'right actions'.

In contrast, a serious dilemma faces individuals in an organization who feel that their managers are pursuing unethical practices. There are several examples of individuals who have

Critical reflection 6.3

Three Ethical Dilemmas

ONE A well-established European pharmaceutical company (X), in a country with a moderate but not large Catholic community, has developed and patented a new drug which safely induces abortion and has demonstrable health-care benefits for women seeking an abortion. For a variety of reasons, largely economic (health-care savings, benefit reductions and corporation tax revenues), its government is encouraging it to launch the drug in the home country and around the world at the earliest opportunity. Profits to the company would be good, but they would not have a dramatic impact on the company's overall profits. They would, however, ensure the future viability of a small production plant in an area of high unemployment. However, a sizeable block of the company's shares (but not a controlling interest) has recently been acquired by a foreign mini-conglomerate whose chief executive is a Catholic and opposed to the drug on religious grounds. As X's managing director you also know from your personal experience that if you launch the drug in America, one of your key export markets, you can expect protests from demonstrators opposed to abortion. What should you do?

TWO A business manager for a well-known high street bank is told by her manager that her function is shortly to be moved to a new regional centre some 25 miles away and that her own position is secure. She is personally delighted as her travel-to-work commute will be reduced, but she knows that there will be redundancies. Under instruction that for the moment the news is embargoed from other staff, she is concerned when her personal assistant approaches her a few days later. She has heard unsubstantiated rumours on the bank's grapevine and she would, for family reasons, be unable to move. She wants to know what she should do as she is about to pay a deposit on a new house. What should the business manager do? What is 'right by her employer' and what is 'right by her subordinate'?

THREE A young consultant with a relatively new and small but fast-growing management consultancy is invited out of the blue to be joint presenter (with the senior partner) of a bid to a potentially very large client. He is surprised; he has had no involvement in preparing the bid. Moreover, it is not in his area of expertise. Flattered with the wonderful opportunity, but at the same time concerned, he discusses the request with his mentor in the consultancy. He is informed that the contact person in the client organization is, like him, from an ethnic minority background. The senior partner felt that the client would like to see that the consultancy's only non-white consultant was a key member of the team. How should he react?

Developed from material in Badaracco, JL Jr (1997)
Defining Moments – When Managers Must Choose
Between Right and Right, Harvard Business School Press.

acted and suffered as a result of their actions. An accountant with an insurance company exposed a case of tax evasion by his bosses and jeopardized his career. Stanley Adams, an employee of Hoffman la Roche, the Swiss drug company, believed that his firm was making excessive profits and divulged commercially sensitive information to the European Commission. He also lost his career and suffered financially. There are similar examples of engineers who felt that design compromises were threatening consumer safety, complained, and lost their jobs. When the UK government started to probe, in greater detail, the banking crisis, it emerged that one ex-employee of HBOS, Paul Moore, a senior Risk Manager, was claiming to have warned the bank's CEO, Sir James Crosby, that the level of exposure was dangerous. He was sacked, he claims for this intervention. Crosby himself left but became a government adviser and later Deputy Director of the FSA (Financial Services Authority). Protesting that he had done nothing wrong, but wished to clear his name, Crosby then resigned from the FSA in February 2009.

Many of the ethical issues that affect strategic decisions are regulated directly by legislation. Equally, many companies do not operate in sensitive environments where serious ethical issues require thought and attention – an issue addressed in Case 6.6 on BAE Systems. However, some companies and their strategic leaders do need a clear policy regarding business ethics. Often they have to decide whether to increase costs in the short run, say to improve safety factors, on the assumption that this will bring longer-term benefits. Short-term profitability, important to shareholders, could be affected. Increased safety beyond minimum legal requirements, for example, would increase the construction costs of a new chemical plant. If safety were compromised to save money, nothing might actually go wrong and profits would be higher. However, an explosion or other disaster results in loss of life, personal injury, compensation and legal costs, lost production, adverse publicity and tension between the business and local community. The long-term losses can be substantial.

Reidenbach and Robin (1995) have produced a spectrum of five ethical/unethical responses:

- *Amoral companies* seek to 'win at all costs'; anything is seen as acceptable. The secret lies in not being found out.

- *Legalistic companies* obey the law and no more. There is no code of ethics; companies act only when it is essential.

- *Responsive companies* accept that being ethical can pay off.

- *Ethically engaged companies* actively want to 'do the right thing' and to be seen to be doing so. Ethical codes will exist, but ethical behaviour will not necessarily be a planned activity and fully integrated into the culture.

- *Ethical companies* such as Body Shop have ethics as a core value, supported by appropriate strategies and actions which permeate the whole organization.

Because ethical standards and beliefs are aspects of the corporate culture, they are influenced markedly by the lead set by the strategic leader and his or her awareness of behaviour throughout the organization. If a proper lead is not provided, managers will be left to 'second guess' what would be seen as appropriate behaviour. Power, then, can be used ethically or unethically by individual managers.

Frederick (1988) contends that the corporate culture is the main source of any ethical problems. He argues that managers are encouraged to focus their professional energies on productivity, efficiency and leadership, and that their corporate values lead them to act in ways which place the company interests ahead of those of consumers or society.

To guard against this it can be useful for a company to publish a corporate code of ethics, which all managers are expected to follow. Typically, large US companies have been more progressive with such codes than those in the UK. In the early 1990s, some 30 per cent of large companies in the UK had published codes, but the number has since been growing all the time.

Case 6.6

BAE Systems   UK

BAE is Britain's largest defence contractor and the leading European arms manufacturer. It is an important foreign currency earner for the UK. In 2008 the company acknowledged that 'it had failed to pay sufficient attention to ethical standards'. This was the outcome of a company-funded investigation begun after BAE was caught up in accusations of alleged payments to an agent to help secure an arms deal with Saudi Arabia. The alleged recipient is a member of the Saudi Royal Family and so the situation was 'political dynamite'. Britain needs Saudi oil and was also negotiating further arms deals with the same country. Prime Minister Tony Blair had called off a formal investigation on security grounds.

BAE's response was to make a senior executive appointment to oversee the implementation of a new Code of Conduct.

The tale raises important issues about the problems faced by the industry worldwide.

The customers for defence products are governments, not private individuals. Some of these governments operate with a culture quite different from the accepted 'corporate responsibility of the West'. Bribery is not always frowned on; it may be expected, it may even be essential, to win orders. One insightful comment made in the past is that there is no decision to make whether or not you offer payment; the real decision concerns who to

pay. You have to find the right person, the one with influence!

It was in 2002 that 'sweeteners' of any kind were made illegal in the UK; previously the rules had been less stringent. And yet BAE and others were still anxious to win orders.

The stakes are huge. As well as foreign currency many thousands of jobs are at stake. Critical mass in the industry matters; it is important not to contract below a certain scale.

Many sales are being made to countries that are in the frontline of the fights against terrorism and drugs, two issues that both pose a major threat to the UK.

It is perhaps ironic that at the same time as the investigation into possible corruption in the arms industry there was a parallel Scotland Yard investigation into alleged corruption in professional football. Specifically whether leading clubs may have paid 'bungs' to players' agents to secure transfers. One might question how similar and how different these cases are.

Question

1   What lessons do you think can be learned from this case?

SOURCE: THIS CASE STUDY WAS PREPARED USING PRIMARILY PUBLICLY AVAILABLE SOURCES OF INFORMATION

The typical issues covered in an ethics code include relationships with employees (the most prevalent factor in the UK codes of ethics), government (more important in the US), the community and the environment.

Drawing on earlier points, attitudes towards bribery and inducement, and the use of privileged information, could also be incorporated in any code. Attention might also be paid to practices which are commonplace but arguably unethical. Examples would include a deliberate policy not to pay invoices on time, and creative accounting, presenting information in the most favourable light. The extent to which audited company accounts can be wholly relied upon is another interesting issue.

Tucker and Maitland (2004) report that the Association of British Insurers (representing shareholders who own 20 per cent of the shares traded on the London Stock Exchange) are putting increasing pressure on businesses to disclose any relevant social, ethical and environmental concerns. Issues that might raise concern would include those linked to pollution and climate change, fast food and obesity and working conditions in developing countries. Perhaps there is an element of enlightened self-interest, a fear of the impact of litigation on share prices if something goes wrong – but perhaps it is the outcome rather than the motive that really matters.

Business ethics is arguably important and worthy of serious attention. However, a consideration of ethical issues in strategic decisions typically requires that a long-term perspective is adopted. Objectives and strategies should be realistic and achievable rather than overambitious and very difficult to attain. In the latter case individual managers may be set high targets which encourage them to behave unethically, possibly making them feel uneasy. Results may be massaged, for instance, or deliberately presented with inaccuracies. Such practices spread quickly and dishonesty becomes acceptable. The longer-term perspective can reduce the need for immediate results and targets which managers feel have to be met at all costs. However, pressure from certain stakeholders, particularly institutional shareholders, may focus attention on the short term and on results which surpass those of the previous year. The longer-term perspective additionally allows for concern with processes and behaviour, and with how the results are obtained. The drive for results is not allowed to override ethical and behavioural concerns.

Houlden (1988) concludes that strategic leaders should be objective about how society views their company and its products, and wherever possible should avoid actions that can damage its image. If an action or decision that certain stakeholders might view as unethical is unavoidable, such as the closure of a plant, it is important to use public relations to explain fully why the decision has been taken. The need for a good corporate image should not be underestimated.

Other chapters (particularly Chapter 4) include discussions on how organizations might achieve competitive advantage. Ethical considerations can make a significant contribution to this. A commitment to keeping promises about quality standards and delivery times, or not making promises which cannot be met, would be one example. If employees are honest and committed, and rewarded appropriately for this, then costs are likely to be contained and the overall level of customer service high, thereby improving profits.

Summary

The corporate *mission* represents the overriding purpose for the business, and ideally it should explain why the organization is different and set it apart from its main rivals. It should not be a statement that other organizations can readily adopt. Its main purpose is communication.

It is useful to separate the mission statement from a statement of corporate *vision* which concerns 'what the organization is to become'.

Both can provide a valuable starting point for more specific *objectives* and strategies. Shorter-term objectives will normally have timescales or end-dates attached to them and ideally they will be 'owned' by individual managers.

It is, therefore, feasible to argue that organizations (as a whole) have a purpose and individual managers have objectives.

Mission, vision and objectives all relate to the *direction* that the organization is taking – the ends from which strategies are derived.

It is not, however, feasible to assume that the organization will always be free to set these objectives for its managers: there may be constraints from key stakeholders. A number of theories and models, mainly from a study of economics, can help us to understand why organizations do the things they do.

In addition, individuals will have *personal objectives* that they wish (and intend) to pursue, which should not be allowed to work against the best interests of the organization.

External *stakeholders* also have expectations for the organization. These will not always be in accord with each other, and important trade-offs and priorities must be established. There is always the potential for conflicts of interest. As a result, the organization will be seen to have a multitude of objectives, but all contributory to a single purpose.

Profit is necessary for profit-seeking businesses; a positive cash flow is essential for not-for-profit organizations. Profit (or cash) can, however, be seen as either a means or an end, and this will impact upon the 'feel' or culture of the organization.

Regardless, there is a virtuous circle of financial returns, motivated employees and satisfied customers.

Issues of *social responsibility* and *business ethics* are important for all organizations. They will be seen by some organizations as a threat or constraint and encourage a strategy of compliance. Other organizations will perceive them as an opportunity to create a difference and in turn a positive image. They are becoming increasingly visible, issues which organizations should take seriously and not ignore.

Online cases for this chapter

Online Case 6.1: New York's Yellow Cabs
Online Case 6.2: National Theatre

Online Case 6.3: Nike

Questions and research assignments

1 Using the Ben and Jerry's case (or another case from Chapter 6 if you prefer) clarify what you think the business model is. How would you define that company's vision and mission?

2 Think of any organization with which you have personal experience. Do you believe that profit (or cash in the case of a non-profit organization) is seen as a means or an end by the key decision-makers? Do they all agree on this?

3 What key issues do you believe should be incorporated in a company statement on ethics?

Internet and library projects

1   From the FT Fast Track website, pick a rapidly growing business of your choice from within the top ten businesses listed. In 400 words or less can you identify the business objectives of that business. **http://www.fasttrack100.uk/**

2   When Tottenham Hotspur became the first English Football League club with a stock exchange listing (in 1983) the issue prospectus said: 'The Directors intend to ensure that the Club remains one of the leading football clubs in the country. They will seek to increase the Group's income by improving the return from existing assets and by establishing new sources of revenue in the leisure field.'

   a   Research the strategies followed by Tottenham Hotspur plc since 1983. Do you believe that the interests of a plc and a professional football club are compatible or inevitably conflicting?

   b   Which other clubs have followed Tottenham? Have they chosen similar or different strategies? How have they performed as businesses?

   c   In view of the comments about social responsibility, how do you view the fact that football clubs generally invest far more money in players (wages and transfer fees) than they do in their grounds (amenities and safety)? For example in the case of Newcastle United, in 2009, the percentage of revenue going on players wages was 72 per cent of club turnover. In 2007/8 turnover was just under £100m.

3   Have the objectives (in particular the order of priorities) of the Natural History Museum changed since the introduction (and later abandonment) of compulsory admission charges in April 1987?

4   In March 2009 it was announced that Cadbury was 'to become the first mass-market chocolate brand to adopt the Fairtrade certification mark'. How significant was this? Do you see this as reactive to changing consumer views or a very smart proactive move – or both? What has been the impact?

5   In January 2009 an investigation by the BBC found that clothes sold in Primark stores were being made in factories in the UK where workers were being paid less than the official minimum wage – and also working very long hours in poor conditions. How did the company deal with this revelation?

Strategy activity

Play Pumps

Play Pumps is a South African social enterprise with a different perspective on children playing and having fun. It is based on the belief their energy can be captured and used to create community value.

In rural areas in developing countries there is no piped water routinely available. The main source of fresh water is boreholes where springs, streams and rivers are missing or unsuitable. Water is raised using hand pumps and many women and children invest hours of time fetching and carrying water for their family's needs. Individually we each need a minimum of five litres a day. If petrol or diesel is available and can be afforded, motorized pumps can be used – as long as they can be maintained for a lengthy period of time – otherwise communities have to rely on hand pumps. Typically a hand pump will deliver 150 litres per hour to ground level, and that water will need using relatively quickly as there is unlikely to be anywhere to store it hygienically. Installing a hand pump costs in the region of 10,000 South Africanrand, something over £1000. For between three and five times that amount a Play Pump could be installed.

The idea of the inventor was to build a special playground roundabout to be the main power source and encourage children to have fun spinning it round and round – which is something young children have always enjoyed doing! Clean borehole water is pumped up and collected in large above ground storage tanks. Because there is no engine, maintenance is straightforward and relatively inexpensive. The equipment used is standard windmill equipment which is readily available and does not require special sourcing. Below the ground is a positive displacement cylinder using rising rods and pipes – which very simply converts the rotational movement of the roundabout into a vertical movement. Each rotation of the roundabout can pump up to four litres of fresh water, allowing for some 1400 litres per hour to be raised into the storage tank if the depth does not exceed 40 metres. The system can support raising water 100 metres but obviously the capacity is substantially reduced. Storage tanks will typically hold up to 5000 litres on a 6-metre high stand. Water is drawn by a simple tap arrangement. The outer skin of the storage tank can also be used for advertising, and the revenue from this will certainly pay for all the maintenance and may, over time, repay the cost of the installation. The advertising works as women will generally be the ones to come and collect the water.

Women do not have to labour as they do with hand pumps. Children have fun. Communities get fresh water. And the project is self-sustaining.

The South African government has funded a project in KwaZulu Natal to install Play Pumps in school playgrounds wherever this is appropriate and water can be harnessed and drawn. Clearly this is an invention that has relevance for other countries in Africa and Asia.

Question

1 Can you find any other examples of such a win-win outcome?

Further reading

Andrews, KR (1989) Ethics in practice, *Harvard Business Review*, September–October.

Campbell, A and Yeung, S (1991) Creating a sense of mission, *Long Range Planning*, August.

Chan Kim, W and Mauborgne, R (2002) Charting your company's future, *Harvard Business Review*, May–June.

Drucker, PF (1989) What business can learn from non-profits, *Harvard Business Review*, July–August.

Simon, HA (1964) On the concept of organizational goal, *Administrative Science Quarterly*, 9 (1).

References

Ackoff, RL (1986) *Management in Small Doses*, John Wiley.

Badaracco, JL and Webb, A (1995) Business ethics: a view from the trenches, *California Management Review*, 37 (2), Winter.

Baumol, WJ (1959) *Business Behaviour, Value and Growth*, Macmillan.

Campbell, A (1989) Research findings discussed in Skapinker, M (1989) Mission accomplished or ignored? *Financial Times*, 11 January. See also:

Campbell, A and Nash, L (1992) *A Sense of Mission: Defining Direction for the Large Corporation*, Addison-Wesley.

Constable, J (1980) The nature of company objectives. Unpublished paper, Cranfield School of Management.

Cyert, RM and March, JG (1963) *A Behavioural Theory of the Firm*, Prentice-Hall.

Deloitte (1999) *Making Customer Loyalty Real – A Global Manufacturing Study*, Deloitte Consulting and Deloitte & Touche, http://www.dc.com/research

Drucker, PF (1974) *Management: Tasks, Responsibilities, Practices*, Harper & Row.

Frederick, WC (1988) An ethics roundtable: the culprit is culture, *Management Review*, August.

Freeman, RE (1984) *Strategic Management: A Stakeholder Approach*, Pitman.

Friedman, M (1979) The social responsibility of business is to increase its profits. *In Business Policy and Strategy* (eds DJ McCarthy, RJ Minichiello and JR Curran), Irwin.

Galbraith, JK (1963) *American Capitalism. The Concept of Countervailing Power*, Penguin.

Galbraith, JK (1969) *The New Industrial State*, Penguin.

Gerber, M (2008) *Awakening the Entrepreneur Within*, Collins.

Hamel, G (2000) *Leading the Revolution*, Harvard Business School Press.

Houlden, B (1988) The corporate conscience, *Management Today*, August.

Kaplan, R and Norton, D (2000) *The Strategy Focused Organization*, Harvard Business School Press.

Marris, R (1964) *The Economic Theory of Managerial Capitalism*, Macmillan.

Martinson, J (1998) Ethical equities perform well, *Financial Times*, 21 July.

Newbould, GD and Luffman, GA (1979) *Successful Business Policies*, Gower.

Penrose, E (1959) *The Theory of the Growth of the Firm*, Blackwell.

Performance Group, The (1999) *Sustainable Strategies for Value Creation*, Oslo, Norway.

Perrow, C (1961) The analysis of goals in complex organizations, *American Sociological Review*, 26, December.

Pfeffer, J (1981) *Power in Organizations*, Pitman.

Porter, ME (1995) Interviewed for the Green Management letter, *Euromanagement*, June.

Public Management Foundation (1999) *Wasted Values*, London.

Reidenbach, E and Robin, D (1995) Quoted in Drummond, J: Saints and sinners, *Financial Times*, 23 March.

Richards, MD (1978) *Organizational Goal Structures*, West.

Simon, HA (1964) On the concept of organizational goal, *Administrative Science Quarterly*, 9 (1).

Taylor, A (1997) Home buyers unaware of contamination, *Financial Times*, 24 October.

Thompson, AA and Strickland, AJ (1980) *Strategy Formulation and Implementation*, Irwin.

Tucker, S and Maitland, A (2004), Business put under pressure to disclose ethical risks, *Financial Times,* 26 February.

Waterman, R (1994) *The Frontiers of Excellence: Learning from Companies that Put People First*, Nicholas Brealey Publishing.

Williamson, OE (1964) *Economics of Discretionary Behaviour: Managerial Objectives in a Theory of the Firm*, Kershaw.

7 Strategic success

Learning objectives

Having read to the end of this chapter you should be able to:

- distinguish between efficiency and effectiveness

- explain how success might be measured and assessed

- explain the significance of financial measures of performance

- appreciate how strategic competency and admiration are important themes in a holistic approach to evaluation

- identify the difficulties involved in measuring the effective performance of many not-for-profit organizations.

The performance of a company, the outcomes of the strategies that it is pursuing, is typically evaluated by financial ratios and other quantitative measures. In this chapter it is argued that while these are an essential element of the evaluation process, alone they are inadequate. We need to take a more holistic perspective which embraces both subjective performance indicators and also recognizes the underlying causes of relative success and failure.

We show how different measures and assessments can provide conflicting conclusions and provide a comprehensive model based on E–V–R (environment–values–resources) congruence.

Financial ratio analysis, however, remains an important aspect of management case-study analysis; consequently a section explaining the main ratios is appended to this chapter.

Case 7.1

Arsenal FC   UK

When its latest financial results were published in September 2007 Arsenal FC was reported by one newspaper to be the UK's richest football club, ahead of both Manchester United and Chelsea. Only Real Madrid was richer. Other presentations of the relevant data would put United ahead. In 2008 according to Deloitte Football Money League, Arsenal was sixth in the European richest clubs league with £209m of revenue just behind Chelsea in fifth position with £212.9m. Conversely in 2008 Arsenal were in debt to the tune of £268.2m (Deloitte). However you look at it Arsenal are one of Europe's richest and high profile clubs. But are they successful?

In 2006 Arsenal had moved across North London from the Highbury to the brand new 60,000 seat Emirates Stadium. The old stadium has been transformed into apartments, earning Arsenal millions of pounds.

Arsenal have never won the coveted Champions' League, the European club championship. But they have won the domestic league and FA Cup double on a number of occasions spanning the original 'First Division' and the Premier League. It is the only club to complete a Premiership season unbeaten. In the 2007/8 season Arsenal trailed Manchester United and Chelsea in third place and didn't play in the final of any major cup competition. For a good proportion of the season Arsenal topped the league but was then affected by a number of disappointing results and injuries. To some this would amount to a poor season – and yet the seventeen clubs below them would have loved to finish third.

Financially Arsenal had turned in revenues of £200 million in 2006/7, yielding operating profits of £50 million. It earns around £3 million at every home match. There is some £70 million in the bank but there are outstanding loans of £250 million on the new stadium. Arsenal is rarely a major buyer in the transfer market, preferring instead to groom young talent. The majority of the squad are overseas players. The manager Arsene Wenger, a French economics graduate, joined in 2000 and is contracted to 2011. He is generally credited with creating and invariably putting out a very skilful and attractive team, whose open and fast-flowing style has received high praise from both pundits and fans. But Arsenal has the second highest wage bill amongst football clubs in the UK. There is an ongoing belief that its young stars will come good and become an outstanding team – but it has still to happen.

In 2008 Manchester United won both the Premiership and the Champions League. In contrast Arsenal had a disappointing season, although they did qualify for the premier European competition in 2008/9. Manchester United was clearly established in second place in the 'rich club' stakes – with Real Madrid topping the list for the fourth consecutive year. Some analysts believed United would have overtaken Real had the pound not weakened against the Euro – they did, after all, dominate the rich list in the 1990s and early 2000s. Chelsea was fifth, Arsenal sixth and Liverpool seventh in the list.

Arsenal's Chairman is Peter Hill-Wood – he, his father and his grandfather have chaired the club for 80 years. Hill-Wood now owns just 1 per cent of the shares in Arsenal, but the Board as a whole controls 45 per cent. There is reported to be foreign interest in a takeover.

Questions

1   Is Arsenal successful? What criteria are you using to make your decision?
2   Is it really the case of the rich getting richer as some commentators believe? In your answer you might consider how the economic recession could affect the relative financial fortunes of top football clubs in Europe.

Reference: **www.sport-magazine.co.uk** (Issue # 109, February 27, 2009)

© DBURKE/ALAMY

7.1   Introduction

Defining success

An organization is successful if it is meeting the needs and expectations of its stakeholders. This implies a mixture of common sense and competency. These two simple, bold statements explain how we should seek to measure the success of an organization. We certainly need to know how well the stakeholder expectations are being met; we also need to understand the 'why' and 'how' behind the 'how well', as otherwise we will not be in a strong position to remedy weaknesses or sustain success.

We may feel that we know instinctively whether an organization is doing relatively well or relatively poorly, but realistically we need to be more precise than this. For one thing, we could be deluding ourselves or misjudging a situation. We could be seduced into feeling complacent and ignoring environmental changes. Success, assuming the success is real and not imagined, can be transient.

See the online "lastminute. com" case for an example of this section's theory in practice

Case 7.1 (Arsenal FC) and Online Case 7.1 (Lastminute.com) address success in two quite different organizations. Arsenal is renowned for the style of football it plays, but is it successful or would it be fair to argue it under-achieves? And how do we evaluate success in the case of the modern-age dot.com businesses?

Figure 7.1 implies that it is essential that organizations and their managers know where, how and why a company is doing relatively well or relatively poorly and that they use this information to sustain success by improvement and change or remedy weaknesses by remedial action. Otherwise, if relative success is taken for granted, or if relative failure is not understood, the organization will experience decline, whether this is slowly or rapidly.

It is quite normal to look for explanations when results or outcomes are disappointing or below target. Attention is quickly focused on failure. This is not always the case with success. It is not unusual for a group of managers proverbially to pat themselves on the back and assume that the success is a result of their personal abilities and brilliance. The reality could be that the success lies more in good fortune and an absence of any strong, threatening competitors. Such advantages can prove very short-lived. Success, when taken too much for granted, can quickly turn to failure. The issues, of course, are a manifestation of the prevailing culture.

It is also necessary to face up to the real issues and not attempt to 'spin' the figures to provide an attractive, but not entirely honest, explanation. Companies like to present and discuss their results in terms of absolute figures for revenue and profits, and the media seem happy to report these figures, frequently headlining any growth. Absolute growth in this form can – and can be used to – hide a deterioration in true performance. Profitability, for instance, is more important than profit per se for understanding how well a company is doing. Growth alone can be a very dubious and misleading measure of success. Always remember – *sales revenue is vanity; cash flow is clarity; profits are sanity.*

Taking this point further, it is also not unusual for companies to concentrate measurement on factors that can be measured most easily or readily. Typically, these will relate to inputs, resources and efficiencies, because outcomes and effectiveness are more difficult to measure. Yet, as we have already seen, satisfying the needs and expectations of key stakeholders is critical for

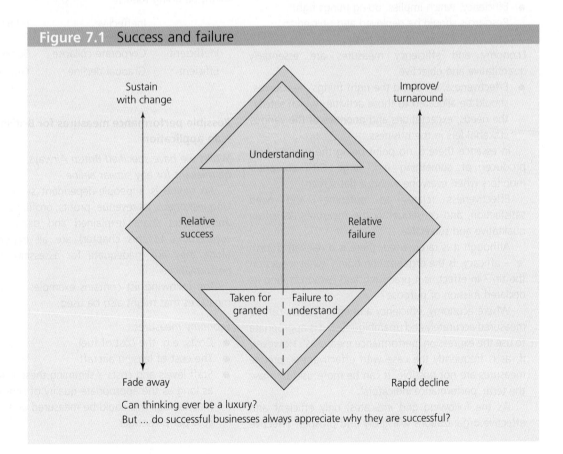

Figure 7.1   Success and failure

Sustain with change

Improve/ turnaround

Understanding

Relative success

Relative failure

Taken for granted

Failure to understand

Fade away

Rapid decline

Can thinking ever be a luxury?
But ... do successful businesses always appreciate why they are successful?

long-term prosperity. Critical reflection 7.1 on efficiency and effectiveness reinforces the point and it incorporates a summary of relevant measures for British Airways. Thompson and Richardson (1996) have shown how generic strategic competencies can be categorized into three broad groups which influence the organization's efficiency and effectiveness and have a relevance for all of its stakeholders. *Content* competencies reflect the ways through which organizations add value, differentiate and manage their costs. They include functional and competitive strategies. *Process* competencies deal with the ways by which these content competencies are changed and improved in a dynamic and competitive environment, while *awareness and learning* competencies inform the change management process. Process competencies relate, for example, to strategy implementation and to quality and customer care; awareness and learning competencies include the ability to satisfy stakeholders, ethical and social issues and the ability to avoid and manage crises.

Critical reflection 7.1

Efficiency or Effectiveness?

There are three important measures of performance:

- Economy, which means 'doing things cost effectively'. Resources should be managed at the lowest possible cost consistent with achieving quantity and quality targets.
- Efficiency, which implies 'doing things right'. Resources should be deployed and utilized to maximize the returns from them.

Economy and efficiency measures are essentially quantitative and objective.

- Effectiveness, or 'doing the right things'. Resources should be allocated to those activities which satisfy the needs, expectations and priorities of the various stakeholders in the business.

In essence there is no point being the world's best producer of something e.g. large CRT computer monitors when everyone wants a flat screen!

Effectiveness relates to outcomes and need satisfaction, and consequently the measures are often qualitative and subjective.

Although it is rarely used, there is a relevant fourth 'e' – efficacy. Is the organization doing 'what it says on the tin'? In effect, is it practising and demonstrating its declared mission or purpose?

Where economy, efficiency and effectiveness can be measured accurately and unambiguously it is appropriate to use the expression 'performance measures'. However, if, as is frequently the case with effectiveness, precise measures are not possible, it can be more useful to use the term 'performance indicators'.

As the following grid indicates, only efficient and effective organizations will grow and prosper. Effective

but inefficient businesses will survive but underachieve because they are not using minimum resources; efficient but ineffective companies will decline as they cease to meet the expectations of their stakeholders – simply, the things they are doing are wrong, however well they might be doing them.

	Ineffective	Effective
Inefficient	Corporate collapse	Survival
Efficient	Gradual decline	Growth and prosperity

Possible performance measures for British Airways – an application

Whilst we have specified British Airways, this list would be relevant for any similar airline.

An airline is a people-dependent service business. Unquestionably its revenue, profits, profitability, liquidity and market share (explained and discussed in the supplement to this chapter) are all important. But alone they are inadequate for assessing the overall performance.

The following list contains examples of appropriate measures that might also be used.

Economy measures
- Costs, e.g. the cost of fuel
- The cost of leasing aircraft
- Staff levels and costs – slimming these is acceptable as long as the appropriate quality of service is maintained. This could be measured as an overhead cost per passenger.

Efficiency measures
- Timekeeping/punctuality
- Revenue passenger kilometres (RPK), the number of passengers carried multiplied by the distances flown
- Available seat kilometres (ASK), the number of seats available for sale multiplied by the distances flown
- The overall load factor = RPK/ASK. (Similar measures for freight are also relevant.)

Solid performance with these measures is essential if the airline is to run at all profitably, but increasing them requires the airline to be more effective in persuading more customers to fly, utilizing marketing and consistently good service.

A related measure is:

- Passenger revenue per RPK. Improving this implies increasing the return from each flight, given that on any aircraft there are likely to be several pricing schemes in operation. We shall see later how BA has changed its strategy to address this issue (Case 11.4).
- Income (from all sources) related to the numbers of employees
- Reliability of the aircraft, i.e. continuous flying without breakdown (as a result of efficient maintenance, see below)
- The average age of the aircraft in the fleet.

Effectiveness
- Ability to meet all legislative requirements
- Image – which is based on several of the factors listed in this section
- Staff attitudes and contributions – both on the ground and on board the aircraft: care, courtesy, enthusiasm, friendliness, respect and efficiency
- The aeroplane – does it look and feel new and properly looked after?
- Other aspects of the on-board service, such as the cleanliness of the seating and toilet areas, food and entertainment
- Innovation – new standards of passenger comfort
- Safety record
- The number of routes offered, the timing of flights and the general availability of seats (this requires good links with travel agents)
- Recognition of, and rewards for, regular and loyal customers, reflected in the accumulation of Air Miles by passengers and the numbers of passengers who become 'gold-card' holders in regular flyer schemes

- Having seats available for all people with tickets who check in. While airlines, like hotels, often overbook deliberately, they must ensure that they are not 'bumping' people onto the next available flight at a level which is causing ill-will and a poor reputation
- The compensation package when people are delayed
- Time taken at check-in
- Reliability of baggage service, particularly making sure that bags go on the right flight. This also involves the issue of bags being switched from one flight to another for transit passengers
- The time taken for baggage to be unloaded (this is partially in the hands of the airport management)
- The absence of any damage to luggage. *Issues of lost and delayed bags plagued the opening of BA's new Terminal 5 at London Heathrow in 2008, an issue discussed further in Chapter 16 – see Case 16.6*
- The systems for allocating particular seats in advance of the flight and at check-in
- The number of complaints; the number in relation to the number of passengers
- The way in which complaints are handled
- The ability to balance the cost of maintenance with the costs incurred if things go wrong. If there is inadequate maintenance there are likely to be incidents or accidents which are costly in lost revenue and goodwill. At the same time airlines could overmaintain to a level where they are no longer able to compete because of too-high costs.

The additional factors below are not wholly the responsibility of airlines as they also involve the airport owners:

- Terminal provisions and comfort – seating, escalators, restaurants, duty-free shopping and toilets
- Security – evidence of security and the perception that it is being taken seriously
- Availability of trolleys and wheelchairs for disabled passengers.

Endnotes

It is also important to consider how all these factors might be measured and evaluated. Observation, passenger surveys, complaints and comparisons with other airlines are all possibilities.

The distinction between indicators – aspects of service which are actually difficult to measure – measures and performance targets – standards to measure against – needs to be recognized.

The following points are also worth noting:

- it is sensible not to be overambitious with both measures and targets

- if something cannot be measured it is perhaps better to leave it out
- the chosen measures must be relevant and easily understood; hopefully the very act of measurement will foster improvements

Improving competency

Where organizations need to become more successful and less crisis prone, it will be necessary for them to improve and/or reprioritize their competencies. Thompson and Richardson (1996) argue that it is necessary, first, to evaluate which competencies are critical for strategic and competitive success and, second, to ensure that the organization possesses these competencies at an appropriate level. To facilitate this, and to ensure that there is improvement and change, it will clearly be necessary for organizations to measure their competencies. Figures 7.2 and 7.3 expand the strategic implications of these points on competency for organizations.

The four-quadrant box on the left of Figure 7.2 has been adapted from May and Kruger (1988), whose ideas on personal competency have been extrapolated to an organizational context. An *unconsciously incompetent* organization does not appreciate just which factors are critical for competitive and strategic success; partly as a consequence of this it is both inefficient and ineffective. It is not deploying the right mix and measure of the generic competencies.

An *unconsciously competent* organization is efficient and effective, satisfying the needs and expectations of its stakeholders. However, there is an implication that it does not fully understand why it is successful, and when it might need to change. Consequently, it has a taken for granted paradigm of competitive and strategic success which may become out of date and no longer appropriate.

Figure 7.2   Conscious and unconscious competency

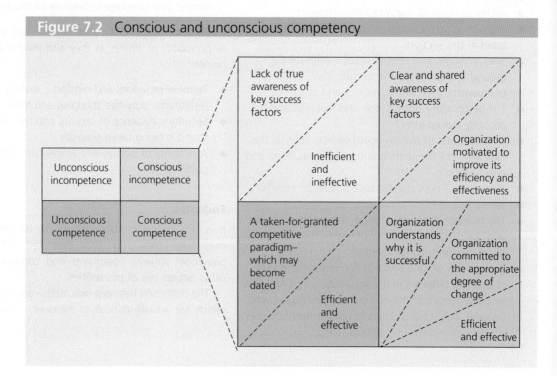

Figure 7.3 Improving competencies

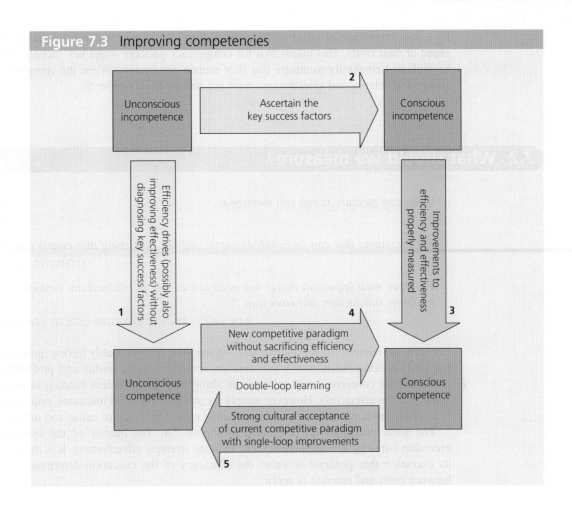

The *consciously incompetent* organization has a clear and shared awareness of key success factors. Managers recognize which issues and competencies are essential for success. Unfortunately, it is less efficient and effective than it needs to be, but it is motivated to improve.

Finally, the *consciously competent* organization understands why it is successful. It is efficient and effective and it is motivated to manage both continuous and discontinuous change as necessary.

Figure 7.3 illustrates the requirements for moving from one quadrant to another. An unconsciously incompetent organization becomes more competent (arrow 1) by efficiency and productivity drives, which may also improve effectiveness to some extent, but it may not become properly effective because it fails to clarify its key success factors. The same organization, alternatively, may become more conscious by attempting to clarify the key success factors (arrow 2). This, later, needs to be accompanied by a determined effort to improve efficiency and effectiveness (arrow 3) to generate competency.

Arrows 4 and 5, linking the bottom two quadrants, indicate an organization with E–V–R congruence. Once an organization has become consciously competent, these competencies and the associated competitive paradigm need to be fully accepted and absorbed into the organization's culture and values. Satisfying the key success factors happens almost automatically and unconsciously (arrow 4), and there is an ongoing commitment to continuous improvement. However, this state of affairs is only satisfactory while the underpinning competitive paradigm remains appropriate. Competitive pressures will at some stage require most organizations to search for a new perspective of effective competition, and ideally reach the new competitive high ground ahead of their rivals. This means that the competency package – and key success factors – should be evaluated constantly to ensure that they remain appropriate. When the competitive strategy is changed, efficiency and effectiveness must not be sacrificed (arrow 5).

7.2 What should we measure?

If you can measure it you can manage it

PETER DRUCKER

Not everything that can be counted counts; and not everything that counts can be counted

ATTRIBUTED TO ALBERT EINSTEIN

The three most important things you need to measure in business are customer satisfaction, employee satisfaction and cash flow.

JACK WELCH, EX-CHIEF EXECUTIVE OFFICER, GENERAL ELECTRIC (US)

The ultimate measure of success for any organization will invariably have a quantitative element. For profit-seeking businesses it will concern revenue growth, profits and profitability. For non-profit-seeking concerns it will relate to an ability to raise sufficient funding to fulfil its purpose and objectives effectively. However, simply focusing on financial measures, important as they are, is woefully inadequate as they pay insufficient regard to issues of cause and outcome.

The basic principles are explained in Figure 7.4. The quality of the opportunity and its execution (strategy and implementation) indicate strategic effectiveness. It is the opportunity and its execution that generate revenue; the efficiency of the execution determines costs. The gap between costs and revenue is profit.

Figure 7.4 Strategic and financial success

A holistic model

Accepting these reservations, it is next important to look at performance measures within a comprehensive cause and outcome framework. Manfred Kets de Vries (1996) argues that strategic leaders have two key roles to play. First, a charismatic one, through which they ensure that the organization has an understood vision and direction, people are empowered and as a consequence they energize, stimulate and galvanize change. Second, an architectural role of establishing an appropriate structure and style for both control and reward. Effective leaders succeed when strategies are owned by those who must implement them, customers are satisfied, people enjoy their work and things happen in the organization – specifically, the necessary changes are quick and timely. These issues will be explored more fully in Chapter 9.

Extending the themes, Figure 7.5 reinforces earlier comments about how strategic leadership is crucial for establishing (and changing) both competency and the corporate strategic logic of the organization. With the latter we are considering whether or not the organization's corporate portfolio and its competitive strategy or strategies make sense and can be justified, or appear to be a recipe for poor or disappointing performance.

A strong and well-managed portfolio will be reflected in successful and effective competitive and functional strategies and in operating efficiency. Equally important and relevant manifestations are the image, visibility and reputation of the organization, its strategic leader and its products and services, factors which can be managed and can have a bearing on many things, but which are tricky to evaluate and measure, particularly by the organization itself. Largely, they are the subjective opinion of external experts and stakeholders.

There are three distinctive broad approaches to measuring outcomes. These are:

- *Financial results* and other market-driven quantitative measures such as market share
- *Stakeholder satisfaction*, reflected in the Balanced Scorecard and similar packages
- *Admiration*, for example the annual reviews carried out by *Fortune* in the US and *Management Today* in the UK.

Figure 7.5 Strategic performance evaluation

This chapter now looks briefly at corporate logic, and then at admiration, image and reputation, financial measurement and stakeholder measures, to explain the linkages in Figure 7.5.

Corporate strategic logic

Caulkin (1995) stresses that the average life expectancy of successful UK companies is some 40–50 years. He has shown how only nine of the 30 companies used to make up the first *Financial Times* share index in 1935 still existed in their own right 60 years later. Several others were still in existence, but under new ownership. Some had been liquidated; many had been acquired and absorbed by their new corporate parents. It is inevitable that every one of the companies will have seen major strategic and/or structural changes of some kind.

Sadtler *et al.* (1997) defend the case for a clear focus built around a defensible core of related activities, and in this they reflect current practice. These issues are debated further in Chapters 11 and 16.

Admired companies

Sound profits and a strong balance sheet are very important, but alone they will not necessarily lead to a company being 'admired'. In the 1980s, and based on research in the USA by *Fortune*, *The Economist* began to investigate which companies are most admired by other business people, particularly those with whom they compete directly. More recently, *Management Today* has taken over the project in the UK and the *Financial Times* in association with Price Waterhouse later initiated a parallel European and then a global study. Business people are asked to allocate marks against certain criteria for their main rivals. The criteria used in the UK survey are as follows: quality of management; financial soundness; value as a long-term investment; quality of products and services; the ability to attract, develop and retain top talent; capacity to innovate; quality of marketing; and community and environmental responsibility. These reflect multiple perspectives and stakeholder interests; and consequently *The Economist* (1991) argues that admiration encourages customers to buy more and to stay loyal, employees to work harder, suppliers to be more supportive and shareholders also to remain loyal.

The 2008 UK *Management Today* top ten is listed below, with any relevant 2007 placings in the right:

1 Diageo (spirits) — 9th
2 Johnson Mathey (chemicals and metals) — 5th
3 Unilever (foods and detergents)
4 BskyB (media) — 3rd
5 Tesco (grocery retailing) — 2nd
6 Stagecoach (bus and rail travel)
7 Rolls-Royce (aircraft engines) — 10th
8 Man Group (investment products)
9 Kingspan (building products)
10 3i (private equity funding)

In 2007 the other five winners in the top ten (not there a year later) were: Marks & Spencer (first), Serco (support services), ICAP (finance), Sainsbury's and Capita (support services again). Sir Terry Leahy of Tesco was the most admired strategic leader in both years. Interestingly, given the ranking for the business, Sir Stuart Rose of Marks & Spencer was runner up in both years. In 2007 third place went to the now disgraced banker, Sir Fred Goodwin, CEO of Royal Bank of Scotland; a year later this honour went to Sir John Rose of Rolls-Royce. In 2007 RBS and HBOS (another bank that collapsed in 2008) were ranked first and fourth in the banking section.

Table 7.1 features a selection of the most admired British companies for the period 1994–2002, tracking the relative progress in the charts of the top five businesses in 2002. Tesco stands out as the one business which was ranked consistently over this period of years; the other winners have enjoyed more mixed fortunes, although BP was particularly strongly regarded in the later years. In 2002 (and for a number of successive years) BP's CEO, Lord (John) Browne was also recognized as Britain's most admired corporate leader. It is very unusual for a company and its leader to receive such joint honours. That said, Lord Browne resigned as CEO of BP in May 2007 over issues connected to his private life and possible perjury in a libel case. In contrast, Marks and Spencer declined dramatically. Positioned between 3 and 7 between 1994 and 1997, M&S dropped to eleventh place in 1998 and then fell out of the top 100. The explanation can be found in Chapter 1. In general, British service businesses also tend to score very highly in the European poll but, significantly, the manufacturing sections are normally dominated by German, Swedish and Swiss companies.

Listed below are the ten most admired American companies in 2008 on the *Fortune* website – their placing in 2007 is alongside to the right:

1	Apple	7th
2	Berkshire Hathaway	4th
3	General Electric	1st
4	Google	8th
5	Toyota	3rd
6	Starbucks	2nd
7	FedEx	6th
8	Procter & Gamble	10th
9	Johnson & Johnson	9th
10	Goldman Sachs	11th

A number of observations can be made about the American polls:

● In an era of strategic focus, an extensively diversified company, GE, was the most admired – and globally the most respected – for a number of years. GE was only deposed when its highly regarded chief executive, Jack Welch, retired. The important contribution made by Jack Welch, in ensuring that there is a cohesive and synergistic link between strategy, structure and style will emerge throughout this book.

● In 2000 the chart of winners was dominated by computing, networks and semiconductor companies, of which there were five in the top ten. Cisco, Intel and Lucent have since

Table 7.1 Britain's most admired companies, 1994–2002. Selected results for the 2002 Top 5

	1994	1995	1996	1997	1998	1999	2000	2001	2002
Tesco	31	4	1	2	1	1	5	4	3
BP							2	3	1
Glaxo Wellcome	2	13	11	4	6	3			
Glaxo SmithKline							1	5	5
SmithKline Beecham	4	14	7	8	5	2			
Cadbury Schweppes	7	1	5	16	2	5	4	7	2
Unilever	5	2	16	6	7	7		13	4

disappeared and were replaced by a mixture of service businesses and long-established manufacturers. Later Apple and Google came into the top ranks – but there is no top ten place for Microsoft.

- The extremely successful and remarkable Berkshire Hathaway is included. Run by entrepreneur Warren Buffett, Berkshire Hathaway is neither a manufacturing nor a service business; instead it is an investment vehicle for its shareholders' funds. Minority shareholdings in a range of companies, including Coca-Cola, are typically held for the long term. Notably, high-technology companies are avoided because of their perceived inherent uncertainty.

An earlier survey in the UK by BMRB/Mintel (see Summers 1995) asked a sample of consumers which companies they perceive offer good value for money, understand their market, are trustworthy and care about the environment. Boots won every category except for environmental concern, where it came second to the Body Shop. Inevitably, the winning companies in a poll such as this will be those with high visibility and presence, especially retailing organizations, reflecting the value of a good corporate image. Ironically, Marks and Spencer did not appear in the top ten in any category.

Yet another related survey is the British Quality of Management awards (see Houlder, 1997), where Marks and Spencer were again placed first for three consecutive years in the mid-1990s, this time followed by British Airways and Glaxo Wellcome. The polling here is conducted by MORI, who seek opinions on a selection of key issues from institutional investors, company chief executives and business journalists. One significant fact to emerge is that different categories of judges prioritize the significant issues in different ways. Journalists see innovation as vitally important, whereas it receives much lower priority from industrialists in the MORI poll. By contrast, Price Waterhouse concluded that both industrialists and analysts see innovation as the most important factor of all.

Interestingly, strategic leadership is not recorded as a particularly high priority for fund managers by MORI but the following comment was made about ABB's success in the European poll for several years in the 1990s:

The biggest asset may well be the charismatic figure of its chairman [Percy Barnevik] ... who is identified as an outstanding business leader.

ASEA BROWN BOVERI (ABB) IS A SWEDISH–SWISS ENGINEERING CONGLOMERATE

Financial success alone certainly does not guarantee admiration from competitors and popularity with all the stakeholders; at the same time, as evidenced by the Body Shop over a period of years, deteriorating financial returns will bother shareholders far more than customers! Fisher (1996) has argued that admiration placings in the US can certainly affect the stock price both positively and negatively, yet the extent to which financial performance affects the admiration marks remains less clear.

While several tentative conclusions might be drawn from these polls, prolonged debate is outside the scope of this book. However, it is worth emphasizing three points: first, fortunes can change very quickly; second, admiration seems to be affected by short-term changes of fortune; and third, the various polls on the same themes are themselves not always consistent, although some patterns can be traced.

Image and reputation

A well-recognized and positive image and reputation appear to improve the admiration rankings; and, correspondingly, linkage with a major corporate mistake or mishandled crisis has a negative effect, especially if social and ethical responsibilities are involved.

The next issue to be addressed, therefore, concerns the relative value of a good reputation and high visibility. Could reputation, inevitably a subjective judgement, actually help to cover up a relatively poor financial performance, itself a more objective measurement? Fombrum (1996) contends that reputations create economic value, and that image, because it embodies the company's uniqueness, is a key competitive tool. He uses this as an argument in favour of benchmarking those companies perceived to be the leading performers, to ensure that no critical gaps are left open.

Brands can give a company visibility, sometimes international visibility. When a prominent brand becomes associated with trust and quality, its corporate owner should be in a position to command premium prices, although some of this is needed to cover the extra promotional costs required to sustain the brand's visibility. Companies are increasingly including their brands as balance-sheet assets and attempting to place a value on them. Usefully for consumers, sensible companies will invest in their brands in order to improve them and sustain their competitive leadership.

> *Virgin may be innovative and Body Shop may be ethical, but the main thing that distinguishes these companies from the pack is how hard they shout about their achievements.*
>
> COLUMNIST LUCY KELLAWAY WRITING IN THE *FINANCIAL TIMES*, 23 SEPTEMBER 1996

The relative value of a charismatic, high-profile and media-friendly – or even media-chasing – strategic leader such as Richard Branson is more difficult to quantify, although the reality of their impact is not in question.

Financial measures

A plethora of financial performance measures has long been used to help evaluate the relative success and progress of a business; there is no suggestion here that this should cease to be the case. These measures include ratios such as return on capital employed and return on shareholders' funds, earnings per share, the share price itself and the price to earnings ratio. Typically, a company's share price performance will be evaluated against the relevant industry average and against one of the *Financial Times* indices. While these are objective within the constraints of accounting practice and convention, there are two points to note. First, although analysts always seem to stress profitability, relating pre- or after-tax profits to either sales, capital employed or shareholders' funds, press headlines are more likely to focus on the specific growth or decline in revenues and actual profits made. Second, share prices are also affected by future expectation, and a plausible and convincing strategic leader can be persuasive about 'better times being on the way'.

An analysis of financial ratios is useful for a number of reasons.

- It enables a study of trends and progress over a number of years to be made.
- Comparisons with competitors and with general industry trends are possible.
- It can point the way towards possible or necessary improvements – necessary if the organization is performing less and less well than competitors, useful if new opportunities are spotted.
- It can reveal lost profit and growth potential.
- It can emphasize possible dangers – for example, if stock turnover is decreasing or ratios affecting cash flow are moving adversely.

Financial analysis concentrates on efficiency rather than effectiveness unless the objectives are essentially financial or economic ones. The real measures of success, as far as the strategic leader and the various stakeholders are concerned, is whether or not the objectives that they perceive as important are being achieved.

Outside analysts, such as students and interested readers, can gain some insight into the apparent objectives of an organization by reading annual reports, articles, press releases and so on, but only the people involved in decision-making know the real objectives and whether they are being achieved. Financial analysis from the published (and easily obtained) results can be very informative and lead to conclusions about how well a company is performing, but certain aspects remain hidden. Decision-makers inside an organization use financial analysis as part of the wider picture, but outsiders are more restricted. Financial analysis, then, is a very useful form of analysis, and it should be used, but the wider aspects should not be overlooked.

More recently, *economic value added* (EVA; see, for example, Lynn 1995) has been adopted as another measure. EVA compares a company's after-tax operating profits with its cost of capital.

A more detailed treatment of financial measures is included as a Finance in Action appendix to this chapter.

Stakeholder measures

The important *Tomorrow's Company* report (RSA 1995), written in an attempt to improve the competitiveness of UK industry in global markets, concluded that there was:

- complacency and ignorance about world-class standards
- an over-reliance on financial measures which often focus attention on the short rather than the long term
- a national adversarial culture which fails to integrate stakeholders into a cohesive network of interdependent organizations.

We might ask: has much changed in the fifteen years since this research?

We believe the preferred solution lies in a more holistic approach which incorporates the interests of multiple stakeholders. Implicit here is a clear realization that both measurement and organizational learning must encompass both what is happening inside an organization and what is emerging in the outside environment. This accords with the ideas behind the '*Balanced Scorecard*' approach of Kaplan and Norton (1992, 1996).

Kaplan and Norton suggest that organizations should focus their efforts on a limited number of specific, critical performance measures which reflect stakeholders' key success factors. In this way managers can readily concentrate on those issues which are essential for corporate and competitive success.

We saw in Chapter 6 that Kaplan and Norton use the term 'Balanced Scorecard' to describe a framework of four groups of measures, and argue that organizations should select critical measures for each one of these areas. The four groups, and examples of possible measures, are:

- financial – return on capital employed; cash flow
- customers – perceived value for money; competitive prices
- internal processes – enquiry response time; enquiry to order conversion rate
- growth and improvement – number of new products/services; extent of employee empowerment.

These measures encapsulate both efficiency and effectiveness. Figure 7.6 illustrates the synergistic dependencies and linkages between the four groups of measures. These have a close relationship with the competency linkages mentioned in the Introduction to this chapter, and featured on the right-hand side of the figure.

Measuring effectiveness requires a recognition that quality does not mean the same things for every customer. Organizations must determine what will generate repeat business and seek to provide it. Supermarkets, for example, can offer service in the form of a wide range of products, brand choice for each product in the range, low prices, fast checkout and ample car parking.

Figure 7.6   Stakeholder measures

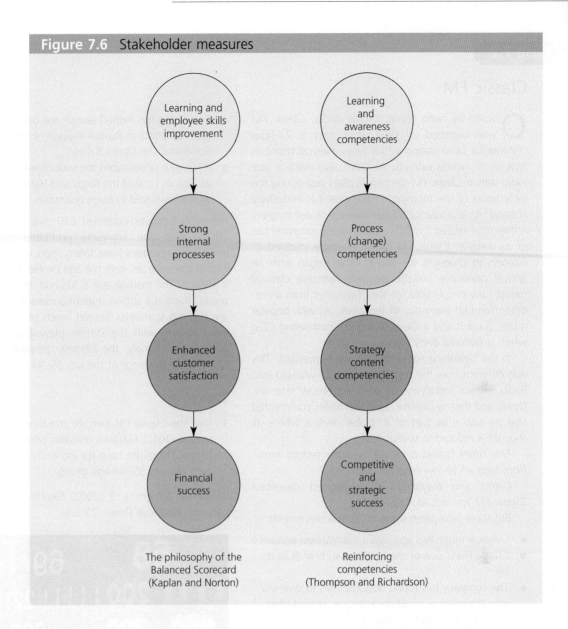

The philosophy of the
Balanced Scorecard
(Kaplan and Norton)

Reinforcing
competencies
(Thompson and Richardson)

Stores can focus aggressively on one or more of these or seek a balanced profile. The major chains will have a basic competitive posture and then tailor each store to meet local conditions.

Case 7.2 – Classic FM – describes how a radio station has introduced classical music to millions of new listeners, and caused an increase in classical CD sales, whilst not meeting all its own financial expectations. It has also been criticized by 'musical purists'.

7.3   The measurement of success in not-for-profit organizations

It was suggested in Chapters 1 and 6 that the objectives of not-for-profit organizations are often stated in terms of resource efficiency because of the difficulty of quantifying their real purpose. As a result, the measures of their success that are used in practice may not be closely related to their real mission and purpose. Where this happens, financial and other quantitative measures are being used

Case 7.2

Classic FM   UK

Owned by radio group, Global Radio, Classic FM was launched in 1992. It is now a 24-hour commercial radio station which plays classical music in typically 4 minute extracts. As GWR also owns a jazz radio station Classic FM sometimes plays jazz during the early hours of the morning – otherwise it is exclusively classical. As its audience ratings have continued to grow – they now exceed 7 million – and making extensive use of its website, Classic FM has increasingly involved its listeners in choosing the playlist. This began with an annual popularity poll for people's favourite classical music; now people vote for their favourites from a pre-determined list every day of the week. As with popular music, there is also a Classical Top 20 (best-selling CDs) which is featured every week.

In the beginning some 'purists' were incensed. This was different from the approach of the 70-year-old BBC Radio 3 which had always targeted 'high-brow' listeners. Opera and theatre director, Jonathan Miller commented that he saw it as part of a 'global decline where all thought is reduced to soundbites'.

The Times feared it would 'relegate serious music from high art to low entertainment'.

Diarist and playwright Alan Bennett described Classic FM listeners as 'Saga-louts'.

But there have been some notable achievements:

- Classical music has acquired a mainstream audience
- Classic FM is one of the best-known brands in the UK
- The company has found opportunities to diversify – into a magazine, retail organization, record label, credit card and dating agency
- Compilation albums of favourite classical music have been spawned and sold in large numbers by both Classic FM and mainstream labels
- Record stores feature classical music more extensively, especially the chart albums

- Classic FM has helped launch the careers of such popular artists as Russell Watson, Andrea Bocelli, Bond and The Opera Babes
- It has also popularized the soundtracks of films such as *Titanic*, *Lord of the Rings* and *Harry Potter* – all of which have sold in huge quantities.

Although turnover exceeded £30 million by the early 2000s, with the company profitable from 1997, advertising revenues have fallen short of early targets. Part of the issue lies with the age profile of the listeners it attracts. The median age is 52; half are over 45, half under. There is a strong student audience, but students are not big spenders! Indeed much of this book has been written with the station playing quietly in the background. Simply, the biggest spending advertisers want to see evidence of the key 35–44 age group.

Question

1 Visit the Classic FM website and tune into the station (101.1 FM) and consider what options Classic FM might have for increasing its popularity with the key 35–44 age group.

Reference: Sanghera, S (2002) Gentle ways to make ears pay, *Financial Times*, 23 July.

SOURCE: THIS CASE STUDY WAS PREPARED USING PRIMARILY PUBLICLY AVAILABLE SOURCES OF INFORMATION FOR THE PURPOSES OF CLASSROOM DISCUSSION; IT DOES NOT INTEND TO ILLUSTRATE EITHER EFFECTIVE OR INEFFECTIVE HANDLING OF A MANAGERIAL SITUATION.

as the measures of performance, and efficiency, not effectiveness, is being evaluated. In other words, performance and success is being measured, but despite the usefulness of, and need for, the measures being used, they may not be assessing strategic performance directly in relation to the mission. These points are expanded below.

Drucker (1989) comments that many not-for-profit organizations are more money conscious than business enterprises are because the funding they need is hard to raise. Moreover, they could invariably use more money than they have available. Money, however, is less likely to be the key element of their mission and strategic thinking than are the provision of services and the satisfaction of client needs. Given this premise, the successful performance of a not-for-profit organization should be measured in terms of outcomes and need satisfaction. Money then becomes a major constraint upon what can be accomplished and the appropriate level of expectations.

The outcomes, in turn, must be analysed against the expectations of the important stakeholders. For many organizations in this sector this involves both beneficiaries of the service and volunteer helpers as well as financial supporters and paid employees. Typically their personal objectives and expectations will differ.

But what is the case in reality?

The performance and effectiveness of the education system relates to the impact on pupils after they leave the system, their parents, the taxpayers who fund education and future employers. Their perspectives will differ, and their individual aspirations and expectations will be difficult to quantify and measure. It is far easier to measure efficiency in the way that resources are utilized, for example by class sizes, staff/student or staff/pupil ratios, building occupancy and examination performance.

Similarly, local authorities exist to serve local residents, and their mission is concerned with making the area a better place in which to live. Would all the residents agree on what is implied by 'a better place in which to live', and could changes be objectively measured and evaluated? Because of the difficulties, value for money from the resources invested is more likely to be considered, and improvements in the efficiency of service provision sought.

If a charity seeks to save money by minimizing administration and promotion expenditures it is focusing on short-term efficiency. If it concentrates on long-term effectiveness it may well be able to justify investing in marketing and administration in order to raise even more money. A charity that spends some 60 per cent of its current income on administration and marketing (and the rest on its directly charitable activities) could well, in the long run, be more effective than one that spends only 20 per cent in this way. The aim is to establish the most appropriate structure, administration network and promotional expenditure to achieve the purpose, and then run it efficiently.

The not-for-profit sector is increasingly attempting to measure effectiveness in terms of impacts and outcomes rather than efficiency alone. The task is not straightforward.

Value for money looks at the relationship between the perceived value of the output (by the stakeholders involved) and the cost of inputs. Essentially it is used as a comparative measure. There are too many uncertainties for there to be any true agreement on the magnitude of 'very best value', and consequently one is seeking to ensure that good value is being provided, when measured against that of other similar, or competitive, providers.

If we consider both inputs and outcomes then we are considering the efficiency and effectiveness of the organization's transformation processes, its ability to add value. With certain non-profit organizations, such as the UK National Health Service (NHS), it is also tempting to make international comparisons. How much per head of the population is spent on health care? What percentage of gross domestic product does this represent? Again, these are input measures when it is outcomes that matter. The life expectancy of British people and the infant mortality rate are critically important outcomes but, while health care makes an important contribution, it is not the only causal factor. Case 7.3 discusses the issues in measuring performance in the NHS in greater detail. This is, incidentally, the first of three cases on the NHS.

Jackson and Palmer (1989) emphasize that if performance is to be measured more effectively in the public sector, then the implicit cultural and change issues must also be addressed, a point that was addressed in Chapters 1 and 6. The climate must be right, with managers committed to thinking clearly about what activities should be measured and what the objectives of these activities are. This may well involve different reward systems linked to revised expectations. This

Case 7.3

The UK National Health Service - I   UK

Evaluating outcomes and performance   UK

This is the first of three short cases on the UK NHS included in this book. It can be read in isolation or in conjunction with the others which appear in Chapters 14 and 15.

At the simplest level, we might argue the UK NHS is concerned with the funding and the provision of health care. Most of the NHS funding comes from the government and thus from taxation and national insurance payments. We would normally associate its employees, in particular doctors and nurses, with a 'caring profession'. But these staff have some very difficult decisions to make and some patients would see themselves as low priority but wish it were otherwise. Simply the funding available cannot meet all the demand that exists.

Basic economic theory states that when demand exceeds supply, prices will normally rise to bring the two into some form of equilibrium. But when patients don't actually pay directly for their services, prices can't actually increase. Instead the perceived levels of inconvenience and dissatisfaction rise.

Successful practice is linked to meeting targets, and, as is generally the case anywhere, 'what gets measured gets done'. Decisions about what to target and measure are therefore critical. It is not unusual to see things that capture the attention of the media – such as high waiting lists in the past – get prioritized. In recent years there has been evidence that certain hospitals have in part managed their waiting lists by diverting some operations to the private sector – and paying a price that is greater than the cost of providing the same treatment under the NHS. One might query whether this is an effective use of scarce resources – but it can bring results against critical targets!

In 2006, and following a number of years of record levels of investment by the government, the NHS recorded its highest ever level of overspend against budget. As a consequence some hospitals had to be told not to treat any more patients in 2007 than they had in 2006.

In this contextual environment, the following is a selection of relevant challenges and issues; it is by no means exhaustive. But it does allow reflection upon the difficulties of measuring the performance of an organization of this size and complexity:

- Should government focus its investment in the NHS in buildings, equipment or staff? How should it balance these conflicting priorities? In reaching a decision it is important to flag that doctors and nurses are part of an international industry; although there may sometimes be a need to re-qualify, they can (and often do) migrate from country to country.

- Similarly, to what extent should the NHS be about 'health care' when people are ill and also about 'advice' to try and reduce people's need for care in the first place?

- To what extent should patient preferences be a factor in prioritization? After all, they are not paying directly for their service and find it difficult to go elsewhere for treatment.

- In recent years general practitioners have been awarded new contracts. As a consequence their remuneration has improved but some critics argue that many patients find it difficult to get surgery appointments in the evening or at weekends. Doctors seem to be working fewer hours. If there is a desire to change this, is a 'carrot' or a 'stick' the better approach? It has been reported, for example, that the government has considered fines for GPs whose patients end up needing care from an Accident and Emergency Department in a hospital if that is something that should have been available from their GP.

- If we benchmark every area of care against the best practice in the world is this a positive or negative approach? Whilst we might wish to provide a truly high quality service, is it remotely realistic to provide the best in the world in every area?

© PAULA SOLLOWAY / ALAMY

- If people can expect 'free' treatment from their GPs and hospitals, as part of the NHS, what is an appropriate expectation when it comes to eye care, dentistry and physiotherapy?
- On what basis should decisions about the drugs that are available for patients be made? In 2008 four kidney cancer drugs – all of them properly tested and licensed around the world – were turned down by NICE (National Institute for Clinical Excellence), that makes these decisions. Simply they were not deemed cost effective. They came out at some £30,000 per patient per year but they are not a cure for kidney cancer – rather they extend a patient's life by months or a few years in more exceptional cases.

Question

1 How difficult is it to determine desired outcomes and targets for the NHS? Are the various stakeholder preferences simply too complex for there to be any consensus? What are your views on the issues raised in the case? Can you think of other relevant dilemmas?

approach, they suggest, leads managers to move on from measuring the numbers of passengers on the railway network to analysing how many had seats and how punctual the trains were; and measuring and analysing the numbers of patients readmitted to hospital after treatment, rather than just the numbers of patients who are admitted and the rate of usage of hospital beds. Jackson and Palmer also emphasize the importance of asking users about how effective they perceive organizations to be.

7.4 A holistic framework of measures

Figure 7.7 offers an outline framework for reflecting on the measurement demands facing an organization. It is based on the premise that a competitive and strategically successful organization will achieve and, with changes, sustain, a congruency among its environment (key success factors), resources (competencies and capabilities) and values (the ability to manage appropriate and timely continuous and discontinuous change). A small reminder of this E–V–R congruence model is provided in the top right corner.

While corporate strategic success is concerned with the mission and purpose of the organization, it will frequently be assessed by financial measures of some form, as highlighted earlier. Long-term strategic success requires that the interests of stakeholders are met, and are seen to be met, that this is accomplished efficiently with capable resources, and that there is a commitment to the mission reflected in organizational values. The implication is that in addition to resource efficiency and stakeholder satisfaction, organizations should attempt to measure values to ensure that the culture is appropriate. However, the true complexity of this task is realized when we question whether we really know what the culture of an organization in an era of continuous change – and incorporating periodic restructurings and downsizings – should be like.

> *In a very turbulent, rapidly changing time what we need to give people is something they can depend on, something lasting. Every company needs to rethink what are the values and what are the operating principles that will be unchanging in time so that we can truly establish a new contract with all employees.*

GEORGE FISHER, CHAIRMAN, EASTMAN KODAK

Research can capture a snapshot of currently held values and the extent to which particular behaviours are being manifested. Some organizations will prefer to use volunteers from among the workforce rather than select a sample. The findings should be evaluated against a set of

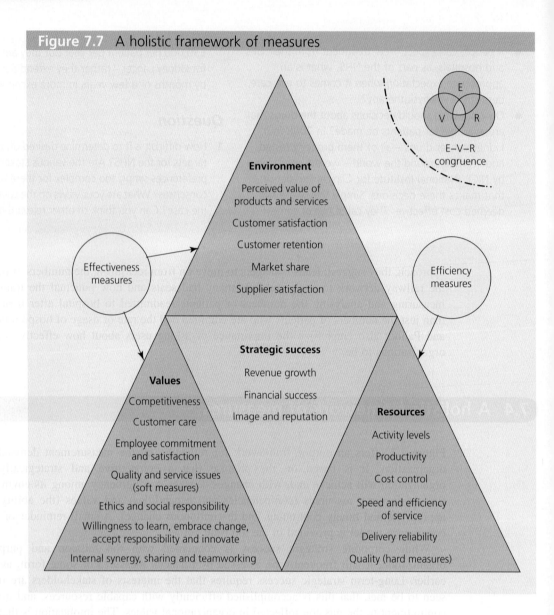

Figure 7.7   A holistic framework of measures

expectancies, and follow-up research can track both positive and negative developments. The organization must then decide what action to take if there is any deterioration or the initial absence of a critical value or behaviour pattern. Changing the culture of the organization is dealt with later in this chapter.

It will, therefore, be realized that the Figure 7.7 framework implies a series of both hard and soft measures and indicators. Some will be straightforward, others far more difficult and subjective. Arguably the real key to success lies in those issues that are most difficult to assess. This is no excuse for not attempting a robust assessment of some form, even though it is sometimes easy to argue a case based on unsubstantiated opinion which, when rigorously probed, turns out to be a delusion. It is all too easy for senior managers to argue for what they would like to believe is a reality: that their company is competitive, that it is committed to quality and service, and that their employees are committed and supportive. They need to check these things out!

Summary

At a most basic level of argument, an organization is successful if it is meeting the needs and expectations of its stakeholders, such that their support and commitment are maintained.

Strategically, this will imply a clear direction, from which are derived corporate, competitive and functional strategies, the implementation of which brings about the desired results. This needs both common sense and strategic competency.

Measurement matters. Apparent success cannot, and must not, be taken for granted. Nor must weaknesses be overlooked. We must measure those issues which really matter. The act of measurement focuses attention and endeavour on that which is being measured: being brilliant at things that do not really matter to stakeholders will not add and build value.

Some key elements will, through their very nature, be difficult to measure. They are essentially subjective and qualitative issues rather than objective and quantifiable. This is no excuse to avoid tackling them; instead we have to rely on indicators rather than measures of performance.

In some cases attention is focused on efficiency measures, which largely concern the utilization of resources. We are evaluating whether or not we are 'doing things right'. Measures and indicators of effectiveness look more at outcomes (for stakeholders) and provide a check on whether we are 'doing the right things'.

Most organizations use a raft of quantitative measures, embracing sales and production. Analysts external to the organization, such as students – and lecturers, come to that – will not normally have access to this information to draw conclusions from. However, financial data have to be published and can be used to calculate a number of valuable ratios which provide some insight into organizational performance. In the appendix to this chapter investment, performance, solvency and liquidity ratios are explained.

The balanced scorecard approach provides a more comprehensive set of measures which cover stakeholders. The four categories for measurement are: finance; customers; internal processes; and growth and improvement.

It is also relevant to look at issues of admiration, image and reputation. These evaluations are normally by people inside the relevant industries and therefore provide an insight into how organizations are rated by their competitors and peers. There is, however, a short-term focus in this approach. Companies that are highly regarded will not necessarily be those with the strongest financial results. Although there is some link between the most admired American and the most respected global companies, those British companies that enjoy the greatest international admiration are not those held in the highest regard at home.

In isolation, therefore, any single measure or type of measure must be treated cautiously.

Online cases for this chapter

Online Case 7.1: Lastminute.com

Online Case 7.2: BTA – British Tourist Authority

Questions and research assignments

1 The purpose of the Metropolitan Police Service is to: 'uphold the law fairly and firmly; to prevent crime; to pursue and bring to justice those who break the law; to keep the Queen's peace; to protect, help and reassure people in London; and to be seen to do all this with integrity, common sense and sound judgement'.

   How might they measure their success?

2 The Royal Charter for the Royal National Institute for the Blind (RNIB), granted originally in 1949, states that the RNIB exists in order to:

   - 'promote the better education, training, employment and welfare of the blind;
   - protect the interests of the blind; and
   - prevent blindness.'

   How might they assess how well they are doing?

Internet and library projects

1 In early 2000 Microsoft was judged by the American courts to have been operating as a monopoly and stifling competition. How have its reputation, respect and admiration been affected by this judgement and also by subsequent moves by both the company and the competition authorities in both America and Europe?

Microsoft **http://www.microsoft.com**

2 Select a number of organizations from the 'Admired Company' section of this chapter, picking out ones that interest you personally. Obtain their financial results for at least two years which correspond with the admiration rankings. To what extent are financial performance and admiration linked? By also checking the movements in the company's share prices over the same period, does the company's market valuation more closely reflect financial performance or a wider perception of its relative performance?

3 The National Health Service

British Prime Minister John Major announced a new Citizen's Charter in July 1991. This implied a change of attitude for the NHS: patients should be seen as customers with rights, rather than people who should be grateful for treatment, however long the wait. From April 1992 hospitals would have to set standards for maximum waiting times.

This followed on from the 1989 NHS White Paper, Working for Patients, which was designed to achieve:

- raising the performance of all hospitals and general practitioners (GPs) to the level of the best (significant differences existed in measured performances)

- patients receiving better health care and a greater choice of services through improved efficiencies and effectiveness in the use of NHS resources

- greater satisfaction and rewards for NHS staff.

In subsequent years, how did this impact on NHS strategies?

In 1997 a Labour government was elected and it set about changing the Conservative philosophy, dismantling and replacing a number of strategies.

What was the Labour approach? How have these changes impacted upon performance measurement? Can the relative success of the NHS ever be evaluated effectively without imputing political concerns?

4 Research how profitable John Lewis and Waitrose have been in comparison with their major competitors in the last ten years. What conclusions can you draw?

John Lewis Partnership **http://www.johnlewis .co.uk**

Waitrose **http://www.waitrose.com**

5 Find out where your nearest John Lewis or Waitrose store is and if possible visit it. Can you detect any differences in attitude between the John Lewis staff and those who work in similar stores?

John Lewis Partnership **http://www.johnlewis .co.uk**

Waitrose **http://www.waitrose.com**

6 In conjunction with the financial analysis exercise at the end of the following Appendix, determine just how successful in a relative and competitive sense you believe Shepherd Neame to be.

Strategy activity

Apple

The following short case introduces Apple – which is featured in a longer case towards the end of the book.

In the 1970s, Apple ignited the personal computer revolution with the Apple II and reinvented the personal computer revolution in the 1980s with the Macintosh. It now has the very successful Mac Book range despite the high price tag. Apple continues to launch the latest versions of its pocket sized iPods, which are linked to Apple's iTunes Music Store. Co-founder Steve Jobs revealed in early 2008 that there had been 675million iTune downloads in 2007. The iPod and iTunes combination looks set to help Jobs and Apple reach their goal of getting iPods and iTunes into the hands of every music lover around the world. Jobs is the original 'comeback kid'. He was only 13 when he teamed up with Steve Wozniak to invent the world's first PC in Jobs' stepfather's garage. The rest, as they say, is history. Some argue Jobs left Apple in 1986 to set up a new computer company to do it all again. The alternative version is that Jobs was booted out because Apple was a proverbial managerial mess. He called his new company NeXT. Although it was not successful, Jobs' other development was the hugely influential Pixar Studios. He returned to Apple as chief executive in 1997 at the request of a board desperate for innovation and for someone to salvage their fortunes. Jobs' new gamble was taking Apple into digital music. It was considered to be both hugely risky and highly profitable for someone who could get it right.

'Innovate', an unshaven Jobs bellowed from the stage to a gathering of French elite at a swell party in the Musée d'Orsay in Paris in September 2003. 'That's what we do – we innovate'. Of course, he is right and that may be the trouble. It is possible to innovate pointlessly. Darwin and others described the virtues of creative destruction. At Apple, it may have an evil twin: destructive innovation. *Scotland on Sunday*, Business Agenda, January 11, 2004

Questions

1 What do you think is the current position with Apple under Steve Jobs? There are concerns now for his health. So is the business fully ready to go on without Jobs (for the second time) should he have to pull out?

APPLE **http://www.apple.com**

Further reading

Atkinson, AA, Waterhouse, JH and Wells RB (1997) A stakeholder approach to strategic performance management, *Sloan Management Review*, Spring.

Bourantes, D and Mandes, Y (1987) Does market share lead to profitability?, *Long Range Planning*, 20 (5).

Huffman, B (2001) What makes a strategy brilliant?, *Business Horizons*, 44 (4).

Kaplan, RS and Norton, DP (1992) The balanced storecard – measures that drive performance, *Harvard Business Review*, January–February.

Kaplan, RS and Norton, DP (1996) Using the balanced scorecard as a strategic management system, *Harvard Business Review*, January–February.

Kaplan, RS and Norton, DP (2000) Having trouble with your strategy? Then map it, *Harvard Business Review*, September–October.

References

Brady, G (1999) The new rules for start-ups, *e-business*, December

Caulkin, S (1995) The pursuit of immortality, *Management Today*, May.

Drucker, PF (1989) What businesses can learn from nonprofits, *Harvard Business Review*, July–August.

Fisher, AB (1996) Corporate reputations, *Fortune*, 4 March.

Fombrum, CJ (1996) *Reputation – Realizing the Value from the Corporate Image*, Harvard Business School Press.

Hill, R (1990) Nissan and the art of people management, *Director*, March.

Houlder, V (1997) What makes a winner? *Financial Times*, 19 March.

Jackson, P and Palmer, R (1989) *First Steps in Measuring Performance in the Public Sector*, Public Finance Foundation, London.

Kaplan, RS and Norton, DP (1992) The balanced score-card – measures that drive performance, *Harvard Business Review*, January–February.

Kaplan, RS and Norton, DP (1996) *The Balanced Scorecard*, Harvard Business School Press.

Kets de Vries, M (1996) Leaders who make a difference, *European Management Journal*, 14 (5).

Leadbeater, C and Rudd, R (1991) What drives the lords of the deal? *Financial Times*, 20 July.

Lynn, M (1995) Creating wealth: the best and the worst, *Sunday Times*, 10 December.

May, GD and Kruger, MJ (1988) The manager within, *Personnel Journal*, 67 (2).

Peters, TJ and Waterman, RH Jr (1982) *In Search of Excellence: Lessons from America's Best Run Companies*, Harper and Row. Original article: Peters, TJ (1980) Putting excellence into management, *Business Week*, 21 July.

Prahalad, CK and Hamel, G (1985) Address to the Annual Conference of the Strategic Management Society, Barcelona, October.

Reid, W and Myddelton, DR (1974) *The Meaning of Company Accounts*, 2nd edn, Gower. The quotation in the supplement was taken from this second edition, but there are later editions.

RSA (1995) *Tomorrow's Company: The Role of Business in a Changing World*, Royal Society of Arts.

Sadtler, D, Campbell, A and Koch, R (1997) *Break-up. When Large Companies are Worth More Dead Than Alive*, Capstone.

Summers, D (1995) Boots comes top in corporate image poll, *Financial Times*, 23 October.

Thompson, JL and Richardson, B (1996) Strategic and competitive success – towards a model of the comprehensively competent organization, *Management Decision*, 34 (2).

Chapter 7 appendix

Learning objectives

Having read to the end of this section you should be able to:

- describe the key parts of a balance sheet, profit and loss account and cash flow statement

- calculate and evaluate a number of ratios relating to investment, performance and financial status

- discuss how profitability might be improved.

This supplement is a simple guide to aspects of financial accounting. For those readers familiar with the subject it serves as a short reference guide: for others, it provides a brief and straightforward summary of the critical issues.

The purpose of including it is to enable readers to be able to analyse and make sense of published financial data and the financial appendices which accompany many strategy case studies.

The content is:

- Financial statements – profit and loss accounts; balance sheets; cash flow statements

- Investment, performance, solvency and liquidity ratios.

Financial analysis

The published financial accounts of a company, as long as they are interpreted carefully, can tell a good deal about the company's activities and about how well it is doing. This section concentrates on three main aspects, examining the financial measures and what they can tell us, and considers the strategic implications. The three aspects are as follows.

- *Investment*: How do the results relate to shareholders and the funds they have provided, and to the company's share price?

- *Performance*: How successfully is the business being run as a trading concern? Here we are concerned not so much with profit as with profitability. How well is the company using the capital it employs to generate sales and in turn profits?

- *Financial status*: Is the company solvent and liquid? Is it financially sound?

The ratios calculated in each of these categories have relevance for different stakeholders. Shareholders, and potential investors, are particularly concerned with the investment ratios. Performance ratios tell the strategic leader how well the company is doing as a business. Bankers and other providers of loan capital will want to know that the business is solvent and liquid in addition to how well it is performing.

This form of analysis is most relevant for profit-seeking businesses, although some of the measures can prove quite enlightening when applied to not-for-profit organizations.

Ratios are calculated from the published accounts of organizations, but an analysis of just one set of results will only be partly helpful. Trends are particularly important, and therefore the changes in results over a number of years should be evaluated. Care should be taken to ensure that the results are not considered in isolation from external trends in the economy or industry. For example, the company's sales may be growing quickly, but how do they compare with those of their competitors and the industry as a whole? Similarly, slow growth may be explained by industry contraction, although in turn this might indicate the need for diversification.

Hence, industry averages and competitor performance should be used for comparisons. One problem here is that different companies may present their accounts in different ways and the figures will have to be interpreted before any meaningful comparisons can be made. Furthermore, the industry may be composed of companies of varying sizes and various degrees of conglomeration and diversification. For this reason certain companies may be expected to behave differently from their competitors.

In addition, it can be useful to compare the actual results with forecasts, although these will not normally be available to people outside the organization. The usefulness is dependent on how well the forecasts and budgets were prepared.

Financial statements

The two most important statements used for calculating ratios are the profit and loss account and the balance sheet, simplified versions of which are illustrated in Tables 7.2 and 7.3. The full accounts may be required in order to make certain adjustments.

From the profit and loss account (Table 7.2) we wish to extract a number of figures. Gross profit is the trading profit before overheads are allocated. It is the difference between the value of sales (or turnover) and the direct costs involved in producing the product(s) or service(s), which is known as the contribution. In the case of multiproduct or multiservice organizations, where it may be difficult to attribute overheads to different products and services accurately, comparison should be made between the contributions from different divisions or strategic business units.

When depreciation and selling and administrative overheads are subtracted from gross profit the remainder is profit before interest and before tax. This is the net profit that the organization has achieved from its trading

activities; no account has yet been taken of the cost of funding. This figure is not normally shown in published accounts; it has to be calculated by adding interest back onto profit before tax.

Profit before tax is the figure resulting when interest charges have been removed. Tax is levied on this profit figure, and when this is deducted profit after tax remains. This represents the profits left for shareholders, and a proportion will be paid over to them immediately in the form of dividends; the remainder will be reinvested in the future growth of the company. It will be transferred to the balance sheet as retained earnings (or profit and loss) and shown as a reserve attributable to shareholders.

This simplified outline excludes the need to, and value of, clearly separating the revenue and profits from ongoing businesses or continuing activities, recent acquisitions and discontinued activities.

Balance sheets are now normally laid out in the format illustrated on the right in Table 7.3. Assets are shown at the top and the capital employed to finance the assets below.

Fixed assets comprise all the land, property, plant and equipment owned by the business. These will be depreciated annually at varying rates. Balance sheets generally reflect historical costs (the preferred accounting convention), but occasionally assets may be revalued to account for inflation (land and property values can increase significantly over a number of years) and any ratios calculated from an asset figure will be affected by this issue of up-to-date valuations.

Current assets, assets which are passing through the business rather than more permanent features and which comprise stocks (raw materials, work-in-progress and finished goods), debtors (customers who are allowed to buy on credit rather than for cash), investments and cash, are added on. Current liabilities, short-term financial commitments, are deducted. These include the overdraft, tax payments due and trade creditors (suppliers who have yet to be paid for goods and services supplied).

The left-hand column of Table 7.4 shows the resultant figure as net assets, which is equal to the total capital employed in the business, or the sum of long-term loans and shareholders' funds. The right-hand column differs slightly and presents net assets as total assets minus the sum of current liabilities and long-term loans – and therefore equal to shareholders' funds. This is the normal way in which a company will present its accounts, leaving us to calculate a figure for total capital employed.

Long-term loans are typically called 'creditors: amounts falling due after more than one year'.

Table 7.2 Simplified profit and loss account

Sales/Turnover

less:	Costs of goods sold	= Gross profit
less:	Depreciation, Selling costs and Administration costs	= Profit before interest and tax*
less:	Interest on loans	= Profit before tax
less:	Tax	= Profit after tax
less:	Dividends	= Retained earnings (transferred to balance sheet)

* In published accounts this figure will not always be shown. It is required, however, for the calculation of certain ratios.

Table 7.3 Simplified balance sheet

	Information required for ratio calculations			Conventional presentation of figures in published accounts
	Fixed assets	Land; property buildings; plant and equipment		Fixed assets
+	Current assets	Stock; debtors; cash and investments	+	Current assets
Less	Current liabilities	Creditors: amounts falling due within one year; specifically trade creditors, overdraft, taxation not yet paid	less	Current liabilities
=	Net assets		=	Total assets less Current liabilities
	Long-term loans	Generally termed creditors: amounts falling due after more than one year		plus long-term loans
			=	Total net assets
+	Shareholders' funds	Called-up share capital: share premium account; revaluation reserve; profit and loss account		Shareholders' funds
=	Total capital employed			
Net assets	=	Total capital employed		Total net assets = Shareholders' funds

Shareholders' funds are made up of the called up share capital (the face value of the shares issued), the share premium account (money accrued as shareholders have bought shares for more than their face value, dependent on stock market prices at the time of sale), any revaluation reserve (resulting from revaluation of assets) and retained earnings (past profits reinvested in the business).

Balance sheets balance. Net assets are equal to the capital employed to finance them.

Investment ratios

The five key investment ratios are explained in Table 7.4, and the linkages between four of them are illustrated in Figure 7.8.

The return on shareholders' funds deals with the profit available for ordinary shareholders after all other commitments (including preference share dividends) have been met; and it is divided by all the funds provided both directly and indirectly by ordinary shareholders.

The return on shareholders' funds is probably the most important single measure of all. It takes into account the return on net assets, the company's tax position, and the extent to which capital employed has been supplied other than by the ordinary shareholders (for example by loans).

REID AND MYDDELTON, 1974

Earnings per share indicates how much money the company has earned in relation to the number of ordinary shares. Taken in isolation this measure is useful if considered over a number of years. Companies can be compared with each other if the ratio is linked to the current market price of shares. This calculation provides the price-to-earnings ratio – P/E.

The P/E ratio indicates the amount (how many times the current earnings figure) that potential shareholders are willing to pay in order to buy shares in the company at a particular time. It is affected by previous success and profits, but really it is an indication of expectations. The more confidence the market has in a company, generally the higher will be its P/E. It can also indicate relatively how expensive borrowing is for the company.

Table 7.4   Investment ratios

Ratio	Calculation	Comments
Return on shareholders' funds (%)	$\dfrac{\text{Profit after tax}}{\text{Total shareholders' funds}}$	Measures the return on investment by shareholders in the company. The more unstable the industry and the company, the higher this will be expected to be
Earnings transpose per share (pence)	$\dfrac{\text{Profit after tax}}{\text{Number of ordinary shares issued}}$	Profit after tax represents earnings for the shareholders. It can be returned to them immediately as dividends or reinvested as additional shareholders' funds (retained earnings)
Price-to-earnings ratio (P/E)	$\dfrac{\text{Current market price of ordinary share}}{\text{Earnings per share}}$	Indicates the multiple of earnings that investors are willing to pay for shares in the stock market. The higher the ratio, the more favourably the company is perceived
Dividend yield (%)	$\dfrac{\text{Dividend per share}}{\text{Market price per share}}$	Equivalent to rate of interest per cent paid on the investment. Shareholders will not expect it to equal say building society rates – reinvested profits should generate longer-term increases in the share price
Dividend cover (number of times)	$\dfrac{\text{Earnings per share}}{\text{Dividend per share}}$	The number of times the dividends could have been paid from the earnings: the higher the better

Figure 7.8 Linkages between four investment ratios: the squares represent the investment ratios; the circles represent the figures required for calculating ratios. (Note: the two figures required to calculate each ratio are shown leading into the box.)

If the company opts to raise money from existing shareholders by offering new shares in a rights issue (the shareholders are invited to buy new shares in fixed proportion to those they already hold) the higher the P/E is, the cheaper is the capital. A high P/E implies that shareholders will pay many times current earnings to obtain shares.

The P/E ratio is also very important in acquisition situations. Consider two companies as an example. Company A has issued 500,000 ordinary shares with a face value of 25p and their current market price is 600p. Current earnings per share are 20p (£100,000 in total). Hence, the P/E is 600/20 = 30. Company A looks attractive to the shareholders of company B when it makes a bid for their shares. B also has 500,000 shares issued, again with a face value of 25p, but they are trading at only 150p as company B has been relatively sleepy of late and growth has been below the average for the industry. With earnings per share of 10p (£50,000 in total) the P/E is 15. A offers one new share in company A for every three shares in B (perhaps more generous than it need be), and the shareholders in B accept. A–B now has 666,667 shares issued; at the moment the combined earnings are £150,000. If the stock market, and the shareholders, are confident that A can turn B round and increase earnings significantly the current P/E of 30 could remain. If so, the new price of shares in the combined A–B is 675p. Earnings per share are 22.5p (£150,000/666,667 shares).

A's share price has in effect risen, possibly making it appear an even more successful company. Any company wishing to acquire A will now have to pay more. Equally, A's ability to acquire further companies on the above lines has been enhanced.

The price-to-earnings ratio and earnings per share are measures which are most applicable to companies whose shares are traded on the stock market.

Two dividend ratios

The dividend yield provides the rate of interest that shareholders are receiving in relation to the current market price for shares. It must be used cautiously as it takes no account of the price that people actually paid (historically) to buy their shares; and in any case shareholders are often more interested in long-term capital growth.

The dividend cover indicates the proportion of earnings paid out in dividends and the proportion reinvested. Company dividend policies will vary between companies and, for example, a decision to maintain or reduce dividends in the face of reduced

earnings will be influenced by the predicted effect on share prices and in turn the valuation of the company, which as we saw above can be an issue in acquisitions.

Quoted companies can also be analysed by considering the movement of their share price against the *Financial Times* 100 Shares Index or the All Shares Index, and against the index of shares for their particular industry. Under- and overperformance of the shares are further reflections of investors' confidence and expectations.

Performance ratios

Table 7.5 explains the various performance ratios.

Profitability

The return on net assets or the return on capital employed uses profit before interest and before tax and compares it with the assets, or capital employed, used in the business to create the profit. Actual profit is important as it determines the amount of money that a company has available for paying dividends (once interest and tax are deducted) and for reinvestment. But it is also important to examine how well the money invested in the business is being used – this is profitability. This particular ratio ignores how the business is actually funded, making it a measure of how well the business is performing as a trading concern. It was mentioned earlier that contributions from different products or strategic business units should be compared in the case of multiproduct organizations. The return on net assets should also be used to compare the profitabilities of products and strategic business units. In this way the ratio can be used for evaluating particular competitive strategies and the relative importance to the business of different products. However, this measure should not be used in isolation from an assessment of the relative importance of different products in terms of turnover. High-volume products or divisions may be less profitable than smaller volume ones for a variety of reasons, which are examined in the section on **portfolio analysis** in Chapter 8.

This ratio is particularly useful when it is examined in the light of the two ratios that comprise it. The return on net assets is equal to the profit margin times the net asset turnover. The profit margin is the proportion of sales revenue represented by profits (before interest and tax); the net asset turnover illustrates how well the company is utilizing its assets in order to generate sales.

Table 7.5 Performance ratios

Ratio	Calculation	Comments
Return on net assets Return on capital employed (%)	$$\frac{\text{Profit before interest and before tax}}{\text{Total capital employed in the business}}$$	Measures the relative success of the business as a trading concern Trading profit less overheads is divided by shareholders' funds and other long-term loans Useful for measuring and comparing the relative performance of different divisions/strategic business units
Profit margin (%)	$$\frac{\text{Profit before interest and before tax}}{\text{Sales (turnover)}}$$	Shows trading profit less overheads as a percentage of turnover Again useful for comparing divisions, products, markets
Net asset turnover (number of times)	$$\frac{\text{Sales}}{\text{Total net assets or capital employed in the business}}$$	It measures the number of times the capital is 'turned over' in a year Or: the number of pounds of sales generated for every pound invested in the company

Certain companies will adopt strategies that are designed to yield good profit margins on every item sold, and as a result probably add value into the product or service in such a way that their assets are not producing the same amount of sales per pound sterling as is the case for a company which uses assets more aggressively, adds less value and makes a lower profit margin. Particular industries and businesses may offer little choice in this respect; others offer considerable choice.

If a decision is reached that for the business as a whole, or some part of it, the return on net assets (profitability) must be improved, there are two approaches. Either profits must be increased, or assets reduced, or both. Figure 7.9 illustrates the alternatives available to the organization, and at the bottom the functional responsibilities. Hence, a corporate or competitive strategy change will result in changes to functional strategies.

Other useful performance ratios

Table 7.6 explains stock turnover and debtor turnover, which both indicate how well the company is managing two of its current assets. The stock turnover will depend on how the company is managing its operations – different strategies will lead to higher or lower stocks. Low stocks (high stock turnover) save costs, but they can make the business vulnerable if they are reduced to

too low a level in order to save money and result in production delays. Debtor turnover, for certain types of business, looked at over a period can show whether the company is successful at persuading credit customers to pay quickly. This can affect the marketing strategy if decisions have to be taken not to supply certain customers who are slow payers.

The gross profit margin and the selling and administration costs to sales ratio are useful for indicating the percentage of turnover attributable to overheads. If a company has a high gross profit margin but is relatively unprofitable after accounting for overheads it is a sign of poor management. The product or service is able to command a price comfortably in excess of direct costs (direct labour and materials) but this contribution is being swallowed by overheads which are possibly too high and in need of reduction. Such a company is appropriate for restructuring and perhaps acquisition. Again, these ratios should be examined over a period of years to ensure that the overhead burden is not creeping up without just cause. In terms of increasing profits (to improve profitability; Figure 7.9) it may be easier to reduce overheads than to reduce direct costs.

Measures of financial status

Measures of financial status can be divided into two groups: solvency and liquidity. The ratios are explained in Table 7.7.

Figure 7.9 Improving profitability

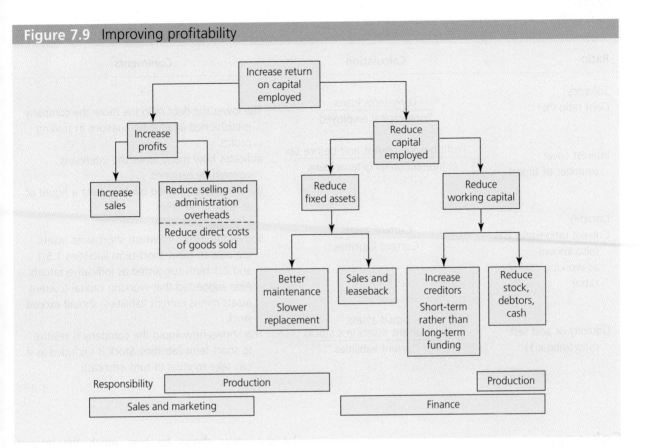

Responsibility		
Production		Production
Sales and marketing		Finance

Table 7.6 Other useful performance ratios

Ratio	Calculation	Comments
Stock turnover (number of times)	$\dfrac{\text{Turnover}}{\text{Stock}}$	Shows how quickly stocks move through the business. Logically the quicker the better – as long as it does not result in stock shortages Most accurate measurement from average stock level over the year rather than the balance-sheet figure
Debtor turnover (number of times; or days of credit given)	$\dfrac{\text{Turnover}}{\text{Debtors}}$	Shows how quickly credit customers pay. Again, use average debtors. Retail organizations, such as Marks and Spencer, sell mostly for cash, or charge interest for credit through their credit cards
	$\dfrac{\text{Debtors}}{\text{Turnover} \times 365}$	A similar measure, credit purchases/average creditors, shows how much credit time is received by the company
Gross profit margin (%) and	$\dfrac{\text{Gross profit}}{\text{Turnover (sales)}}$	Indicates percentage profit before overheads
Selling and administration costs to sales (%)	$\dfrac{\text{Selling and administration cost}}{\text{Turnover (sales)}}$	Shows overheads (indirect costs) in relation to turnover

Table 7.7 Measures of financial status

Ratio	Calculation	Comments
Solvency		
Debt ratio (%)	$$\frac{\text{Long-term loans}}{\text{Total capital employed}}$$	The lower the debt ratio the more the company is cushioned against fluctuations in trading profits
Interest cover (number of times)	$$\frac{\text{Profit before interest and before tax}}{\text{Interest on long-term loans}}$$	Indicates how many times the interest is covered by earnings It is sometimes argued banks expect a figure of at least three times
Liquidity		
Current ratio (ratio x:1) (also known as working capital ratio)	$$\frac{\text{Current assets}}{\text{Current liabilities}}$$	Shows the extent to which short-term assets are able to meet short-term liabilities 1.5:1 and 2:1 both suggested as indicative targets. Also suggested that working capital (current assets minus current liabilities) should exceed stock
Liquidity or acid test ratio (ratio x:1)	$$\frac{\text{Liquid assets (i.e. current assets less stock)}}{\text{Current liabilities}}$$	This shows how liquid the company is relative to short-term liabilities. Stock is excluded as it can take months to turn into cash

Solvency

The major ratios are the debt ratio and interest cover. The debt ratio relates to the company's gearing – how much it is funded by equity capital (shareholders' funds) and how much by long-term loans. Loans generally carry fixed interest payments, and these must be met regardless of any profit fluctuations; a company can elect not to pay dividends to shareholders if profits collapse, which gives it more flexibility.

Managers and investors will both be wary of the debt ratio creeping up, as it does when companies borrow money from the banking system to finance investment or acquisitions. In fact, acquisitive companies must relate their acquisition strategies to their ability to finance them. Sometimes money can be raised from shareholders, but the company must be confident that shareholders will subscribe to rights issues. If not, and the shares have to be sold to the banks who underwrite the issue (who then sell them when the price is appropriate), blocks of shares can be bought up by other acquisitive companies and this can pose a threat. The alternative is long-term loans, and the higher the proportion these constitute, the more stable profits need to be. This is taken up later in the book (in a Finance in Action supplement to Chapter 10).

Interest cover shows by how much the interest payments are covered by profits.

Liquidity

The two main liquidity ratios, the current ratio and the acid test (liquidity) ratio, relate to working capital. Has the company sufficient money available to meet its short-term commitments? They are determined by the flow of cash in and out of the business. A shortage of cash, and commitments to meet, will push the company towards increased borrowings (say a larger overdraft), and this will increase interest commitments.

While targets of 1.5:1 and 2.0:1 are sometimes quoted for the current ratio, these should be treated with some caution. Companies who trade mainly in cash, rather than allow credit, are likely to have a ratio much nearer 1:1 and still be perfectly liquid. Retailers and breweries are cases in point.

A company will experience liquidity problems if it invests in stock and then fails to win orders or if it fails to control its debtors. Conversely, a successful company can have cash problems. Success at winning orders may require investment in machinery or stocks and labour, and these may have to be paid for before and during production and before the goods are delivered and paid for by customers. This can lead to temporary illiquidity, and is known as overtrading.

Managing cash

Cash flow, therefore, can be just as important as profitability. Where demand is seasonal for certain products production may take place when sales are low, in advance of peak demand. This puts pressure on cash flow in the way outlined above. A perfect example of this is Standard Fireworks, a largely focused business, whose sales are concentrated in the weeks before bonfire night (5 November), but who produce all through the year.

Cash reserves built up in good years can be run down to finance a company during lean years or a recession.

Cash-flow issues affect corporate strategy in terms of the range of products, services and businesses selected, competitive strategies in terms of the way they are marketed (to avoid the worst implications of seasonal fluctuations) and functional production, marketing and financial strategies.

It is not unusual for companies to be slow in paying their bills when their performance is poor. This impacts upon their suppliers, and highlights the importance of cash flow, particularly in a recession. Table 7.8 shows how cash is generated and spent.

Cash flow can be improved in a number of ways, for example, by

- increased turnover – but only if linked to
- effective management of debtors and creditors

Table 7.8   A typical cash-flow statement

Cash generated by operating activities (including operating profits, changes in stocks, debtors, and creditors and depreciation charged in the accounts)

Add:	Interest from investments
	Proceeds from any share issues
	Receipts from any asset sales
	New loans taken out
Deduct:	Interest paid on loans
	Loans repaid
	Tax paid
	Dividend paid
	Fixed assets purchased
Leaving:	Money available for further investment

- higher operating profit margins
- reduced tax payments
- reduced investment in working capital and/or fixed assets
- improved gearing to reduce interest payments.

Simply, a company must be able to produce cash in order to finance future investments and acquisitions, meet outstanding payments on earlier acquisitions and cover any unexpected events requiring extraordinary charges.

Accounting for inflation

It is an accounting convention to use historical costs, and within the accountancy profession there is ongoing debate and disagreement about how best to treat inflation. This topic is outside the scope of this book. However, it is important to take some account of inflation when looking at growth rates for actual data such as turnover and profits as otherwise companies appear to be doing far better than in reality they are.

Other quantitative performance indicators

In addition to all of these financial ratios, businesses will typically collect and evaluate information concerning the performance of all the activities being undertaken. For each functional area there will be a number of measures, such as the value of orders acquired by every salesperson, machine utilization, turnover at every retail outlet, output per shift, productivity per employee and absenteeism. Performance will be evaluated against targets or objectives agreed with individual managers who should be held accountable. These **performance indicators** are measures of resource efficiency. They are important control measures which evaluate the efficiency of each functional area of the business.

Similarly, individual sectors will favour particular measures. Retailers will typically consider sales per square foot of trading space, sales per employee, average shopping spend per trip and the number of new store openings or refits.

Improvements can strengthen the company's competitive capability. In isolation, however, these measures do not indicate how successful the company is strategically. This particular issue is very significant for not-for-profit organizations which cannot use the traditional profitability ratios sensibly and at the same time cannot readily measure their effectiveness in relation to their fundamental purpose. Consequently, they often rely more on quantitative measures of efficiency.

These measures are not developed in the same detail as the financial ones in this chapter and appendix as they will not be available to students tackling management case studies, whereas key financial data are normally obtainable.

Service businesses

In addition to the above measures, the ability to retain customers is a key requirement for service businesses.

Retention implies customer satisfaction and probably word-of-mouth recommendation. It is likely to result in higher profits because of the high costs incurred in attracting new business. Moreover, customers are likely to increase their level of spending over time. For insurance companies the cost of processing renewals is far cheaper than the cost of finding new clients; and many people will take out additional policies with a company on which they feel they can rely.

Key performance measures for solicitors are their ability to achieve results for their clients, and the service they offer, measurable by, for instance, the speed with which they respond to letters and telephone calls.

Internet and library projects

Applying the ratios

Table 7.9 provides selected financial data for Shepherd Neame in 2008, and Table 7.10 is a worked analysis of some of the key ratios described in this Finance in Action supplement. This Kent-based brewery is the oldest independent brewer in the UK. It was formed in 1698. As well as brewing, the company imports and distributes wines and spirits and operates a number of pubs and restaurants.

Check how these ratios have been calculated and consider how strong you think Shepherd Neame's

Table 7.9 Shepherd Neame: Extracts from profit and loss account and balance sheet, 28 June 2008

	£ million		£ million	£ million
Turnover	101.7	Fixed assets	171.5	
		Investments	2.0	
Cost of sales	65.1			173.5
Gross profit	36.6	Current assets		
		Stock	5.9	
Overheads/administration	25.9	Debtors	16.3	
Operating profit	10.7	Cash	0.1	
Other income	1.3			22.3
Interest	3.5	Current liabilities		
		Creditors	19.0	
Tax	2.4	Working capital	1.6	
Profit after interest and tax	6.1	Total net assets		175.2
Dividend paid	2.3	Long-term loans	59.4	
Retained profit	3.8	Provisions for charges	4.6	
		Shareholders' funds	111.2	
Number of ordinary shares				
Year-end share price		Total capital employed		175.2

Table 7.10 Shepherd Neame – worked ratio analysis for 2008

Investment ratios

Return on shareholders' funds	=	6.1/111.2	=	5.5%
Earnings per share	=		=	*49.3 pence*

Performance ratios

Return on net assets	=	10.7/175.2	=	6.1%
Profit margin	=	10.7/101.7	=	10.5%
Net asset turnover	=	101.7/175.2	=	0.58 times
Stock turnover	=	101.7/5.9	=	17.2 times
Debtor turnover	=	101.7/16.3	=	6.2 times
Gross profit margin	=	36.6/101.7	=	36%

Solvency ratios

Debt ratio	=	59.4/175.2	=	34%
Interest cover	=	12.0/3.5	=	3.4 times

Liquidity ratios

Current ratio	=	22.3:20.6	=	1.08:1.0
Liquidity ratio	=	22.2:20.6	=	1.08:1.0

performance was at this time. Do you believe the figures to be 'roughly in line with what you would expect' for a brewery chain? Then update the figures for intervening years and bring your performance evaluation up to date. Where has it improved? Deteriorated?

What factors have affected the company's performance in any meaningful way? You might also like to compare Shepherd Neame with one of the larger breweries.

Chapter 8

An introduction to strategy creation and planning

PART 1
Understanding strategy

1 Introducing strategy and strategic management

PART 2
Strategic positioning

2 Strategic thinking, environmental analysis, synergy and strategic positioning

3 Resource-led strategy

4 The dynamics of competition

5 Introducing culture and values

STRATEGIC MANAGEMENT: AWARENESS AND CHANGE

PART 3
Strategic analysis and choice

6 Strategic purpose

7 Strategic success

8 An introduction to strategy creation and planning

9 Strategic leadership, entrepreneurship and intrapreneurship

10 Strategic alternatives, strategy evaluation and strategy selection

PART 4
Issues in strategic growth

11 Strategic growth

12 International strategy

13 Failure, consolidation and recovery strategies

PART 5
Strategic management

14 Strategy implementation

15 Leading change

16 Managing strategy in the organization

17 Final thoughts – the purpose of strategy

Learning objectives

Having read to the end of this chapter you should be able to:

● distinguish between three broad modes of strategy creation – the planning, visionary and emergent approaches

● describe how emergent strategy includes adapting to new opportunities and changing intended strategies incrementally as they are implemented

● show how an overreliance on formal planning systems can bring about a strategic crisis

● appreciate the relevance of military planning for understanding business strategy creation

● distinguish between planning as a cerebral activity carried out by all managers and systematic strategic (or corporate) planning

● describe a number of approaches to corporate planning and, in relation to these, discuss who should be involved in planning

● explain the concept of the planning gap

● discuss what is involved in a contemporary approach to planning

● assess the contribution of a number of planning techniques

● discuss how corporate planning would be used in the public sector

● explain the idea of spheres of influence.

The following chapters show why it is the case that every manager can be a strategy maker, although it should be said that not every manager can be either a leader or an entrepreneur. Chapter 8 provides a short introduction to the whole topic of strategic creation and strategic planning. It recaps on themes introduced in Chapter 1. Figure 1.10 summarized the situation, by showing the linkages between the ideas of intended strategy (through strategic planning and entrepreneurial leadership) and emergent strategies when intended strategies are changed incrementally as they are implemented and new strategies are created as managers adapt in a changing environment.

We're not necessarily great overall strategists [at Virgin] ... we often do things and then work out afterwards what the overall strategy was.

SIR RICHARD BRANSON, CHAIRMAN, VIRGIN GROUP

If you're in the penalty area and aren't quite sure what to do with the ball, just stick it in the net and we'll discuss your options afterwards.

BILL SHANKLY (1914–1981), ONCE MANAGER, LIVERPOOL FOOTBALL CLUB

8.1 Introduction

Football, or really any professional sport, provides a useful metaphor for understanding strategy creation. Teams or, in the case of sports such as tennis, individuals will begin all important

Case 8.1

EasyGroup

UK

The founder

Entrepreneur Stelios Haji-Ioannou was born in Athens in 1967 – his business card describes him as a 'serial entrepreneur'. His father was a successful businessman. After completing two degrees (in London), and work experience in his father's shipping company, he used family money to start Stelmar Tankers (another shipping company) in 1992. Three years later he established EasyJet. Both companies have been very successful and continue to prosper.

Case 1.1 on the Low Price, No Frills Airlines discusses the growth of EasyJet, bringing out its rivalry with Ryanair in the quest to be Europe's leading no frills airline. EasyJet has a clear business model, borrowed in many respects from the pioneering Herb Kelleher and Southwest Air in America. Its growth has been supported by television exposure (a long-running 'docusoap') and the acquisition of Go after this spin-out from British Airways had itself been bought by its managers with substantial venture capital funding.

In 1998 Stelios set up EasyGroup as a holding company and private investment vehicle to facilitate the exploration of new venture opportunities through which the Easy brand could be extended. Once he has established a new business, licensing, franchising and alliances have all featured in the growth strategies. Although there are clear differences of style and approach, in many respects this was not dissimilar to the growth path trodden earlier by Richard Branson with his Virgin brand.

Meanwhile EasyJet was floated successfully as a public company (2000) and Ray Webster, an experienced airline executive from Air New Zealand, came to the UK to run it for Stelios. Stelios himself began to withdraw from the management of the airline and in 2002 he left completely to concentrate on his new ventures. Because his name is associated with the founding of EasyJet, and because he remains a major shareholder, many people would imagine he still runs it, but this is not the case.

Stelios argues he looks for business opportunities where 'he can rip the frills out of the industry' and sums up his own contribution as follows:

'I am best at doing research and deciding on the business model .. .. as soon as I've found the business model I hire a manager to run it … I learn by doing more and more myself and getting the right people to help.

The EasyGroup website clarifies that there are eight stated brand values:

1   Great value
2   Taking on the big boys
3   For the many not the few
4   Relentless innovation
5   Keep it simple
6   Entrepreneurial
7   Making a difference in people's lives
8   Honest, open, caring and fun.

But does he typically get the business model right?

The emergence of Stelios' other businesses

The second Easy business was originally called EasyEverything, but it has since been renamed **EasyInternetcafé**, which better describes its purpose. The first café was opened in Central London in 1999 but others soon followed in other leading European cities. The idea was fast access to the Internet at any time, night or day, seven days a week. The business model was price driven: basically £1 for 1 hour. Keyboards and screens were provided side-by-side in wide rows. Tutors were available if required and there were also 'porn patrollers' monitoring site access. This did not prevent EasyGroup losing a court case in 2003 when it was held liable for customers downloading copyright music illegally. Coffee and snacks could be bought and consumed on site. EasyInternetcafés turned out to have a high cash burn. There were interest charges on the debt capital required for the top-range computers. The sites were centrally located in high lease areas. Salaries had to be paid. Customers may have been plentiful but they did not provide enough revenue to meet the costs. The business was unprofitable and Stelios has had to inject additional personal funding to support it. Moreover the business model has been recrafted. Now Stelios focuses on smaller sites by renting space in other retail properties; he is not concerned to be the leaseholder. In larger sites he has retained, space has been sub-let to other retailers and fast food providers.

EasyCar followed in 2000. This rental car company began by focusing on airport locations and a single model of car – small A series Mercedes. The basic rental charges were way below those of leading names such as Avis and Hertz. But higher personal and car insurance premiums soon closed the gap. Customers had to pay a credit card 'damage-waiver' deposit which was only refunded after the rental period and which provided EasyCar with a steady cash flow through the business. Customers who were alleged to have scratched their cars (but disputed this fact) and who had their deposits retained complained to television consumer programmes – which inevitably brought adverse publicity to the company. Again the cost base has proved too high for the income generation and the business has been unprofitable. In 2003 plans were being drawn up for a new strategy when the managing director left. The new business would be based on pools of cars which would be parked up in relatively quiet areas and unattended. Customers would book over the Internet and then make their own way to the pool, where they would contact a service centre by mobile phone. The car would be unlocked remotely by radio signal; the keys would already be inside. This business went 'worldwide' in 2004 and **EasyVan** was added in 2007.

EasyValue is an Internet cost-price comparison engine. It is an alliance with Kellkoo and it originally struggled to raise sufficient revenue from advertising to break-even.

EasyMoney, begun in 2001, is a credit card operation linked to Lloyds TSB. Customer numbers were intially disappointing in a very competitive industry.

Stelios launched **EasyBus** in 2004, to provide short haul low fare services using orange (the traditional Easy colour) minibuses. The target fare was £1. Interestingly Stagecoach, a leading operator, also launched a no-frills cut price service on longer routes and using double decker buses. Brian Souter, founder of Stagecoach, said he was doubtful that Stelios has a profitable business model as his required revenue per seat mile (to cover costs) is way in excess of the Stagecoach model.

In 2005 Stelios launched **EasyPizza**, a pizza delivery service probably similar to the Domino's Pizza model, in Milton Keynes – where he had opened a cinema, a story described below. The Pizza business has been franchised to other locations in the south of England.

The other businesses include:

EasyHotel which started as a booking system for low price hotel rooms around the world. But the concept has grown to include Easy hotels with cut price rooms. Started in London this business has also been franchised, but this time overseas.

Easy4Men is a range of men's cosmetics distributed through selected Boots stores.

EasyJobs is a website for UK job seekers.

EasyMusic provides music downloads cheaper than Apple's iTunes.

EasyCruise provides a hop-on hop-off cruise package – there are two bright orange ships – calling at various ports in the Mediterranean (summer) and Caribbean (winter). Customers pay for a cabin at a daily rate and then everything else on board is chargeable if consumed. The ships follow the same route for several weeks at a time.

EasyMobile sells simcards and air time.

EasyWatch markets watches on line.

EasyOffice provides serviced office space – and, unlike normal rentals, will sell space for periods as short as a single week. Rents are payable in advance.

Some businesses have worked out better than others – there is always a risk in trying something new – as the following example illustrates.

EasyCinema

It was always intended that EasyCinema might eventually grow into a chain but it began as a single multiplex cinema in Milton Keynes. Cinemas are attractive to Stelios because they are sometimes full and with rows of empty seats at other times. Popularity is affected by time of day, day of the week and certainly by the film itself. Some blockbusters play in several cinemas in a multiscreen at any one time and run for weeks if not months. Other films last just one week before they are dropped. Whilst there are discounted matinee prices (and, of course, concessions for children and pensioners), unlike the theatre, the prices tend to be standardized and do not vary between different films, Stelios believed there were wasted opportunities for price differentiation. As well as day and time, different film titles and the number of weeks since a film's release are relevant – and naturally cheaper prices could be offered for booking a number of weeks in advance. However, if schedules are not available weeks in advance there could be an element of lottery in this. He believed low prices would stimulate high demand and he wanted 20 pence prices for Internet bookings one month in advance to be his baseline.

Stelios – assisted by Stuart Niblock, his Head of New Enterprises at the time and, in effect, a project manager – set out to find a suitable venue to trial his business model. Once they found somewhere, they would 'work out how to do it'. They came across The Point in Milton

Keynes, which was closed but which had been a thriving UCI multiplex cinema after it opened in 1985. It had lost out when competitors opened new complexes. They took it on in 2003 and in a matter of weeks it would be refurbished and open for business.

There was to be no box office and no ice cream, soft drinks or popcorn for sale. People would be asked to carry out and deposit all their rubbish so the downtime between screenings could be minimized. Customers would book in advance on the Internet and once they had paid with their credit card they would be able to print off a bar code on a sheet of paper. When passed over a scanner at the entrance to the relevant cinema screen they would be allowed through a turnstile. Staff would be present to help anyone in difficulty and generally watch over things.

All Stelios needed now was popular films at the time of their release. Six leading distributors control some 90 per cent of film releases and every one of them was sceptical about the sustainability of the EasyCinema business model. They all refused to supply him with films. Normally they receive a figure approximating to £1.30 per person viewing for the films they supply. Pathé, not one of the six, did agree to supply him with films so he could open his cinema, but they were not the latest mainstream titles. Would people be attracted by 20p prices for films that had been around for a while and that had never been stunningly popular? Stelios offered the leading distributors up-front cash payments and when they refused this he argued they were acting as a cartel to exclude him from the industry. He decided to sue them in America.

Staff were recruited and trained in Easy procedures. Stelios himself was on hand and he walked around Milton Keynes – and in rival cinemas – with a sandwich board promoting the venture. [He had adopted a similar approach when the airline Go started up and challenged EasyJet. He had bought tickets, organised photographers and turned up in an orange EasyJet sweater and carrying a promotional banner.] One cinema threw him out – whereupon he complained to the police. The scanners did not work altogether smoothly on opening night, but plenty of customers turned up! To the amazement of some of them Stelios went around with a bucket and asked them for more money 'to help him fight his campaign against the leading distributors'. Afterwards he said the money would be topped up by him and given to charity; he just wanted to draw people's attention to the issue.

Stelios attracted a steady stream of customers with his very low prices for non-mainstream films but the venture was not profitable. In Spring 2004 the leading distributors had partly capitulated, but he was still only able to secure films a month after their initial release. He recruited Charles Wesocky to run EasyCinema for him. Wesocky was a 'veteran of the industry'; indeed he had opened The Point for UCI some twenty years earlier. His main role: improve relations with distributors.

But the business model was never right and EasyCinema has become a rental site for DVDs.

Questions

1 Making use of the Internet, pick up on the earlier comment, and consider whether Stelios *generally* 'gets the business model right'?
2 How much is Stelios an entrepreneurial visionary?
3 Is there sufficient planning of the right type?
4 Is too much left to chance?

© JIRI REZAC/ALAMY

matches with a game plan. They will have studied their opponents, assessed their relative strengths and weaknesses, thought about their natural game and about how they might approach this particular match, and worked out how they might be beaten. In a football game, coaches will have helped the players with the analysis and the tactics. Normally, the objective will be about winning. In some instances it can be about not losing (a subtle difference) or winning might be qualified by adding a 'means' objective related to approach and style. These game plans will undoubtedly *inform* the players, but it may be impossible to carry them out to the letter. Unexpected tactics from their opponents will ensure that this is the case.

Once the game is underway, the intended plans and strategies will be adjusted – there will be incremental changes. Broadly, however, they may well be implemented, certainly as long as the game is being won and not lost. At the same time, new, unexpected opportunities will be presented during the game, and good teams will be able to adapt.

Of course, 'the best laid plans o' mice and men gang aft a gley' (Robert Burns). The opponents may prove stronger and more disciplined than predicted. They may take the lead in the first minute and seize control of the game. In this case, there will be a need to adapt to the threats and change the tactics. When this happens, the ability to remain cohesive and disciplined as a team is essential. In football pundit terminology this is usually described as 'keeping your shape'. In other words, don't panic.

At any time there is always the opportunity for individuals to show initiative and to shine. A strong, experienced and maybe visionary team manager (the strategic leader in this example) can act as a master tactician and an inspiration both beforehand and from the sidelines during the game. Talented players, with individual goals, spectacular saves or important tackles at key moments, will often make important contributions and, by doing so, encourage their colleagues also to make the extra effort that tips the balance. As they always say, a game is not lost until the final whistle: teams often do go one or two goals down before recovering to win.

It is useful to contrast this metaphor with others. American football resembles rugby (league) in some ways, but it remains a very distinctive game. At any one time a team will be attacking or defending in a series of moves, designed to advance a fixed number of yards – or stop the opposing team advancing. The player pool will contain both attackers and defenders, and players will enter and exit the fray depending on the state of the game. Specialist kickers will only be on the field when a kick needs taking. Coaches can call time-outs and provide tactical advice between plays as players come on and off the field. Tactics and planning clearly have a different role.

Warfare is also a competition in its own way. There are clearly objectives for the conflict. There are plans and tactics. There are visionary leaders and historically there has been considerable emergence, with a reliance on the bravery of men in the field. In the past warfare has often involved a serious degree of slaughter in the attempt to defeat the enemy systematically over a period of time. More recently the strategic intent has been based on demoralization. Combatants will endeavour to make a very powerful early strike of such enormity it destroys the enemy's belief that they can win. This is now termed 'shock and awe'. This implies an emphasis on vision (the way to achieve this), planning (the tactics) and speedy execution. There is, then, less reliance on emergence and more reliance on technology and resources.

8.2 Strategy creation

Chapter 1 explained how strategy creation involves three strands:

- *planning*, both systematic and formal strategic planning systems and informal, cerebral planning
- *vision* and visionary leadership, and

- *emergent strategies* – incremental changes to predetermined, intended strategies and adaptive additions with learning and responsiveness to opportunities and threats.

Figure 8.1 reiterates that strategy and strategic management embrace the corporate portfolio of businesses and the search for competitiveness and competitive advantage with each business, product and service, and that this competitiveness arises from the functional activities that an organization undertakes. Visionary ideas *pull* the organization forward. Where these result in significant changes, they will often be associated with the strategic leader. Planning *pushes* everything forward. Emergent changes, improvements and adjustments – intrapreneurial changes initiated and implemented by individual managers throughout the organization – *support* and complete the process.

If all strategies were planned formally, then organizations would be able to look back and review the decisions that they had made over a period of time. At some stage in the past there would have been a clear recorded statement of intent which matched these events closely. In reality, stated plans and actual events are unlikely to match closely. In addition to strategies that have emerged and been introduced entrepreneurially, there are likely to have been expectations and planned possible strategies that have not proved to be viable. However, broad directions can be established and planned and then detailed strategies allowed to emerge as part of an ongoing learning experience within the organization.

Idenburg (1993) presents these ideas in a slightly modified way, distinguishing between the following strategies.

- Formal planning systems, through which clear objectives should lead to intended strategies.

- Learning or real-time planning, which represents a formal approach to adaptive strategy creation. Managers meet regularly, both formally and informally, and debate how key strategic issues are changing and emerging. Objectives and strategies will be changed in a turbulent environment.

- Incremental change and logical incrementalism. The organization will have a clear mission and directional objectives, and it will be recognized that pursuing these requires flexibility. Managers will be encouraged to experiment with new ideas and strategies, learning and adapting all the time. Internal politics and systems will play an important role in this mode.

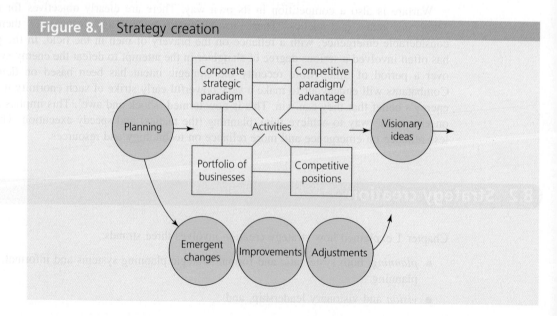

Figure 8.1   Strategy creation

thousands of franchisees worldwide. In the late 1990s its annual rate of global expansion grew to over 3000 new restaurants although this has been trimmed back after some misguided expansion; this required careful planning. This planning, together with arrangements with building contractors and suppliers, has also allowed McDonald's to cut 30 per cent off the cost of opening every new restaurant, through the use of more efficient building systems, standardized equipment and global sourcing. As a consequence, it can now afford to open restaurants in locations which, in the past, had been seen as uneconomical. Given the intense competition in the fast-food industry, it is also essential for McDonald's to remain flexible and responsive, internationally, nationally and locally.

Case 8.1 applies these themes to EasyGroup, the collection of businesses started by Stelios Haji-Ioannou on the back of the success of EasyJet, which we featured in Case 1.1. Stelios had a vision for the airline opportunity and executed it effectively. None of his other businesses have achieved the same level of success. Is he getting the vision and the business model wrong? Is there inadequate preparation and planning? Is there an over-reliance on 'everything working out'? Interestingly, and maybe significantly, this serial entrepreneur continues to start new ventures before his last one has broken even. It could however mean he is just easily bored or he really does not have the new killer idea that he had with the airline. Alternatively it might mean that he is acting as the true entrepreneur, whose skill is based on seizing the perceived opportunity, starting up only to move on. Essentially the skill set that Stelios has is not that of the corporate manager. Chapter 9 will look at this topic of the role of the entrepreneur in greater detail.

Chris Gorman, operates very much within the entrepreneur strategic leader role. Immediately prior to his involvement with the Gadget Shop (unfortunately an unsuccessful acquisition for him), Gorman had the very interesting title of 'Chief Entrepreneur' within Great Universal Stores. GUS had bought the Reality Group from Gorman, and after the acquisition Gorman had this new role. However, Gorman did not stay long within GUS because 'it was not my skill set … I am not someone who is comfortable as a manager working through the layers that make up a large PLC'.

Table 8.1 further relates these themes to the three levels of strategy: corporate, competitive and functional. In large organizations much of the responsibility for corporate strategic change will be centralized at the head office, although the businesses and divisions can be involved or consulted. Competitive and functional change decisions are more likely to be decentralized, but again, not exclusively. Corporate policies can require or constrain changes at these levels.

Planning and strategy creation

Mintzberg (1989) contends that the strategic leader should be the chief architect, in conjunction with planners, of corporate plans; the process should be explicit, conscious and controlled; and

Table 8.1 Levels of strategy and modes of strategy creation

Modes of strategy creation	Levels of strategy	
	Corporate strategy	Competitive and functional strategies
Planning	Formal planning systems	Planning the detail for implementing corporate strategies
Visionary	Seizing opportunities – limited planning only	Innovation throughout the organization
Adaptive/incremental	Reacting to environmental opportunities and threats, e.g. businesses for sale; divestment opportunity	Reacting to competitor threats and new environmental opportunities. Learning and adjustment as planned and visionary strategies are implemented

issues of implementation should be incorporated. Essentially, analysis leads to choice, which leads on to implementation. The process is sequential:

$$Analysis \rightarrow Choice \rightarrow Implementation$$

Certain organizations might claim that detailed long-term planning is essential for them. An airline, for example, must plan capacity several years ahead because of the long delivery lead times for new aeroplanes and the related need to manage cash flow and funding. In addition, resources must be co-ordinated on an international scale. While planes are utilized on most days and fly as many hours in the day as possible, crews work only limited hours, and typically finish a flight or series of flights in a location which is different from their starting point.

However, Mintzberg argues that this is planning the implications and consequences of the strategic perspective, not necessarily the perspective itself. Detailed planning of this type should not inhibit creativity concerning the perspective.

Planning of some form will always be required in large organizations. It forces thinking and enables and supports resource allocation and budgeting. However, the extent and nature of the overall planning contribution will relate to the industry and the environment and be affected by both leadership and culture.

The visionary mode

A visionary strategic leader who formulates strategic change in his or her mind may only be semiconscious of the process involved. He or she will clearly understand the current and desired strategic perspective, and ideally the culture of the organization will be one in which other managers are receptive of the changes in perspective. The personality and charisma of the leader, and the ability to sell his or her ideas, will be crucial issues, and as speed of action, timing and commitment are typical features the strategy can prove highly successful.

The visionary or entrepreneurial approach suggests that the strategic leader is very aware of the strengths, weaknesses and capabilities of the organization; the current matching with the environment; a wide range of possibly diverse opportunities for change; and the likely reaction of managers to certain changes. Similar to the '**bird approach**' where unlimited opportunities make the final decision arbitrary, the selection is made somewhat arbitrarily without careful and detailed planning, and therefore an element of risk is involved. This informality in the process is important to allow for creativity and flair. The strategic leader then sells the idea to other managers, and the strategy is implemented and changed incrementally as experience is gained and learning takes place. In other words, the vision acts as an umbrella and within it specific decisions can be taken which lead to the emergence of more detailed strategies.

With this mode it is difficult to separate analysis and choice, so that:

$$Analysis\ (in\ the\ form\ of\ ongoing\ awareness)\ and\ choice \rightarrow Implementation$$

Dangers The success of this mode in the long term depends on the continued strategic awareness and insight of the strategic leader, particularly if the organization revolves around a visionary leader and becomes heavily dependent upon him or her. People may be visionary for only a certain length of time, and then they become blinkered by the success of current strategies and adopt tunnel vision, or they somehow lose the ability to spot good new opportunities. It might also be argued that, if luck is involved, their luck runs out. The problems occur if the strategic leader has failed to develop a strong organization with other visionaries who can take over.

On a current basis the strategy requires management as well as leadership. In other words, managers within the organization must be able to capitalize on the new opportunities and develop successful competitive positions within the revised strategic perspective. This might involve an element of planning; equally it might rely more on the adaptive approach described below.

The adaptive and incremental modes

Under the adaptive and incremental modes strategies are formed and evolve as managers throughout the organization learn from their experiences and adapt to changing circumstances. They perceive how tasks might be performed, and products and services managed, more effectively, and they make changes. They also respond to pressures and new strategic issues. There will again be elements of semiconsciousness and informality in the process. Some changes will be gradual, others spontaneous, and they will act collectively to alter and improve competitive positions. As individual decisions will often involve only limited change, little risk and possibly the opportunity to change back, this is essentially the '**squirrel approach**' described in Chapter 1, Box 1.3. Managers learn whether their choice is successful or unsuccessful through implementation.

Hence this mode implies limited analysis preceding choice and implementation, which are intertwined and difficult to separate. A proper analysis follows in the form of an evaluation of the relative success:

Analysis (limited) → Choice and implementation → Analysis

Adaptive strategic change requires decentralization and clear support from the strategic leader, who also seeks to stay aware of progress and link the changes into an integrated pattern. It is often based on setting challenges for managers: challenging them to hit targets, improve competitiveness and stretch or exploit internal systems and policies to obtain the best possible returns. The greater the challenge, the more care needs to go into establishing a suitable reward system. When the structure enables effective adaptive change, then **intrapreneurship** can be fostered throughout the organization and individual managers can be allowed the necessary freedom. However, if adaptive changes are taking place in a highly centralized organization, and despite rigid policies, there is a problem which should be investigated. The major potential drawbacks concern the ability of the organization and the strategic leader to synthesize all the changes into a coherent pattern, and the willingness and ability of individual managers to take an organization-wide perspective. This latter point is examined later in Chapter 9.

Information technology provides opportunities for collecting and co-ordinating information and should be harnessed to support decentralization. In addition, team briefing can prove useful. Here, a strategic leader would regularly brief his or her senior executives, discussing progress and any proposed changes to the corporate strategy and policies. On a cascading basis managers would quickly and systematically communicate this information downwards and throughout the organization by meeting teams of people responsible to them. The secret lies in also using team briefing meetings to communicate information upwards by reporting on new strategic issues and how they are being handled.

Figure 8.3 provides a short summary of the processes. Planning is shown at the top as a 'closed funnel' activity. The entrepreneurial, visionary style is more one of diverging and opening things up, widening the scope of the ideas considered. Adaptive strategy (responding to new opportunities) is, conversely, illustrated as a convergent process. Here, learning and synthesis are required to form cohesive patterns which bind the emerging strategies. In the entrepreneurial mode, planning is required during implementation; and in the adaptive mode, individual managers are doing their own planning, sometimes informally, sometimes more formally.

8.3 Changing strategies

Two important strategic pressures can leave the unprepared organization weakened: competitive and other environmental pressures, and focusing too much on controls at the expense of flexibility.

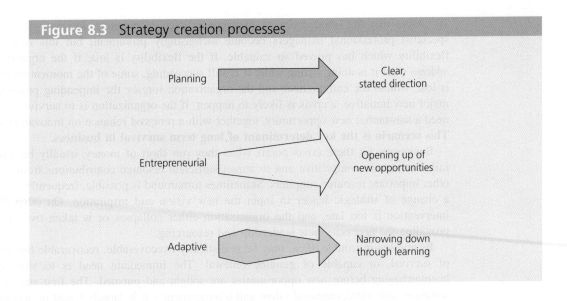

Figure 8.3 Strategy creation processes

Planning → Clear, stated direction

Entrepreneurial → Opening up of new opportunities

Adaptive → Narrowing down through learning

Hurst (1995) has shown how management and control becomes increasingly necessary as organizations grow and become more complex, but that this development contains the seeds of potential failure. Figure 8.4 shows that organizations often start life with an **entrepreneurial vision** but that the significance of this vision soon gives way to learning and emergence as the entrepreneur and the organization learns to cope with the pressures of a dynamic and competitive environment. This flexibility maintains the momentum and the organization grows and prospers.

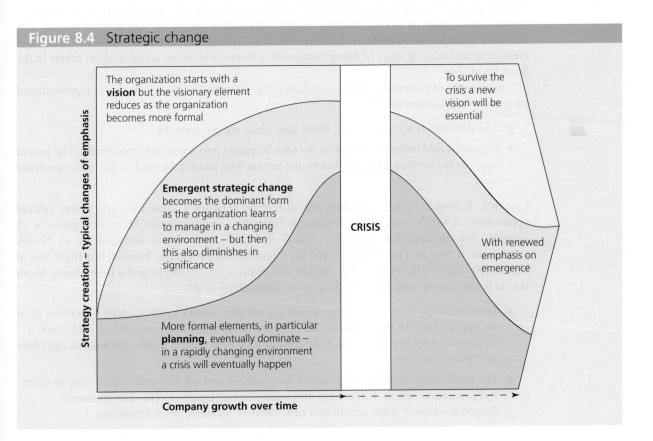

Figure 8.4 Strategic change

The organization starts with a **vision** but the visionary element reduces as the organization becomes more formal

To survive the crisis a new vision will be essential

Emergent strategic change becomes the dominant form as the organization learns to manage in a changing environment – but then this also diminishes in significance

CRISIS

With renewed emphasis on emergence

More formal elements, in particular **planning**, eventually dominate – in a rapidly changing environment a crisis will eventually happen

Strategy creation – typical changes of emphasis

Company growth over time

To ensure that the organization is managed efficiently, planning and control systems run by specialist professional managers become increasingly prominent, but this often reduces the flexibility which has proved so valuable. If the flexibility is lost, if the organization fails to address what it is doing wrong while it is still succeeding, some of the momentum for innovation is lost. Unless the entrepreneur and the organization foresee the impending problem and find a major new initiative, a crisis is likely to happen. If the organization is to survive the crisis it will need a substantial new opportunity, together with a renewed reliance on innovation and learning. **This scenario is the key determinant of long term survival in business.**

Businesses hit these crisis points when they run short of money, usually because they have failed to remain competitive and to attract sufficient resource contributions from customers and other important resource suppliers. Sometimes turnaround is possible, frequently accompanied by a change of strategic leader to input the new vision and inspiration. On other occasions the intervention is too late, and the organization either collapses or is taken over as a means of providing the necessary new leadership and resourcing.

Businesses in trouble, then, may be realistically irrecoverable, recoverable but only to a level of survival, or capable of genuine renewal. The immediate need is to stop any financial haemorrhaging before new opportunities are sought and pursued. The first step does not need someone with entrepreneurial talent and temperament – it is largely based on technique, backed by a willingness to take tough decisions – but the second stage does.

Hurst further argues that on occasions it can be valuable to engineer an internal crisis and upset in order to drive through major changes in an organization that has lost its dynamism and become too resistant to change. A controlled crisis is better than one resulting from external events as it can be used for positive change rather than constitute a more desperate reaction.

Stasis is less likely to happen if the company employs and encourages creative people who drive innovation and intrapreneurship. But if momentum is lost, the company may need more than creative people: it may need a 'maverick', perhaps someone who is normally ill-at-ease in a typical organization or a new strategic leader who will come in for just a short period. The maverick manager is unorthodox, individualistic and outspoken, someone who will challenge mediocrity and existing ways of doing things and someone who is not afraid to upset others in the drive for change.

Another way of presenting these arguments is the following four-stage model of organizational progression and development:

- The first step is a *creative* one, when new ideas are put forward.

- *Reflection and nurturing* follow as the idea is crafted into a winning opportunity. The person who has the original idea may not be the person who takes it forward in the most opportune way.

Case 8.2, Eclipse Aviation, examines the difference between a great idea and a true market opportunity. A similar idea is the Terrafugia Transition, a road car that becomes a plane in 15 seconds. The airplane that becomes a car – and vice versa – was designed by ex NASA technicians; it runs on a petrol engine and fits into a normal car garage. Its main test flight was in March 2009 and it sells for $195,000. Would you invest in this? It might be the future and it might not. Is it also a great idea but what kind of an opportunity is it?

- The third stage is an *action* stage as the organization grows by developing a business from the opportunity. As the business takes off, and more and more products are sold, some element of order becomes vital if the organization is to control events, manage its cash flow and deliver on time.

- The fourth stage then becomes one of *management* and administration with clear policies and procedures which deliver smooth running and efficiencies. This can become a dangerous stage if stasis sets in and new, creative ideas are not forthcoming.

Case 8.2

Eclipse Aviation – Great Opportunity or Just a Great Idea?   US

A new jet aeroplane, the Eclipse 500, made its first – and successful – test flight in America in August 2002. Eclipse Aviation was attempting an 'aviation first' with this new aircraft – the first commercial jet priced at under $1 million (approximately £650,000). At this price it would be 75 per cent cheaper than a near rival, the Cessna Citation. To achieve this price, Eclipse would have to sell 1000 aircraft a year. The intention was full airworthiness certification in 2003 with deliveries from 2004. Four separate certifications were required – the aircraft, the engine, the welding technique being used and the avionics.

The first Eclipse 500 may have tested successfully – but it had not been built with the production tooling that has been put in place subsequently.

Any one of the four areas could fail certification and thus delay the project. Any delay would require even more investment capital to bring the project to market. The first plane (after full certification) was actually delivered for service at the end of 2006. Industry experts were always sceptical about the proposal, but non-experts were generally in favour of the entrepreneurial venture.

The entrepreneur behind Eclipse

Vern Raburn had a background in technology, not aviation. He was, in fact, the eighteenth person to join Microsoft in its early days. He believed he could use his experience in improving value to drive new sales and also drive down costs and prices.

The specification

The aircraft has 6 passenger seats but no toilet. Its flying speed is 400 miles an hour and its range is 1300 miles. It is powered by a new single Williams engine (which, like the plane, had to be certified) with double the thrust-to-weight ratio of rival engines. Eclipse had found a suitable supplier for its avionics, which it believed it could purchase for $50,000, whilst Cessna pay $700,000. Manufacturing processes are based on high volume techniques, and a new type of welding was being adopted. Sceptics believe the overall extent of technological change is too ambitious.

The aims of the business model

Eclipse hopes to expand jet travel beyond 'executive elites and to open up a new market opportunity for 'taxis in the sky'.

The idea for a taxi service would require an independent operator to create a service which links hundreds of small airports. As a concept it is unproven. Fractional, part-ownership share schemes have been tried out, but they have been largely unprofitable, as much as anything because of the complex logistics. Forecasting demand and dealing with planes flying return or collection journeys without passengers are a big issue.

Funding

By 2003 some $240 million had been invested in the development. Investors included Bill Gates and an ex-Ford CEO. There had been $25 million in customer deposits which was used for working capital. Through the development phase the business was burning at least $5 million every month and needed more funding to see it through certification.

In 2008 control of the business fell to the Etirc Fund controlled by entrepreneur, businessman and financier Roel Pieper – who was something of a veteran of the computing and IT industries. The fund is based in Luxembourg and Pieper had links with Russia. His intent was to move production there, to a new custom-built factory. Etirc already owned the distribution rights to Russia, Asia and Eastern Europe.

The market

2001 was a record year for business jet manufacture. 738 were built. *Forecast International* suggested a market of 1900 between 2002 and 2011, with Eclipse perhaps achieving 400 of these.

Eclipse aimed for sales of 140 in 2004, 500 in 2005, 900 in 2006 and then 1500 by 2007 from the replacement of existing jets as well as new sales and air taxis. It claimed it already had 1350 firm orders. By the end of 2007 just 104 had been produced, and this caused the financial strains which led to the takeover by Etirc. But mysteries always abounded.

SOURCE: THIS CASE STUDY WAS PREPARED USING PRIMARILY PUBLICLY AVAILABLE SOURCES OF INFORMATION FOR THE PURPOSES OF CLASSROOM DISCUSSION; IT DOES NOT INTEND TO ILLUSTRATE EITHER EFFECTIVE OR INEFFECTIVE HANDLING OF A MANAGERIAL SITUATION.

A Russian entrepreneur, who had built a substantial perfume chain, said he had a company called Nimbus which had access to $1.2 billion for an air taxi service with 1000 aircraft. Nimbus turned out to be an on-line auction business. Another Swiss entrepreneur announced that Aviace would acquire 112 planes to start a business in Europe. Aviace paid a deposit but the rest of its funding was never put in place.

Early in 2008 there were still 1950 'firm orders' – apparently.

The underlying risk

Since 1960 only one new entrant to the market – Embraer of Brazil – has managed to deliver more than one new business jet per month.

Questions

1 Eclipse has been described as 'the last great dream in aviation' … but does this imply a 'half full' or a 'half empty' perspective?
2 Is it a good dream or a bad dream?

Task

Use the Internet to determine what has happened with the venture and with the Terrafugia Transition.

Clearly, each stage has a downside. A constant stream of new ideas may not constitute entrepreneurial opportunities. Too much deliberation may inhibit action. An overemphasis on 'doing' and competitiveness may mean that inadequate attention is given to structural necessities. Finally, too much bureaucracy can mean missed opportunities. The organization begins to need a fresh input of creative ideas. Individually, we are all different and our affinity and fit with each of these stages varies; some of us are not able to switch styles. While the most successful and habitual entrepreneurs will ensure that there is a constant flow of activity between these stages and the potential downsides do not materialize, other strategic leaders will need to recognize their relative strengths and weaknesses and recruit other people carefully to ensure that there is a balance of skills and constant progression. Moreover, the positive organization implied here will be in a better position to exploit and retain its most talented intrapreneurial managers.

Changing strategies and strategy drivers

So far we have seen how opportunities, resources and competition are key drivers of strategy – and we have also seen that the organization's culture can be either a facilitator or an inhibitor of change. These are drawn together in Figure 8.5, where we might think of resources and competition as 'push' forces and opportunities and aspiration as 'pull' factors.

Figure 8.6 presents these themes in an alternative form. It combines the market- and resource-based views of strategy with the analytical (planning in a competitive environment) and aspirational (visionary and emergent) approaches to strategy creation that we introduced and explained in Chapter 1. The market-based approach can be manifest in either an analytical insight into the competitive environment or an endeavour to envision new opportunities for building value through an instinctive understanding of customers and their needs. The resource-based approach can build analytically on core competencies and capabilities. At the same time, real breakthroughs in processes or technologies can help to rewrite the rules of competition in an industry.

8.4 Military strategy revisited

As a conclusion to this part of the chapter we return to the military metaphor we introduced in Chapter 1 and consider how strategy is planned by the armed forces. This provides a valuable link to the next section on strategic planning.

Figure 8.5 Strategy drivers

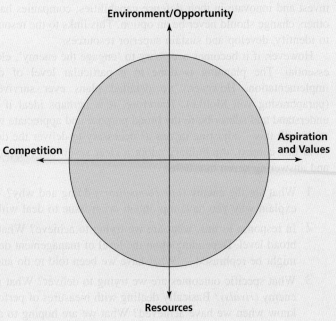

Figure 8.6 Changing strategies

Analysis * – includes strategic planning systems and routine decision-making.
Aspiration ** – ranges from entrepreneurially visionary inputs to new ideas which result in emergent change.

In today's world the armed forces prefer to win without ever firing a shot. This implies being able to scare the enemy with superior force. Pure strength and hold over a market (or niche) can similarly provide a barrier to entry and is clearly valuable to have. To retain such strength, nations invest and innovate in their defence capabilities; companies have to do the same. Sitting back as others change should never be an option. This links to the resource-based view as you are looking to identify, develop and sustain superior resources.

However, if it becomes necessary to 'engage the enemy', clear operational/tactical planning is essential. The planning is done to a particular level of detail and then handed over for implementation. However, 'no detailed plans ever survive engagement with the enemy' (paraphrasing von Moltke). Therefore, it is perhaps ideal if those carrying out orders clearly understand and subscribe to the broad purpose and appreciate what they are trying to achieve and stick with this – adjusting tactics as necessary to deliver the desired outcomes.

In this context, the military adopt a clear seven-stage approach to planning, based on asking and answering seven questions:

1 What are the enemy (*our competitors*) doing and why? The answer to this will broadly explain why you have a problem or an issue to deal with.

2 In response to this, what are we trying to achieve? What are our desired outcomes – at a broad level. Depending upon the level of management dealing with a problem or issue, this might be rephrased – 'What have we been told to do and try to accomplish?'

3 What specific outcomes are we trying to deliver? What impact do we want to have on our enemy *(rivals)?* Basically dealing with measures of performance and success. How will we know when we have achieved? What we are hoping to achieve?

    This is a 'bridge' level. These issues remain a given. Further, more detailed planning will take place, but these plans will be flexible and adjustable within this context.

4 Where and how should we act to fulfil these ambitions? Generally these will be based on a series of verbs – military examples might include *find* (the enemy); *deny* (something); *destroy* (either something the enemy has or some part of the infrastructure as a diversion); *block* (and thus prevent the enemy doing something); *protect* (something strategic or valuable); *defeat* (not destroy, thus setting back in some way).

5 What resources are required for each of these actions and deliverables? Typically the view will always be that they are inadequate and more would be desirable.

6 When and where should the actions take place. This is clearly tactical and it implies sequencing and appreciating dependencies. It is (in part) about project planning. Contingencies are required for when setbacks or unexpected events occur. After all, the enemy is also working to something of a game plan, even if they might have inferior resources. Within the time available, as much conceptual planning as possible should take place, but clearly not every eventuality can be accounted for in advance.

7 What control measures need to be put in place?

The military would see 1, 2 and 3 as strategic planning.
    4 and 5 are operational planning.
    6 and 7 are then tactical planning.
    The seven stages are based on the premise that:

$$\text{Capability} + \text{Intent} = \text{Credibility}$$

In drawing up clear and strong plans there are three clear issues:

● The moral case for what you are doing – this affects people's will as it is, in effect, the quality of the case or cause

- The broad concept – people's ability to grasp the issues and significance. It often relies significantly upon communication from the top

- The physical aspects – having or acquiring the resources that are going to be required. Only if you have them can you plan how you are going to deploy them to achieve the outcomes.

Achieving outcomes in a military sense can often be the easy part. The invasion of Iraq by the US and UK in 2003 and the toppling of Saddam Hussein was comparatively easy from a military point of view. Post the invasion and declared ceasefire, the reconstruction of Iraq in social, economic and technical terms followed – it is still ongoing at great cost both in human lives and money. What seemed to be a straightforward preferred objective, the ending of Saddam's regime, proved to be the simplest objective; strategic planning post 2003 is much more complex. Although the military planning and operation might be deemed a success, we might question whether or not the protagonists had prepared for the consequences of the war. There is a saying: 'fail to plan and you plan to fail'. Yes, planning does matter – but what exactly do we mean by 'planning' in strategy?

8.5 Strategic planning

Planning the future – thinking about the most appropriate strategies, and changes in strategic direction – is essential for organizations, particularly those experiencing turbulent environments. Rigid systematic planning, based on techniques and formalized procedures is, however, no longer as fashionable as it was, nor is it the only way in which strategic change decisions are made. There are dangers if organizations become reliant upon professional planners and where the only outcome of planning is a plan. This may not allow for effective strategic thinking, and may not result in a clear direction for the future.

There are dangers, then, in thinking that all strategic changes can be planned systematically and procedurally. Whether it is the result of formal and systematic planning, or much more informal and ad hoc leadership and management – which, paradoxically, still implies an element of planning – an organization will have strategies and processes whereby these strategies are changed. The processes need to be understood, and in many cases improved. It is important to assess where and how the organization should change and develop in the light of market opportunities and competitive threats, but there are lessons to be learnt about their appropriateness to certain strategic opportunities. Managers should know clearly where the organization is, and where it might sensibly go, and start making appropriate changes. They should then monitor progress and be aware of changes in the environment; in this way they can be flexible and responsive. After all, all managers are strategy makers.

In this context, this chapter now considers what is meant by the term planning, and what is involved in the systematic planning cycle approach to the management of strategic change. The contribution of a number of planning techniques will be evaluated, and possible pitfalls and human issues in planning will be pinpointed.

Readers may notice that a number of the references in this chapter are rather dated. There is a very good reason for this – whilst at one time strategic planning and strategic management were almost synonymous, this is no longer the case. Relatively little is being written on strategic planning that improves on earlier material. The earlier writings on the topic, however, remain important and valid. The points they make have not changed, although it is imperative that we place strategic planning within the wider context of strategy creation.

Planning is one of the most complex and difficult intellectual activities in which man can engage. Not to do it well is not a sin; but to settle for doing it less than well is.

RUSSELL ACKOFF, 1970

8.6   Strategic thinking and strategic planning

The Case 8.3 story on FedEx shows two key elements of strategy creation in action and working together – visionary ideas and planning. The planning focuses on the project management and the implementation of a visionary idea. Without sound planning the venture could not possibly have worked. But when we talk about 'strategic planning' this is not exactly what we mean. Planning can also be used to identify future strategies, although it is only one way of identifying future opportunities. This section looks at planning's contribution to strategy making.

Case 8.3

Federal Express   US

Federal Express provides an excellent example of an organization (and an entrepreneur) that opened up an unrealized market opportunity and began a new industry. 'The greatest business opportunities arise when you spot things your customer didn't have a clue they needed until you offered it to them.'

The idea behind FedEx is simple. It is to provide a speedy and reliable national and international 'overnight' courier service for letters and parcels based upon air cargo. FedEx rightly claim to have invented the concept of overnight delivery, creating a whole new market where previously there was none. The company had a peripheral but significant role in the film *Castaway*, which featured Tom Hanks as a FedEx manager who survived the crash of a FedEx airplane only to spend several years marooned on a desert island. He held on to one of the packages from the plane and finally succeeded in delivering it.

FedEx is, however, unusual in a number of ways. Before it could even begin, FedEx needed a nationwide (North American) distribution system with a fleet of planes and trucks – a huge investment in planning and resources.

The business was the idea of Fred Smith, whose father was also an entrepreneur who had founded and built a successful bus company. When Fred was a student at Yale in the 1960s he wrote a paper outlining his idea for a freight-only airline which delivered and collected parcels to and from a series of hubs. Traditionally parcels were shipped on scheduled passenger airlines as normal mail, whilst Smith proposed flying at night when the skies were relatively quiet. His paper was graded as a C. After graduating, Smith served as a pilot in Vietnam before he bought a controlling interest in Arkansas Aviation Sales, a company which carried out modifications and overhauls. Determined to implement his idea for a courier service he invested a $10 million family inheritance and raised a further $72 million from various sources based on a number of independent but positive feasibility studies.

FedEx took to the skies in 1973, offering a service in and out of 25 East coast cities with 14 jet aircraft. The demand was there, as he had forecast. Unfortunately the rise in the OPEC oil price made FedEx uneconomical almost as soon as it started. Two years of losses and family squabbles – Smith was accused of 'squandering the family fortune' – were followed by profits and Smith's belief, courage and persistence were rewarded.

FedEx opened a hub in Paris in 1999 and opted for a standard price across the eurozone; and in 2006 it acquired UK-based competitor ANC – which it rebranded FedEx UK. In 2004 FedEx acquired Kinko's, an American high street franchise that provides a range of office services. This allows customers to more readily access FedEx services.

FedEx is successful because it delivers on time and speedily, and because it has a sophisticated tracking system – SuperTracker which it introduced in 1986 – for when something does go astray. It uses as a slogan 'The World on Time'. There are now nearly 700 FedEx aircraft flying over one million miles every two days. The central hub remains in Memphis in the US but the flights are international. Six million packages from 220 countries are handled every night. FedEx's courier vans cover another two million miles every day collecting and delivering these parcels. To ensure FedEx can maintain its service it flies empty aircraft every night, which track close to the pick-up airports and which are brought into service if they are needed.

Its success has, of course, spawned competition. But with learning and emergence FedEx has stayed at the forefront of the industry it invented.

Questions

1   What role did planning play in the beginning of the FedEx story and how do you think it is utilized now?

2   Is it more or less significant than visionary ideas and emergent strategy?

Task

Use the Internet to compare and contrast FedEx with UPS.

Robinson (1986) argues that the role of the planner should be not to plan but to enable good managers to plan. It is not the task of the planner to state the objectives; rather he or she should elicit and clarify them. Planning should concentrate on understanding the future, which is uncertain and unpredictable, and helping managers to make decisions about strategic changes. Thus, the aim of planning should be to force people to think and examine, not to produce a rigid plan.

It is worth reinforcing here that the real value of planning is not the plan which emerges, and which might be produced as a summary document which is worth little more than the paper it is printed on! Rather, the value lies in the thinking that the act and process of planning forces people to do.

Undoubtedly, planning techniques, used carefully, can help to provide a valuable description and analysis of where the organization is 'now'. But for managing the future and its inherent uncertainties, vision and flexibility will also be essential, alongside a clear direction and purpose. New thinking is essential for reaching the new competitive high ground first.

Strategic planning systems, popular and dominant in the 1960s and 1970s, became less fashionable in the 1980s and 1990s. They were often seen as too time consuming and mechanistic, unable to keep up with the changes going on in business. In most companies planning had not contributed to strategic thinking and, because strategic thinking is essential, a new role has had to be found for strategic planning.

Strategic planning became fashionable for two basic reasons. First, it provided a means for allocating resources and managing budgets in the new complex multiproduct organizations and, second, it helped to pull together the disparate activities and businesses in organizations. These needs remain.

The outcome for many organizations was formal planning systems, heavily reliant on financial data, and supported by thick planning manuals and too many staff at the centre. This was the downside.

On the positive side, planning can encourage managers to think about the need and opportunities for change, and to communicate strategy to those who must implement it. This was particularly important in the 1960s and early 1970s when there was an abundance of investment opportunities and a dearth of capital and key priorities needed to be established. In complex multi-activity organizations, decisions have to be made concerning where to concentrate investment capital in relation to future earnings potential, and this has generated a number of portfolio analysis techniques, some of which are studied later in this chapter. Rather than use these techniques for gaining greater awareness and insight, for which they are well suited, managers sought to use them prescriptively to determine future plans.

Formal strategic planning had become unfashionable by the 1980s for a number of reasons:

● Planning was often carried out by planners, rather than the managers who would be affected by the resultant plans.

● As a result, the outcome of planning was often a plan which in reality had little impact on actual management decisions, and therefore was not implemented.

● The planning techniques used were criticized primarily because of the way in which they were used.

● The important elements of culture and total quality management were usually left out.

However, many industries continue to experience turbulent environments caused by such factors as slower economic growth, globalization and technological change, and consequently strategic thinking is extremely important. The following questions must be addressed:

● What is the future direction of competition?
● What are the future needs of customers?
● How are competitors likely to behave?
● How might competitive advantage be gained and sustained?

Organizations must ensure that these questions are constantly addressed rather than addressed occasionally as part of an annual cycle. Line managers who implement plans must be involved throughout the process. Every executive needs to understand how to think strategically. Rigorous frameworks and planning manuals are not necessary as long as the proper thinking takes place.

There should be a strategic plan for each business unit in a complex organization, i.e. clear competitive strategies built around an understanding of the nature of the industry in which the business competes, and sources of competitive advantage. Chosen strategies must have action plans for implementing them, including an assessment of the needs for finance and for staff training and development. This is generally less difficult than formulating a corporate strategy for the whole organization.

8.7 Planning and planning systems

What do we mean by planning?

All managers plan. They plan how they might achieve objectives. However, a clear distinction needs to be made between the cerebral activity of informal planning and formalized planning systems.

A visionary strategic leader aware of strategic opportunities and convinced that they can be capitalized upon, may decide independently where the organization should go and how the strategies are to be implemented. Very little needs to be recorded formally. Conversations between managers may result in plans which again exist only in individual managers' heads or in the form of scribbled notes. Equally, time, money and other resources may be invested by the organization in the production of elaborate and formally documented plans.

In all cases planning is part of an ongoing continuous activity which addresses where the organization as a whole, or individual parts of it, should be going. At one level a plan may simply describe the activities and tasks that must be carried out in the next day or week in order to meet specific targets. At a much higher level the plan may seek to define the mission and objectives, and establish guidelines, strategies and policies that will enable the organization to adapt to, and to shape and exploit, its environment over a period of years. In both cases, if events turn out to be different from those which were forecast, the plans will need to be changed.

The value of strategic planning

When managers and organizations plan strategies they are seeking to:

● be clearer about the business(es) that the organization is in, and should be in
● increase awareness about strengths and weaknesses
● be able to recognize and capitalize on opportunities, and to defend against threats
● be more effective in the allocation and use of resources.

Irrespective of the quality or format of the actual plans, engaging in the planning process can be valuable. It helps individual managers to establish priorities and address problems; it can bring managers together so that they can share their problems and perspectives. Ideally, the result will be improved communication, co-ordination and commitment. Hence there can be real benefit from planning or thinking about the future. What form should the thinking and planning take? Should it be part of a formalized system making use of strategic planning techniques?

Corporate and functional plans

Corporate and strategic plans concern the number and variety of product markets and service markets in which the organization will compete, together with the development of the necessary resources (people, capacity, finance, research and so on) required to support the competitive strategies. Strategic plans, therefore, relate to the whole organization, cover several years and are generally not highly detailed. They are concerned with future needs and how to obtain and develop the desired businesses, products, services and resources. The actual timescale involved will be affected by the nature of the industry and the number of years ahead that investments must be planned if growth and change are to be brought about.

Functional plans are derived from corporate strategy and strategic plans, and they relate to the implementation of functional strategies. They cover specific areas of the business; there can be plans relating to product development, production control and cash budgeting, for example. Functional plans will usually have shorter time horizons than is the case for strategic plans, and invariably they will incorporate greater detail. However, they will be reviewed and updated, and they may very well become ongoing rolling plans. While strategic plans are used to direct the whole organization, functional plans are used for the short-term management of parts of the organization. It is easy to imagine how this would apply to Federal Express.

Competitive strategies and functional strategies and plans are essential if products and services are to be managed effectively, but they should be flexible and capable of being changed if managers responsible for their implementation feel it necessary.

Ohmae (1982) emphasizes that individual products must be seen as part of wider systems or product groups/business units, and that although short-term plans must be drawn up for the effective management of individual products, it is important to ensure that thinking about the future is done at the appropriate level. As an example, a particular brand or type of shampoo targeted at a specific market segment would constitute a product market. The company's range of shampoos should be produced and marketed in a co-ordinated way, and consequently they might constitute a strategic planning unit. The relevant strategic business unit might incorporate all of the company's cosmetics products and there should be a competitive strategy to ensure that the various products are co-ordinated and support each other. In terms of strategic thinking, Ohmae suggests that it is more important to consider listening devices as a whole than radios specifically, and that this type of thinking resulted in the Sony Walkman and similar products. In the same way, the Japanese realized a new opportunity for black and white television receivers in the form of small portable sets, when other manufacturers had switched all of their attention to the development of colour sets. If the level of thinking is appropriate, resources are likely to be allocated more effectively.

Alternative approaches to planning

Taylor and Hussey (1982) feature seven different approaches to planning which are detailed briefly below.

- *Informal planning* takes place in someone's head, and the decisions reached may not be written down in any extensive form. It is often practised by managers with real entrepreneurial flair, and it can be highly successful. It is less likely to be effective if used by managers who lack flair and creativity.

- *Extended budgeting* is rarely used as it is only feasible if the environment is stable and predictable. Extended budgeting is primarily financial planning based on the extrapolation of past trends.

- *Top-down planning* relates to decisions taken at the top of the organization and passed down to other managers for implementation. These managers will have had little or no input into the planning process. Major change decisions reached informally may be incorporated here, and then a great deal depends upon the strength and personality of the strategic leader in persuading other managers to accept the changes. At the other extreme, top-down plans may emanate from professional planners using planning techniques extensively and reporting directly to the strategic leader. These are the type of plans that may not be implemented.

- *Strategic analysis/policy options* again uses planning techniques, and involves the creation and analytical evaluation of alternative options. Where future possible scenarios are explored for their implications, and possible courses of action are tested for sensitivity, this form of planning can be valuable for strategic thinking. It is an appropriate use of planning techniques, but it is important to consider the potential impact on people.

- *Bottom-up planning* involves managers throughout the organization, and therefore ensures that people who will be involved in implementing plans are consulted. Specifically, functional and business unit managers are charged with evaluating the future potential for their areas of responsibility and are invited to make a case for future resources. All of the detail is analysed and the future allocation of resources is decided. In an extreme form thick planning manuals will be involved, and the process may be slow and rigid. Necessary changes may be inhibited if managerial freedom to act outside the plan is constrained. A formal system of this nature is likely to involve an annual planning cycle.

- *Behavioural approaches* can take several forms, but essentially the behavioural approach requires that managers spend time discussing the future opportunities and threats and areas in which the organization might develop. The idea is that if managers are encouraged to discuss their problems and objectives for the business freely, and if they are able to reach agreement concerning future priorities and developments, then they will be committed to implementing the changes. However, it is quite likely that not all of the conflicts concerning resource allocation and priorities will be resolved. Clearly, scenario planning can be very useful here.

- The term *strategic review* was coined to take the best features of the other six approaches and blend them together into a systematic and comprehensive planning system. All of these approaches have individual advantages and disadvantages, and they are not mutually exclusive. The approach adopted will depend on the style and preferences of the strategic leader, who must:

- clarify the mission and corporate objectives and establish the extent and nature of changes to the corporate perspective

- approve competitive and functional strategies and plans for each part of the business, however they might be created, and

- establish appropriate control mechanisms, which may or may not involve substantial decentralization.

It has been established that planning may be either informal or formal. Informal planning, as such, cannot be taught; but formal planning systems can. These are the subject of the next sections.

The planning gap

Authors such as Argenti (1980), Hussey (1976), Cohen and Cyert (1973) and Glueck and Jauch (1984) have developed a number of essentially similar models of systematic planning. All of these models use the concept of gap analysis, which is extremely useful for strategic thinking purposes and which is explained in Critical reflection 8.1.

The concept of the **planning gap** can be summarized as 'project the known – develop the new' (see Garvin and Levesque, 2006) and it addresses the following questions:

- Where do we want to go?
- Where can we go realistically?

When considering where and how an organization might develop in the future, both the desired and realistic objectives are essential considerations. Desired objectives relate to where the strategic leader and other decision-makers would like to take the organization if it is possible to do so. Realistic objectives incorporate the influence of the various stakeholders in the business, and their expectations; the existence of suitable opportunities; and the availability of the necessary resources. The issue of the risk involved in the alternative courses of action that might be considered is crucial. The discussion of the planning gap in Critical reflection 8.1 draws attention to the increasing risk typically associated with certain strategic alternatives, in particular diversification, which is often implemented through acquisition. Failure rates with diversification are high, as will be discussed in Chapter 13. However, diversification may be the only feasible route to the achievement of high growth targets or the maintenance of present rates of growth in profits and sales revenues. The strategic leader, perhaps under significant pressure from City investors, shareholders and analysts who expect growth rates to be at least maintained, may be forced to pursue high-risk strategies.

Table 8.2 looks at how two well-known organizations, specifically Virgin and Sony, have pursued several different strategies over a period of years.

While undue risk should be avoided wherever possible, it is always important to accept a certain level of risk and set stretching targets for managers and businesses.

Table 8.2 Applications of the simple growth vector

	Virgin	Sony
Market penetration	Publicity, self-publicity and exploitation of Virgin name, e.g. Branson's balloon challenges	Sony as a brand
Market development	Before divesting the businesses: opening Virgin Megastores around the world and a music business in the US	The Sony Walkman and associated derivatives: existing products repackaged
Product development	Music retailing led to music production and publishing and later music videos	Tape recorders to videos; televisions; compact discs (some limited diversification involved)
Related diversification	Films, computer games	Computers, Sony Playstation (related technologies e.g. PDAs)
Unrelated diversification	Virgin Atlantic Airways, Virgin Holidays, Virgin Cola, Virgin Financial Services	CBS Records, Columbia Pictures (vertical integration that some would argue was related diversification for Sony. The fact it happened facilitated the development of PlayStation.

Critical reflection 8.1

The Planning Gap

The planning gap should be seen as an idea which can be adapted to suit particular circumstances, although gap analysis could be regarded as a planning technique.

An example of the planning gap is illustrated in Figure 8.7. The horizontal axis represents the planning time horizon, stretching forward from the present day; either sales volume or revenue, or profits, could be used on the vertical axis as a measure of anticipated performance. The lowest solid line on the graph indicates expected sales or profits if the organization continues with present corporate, competitive and functional strategies; it does not have to slope downwards. The top dashed line represents ideal objectives, which imply growth and which may or may not ultimately be realized. The difference between these two lines is the gap. The gap is the difference between the results that the organization can expect to achieve from present strategies continued forward and the results that the strategic leader would like to attain.

The example illustrated in Figure 8.7 shows the gap filled in by a series of alternative courses of strategic action ordered in an ascending hierarchy of risk. Risk is constituted by the extent to which future products and markets are related to existing ones; and this idea of increased risk and strategic alternatives is developed further in Figures 8.8 and 8.9.

The lowest risk alternative is to seek to manage present products and services more effectively, aiming to sell more of them and to reduce their costs in order to generate increased sales and profits. This is termed market penetration in the simple growth vector developed by H Igor Ansoff and illustrated in Figure 8.8. It can be extended to strategies of market and product development, which imply, respectively:

● new customers or even new market segments for existing products, which might be modified in some way to provide increased differentiation; and
● new products, ideally using related technology and skills, for sale to existing markets.

(In this context 'new' implies new to the firm rather than something that is necessarily completely new and innovative, although it could well be this.) Figure 8.5 distinguishes between market and product development strategies that are already under way and those that have yet to be started.

Figure 8.7   An example of the planning gap

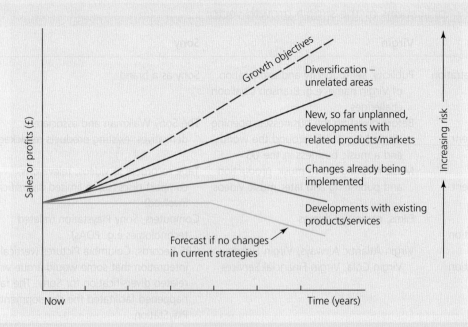

Figure 8.8   Ansoff's growth vector

ANSOFF, HI (1987) CORPORATE STRATEGY, REVISED EDN, PENGUIN

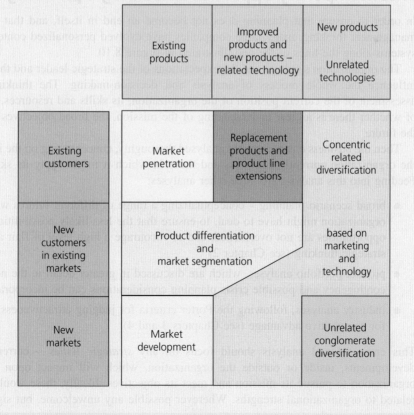

Figure 8.9   An extended growth vector

The highest risk alternative is diversification because this involves both new products and new markets. Figure 8.9 develops these simple themes further and distinguishes between the following:

- replacement products and product line extensions based on existing technologies and skills, which represent improved products for existing customers
- new products based on new or unrelated technologies and skills, which constitute concentric diversification (these may be sold to either existing or new customers)
- completely new and unrelated products for sale to new customers. This is known as conglomerate diversification and is regarded as a high-risk strategic alternative.

Using the planning gap

Thinking about the extent of the initial gap between present strategies and ideal objectives enables managers to consider how much change and how much risk would be involved in closing the gap and achieving the target objectives. Some of the strategies considered might be neither feasible nor desirable, and consequently the gap might be too wide to close. Similarly, the degree of risk, especially if a number of changes is involved, might be greater than the strategic leader is willing to accept. In these cases it will be necessary to revise the desired objectives downwards so that they finally represent realistic targets which should be achieved by strategic changes that are acceptable and achievable.

This type of thinking is related to specific objectives concerning growth and profitability. It does not follow, as was discussed in Chapter 6, that either growth or profit maximization will be the major priority of the organization, or that the personal objectives of individual managers will not be an issue.

A contemporary approach to strategic planning

In order to ensure that planning does not become an end in itself, and that planners facilitate management thinking, many large companies have evolved personalized contemporary planning systems along the lines of the one illustrated in Figure 8.10.

The organization's culture and the expectations of the strategic leader and the key stakeholders influence the whole process of analysis and decision-making. The thinking starts with an assessment of the current position of the organization, its skills and resources, and an evaluation of whether there is a clear understanding of the mission, the broad objectives and directions for the future.

Then the business environment is analysed thoroughly, concentrating on the industries in which the organization currently competes and those in which it might apply its skills and resources. Feeding into this analysis are three other analyses:

- broad scenario planning – conceptualizing a range of different futures with which the organization might have to deal, to ensure that the less likely possibilities, threats and opportunities are not overlooked, and to encourage a high level of flair and creativity in strategic thinking (see Chapter 2)
- product portfolio analyses, which are discussed in greater detail in the next section; contingency and possible crisis planning considerations can be incorporated in this
- industry analyses, following the Porter criteria for judging attractiveness and opportunities for competitive advantage (see Chapters 3 and 4).

This environmental analysis should focus on any *strategic issues* – current or forthcoming developments, inside or outside the organization, which will impact upon the ability of the organization to pursue its mission and meet its objectives. Ideally, these would be opportunities related to organizational strengths. Wherever possible any unwelcome, but significant, potential

Figure 8.10   A contemporary approach to strategic planning

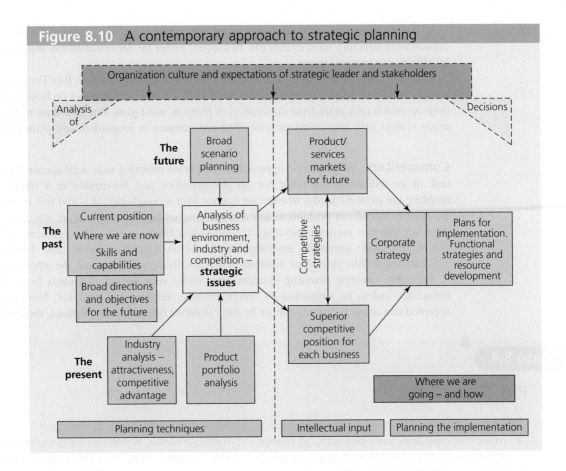

threats should be turned into competitive opportunities. The band across the bottom of Figure 8.8 shows how this contemporary approach blends planning techniques with an intellectual input and later action plans for implementing strategic choices.

It will be seen that the identification of strategic issues is the transition point from analysis to decisions regarding future strategy: it is where techniques give way to more intuition and intellectual inputs before implementation issues are explored.

From these analyses competitive strategy decisions must be reached concerning:

- the reinforcement or establishment of a superior competitive position, or competitive advantage, for each business within the existing portfolio of products and services

- product markets and service markets for future development, and the appropriate functional strategies for establishing a superior competitive position.

Amalgamated, these functional and competitive strategies constitute the corporate strategy for the future, which in turn needs to be broken down into resource development plans and any decisions relating to changes in the structure of the organization – i.e. decisions that reflect where the organization is going and how the inherent changes are to be managed.

Simply, planning techniques and analyses are used to clarify the key strategic issues. Discerning the issues and deciding what should be done to address them requires creativity (the search for something different) and hence a more intellectual input. Once broad strategic directions are clarified, detailed implementation planning will follow. Like the strategies, these detailed implementation plans should not be seen as inflexible.

It is important that new strategic issues are spotted and dealt with continuously, and the organization structure must enable this to happen, either by decentralization and empowerment or by effective communications.

Case 8.4 looks at the issues that international mining conglomerate Rio Tinto has had to deal with in 2008 and 2009. An organization such as Rio Tinto, which relies on huge investments and projects which take years from conception to fruition, must plan. But how does it stay flexible and ready to deal with issues and surprises that can threaten to jeopardize any plans it has?

Commentary A systematic approach to corporate planning may well succeed in the essential task of co-ordinating the plans for all the divisions and businesses in a large organization, enabling the strategic leader to exercise control over a conglomerate – and this is good. However, the system should not prohibit vision and learning within the corporation, which is important as these are the two modes of strategy creation most likely to take the organization forward in a competitive and uncertain environment. Unfortunately, the vision and learning may be concentrated within individual divisions when ideally, it will permeate the whole organization.

Typically, strategic planning systems grew to be very formal. All ideas from the individual businesses had to be supported by comprehensive, documented analyses. Now it is frequently accepted that many proposals cannot be fully justified quantitatively; instead, the assumptions and

Case 8.4

Rio Tinto

AuS

This case illustrates the speed at which the strategic issues that companies must deal with can change.

Rio Tinto is one of the world's leading mining groups and the second largest producer of iron ore. It is also involved in coal mining as well as uranium, copper and gold. It owns Alcan, the Canadian aluminium producer, which it bought in 2007. Its main base is in Australia, but it has other operations as far afield as Indonesia and Chile. A Chinese metals (mainly aluminium) group, the Chinese state-owned Chinalco, has for a while owned a 9 per cent stake.

In early 2008 Rio Tinto was looking for partnerships with Chinese steel and construction businesses to help with the development with a new iron ore mine in Guinea, Africa. With anticipated production of around 170 million tonnes every year this could become the third largest iron ore mine in the world. The problem is that it is in a remote location some 750 kms. from the sea. There is no infrastructure of consequence and a new railway will have to be constructed. This implies an alliance between a mining company and its customers further down the supply chain.

The issue is a complex one. Guinea is not Australia, but the challenge of mining development is similar. BHP Billiton, a rival Australian mining corporation with interests in iron ore and aluminium, built and operates a private railway line in Western Australia to move

material from its mines to the coast. A smaller rival, Fortesque Metals, wanted access to move its ore – which BHP refused – but, in 2008, Fortesque's claim was supported by the courts. BHP had argued that the track was an integral part of its production system and never meant to be a freely available resource for others to access, and that it was running 'close to capacity'. But this argument was not accepted.

At roughly the same time in early 2008 two global businesses were considering bidding to buy Rio Tinto. One represented vertical integration, the other horizontal integration. Whilst the price – at around $70 billion – would be an issue in any decision by Rio Tinto's shareholders, which would make the better strategic sense? BHP was one bidder; the other was Lakshmi Mittal, an Indian steelmaker with interests in Europe and thus an iron ore customer. The steel industry generally was concerned with the implications of a possible merger between BHP and Rio Tinto. This may just have been a defensive spoiler bid. But demand for steel fell in 2008 as car production and other key industries declined. Later in the year, when everyone's share prices fell, interest in the acquisition disappeared. Rio Tinto had determinedly opposed both bids.

By October 2008 the demand for iron ore and other natural resources had changed. China was not exempt from the economic slowdown and demand for steel and hence iron ore was falling. Once this downward trend in demand took hold, commodity prices also started to fall from a record high level in the summer of 2008 – simply compounding the problem for the mining businesses. Rio Tinto found it necessary to revise all its capital investment and expansion plans. That said, Rio Tinto was still trading profitably – but for how long? Rio Tinto's problem was relatively high debt of nearly $40 billion; it needs a strong cash flow to fund the interest payments. As demand fell it was able to save money by laying people off – in December the loss of 14,000 jobs was announced; and quite quickly it was clear that offers for asset sales would be considered. BHP, of course, could well be a bidder for selected interests.

Companies can always look to try and raise money through rights issues of new equity. Rio Tinto is dual listed in London and Sydney. Was this a real possibility in the credit crunch and recession – on the promise of guaranteed future growth once demand for minerals takes off again and commodity prices increase, as they inevitably will? In February 2009 Chinalco announced plans to double its stake from 9 per cent to 18 per cent by investing $19.5 billion. This happened just three days after one senior non-executive director resigned over disagreements about how to deal with the debt burden.

However many investors were opposed to Chinalco taking a larger stake and actively campaigned against it.

The Australian government also expressed concern. By June the deal looked unlikely to happen. Without this Rio Tinto would probably need a rights issue – in a depressed market. And in the meantime Rio Tinto and BHP Billiton had been discussing the possibilities for a joint venture of their iron ore interests in Western Australia. Also in 2009 Rio Tinto and its Chinese customers had been struggling to reach an agreement over future iron ore prices.

Questions

1 What does this case teach us about long term strategic intent and the need to respond to shorter term opportunities and threats?
2 Is it possible to run a business such as Rio Tinto without long term investment planning?
3 Would you expect planning to be the dominant mode of strategy creation?

© TIM WIMBORNE/REUTERS/CORBIS

justifications will be probed and challenged by divisional boards. Care must also be taken to ensure that the evaluation and resource allocation processes do not create too high a level of internal competition. Divisions and businesses should have to justify their intentions and proposals, and it is inevitable they will be competing for scarce resources. Nevertheless, the real enemy is external competitors, not other parts of the organization, and this must never be forgotten.

In addition, some organizations still tend to use the performance targets as the primary means of control, which sometimes results in short-term thinking. Once a business drops below its target it is put under considerable pressure to reduce costs, and this may restrict its ability to be creative and innovative. Many strategic planning systems could be improved if the head office corporate planners had more contact and involvement with the businesses; they sometimes tend to be remote and detached.

In summary, formalized planning systems may be imperfect, but a system of some form remains essential for control and co-ordination. Alone it cannot enable the company to deal with competitive uncertainties and pressures – vision and learning are essential, but planning must not be abandoned.

This section has considered the important role and contribution of strategic planning in large, and possibly diverse, organizations. The next section considers strategic planning in small businesses. Strategy in action 8.1 examines a number of relevant planning issues in local government.

Strategy in action 8.1

Strategy and Local Government

A typical UK local authority is likely to perceive the aim of the activities it carries out as the provision of more, and ideally better, services for the local community. These services fall into three broad categories: front line (housing, education and leisure), regulatory (environmental health, planning and building control), and promotional (economic development and tourism).

How does local government 'work' strategically? Strategic decisions at the top policy level demand an input from two groups of people: the elected councillors who exert a controlling influence, and the salaried managers. The councillors may be politically very experienced and, working on behalf of their constituents, they should be in a position to reflect local needs. The specialist expertise is more likely to come from the salaried staff, although there are some very well qualified and expert councillors. There are, therefore, two strategic leaders – the Leader of the Council and the Chief Executive – who ideally will be able to work together harmoniously and synergistically. On occasions there will be clear evidence of visionary leadership. Some leaders, either individually or in partnership, will transform the character and infrastructure of a town or city. At the other extreme, other leaders really do little more than manage budgets and carry through central government initiatives.

There is an obvious role for strategic planning as local authorities have to work within guidelines and budget restraints set by central government. They have to decide upon how, at least, to maintain local services, improve efficiencies and implement any central government requirements.

Councillors will form into policy-making groups, with the head of each group holding a place in the Cabinet – which is akin to the Cabinet in Central Government. The salaried employees will operate with some degree of delegated authority in discrete service areas. Each service will have policy guidelines, output targets and a budget. Normally they will be free to develop and adapt strategies and programmes as long as they operate within their budget and achieve their outputs.

Many councils will want to increase spending wherever possible, as more or better services are popular with the electorate. In simple terms, spending minus income (including grants from central government) equals the sum to be raised from householders and businesses, and generally more spending is likely to lead to higher local taxes. The freedom to increase these is constrained by central government. Borrowing is used primarily to fund new capital programmes and for managing the cash flow on a temporary basis. It is, for example, still being suggested that in the future many more local councils will borrow money to build new roads, or improve existing ones, and repay the money with congestion charges on motorists, at least in part following the lead of London. Since the residents of Manchester were allowed a vote on this possibility in early 2009 – and rejected it even though it would open the door to external public investment – the future remains uncertain. Some councils establish partnerships with specific developers. An independent company might, for example, develop a new shopping centre in partnership with a local authority. Together they will put up or raise substantial sums of development capital which will be repaid later through rents and business rates.

It is very difficult to measure quantitatively the benefits that accrue from certain services, such as parks and gardens for public recreation. Information from the Audit Commission enables one authority to compare its costs and spending in total, and per head of the population, for individual services with those incurred by similar authorities in the UK. Where this is utilized it is basically a measure of efficiency, rather than an assessment of the overall effectiveness of the service provision, as shown in Chapter 7.

Until the 1980s it was usual for a local authority to carry out most of its activities in-house. External contractors were used for some building and engineering work, and in other instances where very specialized skills were required. However, the first Thatcher government required that councils put out to tender all major new build projects, together with significant projects in housing and highways maintenance. Later in the 1980s school catering, refuse collection, street cleaning and most white-collar services were also subject to compulsory competitive tendering (CCT). Where services were put out for tender an authority continued to determine the specific level of service to be provided, and then sought quotations for this provision. Tendering organizations neither suggested nor influenced the actual level of service. This power remained firmly with the local authority. As more and more services were compulsorily put out to tender, local authorities essentially became purchasers of services on behalf of the local community.

The Blair led Labour government, elected in 1997, was determined to abolish CCT and replace it with 'Best Value'. CCT was abandoned in 2000. Best Value requires a local authority to review each of its services over five-year periods, assessing whether it should be provided in-house, via social enterprises and the voluntary sector or by private-sector contractors. There are four key themes:

- challenge
- consult (stakeholders)
- compare (by benchmarking external and other local authority providers)
- compete (with the best providers that can be identified).

In recent years the contribution of social enterprises and the voluntary sector in providing services that local (and national) government cannot or will not provide has grown – without this contribution many individuals and communities would be far worse off.

Some councils have spun-out services they once ran into private ownership in the form of management buy-outs. Building maintenance for council houses would be a typical example. The new business must tender for the work periodically, but it is free to seek other work and contracts as well. The assumption is a blend of public service and entrepreneurship.

Local councils are constrained by both central government financial rules and by legislative requirements. Since the Blair Labour government came to power in 1997 it has tightened up on the rules that

govern residential care homes for the elderly. Room sizes and facilities must meet certain minimum standards. As a result many have closed, although some have been rebuilt, making homes with fewer but better rooms. In some communities it is significant that it is the public sector homes, rather than those run by the private sector, that have closed down.

© CHESTERT/DREAMSTIME.COM

Strategic planning and small businesses

Many small companies stay focused and do not diversify or acquire another business. Their corporate perspective stays the same, but they still need to create some form of competitive advantage and develop and integrate functional plans. In this respect, small business planning is similar to that for an individual business inside a conglomerate. Unfortunately, many small owner–managers misguidedly believe that:

- strategic planning is too expensive and only belongs in large organizations
- formalized processes, requiring expert planners, are essential
- the benefits are too long term and there are no immediate pay-offs.

As a result they adopt a more seat-of-the-pants reactive approach. Both vision and flexibility are important features of most successful small businesses, but these can be built on to provide greater strength and stability. Simply, and reinforcing points made earlier in the chapter, small companies can benefit in the same way as large ones from discerning the important *strategic issues* and from involving managers from the various functions in deciding how they might best be tackled.

Small companies should involve all relevant managers in discussions about priorities, opportunities, problems and preferences. They should look ahead and not just consider immediate problems and crises. Objective information and analyses (albeit limited in scope) are required to underpin the process, which must be actively and visibly supported by the owner–manager or strategic leader, who, in turn, must be willing to accept ideas from other managers. Adequate time must also be found, and sound financial systems should be in place to support the implementation of new strategies and plans.

It is, of course, important to remember that small companies which needed to raise finance from the banking system or elsewhere would have had to draw up a business plan to support their request. All too often these plans are then put in a drawer and largely forgotten rather than being used as a framework for budgeting and monitoring performance. Some small company managers never really develop a discipline of planning.

8.8 Strategic planning issues

Who should plan?

Among the various authors on corporate planning who have been referred to earlier in this chapter, there is a consensus of opinion that strategic planning should not be undertaken by the chief executive alone, planning specialists divorced from operating managers, marketing executives or finance departments. An individual or specialist department may be biased and fail to produce a balanced plan. Instead, it is important to involve, in some way, all managers who will be affected by the plan, and who will be charged with implementing it. However, all of these managers together cannot constitute an effective working team, and therefore a small team representing the whole organization should be constituted, and other managers consulted. This will require a schedule for the planning activities and a formalized system for carrying out the tasks. As discussed above, it is important that planning systems do not inhibit ongoing strategic thinking by managers throughout the organization. Threats must still be spotted early and potential opportunities must not be lost.

Planning traps Ringbakk (1971) and Steiner (1972) have documented several reasons why formal planning might fail and have discussed the potential traps to avoid. Among their conclusions are the following:

- Planning should not be left exclusively to planners who might see their job as being the production of a plan and who might also concentrate on procedures and detail at the expense of wide strategic thinking.
- Planning should be seen as a support activity in strategic decision-making and not a once-a-year ritual.
- There must be a commitment and an allocation of time from the strategic leader. Without this managers lower down the organization might not feel that planning matters within the firm.
- Planning is not likely to prove effective unless the broad directional objectives for the firm are agreed and communicated widely.
- Implementers must be involved, both in drawing up the plan (or essential information might be missed) and afterwards. The plan should be communicated throughout the organization, and efforts should be made to ensure that managers appreciate what is expected of them.

- Targets, once established, should be used as a measure of performance and variances should be analysed properly. However, there can be a danger in over-concentrating on targets and financial data at the expense of more creative strategic thinking.

- The organizational climate must be appropriate for the planning system adopted, and consequently structural and cultural issues have an important role to play.

- Inflexibility in drawing up and using the plan can be a trap. Inflexibility in drawing up the plan might be reflected in tunnel vision, a lack of flair and creativity, and in assuming that past trends can be extrapolated forwards.

- If planning is seen as an exercise rather than a support to strategy creation, it is quite possible that the plan will be ignored and not implemented.

The impact of planning on managers

Unless the above traps are avoided and the human aspects of planning are considered, the planning activity is unlikely to prove effective. Abell and Hammond (1979) and Mills (1985) highlight the following important people considerations:

- Ensure the support of senior executives.

- Ensure that every manager who is involved understands what is expected of them and that any required training in planning techniques is provided.

- Use specialist planners carefully.

- Keep planning simple, and ensure that techniques never become a doctrine.

- Particularly where detailed planning is involved, ensure that the time horizon is appropriate. It is harder to forecast and plan detail the further into the future one looks.

- Never plan for the sake of planning.

- Link managerial rewards and sanctions to any targets for achievement which are established.

- Allow managers of business units and functions some freedom to develop their own planning systems rather than impose rigid ones, especially if they produce the desired results.

In summary, planning activities can take a number of forms, and organizations should seek to develop systems that provide the results they want. Ideally, these should encapsulate both strategic thinking and the establishment of realistic objectives and expectations and the strategies to achieve them. Planning techniques can be used supportively, and their potential contribution is evaluated in the next section. Systematic corporate planning, though, should not be seen as the only way in which strategic changes are formulated.

The role of planning and planners

In the light of the comments above on strategy formulation, this section concludes by considering further the role of planning and planners. Planning and strategy creation are different in the sense that planners may or may not be strategists but strategists might be found anywhere in the organization. Mintzberg (1989) suggests that planning activities are likely to involve a series of different and very useful analyses, but it does not follow that these must be synthesized into a systematic planning system. Planners can make a valuable contribution to the organization and to strategic thinking by:

- programming strategies into finite detail to enable effective implementation (this will involve budgeting and ensuring that strategies are communicated properly, plus the establishment of monitoring and control processes)

- formalizing ongoing strategic awareness – carrying out SWOT analyses and establishing what strategic changes are emerging at any time
- using scenarios and planning techniques to stimulate and encourage thinking
- searching for new competitive opportunities and strategic alternatives, and scrutinizing and evaluating them.

In other words, all of the activities incorporated in the planning systems discussed earlier in the chapter are seen to be making an important contribution, but they need not be component parts of a systematic model. Rather, they are contributors towards strategic thinking, awareness and insight.

Johnson (1992) further points out that on occasions plans are documented in detail only because particular stakeholders, say institutional shareholders or bankers, expect to see them as justification for proposals. There is never any real intention that they should be implemented in full.

Figure 8.11 draws together a number of these themes and illustrates the various contributions that planning and planners can make. In conjunction with this, the next section considers the relative value and contribution of selected planning techniques.

The key macro and micro variables of our business are so dynamic that poker becomes more predictable than planning and reactivity more profitable than rumination.

DR JOHN WHITE, EX-MANAGING DIRECTOR, BBA, WHOSE CUSTOMERS WERE INVOLVED IN THE MOTOR VEHICLE INDUSTRY

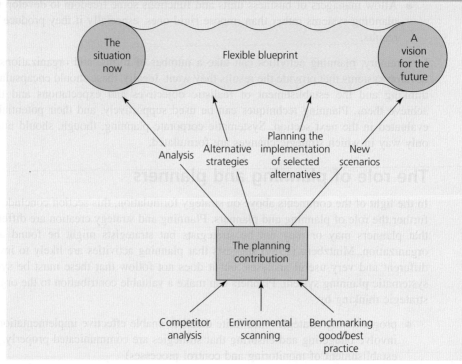

Figure 8.11 The planning contribution
Systematic planning (in isolation) will not create a vision – but you can plan your own way towards a vision. Ideas generated through planning may well change the vision

I have a saying: 'Every plan is an opportunity lost' ... because I feel that if you try to plan the way your business will go, down to the last detail, you are no longer able to seize any opportunity that may arise unexpectedly.

DEBBIE MOORE, FOUNDER CHAIRMAN, PINEAPPLE (DANCE STUDIOS) LTD

8.9   Strategic planning techniques

It has already been explained that different strategists and authors of strategy texts adopt different stances on the significance of vision, culture and strategic planning techniques in effective strategic planning. In this book the view is held that the role of the strategic leader, styles of corporate decision-making and organization culture are key driving forces in strategy creation and implementation. However, strategic planning techniques, which rely heavily on the collection and analysis of quantitative data, do have an important contribution to make. They help to increase awareness, and thereby reduce the risk involved in certain decisions. They can indicate the incidence of potential threats and limitations which might reduce the future value and contribution of individual products and services. They can help in establishing priorities in large complex multiproduct multinational organizations. They can provide appropriate frameworks for evaluating the relative importance of very different businesses in a portfolio.

However, their value is dependent on the validity and reliability of the information fed into them. Where comparisons with competitors are involved, the data for other companies may well involve 'guesstimation'.

Judgement is required for assessing the significance of events and competitor strategies; vision is essential in discontinuous change management.

In the author's opinion strategic planning techniques should be used to help and facilitate decision-makers. They should not be used to make decisions without any necessary qualifications to the data and assumptions.

Portfolio analysis   The Boston Consulting Group growth-share matrix (Strategy in action 8.2) can be very useful for positioning products in relation to their stage in the product life cycle as long as one is both careful and honest in the use of data. In part its value lies in its simplicity – but it must be seen for what it is. It can provide insight into the likely cash needs and the potential for earnings generation. However, while a particular matrix position indicates potential needs and prospects, this should not be seen as prescriptive for future strategy. In certain respects, all competitive positions are unique, and it is very important to consider the actual industry involved and the nature and behaviour of competitors. Business unit and product managers are likely to be able to do this with greater insight than specialist planners as they are in a better position to appreciate the peculiarities of the market.

The product portfolio suggests the following strategies for products or business units falling into certain categories:

- cash cow – milk and redeploy the cash flow
- dog – liquidate or divest and redeploy the freed resources or proceeds
- star – strengthen competitive position in growth industry
- question – invest as appropriate to secure and improve competitive position.

Strategy in action 8.2

The Boston Consulting Group (BCG) Growth-share Matrix

Basic premises

Bruce Henderson (1970) of BCG has suggested first that the margins earned by a product, and the cash generated by it, are a function of market share. The higher the market share, relative to competitors, the greater the earnings potential; high margins and market share are correlated. A second premise is that sales and revenue growth requires investment. Sales of a product will only increase if there is appropriate expenditure on advertising, distribution and development; and the rate of market growth determines the required investment. Third, high market share must be earned or bought, which requires additional investment. Finally, no business can grow indefinitely. As a result, products will at times not be profitable because the amount of money being spent to develop them exceeds their earnings potential; at other times, and particularly where the company has a high relative market share, earnings exceed expenditure and products are profitable.

Profitability is therefore affected by market growth, market share, and the stage in the product life cycle. A company with a number of products might expect to have some that are profitable and some that are not. In general, mature products, where growth has slowed down and the required investment has decreased, are the most profitable, and the profits they earn should

not be reinvested in them but used instead to finance growth products that offer future earnings potential.

The matrix

The matrix is illustrated in Figure 8.12. Chart (a) shows the composition of the axes and the names given to products or business units which fall in each of the four quadrants; chart (b) features 15 products or business units in a hypothetical company portfolio. The sterling-volume size of each product or business is proportional to the areas of the circles, and the positioning of each one is determined by its market growth rate and relative market share.

The market growth rate on the vertical axis is the annual growth rate of the market in which the company competes, and really any range starting with zero could be used. The problem is where to draw the horizontal dividing line which separates high-growth from low-growth markets.

The relative market share on the horizontal axis indicates market share in relation to the largest competitor in the market. A relative market share of 0.25 would indicate a market share one-quarter of that of the market leader; a figure of 2.5 would represent a market leader with a market share that is 2.5 times as big as that of the nearest rival. The vertical dividing line is

Figure 8.12   The Boston Consulting Group growth-share matrix

normally 1.0, so that market leadership is found to the left-hand side of the divider. It is important to consider market segmentation when deciding upon the market share figure to use, rather than using the share of the total market.

The growth-share matrix is thus divided into four cells or quadrants, each representing a particular type of business.

- Question marks are products or businesses which compete in high-growth markets but where market share is relatively low. A new product launched into a high-growth market and with an existing market leader would normally constitute a question mark. High expenditure is required to develop and launch the product, and consequently it is unlikely to be profitable and may instead require subsidy from more profitable products. Once the product is established, further investment will be required if the company attempts to claim market leadership.
- Successful question marks become stars, market leaders in growth markets. However, investment is still required to maintain the rate of growth and to defend the leadership position. Stars are marginally profitable only, but as they reach a more mature market position as growth slows down they will become increasingly profitable.
- Cash cows are therefore mature products which are well-established market leaders. As market growth slows down there is less need for high investment, and hence they are the most profitable products in the portfolio. This is boosted by any economies of scale resulting from the position of market leadership. Cash cows are used to fund the businesses in the other three quadrants.
- Dogs describe businesses that have low market shares in slower growth markets. They may well be previous cash cows, which still enjoy some loyal market support although they have been replaced as market leader by a newer rival. They should be marginally profitable, and should be withdrawn when they become loss makers, if not before. The opportunity cost of the resources that they tie up is an important issue in this decision.

BOSTON CONSULTING GROUP **http://www.bcg.com**

Given that a dog represents a product or service in a relatively low-growth industry sector, and one which does not enjoy market segment leadership, it follows that many companies will have a number of dogs in their portfolios. **Liquidation** or divestment will not always be justified. Products which have a strong market position, even though they are not the market leader, and which have a distinctive competitive advantage can have a healthy cash flow and profitability. Such products are sometimes referred to as cash dogs. Divestment is most appropriate when the market position is weak and when there is no real opportunity to create sustainable competitive advantage, as long as a buyer can be found. Turnaround strategies for products which are performing very poorly are examined further in Chapter 14.

According to Hamermesch (1986) many businesses that are classified as cash cows should be managed for innovation and growth, especially if the industry is dynamic or volatile, or can be made so. In other words, strategies that succeed in extending the product life cycle can move it from a state of maturity into further growth. One example quoted is coffee. This market experienced renewed growth when the success of automatic coffee makers increased demand for new varieties of fresh ground coffee. The success of Starbucks (Case 8.5) shows how a single organization or entrepreneur that spots and seizes an opportunity can change an industry and provide an impetus for growth.

When 'milking' products care also has to be taken not to reduce capacity if there is a chance that demand and growth opportunities might return as a result of scarcities or changes in taste. When restrictions on the import of Scotch whisky into Japan were eased in the late 1980s, the product enjoyed star status, even though it was seen as a cash cow in the UK.

Strategic decisions based on portfolio positions may also ignore crucial issues of interdependence and synergy. Business units may be treated as separate independent businesses for the purposes of planning, and this can increase the likelihood of the more qualitative contributions to other business units, and to the organization as a whole, being overlooked when decisions are made about possible liquidation or divestment.

Case 8.5

Starbucks   US

In around 20 years Starbucks grew from a single store on the Seattle waterfront to a chain of over 15,000 stores throughout the world, spawning competitors in the USA and elsewhere. The company has never made any headway in Italy, which many see as the home of decent coffee bars. As part of its drive to expand internationally, Starbucks bought its smaller UK rival, The Seattle Coffee Company, in 1998. Starbucks succeeded because it found the right way to blend sales of top-grade fresh coffee beans with sales of cups of coffee to drink.

Coffee bars have existed for a very long time, but rarely have they featured the strong and distinctive aroma found in stores that sell fresh coffee. The individual drinks in Starbucks are relatively expensive, but they are individualized and made to order. There is a wide range of piping-hot and ice-cold variants to choose from. Although coffee to drink is very much the leading product, fresh coffee beans and a range of related products, such as cakes, biscuits, mugs, coffee makers and special Starbucks music CDs are also on offer. Customers include shoppers and working people from local stores and offices at lunchtime and teatime on their way home – people who take time to relax and converse over their coffee, as well as people who pop out from work to their nearest outlet when they have a short break because the coffee is perceived to be superior to the instant that they might otherwise have to drink. Outlets can also be found at airport terminals and in those bookstores where people go to browse and relax. Essentially, Starbucks 'sells an emotional experience' and not just a commodity product. It thus adds value.

The success is down to Howard Schulz, the son of a blue-collar worker in Brooklyn. Schulz became a salesman, and when he was working for a houseware products company he visited Seattle and was introduced to the Starbucks Coffee Company, a business that sold imported coffee beans. He joined the business in 1982 with the title of Marketing Director. Enthused by espresso bars on a business trip to Italy, and convinced that a similar concept could be developed for the USA, he attempted to sell the idea to his bosses. The family declined to go along with him and he left to start up on his own. He managed to raise enough money to open one outlet and within two years he was in a position to buy out Starbucks.

Schulz claims that his mission has always been to 'educate consumers everywhere about fine coffee'. Customers who visit Starbucks must feel relaxed and enjoy 'a sense of wonder and romance in the midst of their harried lives'. People will pay 'arguably outrageous prices' for their coffee as long as it is seen as an indulgence. If this is to be achieved, staff attitudes and behaviours are critical. Service, therefore, is everything. Schulz has created Starbucks as 'living proof that a company can lead with its heart and nurture its soul and still make money'. Employees are seen as partners. Including part-timers, they all enjoy free health insurance, stock options (known as bean stock) training programmes and wages above the industry average. Although many are young and fit, students who will not stay long enough to earn stock options and who will not need health care, they feel valued and consequently deliver the desired service. They matter. In addition, all unsold beans over eight days old are given away free to local food banks. Nevertheless, the company has also been criticized for exploiting cheap labour in coffee-growing countries.

In 2007 Starbucks was opening three new outlets every day, roughly 1000 in the year – the same number as in 2006. In 2008 this reduced to 650 and the target for 2009 was 200. In 2008 some 600 poorly performing outlets were closed. The number of American outlets had grown to over 10,000, of which around 6600 are self-standing stores and the remaining 4000 concessions in bookstores and other outlets.

Recent developments include selling bags of Starbucks coffee beans in supermarkets – the beans had been

© RYNO 67/STOCK.XCHNG

available for purchase in Starbucks' own stores for several years – and entering China. Fruit smoothies were introduced, reflecting the growing popularity of these drinks. In doing this Starbucks replicated McDonald's, Dunkin' Donuts, Taco Bell and Jack in the Box. Also in 2008, having failed to truly penetrate the market, Starbucks closed 61 of its 84 outlets in Australia. Interestingly there are some excellent Italian-owned coffee bars in Australia.

Questions

1 How would you summarize the opportunity that Starbucks has identified and exploited?
2 How has Starbucks developed and changed its business model as new competitors have entered the attractive market?

STARBUCKS **http://www.starbucks.com**

Directional policy matrices

Directional policy matrices were a development of this simpler approach. They were popular when systematic planning systems were more popular than they are now. The best-known directional policy matrices were developed in the 1970s by Shell and General Electric and the management consultants McKinsey. They are all broadly similar and aim to assist large complex multi-activity enterprises with decisions concerning investment and divestment priorities. In using such a matrix there is an assumption that resources are scarce, and that there never will be, or should be, enough financial and other resources for the implementation of all the project ideas and opportunities which can be conceived in a successful, creative and innovative organization. Choices will always have to be made about investment priorities. The development of an effective corporate strategy therefore involves an evaluation of the potential for existing businesses together with new possibilities in order to determine the priorities.

Typically the matrix would be constructed within two axes: the horizontal axis representing industry attractiveness, or the prospects for profitable operation in the sector concerned; the vertical axis indicating the company's existing competitive position in relation to other companies in the industry. It will be appreciated that Michael Porter's work links closely to this (Chapters 2 and 4). Products and potential new products can both be evaluated initially along the vertical axis by considering their likely prospects for establishing competitive advantage. The directional policy matrix, like other matrices, is only a technique which assists in determining the industry and product sectors that are most worthy of additional investment capital. Issues of synergy and overall strategic fit require further managerial judgement before final decisions are reached.

Case 8.6 shows how Unilever has utilized portfolio management to focus attention on selected brands with high growth potential.

SPACE (strategic position and action evaluation)

Rowe *et al.* (1989) have developed a model based on four important variables:

- the relative stability/turbulence of the environment
- industry attractiveness
- the extent of any competitive advantage
- the company's financial strengths – incorporating profitability, liquidity and current exposure to risk.

Scores are awarded for each factor, and then put into a diagram (see Box 8.1 on page 387). This particular illustration features a financially strong company (or division or product) enjoying competitive advantage in an attractive industry with a relatively stable environment. The appropriate strategy is an aggressive one. The table shows the appropriate strategies for four clearly delineated positions, and judgement has to be applied when the situation is less clear cut.

Case 8.6

Unilever   Int

Unilever is an Anglo-Dutch multinational corporation with manufacturing activities and markets all round the world. In 1999 50 per cent of Unilever's turnover came from food products, 23 per cent from personal care products and the remaining 27 per cent from home care products and dry cleaning services. In 1999 the portfolio was restructured into 13 categories, with different priorities, and these are listed later. The main brands at the time included:

Food products	– Wall's ice cream, sausages, etc.; Birds Eye and Findus frozen foods; Stork, Flora and other margarines and spreads; Brooke Bond (PG Tips) and Lipton teas
Personal care	– Timotei and Sunsilk shampoos Sure deodorants Signal and SR toothpastes Elizabeth Arden, Brut, Karl Lagerfeld, Fabergé and Calvin Klein fragrances
Home care	– Persil, Lux, Fairy and Dove branded products.

Many of the products are subject to constant innovation. Persil washing powder, for example, lost its market leadership position to Procter & Gamble's Ariel brand in the 1980s and Unilever was determined to fight back. Liquids and concentrates had already taken market share from traditional powders when Unilever launched its new Persil Power in 1994 (branded Omo Power in Continental Europe). This new powder product was claimed to wash clothes cleaner than rival brands, which it did. Unfortunately, the special cleaning agent was particles of manganese, and Unilever misjudged the amount. Procter & Gamble was able to demonstrate that some clothes were damaged after multiple washes, and finally the product was abandoned. Other Persil products, specifically for colour and fine wool and silk garments, followed before Unilever pioneered its new – and this time very successful – Persil tablets.

In 1998 Unilever had charged 20 of its younger managers (their average age was 32) to spend six months on a special project designed to identify new opportunities:

- One outcome was a new way of thinking about products and brands. Unilever, they concluded, was in 'the business of selling dreams of healthy eating, clean living and fragrant sex appeal'. People no longer really want soap powder, instead they want clean clothes, ideally without the hassle of using a washing machine! Unilever's future might well be in services rather than products.
- It was decided that Unilever should be seen as a brand marketing group that makes some of its products, as distinct from a manufacturing organization. Did this imply a new business model?
- The divestment of non-core products was completed. Over a period of years, Unilever has divested plantations, shipping lines and speciality chemical companies.
- The number of global manufacturing sites was reduced from 400 to fewer than 300. Of these 150 were designated key sites; the rest are ancillary. Most divestment was in food processing.
- At the same time, the number of suppliers was reduced to provide a more streamlined supply chain.
- The number of global brands was to be reduced from 1600. The top 400 (which, in classic 'Pareto' style, contribute 90 per cent of annual turnover) would receive serious investment to generate a targeted annual growth rate of 6 per cent (although this would later be reduced for particular years) and higher profit margins. Of the remaining 1200, some would be dropped altogether, some harvested and abandoned when they are no longer profitable, and others marketed without promotion of any consequence. This strategy was known as 'The Path to Growth'.

The 13 new product groups were classified as offering either superior growth (number 1 in the table below), steady growth (number 2) or selective growth only (number 3).

Activity	Product category	Growth prospects
Food	Tea	1
	Culinary products	1
	Ice cream	1
	Spreads and cooking products	2
	Frozen foods	3

Activity	Product category	Growth prospects
Personal care		
	Hair care products	1
	Skin care products	1
	Deodorants	1
	Toothpaste and oral products	2
	Fragrances	3
Home care		
	Laundry products (soap powders, etc.)	2
	Household care products	2
	Professional cleaning	3

In 2000 Unilever announced that it would split its businesses into two separate companies: foods and home products. Unilever then started a new round of acquisitions and divestments. First it acquired Slimfast Foods, and followed this with Ben and Jerry's premium ice-cream business. Later it agreed to buy the American Bestfoods, which constituted the biggest global acquisition in the food industry for 12 years. With an annual turnover of $8 billion, Bestfoods was approximately one-fifth the size of Unilever. Bestfoods provided a number of important brands to complement Unilever's portfolio: Knorr soups, Hellmann's mayonnaise, Mazola oils and Bovril stock cubes and concentrate. To ensure that the acquisition was not blocked by the European competition authorities, Unilever agreed to seek a buyer for its Batchelor's and Oxo branded products. With these acquisitions Unilever became the world's second largest food business, second only to Nestlé. At the same time as acquiring new food brands, Unilever divested its main bakery business for £440 million. As Bestfoods also owned bakeries (producing, for example, Entemann's cakes) it was assumed these might later be sold as well. It also sold the Elizabeth Arden cosmetics business. Unilever was now far more exposed to the food industry than in the past; it had to exploit the brands it owned.

In 2001 professional cleaning services were divested. Unilever had experimented with MyHome domestic cleaning services (using its own branded products of course) but was unhappy with the outcomes. Mazola cooking oils also went. The remaining perfume brands were offered for sale in 2002, but there were no immediate takers. Ambrosia (creamed rice) was sold in 2003.

At the same time certain brands were being deliberately extended. The Dove name belonged to a mild cleansing bar launched in the 1950s – it was now extended to shampoos, conditioners and a deodorant. Ice cream was also an investment priority. Unilever was already the leading company in this industry around the globe, with a 17 per cent share. Its main brands were Magnum and Cornetto as well as the ubiquitous Walls – plus Ben and Jerry's premium ice cream. There were to be 1000 new ice cream cabins on popular beaches around the world, and new Ben and Jerry's parlours would be built. Advertising would be stepped up and a clothing range (featuring the Wall's heart-shaped logo) launched.

In 2003 ice cream did well – but Knorr hot foods suffered – with the record hot temperatures across Europe. With a cooler and wetter summer in 2004, ice cream did much less well. Frozen foods and fragrances were also disappointing in 2003 – both of course were relatively low priority groups. One problem with frozen foods is that customers now perceive chilled foods to be fresher and healthier and Unilever has recognised it must act to try and redeem their image. But the worst fall was suffered by the recently acquired Slimfast products, where sales fell by 30 per cent. The problem – the popularity of the Atkins diet which recommends a low intake of carbohydrates but regular consumption of meat and protein. The general view was that Unilever had failed to generate the returns it had hoped for from the Bestfoods brands it had acquired.

In summary: Unilever certainly seemed able to slim down its portfolio of brands, shed staff and shut factories, but its ability to increase sales to the targets it originally set was more questionable. The recorded growth rates for sales of its leading brands was as follows:

1999	3.8 per cent
2000	3.8 per cent
2001	5.3 per cent
2002	5.4 per cent
2003	3.0 per cent

The target for 2004 was 2.5 per cent but halfway through the year, when Unilever was coming up to the end of five years of its 'Path to Growth', this was already looking very optimistic, maybe too optimistic. Within a year, Unilever's revenue was overtaken by Procter & Gamble when that company acquired Gillette. This would have a more psychological rather than material impact as these two companies are great rivals. So, what would the company 'that moves at the speed of rock erosion' do?

SOURCE: THIS CASE STUDY WAS PREPARED USING PRIMARILY PUBLICLY AVAILABLE SOURCES OF INFORMATION FOR THE PURPOSES OF CLASSROOM DISCUSSION; IT DOES NOT INTEND TO ILLUSTRATE EITHER EFFECTIVE OR INEFFECTIVE HANDLING OF A MANAGERIAL SITUATION.

The company had been working on plans for a restructuring, which it implemented. The company had retained two head offices for years, one in London and the other in Rotterdam – the product of history. This no longer seemed to make sense and one was closed – and Unilever also chose to operate with just one Chief Executive rather than one in each head office. Allegedly there were also several control systems that needed to be rationalized and better communications between the various divisions were desirable. Some analysts speculated that Unilever might split into two separate companies rather than two divisions in a single conglomerate – whilst others suggested it needed to go out and buy new brands to strengthen key parts of its portfolio.

Later that year Unilever sold the remaining brands in its global perfumes business to Coty, a German-owned US business. It was also announced that Birds Eye and Findus frozen foods would be sold if a suitable buyer could be found. It took over a year to engineer this sale, but these frozen foods businesses were sold in August 2006 to private equity firm Permira. Even though it is a frozen food, ice cream was not on the sale agenda.

It has been reported in 2008 that Unilever had received two bids for its American detergents businesses. Could it be tempted to sell? The answer was yes – but Unilever was determined to hold on to its European and other detergents brands. Boursin cheese and Bertolli olive oil were also sold.

Palm oil plantations in the Ivory Coast were sold and the proceeds used to buy a business in the Ivory Coast that manufactures soaps, palm oil and butter. Unilever was expressing a desire to focus on emerging markets but preferred the consumption end of the supply chain. To illustrate this point, Unilever brands now control 80 per cent of the laundry markets in Argentina and South Africa, 70 per cent in Brazil and 40 per cent in India. Some two-thirds of Unilever laundry products sales are generated in emerging markets.

In January 2009 a new CEO, Dutchman Paul Polman, took over as CEO. He had previously been the Finance Director at Nestle and worked for Procter & Gamble for a number of years. He expressed concern at the extent of the decentralization he found and said he wanted to explore how he might ensure the business was controlled effectively whilst capitalizing on the opportunities for synergy across brands. 'Some of the technologies developed for tea and ice cream products have obvious applications in skin creams.' His desire, he claimed, was for fewer new products – brought to market faster.

He also stated that it was his intention to promote sales growth, to place less emphasis on financial targets and milestones and to strengthen performance-related rewards for managers. Lower price, 'good value' brands would be essential.

Questions

1 In the light of its new product and market prioritization, and with hindsight, do the acquisitions of Ben and Jerry's and Bestfoods (still) make strategic sense?
2 Can you identify any problems or risks in Unilever's strategy of focusing on just 400 of its previous 1600 brands?
3 Do you agree with the decision to split the business into two quite separate divisions or would you have gone further and created two businesses?
4 How might a company like this deliver synergies whilst making sure that those managers responsible for individual brands – and logically close to their customers – have the freedom to manage their brands effectively?

UNILEVER **http://www.unilever.com**

© CHRISTOPHER PLEDGER/ALAMY

This technique usefully incorporates finance, which will affect the feasibility of particular strategic alternatives and the ability of a company to implement them. It has similar limitations to directional policy matrices. Box 8.1 can be applied very effectively to the banking industry in the UK.

Scottish and Newcastle was a large UK brewing business which in 2003 sold its 1450 pubs in the UK to Spirit for £2.5 billion. It then followed a strategy of concentrating on brewing rather than be diversified by owning the outlets for its products. It also rationalized the location of its brewing activities and entered into partnerships with smaller scale real ale brewers such as the Caledonian Brewing company in Edinburgh, who brew the award-winning Deuchar's IPA. At the same time S&N (Tony Frogatt) pursued a strategy of 'turning its back on acquisition activity and focusing on operational efficiencies, increased marketing investment and improved utilization of capital'. (Source: Ian Shackleton, Credit Suisse First Boston.) It could be argued that S&N was pursuing all four of the strategic thrusts identified above. As we saw in Case 2.7 S&N was sold to Heineken and Carlsberg in 2007.

8.10 Spheres of influence

According to D'Aventi (2001), **spheres of influence** relate to the building of an arsenal of products and services that enable and support real influence across a wide range of critical interests – they imply consideration of the so-called wider picture. Building this bigger picture implies planning linked to a vision. Although companies may focus on a core (or heartland) of activities, they must not neglect to build a portfolio of logically-related interests, even if some of them are clearly peripheral. The basic idea is to create or restore order in an industry in times of complexity and chaos. After all, more chaos and uncertainty equates to lower profits. It is about strategic logic and it mimics how nations have behaved historically. Under traditional portfolio theory, investment decisions do not require a consideration of the strategic logic for supporting a

Box 8.1

SPACE: Strategic Position and Action Evaluation

Figure 8.13   SPACE

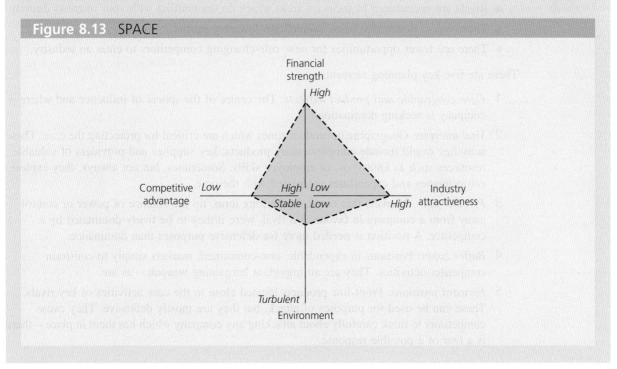

Table 8.3   SPACE

Strategic thrust	Aggressive	Competitive	Conservative	Defensive
Features:				
Environment	Stable	Unstable	Stable	Unstable
Industry	Attractive	Attractive	Unattractive	Unattractive
Competitiveness	Strong	Strong	Weak	Weak
Financial strength	High	Weak	High	Weak
Appropriate strategies	Growth, possibly by acquisition	Cost reduction, productivity improvement, raising more capital to follow opportunities and strengthen competitiveness	Cost reduction and product/service rationalization	Rationalization
	Capitalize on opportunities			Divestment as appropriate
	Innovate to sustain competitive advantage	Possibly merge with a less competitive but cash-rich company	Invest in search for new products, services and competitive opportunities	

ROWE, AJ, MASON, RO, DICKEL, KE AND SNYDER, NH (1989) STRATEGIC MANAGEMENT:

business, even though it could be relatively low profit, whereas spheres of influence looks at why organizations might choose to be in particular businesses.

The desired outcomes are:

- Competitors are manoeuvered into corners
- Rivals are encouraged to focus on areas which do not conflict with your interests directly
- There is less destructive price competition lowering profits
- There are fewer opportunities for new, rule-changing competitors to enter an industry.

There are five key planning elements:

1 *Core geographic and product markets.* The centre of the sphere of influence and where a company is seeking domination.

2 *Vital interests.* Geographic or product zones which are critical for protecting the core. These activities would include complementary products, key supplies and providers of valuable resources such as know-how or employee skills. Sometimes, but not always, they exploit competencies and capabilities associated with the core.

3 *Pivotal zones.* Markets that could, in the long term, tip the balance of power or control away from a company in favour of a rival, were it/they to be freely dominated by a competitor. A position is needed more for defensive purposes than dominance.

4 *Buffer zones.* Positions in expendable, non-committed, markets simply to constrain competitor activities. They are an important bargaining weapon – as are

5 *Forward positions.* Front-line products located close to the core activities of key rivals. These can be used for purposes of attack, but they are mostly defensive. They cause competitors to think carefully about attacking any company which has them in place – there is a fear of a possible response.

We can apply these five elements to Microsoft as follows:

- *Core* – desktop operating systems; graphical user interfaces; Internet browsers.
- *Vital interests* – where it seeks to be a winner – operating systems for networks and for portable devices.
- *Pivotal zones* – e-portals and e-commerce businesses.
- *Buffer zones* – computer games and the X-Box, because rivals might use their dominance of this sector to develop operating systems.
- *Forward positions* – initially bundling Explorer with Windows was a forward position, partly synergistic, partly competitive, to deter Netscape – but it became core.

It is interesting that much of Microsoft's history – and phenomenal success – is characterized by 'catch-up' strategies where it has been quick to capitalize on rival initiatives, but then overtake them with alternative products and services. The Windows computer operating system lagged behind – but grew to dominate – Apple's MacIntosh, which at one time was market leader. Whilst it remains the system of choice for some, especially designers, MacIntosh now has only a fraction of the market share of Windows. Word similarly grew to dominate and displace WordPerfect. Its commercial database SQL was developed to take on Oracle; Windows (Internet) Explorer eventually sidelined Netscape's Navigator although some believe there was an element of 'foul play' in the way Explorer was bundled with other Microsoft products. The Pocket PC was launched as a rival to the Palm hand-held organiser, and its Internet portal MSN was a follower of AOL. X-Box, of course, was designed to rival the Sony PlayStation, but realistically Microsoft has so far failed to seize market leadership. Microsoft has bought a minority stake in Facebook and attempted (unsuccessfully) to acquire Yahoo. In large part these decisions are affected by the strong position of Google and that company's ability to attract billions of dollars in on-line advertising revenue.

Other examples   Wal-Mart focuses on establishing and sustaining dominance of key product markets and territories around the world by, in part, establishing and nurturing relationships with key suppliers, which it then exploits through its huge buying power to force its rivals into niches that are either unoccupied or in which Wal-Mart is not particularly interested. This, of course, is a very typical retail strategy.

Disney retains a presence in children's book publishing and in branded retail stores to give it countervailing bargaining power against potential rivals should it ever need to use it.

Johnson & Johnson (J&J) is perhaps describable as 'The Baby Company' and Procter & Gamble (P&G) 'The Soaps and Shampoo Business'. These two businesses have activities and interests which overlap, but they avoid destructive rivalry. J&J opts not to compete directly with P&G's diaper business and its powerful Pampers brand, a massive baby product; and, similarly, P&G focuses on adult soaps and shampoos and does not address the children's market. Why? Because J&J owns the Neutrogena brand of mild adult soaps and shampoos, which are tightly niched and not mainstream – but they provide the company with competencies and capabilities which it could use to expand if it wished. Equally P&G has the competencies and capabilities to produce children's soaps and shampoos. Competition from powerful rivals in core areas could destroy position and power; there would be no winner as any victory would be pyrrhic. Simply, potential threats are keeping rivals at bay.

Summary

Some strategies are intended; others are emergent in real time. Intended strategies can emanate from planning and also from ideas input by key decision-makers or influencers, typically an owner-manager or a visionary strategic leader. Emergent strategies happen when intended strategies are changed incrementally as they are implemented or when organizations respond to environmental opportunities and threats. We would expect to find at least some evidence of all of these modes in every organization – simply the relative significance of each one will vary.

As organizations grow and become more complex, then it is not unusual to find an increasing reliance on planning at the expense of the other modes. This is understandable as there is an increasing need for effective control mechanisms. However, the risk is that bureaucracy and stasis accompanies the reliance on planning, and this must not be allowed to happen.

The section on military strategy and planning highlights the value of preparation whilst retaining the ability to be flexible. There is, however, one typical difference worth mentioning. Military officers and planners will invest time and energy in planning possible campaigns and in establishing contingencies for how they might respond when the unexpected happens after they engage the enemy. Business leaders might well be expected to do the same. However, in the services, once a decision has been reached all personnel will be expected, if not required, to 'own' the strategies, set off to carry them out, passing them on to others without any question or criticism. Of course, they will have authority to change tactics if and when necessary. In business we would not expect to see this happen in quite the same way. It is not unusual to hope that strategies can be sold to others and that the people who must implement them will feel some ownership of them – but we would not expect to find that people don't question them if they remain sceptical. Later in the book, therefore, we will look in greater depth at the whole issue of strategic change.

Planning techniques, then, can be extremely useful, particularly as they force managers and organizations to ask themselves many relevant and searching questions and compile and analyse important information. But the techniques do not, and cannot, provide answers: they merely generate the questions. The danger is that some managers may perceive the output of a technique such as matrix analysis as an answer to strategic issues.

Strategic planning – using techniques and formalized procedures – is just one of the ways in which strategies are created. Strategies can also be provided by the strategic leader and be decided by managers in real time. Intended strategies, say those selected by the leader or a formal planning system, have to be implemented, and during this implementation they may well be changed incrementally. After all, intended strategies imply forecasting, and, to some extent, all forecasts are wrong. In addition, flexible organizations will adapt all the time by responding to new opportunities and threats.

In the 1960s and 1970s the predominant view with academics and organizations was that formalized strategic planning was at the heart of strategy creation, and should be used to manage future direction. It became clear, however, that a planning approach that relies on quantitative data, forecasts and manuals, can restrict creativity, thinking, flexibility and, critically, the support and engagement of the managers who must implement strategy. Many organizations fell into the trap of believing the key outcome of planning is the plan!

Nevertheless, it is important to realize that all managers plan, all the time. Evaluating the current situation, and discussing possible changes and improvements with colleagues, implies planning. Simply, this is informal planning rather than the formalized systems implied by the term strategic planning.

There are at least seven approaches to planning, which should not necessarily be seen as mutually exclusive. Formal planning is separate from informal planning. The process can be largely top-down or bottom-up. It can take the form of extended budgeting and be numbers driven, or be more behavioural in approach, possibly using scenarios.

The '*planning gap*' is a very flexible concept and technique which can be used in a variety of ways. Broadly, it is used to clarify the extent of the revenue or profits gap that might emerge if current strategies are left largely unchanged. The more ambitious the objectives set by the company, the greater the risk that is likely to be involved in the strategies required to close the gap.

Our contemporary approach to strategic planning is based on a mixture of planning techniques, intellectual input and action plans for implementing strategies; and central to the whole process are current strategic issues.

With any form of strategic planning it is important to decide upon who should be involved and what they should contribute. Professional or specialist planners have an important role to play, but others must be involved as well. Where there is an over-reliance on planners, or where there is inadequate flexibility with the plan itself, the organization is likely to fall into one of the obvious planning traps.

Planning has a number of important contributions to make and individual organizations will not all adopt the same approach.

There is a number of useful planning techniques, specifically:

- The Boston Consulting Group (BCG) 2 × 2 matrix
- Directional policy matrices
- SPACE.

In various ways all of these techniques can be valuable. They will always be dangerous if they are used too rigidly and allowed to drive decisions without reference to, or qualification by, managerial judgement.

The thinking behind spheres of influence concerns the big picture, and contends that companies should look to develop a portfolio of products that strengthen its all-round ability to compete by opening up competitive fronts both proactively and reactively.

Online cases for this chapter

Online Case 8.1: Strategic Issues and High Street Banking

Questions and research assignments

1 What is the difference between planned strategy, visionary strategy and emergent strategy? Distinguish between adaptive and incremental change.

2 Thinking about any project or sporting event you have been involved with, how relevant are the introductory comments on professional football? What have you learned about strategy creation from your own experiences in either a business or other context?

3 Mintzberg has distinguished between 'grass-roots' strategies (which can take root anywhere in the organization but eventually proliferate once they become more widely adopted) and 'hothouse' strategies which are deliberately grown and cultured. What do you think he means?

4 A manufacturer of industrial products is structured around five separate strategic business units (SBUs). Use the data below to construct a Boston matrix and assess how balanced the portfolio seems. Where are the strengths? Where are the weaknesses?

SBU	Sales (£ million)	Number of competitors	Sales of top three companies (£ million)	Market growth rate (%)
A	0.4	6	0.8, 0.7, 0.4	16
B	1.8	20	1.8, 1.8, 1.2	18
C	1.7	16	1.7, 1.3, 0.9	8
D	3.5	3	3.5, 1.0, 0.8	5
E	0.6	8	2.8, 2.0, 1.5	2

5 In the context of the Boston matrix, is the Big Mac a cash cow? What do you feel McDonald's competitive strategy for the Big Mac should be?

6 For an organization of your choice, ideally one with which you are familiar:

a Ascertain how the planning, entrepreneurial and emergent modes might apply currently to strategic change in the organization. Which mode is predominant? Why do you think it is the preferred mode? How successful is it?

b What would be the opportunities and concerns from greater utilization of the other modes?

Internet and library projects

1 Use the Internet to look at all Stelios' businesses – other than EasyJet – and consider where he might have made a visionary impact. What do you think are the main contributions planning might make to the business? How much have the strategies changed as Stelios has striven to make these various businesses profitable?

2 Follow up the web case on UK high street banks. Take any one of the leading banks and examine its portfolio of activities – including the investment banking, international and other financial services businesses. In the current climate do you believe the structure makes sense?

Strategy activity

The Channel Tunnel

The Channel Tunnel between England and France was named the greatest construction achievement of the twentieth century. Passenger and freight shuttles began operating in 1994; Eurostar passenger services began a short while later, but growth was constrained until the fast access route between London and Folkestone began opening (in stages) in 2003. Freight trains also use the tunnel. The tunnel operator, Eurotunnel, has made operating profits since 1997 but other charges have meant net losses. In 2003 Eurotunnel identified the following strategic issues:

- the expensive infrastructure was underutilized
- operator access charges were too high
- there were conflicts between the various stakeholders, many of them caused by the financial losses.

Eurotunnel decided to reduce access charges to stimulate demand. There was a belief that demand was sufficiently price-elastic for this to improve profitability. Debts would have to be restructured –

and not for the first time. There would be fresh investment in the Folkestone freight terminal to allow it to handle Continental gauge trains for the first time. And the terminal areas of Kent and the region around Calais would be promoted to stimulate tourism.

There have been two serious fire incidents. Both resulted in major disruptions which Eurotunnel had to deal with at immediate notice. The company has been restructured financially yet again, the shares are worth very little, and the business is controlled from France.

Questions

1 Overall, has the Channel Tunnel been a success or a failure?

2 Can you identify additional strategic issues to those listed here?

3 What alternative strategies might be considered to improve the fortunes of Eurotunnel?

EUROTUNNEL **http://www.eurotunnel.com**

Further reading

Abell, D (1978) Strategic windows, *Journal of Marketing*, 42, July.

Bryson, JM (1988) A strategic planning process for public and non-profit organizations, *Long Range Planning*, 21 (1).

Hamel, G and Prahalad, CK (1989) Strategic intent, *Harvard Business Review*, May–June.

Haspeslagh, P (1982) Portfolio planning – uses and limits, *Harvard Business Review*, January–February.

Hedley, B (1977) Strategy and the 'business portfolio', *Long Range Planning*, 10.

Idenburg, PJ (1993) Four styles of strategy development, *Long Range Planning*, 26 (6).

Mintzberg, H and Waters, JA (1985) Of strategies deliberate and emergent, *Strategic Management Journal*, 6.

Mintzberg, H (1987) Crafting strategy, *Harvard Business Review*, July–August.

Mintzberg, H (1999) Reflecting on the strategy process, *Sloan Management Review*, 40, Spring.

Peters, T (1993) The transformation of positively everything, *Director*, March.

Ringbakk, KA (1971) Why planning fails, *European Business*, Spring.

Sahlman, WA (1997) How to write a great business plan, *Harvard Business Review*, July–August.

Stacey, R (1993) Strategy as order emerging from chaos, *Long Range Planning*, 26 (1).

Williamson, PJ (1999) Strategy as options on the future, *Sloan Management Review*, 40, Spring.

References

Abell, DF and Hammond, JS (1979) *Strategic Market Planning*, Prentice-Hall.

Ackoff, RL (1970) *A Concept of Corporate Planning*, John Wiley.

Ansoff, HI (1987) *Corporate Strategy*, revised edn, Penguin.

Argenti, J (1980) *Practical Corporate Planning*, George Allen & Unwin.

Bailey, A and Johnson, G (1992) How strategies develop in organizations. In *The Challenge of Strategic Management* (eds G Johnson and D Faulkner), Kogan Page.

Buzzell, RD and Gale, BT (1987) *The PIMS Principles – Linking Strategy to Performance*, Free Press.

Cohen, KJ and Cyert, RM (1973) Strategy formulation, implementation and monitoring, *Journal of Business*, 46 (3), 349–67.

D'Aventi RA (2001) *Strategic Supremacy – How industry leaders create growth, wealth and power through spheres of influence*, The Free Press.

Garvin, DA and Levesque, L C(2006) Project the known – deliver the new, *Harvard Business Review,* October.

Glueck, WF and Jauch, LR (1984) *Business Policy and Strategic Management*, 4th edn, McGraw-Hill.

Hamermesch, R (1986) Making planning strategic, *Harvard Business Review*, July–August.

Henderson, B (1970) *The Product Portfolio*, Boston Consulting Group.

Hurst, DK (1995) *Crisis and Renewal – Meeting the Challenge of Organizational Change*, Harvard Business School Press.

Hussey, D (1976) *Corporate Planning – Theory and Practice*, Pergamon.

Idenburg, PJ (1993) Four styles of strategy development, *Long Range Planning*, 26 (6).

Johnson, G (1992) Strategic direction and strategic decisions, presented at 'Managing Strategically: Gateways and Barriers', Strategic Planning Society Conference, 12 February.

Mills, DQ (1985) Planning with people in mind, *Harvard Business Review*, July–August.

Mintzberg, H (1973) Strategy making in three modes, *California Management Review*, 16 (2), Winter.

Mintzberg, H (1989) Presentation to the Strategic Planning Society, London, 2 February. Further details can be found in Mintzberg, H (1973).

Mintzberg, H and Waters, JA (1985) Of strategy deliberate and emergent, *Strategic Management Journal*, 6 (3).

Ohmae, K (1982) *The Mind of the Strategist*, McGraw-Hill.

Ringbakk, KA (1971) Why planning fails, *European Business*, Spring.

Robinson, J (1986) Paradoxes in planning, *Long Range Planning*, 19 (6).

Robinson, SJQ, Hitchens, RE and Wade, DP (1978) The directional policy matrix – tool for strategic planning, *Long Range Planning*, 21, June.

Rowe, AJ, Mason, RO, Dickel, KE and Snyder, NH (1989) *Strategic Management: A Methodological Approach*, 3rd edn, Addison-Wesley.

Steiner, G (1972) *Pitfalls in Long Range Planning*, Planning Executives Institute.

Taylor, B and Hussey DE (1982) *The Realities of Planning*, Pergamon.

Chapter 9

Strategic leadership, entrepreneurship and intrapreneurship

PART 1
Understanding strategy
1 Introducing strategy and strategic management

PART 5
Strategic management
14 Strategy implementation
15 Leading change
16 Managing strategy in the organization
17 Final thoughts – the purpose of strategy

STRATEGIC MANAGEMENT: AWARENESS AND CHANGE

PART 2
Strategic positioning
2 Strategic thinking, environmental analysis, synergy and strategic positioning
3 Resource-led strategy
4 The dynamics of competition
5 Introducing culture and values

PART 4
Issues in strategic growth
11 Strategic growth
12 International strategy
13 Failure, consolidation and recovery strategies

PART 3
Strategic analysis and choice
6 Strategic purpose
7 Strategic success
8 An introduction to strategy creation and planning
9 Strategic leadership, entrepreneurship and intrapreneurship
10 Strategic alternatives, strategy evaluation and strategy selection

Learning objectives

Having read to the end of this chapter you should be able to:

● define the term strategic leadership

● compare and contrast the role of the strategic leader with the role of the entrepreneur

● identify factors which contribute towards effective strategic leadership

● differentiate between a number of different leader styles

● discuss a number of critical leadership issues such as finite shelf-lives and succession

● explain visionary leadership, entrepreneurship and intrapreneurship

● describe the conditions for making an organization intrapreneurial

● reflect on the nature of ambition and the success or otherwise of various chief executives.

Strategic leaders 'come in all shapes and sizes'. They have to be able to think, make things happen, engage the support of other people and, on occasions, be the public face of the organization. It is optimistic to believe that all strategic leaders will be good at all four of these tasks. Some, such as Sir Richard Branson and Sir Alan Sugar, are very visible and have an influence which extends well beyond the organizations that they run even into fronting, in the case of Sir Alan Sugar top rated business related television shows. Others are far more anonymous as far as the public are concerned but are excellent leaders of their organizations. There is no 'right' style or personality but there are certain roles that must be fulfilled effectively, regardless of the type or size of organization. The strategic leader has an overall responsibility for clarifying direction, for deciding upon strategies by dictating or influencing others around them and for ensuring that strategies are implemented through the decisions that he or she makes on structure, style and systems.

There is a case to be made that the basic nature of the strategic leader will have an impact on the style and culture of an organization, certainly over a period of time. Companies will become dull if they have dull leaders, belligerent leaders could well encourage (perhaps indirectly) a bullying culture, adventurous leaders may well preside over adventurous companies and equally risk averse leaders will rarely be found running risk oriented businesses.

Some leaders are entrepreneurial and visionary, but this is not a requirement. In turn these visionary leaders may be very effective entrepreneurs but they may not be the people to manage the business at a particular point in time. This requirement to try and balance the leadership needs of a business with the need for effective management is at the heart of the success or failure of any business.

Our opening case on Innocent Smoothies features the growth and success of an entrepreneurial business, but one started and run by a team of three friends who share the strategic leadership role and responsibilities.

As well as leading from the front it is also important for a leader to create a climate that facilitates emergent change – appropriate employees should be empowered, encouraged and energized. Intrapreneurs then lead the emergent change initiatives. Leadership is both a job and a process – a process concerned with influence and change. It requires both personal characteristics and leadership skills. The skills can be learned, but effective leaders need to possess certain characteristics in the first place. Successful leaders also tend to build effective teams to support them. Before reading on, readers might wish to revisit Chapter 5 and re-read the sections on empowerment and learning organizations.

In exploring these issues, this chapter also looks at how some leaders are perceived to fail and fall from grace, and at the vital issue of leadership succession.

> *The most important quality of a CEO (Chief Executive Officer) is communicating a clear vision of the company's strategy – and the reputation of the CEO directly contributes to the company's ability to attract investment, recruit talent and survive crises.*

BURSON-MARSTELLER, US PUBLIC RELATIONS BUSINESS

Case 9.1

Innocent Smoothies   UK

Innocent Smoothies was started in 1998 by three friends who had met when they were students at St John's College in Cambridge. They had graduated in the early 1990s. On a snowboarding holiday – which they still enjoy – they decided to start a business, but didn't immediately plan to 'give up the day job'. They had run events together at University and stayed close friends.

Adam Balon was the son of an ENT surgeon. Brought up in Surrey he read economics at Cambridge and afterwards worked for Virgin Cola. Richard Reed's father was a manager with the Yorkshire Rider bus company. Reed read geography and then worked in advertising. Jon Wright was a Londoner, son of an IT manager and he read engineering before becoming a management consultant.

After discarding a number of ideas the trio decided to invest £500, buy some fresh fruit, crush it, bottle it and sell it from a stall at a music festival. They had decided none of them really lived a healthy lifestyle and truly fresh fruit drinks would be one answer. They placed two large baskets on their stall and erected a large sign – *Should we start this business?* It was the philosophy that 'if there's something I want and can't readily get, and other people are saying the same thing, there must be an opportunity'. The 'yes' bucket was quickly filled! They resigned from their jobs and embarked on the journey. They were about to start one of the UK's fastest growing food and drink businesses which would be turning over £10 million after five years. Turnover in 2007 exceeded £100 million; Innocent had 70 per cent of the UK market for smoothies.

Money to establish a 'proper' business was hard to come by until they decided to e-mail all their contacts with a simple question – *Do you know anyone who is rich?* One did, and after some discussions the three were offered £235,000 for 18 per cent of the equity in the business. Their investor is a veteran American serial entrepreneur who had spent some time on the staff at London Business School and become a private venture capitalist. Until 2008 they retained 70 per cent, with the remainder split amongst their colleagues in the business, a number of whom also knew them at Cambridge. Because of the need to comply with legislation and restrictions over manufacture and distribution, things did not go smoothly at first. There were a number of 'false starts' but the trio persisted.

The three have separate roles in the business, concerned with production (Wright), trade sales (Balon) and consumer marketing (Reed) but there is no designated leader or chief executive. They recognize each other's strengths and work as a team.

Although there are now more bottle and package sizes and blends than in the early days, with some flavours now targeted specifically at children, the business remains focused on crushed fruit juices, fruit flavoured water and yoghurt-based fruit smoothies. They only use natural fresh products – with no additives or concentrated juices. The ingredients are sourced carefully from around the world – 'only the best' approach linked to ethical and environmental concerns. They are not, however, organic. They charge premium prices.

The products can be bought widely – in Tesco, Sainsbury and Waitrose, for example. Their markets extend to Dublin, Paris and Hong Kong. Their early success pioneering bottled fruit smoothies provoked competition. Established 'giants' such as Del Monte and Ocean Spray (part of Gerber, itself recently acquired by

Nestlé) have been unable to dislodge them from their market position.

The company has always maintained a fun image and the trio dress casually. Their offices in South London are called 'Fruit Towers'. They are very creative and their logo is distinctive. It comprises an apple shape face with two eyes and a halo above. They want to be seen as fun and funky. They proclaim that their staff, with an average age of 27, are empowered and constantly on the look-out for new ideas. Their website has been likened to a student blog and they regularly e-mail their on-line subscribers. They push the health message and feature mentions of daily fruit and vegetable intakes on their packages. In 2007 they launched new bottles made from polyactic acid which are fully degradable. Ten per cent of Innocent's annual profits are given over to aid projects in Bangalore, Africa and Brazil; and they maintain a 'Sustainability Squad' to monitor environmental issues. Innocent are on record as saying that try to 'leave things better than they find them'. Richard Reed, who has become the public face of Innocent was once asked whom he most admired. Instead of a business leader he chose 'a guy named Paulo who is running a Greenpeace campaign to save the Amazon rainforest'.

Balon, Reed and Wright have registered the Innocent name for categories other than juices and smoothies. Might we, in the future, see bodycare or cosmetic products under the brand?

There has been speculation that the business might be sold but this has yet to happen. In 2008, however, the founders sold a further stake to raise £35 million to help fund the development of new food products. Sales fell back in the second half of the year and there appeared to be some concern that smoothies, very much a discretionary consumer purchase, might suffer in the anticipated economic recession. At this time Innocent were seeking to expand in selected overseas markets – especially in Europe. In April 2009 Coca-Cola bought a 20 per cent stake for £30 million. Press reports stated the founders would continue to run the business and they remained confident the socially

and environmentally-aware stance of Innocent was not under threat. The logic of the investment is that Coca-Cola can help secure new distribution opportunities.

Questions

1   What are the key determinants of the success of Innocent Smoothies?
2   Visit one local supermarket and check out the presence of Innocent drinks and the competition. Can you see any visible threats to the business?
3   Do you see any longer-term risks to the idiosyncratic nature of this business from the investment by Coca-Cola?

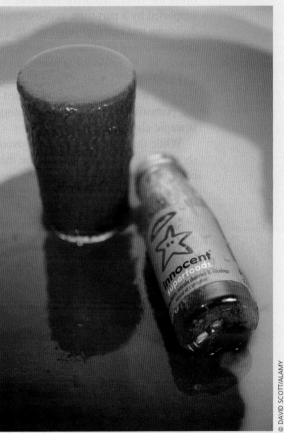

© DAVID SCOTT/ALAMY

9.1   Introduction

The task of leadership, as well as providing the framework, values and motivation of people, and allocation of financial and other resources, is to set the overall direction which enables choices to be made so that the efforts of the company can be focused.

In this quotation, Sir John Harvey-Jones emphasizes the need for a clear direction for the organization.

It is the responsibility of the chief executive to clarify the mission and objectives of the organization, to define the corporate strategy which is intended to achieve these and to establish and manage the organization's structure. Personal ideas, vision and planning systems are all involved in defining the strategy.

The corporate strategy will be implemented within the structure, and the ways in which people behave – and are allowed to behave – within the organization structure will impact upon changes in competitive and functional strategies. The chief executive will also be a major influence on the organization's culture and values, which are key determinants of the ways in which strategies are created and implemented.

However, the chief executive is not the only creator of strategic change. Managers who are in charge of divisions or strategic business units (normally referred to as 'general managers') are also responsible for strategic changes concerning their own products, services or geographical territories. Functional managers will make and carry out decisions which result in strategic change. In many firms the chief executive will also act as chairman of the board, but in others he or she will be supported by a part-time, non-executive chairman who will contribute actively to corporate strategy decisions and external relations. In a limited number of large companies, particularly those which are diverse and multinational, a chief operating officer will report directly to the chief executive. He or she will be responsible for ensuring that the operating parts of the business perform effectively, and consequently will influence changes in competitive and functional strategies. Throughout this book the term *strategic leader* is used to describe the managers who head the organization and who are primarily responsible for creating and implementing strategic change, particularly corporate strategic change.

While the strategic leader has overall responsibility for managing strategy in the organization, it should not be thought that they are the sole source of thoughts and ideas. All employees can make a contribution, and should be encouraged to do so. The more that people are invited to participate in debate and discussions concerning products, services, markets and the future, the more likely they are to accept changes. Where people accept empowerment, emergent strategies can make the organization a strong competitor. Simply, leaders should not – and realistically cannot – do everything themselves, but they remain the catalyst for what does happen.

The strategic leader is in a unique position to gather and receive information about all aspects of the business, and it is incumbent on him or her to monitor the environment and the organization and watch for important opportunities and threats that could affect the whole business. He or she will need both analytical skills and insight (or awareness) to provide an intuitive grasp of the situation that faces the organization.

The way in which the organization manages to grasp opportunities and overcome potential threats will be very dependent on the personal qualities and values of the strategic leader.

Power is irrevocably associated with leadership. Strategic leaders are put in a position of power, but they have discretion over how they use this power. Some leaders, but not all, will be very motivated by the power that the position gives them. However there are many sources of power and many ways in which it can be obtained and used. Some strategic leaders will use it to impose their own ideas; others will seek to share power and responsibility with others, empowering them and encouraging them to make decisions without always referring back for advice and guidance. It is said that the style of Sir Fred Goodwin at Royal Bank of Scotland was to impose his style ('Fred the shred' – the cost cutter) on his fellow managers. Offering up a different viewpoint was not well received at RBS and apparently the same imposing style applied at HBOS under Sir James Crosby. Both banks were affected by the credit crunch and recession as we have seen earlier – and the reputations of both these strategic leaders have been tarnished.

Everyone who becomes a strategic leader will have some experiences and expertise on which they call. The nature of their background and experience will have some impact upon their relative preference for analysis and planning or for working through people and allowing them individual freedom in strategy creation.

These are the key themes of this chapter.

The strategic leader is responsible directly to the board of directors of the organization, and through the board, to the stakeholders in the business. The responsibilities of the board and, in effect, the strategic leader, could be summarized as follows:

1 Manage the business on behalf of all the stakeholders (or interested parties).

2 Provide direction in the form of a mission or purpose.

3 Formulate and implement changes to corporate strategies.

4 Monitor and control operations with special reference to financial results, productivity, quality, customer service, innovation, new products and services and staff development.

5 Provide policies and guidelines for other managers to facilitate both the management of operations and changes in competitive and functional strategies.

Responsibility 5 is achieved through the organization structure; 2 and 4 are dependent on an effective communications network.

Figure 9.1 summarizes these points by explaining that, essentially, the strategic leader has a meta-level responsibility for deciding how strategies are to be created and implemented to pursue the mission and direction. He or she may impose strategies and at the same time decide upon the nature, scope and significance of strategic planning systems. The choices of structure and management style will affect emergent strategy making, as will be seen in Chapters 15 and 16. The structure, style and management systems provide the implementation framework, a subject explored in detail in Part 5.

Hooper and Trompenaars (2009) offer a view on how we might define a leader and his (her) contribution. They emphasize results – the outcomes of the contribution. These results will be, at

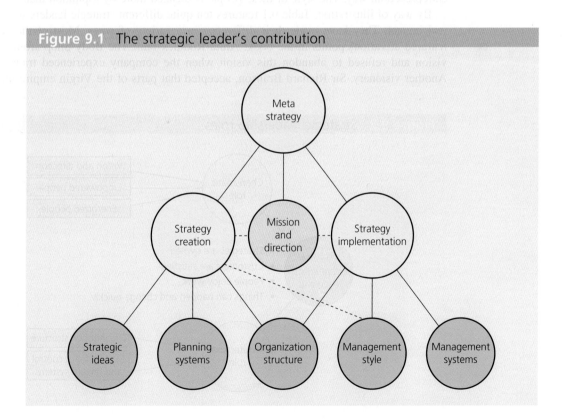

Figure 9.1 The strategic leader's contribution

least in part, driven by personal motives and ambitions, which also affect a second factor – personal values and the specific concerns these bring to the organization. This point is very relevant for leaders such as Anita Roddick at The Body Shop. There are also two issues of style. First, is the leader by nature more analytical or more intuitive? We discuss entrepreneurs in this chapter and this is very relevant here. And second, how effective is the leader at communicating – is he trusted, and, does he trust those that work for him?

9.2 Strategic leaders and strategic leadership

Kets de Vries (1996) concludes that the most successful strategic leaders perform two key roles, a charismatic role and an architectural one, effectively (see Figure 9.2). As a result, their strategies are owned, customers are satisfied, employees enjoy work and things can, and do, happen and change quickly. The charismatic role involves establishing and gaining support for a (winning) vision and direction, empowering employees and energizing them, gaining their enthusiastic support for what has to be done. The architectural role concerns building an appropriate organization structure, together with systems for controlling and rewarding people. We can see that these arguments embrace visionary leaders, entrepreneurs and a process of intrapreneurship within the organization.

Related to this latter point, Hamel (1999) distinguishes between stewardship and entrepreneurship. Stewardship concerns the continued exploitation of opportunities spotted in the past. Costs will be managed for efficiencies; some incremental changes and improvements will be made to reinforce the strategic position in a competitive environment. On its own, however, in an increasingly dynamic environment, this may well prove inadequate. Hamel uses the metaphor of Silicon Valley to contend that organizations need to bring together new ideas, talented and entrepreneurial managers, and the resources that they need in order to exploit new opportunities in an entrepreneurial way. The style of these people is dictated more by aspiration than it is by analysis.

By way of illustration, Table 9.1 features ten quite different strategic leaders who have made a real impact. They have made their difference in a variety of ways. Most of the companies are featured at various points in the book. Anita Roddick built The Body Shop around her personal vision and refused to abandon this vision when the company experienced trading difficulties. Another visionary, Sir Richard Branson, accepted that parts of the Virgin empire that he built up

Figure 9.2 Strategic leadership roles

Table 9.1 Ten strategic leaders, each of whom has or had a vision, and is linked irrevocably with their company's strategy, structure and performance

Anita Roddick	The Body Shop	Built up and 'stuck with it'
Richard Branson	Virgin	Built up and sold parts
Alan Sugar	Amstrad	Built up and split up
Tim Waterstone	Waterstone's	Built up, sold off and started again
Archie Norman	ASDA	Turned around and rejuvenated
Jack Welch	General Electric	Transformed
James Dyson	Dyson	Built up and remains in control
Gerald Ratner	Ratner's	Inherited, grew and lost
Freddie Laker	Laker Airways (Skytrain)	Built up, lost and retired eventually
Stelios Haji-Ioannou	EasyGroup	Built up; stepped down from original business

needed to be sold off at different times, partly to secure the future for that particular business and also to provide funding for new business ideas which he wished to pursue. Sir Alan Sugar similarly chose to separate Viglen from Amstrad, the company he founded – but this was a corporate split, not a sale, and he retained an influence over both businesses. Tim Waterstone, having been made redundant by WH Smith, opened the first Waterstone's store using ideas he spotted in the US. Having built up a chain of bookshops he sold them all to WH Smith, with whom he stayed for a period of years. He resigned and, in true entrepreneurial fashion, began a series of new ventures. When Waterstone's was merged with EMI's Dillons and HMV music stores, and then floated off as a separate business, Tim Waterstone returned as Chairman. He later tried to separate Waterstone's from the group and take it independent again – but he was unsuccessful in this.

Archie Norman was recruited to ASDA when it was in trouble. Together with Allan Leighton, whom he recruited, ASDA was turned around and rejuvenated before being sold to Wal-Mart. Jack Welch similarly transformed General Electric in the US, and, after his retirement, GE remains a hugely successful diversified conglomerate in an era when such conglomerates continue to be unfashionable. James Dyson remains the driving force and public face of Dyson the business. Gerald Ratner inherited a family business, built it up rapidly and then fell from grace when he spoke out of turn at a conference and rubbished his company's products. Sir Freddie Laker built his Skytrain business and then went out of business through a series of strategic misjudgements and very aggressive competition. Stelios Haji-Ioannou built up EasyJet but 'had to step down' from being the chief executive once it was floated on the London Stock Exchange. Ratner, Laker and Stelios, again typical of a true entrepreneur, have all sought to made comebacks with ambitious ventures. For Stelios and his EasyGroup see Case 8.1.

The problem is not to get people to work. It is to get them working together for the same damn thing.

SIR JOHN HARVEY-JONES, RETIRED CHAIRMAN, ICI

Strategic awareness and change involves: becoming aware – listening, being on the shop floor more than in the office whilst, most important of all, staying humble – and taking action – sharing with others.

MICHEL BON, PDG, CARREFOUR SA

As a strategic leader ... one must organize oneself to have as much time as possible to see colleagues in the firm, and to be known to be available to them, for talking face-to-face is more valuable than a long memo. One must go and see others in their offices. This is the only way to stay in touch with what is going on and to ensure that an agreed plan is being carried out.

FRANÇOIS MICHELIN, PDG, MICHELIN ET CIE

The role of the strategic leader

The strategic leader must *direct* the organization and must ensure that long-term objectives and strategies have been determined and that they are understood and supported by managers within the organization who will be responsible for implementing them. The more feasible and achievable the objectives and strategies seem, the more likely they are to be supported.

These intended strategies will be implemented through the *organization structure* adopted by the strategic leader. Some intended strategies will prove not to be feasible, as the assumptions on which they are based may be wrong, and circumstances can change, and they will be discarded or postponed. Decisions taken by general and functional managers within a decentralized structure will lead to new, incremental and adaptive changes in competitive and functional strategies. A third major responsibility of the strategic leader is a system of *communications* which first enables managers throughout the organization to be strategically aware, and second ensures that the strategic leader stays informed of the changes that are taking place.

Strategic vision – thinking At the heart of everything is the need for a clear, understood and supported mission for the organization. Employees must appreciate the fundamental purpose and be committed to its achievement; the mission will provide guidance and direction when managers make decisions and implement strategies determined by others. The mission and vision may be those of the current strategic leader; equally they may have been established by a predecessor. Similarly, the actual strategies – corporate and competitive – for achieving long-term objectives may be created personally by a strong or visionary strategic leader, or they may be ideas from anywhere inside the organization.

It is important to appreciate that strategic leaders need not be personally visionary, the type of visionary leader discussed later, but they must ensure that the organization has a clear direction and resources are committed to its achievement.

Figure 9.3 develops the ideas behind the E–V–R (environment–values–resources) congruence framework introduced in Part 1. Effective strategic positioning is seen as being central and reflecting competitive advantage. It has to be recognized that positions have to be changed. Sometimes the

Figure 9.3 Strategic leadership and E–V–R congruence

situation will be improved with innovation and incremental changes, and functional upon the culture and values, and the ways in which managers work and make decisions about possible changes. On other occasions the changes will be more dramatic and discontinuous and reflect a change in the vision. Hence, the strategic leader dictates changes to both the vision and values.

Until kings become philosophers and philosophers kings, things will never go well in the world.

PLATO

Pragmatism – doing This is the ability to make things happen and bring positive results. This implies that the organization's resources are managed efficiently and effectively. Some strategic leaders will be *doers*, active in carrying strategies through; others will be delegators who rely instead on their skills for motivating and inspiring. Control systems for monitoring results and strategic effectiveness are also important.

Some corporate leaders, then, will be strategic visionaries who are also active in operations; others will contribute ideas and leadership but be happy to devolve operational responsibility. It is possible for pragmatic but non-visionary leaders to be highly effective as long as they ensure that the organization has a clear and appropriate purpose and direction. The dangers here are, first, that short-term success can sometimes be the result of efficient management against a background of friendly market forces (which can, of course, quickly become less friendly) and, second, that when previously successful strategies are in need of renewal, a non-visionary may fail to provide the appropriate leadership and champion the necessary changes. Consequently, Bennis (1988) suggests that vision is crucial and that the most effective leaders are those with ideas. This accords with the view of Sir Winston Churchill, who believed that the 'emperor of the future will be the emperor of ideas'. Churchill was the leader Britain needed to win the World War II. In terms of the appropriate leadership style his stakeholders, the public, did not think he had the leadership style for the peace and voted him out of office post 1945.

The current US President, Barack Obama, was elected on a platform based on change and his vision for a new America. It is his ideas based on the theme of change that have galvanized America. He now has to deliver that promised change.

The strategic leader's vision and his or her record of achievement are critical for obtaining and maintaining the confidence and support of influential stakeholders, especially the very important institutional shareholders. The willingness of large shareholders to hold or sell their shares, and their expressed support for company strategies, are essential for maintaining a healthy share price and reducing the likelihood of a takeover. Their confidence in the ability of the leader is a major determinant; on occasions it is shareholder pressure which forces a change of leadership.

As well as vision and pragmatism it is necessary for the leader to build a structure and culture that captures the abilities and contributions of other managers and employees.

Structure and policies It is the strategic leader who decides on the appropriate structure for carrying out existing strategies and ensuring that there is proper momentum for change.

The issues are as follows:

- Should the organization be relatively flat and informal or have several layers of management and more formality?
- Should it be split into individual businesses or divisions?
- How much power and responsibility should be delegated and decentralized?
- What is the appropriate role for the corporate headquarters?
- How might planning systems be used to direct and co-ordinate the various parts of the organization?
- To what extent should managers and other employees be empowered to take more responsibility?

- What structures and mechanisms are required to ensure that managers in different business areas and different functions integrate and plan how they can help each other? In other words, planning synergies through effective organizational teamworking.

- What policies are necessary and appropriate for guiding and directing decision-making?

Culture To a great extent the culture of the organization is dictated by the strategic leader. The attitudes and behaviours of people are affected, as well as their willingness to accept responsibility and take measured risks.

The strategic leader may have very clear or specific values which influence his or her style, and the culture of the organization. For example, if the leader has a financial background and orientation, this may prove important. Financial targets and analysis may be crucial elements in the management of strategy. Similarly, if the leader has a marketing background this could result in a different style of leadership, with perhaps more concentration on consumers and competition. An engineer may be very committed to product design and quality. These comments are generalizations, and will not always prove to be true; over a period of time a strategic leader is likely to become more of a generalist and less of a specialist. If a new strategic leader is appointed from another company it is inevitable that he or she will bring values which have been learned elsewhere, and these may involve change. Logically, the person will be chosen because of his or her successful record in one or more previous companies, and the newcomer may be determined to establish his or her presence by introducing changes.

Figure 9.4 delineates six key leader styles, each of which makes an important contribution. It may be argued that every leader will have a dominant style, but must make sure that the others are not neglected because all of the contributions are required. The balance between the six, which ones are strong relative to the others, will affect the culture and management style of the whole organization. Arguably, use of this framework can help us to understand why things happen as they do in any organization being analysed. It will certainly help to explain the relative balance between visionary, planned and emergent strategy creation.

Figure 9.4 Strategic leadership style

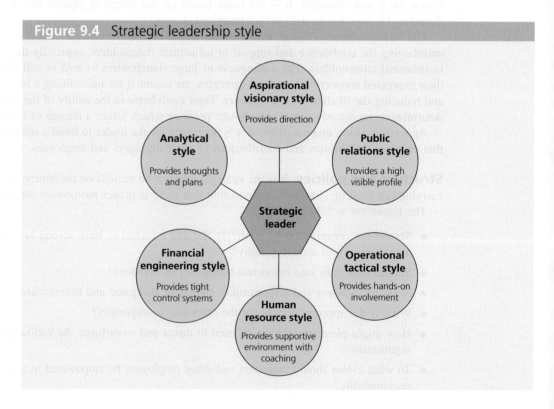

The communications network Effective communication systems, both formal and informal, are required to share the strategic vision and inform people of priorities and strategies and to ensure that strategies and tasks are carried out expeditiously. Where the organization is decentralized an effective communications network is vital for feeding information *upwards and laterally* inside the organization; without this control will be lost. In quite different ways, both 'managing by wandering around' and budgetary control systems can help to achieve this co-ordination. Good lateral communications also help managers to learn from other parts of the business; this in turn can lead to best practices being shared.

In addition, the strategic leader must champion the relationships between the organization and its important stakeholders, particularly its financiers, suppliers and major customers. Effective communications with government agencies and the media may also prove to be critically important.

> *Two-way communication is at the heart of successful management of change. Top management must beware of the conceit that it has all the answers. Having identified a problem, it will often be very rewarding to put to those in middle management a challenge to suggest a solution. Being nearer to the 'sharp-end' of the business in practical terms, it is surprising how frequently and rapidly they will provide an answer; and, since it comes from the heartland of the business, its implementation will find easier acceptance.*
>
> PETER SMITH OBE, WHEN CHAIRMAN, SECURICOR GROUP PLC

Governance and management Corporate governance relates to the location and exercise of power and responsibility at the head of the organization. The complex issues are beyond the scope of this book, but in simple terms, it is vital that the strategic leader ensures that there is a strong, competent and balanced executive team at the head of the organization. It is normally expected that the roles of chairman (often a part-time post) and chief executive are split to provide a check on leader power, but some companies choose to resist this splitting of the corporate leadership role. Another key issue is the role and contribution of part-time non-executive directors, who also provide reality checks as well as bringing experience and expertise. Topics of **governance** controversy frequently involve senior management remuneration packages.

Managing change The importance attached to formal planning processes and emergent strategy creation in an organization will depend upon the personal preferences and the style of management adopted by the strategic leader. The organization must be able to respond to the change pressures of a competitive environment. Curiosity, creativity and innovation become critically important values, and it is important for the strategic leader to ensure that they become part of the corporate culture. However, while learning and incremental change are crucially important, they may not be sufficient. Discontinuous change and strategic regeneration will be necessary for organizations at certain stages in their life cycles. When this is the case, and strategies, structures and styles of management need reinventing simultaneously, an effective, visionary leader will be essential.

The importance of an *effective* strategic leader cannot be stressed too highly, but an individual leader cannot and should not attempt to do everything. An important skill is the ability to understand personal strengths and limitations and to appreciate the most appropriate ways of contributing.

There is no single, recommended behaviour for effective strategic leadership. Some leaders are autocratic, others democratic in the way they make decisions. Some rely on planning and analysis, while others are more intuitive and visionary. Leaders vary in the degree of risk they will accept willingly. Some look for consistency as far as is practicable in today's dynamic environments, while others are constantly opportunistic and driving change. Some pursue growth through efficiency and cost savings, others by adding new values in an innovatory climate. Some set very ambitious growth objectives, and others are more modest. All of these styles can prove effective; the challenge lies in creating and maintaining E–V–R congruence.

It is always important to evaluate the leader's position and situation. A strategic leader may be the founder of an organization and still in control, or they may be a later family generation. The leader may have 'risen through the ranks' to take control, or may have been brought in specially, possibly to turn around a company in difficulty. The leader may be relatively new or have been in post for some time. The style of leadership adopted will depend upon the leader's preferred style, their background and the situational circumstances.

Case 9.2, Wynn Las Vegas, describes an entrepreneur who was able to learn by working in his father's leisure business before branching out on his own. He has been able to change the industry he is in – and he is also having to change continuously to maintain his competitive edge.

Critical reflection 9.1 provides a summary of the qualities and skills required for effective leadership, together with a list of the factors that typically characterize ineffective leadership. Figure 9.5 features those requirements that will determine the extent of the impact made by a strategic leader. The model presents the issues in three clusters:

- Drive – concerns motivation and ambition and a person's ability to accept demanding targets and achieve results

- Judgement – related to decision-making style and abilities. The softer or more conceptual issues of opportunity spotting and problem framing (awareness and insight into a situation) blend with harder analytical abilities

- Influence – a person's appreciation of how others might be influenced and their way of doing it. Networks and contacts are an important element of this.

Case 9.2

Wynn Las Vegas   US

'Wynn' is the name of one of the newest casino resorts in Las Vegas; it is named after its owner, Steve Wynn. It was perhaps coincidental that it opened in 2005, exactly 100 years after Las Vegas got off the ground as a city in the middle of the Nevada desert. Today, of course, it is the gambling capital of the US and renowned all round the word.

Las Vegas today is built around the legendary Strip with its numerous casino resorts, many of them themed around exotic places in the world – Luxor, Paris, Venice (The Venetian) and Mandalay Bay, for example. In 2004 there were 37.4 million visitors who spent $33.7 billion on pleasure. Two-thirds of the total came from hotels, spas, shops, restaurants and entertainment – the rest from gambling. They 'need each other'. Hotel occupancy exceeded 90 per cent (against a national average of 60 per cent). Major boxing matches are staged in Vegas; entertainers such as Elton John and Celine Dion play long runs; there is a multitude of Elvis

Presley impersonators reminding people that 'The King' was once a leading entertainer there himself. Cirque du Soleil has a permanent presence and develops special shows for Vegas. There are, of course, the ubiquitous wedding chapels as well. One downside for some is the burgeoning sex industry alongside the rest of the entertainment.

Steve Wynn's father ran bingo parlours and he worked in this business before striking out on his own and relocating to Vegas in 1967, where he was able to purchase a stake in a small casino. It was some twenty years later (in 1989) that he really began to make his mark – he built and opened the Mirage which would be sold to MGM in 2000; it is now the MGM Grand. He followed with Treasure Island (known for its pirate ship at the front) in 1993 and the more up-market Bellagio in 1998.

Wynn offers 2700 hotel suites and rooms, a golf course, a shopping mall, Ferrari and Maserati dealerships and 22 restaurants – as well as a huge casino.

The challenge for any developer such as Steve Wynn is to come up with something different that can attract people away from the other resorts. There is certainly no shortage of competition in Vegas – and serious competitors such as MGM and Harrah, which, amongst others, owns and runs Caesar's Palace.

Committed gamblers do not need to spend time in the relatively expensive Las Vegas and its resort casinos. If they are further east there is always Atlantic City in New Jersey; more locally Reno, Nevada and other similar places offer lower all-round cost gambling in casinos that don't boast the entertainment spectacles.

Many people from Asia come to Vegas for the gambling, upon which they seem hooked. But they could go to Macao, which is opening more and more super casinos. In addition there is the growing on-line gambling opportunity.

Question

1 What leadership style and approach do you think might be most appropriate for this industry and the challenges someone like Steve Wynn will face?

SOURCE: THIS CASE STUDY WAS PREPARED USING PRIMARILY PUBLICLY AVAILABLE SOURCES OF INFORMATION FOR THE PURPOSES OF CLASSROOM DISCUSSION; IT DOES NOT INTEND TO ILLUSTRATE EITHER EFFECTIVE OR INEFFECTIVE HANDLING OF A MANAGERIAL SITUATION.

Critical reflection 9.1

Effective and Ineffective Leadership

Qualities and skills for effective leadership

- A vision – articulated through the culture and value systems.
- The ability to build and control an effective team of managers.
- Belief in success and in corporate strengths and competencies that can be exploited.
- The ability to recognize and synthesize important developments, both inside and outside the organization. This requires strategic awareness, the ability to judge the significance of an observed event and conceptualization skills.
- Effective decentralization, delegation and motivation (the appropriate extent will vary).
- Credibility and competence. Knowing what you are doing and having this recognized. This requires the abilities to exercise power and influence and to create change.
- Implementation skills; getting things done, which requires drive, decisiveness and dynamism.
- Perseverance and persistence in pursuing the mission or vision, plus mental and physical stamina.
- Flexibility; recognizing the need (on occasions) to change strategies, structures and style. Some leaders are single style and inflexible.

Characteristics of ineffective leadership

After a period in office some leaders appear to coast, enjoying their power and status, but no longer adding any real value to the organization. Specifically:

- There are few new initiatives; instead there is a reliance on tinkering with existing strategies to try and update past successes.
- Good new products and services are not developed.
- The leader surrounds himself or herself with loyal supporters, rather than enjoying the stimulus of newcomers with fresh mindsets.
- Moreover, discordant views are either ignored or not tolerated.
- Cash reserves, beyond those needed to sustain a period of depressed sales, are allowed to accrue.
- The leader becomes out of touch with the views of customers and the activities of competitors.
- Too much time is spent by the leader on external activities, without ensuring that other managers are dealing with important organizational issues.

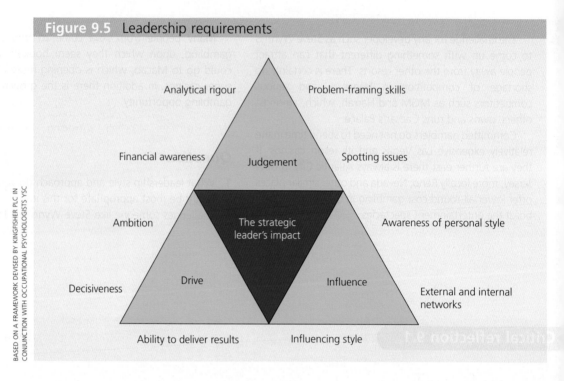

Figure 9.5 Leadership requirements

A number of these themes are also illustrated in Case 9.3 on Sir Tom Farmer, founder of Kwik Fit. Tom Farmer imported his vision for Kwik Fit from the US; success has involved opportunism and innovation backed up by sound business sense.

Sir Tom Farmer could legitimately be described as an entrepreneur. The next section looks at the link between entrepreneurs and strategy before examining visionary strategic leadership.

Leadership skills

Charan (2006) identifies what he believes it takes to be an effective strategic leader in today's world. He argues leadership is hard work and is suspicious that some high profile, charismatic leaders may not really demonstrate all the necessary qualities and know-how, which, he argues, are:

- The ability to position the business in order to make money – which implies an ability to satisfy customers and respond to environmental changes
- Connecting external events to the internal workings of the business – in order to drive the change agenda
- 'Managing the social system' of the organization so that there are effective networks and communications
- Judging, selecting and developing both other and future leaders – and –
- Moulding an effective leadership team
- Deciding upon and pursuing realistic but stretching goals – obviously linked to direction
- Clarifying priority issues – which will affect the likelihood of achieving the desired outcomes
- Finally, dealing with the inevitable, ubiquitous and unexpected challenges. The world is uncertain.

To be fair, Charan does argue it is unlikely any one person will be outstanding in all of these abilities!

Case 9.3

Sir Tom Farmer and Kwik-Fit   UK

Tom Farmer was born into a working-class family in Edinburgh, Scotland, in 1940; he was the seventh child. Brought up a Roman Catholic in a largely Protestant city, he left school at the age of 15 and began working in a tyre company. In 1964 he set up his own business, retailing tyres at discount prices. New legislation on minimum tyre depths opened a window of opportunity and he quickly expanded from one to four outlets. After four years he sold the whole business for £450,000 to Albany Tyres, 'retired' and went to live in California. Within three years he and his wife were bored. He returned to Scotland but, because of his agreement with Albany, he could not start a new tyre-retailing business until a number of years had elapsed.

Instead, he brought over an idea he had seen in the US: a fast-change exhaust shop. Again, he quickly expanded from one to four outlets, so that he could re-employ a number of his old friends! Tyres were added later. As for the Kwik-Fit name, he just dreamed it up. The distinctive blue and yellow colours, pervasive to this day, were chosen because these were the colours of some paint that someone gave him free of charge!

Farmer is a workaholic and was always very committed to his business and his employees. He is also very religious. All of Tom Farmer's employees were put on profit-share schemes; about half became individual shareholders in the business. Private garages and repair shops are often thought to involve dubious commercial practices; one of Tom Farmer's major achievements has been to bring a high level of perceived (and real) integrity into the industry. He places a strong emphasis on good customer service and friendliness, attributes which are featured in distinctive Kwik-Fit advertisements.

By the early 1980s there were 200 depots; arguably the business grew too quickly. Inadequate management control left the company vulnerable to takeover for a while, but it managed to retain its independence. For 29 years the company grew organically and stayed focused. There was some geographical expansion, successfully in Belgium and the Netherlands, but Kwik-Fit entered and then withdrew from France. 'There are cultural differences. The French want to close for lunch. French managers are reluctant to bond with their employees. These are key Kwik-Fit values.'

In 1994 Kwik-Fit acquired 95 Superdrive Motoring Centres from Shell, a related business. In 1995 Kwik-Fit Insurance was launched, exploiting Kwik-Fit's large customer database. Farmer argues that it is based on the same principles: high service using someone else's products. In 1999 Kwik-Fit was sold to Ford for £1 billion. By this time there were 1900 outlets, 9000 employees and 8 million customers a year. Tom Farmer, by this time Sir Tom, stayed active in the business for a some time after the sale to Ford, before effectively retiring for a second time. In August 2002, Ford sold Kwik-Fit to the private equity group CVC Partners for £330m. In 2001–2 Ford had global losses of $5billion and needed to raise cash by selling off non-core activities. Kwik-Fit continues to thrive with over 2500 service centres and 11,000 employees. This time there was no going back to Kwik-Fit for Sir Tom. But he remains active, encouraging other young entrepreneurs.

Yet Farmer has always been seen as a demanding man to work for, and many employees have been 'rather frightened of him'.

In an interview with *Management Today* (August 1995) Tom Farmer made the following comments.

If the customer is king, the staff are emperors.

We don't have a head office; we have a support office. We don't have senior management; we have support management.

All sound businesses are built on good Christian ethics: don't steal, don't exploit your customers or your people, always use your profits for the benefit of your people and the community.

We are in business to make a profit and we should not be ashamed of that, provided we stick to sound principles, and, at the end of the day, do proper things with that profit.

Questions

1 Why was Kwik-Fit so successful?
2 Is Tom Farmer a visionary leader, an entrepreneur or both?
3 Does the fact that he lives in a large house and owns both a corporate jet and a helicopter contradict any of his stated beliefs?

KWIK-FIT **http://www.kwik-fit.com**

SOURCE: THIS CASE STUDY WAS PREPARED USING PRIMARILY PUBLICLY AVAILABLE SOURCES OF INFORMATION FOR THE PURPOSES OF CLASSROOM DISCUSSION; IT DOES NOT INTEND TO ILLUSTRATE EITHER EFFECTIVE OR INEFFECTIVE HANDLING OF A MANAGERIAL SITUATION.

9.3 Entrepreneurs and entrepreneurship

Bolton and Thompson (2000) define an entrepreneur as a person who 'habitually creates and innovates to build something of recognized value around perceived opportunities'. Entrepreneurs can be found starting organizations, running organizations and working in organizations as employees. In the latter case they are typically called intrapreneurs, i.e. internal entrepreneurs. Two issues now need to be examined:

- the strategic leader as an entrepreneur
- whether the strategic leader has built an organization which fosters intrapreneurship.

Strategic management is concerned with environmental fit and it is important to achieve congruence between environment, values and resources for both existing and potential future products and services. Figure 9.6 revisits the model of E–V–R congruence and presents it in a marginally different way, one which implies action rather than being an expression of a state. The environment is presented as a number of windows of opportunity, and resources are represented by organizational competencies and capabilities. The argument is that entrepreneurship in the organization, both at the level of the leader and throughout the whole organization, is required to ensure that resources are developed and changed and used to exploit the windows of opportunity ahead of rival organizations.

The management of existing businesses should ensure that attention is focused on costs and prices (as they determine profits) and on ways of reducing costs by improving productivity. Technology changes and new operating systems may reduce costs; equally they may improve product quality, for which premium prices might be charged.

Future developments might concern new products (or services) or new markets or both, and they might involve diversification. For different alternatives the magnitude of the change implied and the risk involved will vary.

For both areas the changes that take place can be gradual or incremental, or they can be more dynamic or individually significant. Real innovation can be costly in terms of investment required, and consequently can involve a high level of risk, but sometimes it is necessary.

Figure 9.7 shows alternative development paths for a business. We normally think of entrepreneurs as the people who develop new ideas and new businesses, but there are different views on the implications of an entrepreneurial start-up. Schumpeter (1934), for example, argues that entrepreneurs bring innovative ideas into a situation of some stability and create

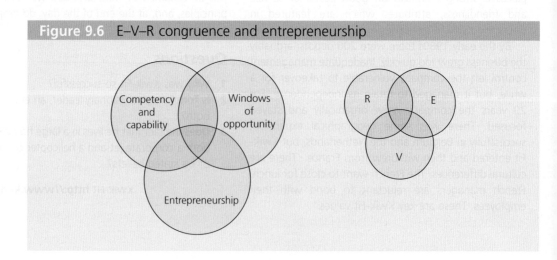

Figure 9.6 E–V–R congruence and entrepreneurship

Figure 9.7 Business development paths

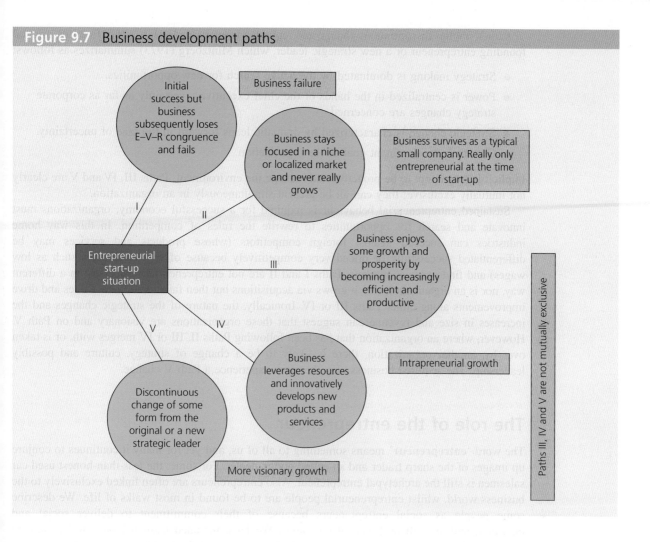

disequilibrium. The so-called Austrian School of economists (see Kirzner, 1973) suggests that entrepreneurs create equilibrium (in the form of E–V–R congruence) by matching demand and supply in a creative way. However, it is the path of future progress that really matters.

From its initial position the business could at first be successful but then fade away without further innovation and renewal (Path I). The original window of opportunity closes and the business fails to find or capitalize on a new one.

Some businesses never really improve and grow (Path II), sometimes by deliberate choice, sometimes through lack of insight and awareness; however, they survive as long as they can satisfy a particular niche or localized market. If one window of opportunity closes they find a new one, but in this respect they are more likely to be reactive rather than proactive. It is quite feasible for Path II businesses to *expand*, as distinct from true growth based on improvement and excellence. In reality, many businesses fall in this category. They are the archetypal small business – and they are not run by 'real' entrepreneurs as they fail the 'habitual' requirement included in the definition. They can legitimately be called lifestyle businesses and their founders are sometimes described as lifestyle entrepreneurs.

Paths III and IV feature more proactive entrepreneurial businesses which *grow* via productivity improvements and/or by leveraging their resources to develop new products and service opportunities. Sometimes, but certainly not always, such businesses will be decentralized, empowered and *intrapreneurial*.

Path V implies discontinuous change and requires visionary leadership, either from the original founding entrepreneur or a new strategic leader, which Mintzberg (1973) summarizes as follows:

- Strategy making is dominated by the active search for new opportunities.
- Power is centralized in the hands of the chief executive – certainly as far as corporate strategy changes are concerned.
- Strategic change is characterized by dramatic leaps forward in the face of uncertainty.
- Growth is the dominant goal of the organization.

Implicit is an attempt to be proactive and manage the environment. Paths III, IV and V are clearly not mutually exclusive; they can all be present simultaneously in an organization.

Sustained entrepreneurial behaviour is required for a successful economy; organizations must innovate and search for opportunities to rewrite the rules of competition. In this way home industries can succeed against foreign competitors (whose products and services may be differentiated successfully or priced very competitively because of cost advantages such as low wages) and find overseas markets. Paths I and II are not entrepreneurial businesses; in a different way, nor is an organization which grows via acquisitions but then fails to add new values and drive improvements along either Paths III or IV. Ironically, the nature of the strategic changes and the increases in size and revenue can suggest that these organizations are visionary and on Path V. However, where an organization that has been following Paths II, III or IV merges with, or is taken over by, another organization, there is likely to be a change of strategy, culture and possibly leadership. The acquired business may therefore experience a Path V change.

The role of the entrepreneur

The word '**entrepreneur**' means something to all of us, and yet for many it continues to conjure up images of the sharp trader and so-called dodgy dealer. For some, the less-than-honest used car salesmen is still the archetypal entrepreneur. Also entrepreneurs are often linked exclusively to the business world, whilst entrepreneurial people are to be found in most walks of life. We describe some people as social entrepreneurs because of their commitment to deliver social and environmental as well as financial outcomes. We have included Case 9.4 on J K Rowling to query whether you would agree that – given the definition at the beginning of Section 9.3 – she can be legitimately described as an entrepreneur as well as an author. In this section we explore how out understanding of the term has developed in the last 250 years.

Cantillon (1755) cites the entrepreneur as any individual who operates under conditions where expenditures are known and certain, but incomes (sales revenues) are unknown and uncertain. The unique characteristic of Cantillon's entrepreneur is foresight and the confidence to operate under conditions of uncertainty. The main qualities of the Cantillon entrepreneur are the creation of entrepreneurial income through decision making and risk taking rather than orthodox effort.

Cantillon was a natural trader and dealer with a relatively shrewd approach to opportunistic profit. His success as a speculator was said to have been based on his ability to perceive and predict the actions and reactions of other speculators better than they could predict his own. This reveals a character that combines intelligence and perceptiveness with a willingness to take risks 'to buy at a certain price and sell at an uncertain price'.

However, the entrepreneur was not just a 'wheeler-dealer'. The word 'Entrepreneur' was first applied to Frenchmen who 'entered and took charge' of royal contracts. Typically, the King would grant some nobleman the right to build a road or bridge and to collect the tolls, in return for a suitable donation to the royal treasury or some other favour. The nobleman would appoint an entrepreneur, who would arrange finance, supervise construction and manage the complete facility. The entrepreneur guaranteed the nobleman a fixed annual payment and kept everything that was left over. Noblemen generally wished to earn a steady income without getting their hands

Case 9.4

J K Rowling

UK

When *Harry Potter and the Deathly Hallows* was published in 2007, sales of the previous six books stood at some 325 million worldwide, 21 million of these in the UK. J K Rowling's books are a global phenomenon, and it had all happened over a ten year period. Her book, film, games and other royalties had earned her some £500 million.

Rowling was a nearly penniless single mother when she wrote the first book – she always said she had written the plot for all seven stories when she began the first one. It was rejected by several publishers before Bloomsbury took it on. Rowling has always paid great attention to detail and sought to protect her intellectual property, but the marketing of Harry Potter has been controlled effectively and this has contributed to the phenomenon.

Launch dates are publicized well in advance and to the day, and it is made clear that anyone involved in the publication who releases the plot will be sued. The books are available from stores at midnight on the launch date and many bookshops open specially. It is not at all unusual to see a long snake of children with their parents wanting to buy a book in the first few minutes it is on sale. Moreover many of the children will be dressed as witches and wizards. In addition the story of the new book is hyped: we all know in advance that one of the main characters is to be killed … but which one?

The books are translated into 65 different languages, but translation cannot start anywhere until the book is launched in its English version. Translators work around the clock across the world to produce foreign versions before sales of English copies take too much of a hold in local markets.

Because adults are avid readers, as well as their children, there are two different covers. The text is identical but there are adult and child versions. Prices are discounted heavily by bookstores and supermarkets – such that no retailer makes any serious money from the biggest book launch in the world.

Question

1 Using the definition of an entrepreneur (Section 9.3 in the text) do you agree J K Rowling is an entrepreneur as well as an author?

© MARCO SECCHI/ALAMY

dirty. They could do this by engaging an entrepreneur. The entrepreneur accepted the uncertain income in return for the chance of earning a profit. Since these entrepreneurs tended to be smart and closely involved with the project, and the noblemen who nominally owned the projects were usually neither, the profits were often substantial.

From this point in history it is clear that the role of the entrepreneur is to accept some form of risk. They however seek to manage that risk by their knowledge of both the process and of the market. The entrepreneur in the project not only accepts risk in return for reward. The project described required the entrepreneur to have the ability to manage the factors of production: land, labour and capital. It is this wider definition of entrepreneurship we will seek to build on and show.

In the German–Austrian Tradition, the entrepreneur is characterized as someone who manages the inputs into the process whereby the outcome is higher level outputs. Essentially, trying to manage demand and supply. In this the entrepreneur has to cope with uncertainty and is as a result a risk-bearer.

Schumpeter (1934) saw the role of the entrepreneur as driving through innovation. Innovation will lead to creation of new firms and to demise of old firms. The survival of the fittest process will lead to the creation of wealth. Schumpeter believed that only large firms would have the resources to both innovate and prevent the competition from new entrepreneurs threatening them. However, we know that small firms continue to be the engine of innovation in any economy and that these firms are led by people we call entrepreneurs.

The Chicago tradition, outlined in the work of Frank Knight (1921), indicates that the entrepreneur does take risks. This is the fundamental characteristic of the entrepreneur. This is linked to the level of uncertainty that exists within any economy. The entrepreneur needs to be able to deal with uncertainty.

The work of Schultz (1962) sought to provide for a bigger role for the entrepreneur in that the entrepreneur should not have a limited role as a business man. The entrepreneur should be the agent of economic change driving the economy forward.

The Modern–Austrian Tradition seeks to portray the entrepreneur as someone who must demonstrate "great ingenuity" and in so doing reaches the higher level of promoting economic change. This means that the entrepreneur can be someone who can contribute much more to the economy and is much more than just an effective manager: the entrepreneur must be alert to opportunity.

For Kirzner (1973) the entrepreneur is not interested in routine managerial tasks. Kirzner's entrepreneur is concerned to demonstrate qualities of creativity and perception. The entrepreneur is alert to changes in the economy and takes advantage of this. This view could return the perception of the role of the entrepreneur as a wheeler dealer who creates nothing except for spotting and taking profitable opportunity. To some extent it will depend on what form opportunity takes. Is it the opportunity to asset strip or the opportunity to innovate? Both might create wealth but whom for and how will the wealth be used?

With the work of Harvey Liebenstein (1966) we are moving towards confirming the more complex profile of the effective entrepreneur. The theory of x-inefficiency and x-efficiency highlights the basic concept that only through innovation will firms progress. Liebenstein identifies two types of entrepreneurs. The first is a routine or managerial figure allocating inputs to the production process in a traditional manner. The other is the Schumpetarian entrepreneur who can produce a new product or process through innovation.

At this point we can link in the work of the Classicists and particularly of J.B. Say (1815) who perceived the entrepreneur as someone who can effectively manage all of the factors of production such as: materials, labour, finance, land and equipment. For example say the entrepreneur is someone who has mastered the art of administration and superintendence. This type of entrepreneur is a real team player and capable of managing the growth of a larger organization. Again we can observe that few entrepreneurs show these capabilities and many have no desire to manage, co-ordinate and combine all of the factors of production. Yet say we believed that if this was not the case, the organization would ultimately fail. Therefore the qualities of the entrepreneur are crucial and this gives added importance to the concept of the entrepreneur team who can provide the wide range of skills needed.

As well as sustained entrepreneurial behaviour, new entrepreneurs are required to start new businesses to replace the jobs which are lost when other companies collapse and certain industries decline, as have coal mining, steel-making and shipbuilding, for example. Typically, a different type of business, with dissimilar labour requirements, will emerge. In general, the issue is not so much in stimulating business start-ups, but in encouraging them to grow. However, growth demands changes in structure and style and requires the owner-manager to relinquish some power and control. Case 9.5 features two interesting examples of visionary entrepreneurs, James Watt and William Chase, and the businesses they have helped to create. Case 9.6 looks at a completely different entrepreneur, Philip Green, who has bought and turned around a number of prominent high street retail chains.

It is, therefore, important for us to understand the motivation of entrepreneurs and how they see and activate opportunities.

Case 9.5

James Watt & BrewDog and William Chase & Tyrrell Chips UK

James Watt grew up in the North East of Scotland in a small fishing village called Gradenstown near Fraserburgh. James would help his father run and maintain his fishing boat. This exposure to hard labour is something that James Watt felt was a good beginning to his business career. After leaving school, Watt moved to Edinburgh to study law and economics at Edinburgh University. Following his graduation, Watt obtained a job in an Edinburgh law office. Pretty soon after joining the law firm, James realized he hated the job and discovered he actually had little real interest in his law career. At this point Watt moved back to his home village and to temporary work on his father's boat.

During this period his friend Martin Dickie (who James had met at Peterhead Academy) had completed a degree in brewing at Heriot Watt University. After graduation, Dickie had obtained employment as head brewer at Thornbridge Brewery in Derbyshire. However, the two friends had kept in touch and shared a passion for beer especially what Watt describes as 'real, honest natural beer not all that mass produced beer that is full of junk and additives with marketing onslaughts designed to change your life'.

BrewDog was founded in 2006 by James Watt and Martin Dickie. The two friends started the business with £120,000 obtained from many sources including their savings and loans from many sources including the Prince's Scottish Youth Business Trust (PSYBT). No external equity was given away, thus leaving the two partners firmly in control.

The brewery at the Kessock Industrial Estate in Fraserburgh produced its first brew in April 2007 and would go on within one year to become Scotland's largest independently owned brewery producing about 120,000 bottles per month for export all over the world. This has now grown to over 200,000 bottles per month with 80 per cent for export to the US and Scandinavia supported by sales in Tesco and Sainsbury in the UK. The BrewDog promise states that they will:

● Only use the finest natural ingredients
● Not include preservatives or additives within their beer
● Always make great tasting beers and promote them in a way which makes people smile.

What is clear about the business is the fervour and style that the two friends have brought to the start-up. Watt is particularly the driving force behind the marketing of the beers with Dickie happy to brew beer rather than sell beer. Watt has recognized that there is a gap in the market between traditional real ale drinkers who were mainly male and over 50, compared with the new beer drinker who is aged 18 to 30 and either male or female. In realizing there was a profit to be made from changing consumer tastes Watt demonstrates the typical entrepreneurial trait of taking advantage of change for profit.

The nature of the different approach to brewing bottled beer that BrewDog has is very well demonstrated in the names given to their beer:

● Hop Rocker (Lager)
● Punk IPA (India Pale Ale)
● The Physics (Amber Ale)
● Rip Tide (Stout)
● Hardcore IPA (India Pale Ale)
● Paradox Imperial Stout, matured in various malt whisky casks

The quirky nature of how BrewDog is run and their attitude to business, customers, beer creation and development can be examined through the company website: **www.brewdog.com**

In 2008 Paradox won the Gold Medal from the Brewers Association of the United States in the strong beer category, beating 53 other entries. This award is generally regarded as the most prestigious one that can be won worldwide for the brewing of beer. In 2008 BrewDog and James Watt won a number of other accolades, including Entrepreneur of the Year in the National Business Awards for Scotland; BrewDog was runner-up for the HSBC 2008 Start-Up Stars Award.

It is not however all 'plain sailing' for BrewDog. Their Fraserburgh location, to which they are fiercely attached, makes it difficult to recruit the staff they need for expansion and it will inevitably add to their distribution costs.

In 2008 BrewDog was challenged by UK drinks industry watchdog, the Portman Group. Portman claimed BrewDog was in breach of their Code of Practice on the Naming, Packaging and Promotion of

SOURCE: THIS CASE STUDY WAS PREPARED USING PRIMARILY PUBLICLY AVAILABLE SOURCES OF INFORMATION FOR THE PURPOSES OF CLASSROOM DISCUSSION. IT DOES NOT INTEND TO ILLUSTRATE EITHER EFFECTIVE OR INEFFECTIVE HANDLING OF A MANAGERIAL SITUATION.

Alcoholic Drink. BrewDog refuted these allegations and countered that Portman was impeding the development of smaller brewing companies.

After an 8 month long dispute and a preliminary adjudication which had ruled against the company, BrewDog was cleared of all breaches of the Code of Practice in December 2008, and was permitted to continue marketing their brands without making any changes to the packaging.

In February 2009, BrewDog announced plans to sell their beer in pubs and clubs up and down the UK stating that 'world domination is very much on the agenda'.

Questions

1 In terms of the theory and practice of entrepreneurship, what theories best explain the actions of James Watt in the creation of BrewDog?
2 What type of entrepreneur is James Watt?

FOR FURTHER DETAIL ON JAMES WATT
**http://www.bbc.co.uk/lastmillionaire/
entrepreneur/jamesw.shtml**.

William Chase

At the ripe old age of 20, William Chase purchased the Tyrrell Court Farm from his father in 1984. Poor sales and a recession saw his investment turn sour with Chase being made bankrupt. However, not to be put off, William Chase fought back. He leased his farm back from the lenders and eventually bought the farm back and moved on to become a successful potato farmer in his own right.

However, Chase believed that the only people making any money out of farming were the supermarkets who were forever forcing down the prices they gave to the farmer. On this basis Chase felt that his business of supplying potatoes would not be profitable for much longer. As with many examples of business change the new direction for William Chase came about through circumstance. A batch of his potatoes scheduled to be turned into oven ready chips by McCain were rejected. Chase quickly found an alternative customer for the potatoes and sold them to a crisp maker. Upon tasting the final product Chase thought he could do better. In 2002 he decided to do market research by going to America to taste as many hand made potato chips as he could. Upon returning he set about making his own hand made potato chips. He knew that success of his chips had to be based upon selling them as a new innovative product. He invested a great deal of money in marketing and packaging to put across the quality hand made image Chase felt was crucial to the success of his chips.

Over the next few years Chase built up his hand made potato chip business by selling firstly to independent retail stores, farm shops and to delicatessens rather than to the big supermarkets who he would not let dictate to him. In September 2006, Chase won a legal battle against Tesco preventing them from stocking his products without his permission. He does however sell to other supermarkets whom he is happy to deal with and they include, Waitrose, Sainsbury's and the Co-op. By 2007 the turnover of the business had reached £8.5 million selling not only the original potato chip but also flavoured potato chips such as Strawberry Sweet Chili and White Wine potato chips. His next great product idea is to launch in 2008 the first British pure potato vodka.

Chase personifies the business. Whilst very ambitious, he is very keen on keeping the business based around the Tyrrell Farm and he is a firm believer in the happy personalized team approach to doing business.

Questions

1 To what extent is business development of this type very much a rare example of how to succeed in business?
2 Profile William Chase. Is he part of a new breed of businessman?

www.tyrrellspotatochips.co.uk

Achievement and power motivation

McClelland and Winter (1971) have argued since the 1950s that all managers, in fact all workers, are influenced and motivated by three desires: the desire to achieve, the desire for power, and the desire for affiliation at work. The relative strength of each of these three desires or motives will vary from individual to individual, and what matters as far as management is concerned is to understand what does motivate people, rather than to believe that all people can be motivated in the same way.

Case 9.6

Philip Green UK

Philip Green is 'Britain's biggest private retailer', having completed a number of very successful deals, using largely his own money.

His business career began in 1973, when, at the age of 21, he took over the family property company. His move into retailing came in 1985, when he invested £65,000 to buy the Jean Jeanie chain of shops. He sold it five months later for £3 million. Three years later he invested in the Amber Day retail chain, a quoted company. After running the business for four years he resigned when he was under pressure following a profits decline. He later bought the Owen Owen department store chain (1994) and Mark One discount clothing (1996), of which he still owns 50 per cent of the shares.

In 1997 he bought Shoe Express from Sears for £8.3 million, and followed this up by purchasing the whole Sears empire for £550 million in 1999. He set about splitting the Sears retail conglomerate and ended up with a profit of some £180 million. When Marks and Spencer was in difficulty in 1999/2000, Philip Green was clearly interested – but never made a formal bid. Instead, and using £50 million of his own money, he bought British Home Stores for £200 million. By 2002 BHS was estimated to be worth £1.2 billion – 'the fastest billion pounds ever made in retailing'. In 2002 Philip Green bought Arcadia for £850 million. Arcadia had divested the Debenhams chain but it still comprised the Topshop, Topman, Miss Selfridge, Dorothy Perkins, Wallis, Evans and Burtons brands.

Green was rebuffed by Marks and Spencer in 2000, but four years later he returned. This time he did make a formal proposition to the Board and asked that they recommend it to their shareholders. He was not minded to enter a hostile takeover situation. The M&S Board responded by replacing their Chairman and Chief Executive. They refused to support Green's bid, although the largest institutional shareholder had agreed to sell to Green if the bid was recommended by the Board.

In 2005 Philip Green took a personal dividend of £1.2 billion from Arcadia – but within a year he was facing criticism for his leadership of his retail empire. The sales and profit figures, particularly for BhS, tell their own story …

		2002	2005	2006	2007	2008
ARCADIA	Sales - £m	2019	1770	1767	1858	1840
	Pre-tax Profits £m	100	254	289	293	275
BHS	Sales - £m	876	889	861	873	860
	Pre-tax Profits £m	172	114	51	50	30

At the same time, M&S was enjoying something of a revival of fortunes. Green stated that with his stores (he) had 'made stupid mistakes'. After all, retail is detail and he seemed to have taken his proverbial eye off the ball. Moreover, fashion changes fast. He was determined to take a serious look at his stores and their products and reverse the trend, which generally he has done. However when his Brand Director at Top Shop resigned there was speculation it was linked to Green signing up Kate Moss to design a fashion range and to model it. Other key executives left Top Shop. One retail rival has commented that 'Philip is brilliant at haggling on prices and bringing costs down, but he is not a brand builder; he doesn't look enough at investing in his brands and people'.

In 2006, and in partnership with one of the UK's leading costume jewellers, Green started Muse, a new chain of jewellery stores.

The retail slowdown and credit crunch late in 2008 seemed to offer a timely possibility for Philip Green – as much as anything because he had a considerable amount of his personal wealth readily available to invest in any attractive retail opportunities. The Icelandic Baugur Group was in difficulty when the Iceland banks were found to be in risk of folding. Baugur owned the House of Fraser department store chain, fashion retailers including Oasis, Warehouse, Principles and Coast, Hamley's toy store in London, Goldsmiths, Mappin and Webb and Watches of Switzerland, Wyevale Garden Centres and the chain of

SOURCE: THIS CASE STUDY WAS PREPARED USING PRIMARILY PUBLICLY AVAILABLE SOURCES OF INFORMATION FOR THE PURPOSES OF CLASSROOM DISCUSSION; IT DOES NOT INTEND TO ILLUSTRATE EITHER EFFECTIVE OR INEFFECTIVE HANDLING OF A MANAGERIAL SITUATION.

Iceland supermarkets. Philip Green was willing to invest his own money to secure part of this business – but he would inevitably have competition. In November 2008 Green acquired from Baugur the 28.5 per cent shareholding it held in Moss Bros, the high street tailoring chain, and was said to be considering a bid for the whole business. Baugur had previously failed to acquire Moss Bros. Green commented that if he did acquire the business he may well keep it as a public company rather than own it privately, the way that he owns Arcadia and BhS. In the event he did not acquire Moss Bros.

Green has been described as a 'born trader'. He is clearly enthusiastic and energetic; and he believes businesses are built on relationships and a small top team. As far as he can, he shuns the services of 'so-called experts'. He is incredibly focused and he understands customers and their expectations. Somewhat predictably he has strong self-belief and (like Kwik Fit's Tom Farmer) is rumoured to be a hard man to work for. Very hands on, he is always likely to turn up unannounced at one of his stores.

His leadership style involves tight control and centralization of key decisions. Each store group, such as Burtons, is a profit centre. It has its own Brand Director and Finance Director and these two are largely in control. Whilst the Brand Director will control styles, designs and ranges, he or she will be required to buy from approved suppliers wherever possible – and these suppliers will also supply other groups in the Green empire, thus enabling substantial discounts and scale economies. Information technology, human resources and financial services are all centralized.

It is, of course, impossible to say what he might have done with Marks and Spencer had he been able to take it over. Some critics of M&S, who believed the company had lost its way, thought he should be given a chance. Others felt he was simply not 'the right person' for M&S; he was culturally inappropriate. On a separate note, Green was instrumental in establishing a new Retail Academy in London, where his wife has a key role.

Questions

1   Use the Internet to help determine why Philip Green has been as successful as he has. How have the fortunes of all the businesses he has owned in recent years fared under his leadership?
2   Can you identify other retail chains that might benefit from the 'Philip Green touch'?

RUNE HELLESTAD/CORBIS

Entrepreneurial behaviour is characterized by high achievement motivation, supported by a power motive, and with affiliation very much third.

Achievement motivation is characterized by concern to do a job well, or better than others, with the accomplishment of something unusual or important, and with advancement. Such managers thrive where they have personal responsibility for finding answers to problems, and they tend to set moderate achievable goals and take calculated risks. If the targets are too modest, there is little challenge and little satisfaction, but if they are too high they are too risky.

Actually achieving the goal is important. They also prefer constant feedback concerning progress. Achievement motivation is closely linked to the desire to create something.

Entrepreneurial behaviour also features a desire for power, influence and independence.

Entrepreneurs need both creativity and confidence if they are to seek out and exploit new ideas; and they must be willing to take risks. While McClelland and Winter describe achievement-motivated people as those who take very measured risks, there are some entrepreneurs who thrive on uncertainty and are successful because they take chances and opportunities that others would and do reject. They will not always succeed, however.

In contrast with this business analysis, one might expect to see people who aspire to be leaders to be driven more by a desire for power.

9.4 Intrapreneurship

Entrepreneurial activity, innovation and growth are affected greatly by the ambition and style of the strategic leader, their values, and the culture that they create, but arguably they should be spread throughout the organization. Intrapreneurship is the term given to the establishment and fostering of entrepreneurial activity within large organizations. Many new ideas for innovation, for product or service developments, can come from managers within organizations if the structure and climate encourage and allow them to contribute. There are a number of ways. Special task forces and development groups are one alternative. Allowing individual managers the opportunity, freedom and, if necessary, the capital to try new ideas is another. Success requires that change is perceived more as an opportunity than a threat, that the company is aware of market opportunities and is customer orientated, and that the financial implications are thought through.

In times of discontinuity and accelerated change, survival depends on flexibility, on our ability to learn to adapt. Organizations which learn fast will survive. Management must take the lead. We must mobilize our greatest asset, our people, invest in their training and orchestrate their talents, skills and expertise. Their commitment, dedication, quality and care will build the competitive advantage of a winning team. Only they can provide our customers with the best product and service in the industry. The management of change takes tenacity, time, talent and training.

JFA DE SOET, PRESIDENT, KLM ROYAL DUTCH AIRLINES

Building the organization

Effective leaders possess a number of characteristics, they set direction and they inspire others. However, their strong leadership should not throttle flexibility and learning by a resistance to trusting other managers and involving them in key decisions. The most successful strategic leaders realize that they cannot do everything on their own and build a team to whom they can delegate important decisions and contributions. While some of these people will, by necessity, be specialists, professionals and technocrats, Horovitz (1997) stresses the importance of also recruiting or developing entrepreneurial managers to ensure the flow of innovation and change and prevent entropy. He argues that one of the reasons for Club Méditerranée losing momentum in the 1990s was the result of a failure to accomplish this back-filling effectively (see Case 5.3). Quinn (1980) also emphasizes the importance of innovation and ongoing learning by this team because not all of the issues and difficulties that will have to be faced can be foreseen.

The aim in a global business is to get the best ideas from everywhere. [In General Electric] each team puts up its best ideas and processes – constantly. That raises the bar. Our culture is designed around making a hero out of those who translate ideas from one place to another, who get help from somebody else. They get an award, they get praised and promoted.

JACK WELCH, CHIEF EXECUTIVE, GENERAL ELECTRIC

Horovitz (1997) contends that organizations should look for the problems before they even arise, by questioning what the (possibly very successful) organization is doing wrong. At times it is important to abandon products, services and strategies which have served the organization well in the past, as they are not the future. De Geus (1997) contends that businesses need to become 'living organizations' if they are to enjoy long and sustained success. This requires that the company:

- knows 'what it is about'
- understands where 'it fits in the world'
- values new ideas, new people, and fresh views and opinions
- manages its resources (especially financial resources) in a way which places it in a position to govern its own future; in other words, it is prudent and does not spend beyond a level it can earn.

These requirements are manifest in:

- clear direction and purpose (awareness of its identity)
- strategic positioning (its sensitivity to its environment)
- the management of change (its tolerance of new ideas) and
- the efficient use of its capital investment.

People, then, must be seen as key assets and managed accordingly; controls must have some element of looseness and flexibility; and constant learning must be possible.

Rosabeth Moss Kanter (1989) clearly supports this view when she argues that the whole organization holds the key to competitive advantage. She suggests that five criteria are found in successful, entrepreneurial organizations:

- *focused* on essential core competencies and long-term values
- *flexible* – searching for new opportunities and new internal and external synergies with the belief that ever-increasing returns and results can be obtained from the same resources if they are developed properly and innovative
- *friendly* – recognizing the power of alliances in the search for new competencies
- *fast* and able to act at the right time to get ahead and stay ahead of competitors
- *fun* – creative and with a culture which features some irreverence in the search for ways to be different; people feel free to express themselves.

For example at an Apple October 2008 product event it was notable that when Steve Jobs handed over the presentation to his executive vice president Tim Cook both men dressed the same casual way and used the same adjectives to describe Apple products.

In her earlier work, Kanter (1983) warned about the potential for stifling innovation by:

- blocking ideas from lower down the organization, on the grounds that only senior or very experienced managers are in a position to spot new opportunities. On the contrary, she argues, younger people with fresh minds are in an excellent position to question and challenge the status quo
- building too many levels in the hierarchy so that decision-making is slowed almost to a point of non-existence
- withholding praise from people who do offer good, innovative ideas, and instilling a culture of insecurity so that people feel too terrified even to question authority, policies or procedures

- being unwilling to innovate until someone else has tried out the idea – a fear of leading change.

Case 9.7, Richer Sounds, illustrates an organization that has benefited substantially from involving employees widely in new strategy creation.

While robust questioning and assumption-testing of new ideas is crucial, it is particularly important to remember that many people fear change, partly because of uncertainty about its impact on them personally. As a result, some people will seek to resist valuable change initiatives, and may even attempt to mount an active and orchestrated opposition. Managing change effectively, therefore, requires continuous effort and sometimes patience, reinforcing the significant contribution made by the project champion.

Case 9.7

Richer Sounds   UK

Electrical goods retailers are not new. The dominant names in the UK are Comet and Curry's, but Richer Sounds is different, and very successful. Richer is more focused than its main rivals, specialising in hi-fi, especially separate units. According to the *Guinness Book of Records*, Richer achieved the highest sales per square foot of any retailer in the world. Sales per employee are also high. Stock is piled high to the ceilings in relatively small stores in typically low-rent locations. All the main brands can be found; the latest models feature alongside discontinued ones, these at very competitive prices. 'We just aren't that ambitious [to justify diversifying] … we feel that by staying with what we know best we can concentrate our effort and resources in one field and hopefully do it well.'

Julian Richer was born in 1959; his parents both worked for Marks and Spencer. He was just 19 when he opened his first shop at London Bridge: 'seventy thousand commuters passed the shop every day'. He now owns some 50 stores in the UK and Eire and two more in The Netherlands. Apart from Christmas, Richer will not open on Sundays. His employees are known as colleagues and they are empowered to work 'The Richer Way'. He claims that his suggestion scheme has generated the highest number of suggestions per employee of any scheme anywhere in the world, and the best ideas are rewarded with trips on the Orient Express. The most successful employees (in terms of sales) can win free use of a holiday home; the most successful shops earn the free use of a Bentley or Jaguar for a month. Every employee is allowed £5 per month 'to go to the pub and brainstorm'. Julian Richer has advised ASDA on suggestion schemes, and ex-ASDA Chairman, Archie Norman, has said: 'Julian has gone to great lengths to create a system that works without him, but, to a great extent, his business is his personality'.

Richer has established a parallel consulting arm, with eight consultants who offer 'The Richer Way as a philosophy for delighting customers'. Consultancy is provided free to charities and good causes. Richer has also established a foundation to help selected good causes, and he owns a number of other small businesses. These include a retail recruitment agency, a property portfolio, and an award-winning tapas bar in Fulham. He has, however, 'one business and a number of hobbies'. He has, he says, stayed focused because of the perpetual threat from Internet sales.

Questions

1 Is 'The Richer Way' a key to sustained competitive advantage?
2 Why do you think it has been successful?

RICHER SOUNDS **http://www.richer-sounds.co.uk**

The process of intrapreneurship

Bridge *et al.* (2009) highlight the importance of recruiting, spotting and using people with entrepreneurial talent who are motivated to use their abilities and initiative and do something on their own, but who may not want to start their own business. These internal entrepreneurs have been called *intrapreneurs* by Pinchot (1985). Intrapreneurship, then, is the term given to the establishment and fostering of entrepreneurial activity in large organizations which results in incremental improvements to existing products and services and occasionally to brand-new products. Strategy in action 9.1 presents an idealized version of this situation, and an example of one large company's approach.

Figure 9.8 shows that both entrepreneurship (creating outcomes which imply a real difference) and intrapreneurship (less ambitious changes which are more likely to be based around improvements than major changes of direction) are broadly similar. They both begin when someone has a personal vision from which an idea and a related opportunity emerge. The opportunity must then be engaged and resources acquired as prerequisites to action and implementation. Intrapreneurship happens as individual managers promote and sell their ideas inside the organization and build a team of supporters. They drive change.

This was illustrated with the example of 3M and Post-it Notes, but realistically this is an extreme case. The innovation is more likely to be a minor, but significant improvement to a product or service or process: anything that makes a valuable difference. Strategy in action 9.1 illustrates how Shell has attempted to foster intrapreneurship with a special programme.

Intrapreneurs, typically, are strategically aware, ideas-driven, creative, flexible, innovative, good networkers, individualistic but also able to work well in a team, persistent and courageous. If frustrated by a lack of freedom they will underachieve or possibly leave. But they are volunteers; intrapreneurship is not right for everyone.

According to Pinchot (1985), the key lies in engaging people's efforts and energy for championing, capturing and exploiting new ideas and strategic changes. This must stretch beyond the most senior managers in the organization, who do not have a monopoly on good ideas. On the contrary, the potentially most valuable and lucrative ideas are likely to come from those people who are closest to the latest developments in technology or to customers. Suggestion schemes are linked in, but on their own do not constitute intrapreneurship. The ideas need to be taken forward, and they can only be developed if the potential intrapreneurs are able to obtain the necessary internal resources and, moreover, they are willing to do something. This in turn requires encouragement and appropriate rewards for success. People must feel involved in the process and comfortable that they are being supported. To Pinchot's list Morris and Kuratko (2002) added that intrapreneurs should manage expectations and never over-promise.

Intrapreneurship cannot work where people feel frozen out or dumped on. Churchill (1997) summarizes the philosophy as skills following opportunities. People in entrepreneurial businesses see the opportunities and set about acquiring the necessary resources. The whole process of change then becomes gradual and evolutionary. The momentum for change and improvement is never lost and the organization is less likely to be exposed and weakened by its competitors, resulting in it having to cross a 'bridge too far'.

Maitland (1999) has described how Bass developed new pub brands. In the early 1990s Bass' traditional customers (older people, and more working than middle class) were deserting pubs; young people became the new target. '[Bass] needed a radical 'break-out' strategy of new product development and concept innovation.' Bass spotted the new It's A Scream format, conceived by entrepreneur David Lee and popular with students. Lee was a builder in Farnham who had been given a pub in lieu of an unpaid debt and had transformed it. Bass bought the pub and the concept and recruited Lee as a consultant with a profit-share and a fixed fee for every new It's A Scream pub which opens. The All Bar One theme pubs, an upmarket, well-lit, city-centre chain with large windows which attracts groups of young female drinkers, reflects a similar story. Other initiatives have been developed from ideas put forward by existing managers, who have been offered

Strategy in action 9.1

Jack's Dream

I'm Jack Dupont. I work for Sunlite PLC, one of the world's largest fruit juice manufacturers. I am an assistant manager in the staff canteen. I was having a shower after a hard game of squash when it suddenly hit me. If you can put shampoo in a sachet, why not fruit juice? When the sun is beating down, as it nearly always does in most countries of the world, what better than a quick squirt of juice to lubricate the tonsils? No cumbersome bottles or glasses, it can be carried in a shirt's top pocket or in a handbag.

I became excited. We could put, say, 100 millilitres of juice in each sachet. 10 to a litre. Each sachet could be sold for 20p – £2 per litre of juice compared to 50p for a full litre pack. I rushed to see Jim McIlroy, my boss. Mary Dignum, his secretary, gave me her usual friendly smile. 'Want to see Jim? He is very busy but I will see what I can do.' She came back with a twinkle in her eye. 'He can fit you in between appointments at eleven.'

I explained my idea. 'Hum' beamed Jim. 'Let's get it off the ground at once. We need a proper business plan of course, to convince the board we have done things properly. Ring James Petrie at Price Waterhouse (Mary has the number) and ask him to do a market assessment for us. Harry in Packaging will know who to contact for the machinery to sachet the juice. You'll need money. We were about to launch a campaign to expand our market in Singapore, but I am sure they would not miss a few grand to help start your new venture. While you develop this idea, I will instruct Catering to buy in a substitute for you for one year. There are some spare rooms in 'D' division where you can pilot some juice sachets. If the piloting is successful, come back to help me arrange further finance. That's all for now, except to say, well done. There will be a rise for you in this.'

I felt inspired as I launched into the project with all the energy I could muster. There were, of course, many problems to overcome, but I had so many experts to help me. I had the full support of Jim and the board, with all the resources of Sunlite behind them. The first sachet rolled off the production line within a year, and is now being sold worldwide under the brand name 'KOOOL'. I never did go back to the catering department. I am currently working on a new project putting gin into small plastic sachets.

Interim question: Have you ever had an idea and a dream like Jack's? If so, how did you feel? What were you minded to do about it? Read the following story of Shell's GameChanger project and consider the parallels.

Royal Dutch Shell, with revenues of around £85 billion and over 100,000 employees worldwide, is an industrial giant in an established industry: petroleum. Historically, access to capital has been carefully controlled and radical ideas from internal entrepreneurs have been rare. Managers switch between divisions and countries for experience and promotion, but they are generally disciplined and loyal to corporate policies and procedures. In 1996, Tim Warren, Director of Research and Technical Services in Exploration and Production (Shell's largest division), was determined to change this, and to free up ideas, talent and resources. He was concerned that competition was intense in the dynamic and turbulent oil industry and Shell was 'not inventing radically new businesses'. Moreover, he firmly believed that Shell possessed the talent to drive a different behaviour.

© COOKELMA/DREAMSTIME.COM

In November 1996 he secured the resources to launch *GameChanger* and £12.5 million was set aside to fund radically new ideas submitted by employees. A group of key people would evaluate the ideas put forward by their peers. Consultants were brought in to run a series of creativity laboratories for volunteers; 72 turned up to the first one.

The focus was on:

- identifying and challenging industry conventions
- identifying emerging discontinuities
- leveraging and exploiting existing competencies to create new competitive opportunities.

The ideas began to flow from the laboratories and their interactive sessions. Some of the money set aside was used to ensure that the ideas which passed the first selection and screening were put into action. The creativity laboratory was supplemented by further work on project management.

As the programme developed, Shell's intranet was used increasingly to move ideas around the organization. Initial funding averaged some £60,000 per project selected, but it has been as high as £350,000. Employees were encouraged to stay involved. Once the concept was proven, further funding could be arranged. A number of important new Shell initiatives have emerged from *GameChanger*.

Follow on questions

Why do you think many large organizations ignore the potential of initiatives such as this?

What are the dangers in their approach?

Developed from:
Hamel, G (1999) Bringing Silicon Valley inside, *Harvard Business Review*, September–October.

secondment to champion their project ideas. Bass recognized the importance of visible support and encouragement from the top, so this became an engineered and not a random process. Bass ensured that adequate financial resources were available and also utilized sophisticated computer mapping systems to help with location issues. The two parallel questions are: Where are the ideal places for locating a particular format? What would be the best format for a site they already own? The key variables are age, affluence and car ownership, linked to how far people are willing to travel to eat or drink out. In other words, Bass brought together ideas, talented intrapreneurs and the resources that they needed.

To summarize these points, Hurst (1995) likens entrepreneurial strategic leaders to gardeners. They prune. They clear out. They plant, by recruiting other entrepreneurial managers. They feed, by encouraging and rewarding managers for being creative and innovative. Simply, they nurture and manage the organization as they would a garden. Paradoxically, many good ideas begin in the same way that weeds emerge in a garden, i.e. randomly. They then need spotting and looking after – the equivalent of transfer to a hothouse?

The intrapreneurial organization

Fradette and Michaud (1998) describe four main elements to an organization which succeeds with intrapreneurship. First, the strategic and structural environment is 'right'. The purpose and direction implies a realistic vision and it is widely understood and shared. Formal systems and controls do not stifle innovation and people are free to make limited changes. Inhibitive internal chimneys are pulled down so that people can collaborate and share ideas readily. Second, an appropriate workforce has been built. Enterprising people have been recruited. They have been trained in key skills and there is an appropriate reward system. The organization's main heroes are the entrepreneurial ones. Third, the workforce is backed by the necessary support systems. Teamworking is commonplace, people collaborate and network naturally, information is shared and learning is fostered. After all, several people in the organization may be thinking along the same lines at the same time concerning future possibilities. Fourth, successes are visibly rewarded

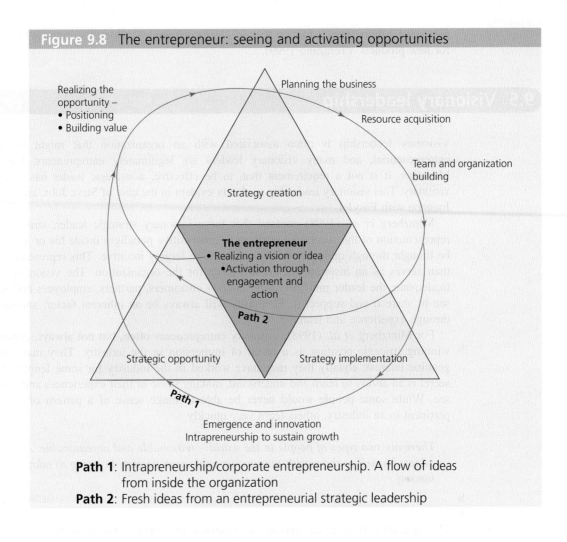

Figure 9.8 The entrepreneur: seeing and activating opportunities

Path 1: Intrapreneurship/corporate entrepreneurship. A flow of ideas from inside the organization

Path 2: Fresh ideas from an entrepreneurial strategic leadership

and mistakes are not sanctioned so harshly that people are dissuaded from further initiatives. These points are discussed further later in this chapter.

An intrapreneurial organization will often feature a relatively flat structure with few layers in the hierarchy; too many layers tend to slow decision-making down. The culture and atmosphere will be one of collaboration and trust. The style of management will be more coaching than instructional, and mentoring will be in evidence. Ideally it will be an exciting place to work. The entrepreneur's enthusiasm will have spread to others. In other words, it will be have to be 'contagious'.

Terazano (1999) also reminds us that effective intrapreneurship is not that easily achieved, and that many organizations set off down the road but fail to reap the anticipated rewards. Balancing control (to ensure that current activities and strategies are implemented efficiently) with flexibility (to foster and embrace changes to the same strategies) can imply different cultures, which are difficult to achieve without tension and conflict. Another difficulty frequently lies with finding the appropriate reward and remuneration systems to ensure fairness. It is a brave organization which only awards bonuses to the visibly entrepreneurial people. Managers in established companies often find it difficult to handle setbacks and disappointments when initiatives fail. But there always has to be the risk of failure, albeit temporary, when experimenting with new and unproven ideas. While intrapreneurs often have the security of large company employment, such that the penalty for failure is to some extent reduced, the rewards for real success are unlikely to equal those of the true entrepreneur. Nevertheless, 'increased competition in global markets and the pressure for innovation is forcing Britain's large companies to look for methods to stimulate ideas for new products' (Terazano 1999).

9.5 Visionary leadership

Visionary leadership is often associated with an organization that might be described as entrepreneurial, and many visionary leaders are legitimately entrepreneurs, but not always. Moreover, it is not a requirement that, to be effective, a strategic leader has to be personally visionary. This visionary leadership is clearly evident in the case of Steve Jobs, and in Stelios Haji-Ioannou with EasyJet.

Mintzberg *et al.* (1998) contend that for a visionary strategic leader, strategy is a mental representation of the successful position or competitive paradigm inside his or her head. It could be thought through quite carefully or it could be largely intuitive. This representation or insight then serves as an inspirational driving force for the organization. The vision or idea alone is inadequate; the leader must persuade others – customers, partners, employees and suppliers – to see it, share it and support it. Flexibility will always be an inherent factor, and detail emerges through experience and learning.

For Mintzberg *et al.* (1998), visionary entrepreneurs often, but not always, conceptualize the winning strategic position as a result of immersion in the industry. They may simply have a genuine interest; equally they may have worked in the industry for some length of time. Their secret is an ability to learn and understand, making sense of their experiences and the signals they see. While some people would never be able to make sense of a pattern of strategic signals pertinent to an industry, others learn very quickly.

> *There are two types of people in the world – reasonable and unreasonable. A reasonable man adapts himself to the world; the unreasonable man persists in trying to adapt the world to himself.*

GEORGE BERNARD SHAW

This quotation from Shaw appears to reinforce the relative merits of two schools of thought concerning what entrepreneurs are actually doing: Schumpeter's (1934) belief that entrepreneurs disturb the existing market equilibrium and stability with innovation, contrasted with the Austrian contention that entrepreneurs actually create equilibrium and market stability by finding new, clear, positive strategic positions in a business environment characterized by chaos and turbulence. The Austrian perspective is that of the reasonable man who observes chaos and uncertainty and looks for an opportunity gap that others have missed. Schumpeter's innovators are unreasonable; they are trying to disturb the status quo, turn things upside down, find new strategic positions and make life hard for any existing competitors. Blanchard and Waghorn (1997) claim that Ted Turner (with CNN 24 hour network news) and Steve Jobs are unreasonable men who, like entrepreneurs in the mobile phones business, have been instrumental in changing the world we know.

Successful visionary, aspirational leaders and entrepreneurs are clearly not all from the same mould. The authors believe that there is a hypothetical well of talent and as individuals we possess the potential most suitable for us to become either a leader, an entrepreneur, an intrapreneurial manager, an inventor, a follower or whatever. We remain in the well until we are released. We can, of course, propel ourselves out with sheer determination; equally, if we are fortunate, we can be spotted, nurtured and encouraged. It is not inconceivable that our true talents will lie buried for many years. The point is that when people with entrepreneurial talents emerge from the so-called well, they follow different paths. In Figure 9.9, hard entrepreneurship represents the paradigm of the independent, pragmatic, opportunistic and competitive entrepreneur. These achievement-orientated people are the typical managed risk-takers and natural networkers in search of a deal.

Figure 9.9   Four dimensions of entrepreneurship

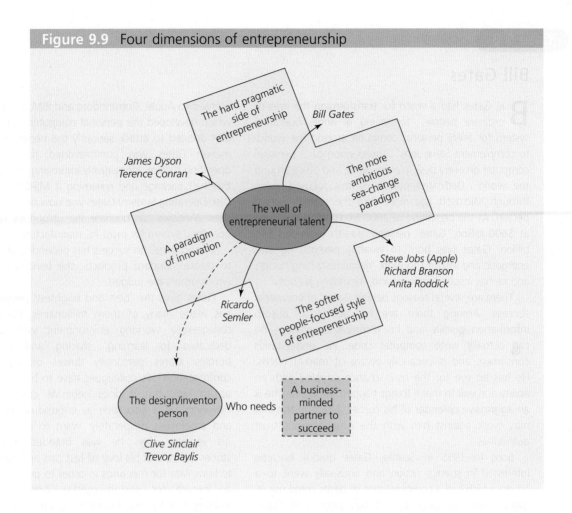

Not every entrepreneur fits this pattern. Some present a softer image. They operate in a more informal manner; they are strong on communication and they sell their vision to engage and motivate others. The hard and soft approaches lead to quite different cultures.

Some visionary, adventurous entrepreneurs set out to change the world. These are people with a real ability to galvanize others; they work hard, play hard and operate at the leading edge. They have to have enormous energy and generally they would be described as 'having a presence'. Again, this approach is not, and need not, be ubiquitous. The fourth arm, innovation, still requires imagination, creativity, passion and a commitment to bring about change (see Lessem, 1986, 1998).

> *Entrepreneurs are risk takers, willing to roll the dice with their money or reputation on the line in support of an idea or enterprise. They willingly assume responsibility for the success or failure of a venture and are answerable for all its facets.*
>
> VICTOR KIAM (REMINGTON RAZOR)

It may be suggested that Bill Gates (Case 9.8) is a typical hard adventurer – Microsoft has literally changed the world of computing – while James Dyson (Case 3.1) is a hard innovator. Steve Jobs (Apple Case 15.1 later), Richard Branson (Case 1.6) are certainly visionaries, whose products have again had a major impact on our lives, but they have all adopted a softer style and approach. Ricardo Semler (Case 3.4) is a visionary as far as management style is concerned, but Semco's engineering products, including pumps and industrial dishwashers, are hardly revolutionary. He appears to typify the soft innovator.

Case 9.8

Bill Gates   US

Bill Gates had a vision for transforming the lives of ordinary people, 'foreseeing a single operating system for every personal computer around the world' to complement Steve Jobs' (Apple) vision of 'a personal computer on every desk in every home and office around the world'. Dedicated pursuit of this focused vision through Microsoft has made him the world's richest person. At the beginning of 2000 Microsoft was valued at $600 billion; Gates' personal wealth exceeded $85 billion. Gates was born to wealthy parents; he was energetic and inspired to work 'ridiculously long hours', and he has inspired criticism and, inevitably, jealousy.

There are several reasons behind Gates' phenomenal success. Among them are his ability to absorb information quickly and his technical expertise – he can actually write computer code. He understands consumers and is uncannily aware of market needs. He has an eye for the main chance coupled with an ability and will to make things happen. Moreover, he is an aggressive defender of his corner, which in the end may work against him with the American anti-trust authorities.

Born in 1955 in Seattle, Gates quickly became interested in science fiction and unusually went to a school which had a computer that students could use. A 'nerd' from an early age, it has been said Gates 'preferred playing with computers to playing with other children'. He nevertheless teamed up with his friend, Paul Allen, and together they 'begged, borrowed and bootlegged' time on the school computer, undertaking small software commissions. Gates and Allen went to Harvard together, where Gates proved to be an unpopular student because of his high self-opinion. Surreptitiously using Harvard's computer laboratories they began a small business on the campus. Gates later left Harvard to start Microsoft, never completing this formal part of his education. Allen was his formal partner in the venture, but Gates always held a majority control. Bill Gates' visionary contribution was the realization that operating systems and software (rather than the computer hardware) held the key to growth and industry domination.

Gates took risks in the early days but, assisted by some good luck, his gambles largely paid off. When the first commercial microcomputer (the Altair) needed a customized version of the BASIC programming language, Gates accepted the challenge. His package was later licensed to Apple, Commodore and IBM, the companies which developed the personal computer market. When IBM decided to attack seriously the personal computer market Gates was commissioned to develop the operating system. Innovatively improving an existing off-the-shelf package and renaming it MS-DOS (Microsoft Disk Operating System) Gates was now on his way. Since then Windows has become the ubiquitous first-choice operating system for most PC manufacturers.

By and large, his success has depended on his ability to create standard products, the benchmark against which others are judged.

Gates hires the 'best and brightest' people and he has made many of them millionaires. He prefers a college-style working environment with a culture dedicated to learning, sharing and overcoming hurdles. Gates personally thrives on combat and confrontation. His colleagues have to be able to stand up to him, but it does generate creative energy. However, he is also seen as enormously charismatic, and employees desperately 'want to please him'. In his younger days he was branded a risk-taker; stories are told of his love of fast cars and his tendency to leave late for meetings in order to provide him with an excuse for driving quickly. After a two-year investigation by the American anti-trust authorities it was ruled (in 2000) that Microsoft should be split into two businesses – one for operating systems and one for applications, including the Internet – and should also be required to give away some of its coding. Gates and Microsoft had been found guilty of exercising monopoly power to the detriment of their competitors. Gates was incensed and appealed against the verdict, which was largely overturned in a higher court. In 2004 the European Competition Commission also ruled against Microsoft, arguing that it had created an effective monopoly by bundling its own Media Player with Windows. Microsoft said that again it would appeal the verdict.

Since the US ruling Gates has announced two key things. First, in the future Microsoft will focus its resources and energies on developing software that will be delivered as services via the Internet rather than loaded into individual PCs. Second, he was standing down as chief executive. He would continue as chairman and adopt a new role as the company's top software architect. He was returning to his roots.

I'm returning to what I love most – focusing on technology. These are dramatic times in our industry. We recognize that we must refocus and reallocate our resources and talents.

In July 2008, Gates left Microsoft in terms of day to day involvement but remained Chairman. Between 2006 and 2008 what is described as a top management transition took place at Microsoft. The new role for Gates will allow him to spend more time on his health and education work through the Bill and Melinda Gates Foundation.

The CEO is Steve Ballmer, who had joined Gates during the Harvard days, where he was a fellow student. Having been a successful vice president for sales, support and marketing he had later been appointed president. Ballmer is recognized as an aggressive hardliner who will have the tricky job of trying to keep the growth of Microsoft going.

Questions

1 What are the strategic issues that confront Microsoft today?
2 What exactly did the European Competition authorities decide and what has developed since the announcement in March 2004?

MICROSOFT **http://www.microsoft.com**

SOURCE: THIS CASE STUDY WAS PREPARED USING PRIMARILY PUBLICLY AVAILABLE SOURCES OF INFORMATION FOR THE PURPOSES OF CLASSROOM DISCUSSION. IT DOES NOT INTEND TO ILLUSTRATE EITHER EFFECTIVE OR INEFFECTIVE HANDLING OF A MANAGERIAL SITUATION.

There is, however, one final category: the designer–inventor who lacks the necessary business acumen or interest to build the business on his or her own, but who can, with help, be part of a successful and entrepreneurial business. Sir Clive Sinclair is a designer–inventor who has come up with a number of truly innovative ideas and products, but he never found the right partner and built a winning business. Trevor Baylis also fits here. He did find the right partner and his BayGen radio has provided the foundation for a successful business.

Visionary leadership and strategy creation

Visionary leadership, then, implies a strategic leader with a personal vision for the future of the organization and at least a broad idea of the strategies for pursuing the vision. Such leadership often appears to be based on intuition and possibly experience rather than detailed analysis, but truly visionary leaders possess strategic awareness and insight, and do not require extensive analyses to understand key success factors and how the organization can use its abilities and competencies to satisfy needs and expectations. There is a 'feel' for which strategies will be appropriate and feasible and for the potential of the opportunity.

When a visionary leader pursues new opportunities and introduces changes the detailed plans for implementing the new strategies are unlikely to be in place; instead, there will be a reliance on incremental learning, flexibility and adaptation. For the approach to succeed, the leader must be able to inspire others and persuade them of the logic and merits of the new strategies. This is true for all important strategic changes, but when new proposals have emerged from a more formal strategic planning system there will be substantive detail and analysis to justify the case instead of a strong reliance on vision and intuition.

Where major changes to the corporate strategy are being considered it may be necessary for the strategic leader to convince other members of the board of directors and, if new funding is needed, the institutional shareholders and bankers.

The strategy cannot be successful until it has been implemented and has brought the desired results and rewards. Such outcomes require the support and commitment of other managers, and consequently effective visionaries are often articulate, communicative and persuasive leaders.

In simple terms, then, visionary strategic leadership implies three steps: step one is the vision, step two is selling it to other stakeholders and managers; and step three is making sure it happens – aspects of vision, communication and pragmatism.

Richardson (1994) suggests that the following factors are typical of visionary leadership:

● 'covert' planning – planning is often cerebral rather than formal and systematic, such that planning *systems* are not a major aspect of strategy creation

- a passion about what they are doing and their business
- they are instrumental in creating and fostering a particular culture
- they are highly persuasive when encouraging others to implement their ideas and strategies
- they rely on charisma and personal power.

Although visionary leaders are sometimes entrepreneurs, and some entrepreneurs are visionary leaders, the two terms are not synonymous. In this book a visionary strategic leader is seen, typically, as someone who is a persuasive and charismatic agent of change, either starting a new, differentiated business which takes off, or changing the direction and corporate strategy of a business in order to maintain or improve its rate of growth. Major, discontinuous change is implied. The growth can be fuelled by astute acquisition. While entrepreneurship again implies growth, the growth need not always be visionary or discontinuous. Equally, many entrepreneurs are not, and need not be, charismatic figures. The key element of visionary strategic leadership is a visionary impact on strategy creation.

Remember, however, that a strategic leader who succeeds in turning around a company in crisis and *restores growth* – a process sometimes called corporate entrepreneurship – can be a visionary. At the same time, it does not follow that visionary leadership is necessary for either new ventures or successful turnaround situations. When a company is in trouble, a good, analytical 'company doctor' who can restructure, rationalize and refocus the business can be very effective. An example of this can be found in the management buy-in to Clyde Blowers plc orchestrated by Jim McColl OBE, provided as Case 9.9.

Narcissistic leaders

Maccoby (2000) has highlighted how strategic leaders, especially those whom we would describe as visionary, are typically more visible today than they ever have been in the past. Some are excellent self-publicists to begin with, and the media are generally more interested in business stories, especially where they concern new industries. Partly as a result of this, Maccoby concludes

---

Case 9.9

Jim McColl   UK

SOURCE: THIS CASE STUDY WAS PREPARED USING PRIMARILY PUBLICLY AVAILABLE SOURCES OF INFORMATION FOR THE PURPOSES OF CLASSROOM DISCUSSION; IT DOES NOT INTEND TO ILLUSTRATE EITHER EFFECTIVE OR INEFFECTIVE HANDLING OF A MANAGERIAL SITUATION.

Jim McColl had spent 17 years (1968–1985) working as an engineer in various UK companies. He followed this with a period of three years as a senior consultant with Coopers and Lybrand working mainly in corporate care work. From 1987–1992 he worked as an independent company doctor. In his own words 'all the time looking for an opportunity to buy into an engineering business'. In 1992 he was offered that opportunity when he bought a 29.9 per cent stake in Clyde Blowers a public listed engineering company whose principal business activity was sootblowing from coal fired boilers. Established in 1924 as a family firm, Clyde Blowers was still controlled and run by the orginal family in 1992. Instead of being an engineering business, Clyde Blowers had become a property company which also earned some revenues from

sootblowing. McColl set about 'realizing the value in the engineering business' by selling off the property interests and investing the cash in the engineering business which had been starved of investment. Additionally, he set about building up the business through a series of acquisitions. During the period 1992–1997, seven companies were acquired worldwide which took the market share enjoyed by Clyde Blowers to over 25 per cent of the world market for sootblowing. In 1992, the turnover of Clyde Blowers was £3.3m and 100 per cent within the UK. By the year 2000, the geographical spread of sales was: 56 per cent US, 34 per cent Europe, 7 per cent UK and 3 per cent China on a total turnover of £70m. McColl describes his strategy for Clyde Blowers as a classic example of textbook consolidation involving: rationalizing of activities; simplfied product lines; 43 per cent reduction in manpower, elimination of the competition; and internationalizing the business.

Described thus it all looks very simple. However, it was McColl who spotted the opportunity and had the vision and drive to see the strategy through to completion including delisting Clyde Blowers from the London Stock Exchange and taking the company private when the share price of the business was marked down by analysts.

Questions

1 What has happened to Jim McColl and Clyde Blowers in recent years?

http://www.clydeblowers.co.uk/

that an increasing number of strategic leaders are narcissists, inspirational personalities who have a major impact upon culture and style, who enjoy the visibility and notoriety, and who often believe that they are 'something special'. Prior to his retirement (in 2001), Jack Welch, who we mentioned earlier and who we also talk about later in this chapter, negotiated an advance of several million dollars for his autobiography. Richard Branson published his own best-selling autobiography and Bill Gates wrote a successful book on how digital processes can solve business problems.

A lot of people want to be led – yet there are very few leaders in life. When people have a good leader who instils team spirit, and they work in an environment that demands excellence, energy, and the keeping of momentum in order to achieve a goal, then they want to stay ... or, if they leave, they want to come back!

LINDA J WACHNER, WHEN CEO, WARNACO (US)

To be effective, leadership has to be seen, and it is best seen in action. Leadership must be communicated in words, but even more importantly in deeds. Leaders must be seen to be up-front, up to their jobs and up early in the morning.

LORD SIEFF OF BRIMPTON, CHAIRMAN, MARKS AND SPENCER, 1972–1984

What we have in these three cases are big-picture visionaries who are associated with risks and who also come across as being charming personalities. They are typically entrepreneurial and competitive.

There is, however, a potential downside to the narcissist. He or she can be an unrealistic dreamer who has delusions of grandeur. They might also be a poor listener and a relatively isolated loner who is uncomfortable with challenge or criticism.

Richard Branson, for example, has sued the author of an unauthorized biography which questions some of his strategies and claims.

9.6 Issues in strategic leadership

A precarious position?

Chief executives of large UK businesses (ones in the top 90 in the *Financial Times* index) stay in post for an average of just four years, while their equivalents in the US last, on average, a year longer. Simply, partly because of the visibility mentioned above, perceived poor performers are dismissed more readily than in the past. A price has to be paid for perceived failure. Although, as it would appear with the collapse of banks, the price is not necessarily financial but more in terms of their reputation amongst the general public.

Charan and Colvin (1999) suggest that these people are normally bright and experienced executives who can articulate a vision and strategy for their organization. This is not their failing.

Instead, their shortcomings lie in an inability to implement strategy. This makes sense. In an age of visibility, visions and broad strategies soon become public property. Rivals can attempt to copy them if they wish. Hence, as was shown earlier (see, for example, Chapter 4, Figure 4.9) sustained competitive advantage lies not in ideas and strategic positions, but in the way strategies are executed.

Charan and Colvin specify a number of typical strategic leader misjudgements:

- underestimating the importance of people – a topic we discussed in Chapter 3

- failing to put people in the right jobs – Buckingham and Coffman (1999) emphasize the importance of ascertaining people's individual strengths and natural behaviours and using these to judge where they are most likely to make their best contribution

- failing to deal with underperforming managers, especially if they are people they have appointed and who remain loyal

- not stretching people to the highest levels of performance that they can reach

- failing to put in effective decision-making processes – such that important decisions are either not made or not carried through. This relates to empowerment, another topic discussed in Chapter 3.

- misjudging the balances between strategy and operations and between the external and internal focus of their efforts. Often this is linked to poor corporate governance, a topic taken up at the end of the chapter. The outcome may well be that a good vision and broad strategy is neither implemented effectively nor updated in changing circumstances.

In the remainder of this section several of these points are taken up.

Finite shelf lives?

All leaders, including the most successful, have finite shelf lives, periods of time when they can contribute effectively to an organization. Some know when to step down and either retire or move on, before they cease to be effective. Others stay too long and risk being remembered for their later shortcomings rather than their earlier successes. Churchill was at his peak at the end of the World War II; Margaret Thatcher achieved her zenith once the main planks of Thatcherite reform were in place. When she stayed on, opposition to her later policies began to ferment, and the details of her downfall will be remembered at least as much as her achievements.

In recent times the departure of Tony Blair as Labour Prime Minister may prove to have been another example of someone staying too long and thus tarnishing their reputation.

Case 9.10 (Volvo) looks at another longstanding strategic leader who eventually lost the confidence of his board.

Kets de Vries (1994) argues that chief executives who fail to make a timely exit go through a three-phase life cycle. As we progressed through the 1990s, the length of this life cycle was shortening. The first stage is the entry of a new strategic leader into the organization, which is followed by experimentation with new strategies. Downsizing, acquisitions, re-engineering and a drive for improved service and quality are likely. The newcomers make their mark; results improve, certainly in the short term. This becomes the second stage of consolidation, when it is likely that the changes are cemented in a new culture. If an organization was in crisis, the risks are now perceived to have fallen back, and herein can lie the seeds of a new crisis. The third stage, then, is one of decline and a new crisis.

The appropriate style

Visionary leadership is frequently associated with entrepreneurial strategies for companies enjoying prosperity in growth markets. As the organization continues to grow, a more formal structure, together with robust control systems, will be required. The leader must therefore be

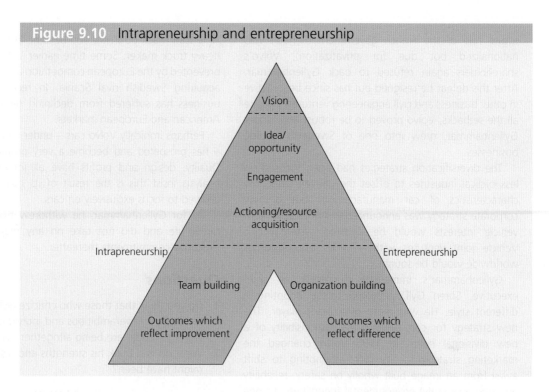

Figure 9.10 Intrapreneurship and entrepreneurship

flexible, capable of adapting and willing to relinquish some personal control. Ideally, other managers will be empowered and encouraged to be entrepreneurial and visionary.

This will not always happen, as some visionary leaders tend to be inflexible. In such circumstances a change of leader would benefit the organization.

Similarly, companies in trouble, facing a strategic crisis or which need rationalizing require a leader who is skilled at managing detail and resources to generate productivity

Case 9.10

Volvo   Eur

Volvo was led from 1971 to 1993 by Pehr Gyllenhammar, a lawyer who was married to the daughter of the previous chief executive. Gyllenhammar has been credited as a visionary leader who failed to implement many critical strategic proposals.

In the early 1970s he concluded Volvo was reliant on a limited product range (essentially large cars, trucks and buses) and constrained by Sweden not being a member of the European Union. He acquired Daf from the Dutch government; a prolonged period of learning was required before Volvo's subsequent range of small cars proved successful. He began to build the first foreign-owned car assembly plant in the US, but production never started. He opened the revolutionary Kalmar assembly plant in Sweden in 1974, based on autonomous work groups rather than the traditional

assembly line; the idea was successful, but not outstandingly so, and Kalmar was closed in 1993. In 1977 a proposed merger with Saab-Scania was abandoned when Saab had second thoughts. In 1978 Gyllenhammar agreed to sell 40 per cent of Volvo to the Norwegian government in exchange for oil rights, but Volvo's shareholders revolted.

In the 1980s Volvo acquired the US White truck business and diversified into the food and drug industries in Sweden, but not without some friction with the Swedish government. Throughout this period Volvo's car subsidiary enjoyed continuing success, albeit with its relatively staid image and reputation.

In 1989 Volvo and Renault cemented a strategic alliance with the exchange of minority shareholdings, and in 1993 a full merger was proposed. Fearing the

SOURCE: THIS CASE STUDY WAS PREPARED USING PRIMARILY PUBLICLY AVAILABLE SOURCES OF INFORMATION FOR THE PURPOSES OF CLASSROOM DISCUSSION; IT DOES NOT INTEND TO ILLUSTRATE EITHER EFFECTIVE OR INEFFECTIVE HANDLING OF A MANAGERIAL SITUATION.

future role of the French government (Renault was nationalized but due for privatization), Volvo's shareholders again refused to back Gyllenhammar. After this defeat he resigned but has since been active in other business and civil engineering ventures. Despite all the setbacks, Volvo proved to be robust and, under Gyllenhammar, grew into one of Sweden's leading businesses.

The diversification strategies had been focused on less cyclical industries to offset the uneven cash flow characteristics of car manufacturing, but a new corporate strategy was announced in April 1994. Non-vehicle interests would be divested systematically. Vehicle joint ventures with a series of companies worldwide would be sought.

Gyllenhammar's immediate successor as chief executive, Sören Gyll, appeared to be adopting a different style. He was more of a team player. The new strategy for cars became the responsibility of a new divisional head. In 1995 Volvo changed the marketing strategy for its cars, attempting to shift away from an image built wholly on safety, reliability and (more recently) environmental friendliness, to one of 'safe but sexy'. Advertisements claimed that (when accelerating in top gear) a Volvo 850 could outpace a Ferrari. The aim was to attract younger 'pre-family' and older 'post-family' buyers without losing the core family customers, and increase output by one-third.

In 1999 Volvo's car division was sold to Ford, which was concerned that 'Volvo had failed to attract younger buyers' and this needed addressing urgently. There would be further changes of management. The sale was possibly inevitable – the group was no longer generating an adequate cash flow for sustainability.

In 2000 Volvo – which by now was largely trucks – bought Renault's truck businesses (which included the American Mack business) and became Europe's largest heavy truck maker. Some time earlier Volvo had been prevented by the European competition authorities from acquiring Swedish rival Scania. In recent years the business has suffered from declining demand in key American and European markets.

Perhaps ironically Volvo cars – under Ford ownership – has prospered and become a very profitable brand. Quality, design and profits have all improved. Some analysts insist this is the result of its managers being allowed to focus exclusively on cars.

As for Gyllenhammar, he withdrew from Swedish public life and did not take on any major business executive commitments thereafter.

Questions

1 Do you think that those who criticize Gyllenhammar for being an overambitious and individualistic strategic leader are being altogether fair?
2 What do you think his strengths and his failings might have been?

VOLVO **http://www.volvo.com**

LEXANDDREAMSTIME.COM

improvements – again different characteristics from the visionary. However, as highlighted earlier, once such an organization has been successfully rationalized, fresh growth requires vision, and here a more visionary leader can again prove ideal.

Succeeding a visionary

Unless proper plans are made, succession can be a critical issue. Unfortunately, many visionary leaders are driven by personal ambition and a personal vision; they are difficult to work with and they do not share their game plan. As a consequence, they fail to build a pipeline of managers ready for succession. This raises a number of possible problem scenarios:

● owner-managed businesses may need to be sold, but once an entrepreneurial leader has left, what is the true value of the remaining assets?

- on a visionary's retirement a complete outsider may be needed, implying major change
- the leader could have an accident or illness, leaving a yawning gap which cannot be filled in time to prevent a crisis.

The very successful diversified American conglomerate, General Electric (GE), is discussed at various points in this book. Comments from its visionary strategic leader, Jack Welch, also appear regularly. One apocryphal story of Welch concerns an alleged conversation with a New York yellow cab driver, who claimed he sold his GE shares every August and bought them back in September. 'Jack goes on holiday in August and who knows what might happen when he's away.'

When Welch gave GE advance notice that he would retire in April 2001, succession planning got underway. Three internal divisional heads, those for GE Medical Systems, GE Power Systems and GE Aircraft Engines, were identified as possible successors. They were all interviewed by GE main board members, as were the key staff who reported to them, to assess their style and suitability. To ensure that one of them could be moved up without leaving a gap at the top of their division, a new chief operating officer was appointed in each case, to provide for a second-stage orderly succession. 'Few large companies approach their succession planning with such care.' Of course, they do not always have as much notice!

Welch's successor has proved to be effective – but in a different way. The two disappointed executives both left to take up CEO roles at other companies, both in retailing: Albertson's and Home Depot. Both businesses were in trouble and have been turned around successfully by their new strategic leaders.

In contrast, Online Case 9.1 looks at how succession issues have contributed to the declining fortunes at Boots.

In the context of succession Bower (2007) argues strategic leaders must engage three challenges: judging where the world is going, identifying managerial and leadership talent and engaging that talent. Planning for succession is integral to the talent challenge; it should not be an occasional decision but an ongoing issue. The implication, that Bower supports, is that succession should come from within; external appointments can be too disruptive. He would argue that GE plan for succession by appointing business heads and making sure they are put to the test as strategic leaders.

When a new strategic leader is appointed, things may not be the same, strategically, culturally and stylistically. This can be good or bad. If real changes are required because the company has lost momentum or is in difficulty, then logically a new leader with a different style is being brought in to make changes. Where a company is successful, then 'change for the sake of change' may be a mistake. But it would not be unusual for a new leader to want to be seen to be his or her own person and to make an early mark. Returning to Figure 9.4, it is quite normal for any new leader to have a different preferred style.

See the online "Boots" case for an example of this section's theory in practice

Leadership and corporate failure

Businesses 'fail' when they fail to meet the needs and expectations of their key stakeholders, or when decisions that they take lead to outcomes which are unacceptable to the stakeholders. These failings may generate crises with which the business is able to deal, usually at a cost; they may also lead to the ultimate collapse of the organization. The outcomes can take a variety of different forms, but authors such as Slatter (1984) have clearly identified three main, direct causes of corporate failure and collapse:

- weak or inappropriate strategic leadership
- marketing and competitive failings
- poor financial management and control.

It can be seen how these failings imply an *incongruency*, or lack of fit, between environment, values and resources, resulting from a lack of strategic awareness. Leadership issues also underpin the marketing and financial weaknesses.

Richardson *et al.* (1994) have identified a number of discrete failure crisis situations, against which we can consider strategic leadership.

A *niche becomes a tomb* when a small company, locked into a successful product or service, lives in the past and fails to change. This is invariably a sign of poor leadership, and quite frequently it will be tied in to succession problems. When *markets are not understood* small companies will fail to establish a position in the market they have targeted and simply not take-off and grow. Sometimes this will be the result of attention being concentrated on the production aspects of the business, where the would-be entrepreneur may have expertise but may not satisfy customer needs and expectations. Equally, sales may be achieved, but not in sufficient volume.

Strategic drift with larger organizations is the result of introversion and inertia in a changing environment. Complacency from past success, or a concentration on day-to-day reactive or crisis management, can lead to a failure situation. Online Case 9.1 on Boots provides a clear example of a previously successful large business having problems adapting to a changing environment.

Overambition can be seen in the guise of the failed entrepreneur and the failed conglomerate kingmaker. The former enjoys early success and rapid growth on the back of a good product or service, but the desire to maintain high growth encourages the entrepreneur to diversify into less profitable areas. A downward spiral begins. The conglomerate kingmaker wants to build a large and powerful corporation and is tempted to acquire businesses that cannot be justified financially. Specifically, they pay a price which either overvalues the assets or which cannot be recouped from earnings, or they overestimate the potential for synergy with the existing businesses. In this regard the failure of the Royal Bank of Scotland is put in part down to the aggressive takeover strategy driven through by Sir Fred Goodwin, RBS's chief Executive. He had joined RBS in 1998 and took over the top job in 2000. In 2002 RBS jumped into the 'big league' through the £22bn hostile takeover of its London based rival NatWest which was three times the size of RBS. Over the next 3 years the group did well with rigorous cost cutting and integration. After that Sir Fred completed a further 23 acquisitions including a US bank, Charter One for $11bn. At that point Sir Fred's reputation was sky high. However, in April 2007 RBS joined with Fortis and Santander of Spain to bid for the Dutch bank ABN Amro for €71bn at the height of the boom. It proved to be a bank too far.

Failures of this nature are frequently characterized by strong, powerful strategic leaders and inadequate attention to critical financial measures and controls. In some instances the result is inadequate governance. The business does not appear to be looking after the interests of all its stakeholders, but instead is driven by the strong, selfish and personal motives of the leader who will sometimes borrow money on the strength of the business. Others may enjoy total control and their judgement may not be questioned.

In October 2008, the Baugur Investment Group (based in Iceland and founded by Jon Asgeir Johannesson) was facing meltdown. It had built up a mountain of debt buying top retail assets in the UK, for example House of Fraser, Hamleys, Mappin & Webb and Oasis. With the credit crunch and the collapse of the Icelandic banks Baugur owed at least £2bn to these banks. What seemed like an integrated strategy of buying related assets including department stores, fashion stores, speciality businesses and food retailers such as Iceland has now all unraveled. Waiting in the wings is Sir Philip Green (Case 9.6) with his eyes on House of Fraser and any other good assets to be bought at a knockdown price.

In the early part of the twenty-first century a number of so-called corporate scandals have been widely publicized and generated considerable cynicism about the world of business and especially about high-profile, celebrity leaders. Creative accounting practices at Enron, alleged greed at Tyco, and convicted insider dealing by author and TV presenter Martha Stewart and now the huge illegal pyramid (Ponzi) scheme designed by Wall Street trader Bernard Madoff, with losses of $50bn or more, are examples. Trust is becoming an increasingly significant issue in leadership and business in general.

'Don't panic, Mr Mainwaring'

Some readers will be familiar with the TV series *Dad's Army* and remember this phrase. We conclude this chapter with comments from Sonnenfeld and Ward (2007), who believe that the most effective strategic leaders are those who can deal with adversity, crises and setbacks – a topic we debate further in Chapter 16. The courage to sort things out when they go wrong is, of course, an important characteristic of the entrepreneur. Those that fail to deal with such challenges will end up as failures. It is a commonly held view that the US and UK view failure in a different way and that for many American entrepreneurs it is basically an invitation to get up and do something else. Success here is in part an issue of temperament, but it also involves an ability to learn from events and mistakes. Sonnenfeld and Ward also comment that a network of supporters can be a great help in rebuilding trust. It is interesting that Martha Stewart, who we mentioned above, has managed to revive her business career after serving her jail sentence, for example. Jimmy Carter was in the minority of US Presidents who stand but fail to get elected for a second term. But rather than retire gracefully, so to speak, he is now a respected humanitarian and a Nobel Peace Prize winner. He found a new mission and pursued it.

Summary

The *strategic leader* of an organization affects both strategy creation and strategy implementation. He or she is responsible for establishing the basic direction of the organization, the communications system and the structure. These influence the nature and style of decision-making within the firm. In addition, decision-making and change is affected by the personal ambitions of the strategic leader, his or her personal qualities such as entrepreneurialism and willingness to take risks, the style of management adopted and the management systems used. Power – how it has been obtained and how it is used – will also affect the style and approach of the strategic leader.

Strategic leaders come in 'all shapes and sizes'. Some are personally visionary, but this is not a prerequisite for effective leadership. It is, however, incumbent on the strategic leader to ensure that the organization has a vision and clear direction and that resources are committed towards its achievement.

Strategic leaders must perform four key tasks or, at least, ensure that they are performed by someone. They must ensure that the organization thinks strategically, that people are engaged and committed and that as a result there is positive action, and that the organization has an appropriate public face and visibility.

The leader can contribute by starting a new business or venture, by turning around a company in trouble, by transforming an already successful company or even by splitting up a company to exploit the true value of its subsidiary parts.

Six different *leadership styles* were identified, often related to past experiences. The leader's natural or preferred style will have a major impact upon the culture of the organization. The six are: analytical, aspirational, public relations, financial engineering, operational and people-based.

Visionary leaders typically provide a strategic vision and rely less on formal planning systems. They are persuasive and charismatic and operate through the culture.

Entrepreneurs are similar in many respects, but they are different. Entrepreneurs build value around opportunities. Internal entrepreneurs (intrapreneurs) will be provided with opportunity and encouragement in some organizations where they will drive emergent strategic change.

Clearly, some strong leaders are instrumental in the success and prosperity of organizations. On other occasions they are perceived to fail. In reality, the shelf-life of many large company chief executives is relatively short. Where they are seen to fail it is often the result of poor implementation, which implies that leaders are more likely to know what they would like to achieve than how to do it. This has a further implication: it suggests that it is easy to think that success lies in a good idea, in a strategic position; but ideas and positions can be copied. Sustained competitive advantage lies in the ways in which things are done. Processes and behaviours are harder to replicate.

Succession is a crucial issue, particularly succession for someone who has been especially successful or charismatic. It would not be unusual for a newcomer to want to make changes, possibly for no other reason than to stamp his or her personality and preferences on the organization.

Online cases for this chapter

Online Case 9.1: Boots
Online Case 9.2: David Bruce

Online Case 9.3: Michelle Mone and MJM International
Online Case 9.4: Pilgrim Jewellery

Questions and research assignments

1 Using the Volvo case (Case 9.10) as a background, discuss why effective leadership involves both strategy creation and strategy implementation. From your experience and reading, which other well-known strategic leaders do you believe are strong on

  a creation
  b implementation
  c both?

2 Research the real ale sector. What might the further development of BrewDog entail?

3   Where do the entrepreneur and the visionary leader overlap and where are they different?

4   Apply Figure 9.4 (alternative styles of leadership) to any strategic leader whom you are in a position to evaluate.

Internet and library projects

1   What has happened recently with respect to the ambitions of Sir Philip Green the owner of BHS and Arcadia? Will he ever get his hands on M&S?

2   Re-examine Figure 9.4 Can you attach a particular entrepreneur to each one of the six key leader styles?

3   How effectively has the General Electric succession issue been resolved?
    General Electric **http://www.ge.com**

4   Go back over the period 2000–2009, and reflect on the career of Sir Fred Goodwin. There was a time when Sir Fred was lauded by everyone including the UK government and the business press. Was he a visionary leader then? What went wrong? Sir Fred paid a price for failure – he left RBS – but he left with a colossal and controversial pension.

Strategy activity

Friends Reunited   UK

In 1999 Julie Pankhurst was pregnant and walking near where she lived in Barnet, North London. She had an idea that it would be interesting to get back in touch with people she had known at school to check which ones were now parents. She shared her thoughts with her husband, Steve, a computer programmer. They came up with the idea for a website and enlisted the additional expertise of Jason Porter, an IT developer.

The site was launched in 2000; the business was being run from the Pankhursts' home. They gained publicity and people soon started clicking on the site and became subscribers. After six months Friends Reunited was talked about on Radio One and this had an immediate impact. Daily subscriptions doubled overnight. Eventually 'half the online population signed up'.

The Pankhursts held 30 per cent of the shares and Porter another 30 per cent. The remaining shares were distributed amongst the managers who joined the growing business. When it was sold to ITV in 2005 the founders became multi-millionaires. ITV paid £175 million – but interest in Friends Reunited then started to fade and by early 2009 the business was valued at £40 million *maximum*, possibly quite a bit less. ITV sold it to DC Thomson for just £25 million in August 2009.

The idea is incredibly simple. It is in effect an alumni society for schools, colleges and universities which goes way back and supplements anything the schools and universities might organize themselves. In fact many universities use Friends Reunited to track their alumni!

There are obvious benefits and outcomes – such as getting to rekindle friendships from way back and organizing reunions – but there have been negative impacts. There are cases of people being libelled on the site. In the end the competition from Facebook and others was too strong.

Questions

1   Why would Friends Reunited be attractive to a business like ITV?

2   Revenue comes mainly from subscriptions, but is this business so much more than that?

3   Were the founders right to sell out whilst they could get a deal?

4   Is Friends Reunited a genuinely entrepreneurial business or what we might call a 'one trick pony'?

Further reading

Brody, P and Ehrlich, D (1998) Can big companies become successful venture capitalists?, *McKinsey Quarterly*, 2.

De Geus, A (1997) The living company, *Harvard Business Review*, March–April.

Eisenhardt, KM (1999) Strategy as strategic decision making, *Sloan Management Review*, 40, Spring.

Ginsberg, A and Hay, M (1994) Confronting the challenges of corporate entrepreneurship, *European Management Journal*, 12 (4).

Goffee, R and Jones, G (2000) Why should anyone be led by you?, *Harvard Business Review* September–October.

Hamel, G (1999) Bringing Silicon Valley inside, *Harvard Business Review*, September–October.

Hansen, MT (1999) What's your strategy for managing knowledge?, *Harvard Business Review*, March–April.

Kets de Vries, M (1994) CEOs also have the blues, *European Journal of Management*, September.

Kets de Vries, M (1996) Leaders who make a difference, *European Management Journal*, 14 (5).

Maccoby, M (2000) Narcissistic leaders, *Harvard Business Review*, January–February.

Morris, E (1988) Vision and strategy – a focus for the future, *Journal of Business Strategy*, 8 (2).

Pearson, EA (1994) Tough minded ways to get innovative, *Harvard Business Review*, May–June.

Richardson, W (1988) Towards a profile of the visionary leader, *Small Business Enterprise and Development*, 1 (1).

Weinshall, TD and Vickery, L (1987) Entrepreneurs: a balanced view of their role in innovation and growth, *European Management Journal*, 5 (4).

Zack, MH (1999) Developing a knowledge strategy, *California Management Review*, 41 (3).

References

Bennis, W, Interview recorded in Crainer, S (1988) Doing the right thing, *The Director*, October.

Blanchard, K and Waghorn, T. (1997) *Mission Possible*, McGraw Hill.

Bolton, WK and Thompson, JL (2000) *Entrepreneurs: Talent, Temperament, Technique*, Butterworth-Heinemann.

Bower, JL (2007) *The CEO Within: Why Inside Outsiders are the Key to Succession Planning,* Harvard Business School Press.

Bridge, S, O'Neill, K and Martin, F. (2009) *Understanding Enterprise, Entrepreneurship and Small Business*, Third Edition, Palgrave.

Buckingham, M and Coffman, C (1999) *First, Break all the Rules*, Simon and Schuster.

Cantillon, R. (1755) Essai sur la Nature du Commerce en General, London and Paris.

Charan, R and Colvin, G (1999) Why CEOs fail, *Fortune*, 21 June.

Charan, R (2006) *Know-How: The eight skills that separate people who perform from those who don't*, Random House.

Churchill, NC (1997) Breaking down the wall, scaling the ladder. *In Mastering Enterprise* (eds S Birley and D Muzyka), Financial Times/Pitman.

De Geus, A (1997) The living company, *Harvard Business Review*, March–April.

Derr, CB (1982) Living on adrenaline – the adventurer entrepreneur, *Human Resource Management*, Summer.

Ettinger, JC (1983) Some Belgian evidence on entrepreneurial personality, *European Small Business Journal*, 1 (2).

Fradette, M and Michaud, S (1998) *The Power of Corporate Kinetics – Create the Self-adapting, Self-renewing, Instant Action Enterprise*, Simon and Schuster.

Hamel, G (1999) Bringing Silicon Valley inside, *Harvard Business Review*, September–October.

Hooper, L and Trompenaars, F (2009) *The Enlightened Leader,* Jossey Bass.

Horovitz, J (1997) Growth without losing the entrepreneurial spirit. In *Mastering Enterprise* (eds S Birley and D Muzyka), Financial Times/Pitman.

Hurst, DK (1995) *Crisis and Renewal – Meeting the Challenge of Organizational Change*, Harvard Business School Press.

Kanter, RM (1983) *The Change Masters – Innovation and Entrepreneurship in the American Corporation*, Simon and Schuster.

Kanter, RM (1989) *When Giants Learn to Dance*, Simon and Schuster.

Kets de Vries, MFR (1996) CEOs also have the blues, *European Journal of Management*, September.

Kets de Vries, M (1994) Leaders who make a difference, *European Management Journal*, 14 (5).

Kirzner, IM (1973) *Competition and Entrepreneurship*, Cambridge University Press.

Knight, F. (1921) Risk, Uncertainty and Profit, Chicago, University of Chicago Press.

Lessem, R (1986) *Enterprising Development*, Gower.

Lessem, R (1998) *Managing Development Through Cultural Diversity*, Routledge.

Liebenstein, H (1966) Allocative efficiency vs. "x-efficiency", *American Economic Review*, June.

Lieberstein, H (1968) *Entrepreneurship and Development, American Economic Review* 58 (2):72–83.

Maccoby, M (2000) Narcissistic leaders, *Harvard Business Review*, January–February.

Maitland, A (1999) Strategy for creativity, *Financial Times*, 11 November.

McClelland, D and Winter, D (1971) *Motivating Economic Achievement*, Free Press.

Morris, H.M. and Kuratko, D.F. (2002) Corporate Entrepreneurship, Fort Worth: Harcourt College Publishers.

Mintzberg, H (1973) Strategy making in three modes, *California Management Review*, 16 (2).

Mintzberg, H, Ahlstrand, B and Lampel, J (1998) *Strategy Safari*, Prentice-Hall.

Pinchot, G (1985) *Intrapreneuring*, Harper and Row.

Pinchot, G III (1994) *Intrapreneuring*, Harper and Row.

Quinn, JB (1980) *Strategies for Change: Logical Incrementalism*, Irwin.

Richardson, B (1994) Towards a profile of the visionary leader, *Small Business Enterprise and Development*, 1 (1).

Richardson, B, Nwanko, S and Richardson, S (1994) Understanding the causes of business failure crises, *Management Decision*, 32 (4).

Say, JB (1815) Catechisme d'Economie Politique, translated (19210 by John Richter, Catechism of Political Economy.

Schultz, TW (1962) Investment in human beings, Chicago, University of Chicago Press.

Schumpeter, J (1934) *The Theory of Economic Development*, Harvard University Press; original German edition, 1911.

Slatter, S (1984) *Corporate Recovery: Successful Turnaround Strategies and their Implementation*, Penguin.

Sonnenfeld, J and Ward, A (2007) *Firing Back: How Great Leaders Rebound After Career Disasters,* Harvard Business School Press.

Terazano, E (1999) Fresh impetus from the need to innovate, *Financial Times*, 25 June.

Strategic alternatives, strategy evaluation and strategy selection

Learning objectives

Having read to the end of this chapter you should be able to:

- identify and describe a number of possible strategic alternatives, separated into limited growth, substantive growth and retrenchment clusters

- define and discuss innovation and show how it is essential for sustaining competitiveness

- explain how selected strategies might be implemented through internal or external growth

- show how organizations pursue different strategic alternatives and means at various times in their development

- define the key criteria for evaluating the appropriateness, feasibility and desirability of a particular strategic alternative

- discuss why there might be a trade-off between these factors

- explain the contribution to this evaluation of techniques described earlier in the book

- summarize a number of alternative theories of decision-making and explain why subjectivity can sometimes result in poor decisions

- explain the role of judgement in strategic choice.

This chapter outlines the various strategic alternatives that might be available to an organization in thinking and deciding where it wants to go, and for helping to close the planning gap. The attractiveness of particular alternatives will be affected by the objectives of the organization. While a whole range of options is discussed, it does not follow that they will all be available to an organization at the same time. Because of the costs or risks involved, particular alternatives might be quickly rejected. The appropriate strategy always matches the environment, values and resources congruently.

As shown in Case 10.1, Diageo, organizations change their strategies over time, and from this the corporate profile takes a new shape.

In their consideration of strategic alternatives, some organizations will be entrepreneurial and actively search for opportunities for change. Others will only consider change if circumstances dictate a need. Some organizations will already have sound and effective strategies that are producing results with which they are satisfied. Others may ignore the need to change. Some texts have quoted the example of the typewriter companies who thought they knew instinctively that electric typewriters, let alone word processors, would never catch on.

The essential criteria for strategy evaluation and selection are appropriateness, feasibility and desirability. These involve a mixture of objective and subjective factors. Not every strategic decision will be objective and consequently we need to understand how managers (and in turn organizations) make decisions and the impact of uncertainty and judgement on these decisions.

Case 10.1

Diageo
UK US

By the early 1990s Grand Metropolitan (GM) had become the world's leading manufacturer and distributor of spirits, through its IDV (International Distillers and Vintners) subsidiary, and an important manufacturer of foods, particularly in the USA. GM owned Pillsbury, the Jolly Green Giant foods company. The strategic perspective had changed dramatically in the previous 25 years, influenced markedly by three strategic leaders, and it was about to change again!

In the early 1960s, led by Sir Maxwell Joseph, GM, then known as Grand Metropolitan Hotels, was a leading hotel company and was specialized. Through a series of acquisitions GM then diversified into restaurants, dairies and supermarkets, leisure activities, brewing and spirits. Additional hotel chains were also acquired. This external growth activity slowed down in the 1970s because GM had become highly geared and was affected by the international oil crisis and high interest rates. When Joseph retired in 1980 three strategic problems could be identified:

- GM was overreliant on the UK (90 per cent of turnover)
- IDV was inadequately represented in the USA, a key market for spirits
- many hotels needed upgrading if they were to capitalize upon the increase in tourism, especially from the USA.

The new chief executive, Stanley Grinstead, sought mainly to consolidate and build, concentrating on the USA. GM acquired its US spirits distributor, Liggett and Myers, in 1980. Liggett also manufactured cigarettes but the tobacco interests were quickly sold off. GM bought Inter-Continental hotels from Pan American and adopted a strategy of repositioning its hotels. Lower grade properties were divested. GM concentrated on exploiting its major brand names and also bought Pearle Health Products in the USA. By the mid-1980s hotels contributed 19 per cent of turnover and 6 per cent of profits. The breweries were suffering as lager became more popular at the expense of bitter beers.

Sir Allen Sheppard, who took over in 1986, chose to focus on those businesses where GM could obtain world market strength and divest everything else. The major acquisitions were Heublein (1987), owners of Smirnoff Vodka, the world's second largest spirits brand, Pillsbury, whose main brands are Green Giant,

Burger King and Häagen Dazs ice cream, and Pet, which includes Old El Paso Foods (USA) and Shippam pastes in the UK. Mexican food is an important growth sector in the USA. After divestments over half of GM's revenue was now being earned in the USA.

The true synergy potential of food and drinks was always debatable – while food is essentially a necessity, drinks are more aspirational – but both businesses feature strong, international brands. GM essentially had developed competencies in people, management and control systems, and operational effectiveness, and used these to add value to its businesses.

Sir Allen Sheppard retired as chief executive in 1996 and was replaced by George Bull, an internal promotion. One year later, Grand Met merged with Guinness, and the group was subsequently renamed Diageo. The name was a combination of the Latin *dia*, meaning day, and the Greek *geo*, meaning world. Diageo therefore symbolized 'everyday pleasure, everywhere'.

A number of important changes happened in 2000. Principally, Burger King (which had been acquired with Pillsbury) was floated off as an independent business, and the remaining food businesses (Pillsbury and Pet primarily) were sold to General Mills. It was then speculated that if a suitable joint venture partner could be found (as a way of overcoming potential resistance from the relevant competition authorities) Diageo would bid for the drinks businesses owned by the Canadian conglomerate Seagram. These included Chivas Regal brandy. In the event Diageo joined forces with Pernod of France to follow up this opportunity. The joint bid was successful, but Pernod acquired Chivas Regal – Diageo obtained Captain Morgan rum and several prominent American and Canadian whiskies.

Paul Walsh replaced George Bull as chief executive.

In essence, this left Diageo more focused as the world's leading spirits business together with additional interests in wine and brewing (Guinness). IDV's leading brands are: J&B and Bells (whisky), Smirnoff (vodka), Gilbey's (gin), Jose Cuervo tequila, Captain Morgan rum, Bailey's and Piat d'Or. The merger with Guinness added UDV (United Distillers and Vintners) and the following brands: Dewar's and Johnnie Walker (whisky) and Gordon's gin. IDV has 16 of the top 100 global spirits brands – including five of Europe's top ten and four of America's top ten.

In 2005 Pernod acquired Allied Domecq to become the clear Number Two spirits company. At this time IDV was shipping 91 million cases a year, 14 million ahead of Pernod. Diageo did not oppose the merger and in return was sold Bushmills Irish whiskey.

The following time-line traces the main acquisitions (normal case) and *disposals* (shown in italics).

1957	Origin of Grand Metropolitan in hotels
1966	Chef and Brewer (restaurants)
1969	Express Dairies (Eden Vale and Ski products)
1970	Berni Inns (restaurants)
	Mecca (including William Hill) – leisure activities (bingo), casinos and betting shops
1971	Truman Hanbury Buxton (brewers)
1972	Watney Mann (brewing)
1973	IDV (spirits)
1980	Liggett and Myers (US) – tobacco plus spirits distribution
	Liggett and Myers tobacco interests
1985	Pearle Health Care (US) – eye products
1987	Heublein (US spirits, including Smirnoff)
	Beginning of divestment of hotel portfolio
1988	Pillsbury – including Green Giant foods, Häagen Dazs ice cream and Burger King
1989	Wimpey restaurants
	Mecca and William Hill
1990	20 per cent stake in Rémy Cointreau
	Pubs put into Inntrapreneur, a joint venture with Courage
	Brewing interests sold
	Wimpey restaurants
	Berni Inns
1992	Cinzano
	Express Dairies
1993	Glen Ellen – US wineries
	Chef and Brewer
1995	Pet (US foods, including Old El Paso and Shippam's pastes)
1996	*Pearle Health Care*
1997	Merger with Guinness and creation of Diageo
1999	*Cinzano*
2000	*[Unsuccessful attempt to float off Burger King]*
	Pillsbury and Pet (to General Mills).
	Spirit brands from Seagram – including Captain Morgan Rum and Seagram's whiskies
2001	Bid for Californian wine business, Kendall Jackson
2002	*Malibu auctioned off – a regulatory outcome of the Seagram acquisitions*
	Burger King also auctioned off
2003	New joint venture with Jose Cuervo on Tequila developments
2004	Chalone Wine (California)
2005	Bushmills Irish whiskey
	Diaego is voted top of consumer section in *Management Today* in terms of Britain's most admired brands
2006	Joint venture agreement to distribute Chinese spirits globally
	Joint venture in India with Radico Khaitan Ltd. New exclusive distribution deal with Smirnoff vodka
2007	Promoting Guinness in Africa to counter falling domestic sales
2008	Rosenblum Cellars (Californian wine)
	Bid for Absolut vodka (owned by Sweden's Vin & Spirit)

Questions

1 Is a focused spirits business with brewing interests strategically more defensible than a diversified food and drinks business? In answering this consider the impact of the UK government's introduction of 24 hour drinking laws and the possible link to binge drinking.

2 Was synergy between food and drinks – two consumer products sold through overlapping outlets – realistic or opportunistic? In what direction does Diaego seem now to be headed?

DIAGEO **http://www.diageo.com**

© PETER MACDIARMID/REUTERS/CORBIS

10.1 Introduction

Figure 10.1 provides a summary of the main strategic alternatives, which are separated into three clusters: limited growth, substantive growth and **retrenchment**. In addition, an organization can opt to do nothing; and on occasions the whole business will be sold or liquidated.

From origins in a single business concept, **market penetration** and product and **market development** are shown as limited growth strategies as they mainly affect competitive strategies rather than imply major corporate change. Invariably they involve innovation. The substantive growth strategies imply more ambitious and higher risk expansion which is likely to change the corporate perspective or strategy. These options, explained below, may involve either a strategic alliance or an acquisition, and these *strategic means* are discussed later in the chapter. It was established in Chapter 1 that it is important for organizations to seek competitive advantage for each business in the portfolio. Consequently, once an organization has diversified, it will be necessary to look for new competitive opportunities, or limited growth strategies, for the various individual businesses.

The bottom section of Figure 10.1 shows the main strategies for corporate reduction, namely turnaround and divestment. They are discussed in detail in Chapter 13.

Figure 10.2, market entry strategies, summarizes the various ways in which an organization might implement its chosen strategies. It should be appreciated that any strategic alternative can be international in scope, rather than focused on a single country or market, and that as we move from the top to the bottom of the chart the inherent scope, risk and potential benefits all increase. The content of Figure 10.2 is discussed in this chapter and in Chapters 11 and 12.

The choice must take into account the risk that the strategic leader considers acceptable given any particular circumstances, and the ability of the organization to deal with the risk elements. Some organizations will not select the most challenging and exciting opportunities because they are too risky.

The options should not be thought of as being mutually exclusive – two or more may be combined into a composite strategy, and at any time a multiproduct organization is likely to be pursuing several different competitive strategies.

Figure 10.1   Strategic alternatives

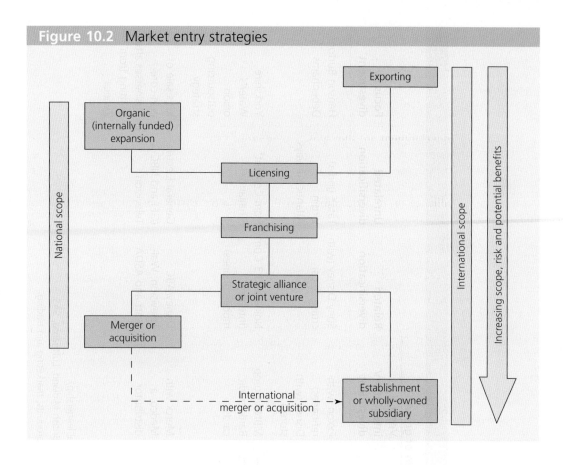

Figure 10.2 Market entry strategies

Table 10.1 combines the themes of this chapter. It provides examples of seven growth directions related to three alternative means of pursuing each of these strategic alternatives. Many of the examples included are discussed in greater detail throughout the book. The one strategy not discussed in detail here is inventing a new way of doing business. On relatively rare occasions a newcomer to an industry or market will have a disruptive influence through real innovation and, in effect, rewriting the rules of competition. They thus force other competitors into a defensive reaction. The prime example of this is Ryanair and EasyJet forcing British Airways and other major European carriers into a whole series of actions including setting up their own budget airlines such as Go, Buzz, bmi baby, of which only the last named has survived. While the real significance of this possibility is recognized, and discussed in other chapters, it is not realistically an alternative open to a normal organization.

10.2 Limited growth strategies

The do-nothing alternative

This do-nothing alternative is a continuation of the existing corporate and competitive strategies, whatever they might be, and however unsuccessful the company might be. The decision to do nothing might be highly appropriate and justified, and the result of very careful thought and evaluation. However, it can also be the result of managers lacking awareness, being lazy or complacent, or

Table 10.1 Examples of strategic growth and change

	Direction of growth						
Means of growth	Inventing a new way of doing business	Market penetration/ divestment	Globalization	Vertical integration/ divestment	Related diversification	Unrelated diversification	Focus by divestment
Organic/ internal	Southwest Air Amazon.com Hotmail	Toyota (with Lexus)	McDonald's Canon	Exxon (with refineries) Disney (with stores)	Sony Disney (with cruise ships)	Tata* (India) Virgin Atlantic Airways	Hanson Burton/ Debenhams
Strategic alliance	Bennetton and IKEA (with their supply chains)	General Motors and Saab	Star Alliance† Coca-Cola and its bottlers	MBNA/Co-op Bank credit cards	Nokia and 3 Com (Internet mobile phones)	Siam Cement‡ (Thailand)	Yorkshire Water's onion outsourcing strategy
Merger, acquisition takeover	Royal Bank/ Direct Line	Ford with Jaguar, Land Rover, Volvo, Daewoo	Astra/Zeneca	Merck with Medco, a distributor	Disney/ABC Television; Wal-Mart and ASDA	General Electric (GE) and NBC Television	ICI's sale of non-core businesses after splitting from Zeneca

* Tata: steel, construction machinery, engineering, locomotives; tea (where it has global leadership).

† Airline code sharing alliance: includes United Airlines, Air Canada, Air New Zealand, British Midland, Lufthansa, SAS.

‡ Siam Cement: also pulp and paper, construction materials, machinery and electrical products, marketing and trading.

deluding themselves into believing that things are going well when in fact the company is in difficulties. Doing nothing when change is required is a dangerous strategy.

A company might appear to an outsider to be doing nothing when in reality it is very active. Some companies, for example, prefer not to be the first to launch new product developments, especially if they know that their competitors are innovating along similar lines. A product may be developed and ready to launch but be held back while another company introduces its version into the market. This allows the initial reaction of consumers to be monitored and evaluated, and competitive and functional strategies reviewed before eventual launch. Timing is the key to success with this strategy. A company will want sufficient time to be sure that its approach is likely to prove successful; at the same time it must react sufficiently quickly that it is not perceived to be copying a competitor when that competitor has become firmly established. In general, the rather more theoretical than realistic do-nothing alternative could conceivably be viable in the short term but is unlikely to prove beneficial or plausible in the long term as environmental factors change. Marks and Spencer has been trying to change to cope with the severe competition it now faces. However, the changes have been criticized as essentially reactive. Named fashion ranges Per Una and Autograph, store cards and mainstream credit cards, contemporary store fit-outs, adding furniture to the mix and cutting food prices with special offers are all reactions to what the competition is doing. One notable and recent success M&S has had is with their well regarded television advertising based around Twiggy and a number of other high profile models – and this from a company that historically chose not to advertise in major media.

We next discuss internal growth strategies – market penetration, market development, product development (all of them dependent upon innovation) and **combination strategies**. It should be appreciated that the strategies described are typically organic in nature (namely, growth from within) and they are not fully discrete and independent of each other. The ideas behind them are closely linked, and it may be very difficult to classify a particular strategic change as one of these strategies rather than another. They can all be linked to the idea of the product life cycle, for they provide suitable means of extending the life cycle once it reaches a stage of maturity and potential decline. It will also be appreciated that they are the key elements of the Ansoff grid. At the heart of all these competitive strategies are customers. It is essential that organizations develop strategies for:

- simply retaining existing customers, which may itself require innovation in a competitive market or industry
- expanding the relationship with existing customers by providing them with additional products or services. Direct Line began with car insurance, but soon realized that there was an opportunity to provide home and contents insurance for its existing client base. Kwik Fit also realized that it had a valuable database of motorists and diversified into providing them with insurance as well as tyre and exhaust services. Sometimes the relationship can be expanded by providing more specialized product and service alternatives to target quite narrow niches
- winning new customers (and hence market share) from competitors.

Consequently, the important issue is the line of thought and the reasoning behind the strategy in question, and the objectives.

Market penetration

This strategy can have one of two broad objectives. First, to seek assertively to increase market share; and second, and more defensively, to hang on to existing customers by concentrating, specializing and consolidating, which implies what Peters and Waterman (1982) designated 'sticking to the knitting' in their book *In Search of Excellence*.

It involves concentrating on doing better what one is already doing well, and quite frequently involves an investment in brands and brand identity. Although it may seem similar to doing nothing, growth is an objective and there is an implicit search for ways of doing things more effectively. In this respect, and because market environments are invariably dynamic, it overlaps with the ideas of market and product development described below.

Resources are directed towards the continued and profitable growth of a 'single' product in a 'single' market, using a 'single' technology. This is accomplished by attracting new users or consumers, increasing the consumption rate of existing users and, wherever possible, stealing consumers and market share from competitors. The word *single* needs careful interpretation, in the context of the limited growth strategies, as companies such as Kellogg (breakfast cereals) and Sony (music) would be classified as organizations which have succeeded with specialization strategies based around a core brand identity. An extensive product line of differentiated brands designed to appeal to specific market segments would periodically have new additions and withdrawals.

At the same time, productivity and more effective cost management can make significant contributions. Sometimes this will be achieved by investing in new technology at the expense of labour.

The two main advantages are, first, that the strategy is based on known skills and capabilities and in this respect it is generally low risk. Second, because the organization's production and marketing skills are concentrated on specialized products and related consumers, and not diversified, these skills can be developed and improved to create competitive advantage. The company has the opportunity to be sensitive to consumer needs by being close to them, and may build a reputation for this.

Market penetration strategies generally have a high likelihood of success, greater in fact than most other alternatives. There are important limitations, however. Alone they may be inadequate for closing an identified planning gap.

Whilst market penetration is a growth strategy, the long-term growth is likely to be gradual rather than explosive. This should not be seen as a disadvantage, because steady growth can be more straightforward in managerial terms. Any firm pursuing this strategy is susceptible to changes in the growth rate or attractiveness of the industry in which it competes, and therefore the strategy can become high risk if the industry goes into recession. There is also a constant need to monitor competitors and ensure that any innovations do not constitute a major threat.

This strategic alternative is particularly applicable to small businesses which concentrate their efforts on specific market niches.

The long tail

In some respects it is easy to overlook the extent to which consumer behaviour has been affected by new supply opportunities which have provided market penetration opportunities. Buying products on-line and physically unseen, and watching television programmes when we want to see them not when they are broadcast, by making use of modern recording and storage technology, are perfect examples.

The traditional product life cycle suggests that sales of new products take off slowly and then grow rapidly before flattening out and then declining. With innovation the life cycle can be extended and extended again and the ultimate decline delayed for possibly many years. Some fashion and fashionable products thus have a very short lifespan whilst others can continue for decades, albeit with changes and improvements at various intervals. The theory would imply that once a product is experiencing a decline in popularity it should be scrapped. Production, storage and distribution have become too expensive for the potential return. The assumption has been that products sell if they are available where and when people expect to find them – at appropriate prices. For many products this means widespread distribution and retail visibility, with the consequential cost implications of the inventory making this no longer feasible. Of course this would make a 'tipping point' of the type outlined by Gladwell (2000) very unlikely as it may not be realistically possible to resurrect production once it has ceased.

Anderson (2006) contends that for some products these principles no longer apply, as much as anything because of changes in distribution and channel preference.

The growth of the Internet and of on-line retailers such as Amazon means that products can continue to be supplied without any consequential major investment in inventory. The actual producer would have to retain some level of stock or be in a position to produce more at short notice, and for certain products such as books, CDs and DVDs, this is realistic. As a consequence so-called back-catalogue items can remain available for years and years, even though their sales have reduced to a fraction of what they were at the height of the product's popularity.

In this context Anderson quotes one Amazon employee as saying 'we sold more books today that didn't sell at all yesterday than we sold today of all the books that did sell yesterday'. A breakdown of sales would therefore be revealing and reinforce the Pareto principle, even if the numbers were not strictly 80:20. In other words a limited number of current best sellers would amount to X per cent of total sales. Very small individual sales of a very long tail of almost-forgotten-about but previously popular items would constitute Y per cent – and Y would be greater than X. We might be tempted to think of what is currently available and on display in high street stores – when we should also factor in all the back catalogue items which will still be featured and listed on Internet sites.

Whilst this is a forceful and persuasive argument it will not affect the need for new products which do have a chance of high sales over a short period of time. It is simply that we realize there are now opportunities to continue to sell them and buy them. But it could also be the point that some new books and music that would previously have been seen as a 'miss' rather than a 'hit' can make money over their life, albeit an extended life. In the past this would have been more difficult to achieve. Arguably it allows producers more freedom to release products they are less convinced about and give them a chance to see if they find favour.

There are other implications of 'new retailing'. It is not many years ago that music sales were concentrated on CDs – which had replaced vinyl and cassettes. Piracy was an issue as people copied their friends' music. But digital music downloading is growing in popularity all the time, as the hardware, software and customer comfort expands. Discerning customers can choose exactly which tracks they want to pay to download and select only those they like and ignore ones they don't like. With CDs you have to buy every track and thus in effect pay for those you are not at all bothered about. Different listeners will react differently to the various tracks – probably every one will be someone's favourite. To this we can add the new potential saviours of the music industry the over-50s age group who have, by buying CDs, relaunched the careers of bands such as the Searchers who have confounded the music industry by selling 70,000 albums in 2008. This older age group are not that interested in downloading preferring the actual product which they can easily buy cheaply in a supermarket such as Asda.

Market development

Market development, together with product development which is considered next, is very closely related to a strategy of specialization. All of these strategies build on existing strengths, skills, competencies and capabilities. Market development is generally another relatively low-risk strategy; and the idea behind it is to market present products, with possible modifications and range increases, to customers in related market areas. This may imply broadening a product range to increase its attractiveness to different customers in different market segments or niches. Clearly, therefore, this strategy is about modifications to strategic positioning. Changes in distribution and advertising will also typically support this strategy.

In summary, the key themes are:

- modifications to increase attractiveness to new segments or niches
- new uses for a product or service
- appropriateness for different countries with particular tastes or requirements.

One example of a market development strategy, then, would be a firm which decided to modify its product in some minor way to make it attractive to selected export markets where tastes and preferences are different. This would be supported by advertising and require the opening of new channels of distribution.

In the last 20 – 25 years China has become an increasingly attractive market for specialized children's products, including nutritional supplements and certain up-market toys. This is the period during which the Chinese government restricted families to a single child as a form of population control. Two parents and four grandparents for each child amounts to significant purchasing power. And 20 million babies are born in China every year.

Product development

Product development implies substantial modifications or additions to present products in order to increase their market penetration within existing customer groups. It is often linked to an attempt to extend or prolong the product life cycle, and typical examples would include the second and revised edition of a successful textbook, or the relaunch of a range of cosmetics with built-in improvements which add value. As product life cycles contract and time becomes an increasingly important competitive issue, this strategy becomes more significant.

Case 10.2 shows how BUPA has developed a new business in care homes – but divested hospitals.

Case 10.2

BUPA   UK

SOURCE: THIS CASE STUDY WAS PREPARED USING PRIMARILY PUBLICLY AVAILABLE SOURCES OF INFORMATION FOR THE PURPOSES OF CLASSROOM DISCUSSION; IT DOES NOT INTEND TO ILLUSTRATE EITHER EFFECTIVE OR INEFFECTIVE HANDLING OF A MANAGERIAL SITUATION.

Many people in the UK would say 'private health care' if asked to explain what BUPA provides. BUPA has in fact been a lead player in this industry for many years. It established its position by both providing the care – in its own hospitals – and also providing health care insurance. Typically private hospitals are ideal for non-critical procedures; they do not have accident and emergency rooms and they would not normally have intensive care facilities. The operations are generally, but not exclusively, carried out by consultants who also have contracts with the NHS (the National Health Service). It has long been recognized that this implies a dual culture. Insurance is driven by numbers – income from premiums must exceed payments to claimants – and it is very competitive. Customers can be corporate clients (insuring their workforce) or private individuals. Hospitals might be expected to exhibit a caring culture, even though they have to be financially viable.

In the UK some 7.5 million people are covered, around 12 per cent of the population. This may, of course, be partial cover rather than the complete package.

Over the years BUPA had acquired a national network of care homes – both residential care and the more specialized nursing care. This is again a competitive industry and one that is very tightly regulated. Homes are individual but there are clearly scale economies in a group. Like hospitals one might expect a manifest caring culture but in a context of financial viability.

In 2008 the current CEO stepped down. Val Gooding had been in post for ten years and had executed a number of major changes. In her ten years she had doubled BUPA's revenues but increased profits by a factor of nine. From a zero base, overseas income now accounted for a third of the total. She had invested in insurance businesses in Australia and the Middle East and nursing homes in Australia and New Zealand.

In 2007 Gooding decided BUPA did not need to own its 26 UK hospitals and sold them to Cinven for almost £1.5 billion. The insurance part of BUPA could direct clients to any UK provider. That said, Gooding bought the Cromwell Hospital in London in early 2008 – but claimed this was not a strategy reversal. It was a one-off investment.

BUPA's hospitals have been rebranded 'Spire' and they have benefited from being able to actively promote their services to NHS patients as the UK government has been willing to allow the NHS to pay money over to the private sector if they can help reduce the waiting lists and thus meet government targets.

Questions

1 Do you see these changes as positive moves by BUPA?

2 Do you believe they leave the organization stronger?

Innovation

Innovation is linked to the three strategies described above but it often involves more significant changes to the product or service. It is explored further in critical reflection 10.1. As a strategy it can imply the replacement of existing products with ones which are really new, as opposed to modified, and which imply a new product life cycle. An excellent example of this is Smirnoff Ice from Diageo (Case 10.1) in 1998. This still-popular vodka-fruit mix 'alcopop' exploits the Smirnoff brand and also takes sales away from bottled beers. The original target market was young female drinkers who wanted to drink from a bottle rather than a glass (which is easier for someone to 'spike' with a drug) but who didn't particularly like beer. Other successful alcopops – or RTD's (Ready to Drink) as they are more properly known – include Bacardi Breezer and Archer's Aqua. Diageo also tried Gordon's Edge (made from gin) but it was withdrawn. One problem is that these innovative drinks have been linked to young 'binge drinkers'. As a consequence some European governments have increased the tax on them, thus hitting sales.

The line which differentiates a really new product from a modification is extremely difficult to quantify. In the case of cars such as the Ford Focus or Ford Fiesta, for example, which appeared in new forms every few years, the changes for each new model were typically marked differences rather than essentially cosmetic. Each new model was very different from the existing model, simply the name was the same.

Similarly, it is important to consider which product life cycle is being addressed. The Sony Walkman and similar personal cassette players have enjoyed their own successful life cycle; at the same time they have extended the product life cycle of cassette players in general far beyond their technical life. As shown in Table 10.1, innovation can be behind the invention of a new way of doing business. Case 10.3 shows how Lego has largely (but not exclusively) stayed focused on building bricks but innovated constantly.

It can be risky not to innovate in certain industries as a barrier against competition. Innovatory companies can stay ahead by introducing new products ahead of their rivals and concentrating on production and marketing to establish and consolidate a strong market position. All the time they will search for new opportunities to innovate and gain further advantage by limiting the market potential for retailer own-brands.

Critical reflection 10.1

Innovation

Innovation takes place when an organization makes a technical change, e.g. produces a product or service that is new to it, or uses a method or input that is new and original. If a direct competitor has already introduced the product or method then it is imitation, not innovation. However, introducing a practice from a different country or industry rather than a direct competitor would constitute innovation.

Innovation implies change and the introduction of something new. Creating the idea, or inventing something, is not innovation but a part of the total process. While at one level it can relate to new or novel products, it may also be related to production processes, approaches to marketing a product or service, or the way in which jobs are carried out within the organization. The aim is to add value for the consumer or customer by reducing costs or differentiating the product or total service in some sustainable way. In other words, innovation relates to the creation of competitive advantage; and, to summarize, there are four main forms of innovation:

- new products, which are either radically new or which extend the product life cycle
- process innovation leading to reduced production costs, and affected partially by the learning and experience effect

- innovations within the umbrella of marketing, which increase differentiation
- organizational changes, which reduce costs or improve total quality.

Where the innovation reflects continuous improvement, product or service *enhancement*, and only minor changes in established patterns of consumer behaviour, the likelihood of success is greater than for those changes that demand new patterns of usage and consumption. Examples of the latter include personal computers and compact disc players. Discontinuous innovations such as these are more risky for manufacturers, but if they are successful the financial payoffs can be huge. By contrast, continuous improvements – which, realistically, are essential in a dynamic, competitive environment – have much lower revenue potential.

Innovation can come about in a variety of ways:

- Ideas can come out research and development departments, where people are employed to come up with new ideas or inventions. Some would argue that there is a risk that departments such as this are not in direct touch with customers; however, while customers may sense that a product or service has drawbacks, they may have no idea how it might be improved. This requires a technical expert.

- People from various parts of an organization working on special projects.
- Employees being given freedom and encouragement to work on ideas of their own, e.g. the 3M approach.
- Everyday events as people interact and discuss problems and issues.

There is a mix of routine, structured events and unstructured activities.

Changes in the service provided to customers and the development of new products and services imply changes in operating systems and in the work of employees, and some of the proposed changes may well be the result of ideas generated internally. However, many of the ideas for innovations come from outside the organization, from changes in the environment. This emphasizes the crucial importance of linking together marketing and operations and harnessing the contribution of people. For example, Ford in the US realized some years ago that a number of its engineers had a tendency to 'over-engineer' solutions to relatively simple problems. As a result, its costs were higher than those of its rivals, particularly Japanese and Korean companies, and its new product development times were considerably longer. Instead, the company needed 'creative engineers' with a fresh perspective and greater realization of customer expectations.

Combination strategies

A firm with a number of products or business units will typically pursue a number of different competitive strategies at any time. Product development, market development and innovation may all be taking place.

The internal growth strategies discussed in this section are primarily concerned with improving competitive strategies for existing businesses. Such changes may not prove adequate for closing the planning gap, and consequently higher risk external growth strategies may also be considered. They are also likely to involve a new strategic perspective.

Case 10.3

Lego   Eur Int

In a volatile and competitive environment we have concentrated and used our strength to go deeper into what we know about.

(Kjeld Kirk Kristiansen, Deputy Chairman and grandson of the founder)

Lego, the brightly coloured plastic building bricks, was launched in 1949, and has always proved popular in an industry renowned for changing tastes and preferences and for innovation. The name was derived from Leg Godt, which is Danish for 'play well'.

Ironically Lego in Latin means 'I put together'. On the strength of this one product Lego has become Europe's largest and the world's fourth largest toy maker. Lego is Danish, family owned and based on strong principles. For example, no toys will be developed that have a military theme. Lego has five stated values: creativity, innovation, learning, fun and quality. Historically it has been relatively secretive, hiding its actual sales and profit figures. The company admits to exceeding sales of 10 billion Danish Kroner (£830 million) in 2002.

The basic strategy is one of product development, with Lego developing an enormous number of variations on its basic product theme. Wheels and electric motors were added in the 1960s. By the mid-1990s some 300 different kits (at a wide range of prices) were available worldwide. There were 1700 different parts, including bricks, shapes and miniature people, and children could use them to make almost anything from small cars to large, complex, working space stations with battery-operated space trains. Brick colours were selected to appeal to both boys and girls; and the more complex Lego Technic sets were branded and promoted specially to make them attractive to the young teenage market. Over 200 billion plastic bricks and pieces had been produced since Lego was introduced.

In a typical year Lego has replaced one-third of its product range, with many items having only a short lifespan. New ideas are developed over a two- to three-year period and backed by international consumer research and test marketing. Lego concentrates on global tastes and buying habits. The Pacific Rim was perceived to offer the highest growth potential during the 1990s. 'If you differentiate too much you start to make difficulties for yourself, especially in manufacturing.' Competition has forced Lego to act internationally and aggressively. One US company, Tyco, markets products that are almost indistinguishable from Lego. Lego has attempted unsuccessfully to sue for patent infringement and now views this competition as undesirable but stimulating. More recently new competition has come from another rival construction product, K'Nex, again American.

In the mid-1990s sales were being affected adversely by changing tastes and by the growing popularity of computer games. In 1997 Lego opted for a new range extension. A new kit, especially for girls, was launched – a doll's house series complete with miniature dolls and furniture. Using technology as an enabler, Lego also began to market construction kits with microchips and instructions on CD-ROMs. In 1998 the company introduced a new Mindstorms range, built around a brick

powered by AA batteries, which could be incorporated into a variety of different models that could then be instructed to move with the aid of an infra-red transmitter and a typical personal computer. Lego had had the technology for some while but had been waiting until it could reduce costs to a realistic level. More recently, Lego has ventured into the computer games market with CD-based products enabling users to 'build' train sets, vehicles, etc., on screen. It has also agreed licensing deals for kits based on Bob the Builder, Star Wars and Harry Potter.

When Lego launched Serious Play in 2002, a corporate training package, it was capitalizing on Lego-based activities developed by independent trainers over many years. Vision Lab is a new research centre built in 2002 to develop scenarios on future families and play.

Lego has manufactured in Switzerland, the Czech Republic, South Korea and the USA as well as Denmark, making its own tools for the plastic injection moulding machines. Bricks were only moulded in Denmark and Switzerland but there were finishing factories in other countries. Tool making could easily be concentrated in one plant, but took place in three to engender competition and to emphasize quality. Lego deliberately maintained strong links with its machinery suppliers. In this and other respects Lego sees itself as being closer culturally to a Japanese company than a US one. Investments in production and improvements are thought to have been in the region of at least £100 million per year. In 2006 production was outsourced to Flextronics, a Singapore-based company – manufacture would take place in Mexico and eastern Europe.

Some years ago, in 1968, Lego diversified with a theme park, featuring rides and displays built with Lego bricks, in Denmark. This has been followed with a similar development on the site of the old Windsor Safari Park in the UK and followed by a third in San Diego, USA, and a fourth in Gunzburg, Germany. In the late 1990s the UK park was attracting 1.5 million visitors every year.

Lego recorded record trading losses in 2000 and set about restructuring. Jobs and plants were lost. There was a new logo – with a new strapline, 'Play On' – and new packaging. Diversification trials for clothing, bags and accessories were abandoned. In 2001 the company was profitable again. Unfortunately this would only last two years, before Lego plunged into loss again. Many believed it had been over-ambitious with its licensing agreements as many of these were only short-term windows of opportunity. There has been further restructuring 'in a drive to remain independent'.

Kjeld Kirk Kristiansen, grandson of the founder, stepped down as CEO, but remained as Deputy

Chairman. Sales revenues had fallen some 20 per cent from their 2002 high point of 10 billion Kroner. In 2006 Lego employed 1500 people in Denmark (it had once been as high as 5000) and 3000 worldwide (down from 8300). But there was no corporate debt. One shining light was the range of robot toys, including Spike, AlphaRex, TriBot and RoboArm, all part of the Mindstorms range. With packs selling for as much as US$250 the appeal was to older children and even some adults.

Some believe Lego brought problems on itself by taking some focus away from traditional bricks and experimenting with other products and activities. Yet in 2009 Lego is reported to be planning the launch of a mobile phone with a casing that looks like Lego bricks. Parts can be removed and replaced to allow for colour changes to suit different moods. The target market is children in the US and Asia. There are also reported plans for a Lego MP3 Player and digital camera.

Lego is not a lifestyle brand.

Jorgen Vig Knudstorp, the new CEO

Questions

1 Can Lego realistically anticipate further growth and prosperity if it relies on its focused strategy or will it become increasingly vulnerable to competitive threats?
2 What would you recommend?
3 Should Lego consolidate or continue to seek to grow?

LEGO **http://www.lego.com**

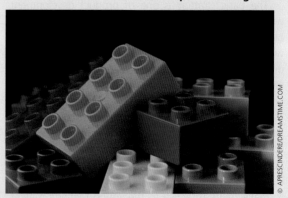

10.3 Substantive growth strategies

While this section provides an overview of four substantive growth strategies – **horizontal integration**, vertical integration, related and unrelated diversification – many of the key issues are discussed in more detail in Chapter 11.

Substantive growth strategies are frequently implemented through acquisition, merger or joint venture rather than organic growth. Franchising can provide another means of generating external growth, but it is only likely to be applicable for certain types of business.

External growth can involve the purchase of, or an arrangement with, firms that are behind or ahead of a business in the added value channel, which spans raw material to ultimate consumption. Similarly, it can involve firms or activities that are indirectly related businesses or industries, those which are tangentially related through either technology or markets, and basically unrelated businesses. The key objectives are additional market share and the search for opportunities that can generate synergy. The outcome from this will be larger size and increased power, and ideally improved profitability from the synergy. In reality, as will be explored in greater depth in Chapter 11, the outcome is more likely to be increased size and power than improved profitability. Synergy often proves to be elusive.

Horizontal integration

Horizontal integration occurs when a firm acquires or merges with a major competitor, or at least another firm operating at the same stage in the added value chain. The two organizations may well appeal to different market segments rather than compete directly. Market share will increase, and pooled skills and capabilities should generate synergy. Horizontal integration is, therefore, concerned with issues of **critical mass**, which are discussed later in this chapter.

See the online "Adidas, Nike and Umbro" case for an example of this section's theory in practice

Brewing, motor cars, banking and insurance are all industries where there has been extensive horizontal integration – where it has been allowed by competition authorities. As we saw earlier the competition rules were 'relaxed' to allow the 2009 creation of the Lloyds Group from the old Lloyds TSB and HBOS. In the oil industry in recent years there have been mergers between Exxon and Mobil, Fina and Elf, BP and Amoco and between Texaco and Chevron.

Case 10.4, Electrolux, is an example of international horizontal integration and it shows how difficult it can be to pull everything together and achieve synergy, despite broadly similar competencies and products. Online Case 10.1 (Adidas, Nike and Umbro) also looks at horizontal integration but incorporates the role of a 'spoiler' determined to stop others merging.

Case 10.4

Electrolux

Eur

In 1970 Electrolux was a Swedish-based manufacturer of mainly vacuum cleaners, supported by refrigerators. A new chief executive introduced a strategy of horizontal integration and acquisition, and within 20 years Electrolux became the world's leading manufacturer of white goods: refrigerators, freezers, washing machines, tumble dryers and dishwashers. The company also owns Flymo (garden products) and Husqvarna (chain saws).

Major acquisitions included:

1984	Zanussi (Italy)
1986	White Consolidated (third largest US producer)
1987	Tricity (UK, from Thorn-EMI)
1988	Corbero/Domar (Spain)
1991	Lehel (largest producer of white goods in Hungary – providing a base for expansion in Eastern Europe)
1994	AEG.

Electrolux bought 400 companies over 20 years, with unrelated businesses and surplus assets often being sold off to recoup part of the purchase price.

Production has been rationalized, with many parts standardized, in an attempt to reduce costs, but Electrolux remains a global manufacturer. Wherever possible the best practices from new acquisitions are shared across frontiers, and clearly Electrolux has faced a series of challenges in integrating the new businesses with their distinctive, national cultures. The integration strategy is based upon speed and the immediate input of a small task force to search for synergy and divestment opportunities.

The ultimate success will depend upon the ability of Electrolux to integrate its marketing, particularly in Europe, which accounts for some two-thirds of the sales. In fact 90 per cent of the sales come from mature European and US markets. Product differentiation is possible, but the fact that competing white goods invariably look alike in many respects adds difficulties. In addition, tastes and preferences concerning particular features vary from country to country.

In 1991 products carrying the Electrolux brand name were relaunched as a pan-European upper mass-market brand, with new design features and common advertising and promotion. A similar strategy, but with a more down-market image, was to follow for Zanussi-branded products. Local brands have also being retained, targeted at individual country preferences: for the UK this means Tricity and Bendix, and for the USA, Frigidaire. This dualistic strategy, involving up to four distinct brands in most countries, differs from that of Whirlpool, the US company which acquired Philips' white goods business, and is Electrolux's main rival. Whirlpool is more reluctant to differentiate between countries.

In June 1992 Electrolux agreed a joint venture with AEG, a smaller European competitor and a subsidiary of Daimler-Benz. Electrolux then acquired the whole AEG appliance business in 1994. The AEG brand is particularly strong in Germany, and this final acquisition gave Electrolux individual country shares of some 35 per cent in France, Germany, Italy and the UK. The Electrolux brand is most popular in northern Europe and Zanussi in southern Europe.

However, the concentrated white goods industry has oversupply and fierce price competition; in 1997 Electrolux announced the closure of 25 plants around

SOURCE: THIS CASE STUDY WAS PREPARED USING PRIMARILY PUBLICLY AVAILABLE SOURCES OF INFORMATION FOR THE PURPOSES OF CLASSROOM DISCUSSION; IT DOES NOT INTEND TO ILLUSTRATE EITHER EFFECTIVE OR INEFFECTIVE HANDLING OF A MANAGERIAL SITUATION.

the world and a workforce reduction of 11 per cent. Electrolux admitted that Whirlpool was enjoying higher operating efficiencies because it had fewer brands. One analyst commented that 'Electrolux has been good at acquiring companies but not so good at integrating them into one unit'. While the challenge seemed to be one of reducing the number of different brands, the trick is to find the right number. Whirlpool had attempted to design a 'world washing machine' to a single specification, and failed. Of course, it doesn't help that the Electrolux brands convey different messages to customers. AEG is associated with German engineering efficiency; Zanussi with Italian style; whilst Electrolux 'conjures up the 1940s and 1950s'.

In 1999 Electrolux settled on a reduced number of global platforms. Dishwashers were reduced from 4 to 1; refrigerators from 46 to 17; and washing machines from 13 to 6. Ovens for much of Europe would be to a common size, but have special features for individual countries. Italians insist on a special pizza setting, for example. Similarly, in France refrigerators have special compartments for fish and shellfish. Design preferences for washing machines vary between European countries, with some preferring front load and others top load, and with some using a hot water feed as well as cold water.

There would be fewer brands and the Electrolux name would be featured on every appliance. But which should be retained, and which could be abandoned?

Production is increasingly being switched to lower labour cost countries whilst designers are being challenged to be more innovative. The production target for 2009 was 40 per cent manufactured in the US and Eastern Europe, down from 85 per cent in 2002. A talking washer – the 'Washy Talky' – has been developed for India. There are refrigerators which can contain smells in separate compartments. The so-called 'Holy Grail' is a washer/dryer that washes clothes but finishes them in such a way that ironing is not required. Electrolux is very aware that if its products are ever seen as commodities its margins will reduce dramatically.

Questions

1 Are the barriers to global products insurmountable in this industry?
2 Are the preference differences too great to overcome?
3 Has Electrolux found an ideal compromise?
4 Can you see any parallels with motor cars?

ELECTROLUX **http://www.electrolux.com**

Vertical integration

Vertical integration is the term used to describe the acquisition of a company which supplies a firm with inputs of raw materials or components, or serves as a customer for the firm's products or services (a distributor or assembler). If a shirt manufacturer acquired a cotton textile supplier this would be known as **backward vertical integration**; if the supplier bought the shirt manufacturer, its customer, this would constitute **forward vertical integration**.

At times firms will reduce the extent to which they are vertically integrated if they are failing to obtain the appropriate benefits and synergy from the fusion of two sets of skills and capabilities. In 1988 the UK clothing retailer Burton Group sold the last of its suit-making factories in order to concentrate on retailing. At one time Burton had been one of the leading clothing manufacturers in Europe, but that was before made-to-measure suits were substantially replaced in popularity by ready-made suits.

Backward vertical integration aims to secure supplies at a lower cost than competitors, but after the merger or acquisition it becomes crucial to keep pace with technological developments and innovation on the supply side, or competitive advantage may be lost.

In 1987 Rover divested its parts distribution business, Unipart – an example of vertical disintegration. Eight years later, after its acquisition by BMW, Rover sought unsuccessfully to buy Unipart back, arguing that it needed to control its parts distribution to support its increasingly international role. Is this good business thinking or just strategic fashion?

Forward vertical integration secures customers or outlets and guarantees product preference, and it can give a firm much greater control over its total marketing effort. At the consumer end of the chain, retailers generally are free to decide at what final price they sell particular products or services, and their views may not always accord with those of the manufacturer. However, greater control over distribution might mean complacency and a loss of competitive edge through less effective marketing overall. In addition, manufacturing and retailing, if these are the two activities involved, require separate and different skills, and for this reason synergy may again prove elusive.

Many of the benefits of vertical integration can be achieved without merger or acquisition. Joint ventures, discussed later, are one option. In addition, there may simply be agreements between companies who appreciate that there can be substantial gains from proper co-operation. Marks and Spencer provide an excellent example historically. Marks and Spencer have benefited from long-term agreements with their suppliers with whom they have worked closely. Many suppliers of a wide variety of products sold by Marks and Spencer rely very heavily upon them, as they are their major customer. At the same time Marks and Spencer set exacting standards for cost, quality and delivery, and guarantee to buy only when these standards are met continuously; and there will always be competitors who would like them as a customer.

The effect of vertical integration can be created organically, without merger or acquisition, but this is likely to be more risky. New skills have to be developed from scratch. Examples of this would be a manufacturer deciding to make components rather than buying them from specialist suppliers, or starting to distribute independently rather than relying on external distributors.

Because new and different skills are involved, vertical integration really implies diversification, but normally these strategic change options are considered separately. The growth and development – and later contraction – of Airtours (now called My Travel) as a vertically integrated holiday company is outlined in Case 10.5.

Case 10.5

Airtours/My Travel   UK

In 2000 Airtours was Europe's second largest tour operator, some way behind Germany's Preussag which had recently acquired the UK market leader, Thomson. Founded in 1972 by David Crossland, who remained Chairman and Chief Executive, Airtours could boast 900 customers in 1980. In 2000 that number exceeded 15 million. But things were about to change.

Ten years before, in 1990, Airtours was still a relatively small but fast-growing package tour operator. Based in Lancashire, it offered low-price holidays in cheaper resorts and for a while had a reputation for carrying rowdy youngsters. Most of its customers were based in the north, and Airtours benefited competitively when the impact of the recession was felt first in the south. When bookings fell dramatically before and during the Gulf War (in Airtours' case, by 40 per cent), the company pulled out of selected markets, slowed down its planned move to new premises and froze capital expenditure on new information technology. Airtours was, however, building an airline, and was committed to taking delivery of five McDonnell Douglas aircraft (on lease) which would operate from Manchester (three planes), Birmingham and Stansted.

Airtours successfully predicted the collapse of International Leisure Group, which included Intasun, the second largest package tour operator. When ILG ceased trading in March 1991 Airtours had agents in place in targeted resorts (the Balearic and Canary Islands, Portugal and Greece) who were ready to buy up all of the released Intasun beds. Striking early, and with the Gulf War still an issue, Airtours obtained good price deals. Within just one week Airtours booked 90,000 new holidays and quickly became the third largest package tour operator. The company had no debt. In 1992 Airtours bought Pickfords, the third largest travel agency in the UK with 333 branches, using its own cash reserves.

In 1993 Airtours narrowly failed to acquire Owners Abroad, then marginally the second largest UK package tour operator ahead of Airtours. Together the two businesses would have been bigger than the existing market leader, Thomson. However, Airtours did buy the 214 Hogg Robinson travel agencies to add to Pickfords, giving it number two position in this sector of the market – the travel agency sector leader was Thomson subsidiary Lunn Poly. Pickfords and Hogg Robinson have subsequently been combined and renamed Going Places.

SOURCE: THIS CASE STUDY WAS PREPARED USING PRIMARILY PUBLICLY AVAILABLE SOURCES OF INFORMATION FOR THE PURPOSES OF CLASSROOM DISCUSSION; IT DOES NOT INTEND TO ILLUSTRATE EITHER EFFECTIVE OR INEFFECTIVE HANDLING OF A MANAGERIAL SITUATION.

Further acquisitions of small UK tour operators soon gave Airtours second position in the package tour market; the company also expanded in Europe by buying the leisure activities of SAS (Scandinavian Airline Systems). At the time of acquisition, SAS Leisure owned or managed 14 resort hotels and also had a substantial interest in its own charter airline.

Airtours diversified into the cruise business in 1994 when it bought two cruise ships and began to provide its own holidays in the Mediterranean and Canaries. In 1996, Carnival, the leading US cruise company, set out to acquire a 29.6 per cent stake in Airtours, firmly linking the two businesses. Together, as a joint venture, Airtours and Carnival bought the Italian cruise line Costa.

In 1997 Airtours bought Belgium's largest tour operator and continued to strengthen its presence throughout Europe. A year later it took a 30 per cent stake in one of Germany's largest tour operators, for example. Also in 1998 were acquisitions in Ireland and America and of a Glasgow-based telephone sales business, Direct Holidays.

1999 saw a major setback. Airtours launched a hostile bid for First Choice, the fourth largest UK tour operator, but was thwarted by the European competition commissioner. At this time Airtours was credited with an 18 per cent market share, Thomson had 23 per cent, Thomas Cook/Carlson 16 per cent and First Choice 15 per cent.

However, in 2000 Airtours bought an American Internet travel company – a specialist in cruise holidays – to complement its increasing Internet booking in Europe. The company has opted not to supply other competing Internet businesses: 'Airtours is only willing to work with agents who can bring something to the table'. The company also opened a call centre in Majorca to deal with all of its customers and their needs and queries.

In 2001 Airtours' performance deteriorated markedly as a result of problems with its German operations. Carnival decided to sell its (by then) 25 per cent shareholding; Airtours' partial shareholding in Costa Cruises had already been sold to Carnival.

David Crossland announced he would step down as Chairman when he reached 55 late in 2002. Tim Byrne had already taken over from him as CEO in 2000. The company would be renamed My Travel at the same time. A new budget airline, MyTravel Lite began flying from Birmingham. But trading difficulties continued, affected in no small part by the reluctance of many people to fly after 9/11 the year before. Rivals had cut capacity; Airtours did not. There was a series of profits warnings

and a realization that the company's auditors were querying the way certain transactions were booked in the accounts. The share price was collapsing. From a price of over £5.00 per share in 1999 it was soon down at 90 pence.

Crossland deferred his retirement and Tim Byrne left the company. The new CEO was Peter McHugh who had been running the businesses in America. The accounts were published in November; the company recorded its first ever loss. There was also a change of Finance Director.

David Crossland did finally depart in March 2003, although he remained the largest shareholder. Unfortunately the share price had now fallen to 14 pence. My Travel had to make disposals. The US Internet travel businesses were divested, along with the German and Polish businesses. To make matters worse a computer error that had caused incorrect (low) prices was discovered. Trading losses continued and another substantial loss was recorded for the year.

Early in 2004 My Travel sold its cruise ships, reduced the number of hotel beds it controlled and cut back the number of planes it was leasing. Continuing losses kept the share price down at around 10 pence.

The company managed to survive and some growth was restored – but there were fresh problems in 2006. Sales were affected by the fear of terrorism, the football World Cup in Germany and a summer heatwave in the UK. The industry was also very volatile as customers were waiting until 'the eleventh hour' in the hope of last minute bargains. In 2007 My Travel merged with the larger Thomas Cook, which is now owned by the German travel business, Karstadt Quelle. The fourth main holiday company in the UK, First Choice, has been absorbed by Tui, the current parent company of Thomson and Europe's largest tour operator.

Questions

1 Given that for many customers a holiday essentially comprises the sale and provision of a 'package' of services, such as hotel beds, apartments, flights and resort services, how much of the supply chain does a company like My Travel need to own?

2 In the case of Airtours do you think the problem was fundamentally one of strategic misjudgements (the wrong strategy) or setbacks in implementation?

3 Was European integration on this scale perhaps inevitable, given the difficulties that tour operators have in differentiating their product and also given the potential for economies of scale?

Related (or concentric) diversification

Any form of diversification involves a departure from existing products and markets. The new products or services involved may relate to existing products or services through either technology or marketing; where this is the case, the diversification is known as concentric rather than conglomerate. A specialist manufacturer of ski clothing who diversified into summer leisure wear to offset seasonal sales would be an example. Potential consumers may or may not be the same; distribution may or may not change; the existing production expertise should prove beneficial.

Similarly, when retailers such as WH Smith add new and different lines and products, they are seeking to exploit their resources and their retailing skills and expertise (core competencies) more effectively.

There is an assumption that synergy can be created from the two businesses or activities; and ideally the new, diversified, company enjoys strengths and opportunities which decrease its weaknesses and exposure to risks.

Any organization seeking concentric diversification will look for companies or opportunities where there are clearly related products, markets, distribution channels, technologies or resource requirements. The related benefits should be clear and genuinely capable of generating synergy. However, diversification might be adopted as a means of covering up weaknesses or previous poor decisions. Benefits will not be expected immediately, and the change involved may divert interest and attention away from existing problems or difficulties. Case 10.6 tells the story of Mars' acquisition of Wrigley, an example of related diversification.

Case 10.6

Mars' Diversification into Chewing Gum   US

Mars, the company behind Mars Bars, Milky Way and Snickers, is around one hundred years old. It was started in America by Frank Mars, who, together with his son, Forrest, created Milky Way as its first important product. Frank and Forrest fell out. Forrest came to the UK and established an independent chocolate business manufacturing the Mars Bars we still buy today. By the end of the 1930s, and the outbreak of the World War II, Mars Bars were the third most popular confectionery brand in the UK. Some time later, in the 1960s, Forrest was able to reclaim the American business.

In 2002 Pfizer put its Adams chewing gum business up for sale. Adams is Number Two to Wrigley; its brands include Chicklets and Trident. Mars considered a bid but did not go ahead. Instead the business was sold to Cadbury Schweppes. Six years later Mars bought the market leader, Wrigleys, for $23 billion.

Mars argued this was related product diversification, with linked customers and distribution. Chewing gum also has a more favourable image than chocolate, because of the links to dental care and an alternative to smoking. Mars had already taken steps to ensure its products are not advertised to children under twelve; it promoted nutritional values and it had abolished the use of trans-fatty acids in its products.

Questions

1 Can you see the logic in this diversification?
2 Do you think Mars might have made a strategic error in not acquiring Adams or was 'the waiting game' strategically very smart?

Unrelated (or conglomerate) diversification

In the case of conglomerate diversification there is no discernible relationship between existing and new products, services and markets. The diversification is justified as a promising investment opportunity. Financial benefits and profits should be available from the new investment, and any costs incurred will be more than offset. Financial synergy might be obtained in the form of greater borrowing capacity or acquired tax credits.

The strategy is regarded as high risk because the new technologies, new skills and new markets involved constitute unknowns and uncertainties. Moreover, because the change is uncertain and challenging, it can be tempting to switch resources and efforts away from existing businesses and areas of strength, and this compounds the element of risk involved.

Conglomerate diversification is often linked to portfolio analysis, and sometimes the search for businesses which might remedy any perceived strategic weaknesses. A company with reserves of cash to invest, because it has a number of cash cow businesses, might seek to buy businesses with growth potential in new industries. Some acquisitive and financially orientated companies diversify in this way with a view to rationalizing the businesses that they buy. Parts will be retained if they feel they can add value and benefit accordingly; other parts will be divested. In such cases, the critical issue should be the opportunity cost of the money involved. In other words, the long-term return on capital employed should exceed alternative uses for the money, including simply keeping it banked! While some companies build up substantial capital reserves to ensure that they have the resources to manage during the recessionary stage of a business cycle – as was the case with GEC under Arnold (Lord) Weinstock – others will use the cash to buy back equity. Shareholders will like to see a company enjoying sound financial health but may well feel that a 'cash mountain' should be used for something such as picking up bargains in a recession! It can be a difficult balance. Referring to points made earlier, where a company is anxious to grow, it might initially look for closely related acquisitions but find such routes blocked by competition authorities who feel that customers might be disadvantaged. When such companies opt for unrelated acquisitions they are very likely to argue that there is more relatedness than there is in reality!

See the online "Granada/ITV" case for an example of this section's theory in practice

Unrelated diversification became less popular in the 1990s, especially under the onslaught of management guru thinking that favoured focus. We develop this later in this chapter as well as in Chapter 16. The real issue concerns whether the strategic leadership can deliver value for all key stakeholders from the diversification. See Online Case 10.2 on Granada.

Some conglomerates and their strategies can work successfully because they targeted underperforming companies and turned them around – linkages and synergies were not high on the agenda. Such strategies are only feasible when poorly performing companies are there to be acquired. Sooner or later the opportunities become fewer and fewer. At this time General Electric (GE) remains a highly successful diversified conglomerate which achieves synergies across unrelated businesses through its ability to operate as a 'learning organization' which exchanges skills and ideas.

Some companies diversify to build a bigger business and thus reduce the likelihood of being acquired by an unwelcome outsider. The argument is, the bigger they become, the fewer companies can afford to buy them. Paradoxically, if they fail to achieve synergy, they may look attractive to an outside bidder who sees value in buying them to split them up.

10.4 To diversify or not – and how

The introduction to this topic begins by defining key terms and looking at diversification and acquisition in a wider context.

Figure 10.3 demonstrates that the growth challenge is to find opportunities for developing and deploying technologies, processes and competencies in ways that generate a more effective and

Figure 10.3 The growth challenge

Products and services — Technologies Processes and alliances Competencies — Customers and markets

beneficial match between the organization's products and services and its customers and markets. Some of the key themes are:

- the potential for synergy from internal and external linkages and alliances
- the diversification/focus dilemma
- opportunities for, and abilities in, transferring skills and competencies
- opportunities to benefit from the exploitation of a successful corporate brand name.

Table 10.2 provides a brief summary of the advantages and drawbacks of the main growth options, namely:

- organic growth – growth from within, utilizing the organization's own resources and developing new competencies as required
- acquisitions – an umbrella term to encompass the friendly purchase of one company by another, an unfriendly purchase (a takeover) and a straightforward merger of the assets of two or more organizations
- strategic alliances – some form of agreement between two or more companies
- joint ventures – alliances, but where there is the exchange of minority shareholdings between the companies involved or the establishment of an independent company, jointly owned by the organizations who start it.

A merger of two organizations will always be agreed mutually, and in some cases acquisition of one firm by another is friendly and agreed. In other cases proposed acquisitions are opposed and fought bitterly by managers in the threatened firm who try to persuade their shareholders that the company would be better off remaining under their control. These are referred to as takeovers; and when the bid succeeds a premium price is often paid. Although not all acquisitions are aimed at bringing about diversification, the majority appears to represent some form of diversification, related or unrelated.

There is another important reason, a financial one, for differentiating between the types of acquisition. When a business is acquired by another, be it in a friendly or hostile manner, the assets of the acquired business are revalued before they are absorbed into the balance sheet of the acquirer. Any difference between the new valuation and the price paid to buy the business would be reflected in the value of goodwill. Because of this revaluation and possible price premium, the

Table 10.2 Alternative growth strategies

	Advantages	Possible drawbacks
Organic growth	Lower risk Allows for ongoing learning More control	Slow Lack of early knowledge – may be misjudgements
Acquisition	Fast Buys presence, market share and expertise	Premium price may have to be paid High risk if any misjudgement Preferred organization may not be available May be difficult to sell unwanted assets
Strategic alliance	Cheaper than takeover Access to market knowledge Useful if acquisition impractical	Possible lack of control Potential managerial differences and problems
Joint venture	As for strategic alliance plus: ● Greater incentive and closer contact ● Can lock out other competitors more effectively	As for strategic alliance

capital employed of the acquiring business may increase quite substantially, and in turn affect (detrimentally) its profitability ratios and return on capital employed for a number of years into the future. In a merger situation, no price is paid and therefore the assets of the two businesses are simply pooled together. Wherever they can, businesses will seek to treat any form of acquisition as a merger for the balance sheet.

Many acquisitions and mergers lead to disappointing results: profitability is reduced and synergy does not emerge. It is difficult to predict success or failure in advance, as issues of both strategy creation and implementation are involved. Changes in corporate strategy are generally more unpredictable and risky than those that concentrate on improving competitive and functional strategies. However, growth opportunities for the present products and markets may be limited and insufficient to fill the planning gap. Few products and ideas cannot be copied and so a company must build and retain a superior competitive position. Experience, applied properly, is of great importance in this. Nevertheless, well-executed acquisitions and diversifications can be sound and very good strategic moves. However, some organizations will turn to strategic alliances or joint ventures as an alternative approach in their attempt to achieve the potential benefits, but avoid some of the potential drawbacks, of acquisitions. In Chapter 11 it is shown that strategic alliances bring their own problems and challenges.

Online Case 10.2 brings out a number of these issues. The acquisition of Forte by Granada represented diversification; the approach was hostile but successful. The subsequent divestment of assets was less extensive than had been predicted and some analysts quickly began to suggest that the new Granada should be split up. The hotel and catering businesses have now been separated from Granada's media activities, which are being expanded with related acquisitions in a changing legislative and competitive environment.

In May 2004 Sir Clive Thompson was ousted as chairman of Rentokil, a company whose growth he had championed over a number of years. He was previously CEO. The apparent reason: disagreements over strategy. His successor as CEO and other executives favoured investing in organic growth, while Sir Clive wanted 'more focus'. By this he meant disposing of certain businesses in order to return some money to shareholders and also to fund 'bold acquisitions'. He was perceived to be thinking more short term than the others in a clear strategic choice between organic growth versus acquisition growth. Much of this is about timing and judgement!

The increasing tendency to diversify

Some twenty five years ago, Channon (1983) analysed the extent to which the largest firms in the UK had become increasingly diversified over a 30 year period from the early 1950s. He used *The Times'* Top 200 companies as his database and categorized them as follows:

- *Single-product companies* – Not less than 95 per cent of sales derived from one basic business
- *Dominant-product companies* – More than 70 per cent, but less than 95 per cent, of sales from one major business
- *Related-product companies* – Companies whose sales are distributed among a series of *related* businesses, where no single business accounts for 70 per cent of sales. This would include companies who had pursued strategies of vertical or horizontal integration or concentric diversification
- *Conglomerate/unrelated-product companies* – Companies whose sales are distributed amongst a series of *unrelated* businesses, again where no single business accounts for 70 per cent of sales.

Channon contends that typically a company would start life as a single-product enterprise and then graduate through the dominant-product stage to become a related business, before finally emerging into a conglomerate. However, he emphasizes that companies do not have to follow this particular growth pattern. Some will miss one or more of the natural stages; others will choose to stay in one form and not change. This trend continued through the 1980s but since then there has been an increasing tendency for organizations to stay more focused.

> *The minimum scale for effective survival is always rising. A niche can easily become a tomb.*
>
> THE LATE LORD WEINSTOCK, WHEN CHIEF EXECUTIVE, GEC

Critical mass

As markets and industries become increasingly global a certain minimum size and market share is often thought to be necessary for competitive viability. This is known as critical mass, and it is one explanation for the growing incidence of mergers and alliances between related and competing organizations. Critical mass is important to ensure that:

- there is sufficient investment in R&D to keep pace with the market leader
- the important cost benefits of the experience curve can be achieved
- marketing activities achieve visibility and a competitive presence. This might require a wide product range and good coverage globally.

As we have seen Lloyds Bank systematically acquired fellow organizations TSB, the Cheltenham and Gloucester (C&G) Building Society and Scottish Widows (life insurance) to give it a comprehensive geographical coverage in UK financial services; critical mass and cost-reduction opportunities were used to justify the acquisitions. The new company was one of the top three in all of the financial services sectors that it targets. Mortgages were marketed through C&G; Lloyds was already strong in this segment. Lloyds also became a key player in the small business lending market and TSB has always been very popular with savers. TSB included an important insurance underwriting business to merge with Lloyds Abbey Life. Now the Lloyds Group is even bigger in terms of its grip of the high street with the takeover of HBOS (combination of the Halifax Building Society and the Bank of Scotland) in 2009. It is however in financial difficulty and essentially state owned but this should only be a temporary problem given the power it has in the high street to generate profitable new business.

Critical reflection 10.2 discusses critical mass in greater detail. As stated at the beginning of this chapter, much of the post-World War II growth and diversification by UK companies has been brought about by merger and acquisition. Some of this has been outside the UK, for a long time, mostly in the US. Statistics from JP Mervis, London-based corporate finance advisers, suggest that, of acquisitions by UK companies in Europe and the USA in the late 1980s, over 90 per cent of the spending was in the USA. During the 1990s and 2000s links with European companies have inevitably grown in popularity. Because of both competitive requirements and regulatory and cultural issues many of these links are between existing competitors, and they often take the form of joint ventures and strategic alliances rather than mergers or acquisitions. On occasions there

Critical reflection 10.2

The Significance of Critical Mass

The reality

The recent trend has been for horizontal and cross-border integrations:

- to establish critical mass and
- as industry rationalization to create global players.

Examples:

- Airbus (combining the relevant British, French and German interests to create a single business that can compete with Boeing)
- oil companies (as mentioned earlier and driven by scale economies)
- pharmaceuticals companies (prompted by high research costs)
- banking
- telecoms – Vodafone/Mannesmann – for European/world power and economies.

Points of debate

There is clear evidence that 'big can be best'?

Dominant companies such as Shell, Exxon and Coca-Cola, for example, are long-term survivors. For example at the end of the 1990s, the powerful Lloyds TSB bank *was* the best performing British bank. But do they always stay the best? Are they more vulnerable to the external rule changer? After all, size is no protection against lost competitive advantage. The share price of the new Lloyds Group in early 2009 tells an interesting story.

Glaxo grew from semi-obscurity to become the top pharmaceuticals company in the world on the back of a single new drug, Zantac, but arguably the rules in this industry have changed since then. Governments are cutting back their spending; generic drugs are becoming more popular all the time; and smaller, entrepreneurial biotechnology companies are having an impact on the industry giants.

On the other hand, privatization and the splitting up of the utilities has improved efficiencies – although these improvements may sometimes have resulted in higher profits rather than lower prices.

At the same time, many dominant industry leaders do falter and fail. United Steel was once the world's largest company and is now 'nowhere in sight'.

Sometimes an industry declines, but sometimes large organizations become sluggish with power. Others diversify and get it wrong strategically, and then get taken over and possibly split up.

What, then, goes wrong?

- loss of control
- lack of co-ordination and communication
- lost momentum/motivation/hunger.

The key issue

Big must think and behave small! Because:

- speed is critical as product life cycles are getting shorter
- information can be dispersed quickly and electronically.

The final question

Do alliances make more sense than mergers?

will be clear arguments in favour of linking two organizations, but pressure from shareholders, managers or governments may mean that acquisition is not feasible.

Introducing the diversification/focus debate

Although their popularity has waned in the 1990s, research evidence confirms that *successful* diversified conglomerates have been very profitable at certain times and in certain circumstances. Hanson (whose history is discussed in greater detail in Chapter 16) has been a notable example. Generally these conglomerates succeeded because they:

- carefully targeted their acquisitions
- avoided paying too much (normally)
- adopted an appropriately decentralized structure and control systems; and
- corporately added value.

Implementation is critical. These two conglomerates were structured as holding companies with very slim head offices; individual businesses enjoyed considerable autonomy; and tight financial control systems prevailed. Financial improvements took precedence over a search for skills transfer and synergies. Businesses were sometimes acquired (and divested) more on the logic of their financial contribution than on arguments concerning strategic fit.

Head-office capabilities and contributions for adding value included low-cost financing for the subsidiaries and skills in trading assets and improving operating efficiencies. In simple terms, these organizations developed a strategic expertise in running a diversified conglomerate, skills not matched by many organizations which choose this strategic alternative. During the late 1990s Hanson was split into five parts. Their particular strategies – which relied on finding acquisitions of a suitable size at a favourable price – became increasingly inappropriate as the British economy revived and weak, underperforming companies either became more productive or disappeared. However, as will be seen in later cases, the American General Electric (GE) has remained a very successful diversified conglomerate with a completely different style of management. GE does look to transfer ideas and skills to generate synergy between its businesses.

Goold *et al.* (1994) use the term *heartland* to describe a range of business activities to which a corporation can add value rather than destroy value by trying to manage a conglomerate which is too diverse. Key constituents are:

- common key success factors – often market driven
- related core competencies and strategic capabilities
- related technologies.

These issues are debated further in Chapter 16, but, as a final comment here it should not be forgotten that a strategy of focus is not immune from the risk of over-dependency.

As soon as things go wrong, companies start talking about focus. Focus is the crutch of mediocre management ... If you are trained in the techniques of management ... you should be able to apply them across a range of companies. Diversified companies possess both defensive qualities in recession and a springboard for new ventures in more expansive times.
A COMMENT IN DEFENCE OF CONGLOMERATE DIVERSIFICATION BY SIR OWEN GREEN, PREVIOUSLY
A SUCCESSFUL CHAIRMAN OF BTR
SOURCE *MANAGEMENT TODAY*, JUNE 1994

Case 10.7 – Nokia – discusses how Nokia successfully divested a number of businesses to focus and grow once it realized the potential of the mobile phone opportunity.

Case 10.7

Nokia

In the early 1990s Nokia of Finland decided to focus on the telecommunications industry. Four key strategic themes were identified: telecommunications orientation, globalization, focus, and value-added products.

Nokia grew rapidly and profitably during 1992–1994 by concentrating on becoming a major player in mobile telecommunications (where it achieved a 20 per cent share of the world market, second only to Motorola) and digital cellular equipment, where it became second to Ericsson of Sweden. The company's origins are in paper and other Nokia products have included televisions, tyres and power, but telecommunications grew from 14 per cent to 60 per cent of the total. Nokia was very successful with its small, lightweight portable telephones; one range competed with Japanese phones by including Japanese numerical characters. Its phones were successful for a number of reasons:

● Small, neat designs
● More user friendly than many rival products
● Good battery life
● Arguably Nokia segmented the market very effectively
● Economies of scale in production and distribution
● Tight control over costs.

Some of the growth was due to weaknesses with two leading rivals, Motorola and Ericsson, but this would not last forever! In 1996 there was a profits warning and a collapsing share price. The growth in demand for mobile phones had led to production bottlenecks, compounded by component supply issues. Nokia was experiencing problems in training its new recruits quickly enough. World prices for analogue phones were falling rapidly; even though market demand was growing healthily, new competitors such as Siemens and Alcatel (Germany and France) were causing supply to exceed demand. Nokia undertook drastic cost reduction programmes and sought to become even more focused on telecommunications. Television manufacture was just one divested activity. The target was for 90 per cent of sales to relate to telecommunications.

By 2000 Nokia was focused on mobile phones together with (a much smaller) networks division. It

was the world's leading manufacturer of mobile phones (with a 28 per cent market share) – Motorola (16 per cent) and Ericsson (12 per cent) were some way behind. However, Nokia announced a delay with new models. In this industry, innovation is critical. The original mobile phones remain, but they are much smaller and lighter than they used to be. Camera phones have helped grow the market overall, especially as picture quality has improved. There is a market for phones that provide effective Internet access and others which allow game playing. There are various views on the market potential for these more sophisticated (and expensive) alternatives. Nokia's 2003 pocket-size folding clam-shell phone (with a picture in the top half and the keys in the bottom half) proved particularly successful. As the market grows, prices continue to fall in both real and relative terms. The experience curve has had an effect. After many years of rapid growth there were signs that 2004 might see some reduction in the rate of growth as the market started to look saturated. In a number of countries there are now more mobile phones than land lines, despite a considerable differential in call costs.

Between 2002 and 2003 Nokia's market share increased from 32.5 to 34 per cent. Motorola was consistent with 15 per cent in second place. Samsung grew from 8 to 11 per cent; Siemens from 8 to 9 per cent. Sony Ericsson (a joint venture discussed separately in this chapter) fell from 6 to 5 per cent. But Sony Ericsson's products are higher price, higher value products; Nokia was particularly strong with lower price phones.

By 2004 Nokia was focused on mobile phones, multimedia, networks and enterprise solutions. In 2005 it struck a deal with Microsoft to use its software to allow music downloads on its phones. At roughly this time Jorma Ollila, who had been CEO for thirteen years and architect of the company's transformation, stepped down and became non-executive chairman. He also accepted a similar role at oil giant Shell. His replacement was an internal promotion, Olli-Pekka Kallasvuo, the existing head of mobile phones.

In 2006 Nokia remained clear market leader for mobile handsets, with a 35 per cent market share. It speeded up its programme of moving production away from Finland. This was of some concern to Finns as the country had become very dependent on the industry and on Nokia. Nokia was all the time growing stronger in multimedia (evidenced with MP3 phones, camera phones and Internet phones). Nokia developed one phone which would switch seamlessly between wireless and network Internet access. One new target was phones which would accept a television signal via satellite. It was clear that the market was segmenting more with low cost basic handsets separate from the higher added value growth area, where Nokia was also becoming a strong competitor. It was doing particularly well in the key emerging markets of China and India.

In 2007 Nokia abandoned in-house development of basic semi-conductor chips and opted to outsource these from four suppliers. Instead it would focus R&D on more sophisticated chips to drive the IT end of the market. Nokia was also looking to develop its own music download alternative to iTunes.

Nokia now had a 39 per cent global market share. Samsung, second in the market, was way behind at 15 per cent. Motorola accounted for 13 per cent, Sony Ericsson 10 per cent and LG 8 per cent. However, Nokia was only fourth in the US. In 2008 there was further restructuring, with German production moved to Romania. In the previous year Nokia had manufactured 165 million phones in China, 85m in Finland, 40m each in Brazil and Hungary, 35m in Germany, 25m in India, 20m in Mexico, 15m in South Korea and 10m in Taiwan. It was a truly global business. Its challenge was to stay relevant for all sectors of the market: newcomers (in emerging countries), replacers and traders up.

Questions

1 Can you fault the strategy pursued by Nokia?
2 Given the change of leadership, do you see the company to be truly consolidated as an industry leader?
3 What do you think the future developments in this industry might be?

NOKIA **http://www.nokia.com**

© JOHN ROBERTSON/ALAMY

ILLUSTRATE EITHER EFFECTIVE OR INEFFECTIVE HANDLING OF A MANAGERIAL SITUATION.

Causes and effects of diversification activity

Constable (1986) argues that the UK experienced the highest rate of diversification among the leading industrial nations between 1950 and 1985, and as a result developed the most concentrated economic structure. Coincidentally, this concentration was accompanied by a trend to the weakest small company sector.

The process of diversification was achieved largely through acquisitions and mergers, which have taken place at a higher rate than that experienced in other countries, especially Japan where there are few large-scale acquisitions. Constable contends that Japan, the US and Germany have concentrated more on product and market development and on adding value to current areas of activity, and that partly as a result of this they have enjoyed greater economic prosperity. Hilton (1987) has suggested that one reason behind this is that in Germany and Japan there is a greater

See the online
"Kodak" case for
an example of this
section's theory
in practice

emphasis on the respective banking systems providing funding, rather than shareholders, and this has influenced both the number of takeover bids and expectations of performance.

Diversification and acquisition strategies and tests to establish whether or not a proposed diversification seems worthwhile will be considered further in Chapter 11.

This section of Chapter 10 concludes by emphasizing that organizations change their strategies, either regularly or occasionally, to pursue different alternatives at different times. Online Case 10.3 explains how Kodak has had to shift its focus as the demand for 'traditional' film has dropped significantly.

Figure 10.4 tracks a range of possible moves. For many, the most logical strategic choices are built around relatedness and the consequent synergy. The central spine of the chart shows that product and market development are used to extend a single product range while retaining a clear focus. Chapter 16 looks in greater detail at the idea of a 'heartland' of related businesses which all benefit from belonging to one particular organization. On occasions, acceptable diversification strategies will also be followed, but sometimes these will later be reversed as the organisation returns to a more focused alternative. Returning to Case 10.1, Diageo – when it was Grand Metropolitan – diversified before refocusing, but it refocused on a new heartland, one quite different from where the company had begun. The three tests – appropriateness, feasibility and desirability – listed at the bottom of the chart are the subject of the next part of this chapter.

10.5 Introducing strategy evaluation

There is no single evaluation technique or framework as such that will provide a definite answer to which strategy or strategies a company should select or follow at any given time. Particular techniques will prove helpful in particular circumstances.

Figure 10.4   Changing strategies

Growth drivers: – Organic investments – Merger, acquisition, takeover

Reduction drivers: – Cut backs – Divestments

- Focused 'heartland' of closely related businesses B
- Diversification into unrelated businesses
- Product and market development
- Diversification into (loosely) related activities
- Vertical integration
- Focused (single) product/range

Routes
⟶ Logical
--→ Acceptable
·····→ Sometimes necessary

The tests: – Appropriateness – Feasibility – Desirability

A sound choice will always address four issues:

1 competitiveness and competitive advantage
2 strategic logic and synergy
3 the financial returns, which should normally exceed the cost of capital
4 the ability to implement.

Several frameworks and techniques which are often classified as means of evaluating strategy have been discussed in earlier chapters and are listed in Box 10.1, together with a number of additional financial considerations which are explained and discussed in the Finance in Action supplement at the end of this chapter.

Certain essential criteria, however, should be considered in assessing the merits and viability of existing strategies and alternatives for future change. This chapter considers how one might assess whether or not a corporate, competitive or functional strategy is effective or likely to be effective. The issues concern *appropriateness*, *feasibility* and *desirability*. Some of the considerations are likely to conflict with each other, and consequently an element of judgement is required in making a choice. The most appropriate or feasible option for the firm may not be the one that its managers regard as most desirable, for example.

In many respects the key aspects of any proposed changes concern the *strategic logic*, basically the subject of this book so far, and the *ability to implement*. Implementation and change are the subject of the final chapters.

Strategic logic relates to:

- the relationship and fit between the strategies and the mission or purpose of the organization; and the current appropriateness of the mission, objectives and the strategies being pursued (synergy is an important concept in this)
- the ability of the organization to match and influence changes in the environment
- competitive advantage and distinctiveness
- the availability of the necessary resources.

Figure 10.5, which recrafts the earlier model of E–V–R (environment–values– resources) congruence, shows that organizations must seek and exploit opportunities for adding value in ways that are attractive to customers. This can be at both the corporate and competitive strategy levels. At the corporate level, the organization is looking to establish a heartland of related businesses and activities; at the competitive level, the challenge is to create and sustain competitive

Box 10.1

The Main Strategy Evaluation Techniques

SWOT analysis
E–V–R congruence
Planning gap analysis
Porter's industry analysis and competitive advantage
    frameworks
Portfolio analyses
Scenario modelling
Break-even analysis

Investment appraisal techniques using discounted
    cash flows
Net present value
Internal rate of return
Payback
Cash-flow implications
(The public sector often also uses cost–benefit analysis)

Figure 10.5 E–V–R congruence restated

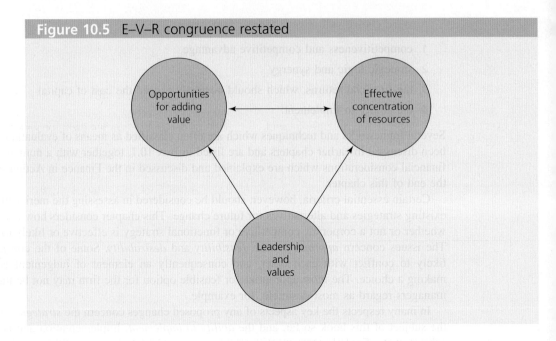

advantage. Resources must be deployed to exploit the new opportunities, and this is driven or, in some cases, frustrated by strategic leadership and the culture of the organization.

Implementation concerns the management of the resources to satisfy the needs of the organization's stakeholders. Implicit in this is the ability to satisfy customers better than competitors are able to do. Matching resources and environmental needs involves the culture and values of the organization, and decisions about future changes involve an assessment of risk. Relevant to both implementation and strategic logic is the role and preference of the strategic leader and other key decision-makers in the organization.

This chapter addresses the following questions:

- What constitutes a good strategic choice?
- What can the organization do and what can it not do?
- What should the organization seek to do and what should it not seek to do?

The last question should not be treated lightly. There will always be options available which are not appropriate for the organization as a whole, even though they might be attractive to some managers and could be readily implemented.

When evaluating any corporate, competitive or functional strategy it is worth considering ten strategic principles, all of which are discussed in detail elsewhere in the book. Where these principles, which are listed in Box 10.2, are evident, and particularly where they are strong and powerful forces, the likelihood of strategic success and effectiveness is enhanced. In addition, the financial returns should always exceed the costs involved, unless there is a defensible strategic reason for cross-subsidization.

Corporate strategy evaluation

Rumelt (1980) argues that corporate strategy evaluation at the widest level involves seeking answers to three questions:

- Are the current objectives of the organization appropriate?
- Are the strategies created previously, and which are currently being implemented to achieve these objectives, still appropriate?

Box 10.2

Ten Principles of Strategy

1 Market orientation and customer relevance
2 Innovation
3 Distinctiveness – relating to differentiation and competitive advantage
4 Timeliness (appropriate for the current situation) and
5 Flexibility (capable of change)
6 Efficiency – relating to cost control and cost efficiency, particularly in production and operations

7 Building on strengths and competencies
8 Concentration and co-ordination of resources (rather than spreading them too widely) to achieve synergy
9 Harmonization of strategy creation and implementation
10 Understanding – remembering that if a strategy is to be supported by employees who are motivated and enthusiastic it must be communicated and understood.

- Do current results confirm or refute previous assumptions about the feasibility of achieving the objectives and the ability of the chosen strategies to achieve the desired results?

It is therefore important to look back and evaluate the outcomes and relative success of previous decisions, and also to look ahead at future opportunities and threats. In both cases strategies should be evaluated in relation to the objectives that they are designed to achieve. A quantitative chart along the lines of Table 10.3 could be devised to facilitate this. In this illustration, and in order to evaluate current and possible future strategies and help to select alternatives for the future, the objectives are listed at the top of a series of columns. It will be appreciated from the

Table 10.3   Evaluating strategies in terms of objectives

Strategic alternative	Objectives*					
	Ability to achieve specific revenue or growth targets	Ability to return specific profitability targets	Ability to create and sustain competitive advantage	Synergy potential – relationship with other activities	Ability to utilize existing (spare) resources and skills	and so on
Existing competitive strategies for products, services, business units	Score out of say 10					
and Possible changes to corporate and competitive strategies	*or* Rank in order of preference					

* For evaluation purposes, each objective could be given a relative weighting.

sample objectives provided that some can have clear and objective measurement criteria, while others are more subjective in nature. The alternatives, listed down the left-hand side, could be ranked in order of first to last preference in each column, or given a numerical score. In making a final decision based on the rankings or aggregate marks it may well prove appropriate to weight the objectives in the light of their relative importance. This table could simply be used as a framework for discussion without any scoring or ranking, if this approach is preferred. In terms of assessing the suitability of strategic alternatives in particular circumstances, Thompson and Strickland (1980) suggest that market growth and competitive position are important elements.

Table 10.4 summarizes their argument. Concentration, for example, is seen as an appropriate strategy where market growth is high and the existing competitive position is strong. By contrast, where market growth is slow and the competitive position is weak, retrenchment is likely to be the most suitable strategy for the organization. Where 'not material' is listed in a column, the contention is that the strategy is appropriate for either high or low growth or strong or weak competitive positions.

10.6　Criteria for effective strategies

When assessing current strategies, and evaluating possible changes, it is important to emphasize that there is no such thing as a right or wrong strategy or choice in absolute terms. However, certain factors will influence the effectiveness of strategies and the wisdom of following certain courses of action. A number of authors, including Tilles (1963) and Hofer and Schendel (1978), have discussed the factors that determine the current and future possible effectiveness of particular strategies.

The factors that they suggest, and others, are considered in this chapter in three sections: appropriateness, feasibility and desirability. This categorization has been selected for convenience, and it will be appreciated that there is some overlap between the sections.

The major issues are summarized in Figure 10.6 and are discussed below. It is important to flag that a number of factors have been linked to each of the three main criteria or sections, largely for convenience. These linkages are not fully cut-and-dried. Some of the factors clearly impact upon

Table 10.4　Strategic alternatives: their appropriateness in terms of market growth and competitive position

Strategy	Market growth	Competitive position
Concentration	High	Strong
Horizontal integration	High	Weak
Vertical integration	High	Strong
Concentric diversification	Not material	Not material
Conglomerate diversification	Low	Not material
Joint ventures into new areas	Low	Not material
Retrenchment	Low	Weak
Turnaround	High	Weak
Divestment	Not material	Weak
Liquidation	Not material	Weak

Source: Developed from ideas in Thompson, AA and Strickland, AJ (1980) *Strategy Formulation and Implementation*, Irwin.

Figure 10.6 Criteria for effective strategies

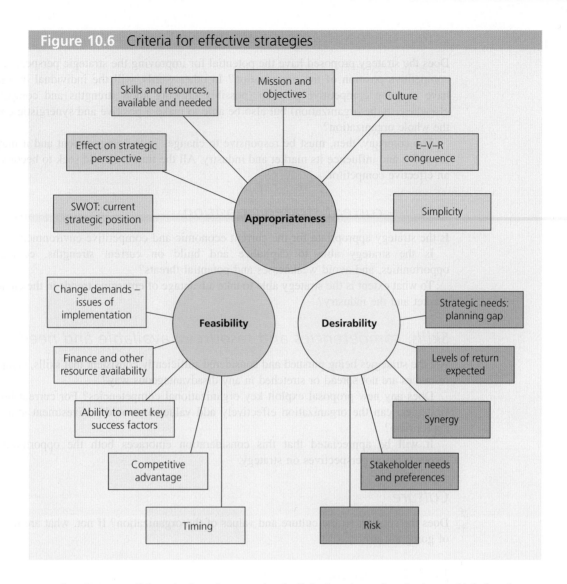

more than just one of the criteria – they are simply linked to the main criteria to which they have a strong link.

Appropriateness

In reviewing current strategies, assessing the impact of adaptive incremental changes that have taken place and considering strategic alternatives for the future it is important to check that strategies are consistent with the needs of the environment, the resources and values of the organization, and its current mission. These general points are elaborated below. For the rest of this section the term 'the strategy' is used to refer to each particular strategy being considered, be it a current one or a proposed change or addition.

Mission and objectives

Does the strategy fit the current mission and objectives of the organization? Is it acceptable to the strategic leader and other influential stakeholders? (This issue is developed further in the Desirability section below.)

Effect on the strategic perspective

Does the strategy proposed have the potential for improving the strategic perspective and general competitive position of the organization? In other words, will the individual business not only have a strong competitive position (possibly drawing upon strengths and competencies from elsewhere in the organization) but also be able to make a positive and synergistic contribution to the whole organization?

The company, then, must be responsive to changes in the environment and it may wish to be proactive and influence its market and industry. All the time it should seek to become and remain an effective competitor.

SWOT – current strategic position

Is the strategy appropriate for the current economic and competitive environment?

Is the strategy able to capitalize and build on current strengths, competencies and opportunities, and avoid weaknesses and potential threats?

To what extent is the strategy able to take advantage of emerging trends in the environment, the market and the industry?

Skills, competencies and resources: available and needed

Are the strategies being pursued and considered sufficiently consistent that skills, competencies and resources are not spread or stretched in any disadvantageous way?

Does any new proposal exploit key organizational competencies? For current businesses and strategies: can the organization effectively add value, or would a divestment strategy be more appropriate?

It will be appreciated that this consideration embraces both the opportunity-driven and resource-based perspectives on strategy.

Culture

Does the strategy fit the culture and values of the organization? If not, what are the implications of going ahead?

E–V–R congruence

Summarizing the above points, is there congruence between the environment, values and resources?

Simplicity

Is the strategy simple and understandable? Is the strategy one which could be communicated easily, and about which people are likely to be enthusiastic? These factors are also aspects of desirability.

Feasibility

Change demands – issues of implementation

Is the strategy feasible in resource terms? Can it be implemented effectively? Is it capable of achieving the objectives that it addresses?

Can the organization cope with the extent and challenge of the change implied by the option?

Finance and other resource availability

A lack of any key resource can place a constraint on certain possible developments. The cost of capital is explained in the Finance in Action supplement at the end of this chapter.

The ability to meet key success factors

A strategic alternative is not feasible if the key success factors dictated by the industry and customer demand, such as quality, price and service level, cannot be met.

Competitive advantage

The effectiveness of a strategy will be influenced by the ability of the organization to create and sustain competitive advantage. When formulating a strategy it is important to consider the likely response of existing competitors in order to ensure that the necessary flexibility is incorporated into the implementation plans. A company which breaks into a currently stable industry or market may well threaten the market shares and profitability of other companies and force them to respond with, say, price cuts, product improvements or aggressive promotion campaigns. The new entrant should be prepared for this and ready to counter it.

Timing

This is related to opportunity on the one hand and risk and vulnerability on the other. It may be important for an organization to act quickly and decisively once an opening window of opportunity is spotted. Competitors may attempt to seize the same opportunity.

At the same time managers should make sure that they allow themselves enough time to consider the implications of their actions and organize their resources properly. Adaptive incremental change in the implementation of strategy can be valuable here. An organization may look to pursue a new strategy, learn by experience and improve by modification once they have gone ahead.

Strategic leadership and the structure, culture and values of the organization are therefore important.

Timing is also an implementation issue; the retailer Next provides one illustration of its significance. Next introduced a number of successful strategic changes which resulted in growth and increased profitability, but then overstretched themselves by pursuing strategies for which they had insufficient resources at the time. This story is explained in detail in the case on the website and this theme relates to the theory of growth and the existence of the receding managerial limit suggested by Edith Penrose (1959), which was discussed earlier.

There is an important paradox of resource management. Resources must be stretched if they are to achieve their full potential, but if the targets set for them imply a 'bridge too far' there is a real danger of both underachievement and damage to the rest of the organization. Here, resources might have to be redeployed, which will have consequences for the business from which they are taken. The reputation of the organization might easily be tarnished. Clearly, the decisions reached will reflect the risk perspective of the managers concerned.

Desirability

Strategic needs – the planning gap

The ability of the strategy to satisfy the objectives of the organization and help to close any identified planning gap are important considerations. Timing may again be an important issue. The ability of the strategy to produce results in either the short or the longer term should be assessed in the light of the needs and priorities of the firm.

The level of returns expected

Decisions concerning where a company's financial resources should be allocated are known as investment or capital budgeting decisions. The decision might concern the purchase of new technology or new plant, the acquisition of another company, or financing the development and launch of a new product.

Competitive advantage and corporate strategic change are both relevant issues.

The ability to raise money, and the cost involved are key influences, and should be considered alongside two other strategic issues:

- Does the proposed investment make sense strategically, given present objectives and strategies?
- Will the investment provide an adequate financial return?

The latter question is partly answered by the company's cost of capital and the whole topic of investment decisions is explored in the Finance in Action section at the end of this chapter. Strategic fit is a broad issue and is addressed in the main part of the chapter.

Synergy

Effective synergy should lead ideally to a superior concentration of resources in relation to competitors. The prospects for synergy should be evaluated alongside the implications for the firm's strategic perspective and culture, which were included in the section on Appropriateness. These factors in combination affect the strategic fit of the proposal and its ability to complement existing strategies and bring an all-round improvement to the organization. Diversification into products and markets with which the organization has no experience, and which may require different skills, may fit poorly alongside existing strategies and fail to provide synergy.

Risk

It has already been pointed out that risk, vulnerability, opportunity and timing are linked. Where organizations, having spotted an opportunity, act quickly, there is always a danger that some important consideration will be overlooked. The risk lies in these other factors, many of which are discussed elsewhere, which need careful attention in strategy formulation:

- the likely effect on competition
- the technology and production risks, linked to skills and key success factors. Can the organization cope with the production demands and meet market requirements profitably? Innovation often implies higher risks in this area, but offers higher rewards for success
- the product/market diversification risk – the risk involved in overstretching resources through diversification has been considered earlier in this chapter
- the financial risk – the cash flow and the firm's borrowing requirements are sensitive to the ability of the firm to forecast demand accurately and predict competitor responses
- managerial ability and competence – the risk here involves issues of whether skills can be transferred from one business to another when a firm diversifies, and whether key people stay or go after a takeover
- environmental risks – it is also important to ensure that possible adverse effects or hostile public opinion are evaluated.

Many of these issues are qualitative rather than finite, and judgement will be required. The ability of the organization to harness and evaluate the appropriate information is crucial, but again there is a trade-off. The longer the time that the organization spends in considering the implications and assessing the risks, the greater the chance it has of reducing and controlling the risks. However, if managers take too long, the opportunity or the initiative may be lost to a competitor who is more willing to accept the risk. The subject of risk is revisited in Chapter 16.

> *In my experience those who manage change most successfully are those who welcome it in their own lives and see it as an opportunity for stimulation and learning new things. Implicit is the willingness to take risks, including making intelligent mistakes.*
>
> *I am much more interested in important failures that prepare the way for future success than I am in cautious competence and maintaining the status quo.*

ROBERT FITZPATRICK, WHEN PRESIDENT DIRECTEUR GÉNÉRAL, EURO DISNEYLAND SA

Stakeholder needs and preferences

This relates to the expectations and hopes of key stakeholders, the ability of the organization to implement the strategy and achieve the desired results, and the willingness of stakeholders to accept the inherent risks in a particular strategy.

Strategic changes may affect existing resources and the strategies to which they are committed, gearing, liquidity and organization structures, including management roles, functions and systems. Shareholders, bankers, managers, employees and customers can all be affected; and their relative power and influence will prove significant. The willingness of each party to accept particular risks may vary. Trade-offs may be required. The power and influence of the strategic leader will be very important in the choice of major strategic changes, and his or her ability to convince other stakeholders will be crucial.

10.7 Decision-making

It has already been emphasized that strategies can form or emerge as well as be formulated or prescribed. Strategic change results from decisions taken and implemented in response to perceived opportunities or threats. The management of change therefore requires strategic awareness and strategic learning, which implies the ability to recognize and interpret signals from the environment. Signals from the environment come into the organization all the time and in numerous ways. It is essential that they are monitored and filtered in such a way that the important messages reach decision-makers. If strategic change is to some degree dependent on a planning system, then that planning system must gather the appropriate data. Equally, if there is greater reliance on strategic change emerging from decisions taken within the organization by managers who are close to the market, their suppliers and so on, these managers must feel that they have the authority to make change decisions. In both cases appropriate strategic leadership is required to direct activity.

This section looks at decision-making in practice, at how decisions are taken and might be taken, and at why some bad decisions are made.

Decision-making and problem-solving

Decision-making is a process related to the existence of a problem, and it is often talked about in terms of problem-solving. A problem, in simple terms, exists when an undesirable situation has arisen which requires action to change it. In other words, a problem exists for someone if the situation that they perceive exists is unsatisfactory for them. They would like to see something different or better happening and achieving different results.

However, in many instances the problem situation is very complex and can only be partially understood or controlled, and therefore decisions are not so much designed to find ideal or perfect answers but to improve the problem situation. In other instances, managers may find themselves with so many problems at any time that they can at best reduce the intensity of the problem rather than systematically search for a so-called right answer.

Russell Ackoff (1978) distinguishes between solving, resolving, dissolving and absolving problems. A *solution* is the optimum answer, the best choice or alternative, and rational decision-making (developed below) is an attempt to find it. A *resolution* is a satisfactory answer or choice, not necessarily the best available, but one that is contingent upon circumstances, such as time limitations or lack of real significance of the problem. This will again be developed below. A *dissolution* occurs when objectives are changed in such a way that the problem no longer seems to be a problem. Feelings about what *should* be happening are changed to bring them in line with what *is* happening; current realities are accepted. Typically managers accept new, weaker objectives which allow them to feel that there is no longer a problem. For example, achieving a target revenue growth of 5 per cent in a static market might be proving difficult; a revised (downwards) figure of 2 per cent would be much more achievable! *Absolution* happens when problems are simply ignored in the hope that they will rectify themselves. Some people tend to treat minor illnesses in this way.

While there will always be an objective element in a strategic decision, other more subjective influences will also play a part. Figure 10.7 shows that the ultimate decision will have been affected by three elements:

- the results of whatever analyses have been used to evaluate the data available
- the intuition and perspective of the person or people involved. Past experiences and their willingness to trust the reliability and validity of the information that they have will both be influential issues. Some managers and strategic leaders, particularly those whom we would describe as entrepreneurial, often have an uncanny and difficult-to-explain

understanding of a market or industry and of which strategy would work. They do not appear to carry out any formal analysis or use any of the techniques described here. But such managers are a minority and others are well advised to use formal analysis!

- the political realities of the various alternatives. The contingent decision is the one that people believe can be implemented. It is not necessarily the alternative that on paper promises the highest rewards. To be effective, all managers must be able to handle the relevant political issues, as discussed in Chapter 15.

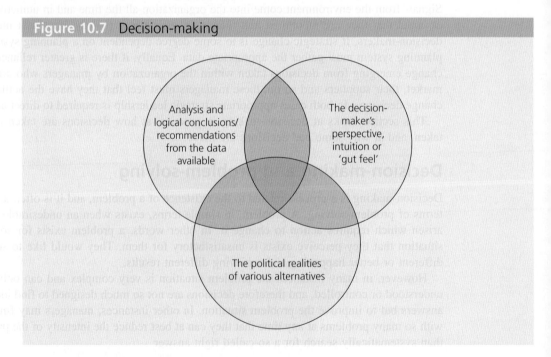

Figure 10.7 Decision-making

Analysis and logical conclusions/ recommendations from the data available

The decision-maker's perspective, intuition or 'gut feel'

The political realities of various alternatives

Figure 10.8 Key issues in decision-making

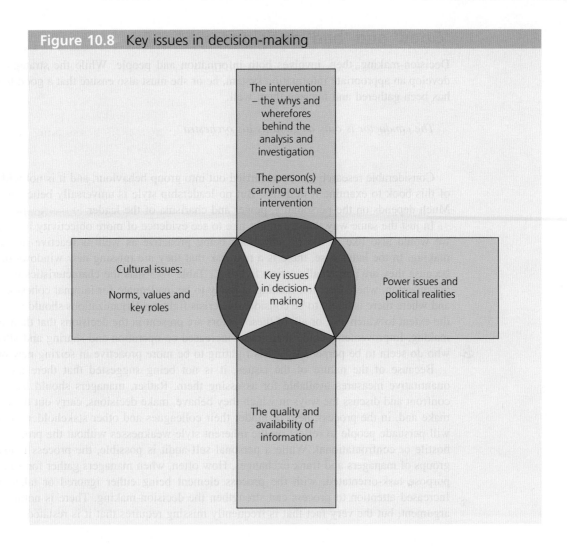

Figure 10.8 presents these themes in a different way by illustrating the four key issues in any decision:

1 the nature of the actual intervention. The idea of 'meaning systems' means that the person or people involved will be involved for a reason. Maybe it is their direct responsibility. Perhaps they have been asked to advise and help. Possibly they have been brought in because those whose responsibility the problem is are simply not coping. Regardless, they bring their own perspective, interpretation and objectives to the situation. Naturally this will have an important bearing on:

2 the relevant power issues and political realities

3 the quality and reliability of the information available

4 cultural issues, in particular norms, values and key roles. The decision taken should never ignore the likelihood of it being implemented successfully. If people oppose the changes or strategy proposed, for whatever reason (again discussed in Chapter 15), they may be minded to try and block its implementation. Where the change complements existing values and practices it should be more acceptable than if it implies a change of culture and behaviour. Radical change is sometimes essential, and should not be avoided simply because it is likely to attract opposition. However, it must be realized that it will take longer to implement.

'Good' and 'bad' decisions

Decision-making, then, involves both information and people. While the strategic leader must develop an appropriate information system, he or she must also ensure that a good team of people has been gathered and manage them well.

The conductor is only as good as his orchestra

ANDRÉ PREVIN

Considerable research has been carried out into group behaviour, and it is not within the scope of this book to examine it in detail. But no leadership style is universally better than the others. Much depends on the personality, power and charisma of the leader.

In just the same way that we might like to see evidence of more objectivity in some decisions, we would also like to see organizations being proactive as well as reactive in their decision-making. In the latter case, there is a real risk that they are missing new windows of opportunity because they are perpetually 'crisis fighting'. Table 10.5 lists the characteristics of a fragmented organization, where decision-making is likely to be inadequate for internal cohesion and synergy and where there is likely to be considerable crisis fighting. Organizations should usefully evaluate the extent to which any, or all, of these factors are present in the decisions that their managers are making. Improvements could then foster increased co-operation and sharing and allow managers who do seem to be perpetually crisis fighting to be more proactive in seizing new opportunities.

Because of the nature of the issues, it is not being suggested that there are obvious and quantitative measures available for assessing them. Rather, managers should be encouraged to confront and discuss the ways in which they behave, make decisions, carry out the decisions they make and, in the process, help or hinder their colleagues and other stakeholders. Hopefully, this will persuade people to reflect on the inherent style weaknesses without the process being either hostile or confrontational. While a personal self-audit is possible, the process is enhanced with groups of managers and frank exchanges. How often, when managers gather for a meeting, is the purpose task-orientated, with the process element being either ignored or taken for granted? Increased attention to process can strengthen the decision-making. There is nothing new in this argument, but the very fact that is frequently missing requires that it is restated.

Table 10.5   Manifestations of a fragmented organization

- Irrational decision-making (processes)
- Weak decision-making/leadership (people)
- Rigidity, reluctance to change and negative politics
- Conflicting perspectives and interests
- Over-hasty decisions (decisive!) which are difficult to implement
- Lack of clear purpose
- Dissolution and absolution (of problems) instead of resolution and solution
- Unhelpful personal objectives
- Stakeholder conflicts
- Poor information
- Inadequate measurement and control
- Managerial inability to take a holistic perspective

Irrational decision-making

The notion of a rational decision-making process would include the following stages, not necessarily in this sequential order:

- clarify the problem, which implies more than a statement of the obvious symptoms and manifestations
- establish clear objectives for the desired outcome
- generate possible alternative courses of action
- assess the probable outcomes for each alternative
- select a course of action, by considering likely outcomes and desired objectives
- implement this choice and
- monitor and evaluate progress.

It is clear that most decisions and managerial actions do not follow a sequence such as this, or incorporate all of these stages. Short-cuts are taken, often because of a lack of time or a lack of information, and sometimes through laziness. A number of explanations for this is available. Simon (1976) offers the idea of 'satisficing', the acceptance of a satisfactory course of action (not necessarily the best solution) which at least deals with the problem. Lindblom (1959) and later Quinn (1980) offer alternative theories based around the concept of trial and error in incremental, learning stages as distinct from a more hands-off decision. Etzioni (1967) argues that managers make a judgement on the relative importance and priority of an issue or problem, and then base the time and attention that they give to the issue on this judgement. All of these are logical and defensible. The issue concerns the extent to which managers are avoiding – consciously or unconsciously – the elements of the rational approach, especially in the case of major, serious problems and, in the end, making poor decisions which fail to deal adequately with the problem.

Weak decision-making

Here we are looking for managers to realize and discuss the extent of their:

- tunnel vision, leading to a lack of internal synergy
- information flows and communications which prevent the right information reaching the people who need it when they can make best use of it
- personal objectives and agendas which lead to subjectivity, selfishness and internal tensions
- willingness to ignore the potential downside impact of their actions on other managers and other parts of the organization
- unwillingness to compromise to reach an accommodation with other managers.

Many of these issues are always likely to be present. Are they being ignored – causing frustration and maybe even despair – or dealt with? It is important here to stress the idea of *accommodation* among managers, as distinct from consensus, where multiple objectives and perspectives are present.

Resistance to change

Heirs and Farrell (1987) identify three 'destructive minds', the impact of which organizations must minimize if they are to manage change effectively:

- the rigid mind which stifles originality and creativity and ignores the need to change
- the ego mind which fosters subjectivity and makes collaboration very difficult
- the 'machiavellian mind' which uses political activity to achieve personal objectives at the expense of others.

All effective managers will be political; they will use their power and influence to bring about decisions and actions which serve the needs and interests of the organization. Negative politics occurs when this power and influence is used against the best interests of the organization.

How many of these minds are evident in a crisis fighting organization that is largely reactive to events?

Over-hasty decisions

Crisis fighters are typically pragmatic and decisive. Sometimes, though, decisions taken in haste prove difficult to implement, as valuable time is spent trying to justify the decision. Taking time initially to search for support and agreement, involving a range of people and opinions in the process, can be hard to justify when time pressures are tight. However, if decisions enjoy people's support because they have been consulted and understand the background, implementation can be smoother, actually saving time in the end. We can learn a great deal from the Japanese here – but in many organizations, are managers listening and learning?

Stakeholder conflicts – the need for a holistic perspective

It is unlikely that all the preferences of every internal and external stakeholder can be met in full and, as we saw earlier, accommodation is necessary. The issue here concerns the ability of managers to appreciate and accept that different people have different perspectives, and they do not see problems and issues in the same way. There is a saying: 'the way we see the problem is the problem'. Too narrow a perspective leads to a poor decision with adverse impacts on others. Taking account of different perspectives demands dialogue and sharing.

Finkelstein *et al.* (2009) argue that bad decisions come in two stages. In the first instance an individual or group exercises poor judgment; but then, and second, there is a failure to correct the mistake. They cite four key causes: misleading experiences; misleading prejudgments; inappropriate self-interest; and inappropriate attachments. Sometimes emotional attachments get in the way of logic. They see the Sinclair C5 (electric car) and the acquisition of ABN Amro by Royal Bank of Scotland as 'bad mistakes'. They comment that managers post-event will often argue that 'it seemed like a good idea at the time'. It perhaps did – because of the causal factors involved. After all, more often than not, the managers involved are not stupid and they are not setting out to destroy their organizations. They simply make mistakes. The risks they take do not work out for them.

Implementing decisions

The implementation aspects of the decision are of vital importance. Simply, a decision can only be effective if it is implemented successfully and yields desirable or acceptable results. It may prove very sensible to spend time arriving at a decision by, say, involving the people who must implement it, aiming to generate a commitment at this stage even though it may be time-consuming. Such a decision is likely to be implemented smoothly. One alternative to this, the speedy decisive approach, may prove to be less effective. If it is not supported, the alternative chosen may result in controversy and reluctance on the part of others to implement it. Vroom and Yetton (1973) have developed a model of five alternative ways of decision-making.

Vroom and Yetton's model   A short summary of the five approaches is as follows.

1   The leader solves the problem or makes the decision him or herself using information available at the time.

2   The leader obtains necessary information from subordinates and then decides on the solution to the problem him or herself. Subordinates are not involved in generating or evaluating alternative solutions.

3 The leader shares the problem with relevant subordinates individually, obtaining their ideas and suggestions without bringing them together as a group. Then the leader makes the decision, which may or may not reflect the influence of subordinates.

4 The leader shares the problem with the subordinates as a group, collectively obtaining their ideas and suggestions. Then he or she makes the decision, which again may or may not reflect their influence.

5 The leader shares the problem with the subordinates as a group, and together the leader and subordinates generate and evaluate alternatives and attempt to reach an agreement on a solution.
(Vroom and Yetton use the expression 'solve' throughout.)

Vroom and Yetton contend that the choice of style should relate to the particular problem faced, and their model includes a series of questions which can be used diagnostically to select the most appropriate style. While the model is useful for highlighting the different styles and emphasizing that a single style will not always prove to be the most appropriate, it is essentially a normative theory – 'this is what you should do' – and in this respect should be treated with caution.

I make every decision, but get lots of advice. I don't delegate. It's 'What do you think?' 'What do you think?' 'What do you think?' Then boom, I decide.

JEFF INMELT, CEO, GENERAL ELECTRIC

10.8 Judgement

The judgement dilemma

Judgement, per se, cannot be taught or learned; instead it comes from experience. Experience is gained by making mistakes, which, of course, are the result of poor judgement! Managers exercise poor judgement because it cannot be taught or learned.

Strategic changes can be selected by an individual manager, often the strategic leader, or a team of managers, and Vickers (1965) stresses that three contextual aspects have a critical impact on the decision:

● the decision-makers' skills and values together with aspects of their personality (*personal factors*)
● their authority and accountability within the organization (*structural factors*)
● their understanding and awareness (*environmental factors*).

Related to these, the decisions taken by managers are affected by their personal judgemental abilities, and understanding judgement can, therefore, help us to explain why some managers appear to 'get things right' while others 'get things wrong'.

Vickers suggests that there are three types of judgement:

1 *Reality judgements* – Strategic awareness of the organization and its environment and which is based upon interpretation and meaning systems.
2 *Action judgements* – What to do about perceived strategic issues.
3 *Value judgements* – Concerning expected and desired results and outcomes from the decision.

Figure 10.9 shows how these are interconnected. Decision-makers need to understand 'what is' (*reality*), 'what matters' (*values*) and 'what to do about it' (*action*). Their choice will be based upon a conceptualization of what might or what should be a better alternative to the current

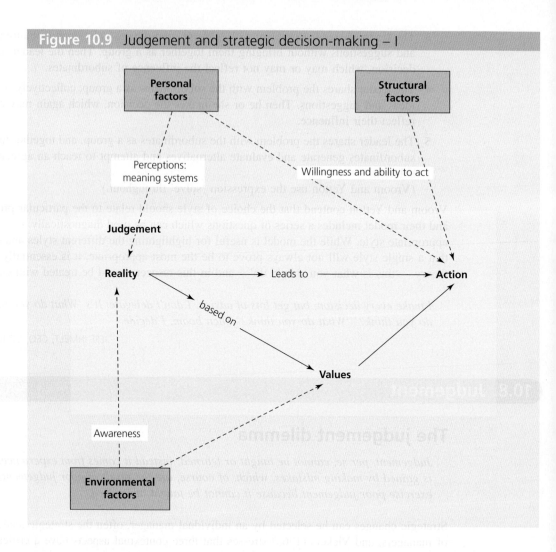

Figure 10.9   Judgement and strategic decision-making – I

situation. Ideally, it will incorporate a holistic perspective, implying either an understanding or a personal interpretation of the organization's purpose or mission, and it also requires an appreciation that what matters is a function of urgency and time horizons. A company with cash difficulties, for example, might need a strategy based upon immediate rationalization or consolidation; a liquid company evaluating growth options has greater flexibility. The choice will also be affected by managers' relative power and influence, their perception of the risks involved, and their willingness to pursue certain courses of action.

Tichy and Bennis (2007) suggest managers and leaders must exercise good judgement in three critical areas: the selection of key people, the choice of strategy to follow, and how to handle crises when something unexpected happens. Effective leaders, they argue, are better briefed and better prepared and they 'make good calls'. It is, they say, all too easy for a leader to be 'dazzled by an exciting strategy without thinking hard enough about how achievable it is, given the resources available'. Tichy and Bennis include one comment from a strategic leader in a large corporation who says 'things seem very different now it's my ultimate responsibility than they did when I was a McKinsey consultant in the past'.

To conclude this chapter, Figure 10.10 draws together key points from the sections on decision-making and judgement. The top part of the diagram explains that managers have to assess any problematical situation and determine the extent to which it is normal or unusual. This is their reality judgement of the situation. Where they perceive that there is a real degree of normality to

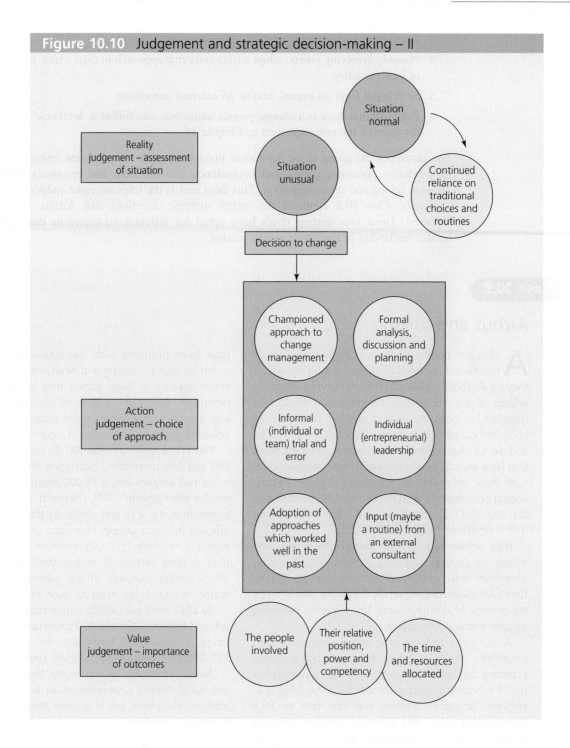

Figure 10.10 Judgement and strategic decision-making – II

the events, the likelihood is that they will continue to rely on traditional routines and approaches. However, where the situation is seen as more unusual a decision has to be made about how to deal with it. This choice reflects action judgement, and there are six (and possibly more) alternatives to choose from:

1 Continue to rely on approaches which have worked well in the past.

2 From a position of leadership, take decisive action – reflecting an entrepreneurial style.

3 Involve others in formal analysis, discussion and planning.

4 Possibly involving others, adopt a trial-and-error approach to craft a new strategy adaptively or incrementally.

5 Seek input from an expert, maybe an external consultant.

6 Establish that there is a change project under way and follow a 'textbook' approach – along the lines of the one explained in Chapter 15.

The outcomes are going to be dependent upon the people who become engaged and involved, their relative positions, power and competency and the time and resources allocated to the decision taking and implementation. This final part is the relevant value judgement.

Finally, Case 10.8 contrasts the recent strategic directions that Airbus and Boeing have followed. These two leading rivals have opted for different strategies as they both strive for market leadership in the future airline market.

Case 10.8

Airbus and Boeing   EU US

SOURCE: THIS CASE STUDY WAS PREPARED USING USING PRIMARILY PUBLICLY AVAILABLE SOURCES OF INFORMATION FOR THE PURPOSES OF CLASSROOM DISCUSSION. IT DOES NOT INTEND TO ILLUSTRATE EITHER EFFECTIVE OR INEFFECTIVE HANDLING OF A MANAGERIAL SITUATION.

Airbus and Boeing are the two leading suppliers of commercial airplanes to airlines around the world; they are also both suppliers of military planes. Historically Boeing of the US (which absorbed rival McDonnell Douglas) has been the leading supplier, but Airbus, a European consortium involving France, Germany, Italy and the UK, has made serious progress. In recent years they have been following quite different strategies – and both have struggled to implement their strategies. Boeing provided the world with the 747 'Jumbo' and the 737, the favourite plane of the low frills carriers. Airbus pioneered fly-by-wire technology.

New airliners require huge investments in time and money to develop and test. Airlines will, however, sometimes order well ahead and pay deposits to help fund such investment – but only if they are convinced by the promise of the new plane. Consequently delivering on time is critically important.

Airbus chose to focus on a new 'Superjumbo' with passengers on two levels. A typical first-business-economy configuration would imply 555 passengers – but all economy it could easily seat 840. This A380 is 4-engined. Singapore Airlines was the first to take delivery of a plane and generally deliveries are way behind schedule. One added complication is that this plane is so big only certain runways and terminals can handle it. Boeing has provided a stretch version of the 747 but has opted not to compete with a genuinely new plane in this sector of the market.

Instead Boeing has been developing its 787 Dreamliner plane – which is also behind schedule. First deliveries – promised 2008 – will be in 2009. There have been problems with the supply chain. Boeing opted for global sourcing and what was meant to be a virtue appears to have turned into something of a nightmare. Before the economic recession started to bite Boeing had a strong order book, with the first deliveries going to All Nippon of Japan.

The first Dreamliner (the 787-8) can seat between 210 and 250 passengers, depending on configuration. It has two engines and a 15,000 kilometer range. It is smaller than Boeing's 747, 767 and 777 planes but bigger than the 737 and similar to the 757. It is fuel efficient (offering savings of around 20 per cent) and boasts a relatively low CO_2 emission figure. Carbon fibre is used extensively in the construction. It also offers greater humidity in the cabins and, for this reason, is seen as less likely to cause jet lag.

By 2012 there will be two further models. The 787-3 will seat between 290 and 330 passengers with a flying range of some 6000 kilometers; the 787-9 will seat 250-290 and have a range of 8500 kilometers.

Airbus, which has grown on the back of the A320 and A340 models is working on an A350 long range medium size plane, but it is some three years behind Boeing's Dreamliner.

Question

Airbus and Boeing both developed their strategies when economies were healthy around the world. When demand started falling in 2008, and passengers were being asked to pay fuel surcharges, which of the two strategies would look to be the more appropriate?

Summary

There is a range of strategic alternatives and strategic means that organizations might review and possibly choose at any time. Organizations will change their directions and strategies and they do not always pursue the same strategy in the same way. Normally, they will aim to be proactive and purposeful about this. Sometimes, however, they are constrained: an option that they would like to pursue is unrealistic. This would be the case if the Competition Commission blocked a proposed acquisition. Similarly, the Commission might insist on a particular divestment in return for permission to proceed with a merger.

Over time, the corporate portfolio migrates. It should be built around a defensible heartland of related businesses, accepting that at times there will be diversification into related and unrelated activities. We cannot finally judge the worthiness of a particular choice until we take account of the organization's ability to implement the strategy that it has chosen.

The key strategic alternatives are limited growth, substantive growth and retrenchment.

Limited growth

- market penetration, either in a deliberate attempt to build market share or as a form of consolidation to protect a customer base
- market development – opening up new opportunities with different customers, possibly in overseas markets
- product development – extending the range in order to expand the level of business with existing customers.

Substantive growth

- horizontal integration – generally merging with a direct or indirect competitor, again to increase market share
- vertical integration – linking with another company in the same supply chain
- related diversification – moving into an area where either marketing or technology issues are similar, often by acquisition, merger or strategic alliance
- unrelated diversification – the higher risk strategy involving new markets, new products and new technologies.

The key strategic means (which are discussed next) are:

- organic growth – internal investment to develop new competencies

- acquisition (friendly purchase), merger (two companies simply joining together) and takeover (hostile purchase)
- strategic alliances (partnerships, whatever the form) and joint ventures (alliances which involve a major financial investment by the parties concerned).

When evaluating and selecting strategies, it is important for organizations to address the following questions:

- What constitutes a good strategic choice?
- What can the organization do and what can it not do?
- What should the organization seek to do and what should it not seek to do?

An effective strategy is one that meets the needs and preferences of the organization, its key decision-makers and influencers – ideally better than any alternatives – and can be implemented successfully.

The techniques introduced in earlier parts of the book can all make a contribution, but there are likely to be subjective elements as well.

There are three broad criteria for evaluating strategies:

Appropriateness

- Does the proposal fit – and strengthen – the existing portfolio of activities?
- Is it compatible with the mission of the organization?
- Does it address any targeted opportunities or help redress any critical weaknesses?
- What impact would the change have on E–V–R congruence?
- Is this an opportunity for stretching the organization's resources and exploiting core competencies further? Or does it imply diversification?

Feasibility

- Can the strategic change be implemented successfully – and without any detrimental impact upon present activities?
- Does the organization possess the skills and competencies required? If not, can they be acquired in a relevant timescale?
- Can the implied costs be met?
- Is there an opportunity to build and sustain a strong competitive position?

Desirability

- Does the option truly help to close the planning gap?
- Is the organization comfortable with the risks implied?
- Is this a justifiable (and, in certain cases, the most profitable) use of organizational effort and resources?
- Is there potential synergy?
- Which stakeholder needs will be met and satisfied?

When reviewing options, it is unlikely that one will turn out to be the most appropriate, the most feasible and the most desirable. Trade-offs will have to be made.

The decision-making processes used will inevitably have elements of subjectivity. Judgement will have to be applied alongside any technique-driven strategic analyses. Decision-making, therefore, must embrace issues of intuition and political reality alongside the available information and analyses. There are a number of explanations – all easily appreciated – for 'poor' decision-making.

Judgement comprises three key elements:

- a *reality judgement* of the situation and the implied problem
- an *action judgement* about what to do
- *value judgements* concerning expected and desired outcomes.

Online cases for this chapter

Online Case 10.1: Adidas, Nike and Umbro
Online Case 10.2: Granada/ITV: Granada's Acquisition of Forte

Online Case 10.3: Kodak
Online Case 10.4: Next

Questions and research assignments

1 For each of the following strategic alternatives, list why you think an organization might select this particular strategy, what they would expect to gain, and where the problems and limitations are. If you can, think of an example of each one from your own experience:

- do nothing; no change
- market penetration
- market development
- product development
- innovation
- horizontal integration
- vertical integration
- concentric diversification
- conglomerate diversification.

2 What are the relative advantages and disadvantages of organic growth as opposed to external growth strategies?

3 Which of the evaluation techniques listed in the chapter (Box 10.1) do you feel are most useful? Why? How would you use them? What are their limitations?

4 From your experience and reading, which evaluation criteria do you think are most significant in determining the effectiveness of strategies? List examples of cases where the absence of these factors, or the wrong assessment of their importance, has led to problems.

Internet and library projects

1 For an organization of your choice, trace the changes of strategy and strategic direction over a period of time. Relate these changes to any changes in strategic leadership, structure and, wherever possible, culture.

2 Walt Disney Corporation became hugely successful and influential on the back of cartoon films, beginning with Mickey Mouse. In more recent years theme parks and 'straight' movies have also been vitally significant. In addition a number of

proposals have bitten the dust. As a consequence, in 2004, the CEO Michael Eisner was under considerable pressure from some shareholders to resign. Research and evaluate the various strategic options pursued by Disney. Where should it seek to develop next?

3 Mumtaz started life as an Indian restaurant in Bradford, West Yorkshire, in the UK. It was started by a son and his mother in 1979. A second brother – who was a medical doctor – later opted to join the business. Mumtaz boasts Sir Alex Ferguson, various high-profile footballers and other celebrities as its customers. Her Majesty the Queen has eaten their food. There is now a second restaurant in Leeds and the business has diversified into Halal baby food (with 50 per cent of the sales going to non-ethnics) and a range of supermarket meals – starters, mains desserts and breads.

Why has Mumtaz been as successful as it has with its strategic choices when there are numerous Indian restaurants in the UK?

4 In 1983 Tottenham Hotspur became the first English football club to be listed on the Stock Exchange. Subsequently, the club diversified, acquiring a number of related leisure companies. The intention was to subsidize the football club with profits from the new businesses. Initially this happened, but in the recession of the late 1980s football had to prop up the other activities. Businesses were closed or divested, and the ownership of Tottenham Hotspur changed hands in 1991. During the 1990s entrepreneur Alan Sugar acquired the club, only to relinquish control when he proved unpopular with many Spurs fans. Sugar claimed the Club forced him to take his eye off the ball with his business. Since then, despite several changes, including a new owner and several new managers (the most recent being Ramos and now Redknapp) and spending £70m on new players during 2008, Tottenham Hotspur has struggled to retain its place in the Premiership. Research the various changes and evaluate the strategies. Was it appropriate and desirable for Tottenham to become a public limited company at the time it did? How different was the approach taken some years later by Manchester United? What strategies have made Manchester United the richest football club in the world?

Tottenham Hotspur plc **http://www.spurs.co.uk**

Manchester United FC **http://www.manutd.com**

Strategy activity

Reuters

Started in 1850 by a German living at the time in Belgium, Reuters is prominent and well-known as a news agency; it has employed journalists to report conflicts and events across the world.

But 'news' has never been Reuter's main revenue earner! The provision of financial data has always been the principal business, and for this it is the current world leader. In the early days pigeons were used to fly data from one stock exchange to another across Europe and further afield.

In 2001, and some 150 years old, Reuters was though to be near to collapse because of the growing prominence of US rival, Bloomberg, which runs its own satellite TV channel and also owns Thomson Financial.

Reuters' main customers are banks, brokerages and fund managers. It opted to rationalize its product range and to target these customers more effectively. It would look to provide data and analysis packages suited to specific needs in a more differentiated way. This implied higher added value products and in some cases premium prices. There was a downside risk that some customers would 'trade down' for a cheaper, more generic, package. There would also be fewer global centres. This would save on overheads; but, thanks to IT, customers were unlikely to be affected. In 2008 Thomson and Reuters merged.

Question

Do you think this more focused approach and the merger were perhaps risky in the economic recession and credit crunch of 2008 and 2009?

Further reading

Markides, CC (1999) A dynamic view of strategy, *Sloan Management Review*, 40, Spring.

Tilles, S (1963) How to evaluate corporate strategy, *Harvard Business Review*, July–August.

References

Ackoff, R (1978) *The Art of Problem Solving*, John Wiley.

Anderson, C (2006) *The Long Tail*, Hyperion

Channon, DF (1983) *Strategy and Structure in British Industry*, Macmillan.

Constable, CJ (1986) Diversification as a factor in UK industrial strategy, *Long Range Planning*, 19 (1).

Etzioni, A (1967) Mixed scanning: a third approach to decision making, *Public Administration Review*, 27, December.

Finkelstein, S, Whitehead, J and Campbell, A (2009) *Why Good Leaders Make Bad Decisions and How to Keep it From Happening to You*, Harvard Business School Press.

Gladwell, M (2000) *The Tipping Point – How Little Things Can Make a Big Difference*, Little Brown.

Goold, M, Campbell, A and Alexander, M (1994) *Corporate Level Strategy*, John Wiley.

Heirs, B and Farrell, P (1987) *The Professional Decision Thinker*, Sidgwick and Jackson.

Hilton, A (1987) Presented at 'Growing Through Acquisition', Conference organized by Arthur Young, London, 31 March.

Hofer, CW and Schendel, D (1978) *Strategy Evaluation: Analytical Concepts*, West.

Lindblom, CE (1959) *The Science of Muddling Through*, reprinted in *Organization Theory*, Pugh, DS (ed.) 2nd edn (1987) Penguin.

Penrose, E (1959) *The Theory of the Growth of the Firm*, Blackwell.

Peters, TJ and Waterman, RH Jr (1982) *In Search of Excellence: Lessons from America's Best Run Companies*, Harper and Row.

Quinn, JB (1980) *Strategies for Change: Logical Incrementalism*, Richard D Irwin.

Rumelt, R (1980) The evaluation of business strategy. In *Business Policy and Strategic Management* (ed. WF Glueck), McGraw-Hill.

Simon, HA (1976) *Administrative Behavior: A Study of Decision Making Processes in Administrative Organizations*, 3rd edn, Free Press.

Thompson, AA and Strickland, AJ (1980) *Strategy Formulation and Implementation*, Richard D Irwin.

Tichy, N and Bennis, WG (2007) *Judgment – How Winning Leaders Make Great Calls*, Portfolio.

Tilles, S (1963) How to evaluate corporate strategy, *Harvard Business Review*, July–August.

Vickers, G (1965) *The Art of Judgement: A Study of Policy Making*, Chapman & Hall.

Vroom, V and Yetton, P (1973) *Leadership and Decision Making*, University of Pittsburgh Press.

Chapter 10 appendix

Finance in action: Financial management

Learning objectives

Having read to the end of this supplement you should be able to:

- discuss the advantages and disadvantages of different sources of investment capital

- apply a number of different investment appraisal techniques and evaluate their contribution to investment decisions

- calculate the optimal capital structure for a firm and its weighted average cost of capital

- describe the capital asset pricing model

- explain how a company might be valued, say for acquisition purposes.

Financing the business

The various sources of funds to support a growing business and their relative cost. Calculating the cost of capital, taking into account the various funding sources.

Investments and capital budgeting

Alternative ways of calculating the real cost and returns from investment opportunities.

Financing the business

Sources of funds

Most funds used by established UK organizations are normally generated internally through retained profits, but from time to time it is necessary to raise funds externally. This applies to both the public and the private sectors. In general, loan capital or borrowing has been used more extensively than equity, which might take the form of new equity issued openly or rights issues to existing shareholders.

At present in the UK and USA, equity funding is proving more significant than borrowing; the reverse is the case for Germany, France and Japan, partially as a result of different regulations. In the 1990s some UK companies used new equity to compensate for reduced cash flows and retained earnings, and US companies bought back shares and returned funds to their shareholders. This strategy is a form of defence against possible unwelcome bids. Regulations reduce the likelihood of German, French and Japanese companies being acquired by unwelcome predators. Investment funding, then, is available through borrowing or increased equity, but assets can be increased without investing to the same extent. This is accomplished by leasing them rather than purchasing them.

Equity capital In general, equity capital would be increased by a rights issue of ordinary shares to existing shareholders. As an example, holders of ordinary shares might be offered one new share for every two or three that they already own, at a price equal to or below the current market price. At a higher price people would be unlikely to purchase. If all shareholders take up the offer then the percentage breakdown of the shareholders' register will remain the same; if they are not taken up by existing shareholders they will be offered to the market by the institutional underwriters, and the share register profile may change. Blocks of shares could be built up quite readily, and at a price below the current market price; and depending upon who was buying them, threats to the organization from powerful shareholders could emerge.

Rights issues will not be successful without the support of institutional shareholders. This requires investor confidence in the company's strategy and strategic leadership.

Although many shareholders buy and retain shares with a view to a long-term capital gain, resulting from their sale at a price higher than the one at which they were bought, dividend policy is important. Dividends represent a rate of return on shareholders' investments. Although dividends are not fixed and can theoretically be raised or lowered freely and in relation to increases or decreases in profits, and to any changing need for retained earnings for investment, companies generally seek stability.

Loan capital There are various forms of loan capital, but they all have one essential characteristic. They do not carry ownership, which ordinary shares do. Loans might well be for a definite period, after which they are repayable, and with a fixed rate of interest for each year of the loan. Hence, interest payments come out of profits, but they cannot be reduced if profits decline through unfavourable trading conditions. Overdrafts provide flexible short-term funding up to an agreed limit, and their cost will vary both up and down as the prevailing market rate of interest changes. Loans are invariably secured against assets, which reduces the risk for the lender. If interest payments are not met, the bank, or whoever has loaned the money, is free to appoint a receiver and effectively take over day-to-day control of the company. Interest is paid out of profits before they are assessed for taxation, and they can thereby reduce the company's tax burden; dividends for ordinary shareholders are paid after tax.

Generalizing, the cost of borrowing can be expected to rise as the degree of risk for the lender increases. Lenders will expect higher returns from higher risk investments. Government securities are considered very safe, for example, and consequently the anticipated rate of return will typically be lower than for other investments. Secured loans are safer than ordinary shares, as mentioned above, and therefore borrowing should normally prove cheaper than equity.

The ability to obtain either – and the cost – are likely to be dependent on how well the company has been performing, and how well it has been perceived by the market to have been performing. Opportunity, ability and cost are therefore essential criteria in deciding upon a preference between equity and loan funding, but this decision should be related to the decision concerning whether to invest at all. Investments, which are discussed later in this Appendix, should be analysed by comparing their returns, discounted for the period they are earned, with the cost of financing them, or the opportunity cost of the money being used. The viability of an investment is therefore dependent upon the cost of the capital used.

The cheaper the cost of capital, the more likely it is that an investment is viable and profitable. Hence if the cost of obtaining investment funding is high, opportunities might be lost.

Moreover, the capital structure of the company determines the impact of profit fluctuations on the money available after tax for paying dividends and for reinvestment. Large loans and high interest payments absorb profits, and this can be crucial if profits fluctuate significantly for any reason. The more that is paid out in dividends, the less is available for reinvesting, and vice versa. In turn, dividend payments are likely to affect the view held by shareholders and the market of the company's performance, and this will affect their willingness to lend more.

Leasing In many cases organizations are more concerned with using assets than actually owning them. Leasing assets is one way of acquiring them without paying their full price at any one time; the popularity of leasing has grown since the late 1970s.

When an asset is leased there will normally be an agreed annual charge for a fixed number of years, and possibly there will be an arrangement whereby the company obtains ownership of the asset for a residual price at the end of the period of the lease. In aggregate terms leasing is unlikely to be cheap, but it can have a significant effect on cash flow. In addition, there have been advantageous tax regulations. Leasing is generally low risk for the lessor, who retains legal ownership of the asset and can reclaim it if the lease payments are not met.

Leasing has offered strategic opportunities, as well as financial benefits, for certain organizations. Some companies have chosen to sell and lease back property that they owned, for example, finding willing partners in property companies and institutional investors. The funds released have then been available for other investments.

The cost of capital

The optimal capital structure In theory there is an *optimal capital structure* (OCS) in terms of debt and equity for any firm, and it will depend on:

● the amount of risk in the industry

● the riskiness of the company's corporate and competitive strategies, and their potential impact on profits

● the typical capital structure for the industry, and what competitors are doing – the cost of funding can provide competitive advantage

- management's ability to pay interest without too serious an impact on dividends and future investment
- both the owners' and the strategic leader's preference for risk, or aversion to it.

The weighted average cost of capital In considering, or attempting to decide, the OCS it is important to evaluate the *weighted average cost of capital* (WACC). The WACC, again in theory, is the average rate of return that investors expect the company to earn. In practice it is the average cost of raising additional investment funding. If a company used only loan funding the WACC would be the after-tax cost of borrowing more; but most organizations have a complex structure of debt and equity, each of which carries a different cost. The WACC is therefore an attempt to approximate what more funding would cost if it were raised proportionately to the percentages of debt and equity in the OCS. In practice it will relate to the current capital structure.

Determining the weighted average cost of capital The formula is:

$$WACC = (\text{Percentage of long term debt in the OCS} \times \text{After tax cost of debt}) \text{ plus}$$

$$(\text{Percentage of ordinary shares in the OCS} \times \text{After tax cost of equity})$$

As mentioned above, the WACC will normally be calculated in terms of the firm's current capital structure rather than the theoretical OCS.

The *cost of long-term debt* is the weighted average of the various interest rates incurred on existing loans, after accounting for tax. Hence, for a company which pays 10 per cent interest on 40 per cent of its loans, 12 per cent on the other 60 per cent and tax at an effective rate of 30 per cent, the cost of long-term debt is:

$$((10\% \times 40) + (12\% \times 60)) \times (1 - 0.3) = 7.84\%$$

The *cost of equity* is more difficult to calculate. One popular model for estimating it is the capital asset pricing model (CAPM), which is described here only in outline.

The capital asset pricing model In theory the cost of equity for an individual company should equal the rate of return that shareholders expect to gain from investing in that company. This is based on their

perception of the amount of risk involved. The CAPM attempts to capture this. The formula is:

$$R = F + \text{beta}(M - F)$$

R is the expected earnings or return on a particular share and F represents the risk-free rate of return expected from the most secure investments such as government securities, where the likelihood of default is considered negligible. The expected risk-free rate is determined by the current interest rate on these securities and expected inflation. M is the average rate of return expected from all securities traded in the market and beta is a measure of risk based on the volatility of an individual company's shares compared with the market as a whole. A beta of 1.6 (empirically high) means that a company's share price fluctuates by 1.6 times the market average. In other words, if the market average rises or falls by 10 per cent, the company's share price increases or decreases by 16 per cent. A low beta might be 0.3. Low beta shares in a portfolio reduce risk, but in general high beta shares do little to reduce risk.

Research at London Business School yielded the following betas in the mid-1990s:

Hong Kong and Shanghai Banking Corporation	1.6
J. Sainsbury	0.6
Manchester United Football Club	0.4

As an example, assume that the risk-free rate is 10 per cent, the market as a whole is returning 18 per cent and a company's beta is 1.2:

$$R = 10 + 1.2(18 - 10) = 19.6\%$$

In other words, the market would be expecting the company to achieve 19.6 per cent earnings on shareholders' funds. This is earnings after interest and tax divided by total shareholders' funds, including reserves.

By contrast, if a company's beta was 0.5:

$$R = 10 + 0.5(18 - 10) = 14\%$$

The CAPM is useful for estimating the cost of equity, but there are certain problems in implementing it. Primarily, all of the data will be adjusted and extrapolated historical data, when really it is realistic forecasts of future earnings and returns that matter. F and M theoretically represent expected future returns, and beta should be based on expected future fluctuations, but normally historical data will be used in the model on the assumption that trends continue. The prevailing and predicted rates of interest in the economy will be used to increase or decrease past return figures.

The WACC can now be calculated. Assume that a company has £1.2 million equity funding and £800,000 in long-term debt, and that the relative costs of each are 16 per cent and 8 per cent, respectively:

Source of funding	Total £ million	Percentage of total	Cost %	Weighted cost
Equity	1.2	60	16	9.6
Loans	0.8	40	8	3.2

Thus WACC = 12.8 per cent.

Of course, retained earnings that can be reinvested in the company could alternatively be paid out as dividends, which shareholders could themselves invest wherever they chose. Consequently, the return on such reinvestments in the company should be at least the same as that which investors expect from their existing shares. Given that all shareholders' funds are incorporated in the CAPM, this is taken into account.

This whole area is extremely complex, but nevertheless the cost of capital is an important consideration alongside availability. The cost of capital can affect the viability of a proposed investment, and it can affect the overall costs of producing a product or service and thereby influence competitive advantage. Investments, and how they might be evaluated, are the subject of the next section.

Investments and capital budgeting

In simple terms, an investment represents the commitment of money now for gains or returns in the future. The financial returns are therefore measured over an appropriate period. Estimating these returns relies substantially on forecasts of demand in terms of both amount and timing; and generating the returns further relies upon the ability of managers to manage resources in such a way that the forecasts are met. Uncertainty is therefore an issue.

In general, any investment should be evaluated financially on at least the following two criteria:

- Individually, is it worth proceeding with?
- Is it the best alternative from the options the company has, or if money is reasonably freely available to the company, how does the proposal rank alongside other possibilities?

In the financial evaluation of a proposed investment which produces a cash flow over a period of time, it is necessary to incorporate some qualification for the fact that inflation and other factors generally ensure that a 'pound tomorrow' is worth less than its current value. This is achieved by discounting the cash flow.

Analysing proposed investments

The background to discounted cash flows

If the prevailing rate of interest on bank deposit or building society accounts is 10 per cent, an individual or organization with money to invest could save and earn compound interest with relatively little risk. If the rate stayed constant, £100 today would be worth £110 next year and £121 the year after if the interest was not withdrawn annually. To calculate future values simply multiply by $1 + r$ each year, where r is the rate of interest. Therefore, in ten years' time £100 is worth $£100 (1 + r)^{10}$.

Reversing the process enables a consideration of what money earned in the future is worth in today's terms. In other words, if a company invests now, at today's value of the pound, it is important to analyse the returns from the investment also in today's terms, although most if not all of the returns from the investment will be earned in the future when the value of the pound has fallen. This is known as *discounting future values*. So £100 earned next year is worth $£100/(1 + r)$ today, i.e. £90.90.

Similarly, £100 earned ten years' hence would be worth in today's terms $£100/(1 + r)^{10}$. This is known as *net present value*.

In discounting cash flows and calculating net present value, discount tables are used for simplicity.

An example   Assume that a company invests £1 million today and in return earns £250,000 each year for five years, starting next year. Earnings in total amount to £1.25 million, but they are spread over five years. The company's estimated cost of capital is 10 per cent:

Year	Cash-flow receipts £ thousand	Discount factor at 10%	Net present value £ thousand
1	250	0.909	227
2	250	0.826	206
3	250	0.751	188
4	250	0.683	171
5	250	0.621	<u>153</u>
			945

Hence £1 million is invested to earn £945,000 in today's terms – a loss of £55,000. Logically, a positive figure is sought; and if the investment is required to show a return which is higher than the cost of capital, this target return rather than the cost of capital should be used as the discount rate and a positive net present value should be sought at this level.

Financially, this investment would only be viable with a lower cost of capital. Logically, all projects look increasingly viable with lower capital costs. The calculation which follows is of the cost of capital at which this particular project becomes viable.

The internal rate of return

The next step would be to discount at a lower rate, say 5 per cent:

Year	Cash-flow receipts £ thousand	Discount factor at 5%	Net present value £ thousand
1	250	0.952	238
2	250	0.907	227
3	250	0.864	216
4	250	0.823	206
5	250	0.784	196
			1083

This time a positive net present value of £83,000 is obtained.

The following formula is used to calculate the internal rate of return:

$$\frac{83,000}{138,000} \times \frac{5}{100} = 3\%$$

(£83,000 is the positive net present value at a 5 per cent cost of capital, £138,000 is the difference in net present value between the 5 per cent and 10 per cent rates, and the 5/100 represents the percentage difference between the 5 and 10).

This 3 per cent is added to the 5 per cent to give 8 per cent, which is the yield or internal rate of return from this investment.

Check:

Year	Cash-flow receipts £ thousand	Discount factor at 8%	Net present value £ thousand
1	250	0.926	232
2	250	0.857	214
3	250	0.794	198
4	250	0.735	184
5	250	0.681	170
			998

In other words, this investment gives a yield of 8 per cent. This is also known as the internal rate of return, the discount rate which makes the net present value of the receipts exactly equal to the cost of the investment. In the same way that one might look for a positive net present value, one would be looking for an internal rate of return that exceeded the cost of capital.

Payback Payback is simply the length of time it takes to earn back the outlay; and obviously one can look at either absolute or **discounted cash flows**, normally the former. In the example above the payback is four years exactly. The outlay was £1 million, and the receipts amounted to £250,000 each year.

Payback is quite useful. For one thing it is relatively simple. For another it takes some account of the timing of returns, for returns can be reinvested in some way as soon as they are to hand.

Evaluating proposed investments

If an organization wishes to be thorough and objective, investments could usefully be analysed against the six criteria listed below. The first three of these are essentially quantitative; the second three incorporate qualitative issues. Sometimes the strategic importance of a particular proposal may mean that, first, the most financially rewarding option is not selected or that, second, an investment is not necessarily timed for when the cost of capital would be lowest. As an example of the first point consider a firm in a growing industry which feels that it has to invest in order not to lose market share, although the current cost of capital may mean that the returns from the investment are less than it would wish for or that it could earn with a strategically less important option. An example of the second point would be a firm whose industry is in recession but predicted to grow, and where investment in capital in readiness for the upturn might result in future competitive advantage. At the moment the cost of capital might be relatively high, but the strategic significance of the investment might outweigh this.

The six criteria for evaluating a proposed investment are as follows:

1. the discounted present value of all returns through the productive life of the investment

2. the expected rate of return, which should exceed both the cost of capital (the cost of financing the investment) and the opportunity cost for the money (returns that might otherwise be earned with an alternative proposal)

3   payback – the payout period and the investment's expected productive life – which is a very popular measure as it is relatively easily calculated

4   the risk involved in not making the investment or deferring it

5   the cost and risk if it fails

6   the opportunity cost – specifically, the potential gains from alternative uses of the money.

Discounting techniques are theoretically attractive and used in many organizations, although more in the USA than Europe, and particularly where the proposal is capital intensive. However, the technique must involve uncertainty if the cash flows cannot be forecast accurately, as is often the case. In addition, the net present value is dependent on the discount rate used, and this should relate to the weighted average cost of capital, which again may be uncertain.

There will always be some important element of managerial judgement, and one might argue that this managerial intuition will be preferred in some smaller firms which place less emphasis on planning than do larger firms, and in those companies that are more entrepreneurial and risk orientated. However, if the decision-maker really understands the market and the strategic implications of the proposed investment, this may not be detrimental.

Large organizations evaluating possible investments for different divisions or business units should consider the estimated rate of return from each proposal, the current returns being obtained in each division and the company's average cost of capital, as well as any strategic issues. Take the following two possibilities:

	Division A	Division B
Rate of return on proposal	20 per cent	13 per cent
Current returns	25 per cent	9 per cent

Division A's proposal could seem unattractive as it offers a lower return than existing projects, while B's investment offers an improvement to current returns. If the company's cost of capital is 15 per cent, A's proposal is profitable and B's proposal is not.

Questions and research assignments

1   Calculate the weighted average cost of capital given the following information:
Optimal capital structure 50:50
Debt funding: half is at 10 per cent interest, half at 12 per cent
Effective tax rate 30 per cent
Risk-free rate 8 per cent
Return expected in the stock market 12 per cent
Company's beta 1.2.

2   A firm has two investment opportunities, each costing £100,000 and each having the expected net cash flows shown in the table below. While the cost of each project is certain, the cash-flow projections for project B are more uncertain than those for A because of additional inherent risks. Those shown in both cases can be assumed to be maxima. It has

therefore been suggested that while the company's cost of capital is of the order of 10 per cent, B might usefully be discounted at 15 per cent.

3   For each alternative calculate the net present value, the internal rate of return and the payback.

4   On the data available what would you advise the firm to do?

5   How limited do you feel this analysis is?

Expected cash flows

	Project A (£)	Project B (£)
Year 1	50,000	20,000
Year 2	40,000	40,000
Year 3	30,000	50,000
Year 4	10,000	60,000

4

Issues in strategic growth

This part of the book is about choices.

Chapter 11 concentrates on managing growth by discussing diversification, acquisition strategies and strategic alliances.

Chapter 12 covers the broader topic of international strategy. It is broader in the sense that all of the growth strategies discussed in Chapter 11 can have an international dimension. Therefore internationalization needs to be examined as a strategic action in its own right.

Finally, Chapter 13 looks at business failure, consolidation and recovery strategies. If anything in human life is certain then it is death. This applies to many businesses. At some point in the life of any business, elements of Chapter 13 will be relevant. Corporate level failure is a fact of life; no business of any size is immune to this possibility and just as failure can happen so can it be avoided or recovered from by the correct strategic actions.

It is, therefore, important to consider strategic growth in the wider context of strategic development. The figure on the next page shows (moving left to right) that organizations can choose a path of (sustained) growth or seek (with constant innovation) to maintain and sustain their position in an industry. From time to time there will be some need to rejuvenate strategies – or otherwise there is the serious risk that what has been created and nurtured will drain away and be lost. In Chapter 11 we will explore the logic of constantly seeking to grow, which, as we have seen in Chapter 10, sometimes implies serious risk.

Strategic development paths

Chapter 11
Strategic growth

PART 1
Understanding strategy

1 Introducing strategy and strategic management

PART 5
Strategic management

14 Strategy implementation

15 Leading change

16 Managing strategy in the organization

17 Final thoughts – the purpose of strategy

PART 2
Strategic positioning

2 Strategic thinking, environmental analysis, synergy and strategic positioning

3 Resource-led strategy

4 The dynamics of competition

5 Introducing culture and values

STRATEGIC MANAGEMENT: AWARENESS AND CHANGE

PART 4
Issues in strategic growth

12 International strategy

13 Failure, consolidation and recovery strategies

PART 3
Strategic analysis and choice

6 Strategic purpose

7 Strategic success

8 An introduction to strategy creation and planning

9 Strategic leadership, entrepreneurship and intrapreneurship

10 Strategic alternatives, strategy evaluation and strategy selection

Learning objectives

Having read to the end of this chapter you should be able to:

- identify the typical growth patterns of large companies

- debate the issues involved in the key focus–diversify dilemma

- discuss the extent of diversification in various countries, highlighting how the extent of diversification has changed in recent years

- list why organizations might seek to diversify, often by acquisition

- discuss the risks involved in this strategic alternative

- explain why acquisitions often fail to bring the desired level of benefits

- summarize the stages involved in designing an effective acquisition strategy

- explain why strategic alliances and joint ventures might be preferred to acquisition or takeover as a strategic means of growth

- describe alternative forms of strategic alliances and joint ventures, giving examples of each

- discuss the key issues involved in implementing such strategies effectively

- appreciate the potential value of franchising and licensing in supporting growth

- explain the role of private equity funding in the strategic development of certain organizations.

External growth strategies continue to be popular alternatives for many companies, particularly larger ones, but research suggests that they often fail to meet expectations. Growth strategies need careful, thorough and objective analysis before they are pursued, and care and attention in implementation. This chapter explores diversification and acquisition strategies adopted by UK companies and considers how to manage these strategies effectively.

Acquisitions happen for a number of reasons, some strategic, others more personal to a strategic leader. There is a strongly held view that the strategic argument of synergy should only be used to justify an acquisition which implies real diversification if the companies concerned are somehow blocked from working together in some form of partnership, alliance or joint venture. Simply, there is an argument that alliances and joint ventures are often a better alternative than a full acquisition, merger or takeover for generating synergy and fuelling growth. Alliances and joint ventures are not, however, without risks and they can sometimes be problematical in the implementation stages. However, they will generally offer more flexibility. Their downside for many strategic leaders is that they do not create a larger and more powerful organization.

This relatively short chapter explores these issues by looking at different forms of partnering and the various reasons for doing so. Franchising and licensing are also considered briefly.

Strategies can only be judged to be relatively successful or unsuccessful when implementation issues are also considered. Therefore, corporate strategy is explored here in the context of both the strategy and its implementation.

Case 11.1

Daimler-Chrysler

Eur

This case charts the German Daimler-Benz's search for synergy in its quest to create an integrated transport company. The story is peppered with a number of questionable and sometimes controversial choices.

Daimler-Benz has long been renowned for engineering excellence, product quality and marketing. At the beginning of the 1990s it was Europe's largest manufacturing group, and comprised:

Mercedes-Benz	– commercial vehicles
	– passenger cars
AEG	– electrical and electronic products
Dasa	– aerospace
Debis	– financial and information services

Vehicles were responsible for two-thirds of annual sales revenue; AEG and Dasa each generated approximately 15 per cent.

The majority of the non-vehicle businesses had been acquired systematically during the 1980s; the intention had been to create an 'integrated technology' group. Daimler-Benz's stated objectives for the acquisitions were, first, to offset stagnating vehicle sales by expanding into high-technology growth markets, and secondly, to strengthen the automotive businesses by applying advanced technologies from the new acquisitions. The challenge was always to achieve this potential synergy; the time-scale to realize the benefits was set at ten years, and the important institutional shareholders allegedly pledged their support for the strategy.

Initially, vehicles had to subsidize the new businesses; but critics argued that the second of the two objectives did not require ownership and that in reality the synergy argument was being used as an afterthought to justify the diversification.

Daimler-Benz's strategic dilemma was that both AEG and Dasa required turning around at the same time that vehicles were under threat from Japanese car manufacturers, who were becoming increasingly competitive in the more up-market sectors. Mercedes needed new, more competitive models to prevent being squeezed into too small a niche. An alliance with Mitsubishi was mooted as one suitable way forward.

AEG, which Mercedes had rescued from near bankruptcy, was already diversified (it included white goods, typewriters and traffic-control systems) and was itself searching for synergies. Some AEG business areas were losing money, and in 1994 AEG's appliance business was sold to Electrolux. AEG's railway equipment division became a 50:50 joint venture with ABB, Asea Brown Boveri. Daimler-Benz actually had to pay ABB as AEG's division was currently losing money and its new partner was profitable. The two businesses complemented each other well: ABB focused on heavy locomotives, high-speed trains and signalling; AEG was concentrated on light and urban railways and airport transit systems.

Dasa (Deutsche Aerospace) comprised a number of separately acquired companies and there was some duplication of activities. Messerschmitt has always been a major supplier to the European Airbus project, but its contribution, rear fuselages, is technically less sophisticated than Aerospatiale's forward fuselages and flight decks and British Aerospace's wings. Further alliances with other members of the Airbus consortium, to develop commuter aircraft and helicopters, were discussed. In 1992 Daimler-Benz added to this division when it acquired a 78 per cent shareholding in the Dutch aerospace company, Fokker. The Dutch government held the remaining shares but, again, the company was already in difficulty.

The promised synergies simply did not materialize as Germany suffered its deepest recession in manufacturing since 1945. Mercedes-Benz began to trade at a loss in 1993, and this led to job reductions and investment in plants outside Germany (to avoid the difficulties of high domestic wage rates and a strong Deutschmark). Development work on new four-wheel drive vehicles and a micro-car (eventually launched as the Smart car) were already underway, the latter in conjunction with SMH of Switzerland, best known as the manufacturer of Swatch watches.

A new CEO (Jurgen Schrempp) was appointed in Summer 1995 and later that year Daimler-Benz announced a trading loss equivalent to £2.7 billion, 'the worst non-fraudulent result ever recorded by a German company'. A leading analyst commented that the company was 'so bogged down with aerospace and AEG it had missed important opportunities in the automotive arena'. Drastic action was anticipated.

In January 1996 further AEG divisions were sold to Alcatel Alsthom (France); the remainder were to be fully absorbed into Mercedes-Benz. Daimler-Benz also announced the withdrawal of further financial support for Fokker, making its collapse inevitable unless a new buyer came forward.

Daimler-Benz redefined itself as a 'transportation group' and restructured into 25 operating units in seven main divisions. All operating units had to fit the core strategy and achieve a target return of 12 per cent return on equity. Failure to achieve would result in sale or closure. The future of Dornier (manufacturer of regional aircraft) and MTU (Daimler aero engines) thus looked particularly precarious unless alliance partners could be found to help.

In 1997 Daimler-Benz increased its already dominant presence in the global heavy trucks industry by acquiring Ford's activities. Also in that year Mercedes launched its first small car, the 'A' class hatchback. Almost immediately the car was withdrawn from sale when a motorist, admittedly driving in unusual and extreme conditions, had turned one over. The car was redesigned and relaunched. The launch of the even smaller Smart micro car was also delayed for safety reasons. As a consequence Mercedes bought out its partner in this venture to take total control. Over time the two-seater Smart car has been very successful, but the larger four seat model has not proved as popular.

In 1998 Daimler-Benz announced a 'merger of equals' with America's third largest, and most profitable car manufacturer, Chrysler. The new company would be called Daimler-Chrysler, but ownership was split 57:43. It would be the fifth largest in the world, after General Motors, Ford, Toyota and Volkswagen. There was no product overlap, as Chrysler's Dodge and Plymouth cars were less luxurious than Mercedes, which also had the monopoly on small cars. Chrysler was prominent in pick-up trucks and four-wheel drive vehicles (the Jeep brand), which were new to Mercedes. However, it was arguable that together the two companies would have too many platforms and some rationalization would be required. The intention was to retain separate brands, plants and dealerships. The synergy would come from administration, shared skills and (later) common platforms. Chrysler, however, was less global than Daimler-Benz and the cultures of the two companies were very different. Daimler-Chrysler subsequently bought minority stakes in Mitsubishi and Hyundai. However, towards the end of 2000 it was clear that there were significant implementation problems with

the Daimler-Chrysler merger, Meanwhile, Dasa had been merged with British Aerospace, its partner in the Airbus project.

In 2000 Kirk Kerkorian, a US billionaire who had been the largest individual shareholder in Chrysler and who remained the third largest shareholder in Daimler-Chrysler, began a legal action against three Daimler-Benz executives. He alleged fraud in the takeover – which he claimed was not a merger of equals. A structure which reflected equality had been promised; in the end the business was controlled from Germany.

Meanwhile restructuring continued. Chrysler was being dramatically rationalized on the grounds it had ageing product lines which had to be axed. Before the merger the company had been discounting heavily and investing significantly in new products at the same time. Financially it was weak. The intention was to replace 80 per cent of its product range over 5 years. Jobs were lost and the ex-Chrysler shareholders had seen the value of their investments collapse. By 2002 it was clear that Chrysler was refocusing on saloon cars at the expense of light trucks and SUVs – sports utility vehicles. Both of these had been growing but competition, especially from Japan, had intensified. Larger vehicles remained as Chrysler's core business, though, and so the company would be hit hard when fuel prices rose, as they did.

In 2003 BMW cars outsold Mercedes for the first time in six years. Customer complaints were increasing. Jeremy Clarkson even described a new Mercedes as 'crap' on a UK *Top Gear* television programme. Why? The smaller car strategy had failed to meet hopes and expectations. The new BMW Mini was more popular than the Smart car. Sales of new Mercedes SUVs were also below target.

By 2004 Mitsubishi Motors (in which Daimler-Chrysler retained a minority stake) was in trouble. Daimler-Chrysler declared they had no resources to invest to help it out. The company also decided to sell its stake in Hyundai. Mercedes were also to be assembled in China for the first time.

In 2005 Jurgen Schrempp stepped down as CEO after 'ten turbulent years' in charge. He had refocused the business on automobiles but 'destroyed value in the process' proved to be the verdict of his critics. A year later, with new leadership, Daimler-Chrysler admitted it had paid bribes, but that the employees concerned had left the organization.

In 2007 Chrysler was divested. 80 per cent of the shares were sold to Cerberus Capital Management, a New York private equity group. Cerberus appointed Bob Nardelli as the new CEO. Nardelli had been an executive at General Electric before taking over at Home Depot, where he was seen as a successful turnround leader. Given the problems of the US auto industry (discussed in a separate case on Ford & General Motors), Chrysler and Nardelli had a steep hill to climb! However, in January 2009, Fiat announced plans to acquire a 35 per cent stake in Chrysler and an alliance was forged between the two companies. Chrysler would gain investment and Fiat expertise, Fiat an entry into the American market.

Chrysler was nevertheless still in trouble because of falling sales worldwide. When the US government offered conditional loans it asked for US$4 billion. In early 2009 it was clear that at least 3000 jobs were going to be lost and three plants closed.

At the beginning of May 2009 Chrysler filed for bankruptcy in America. This was intended to be relatively short term to allow for a restructuring under protection from creditors. A new slimmer Chrysler would emerge with the models and plants it wanted to keep and for which there was believed to be a future. The remainder would probably have to close unless a buyer could be found. The US and Canadian governments would together own a substantial stake, possibly a majority of the equity; the Union of Auto Workers would also own shares. Fiat would take 20 per cent. A large number of Chrysler dealerships, maybe as many as 800, would be lost.

Since 2007 Daimler-Chrysler has been known as Daimler, although some insiders preferred Benz. The rebranding cost some 50 million Euros. Daimler sold the remaining 20 per cent of Chrysler to Cerberus in 2008. In early 2009 the company posted losses 'in excess of expectations'. In the last fifteen months its shares had fallen by two-thirds.

Questions

1 Where do you think the key problems and difficulties with the Daimler and Chrysler merger might lie? How difficult might it be for a European

car manufacturer to merge with an American producer rather than, say, invest in manufacturing in the US – a more common strategy? Reviewing issues discussed in Chapter 5 what do you think might have been the cultural challenges involved in a German-US merger that would be difficult to reconcile?

2 Do you believe Chrysler is now in a stronger position to weather the decline in demand for cars in America?

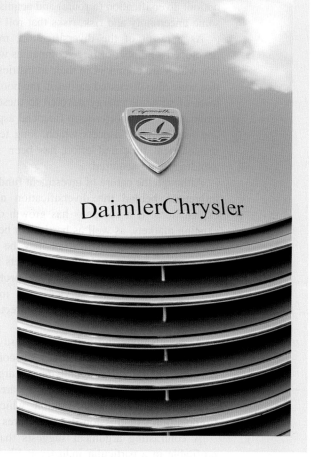

You will note, again, that a number of the references in this chapter are rather dated and summarize research from several years back. They are used deliberately, as this foundation research in this important topic has been reinforced rather than questioned by later work.

11.1 Introduction

Organizations can opt to grow organically, by investing their own resources to develop new competencies and capabilities and open up new market opportunities, but this is always going to take time. There is also an implicit assumption that the necessary competencies can actually be developed. It could be that aspects of the intellectual property involved are elusive. Equally, potential customers have to be persuaded to buy from a new and possibly unproven provider. Again this may prove elusive. Acquisitions, joint ventures or strategic alliances have the advantage of linkages with a proven supplier who has already developed the appropriate competencies and the necessary customers. They will also typically be faster – but they are often going to imply higher risk because they involve partnerships that have to be worked out. The successful implementation of an acquisition can easily take longer than anticipated. These themes, together with the issue of diversification, were introduced in Chapter 10 and they are illustrated in Case 11.1 on Daimler-Chrysler, where we see a need to unscramble a cross-border merger. Cultural differences (see Chapter 5) were one of the key issues in the failure to reap the projected benefits. Because many organizations continue to prefer 'external' means to the internal, organic option, diversification (a route) and acquisition (a means) often go hand-in-hand. They both imply some uncertainty and risk, risks that roll together.

As a result of the diversification, merger and acquisition activity the UK (for one) has developed a number of large companies with sizeable asset bases and domestic market shares, but few which are dominant in their industries or sectors at a world or even a European level – points that were also discussed earlier in the book (see Chapter 7). Constable (1986) argues that the high level of strategic energy devoted to these strategies created an illusion of real growth, with an emphasis on the shorter-term financial aspects of strategic expertise as opposed to the operational and market-based aspects which, long term, are of great significance. Arguably, too much top management time and effort has been spent on seeking and implementing acquisitions, and avoiding being acquired.

Although the nature of investment funding and stock market expectations have been significant influences behind the diversification and acquisition activity in the UK, there are other explanations. If a company has growth objectives and there are finite limits to the potential in existing markets, as well as barriers to becoming more international in order to penetrate related markets abroad, diversification may be an attractive option. However, there may already be intense competition in domestic markets which the company considers entering, especially if the industries involved are attractive and profitable. The competition may be both UK producers and imported products and services and may be compounded by active rivalry for share and dominance. In such circumstances, direct entry may seem less appropriate than acquisition of an existing competitor.

As acquisitions and mergers increase industrial concentration and the power of certain large organizations, government policy on competition may act as a restraint on particular lines of development for certain companies. Large firms may be encouraged to diversify into unrelated businesses where there is little apparent threat to the interests of consumers, rather than attempting horizontal integration which might be prevented by the intervention of the Competition Commission. Joint ventures offer another way round this constraint.

A contrasting argument suggests that a company which has grown large, successful and profitable in a particular industry is likely to seek diversification while it is strong and has the resources to move into new business areas effectively. The benefits of such a move are likely to seem more realizable by the acquisition of an existing organization than by the slower build-up of new internal activities. This type of growth requires finance, which generally has been available for successful companies.

When companies are acquired then both sales and absolute profits increase quickly, and sometimes markedly. But does profitability also increase? Are assets being utilized more effectively in the combined organization? Is synergy really being obtained? Or are the increased sales and profits merely an illusion of growth?

Finally, Constable offers two further arguments to explain the strategic activity in the UK. First, strategic leaders of large organizations are typically aggressive in nature, and acquisition is an expression of aggression. Second, there is a commonly held belief that the larger a company becomes the less likely it is to be a victim of a takeover bid. Hence, while diversification is essentially offensive and designed to bring about expansion and growth, it could be argued that on occasions it is a defensive strategy.

In choosing whether to diversify or not, Markides (1997) recommends that organizations should address five key questions:

1 What can we do better than our competitors? This, of course, is the area around which to focus and build.

2 What strategic resources are required in the possible new areas? What are the implications of this?

3 Can we beat the competition and become a strong player?

4 Is there a downside risk? In particular, might existing businesses be affected in any detrimental way?

5 What learning potential is there? Can the new business enhance synergy and improve our existing businesses and the organization as a whole? This assumes, of course, that the organization is able to exploit the learning potential.

Campbell and Park (2005) – reinforcing points made by Harding and Rovit (2004) – argue that endless (high) growth is really a delusion and that low growth has become the norm and not the exception. This will have been reinforced during 2008 and 2009! Managing growth wisely, they contend, is a key managerial skill for organizations – new business areas should be entered cautiously. Campbell and Park put forward four key issues that determine the wisdom of acquisitions designed to engineer growth, points we will see reinforced in the next sections. The four are: first, the potential for creating new value, both for the acquirer and the acquired business; second, the potential for profit (initially to repay the cost of the acquisition; third, the managerial and financial capacity of the acquiring business to absorb the newcomer; and fourth, the potential impact on existing businesses – especially given they could lose key managers who are moved over and there may be consequentially fewer investment funds for them.

Reasons for diversification and acquisition

There are, then, a number of sound and logical reasons why a firm might seek to diversify through acquisition. Some of these have been mentioned above; others are discussed below. Most are economic. The fact that diversification and acquisition strategies often prove less successful than the expectations for them is more likely to result from the choice of company to acquire and from issues and problems of implementation than the fact that the idea of diversification was misguided. This will be explored further later in the chapter.

Diversification may be chosen because the existing business is seen as being vulnerable in some way: growth potential may be limited; further investment in internal growth may not be justified; the business may be threatened by new technology. Some businesses are undervalued by the stock market, making them vulnerable to takeover if they do not diversify. Some products and businesses may currently be valuable cash generators, but with little prospect of future growth. In other words, they may be cash cows generating funds that need to be reinvested elsewhere to build a future for the company. Leading on from this, the company may have growth objectives that stretch beyond the potential of existing businesses.

Diversification may occur because a company has developed a particular strength or expertise and feels that it could benefit from transferring this asset into other, possibly unrelated, businesses. The strength might be financial (high cash reserves or borrowing capacity), marketing, technical or managerial. If genuine synergy potential exists, both the existing and newly acquired businesses can benefit from a merger or acquisition.

A company which has become stale or sleepy, or which has succession problems at the strategic leader level, may see an acquisition as a way of obtaining fresh ideas and new management, and this may seem more important than the extent to which the businesses are related.

Some diversification and acquisition decisions are concerned with reducing risk and establishing or restoring an acceptable balance of yesterday's, today's and tomorrow's products in a complex portfolio. This will be especially attractive where a company is relying currently on yesterday's products.

Some strategic changes in this category will result from the ego or the ambitions of the strategic leader, who may feel that he or she can run any type of business successfully, regardless of the degree of unrelatedness. Some may be very keen to grow quickly, possibly to avoid takeover, and acquisitions may happen because a company is available for purchase rather than as the outcome of a careful and detailed analysis.

It will be suggested later that the major beneficiaries of an acquisition are often the existing shareholders of the company being acquired. Consequently, it is sometimes argued that the self-interest of the City and large institutional shareholders might be behind certain mergers and acquisitions.

Figure 11.1 provides a useful summary of related and unrelated diversification opportunities. The top part of the diagram suggests that the degree of unrelatedness increases when:

- the **tangible resources** involved, both plant and equipment and intangible brands are different rather than similar, and

- the processes – the ways in which these resources are deployed and utilized – also change.

The bottom part provides examples of each situation. It will be appreciated that the strategic risk increases as the extent of the newness and learning increases.

11.2 Research into diversification and acquisition

The relative success of diversification and acquisition

A number of research studies have been carried out in both the UK and the US on the relative success of diversification and acquisition strategies. There are some general conclusions as well as specific findings, and the major ones are documented here. In the main, most of the findings are consistent.

It is important to emphasize, however, that this is a particularly difficult area to research because of problems with data availability. If, for example, one is attempting to study the change in a company's performance before and after an acquisition, then one needs several years of data to ensure that longer-term effects are studied once any teething problems of early implementation are overcome. However, company W may have acquired company X in, say, 1995 and as a result been included in a research study which began in the same year. Ideally, the performance of the combined company WX would be compared with the previous performance of W and X as independent companies. If company W is naturally acquisitive it may divest some unattractive businesses from X during 1996 in order to raise money to help to finance the purchase of company Y in 1998 and company Z in 1999. An ongoing programme of this nature means that it is impossible to compare the long-term effects of one particular acquisition on an organization. The original sample continually reduces. In the same way, a comparison of the performance over a period of time of companies which might be classified as single, dominant, related and unrelated product (terms explained in Chapter 10) will be affected by firms which change category as a result of the strategies they follow. The relevance of these points can be seen in online Case 10.2, Granada.

Figure 11.1   Diversification alternatives

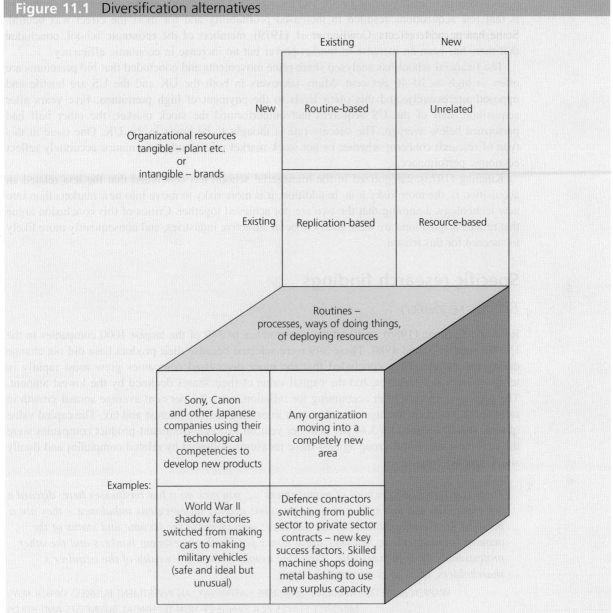

General conclusions from the research suggest that no more than 50 per cent of diversification through acquisition strategies are successful. Quite simply, the synergies that were considered to exist prior to acquisition are frequently not realized. There is also agreement that shareholders in a company which is taken over or acquired benefit from selling their shares to the bidder, who often pays an unwarranted premium. Shareholders who accept shares in the acquiring company instead of cash, together with the existing shareholders in that company, tend to be rewarded less in the longer term using share price appreciation as a measure. As mentioned earlier in the chapter, the research findings also support the contention that the profitability gains attributable to internal investments in companies are generally much greater than those accruing to acquisition investments.

Lorenz (1986) suggests that research in this field can be classified into four schools: accounting, economic, financial and managerial. The accounting school have concentrated on post-merger profitability in the 1970s, and their general conclusion, accepting sampling problems, is that few acquisitions resulted in increased profitability and for most the effect was neutral. Some had negative effects. Cowling *et al.* (1979), members of the economic school, concluded that there has been an increase in market power but no increase in economic efficiency.

The financial school has analysed share price movements and concluded that bid premiums are often as high as 20–40 per cent. Many takeovers in both the UK and the US are hostile and opposed aggressively, and this often leads to the payment of high premiums. Five years after acquisition, half of the US acquirers had outperformed the stock market; the other half had performed below average. The success rate is thought to be lower in the UK. One issue in this type of research concerns whether or not stock market prices and performance accurately reflect economic performance.

Kitching (1973), categorized in the managerial school, has concluded that the less related an acquisition is, the more risky it is. In addition, it is more risky to move into new markets than into new technology, assuming that the two are not achieved together. Critics of this conclusion argue that related acquisitions are more likely to be in attractive industries, and consequently more likely to succeed for this reason.

Specific research findings

British research

Reed and Luffman (1986) analysed the performance of 349 of the largest 1000 companies in the UK between 1970 and 1980. These 349 were selected because their product base did not change during the decade. They concluded that the more diversified companies grew most rapidly in terms of sales and earnings, and the capital value of their shares declined by the lowest amount. The respective figures, after accounting for inflation, were 2.1 per cent average annual growth in sales and 1.3 per cent average annual growth in earnings before interest and tax. The capital value of their shares declined by 3.44 per cent per year on average. Dominant-product companies were the next most successful group against these measures, followed by related companies and finally single-product companies.

> There is a 'gin rummy school of management' ... you pick up a few businesses here, discard a few there. The sad fact is that most acquisitions display an egregious imbalance – they are a bonanza for the shareholders of the acquiree; they increase the income and status of the acquirer's management; and they are a honey pot for the investment bankers and the other professionals on both sides. But, alas, they usually reduce the wealth of the acquirer's shareholders, often to a substantial extent.
>
> WARREN BUFFETT, CHAIRMAN, BERKSHIRE HATHAWAY, AN INVESTMENT BUSINESS WHICH BUYS
> MINORITY STAKES IN A RANGE OF NON-TECHNICAL BUSINESSES AND HOLDS
> THEM FOR RELATIVELY EXTENDED PERIODS

However, the return on capital employed ratios were not consistent with the growth figures. Dominant-product companies were the most profitable (19.1 per cent on average), followed by single-product companies (18.1 per cent), related-product companies (16.9 per cent) and finally unrelated-product companies (16.7 per cent). Reed and Luffman conclude that this is a result of the complexities of the inherent changes rather than of the strategy itself.

These findings replicated earlier US research by Rumelt at the Harvard Business School (1974), and they suggest that the contention by Peters and Waterman (1982) that successful companies 'stick to the knitting' is justified.

Meeks (1977) looked at post-merger profitability during the late 1960s and early 1970s. He started with a sample of 213 firms, reducing the sample size annually as the organizations concerned changed their strategies again in some significant way. In four years the sample halved; and after seven years there were only 21 companies left from the original 213. Meeks looked at the percentage of remaining firms each year and considered whether their profitability had increased or decreased. In the first year after the merger 34 per cent of the firms exhibited lower combined profitability than they had enjoyed previously as independent companies. This percentage increased during the first four years to a high of 66 per cent, with half the original sample left. At the end of seven years of research, 62 per cent of the remaining 21 companies were showing reduced profitability.

Meeks concluded that mergers which involved related businesses increased market power, but this was not the case for conglomerate mergers. All types experienced lower profitability and reflected reduced efficiency as a result of the merger activity. Greater size primarily yields higher salaries for executives, a generally more stable corporate performance and increased immunity from takeover.

Houlder (1997) reports on research from Warwick University which concludes that acquisitions are prone to fail where the acquirer neglects the new business after the acquisition. In such cases, the managers in the acquired business become frustrated and depressed – they feel that they have been left to 'operate in a vacuum'. Their subsequent underperformance increases the likelihood that the business will be sold again. Therefore, a careful balance needs to be struck between independence and 'arm's-length freedom' and determined integration with the parent. The appropriate style will depend upon the extent and the nature of the fit between the two. The research also distinguishes between repeat acquirers, who have learned about integrating new businesses into a corporate whole and have developed key implementation skills, and occasional, even first-time, acquirers who are at the start of a learning curve.

US research   Salter and Weinhold (1982) studied 36 widely diversified US companies between 1967 and 1977 and concluded that 'diversification strategies designed to raise performance actually brought return on equity down'. In 1967 the companies concerned were producing returns which were 20 per cent above the *Fortune* 500 average, and consequently they could afford to diversify. In 1977 they were 18 per cent below average.

Porter (1987) analysed the strategies and performance of 33 large US conglomerates during the 1970s, and based his general conclusions upon the pattern of later divestment of the acquisitions. Well over half his sample divested at least some of their acquisitions, and a typical retention period seemed to average five to six years. Companies which moved into related activities generally performed better than those which diversified into unrelated areas. From this research Porter suggested three tests for successful diversification, and these are discussed later in this chapter (see p. 518).

McKinsey, in research published in 1988, documented the performance of 116 large UK and US companies since 1972. Sixty per cent had failed to earn back the cost of capital on the funds invested in acquisitions, and this figure rose to 86 per cent for large unrelated acquisitions.

Nesbitt and King (1989) examined the progress of 1800 US companies between 1978 and 1988 and concluded that corporate performance is dependent on strategy implementation rather than the strategy itself. The degree of diversification as opposed to specialization, taken in isolation, has little impact.

Burgman (1985) studied 600 US acquisitions which took place between 1974 and 1978 and concluded that:

- the higher the premium paid to acquire a company, the less likely it was to be successful
- prospects for success were greater where the acquirer had a functional appreciation of the business being acquired
- success depended upon the ability to retain key managers in the acquired company
- larger acquisitions were often more successful, possibly because the sheer size and financial commitment necessitated a thorough appraisal beforehand.

Further research, some of it more recent, confirms these key findings.

These research programmes and papers by Biggadike (1979) and Kitching (1967) suggest a number of reasons why acquisitions fail, and these are considered below.

Why acquisitions fail

It has been mentioned previously that a key reason why acquisitions fail is that they do not generate the synergy that was anticipated or at least hoped for. This is particularly true for conglomerate rather than concentric diversification. Case 11.1 looks at the search for synergy by Daimler-Benz. In general, it is easier to gain synergy from production and operations than it is from marketing. It is difficult to gain real additional benefit from selling more than one product or service into one market.

Linked to this issue is the reality that in many cases the real weaknesses of the acquired company are hidden until after the acquisition, and consequently are underestimated. Also underestimated are the cultural and managerial problems of merging two companies and then running them as one. As a result insufficient managerial resources are devoted to the process of merging, and hence the hoped-for synergy remains elusive.

This problem typically arises because the acquiring company concludes that the skills which were to be transferred to the new acquisition in order to generate the synergy are in reality not available. They are already fully committed and in the end are not transferred.

Key managers who have been responsible for the past growth and success of the company being acquired may choose to leave rather than stay with the new conglomerate. Where this happens, and depending on the extent of the contribution of these managers, past successes may not be repeatable.

Further reasons concern the amount paid for the acquisition, and the extent of the premium. For a contested takeover in particular, the bidding company may become overenthusiastic and optimistic about the prospects, overstretch itself financially and then not be able to afford the necessary investment to generate benefits and growth in the new company. When a premium is paid the acquirer is likely to set high targets initially for the new company in order to try and recover the premium quickly. When these targets are missed, because they are unrealistic, enthusiasm is lost and feelings of hostility may develop. It can be argued that if synergy really is available, price is less significant as an issue, and a premium may well be justifiable. However, if an acquisition is fundamentally misconceived a low or a cheap price will not make it successful at the implementation stage.

Finally, the reaction of competitors may be misjudged.

The difficulties apply in service businesses as well as manufacturing, as the following examples illustrate. Some years ago the long-established and family-owned Cadbury was persuaded by management consultants to believe that 'successful managers can manage anything' and diversified into Schweppes soft drinks (related distribution channels) and the unrelated Jeyes (disinfectants). Jeyes was quickly divested when it became clear that the core chocolate business was suffering as managers became preoccupied with the new activities. Interestingly, the same consultants also persuaded Cadbury to abandon its paternalistic style of management, manifested in the Bourneville village and community which the Quaker family had built for its workforce. When it was still independent, General Accident acquired a related insurance business in New Zealand in 1988 and as part of the purchase inherited the NZI Bank. The loan book deteriorated in the worldwide recession and, lacking the necessary turnaround skills, General Accident decided to close the bank. The Prudential similarly chose to exit estate agencies after incurring huge losses. They had overpaid for their acquisitions and the anticipated learning and synergy was slow to materialize. Some would argue that the strategy of linking insurance with estate agencies was misjudged; others that the problems were really those of implementation. In particular, the Prudential attempted to exercise central control over a disparate group of acquisitions.

In reality, acquisition is an uncertain strategy. However sound the economic justification may appear to be, implementation or managerial issues ultimately determine success or failure. These issues are the subject of the next section.

Issues in diversification and acquisition

Where two companies choose to merge there is the opportunity for a reasonably comprehensive assessment of relative strengths and weaknesses, although it does not follow that one or both will not choose to hide certain significant weaknesses. In the case of a contested takeover less information will be available. UK takeover law requires that once a company has built up a shareholding of a particular size in another company it must offer to buy the remaining shares, at which stage, the targeted company must make certain information available through the process of due diligence. (Since 1989 one company must inform another if it builds up a share of three per cent or more. When the ownership reaches 10 per cent a company has to declare its intent – preparation for a later bid or a mere investment. Companies will be held to this declaration. If one says that it is merely investing it will not then be able to launch a bid for at least one year. A company can own up to 29.9 per cent without making a bid for the remainder, but once this figure is exceeded a bid for the rest must follow.) Crucially, however, the information that will affect the ease or difficulty of merging the two cultures and organizations, and implementing the changes, is less freely available than financial data.

It is never easy to determine from outside an organization what the style of management is, its managers' attitude to risks, how decisions are made and whether managers are largely self-reliant. In the final analysis, the success of an acquisition or merger will be influenced markedly by the way the companies fit (or do not fit) together as well as by the logic used to justify the strategy (see Figure 11.2). As a result financial analysis may be used to justify the acquisition, but it will not answer questions relating to implementation. Table 11.1 highlights the significant information that is unlikely to be available until after the acquisition.

The following list of questions and issues indicates the key considerations which should be addressed by a company before it acquires another:

- how the acquiring company should restructure itself in order to absorb the new purchase, and what implications this will have for existing businesses and people
- what acceptable minimum and maximum sizes are for proposed diversifications in relation to present activities
- what degree of risk it is appropriate for the company to take
- how to value a proposed acquisition and how much to pay

Figure 11.2   Strategy creation and implementation

BASED ON A MATRIX DEVISED BY BOOZ, ALLEN AND HAMILTON

Table 11.1 Information available before and after an acquisition	
Before	**After**
Organization charts	Inner philosophy and culture
Data on salaries of top management	Real quality of staff in decision roles
Reasonably detailed information on board	Salary and reward structures and systems
members and key executives – but only brief	Decision processes
details on middle management	Interrelationships, power bases, hidden conflicts and
Products	organizational politics
Plants	Individual objectives being pursued
Corporate identity, image and reputation	
Past record, especially financial	

- how to maintain good relationships with key managers during negotiations to try to ensure that they stay afterwards
- how to maintain momentum and interest in both companies after a successful offer
- how quickly to move in merging organizational parts and sorting out problems
- reporting relationships and the degree of independence allowed to the acquired company, particularly where the business is unrelated
- whether and how to send in a new management team.

Some of these issues are considered in the next section where effective acquisition strategies are discussed, but many of them are taken up in later chapters which consider the implementation aspects of strategic change. Figure 11.2 illustrates that an effective strategy is one that is based upon good vision and sound implementation prospects. Vision is in relation to the organization's strengths and market opportunities, and an effective strategy will match these. In the context of diversification and acquisition, implementation relates to a consideration of how the two organizations will be merged together and the changes required to structures, cultures and systems in order to ensure that potential synergy is achieved. Poor vision and poor implementation will both cause strategic management to be less than effective. If the logic behind an acquisition is poor, then the merged corporation is likely to underperform, however well the two companies might be managed as one corporate whole. If the vision is good but implementation is weak, under-performance is again likely because synergy will not be created.

If companies develop by a series of acquisitions it is quite typical for several banks to become involved. These could be spread worldwide; their cultures and lending philosophies may differ; their levels of exposure will vary; the assets securing the loans will not be the same; and certain banks may see themselves as lenders to just one company rather than the whole organization. Problems are likely to arise if one of the banks gets into financial difficulties or if the company seeks to extend a loan or adjust the terms.

11.3 Effective acquisition strategies

A number of authors have suggested ways of improving the effectiveness of acquisition strategies. Drucker (1982), for example, argues that there are five rules for successful acquisitions.

1 It is essential for the acquiring company to determine exactly what contribution it can make to the acquired company. It must be more than money.

2 It is important to search for a company with a 'common core of unity', say in technology, markets or production processes.

3 The acquiring company should value the products, services and customers of the company that it is taking over.

4 Top management cover for the acquired company should be available in case key managers choose to leave after the acquisition.

5 Within a year managers should have been promoted across company boundaries.

These points can be usefully applied to the merger between Delta and Northwest Airlines, described in Case 11.2. Do you see this as a defensive or an offensive merger? Was it driven by expediency and a desire to save costs or a genuine belief new value could be created?

In a report entitled *Making Acquisitions Work: Lessons from Companies' Successes and Mistakes*, Business International (1988) offers the following guidelines:

● *Plan first* – As a company, know exactly what you are going to do. Ascertain where the company being acquired has been, and maybe still is, successful, and ensure that it can be maintained – taking special account of any dependence on key people. Appreciate also where it is weak. It is quite possible that it will have good products but overheads which are too high.

● *Implement quickly* – People in the acquired company expect decisive action, and delay prolongs speculation. At the same time it is important not to act without thinking things through first.

Case 11.2

Delta and Northwest Airlines   US

Highlighting the global nature of the airline industry a major acquisition in America posed some interesting issues for the leading European airlines.

The acquisition of Northwest Airlines by Delta was confirmed in October 2008. With 75,000 employees and serving 375 cities worldwide, the new airline would not just be the largest in America, it would be the largest in the world. The economic recession, falling demand and high fuel prices were causing difficulties for the industry and this acquisition was allowed to go ahead by the competition authorities when, in different economic circumstances, one might imagine it would have been stopped.

In terms of revenues, Delta would now be Number One in the US. Second would be United (part of the powerful Star Alliance), third American, fourth Continental and fifth US Air (another member of the Star Alliance). Northwest was already allied with Air France, which, in recent years, had acquired the Dutch national carrier, KLM, with which it had been previously allied. Would Air France and Delta now develop co-operation?

There were, then, some interesting issues for British Airways to deal with. BA was already allied with American Airlines, as part of the One World alliance, but discussing tighter tie-up prospects. At roughly the same time Sir Michael Bishop, founder of British Midland International, chose to exercise an option he had to ask Lufthansa to buy out his 50 per cent personal shareholding in BMI. Lufthansa already owned 30 per cent of BMI, with SAS (Scandinavian Airline Systems) owning the remaining 20 per cent. Through this deal Lufthansa would become the second largest operator (behind BA) at London's Heathrow Airport. In the recent past Lufthansa had acquired Swiss Airlines and taken a 45 per cent stake in Brussels Airlines. BA was in the process of merging with Iberia of Spain.

Questions

1 Would you see this as a defensive merger of convenience or something more positive?

2 Does it pose a serious threat to British Airways?

SOURCE: THIS CASE STUDY WAS PREPARED USING PRIMARILY PUBLICLY AVAILABLE SOURCES OF INFORMATION FOR THE PURPOSES OF CLASSROOM DISCUSSION; IT DOES NOT INTEND TO ILLUSTRATE EITHER EFFECTIVE OR INEFFECTIVE HANDLING OF A MANAGERIAL SITUATION.

- *Communicate frankly* – Explain the acquisition or merger, the expected benefits and the changes which will be required. In addition, it is useful to ensure that there is an understanding of the values and expectations of the acquiring company.
- *Act correctly*, particularly as far as redundancy is concerned.

Ramsay (1987) argues that effective acquisition strategies have four stages, which are illustrated in Figure 11.3:

- the need to formulate a clear strategy
- the search for possible acquisitions
- the acquisition
- the merger of the organizations following acquisition.

These four stages are now discussed in detail.

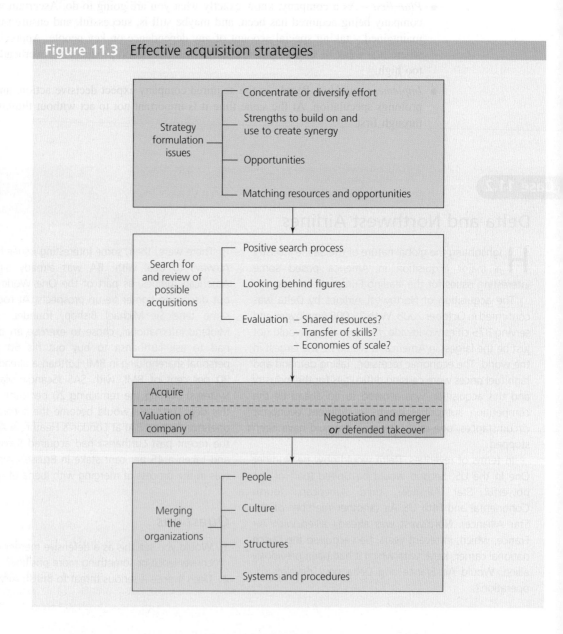

Figure 11.3   Effective acquisition strategies

Strategy formulation issues
- Concentrate or diversify effort
- Strengths to build on and use to create synergy
- Opportunities
- Matching resources and opportunities

Search for and review of possible acquisitions
- Positive search process
- Looking behind figures
- Evaluation – Shared resources?
            – Transfer of skills?
            – Economies of scale?

Acquire
Valuation of company   Negotiation and merger *or* defended takeover

Merging the organizations
- People
- Culture
- Structures
- Systems and procedures

The formulation of a clear strategy

An effective, well thought through diversification and acquisition can constitute real strategic growth by providing entry into a new market, a new opportunity to build on competitive strengths, an opportunity to create and benefit from synergy, and the possibility of removing some element of competition. This, however, implies more logic behind the acquisition than mere sales growth or the purchase of a profit stream. Hence there are a number of issues to consider in attempting to formulate an effective strategy for acquisition.

- First, the issue of how much to concentrate and how much to diversify must be examined. We mentioned earlier that research indicates that concentration is generally superior but that the opportunities available may not be sufficient to fill the planning gap. A major advantage of concentration, and a limit on diversification, is that experience is difficult to copy. Learning and experience can lead to superior competitive positions through an understanding of customers and how to satisfy their needs through production and service. Horizontal integration and concentric diversification can both provide opportunities to capitalize on learning and experience.

- Second, a good strategy will build on existing strengths and develop synergy around them. This requires an opportunity to transfer skills and competencies and achieve economies of scale. This issue is discussed further below.

- Third, it is important to be able to spot an opportunity and act quickly and decisively to capitalize on it. It has been argued, for example, that, once legislation permitted it in the mid-1980s, the building societies that moved quickly into estate agencies benefited far more than those that lagged behind, because the cost per site increased with the acquisition activity. Such a strategic move would be classified as vertical integration because an estate agency is really a channel of distribution for mortgages.

- Fourth, resources (strengths) and opportunities need to be matched. The ability to do this effectively relates to the way the company is managed, and to the culture and values.

The search for, and review of, possible acquisitions

- There should be an active and positive search process. Acquisitions are difficult, diversification is risky, and the decisions can prove expensive if they are wrong. Strategic leaders should track and carefully analyse possible acquisitions rather than rely on opportunities which might arise.

- It is essential to be realistic. Where there is a friendly merger, or the acquisition of a company in difficulties, it is possible that certain key weaknesses may be hidden; and in the case of a hostile bid situation it is important not to become unrealistic through determination and, as a result, pay too much.

- Before acquiring it is crucial to assess just how resources are going to be shared, where and how skills are going to be transferred, and where and how economies of scale are going to be obtained. If such an analysis is left until after an acquisition, synergy is likely to prove more elusive.

The price paid to acquire a company relative to its earning potential, and the ability to generate synergy through shared activities or transferred skills, are the key determinants of likely success.

Porter (1987) contends that a portfolio of unrelated companies is only a logical corporate strategy if the aim is restructuring. Restructuring is the strategy pursued by conglomerates such as Hanson, and it requires the identification of companies which are underperforming and which can be transformed with new management skills. Ideally, they are valued below their real potential when acquired. The new owner seeks to improve the competitive position of the organization and improve its profitability. Logically, companies or business units are sold when they no longer have potential for increasing earnings further. The opportunity to pursue this strategy effectively lies in the ability to spot and acquire undervalued companies cheaply and to manage unfamiliar businesses better than the existing managers.

In any acquisition, Porter argues, three tests should be passed.

1 The industry involved should be or could be made structurally attractive. In other words, the potential returns exceed the company's cost of capital.

2 The entry cost should not be so high that future profit streams are compromised. As well as the purchase price, the cost must also take account of professional fees involved in the merger or acquisition.

    Granada incurred professional fees exceeding £100 million for its takeover of Forte. Forte's defence costs, post-acquisition divestment fees, together with other payments and provisions, built up an accumulated total of some £250 million. Granada paid £9 billion for Forte.

3 One of the companies should be able to gain competitive advantage, and the newly acquired business should be better off in the new corporation than elsewhere. In other words, the interrelationships, based on shared activities and transferred skills, must give added value which outweighs the costs incurred. These benefits are often not gained for two main reasons. The new, more diverse, more complex, organization is likely to be decentralized, but the business units may be independent in practice rather than interdependent. Managers may not be able to understand and implement the interrelationships.

Van de Vliet (1997) reports on research from Mercer Consulting which confirms the switch during the 1990s from conglomeration to mergers with a more defensible strategic logic, but also confirms a concurrent increase in hostile takeovers. The implication is that higher premiums are being paid. This seems to be a situation of gain against one test and deterioration against another!

Some commentators have also argued that a fourth test should be added to Porter's three: how much will have to be invested in the future, post-acquisition? The experience of BMW with Rover is testimony to the significance of this test. BMW underestimated the investment requirements and eventually sold the business 'for a song' to avoid further spending.

Figure 11.4 attempts to pull these points together diagrammatically.

Hence companies that are seeking to grow through acquisition and the consolidation of the acquired and existing businesses should ensure either that skills can be transferred or that activities can be shared, i.e. clear interrelationships can be identified.

These can relate to any part of the value chain. The aims are greater economies of scale, lower costs or enhanced differentiation through sharing activities, know-how or customers, or transferring skills and know-how. The research findings quoted earlier suggest that these opportunities are more likely to be found in industries which are in some way related. Tobacco companies in both the UK and the US, for example, when faced with declining demand and hostile pressure groups, realized that they would have to diversify if they were to avoid decline. They chose such industries as food, wine and brewing initially because they felt that they could transfer their skills and expertise in marketing consumer products.

Acquisitions are likely to prove disappointing if the opportunity for such synergy is not evaluated objectively in advance, or if the companies convince themselves that synergy must be possible without establishing where and how.

One final point worth making is on timing. It is or should always be the case that 'timing is everything' in an acquisition. It is not often that the opportunity to achieve a good price for a business comes along. Irrespective of expensive accountants and due diligence, the seller should really take the money on offer in most cases. There are far more cases where the seller, who did not close the deal, wished he had as the timing turns against him and the price on offer is no longer on the table.

Figure 11.4   The effective acquisition

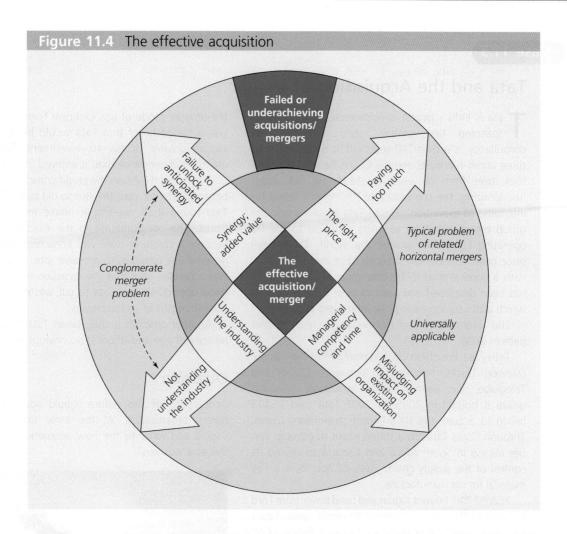

In the context of these arguments, did the acquisition of Jaguar-Land Rover by Tata (Case 11.3) make strategic sense? We might also question whether the previous acquisition of the businesses by Ford also made strategic sense.

Acquiring the company

The key issues involved in the acquisition itself have been discussed earlier; alternative ways of valuing a business – in order to determine an appropriate bid price – are described in Strategy in action 11.1.

It was emphasized above that it is important to look for hidden weaknesses in friendly mergers and avoid paying too much in a contested takeover bid. It was also mentioned earlier that if too high a premium is paid the acquisition is less likely to be successful (Burgman 1985), and a vicious circle of disillusionment can easily be created. If the acquisition is overvalued or a substantial premium is paid, the expected early returns on the investment will be very high. An acquisition involves an investment that must be paid back by generating returns which exceed the cost of capital involved. If targets are missed the possible disillusionment and loss of confidence may mean that additional investment to develop the business, which really is needed, will not be forthcoming. Consequently, performance will deteriorate further and the business will run down. A likely outcome of this will be its sale at a discounted price, and the acquirer will have lost money from the acquisition. The payment of any premium should be related to the ability of the acquirer to add value by sharing activities or transferring skills.

Case 11.3

Tata and the Acquisition of Jaguar   Int

Tata is India's largest conglomerate, with interests spanning tea, motors, steel and software consultancy. It is over 140 years old. It is controlled by three family-run trusts and the CEO is Ranan Tata, who took over from an uncle in 1991. He set about 'modernizing' the conglomerate to 'make it ready for international expansion'. Ranan Tata initially made the group more centralized to bring cohesion to the 90 operating companies around the world. There have since been selective investments – but also disposals – with a general drive to become more international. IT has been developed and used to drive control systems which allow for increasingly decentralized authority.

The international strategy began to really gather pace in 2000.

Tetley tea, bought in 2001, is now part of Tata, as are Daewoo Trucks, NatSteel of Singapore (2004) and Teleglobe, the Bermuda-based wholesale telecoms group it bought in 2005. In 2007 Tata paid US$13 billion to acquire the UK's largest steelmaker, Corus. Through Corus Tata has a stated intent to develop iron ore mining in South Africa and Canada to extend its control of the supply chain. Steel, of course, is a key material for car manufacture.

In 2007 Tata bought Jaguar and Land Rover from Ford of America. This was an interesting move, given Tata's parallel strategy of developing the so-called People's Car, the Tata Nano, the truly low price car discussed in a separate case. Tata really had no previous experience of luxury brands. There were commentators who expressed the view that they could not understand this move. After all, Tata was more used to building rudimentary trucks for relatively poor roads across India.

Jaguar was thought to be in need of repositioning – it had lost some of its edge through association with the broader range of less exclusive Ford models. There was a stated belief that Tata would be able to offer Jaguar greater access to investment funding and greater independence than it enjoyed at Ford.

But would it? When the credit crunch and recession began to bite car sales fell. But so did steel demand and Tata found itself needing to make major savings at Corus. The conglomerate in the ex-colony that had become a colonizer itself was enquiring about foreign government subsidies to preserve jobs. However there was a parallel view that the recession would provide a good opportunity for Tata to cut waste and build the core strengths of its businesses.

Another problem is that Ranan Tata is past normal retirement age and 'there is no obvious successor'.

Question

Acquisitions of this nature should add value to the parent organization. At the same time the parent should add value to the new acquisition. Do you see this as a win-win?

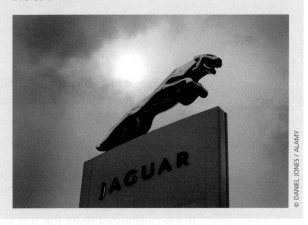
© DANIEL JONES / ALAMY

Strategy in action 11.1

Valuing a Company

Acquisition of another company constitutes an investment, although one major strategic objective might be to avoid being taken over by another firm.

Whatever the strategic reason, the current value of an organization is important. Assuming that we are not talking about a merger (of assets), a company will normally be acquired when another company buys an appropriate percentage of its shares. While the bid price will always be influenced substantially by their current market price in trading, the likely purchase price in both a hostile and a bidding situation (where more than one prospective buyer is in evidence) will reflect a premium. However, the market price at any time may or may not reflect the value of the organization.

Alternative valuation methods

Rule of thumb

A typical rule of thumb valuation of a company would be to multiply the most recent annual profits (or an average of the last few years) times an x factor. Relatively small xs will be selected for small companies (which have fewer customers and fewer key people) and service businesses, where it is easier for key people to be lost during or after the acquisition. The x factor might vary from 3 up to 13 for large, established manufacturing businesses.

The balance sheet valuation

The balance sheet value of a company is normally taken from the value of the net assets. Divided by the number of ordinary shares issued, this yields the asset value behind every ordinary share, and it can therefore be useful in assessing what an appropriate bid price for the ordinary shares might be. However, caution is needed because the balance sheet traditionally records historical costs rather than present values, and this can be misleading in the case of property. In addition, although some companies do account for this, the value of such intangible assets as brand names is rarely reflected in the balance sheet.

The market valuation

The market valuation of a company is the number of ordinary shares issued multiplied by their present price plus the inherited debt. This will reflect the likely lowest cost to a buyer, as any bid for shares at a price below their existing price is unlikely to succeed. In reality, the price of shares is likely to increase during the period between when current shareholders realize that a bid is likely, or when one is announced, and when control is finally achieved by the bidder.

The current share price and the asset value of shares should be looked at together.

Earnings potential

Many contend that it is future earnings potential that determines how valuable a company is, not historical results – see, for example, Allen (1988). An analysis of past and current performance is therefore limited in its usefulness. In isolation, a high return on capital employed, for example, can hide the reality of an asset base which is declining in real terms. Therefore, one should estimate the future cash flows that the company is capable of generating and discount these by the cost of capital. The current value of the company is determined by this net present value calculation.

The decision to acquire a company, however, will not be based solely on the discounted future earnings, nor the purchase price, but both of these are very important. Future earnings potential for both the acquiring and the acquired companies could be improved with a merger if valuable synergy of some form is derived, and for this potential a premium price might be justified. To a large extent the price will often be determined by what improvements to the bottom line the acquiring management believe they can achieve.

© ESPION / DREAMSTIME.COM

A multifactor approach

Consequently, Copeland *et al.* (1990) recommend a five-level valuation approach:

- The first level is the current market value, described above.
- The second level is the earnings potential, the value of the projected cash flow, discounted.
- The third level projects a value once internal improvements have been undertaken. New business processes, for example, could improve the cash flow.
- The fourth level is the value after restructuring, when non-core or poorly performing activities have been sold or divested.

- The fifth level combines level three and four benefits. Significantly, the improvements implied in these three levels may require a fresh management team and style.

References

Allen, D (1988) *Long Term Financial Health – A Structure for Strategic Financial Management*, Chartered Institute of Management Accountants (CIMA).

Copeland, T, Kotter, T and Murrin, J (1990) *Valuation: Measuring and Managing the Value of Companies*, John Wiley.

There are a number of ways of *paying for the business*. Clearly cash is one alternative. In this case, the likely return should exceed either the return that could be earned if any surplus cash were invested elsewhere, maybe in government securities, or the cost of borrowing the cash required for the purchase. The other option is to use equity, whereby a predator or acquirer simply offers its shares in exchange for those in the targeted business. This is perfectly feasible as shares normally have a trading value, but invariably it will be necessary to offer more than the current value of the shares in the business being acquired. Sometimes a mixture of shares and cash will be chosen. The decision will be influenced by:

- whether there is surplus cash in the balance sheet
- the prevailing rate of interest
- the impact on the acquirer's debt ratio and gearing.

In the UK a company cannot use the assets of a targeted business as collateral for a loan, although this is permissible in the US. It is also legal in the US to buy shares in another business with the later intention of selling them back to the company for a profit, an action sometimes called 'greenmail'.

Unwelcome bids

Organizations which find themselves the object of an unwelcome bid can defend themselves in a number of ways. A revised profit forecast, promising improvements, can prove effective – but subsequently the improvement must be delivered. This will sometimes be linked to a promise to restructure and divest parts of the business which are not core and not contributing synergy. An appeal to regulatory bodies may at least impose a delay; and finally, the company can seek a white knight, a preferred friendly bidder. Jenkinson and Mayer (1994) have shown, first, that white-knight interventions normally succeed but, of course, the company's independence has still been lost and, second, that where there is no white knight cash bids are more difficult to defend against than equity bids.

On other occasions a targeted company will seek the support of its employees or trade unions, on the grounds that it is their jobs that could be affected detrimentally. The outcome of this strategy is variable and unpredictable. Another popular strategy is to acquire fresh assets which make the acquisition less attractive to the predator but, of course, there might be a strategic price to pay later if the bid does not go through and if this is purely defensive in nature! A number of defensive strategies by Forte were evident in its attempt to avoid takeover by Granada (Online Case 10.2).

In the case of the hostile takeover of Arcelor of Spain in 2006 by the Indian steel company Mittal, the bid process involved the efforts of several European governments in France, Spain and Luxembourg – who all sought to block the bid. It led to Mittal putting together a road show to demonstrate the potential synergies in terms of product line between the two businesses, with very limited overlap between the two steel giants. Mittal Steel had come into existence in 1989 and up until the proposed takeover of Arcelor, Mittal had the best performance of any steel company in the world through its acquisition strategy. Another factor to consider was the fact that the Mittal family held 88 per cent of the shares of Mittal Steel. There were also concerns regarding a clash of cultures between the Indian steel company taking over a European steel company. There is a useful cross-reference to the issues in the Daimler-Chrysler Case, 11.1. The offer to Arcelor shareholders involved shareholders exchanging 12 Arcelor shares for 13 Mittal shares plus a sum in cash of £150.60. In essence the low key approach of Mittal, putting forward the gains to be had from a merger of equals offering global integration and consolidation, won the day. Arcelor Mittal became the largest steel company in the world with 320,000 employees with revenues in 2007 of $105 billion.

These issues are explored further in Strategy in action 11.2.

Strategy in action 11.2

Hostile Takeovers

In a research sample year (1989) in the UK there were 161 bids for publicly listed companies; 35 of these were hostile takeover attempts as distinct from agreed or friendly acquisition bids. In one sense the year was seen as typical: some 70 per cent of the largest acquisitions/takeovers were hostile. Of these about half will normally succeed; in the other cases the target company will be able to mount an effective defence strategy.

By contrast, Germany had experienced just three hostile takeover bids since 1945. They are equally rare in France and almost unheard of in Japan. They remain popular in the US, where a larger number of defence mechanisms are available than is the case in the UK.

Alternative defence strategies

(Listed in order of popularity in the UK)

1 *Financial responses* Companies will hope to be able to announce forthcoming profit improvements – they have been targeted because, although fundamentally competitive and sound, recent profits have been disappointing. They may also seek to revalue their assets to make the bid appear to be undervaluing the true worth of the business.

2 *Legal and political tactics* Political lobbying and attempts to get a bid referred to the competition authorities, the latter to, at the very least, buy time and allow a company to mount a stronger defence.

3 *Attempted white-knight bids* An alternative, preferred, outside bidder is sought.

4 *Corporate restructuring* As seen in Case 10.8, disposals are announced. Bidders will claim that attempts to rationalize and downsize, while appropriate and desirable, have been provoked by the bid and are indicative of reactive senior management. Sometimes the strategic leadership will attempt to mount a management buy-out as an alternative to the outside bid.

5 *Poison pills* This strategy, most popular in the US, describes shareholder rights plans which effectively increase the price to the bidder. An example would be preferentially priced stock being available to existing shareholders, giving them a later right to new ordinary shares. Similarly, the term *golden parachutes* describes special departure terms for directors in the event of an unwelcome acquisition.

In 1999, for example, American Airlines (linked to Canadian Airlines and allied with British Airways in the Oneworld alliance) was interested in bidding for Air Canada, which was experiencing financial difficulties. However, Air Canada was part of the Star Alliance, dominated by American's main rival, United Airlines. A poison pill was in evidence – whoever might own Air Canada, it would remain a member of the Star Alliance for ten years or United and its partners would be entitled to huge damages.

The presence of this arrangement was sufficient to deter American.

Outcomes

In general a well-formulated and strategically logical bid for a poor performer should succeed; a strong performer will clearly be in a stronger position to defend itself and its record. However, in isolation, a strong financial performance is not everything – simply, there may appear to be more strategic logic in the business being parented by the bidder instead of staying as it is.

Cash bids have the greatest likelihood of success. In 1989, 21 per cent of the 161 bids were equity based and just 11 per cent of these succeeded; 43 per cent were cash only with a 56 per cent success rate; the remaining 36 per cent were mixed cash/equity bids and 53 per cent of these succeeded. Normally, the value of a hostile bid will be increased once the nature and robustness of the defence is revealed.

Cash bids are most likely to fail if an alternative white knight bidder is found. The likelihood of the success of equity and mixed bids appears to depend upon the quality of the financial defence.

Source

Jenkinson, T and Mayer, C (1994) *Hostile Takeovers: Defence, Attack and Corporate Governance*, McGraw-Hill.

© THAYYILANI / DREAMSTIME.COM

Abandoned discussions

There are occasions when merger talks fail and are abandoned. Walton and McBride (1998) provide a number of possible reasons for this, few of which relate to the actual strategic logic of the merger:

- There is a reluctance on the part of one company to accept that they are in reality number two and that it is not a partnership of equals.
- There is disagreement on future strategic leadership – who will run the new merged company. Egos get in the way. There was a delay in the merger between Glaxo Wellcome and SmithKline Beecham for exactly this reason.
- There is inadequate consultation with key shareholders – typically institutions – who then intervene.
- There is an insistence on preserving too many elements from the past – often things related to a strategic leader who is reluctant to let them go.
- Relationships and trust simply break down as negotiations proceed.

Implementation issues

Ernst and Young (1995) argue that the nature of the post-acquisition challenge depends upon the type of acquisition and the objectives behind it. They identify four alternatives:

1 *Financial acquisitions* are companies brought into a **holding company**, sometimes for the purpose of restructuring. The main objectives for the acquisition are the financial opportunities from cost (overhead) eradication, cost reduction and improved efficiencies. Those parts of the business which do not offer these opportunities are likely to be offered for

sale; and, in fact, any part of the business is likely to be available for sale to a buyer offering a premium price. The critical implementation issues concern timing and decisiveness.

2 *Geographical acquisitions* are intended to expand the acquirer's core business across new frontiers. Merging different country cultures is the key challenge, but this is generally regarded as manageable as long as the strategic logic for the merger is sound. One dilemma concerns cuts and job losses in the acquired business; alleged national bias may well cause resentment.

3 *Symbiotic acquisitions* describe situations where newly acquired products and competencies are absorbed into the parent's business but the acquired company retains some independence. Abbey National's purchase of Scottish Mutual is an example. The establishment of an appropriate new structure, culture and communications system are the implementation issues.

4 *Absorption acquisitions* imply that the two businesses are fully integrated, with one effectively losing its identity. Such acquisitions are particularly challenging to implement as really everything changes.

For any acquiring company to gain financially, sales must be increased and costs reduced to a level which compensates for any price premium paid. Researchers suggest that this is rarely less than 20 per cent. Easy savings are rare, particularly in the case of many hostile bids, where the target is often a high, rather than a poor, performer. Too many companies, apparently, pursue the elusive synergistic opportunities and do not act on the cost base quickly and decisively. They also tend to postpone the difficult issues relating to culture and style. Successful acquisitive companies such as Hanson did act quickly, concentrating on cost eradication and reduction; they also imposed their own style of management on their new businesses, top-down from the centre.

Clearly, the type of acquisition and the rationale behind it must influence the appropriate implementation strategy; as noted already, Hanson was a restructuring organization. Where genuine synergy potential exists, a more participatory style is likely to prove appropriate and foster the necessary learning and skills transfer.

Merging the two organizations

Merging two organizations involves decisions about the integration of strategic capabilities, in particular:

- operating resources – sales forces, production facilities
- functional skills – product development, R&D
- general management skills – strategy development, financial control, human resource strategies.

The speed and pattern of the integration will be dependent on the desired interde-pendency of the businesses, and the opportunities for synergy. It is essential that there is a strategy for the implementation, and ideally this will be developed after the merger or acquisition when fuller details are available. Moreover, important issues concerning people, culture, structure, systems and procedures must be thought through.

- *People* – It is accepted that many chief executives and other senior managers leave acquired companies either immediately or within one to two years after the acquisition, especially where the acquisition was contested. This may or may not be significant, depending on the strengths of the acquiring company. In some cases it will prove crucial, particularly where the managers have been the major source of competitive advantage. The managers in the two organizations being merged may well have different values, ethics and beliefs in quality and service, and these will somehow have to be reconciled.

- *Culture* – It is quite possible that the two organizations will have different cultures, which also must be reconciled. One may be a large company and the other small, with typical role and power cultures, respectively. Managers will be used to different levels of responsibility. One may be much more formal and procedural than the other. One may be entrepreneurial and risk orientated, and the other cost conscious and risk averse. These cultural issues should be considered when the post-acquisition structure is designed, and in the new systems and procedures.

- *Structure, systems and procedures* – While mentioned here, this issue is the subject of Chapter 16, and it concerns the degree of decentralization. As companies become larger and more complex they must be broken down into business units, and managers must be given some degree of independence – to motivate them and to ensure that functional and competitive strategies can be adapted in response to environmental changes. However, if activities are to be shared, or skills transferred, it is essential to ensure that independence does not inhibit, or even prohibit, the implementation of the necessary interdependencies.

McLean (1985) contends that six factors determine whether the integration of two or more companies is a success or a failure:

- first, active leadership by the strategic leader of the acquiring company in conveying objectives and expectations, and in redesigning the structure of the organizations

- second, the conscious development of shared values and a transfer of the important aspects of the culture of the acquiring firm

- third, an appropriate interchange of managers between the firms, which can be one way of retaining valuable managers from the acquired company

- fourth, proceeding with caution (although some changes may have to be implemented quickly, say to reduce costs in certain areas, others will be less urgent; this provides an opportunity to learn about the underlying strengths of the new business which might be capitalized on)

- fifth, relationships with customers must be protected until decisions about future products and market priorities are taken

- sixth, rigid new systems, which might be inappropriate for the new business, should not be imposed too ruthlessly or too quickly. Where there are differences in, in particular, culture, technology and marketing needs, managers in the acquired company should be allowed the necessary freedom to manage the competitive and functional strategies and respond to market pressures.

To summarize this section, it could be argued that:

- the price paid for an acquisition should reflect the ability of the acquirer to add value, share resources and transfer skills

- the strategy for achieving this should be soundly based, and the potential synergy real rather than imagined

- post-acquisition management should recognize that, while changes will have to be made in order to add value, two cultures have to be integrated if the strategy is to be implemented effectively.

Finally, five factors for implementing acquisitions and mergers successfully can be identified:

1 Tread warily and carry out sufficient analysis – especially where there is a hostile reaction from the target.

2 Evaluate any prospective partner fully, carrying out a culture and style assessment as well as a financial evaluation.

3 Take on board the best practices from both (all) businesses to increase the prospects for synergy. It is highly unlikely that one partner will have a monopoly on good ideas.

4 Communicate with those people affected to the maximum extent that is expedient.

5 Ensure that key people are identified and stay.

11.4   Strategic alliances – an introduction

While some form of partnership can be one of the quickest and cheapest ways to grow or develop a new and maybe global strategy, it is also one of the toughest and most risky. Many alliances fail. The needs of both partners must be met, and consequently three important questions must be answered satisfactorily:

1 *Why* use an alliance?

2 *Who* to select as a partner?

3 *How* to implement the agreement?

Garrette and Dussauge (1999) argue that many European companies have tended to think about alliances from a defensive perspective rather than as a proactive growth opportunity. All too often they are a fall-back when the competition authorities stand in the way of a merger or acquisition. Many of the examples referred to throughout this chapter indicate that several successful American and Japanese companies have adopted a different perspective. In the late 1990s, for example, research into the largest 1000 American companies revealed that 20 per cent of their revenues came directly from alliances.

Online Case 11.1 shows how British Airways (BA) has mixed mergers and alliances, together with both positive and reactive strategies for its alliances, in an attempt to create the world's first truly global airline. BA has not succeeded in its quest.

There is evidence of some disagreement amongst strategy authors concerning the meaning of the terms 'joint venture' and 'strategic alliance'. Here, *strategic alliance* is used to encapsulate all forms of agreement between partners, and *joint venture* for those agreements which involve either the establishment of a new, independent company owned jointly by the partners, or the minority ownership of the other party by one or both partners.

The term 'consortium' is also used in this context. One instance would be where companies in an industry generally collaborate or share, maybe through a trade association. The Japanese *keiretsu* (or family of businesses) is another, but quite different, example. Here companies, often in a geographical cluster, own stakes in each other and share and collaborate wherever possible. This might take the form of intertrading; it might equally be by seconding staff to help with a particular problem or difficulty.

An alliance (or joint venture) could involve:

1 direct competitors, maybe sharing common skills, and with the objective of increased market share

2 less direct competitors with complementary skills – where the intention is more likely to be benchmarking and learning for mutual benefit, and the possible development of new ideas

3 related companies sharing different skills and competencies. Here organizations might well be linked in the same added-value chain (e.g. a manufacturer and either a supplier or a distributor). Such an alliance should generate synergy through cooperation, innovation and lower costs while allowing each partner to concentrate on its core competencies.

The intention will invariably be to increase competitive advantage without either merger or acquisition. As we move from an alliance to a joint venture and from 1 to 3 in the above

http://www.

See the online "British Airways" case for an example of this section's theory in practice hierarchy, the significance increases for the partners involved. Some companies will be involved in several alliances with different companies at the same time – this is not a one-off strategy for them. As an example, Toshiba (Japanese manufacturer of heavy electrical apparatus, electronic devices, information systems and consumer products such as televisions, videos, kitchen appliances and white goods) has created a global network of allies for different products and technologies, including Alstom, Siemens, Ericsson, General Electric, Motorola, Time Warner and Apple. Toshiba sees this 'circle of friends' as an opportunity for sharing ideas to obtain the latest technology and to gain competitive advantage through learning.

Case 11.4 describes how Yorkshire Water adopted an onion strategy to allow it to concentrate more on its core service competencies – and the necessary learning curve it faced. The company needed to form a network of partnerships and develop capabilities in managing such a network.

Case 11.4

Yorkshire Water's Onion Strategy   UK

Since being privatized in 1989 most of the ten water companies in the UK have pursued diversification strategies. The core business activities are water supply and the management of waste water (i.e. sewage treatment). Prices and quality standards are closely regulated, and consequently the diversification is aimed at offsetting the perceived risks and constraints inherent in regulated businesses. The most popular activity has been waste management, the collection and disposal of industrial and domestic waste. For example, Severn Trent Water acquired Biffa, and Wessex formed a joint venture with Waste Management of the US, one of the world's largest companies in the industry. South Staffordshire diversified into Homeserve, which organizes plumbing services for clients who take out insurance policies with them. Yorkshire Water developed a similar business but sold it to South Staffs. Homeserve has been split off from its original parent and is thriving.

After privatization Yorkshire Water (YW) basically created two separate, but linked, businesses: Yorkshire Water Services to control the core businesses, and Yorkshire Water Enterprises, later renamed Yorkshire Environmental Solutions, for other commercial ventures. Eventually these would become a £1 billion business. In recent years Yorkshire Water has been renamed Kelda and acquired by a private equity company. The holding company has three subsidiaries: Yorkshire Water itself (turning over some £700 million); Kelda Water Services (what was Yorkshire Water Enterprises and turning over some £100m); and Keyland Development (property, £20 million). A fourth

company, Aquarion, has been divested – as explained below.

Kelda continues to be focused on water and waste management, with Yorkshire Water providing core services in the Yorkshire Region and Kelda Water Services operating water and waste management contracts and private finance initiatives primarily for other water companies throughout the United Kingdom.

Yorkshire Water Enterprises (now Kelda Water Services)

This business became active in the following areas:

- *Waste management* – Industrial effluents and clinical waste. This was sold in 1998 to Waste Recycling, but Yorkshire Water retained a 49 per cent shareholding in the enlarged Waste Recycling business – until it was sold off completely.
- *Engineering consultancy and support* – A joint venture with Babcock International. Since 1989 YW have been investing in treatment plants (mainly) and water-distribution networks, the latter to free up engineering resources which the joint venture would seek to deploy and exploit. This was sold to Earthtec.
- *'Pipeline Products'* – The sale of existing stores items to external customers – now a ceased activity.
- *'Waterlink'* – A network of approved subcontractor plumbers. YW provided an arrangement service before selling the business to South Staffordshire Water. This business is now part of Spice Holdings which also embraces a number of other related activities.

- *Laboratory services* – Providing analytical services and environmental testing to a range of businesses and agencies – before being sold.
- *Loop* – A separate subsidiary to provide customer service management, billing, payment and debt collection. Services are sold to external customers; control lies with Yorkshire Water.
- *Management training* – Primarily exploiting existing markets and competencies. This has also been stopped.
- Keyland Developments – Property development and representing 'real' diversification. This continues and is focused on maximizing the value of Kelda and Yorkshire Water assets.

The Director General of OFWAT, the industry regulator, always emphasized that he was not going to ignore these strategic developments. 'Customers of core services must not be affected adversely.' For example, the water companies were prevented from selling services from the associated businesses to the core at contrived prices which benefited shareholders at the expense of captive water customers. In addition, 'the required investment funds for the water supply services must not be put at risk'.

Yorkshire Water Services

YW stated quite early that it did not intend to build and then manage a diversified corporation. Once the appropriate business had been constructed, with YW's resources deployed effectively, the layers would be peeled away systematically – an onion focus strategy – until only the core business remained. The defined core activity was *water delivery*, which incorporated the removal of sewage and water treatment. The pursuit of this strategy entailed divesting certain non-core or support activities into either wholly owned subsidiaries or independent contractors (in properly negotiated alliances), and possibly more joint ventures, but only where there were providers able to deliver the range and quality of services.

Four alternative implementation approaches for this strategy are illustrated below.

The services divested by YW are also highlighted. Where there were agreements with multiple outside contractors (Approaches 2 and 3), separate geographical regions were typically the predominant logic. For example, the pipework to sewage treatment works was initially divested to individual local authorities.

This corporate onion strategy aims to improve a company's competitiveness with the premise that non-core services can invariably be acquired more effectively from an experienced outside provider, selected because it already has competitive advantage. It is essential to define the core carefully and to establish the appropriate ongoing relationships in order to minimize risk. The order and timing of each divestment is also an important issue. The company benefits because it can concentrate on its core activities; it has access to a wider skill and resource base, which should promote best practice, enable greater service flexibility and lead to overall quality improvements. Resources should match needs more effectively. In addition, clearer accountability should foster cost reductions, and the introduction of controlled competition should enhance the quality of in-house service provision and act as a catalyst for change throughout the organization. YW, for example, set up contracts to buy all the pipes that would be needed by its contractors. The contractors were then able to take advantage of the favourable prices negotiated, but they bought the pipes and held the inventory. To implement this strategy successfully the central organization must develop competency in network management. Effective partnership sourcing such as this requires unambiguous long-term agreements, clear performance measures and shared risk. It is most appropriate where the service is a core activity for the contracted supplier. The partners should engage in ongoing dialogue and maybe even exchange personnel periodically.

However, in the mid-1990s a summer drought caused Yorkshire Water considerable embarrassment. Public relations were clumsy; the managing director suggested people could easily wash with just a basin of water as opposed to having a bath, for example. The company ended up hiring road transporters to move water from different parts of Yorkshire to its own reservoirs, but supplies were never cut off. In the end the chairman and managing director both retired and, with a new strategic leader, the parent company was then renamed Kelda. The company bought Aquarion, an American water company, in 2000. Since then this New England business was active acquiring related businesses in other New England states. However the potential returns were always limited by US regulations and the business was consequently sold on.

When YW started with this onion strategy the supplier market was relatively immature and considerable learning took place. YW came to realize that it was difficult to drive innovation when it relied extensively on independent suppliers, and so it needed to rethink aspects of the strategy to make sure this could happen. It also became apparent that if efficiency improvements were to be driven then it needed YW to find ways of rewarding 'high performers' at the expense of poorer performers. YW also realized that it needed to be able to exercise some control over work planning and scheduling of critical activities, even if they were provided by external organizations and this also had to be tackled as an issue. In recent years most other water companies have followed a similar route and the market has become more mature. There have been new entrants and consolidation. Basically the trend over the time this onion strategy has evolved has been to reduce the number of contractors, to enable stronger, and more strategic, alliances to be developed.

Four alternative onion-focus strategies applied in Yorkshire Water Services

Strategy 1

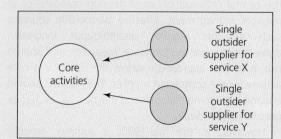

Examples: Fleet services and laboratory services

Strategy 2

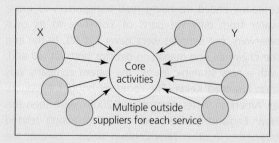

Examples: Electrical and mechanical maintenance; repair and maintenance

Key success factor: Partnership sourcing, establishing firm alliances with each supplier

The suppliers were generally based in specific geographic locations and looked after a 'territory'. The most efficient were rewarded in two ways. First any financial benefits from beating agreed targets were shared with Yorkshire Water. Second their territory was increased in size at the expense of poorer performers.

Strategy 2 became the dominant and preferred model of the four alternatives.

Strategy 3

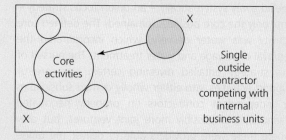

Objective: Develop the in-house capability into a centre of excellence

Example: Waste detection.

This model was only applied sparingly. Sewage management – the pipework to the sewage treatment works – was given over to local authority control, but it has since been taken back in-house.

Strategy 4

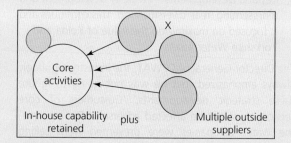

Objective: Form an alliance with an outside expert and benchmark to drive internal improvement.

In the end this model was abandoned quite quickly and absorbed into Strategy 2.

In 2000 Kelda announced a radical proposal. It indicated an intent to sell all of its physical assets (pipes, sewage works and reservoirs) to a new mutual company, which would be owned by Kelda's customers and financed with debt capital. Kelda would simply lease back the assets and employ contractors. Other activities would also be sold to leave a water *services* company. Environmental groups, customers and the water regulator all opposed the plan, which was subsequently abandoned.

Water meter reading is one key activity that was contracted out but has been brought back in-house – as much as anything to drive improvement and innovation. Yorkshire Water has also used its experience to form relevant alliances outside the water industry. For example it has looked to expertise developed for the oil industry to drive innovations in water leak detection.

Questions

Can alliance-based networks such as the one developed (and proposed) by Yorkshire Water deliver the equivalent or even greater value to customers than a company which owns and manages all of its activities?

Footnote

Michael Smith, retired Director of Human Resources, has provided invaluable support in clarifying the specific details described in this case.

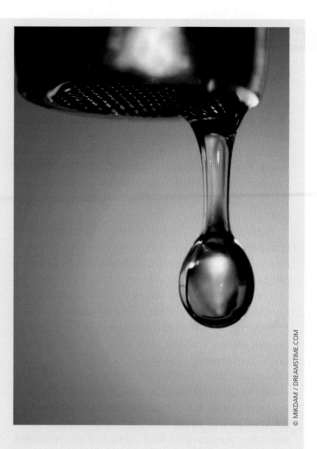

© MIKDAM / DREAMSTIME.COM

Reasons for joint ventures and strategic alliances

- The cost of acquisition may be too high.
- Legislation may prevent acquisition, but the larger size is required for critical mass.
- Political or cultural differences could mean that an alliance is more likely to facilitate integration than would a merger or acquisition.
- The increasing significance of a total customer service package suggests linkages through the added value chain – to secure supplies, customize distribution and control costs. At the same time individual organizations may prefer to specialize in those areas where they are most competent. An alliance provides a solution to this dilemma.
- The threat from Japanese competition has driven many competitors into closer collaboration, but they may not wish to merge. For example, American and European car manufacturers have taken stakes in Japanese businesses, where outright acquisition is unlikely.
- Covert protectionism in certain markets necessitates a joint venture with a local company. This has been particularly true in China, one of the world's fastest growing economies.

Developing these points, Case 11.5 contrasts the acquisition approach of Ford with the alliance strategy of General Motors as they have both become increasingly global in their endeavours to remain the world's largest car manufacturers. In some respects neither strategy has succeeded particularly well – both companies have made mistakes with their model development priorities.

Case 11.5

General Motors and Ford   US

When Barack Obama was elected as the new President of America in November 2008 he knew that the auto industry was one of the main industrial issues he would have to deal with. The so-called Big Three, General Motors (GM), Ford and Chrysler – Chrysler was discussed in a separate case (11.1) earlier in the chapter – were asking for emergency funding.

General Motors (GM) remains the world's largest car manufacturer; Ford was for a long time second but is now third. Toyota is the most profitable and threatening GM as the leading producer measured by the number of cars produced. The third largest US car manufacturer is Chrysler. In the early 2000s GM has enjoyed higher operating margins than its leading US rival, Ford, but this has not always been the case. Over the last 30 years GM's performance has been steadier and more predictable than Ford's. In some years Ford has exceeded GM's operating profits; in other years it has lagged markedly. It was thought the US car industry was between 20 and 30 per cent over-capacity late in 2008 when the recession took hold – jobs and plants needed to go.

Both GM and Ford have their corporate headquarters in Detroit, Michigan. In fact they are less than 10 miles apart. But these two companies have followed quite different strategies in their quest for globalization.

GM and Ford have followed what Porter would describe as a classic differentiation strategy for a wide cross-section of the market. Toyota is the established cost leader as it is the most efficient and most productive. But arguably both GM and Ford have misjudged demand patterns and their ranges have become unbalanced. Both focused on higher-price SUVs (sports utility vehicles) and pick-up trucks at the expense of smaller cars, but when gas prices increased rapidly they saw overall demand fall. Late in 2008 Toyota was also reducing capacity – no producer was unaffected by the fall in demand.

General Motors

GM – which owns Opel in Germany and Vauxhall in the UK – opted to form a loose network of international partners arguing 'we can realize synergies faster than in

a full buy-out situation – we get most of the gain and less of the pain'.

GM's joint ventures have included the following:

- GM bought 20 per cent of Fiat Auto (Italy) with an option to buy the remaining 80 per cent should it so wish – at the time a reflection of Europe's overcapacity. As part of the deal, GM helped Fiat to market its Alfa Romeo brand in America, but the expensive Ferrari and Maserati brands were always excluded from the alliance. This happened when Fiat was struggling, although some recent models have proved very successful. When it came to decision-time in 2005, GM did not want to buy out Fiat and had to pay a penalty to back out of the arrangement!
- GM also bought 20 per cent of Fuji Heavy Industries, which includes Subaru cars and major components businesses.
- GM has 10 per cent of Suzuki and 49 per cent of Isuzu (trucks as well as cars). Suzuki sells GM products in Japan.

In all of these cases, GM gained access to technology and platforms that would have been hugely expensive to develop in-house.

- GM has bought the remaining 50 per cent of Saab it did not own to give it total control – it had held the first 50 per cent for over ten years. Subaru helped Saab to develop its newest models.
- In 2002 GM acquired 67 per cent of Daewoo (South Korea). Ford had been the preferred bidder for Daewoo at one stage, but had withdrawn.
- The most recent alliance has been with Shanghai Automotive to develop hybrid cars, which would be marketed in China as well as the US and other countries.

GM's philosophy for these alliances has been one of accord and it is generally opposed to hostile take-overs, but GM remains on a learning curve for yielding the potentially elusive synergistic benefits of these alliances.

As well as being too dependent on trucks and SUVs, it also became apparent that GM was making too many different marques – it was perhaps over-differentiated! Companies with more limited ranges have performed better in recent years. The company decided it would re-emphasize small cars, and also develop seriously its Volt plug-in electric car, which it would sell in Europe as well as the US. Its Hummer division (larger gas-guzzlers) and Saab were both offered for sale.

Ford

Ford is different in many ways. Started by the legendary Henry Ford, it is renowned for its introduction of the Model T, produced on the first vehicle assembly line. The Ford family retain 40 per cent of the voting shares in the business but just 4 per cent of the equity. Ford's descendants have sometimes run the company, but this has certainly not always been the case.

After many years of fundamentally organic growth, Ford made a series of acquisitions in the late 1990s: Jaguar, Land Rover, Aston Martin and Volvo. Ford also bought Kwik Fit, the tyre and exhaust replacement specialist, but relatively quickly sold it at a substantial loss – it was a diversification that did not pay off.

Ford's strategy had been to buy and own *strong brands*, which it could position and market as it liked to complement the complete Ford portfolio. Chief Executive in the 1990s, Jacques Nasser, claimed that GM would also have bought brands like these if it had been able. Ford dismissed Nasser and replaced him with Bill Ford Jr., a direct descendant of founder Henry Ford. He was later replaced by Alan Mulally, recruited from Boeing, in 2005.

There is, though, a number of parallel alliances. Ford is allied with Peugeot-Citroën for diesel engine development, and with Yahoo!, Oracle and Microsoft for Internet services of various forms. It also has joint ventures in China, India and Turkey.

An earlier alliance with Volkswagen to build people carriers on a common platform failed to deliver the anticipated results and was abandoned. In addition, Ford took a 33 per cent shareholding in Mazda (in 1996) and accepted a major role in the control and running of the Japanese company. Importing American techniques into Japan is difficult, and Mazda's fortunes have fluctuated. Ford's dilemma concerned whether the Mazda brand should stand apart or be integrated into the rest of the Ford portfolio.

In 2006 Ford recorded a record loss of US$12.6 billion – which the *Financial Times* stated was the result of 'incompetent management, chaotic product development and lax cost control'. It had ended up making the cars it wanted to make which were not necessarily those that customers were looking to buy. In just a few years its share of new cars being driven out of showrooms had fallen from 1 in 4 to 1 in 7. Two-thirds of its sales were trucks and SUVs, which were declining in popularity. Bill Ford, said the *Financial Times*, cared passionately but he was 'not the right man for the job'.

Mulally auctioned Aston Martin and sold Jaguar and Land Rover to Tata of India. (See Case 11.3.) In 2008 he reduced the stake Ford held in Mazda. This was a reluctant decision, but Ford needed the money. Mazda and Ford shared car platforms for selected models and so an alliance, albeit a quite different one, would continue. There would (like GM) be a renewed focus on smaller cars; design and development would be more centralized. Ford would look to standardize platforms more and instead compete on external aesthetics.

Ford, which is generally perceived to have fallen behind GM, is rationalizing its ranges and platforms and new product development. For a while its (acquired) luxury brands subsidized the 'mainstay' Ford product ranges. It was perhaps ironical that integrating the acquisitions was not easy (and it maybe diverted attention away from the more serious issues with Ford cars and trucks) but the acquired up-market brands were for a time the most profitable parts of the group. But a major and high profile recall of Ford Explorers – SUVs – because of problems with its standard Firestone tyres, was embarrassing and again diverting.

So, should the US government provide special financial support for GM, Ford and Chrysler? Some would argue that this is an industry that is too important to be allowed to collapse; it must be protected in some way. Critics, however, argue this type of support would be rewarding failure, preserving over-capacity in the US and subsidizing the Big Three's relatively expensive car plants in Detroit at the expense of the lower cost and more efficient plants in the Southern states making cars for the leading Asian manufacturers such as Toyota. But there are over 100 car plants in the US employing nearly a quarter of a million people. Moreover there are 13,000 car dealerships employing on average some 50 people each. There is a great deal at stake.

The discussions became a classic illustration of game theory – the decisions and choices would be based on the decisions and expectations of other 'players' or interested parties. The companies, their creditors, the government and the unions all kept pushing for a deal that was more favourable to them, but there was an element of brinksmanship. Ironically it is not unusual for the party with the weakest case to win through – if they can hold out long enough! There was always a feeling the US government had the most to lose – and there was to be a change of President.

In the event some $17 billion has intially been made available to support the industry. But there were conditions. It would only be available when a sustainable business plan was forthcoming from the car makers, one which demonstrated reduced wages and pension payments to make the companies more competitive. Despite the dangerous positon of the companies, the relevant unions opposed the terms and conditions. GM and Chrysler were always thought to be the most likely to strike a deal, but soon afterwards Chrysler formed its alliance with Fiat – described briefly in the separate case on Daimler Benz. In the event GM sought to borrow some US$10 billion and Chrysler $4billion. The loans would not save jobs but they might well save the industry – ready for when demand started to grow again.

This American deal was offered in December 2008; in January 2009 the UK government pledged it would provide support for UK car companies to try and ensure that even though workers were being given paid leave of absence to stay away from work for periods of several weeks (there were too many unsold cars in compounds) there would be jobs for them to return to once demand took off again.

In January 2009 it was announced that before the end of the year GM planned to lose 10,000 jobs in its workforce, a third of these in the US. Employees would also be taking pay cuts. A month later this figure was increased substantially. Sales were still very depressed. Saab was still for sale and in deep trouble; there were rumours GM might seek equity funding for stakes in Opel and Vauxhall. Soon afterwards GM CEO Rick Wagoner resigned when it was clear that both GM and Chrysler needed yet more money. President Obama was said to be 'frustrated' that the firms were not yet making an effective case to justify the aid – their proposals for changing practices were 'inadequate'. Wagoner had worked for GM for 30 years and had been CEO since 2000. Some commentators were starting to argue that bankruptcy and a completely fresh start might be the best option.

Like Chrysler earlier (Case 11.1) GM filed for bankruptcy in June 2009 – the largest industrial bankruptcy in history. The 'new GM' would have fewer brands and plants. The US and Canadian governments would own at least 60 per cent of the business (an exchange for the loans they had already made) and the Union of Auto Workers perhaps 17.5 per cent. Existing shareholders would get very little. Jobs would go and dealerships would have to close.

Meanwhile GM Europe looked likely to be acquired by a Canadian-Austrian auto parts business, Magna. Fiat had been a rival bidder but had pulled out. It seemed unlikely that all the Opel and Vauxhall plants could survive intact, but where would any closures happen?

GENERAL MOTORS **http://www.gm.com**
FORD MOTOR COMPANY **http://www.ford.com**

Questions

1   Whose strategic approach do you believe is the better one? Why?
2   Do you agree that the US (and UK) auto industry should receive 'special treatment'? Are they genuinely too important to be allowed to fail?

GM has had to accept emergency funding from the US government and the resignation of its CEO as a condition of further support.

The likely outcomes

● In simple terms, increased competency, synergy and a stronger global presence are the potential outcomes targeted most frequently by alliance and joint venture partners.

● Greater innovation could well accrue from the pooling and sharing of ideas and competencies, which in turn enables greater focus (by each partner) combined with resource leverage.

● The partnership and sharing could also result in lower costs. A virtual circle of learning, where each partner learns new skills and competencies from the other, contributes to this.

● Finally, the linkage could provide access to new markets and technologies.

● Simply, an alliance is a means to an end. It is not necessarily going to be seen as a permanent arrangement, and it most probably can be changed as time goes on.

Developing these outline points, Connell (1988) contends that companies collaborate strategically for primarily three reasons:

1 To gain access to new markets and technologies as markets become increasingly international.

In 1989 Pilkington, the UK float glass manufacturer and world market leader, sold 20 per cent of its US vehicle glass subsidiary to Nippon Sheet Glass of Japan. Pilkington had 17 per cent of the world market for vehicle glass at the time, Asahi of Japan 19 per cent. Nippon already had 9 per cent and manufactured float glass under licence from Pilkington. Nippon gained access to the US market; Pilkington was looking to build a customer base in Japan, arguing that as car manufacture becomes increasingly global they needed a presence in all major markets. Pilkington already supplied the Toyota plant in the US.

2 To share the costs and risks of increasingly expensive research and development.

Nippon Steel (a related business) developed another strategic alliance – designed to cut production costs – with Posco (South Korea's Pohang Iron and Steel). Nippon and Posco were the world's largest steelmakers (a joint market share of just 7 per cent, nevertheless) and wished to retain their positions of leadership. Research and development resources were pooled but there was no collaboration on either production or marketing. Suppliers expressed concern that the partners might use their alliance to drive down prices.

3 To manage innovation more effectively. This is important because of high R&D costs and greater globalization, which together often ensure that any competitive advantage gained from technology is relatively short-lived. Both the opportunities and threats require that companies are able to be flexible and change quickly.

In 1995 Motorola joined with IBM, Siemens and Toshiba (an existing alliance) to develop the next generation of advanced memory chips, which are highly complex and extremely costly to develop and make.

Two more recent alliances appear to address all three reasons. In 2008 Peugeot and Mitsubishi started working together on the development of motors for electric cars. In the same year Bosch and Samsung formed a 50:50 joint venture to develop, manufacture and sell automotive lithium-ion batteries.

There is arguably a fourth reason – an attempt to regain lost competitiveness in a marketplace. This is thought to be the cause of a series of agreements among European electronics manufacturers, and links between them and Japanese and US competitors.

While there are a number of reasons and justifications for such strategic alliances, they can again be difficult strategies to implement effectively, as shown later in the chapter.

11.5 Forms and examples of strategic alliances and joint ventures

Strategic alliances and joint ventures can take a number of forms. The six categories which follow should not be seen as mutually exclusive; some joint ventures will cover more than one.

Component parts of two or more businesses might be merged

In Case 9.9 we discussed the opportunity that Jim McColl grasped to conduct a management buy-in to Clyde Blowers. The industry that Clyde Blowers was in was highly fragmented, with a large number of companies competing for a share of the soot blowing business. Essentially this made many of them loss making. Over the period 1993–1998, Clyde Blowers, funded by their bank, acquired a total of six of their world wide competitors, including their major US rival Bergemann, for a total of £33.2m. This achieved for Clyde a new market share of over 50 per cent when the market share had previously been 8 per cent. In parallel to this, Clyde Blowers acquired a number of materials handling businesses, synergistic to the movement of coal into the power stations. This led to the creation of a new division, Clyde Bergemann Power, with a total spend of £25.7m. For Clyde Blowers the classic benefits were a rationalization of activities, simplified product lines and a 43 per cent reduction in manpower, what McColl described as 'a classic MBA text book strategy'.

Companies might agree to join forces to develop a new project

Club Méditerranée and Carnival Cruise Lines (US) joined forces to provide cruise-based holiday packages for Europe and Asia.

Philips and Nintendo jointly developed a new generation of video games on compact discs compatible with Philips' CD-i (compact disc-interactive) players which linked up to high-definition televisions. Nintendo has gone on to develop the Wii with its wireless controller and the Wii remote which can be used as a hand held pointing device to detect movement in three dimensions.

Airbus Industrie was formed because no partner alone could afford the development costs of large passenger aircraft, and because of pressure from European governments who wanted to reduce the predominance of the large US companies.

Psion, UK manufacturer of palm-size computers and electronic organizers, joined forces with the world's largest mobile telecommunications companies, Nokia, Motorola and Ericsson, to develop Internet-linked mobile phones and other products which use WAP (wireless application protocol) technology. This alliance was seen as a means of counteracting the power of Microsoft in one of the fastest growing areas of the computing industry.

Sony has been an innovative company throughout its 50-plus years of existence. Using its competencies in miniaturization it has developed a vast range of home electronics products, including the Walkman (in its many variants) and the PlayStation games consoles, sales of which now exceed 75 million units worldwide. Sony has recently joined forces with Intel (manufacturers of sophisticated memory chips) to develop applications that can again be linked to the Internet. One example is the memory stick, which stores images, music and computer files and then allows them to be used in various electronic devices. Sony is also partnered with DoCoMo, another Japanese company which has 17 million subscribers and specializes in delivering computer games and other services directly over the Internet.

Companies might agree to develop a new business jointly

Sony Ericsson is a 50:50 joint venture for developing upmarket mobile phones. There have been problems integrating teams from two distinct backgrounds and cultures, but the business is beginning to develop products that can compete effectively in this very competitive industry. Some phones are being assembled in China, which has, of course, introduced new issues to deal with.

Cereal Partners World-wide is a joint venture designed to strengthen market access for the two companies involved. General Mills, an American rival to Kellogg, had developed a number of popular products (particularly Cheerios), but was not geared up to distribute them outside America. Nestlé owned a formidable distribution network and could provide access to most of Europe. Nestlé had earlier tried to break into this industry without any marked success.

There might be specific agreements between manufacturers and their suppliers

American Express (AMEX), like many other large corporations, had a travel department which organized the global travel arrangements for its managers. They developed a competency which they now provide as a service to other corporations who prefer to outsource this task when they can find someone with the appropriate expertise. AMEX developed this competency further and moved into consumer travel as well.

A company might make a strategic investment in another firm

Several years ago Guinness and LVMH exchanged shareholdings and formed a whole series of distribution joint ventures around the world. There were efficiency savings and marketing advantages from combining, in particular, the spirits brands of the two companies. LVMH owns the world's leading cognac brand, Hennessy, as well as its leading champagnes; Guinness, through its United Distillers subsidiary, owned a portfolio which includes Johnnie Walker, the world's best-selling Scotch whisky, and Gordon's gin, another international best-seller. However, Guinness merged with Grand Metropolitan (see Diageo – Case 10.1) and this put enormous stress on the joint venture. In fact, LVMH was able to dictate certain terms of the merger agreement.

British Telecom (BT) sees minority stakes and joint ventures as its path to a global presence. It has used this strategy to become the second largest competitor in several European countries, namely Sweden, France, Germany, the Netherlands, Spain, Portugal and Italy. BT, which has the most extensive portfolio of assets in the European telecommunications industry, claims that acquisitions were 'never on the cards' but does not rule out increasing its stake in the partner organizations.

Companies might form international trading partnerships

Disney Corporation, McDonald's and Coca-Cola, owners of three of the most important brands in the world, have a loose partnership which varies from country to country, depending upon how local managers wish to exploit its potential. There are several aspects to the partnership:

- McDonald's is Coca-Cola's largest customer and buys its soft drinks exclusively from Coca-Cola
- McDonald's sponsors activities and exhibits at Disney attractions as well as running restaurants on site
- Disney collaborates with McDonald's on special worldwide promotions which feature Disney characters, especially when new movies are released
- Coca-Cola is also the sole supplier of soft drinks to Disney's theme parks.

11.6 Key issues in joint ventures and strategic alliances

This concluding section summarizes the views of a number of key authors who have examined the relative success of alliances and joint ventures.

Kanter (1990) offers the following criteria as key determinants of their success:

- The alliance or joint venture must be important strategically for both partners.
- Ideally they should bring complementary, rather than exactly the same, competencies to the arrangement.

- Information must be shared openly.
- There should be genuine integration to create linkages, even though this may be across divergent cultures. Trust becomes essential.
- The arrangements should become institutionalized into some framework which can demonstrate a clear identity and a position of importance.

Kanter reinforces the point that alliance management needs to become a key strategic capability.

Ohmae (1989) argues that the following issues are significant and help to determine whether the agreement is likely to prove effective:

- Successful collaboration requires commitment on both sides. Without sufficient management time, trust and respect the agreement is likely to fail. In reality, all the required resources must be committed. Either for managing linkages, or for managing a new joint venture company, capable managers must be transferred or seconded. The outcome of the alliance will depend upon both the commitment of the partners and the emergent power and influence they exert.
- There must be mutual benefits, the attainment of which may well involve sacrifices on both sides. Both partners should appreciate clearly what the other party wants from the agreement, and their objectives. If the commitment of each ally is uneven, the keener partner or the faster learner is likely to assume control. This might mean that the interests of the weaker partner are either bought out or simply taken over.
- If circumstances change during the period of the alliance, flexibility may be required as the objectives and priorities of either or both partners may change.
- Cultural differences, which might be either geographic or corporate in origin, will have to be reconciled.

In addition, it is sensible if alliance partners see their joint involvement as an opportunity to learn new skills and good practices. Partners are not simply there to plug gaps or weaknesses. Analysts acknowledge that the Japanese have been very good at learning from their alliances, and that Western companies have been slower to exploit the learning opportunities.

Badaracco (1991) differentiates between:

- migratory knowledge – easily transferred technical skills, and
- embedded knowledge about how a company does business, which is particularly useful for deepening insight into new markets.

Where companies do enter an alliance through weakness rather than strength, it is vital that they use the partnership for learning and development. In 1991 Ford formed an alliance with Yamaha to develop a new engine for its Fiesta and Escort ranges. While such high-performance engines as the Ford Cosworth are the outcome of past joint ventures, this was the first incidence of an alliance for mainstream car engines. Analysts have commented that Ford needed an agreement because they had become weak in a rapidly changing industry, stimulated by new materials, higher fuel consumption expectations and tighter emission standards. 'Ford must learn from the deal, and not subcontract their engine technology for the long term.' Ford prefers acquisition to alliances (see Case 11.5 earlier).

Acquisitions should be evaluated in terms of their ability to generate synergy. Joint ventures and strategic alliances should be regarded in the same light. Devlin and Bleackley (1988) argue that the key issues are the strategic wisdom behind the decision to form an alliance in the first place, the choice of partner, and the management of the alliance once it has been agreed. The position of both parties to the agreement should be improved from the alliance. If there is a real opportunity for synergy, joint benefits and mutual trust and commitment by both parties, joint ventures can be an effective means of implementing strategic change. However, although some of the inherent difficulties of acquisition are avoided by this type of agreement, there will still be implementation issues. Unless these are tackled properly, the joint venture is likely to prove expensive and tie up resources which might otherwise be deployed more effectively.

Alliances can fail and/or be dismantled for a number of reasons; consequently the extent to which any organization is dependent upon its alliances should be carefully monitored.

11.7 Franchising and licensing

Next in this chapter we look at two other means of growing the organization which avoid the risks and pitfalls of acquisitions and joint ventures, but which still require relationship building and trust.

Franchising

Franchising again takes many forms, and it provides an opportunity for rapid growth for established businesses and a relatively low risk means of starting a small business. Service businesses are more common than manufacturing in franchising, and as the UK continues to switch from a manufacturing to a service economy they may well become even more important. Tie Rack is one example of a retail organization which has concentrated on specific market segments and grown rapidly with franchising. Thornton's chocolate shops, Fastframe picture framing, Prontaprint printing and copying shops, Body Shop and the British School of Motoring are other examples. Although McDonald's is franchised throughout the US, many restaurants in Britain are owned by the company. Subway, Kentucky Fried Chicken, Burger King and Spud-U-Like, however, are franchised.

A company which chooses franchising as a means of strategic growth enters into contractual arrangements with a number of small businesses, usually one in each selected geographical area. In return for a lump sum initial investment and ongoing royalties the typical franchiser provides exclusive rights to supply a product or service under the franchiser's name in a designated area, know-how, equipment, materials, training, advice and national support advertising. This allows the business in question to grow rapidly in a number of locations without the investment capital which would be required to fund organic growth of the same magnitude. Another advantage for the franchiser is the alleviation of some of the need for the development of the managers, skills and capabilities required to control a large, growing and dispersed organization. Instead efforts can be concentrated on expanding market share. It is essential, though, to establish effective monitoring and control systems to ensure that franchisees are providing the necessary level of quality and service.

The small business franchisee needs sufficient capital to buy into the franchise, but the risk is less than most independent starts because the business is already established. As a result a number of small independent businesses operate as part of a chain and can compete against larger organizations.

Franchising would appear to offer valuable opportunities to Ajisen Ramen (Case 11.6).

Case 11.6

Ajisen Ramen (China)   Cn

Ajisen Ramen (China) Holdings Limited is based in Hong Kong and is one of the biggest fast food noodle restaurant chains in China, selling Japanese ramen noodle soup dishes. The 120 plus chain of outlets is mainly to be found in the Far East but also as far away as Australia and Canada and, in the US, in California and New York. Originating from Kumamoto in western Japan, Ajisen was a moderately successful family owned Ramen chain best known for its white broth, which is made by simmering different kinds of bones including fish bones for many hours. Ajisen (China) Holdings is the Hong Kong-based holder of the Japanese brand's Chinese franchise. In Japan the ramen industry as a whole has been facing declining demand, mainly due to the falling birth rate in Japan. For the business the growth market now is China.

Rapid growth

The first bowl of Ajisen Ramen noodle was sold in Shenzhen, China some 12 years ago in 1997. The Chinese diet at this time very much favoured a fast food noodle business, as opposed to what might be considered as Western fast food. The Japanese Ramen noodle is served in a wooden bowl and is much more refined than the Chinese 'la mian' equivalent and is considered by the Chinese customer to be a better quality, more fashionable and desirable taste – despite being more expensive. This made the Ramen noodle more attractive to younger white collar workers in China. The rapid growth enjoyed by Ajisen was based on the perception that the Ramen noodles were a healthier casual food, as opposed to a western style fast food. Ajisen (which means 'a thousand tastes' in Japanese) design their outlets with their own distinctive lantern style ambience based on the original Japanese restaurant look; this includes the 'byobu' screen which is illustrated with pictures and a good evening in Japanese from the Chinese waitresses as you enter the restaurant.

The business model behind the success of Ajisen Ramen was this casual food positioning allied to the creation of a chain of noodles outlets that were set-up based on unified purchase of raw materials and unified methods of production which has the aim of keeping the noodle taste consistent across the chain. In contrast the Chinese 'la mian' is varied in its taste, depending on what area the outlet is based and the type of noodle that is being used. The standardization of the products of the Ajisen Ramen noodle bar enabled each outlet to serve its customers very quickly. The standardization also gave Ajisen Ramen large cost advantages.

In 2006, Ajisen (China) had profits of $16.3 million compared to $6.6 million in 2005. Sales in 2007 were up by 33 per cent at $81.6 million. In March 2007 Ajisen (China) had a successful listing on the Hong Kong stock exchange that raised $210 million and saw the stock valued at $1.4 billion. Ajisen has now successfully built a brand in China on the back of being seen as representatives of high quality Japanese Ramen and Japanese fast food.

Ajisen Ramen (Holdings) Limited is now committed to rapid growth. 'The potential for the company is so great,' argues Alan Zheng, Ajisen's Shanghai-based Chief Financial Officer. 'A year ago (2006), the company had 120 restaurants in China, and by the end of this year it will be 200'. And the growth is set to continue. 'For the coming year, we feel confident that we will be better than 320', says Zheng. All of this is on the back of a major expansion in factory capacity in China, where a new $13.7 million noodle factory in Shanghai will be big enough to supply noodles for 500 restaurants.

Questions

What are the key features of the success of Ajisen Ramen in China?

Do you believe the urbanization and wealth development amongst the Chinese population will actually detract or encourage the growth of the noodle restaurant chain? What role can you see for franchising?

www.ajisen.com.hk

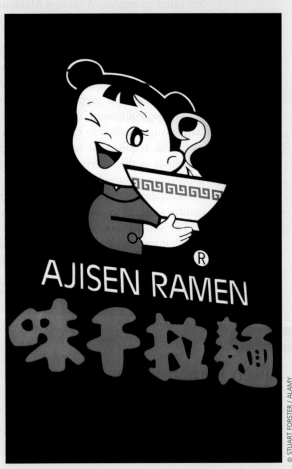

Licensing

Licensing is an arrangement whereby a company is allowed to manufacture a product or service which has been designed by someone else and is protected by a patent. Companies in different countries are often involved. Pilkington, for example, patented float glass and then licensed its production throughout the world. Pilkington earned money from the arrangements and established world leadership; they would not have been able to afford to establish production plants around the world. In contrast Mary Quant, designer of cosmetics, tights, footwear, beds and bed linen, never manufactured the products she designed. They were all licensed; and some were marketed under the Quant name and some under the manufacturer's name (Myers beds and Dorma bed linen, for example). Licensing also provides an ideal opportunity for the owners of valuable **intellectual capital** (such as Disney with their characters) to earn revenues from their knowledge-based resource without having to invest in manufacturing. One argument in favour of this arrangement has been that production and labour relations problems are avoided, enabling the business to concentrate on the areas in which it has expertise and competitive advantage.

11.8   The role of private equity funds

It has been suggested that private equity funds are the new conglomerates. They look to acquire struggling businesses (usually as a whole) or buy selected parts of existing businesses that the current owners are happy to divest, put in a new management team (often described as a management buy-in – which we discuss further in Chapter 13), turn them around and prepare them for flotation. Their logic is to borrow money at competitive rates and seek to earn a handsome return from the flotation in a relatively short period of time. There are a number of success stories that bear out the logic of this approach. The Debenhams Strategy activity below (Debenhams) provides a valuable example.

But private equity funders have been criticized and accused of 'job cutting and asset stripping'. Is this altogether fair, especially given the fact that many of the businesses they target are under-performing – which makes them a target in the first place? There is evidence that contradicts this view. Analysis reported by the *Financial Times* (see Arnold, 2009) looked at the largest businesses currently owned by private equity funds at the end of 2007 and tracked back to when they had been acquired. This analysis showed that they had actually created jobs and increased the investment in fixed assets. More significant, though, was the impressive increase in productivity and value added – well ahead of the UK average.

This particular strategy depends upon equity funds being able to access money for investment – when the credit crunch took hold in 2008 this, inevitably, became more difficult – and on being able to find under-performing businesses that it makes sense to buy because they have hidden growth prospects.

Summary

Periodically, organizations must make decisions about how focused and how diversified they wish to be. Horizontal integration, such as acquiring or merging with a competitor, will engender critical mass but may be restrained by the relevant competition authorities. Diversification can be into related or unrelated businesses, or vertically forwards or backwards in the supply chain.

Where a company does choose to diversify it is more likely to implement this strategy through acquisition (friendly purchase), merger (bringing together the assets of two businesses) or takeover (hostile purchase) than it is through organic growth.

Unrelated diversification is invariably high risk, but it may be justified or chosen for one of the following reasons:

- weakness of the present businesses
- existing businesses having strengths and competencies that could be exploited in other industries
- the ambitions of the strategic leader.

Research in both the UK and US consistently indicates that diversification through acquisition has only a 50 per cent likelihood of success, specifically delivering the hoped-for benefits. The typical reasons for failure are:

- the synergy potential is overestimated
- managerial problems and issues are underestimated
- key managers leave after the acquisition
- hidden weaknesses are not spotted until it is too late
- too much money is paid and the premium cannot be recovered.

The companies that succeed with this strategy tend to follow a number of simple rules:

- they carefully target their acquisitions
- they learn from previous experiences and become 'professional acquirers'
- they avoid paying too high a premium
- they adopt an appropriate post-acquisition structure and style and ensure that the businesses are integrated effectively
- corporately, they add value.

Strategic alliances and joint ventures (a stronger type of alliance where shares are exchanged or an independent company is set up) provide an alternative to an acquisition or merger. While they are designed to deliver synergy, cost savings and access to either technology or markets, they are not without their own implementation challenges.

It is generally acknowledged that the Japanese in particular have developed real capabilities in alliance management and that many Western companies have looked upon them from a more defensive perspective. For example, they are an alternative when an acquisition is not feasible for whatever reason.

There are three main reasons behind this strategy:

- to gain access to new markets and technologies
- to share expensive research and development costs
- to manage innovation more effectively.

Clearly these reasons overlap.

There are six particular, and again overlapping, forms of alliance and joint venture:

1 the merging of component parts of two or more businesses
2 companies joining forces to develop a new project
3 companies joining forces to develop a new business together
4 agreements between partners in the same supply chain
5 where companies purchase a stake in another business for strategic, rather than purely financial, reasons
6 international trading partnerships.

For alliances and joint ventures to work successfully, commitment from all parties is required. Everyone must appreciate that they can benefit and commit accordingly. Trust, sharing and collaboration become essential, even though different cultures and languages might be involved.

Franchising and licensing can sometimes provide valuable means of growing. The risks are different but the capital required is considerably less.

Private equity funding, described as the 'new conglomerate' can result in strategic renewal in the case of under-performing companies. New ways are often found to add value and engineer growth.

Online cases for this chapter

Online Case 11.1: British Airways
Online Case 11.2: **Asda–MFI.** This case was originally written to illustrate the three tests described in the section entitled 'The search for, and review of, possible acquisitions'?. The anticipated synergy was not achieved. Asda, of course, is now owned by Wal-Mart. MFI went into administration in December 2008 and all of its branches closed.

Questions and research assignments

1 From the various points and issues discussed in this chapter list the possible advantages and disadvantages of diversification and acquisition strategies, and from your experience list one successful and one unsuccessful example of this strategy. Why have you selected these particular cases?

2 What are the key arguments for and against strategies of unrelated diversification and focus? Again, from your own experience, list examples of each.

3 What exactly is the difference between a strategic alliance and a joint venture? Can you provide examples of each – in addition to those included in the text?

4 Do you agree with the view that, if they are established and managed carefully, strong alliances can provide all the benefits of an acquisition or merger without most of the drawbacks?

Internet and library projects

1 Obtain statistics on either a selection of large companies which interest you, or the largest 20 companies in the UK, and:

   a ascertain the extent to which they are diversified and classify them as either single, dominant, related or conglomerate product companies
   b determine their relative size in relation to their competitors in the US, Japan and Europe.

2 In 2003 Cadbury Schweppes became more diversified – albeit relatedly – when it acquired Adams Confectionery, a leading manufacturer of chewing gum. We saw in Case 10.7 that Mars had considered buying Adams – and that it eventually bought Wrigley instead. Was this a justifiable move by Cadbury Schweppes? Why? Why not? Has it turned out to be a successful strategy? Did it force the hand of Mars?

3 Take any well-known Japanese manufacturer, such as Toshiba or Sony, and determine how many alliances and joint ventures they have and what they are designed to contribute strategically.

4 Using actual examples as your base point, could the high-technology things we currently take for granted (such as mobile phones, personal computers and the Internet) have been developed to the stage they have if companies had worked in isolation? Has the co-operation approach been more sensible and realistic than a series of cross-border mergers?

5 Take any leading investment by private equity funders and explore the impact of the intervention. You might, for example, choose from Fitness First, Madame Tussauds, National Car Parks or Travelodge – depending on your personal interests.

Strategy activity

Debenhams

The hostile acquisition of Debenham's department stores by Burtons – which later changed its own name to Arcadia – took place in 1985. Debenhams was then owned by Burton for 12 years until 1997 before it was demerged as an independent company with a separate listing on the Stock Exchange. It was generally acknowledged that it had not been able to prosper as part of the larger group. At this time sales exceeded £1 billion from the 92 stores. The managing director in post at the time, Terry Green, stayed on until 2000, when he left to run BHS (British Home Stores).

Belinda Earl was then promoted to the top job. 38 years old, she had extensive experience in 'trading' but was less experienced in the property and financial aspects. Her strategy was focused on improving customer service and introducing a wider, more differentiated product range. The ranges would not be the same in every store; she wanted the individual units to be as flexible as possible and able to respond to regional taste variations. She also wanted to increase the number of stores to 150 – but gradually over a period of time. She also opted to join Barclaycard, BP and Sainsbury in the Nectar loyalty card scheme.

Prices were reduced in 2001 and 2002 to boost sales; and by 2002 turnover had risen to £1.7 billion. Pre-tax profits were £150 million. Many analysts believed Debenhams was being set up for sale.

In 2003 two prospective external buyers came on the scheme. Both were venture capitalists, anxious to buy a successful business. First to bid was Permira, once called Schroder Ventures. It offered 425 pence per share, valuing the business at £1.54 billion. Permira were experienced in these deals, having bought Homebase from Sainsburys before strengthening it for sale on to Great Universal Stores (GUS). In two years Permira had generated a cash return of six times its original investment. Belinda Earl and her Finance Director were given permission by the Debenham's Board to co-operate fully; and it was assumed that if Permira were successful, Earl would stay on as Managing Director and as a substantial shareholder.

The alternative bidder was CVC Capital Partners in association with Texas Pacific Group. They bid 455 pence per share, valuing the business at £1.65 billion. Some independent non-executive directors on the Debenhams Board backed them, but it was clear CVC would not be retaining Belinda Earl if they succeeded. CVC were successful and they installed a new management team. In charge was Rob Templeman, who was currently the Chairman of Halfords, which CVC had bought from Boots. He had also been in charge of Permira's turnaround of Homebase after its purchase from Sainsbury.

The business changed hands in December 2003. The CVC buy-in team had four main planks to its strategy: improve cash management; cut costs; increase top-line sales – the new target audience was to be young females interested in fashion – and better supply-chain management. Templeman commented that Debenhams 'is a good business with a good brand – but we think we can do it better'. Head office staffing levels were soon reduced and supply chain costs saved through inventory reductions of £50 million, coupled with an increased stock turn. The number of suppliers was reduced. Stores were remortgaged and bonds issued to replace expensive debt capital. Prices for some slow-moving items were slashed to clear stocks. By mid 2004 sales were running some 5.5 per cent ahead of 2003 levels; profits were up by round 14 per cent. Five new outlets were planned for 2005. New overseas suppliers were being targeted. It seemed only a matter of time before Debenhams followed Halfords and Homebase as a sale or flotation business in a relatively short space of time.

The IPO took place in 2006. When this was complete the business had generated well over £1 billion for the new investors. The company was being valued around £3 billion. Templeman stayed on as CEO after the flotation. CVC and Texas Pacific still held (smaller) stakes.

Some of the new Debenhams early success had coincided with problems at Marks & Spencer, but, and like John Lewis, this business started to improve its performance. Moreover key staff left Debenhams for other retailers. 2007 saw the share price fall and there was a series of profit warnings. Capital expenditure for new stores and refurbishments would have to be curtailed which would hit performance further. The question was – **could Templeman be as effective at building new value as he was at cost cutting and retrenchment?**

Christmas trading at the end of 2007 was also disappointing – although Debenhams was not alone in this – and in 2008 the share price continued to fall. At the beginning of the year Angela Spindler joined the business from Asda, where she had been in charge of the George clothing range. She had the title Managing Director and was being talked about as a future CEO. But she left before completing twelve months. Under Templeman the trading position of Debenhams continues to fluctuate.

When Principles, the fashion chain that was owned by collapsed Icelandic investor Baugur, went into administration in 2009 Debenhams took on the in-store concessions it already had. High Street Principles stores closed. Debenhams was able to acquire the name and any stock it wanted. Debenhams has also announced plans to open more stores. However, the shares have slumped due to worries over the debt pile.

In June 2009 CVC Capital Partners made its exit. Texas Pacific remained involved, reiterating its confidence in the business and its management team. That said, Debenhams' debt burden still stood at £925 million.

Question

1 Clearly when strategic leaders fail, their replacement by someone capable of turning around the business can be justified. But Belinda Earl was successful. In whose interests is a management buy-in along the lines described here?

Project

1 By either visiting a Debenham's store or using the Internet (or both) try and ascertain what benefits have accrued from this change of ownership and management. Can you see ways in which they might create new value for customers?

Further reading

Biggadike, R (1979) The risky business of diversification, *Harvard Business Review*, May–June.

Caulkin, S (1996) Focus is for wimps, *Management Today*, December.

Clarke, CJ and Brennan, K (1990) Building synergy in the diversified business, *Long Range Planning*, 23 (20).

Devlin, G and Bleackley, M (1988) Strategic alliances – guidelines for success, *Long Range Planning*, 21 (5).

Kanter, RM (1994) Collaborative advantage: the art of alliances, *Harvard Business Review*, July–August.

Markides, C (1997) To diversify or not to diversify, *Harvard Business Review*, November–December.

References

Arnold, M (2009) Brickbats and bouquets for private equity, *Financial Times*, 15 January.

Badaracco, JL (1991) *The Knowledge Link: How Firms Compete Through Strategic Alliances*, Harvard Business School Press.

Biggadike, R (1979) The risky business of diversification, *Harvard Business Review*, May–June.

Burgman, R (1985) Research findings quoted in McLean, RJ, How to make acquisitions work, *Chief Executive*, April.

Business International (1988) *Making Acquisitions Work: Lessons from Companies' Successes and Mistakes*, Report published by Business International, Geneva.

Campbell, A and Park, R (2005) *The Growth Gamble*, Nicholas Brealey.

Chiesa, V and Manzini, R (1997) Competence-based diversification, *Long Range Planning*, 2 June.

Connell, DC (1988) Strategic partnering and competitive advantage, Presented at the 8th Annual Strategic Management Society Conference, Amsterdam, October.

Constable, CJ (1986) Diversification as a factor in UK industrial strategy, *Long Range Planning*, 19 (1).

Cowling, K, Stoneman, P and Cubbin, J (eds) (1979) *Mergers and Economic Performance*, Cambridge University Press.

Devlin, G and Bleackley, M (1988) Strategic alliances – guidelines for success, *Long Range Planning*, 21 (5).

Drucker, PF (1982) Quoted in Drucker: The dangers of spoonfeeding, *Financial Times*, 15 October.

Ernst and Young (1995) Key success factors in acquisition management, Research project with Warwick Business School, Ernst and Young, London.

Garrette, B and Dussauge, P (1999) Strategic alliances – why Europe needs to catch up, *Financial Times Mastering Global Business*, No. 5.

Harding, D and Rovit, S (2004) Building Deals on Bedrock, *Harvard Business Review*, September.

Houlder, V (1997) Neglect of the new addition, *Financial Times*, 5 February.

Jenkinson, T and Mayer, C (1994) *Hostile Take-overs: Defence, Attack and Corporate Governance*, McGraw-Hill.

Kanter, RM (1990) *Synergies, Alliances and New Ventures*, Harvard Business School video package.

Kitching, J (1967) Why do mergers miscarry? *Harvard Business Review*, November–December.

Kitching, J (1973) *Acquisitions in Europe: Causes of Corporate Successes and Failures*, Report published by Business International, Geneva.

Lorenz, C (1986) Take-overs. At best an each way bet, *Financial Times*, 6 January.

Markides, C (1997) To diversify or not to diversify, *Harvard Business Review*, November–December.

McLean, RJ (1985) How to make acquisitions work, *Chief Executive*, April.

Meeks, J (1977) *Disappointing Marriage: A Study of the Gains from Merger*, Cambridge University Press.

Nesbitt, SL and King, RR (1989) Business diversification – has it taken a bad rap? *Mergers and Acquisitions*, November–December.

Ohmae, K (1989) The global logic of strategic alliances, *Harvard Business Review*, March–April.

Peters, TJ and Waterman, RH Jr (1982) *In Search of Excellence: Lessons from America's Best Run Companies*, Harper & Row.

Porter, ME (1987) From competitive advantage to corporate strategy, *Harvard Business Review*, May–June.

Ramsay, J (1987) The strategic focus: deciding your acquisition strategy, Paper presented at 'Growing Through Acquisition', Conference organized by Arthur Young, London, 31 March.

Reed, R and Luffman, G (1986) Diversification: the growing confusion, *Strategic Management Journal*, 7 (1).

Rumelt, RP (1974) *Strategy, Structure and Economic Performance*, Division of Research, Harvard Business School.

Salter, MS and Weinhold, WA (1982) *Merger Trends and Prospects for the 1980s*, Division of Research, Harvard Business School; quoted in Thackray, J (1982) The American takeover war, *Management Today*, September.

van de Vliet, A (1997) When mergers misfire, *Management Today*, June.

Walton, C and McBride, J (1998) Broken engagements, *Financial Times*, 26 February.

Chapter 12

International strategy

PART 1
Understanding strategy

1 Introducing strategy and strategic management

PART 5
Strategic management

14 Strategy implementation

15 Leading change

16 Managing strategy in the organization

17 Final thoughts – the purpose of strategy

STRATEGIC MANAGEMENT: AWARENESS AND CHANGE

PART 2
Strategic positioning

2 Strategic thinking, environmental analysis, synergy and strategic positioning

3 Resource-led strategy

4 The dynamics of competition

5 Introducing culture and values

PART 4
Issues in strategic growth

11 Strategic growth

12 International strategy

13 Failure, consolidation and recovery strategies

PART 3
Strategic analysis and choice

6 Strategic purpose

7 Strategic success

8 An introduction to strategy creation and planning

9 Strategic leadership, entrepreneurship and intrapreneurship

10 Strategic alternatives, strategy evaluation and strategy selection

Learning objectives

Having read to the end of this chapter you should be able to:

- show how the issues covered in Chapters 11 and 12 can be applied at an international level

- explain what is meant by a global strategy

- appreciate why internationalization is essential for many organizations

- discuss the important considerations in international strategies

- explain a simple stage model of international development

- evaluate the value and relevance of different market entry strategies in an international context

- appreciate how franchising has been behind the growth of a number of well-known international brands

- discuss a number of constraints and outline a selection of possible future influences on international growth.

We have discussed in Chapters 10 and 11 the various strategic alternatives that might be available to an organization in thinking and deciding where it wants to go, and for helping to close the planning gap. In this chapter we look at the issues in the international context. Options range from 'simply' exporting to a fully-fledged global strategy and structure. The attractiveness of particular alternatives will be affected by the objectives of the organization. Some companies will be proactive; others reactive. Not all organizations need to, or should, take advantage of every international opportunity which comes their way. The appropriate strategy always matches the environment, values and resources congruently.

> *In future we will have local [retail] companies and global companies and not much in-between. Globalization pressures will lead to those who are not in the first division and those who are purely national to make alliances.*

> DAVID BERNARD, CHAIRMAN, CARREFOUR HYPERMARKETS

Case 12.1

Tesco's International Strategy   UK

Tesco is the UK's leading supermarket chain and its largest private sector employer– and it is diversified into several non-food lines. It has also expanded overseas in a careful and systematic manner. By 2004 some 20 per cent of its revenue was earned outside the UK. This also represented 15 per cent of total pre-tax profits but from 50 per cent of the floor space. In 2005 Tesco's non-food sales overtook those of Marks & Spencer. In global terms, Tesco is the sixth largest retail group. The five larger supermarket groups are Wal-Mart (including Asda and which earns 21 per cent of its revenues outside America); Carrefour (48 per cent outside France); Ahold (84 per cent outside the Netherlands); Metro (47 per cent outside Germany); and Kroger (entirely US).

By early 2008 Tesco had 2115 stores in the UK, 814 in Asia, 747 in Europe and 53 in the US. Of its overseas expansions, South Korea, Thailand and the Irish Republic have shown the best returns.

Chronologically the Tesco story is as follows:

The first 'foray' overseas was the Republic of Ireland, when Tesco acquired an existing retail chain in 1978 – which it later divested in 1986. In 1993 the company acquired a French rival, Catteau, but never really consolidated the business and sold that in 1997.

Since then it has been more successful. In 1994 Tesco purchased a majority share in the Hungarian retailer, Global (41 supermarkets), and followed that with acquisitions in Poland (1995), the Czech Republic and Slovakia (1996). Prior to these moves, Tesco had employed a Hungarian to do ground research in Eastern Europe. Tesco is now the largest private employer in this part of the world as well. With the exception of Slovakia, it is the market leader, but it wasn't the first overseas grocer to enter the market. Although it has yet to make a move, it has Romania, Bulgaria and Russia 'in its sights'.

Tesco returned to Ireland (both Northern Ireland and the Republic) when it bought the retail interests of Associated British Foods in 1997.

The next ventures were largely in the Far East. An acquisition in Thailand (1998) was followed by a joint venture with Samsung in South Korea in 1999. Tesco opened its own business in Taiwan in 2000, entered into a joint venture with Sime Darby in Malaysia in 2002 and then acquired a chain in Japan in 2003. There has also been an acquisition in Turkey (2003) and a joint venture in the US with Safeway (2001). In 2004 Tesco entered China.

Japan is an unusual retail market in some respects, but it is the world's second largest. Luxury brands such as Louis Vuitton, Prado and Gucci do well, but from the UK both Boots and Prêt a Manger have entered and exited. Operating costs are high and consumers are fastidious. The message has to be right! But in addition it has to be realized that shopping by car is hardly ubiquitous – many people shop on their bikes. Consumers often buy food every day – and they happily visit several stores and shop around.

In 2003 Tesco bought a chain of 80 discount convenience stores in the Tokyo region – not its usual supermarkets-hypermarkets by any means. This approach had already been taken by Wal-Mart in Japan – but Carrefour was operating a limited number of successful hypermarkets. Tesco was able to export its Tesco Metro (small, localized) store format to some degree.

It was clear for a while that Tesco was 'looking to buy' a stake in a Chinese food retail chain, and it found a receptive business (25 hypermarkets) in 2004. Hymall is Taiwanese-owned and concentrated in East, North and North-East China. Ten new stores are in the offing. Tesco acquired a 50 per cent stake at a cost of £140 million. Again Wal-Mart and Carrefour are already there.

Generally, once it has entered a new market, Tesco has looked for opportunities to expand its operations there.

In 2005 it was reported that Tesco was 'looking at' US supermarket group, Albertson's, but none of the commentators seemed to think an acquisition would result – and it didn't. There were also rumours that Tesco would like to pull out of Taiwan, and it agreed a deal with Carrefour, whereby Tesco's Taiwanese stores were exchanged for Carrefour stores in Slovakia and the Czech Republic. In 2006 it was rumoured that Tesco might form a new local alliance to enter the Indian market, but nothing came of this. That year Tesco did acquire a larger holding in Hymall (China) and also introduced the Tesco brand in China.

In late 2007 Tesco entered the US market. This is a chain of neighbourhood convenience stores on the West Coast, predominantly Southern California. The ultimate target is said to be 1000 stores, but this seems a long way off. Tesco's 'Fresh & Easy' is a new retail concept for the company – and really the name says it all – with stores supported by a food processing and distribution centre. During 2008 Tesco had to deal with a series of press articles that claimed it was failing to hit its targets in America.

In 2008 Tesco bought just short of 40 new hypermarkets in South Korea, really consolidating its presence there. It was 'the largest acquisition in Tesco's history'. The company has also moved towards global sourcing, and has established sourcing centres in Hong Kong, India, Thailand and Central Europe. These currently source over 50 per cent of Tesco non-food products, excluding health and beauty products.

Since the mid 1990s Tesco has sent experienced UK managers overseas to work with locals to get the business model right. Whilst each country has a strong element of local taste in the product range and store ambience, they are Tesco stores. There is a common philosophy globally. *Every little helps.* From this stem price discounts and a high level of customer service.

The company appears to be following a classic 'think globally, act locally' strategy, by having a format which is internationally transferable, but which at the same time can be adapted locally. Thus, the stores in Central Europe and Asia tend to have more products on sale, with a higher proportion of non-food ranges. The whole operation is geared towards a single shopping trip. Tesco combines its retailing skills and high service standards to serve these markets, and at the same time acquires local knowledge which it uses to good effect. Tesco's chief executive, Terry Leahy, has stated that successful retailers will be those which can manage changes in domestic and foreign markets to emerge as global forces.

Questions

1 Why do you think that after its earlier disappointments Tesco has managed to develop a strong global strategy?
2 Would it make any sense for Tesco to want stores in countries where it sources products for sale in the UK?
3 Where do you think Tesco should seek to venture next? Should it expand where it is or disperse itself further?

12.1 Introduction

Internal growth, external growth and disinvestment strategies may all involve an international dimension with special complexities. Countries differ economically (variable growth rates), culturally (behaviours, tastes and preferences) and politically. National politics can dictate the appropriate strategy – some markets cannot be penetrated effectively without joint ventures with local companies.

Internal growth might involve exporting to new markets overseas and the development of special varieties of a product or service in order to target it to the specific needs and requirements of overseas customers. External growth can range from the creation of distribution or assembly bases abroad, to joint ventures and licensing agreements with foreign companies, to the establishment of a comprehensive global organization. The latter can be accomplished through both acquisition and strategic alliances. The opening case shows how Tesco's international strategy has emerged over a period of time.

Kay (1990) recommends that organizations should seek to determine the smallest area within which they can be a viable competitor. Whilst a retail newsagent can still succeed by concentrating on a local catchment area, most car manufacturers, in common with many other industries and service businesses, now see their relevant market as a global one. The term 'multinational' is generally applied to any company which produces and distributes in two or more countries; a transnational, global, corporation is one which has a large proportion of its sales, assets, and employees outside its home base. Using these criteria, Nestlé is the most global business in the world.

Porter (1990) believes **global strategies** essentially supplement the competitive advantage created in the home market. Wickham (2001) indicates that there are six main types of competitive advantage:

- A lower price than competitors
- Features or performance that differentiates the product offering
- Better service
- Branding
- Brand imagery
- Better distribution and easier access to the product.

For the advantage to be sustainable it is the view of Lynch (2000) that the success needs to be based on being the low cost producer in the industry and for this to lead to a higher level of profit.

Alternatively an organization can pursue a strategy of differentiation, with more reliable products, better levels of service. Finally the third generic strategy is that of focus where the business seeks to achieve a competitive advantage in specific target segments.

It is the view of Porter (1990) that firms must retain their national strengths when they cross over borders. Ohmae (1990) disagrees and argues that global firms should shake off their origins. Managers must take on an international perspective, avoiding the near-sightedness which often characterizes companies with centralized and powerful global headquarters. Markets, he says, are driven by the needs and desires of customers around the world, and managers must act as if they are equidistant from all these customers, wherever they might be located.

Ohmae is perhaps presenting a futuristic vision of how he believes things will be as global forces strengthen. At the moment, whilst world leaders like IBM, Sony and Nestlé are spread around the world and substantially dependent on non-domestic customers, their underlying cultures and competitiveness remain rooted in the US, Japan and Switzerland, respectively.

Chandler (1990) stresses the continuing importance of economies of scale (cost advantages with large scale production) and economies of scope (the use of common materials and processes to make a variety of different products profitably). This implies carefully targeted investment in large-scale operations and a search for international marketing opportunities.

The growth and internationalization strategies of Galanz and Haier are discussed in Case 12.2. as examples of the application of competitive advantage.

Case 12.2

Galanz and Haier   Cn

Galanz (China) is now one of the world's biggest home appliance manufacturers with in 2007 a total of 36,000 employees spread over three global manufacturing bases: microwaves, air conditioning and home appliances. In 2007 total sales revenues were 18 billion RMB and export sales volumes were $800m. In 2006 global sales of microwaves were a total of 20 billion units. Many of the products are produced for someone else and badged. For example Galanz supplies the French supermarket giant Carrefour with microwaves that have the Carrefour trademark on them.

Galanz has come a long way from when it was established in 1978 as a producer of feather products in a small town within Guangdong Province. Indeed it was only in 1993 that Galanz actually moved to become a producer of microwaves. To achieve this dramatic change Galanz has pursued a strategy of cost leadership in all areas of its business. An example of this attitude to cost leadership is as follows: 'Transformers are an important part of the microwave. One Japanese transformer costs more than 20 dollars. In Europe and in the US the transformer is more than 30 dollars each. We moved an advanced production line from the US to China by agreeing to supply the US company at a unit price of 8 dollars. Once their needs were met the line was ours. We adopted three shift working. Of the 6.5 working days we only spent one day on the needs of the US company. With our superior technology and lower labour costs, one tenth that of the US and Japan, we could supply the transformer at 5 dollars. Eventually the Japanese transformer production line was moved to China and Galanz supplied them at 5 dollars.' (Zhang Jinsong, European Sales Manager).

Galanz follows an internationalization strategy based on being the lowest cost producer and able to sell at the lowest price, coupled with advanced technology to ensure quality. Over time this has developed through attention to branding, product and after sales service – all connected to economies of scale. In 2000 microwave production was 12 million units. By 2006 it was 20 million units with 18 million units going for export. This was around eight times the level of sales of the nearest producer. The same tactic of aggressive pricing, allied to advanced technology (Galanz has an R&D facility in the US to develop proprietary technologies) and economies of scale are also the tactics used by Galanz in its air conditioning and domestic appliance sales both in China and in export markets.

Haier is the fourth largest white household appliance manufacturer in the world. In terms of employment its global workforce (in 2007) approached 50,000. It owns more than 200 subsidiary companies and has established design centres, manufacturing bases and trading companies in more than 30 countries. A crucial role in the development of Haier has been played by one man – Zhang Ruimin, who is the Chairman and CEO of the Haier Group. Born in 1949 he graduated from the Chinese University of Science and Technology and obtained an MBA in 1995. It was in 1984 that Zhang Ruimin took the job of Director of the Qingdao Refrigerator Factory. At that time the products were 'shoddy' and the workers poorly paid if at all. Zhang Ruimin was the fourth Director of the factory to be appointed that year and none of the others had been able to solve the problem. Nobody appeared to care about the quality of the product and this gave rise to a large number of defects. Customers did not trust Haier and in 1984 losses of 1.47 million RMB were incurred driving the business almost to bankruptcy. When a number of defective refrigerators were discovered Zhang Ruimin ordered the workers to destroy the defective products in public using sledgehammers. From now on, he stated, there would be no more defects.

From that particular day major changes in attitude and product development have taken place to the extent that in 2006, Haier Group developed a dual power washing machine without the need to use soap powder. The natural cleansing dual power washing machine features 32 technological patents, and exceeds international standards in saving water and electricity.

Under Zhang Ruimin the Haier Group has successfully implemented a brand strategy, a diversification strategy and an internationalization strategy and is moving on to what it sees as the fourth stage of development, that of a globalization strategy. In 2006 its overseas sales were $28 billion and in 2008 Haier was one of the major sponsors of the Olympic Games. The competitive strategy of Haier is based on product quality. Every employee is educated into the Haier culture of product quality where sub-standard products are not acceptable. The second strategy is that of constant product development. The next key strategy is the 24 hours strategy where support for Haier products is available 24 hours a day. In seeking to enter the European market, Haier first chose to enter the German market because it was the most difficult. Initially this was done with an alliance with Liebherr and from this Haier went on its own with the products meeting the German VDE Certificate.

Haier do not participate in price wars. Instead their strategy is based on their reputation for quality and after sales support. It is the view of Haier that the customer is willing to pay a higher price for a higher technology premium product with the built in quality. Additionally Haier does spend large sums of money on marketing. In overseas markets Haier directly uses the existing distribution and service networks of its foreign partners. This seems to work as Haier is now established in over 31 countries. Haier has also grown through what it terms is its 'stunned fish' strategy, taking over white goods companies who have good products, facilities and distribution channels but poor senior management. Haier regards research and development as very important. In 2007 just over 8 per cent of sales was spent on R&D, double the percentage of ten years before. In 2006 Haier applied for 819 patents of which 415 were classed as inventions.

Questions

1 Using the Wickham model of competitive advantage, compare and contrast the strategies of Galanz and Haier. What are the essential differences in their strategies?
2 What is your opinion of the nature of the strategies adopted by each?

http://www.galanz.com.cn
http://www.haier.com.cn

© LOU LINWEI/ALAMY

Definitions of internationalization

One problem with attempting a definition of internationalization is trying to find one on which everyone can agree. A brief review of the literature will reveal that such a definition does not exist. Instead there are almost as many definitions as there are contributions to the body of research knowledge on this topic. Following a study in 1988, the following useful definition was produced: 'Internationalization may be viewed as an approach to management which allows an organization to integrate domestic and international opportunities with internal resources' (Yanacek 1988).

Alternatively international business can be said to consist of transactions that are devised and carried across national borders to satisfy the objectives of individuals, companies and organizations. Primary types of international business are export-import trade and direct foreign investment. (Czinkota *et al.*, 2005).

Each new study on the topic tends to have a different perspective and so it is difficult to point to a simple coherence in the literature on the subject of internationalization. But then again, why should there be any simple solution to such a complex process?

The origin of much of the work on internationalization stems from studies in the 1960s on the nature of export behaviour, when the promotion of an 'international outlook' or 'internationalization' among managers was identified as a more successful route to increasing exports than any appeal to nationalistic motives. This work became formalized into models of export behaviour, mainly by a number of Swedish researchers including Johanson and Wiedersheim (1975). For them it was the interaction of these attitudes and actual behaviour which describe the internationalization process. These attitudinal and behavioural themes continued to be echoed in the literature by Joynt and Welch (1985). More importantly they also state that a crucial component of the whole internationalization process is the 'internationalization of people and their attitudes'.

One question that is often asked is why can't all the problems of selling across borders not be achieved through management contracts or licensing agreements? Why is it necessary for the firm to establish itself with a physical presence in another country? In essence we are missing the hugely important source of competitive advantage, namely the proprietary information possessed by the firm and its people. We need the physical presence to access this.

Another theme apparent in some of the definitions of internationalization is that it is a gradual process during which firms acquire, integrate and utilize their knowledge about foreign markets and operations. As this happens over time, the firms gradually increase their commitment to international markets. Some research work on this topic has suggested that internationalization evolves as firms gradually increase their commitment and exposure to risk. This is reflected in their market entry mode which may progress through (i) exporting, (ii) agency representation, (iii) overseas licensing, (iv) overseas sales subsidiary, and finally (v) the establishment of an overseas production subsidiary.

Apart from these recurrent themes there remains no one agreed definition. Part of the problem is that few studies use identical methodologies, and therefore cross-cultural or longitudinal studies are rare. Other criticisms of the work into internationalization have included its over-association with the exporting mode, lack of empirical evidence for the stages model (discussed in Section 12.3), discrepancies based on the unit of observation, and a neglect of service-based companies and of purchasing behaviour.

Motives for internationalization

The nature of internationalization is explained in Daniels, Radebaugh and Sullivan (2007) in that internalization is about control through the self-handling of operations internal to the organization. This concept comes from transaction cost theory, which holds that companies should seek the lower cost of handling something internally and contracting another party to handle it for them. In reality it might actually better to let another company handle things for you if they have a significant technology or cost advantage. (Case 12.2 Galanz and Haier relates where Galanz had such a cost advantage in the manufacture of microwave transformers that there is no point in either their US or Japanese counterparts trying to handle operations themselves.)

Generally speaking the first decision to go international is a specific one based on an actual opportunity rather than a decision to look around the globe for investment opportunities (Ghauri, 2000). At this stage the company has limited knowledge but will benefit from its early experiences in its subsequent investment decisions. What is needed is a strong push and/or commitment to go abroad. Ghauri sees the decision to go international as being strongly influenced by three organizational and three environmental factors:

Organizational	The ambitions of the management team
	The objectives and motives of the organization
	The company's success record in its home market
Environmental	Unsolicited proposals
	The bandwagon effect
	Strong overseas competition in the home market

Most of these factors are self-explanatory, but it may be worth noting that the unsolicited proposal can come from a foreign government, distributor or customer. The bandwagon effect can be created by competitors going international or a general belief that a presence in a certain market is somehow a must. Examples of the latter include investment in the former communist states of Eastern Europe post-1989 and the current fascination for China.

In this context, the crucial importance of spending significant amounts of time on relationship building and on being sensitive to the cultural differences in both business and personal relationships cannot be stressed too highly.

Market entry   Firms enter into the international arena, then, for a variety of reasons. No classification can be regarded as inclusive of all possible reasons; instead they act as a shorthand guide to be adapted to all sorts of situations. Likewise, all firms operate within a framework of constraints; not all opportunities can be responded to positively, and they need to be evaluated within the overall context of the businesses aims. Motives are also directly related to the mode of market entry adopted by a company.

There are a range of generally recognized export motives, but ways of classifying them vary and in some cases it is not always clear which category a particular motive belongs in. The traditional way in the literature is to regard export motives as push (internal) and pull (external) factors.

The main *push factors* are:

- Excess capacity
- Having a unique product
- Having a company-specific advantage
- Having a marketing advantage
- Being driven by the ambitions of the strategic leader.

And the main *pull factors* are:

- Receiving an unsolicited order
- A saturated domestic market
- Competitive pressures
- Attractive export development or incentive programmes.

Some find this a difficult classification to endorse, since the difference between a pull and a push can be difficult to judge. For example, a saturated home market could really be seen as both a pull and a push factor. Perhaps greater clarity is offered by the use of the terms proactive and reactive, which can be cross-tabulated against internal and external – see Table 12.1.

Proactive internationalization is then seen as being in line with the ambitions of the strategic leader (the owner–manager in a small organization) and it follows a strong market development in the domestic market that provides finance for international activities. Alternatively the company may internationalize rapidly because of a strong product concept, brand or service. Internationalization in this context is deliberate and planned, reflecting the owner's commitment to the process and the associated risks. Quite often proactive internationalization can be the result of a conscious policy of recruiting people, often younger graduates, who have a positive attitude to international business and to 'dealing with foreigners'.

Reactive internationalization tends to be based, at least initially, on an extension of domestic marketing practice with very little adaptation to local customer needs. The whole internationalization process tends to be more gradual and it emerges in an ad hoc and incremental way. This is often based on a chance order from abroad which the company follows up without any grand design. Market spreading tends to be more common than concentration as opportunities are followed without, at least initially, any strategic plan in mind.

Three examples from the north of Scotland are given below:

Market factors (push) Harris Tweed has been a traditional product unique to Scotland and especially to the island community of Levis and Harris. During the period 1987–2000, sales of Harris Tweed in North America and Europe fell away as it appeared unfashionable. However, promotion and sponsorship amongst textile students has increased the awareness of Harris Tweed amongst a new generation of fashion designers. The product has always been perceived as a high quality cloth, very classic and long lasting but needs to have more focus spent on its potential to be

Table 12.1	A classification of international involvement motives	
	Internal	**External**
Proactive	• driven by owner–manager/key decision-makers • desire to increase profits • to increase market share/market power • having a unique product/service/brand • extend life cycle or seasonality • new product/service development • having a company-specific advantage, e.g. in marketing, technology • to serve customers better by being closer to where they are	• perceived international market opportunities, e.g. removal of trade barriers • export development activity by governments, trade associations, banks • improvements in IT, physical infrastructure e.g. transport links
Reactive	• excess production capacity • spreading costs and risk	• unsolicited order • small domestic market • declining domestic market • saturated domestic market • peer competitive pressure • service existing customers who have gone international

soft and light for modern high fashion garments. This requires an internationalization strategy with the Harris Tweed Association attending major fashion and textile shows in North America such as the New York Textile Show and the Magic Show in Las Vegas funded in part by Highlands and Enterprise. The Harris Tweed industry is extremely important to the economy of the Western Isles directly employing the equivalent of 190 full-time jobs. Over £6m of cloth is exported each year making textiles the sixth most important value generator for the Western Isles economy. The lesson here for a classic almost timeless product is the need to promote the product in such a way as to both take advantage of it being a unique product and the marketing advantage that comes with this needs to be connected to shaping and supporting perception of the product amongst key industry players. These players need to be identified and a focused marketing strategy followed.

Proactive internationalization   A weaving company was founded in the far north of Scotland in 1991 and is involved in the production of fashion accessories. The key influence here on their exporting activity was that a previous company had existed from 1986–1990. Crucially, the international networks developed by the designer associated with the original company were maintained by the new company as a part of their business strategy. This planned use of networks paved the way for the international success and the company now has agents in France, Italy, Japan and the US. Indeed the company's entire turnover has traditionally come from export markets. It is only since 1995 that the domestic market has been given serious marketing consideration.

Reactive internationalization   A second company, founded in 1995, is located north of Inverness and is involved with jewellery design and making. The entry to the export market occurred when the owner attended a trade fair in London. The entrepreneur was approached by a Japanese buyer for a small gallery in Yokohama City. The buyer 'liked the design, then the price'. The gallery has since reordered and the company is seeking to extend its business in Japan. Clearly in this case attending the trade fair was a crucial catalyst for starting exporting, but, from the entrepreneur's point of view, it was an unplanned development.

Case 12.3 explores the drive and motivation behind Bata Shoes' expansion around the world.

Case 12.3

Bata Shoes   Eur

Although not a familiar name in the UK, Bata is one of the world's leading footwear retailers. The company remains family owned and with headquarters in Lausanne, Switzerland. It manufactures and retails all round the world – there is production in 25 different countries and retailing in 50. Approximately one million customers buy Bata shoes every day, and in its life the company has sold 14 billion pairs. The company seeks to stay ahead by innovation in both products and processes. Its shoes are designed for comfort as well as fashion and design. This market position has been brought about because Bata has been able to deal with a variety of environmental shocks.

The company was founded in 1894 in Zlin, which today is in the Czech Republic but then was classified as the Austro-Hungarian Empire. Thomas Bata was a descendant of a family of cobblers who had been shoemakers for centuries. Real growth started during World War I when the company received orders for military boots, which allowed it to move from a small family concern to mass production. Bata has been described as the 'Henry Ford' of Eastern Europe. He was always concerned about his employees and built houses and recreation facilities for them. When Thomas died in a plane crash in 1932 there were 16,500 employees.

His half-brother, Jan, took over the business and he set about expanding throughout Europe – previously the company had been concentrated in the East – and adding new products such as toys and tyres. After ten years of Jan's leadership there would be over 100,000 employees and various overseas subsidiaries.

But Germany occupied Czechoslovakia in 1939 and Jan Bata was forced to leave the country. He was a recognized supporter of the Czech in exile. The Czech factories were handed over to a distant family member and Thomas' grandson, another Thomas, was left controlling all the overseas subsidiaries from a new base in Toronto, Canada. It is reported that during World War II Jan Bata helped many Czech and Slovak Jews to escape the Nazi occupation, finding them work in the various factories.

When the war was finished there were ownership disputes over the Czech factories and eventually they were nationalized in 1945. Jan Bata was put on trial (in absentia) by the new Communist government and convicted; it was clear he would be unable to return. His conviction would eventually be quashed in 2007. Quite soon the family name disappeared from the business in Czechoslovakia, which was renamed Svit.

But the business, known worldwide as Bata Shoe Company, has continued to expand. Private label ranges were added to the basic name in the 1970s: Bubblegummers, Power, North Star and Marie Claire. In the 1980s the retail formats were changed to reflect current trends; there were now city stores, large format stores and speciality sports stores. As was happening with many shoe manufacturers, production in developed countries largely ceased during the 1990s. After the fall of the communists in Czechoslovakia in 1989, named the so-called 'Velvet Revolutions', Thomas Bata, the new CEO, was invited to invest in the ailing Svit business, but it could not be returned to its original ownership. Instead he bought a number of stores and also established partnership agreements with businesses in Russia, Poland, Croatia and Slovenia. The original Czech company was simply unable to compete in a new, free market and it went bankrupt in 2000. There is, however, a shoe museum in Zlin and the Bata family still have a small shoe trading business. The actual business may have gone full circle but the company name is revered in the Czech Republic for what it has achieved.

Questions

1 How well do you think Bata dealt with the challenges and threats it faced?
2 Do you think the enforced trigger caused the development of an international strategy that otherwise might not have happened?

12.2 International strategies

Developing new markets for existing products and diversification are the options most likely to be associated with international business. Diversification is the highest risk strategy since it takes the company furthest away from its core expertise in production and domestic distribution.

For some growth companies, being global is the 'holy grail' and it is a central part of the business strategy from the formation of the company. Going global may seem ambitious but it is also a viable strategy, if it is well managed by the leadership team. This is akin to portfolio management and involves the simultaneous entry in to a number of different markets geographically. Clearly the option is most viable for companies (or entrepreneurs) that have technology- or knowledge-based products that are transferable across international boundaries.

Globalization is a business philosophy that is based on the belief that the world is becoming more homogeneous and that distinctions between national markets are not only fading but, for some products, will eventually disappear. Only the brands will survive in any scale. It is argued that companies need to globalize and standardize their international strategy by formulating it across country markets in order to take advantage of underlying market, cost, environmental and competition factors.

'Companies such as Coca-Cola and Levi Strauss have based their global marketing effort over the past decades on the premise that universal appeal exists. Coke's *'one sight, one sound, one sell'* was a legend among global marketers. But the world is continually changing, and with it the need to revise global marketing strategies. If cultural and competitive differences are less important than similarities, a single advertising approach can exploit the similarities to stimulate sales everywhere. This can be done at far lower cost than if campaigns were developed for each market.

Organizations which develop their corporate strategy internationally have to consider in particular:

- marketing and financial strategies
- the structure of the organization – including location issues
- cultural and people issues.

Before discussing these factors individually, Figure 12.1 endeavours to link them together and implicitly reinforce the notion of E–V–R (environment–values–resources) congruence. The situational factors have to be right for an international strategy to make sense. Specifically, the returns must exceed the investment. We can see this illustrated in Figure 12.2.

Gupta and Govindarajan (1998) argue that the potential pay-off can be assessed by addressing a number of obvious questions:

- Which product lines are (most) suitable for internationalization?
- Which markets should be targeted – and in what order of priority?
- What are the most appropriate ways of entering these target markets?
- How rapidly does it make sense to expand? Does a fast-track approach (such as Glaxo licensing Zantac for production in various countries simultaneously) make more sense than a slower approach (IKEA deliberately restricting the number of new branch openings every year to retain tight control)?

Figure 12.1   International strategy

> **Figure 12.2** The attractiveness of the international opportunity

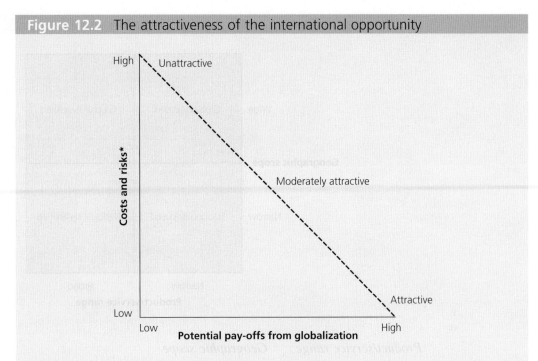

*The costs and risks relate to entry barriers, local regulations (e.g. the need for a local partner) and the extent of investment required to make products/services suitable for individual markets

Marketing

The issue of how global products and services can be made, and the extent to which they have to be tailored to appeal to different markets, is critical. Markets vary from those termed multi-domestic (where the competitive dynamics of each separate country market are distinctive and idiosyncratic) to global (where competitive strategies are transferable across frontiers). Coca-Cola, Levi jeans and the expensive perfumes and leather goods marketed by Louis Vuitton Moët Hennessy (LVMH), do attract a global consumer with identical tastes, but they are more exceptional than normal. The challenge to design the 'world car', for example, remains unresolved. Honda initially hoped to achieve this when it began redesigning its Accord range in the mid-1980s, but concluded that international performance expectations, and in turn components, are irreconcilable. In Japan the Accord is seen as a status symbol car for congested roads where driving is restricted; in the US it is a workaday vehicle for travelling long distances on open highways. Standardizing platforms and hidden components for different models and countries has provided a suitable compromise.

Clearly different competitors in the same industry adopt a variety of competitive strategies. Some owners of premium and speciality beer and lager brands elect to control the brewing of their product and rely on local, individual country brewers for distribution; others license the actual brewing to these national companies. Grolsch, recognizable by its distinctive bottles with metal frame tops, is brewed and bottled in Holland and exported. Most UK premium beers which succeed in the US are similarly exported to that country. Guinness is brewed in Dublin and exported for bottling in the US, whilst Fosters and Budweiser are both brewed under licence in the UK.

There is a follow-up issue concerning the appropriate range of products or services. The following framework (illustrated as a 2 × 2 four quadrant matrix in Figure 12.3) could be a useful starting point for analyzing both opportunities and competitor strategies:

Figure 12.3   Competitor analysis in a global context

Product/service range   *Geographic scope*

1 Narrow   National

2 Broad   National

3 Narrow   Global

4 Broad   Global

Where organizations find it necessary to be located close to customers in order to provide the delivery and other services demanded, this can be achieved with strategic stockholding rather than manufacturing.

Globalization differs from a multilevel domestic approach in three basic ways:

1 The global approach looks for similarities between markets. The multilevel domestic approach ignores similarities.

2 The global approach actively seeks homogeneity in products, image, marketing, and advertising message. The multilevel domestic approach results in unnecessary differences from market to market.

3 The global approach asks: *'is this product or process suitable for world consumption?'* The multilevel domestic approach, relying solely on local autonomy, never asks the question.

In a multilevel domestic strategy, marketing is typically the most localized of the business functions. Even within marketing, however, differences exist in marketing mix elements and between companies. Elements that are strategic – such as positioning – are more easily globalized, while tactical elements – such as sales promotions – are typically determined locally. Interestingly, adaptation is present even at Coca-Cola, which is acknowledged to be one of the world's most global marketers. The key is the worldwide use of ideas and methods rather than absolute standardization.

Globalization, by contrast, means the centralization of decision-making – something that is invariably beyond the resource or management capability of a small fast growth company.

Adaptability – or localization – invariably takes place influenced by three factors:

● The markets targeted and their level of sophistication

- The product and its ability to transfer across boundaries, to include issues of conformity and supply-chain management
- Company culture including factors such as resources and experience in overseas markets.

On this basis it is possible to be a global company, providing that a company has the vision and means to adapt products or services to suit local circumstances. This means that the process of being a global company involves an infinite number of alterations to the marketing mix.

The characteristics of a global business are summarized in Table 12.2.

Finance

The management of currency transfers and exchange rates adds complexity. Floating exchange rates imply uncertainty, although companies can, and do, reduce their risk by buying ahead. The European Exchange Rate Mechanism (superseded by the single European currency, the Euro) was originally designed to minimize currency fluctuations, but economic pressures still cause periodic devaluations. For example the Euro can still fluctuate widely against the pound sterling to such a degree as to make many transactions in Euros very expensive and vice versa. Predictable or fixed rates benefit, for example, a car manufacturer which produces engines and transmission systems in one country, transfers them to assembly plants in a second and third country, each specializing in different cars, and then finally sells them throughout Europe. Costs and estimated profits must be based on predicted currency movements, and any incorrect forecasting could result in either extra or lost profits.

Where such an organization structure is created, transfer pricing arrangements are required. If managers of the various divisions or business units are motivated or measured by their profitability figures there will be some disagreement about the **transfer price** which affects

Table 12.2 Characteristics of a global business

Criteria	Measurement
Mission	Clear mission statement signalling that the company has significant international ambitions
Objectives	Quantifiable objectives showing ambition to operate or market on two or more continents
Size	>£5m turnover
	Minimum 30 per cent turnover from overseas
International markets	Sales: minimum two continents
Overseas operations	On a minimum of two continents:
	Employment or assembly or manufacture or distribution channels
HQ	CEO based in and board meetings held in founding country. Overall operational control there
Strategic independence	Strategic decision-making in 'home' country
Growth	Five year turnover growth
Influence on markets	Global market share. Global brands
Integration of operations	Operational control
	or
	Brand management on at least two continents
International recruitment	Significant numbers of non-home nationals at senior managerial level
International sourcing	Company seeks inputs worldwide

their value added figures. Equally the organization may be seeking to manage transfer arrangements for tax purposes, seeking to show most profit where taxes are lowest.

Companies with a main base in a country whose currency is strong and appreciating may find their international competitiveness weakened. Exported products will become relatively expensive, competing imports cheaper. Such companies may be tempted to invest and relocate elsewhere. In 1995, for example, Toyota, which already had a number of manufacturing plants around the world, began to seriously consider closing down plants in Japan because of the high yen. Given the nature of the global currency fluctuations it may actually be the case that it does not matter where the car is built, what matters is the product strategy and management of the business. Cars are essentially just made of assembled parts that can come from anywhere. It is the nature of the car, its type and design, its cost and the quality of parts, that determine the success of the product.

In two cases in Chapters 11, in particular Case 11.5, we saw the extent to which the US indigenous automakers have major problems in 2009. Demand has been slashed due to the sub-prime induced credit crunch with US automakers unable to compete with their overseas rivals who are also based in the US. The problem for US automakers is the failure to react to changes in what consumers want to buy and the failure of management to change the costs structures of the business to reflect global market conditions. The basic problem is that a Japanese car maker located in the US can produce an equivalent car to a US automaker for significantly less. This is due to the high level of pension and other benefits paid to US autoworkers in GM, Ford and Chrysler and to the failure of the US owned businesses to produce a profitable mid-range and small car.

Structure

The two key questions are:

1 Where to make the various products and services to obtain the necessary people and other resources required, to be as close as appropriate to each defined geographic market and to manage costs efficiently; and

2 How best to structure the organization in order to control it effectively but, at the same time, ensure it is sufficiently responsive to changing environments. The speed and nature of change pressures may be uneven. IT increasingly offers opportunities for more effective control of globally dispersed businesses.

One obvious way for a firm to expand is by offering its existing products in foreign markets. This can be done by exporting from its domestic production base, and employing the services of agents and distributors to handle its products in export markets. Alternatively, and implying greater commitment, the firm may decide to relocate production itself by establishing manufacturing plants in selected overseas markets.

The company may decide to become vertically integrated on a global basis, sourcing some of its raw material requirements and intermediate products from overseas subsidiaries or suppliers, and establishing overseas sales subsidiaries in order to put its international marketing operations on a more dedicated footing. Likewise, the company may choose to diversify its business by acquiring suitable foreign companies. These multichannel strategies are consistent with becoming a global entity.

The structural alternatives available are:

- A globally centralized organization, remote from markets, and relying on exporting. This is likely to prove cost-efficient but possibly out of touch.

- Manufacturing plants located close to markets in order to satisfy local needs and preferences. This structure, known as both international and multi-domestic, could still be controlled centrally, or substantially decentralized into fully autonomous units, in which case the plants may be independent or co-operate in some way. This is a more expensive structure, but one which can offer higher levels of service. Unilever, which relies on localized manufacturing and marketing, is an example. Whilst cement is an international commodity product, companies are structured in this way because there is no benefit to be gained from transporting cement across frontiers.

- Centralized manufacture of key components, possibly in a low-wage country, with final assembly or finishing nearer to markets. Caterpillar Tractors have utilized this strategy.

- An integrated global structure with production locations chosen on resource or cost grounds. Finished goods will be transported to markets. In this structure the organization will have an international presence, but in say Country X its sales could consist mainly of products imported from other locations, whilst most of Country X's production is exported. Marketing, production *control*, purchasing and research and development will all be co-ordinated globally if they are not centralized.

Centres of excellence may be established where cultural values and behaviours are most appropriate. Philips chose to concentrate technology development in the Far East, where a long-term perspective is natural; IBM have established R&D facilities in Italy, which they regard as suitably intuitive and innovative. Lenovo of China when they bought the PC business from IBM, moved the HQ of the new business to New York. However, if national preferences and requirements are markedly different, there is an argument in favour of establishing dedicated R&D facilities in several countries. ICI opened a technical centre in Japan for developing special chemicals and materials in collaboration with the major car and electronics manufacturers. The intention was to sell their products to Japanese plants throughout the world. 'Japanese companies prefer to collaborate with chemicals suppliers which have scientists and engineers in Japan, and a factory to produce material locally.' General Motors strengthened its Opel technical development centre in Frankfurt to spearhead its expansion in all international markets outside the US. Eastern Europe and the Pacific Rim are targets for growth in respect of both production and sales. Meanwhile Ford has sought to integrate product development globally in its search for a range of world cars.

- A global network via strategic alliances.

This alternative has many strategic advantages, but it can be complex to control and costly in overheads. Typical companies are Sony and Coca-Cola. Coca-Cola, based in Atlanta, commands 50 per cent of the world's soft drinks market and 44 per cent of the US domestic market. The key success factor is obtaining distribution and access to markets, and because Coca-Cola is mostly water this is decentralized. Branding and marketing is global and centralized. The strategy is to sell concentrate or syrup to local bottlers, be they independent businesses or joint venture partners. Pricing is based on what can be afforded locally, and a variety of support mechanisms are offered. Coke is frequently promoted with local endorsements, but marketing and advertising also features sponsorship of international sporting events.

International location

The international location decision is affected by a number of key issues, including:

- The existence of any national resources which influence competitive advantage in any significant way. Nike and Reebok have built factories in China, Thailand and the Philippines for labour cost savings. Even small businesses are turning to the use of overseas factories to produce goods at a low price for them but retaining home based R&D and sales and marketing. A number of leading computer and semiconductor businesses are located in California's Silicon Valley because of the pool of skilled labour and acquired expertise to support research and development. Consumer electronics and pharmaceuticals are further examples of industries where the headquarters of the leading companies are concentrated in one or a few countries. Case 12.4 shows how Infosys chose to locate where specialist people resources were available and affordable.

Case 12.4

Infosys

Infosys is a software business based in India, but which targets markets around the globe. It was set up with this strategy in mind.

Infosys was started in 1981 with 10,000 (Indian) rupees, equivalent to some US$1200; it is now one of India's most dynamic wealth generators. The company was floated in 1993; within six years, and after growing by some 50 per cent per year, the share value had increased 85 times. Infosys has become the fifteenth largest company quoted on the New York NASDAQ and the first Indian business to be listed there.

Founder Narayana Murthy, who was around 35 at the time, left an American computing business, together with six Indian colleagues, and they started Infosys in Murthy's home in Poona, near Mumbai. Infosys would write software for established businesses in the G7 countries, and also provide systems integration and consultancy services. Murthy was the son of a teacher, and, although he had been working abroad extensively, particularly in Paris, he was to be the only one of the seven to stay based in India. The others would work in America, close to their key clients. The business would be global from 'day one' there was no local market of any consequence for what they were doing. Their first major client was Reebok.

'The market for the idea did not exist in India…we had to embrace globalization. I believe globalization is about sourcing capital from where it is cheapest, producing where it is most cost-effective and selling where it is most profitable, all without being constrained by national boundaries' (Murthy).

India was able to offer well-educated, English-speaking staff who were proficient in IT. They had a strong work ethic and the prevailing salaries were well below those of their client countries. America has generally provided two-thirds of the company's revenues. Infosys was able to offer very competitive prices for high quality work. But things were not altogether smooth. 'It took one year for a specialist telephone connection, two years to get a licence to import a computer and two weeks every time we needed foreign currency to travel abroad.'

In 1987 Infosys began a joint venture with a management consultancy based in Atlanta. The US staff would seek out business; Infosys would provide the skilled personnel to deliver the product. This gave Infosys market credibility and opened up a host of fresh opportunities. New clients included Nestlé, General Electric and Holiday Inn.

The joint venture was abandoned in 1995 when Infosys felt it was sufficiently established and well-known to open its own offices in the US. In 1991, back in India, Infosys had moved from Poona to a new 55-acre complex in Bangalore, home of India's burgeoning software industry. There was now to be a focus on a broader product range with an extended set of staff skills and competencies; this would involve selective acquisitions. The company was restructured around strategic business units. The emphasis would be on service and customer focus. Additional business from existing clients was sought energetically – it amounted to 80 per cent of revenues – as well as the active search for new clients.

There are a number of reasons why Infosys has been as successful as it has:

- World-class operations and high quality products and service
- A recognition that in software human resources are the core resources and they must be nurtured. Systems and conditions were created which would attract and retain the best. Good young talent was sought and, unusual for India, Western-style stock options offered
- Expertise in project management
- A clear structure (in Bangalore) that was dedicated to servicing overseas clients. However, as relative salaries in India have risen (albeit still well below those of the US and UK!) Infosys has started to set up overseas supply operations. It now employs software writers at its operation in Shanghai, China, for example.

- Ensuring that whilst large clients are sought, Infosys avoids dependency on any single client. At one time GE provided 25 per cent of revenues; this has been reduced to 10 per cent over time as the company has grown.

Infosys has not been without its critics in India. Its 'social perspective' on working conditions and rewards has not endeared it to everyone. Murthy has proclaimed that 'all profitable exporters should give 20 per cent of their earnings before interest and tax to help fund higher education in India', which has detractors as well as supporters.

As for Murthy himself, he has stepped down from the Chief Executive position he held for over twenty years but he remains as Chairman. In 2003 he became the company's 'Chief Mentor' responsible for helping to 'create future leaders' within Infosys.

Questions

1 What factors might threaten the type of global strategy practised by Infosys?
2 What do you think are the most realistic growth options available to Infosys?

Footnotes

In 2008 the global credit crunch and recession hit India's outsourcing industry quite markedly. Infosys slashed its earnings targets by 30 per cent. The main problem: the demise of the US financial sector. Also in 2008 Infosys looked at acquiring Axon, a UK-based specialist in business software. It backed away, saying it was 'no longer prudent' at the existing valuation.

© LYNSEY ADDARIO/CORBIS

Whatever the structural format, a truly international business must develop a global mission and core values (such as consistent quality worldwide), and achieve integration through effective communications. The corporate strategy must be centralized even if the company has a number of independent subsidiaries and operates in several multi-domestic markets. However, the organization must be able to embrace the different national cultural traits and behaviours, and this presents an important managerial challenge. Decisions have to be made concerning the balance of local managers and mobile 'international' managers who are easily transferable between divisions and countries.

Bartlett and Ghoshal (1989) summarized the above points as three potentially conflicting issues which must be reconciled. These are:

- the need for efficiency through global centralization
- the need to respond locally through decentralization
- the need to innovate and transfer learning internationally.

Bartlett and Ghoshal (1992) have also concluded:

- There can be no such thing as a 'universal international manager'. Large global companies will need functional specialists (such as production experts) and national managers (committed to one country and most familiar with that culture) as well as those executives who are able to switch readily between divisions and countries. International managers are responsible for corporate and competitive strategies within the organization, whilst national managers ensure that the needs of local customers, host governments and employees are satisfied effectively. The organizational challenge in respect of functional managers is to ensure that best practices are learned and spread throughout the organization.

● The attempts to integrate all the global operations (products, plants and countries) should be concentrated towards the top of the organizational hierarchy. At lower levels managers should have clear, single-line, responsibilities and reporting relationships.

● One benefit of adopting these recommendations is a limited requirement for international managers, who, inevitably, are in short supply because of the qualities they are required to have. Some industrialists would argue that this supply constraint is the deciding force, and that a successful global matrix structure would be preferable. One such structure is described in a later case on ABB (Asea Brown Boveri). ABB's managers were encouraged to 'think globally but act locally'. Their key measure was profitability and this can be enhanced if managers respond effectively to local employee and customer needs, seeking to satisfy different aspirations and requirements, whilst thinking globally about, say, sourcing and supply flexibility to take advantage of price and currency opportunities.

Culture

It is important to consider cultural issues in the process of globalization from two points of view – a national perspective as well as a policy perspective. The outcome is strategies that allow entrepreneurial companies to think globally and still deliver products and services that are locally suited. One of the key contributions to the understanding of culture and its influence comes from Hofstede (1991) who states that differences, and specifically cultural differences, reveal themselves in various ways through values, rituals, heroes and symbols. Expanding issues we raised in Chapters 5, Hofstede developed five dimensions to describe the culture of 58 countries. These are:

1 *Masculinity* – specifically values associated with earnings, advancement and assertiveness – *versus femininity* – values associated with a friendly atmosphere, nurturing and relationship building.

2 *Individualism* – a concern for oneself – *versus collectivism* – a concern for the priorities of the group or team to which one belongs

3 *Uncertainty avoidance* – preferring formal rules and not tolerating ambiguity

4 *Power distance* – the extent to which hierarchy is a fact of life

5 *Long-term versus short-term orientation.*

In terms of masculinity, for example, it was found that within Europe Austria, Italy, Switzerland, the UK, Ireland and West Germany (as it was at the time) had the highest scores, while feminine cultures where found in Scandinavia, Holland and the former Yugoslavia. Better off nations were found to be more individualistic and the poorer ones more collective orientated. Uncertainty avoidance is higher in the Latin European and Mediterranean countries than in the English speaking countries. Latin countries also score highly on the power distance dimension while most of the countries studied scored highly on the short time dimension.

Separately, colleagues teaching international MBA students have commented that western European students are more comfortable with group working than many people from the former communist Eastern European countries.

Wherever this type of analysis is used, cultural differences must influence the market entry strategies of firms. McAuley (2001) notes that:

the European retailers prefer to enter geographically close countries first and often, but not always, these were culturally close. It was also found that standardized retail formats are first exported to culturally close countries (Ikea). In addition those countries (France, Germany and Belgium) with a high degree of uncertainty avoidance apply entry modes giving them a high degree of control. The same was true for power distance in the case of the examples from France and Germany.

This approach, though, creates a dilemma for firms seeking rapid internationalization – is it better to opt for an efficient distribution network and tackle countries that are closer or better to account for cultural similarities? Whilst it is not possible to be predictive about cultural differences, it can be suggested that geographic proximity and logistics can be overridden by cultural empathy – an understanding of a particular market or a feeling of national closeness.

Case 12.5 touches upon the cultural differences between the so-called 'old world' and the new world wine producers.

Case 12.5

Constellation Wines   US, Aus

This case describes consolidation amongst New World wine producers.

Constellation Wines came about when two of the 'New World's' leading wine producers merged in March 2003. The Constellation Group of California effectively acquired Australia's BRL Hardy Group (which already had interests in New Zealand as well) to create the world's largest producer. Constellation's leading brands include Hardy's, Ravenswood, Nobilo and Banrock Station. However it chose Adelaide for its headquarters. The new CEO was Stephen Millar, an accountant recruited from General Motors. His credo is that 'business culture is the one competitive advantage any business has. Brands and vineyards can be bought and sold.'

Constellation's market position was then as follows:

Australia	1st	24 per cent share
US	2nd	20 per cent share
New Zealand	2nd	14 per cent share
UK	1st	10 per cent share

The BRL Hardy acquisition was followed by the acquisition of Robert Mondavi, a competing and well-respected Californian operation.

The second largest producer was Gallo, another Californian business – reflecting the growing popularity of New World wines in recent years. It is, in fact, these wines that have underpinned the growth in wine drinking around the world. Many consumers see Australian wine as the all-round best value. These New World producers have a radically different business model from the archetypal small French and Italian vineyards that grow and press their own grapes. Here competitive success comes from astute grape buying and blending, efficient processing and distribution and branding based on grape varieties rather than regional or even district origins.

Australia came 'from nowhere' to be the world's fourth largest exporter of wine in a period of some 20 years at the end of the last century. Over this time production tripled. It is particularly famous for its Chardonnay (white) and Shiraz (red) grapes. Its main export market is the UK, followed by the US. Southcorp (brands – Lindemans, Rosemount and Penfold) is another leading producer.

In 2005 Southcorp was looking to consolidate and strengthen its position by merging with Foster's wine division. Foster, which is better known for its beers, had been looking to acquire Southcorp, but this was a hostile takeover bid that did not proceed. 95 per cent of American wine is produced in California, where Gallo is the leading producer and distributor. 75 per cent of the wine drunk in America is home-produced. The leading importer is Italy, followed by Australia. Just 15 per cent of wine production is exported.

The industry has grown remarkably in recent years, but where next? France is a leading producing and drinking country, but French people are fiercely loyal to French wine. Germany is the world's biggest importer,

© DANIELM | DREAMSTIME.COM

but 'the bastion of old world wine'. Countries in the EU continue to produce and consume two-thirds of the world's wine.

Questions

1 What do you think Stephen Millar's strategy should be if Constellation was to reap the potential benefits of the acquisitions described?

2 European wine producers are smaller, their grapes are not always the best by any means and their marketing resources lag behind those of the New World producers – how do you think they will choose to compete in the future?

12.3 Stage models

Stage model frameworks such as the one featured in Figure 12.4 are based on the premise that internationalization is a process. It is viewed as an evolutionary development over time and consists of a number of phases. Two concepts strongly associated with the models are psychic distance and geographic proximity. Psychic distance refers to the tendency for those people involved in first time exporting to trade with countries with which they feel comfortable culturally. So, for example, English speaking nations will be more likely to trade with each other initially, even if the geographic distance is greater than their nearest neighbour. The issue of geographic distance is straightforward in that the initial exporting will take place to countries in close proximity. Both concepts work together to influence the destination of the first export order.

The models draw on organizational behaviour and learning theory to capture both firm behaviour and managerial learning over time – as the following story illustrates.

Ensuring successful market entry

A company was founded in 1981 in Newcastle, England, UK – its set-up was, in itself, an interesting process. It was started by a Swedish entrepreneur and, because of patent protection in

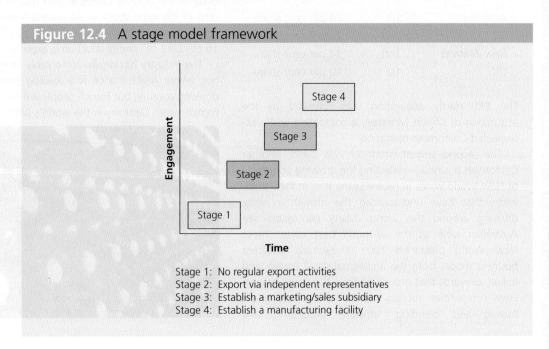

Figure 12.4 A stage model framework

Stage 1: No regular export activities
Stage 2: Export via independent representatives
Stage 3: Establish a marketing/sales subsidiary
Stage 4: Establish a manufacturing facility

the UK, was immediately forced to export – a truly international firm from the outset. Whilst not directly reflecting the classic stages model, its history does help to illustrate stages of gradual market expansion and product development. The first main products which the company marketed were surf boards and surf skis. These were sold into identified markets in France, Australia and the United States. Five years after it was founded, the company acquired a clothing manufacturer in order to develop a range of leisure wear, which it again sold to the same markets where it had successfully marketed its surf boards. This time, of course, it had benefited from the market knowledge and experience gained from the first round of international involvement. Further new product development produced a kayak which again was to be sold into the company's already established key markets.

Much of the conceptual and empirical foundation in this school of research was initiated by Johanson and Wiedersheim-Paul (1975), who developed a model which suggests that internationalization activities occur incrementally, and are influenced by increased market knowledge and commitment. The basic theory is that the perceptions and beliefs of managers both influence, and are shaped by, incremental involvement in foreign markets. This results in a pattern of evolution, from the managers having little or no interest in international markets, to trial initiatives in, and evaluation of, psychically close markets. Managers then pursue active expansion into more challenging and unknown markets, becoming increasingly committed to international growth.

See the online "Volkswagen" case for an example of this section's theory in practice

Since the late 1980s research has shown that many companies are engaging in rapid and more direct forms of internationalization. The stage models are ill-equipped to deal with this dynamic process. Many of the early models were based on very small samples of large firms, whose wider relevance must be questioned. Further, the implied sequential process is not inevitable and there is evidence of companies moving backward and forwards or even jumping stages within the model. Evidence of rapid internationalization by high-technology products, whose window of opportunity on the world market can be quite limited, has further added to the criticism.

Why, then, has this theory survived so long? One reason is that nothing better has come along. The model remains intuitively appealing to our search for order and neat explanations in the chaos of the international environment. However, while elements of the model may provide useful insights to our understanding, it is long past the time when the stages approach should be accepted as the best explanation of the internationalization process.

12.4 Market entry strategies

Selecting international markets in which to operate is a crucial element of international activity. In Online Case 12.1 we can see how Volkswagen has entered different countries to acquire both existing brands and assembly plants and for sourcing components.

Any company will have a number of broad strategic choices which it will have to address including: is a domestic export-based strategy, or a production-based strategy in the host country, more appropriate? It may be that the host country will only welcome the exporter if it involves a presence in the host market. Such a presence will require a commitment, at the very least, to international marketing or a production plant, unlike a pure domestic export-based strategy. For many years China, for example, required joint venture arrangements with a local Chinese company as a condition of market entry. Under such a strategy the responsibility could be devolved to the intermediary being used.

Table 12.3 shows that there are a number of ways to classify the options open to companies, and no one method is correct or perfect. The approach used in this chapter is to look at indirect and direct market entry together with strategies which do or do not involve foreign investment. This is outlined in Table 12.3 and some of the strategies are discussed in greater detail. We

Table 12.3   Classification of modes of market entry

Indirect market entry	Strategies without foreign investment
● Unsolicited orders ● Domestic-based intermediaries Courier/express services Export management companies Export houses Trading companies Piggybacking Brokers Jobbers	● Licensing ● Franchising ● Management contracts

Direct market entry	Strategies with foreign investment
Domestic-based intermediaries ● Freight forwarders ● Consortium exporting ● Export department Foreign-based intermediaries ● Agents ● Distributors	● Marketing subsidiary ● Manufacturing subsidiary ● Joint ventures Joint equity venture Contractual joint venture

concentrate on those not discussed in detail in Chapters 11, although some of these, especially acquisitions, joint ventures and strategic alliances, are very significant in international strategy.

Ensuring successful market entry

Of course nothing can guarantee success; not even a monopoly situation in the long term, as many state-owned businesses have found to their cost throughout the world. The environment does not stand still. Market awareness and knowledge is important, as the following story illustrates.

For one company that attempted to exploit the Dutch market from a base in the UK, failure was based on poor market research. A showroom was opened in Holland to sell female clothing. The company attempted to simply transfer the product to the new market, and in so doing made the mistake in marketing of giving the market the wrong product. Colours and styles which had gone down well in England were found to be unacceptable in the Dutch market. The company also encountered problems with regard to the size of its garments. It did not take into account the difference in stature between customers in the two markets. The company found, too late, that the Dutch customer was taller and larger than its UK market. Formal market research would have revealed the special characteristics of the new market, and allowed the company to adapt its products to the fashion tastes of the Dutch buyers.

In hindsight the company accepted it had learnt a lot:

I think that if the company is going to go into the Dutch market then you have to sort of cater for their way of thinking. You maybe have to hire Dutch designers if you go into things like that because it's so specialized. They're different people – it's like the French, they have a different attitude towards fashion.

However, the very best information-gathering exercise is only as good as the interpretation or spin put upon it by the individuals concerned. There is perhaps a rather understated view, which says that marketing cannot guarantee success, but that an enterprise will fail less badly because of it. Not everything goes smoothly all the time for market entry and the literature is full of famous errors. Failure can occur for all sorts of reasons, e.g. poor intermediaries, poor communication, or not getting paid.

Export readiness

Few companies have the management resources, experience or financial resources to launch products globally. It is therefore inevitable that the choice of market entry options is more restricted for smaller and newer companies. It is also not possible to be prescriptive about the method of entry chosen. Different international markets require different solutions!

The starting point for understanding market entry decisions is the play-off between having a high level of control set against the cost of achieving this status. Most writers on this subject make the distinction between indirect and direct modes of entry. The difference between the two centres on the level of foreign (or direct) investment that is available for overseas expansion. For example, a new firm or a firm new to exporting may, for financial reasons, choose to use domestic intermediaries to respond to unsolicited orders. As these types of order grow in numbers and regularity, the company may then choose to appoint a representative in-country who will be given the task of actively seeking new orders.

Case 12.6, Li Ning, looks at export readiness.

Case 12.6

Li Ning Company   Cn

The Li Ning Sports Wear company was first established in 1989 by Li Ning, one of the outstanding Chinese athletes of the 20th century – at the 23rd Los Angeles Olympic Games Li Ning won three gold medals, two silver medals and one bronze medal. As a gymnast he won over 106 medals in various competitions over a career in sport that lasted 17 years. Li Ning retired in 1989 and by 1990 he had founded the Li Ning Sportswear business. In August 1990, Li Ning Sportswear was selected to provide the designated clothing for the Chinese delegation at the 11th Asian Games and in 1992 for the 25th Barcelona Olympic Games.

Encouraged by this success Li Ning was cross-listed in Hong Kong Stock Exchange in 2004 and was the first Chinese sports good business to do this. Throughout this period Li Ning had been trying to succeed in international markets. He set up within Li Ning Sportswear an international trade department and

signed agreements with European distributors; he also hired designers of sportswear and equipment in Italy and France. The company was represented at European Trade Fairs in major cities such as Munich. All of this activity failed to help the business reach its overall target of sales of 1 billion RMB. The brand simply had not taken off outside China. It appeared that European markets were not ready for a Chinese sportswear business competing head on with Adidas and Nike and other multinational brands.

During this period, when the focus of the company was on developing its international trade, the domestic market had become extremely competitive. Li Ning then decided to concentrate on the domestic market in order to achieve the original sales objective set by the founder, that of sales of 1 billion RMB. 'To some extent China is the world', Li Ning commented. At this point international sales were less than 2 per cent of total sales.

However Li Ning did not give up on his quest to create an international business. In part this was driven by the corresponding success of Adidas and Nike in the Chinese market, where from 2004 they took advantage of the booming Chinese sports goods market to open two stores a day in the major cities. The Chinese brands such as Li Ning, and Anta faced the real possibility of being relegated to second tier businesses. To combat this Li Ning decided to combine the Chinese oriental elements of design into the sportswear, in order to differentiate the business, and also to invest heavily in technology based R&D for its sportswear and equipment. At the same time he adopted the 'best of overseas management practices' in terms of IT, stock control and marketing. European companies were hired to install and implement the management systems needed.

Li Ning had started to sponsor foreign sports groups in 2001. Between 2001 and 2006 this was stepped up, and in 2006 Li Ning successfully sponsored the French gymnastics team and became the designated supplier for the Spanish male and female gymnastics and basketball teams. At the same time Li Ning was investing in the home market with major new stores in Beijing and Shanghai.

Li Ning was now perceived to be a success. This was highlighted in 2008, when, at the Beijing Olympic Games, Li Ning himself flew across the stadium to light the Olympic torch. This fitted in with the company's slogan of 'Anything is Possible'.

Following on from this Li Ning, in March 2009, signed a major sponsorship agreement worth $7.5 million over 5 years with Elena Isinbayeva, the double Olympic gymnastic champion at the Beijing games. Elena is to become the international face of Li Ning as it seeks to combine what they believe is the unique combination of oriental style with advanced technological developments in sportswear and equipment. The aim is to make Li Ning into one of the top five world sports brands at some point between 2013 and 2018. There is still a long way to go for this to be achieved.

Clearly, for a business solely based in China, there is much to do to become a truly international brand.

Questions

1 Research the Li Ning business. What can you learn from this in terms of how the business has developed?

2 What steps are needed for Li Ning to be a truly international business?

http://www.lining.com

© UDEN GRAHAM/REDLINK/CORBIS

Indirect exporting According to McAuley (2001) 'the indirect method of exporting is often referred to as passive exporting or as being a result of an 'export pull' effect, since people outside the company stimulate the activity'. He goes on to suggest that the strategies that come under this category are 'responding to unsolicited or chance orders'. For some companies, this is the first introduction to international markets, which may stimulate them to explore the feasibility of exporting more seriously as the stage models would suggest. It does have that advantage of being new, unexpected business. It illustrates the fact that there are potential, as yet unreached, customers in the world, and it involves no product adaptation costs or promotion costs. The downside of this approach is that the company 'is not geared up for exporting, and therefore there are relatively high costs involved because of the learning curve which has to be gone through. For example, a one-off distribution channel will be relatively expensive as no economies of scale are available. The potential benefits of this initial involvement depend on the company's medium-term response to the unsolicited order.'

Direct entry

The direct approach centres on finding and appointing in-country representatives, usually in the form of agents or distributors. This is an active form of exporting and it relies on using in-country intermediaries. Inevitably the commitment and investment required are greater than in direct exporting, but then again, the rewards are potentially greater.

The options involved are as shown in Table 12.4.

Whilst agents and distributors are the most common form of entry by newer growth firms, this form of representation requires management and control. Sometimes this is learnt the hard way!

The major limitation of working through an intermediary is that a firm will not own its distribution network or its customers within a foreign market. The most significant impact of this is that the exporter can be starved of information on market trends and competitor activities. This is because it is in the interest of an intermediary to control that information.

It is worth noting that in fast-moving markets or with products at the early stages of growth, access to information can be crucial to gaining entry. For this reason, licensing and joint ventures are more common methods of entry for technology-based businesses.

Agents and distributors will usually seek exclusivity for a territory. The difference between an agent and a distributor is that the distributor will, like a foreign customer, be placing orders, holding stock and accepting responsibility for the sale of goods. Despite best intentions, a growth business with a limited track record and product innovation is less likely to attract a distributor who is willing to hold stock. Agency agreements are, initially, the more common form of entry, especially where more than one market is being addressed. In this case, most agreements are set out between sole agents rather than the larger multichannel agency that is more likely to deal with public limited companies.

Table 12.4	Options for direct entry	
Agents	Generate customers for products on a commission basis	Exporter's control is high but the method involves close management if market coverage is to be achieved
Distributors	Take title of goods and earn a profit from the mark-up Handle local distribution and marketing	Low level of initial control but offers rapid coverage
Direct selling	Supply to direct customers who order through catalogues, online or through trade fairs	Potentially high level of control but lack of country presence may limit penetration
Sales office	Exporter's own personnel actively target customers Office handles all sales functions	Country presence helps develop sales but coverage may not be sufficient for larger markets such as the US
Subsidiary	Dedicated sales and operations may range from assemblage to locally sourced manufacturing	High potential control but coverage can be limited

It is always important to find an agent for whom the company's business is significant – such that they will provide adequate support and prioritize the products amongst the range they represent and promote. At the same time it is important to remember that no agent will willingly expose himself to the risk of being supplanted by a branch of the company's own sales organization. Exclusivity is usually central to negotiations for the agency agreement, but many unsuspecting firms give away too much territory to a single agency.

In market situations where there is slow growth for the company's product in an otherwise high growth market – which does happen – there is a real likelihood the agent concerned is either overstretched or the wrong agent. By this we mean someone for whom the products and the business are insignificant or low priority.

On the other hand, high market growth can create pressures within the company to take over the territory or replace the agent. This may often require compensating the agent handsomely, especially where local legislation exists to protect his position. Elsewhere, the situation may arise where the company wishes to expand its product line or else diversify into a quite different product. If the local agent finds himself unable to meet this new expansion, but still holds a company agreement to exclusivity of sales territory, then contracts will need renegotiating or terminating.

These factors may explain why, when entering a new market, it is comparatively easy to find an agent but extremely difficult to find the one that is right for the company. An agent is paid commission only on sales, so loyalty rests purely on the company currently providing him with the greatest earnings. As agents may represent a number of separate companies and product lines, this may be – or it may become – a problem. Meanwhile, the company holds responsibility for whatever unsold inventory is held by the agent, while at the same time being virtually deprived of market information. This can be frustrating and points to the need for preparation when recruiting agents.

Other direct entry choices tend to rely on strategic alliances or partnering relationships, which can take many forms.

Other direct entry choices

Licensing   refers to agreements that provide unilateral technology access, frequently through patents, to a licensee in return for a fee. Cross-licensing is a bilateral form of licensing where companies usually swap packages of patents to avoid patent infringements or to exchange existing, codified technological knowledge.

Second-sourcing agreements   regulate the transfer of technology through technical product specifications in order to produce exact copies of products. In the case of mutual second sourcing this transfer takes place between two or more companies that transfer technical specifications of different products.

Customer–supplier relationships   are co-production contracts and co-makership relations that basically regulate long-term contracts between vertically-related, but independent, companies that collaborate in production and supply. A specific case of customer–supplier relationships are R&D contracts where one company is subcontracted by another company to perform particular R&D projects.

Joint R&D   pacts and joint development agreements are contractual relationships through which companies perform jointly funded R&D projects, or in the case of joint development agreements, jointly work on the development of new products or processes.

Joint ventures are the combinations of the economic interests of at least two separate companies in a distinct organizational entity, where profits and losses are usually shared in accordance with the equity investments by the parent companies. Joint ventures act as separate organizations that have regular company objectives such as production, marketing and sales, but if relevant also R&D, as a specific objective of the partnership.

It is not always possible to distinguish between these alternatives, and experienced companies will often mix and match the methods according to their market and their resources. The characteristic that all the methods share is that they promote collaboration through two or more firms. The main factor which increasingly encourages and enables this form of businesses activity is information communications technology (ICT). This not only allows businesses to trade (electronically) across boundaries, it has also facilitated new forms of organizations such as virtual companies.

It can be argued that the world has become too large and the competition too strong for even the largest multinational corporations to do everything independently! Technologies are converging and markets becoming integrated, making the costs and risks of both product and market development ever greater. Partly as a reaction to and partly in order to exploit these developments, entrepreneurial management has become more pragmatic about what type of alliance it takes to be successful in global markets.

The emerging business model, especially amongst technology-centred companies, favours the formation of strategic alliances with suppliers, customers, competitors, and companies in other industries. These alliances can take many forms, ranging from informal co-operation to joint ownership of plants and operations.

12.5 Franchising

A number of prominent companies have used franchising to open up access to a global market without the financial and other resource implications of, say, acquisitions. We mentioned it earlier in this part of the book and here we explore it in greater detail.

In most developed economies franchising is widely used for operating businesses. It is a system that has enabled organizations to develop some of the largest brands around, for example, McDonald's, Subway (Case 12.7), Dyno-Rod and Holiday Inn. Moreover, the governments of some developing countries e.g. Malaysia actively encourage Malaysian business people to use franchising as a way of fostering entrepreneurship. The franchisor gains national and international distribution for the business idea much more quickly than if the expansion had been undertaken through fully-owned outlets. Also, as self-employed individuals, the franchisees, who supply most of the capital for the expansion, are usually more motivated to work hard at building their businesses.

Franchising is not new; the emergence of the modern concept of franchising occurred in the United States just after the Civil War with the activities of the Singer Sewing Machine Company. However, it was not until the beginning of the twentieth century that this method of business development gained wider acceptance. The automobile industry and the soft drink industry were the first to adopt the so-called product and trademark franchising. These include arrangements in which franchisees are granted the right to distribute a manufacturer's product within a specified territory or at a specific location, generally with the use of the manufacturer's identifying name or trademark, in exchange for fees or royalties.

By the 1930s the petroleum industry was franchising gasoline/petrol service stations. The real expansion of franchising, though, took place in the US in the1950s, with the appearance of 'business format franchising'. This type of franchising is also known as second generation franchising, and it is characterized by an ongoing relationship between the franchisor and the franchisee. This includes the product or service, the trademark and effectively the entire business concept – a marketing strategy and plan, operating manuals and standards, quality control and a

Case 12.7

Subway

US

Many entrepreneurial businesses and fortunes have been built with franchising – McDonald's is an excellent example. However, by 2003, McDonald's had been overtaken by Subway in terms of the largest number of fast food outlets in America. The company is also growing overseas – and all of it through franchising. Worldwide, there are now over 30,000 branches. Annual turnover exceeds $20 billion.

When Subway moved into the UK, for example, CEO Fred Deluca split the country into 18 areas and appointed a manager for each one. Their task was to find suitable locations and franchisees.

The company, which sells freshly made sandwiches and salads to order – its trademark is the long 'submarine' roll – was started in 1965 by the seventeen year old Fred Deluca, in partnership with a family friend – and nuclear physicist – Dr Peter Buck, who invested $1000. They still own the business. The first sandwich shop struggled at the very beginning, but it survived and was joined by a second and then a third. By 1968 Deluca owned five outlets. In 1974 he switched to franchising. Rapid growth followed such that 200 outlets in 1981 became 5000 in 1990 and 11,000 in 1995. In 1983 Subway outlets began baking all their own bread.

Subway is successful for a number of reasons:

- It is simple – an easy model to replicate

- It is innovative. Menus are changed constantly with new breads as well as fillings
- There is distinct advantage in the healthy option sandwiches and salads
- It has a very clear focus and business model. Franchisees are not creators of new ideas; rather they are there to deliver products and service. Their overheads are low because the franchisor supplies most of the equipment they need. Franchisees organize their own local food purchases – which is quite different from the way many franchised fast food outlets are supplied with centrally sourced materials. Local stores and area managers can also negotiate with the UK head office over pricing and sandwich fillings.

Deluca has been asked whether he has plans to sell the business – his response is that 'if we do sell, we'll have money…but we don't need money and what would we do with it'.

Questions

1 Was franchising the most logical growth route for Subway?
2 What do you think are the key competencies and capabilities for managing international growth of this magnitude using franchising?

continuing process of assistance and guidance. In the 1970s companies increasingly saw the international potential of business format franchising.

Under a business format franchise the franchisees operate the franchise in a standard way under a common trademarked name. The kinds of businesses operating under such a system can include fast food restaurants, courier services, cleaning services, employment or estate agents, kitchen or bathroom installers.

Initially the expansion took place in markets which were most accessible or had good market potential, low cultural distance and the existence of a developed service sector. Thus, Canada became a prime target for international expansion, followed later by the UK and Australia. Development of franchising in Japan was facilitated by the use of a master franchise agreement, which reduced the need for direct involvement in the development of operations in what was, especially for Americans, a very unique culture. A master franchisee usually has responsibility for more than one outlet and is commonly totally responsible for the development of the franchised business (through other franchisees) in an area.

There are, then, a number of other models which are dependent on franchise relationships:

1 *Manufacturer-Retailer* – Where the retailer, as franchisee, sells the franchisor's product directly to the public (for example, new motor vehicle dealerships).

2 *Manufacturer-Wholesaler* – Where the franchisee, under licence, manufactures and distributes the franchisor's product (for example soft drink bottling arrangements).

3 *Wholesaler-Retailer* – Where the retailer, as franchisee, purchases products for retail sale from a franchisor wholesaler (typically a wholesale co-operative set up by the franchisee retailers, who are contractually obliged to purchase from it). Examples include hardware and automotive product stores.

4 *Retailer-Retailer* – Where the franchisor markets a service or a produce under a common name and standardized system through a network of franchisees. This is the classic business format franchise.

Why businesses franchise?

Companies can expand in a number of ways, and full ownership of new outlets is perhaps the most obvious way forward. However, having fully assessed the costs and risks of expansion, some organizations decide to follow the franchising route. Why? Three key reasons are resource scarcity, agency theory and risk spreading.

Resource scarcity means that a company needs access to management talent or other knowledge not available to them, and at the same time may not have a large amount of money to invest in the expansion. *Agency theory* is about the way in which those people who manage the outlet are motivated and monitored. Because franchisees have considerable financial investments at stake, and because they receive profits from the outlet, they are more motivated than managers of company-owned units to work hard to make the franchise profitable. *Risk spreading*, compensating for the decisions surrounding any expansion, is accomplished through franchising. The investment risk is lowered through franchising compared with joint ventures, which can involve large capital investments and legal complications. Franchising creates sales and brand recognition at a much lower cost. In international expansion the political risk and the overall risk of failure are primarily borne by the franchisee.

The timescale required by franchising is seen as faster than self-owned expansion, which will often require more monitoring. The process of establishing a chain of franchises increases the knowledge of the franchisor, and the time required for each new outlet is reduced as expertise increases. With experience the franchisor develops sensitivity to site selection, store layout, procurement and operating policies appropriate to particular environmental settings.

12.6 Constraints on internationalization

It is worth bearing in mind that not all companies are in a position to take advantage of all the international opportunities which may present themselves. Indeed, it is possible that not all opportunities will even be recognized by the decision-makers in the company. It is this perceptual variation and ability to process information which helps to create the variability on the map of international activities.

Morgan and Katsikeas (1997) identified four barriers that explain why business owners are discouraged from participating in international business:

- First, an insufficient pool of resources can create strategic obstacles.
- Second, a firm's cost base and margins can lead to operational (and logistical) obstacles.
- Third, a lack of fit between a firm's strategy and its environment may result in limited knowledge of market opportunities, creating informational obstacles.
- Fourth, a firm may be unable to maintain necessary interactions with key parties because of limited resources leading to process-based obstacles.

Little, quoted in Yanacek (1988), has identified ten constraints faced by companies marketing products or services internationally. These are:

- Building distribution networks
- Designing market entry strategies
- Identifying market opportunities
- Dealing with political and commercial risks
- Obtaining information on alternatives to direct exporting
- Securing working capital and export financing
- Collecting foreign receivables
- Providing after-sales customer service
- Dealing with tariff barriers and quotas
- Dealing with export laws, regulations and procedures.

Of course, it is also worth remembering that not all companies wish to become internationally active. This can occur for a variety of reasons, some of which, particularly in smaller companies, can be associated with the personal characteristics of the strategic leader or founding entrepreneur. Some find it difficult to delegate responsibility and, therefore, it is difficult for the company to grow. Others have reached what some authors have called the 'comfort level', and do not wish to see an expansion of the business. While outsiders may wish to see growth, and while it may be frustrating to watch a company effectively underachieve, it is also dangerous to force change upon such a company.

In the Western Isles of Scotland there is a company which produces soft toys, particularly teddy bears. This is a small company operating in a remote area where any employment is welcomed. Production is limited as the toys are hand-made. During a visit to Scotland executives from Disney who had seen the company's products, and liked them, approached the company to investigate the possibility of them becoming a supplier to Disney. The executives were taken aback to find that the person they spoke to had never heard of Disney – nor was the company interested in doing a deal on the grounds the volume Disney required was way beyond their capacity. This story raises a number of interesting points. For one thing, it shows that even a global brand as powerful as Disney can still be taken down a peg or two. More significantly, there is the lost potential for bringing new business to a remote community. Had the motives and personal attitudes been different at the company, then perhaps an opportunity might have been explored to machine-make the teddy bears as a special line for Disney. There could be marketing kudos in the fact that they were linked to a hand-made tradition. This would require knowledge of branding and product line differentiation, but unfortunately this option was never explored.

As well as what might be termed these 'softer' constraints, there are the more traditional ones related to worries about:

- Resources – mainly finance and people
- Time available
- Market uncertainties
- Marketing costs
- Payment terms
- Exchange rates
- The cost of insurance
- Information shortages
- Political uncertainties
- Cultural differences.

Any organization, then, faces many decisions in its attempt to internationalize its activities:

- What volume of trade is desirable?
- How many countries to market in?
- Which countries to select?

The degree of market attractiveness will be influenced by a number of factors related to geographic, demographic, economic, technological and sociocultural characteristics. Once it has evaluated the relative attractiveness of the potential markets in relation to the company's product/service a company should be better placed to select those markets where the 'fit' is apparently best. For each business, the selection of entry mode will then be linked to their international strategy, which in turn is influenced by motives and constraints. For example, the use of export or international production strategies, the use of intermediaries or how much control over marketing activities the business wishes to retain. There will be also issues regarding expected payback on the investment, the degree of flexibility required and how the strategy fits with broader business objectives. All of these issues prepare the way for one of the dominant decisions of the internationalization process, namely, the mode of market entry decision.

In briefly exploring the constraints on internationalization, it is clear that they can act as barriers to the initiation of international activity as well as affecting the process of international business by influencing the choice of market entry.

12.7 Future influences on international business

The international business environment will continue to evolve and the activities of individual firms will be shaped by the interaction of external and internal forces. Within Europe, for example, the current expansion of the EU and the further development of the Russian Federation will have a significant impact. In the recession of 2009 we began to see some evidence of a rise in protectionism. Some decisions taken by the US and certain European countries appeared to be focused on preserving jobs at home. After years of movement towards freer trade and open borders there was now a question concerning whether countries were metaphorically putting the clock back. There is now pressure building to avoid this and for a return to the Doha Development Round which is the trade negotiation forum for the World Trade Organization (WTO). This round started in November 2001 in Qatar but stalled in 2008. The aim of Doha is to lower trade barriers around the world and in so doing increase global trade.

More generally, global trends will include the creation of enterprises based on the knowledge-based economy. The preceding discussion has described the background against which managers and marketers act their part in the global economy. This background, as we have seen, is complex, full of uncertainty and subject to change which is often rapid and unpredictable. Organizations must be alive to the opportunities which come along and be prepared to take advantage of windows of opportunity as they open. This is just as relevant for **small and medium-sized enterprises** as it is for the multinational.

Three decades of constant progress in information and communication technologies have triggered a complex pattern of change in international business relationships. This technological revolution is shaping the process of globalization by providing new tools and infrastructures with which entrepreneurial companies capture global opportunities. Unlike previous transformations, the international economy now encompasses global consumers who have local tastes, preferences and servicing requirements. The concluding section in this chapter looks at both the knowledge economy and corporate social responsibility and their effect on business models and business methods in the coming years. Particular attention is paid to sectors of the economy that are already global in their scope of operations. It also examines the 'virtual firms'. The virtual firm is seen as an embodiment of the entrepreneurial business in a global economy.

The knowledge economy

In 1988, Peter Drucker wrote an article in the *Harvard Business Review* entitled 'The Coming of the New Organisation' in which he defined the term knowledge management as being the criteria that would define companies in the next 20 years. The knowledge economy differs from the traditional economy in several key respects. The most significant influence is that knowledge is measured not of scarcity, but rather of abundance. Unlike most company resources that deplete when used, information and knowledge can be shared, and actually grow through application.

This has the effect of encouraging business alliances across international frontiers. In this sense, the effect of location is diminished. Using appropriate technology and methods, virtual marketplaces and virtual organizations can be created that offer benefits of speed and agility, of round the clock operation and of global reach. These characteristics require new thinking and approaches by entrepreneurial companies, policy-makers, senior executives and knowledge workers alike. To do so, though, requires leadership and risk taking, against the prevailing and slow changing attitudes and practices of existing institutions and business practice.

There are several types of knowledge – 'knowing' a fact is little different from 'information', but 'knowing' a skill, or 'knowing' that something might affect market conditions is something that, despite attempts of knowledge engineers to codify such knowledge, has an important human dimension. It is some combination of context sensing, personal memory and cognitive processes. Measuring the knowledge asset, therefore, means putting a value on people, both as individuals, but, more importantly, on their collective capability, and other factors such as the embedded intelligence in an organization's computer systems. Unlike information, knowledge is less tangible and depends on human cognition and awareness.

Like most assets, knowledge is only valuable if it can be transmuted into goods and services that people will pay for. Here we get into leveraging knowledge, looking at adding value through its development.

Virtual companies

Knowledge management combined with the enabling technology associated with e-business is changing nearly all that companies do, from the procurement of supplies to the delivery of finished products and services. New types of competitors, value-added services and new delivery channels are shifting the boundaries between customers, suppliers, partners and competitors, and profoundly altering industry value chains.

Arguably, web-based organizations exist because market conditions are changing. Customers demand more specialized products which means that companies have to develop a wider range. At the same time they expect a high degree of customization as well as localization to suit conditions that prevail in any particular market. Virtual companies are able to command resources beyond those immediately available to them through collaboration and alliances – a strategy ideally suited to those organizations who wish to cross geographic frontiers.

Specialization and individualization of products leads to shorter production cycles which in turn increase the investment and costs of R&D, production, and sales. As a counter-balance to this trend, information communications technology (ICT) has dramatically improved the speed, quantity and quality of communication and especially the co-ordination of economic actions and transactions. In this respect ICT can be viewed as an enabler and at the same time as a driving force towards the virtual organization. A key objective of a virtual company is to improve its flexibility – the kind of flexibility needed to meet the fast changing market conditions. In order to decrease complexity and increase flexibility companies seek to create, nurture and exploit relevant core competencies. This strategy means that companies concentrate on what they can do best – they specialize in certain areas, they develop and constantly improve their core competencies.

However, as we pointed out in Chapters 3, a core competence on its own does not create any value; therefore, companies have to search internationally for value chains where they can integrate their core competencies. Those core competencies are then flexibly configured in different value chains whereby those value chains are made of many different core competencies provided by different economic actors, which leads theoretically to an optimum value creation process.

In conclusion, the evolution of virtual organizations is forced by changing market conditions: in particular, the increased requirement to offer specialized products, to reduce the time to market process, the increased international competition (globalization), and the need to satisfy individual customer needs to which organizations have to respond. Some commentators expect multinationals to be losers in this world order. Others anticipate that the large global companies will form strategic alliances with the small technology innovators and between them they will have the capability to squeeze out the existing market leaders. This process of change offers an increasing number of opportunities for entrepreneurial firms that are knowledge-based and willing to play on the global stage.

A stakeholder view

The nature of the changing planet we all live in means that firms involved in internationalization must be concerned with the quest for sustainability. Businesses and individuals all have a stake in the planet's survival. The key goal for corporate social responsibility (CSR) is global sustainability, which is defined as 'the ability to meet the needs of the present without compromising the ability of future generations to meet their needs' (Peng, 2009). For Peng this means not only sustainable social and natural environments but also sustainable capitalism that will help address the issues we all face relating to population growth, poverty and inequality on a world scale. Capitalism through the success of international business has a major role to play in this. Businesses are now seeing the benefits of Fair Trade and sustainability. Despite the problem with the banks worldwide capitalism as we know it is not bust. Businesses have a major role to play in the development of what is termed the triple bottom line, the economic, social and environmental performance that simultaneously satisfies the needs of all stakeholders groups. A key element of this is the guidelines for multinational enterprises published by the OECD (**www.oecd.org** and the UN at **www.un.org**).

Summary

All strategic options can have an international dimension – ranging from exporting to a global corporation where products are manufactured in various places around the world and then marketed globally as appropriate.

Some companies will 'go global' with existing products and services they market overseas – others will tailor complete strategies for local markets.

The motivation to 'go international' can be internal (organization-driven) or external and driven by environmental opportunities. The deciding factors can thus be push or pull and involve either a proactive or reactive stance.

The key issues in developing an international strategy concern?

- Products
- Markets
- Entry considerations
- Timing.

The main considerations then are:

- Marketing – the global and multi-domestic approaches
- Finance
- Structure and location – where to produce in relation to market opportunities
- Culture – which differs between countries
- Who are the stakeholders? What are their prime interests.

There are useful stage models which provide some insight into a typical (if not universally adopted) path to internationalization.

Similarly there are a number of market entry opportunities, although sometimes there will be a given element which acts as a constraint.

Entry into a market can be either direct or indirect and it may or may not require foreign investment.

Good overseas agents (a crucial element of the direct approach) are worth their weight in gold, but it is all too easy to appoint the wrong agent.

Strategic alliances can also be very significant in developing internationally.

Franchising is an approach used by many countries to develop internationally. It can allow for controlled investment and more limited resource implications.

Not all options are always going to be available or suitable. Constraints thus limit opportunities – here resources, costs and knowledge may be relevant. The ability to gain market access will always be critical.

Some companies will deliberately avoid the risks and uncertainty associated with internationalization.

Finally, we outlined how e-commerce and the knowledge economy is changing the nature of global strategy by opening up new and exciting opportunities.

Online cases for this chapter

Online Case 12.1: Volkswagen

Online Case 12.2: Matsushita and Canon

Questions and research assignments

1 Revisiting Chapter 10, for each of the following strategic alternatives, list why you think an organization might select this particular strategy as a means of international growth. What would they expect to gain, and where are the problems and limitations? If you can, think of an example of each one from your own experience:

- market development
- product development
- innovation
- horizontal integration

- vertical integration
- concentric diversification
- conglomerate diversification.

2 What are the relative advantages and disadvantages of direct market entry as opposed to indirect entry strategies?

3 What are the essential differences between an export, an international and a global organization?

Internet and library projects

1 Consider the most appropriate strategy for a UK-based company with international ambitions in the following industries (assume that your choice could be implemented):

- men's fashion
- real ale
- baby clothes
- ladies' handbags.

2 For an organization of your choice, trace the changes of international strategy and strategic direction over a period of time. Relate these changes to any changes in strategic leadership, structure and, wherever possible, culture.

3 Sony is renowned as an innovative company within the consumer electronics industry, and its success has depended substantially on televisions, videos and hi-fi equipment. In recent years Sony has followed a strategy of globalization and diversification arguably in related product areas. The international strategy has been called global localization; Sony aims to be a global company presented locally, and this involves devolving authority away from Tokyo and expanding manufacturing and R&D around the world. How does Sony achieve this?
Sony **http://www.sony.com**

4 Abrakebabra is Ireland's premier fast food chain. It has grown rapidly in Ireland through franchising. Can you ascertain why? There are at present, in 2009, no international outlets. How 'international' could this business be? Why do you think there are no international outlets?
Abrakebabra **http://www.abrakebabra.com**

5 Find two businesses that have grown internationally through franchising, one a product business and the other a service business. Compare and contrast their development. To what extent are they similar and to what extent different?

Strategy activity

Sanyo

Sanyo is an innovative and pioneering Japanese electronics company, and a global leader for certain consumer electronics goods. Once best known for its low prices, Sanyo has been described as unusual amongst Japanese businesses – it drops products and businesses that under-perform rather than persisting with them. Sanyo became the world's leading manufacturer of digital still cameras, a very high growth business – it captured a 30 per cent share. This fact would not be realized by looking at the camera displays in stores around the world – the vast majority of the cameras Sanyo makes are marketed with other leading brand names attached. This approach helps overcome the relative weakness of its own brand, when compared with other leading Japanese electronics companies – and also provides a revenue stream to fund research and investment. It is also a leader with optical pick-ups, a key component of CD and DVD players. Some 40 of its various semi-conductor products enjoy niche dominance; and it produces the rechargeable batteries for a large proportion of the world's mobile phones.

Sanyo is successful because it focuses its resources on carefully identified opportunities:

- It concentrates on where it can be 'Number One' globally. 'Unless you choose what to focus on, you will not survive' (*Yukinori Kuwano, CEO*).
- It rates all its businesses by their growth potential and achievable margins – basically following the portfolio approach discussed in Chapters 8 and 16.
- It constantly searches for new opportunities, especially acquisitions that would strengthen critical mass and market (segment) dominance.
- Sanyo has also developed a joint venture in China with Haier (Case 12.2), China's largest consumer electronics group, to provide access to this important and growing market.

Question

1 What do you think are the relative merits and disadvantages of Sanyo's strategy of producing digital still cameras for some of the leading brand names?

Further reading

Bartlett, C and Ghoshal, S (1987) Managing across borders – new organizational responses, *Sloan Management Review*, Fall.

Douglas, S and Wind, Y (1987) The myth of globalization, *Columbia Journal of World Business*, Winter.

Levitt, T (1983) The globalization of markets, *Harvard Business Review*, May–June.

Porter, ME (1990) *The Competitive Advantage of Nations*, The Free Press.

References

Bartlett, C and Ghoshal, S (1989) *Managing Across Borders: The Transnational Solution*, Harvard Business School Press.

Bartlett, C and Ghoshal, S (1992) What is a global manager? *Harvard Business Review*, September–October.

Chandler, AD (1990) The enduring logic of industrial success, *Harvard Business Review*, March–April.

Czinkota, M., Ronkainen, and Moffet, M. (2005) *International Business*, Seventh Edition, Thomson, South-Western.

Daniels, J., Radebaugh, L., and Sullivan, D. (2007) *International Business*, Seventh Edition, Pearson Prentice Hall, Upper Saddle River, New Jersey.

Drucker, PF (1988) The coming of the new organization, *Harvard Business Review*, January–February.

Ghauri, P (2000) Internationalization of the firm, in Tayeb, M (ed.) *International Business – Theories, Policies and Practices*, FT-Prentice Hall.

Gupta, A and Govindarajan, V (1998) How to build a global presence, *Financial Times Mastering Global Business*, No 1.

Hofstede, G (1991) *Cultures and Organization: Software of the Mind*, McGraw Hill.

Johanson, J and Wiedersheim-Paul, F (1975) The internationalization of the firm – four Swedish cases, *Journal of Management Studies*, 12 (3).

Joynt, P and Welch, L (1985) A strategy for small business internationalization, *International Marketing Review*, 2 (3).

Kay, JA (1990) Identifying the strategic market, *Business Strategy Review*, Spring.

Lynch, R. (2000) *Corporate Strategy*, Second Edition, Prentice Hall.

McAuley, A. (2001) *International Marketing – Consuming Globally, Thinking Locally*, John Wiley.

Morgan, RE and Katsikeas, CS (1997) Obstacles to export initiation and expansion, *International Journal of Management Science*, 25.

Ohmae, K (1990) *The Borderless World*, Harper.

Peng, M.W. (2009) *Global Business*, South-Western, Cengage Learning.

Porter, ME (1990) The *Competitive Advantage of Nations*, Free Press.

Wickham, P.A. (2001) *Strategic Entrepreneurship*, Second Edition, Prentice Hall.

Yanacek, F (1988) The Road to Exports, *Transportation and Distribution*, 29 (2).

Chapter 13

Failure, consolidation and recovery strategies

PART 1
Understanding strategy

1 Introducing strategy and strategic management

PART 5
Strategic management

14 Strategy implementation

15 Leading change

16 Managing strategy in the organization

17 Final thoughts – the purpose of strategy

PART 2
Strategic positioning

2 Strategic thinking, environmental analysis, synergy and strategic positioning

3 Resource-led strategy

4 The dynamics of competition

5 Introducing culture and values

STRATEGIC MANAGEMENT: AWARENESS AND CHANGE

PART 4
Issues in strategic growth

11 Strategic growth

12 International strategy

13 Failure, consolidation and recovery strategies

PART 3
Strategic analysis and choice

6 Strategic purpose

7 Strategic success

8 An introduction to strategy creation and planning

9 Strategic leadership, entrepreneurship and intrapreneurship

10 Strategic alternatives, strategy evaluation and strategy selection

Learning objectives

Having read to the end of this chapter you should be able to:

- identify the four possible outcomes of strategic change when companies are in difficulties

- describe a number of retrenchment and turnaround strategies

- discuss the thinking behind divestment strategies and the implementation issues involved

- explain management buy-outs and buy-ins

- explain which strategies are important during a recession

- summarize the possible strategies for individual competitors in declining industries

- explain what is meant by corporate decline and failure

- identify the main symptoms of failure

- describe the most likely causes of decline

Ultimate business failure implies closure or liquidation – the organization has failed to satisfy certain key stakeholders and it has ceased to be financially viable. It is beyond turning around by new management. This happens with many small businesses and it also happens with much larger and established organizations. However, the larger the organization, the greater the general likelihood that at least some part can be rescued. Where the fortunes of a business have sunk to a crisis level, and radical changes of strategy are required, this clearly also represents failure – even if with sound retrenchment and turnaround strategies the business can be rescued. It is a failure of strategic management because mistakes have been made, in the form of either poor judgement or relative inactivity in the face of a need to change. If a business, or a part of a business, is sold because it is unprofitable, this may well represent failure by the current management team. The assumption is that the business has a stronger future in different hands. However, one should not assume that all divestments of this nature imply failure – they may simply represent poor strategic fit and perhaps a past misjudgement. Hence the study of failure here concerns why the performance of a business can sink to a crisis level which demands either drastic remedial action, sale or closure. There is also an argument to be made that under-performance and under-achievement (against potential) is a form of failure.

Poor strategic leadership, insufficient control of the essential aspects of financial management and the failure to be competitive are the key issues behind corporate decline and failure.

Cases 13.1 and 13.2 both tell stories of failure. Jinan Sanzhu failed for a number of reasons; for one thing it grew very quickly and executives 'took their eye off the ball'. Golden Wonder was ultimately beaten by its competitors in an industry where barriers to entry are relatively low.

At any given time certain industries will provide attractive growth prospects for those companies who already compete in them, and for potential newcomers. At the same time, however, other industries will be in terminal decline. This might be taking place slowly or rapidly. In the case of slow decline, profitable opportunities may still exist for those companies that can relate best to changing market needs. Where decline is rapid, prospects are likely to be very limited. A third group of industries might be undergoing significant change, and the companies that can adapt effectively will be able to survive and grow. An example of this can be found in shipbuilding, an industry which has migrated to yards in the Far East. Some European yards have thrived by switching to building modern cruise ships for an industry now flourishing by adapting to changes in holiday patterns and the age profile of the population at large.

Any recovery from a difficult situation will be related to, first, improved marketing effectiveness, competitiveness and revenue, and second, managing the organization more efficiently in order to reduce costs. Where these changes in functional and competitive strategies prove inadequate, something more drastic will be required. Retrenchment strategies aim to increase revenue and reduce costs by concentrating and consolidating – these involve changes in functional strategies. Turnaround strategies relate to changes in competitive strategies and frequently feature repositioning for competitive advantage. Retrenchment and turnaround strategies are often collectively called recovery strategies. Divestment occurs when part of an organization is sold, normally because it is diverting resources which could be used more effectively, but sometimes just to raise money. These result in changes to the company's corporate strategy.

Businesses succeed when a number of things are in place, in particular:

- A sound business and revenue model where there is real demand and an opportunity to earn revenues in excess of costs
- A solid cash flow
- Good relationships with customers and
- Strong relationships with employees.

These themes are particularly relevant when times are tough – such as in a recession – and they point the way to understanding what business should look to achieve and protect all the time.

13.1 Introduction: failure in context

In broad terms it could be argued that a company is failing if it does not meet the objectives set for it by its stakeholders, or if it produces outputs that are considered undesirable by those associated with it. The outcome may not be ultimate failure, closure or liquidation, however. When the failure or the decline reaches a certain level, or continues for a certain length of time: this should act as a trigger for remedial action. Such action might be spurned, of course, or prove inadequate, such that the business deteriorates and is finally liquidated.

A company which polluted or harmed the natural environment in some way would be classified as unsuccessful – and maybe even perceived as a failure – by certain stakeholders, but it would not necessarily fail financially and go out of business. Companies sometimes develop and launch new products that fail because very few people buy them – the Ford Edsel car and Strand cigarettes are well-quoted examples from business history. In recent times Sony have launched recording products that have not caught on with the general public e.g. DAT tapes and the mini disk. In this respect the companies are unsuccessful with particular competitive strategies, but again they may not necessarily experience corporate failure as a result.

Corporate failure, liquidation and the lack of success should not then be seen as synonymous terms. A private-sector, profit-seeking organization would certainly be classified as a failure if it ended up in liquidation and was closed down with its assets sold off piecemeal. A similar company might be unsuccessful and in decline, but able to avoid liquidation. Appropriate strategic action that addresses the causes of the decline may generate recovery. For example, the major shareholders might insist upon the appointment of a new strategic leader, or the financial or competitive weaknesses might be acted upon. Such a company might also be acquired by another, and this may be because the shareholders are happy to sell their shares or because the company has been placed in receivership and the receiver has arranged the sale of the business as a going concern. Receivership occurs when a business is unable to pay its creditors, for example its

Case 13.1

Jinan Sanzhu Group   Cn

The Jinan Sanzhu Group was founded in 1993 by Bingxin Wu. He started the business with the equivalent of £20,000 or RMB 300,000 (RMB conversion of 15 to £1). By 1996 the turnover of the Sanzhu Group had reached RMB 8 billion. The basic product of the business was a health food drink which was claimed to both prolong life and cure a range of diseases. The founder of the business, Mr Wu, was a self-made man who, after the death of his parents and six brothers, had been forced to feed and clothe himself from an early age. He had successfully built up his first business when he was struck down with a serious illness. Fortunately he recovered and it was this brush with cancer that led him to set up his latest venture selling the health food drink. Mr Wu is very typical of the kind of self-made Chinese entrepreneur who, after starting a business from humble beginnings, is able to create a large business by sheer force of their personality and power within the business.

The company grew rapidly, setting up 2000 offices throughout China and with a salesforce of 150,000 people recruited mainly as agents. The advertisements for the product implied that it could cure a range of diseases; and within 3 years the company was selling 0.4 billion bottles of the product per annum. During its period of success the Sanzhu Group diversified very rapidly – entering a range of business sectors including medicine, bioengineering, chemical and cosmetics industries. However, in 1996, a man called Boshun Chen died suddenly at the age of 60 in Hunan province. His family suspected that the health product of Sanzhu

had caused the death of Mr Chen. The event received widespread media publicity within China and within a few months the turnover of the company rapidly declined. A lawsuit was also lost in 1998 and the army of sales agents built up by the group quickly dropped away. Most of the existing health products of the business were now worthless and two modern factories set up to manufacture the product were closed. Unlike many sophisticated multinational businesses, the Sanzhu Group was unable to make effective use of the media to defend the product so as to retain the loyalty of their customers. Within 5 years of start-up the Jinan Sanzhu Group had failed.

Question

1   What are the classic management problems that a careful reading of the Jinan Sanzhu Group situation can identify?

suppliers or bank loan interest. The receiver is normally a professional accountant and is charged with saving the business if it is possible to do so. The alternative to be placed into receivership is the process of 'members voluntary liquidation'. Here the owners are still in control of the business and chose to close it selling off the assets themselves rather than a forced sale of assets by the receiver.

In a similar way a non-profit-seeking organization could be closed down or provided with new leadership and direction on the insistence of its major financial stakeholders or trustees.

Figure 13.1 tracks the potential outcomes once difficulties and potential failure are realized and acted upon. We shall see later that timing of the intervention is critical here. Sometimes businesses can be turned around; sometimes it is too late to undo the effects of weaknesses and poor decisions in the past.

A company might be relatively unsuccessful compared with its competitors for a prolonged period if the key stakeholders allow it, but it is never perceived to be failing. For example, a small private company whose shares are not quoted on the stock exchange might be making only very

Case 13.2

Golden Wonder Crisps   UK

The business was started in Scotland in 1947. It was acquired by Imperial Tobacco in 1961 – and a year later it pioneered flavoured varieties, with the first cheese and onion crisps. By 1966 it was the UK market leader. In 1977 Golden Wonder launched Pot Noodles, which would become a very successful business in its own right. In 1986 Hanson acquired Imperial Group in a hostile takeover and Golden Wonder was sold to Dalgety. In 1995 the business was the subject of a management buy-out; at this point Pot Noodles was separated from the original crisps business. In 2000 Golden Wonder was sold to a venture capital business and in 2002 to a Yemeni business owner. By 2006 the company was in administration; Golden Wonder was finished. Pot Noodles remains strong and popular.

The recent changes of ownership had probably contributed to the demise – in that the business did not receive the investment capital it needed to strengthen itself in the face of stiff competition.

The most obvious competition had come from Walkers Crisps, a business owned by PepsiCo. Walkers had been very successful with different flavours and had benefitted from a long series of advertisements featuring the popular Gary Lineker. But Golden Wonder had also been hit by the growing popularity of higher priced premium products such as Tyrrells chips (vegetable as well as potato chips-see Case 9.5) and Kettle chips.

It has been commented that maybe the product itself was a contributing factor. After all, what can one say when the meat flavoured crisps are promoted as safe to eat by vegetarians?

Question

1   How difficult is it to sustain success when there are few barriers to entry into an industry (the technology involved is simple) and there is a constant risk of successful competitor innovations (such as new varieties and flavours)?

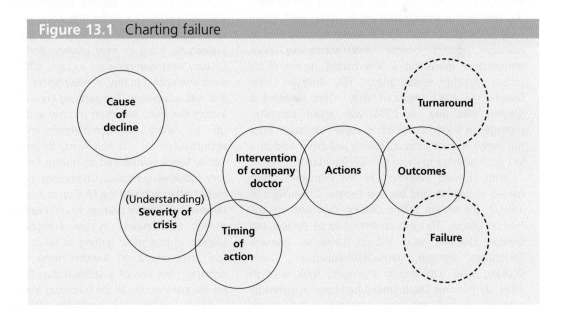

Figure 13.1   Charting failure

limited profits and growing at a rate slower than its industry, but its owners may be happy for it to stay in existence as long as it is solvent. This could be because the owners are drawing substantial earnings and not reinvesting to build a future – for them the business exists to provide them with a lavish lifestyle. In the English football league a large number of clubs, particularly outside the Premier League, fail to make any profit on their footballing activities because their crowds are too low, but other commercial activities, sponsorship, sales of players – and particularly benevolent directors – keep them in business. However, such a lack of success consistently will weaken the company, cause it to exhibit symptoms of decline (discussed below) and may ultimately lead to failure. Top football league clubs in countries such as England, Italy and Spain have all been living beyond their means, particularly in paying players a far greater salary than normal cash flow management would dictate. Once the percentage of money going to pay the players reaches over 60 per cent of turnover a real problem exists. Inflated and unpredictable television and Champions League revenues have all led to potential major failures for clubs such as Leeds United, Barcelona and Lazio. Case 13.3 looks in detail at the rapid collapse of Leeds United.

The forthcoming sections look at what factors typically lead to corporate decline and failure and at how managers might realize that their company is heading for failure unless remedial action is taken. A **turnaround strategy** for companies in trouble will be considered in detail in this chapter.

Case 13.3

Leeds United Football Club   UK

Under manager Don Revie, Leeds United enjoyed their so-called 'Glory Days' in the 1960s and early 1970s, when they were successful in both England and Europe. In 1974 Revie left to become England manager. Six years later – after five changes of manager including Brian Clough's short stay – the club was relegated from the first to the second division. In 1982, with Eddie Gray (a star player from the Revie era) now installed as manager, crowd trouble and continuing poor performance made this a 'low period' in the club's history. Another ex-star player, Billy Bremner, who lasted until 1987, replaced Gray. Gray retained a support role and in 2004 was again caretaker manager as Leeds struggled to avoid relegation from the (now) Premier League, having just been sold in a last ditch attempt to avoid possible liquidation.

With Howard Wilkinson as the manager, Leeds gained promotion and became League Champions in 1991/2, the season before Division One became the Premier League. Fortunes continued to be cyclical and George Graham, who left in 1996 to manage Tottenham Hotspur, replaced Wilkinson. David O'Leary, who was deputy manager, took over in 1998. By this time Leeds United had been acquired by external investors and was, in reality, a PLC, Leeds Sporting. The new Chairman was Peter Ridsdale, a lifelong supporter of the club who had been managing director of the Burton retail chain, which was a major club sponsor. Some commentators were astonished that Ridsdale reportedly offered George Graham a

salary package of £1 million a year in an attempt to persuade him to stay. O'Leary's contract was, however, also worth £6 million over 5 years. Leeds was successful, in part due to a number of young players who had been recruited as youths in the Graham years. However, by 1999, leading players were asking for £50,000 per week salaries. The wage bill was spiralling upwards and the club also began to spend millions of pounds to bring in new players. Both Ridsdale and O'Leary were gambling on success, which, really, they were attempting to buy. In one respect, it made sense – if it was achievable. The winning Premier League clubs attract the most television income and success opens up a variety of commercial and sponsorship opportunities. At the very least, to remain financially viable, Leeds United had to qualify for a place in the very lucrative European Champions League and this meant either winning the FA Cup or finishing in the top three of the Premier League. In 2001 Leeds United were beaten semi-finalists in the European Champions League. In one sense getting as far as they did was a real achievement. In another sense, defeat was a setback – but less of a setback than failing to qualify for the competition in the following season.

Leeds Sporting was profitable until 2000, but the financial situation began to deteriorate in 2001, which coincided with yet another decline in the club's playing success. During this period Manchester United was the dominant club in England, although Arsenal enjoyed some more limited success. Manchester United, of course, is a hugely successful global brand which opens up a myriad of income-generating opportunities. The situation had been made worse for Leeds United in 2000 when two players, Lee Bowyer and Jonathan Woodgate, were charged with assault outside a nightclub in Leeds City Centre.

In 2001 Ridsdale began to receive hate mail from fans who opposed his proposal to move Leeds United out of their Elland Road ground to a new purpose-built stadium. He was now England's highest-paid football club Chairman. Bowyer and Woodgate were acquitted, but Ridsdale disciplined Bowyer, which again angered certain fans. The club was beginning a spiralling cycle of decline.

Results on the field were poor, despite some European success. O'Leary was sacked (with a multi-million pound payoff). Terry Venables and Peter Reid preceded Eddie Gray's second chance as manager. The tendency to replace the manager when results are poor was continuing. Recent signing, Rio Ferdinand was sold to Manchester United for £30 million, yielding a £12 million profit. But he was just one of several players 'divested' to help offset the now unprofitable club's debts, which were growing rapidly as Leeds United was unable to generate an adequate cash flow without European football.

Ridsdale himself resigned in March 2003. To many outsiders he had enjoyed too much power and his willingness to spend money on players and wages had been largely unchecked. Within twelve months, and with debts approaching £100 million, Leeds United's leading creditors accepted a deal and new owners bought the football club from Leeds Sporting, whose shareholders lost everything they had invested. It was now crucial the club avoided relegation at the end of the 2003/4 season. But this was not to happen. Rumours that the club was to be sold again (literally within months) came to nothing when one interested businessman could not secure the necessary funding. Gray was sacked as manager and it was obvious that a number of players would be sold to raise money and reduce the wage bill. What was going to be required now to secure promotion back to the Premier League, let alone to restore the 'Glory Days'?

Ken Bates, who had sold his share in Chelsea FC to the Russian billionaire, Roman Abramavitch, bought Leeds United in January 2005 and took over as Chairman. Leeds competed for two more years in the Championship (one league below the Premier League) but failed to secure promotion in an end-of-year play

off final in May 2006. A year later they were relegated. To make this situation worse the club went into administration with debts of £35 million they could not meet – some of this to the Inland Revenue. Controversially Bates bought the club back from the Administrator, but the debts were not paid in full. Leeds United was required to start the 2007/8 season in a lower division and with a 15 points penalty. They had a remarkably good season and managed to win a place in the play-offs – but they lost again in the final. They would then be ousted from the FA Cup before Christmas 2008 by a non-league team. Managers have continued to 'come and go'. There has also been considerable player movement as the club has tried to keep its debts to a minimum. The most recent appointment generated controversy, yet again. After sacking Gary McAllister, following a run of five defeats, Leeds appointed Simon Grayson, manager at Blackpool, in December 2008. Blackpool accused Leeds of making an illegal approach.

David O'Leary, seen by many as one of the culprits for spending money to build a winning side that failed to deliver results, became manager at Aston Villa for a time – under his leadership Villa almost qualified for a place in the European Champions League in 2004. He is no longer in club management. Peter Ridsdale became Chairman of Barnsley FC, another club that had experienced financial difficulties in recent years, but left for Cardiff City. When Ridsdale left Barnsley the club was in debt. Most Leeds fans always believed Ridsdale had more questions to answer than O'Leary. Before he left the club Ridsdale had had to employ security staff because of threats to the safety of his family.

In 2007 Ridsdale published a book – *United We Fall* – where he maintained the bulk of the blame should lie with O'Leary; he blamed other managers as well. Ken Bates has commented that many of the club's ongoing problems are largely the result of Ridsdale's debt legacy.

Many have opinions, some driven by insight, others by emotion, but will we ever know the truth about exactly what happened? Maybe Peter Ridsdale was right when he commented that 'nobody at Leeds United ever seems to have been honest with one another'.

Questions

1 What exactly had gone wrong?
2 Is it ever possible to apportion blame in circumstances like these?

3   And should we seek to do this anyway?
4   Are there any lessons in this case that might allow other clubs to avoid the same problems, given that ambition demands investment? You might have a look at Newcastle United.

How different is the situation at Chelsea – a club which is also gambling on success by investing huge amounts on players from around the world? Although there is a wealthy benefactor, he could change his mind if the club doesn't win trophies consistently.

13.2 Symptoms of decline

Symptoms of decline are not the causes of failure but indicators that a company might be heading for failure. They will show when a company is performing unsuccessfully relative to what might be expected by an objective outsider or analyst. As mentioned above they will indicate the outcome of poor strategic leadership, inadequate financial management or a lack of competitiveness. Slatter (1984), building on the earlier work of Argenti (1976), analysed 40 UK companies in decline situations which have either been turned around or have failed. He concluded that there are ten major symptoms. In the same way that relative success can be evaluated from financial analysis, several of these symptoms of decline are finance based:

1   falling profitability
2   reduced dividends, because the firm is reinvesting a greater percentage of profits
3   falling sales, measured by volume or revenue after accounting for inflation
4   increasing debt
5   decreasing liquidity
6   delays in publishing financial results, a typical indicator that something is wrong
7   declining market share
8   high turnover of managers
9   top management fear, such that essential tasks and pressing problems are ignored
10   lack of planning or strategic thinking, reflecting a lack of clear direction.

If any of these symptoms are perceived it will be necessary to identify the underlying causes before any remedial action can be attempted. Slatter concluded that a number of causal factors recurred on several occasions in the companies that he studied, and these are summarized below, but categorized in terms of issues of leadership, finance and competitiveness.

Although Slatter's work is over two decades old, it remains definitive. More recent research affirms the arguments. For example, The Society of Practitioners of Insolvency (1995) investigated some 1000 insolvencies in 1994 and determined that the greatest single cause of business failure was loss of market, which was responsible for 29 per cent of the insolvencies. Inadequate cash flow accounted for a further 25 per cent and leadership failings for a further 16 per cent. Earlier analyses by the SPI placed greater emphasis on inadequacies in the financial structure of organizations.

Signals of weak strategic leadership

This list of warning signals has been largely derived from Heller (1998) and Oates (1990) and it relates mainly, but not exclusively, to smaller organizations.

1 *The existence of (too many) 'would-bes'* – Something critical is missing. Possibly the interested people have a will to do something different but lack a good new idea; some key competence is missing, making implementation difficult; or there is a lack of true commitment to an idea, opportunity or venture.

2 *The single-dimension paradox* – The start-up stage for a small business has progressed well, but there is a lack of ability or opportunity to grow the business beyond the initial stages. The idea might only be viable in the short term; there may be inadequate funding; the entrepreneur may be unwilling to let go at the critical time; the initiative could simply run out of steam. The paradox is that the clear focus and individual drive that got the initiative moving in the first place can be what brings it down, through a lack of necessary flexibility.

3 *The business is a half-way house* – In other words it is a franchise or co-operative (or something conceptually similar) and critically dependent upon the continued support and engagement of others who may be outside the business.

4 *The business is impoverished* – Specifically, it fails to achieve, or it loses, a winning strategic position – it is not sufficiently different. Funding is difficult or mismanaged and the business is undercapitalized. Insufficient attention is given to getting the quality right to delight customers. The management team has not developed in the appropriate way, or it has been weakened by people leaving, such that key skills are missing. The business cannot cope when succession becomes an issue.

5 *The business is blinkered* – There is too much self-belief, perhaps driven by an orientation to production rather than customers – the 'we know best' syndrome. The strategic leader is unwilling to accept outside views and advice.

6 *The business is technology shy* – There is a tension here – the business needs capital and technology, but it all costs money. The key questions are just when do you invest and how much do you spend?

7 *The business has become smothered* – Specifically, it has become too bureaucratic, either because of government or even European legislation/rules and regulations, or because it has become bigger and more structured and has lost its creative spark.

8 *The business is (now) run by a crisis manager* – a manager who relies too much on an ability to deal (or not deal!) with setbacks and crises as they arise, often implying the wrong trade-off between reactive and proactive strategies.

9 *The business has started making (too many) mistakes* – Possibly it has become too ambitious, say with misjudged diversification or acquisition. Perhaps it has ignored warning signs such as a cash shortage. Perhaps it is simply too greedy.

The next section discusses how these signals are often the prelude to decline and failure.

13.3 Causes of decline

Inadequate strategic leadership

Poor management

It was shown in Chapter 9 how inadequate strategic leadership can be manifested in a number of ways, which in turn cause key strategic issues to be neglected or ignored. The company could be controlled or dominated by one person whose pursuit of particular personal objectives or style of leadership might create problems or lead to inadequate performance.

The organization might fail to develop new corporate or competitive strategies such that previous levels of performance and success are not maintained when particular products, services or strategies go into decline. This issue can be compounded or alleviated by weak or strong managers, respectively, supporting the strategic leader, and by the quality of non-executive directors on the board.

Poor strategic leadership in terms of building an appropriate organization might mean that key issues or key success factors are ignored or are not given the attention they deserve. A company that is dominated by accountants or engineers might, for example, fail to pay sufficient attention to changing customer requirements and competition. Equally, a company without adequate financial management might ignore aspects of cost and cash-flow management – a factor which will be explored next. Similarly, a company that is undergoing rapid change and possibly diversification might concentrate its resources in the areas of development and neglect the core businesses which should be providing strong foundations for the growth.

Acquisitions which fail to match expectations

As shown in Chapter 11, companies seeking growth or diversification may acquire or take over other companies, or merge with them. Research consistently confirms that in many cases the profits and successes anticipated from the acquisition fail to materialize. This can be the result of a poor choice by the strategic leader, who overestimates the potential, or an inability to manage the larger organization effectively because the problems are underestimated. It is not unusual for companies which fail to have sought fast growth, often following strategies involving major acquisitions.

Mismanagement of big projects

This is related to the previous point, but incorporates a number of other possible strategic decisions. By big projects is meant any really new venture for an organization, including developing new and different products and entering new markets, possibly abroad. It is essential to forecast potential revenues without being unrealistically optimistic, and to control expenditures and costs, but this does not always happen. It seems that companies often:

- underestimate the capital requirements – through poor planning, design changes once the project is under way, and inaccurate estimations of the development time that will be required
- experience unforeseen start-up difficulties – sometimes resulting from lack of foresight and sometimes from misfortune
- misjudge the costs of market entry because of customer hostility or hesitation, or the actions of competitors.

Companies should be careful not to stretch their financial and managerial resources with big projects as they can cause other healthier parts of the business to suffer.

Online Case 13.1 General Electric Corporation (GEC) illustrates these points. Here we see how a previously relatively conservative company (under new leadership) entered new industries and under-estimated the financial and competitive implications of its decisions. The decline was rapid and dramatic.

http://www.

See the online "GEC" case for an example of this section's theory in practice

Dishonesty

There is no doubt that some strategic leaders and businesses take chances and risks which amount to sharp practice and rely on not being found out. However, if there is real dishonesty, and it is found out, then ultimately the business may find survival difficult. The story of the collapse of Robert Maxwell's business empire, after his untimely death by drowning, is well known – he had been using funds from the Mirror Group pension fund to shore up other businesses which needed cash. Once the real extent of the funding needs became known, the whole empire was in danger. A very astute businessman had become too greedy and then turned to desperate measures.

The earlier classic case of the high profile and media-loving American John de Lorean is another example. Supported with money from the UK government he built a car assembly plant on waste land near Belfast and began to manufacture the gull-wing sports car that was featured prominently in the three *Back to the Future* movies. Sadly a series of financial scandals helped finish the venture. De Lorean himself was charged with possessing drugs but the case was eventually dismissed on the grounds of 'Federal entrapment'.

More recent cases in the United States featuring huge businesses such as Enron (creative accounting and unethical trading whereby billions of dollars were earned by exploiting energy shortages in California), Tyco (misuse of corporate funds as well as creative accounting) and Lehman Brothers (improper investments) indicate what can happen when there is a failure of regulation and corporate governance which allows greed and malpractice to occur.

Poor financial management

Poor financial control

This can manifest itself in a number of ways. Particularly important are the failure to manage cash flow and the incidence of temporary illiquidity as a result of overtrading. Inadequate costing systems can mean that companies are not properly aware of the costs of the different products and services that they produce, and as a result they can move from profit to loss if the mix of products that they produce and sell is changed.

If an organization invests in expensive equipment for potentially lower costs or product differentiation, then it automatically increases its fixed costs or overheads. This will increase the break-even point and consequently make the company more volume sensitive. Investments of this nature should not be undertaken lightly and without a thorough and objective assessment of market potential; but some companies do invest without adequate analysis and create financial problems for themselves.

Finally, some companies in decline situations appear not to budget properly. Budgets are short-term financial plans which forecast potential demand and sales revenue, the costs that will be incurred in meeting this demand, and the flow of cash in and out of the business. If budgeted targets are not being met it is essential to investigate why and take any steps necessary to improve the situation. Without proper budgeting companies cannot estimate profits and cash needs adequately and can therefore experience unexpected financial difficulties. Case 13.3 on Leeds United deals with this.

In 2009 a shortage of credit and tight overdrafts hurt small businesses in the UK. They appeared to have healthy order books they were struggling to fulfil. The banks were accused of withholding loans. Whilst it is easy to make this argument, the banks' defence was that they could not be sure the order books would not collapse as the recession deepened.

Cost disadvantages

In addition to the problem of breaking even and covering overheads, described above, companies can experience other cost disadvantages which result in decline.

Companies without scale economies can be at a cost disadvantage relative to larger competitors and suffer in terms of low profit or a failure to win orders because their prices are higher.

Other companies which are vertically integrated and able to exercise control over their supplies, or which are located in areas where labour or service costs are relatively low, can enjoy an absolute cost advantage over their rivals and thereby put pressure on them.

Company structure can yield both cost advantages and cost disadvantages. Large multiproduct companies can subsidize the cost of certain products and again put pressure on their rivals; or conversely they can find that their costs are higher than their smaller competitors because of the overhead costs of the organization structure, say through an expensive head office.

Finally, poor operating management can mean low productivity and higher costs than ought to be incurred, and thereby cause decline. These cost problems all affect competitiveness and they are therefore linked to the additional competition factors discussed below.

Other issues

The debt ratio should be controlled so that companies do not risk embarrassment through not being able to pay interest charges because of low profits. Companies which rely on loan capital may find that in years of low profits they are unable to invest sufficiently and this may lead to decline. Conversely, other companies may decline because they have not invested as a result of conservatism rather than financial inability. This reflects another weakness of strategic leadership.

Competitive forces

Porter's model of the forces that determine industry profitability was discussed in Chapter 2. While all the relevant forces can be managed to create competitive advantage, each of them could cause a weak competitor to be in a decline situation.

The effect of competitive changes

Primarily, companies can find themselves in decline situations if their products or services cease to be competitive. Their effective life and attractiveness to customers might be ending; or their competitors might have improved their product or introduced something new, thereby strengthening their product differentiation and competitive edge and inevitably causing demand for other products to fall. In other words, decline can result from a loss of clear differentiation and in turn a failure to maintain competitive advantage.

If costs increase, say because of increased labour costs which competitors manage to avoid, then pressure will be put on prices or profit margins, and it may no longer be worthwhile manufacturing the product or service. Case 13.2 on Golden Wonder illustrates this.

Resource problems

It was mentioned above and in Case 13.3 (Leeds United) that increased labour costs can render a company uncompetitive; other resources controlled by strong suppliers can have a similar effect. In addition, a company can experience cost problems as a result of currency fluctuations if it fails to buy forward appropriately to offset any risk, and with property rents if leases expire and need renegotiating during a period of inflation.

Inadequate or badly directed marketing

This factor relates to issues of rivalry between competitors. Companies whose competitive strategies rely on differentiation must ensure that customers recognize and value the source of the differentiation. This requires creative and effective advertising and promotion targeted to the appropriate segments and can be very expensive, especially if the industry is characterized by high advertising budgets. Companies who fail to market their products or services effectively may decline because they are failing to achieve adequate sales.

13.4 The feasibility of recovery

When sales or profits are declining because a company is uncompetitive or because an industry is in decline, recovery may or may not be possible. If a company is a single-product firm, or heavily reliant on the industry in question, then it may be in real difficulties and in danger of liquidation unless it can diversify successfully. If profits are declining, such a strategy may be difficult to fund. Where the situation applies to one business unit in an already diversified company, the company as a whole may be less threatened. However, a change of strategy will be required, and the issue concerns whether or not a successful recovery can be brought about and sustained.

The likelihood of a possible recovery improves where:

- the causes of the decline in the firm's sales and profits can be tackled and the problems overcome – this depends upon how serious and deep-rooted they are
- the industry as a whole, or particular segments of the industry which might be targeted, remains attractive
- there is potential for creating or enhancing competitive advantage.

Slatter and Lovett (1999) indicate that there are four steps to turnaround management:

Step 1: Take control and manage the immediate crisis.
Step 2: Rebuild stakeholder support.
Step 3: Fix the business.
Step 4: Resolve future funding.

Recovery situations

Slatter (1984) has postulated that there are essentially four types of recovery situation, and these are illustrated in Figure 13.2(a). Once the profits of the firm or business unit have declined to a crisis stage, then a change in strategy is essential. However, the industry and competitive factors might be such that recovery simply is not feasible. Insolvency is inevitable, whatever alternative strategies might be tried. Successful retrenchment strategies might be implemented and profits improved to a non-crisis level again. However, unless the industry remains in some way attractive and potentially profitable, or the firm retains its competitive advantage, the retrenchment might subsequently fail. A third alternative is a successful turnaround but no real growth and sustained recovery. Possibly in a low-profit industry insufficient funds are generated to finance investment for further growth and diversification. A sustained recovery implies real growth, and possibly further changes in functional, competitive and corporate strategies.

Weitzel and Johnson (1989) drew attention to the issue of timing and highlighted that the later an organization leaves it before it attempts to recover itself from a downward trend, the more difficult the task. Figure 13.2(b) shows that sustained survival or sustained recovery is a much steeper challenge (with less likelihood of success) when remedial action is delayed. There is a point in time – shown as a 'crisis zone' – when recovery is unrealistic.

Non-recoverable situations

Slatter argues that in situations where there is little chance of survival and the likelihood that both retrenchment and turnaround strategies will fail, a number of characteristics are likely to be present.

- The company is not competitive and the potential for improvement is low. This might be the result of a cost disadvantage that cannot be remedied. Certain businesses and industries that

Figure 13.2   The feasibility of recovery

(A) ADAPTED FROM SLATTER, S (1984) CORPORATE RECOVERY, PENGUIN

(B) ADAPTED FROM WEITZEL, W AND JOHNSON, E (1989) DECLINE IN ORGANIZATIONS – A LITERATURE INTEGRATION AND EXTENSION, ADMINISTRATIVE SCIENCE QUARTERLY, 34 (1)

have declined in the face of foreign competition, especially from countries with low wage costs, are testament to this.

- The company is not diversified and lacks both the resources and access to resources to remedy this weakness.
- Demand for the basic product or service involved is in terminal decline.

Temporary recovery

Where a retrenchment strategy is implemented successfully it may or may not be sustained. If new forms of competitive advantage are found and sustained, or the product or service is effectively repositioned, subsequent insolvency may be avoided. However, if costs are reduced or additional revenues are generated in an essentially unattractive and declining industry, the effect will be limited. In such cases it will become important for the company to invest the cash generated from the retrenchment to diversify, if that is possible.

If an organization has captive customers who are in some way dependent and face high short-term exit costs, possibly because of agreed specifications, they can exploit them for a period by charging high prices. There will be a temporary profit improvement, but the customers will be lost in the medium to long term. Companies following this strategy need to use the extra revenue and the time that they buy to develop new strategic opportunities.

Case 13.9 (Arcadia, at the end of this chapter) illustrates a temporarily successful turnaround by the Burton Group which was not sustained. Further retrenchment was required.

Sustained survival

Sustained survival implies that a turnaround is achieved but there is little further growth. The industry may be in slow decline, or generally competitive and unprofitable. Survival potential and limited profit opportunities continue to exist, but little more. Sustained survival would also apply where a company failed to use its increased earnings effectively and did not diversify into new, more profitable opportunities which could provide growth prospects.

Sustained recovery

A sustained recovery is likely to involve a genuine and successful turnaround, possibly new product development or market repositioning. In addition, the turnaround may well be followed by a growth strategy, perhaps acquisition and diversification.

The recovery is helped if the industry is strong and attractive and the company's decline has been caused by poor management rather than because the industry itself is in a decline.

Both a sustained survival and a sustained recovery may involve divestment of assets or part of the business to enable the company to concentrate on selected market segments or products.

Slatter (1984) studied a number of successful and unsuccessful attempts at turnaround, and concluded that there are three main features of a sustained recovery:

1 Asset reduction is invariably required in order to generate cash. Quite frequently this will be achieved by divestment of part of the business.

2 A new strategic leader is usually necessary. The new strategic leader will typically be associated with a restructuring of the organization, the introduction of new strategies and a redefinition of roles and policies.

3 Better financial control systems are also a normal feature.

While retrenchment and initial survival can be achieved by concentrating on improving efficiencies, sustained survival and recovery will invariably require more effective competitive and corporate strategies. Case 13.4 provides an example of a more sustained recovery at Pringle. The strategic leader involved, Kim Winser, then left to try and do the same for Aquascutum.

To summarize this section, the opportunities for sustained recovery, or at least survival, improve where:

- there are fewer causes of the decline
- the crisis is not deep-rooted, perhaps because the decline is the result of poor management rather than an unattractive declining industry
- there is support from key stakeholders for the changes required (this may involve understanding by financiers and the commitment of managers and other employees to the necessary changes)
- strategic opportunities exist to differentiate, refocus and create competitive advantage
- the company has the ability to reduce costs.

Case 13.4

Kim Winser, Pringle & Aquascutum

This case describes the impact Kim Winser has had in reviving the fortunes of two long-established brands. Winser herself has been described as having that 'unnerving mix of friendliness and control that powerful women have'.

Pringle is a long-established clothing and knitwear manufacturer based in the Scottish borders. Formed in 1815 Pringle is believed to be the UK's oldest clothing brand. The company became known for the 'twinset' matching jumper and cardigan for ladies – which was worn and popularized by movie stars such as Audrey Hepburn, Vivienne Leigh and Margaret Lockwood in the 1950s – the shruggie 'ballet cardigan' and the Argyle check sweater worn by golfers.

In 2002 the current owner, Dawson International, a Scottish yarn and clothing manufacturer, was keen to refocus its business around cashmere products, and opted to sell Pringle for £10 million to Fang Brothers Knitting of Hong Kong. At the time Pringle was in decline. A number of reasons were cited. Sales had fallen in key Asian markets; the value of sterling was high; the clothes were staid and unfashionable; the brand had failed to keep up with changing tastes. Dawson had closed the Pringle factory in Berwick and reduced the headcount elsewhere – but the overall health of the business had not improved markedly. New owner Kenneth Fang decided he needed a fresh chief executive if the brand was to be rejuvenated.

He recruited Kim Winser, at the time a marketing director with Marks and Spencer, where she had worked since she was eighteen. Feisty, she had once criticized M&S chief, Lord Sieff, in a meeting, arguing against his plan to appoint a female board director. The argument is that she herself wanted to be the first woman on the M&S Board! She had been promoted through the ranks and was credited with turning around the womenswear business in the 1990s. She came with a reputation for being driven, career-minded and organized. Fang was willing to give her considerable autonomy.

She concluded the brand needed reconceptualizing and repositioning in a short period of time – her target was just three months. She set out to simultaneously lower costs and develop new products and market opportunities. More jobs, including senior management posts, were lost. The long-standing retail concession with Edinburgh Woollen Mills was abandoned in favour of high end/high fashion outlets such as Selfridges and Harvey Nichols. A celebrity endorsement deal with golfer Nick Faldo was terminated.

A new collection was quickly designed – with a more modern look – although the product range overall was being reduced. Aspects of the past – the Argyll check, the twinset and the cashmere yarns – were retained, but new colours, new styles and new ways of displaying the famous Pringle motifs were sought. The range was promoted in glossy fashion and lifestyle magazines; model Sophie Dahl was recruited for the campaign. The effect was instantaneous and sales jumped 30 per cent. A confident Pringle joined the London catwalk for the first time in its history. When Madonna, David Beckham and Robbie Williams were all seen in public wearing Pringle clothes (a hugely valuable free endorsement) the brand was 'hot'. It was now 'nightclub' rather than 'golfclub'.

Winser decided to enter retailing, another first for Pringle. She began with a shop at Heathrow Airport, but with plans for Central London, New York, Tokyo and other European cities. The range has also been extended beyond knitwear into complementary skirts, trousers, dresses, coats, swimwear and accessories. Baby wear and homewear are on the future agenda. It helps that any spare capacity in the Pringle factories can be used to manufacture other products for the Fang Brothers.

In 2006 Kim Winser joined Aquascutum, which she described as a 'sleeping giant of a business'. Aquascutum had also been described as 'Britain's noblest fading brand'. Could she repeat her turnaround achievements?

Aquascutum became a popular choice for consumers willing to pay premium prices for good quality, stylish clothing; it is perhaps best known for its trenchcoat – a distinctive, classic, light tan coloured, belted, double-breasted raincoat with sleeve straps and epaulettes. The company is 150 years old – younger than Pringle! – and now owned by a Japanese business, Renown.

The flagship London store has photographs of Hollywood celebrities wearing the products – the fact that most of these are 'older' rather than 'youthful' stars is indicative of the typical buyer. Annual turnover exceeds £200 million, mainly in the UK and Japan, but the business had been losing money. One question concerned whether it would lend itself to a more youthful appeal with endorsement by models such as Kate Moss or Sophie Dahl.

Winser believed she needed to 'have fun with the style' but not sacrifice the brand's heritage – an interesting challenge. She wanted to attract new customers without losing the existing ones. More accessories were on the cards, especially bags.

In 2009, and after three years of losses, Winser sought to acquire the business as a management buy-out, but her bid failed 'at the eleventh hour'. She resigned and left immediately. Renown continued with its attempt to sell the business and started discussions with a Hong Kong trader who already acted as a wholesaler in the Far East for Aquascutum trenchcoats – but again no deal was concluded. 'The chances of the brand surviving as a British business were fading fast'. It began to appear that Renown might move everything, including design and manufacture, to the Far East.

Meanwhile Kim Winser's name has been linked to a senior post at Versace and also as a possible successor to Sir Stuart Rose as CEO of Marks & Spencer.

Questions

1 How do you perceive the similarities and differences of the two turnaround challenges faced by Kim Winser?

2 Given that in the world of high fashion little stays still for long, what would you recommend Pringle should do in the future to make sure Pringle does not once again switch from growth into decline?

3 Had Kim Winser succeeded in buying Aquascutum what changes do you think she might have made/needed to make?

4 Given her record would she appear to be a likely candidate for the leadership role at M&S?

Rescue, to provide a platform for recovery, could well take 12–18 months and the key themes are:

- making the business cash rich by: selling assets, obtaining a new injection of funding and restructuring debt; and
- tightening operations by: strengthening margins, better cost control, better working capital management and better information.

True renewal and recovery could then require a further 3–5 years.

The skills required for the rescue and recovery stages are different. There may be a requirement or a logic in changing the strategic leader – as happened at Pringle – to find the most appropriate person at any time.

It is worth remembering that a vision for recovery is of little use until the business has been rescued and consolidated; equally, consolidation without a future vision is likely to show only limited and short-term benefits.

Van de Vliet (1998) provides the following list of useful questions for attempting to assess the situation and the recovery potential:

1   Is there some part of the business worth rescuing?

2   What are the key core activities in the business?

3   Does the organization have the people it is going to need, people who truly understand the business at an operational level?

4   Do these managers have the freedom to manage?

5   Are there ways in which the product(s) and/or service(s) could be improved?

6   Can the necessary resources (other than people) that are going to be required be secured?

Case 13.5 – Ministry of Sound – deals with these points.

Case 13.5

Ministry of Sound   UK

Ministry of Sound is a multi-media business founded by ex-Etonian entrepreneur James Palumbo, despite him being described as 'media shy and someone who loathes dance music'. It began in 1991 when a South London warehouse was transformed into London's first 'superclub'. It was located well away from the main London club scene and the bar was non-alcoholic. The sound system was state-of-the-art. The brand was quickly extended and the business diversified into CD compilations, magazines, holidays, a music Internet site and clothes. Ministry of Sound also started an independent record label. Its 'Relentless' label (a joint venture) recorded Daniel Bedingfield.

In 2000 Palumbo was able to sell 15 per cent of the business to 3i for £24 million.

But by 2002 dance music was less popular and the dedicated magazine *Ministry* was closed down. 10 per cent of the staff were made redundant and a planned move into radio was postponed. Palumbo opted to step up to the Chairman role and promoted marketing manager Mark Rodol to be CEO. Rodol was charged with finding a 'focused, long-term, brand-led strategy'; he was seen as closer to the customers than Palumbo himself, who still owns the business.

What had gone wrong? The business had perhaps expanded too quickly in too many directions. It pursued an idea if Ministry 'could make money out of it' regardless of whether it added value to the corporate brand or even had distinctive competitive advantage.

Rodol wanted to focus on clubs, CDs, the popular Internet site, events and relevant licensing deals. The

flagship London nightclub, which was still attracting between 5000 and 7000 'clubbers' every week, was refurbished. A new magazine deal was established with publishers, Condé Nast. Ministry of Sound licensed its

© PEERPOINT/ALAMY

name to electronics company, Bush, for a new range of hi-fi equipment. Annual sales of £20 million were expected.

In the past few years MoS has expanded with a number of franchised clubs in Asia, including Bangkok and Singapore. Another is due to open in Melbourne in 2010. After a tricky period the recording arm has released a number of successful compilation DVDs and expanded with the acquisition of the Hed Kandi record label. Ministry of Sound TV has been introduced to complement the dedicated radio station. In 2007/8 group turnover was £136 million.

Questions

1 Has Rodol found a defensible 'focused, long-term, brand-led strategy'?

2 What future changes/ additions would you recommend?

3 Do you think the problems MoS faced had more to do with strategic ideas or with the implementation of the ideas?

Having considered the background feasibility of recovery, the actual recovery strategies are now examined in greater detail.

13.5 Retrenchment strategies

In this section organizational and financial changes, cost and asset reduction and strategies aimed at generating revenue are considered. Retrenchment strategies are essentially functional, rather than competitive or corporate, and are aimed at making the company more productive and profitable while retaining essentially the same products and services, although there might be some rationalization. By concentrating on financial issues, they often address major causes of the company's decline.

Organizational changes

It was emphasized above that a change in strategic leadership is frequently involved in recovery strategies. In addition, there might be a need to strengthen the management team in other areas. The fact that there are personnel changes is not the important issue. The subsequent changes to strategies, structure and policies, and the effect on the existing staff and their motivation, are what matter. Reorganizations are likely to take place, involving new definitions of roles and responsibilities. Policies and management and control systems may also be changed to give managers new opportunities to achieve, and to convince them that recovery prospects are real.

Financial changes

Poor financial control systems, say a badly managed cash flow, are often a feature of companies in difficulties. In addition, overheads may have been allowed to become too high in relation to direct production costs, and the company may not know the actual costs of producing particular products and services or be able to explain all expenditures. The establishment of an effective costing system, and greater control over the cash flow, can improve profitability and generate revenue.

Another retrenchment strategy is the restructuring of debt to reduce the financial burden of the company. Possibly repayment dates can be extended, or loan capital converted into preference shares or equity, thereby allowing the company more freedom through less pressure to pay interest. Eurotunnel provides an excellent example of this: loans were rescheduled and some were transferred into equity to reduce the interest burden as the company struggled to generate enough revenue to cover its costs. Operationally, Eurotunnel is now a success. Passenger and freight traffic, supported by income from Eurostar, delivers a trading profit – but the cost of its debt, required for the enormous construction project over several years, drastically reduces this.

Cost-reduction strategies

Traditionally highly acquisitive companies such as Hanson looked for companies with high gross margins and relatively low after-tax profitability. These are indications of overheads which have been allowed to grow too much, thereby providing opportunities for improving profits by reducing organizational slack and waste.

Companies can address the overheads issue for themselves, without being acquired, if they recognize the extent of the problem and are determined to reduce their costs in order to improve their competitiveness and profitability. This happened increasingly in the late 1980s and 1990s, reducing the number of attractively priced acquisition targets. By and large those companies that could not reduce their costs were liquidated as the economy tightened.

In terms of reducing costs, the normal starting place is labour costs. In many cases opportunities will exist to reduce labour costs and improve productivity, but if the reductions are too harsh there can be a real threat to the quality of both the product and the overall service offered to customers. One opportunity is to examine working patterns and attempt to manage overtime, part-time arrangements and extra shifts both to meet demand and to contain costs. Companies can slip easily into situations where overtime and weekend working are creating costs which cannot be recovered in competitive prices.

Redundancies may be required to reduce costs and bring capacity more into line with demand. Again this can be implemented well or poorly. In most cases the issue is not losing particular numbers of people and thereby saving on wages, but losing non-essential staff or those who fail to make an effective contribution. There is always the danger in a voluntary redundancy programme that good people will choose to leave or take early retirement.

Costs can be reduced anywhere and everywhere in the value chain. Better supply arrangements and terms can reduce costs; products can be redesigned to cost less without any loss in areas significant to customers; and certain activities, such as public relations, training, advertising and research and development (R&D) might be cut. The argument here is that these activities are non-essential, and this might be perfectly plausible in the short term. It may not be the case for the longer term, and therefore they would need to be reinstated when extra revenues had been regenerated.

Asset-reduction strategies

Divestment of a business unit, or part of the business, is an asset-reduction strategy but is considered in greater detail later. It is really more of a corporate than a functional strategy, and the decision should not be made on financial grounds alone. While the sale of a business can raise money, this gain may be more than offset if there is existing synergy with other parts of the company which suffer in some way from the divestment.

Internal divestment or rationalization can take a number of forms. Plants might be closed and production concentrated in fewer places; production might be rescheduled to generate increased economies of scale. The idea is to reduce both overheads and direct costs.

Assets might be sold and leased back – As far as the balance sheet is concerned, assets have been reduced and in turn cash has been generated. The scope and capacity of the business may be unaffected; the changes are exclusively financial.

Revenue-generating strategies

The marketing strategies considered in the next section on turnarounds are essentially revenue-generating strategies, and they frequently involve changes in competitive strategies. However, revenue can also be generated by improving certain management control systems. If stocks are reduced by better stock management or by a review of the whole production system and a move towards just in time, cash is freed. In the same way, if debtors can be persuaded to settle accounts more speedily, cash flow can be improved.

> We weren't making money at SAS [Scandinavian Airlines System] when I came here. We were in a desperate situation, and that's the worst time to focus on preventing mistakes and controlling costs. First, we had to increase revenues. We had to decide what business we were going to do – before you can start managing effectively you must know who is your customer and what is your product – and go to work on the revenue side. Then we could think about cutting costs, because only then would we know which costs could be cut without losing competitiveness.
>
> JAN CARLZON, WHEN PRESIDENT AND CHIEF EXECUTIVE OFFICER, SCANDINAVIAN AIRLINES SYSTEM

Case 13.6 features three well-known brands, Gap, Gucci and Maserati, and examines their approaches to increasing revenue.

Case 13.6

Gap, Gucci and Maserati   US Int

Gap

Gap is a US clothing retailer which also owns the Old Navy and Banana Republic brands. The business was founded by Don Fisher and throughout the 1990s he continued to work closely with his hands-on CEO, who designed clothes and specified inventory quantities. When Paul Pressler was recruited from Disney in 2002, and appointed CEO, the business was in some difficulty. Sales were falling and Gap appeared to have 'lost touch with its customers'. Could Pressler restore its previous performance levels?

Gap's original target customers were the so-called baby boomers, those born between 1946 and 1964. As they matured, married and had children the brand was extended – with Gap Kids (1986) and Baby Gap (1990). The business did very well with smart casual clothes when 'dress down Fridays' were introduced. But competition from 'more sassy brands' such as Abercrombie & Fitch and American Eagle hit Gap. The company reaction was to target the younger market, but critics felt the focus was more on teenagers than people in their twenties and this was a mistake. Gap had failed to get the range quite

right. Profits were affected because costs were relatively high through inadequate investment in retail systems.

Pressler was more detached in his style and he was determined to 'replace intuition with science'. He repositioned the brands – with Banana Republic the most up-market, followed by Gap and then Old Navy. Products were segmented for discrete groups such as mums, mums shopping for families, fashionable young people and more conservative young people. Considerable work was done on sizing – with sales data used to determine which sizes would feature in different stores. Where sales were inadequate, stores were closed. But three years after his appointment, Gap was still struggling.

Gucci

Gucci began life in Florence in 1923 as a manufacturer of superior quality leather goods – but since 2001 it has been owned by the French business Pinault Printemps Redoute (PPR); it is now based in London. During the 1990s the company had enjoyed something of a revival in its fortunes.

Gucci is perhaps best known for its shoes and handbags – which are sold in boutiques and specialist department stores around the world. Many of its customers are wealthy Asians. The company has systematically diversified and the Gucci *group* also includes Yves Saint Laurent (clothing, perfumes and other luxury items), the Alexander McQueen, Stella McCartney and Balenciaga fashion labels and the French Boucheron jewellery business. YSL had been acquired in 1999. Group sales were in the region of 2.5 billion Euros when PPR acquired the business.

PPR appointed a new CEO, Robert Polet, from Unilever. Although he had been responsible for revenues some three times Gucci's turnover, his main experience was with ice cream.

He targeted a number of things:

- Sales of Gucci-branded products needed to double (from 1.5 billion Euros) by 2010 – by exploiting opportunities in Asia and India
- The group overall should adopt the 'lighter style' of YSL
- Shoes and jewellery sales should be increased
- The specialist fashion labels needed to be lifted to at least break-even performance
- Marketing and customer awareness was not strong enough
- The supply chain should be strengthened to 'best in class' performance levels.

Maserati

Maserati started making cars in 1914; and its success as a sports car manufacturer peaked in the 1950s. There have been six owners of the business, the most recent being Ferrari, itself owned by Fiat. Ferrari bought 50 per cent of the business in 1997 and the remaining half in 1999.

In the early years of the 21st century Maserati was losing money. It was not alone. The two luxury brands owned by Volkswagen – the Italian Lamborghini and the French Bugatti – were also struggling. Ferrari inherited a 'ramshackle factory' making 700 cars a year. It 'wasn't really a business any more' but Ferrari was determined to remedy this. Money was invested and capacity increased to 5000 cars a year. This was 300 cars more than Ferrari itself, which was being kept at that level. The realistic target for Maserati was thought to be 10,000. To put these figures in perspective, the UK's specialist sports car builder, Morgan – albeit a different offering – makes around 700 cars a year. A new CEO, Martin Leach, from Ford, was appointed in 2004.

There was a stated desire to introduce new models, but this takes time. Maserati uses Ferrari engines, as one might expect. The focus of investment would be on the engine, gearbox and electronics – the car must be distinguishable on performance. The most popular model is the sporty Quattro Porte saloon, which competes against the top of the range BMW and Mercedes models. 'The Maserati brand has an intrinsic value that can justify a high price – 10 per cent to 20 per cent above BMW and Mercedes – if the product is right.'

Questions

1 How difficult is it to revive a flagging brand and target new customers in a very competitive market?
2 What has happened to Gap and Gucci during 2008 and 2009 when so many retailers have been struggling?
3 Was the timing of the attempt to rejuvenate Maserati 'right' or 'wrong'?

SOURCE: THIS CASE STUDY WAS PREPARED USING PRIMARILY PUBLICLY AVAILABLE SOURCES OF INFORMATION FOR THE PURPOSES OF

13.6   Turnaround strategies

Retrenchment strategies will usually have short time horizons and they will be designed to yield immediate results. Turnaround strategies are likely to address those areas which must be developed if there is to be a sustained recovery. They involve changes in the overall marketing effort, including the repositioning or refocusing of existing products and services, together with the development of new ones. They are designed to bring quick results and at the same time contribute towards longer-term growth. They overlap with the internal limited growth strategies outlined in Chapter 11, and they may also be a stepping stone to growth through diversification.

Retrenchment strategies do not affect customers directly, but the following turnaround strategies are designed to improve the effectiveness of the company's marketing. Consequently, they are addressing customers and consumers directly, and for this reason some degree of caution is required in implementing the changes involved.

Changing prices

Prices can be changed at very short notice, and price increases or decreases can result in increased revenue. Price rises can increase revenue as long as the elasticity of demand ensures that sales do not decline unacceptably with the price increase. Price decreases can improve demand and hence revenue, again depending on the elasticity of demand. Hence, it is important to have an insight into the demand elasticity for individual products and services, although forecasting the effect of price changes will be subject to some uncertainty. In general, the opportunity to increase prices is related to the extent of existing differentiation, and the opportunity to differentiate further and create new competitive advantage.

It is important to remember that unless particular products and services are regarded as underpriced by customers in relation to their competition, a price rise should be accompanied by advertising support and possibly minor changes and improvements in the product or packaging. The price change must be justified.

It is also important to consider the likely reaction of competitors, which in turn will be influenced by the structure of the industry and the degree and type of competitive rivalry. Markets with an oligopoly structure, an essential feature of UK industry, tend to follow price decreases but not price rises.

In relation to the concept of price changes, discount structures might be altered to favour certain groups of customers at the expense of others. Such a strategic move can both raise revenue and improve the attractiveness of a company to certain market segments. Any negative effect on other customer groups should be monitored carefully.

However, on occasions, some companies will be seen to increase their prices immediately after being acquired by a new parent. When this happens there is often an assumption that existing customers are, at least for a time, committed and locked in – finding a new supplier will take time – and so they can be 'exploited'. The new parent is willing to lose them in the medium term as it has other plans for the business, which it might well involve rationalization and selling on.

Refocusing

The idea behind refocusing is to concentrate effort on specific customers and specific products, relating the two closely together. The strategy requires careful thought and attention in relation to why people buy and opportunities for differentiation, segmentation and competitive advantage. The selection of particular product/market and service/market niches for concentrating effort will depend upon revenue and growth potential, gross margins, the extent and type of competition for the segment or niche, and the potential to create a response to marketing activity, such as advertising.

In the short term products or services that sell quickly and generate cash quickly may be attractive opportunities even if their gross margin is small; and there may well be a group of customers for whom an appropriate package can be created.

New product development

The replacement of existing products with new ones may be required to effect a turnaround if a company has been losing competitiveness in an attractive industry by falling behind competitors in terms of innovation and product improvement. Equally, product improvements, designed to prolong the product life cycle, can be extremely useful in low-growth or declining industries. They can be used to help a company to concentrate on the particular segments of the market that are remaining relatively strong.

Rationalizing the product line

Variety reduction can similarly be useful for concentrating efforts on the stronger market segments and opportunities, particularly where the industry overall is losing attractiveness. Such a strategy needs a proper understanding of costs, and which individual products and services are most and least profitable. In a multiproduct organization, with interdependencies between the business units, for example, transfer price arrangements can distort profitabilities. As mentioned earlier, certain products and services can be vital contributors to overall synergy, but individually not very profitable, and care needs to be taken with these.

Emphasis on selling and advertising

An emphasis on selling and advertising might take the form of selected additional expenditure in order to generate greater revenue, or the examination of all current marketing expenditure in order to try and ascertain the best potential returns from the spending.

Expenditure on advertising, below-the-line promotions and the salesforce is used to promote products and services in order to generate sales revenue. However, all of these activities are investments, and their potential returns should be considered. The increased revenue expected from any increased spending should certainly exceed the additional costs incurred, and there is an argument that the opportunity cost of the investment funds should also be assessed.

While five alternative approaches to improving marketing effectiveness have been considered in this section, a number of them may be used in conjunction at any time. Moreover, these turnaround strategies may also be combined with the retrenchment strategies discussed earlier, the aim being both to reduce costs and to improve revenue at the same time.

It has already been explained that the divestment of products or business units can be useful for reducing assets in retrenchment strategies. Divestments can also be used to rationalize the product line, as discussed above.

Rejuvenating mature businesses

Pulling these points together, Baden-Fuller and Stopford (1992) define a mature business as 'one whose managers believe themselves to be imprisoned by their environment and unable to succeed'. As a consequence they are invariably giving poor service to their customers and achieving financial returns that are barely adequate. Often, with a more creative, entrepreneurial, innovative approach, they can be rejuvenated. The challenge, simply, is to become a stronger competitor. This transformation is likely to require a number of developmental steps over an extended period, rather than can be achieved with a one-off major project; it implies a change of culture and style. Success will not be instantaneous; it will need building. Baden-Fuller and Stopford have developed a four-stage model for rejuvenation, which is summarized in Figure 13.3.

1 *Galvanization* comes when there is a clear recognition of the true state of the business and the establishment of an able management team which is committed to dealing with the problem. This may only need a change of strategic leader; on other occasions the changes will be more extensive. If those managers who are responsible for bringing about the crisis, through poor decisions and judgement, or negligently allowing the situation to deteriorate, stay, they will need to change.

Figure 13.3 Rejuvenating the mature business

ADAPTED FROM BADEN-FULLER, C AND STOPFORD, J (1992) *REJUVENATING THE MATURE BUSINESS*, ROUTLEDGE

Progress then requires resources. Independent businesses are likely to require fresh capital and possibly new owners. Subsidiaries of larger organizations will have to justify new, corporate investment.

2 *Simplification* follows, implying a clearer focus and the concentration of scarce resources on a smaller agenda to build a strong and sustainable core. Strategies, structures and styles may all have to change. This level of change is sometimes termed strategic regeneration, and the demands and implications are looked at further in Chapter 17. The business must next

3 *Build* new competencies and competitive advantages. Because of resource pressures this is again likely to take time and prove highly challenging. Finally, true rejuvenation requires it to

4 *Exert leverage* to extend its new competencies and capabilities into new products, services, markets and opportunities.

These points are illustrated in Case 13.7, where we see the intervention of a turnaround specialist at two businesses: New Covent Garden Foods and Green and Black's Chocolate.

Case 13.7

William Kendall – Turnaround Specialist UK

William Kendall has demonstrated expertise in turning around companies. He will join a company and allow its founder to make an exit; he will then build the business in terms of both scale and profitability before selling it on as a viable concern.

Kendall is the son of a Bedfordshire farming family and he grew up passionate about both food and business. After school he spent a year in the army before reading law at Cambridge. He trained and practised as a barrister before becoming an investment banker. After the crash of 1987 he opted to study for an MBA at Insead.

In 1989 he joined the New Covent Garden Food Company, best known in the UK for its fresh soup in cartons, a product the supermarkets have come to copy with their own branded ranges. The company was not making money when Kendall arrived, and this continued for five years. But with innovation, new products, diversification into fresh gravies, fresh baked beans and fresh sweet sauces, and with more robust management systems, its fortunes were changed around. In 1998 it was sold for £24 million to existing food business, S. Daniels, a related business that had moved from canned to fresh and chilled fruit and drinks products.

His next challenge was Green and Black's chocolate, where he and a business partner bought an 85 per cent stake. He was able to do this at a favourable price because the company was 'losing money thanks to a mish-mash of a product range'. The business had been set up by Craig Sams, an American who had come to the UK from California. Sams had been an early campaigner for organic living and he set up Whole Earth Foods in 1967 to make peanut butter, jams, baked beans and cereals. Whilst on a holiday in Belize he met some Mayan Indians and spontaneously offered to buy organic cocoa from them if they started to grow it. Some time later they took him up on his offer! As a response he started Green and Black's in 1991 and its chocolate became the first product in the UK to feature the Fair Trade kite mark, signalling that a fair price was being paid to the farmers who supplied it. It symbolizes an ethical business. Kendall and Sams knew each other, got on well, but Kendall commented that Sams was not a businessman at heart. 'He has brilliant ideas, but soon moves on to the next thing.' In other words, he starts things but doesn't stay focused and build the business.

Kendall immediately rationalized the product range to focus on chocolate. He set out, as he had at Covent Garden, to build a strong management team so he could step back from operational commitments. To generate funding he negotiated a sale of 5 per cent of the equity to Cadbury Schweppes. The product was clearly a luxury product, not an essential food stuff, and it was priced higher than the main branded chocolate bars. But it was high quality and customers 'get their chocolate hit from eating less than they would of the main brands'. Kendall recognized the importance of supermarkets and targeted them. Supermarket sales of £2 million in the 1990s increased sevenfold in the first four years Kendall was in control, and the annual growth was around 40 per cent through this channel. Margins might be tight but it was a very significant route to market for a confectionery product. Improved marketing, new products and ever-increasing quality standards went hand-in-hand with the supermarket strategy. In 2006 the whole business was sold to Cadbury Schweppes for some £20 million. Inevitably there were sceptics who did not believe the new owner would preserve the strong ethical values of the business. Kendall dismissed this argument and said they had been able to work with Cadbury Schweppes successfully for three years and 'big business is not automatically evil'. Cadbury has since extended its committee to Fair Trade.

Questions

1 Would you think any strategic leader who 'understands the theory' could be a turnaround specialist like William Kendall, or do you think he has certain qualities and skills that make him the expert he is?
2 What is the 'secret of his success'?

SOURCE: THIS CASE STUDY WAS PREPARED USING PRIMARILY PUBLICLY AVAILABLE SOURCES OF INFORMATION FOR THE PURPOSES OF

Total quality management initiatives and **business process re-engineering** programmes can make a major contribution, but alone they will not make an organization more innovatory. The whole enterprise must become more customer focused, committed to efficiency and improvement, and responsive to environmental demands.

It would be useful at this point to return to Figure 3.10. Through double-loop learning an uncompetitive firm has found new opportunities for adding value and creating advantages; it has then used single-loop learning initially to leverage this new advantage.

Turnaround themes

To round off this section, van de Vliet (1998) suggests that the following themes determine the likelihood of turnaround success:

● the existence of 'some fat to live off'. An organization which has reached a certain size, perhaps a turnover of some £10 million, and has a strong customer base, will have a more realistic chance than a much smaller organization without an equivalent customer base

- some identifiable potential, such as market leadership in a niche or segment
- the consistency or focus in the portfolio – and the potential for synergy. If there has been a series of non-synergistic acquisitions, divestments should be straightforward
- the opportunity for a fresh perspective from a new strategic leader
- the existence of a strong management team, or one with potential, even if they are currently underperforming
- the existence of a clear structure and communications
- the ability to eradicate any overtrading quickly to strengthen the cash position.

13.7 Divestment strategies

Divestment can be essentially *internal*, the closure of a plant as part of a rationalization programme, or *external*, the sale of part of the business. The justification will be similar for each, and any resources saved or generated should be reallocated.

Pharmaceutical companies are now divesting non-core assets such as medical devices and manufacturing plants in an effort to cut costs and focus on core strategies, primarily drug development. However, while some Pharma companies are narrowing their focus, targeting specific disease areas for future growth, others are taking a broader approach in an effort to spread risk and return on investment.

Davis (1974) argues that divestments are often sudden decisions rather than decisions reached as part of a continual evaluation process which reviews all of the products and services in the firm's portfolio periodically. Companies that utilize portfolio analysis as part of their planning will be in a position to identify which parts of the business are the poorest performers and possible candidates for divestment. However, Devlin (1989) contends that effective divestment is a skill that few strategic leaders actually possess. This, he suggests, is a critical strategic issue, given that many acquisitions fail to achieve their expected returns. While divestment may suggest an admission of failure, it can be used positively. After Boots divested Halfords (car spares, bicycles etc.) the 'business that did not fit' has thrived under new ownership.

There will be an obvious reluctance to sell a business unit to another company, especially a competitor, who might succeed and transform the business into an effective performer. This will be particularly important if such success could pose a future threat to business units that have been retained. For these reasons divestments are often associated with a change of strategic leader, as an outsider is less likely to feel any loyalty to past decisions.

Issues in selecting a divestment candidate

A number of possible considerations might be relevant in selecting a product, service or business unit for divestment. Both financial and strategic aspects are important:

- the current position in the product life cycle, and the likely future potential for further growth and profitability
- the current market position, and opportunities for competitive advantage
- taking these two points further and considering portfolio analyses, the future potential for cash generation and future investment requirements in order to remain competitive (linked to this is the opportunity cost of the resources being utilized)

- identified alternative uses for the resources which could be freed up, and in certain cases the extent of the need to free up resources for relocation
- the ability to find a suitable buyer willing to pay an acceptable price.

In Chapter 11 we saw how Daimler-Benz decided to withdraw funding from its Fokker aircraft subsidiary. Realistically, a new owner was required for Fokker. One possibility was Bombardier, the Canadian company which had already rescued Shorts (Belfast, and a major subcontractor to Fokker), de Havilland and Learjet. Bombardier's post-acquisition strategy is to invest heavily to restructure, modernize and extend the product line. It weighs the turnaround chances carefully, looking for good management and stable employee relations, sound technologies, products with competitive advantage and long-term growth potential, component orders to offset cyclical downturns and tight cost management. In the event, Bombardier decided that Fokker was not an appropriate purchase.

Issues in the divestment

Once the decision to divest has been taken, there is a number of further considerations.

First, there is the issue of how active and how secretive the search for a buyer should be. It can be argued that there should be an active search for an acceptable buyer who is willing to pay an appropriate premium, on the grounds that it is all too easy to sell a business cheaply. A low price might be expected where the sale is hurried, perhaps because there is a pressing need to raise money or where a first offer is accepted without an exploration of other options. There is also an argument in favour of secrecy and speed as opposed to prolonged and publicized negotiations. Employees may leave if they feel that their company is no longer wanted by its existing parent, and relationships with important suppliers and customers may also be affected.

In addition, simply offering a business for sale may not be productive. Sales must be negotiated and potential buyers must be vetted. The terms of the sale should be financially acceptable, and the buyer should not be an organization that can use the newly acquired business to create a competitive threat to retained activities.

Devlin (1989) suggests that in general speed is of the essence. Long delays are likely to mean lost confidence. However, some businesses may be difficult to sell.

Second, buyers can be categorized into different types, and the potential of the business for them needs careful consideration during negotiations:

- *Sphere-of-influence buyers* might expect immediate synergy from the acquisition. These would include competitors for whom it would be horizontal integration, and buyers and suppliers for whom it would imply vertical integration. These are the buyers who are most likely to pose future threats unless the divestment removes any involvement in the industry in question.

- *Related industry companies* – these might not be current competitors but companies for whom it might be possible to share activities and transfer skills.

- *Management buy-outs*

- *Management buy-ins.*

Management buy-outs involve the purchase of a business from its existing owners by the current managers in conjunction with one or more financial institutions. Some buy-outs occur because family owners have no organized succession and a sale to the existing managers is seen as more desirable than sale to an unknown outsider.

Management buy-ins occur when a group of outside managers is brought in to run a company which is sold to them and their backers rather than to existing managers. The disadvantage is the loss of continuity and the lack of insight and experience in the particular company; a possible advantage in certain circumstances is the influx of fresh ideas.

Financiers are attracted to management buyouts because they offer the potential to earn higher returns than investing in large companies and lower failure rates than traditional start-up businesses. However they will typically look to earn back their investment – normally through a public share offering – in around four years. Banks will normally agree to a higher percentage of debt in relation to equity (gearing) or in relation to total capital employed (the debt ratio) than is conventional, and will look for a cash flow that can both pay the interest and repay the debt after an agreed number of years. It is important that managers are able to make the business more competitive and overcome the constraints imposed by the high debt burden. In addition, they must be able to generate a positive cash flow. The Strategy activity at the end of Chapter 11 shows how private equity was invested in Debenhams and how a handsome return was earned quite quickly.

Third, there is an argument that the cash raised from the sale should be deployed effectively and without undue delay. If a company is decreasing in size, building up reserves of cash, and can find no suitable investment opportunities, it might become vulnerable to acquisition. Ideally, a use for the cash will be determined before the sale, but implementation of a combined sale and investment may prove difficult. Devlin argues that where these changes can be managed effectively, divestment can provide a source of new competitive advantage.

Having explored retrenchment, turnaround and divestment strategies, these strategies are discussed specifically in the context of an economic recession, and this chapter concludes by considering alternative strategies for declining industries and how the most appropriate strategy might be selected.

> We have used the recession as a time to bring new products out.
> It shows you're not demoralized, and it's something new to go to customers with.
> Being private has enabled us to plough our own furrow through the good and the bad times and not be swallowed up. All our capital investment would be looked at in a different way if we were a public company.
>
> SIR ANTHONY BAMFORD, CHAIRMAN, JC BAMFORD (JCB EXCAVATORS),
> QUOTED IN THE *FINANCIAL TIMES*, 2 JUNE 1993

13.8 Managing in a recession

The early 1990s was characterized by an economic recession. This was not unusual; economies experience cycles. Typically, the latter years of the decade provided clear evidence of an economic recovery in the UK, but this time the real beneficiaries were service businesses rather than the manufacturing sector, which was affected by the high value of the pound sterling. This early 1990s recession was global and it affected most countries, industries and businesses, regardless of size or sector. Since then other world economies have performed worse than the UK, which has benefited from low inflation and low interest rates and from investment in the public sector. The UK Labour government seemed to have 'got it right'. It was, though, always highly likely that another recession would occur at some stage in the future, but the unpredictable issue was its possible extent.

In the event it would be a deep recession. America, Europe and Asia would be affected. The falls in these developed economies would then impact upon the developing countries such as China and India that supply them with manufactured goods. The rest of the world then suffered as the fallout from the banking crisis spread worldwide. One problem in the UK was that the government had not saved during the good times and so any spending to get the country out of recession would require borrowing. Unlike the German economy that had saved during the good times.

The recession of 2008/2009 has seen the traditional economic downturn – but this has been accompanied by limited and expensive credit – the so-called credit crunch – brought about by the banks becoming defensive as they try to recover from the imprudent lending that had characterized the previous few years – fuelled, in the eyes of many people, by inadequate policing and regulation of financial services. The government put pressure on the banks to lend but things were slow to happen. In Ireland, the government would only lend money to the (needy) banks if they promised to lend rather than shore up their capital reserves. But this was only likely to happen if the government offered 'guarantees' against loan defaults The latest recession was also particularly volatile and uncertain. The volatility was manifest by the suddenness and steepness of the downturn in orders; the uncertainty by the lack of clarity and agreement on how long it would last. Running a business became very uncertain – but, of course, such uncertainty is a threat to some and an opportunity to others. In the past, for example, the online auction house, eBay, has made a lot of money by helping companies clear their surplus stocks.

For those companies that could survive the recession with their capacity and employees largely intact, the turnaround in the economy would be a genuine opportunity. The issue and the challenge was how to do this. In 2009 some companies – for example, all the leading car manufacturers – were giving their workers extended holidays on part pay. Others were reducing hours and some reduced pay. Large companies – where they were able – took extended credit, something that is always easier if the suppliers are small companies with only limited power and influence. For any that could grant extended credit there was a chance to pick up fresh orders.

Not unexpectedly in a media-driven country such as the UK stories of doom and gloom abounded and people began to question whether the 'world would ever be the same again'.

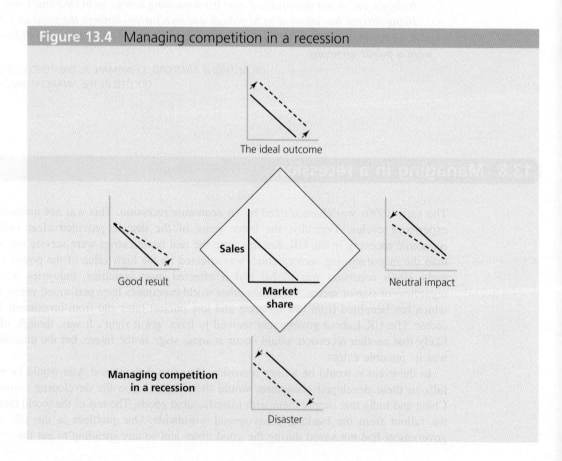

Figure 13.4   Managing competition in a recession

Figure 13.4 illustrates a number of possible competitive outcomes from a recessionary period.

We can see the two key variables are sales and market share. During the recession sales overall in an industry will go down. A neutral effect for all (or any single competitor) would be reduced sales but retained market share. A 'perfect' result would be increased sales and market share – quite possible if some competitors are forced to close. A good result would be constant sales which would imply an improved market share. A reduction in both sales and market share would be a relative disaster and reflect a weak competitor.

In a recession, then, retrenchment strategies are frequently required as demand falls and costs need containing; at the same time there is a need, wherever practical, to invest and prepare the organization to benefit from the recovery when it comes.

Recession alone will not necessarily put a company into a crisis or turnaround situation; rather, it highlights existing weaknesses either created in, or hidden in, boom conditions. The organizations that are best prepared to cope with a recession are those with relatively low borrowings. Highly geared companies may be forced to divest assets in order to raise cash to cover their interest and repayment needs.

Clifford (1977) has suggested that companies that survive a recession most successfully are characterized by superior management which emphasizes the protection of margins, the efficient use of capital, and a concentration on markets or segments where distinctive competitive advantage is possible. Such competitive advantage will result from more effective cost control, innovative differentiation, a focus on service and quality and speedy reaction and change in a dynamic environment. An economic recession will typically force organizations to be creative in their search for cost reductions, especially if productivity drives have already eliminated many operational inefficiencies. Information technology (IT) has provided some valuable opportunities in recent years. Cost savings must then be controlled to ensure that they do not creep up again. The focus of the cost-cutting is critical. Training and R&D, for example, should not be sacrificed unnecessarily because new ideas and service quality are increasingly important for adding value, helping customers to find new competitive opportunities themselves and persuading consumers to buy when their spending power is limited. R&D, then, should be managed better rather than cut, and directed more towards short-term improvements. However, the long-term needs should not be wholly ignored. In particular, the development time for new products and services should be speeded up.

Dividend payments and investment funding may have to be traded off against each other. Some organizations will reduce dividends when profits fall to conserve their resources; others will maintain them to appease shareholders.

Moreover, increasing global competition has forced companies to target markets and niches more effectively and, in many cases, increase their marketing rather than cut expenditure. The emphasis has typically focused on efficiencies and savings rather than luxury – consumers with less discretionary purchasing power have been more selective.

Whittingham (1991) reinforces points made earlier in the book and contends that innovation and product and service improvement is a more effective use of scarce resources in a recession than is diversification, and that cutting back too much leaves companies exposed and under capacity for the recovery. Ideally, organizations will consult and involve employees, looking to, say, negotiate pay freezes and reduce hours rather than make staff redundant. This provides greater flexibility to grow. Nevertheless, many firms will not have sufficient resources to pursue their preferred option.

When companies emerge from a recession and attempt to satisfy increasing demand there is a fresh challenge: the need to control events, monitor the cash flow and guard against overtrading.

Paradoxically, a recession can be an ideal time to invest for the future, to ensure that the organization is in a state of readiness to capitalize fully when the economic recovery begins. This could imply investing in new plant and equipment, in R&D or in new IT at a time when the company is struggling. The secret is money. If a company builds up a cash mountain when its revenues and profits are high, there is a real likelihood that it will be criticized for not finding opportunities to spend it. It may even come under pressure to return some of it to shareholders. It might also be persuaded to diversify or acquire unnecessarily. It is such a cash mountain that helps to pay staff when future revenues and profits are restrained. This can allow an organization to hang on to the people whom it does not want to lose rather than face enforced redundancy programmes.

The Institute of Chartered Accountants in England and Wales (ICAEW, 2009) offers eight key strategies for coming through an economic downturn:

1 Manage risk and uncertainty – which implies understanding where the business might be most exposed. It could be at risk if any key supplier was to close or disappear, or if a major client was lost. Currency movements could also be a huge problem for some.

2 Manage cash – which for some is easier said than done in a credit crunch. A recession is exactly when a business needs cash reserves (which it might have been vilified for not using when times were more prosperous) because these reserve can (a) help pay wages when the order book is thin and (b) be there for investing to seize new opportunities from others who are less able to respond.

3 Try and secure any funding shortfalls that are going to be needed for future investment. It can be useful to sell unwanted or spare assets (assuming a buyer can be found) as the opportunity cost of the money released can be greater.

4 Review the organization structure and its cost base. This could be a good time to outsource non-critical items, for example. The onion strategy we discussed in Chapter 11 can be very relevant here. That said, it is critical not to do things that might damage the long-term interests of the business for short term pragmatism.

5 Ask for professional advice and support if some decisions take the organization into 'unknown territory'.

6 'Manage the year end' by being open and honest about progress – so as not to spring unnecessary surprises on investors.

7 Engage and involve employees. They will know where savings can be made. If painful decisions have to be made then there are 'good' and 'bad' ways of dealing with the problem.

8 Finally, look ahead, plan ahead. The recession will end; new opportunities will arise. Is the company's business model appropriate for the future?

Table 13.1 provides a useful bullet-point summary of these and other points.

Accenture (2003) suggested the following companies as examples of strategic successes during the 1990s recession. Nokia divested a range of businesses and invested in mobile telephones, becoming the world's leading manufacturer of handsets. Southwest Airlines continued to expand through the recession, opening up new routes and cities, but never deviating from its winning competitive formula. It was consistently profitable when other airlines were losing money. Wal-Mart also grew (opening up more and more new stores) and remained focused on its existing strategies, whilst many other rivals changed their strategy in an attempt to boost sales. In contrast Samsung restructured, decentralizing to give managers more autonomy. In every case we can see evidence of investment in a clear business model. The conclusion: successful companies do not spend excessively in boom times; instead they generate cash, reduce debt and build up their resource base. This provides them with flexibility.

But other businesses will perish in a recession. Case 13.8 shows how Woolworths fell into real difficulties, in part because it did not have a sound business model. It was surviving in better times but the business was at risk. Zavvi, what had been Virgin Megastores before they were bought out by their managers, was critically affected by Woolworths' collapse because they relied on them for their supplies.

Table 13.1   Managing in a recession

In a recession, companies should:

- Determine and clarify strategic priorities
- Be willing to act rather than procrastinate with some tough decisions
- Stay fully informed about trends and changes in relevant industries, making use of IT for this and other potential benefits
- Monitor gross profits and cash flow very carefully
- Identify where there is any overcapacity
- Spend carefully
- Seek to extend payment times to creditors
- Look for possibilities to reduce overheads or fixed costs
- Cut back on borrowings if at all possible
- Monitor currency fluctuations if the company trades in foreign currencies, buying forward where appropriate
- Recognize that high prices may be unsustainable and act sooner rather than later
- Keep staff informed of the situation, taking as positive a stance as is realistic
- Tighten staffing levels where appropriate, but not by losing key people
- Make any necessary redundancies all at once
- Invest in training for those who remain and look to retain morale
- Stay in close contact with customers and look for opportunities where both parties can help each other
- Seek out relevant marketing opportunities at home and abroad – recessions are uneven in their impact
- Accept that flexibility and innovation are crucial

Case 13.8

Woolworths & Zavvi   UK

The ubiquitous and universally known high street chain Woolworths went into administration towards the end of 2008. Did it have a future as a going concern, or had the business deteriorated beyond the point of return? If it was finished as a business, there would be a large number of store closures and staff redundancies. Realistically the business had lost focus; it had an image problem and no positive unique qualities.

Various organizations asked for information but no serious buyer came forward and a closing down sale was introduced. The subsidiary business (Entertainment UK) which supplies music and DVDs to supermarkets and independent retailers) would also close down. Some of the retail units enjoy prime high street positions and were eventually likely to be taken up by various rivals and supermarket chains – but this would not save jobs in the short term.

Woolworths was introduced into the UK from America in 1909 when a store was opened in Liverpool. The stores sold a huge range of household goods at very affordable prices. The real growth came between the two world wars when Woolworths arrived in every town or city of any size.

Many of us have very fond memories of Pick 'n' Mix sweets, but that is only part of the story. The stores sold a huge and eclectic range – including toys, music, electrical goods, household items and some food products as well as sweets and chocolate. Recorded music was once a key product, with Woolworth being the leading music retailer in the UK. At one time it had its own range of (cheaper) cover versions of the leading hit records of the day – on the Embassy label.

In the 'old days' the counters were piled high with an incredible array of goods to meet almost any need. But in retail it is critical to get the product range, the displays and the service 'right'. Woolworths didn't and arguably lost focus – thus opening itself to competition from chains such as Wilkinson and Toys R Us, let alone the supermarkets such as Asda and Tesco with their growing ranges of non-food items. Music sales were affected by Amazon and then downloading.

The company was probably too slow to engineer the changes it needed to make. For a lengthy period, and throughout the 1980s and1990s, it had been part of the Kingfisher Group, which also incorporated Superdrug and B&Q DIY – but the group was split up, with Woolworth eventually to be the main loser.

It also had something of an image problem. To many it was always perceived to be relatively 'down-market' when compared to Marks & Spencer, for example. Whilst there might always have been a huge affection for Woolworths – in part this might be because it had always been there – this did not bring in high spending shoppers in sufficient numbers. In the end the company could not service its debts – 'the charm of everything under one roof' had finally worn off.

But the problem did not stop there!

Zavvi is the trading name of the ex-Virgin Megastores that had been a management buy-out in September 2007. Zavvi became the UK's largest independent entertainment retailer with 114 stores – but it was dependent upon Woolworths' Entertainment subsidiary for its supplies. Once this supply route was closed off Zavvi had a problem replenishing its stock – the credit crunch (and the reluctance of the banks to lend money and increase overdrafts) was a key issue. Demand for CDs and DVDs was strong, especially in the run-up to Christmas, and Zavvi was seen as a strong competitor with a good product offering – but this couldn't save it. By early 2009 many of the stores had closed.

Questions

1 Consider the reasons for the failure of these two businesses. Was the demise of Woolworths basically inevitable in a steep recession?
2 Was Zavvi basically unlucky or had it made a strategic error in relying on one chain of supply?
3 What are the key lessons in managing in good times such that recessionary trading conditions are less likely to result in failure?

Footnote: Wellworths

Claire Robertson, manager of the Woolworths branch in Dorchester, Dorset, decided to take her future into her own hands. She approached the landlord for her branch and negotiated a deal; she would re-open the store and trade as Wellworths. The trading space is 6500 square feet and she aimed to re-employ her 22 staff – most chose to join her. The new branch was featured in a television documentary and the radio DJ Chris Evans offered to officially open it in February 2009. The new store does not sell CDs, DVDs or clothing, but it still has Pick 'n' Mix and a large range of household items.

© DAVID ASKHAM/ALAMY

13.9 Strategies for declining industries

Rarely is an industry unattractive for every company competing in it; mature and declining industries can be made attractive for individual competitors if they can find appropriate and feasible opportunities for adding value and creating competitive advantage. Although tea is a more popular drink than coffee in the UK, consumption has been declining for a number of years. Tetley became the market leader in the 1990s and it has adopted a number of strategies to retain its leadership. For example, it promoted more specialist teas such as Earl Grey, Red Bush and Lapsang and it introduced draw-bag tea bags. Tea sales were also boosted by the increasingly popular fruit flavoured infusions. After being bought out by its managers (from

Allied Domecq) in 1995, Tetley formed a joint venture with Indian tea grower, Tata – which is now its new owner.

Some firms experiencing decline in a mature industry will be the cause of their own demise, through their persistence with dated, inappropriate competitive strategies; and in some cases, an innovatory new strategy by one competitor can rejuvenate the whole industry.

When an industry has reached maturity or begun to decline, a number of issues must be faced. Generally:

● while demand overall is declining, the pattern can vary markedly – some sectors or segments may be static or expanding

● consumers will be knowledgeable because the product or service has been around for a while

● many customers will become increasingly price conscious and prices will tend to fall in real terms

● the 'commodity' perception of products will increase

● distribution is likely to become more concentrated.

Companies will again be attempting to find new ways of adding value and differentiating, but as time goes on the opportunities become increasingly limited. Paradoxically, they will often find it harder to justify both R&D spending (to develop new variations) and marketing expenditure to inform and persuade customers of the differentiation. However, as the decline continues and overcapacity emerges, there will be a tendency for the weakest or least profitable producers to withdraw from the industry. This relieves some of the pressure on those who remain.

Harrigan (1980) draws upon the themes outlined when portfolio analysis was discussed in Chapter 8 and considers whether retrenchment, turnaround or divestment is the most appropriate strategy for an individual competitor in a declining industry. Strategies of leadership and **niche marketing** (turnaround), exploiting or harvesting (retrenchment) and divestment are considered in the light of the overall attractiveness of the industry while it is declining and the opportunities for an individual competitor to create and sustain competitive advantage. These are illustrated and defined in Figure 13.5.

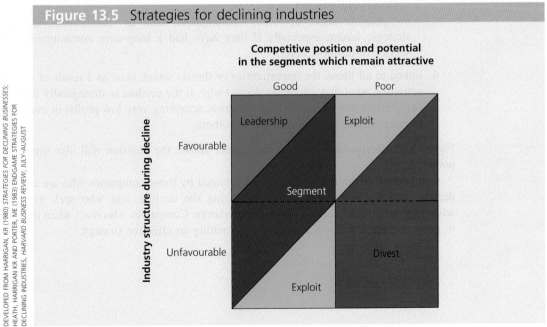

Figure 13.5   Strategies for declining industries

DEVELOPED FROM HARRIGAN, KR (1980) *STRATEGIES FOR DECLINING BUSINESSES*; HEATH, HARRIGAN KR AND PORTER, ME (1983) ENDGAME STRATEGIES FOR DECLINING INDUSTRIES, *HARVARD BUSINESS REVIEW*, JULY–AUGUST

Leadership	Selective investment: turnaround
	Invest as appropriate to give real competitive advantage
	Idea: Become one of the strongest competitors in the declining industry with either the lowest costs or clear differentiation
Segment or niche	Selective investment: turnaround
	Identify one or more attractive segments, those with greatest potential for longer-term survival or short-term returns, and seek a strong position whilst divesting in other segments
Exploit or harvest	Phased withdrawal; retrenchment
	Controlled disinvestment, reducing product alternatives, advertising and so on in order to cut costs
	Problem: losing the confidence of suppliers and buyers as they witness the obvious reduction of commitment
	Must lead eventually to divestment or liquidation
Quick divestment	Immediate sale or liquidation

Harrigan contends that the most appropriate strategy is dependent on four factors:

1 the nature of the decline, and the causes – the speed at which decline is taking place, and whether specific segments are still surviving and offering differentiation and niche marketing opportunities for companies who can create and sustain competitive advantage. These factors affect the attractiveness of the industry

2 the ability of a company to target these market segments effectively and create consumer preference. This is affected by company strengths and weaknesses

3 the exit costs for all competitors. Exit costs influence the degree of urgency that companies feel towards finding a way of remaining competitive rather than simply withdrawing. Exit costs relate to:

   – the inability to find a buyer for the business, and the cost of closure
   – the strategic significance for the company as a whole, particularly if vertical integration strategies are affected
   – the possible effect upon key stakeholders, such as shareholders, managers and the strategic leader, especially if they have had a long-term commitment to the product service or business unit.

4 linked to all these, the opportunities or threats which exist as a result of competitor activities, what they choose to do and why. If the product is strategically significant, certain competitors may choose not to withdraw, accepting very low profits or even no profits, and thereby making it more difficult for others.

Figure 13.5 encapsulates the first two points above; the decision will also involve the last two points.

Competitive advantage is likely to be attained by those companies who are aware early of the decline, and the opportunities present during the decline, and who seek to create the most advantageous positions ahead of their competitors. Companies who react when things have started to go wrong are less likely to succeed in creating an effective strategy.

13.10   Implementing recovery strategies

In Chapter 11 it was stressed that organizational issues and difficulties often result in failure of the diversification and acquisition strategies to yield the desired results. Organizational issues will again be important in the case of recovery strategies. Time is likely to be limited and proposed changes will have to be implemented quickly. The support and co-operation of managers and other employees will be essential, particularly where redundancies, changes in organization structures or changes in working practices are required. Quite possibly changes in attitudes – an issue of organizational culture – will be involved. Although the gravity of the situation may be visible, and the dangers of failing to change clearly understood, the changes will need managing properly if they are to prove effective. The issues involved in managing change are discussed in Chapter 15.

We finish the chapter with Case 13.9 on Arcadia, a retail group that has experienced turbulent times. Attempts to revive the fortunes of once-famous brands have proved how difficult sustained turnaround is. The company is now owned by the entrepreneur Philip Green.

Case 13.9

Arcadia   UK

Arcadia was previously known as the Burton Group of retail outlets.

Origins and diversification

The Burton Group became a retailer of fashionable clothing for men and women through a number of branded outlets. The company was started as a single shop in 1901 by Montague Burton, who had built the company into a vertically integrated organization of factories and some 600 stores when he died in 1952. The main product area had been made-to-measure suits for men.

In the late 1960s the company had problems of management succession and it was basically stagnant with under-utilized assets. Burton was also experiencing a number of specific problems:

- The menswear market was switching in preference from made-to-measure to ready-made suits.
- The company had a large manufacturing base in relation to the falling demand for its products. Moreover, the factories were inefficient and insufficiently capital intensive.
- There was growing competition from such stores as Marks and Spencer.
- The company had an old-fashioned image, made worse by stores which were not designed or fitted for the growing market for ready-made clothes.

A new management team was appointed and their strategy was one of diversification. In the early 1970s Burton acquired five new businesses:

- Evans – outsize fashions for women with fuller figures
- Ryman's – office supplies
- St Remy – clothing stores in France
- Green's – cameras and hi-fi equipment
- Trumps – an employment agency.

Burton also opened a chain of womenswear shops with the Top Shop brand name.

Divestment and turnaround; the acquisition of Debenhams

The diversification strategy failed in overall terms, although parts did prove successful, and divestment began in the mid-1970s.

In addition:

- Branches were modernized and some were enlarged. The aim was to make Burton stores more appealing to younger buyers. Some stores, though, were closed.
- A new chain of Top Man stores was opened to complement Top Shop.
- There was greater emphasis on the womenswear market, with more Top Shops and the acquisition of Dorothy Perkins.
- The Principles chain was developed.

- Manufacturing was pruned and the final factory was disposed of in 1988.

Between 1976 and 1979 the number of employees was reduced from 21,400 to 11,000.

These changes were led by Ralph Halpern, who became chief executive in 1977 (and executive chairman in 1981), and the result was revitalization, new growth and profitability. The Burton Group built up a 12.5 per cent share of the UK clothing market, second only to Marks and Spencer. Halpern was fêted as a retailer of genius, and rewarded with a million pound salary, a knighthood and celebrity status. However, when this expansion required consolidation in the 1980s, a number of strategic misjudgements was made.

- In 1985 Burton took over Debenhams after a fierce and very acrimonious battle. The new department stores required expensive revamping and the payback was slower than anticipated. Moreover, different retailing skills were involved.
- Burton diversified into shopping-centre development, and was financially exposed when property prices fell.
- The growth led to over-expansion and the acquisition of new sites with very high rent and lease charges. These proved too expensive in the retail recession of the late 1980s.

Profits and the share price collapsed and Halpern departed in November 1990, to be replaced as chief executive by his deputy, Lawrence Cooklin. In mid-1991 Burton sought to raise money in a 'desperate rights issue', imposed a pay freeze and looked to rationalize by reducing both the number of stores and head-office administration.

The company traded at a loss during 1991–1992; a new, experimental, out-of-town discount format, branded IS, was introduced and the flagship Harvey Nichols London department store was sold for £51 million in August 1991. (Harvey Nichols was floated on the stock exchange in 1996 with a valuation of £150 million.) Analysts commented that Burton was still searching for a retail format suitable for the 1990s and estimated the odds of a second successful recovery to be no better than 50:50. Cooklin was replaced in February 1992 by American John Hoerner from Debenhams.

A second turnaround

Hoerner was determined to tackle two key strategic issues:

1. The Burton brands/businesses saw themselves in competition with each other; they frequently targeted the same customers
2. The company was too willing to discount its prices when trading levels were disappointing.

Three years later Burton was profitable again. What had happened? Initially:

- Hoerner initiated a cross-formats review of target markets, design, merchandising, pricing strategies, visual marketing and buying.
- The formats were then refocused, some more than others, and new strategies trialled. Top Shop, for example, targeted 16–19-year-olds by experimenting with a 'funky, grungey' look. Those targeted loved the new image; unfortunately Top Shop's other customers did not, and they voted with their feet. Top Shop switched to a less radical look which had appeal for all ages up to 30.
- Locations were reviewed from a corporate perspective. Some sites were closed and replaced with new ones, although not as many. In addition, some formats were exchanged for other Burton brands to try and achieve the most appropriate location for each one.
- The new but unprofitable IS format was abandoned in 1994.
- The head office was reduced in size and numbers. In the branches there was a programme of switching employees from full-time contracts to flexible part-time hours.

Hoerner then turned his attention to supplier relationships and to the links and inter-dependencies between the Burton formats. The future strategy was to be based on building the strength of the various brand names.

During 1996 mail order (or home shopping) began to play a more prominent role in Burton. Two acquisitions: first, the Innovations (unusual and inventive household and leisure products) and secondly, the Racing Green (smart casual clothes) catalogues were added to Hawkshead and McCord which Burton already owned.

Demerger

In July 1997 Burton Group announced that it was to demerge the department store chain Debenhams into an independent business. It was generally acknowledged that it had not been able to prosper in a Burton Group beset with other high-street problems. In recent months Debenhams had been growing much more quickly than Burton's other brands. Burton's menswear sales in particular were being affected by the increasing success of specialist designer menswear brands and branded sportswear companies.

John Hoerner would remain as chief executive of Burton – which was to be renamed Arcadia – and which now comprised the Burton, Dorothy Perkins, Evans, Principles, Top Shop and Top Man high-street stores, together with Burton Home Shopping. The new chief executive of Debenhams was to be Terry Green, who was currently in charge within Burton's. Shareholders should benefit from identified cost savings amounting to £30 million. There would be job losses as the operating and administration systems for all the Burton stores would now be amalgamated and centralized. Each store chain would retain its independence for product sourcing, range building, supplier development and customer relations.

It is invariably possible to reduce costs after a strategic change such as this. The real challenge lies in finding new opportunities for adding value and differentiating to give fresh life to the brands and stores concerned. The prediction was that both Burton Group and Debenhams could benefit and grow after this split. Time would tell.

An argument was put forward that department stores such as Debenhams could prove to be the new retail force for 'thirty-something and forty-something' shoppers as they would be able to offer designer brands (concessions), smart cafés, baby changing rooms and affordable own-label products in a single store, and thus provide convenience for the whole family. In 1999 Burton extended its women's wear chains by buying Wallis, Warehouse and Evans (again) from Sears.

Arcadia/Burton in 2000

In April 2000 Arcadia announced that 400 shops would be closed and 3500 jobs lost. Casualties included all of the Principles for Men and some Top Shop, Miss Selfridge and Principles stores. In addition, Burton stores would be paired with Dorothy Perkins rather than remain as stand-alones. The reason was intense discounting in the clothing sector in late 1999. Arcadia was trading at a loss and could no longer afford the rents and rates that it was paying.

Customer comments reinforced Arcadia's difficulties: it was often difficult to differentiate between the product ranges in the various high-street chain stores. Cut-price warehouses (such as Matalan) were also making real inroads into the market.

In 2002 the entrepreneur Philip Green bought the business for £850 million.

Recent fortunes

Arcadia remains the largest privately owned clothing retailer in the UK with 2500 stores. Each brand – Burton, Dorothy Perkins, Evans, Miss Selfridge, Outfit, Topshop, Topman and Wallis – is distinctive and managed individually. There are also 420 franchised outlets around the world.

The total sales trend for 2006, 2007, 2008 was £1767 million, £1859 million, £1840 million; with operating profits of £289 million, £293 million and £275 million respectively. By late 2008 Philip Green commented that his 'younger' brands – particularly Topshop, Topman and Miss Selfridge – were doing well in the emerging recession but Burton and Dorothy Perkins were finding trading conditions more demanding. Green had recruited the high profile model Kate Moss to be the 'face' of Topshop.

Questions

1 In the face of competition from retail formats such as Matalan and Primark, what is the future for specialist clothing retailers such as Arcadia and its long-established brands?
2 If you were Philip Green, what would you do to try and secure Arcadia's future during the recession of 2009?

Projects

1 What has happened to Harvey Nichols since its sale by Burton in 1991. Are such specialist brands better off with greater autonomy?
2 Ryman was part of Burtons. It is now owned by Theo Paphitis of Dragons' Den fame. Paphitis is an expert at buying failing businesses and reinventing them. Which other businesses is he associated with?

ARCADIA (BURTON GROUP)
http://www.arcadia.co.uk

Summary

Ultimate business failure happens when a business is liquidated or sold. Its managers have made strategic errors or misjudgements; maybe they simply avoided the need to change in a dynamic environment. However, a business can similarly fail to meet the needs and expectations of key stakeholders, experience financial difficulties but be saved. In this latter case, one or more factors might be involved. A new strategic leader might be appointed who succeeds in turning the company around. Part, or all, of the business might be sold.

Companies fail for a variety of reasons, and normally more than one factor is in evidence. The main ones are: poor management; competition; a decline in profits; a decline in demand for the product or service; misjudged acquisitions or other changes in corporate strategy.

At any time certain industries will be declining and others will be relatively unattractive as far as particular companies are concerned, generally because of intense competition. Individual companies might be performing poorly and in need of either a recovery strategy or an appropriate divestment.

When this is the case, the feasibility of recovery will vary from situation to situation, and the four possible outcomes of a change in strategy are:

- a failure to recover
- temporary recovery
- sustained survival, and
- sustained recovery.

The likely outcome is inevitably affected by the timing of the intervention. If a company realizes the gravity of a pending situation at an early stage, it will be better placed to deal with it. Recovery will be more difficult to achieve if the organization waits until it facing a real crisis.

In simple terms, *retrenchment* – to create a platform for possible expansion later on – concerns stronger cash management and tighter operations. Renewal brings in marketing and the search for new opportunities for adding value and differentiating. It is about building new forms of competitive advantage.

Divestment can be an important theme in retrenchment and consolidation. Management buy-outs are sometimes used as a convenient means of divesting a business which has the potential to grow but which is no longer core to its existing parent.

A four-stage model of the process can be summarized as:

1 galvanization – engaging the problem
2 simplifying the situation so it can be dealt with
3 building new competencies
4 exerting leverage to develop and sustain new competitive advantages.

From time to time economies move from boom conditions into recessions, the depth and length of which vary markedly. In a recession company revenues and profits will fall and a number of the issues and strategies discussed in relation to retrenchment and consolidation become relevant. Paradoxically, an economic recession is often an ideal time for a company to invest if it has the appropriate resources. If it can afford to hold on to its staff, the chances are that they will have time to deal with the implied changes. New plant, equipment and technology could then be in place in time for when the economy turns around – placing the organization in a strong position.

There are several possible strategies for individual competitors in mature and declining industries. Some companies will withdraw from the industry. Others will find attractive niches. The fact that an industry is in decline does not automatically make it unattractive for everyone.

Online cases for this chapter

Questions and research assignments

1 Do the causes discussed in this chapter provide an adequate explanation for any corporate failure with which you are familiar?

2 Why might a company wish to remain a competitor in an industry despite low or declining profitability? Classify your reasons as objective or subjective. Can the subjective reasons be justified?

3 What factors do you feel would be most significant to all parties involved in a proposed buy-out during the negotiations? Where are the major areas of potential conflict?

Internet and library projects

1 Chariot has been described as a 'small but brazen' lottery provider. In 2006 it attempted to launch an alternative to Camelot and the National Lottery. It claimed the existing lottery 'gave money to unworthy causes', the opposite of its mission. The business lasted less than six months. What happened to cause it to fail?

2 Coffee Republic was one of the fore-runners with coffee bars providing freshly made and relatively expensive coffees in the UK. Its founders, Sahar and Bobby Hashemi, wrote a book for would-be entrepreneurs – *Anyone Can Do It*. But competitors like Starbucks, Café Nero and Costa Coffee were far more successful. Again, what went wrong? What are the lessons in this particular case?

Strategy activity

Northern Foods

Northern Foods in the UK is best known for certain brands: Fox's Biscuits, Goodfella's Pizza and Dalepak burgers. It had also produced own-label foods for Marks & Spencer and the leading supermarkets. Changes to the M&S supply chain and price demands from the supermarkets had hit its margins. A number of reasons were offered as to why Northern Foods got into difficulties:

- It had been more concerned with sales than cash
- It operated from too many (dispersed) sites
- It was too ready to say 'yes' to its leading customers without examining the implications of the choices this implied
- There had been inadequate innovation – say with healthy option foods

- Across the business there was inadequate learning and sharing.

As a result it faced some difficult decisions in 2009. One concerned the future of Fox's Biscuits. The factories were in need of improvement. There were two key sites, one in Batley (West Yorkshire) and one in Uttoxeter. Neither was adequate. One new factory was needed – but where should it be sited? Wherever was chosen, redundancies were implied.

Question

1 Once Northern Foods is through these difficulties what do you think it should do differently in the future?

Further reading

Clarke, CJ and Gall, F (1987) Planned divestment – a five-step approach, *Long Range Planning*, 20 (1).

Harrigan, KR and Porter, ME (1983) End game strategies for declining industries, *Harvard Business Review*, July–August.

Kanter, RM (2003) Leadership and the psychology of turnarounds, *Harvard Business Review*, May–June.

Stopford, JM and Baden-Fuller, C (1990) Corporate rejuvenation, *Journal of Management Studies*, July.

References

Accenture (2003) *Investing for the Upturn*. Summarized from the Accenture website at the time: **www.Accenture.com/upturn**

Argenti, J (1976) *Corporate Collapse*, McGraw-Hill.

Baden-Fuller, C and Stopford, J (1992) *Rejuvenating the Mature Business: The Competitive Challenge*, Routledge.

Buckley, N and Liu, B (2003) Fixer puts the final touches to a DIY refit, *Financial Times*, 8 July.

Clifford, DK (1977) Thriving in a recession, *Harvard Business Review*, July–August.

Davis, JV (1974) The strategic divestment decision, *Long Range Planning*, February.

Devlin, G (1989) Selling off not out, *Management Today*, April.

Harrigan, KR (1980) *Strategies for Declining Businesses*, Heath.

Heller, R (1998) *Goldfinger – How Entrepreneurs Get Rich by Starting Small*, Harper Collins.

ICAEW (2009) *Surviving the Downturn*, Institute of Chartered Accountants in England and Wales, Publication No. 5760.

Oates, D (1990) *The Complete Entrepreneur*, Mercury.

Slatter, S (1984) *Corporate Recovery: Successful Turn-around Strategies and Their Implementation*, Penguin.

Slatter, S and Lovett, D (1999) Corporate Turnaround, Penguin

Society of Practitioners in Insolvency (1995) *Personal Insolvency in the UK*, SPI, London.

Van de Vliet, A (1998) Back from the brink, *Management Today*, January.

Weitzel, W and Johnson, E (1989) Decline in organizations – a literature extension and integration, *Administration Science Quarterly*, 34 (1).

Whittingham, R (1991) Recession strategies and top management change, *Journal of General Management* 16 (3).

5

Strategic management

Parts 1 and 3 – Understanding Strategy and Strategic Analysis and Choice – have addressed a number of important 'how' questions, in particular, how strategies are created, while Parts 2 and 4 have been more focused on 'what' and 'where' issues. This final part of the book addresses a number of additional 'how' questions regarding the management of strategy.

In particular, the following questions are asked:

- How are intended strategies implemented? (Chapter 14)
- How does emergent strategy actually happen? (Chapter 14)
- How should the organization be structured and designed to ensure that both happen? (Chapter 14)
- How can the strategic leader manage both the organization structure and resources to achieve corporate-level synergy? Are the various functions, activities and businesses co-ordinated and contributing towards clearly understood objectives? (Chapter 15)
- How should the organization seek to deal with the pressures and demands of change, appreciating that cultural and behavioural changes may be required? (Chapter 15)
- How should resources be deployed and managed? (Chapter 16)
- How can the organization manage risk and avoid managing crises? (Chapter 16)

We conclude the book by asking:

- What is strategy? and (Chapter 17)
- What is the purpose of strategy? (Chapter 17)

Strategy implementation

Learning objectives

Having read to the end of this chapter you should be able to:

- clarify the vital significance of strategy implementation

- explain how strategy and structure are linked in a circular process

- discuss the processes involved in the implementation of both intended and emergent strategies

- describe the problems inherent in implementing strategic change effectively

- discuss the advantages and disadvantages of centralization and decentralization

- identify and describe five basic structural forms which an organization might adopt

- explain why structures evolve and change as organizations develop and grow.

It was emphasized in Chapter 10 that to be considered effective a chosen, intended strategy must be implemented successfully. The prospects for effective implementation are clearly dependent upon the appropriateness, feasibility and desirability of the strategy. At the same time, competency in implementation – the ability to translate ideas into actions and generate positive outcomes, sometimes swiftly, can itself be a major source of competitive advantage. Internal processes can add value by creating high levels of customer service and/or saving on costs by, say, removing any unnecessary delays or duplication of activities. In this last section of the book, therefore, we consider issues of strategy implementation and control. Reed and Buckley (1988) suggest that new strategies are selected because they offer opportunities and potential benefits, but that their implementation, because it involves change, implies risk. Implementation strategies should seek to maximize benefits and minimize risks. How might this be accomplished?

The final section examines the linkages between strategy and structure by examining a number of alternative structural forms and by considering the key issues of centralization and decentralization. The forces that influence and determine the structure are discussed. The structural challenges of global and small, entrepreneurial businesses, manufacturing and service companies and organizations in the public sector are also covered.

14.1 Strategy → structure or structure → strategy?

We trained hard, but it seems that every time we were beginning to form up into teams we would be reorganized. I was to learn later in life that we tend to meet any new situation by reorganizing, and a wonderful method it can be for creating the illusion of progress, while producing confusion, inefficiency and demoralization.

GAIUS PETRONIUS ARBITER, ROMAN GOVERNOR AT THE TIME OF NERO

The structure of an organization is designed to break down the work to be carried out – the tasks – into discrete components, which might comprise individual businesses, divisions and functional departments. People work within these divisions and functions, and their actions take place within a defined framework of objectives, plans and policies which are designed to direct and control their efforts. In designing the structure and making it operational it is important to consider the key aspects of empowerment, employee motivation and reward. Information and communication systems within the organization should ensure that efforts are co-ordinated to the appropriate and desired extent and that the strategic leader and other senior managers are aware of progress and results.

It has already been established that in a competitively chaotic environment one essential contribution of the strategic leader is to provide and share a clear vision, direction and purpose for the organization (see Figure 14.1). From this, and taking into account the various ways in which strategies might be created (incorporating the themes of vision, planning and emergence), actions and action plans need to be formalized – the middle column in the figure. These strategies and proposals for change cannot be divorced from the implementation implications, which are shown in the right-hand column. Is the structure capable of implementing the ideas? Are resources deployed effectively? Are managers suitably empowered? Do organizational policies support the strategies? If the answers to these questions contain negatives, then either the strategic ideas themselves, the structure, organizational policies or aspects of resource management will need to be reviewed and rethought. The final decisions will either be determined or strongly influenced by the strategic leader, and affected by the culture of the organization. Online Case 14.1 describes a number of strategic, structural and managerial changes at Amstrad; Amstrad has always been a strategically creative company but it has sometimes been constrained by implementation difficulties. The case documents a number of changes of fortune and potential crises and describes how Amstrad has managed these various challenges.

If appropriate, feasible and desirable strategies that *are* capable of effective implementation are selected and pursued, the organization should be able to establish some order and control in the environmental chaos and avoid major crises – the left-hand column of Figure 14.1. This still requires that strategies, products and services are managed efficiently and effectively at the operational level. Responsibility for operations will normally be delegated, and consequently, to ensure that performance and outcomes are satisfactory, sound monitoring and control systems are essential.

It is important to appreciate that while structures are designed initially – and probably changed later at various times – to ensure that *determined* or *intended* strategies can be implemented, it is

Figure 14.1   Strategy implementation

the day-to-day decisions, actions and behaviours of people within the structure which lead to important *emergent* strategies. There is, therefore, a continual circular process in operation:

Consequently, while issues of structure and implementation are being considered at the end of this book, they should not be thought of as the end point in the strategy process. They may be the source of strategic change.

Figure 14.2 explains the implementation of intended strategies in more detail. The strategic leader is charged with ensuring that there are appropriate targets and milestones, establishing a suitable organization structure and securing and allocating the relevant strategic resources, such as people and money. People then use the other strategic resources, working within the structure, to carry out the tasks that they have been allocated, and their actions should be monitored and evaluated to check that the targets and objectives are being achieved.

Figure 14.3 summarizes the emergent strategy process which, clearly, is less prescriptive. This time the strategic leader provides a broad strategic direction. Empowered managers work within a decentralized structure, but they are constrained by any relevant rules, policies and procedures. The strategies that emerge are affected by the constraints, the extent to which managers accept empowerment and the accumulation, sharing and exploitation of organizational knowledge. The outcome of the strategies is related to the extent to which they deal with the competitive and environmental pressures with which the organization must deal.

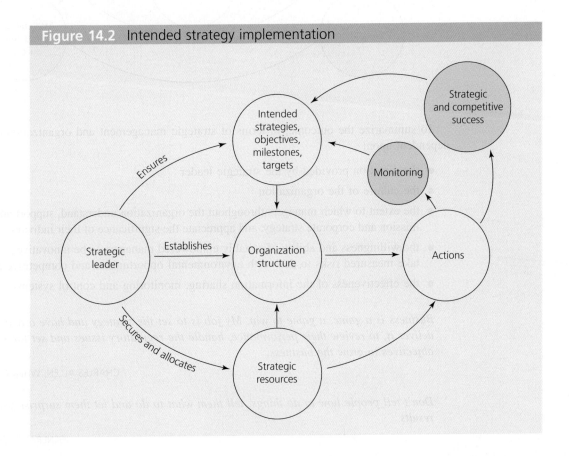

Figure 14.2   Intended strategy implementation

Figure 14.3 Emergent strategy

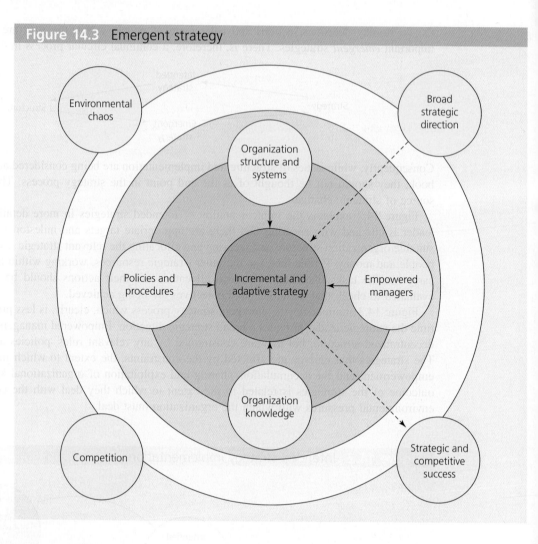

To summarize the outcome, in terms of strategic management and organizational success, is dependent upon:

- the direction provided by the strategic leader
- the culture of the organization
- the extent to which managers throughout the organization understand, support and *own* the mission and corporate strategy, and appreciate the significance of their individual contribution
- the willingness and ability of suitably empowered managers to be innovative, add value and take measured risks to deal with environmental opportunities and competitive surprises
- the effectiveness of the information sharing, monitoring and control systems.

Business is a game, a game to win. My job is to set the strategy and have a team that can deliver it, to review their performance, handle the regulatory issues and set targets and objectives to grow the business.

CHARLES ALLEN, WHEN CHAIRMAN, ITV

Don't tell people how to do things, tell them what to do and let them surprise you with their results.

GENERAL GEORGE S. PATON

14.2   Implementation and change

Implementation incorporates a number of aspects, some of which can be changed directly and some of which can only be changed indirectly. The latter aspects are more difficult for the strategic leadership to control and change. The success of the strategic leader in managing both the direct and indirect aspects influences the effectiveness of:

- the implementation of strategies and strategic changes which are determined through the planning and visionary modes of strategy creation, and
- the ability of the organization, and its managers, to respond to changes in the environment and adapt in line with perceived opportunities and threats.

Aspects of implementation that can be changed directly

- The organization structure (the actual, defined structure, not necessarily the way in which people behave within the structure)
- management systems
- policies and procedures
- action plans and short-term budgets
- management information systems.

Aspects of implementation that are changed indirectly

Communication systems

While the management information system can affect formal information flows, the network of informal communications truly determines awareness. Such communications are affected by, and influence, the degree and spirit of co-operation between managers, functions and divisions.

Managing and developing quality and excellence

Attention to detail, production on time and to the appropriate quality, and the personal development of managers and other employees are all factors in this. As well as developing managers' skills and capabilities generally, it is important to consider the quality of management in particular areas and the cover for managers who leave or who are absent. The organization structure should provide opportunities for managers to grow and be promoted.

Manifested values and the organization culture

This involves the way in which things are done: standards and attitudes which are held and practised.

The fostering of innovation

The willingness of people to search for improvements and better ways of doing things. Their encouragement and reward is very much influenced by the strategic leader, with leadership by example often proving significant.

Those aspects that can be changed directly generally imply physical changes in the way in which resources are allocated. Behavioural aspects, which imply changes in beliefs and attitudes, can only be modified indirectly. Both are considered in the forthcoming chapters.

14.3 Problems of successful implementation

Owen (1982) contends that in practice there are four problem areas associated with the successful implementation of strategies.

1 At any time strategy and structure need to be matched and supportive of each other. Products and services need to be managed independently, or in linked groups or business units, if they are to be matched closely and effectively with their environments. There may be good reasons for having a structure that does not separate the products, services and business units in this way. The strategic leader might prefer a centralized structure without delegated responsibilities, for example. The organization might possess certain key skills and enjoy a reputation for strength in a particular area, and this might be influential in the design of the structure. Equally, certain skills might be absent and have to be compensated for. Related to this might be the willingness or reluctance of managers to change jobs or location within the structure. Structures cannot be created and activated independently of the people involved; their individual skills may provide either opportunities or constraints. Changing attitudes and developing new skills is accomplished indirectly, as pointed out above, and takes time.

   It is also possible that related products may be produced in various plants nationally or internationally, when a geography-orientated structure, which keeps the plants separate, is favoured for other sound reasons. In addition, it may not prove feasible to change the structure markedly every time there is a change in corporate strategy and, instead, acceptable modifications to the existing structure are preferred to more significant changes.

2 The information and communications systems are inadequate for reporting back and evaluating the adaptive changes that are taking place, and hence the strategic leader is not fully aware of what is happening. Hence the performance of the existing structure is not monitored properly, and as a result control mechanisms may be ineffective.

3 Implementing strategy involves change, which in turn involves uncertainty and risk. New skills may have to be developed, for example. While managers may agree in meetings to make changes, they may be more reluctant in practice to implement them. Motivating managers to make changes is therefore a key determinant.

4 Management systems, such as compensation schemes, management development and communications systems, which operate within the structural framework will have been developed to meet the needs of past strategies. They may not be ideal for the changes that are taking place currently, and again it is difficult to modify them continually.

Alexander (1985) argues that additional factors are also significant, especially:

● The failure to predict the time and problems that implementation will involve, such as the time required for a new business or venture to take off, which is invariably underestimated. This may not seem critical, but it can be. In the early months of a new business, more cash is typically spent than revenue is earned. The accumulating debt is a so-called 'valley of death' that the business must come through and out of before it can start earning real money and (eventually and hopefully) enter the land of plenty.

● Other activities and commitments that distract attention and possibly cause resources to be diverted. Paradoxically, one way of coping with the likelihood of disruptive and distracting events is to ensure that the organization has spare resources in readiness for such emergencies; but slack of this sort can appear to imply inefficiency and under-utilized resources, and it can be expensive.

- The bases on which the strategy was formulated changed, or were forecast poorly, and insufficient flexibility to deal with the change pressures has been built in.

All of these problems presuppose that the formulated strategic change is sound and logical. A poorly thought-out strategy will create its own implementation problems.

14.4 Successful implementation

To counter these problems Owen (1982) suggests the following:

- Clear responsibility for the successful outcome of planned strategic change should be allocated.
- The number of strategies and changes being pursued at any time should be limited. The ability of the necessary resources to cope with the changes should be seen as a key determinant of strategy and should not be overlooked.
- Necessary actions to implement strategies should be identified and planned, and again responsibility should be allocated.
- Milestones, or progress measurement points, should be established.
- Measures of performance should be established, as well as appropriate monitoring and control mechanisms.

These, Owen argues, can all be achieved without necessarily changing the structural framework but rather by changing the way in which people operate within it.

In addition, Alexander contends that the involvement and support of people who will be affected by the changes in strategy must be considered, and that the implications of the new strategies and changes should be communicated widely, awareness created and commitment and involvement sought. Incentives and reward systems underpin this.

In the same way that no single evaluation technique can select a best strategy, there is no best way of implementing strategic change. There are no right answers, as such. A number of lessons, considerations and arguments, however, can be incorporated into the thinking and planning; and these are the themes of Part 5.

Three final points need to be mentioned to conclude this introduction. First, although there are no right answers to either strategy formulation or strategy implementation, the two must be consistent if the organization is to be effective. Arguably, how the organization does things, and manages both strategy and change, is more important than the actual strategy or change proposed.

Second, the style of strategic leadership will be very influential. We also argue that the preference of the strategic leader affects the desirability of particular strategic alternatives. The structure of the organization, the delegation of responsibilities, the freedom of managers to act, their willingness to exercise initiative, and the incentive and reward systems will all be determined and influenced by the strategic leader. These in turn determine the effectiveness of implementation. The strategic leader's choices and freedom to act, however, may be constrained by any resource limitations and certain environmental forces.

Third, the timing of when to act and make changes will also be important. In this context, for example, Mitchell (1988) points out that timing is particularly crucial in the implementation decisions and actions that follow acquisitions. Employees anticipate changes in the organization, especially at senior management level, and inaction, say beyond three months, causes uncertainty and fear. As a result, there is greater hostility to change when it does occur. The dangers of hasty action, such as destroying strengths before appreciating that they are strengths, are offset. Mitchell concludes that it is more important to be decisive than to be right, and then learn and adapt incrementally.

14.5 Structural alternatives

We have established in the early pages of this chapter that the organization structure provides the framework through which intended strategies are implemented – or not, as the case may be. However, at the same time, the structure also provides a foundation for emergent strategy creation. By dividing up tasks, the structure places people in certain roles with certain expectations. The accompanying systems, which in part are designed to co-ordinate all of these tasks into a meaningful whole and thus create synergy, help to determine the freedom that individual managers have to change things. It is the style of management, largely dictated by the strategic leader, which finally determines how co-ordinated the efforts are, how co-operative managers, functions and businesses are with each other, and how willing managers are to accept empowerment and make changes.

We now examine the linkages between strategy and structure by examining a number of alternative structural forms and by considering the key issues of centralization and decentralization. The forces that influence and determine the structure are discussed. The structural challenges of global and small, entrepreneurial businesses, manufacturing and service companies and organizations in the public sector are covered.

Lawrence and Lorsch (1967) have argued that the organization should be structured in such a way that it can respond to pressures for change from its environment and pursue any appropriate opportunities which are spotted. Given that strategies are concerned with relating the organization's resources and values with the environment, it follows that strategy and structure are linked. Structure, in fact, is the means by which the organization seeks to achieve its strategic objectives and implement strategies and strategic changes. Strategies are formulated and implemented by managers operating within the current structure. Thompson and Strickland (1980) comment that while strategy formulation requires the abilities to conceptualize, analyse and judge, implementation involves working with and through other people and instituting change. Implementation poses the tougher management challenge.

The essential criteria underpinning the design of the organization structure are:

- first, the extent to which decision-making is *decentralized*, as opposed to centralized, and
- second, the extent to which policies and procedures are *formalized*.

Decentralization to some degree is required if incremental and adaptive strategic change is to take place. Issues of centralization/decentralization are explored in Critical reflection 14.1. Formality is linked to the extent to which tasks and jobs are specialized and defined, and their rigidity, i.e. the period over which jobs have remained roughly the same. The longer the period is, arguably, the greater will be the resistance to changing them. Clearly, communications and formality are linked. In a formal organization there will be a reliance on vertical communications, with instructions passing downwards and information on results passing upwards. In some organizations, there is a tendency for good news to flow upwards quickly and readily and for bad news to be covered up. The greater the informality, the greater the likelihood of strong and effective horizontal communications as people across the organization are encouraged to talk and share.

The challenge for most organizations, then, is to find the appropriate degrees of decentralization and informality, to enable them to maintain control while innovating and managing change in a dynamic and turbulent environment. In turn, this requires that managers are *empowered*. It would not be unusual for an organization to be centralized and informal when it first starts up. Afterwards, as limited power and responsibility is devolved to identifiable managers, the structure becomes more formalized, but the central power of the strategic leader remains strong. As the organization grows beyond a stage where one person can really remain in effective control, the switch is to decentralized with formal controls through policies, procedures and reporting relationships. Three cases are included together at this point. They explore how three quite

Critical reflection 14.1

Centralization and Decentralization

Centralization and decentralization relate to the degree to which the authority, power and responsibility for decision-making are devolved through the organization. There are several options, including the following:

- All major strategic decisions are taken centrally, at head office, by the strategic leader or a group of senior strategists. The size of any team will depend upon the preference of the overall strategic leader together with the size, complexity and diversity of the organization. Strictly enforced policies and procedures will constrain the freedom of other managers responsible for business units, products, services and functional areas to change competitive and functional strategies. This is centralization.
- Changes in the strategic perspective are decided centrally, but then the organization is structured to enable managers to change competitive and functional strategies in line with perceived opportunities and threats.
- The organization is truly decentralized such that independent business units have general managers who are free to change their respective strategic perspectives. In effect they run a series of independent businesses with some co-ordination from the parent headquarters.

The extent to which true decentralization exists may be visible from the organization's charted structure. It is always useful to examine the membership of the group and divisional/business unit boards, regardless of the number and delineation of divisions. The organization is likely to tend towards decentralization where there is a main board and a series of subsidiary boards, each chaired by a member of the main board. The chief executive/strategic leader, who is responsible for the performance of each subsidiary, will not necessarily have a seat on the main board. The organization will tend towards greater centralization where the main board comprises the chairperson/chief executives of certain subsidiaries, generally the largest ones, together with staff specialists. Hence decentralization and divisionalization are not synonymous terms.

The ten main determinants
- the size of the organization
- geographical locations, together with the

– homogeneity/heterogeneity of the products and services
– technology of the tasks involved
– interdependencies
- the relative importance and stability of the external environment, and the possible need to react quickly
- generally, how quickly decisions need to be made
- the workload of decision-makers
- issues of motivation via delegation, together with the abilities and willingness of managers to make decisions and accept responsibility
- the location of competence and expertise in the organization. Are the managerial strengths in the divisions or at headquarters?
- the costs involved in making any changes
- the significance and impact of competitive and functional decisions and changes
- the status of the firm's planning, control and information systems.

Advantages and disadvantages

There are no right or wrong answers concerning the appropriate amount of centralization/decentralization. It is a question of balancing the potential advantages and disadvantages of each as they affect particular firms.

It has been suggested that companies which achieve and maintain high growth tend to be more decentralized, and those which are more concerned with profits than growth are more centralized. The highest performers in terms of both growth and profits tend to retain high degrees of central control as far as the overall strategic perspective is concerned. Child (1977) contends that the most essential issue is the degree of internal consistency.

Advantages of centralization
- Consistency of strategy
- Easier to co-ordinate activities (and handle the interdependencies) and control changes
- Changes in the strategic perspective are more easily facilitated.

Disadvantages of centralization
- May be slow to respond to changes which affect subsidiaries individually rather than the organization

as a whole, depending upon the remoteness of head office
- Easy to create an expensive head office that relies on management information systems and becomes detached from customers, and for which there are too many diverse interests and complexities
- General managers with real strategic ability are not developed within the organization. Instead the organization is dependent on specialists and as a result the various functions may not be properly co-ordinated. Does this achieve a fit between the organization and its environment?

Advantages of decentralization
- Ability to change competitive and functional strategies more quickly

- Improved motivation
- Can develop better overall strategic awareness in a very complex organization which is too diverse for a head office to control effectively.

Disadvantages of decentralization
- May be problems in clarifying the role of head-office central services which aim to co-ordinate the various divisions and business units and achieve certain economies through, and the centralization of, selected activities
- Problems of linking the power that general managers need and the responsibility that goes with the power. General managers must have the freedom to make decisions without referrals back.

Case 14.1

The National Health Service – II   UK

The UK National Health Service (NHS) is one of the largest employers in the world; it may only be exceeded by the Indian railways in terms of numbers of employees. These employees deal with funding, commissioning and the provision of services to patients. This makes it inherently complex. Designing a structure to implement government strategies for health is tricky, and successive governments have been criticized for constant changes in structure and expectations. It is, of course, probably impossible to meet most (let alone all) the expectations of the various stakeholders. In some respects, a fundamental role of the NHS is to ration the resources it has available – and thus satisfy some demands at the expense of others.

When they were in power in the 1980s and early 1990s, the Conservatives pursued a strategy of internal competition to drive efficiencies. The system they inherited was essentially centralized. At the core, GP (General Practitioner) Fundholders now bought services from Hospital Trusts, working alongside Health Authorities who guided priorities and provided quality assessment. They were theoretically free to choose which hospitals they sent their patients to.

When Labour came to power in 1997 it set out to dismantle this internal market at the first opportunity.

GP Fundholders soon became Primary Care Groups which helped Health Authorities purchase services from Hospital Trusts. Over a period of time the higher-tier Regional Health Authorities disappeared, and 95 lower-tier Area Authorities became 28 (larger) Strategic Health Authorities through consolidation and rationalization. In 2002 the Primary Care Groups became Primary Care Trusts – which purchased care themselves. Labour defended this as a different type of internal market. It was different because it was heavily regulated, and much less 'free' than it had been under the Conservatives. This implied the creation of new managerial and administrative posts. But once again money was related directly to activity.

One layer of complexity comes when one sets Primary Care Trusts alongside Hospital Trusts. For some (routine) treatments hospitals are only likely to be commissioned from PCTs in a relatively tightly defined geographical area. But where that same hospital provides more specialist acute care, it can be dealing with PCTs across a much wider region. The bottom line, in theory at least, is that patients end up where they can get the best care.

More recently, and somewhat controversially, Foundation Hospitals have been created. Those

Hospital Trusts that score three stars on a raft of key measures can apply for greater independence within the Health Service. They can, for example, borrow money at their own discretion. The catch is, the Treasury monitor this and, by other withdrawals, make sure no extra money is going into the system, beyond that the Chancellor of the Exchequer has decreed is the appropriate aggregate amount. The star rating is monitored on an annual basis, and any Trust that loses its three-star rating loses its Foundation status. From time-to-time the key measures are changed as well. In 2004, for example, the ability to control the 'super bug' – which leaves hospital patients with secondary infections – became critical for the first time.

Another regulatory arm introduced by Labour has been NICE – the National Institute for Clinical Excellence – which dictates which drugs can and cannot be prescribed. NICE has made many controversial decisions since its creation.

Alongside the NHS itself, the government has allowed and encouraged Fast Track Surgery Centres, sometimes called Polyclinics, where the private sector provides certain procedures – minor operations and diagnostics – on behalf of the NHS at an agreed charge to the system. The relevant costs are typically less than those of the insurance-based private sector itself. Some of these Centres have attracted surgeons from overseas and they are a threat to the poorest-performing hospitals, those that cannot cope with their waiting lists.

In addition, some patients have also been allowed to have treatment in other European countries (paid for by the NHS) where local waiting lists are lengthy. This has sometimes been controversial, as have the discussions on co-payments. Historically patients have either been NHS or private – for a particular course of treatment. They can, of course, be both at various times for different treatments. As a consequence patients have been discouraged from paying for the private sector to supplement or top-up their NHS treatment. With co-payments they could receive treatment from both sectors at the same time.

Practice-based commissioning is another recent initiative. Here funding is made available (against bids) for delivering care in some new, innovatory way. The money can be awarded to GP practices and to private sector providers, for example. It is possible we will see NHS staff on part-time contracts with a hospital and also working for another provider because there are finite skills resources but the financing of the relevant care has been dispersed. Whilst this could drive both cost efficiency and all-round effective care, it could also be confusing. Quality will certainly need measuring and benchmarking. Certain areas, such as specialist acute or secondary care, are likely to be relatively immune, for example.

In summary, centralization gave way to a free market which itself was replaced by regulated devolution.

Questions

1 What do you think might be the advantages and disadvantages of the current system?
2 Could you design a structure that allows greater decentralization without destroying the ethos of a 'national' health service?

Case 14.2

Oxfam – A Structure for Emergent Strategy UK

Oxfam is a well-known international charity engaged in:

- 'doing good' around the world, both through routine operations (such as improving fresh water availability in developing countries) and responding to emergencies such as the tsunami a few years ago with both physical goods and people

- campaigning and lobbying
- fund raising and promotion
- running a chain of charity shops and warehouses.

These activities might be (and clearly are) related, but they are different in respect of key success factors, competencies and culture. The challenge is compounded by the fact that Oxfam operates globally – but it is not one single operation. The charity was started in the UK, in Oxford, in 1942; and whilst the UK operation remains substantially the largest, there are now twelve Oxfams around the world. There are national operations in Spain, Germany, Holland, Hong Kong, Australia and the US, for example – all 'working together' and co-ordinated from Oxford.

Each national operation has something of a distinctive and preferred modus operandi. For example the Dutch Oxfam prefers to ally with local partners whilst the UK is big enough to deploy its own field workers.

When some new disaster or emergency arises and Oxfam's help is needed, there are a number of things to co-ordinate. The delivery of actual aid to various points of need must be overseen. Staff need to be deployed to those areas where they can be of most help – some quite senior staff have to be available on a flexible basis to travel at short notice. Oxfam's efforts overall must link with parallel work by the United Nations and other aid agencies.

Decision making must be speedy and to a genuine degree devolved. Moreover it is important that Oxfam is genuinely responsive – its efforts should be targeted at the needs its clients have, rather than in the pursuit of a provider's agenda.

It was clear not very long ago that sometimes the different national operations were working 'side by side' at least as much as they were behaving as a single operation with joined-up thinking and effort. As a consequence Oxford took on a stronger centralized co-ordination role – helped by (subsidized) investment in new IT systems.

Question

1 Given the nature of the needs and challenges outlined, to what extent do you think Oxfam should be centralized and to what extent decentralized?

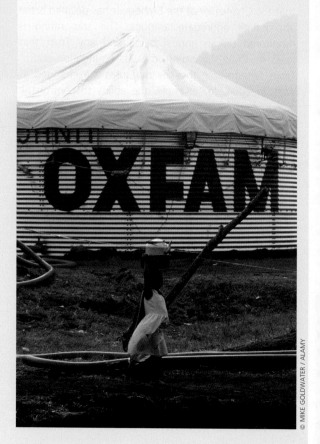

© MIKE GOLDWATER / ALAMY

Case 14.3

Nantucket Nectars   US

Nantucket Nectars is an unusual but very successful business which was started by two friends. When Tom First and Tom Scott graduated from Brown University in Rhode Island they decided they wanted to live on Nantucket Island, off the New England coast, and find some way of earning a living. In the summer of 1989 they started a small business for servicing the yachts belonging to visitors to the island. This was always going to be seasonal. They travelled around the harbour in a distinctive red boat, delivering newspapers, muffins, coffee, laundry and any other supplies for which there was a demand. They also washed boats, emptied sewage and shampooed dogs. This seemed to lead naturally to them later opening the Nantucket

Allserve general store, which still exists. They used the following promotional slogan in the early days: 'Ain't nothing those boys won't do'.

Once the summer was over, demand for their services fell as the yachts disappeared. They decided to experiment with fruit juices, mixed in a household blender. They first sought to replicate a peach-based nectar that they had sampled in Spain. During the following summer they sold their bottled juices from their red boat. They always produced distinctive flavours from the best quality ingredients. By investing their joint savings they were able to hire a bottler to produce 1400 cases. Overall, though, the business merely struggled on for a couple of years, until one wealthy yacht owner offered them a $500,000 loan to develop the business. They seized the opportunity. Nantucket Nectars then expanded quickly to cover a number of states on the American east coast. Initially they did their own bottling, but they switched to subcontracting. As the business has grown they have also switched to independent distribution.

If I were on the outside looking in, I'd say Nantucket Nectars was an overnight success. Being on the inside, it's been a long, long time. We almost went out of business a thousand times.

(TOM SCOTT)

By the late 1990s Nantucket Nectars employed over 100 people and sold in over 30 US states and a number of selected export markets. Values were always a key element. The partners remained determined to 'create the best quality product in the juice market', and yet the company remained enigmatic. The bottle labels stated: 'We're juice guys. We don't wear ties to work'; folksy radio commercials were utilized extensively in America; but the new head office is in an old Men's Club near Harvard University. It is furnished with antiques and managers have private offices instead of the open-plan arrangement which is increasingly popular in many informal organizations. First and Scott typically took their dogs into work. Each week every head-office manager focused on talking personally with one of their salespeople in the field, staff who would otherwise have little contact with head office.

The founders claim that the company was always run on gut instinct and trial and error. Few people had any formal business qualifications. In 1997 Nantucket Nectars

was awarded a contract to provide juice for Starbucks, and later that year Ocean Spray – leading manufacturer of cranberry juices and other products – acquired a 50 per cent stake. The companies believed that they could make extensive savings on supplies if they joined forces. First and Scott continued to run the business that they founded.

One other related diversification is the Juice Guys Juice Bar which sells freshly prepared smoothies made from fruit, yogurt and Nantucket Nectars fruit juices, as well as sandwiches and memorabilia.

Questions

1 How easy would it have been for First and Scott to maintain their informal style and culture as Nantucket Nectars grew?
2 Would more formality really be required?
3 How are strategy and structure linked?
4 What is the balance between intended and emergent strategy?

You might usefully apply Figures 14.1–14.3 to this case.

© KLAUDIA STEINER / ISTOCK

different organizations – The UK National Health Service, the international charity Oxfam and Nantucket Nectars, an entrepreneurial American business – have dealt with the centralization-decentralization challenge. The NHS needs decentralization because of its sheer size; Oxfam needed centralization to achieve co-ordinated effort. It is not difficult to imagine how the need for a formal structure developed and became urgent as Nantucket Nectars grew in size.

These structural types, then, will be evidenced in the organization frameworks and structural designs which are explored in detail in the next section of this chapter. It is important to appreciate that structure involves more than the organization chart or framework which is used for illustrative purposes and to explain where businesses, products, services and people fit in relation to each other. Charts are static; structures are dynamic and involve behaviour patterns.

> *In my experience, the key to growth is to pick good managers, involve them at the outset of discussions on strategy and objectives, and then devolve as much responsibility as they will accept. That's the only way you know if they are any good.*
>
> SIR MICHAEL GRADE, ITV CHAIRMAN, WHEN CHIEF EXECUTIVE, CHANNEL FOUR TELEVISION

> *Autonomy is what you take, not what you are given.*
>
> ROY WATTS, WHEN CHAIRMAN, THAMES WATER

During the World War II the initial success of the German army in 1940, and the speed at which it overcame the French and British armies (known as blitzkrieg), was in no small measure due to the degree of autonomy given to individual officers in the field to make decisions as they went. By the time the German army had become bogged down on the Russian front, especially the Sixth Army at Stalingrad, that individual autonomy for the senior commanders, and the officers in the field, was gone and any major movement required the permission of Adolf Hitler. Organizational flexibility and speed of movement, the hallmarks of the Wehrmacht in the early part of the war, suffered as a consequence.

14.6 Structural forms

A number of discrete structural forms can be adapted by an organization when attempts are made to design an appropriate structure to satisfy its particular needs. The following are described in this section:

- the entrepreneurial structure
- the functional structure
- the divisional structure
- the holding company structure
- the matrix structure.

This is not an exhaustive coverage, in the sense that personalized varieties of each of these alternatives can easily be developed.

Chandler (1962) and subsequent authors such as Salter (1970) have suggested that as firms grow from being a small business with a simple entrepreneurial structure, a more formal **functional structure** evolves to allow managers to cope with the increasing complexity and the demands of decision-making. As the organization becomes diversified, with a multiplicity of products, services or operating bases, a different structure is again required, and initially this is likely to be based on simple **divisionalization**. In other words, there are stages of structural development which evolve as strategies change and organizations grow. Chandler contends, however, that while strategy and structure develop together through a particular sequence, structures are not adapted until pressures force a change. The pressures tend to relate to growing inefficiency resulting from an inability to handle the increasing demands of decision-making. **Matrix organizations** have been designed to cope with the complexities of multiproduct, multinational organizations with interdependencies which must be accommodated if synergy is to be achieved. However, matrix organizations are difficult to manage and control. Large organizations in particular change their structures (at least in part) quite frequently as they search for one that allows effective implementation of intended strategies while permitting emergent strategy creation to a desired level.

It has been emphasized earlier (see Chapter 11) that many organizations fail to achieve the anticipated synergy from strategies of diversification and acquisition, and as a result divest the businesses to which they cannot add value. Implementation difficulties are often linked to a failure to absorb the new acquisition into the existing organization, and this is likely to involve changes in the structure.

It is important to appreciate that the structural forms described in this section are only a framework, and that the behavioural processes within the structure, the way in which resources are managed and co-ordinated, really determines effectiveness. In turn, this is related to the way in which authority, power and responsibility are devolved throughout the organization, and whether generally the firm is centralized or decentralized. These themes were explored in Critical reflectiona 14.1, where it is emphasized that decentralization and divisionalization are not synonymous. The establishment of a divisionalized structure does not necessarily imply that authority to adapt competitive and functional strategies is freely delegated; the firm could remain centralized.

The entrepreneurial structure

The entrepreneurial structure, built around the owner–manager and typically utilized by small companies in the early stages of their development, is illustrated in Figure 14.4. The structure is totally centralized. All key decisions are made by the strategic leader, and employees refer everything significant back to him or her. It is particularly useful for new businesses as it enables the founder, who normally will have some expertise with the product or service and whose investment is at risk, to control the growth and development.

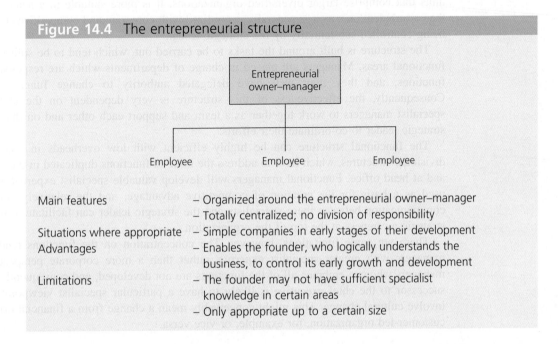

Figure 14.4   The entrepreneurial structure

Main features	– Organized around the entrepreneurial owner–manager
	– Totally centralized; no division of responsibility
Situations where appropriate	– Simple companies in early stages of their development
Advantages	– Enables the founder, who logically understands the business, to control its early growth and development
Limitations	– The founder may not have sufficient specialist knowledge in certain areas
	– Only appropriate up to a certain size

There is an argument that this is not really a formal structure as all responsibility, power and authority lie with one person. However, in some small companies of this nature, selected employees will specialize and be given job titles and some limited responsibility for such activities as production, sales or accounting. In this respect the structure could be redrawn to appear more like the functional organization discussed below. The functional form only really emerges when *managers* are established with genuine delegated authority and responsibility for the functions and activities that they control.

New firms with entrepreneurial structures are likely to be established because the owner–manager has contacts and expertise in a particular line of business and, for whatever reason, wishes to establish his or her own business. While the entrepreneur will want to control the early stages of growth, it does not follow that he or she will have expertise in all aspects of the business. Many start-ups occur because the founder understands the technology and production or operational aspects of the business. Marketing, sales and financial control may well be areas of potential weakness with a consequent reliance on other people together with an element of learning as the business develops. This need can prove to be a limitation of the entrepreneurial structure.

Another limitation relates to growth. At some stage, dependent on both the business and the founder, the demands of decision-making, both day-to-day problem decisions and longer-term planning decisions, will become too complex for one person, and there will be pressure to establish a more formal functional organization. The owner–manager relinquishes some responsibility for short-term decisions and has greater opportunity to concentrate on the more strategic aspects of the business. This can prove to be a dilemma for some entrepreneurs, however, particularly those who started their own business because they wanted total control over something, or because they were frustrated with the greater formality of larger companies.

The functional structure

The functional structure, illustrated in Figure 14.5, is commonplace in small firms that have outgrown the entrepreneurial structure and in larger firms that produce only a limited range of related products and services. It is also the typical internal structure of the divisions and business units that comprise larger diversified organizations. It is more suitable in a stable environment than a turbulent one, as it is generally centralized with corporate and competitive strategies again being controlled substantially by the strategic leader.

The structure is built around the tasks to be carried out, which tend to be split into specialist functional areas. Managers are placed in charge of departments which are responsible for these functions, and they may well have delegated authority to change functional strategies. Consequently, the effectiveness of this structure is very dependent on the ability of these specialist managers to work together as a team and support each other and on the ability of the strategic leader to co-ordinate their efforts.

The functional structure can be highly efficient with low overheads in comparison with divisional structures, which have to address the issue of functions duplicated in the business units and at head office. Functional managers will develop valuable specialist expertise which can be used as a basis for the creation of competitive advantage, and the relatively simple lines of communication between these specialists and the strategic leader can facilitate a high degree of strategic awareness at the top of the organization.

There are some limitations, however. The concentration on the functions tends to lead to managers with greater specialist expertise rather than a more corporate perspective. General managers who can embrace all of the functions are not developed, and consequently any internal successor to the chief executive is likely to have a particular specialist viewpoint, which may involve cultural change. This might conceivably mean a change from a financial orientation to a customer-led organization, for example, or vice versa.

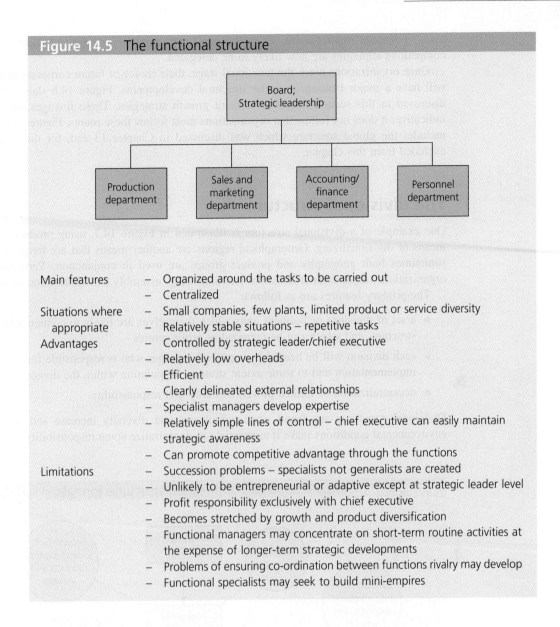

Figure 14.5 The functional structure

Main features	– Organized around the tasks to be carried out
	– Centralized
Situations where	– Small companies, few plants, limited product or service diversity
appropriate	– Relatively stable situations – repetitive tasks
Advantages	– Controlled by strategic leader/chief executive
	– Relatively low overheads
	– Efficient
	– Clearly delineated external relationships
	– Specialist managers develop expertise
	– Relatively simple lines of control – chief executive can easily maintain strategic awareness
	– Can promote competitive advantage through the functions
Limitations	– Succession problems – specialists not generalists are created
	– Unlikely to be entrepreneurial or adaptive except at strategic leader level
	– Profit responsibility exclusively with chief executive
	– Becomes stretched by growth and product diversification
	– Functional managers may concentrate on short-term routine activities at the expense of longer-term strategic developments
	– Problems of ensuring co-ordination between functions rivalry may develop
	– Functional specialists may seek to build mini-empires

Functional organizations are less likely to be entrepreneurial throughout the company than is the case in more decentralized forms, although the strategic leader could be personally dynamic and entrepreneurial. Because corporate and competitive strategy changes are generally the responsibility of the strategic leader, functional managers may concentrate on short-term issues at the expense of longer-term strategic needs. The tendency for profit responsibility to lie primarily with the strategic leader compounds this. Functional managers may seek to build mini-empires around their specialism, and this can lead to rivalry between departments for resources and status and make the task of co-ordination and team-building more difficult.

The structure is stretched and becomes more inefficient with growth and product or service diversification. As the firm grows from a limited range of related products to unrelated ones, co-ordination proves increasingly difficult. Hence, a need grows for some form of divisionalization, together with a revised role for the strategic leader. The strategic leader is now responsible for co-ordinating the strategies of a series of business units or divisions, each with a general manager at their head, rather than co-ordinating specialist functional managers into a cohesive and supportive team. Financial management skills become increasingly necessary. Adaptive changes in competitive strategies are now likely to be delegated.

Once organizations reach the functional stage, their choice of future corporate growth strategy will have a major bearing upon the structural developments. Figure 14.6 shows the structures discussed in this section linked to relevant growth strategies. These linkages must be seen as indicative; it does not follow that organizations must follow these routes. Figure 14.6 additionally includes the global structure which was discussed in Chapter 13 and, for this reason only, is excluded from this chapter.

The divisional structure

One example of a divisional structure is illustrated in Figure 14.7, using product groups as the means of divisionalizing. Geographical regions are another means that are frequently used, and sometimes both geography and product groups are used in conjunction. Vertically integrated organizations might divisionalize into manufacturing, assembly and distribution activities.

The primary features are as follows:

- a set of divisions or business units which themselves are likely to contain a functional structure, and which can be regarded as profit centres
- each division will be headed by a general manager who is responsible for strategy implementation and to some extent strategy formulation within the division
- decentralization of limited power, authority and responsibility.

Divisional structures are found when complexity and diversity increase and where turbulent environmental conditions make it appropriate to decentralize some responsibility for making sure

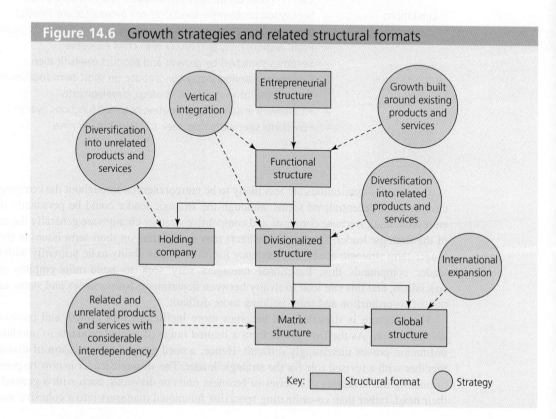

Figure 14.6   Growth strategies and related structural formats

Figure 14.7 The divisional structure. A product divisional structure is illustrated. Geographical divisions, or a mixture of the two, are also used

Main features	– Divisions are likely to be profit centres and may be seen as strategic business units for planning and control purposes
	– Divisions/business units are headed by general managers who enjoy responsibility for their own resources
	– Decentralized
Situations where appropriate	– Growing size and complexity
	– Appropriate divisional/business unit splits exist
	– Organizations growing through merger and acquisition
	– Turbulent environments
	– Product/market divisions/business units most appropriate where there is a diverse range of products
	– Geographic divisions are common where there are cultural distinctions between the company's markets – especially if distances are great
	– Divisionalization may also be a mix of products and geography or based on different production processes
Advantages	– Spreads profit responsibility
	– Enables evaluation of contribution of various activities
	– Motivates managers and facilitates the development of both specialist and general managers
	– Enables adaptive change
	– Chief executive can stay away from routine decisions and concentrate on corporate strategy
	– Growth through acquisition more readily implemented – Can be entrepreneurial throughout the organization
	– Divestment can also be handled relatively easily
Limitations	– Conflict between divisions, say for resources
	– Possible confusion over focus of responsibility (head office and divisions) and duplication of efforts and resources
	– Divisions may tend to think short term and concentrate on profits
	– Divisions may be of different sizes and some may grow very large – evaluation of relative performance may be difficult
	– Co-ordinating interdependent divisions and establishing transfer prices between them

that the organization is responsive and possibly proactive towards external forces in a variety of different industries. They are also useful where there are major differences in needs and tastes in the company's markets around the world.

The major advantage of this structure is that it can facilitate the ability of the organization to manage the strategies of a number of disparate products and markets effectively. The major difficulty lies in designing the most appropriate structure.

There is no one best way of dividing a business into divisions, especially if the composition of the whole corporation changes with acquisitions, divestments and closures. Large companies will change their structures periodically in an attempt to improve both efficiency and effectiveness. Structural changes of this nature imply changes in the power structure, the relative amount of decentralization and managers' jobs, and for these reasons they may prove disruptive. Case 14.4 charts Nestlé's approach.

Case 14.4

Nestlé   Eur

Nestlé began in the 1860s as a condensed milk factory in Switzerland, where it still has its global headquarters. Having developed largely by acquisition (followed by organic growth) Nestlé now produces in 500 factories in 80 countries and sells in over 100 countries, many of which have strong local preferences. Altogether there are some 8000 different brands involved. Only 2 per cent of its sales now originate in Switzerland. It aims to be Number One or Number Two in all the markets it targets, and consequently invests in branding. The main products and brands are as follows:

Beverages – coffee (its Nescafé brand is ubiquitous around the world), mineral water (Perrier (carbonated water) was acquired in 1992 to add to Vittel still water) and fruit juices

Milk products – based on its original brand name, Carnation but also including Libby's and, with the purchase of Gerber in 2007, baby foods

Ice cream, chocolate (Rowntree and Kit Kat, for example, both acquired in 1988) and confectionery (Smarties)

Prepared dishes (Crosse and Blackwell), frozen foods (Findus), sauces and condiments (including Maggi and Buitoni)

Pet foods – Spillers was acquired in 1998 to supplement the existing business

Nestlé also owns a substantial stake of French cosmetics business, L'Oréal.

Its corporate headquarters was slimmed down in the early 1990s in an attempt to be more innovative and more customer-focused. There are now seven strategic business units (namely beverages, foods, dairy products,

confectionery, ice cream, pet care and food services) which have world-wide **strategic** responsibility. They establish the global business strategy and are responsible for R&D. Operations in the various countries are co-ordinated through a regional network. Six business unit head offices are co-located at corporate headquarters in Switzerland; Nestlé's mineral water interests, including Perrier are run from Paris. There were plans to locate the global confectionery business in York (where the Rowntree business was built and based) but these were abandoned because of the travel implications.

Each strategic business unit is free to operate in the most appropriate way – there is no longer a 'central way of doing things'. The style and approach appears to vary with the degree of novelty/maturity of the business, its market share and technological intensity, and the need to be localized. The intention is to establish the most appropriate cost structure and decision making procedures. The requirements for E–V–R congruence vary between the divisions. There are, however, in-built mechanisms to try and spread best practices and to overcome a past tendency to resist adopting ideas developed in other countries.

Nestlé do not believe there is such a person as a 'global customer' and therefore focus on regional and local differences rather than global brands.

Question

1 Does this structure make sense for the scope and diversity of the businesses? Why? Why not?

Other advantages of divisional structures are that profit responsibilities are spread between the divisions or business units. This helps to motivate managers who can be given authority and responsibility for profit, and enables an evaluation of the contribution of each activity to the organization as a whole. Responsibility for changes in competitive and functional strategies can be delegated to the general managers in charge of each division or business unit; and it is feasible for these managers also to have responsibility for changes in the corporate strategy of their divisions. In this way the strategic leader of the corporation can concentrate substantially on corporate strategy and avoid involvement in routine decisions. Acquisitions and divestments can be handled so that only parts of the firm are affected directly. Finally, this structure facilitates innovation and intrapreneurship throughout the corporation if there is encouragement for this by the strategic leader.

In addition to the difficulty of designing an appropriate structure, there are problems of implementation. It was highlighted above that divisions are normally seen as profit centres, and consequently their profit targets will be used as a basis for assessing performance and effectiveness. There may be problems in establishing profit targets which are seen as equitable, given that divisions (a) may well be of uneven sizes, (b) are likely to be operating in markets which differ in their attractiveness, (c) may have strong or weak relative market shares, (d) may be interdependent upon each other, and (e) have to compete with each other for scarce corporate resources. Where there are interdependencies the corporate policy on transfer prices will favour certain divisions at the expense of others, which again can cause conflict. Wherever profits are a key measure, buying divisions will look for discounts and favourable treatment from within the corporation; selling divisions will expect other parts of the company to pay the going market price, or they will prefer to sell outside. Such profit orientation may also encourage divisions to think in terms of short-term financial measures rather than address more strategic issues.

Where an organization has a variety of different products, all of which depend on core skills and technologies, the challenge is to harness and improve the skills (which are, in effect, corporate resources) while ensuring competitiveness and operating efficiency for each product range. Canon, for example, has developed a range of discrete products (cameras, copiers, printers, etc.) around three core competencies: precision mechanics, fibre optics and micro-electronics.

Finally, each division is likely to contain a functional structure, and there is also likely to be functional support from headquarters. The corporation as a whole may be able to negotiate better borrowing terms than an individual division could; personnel policies may need to be consistent throughout the firm; and head-office planners may provide support to divisional planners. Reconciling any conflicts between these divisional and head-office groups, together with the need to minimize the potential waste from duplicate resources, can be a limitation of this structural form. The problem can be more difficult to resolve where there are layers of divisions, as discussed below.

Where organizations grow very large, complex and diversified it may be necessary to establish a number of layers of divisions or business units within larger divisions. Each business unit or subdivision may also be a profit centre with its own general manager.

As organizations develop globally the structural issues are compounded. It was shown in Chapter 12 that Porter (1990) and Ohmae (1990) disagree about how a company should transform itself into a successful global firm. Ohmae argues that it should shake off its origins, whereas Porter thinks they must be preserved. Should all of the high added value activities (such as design, development and engineering) be centralized at a global company's home base or spread around the world? Ohmae advocates decomposing the central head office into a number of regional headquarters, with the control of different functions (marketing, production, etc.) being dispersed to different extents and to different locations.

In essence it can be argued that both Ohmae and Porter are correct. There should in fact be no one correct solution to follow slavishly. What is needed is flexibility to consider the needs of the business and the environment at the time. The decision should be based on this and not what is in fashion at the time.

Case 14.5 (later) discusses ABB, a company which deliberately followed a strategy of devolution when it was growing and diversifying.

The holding company structure

The holding company structure, illustrated in Figure 14.8, is ideal for diversified conglomerates where there are few interdependencies between the businesses. The small head office acts largely as an investment company, acquiring and selling businesses and investing money as appropriate. The subsidiaries, which may or may not be wholly owned, are very independent, and their general managers are likely to have full responsibility for corporate strategy within any financial constraints or targets set by headquarters. It is quite common to find that the subsidiaries trade under individual names rather than the name of the parent organization, especially where they are acquisitions who may at any time be sold again.

The holding company structure is particularly appropriate for companies pursuing restructuring strategies, buying, rationalizing and then selling businesses when they can no longer add further value. The advantages of this structural form are that it implies low central overheads and

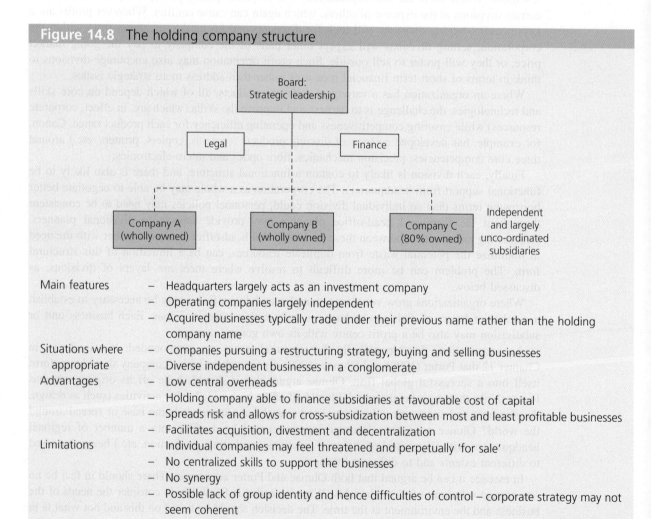

Figure 14.8 The holding company structure

Main features	– Headquarters largely acts as an investment company
	– Operating companies largely independent
	– Acquired businesses typically trade under their previous name rather than the holding company name
Situations where appropriate	– Companies pursuing a restructuring strategy, buying and selling businesses
	– Diverse independent businesses in a conglomerate
Advantages	– Low central overheads
	– Holding company able to finance subsidiaries at favourable cost of capital
	– Spreads risk and allows for cross-subsidization between most and least profitable businesses
	– Facilitates acquisition, divestment and decentralization
Limitations	– Individual companies may feel threatened and perpetually 'for sale'
	– No centralized skills to support the businesses
	– No synergy
	– Possible lack of group identity and hence difficulties of control – corporate strategy may not seem coherent

considerable decentralization but enables the head office to finance the subsidiaries at a favourable cost of capital. In fact, low-cost finance can reduce the total costs for a business and thus help to provide competitive advantage. In addition, risks are spread across a wide portfolio, and cross-subsidization is possible between the most and least profitable businesses. This again raises the issue of ascertaining a fair reward structure for the general managers.

The limitations relate, first, to the vulnerability that general managers may feel if they suspect that their business may always be for sale at the right price. There are fewer centralized skills and resources supporting the businesses, little co-ordination and therefore few opportunities for synergy. In addition, there may be no group identity among the business units and a lack of coherence in the corporate strategy. The potential benefit to headquarters lies in their ability to earn revenue and profits from the businesses, ideally in excess of pre-acquisition earnings, and being able to sell for a real capital gain.

> *The constituent companies [in LVMH, Louis Vuitton Moët Hennessy] have asked for the following: simplified structures, autonomy for the operational units and a method of administration in keeping with their particular culture.*
>
> *I am convinced that the success of our group and its subsidiaries is due to the fact that we trust the operational teams to carry out their own quest for quality.*
>
> *We keep these companies autonomous at middle management level so that they can have the advantages of medium size companies as well as the advantage of belonging to a powerful group that can fund their development.*
>
> BERNARD ARNAULT, GROUP CHAIRMAN, LVMH, LOUIS VUITTON MOËT HENNESSY

Several control issues which face head offices of divisionalized and holding company structures have been mentioned in the above sections, and these will be explored in greater detail in Chapter 16.

The matrix structure

Matrix structures are an attempt to combine the benefits of *decentralization* (motivation of identifiable management teams; closeness to the market; speedy decision-making and implementation) with those of *co-ordination* (achieving economies and synergy across all the business units, territories and products). They require dual reporting by managers to, say, a mix of functional and business unit heads or geographical territory and business unit general managers.

The matrix structure is found typically in large multiproduct, multinational organizations where there are significant inter-relationships and inter-dependencies, as illustrated in Figure 14.9 and Case 14.5, and in small sophisticated service businesses such as a business school. The matrix structure in Figure 14.9 illustrates an organization which is split into a series of divisions, based on both products and geographical territories. The product groups would be responsible for co-ordinating the production and marketing of their particular products in a series of plants which might be based anywhere in the world. The geographical divisions would have responsibility for co-ordinating the sales, marketing and distribution of all of the corporation's products, regardless of where they are manufactured, within their territorial area. The operating units would be the production plants, who were members of one or more product groups, depending upon the range of products manufactured in the plant, and whose products are marketed in more than one territory or geographical region. Consequently, the general manager in charge of each operating unit is responsible in some way to a series of product and territory chiefs (four in the illustration), all of whom will have profit responsibility. The matrix is designed to co-ordinate resources and effort throughout the organization. Structures such as this evolved in the 1960s and 1970s because of the need to establish priorities in multiproduct, multinational organizations. Should the

Figure 14.9　The matrix structure

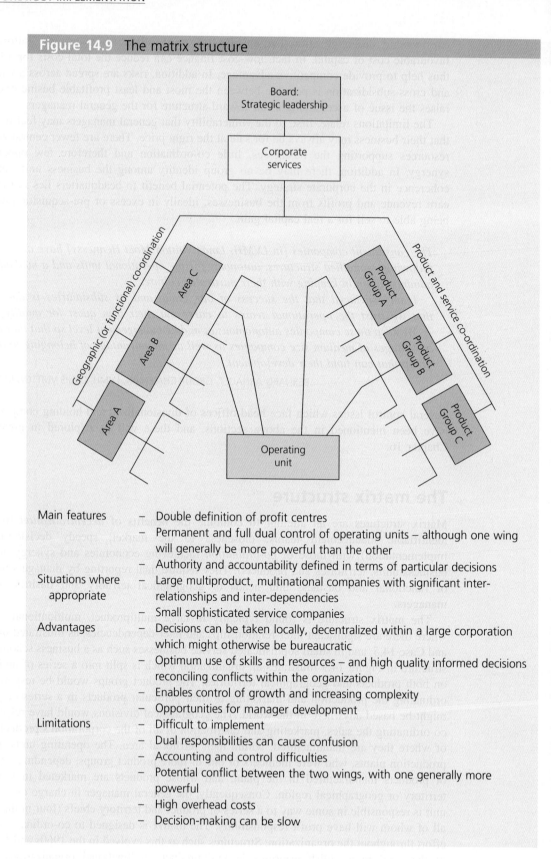

Main features	– Double definition of profit centres
	– Permanent and full dual control of operating units – although one wing will generally be more powerful than the other
	– Authority and accountability defined in terms of particular decisions
Situations where appropriate	– Large multiproduct, multinational companies with significant inter-relationships and inter-dependencies
	– Small sophisticated service companies
Advantages	– Decisions can be taken locally, decentralized within a large corporation which might otherwise be bureaucratic
	– Optimum use of skills and resources – and high quality informed decisions reconciling conflicts within the organization
	– Enables control of growth and increasing complexity
	– Opportunities for manager development
Limitations	– Difficult to implement
	– Dual responsibilities can cause confusion
	– Accounting and control difficulties
	– Potential conflict between the two wings, with one generally more powerful
	– High overhead costs
	– Decision-making can be slow

Case 14.5

ABB (Asea Brown Boveri)   Eur

Barnevik's matrix structure

ABB was formed in 1988 when the Swedish company ASEA merged with Brown Boveri of Switzerland to create a global electrical engineering giant. At the time this was the largest cross-border merger in modern history. ABB would later acquire over 100 additional, but smaller, businesses in Europe and America, all of which have needed integrating effectively. The chief executive who masterminded the merger and consequent restructuring was Percy Barnevik (of ASEA), who realized that he had a major challenge if he was to maintain both drive and dynamism during the integration. He became committed to an individualized matrix structure and his aim was to make ABB the global low-cost competitor. His creation has been declared 'the ultimate global organization' – a decentralized structure with centralized control over information and knowledge development. Simply, ABB became a 'multi-national without a national identity'.

Barnevik was Swedish and he has been described as soft spoken, intense and philosophical. He was noticeably strong on information technology (IT) and he was very committed to the economic development of Eastern Europe and to the fostering of 'clean' energy and transportation. During his eight year reign as Chief Executive revenues doubled and net profits trebled. The share price rose by 20 per cent every year.

Under Barnevik ABB was divided up into 1300 identifiable companies and 5000 profit centres. These were aggregated into eight business segments and 59 business areas. There were over 200,000 employees worldwide.

The eight segments were:

- power plants, further subdivided into

  - gas turbine plants
  - utility steam plants
  - industrial steam plants
  - hydro power plants

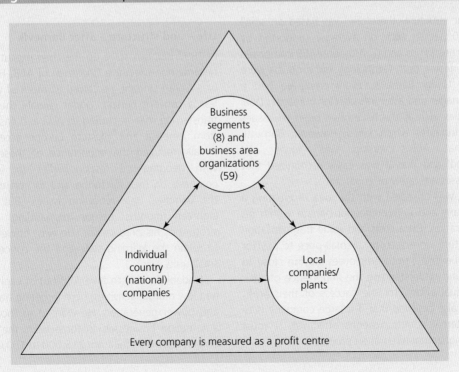

Figure 14.10 Component businesses in the ABB matrix

Business segments (8) and business area organizations (59)

Individual country (national) companies

Local companies/ plants

Every company is measured as a profit centre

– nuclear power plants
– power plant controls

- power transmission
- power distribution
- electrical equipment
- transportation (such as high-speed trains)
- environmental controls
- financial services
- other activities.

The segments were responsible for organizing manufacture around the world and for product development. Horizontally, ABB was divided up into a mix of countries and regions. The figure summarizes the basics of the matrix. There was a 12 member executive board representing products, regions and corporate operations, and a slim head office (under 200 employees) in Zurich. It was not seen as essential that the divisional headquarters for the eight business segments were located in Zurich. Some years earlier ASEA had had a head office staff complement of 2000; Brown Boveri employed 4000 in its head office.

Zurich essentially retained control over:

- acquisitions
- shifting production to Asia and Eastern Europe
- raising and managing corporate finance.

Financial reporting and evaluation was on a monthly basis.

The basic structure, therefore, was based on small units (of 50 people each on average) supported by good communications and IT. Although ABB comprised distinct businesses, both technology and products were exchanged. Under Barnevik, every employee had a country manager and a business sector manager. Dual responsibilities such as this have often been key issues in matrix structures which failed. However, Barnevik insisted that ABB's version was 'loose and decentralized' and that it was easily recognized that the two bosses are rarely of equal status.

Barnevik was obsessed with the idea of creating a small-company and entrepreneurial climate within his large corporation. Extra costs and some fragmentation in the structure were seen as 'a small price to pay for speed and flexibility, with employees staying close to customers and understanding the importance of their own individual efforts for the success of their profit centre'. He also believed that if a large company is to manage internal communications effectively it must develop a 'horizontal integration process'.

The front-line managers, the heads of the 1300 businesses, were no longer implementers of decisions from the strategic leader; instead they were initiators of entrepreneurial action, creating and chasing new opportunities. The role of middle managers – in this flatter structure – concerned coaching and technology and skill transfer. Strategic leadership was about creating purpose, challenging the status quo and setting stretching, demanding targets for front-line managers; it was not simply, as historically it was, to allocate corporate resources and resolve internal conflicts.

Barnevik also commented that the biggest problem was 'motivating middle and lower level managers and entrenching corporate values – particularly a customer and quality focus'. He believed that his executives should see the business as their number one priority and assumed that highfliers would spend up to 30 hours a week (in addition to their regular tasks) travelling, attending conferences and evening seminars and lectures.

It is the responsibility of every manager to network within the family of companies, developing informal relationships and looking for synergistic opportunities.

(BARNEVIK)

Life – and structure – after Barnevik

In 1997 Barnevik gave up the chief executive role and became non-executive Chairman of ABB. His successor was Göran Lindahl, perceived as more of a detail and less a concept person. Under Lindahl the process of transferring manufacturing to Asia and Eastern Europe from America and Western Europe accelerated. He initially reduced the importance of those executives with geographical responsibilities to focus more emphasis on manufacturing and to iron out some of the complex, dual-reporting issues. But he waited eighteen months before dismantling the matrix struture of his predecessor. He was, however, anxious to retain the learning style and the concentration on small units.

Lindahl decided to take ABB out of capital-intensive and low margin activities, here targeting transportation and power generation. He wanted to focus more on automation businesses. In three years the number of employees would fall from 215,000 to 160,000. Lindahl resigned in 2000 after initiating these changes of strategic direction. When he left the share price was half the value when he took over. At this time there were four industrial divisions – power transmission; power distribution; building technologies; and automation.

In fairness to Lindahl, some of ABB's markets had been declining and many agreed the company had diversified too quickly and too far. Adverse interest rate movements affected pre-tax profits and an ill-judged acquisition in America left ABB saddled with asbestos liabilities.

His successor, Jörgen Centerman opted to restructure ABB again, this time around four consumer segments – utilities; process industries; manufacturing and consumer industries; oil, gas and petrochemicals – and two product segments – power technology and automation technology. The product divisions both provided technology support to all the consumer divisions. It took him just one month to instigate this change. In recent years, sales growth had fallen back and Centerman believed ABB had to focus more on its customers. However he also created a stronger central executive team. The general assumption was that he would focus even more on automation and exit power transmission and distribution.

In November 2001 Barnevik resigned as Chairman, 'accepting responsibility for the collapse of the business'. The share price was now back to the 1988 merger value. Barnevik was replaced by Jurgen Doorman, who was recruited from Avensis (created through the merger of German and French chemical/pharmaceutical companies Hoechst and Rhône Poulenc). He was a 'hard-headed numbers man'.

> You may have a brilliant vision ... but if your bottom line is bad, your vision will be called into question very quickly ... you have to implement your ideas
>
> (DOORMAN).

When Centerman also left in September 2002, Doorman took over his role as well.

Almost immediately, ABB's financial services business was sold to General Electric and oil and petrochemicals were put up for sale. An initial deal for part of the business was concluded in 2003. ABB was to be structured around two core activities: automation technologies and power technologies. There would be twelve business areas. Current staff levels of 150,000

would shrink further. ABB was now a 'mid-size engineering group with a lot of debt and a list of disposable assets'.

ABB had once been renowned for its growth and imaginative structure, for which it had sought publicity and notoriety. But 'arrogance and complacency are contagious ... successful organizations have a tendency to become bureaucratic. The company went from the very entrepreneurial spirit under Percy [Barnevik] in his early days to then having become too successful. People felt there was too much power out there and wanted to centralize management control. This went far beyond what should have happened. It's operational excellence that's required now ... and improving operating margins ... some might say that's [more] boring [than in the past].' (Doorman).

ABB began its recovery in 2003, but it was a dramatically different company from when Asea and Brown Boveri were merged. Fred Kindle (from Sulzer) was appointed in 2004 to succeed Doorman as CEO from 1 January 2005. Doorman would progressively reduce his commitment to the business. There were 115,000 employees and the 2003/4 financial year showed a profit after three consecutive trading losses.

In 2004 ABB announced it was to build the world's largest underwater HVSC power cable link, joining Norway and Holland. The asbestos liabilities were finally settled in 2006. At this time a HVSC link between Finland and Estonia was completed. When the final oil and gas interests were sold in 2008, ABB was 'free to focus on power and automation'.

The current interests are:

- Power products – which distribute electricity
- Power systems – such as substations
- Automation products – drives, motors and generators
- Process automation – plant control systems
- Robotics – for industry.

Profits exceeded $1 billion in 2007 – although the global economic downturn would follow, ABB appeared to be once more a robust – if different – organization. But in February 2008 Fred Kindle announced he was leaving – because of 'irreconcilable differences about how to lead the company'. It was announced that these differences did not relate to strategy or to acquisitions, and they did not imply 'problems lurking in the bushes'.

Questions

1 While the idea of a matrix structure is very attractive, it is inherently complex. Why do you think Barnevik's structure was at one time described as the 'ultimate global organization'?

2 How do you think it would feel to work within a structure such as this?

3 Is the swing between decentralization and centralization flagged in the Doorman quote towards the end of the case an inevitability?

© VARIO IMAGES GMBH & CO.KG/ALAMY

resources and efforts be concentrated on the product groups or in the geographical territories? The ideal answer is both.

Figure 14.11 is a more straightforward illustration of how the staff in a business school might be organized. It is assumed that all of the academic staff would have a specialization which would fit into one of the six columns shown, and that expertise and development in their subject specialism would be important to the staff. At the same time the business school would offer a series of products or services, which are shown as four rows. Staff from each subject group would be allocated to each of these areas. Each product group, and possibly each course within the group, would have a leader with responsibility for delivering a quality product and earning revenue; each subject group would also have a leader responsible for allocating resources and ensuring that staff develop academically.

The potential advantages of a matrix are that responsibility and authority are delegated and spread throughout a complex organization and the stifling tendencies of a bureaucracy are avoided. Because of the flows of information, and the establishment of priorities, decisions are informed and quick. Conflicts between the various groups are reconciled within the structure by the establishment of the priorities and objectives. In addition there are numerous specialist and generalist development opportunities for managers.

Figure 14.11   Possible matrix structure for a business school

	Human resources	Marketing	Operations	Finance and accounting	Business policy/ strategy	Information technology
Undergraduate courses						
Postgraduate and post-experience courses						
Research						
Executive courses						

Alternatives to the matrix   In many cases, then, the matrix has proved to be too complicated to be effective. The primary reason has been the inability to deal with the issues of dual responsibility. Henri Fayol (1916) established a number of basic management principles, one of which was 'unity of command', the need to be responsible to only one manager; and the matrix has challenged this premise. Fayol's contention, however, has not been overturned. Decisions have been stifled by confusion, complexity and delay because managers have not been sufficiently sophisticated to operate effectively within this theoretically ideal structure. The need for a structural form which offers the potential advantages of the matrix to large complex multiproduct, multinational organizations, and which can be implemented, remains. If an organization is unable to design and operate a structure that enables the effective linking of a diverse range of related interests to achieve synergy, and at the same time permits the various business units to be responsive to environmental change, the organization may need to be split up.

Hunsicker (1982) quotes Philips, Ciba-Geigy and Texas Instruments as examples of multinationals that introduced and then retreated from the pure matrix structure. ABB (Case 14.5) changed its matrix to adjust the balance of power and then largely abandoned it. Hunsicker argues that matrices were designed to co-ordinate activities, and that the real strategic need has now become the development of new initiatives. This suggests a greater emphasis on temporary project teams, and the development and encouragement of managers within the organization so that they are more innovative and intrapreneurial. This implies that attention is focused more on changes in behaviour than on changes in the structural framework.

Pitts and Daniels (1984) list the following opportunities for obtaining the benefits of a matrix-type structure within more unitary forms:

- Strengthen corporate staffs to look after corporate strategic developments. They might, for example, search for new opportunities that existing business units could exploit.
- Rotate managers between functions, business units and locations. This increases their awareness and provides inputs of fresh ideas.
- Locate those executives responsible for product co-ordination in geographical territories physically closer to those managers responsible for production of the key products. Quite often such territory managers are based in their territories, close to their customers and somewhat divorced from manufacturing.
- Create some form of liaison groups which meet periodically and whose brief is to co-ordinate related issues. Such a group might attempt to co-ordinate the global strategies of a number of related products in a search for synergy and mutual benefits.
- Build the notion of agreed contributions between business units into both the management by objectives systems and the compensation schemes.
- Periodically review and amend the constitution of the divisions without restructuring the whole organization.

These suggestions again concentrate more on the processes within the structure than on the framework itself.

To conclude this section and chapter, it is worth recapping an earlier argument. Drucker (1988) suggested that the organization of the future would have fewer managers and fewer layers in the management hierarchy. He believed that IT would lead to more autonomy for individual managers and more informed decision-making when specialists have decentralized responsibility for key activities within the organization. Strategy co-ordination would still constitute a major challenge, however. We are now in a position to judge his prediction. Virtually every manager has access to a personal computer, an organizational intranet and the Internet. For many, letters, memos and phone calls have been replaced by e-mails. In reality what has really changed? Have e-mails and electronic file transfers led not to better decision making through more autonomy but actually to rushed decision making due to having less time to consider the next move?

Summary

To be successful an intended strategy must be implemented.

This requires that the organization's strategic resources are developed, deployed and controlled appropriately. This is accomplished through the design of the organization (the structure) and the processes encapsulated within the structure.

The structure can be described as the *means* by which an organization seeks to achieve its strategic objectives. However, the structural processes are a reflection of culture, power and political activity, and where people are empowered in a decentralized organization, it is these processes which determine the actual (adaptive and/or incremental) strategies pursued.

Consequently the structure must be capable of both creating and implementing strategy. The key issues which impact upon strategy creation and implementation are the extent of any decentralization, the need for co-ordination and the relative degree of formality–informality.

Organization structures are designed to ensure that intended strategies can be implemented effectively. The processes within the structure also affect and facilitate emergent strategy. Particularly significant for ensuring that both happen is the location of power, responsibility and authority in the organization and the extent to which these are centralized and decentralized. In large organizations the relationship between the head office and the various subsidiaries (businesses or divisions) relates to this issue.

Centralization yields consistency and control, but it can result in an organization being slow to respond to the pressures for change in its external environment. In addition, entrepreneurial managers may feel constrained. *Decentralization* enables flexibility, but control is more difficult. It is dependent upon an effective information system which can gather together the various changes that are taking place as empowered managers make and take decisions.

Centralization/decentralization and formality/informality (the nature of control mechanisms and communications) determine the broad structural type.

There are five main structural forms:

- The *entrepreneurial structure* is found in the typical small business where everything is centred around a key person, often the owner–manager.
- The *functional structure* emerges as departments and managers are created to deal with the increasing number of tasks.
- The *divisionalized structure* is a popular structure for organizations with several products or services which may or may not be related.
- The *holding company* is adopted by a diversified business with largely unrelated activities or businesses which can advantageously be kept separate for control purposes.
- The *matrix structure* – or some variant of it – is most frequently used where there is a need to co-ordinate both products and countries in a business which manufactures and markets worldwide. Because of its inherent complexities alternative forms of integration might be sought.

Organizations change their structures as they grow. They may also be changed in line with alterations to the corporate portfolio to try and keep the two in balance.

The main determinants of structure are: size, tasks to be carried out, environment and ideology.

The basic structure divides up the tasks but, of course, the structure is merely a framework for allocating tasks and roles and positioning people. The real follow-up challenge is one of integration

Online cases for this chapter

Online Case 14.1: Amstrad

Online Case 14.2: Pilkington

Questions and research assignments

1 It was stated in the text that decentralization and divisionalization are not synonymous. What factors determine the degree of decentralization in a divisionalized organization?

2 For an organization with which you are familiar, obtain or draft the organization structure. How does it accord with the structural forms described in the text? Given your knowledge of the company's strategies and people, is the structure appropriate? Why? Why not? If not, in what way would you change it?

3 How uncertain and traumatic might it be to work in a middle or senior management position in a large organization which changes its structure relatively frequently? Despite this, is change inevitable?

Internet and library projects

1 Evaluate the divisionalized or holding company structure of a large, diverse, multiproduct, multinational, considering the main board status of the key general managers. Does this suggest centralization or decentralization? If you are familiar with the company, do your findings accord with your knowledge of management styles within the organization? To what extent is performance determined by structure?

Strategy activity

WH Smith

In the last fifteen years WH Smith has struggled to clarify its strategic position in the retail industry. There is serious competition for all its products. As a consequence its performance has both improved and deteriorated. There have been changes of leadership and rumours of a possible takeover or sale to private equity. The data below provides a summary of the organization structure in 1995, 1999, 2003 and 2008. Research the company's progress over this period. Has the structure merely changed to reflect changes of strategy? Or might the structural changes have been a serious attempt to drive the business both competitively and in fresh directions?

WH Smith: Group Structure, 1995

Retailing: UK and Europe

WH Smith Retail	High street stores – books, sounds, stationery
	Airports and stations
	Specialist Playhouse video stores
Virgin Our Price (75 per cent holding)	Virgin Megastores – *sold 1998*
Waterstone's	Specialist booksellers – large towns and cities – *sold 1998*

Retailing: USA

WH Smith Inc	Gift shops, typically in hotels and airports
The Wall Inc	Specialist bookselling in major cities and airports – *sold 1998*

Distribution: UK and Europe

WH Smith News and Books	Newspaper and magazine wholesaling and distribution
	Book distribution to retailers, schools and libraries
WH Smith Business Supplies	Five acquired suppliers of commercial stationery and office products amalgamated under the Nice Day brand – *sold in 1996 to Guilbert of France*

Do It All

DIY retailers, at this time a 50:50 joint venture with Boots – *sold to Boots in 1996*

WH Smith: Group Structure, 1999

WH Smith High Street	545 stores – books, sounds, stationery in the main
WH Smith Europe Travel Retail	183 station and airport stores
WH Smith USA Travel Retail	412 gift shops mainly in hotels and airports
WH Smith Asia Travel Retail	Hong Kong, Singapore and Sydney airports
WH Smith Direct	Internet retailing, with terminal access in selected stores
Hodder Headline	Consumer books publisher – with an 8.5 per cent share of the relevant market segment
WH Smith News Distribution	51 depots, making WHS the UK's leading wholesaler of newspapers and magazines. (The High Street and Europe Travel Retail included the rebranded John Menzies stores acquired by WH Smith in 1998)

WH Smith: Group Structure, 2003

UK Retailing	The high street, airport and station stores plus WH Smith Direct (on-line sales)
WH Smith Asia Pacific	Stores in Australia (Angus & Robertson) and New Zealand (Whitcoulls) had been acquired.
	The US Travel Retail Business had been sold in 2003
WH Smith News Distribution	
Publishing	Publishers John Murray and Robert Gibson had been acquired to strengthen Hodder Headline.

Publishing was floated off as an independent business in 2004.
Also in 2004 the Asia Pacific business was sold to private equity.
In 2006 the business was split into two and existing shareholders given shares in both –
WH Smith Retail and Smiths News

WH Smith Retail: Group Structure, 2008

WH Smith High Street	557 stores, selling newspapers, magazines, stationery, books and entertainment. There were Post Offices in 82 of these and Bureau de Change facilities in 50 branches.
WH Smith Travel	449 outlets at airports, railway stations, hospitals and motorway services – selling a dedicated range of newspapers, magazines, books and confectionery.
WHS Direct	24 hour internet sales.

Smiths News comprised 44 distribution centres (or 'houses') handling newspapers and magazines for 22,000 large and small retailers.

Further reading

Greiner, LE (1972) Evolution and revolution as organizations grow, *Harvard Business Review*, July–August.

Handy, C (1989) End of the world we know, *Management Today*, April.

Mintzberg, H (1991) The effective organization – forces and forms, *Sloan Management Review*, Winter.

Pitts, RA and Daniels, JD (1984) Aftermath of the matrix mania, *Columbia Journal of World Business*, Summer.

References

Alexander, LD (1985) Successfully implementing strategic decisions, *Long Range Planning*, 18 (3).

Chandler, AD (1962) *Strategy and Structure: Chapters in the History of the American Industrial Enterprise*, MIT Press.

Child, JA (1977) *Organization: A Guide to Problems and Practice*, Harper & Row. (A more recent edition is now available.)

Drucker, PF (1988) The coming of the new organization, *Harvard Business Review*, January–February.

Fayol, H (1916) *General and Industrial Administration*, Pitman, 1949 (translation of French original).

Hunsicker, JQ (1982) The matrix in retreat, *Financial Times*, 25 October.

Lawrence, PR and Lorsch, JW (1967) *Organization and Environment*, Richard D Irwin.

Mitchell, D (1988) *Making Acquisitions Work: Lessons from Companies' Successes and Mistakes*, Report published by Business International, Geneva.

Ohmae, K (1990) *The Borderless World*, Harper.

Owen, AA (1982) How to implement strategy, *Management Today*, July.

Pitts, RA and Daniels, JD (1984) Aftermath of the matrix mania, *Columbia Journal of World Business*, Summer.

Porter, ME (1990) *The Competitive Advantage of Nations*, Free Press.

Reed, R and Buckley, MR (1988) Strategy in action – techniques for implementing strategy, *Long Range Planning*, 21 (3).

Salter, MS (1970) Stages in corporate development, *Journal of Business Policy*, Spring.

Thompson, AA and Strickland, AJ (1980) *Strategy Formulation and Implementation*, Richard D Irwin.

Chapter 15

Leading change

PART 1
Understanding strategy

1 Introducing strategy and strategic management

PART 5
Strategic management

14 Strategy implementation

15 Leading change

16 Managing strategy in the organization

17 Final thoughts – the purpose of strategy

PART 4
Issues in strategic growth

11 Strategic growth

12 International strategy

13 Failure, consolidation and recovery strategies

STRATEGIC MANAGEMENT: AWARENESS AND CHANGE

PART 2
Strategic positioning

2 Strategic thinking, environmental analysis, synergy and strategic positioning

3 Resource-led strategy

4 The dynamics of competition

5 Introducing culture and values

PART 3
Strategic analysis and choice

6 Strategic purpose

7 Strategic success

8 An introduction to strategy creation and planning

9 Strategic leadership, entrepreneurship and intrapreneurship

10 Strategic alternatives, strategy evaluation and strategy selection

Learning objectives

Having read to the end of this chapter you should be able to:

- appreciate the dynamics of change and change management and why organization must be change-oriented if they are to grow and prosper

- describe the major forces for change and types of change situation, and draw up a hierarchy of levels of change

- understand that change can be incremental or more discontinuous and transformational

- explain why people frequently resist change

- summarize alternative ways of overcoming resistance

- identify a number of different approaches to the planned management of change

- assess the importance of power and how it is used in change situations

- describe ways in which managers can improve their political effectiveness in organizations.

Organizations and managers face change on a continuous basis, especially in volatile environments. Some changes are reactions to external threats; others are proactive attempts to seize opportunities and manage the environment. Organizations should seek to obtain and maintain a congruence between their environment, values and resources, making changes when there are pressures from either the environment or their resources. It is crucial that organizations seek to create and sustain competitive advantage, and wherever possible innovate to improve their competitive position. This implies a readiness to change within the organization and the ability to implement the proposed changes.

At times there will be a perceived need to try and change values and culture. Towards the end of the twentieth century the pressures for change in a wide cross-section of businesses were clearly visible. Food manufacturers and retailers were affected by changing consumer attitudes to their diet. Mutual societies and banks were responding to changes in the competitive regulations that directly affect them, generally seeing the changes as opportunities. Technological change is at the heart of upheavals in the film and music industry. Many see the changes as threats; others as opportunities.

This chapter looks at various issues and problems in the management of change.

The first and perhaps most important element in the change process is that of leadership. When a major business organization is under pressure it is the chief executive who feels the heat. Organizations must be reactive to external change pressures and proactive in seeking to take advantage of opportunities and shape their environment if they are to be effective strategically. Cultural and power considerations are important variables in the management of change. It is particularly useful at this point to refer back once again to the earlier discussions of intrapreneurship, empowerment and learning organizations.

The opening case builds on the themes of the previous chapter and looks at a series of strategic, structural and leadership changes at Apple Computers. The case charts the story of Apple over some 30 years and shows how the company has enjoyed mixed fortunes. Sometimes highly innovative and successful, Apple has also been affected by competitor initiatives which have changed the personal computer industry in dramatic ways. Some of the changes documented were therefore reactive while others were more proactive.

There is nothing more difficult to take in hand, more perilous to conduct, or more uncertain in its success than to take the lead in the introduction of a new order of things.

MACHIAVELLI

In this race ... you run the first four laps as fast as you can – and then you gradually increase the speed.

WILLIAM WEISS, WHEN CEO, AMERITECH

Case 15.1

Apple Computers   US

Apple was started in 1976 by a young entrepreneur, Steven Jobs, and his partner, computer nerd Stephen Wozniak. Wozniak was the stronger technically; Jobs was more creative and the entrepreneurial force behind the business. They began by making personal computers (PCs) in a garage. In 1983 the company's turnover, from essentially one model – the distinctive Apple computer – was approaching $1 billion. Apple had ignited the personal computer revolution of the 1970s. At this stage in the company's development Wozniak had already left (after a disagreeement with Jobs over work practices) and Jobs had been quoted as saying that he was no longer able to do what he most enjoyed, working with a small group of talented designers to create new innovative products. To overcome his frustration with an increasingly bureaucratic organization Jobs had formed a new team of designers and set about developing the company's second major product, the Apple Macintosh, away from corporate headquarters and the production plant. The Macintosh was regarded as very user friendly and featured an illustrated screen menu and a hand-held mouse unit for giving instructions. It was launched in 1984 and sold immediately. However, it was launched at a premium price, which remained high as sales took off. This niche-marketing approach left a wide-open gap which was ultimately filled by Microsoft.

Jobs had actually seen the first graphic-user interface being demonstrated at Xerox PARC (Palo Alto Research Center) where it had been developed by a Xerox scientist in the 1970s. At this stage, Xerox failed to appreciate the value of the idea they had; Jobs immediately saw the potential of this new technology and set about developing a PC which used it. Jobs used Bill Gates to help with some of the development work –

and this was the birth of *Windows*. Had Xerox executives been more visionary, they would probably have driven the PC industry instead of Microsoft.

John Sculley, previously CEO of PepsiCo, was recruited by Jobs to be Apple president in 1983 and he took over executive control. Sculley reports that Jobs challenged him: 'Do you want to spend the rest of your life selling sugared water or do you want a chance to change the world?' His initial priorities were to co-ordinate product development activities, which he felt were fragmented, and to integrate these developments with existing programmes. To achieve this, power was centralized more than it had been in the past and was supported by formalized reporting procedures and new financial control systems.

Sculley was regarded as being more marketing orientated than Jobs, and their business philosophies clashed. Jobs resigned in 1985, together with a number of other key employees, deciding to concentrate his efforts on the development of sophisticated PCs for university students in a small, entrepreneurial organization environment.

Despite the increased business discipline, Sculley attempted to preserve important aspects of the original Apple culture. Informal dress codes, a 'fun working environment' and elaborate celebrations when targeted milestones are reached were all considered important. Apple retained a structure with few layers of management, few perks and few status-carrying job titles.

Sculley's challenge was to move the company away from an informal and entrepreneurial management style to a more functional and later (1988) a divisionalized structure, while retaining the important aspects of the culture. In addition, Sculley felt that

Apple needed to be repositioned in the market in order to overcome the competitive threats from the Far East.

With new versions of the Macintosh, Apple moved from an education and home computer base into a business computer company which also sold to schools and universities. Apple was a major innovator in desk-top publishing, pioneering the market in advance of competition from IBM and Xerox.

Apple prospered in the late 1980s, but its strategy began to appear inappropriate for the recession and the 1990s. Apple had concentrated on, and succeeded with, high-margin products which were substantially differentiated. However, Sculley claimed that Apple's ideas were being copied and used in cheaper rival products – Apple began a legal action against Microsoft, alleging that its Windows software used ideas from the Macintosh. Moreover, PCs have become more of a commodity product in a maturing market. Although Apple had sold 22 million Macintosh computers at this time, the continued success of Microsoft has been very damaging to the company.

In 1991 Apple agreed a series of strategic alliances, mostly with IBM, historically its main rival. The alliances concentrated on areas where Apple lacked either development skills or the ability to fund the research and development independently. New PC technology and operating systems software were key areas. Cultural and other differences between Apple and IBM have led to their alliances being relatively unsuccessful.

Coincidental with its agreements with the global IBM Apple's culture had actually been changing. Empowerment, flexibility and freedom remained important, but 'there had to be more discipline. Our cost structure was out of line. We did not know how to meet schedules. We were a benevolent company that sponsored people to work on things they were interested in' (Sculley).

Apple reduced the prices of its existing products, hoping for higher volumes which would more than compensate for the lower margins, and introduced a range of cheaper, lower-performance Macintosh computers. In terms of new products Apple was arguably two years late with its laptop computer. Other new products concentrated on personal electronics devices and included electronic books and a notebook computer. In 1993 Apple launched *Newton*, a $7 \times 4^1/_2$ inches black box with a 5×3 inches screen; users could jot down ideas on the screen and draw sketches as they talked and thought, and record notes and appointments. The machine could translate the images, store and organize. In addition, electronic data, such as a map, could be input. Sales of the Newton were disappointing and it failed to live up to Apple's early expectations.

As market shares and gross margins fell during the early 1990s, Apple's pre-tax profits and share price were both erratic. Sculley, the Newton product champion, was accused of neglecting the main hardware products to push the new idea, and his position was threatened. Sculley was in fact replaced by Michael Spindler in 1993, an internal promotion but, three years later, Spindler also left. Another new strategic leader, Gil Amelio, joined Apple from National Semiconductor in 1996. After his own departure Sculley commented: 'I don't think anyone can manage Apple'.

Amelio decided to halve the Macintosh product range (responsible for 80 per cent of Apple's revenue) in order to reduce costs and help to restore profitability. This controversial cut radically affected Apple's strategy of market segmentation. In addition, six varieties of its software operating system were consolidated into one, which Apple would also seek to license to other manufacturers. Allied with Adobe – which could put on to a laser printer what was appearing on a screen – Apple pioneered desk-top publishing. The Macintosh has always been the preferred machine for designers.

The company was also restructured into seven profit-centre divisions: four for different hardware products, plus software, service and Internet – the Macintosh has always been an ideal machine for creating Internet products.

Amelio recognized that cultural change was again an issue – he believed from one where 'employees felt free to question, and even defy, management decisions' to a more conventional style. Product managers would no longer be 'free to veto the strategic leader'.

Apple's core competency was still its ability to make technology easy to use and Amelio argued that it needed to exploit this in ways that allowed it to move further away from the cut-throat PC market and capitalize upon the new opportunities that were emerging as more and more people worldwide gained access to computers. Currently just 9 per cent of the world's population had access.

Apple's new Macintosh operating system, called Copland, and due around the end of 1996, was being predicted 'to make Windows 95 seem as quaint and feeble as DOS' because of its radical new ability to organize, track and retrieve stored data and files. However, in 1996 Steve Jobs stated:

> 'If I were running Apple I would milk the Macintosh for all its worth – and get busy on the next great thing. The PC wars are over. Done. Microsoft won a long time ago.'

Declining sales and falling profits were a feature of 1996, and Amelio had to shoulder some of the blame. The new Macintosh operating system, Copland, was not launched on time; the development team had been depleted too much by redundancies and resignations. However, in December 1996, Apple attempted to help rectify these weaknesses by acquiring NeXT Software, the company formed by Apple cofounder Steven Jobs after he was ousted by John Sculley in 1985. The assumption was that Apple should now get the new technology it required for updating the Macintosh. In addition, though, it would obtain the part-time consultancy services of Steven Jobs, who would advise on product strategy.

Jobs commented: 'For the past ten years the PC industry has been slowly copying the Mac's revolutionary graphical user interface. Now the time has come for new innovation ....' The key relationships lay with other software developers who typically produced a Windows version first, and only released Macintosh versions some months later.

NeXT's software had generally been highly acclaimed, but it had enjoyed only limited commercial success. Jobs meanwhile had been more successful with his other company venture, Pixar. Pixar is the film animation company which worked with Disney on *Toy Story* and had a ten-year partnership deal with the Walt Disney Corporation. Eventually Disney would buy out the business. More recently Pixar has worked on *Finding Nemo* and *Monsters Inc.* Jobs – who remained active within Pixar as well as Apple – quickly began to make an impact. Executives from NeXT took over senior positions at Apple and a close colleague of Amelio was demoted. Jobs' co-founder at Apple, Steven Wozniak, was also brought back as a consultant. Costs and employees continued to be cut back, however. The workforce of 13,000 was reduced to between 10,000 and 11,000. Product development, sales and marketing were streamlined. It was quickly speculated that the Apple Newton would be floated off as a separate business.

Once Amelio had left it was also speculated that Jobs would take over full-time, although he continually denied any interest in the challenge, emphasizing his commitment to Pixar. While some assumed that he would be able to rejuvenate Apple with his renowned entrepreneurial flair, one analyst was sceptical: 'The idea that they are going to go back to the past to hit a big home run to beat Microsoft is delusional'. In addition, there were fresh rumours that the NeXT software was after all proving to be inappropriate for Macintosh.

So, two questions arose. One, where did Apple currently fit in the PC industry? And two, could it continue to survive in its present form? Sales of Macintosh had declined to a level where Apple had less than a 5 per cent share of the US PC market; just two years ago it had an 11 per cent share. The odds on Apple being taken over began to shorten. After all, IBM had already made two unsuccessful offers (in 1994 and 1995) and Sun Microsystems one (in 1996).

Early in August 1997 Steve Jobs announced that Microsoft was to invest $150 million in Apple and the two companies were forming a partnership. The key terms of the agreement were as follows:

- Microsoft would develop and distribute office applications for the Apple Macintosh
- Apple would bundle Microsoft's Internet browser software, Internet Explorer, in future Macintosh products.

For Apple, the alliance clearly provided a positive new lease of life. For Bill Gates and Microsoft, it was more of a defensive strategy. If Apple collapsed, Microsoft would be a monopoly supplier – between them, Apple and Microsoft accounted for virtually all the sales of PC operating systems software around the world – and this might raise issues for the US anti-trust authorities. Moreover, Microsoft's real competitive threat at this time did not come from Apple's software and PCs, but rather from Netscape's rival Internet browser and Oracle's network computer which could grow at the expense of independent PCs. Consequently, this deal was designed to strengthen its overall position.

Early in 1998 Apple became profitable again. A new range of PCs was beating sales forecasts – the latest G3 version of the Mac was faster and cheaper than equivalent Windows-based PCs, a very different situation from the earlier years. Jobs, now firmly in control again, took the credit. Newton was abandoned. One lingering concern, though, was that sales were still to committed Mac users, who were updating, rather than to new buyers.

In May 1998 Apple announced its radical new iMac, an integrated computer and monitor in a single unit and in a bright, translucent housing. A keyboard and mouse could be attached in an instant. The keyboard was also translucent and the mouse lit up. At its launch in August it 'flew off the shelves'. In 1999 Apple launched a new range of notebook computers in a similar style and packaging to the iMac. Jobs appeared to have tapped into a new market segment – 'the Generation Y buyer that likes individuality'. In the end, though, and however popular its products might be with loyal Apple users, Apple only commands around 3.5 per cent of the PC market.

Apple lauched the Mac Mini in 2005, a compact, stripped-down desktop version. It believed its popularity would be affected positively from a 'halo effect' from the increasingly popular iPod. Apple also started to use Intel processors much more extensively.

Interim questions

At this stage would you have thought that Apple's latest turnaround might be real and sustainable? What would be required for sustainability?

The iPod and iTunes

In recent years Apple's renewed success has been boosted by its leadership of the fast-growing recorded music download industry. The leading music companies (such as EMI, Sony and Time-Warner) have seen sales of recorded music, especially singles, fall – at times quite dramatically. Increasingly consumers were copying CDs and downloading illegally from the Internet. With its innovative iPod and support software, Apple has pioneered legal downloads at 99 US cents per track – which for along time was around 56 pence but increased as the sterling/dollar exchange rate has changed. This coincided with the music companies taking legal action (successfully) against companies such as Napster, which were making the illegal downloading possible.

The iPod is a small, stylish portable digital music player – with a significant memory – that has become the 'Sony Walkman for the J-Lo generation', although Sony might dispute this description! The product range has continued to develop and expand – different finishes, different memory capacities, the iPod Shuffle, the iPod Nano, plus accessories including speakers and car kits. Many accessories are, of course, produced by companies other than Apple who have licence agreements. This time, though, Jobs was determined not to lose the software battle, as he had done with PC

operating systems. By the end of 2000, some 2 million iPods had been sold amounting to a 30 per cent leading share of digital music players.

Supporting the hardware, iTunes is an on-line music store with which iPods work. It is compatible with Windows PCs. It accounts for some 70 per cent of the legal music downloads around the world. In its first year over 50 million tracks were sold and downloaded. By July 2004 Apple was looking for the person who would download the 100 millionth song – he or she was in line for a special prize!

But how profitable is this business? Of the 99 cents, some 65 cents are given back to the record companies and Apple's direct costs for credit card transactions and distribution account for another 25 cents. The gross margin is 9 cents. The pricing strategy, however, is set to promote growth in the market – Apple makes a higher margin on the hardware.

Somewhat inevitably competition would emerge and intensify. In 2004 Sony launched a new 20-gigabyte digital Walkman as a serious competitor to the iPod; and at that time rival products from Philips and Samsung were in the pipeline. More recently Microsoft has launched a media player, Amazon has started to sell music downloads and Nokia provides similar facilities through some of its mobile phones.

By 2005 Apple was shipping some 20 million iPods every year; they now amounted to 40 per cent of the company's revenue. It was commented that it was now the 'most popular consumer electronics gadget in the world'. iTunes was used for 80 per cent of the downloads that were taking place. A year later, and for $4.99, iPod owners could download recent Hollywood movies.

In 2008 the world's leading music companies started to relax their tight rules on downloading and there appeared to be a risk to the continuing dominance of iTunes – another 'watch this space' situation for Apple to deal with. Furthermore, would the recession affect sales of either iPods or downloads or both?

The iPhone

Apple launched the iPhone at the end of 2006. The first models cost $499 and they are a combined mobile phone, music player and web browser. They have an easy-to-use touch-screen interface. To many, their main competition would be the (cheaper) BlackBerry from Research in Motion, but there are other smart phones on the market. The iPhone is seen as relatively expensive but superior to most competitors. Part of the business model for this product is an agreement with mobile phone operators to share a proportion of the call revenues generated – Apple was able to secure this by stating it would not allow the retail price of the iPhone to be subsidized through call charging.

Steve Jobs

Jobs has been involved with Apple for many years now, but, in his early 50s, he is still relatively young. He has, however, survived cancer surgery in 2004, and in early 2009 was taking time away because of a renewed health scare. It has been commented that his shoes are 'big shoes to fill', but clearly only time will tell how difficult this challenge will be. How dependent is the future of Apple, especially in terms of product innovation, on Steve Jobs? This question was asked in the past, of course.

Jobs stepped down from day-to-day control of Apple in June 2008 and handed over to his 'workaholic' Chief Operating Officer Tim Cook. Cook had been with Apple for ten years and was credited with turning around its manufacturing and logistics. He provided a left brain-right brain contrast with Jobs. They have quite different temperaments but appear to work together very well

and complement each other. But that would not make Cook the natural successor.

Questions

1   Do you agree that the music download industry is really still in its infancy?
2   What competitive strategies should Apple explore if it is to continue to stay ahead of its rivals?
3   In the context of Apple, do you agree with the view that 'the right strategy depends upon personal vision, and personal vision depends upon having the right person'?

© APPLE / ALAMY

15.1   Introducing strategic change

Figure 15.1 illustrates the strategic change process. The process is driven by the strategic leader and is affected markedly by the organizational culture. The organization is attempting to both manage in (reactively) and manage (proactively) its external environment. The structure, objectives and the related performance measures are determined by the mission and direction and they, in turn, guide the decisions, actions and outcomes. These outcomes can then be compared with performance expectations. The timing of change is critical. If things are not changed at the appropriate time the organization is likely to be reactive and may well end up perpetually crisis fighting.

Strategies, as we have said earlier, follow life cycles. Throughout the life of a strategy it is assumed there will be innovative, incremental improvements in the face of competition. But when industries, markets or technologies are disrupted, companies must adapt and maybe transform themselves if they are to survive. This may be more pronounced if they have been 'betting' as opposed to 'hedging'. Betting implies having pursued a focus strategy and relied on a limited range of related products rather than diversified to spread the risk across a number of industries – which is hedging.

Effective organizations, then, must be able to *manage change*, with managers and employees supportive rather than resistant or hostile. When strategies change, there are often accompanying

Figure 15.1 The strategic change process

changes in structures and responsibilities, and people are clearly affected. Kotter and Schlesinger (1979) and later Waterman (1987) suggested that most companies or divisions need to make moderate organizational changes at least every year, with major changes every four or five years. In today's world this demand has certainly not relaxed!

While organizational changes can be reactive and forced by external change, effective strategic management really requires *learning*. Managers must be aware of their environment, assessing trends and deciding in advance what should be done about perceived opportunities and threats. Planning activities and systems should ensure that the future is considered, and the resultant plans should encompass the implementation aspects of any proposed changes and the need to be flexible to accommodate unexpected changes. Moreover, innovation should be possible within the organization. Managers should constantly be looking for ways of being more effective and able to proceed with appropriate changes.

Ideally, the organization will seek to develop a culture where people do not feel threatened when they are constantly asked to question and challenge existing behaviours and acknowledged ways of doing things, and change them – a culture that sees innovation and change as normal; a culture that is ideal for dealing with the competitive chaos that characterizes many industries and markets; a culture where people do not automatically ask: 'Who is already doing this?' when someone proposes an innovative change. This cannot happen without strong strategic leadership which fosters, encourages and rewards intrapreneurial and innovative contributions from managers and other employees throughout the organization.

A culture such as this will frequently be based around a working atmosphere of creativity and fun; people must enjoy doing things differently and originally, actively looking for new competitive opportunities, instead of simply copying others.

A change culture is highly desirable for many organizations but very difficult to achieve. Hence, the implementation of change requires:

- *a perceived need for change* – this can originate with either the strategic leader or managers throughout the company who are aware of the possibilities
- *the necessary resources* – this involves aspects of competency as well as physical resources, and the ways in which managers use power to influence the allocation and utilization of resources
- *commitment* – the culture of the organization will influence the extent to which managers are responsive and innovative.

Figure 15.2 takes the concept of E–V–R (environment–values–resources) congruence and restates the idea from the perspective of effective change management. The *environment* provides opportunities for organizations to benefit from innovation and continuous improvement; on other occasions the environment will encourage more dramatic, discontinuous change. This pressure can take the form of a threat (major environmental disturbance) or an opportunity (whereby the organization, 'seeing the future' ahead of its rivals, can shape its environment). The relative strength of the organization's *resources* is reflected in the success of existing strategies; *values* dictate the ability of the organization to manage change effectively. Strategic effectiveness demands congruency. The bottom bars confirm that an organization which enjoys E–V–R congruence is likely to be enterprising and relatively crisis averse, whereas strategic drift and lost congruence are matched with crisis proneness and a relative lack of enterprise.

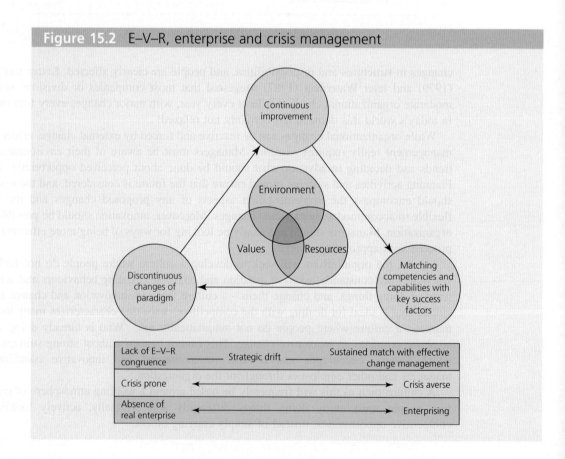

Figure 15.2 E–V–R, enterprise and crisis management

The cycle of growth

Figure 15.3 is based around four stages of organizational development and growth: creativity, nurturing, 'doing' and control. Organizations must be able to accomplish all four elements – if any one is relatively over-abundant or under-achieved, there will be a weakness. Continued progression around and around the loop implies an organization is managing the change agenda; a failure to keep moving perpetually implies a failure to adapt to change pressures.

The model is iterative and systematic. Originally it begins with creativity – new ideas in a somewhat chaotic environment. This active stage should be followed by more passive reflection and nurturing when the idea is crafted into a real opportunity. Often this is where a new business idea springs up. Whilst many organizations and entrepreneurs spend insufficient time carrying out this essential strategic thinking, it is equally possible to become bogged down in planning and not move on to action. Generally it is this action or 'doing' phase that brings about success and growth, demanding proper organization and structure in order that there can be management and control. The danger is that this control can stifle innovation through stasis and a loss of entrepreneurial drive. To ensure the organization can continue to grow, fresh ideas – renewed creativity – is needed once more. We saw earlier in Chapter 8 how some strategic leaders deliberately engineer a (perceived) crisis before a real one takes hold in order to drive the change process.

Ideally an organization will progress from one stage to another and continue around the cycle. However, many people have ideas which never become opportunities, for example. Some opportunities are never enacted; and some entrepreneurial organizations are so involved in the doing stage that they only put in the proper structure when it becomes essential. Once systems, rules and control procedures begin to take hold, fresh creativity can easily be stifled. Naturally creative people may not seem to fit in with the more disciplined approach the organization has adopted. Most of us are capable of being creative, but we need to be working in an appropriate organization culture which encourages us to be creative. Consequently, this progression is unlikely to just happen – movement is likely to require triggers and some clear manifestation of need.

In addition, there are sub-loops in the cycle. Creating and developing an opportunity is often an iterative loop in itself. Strategic thinking and action can be the same. Strategy and structure, as we have seen before, are also linked. Intrapreneurship in large and established organizations is represented by a creativity-reflection-doing sub-loop within an appropriate structure.

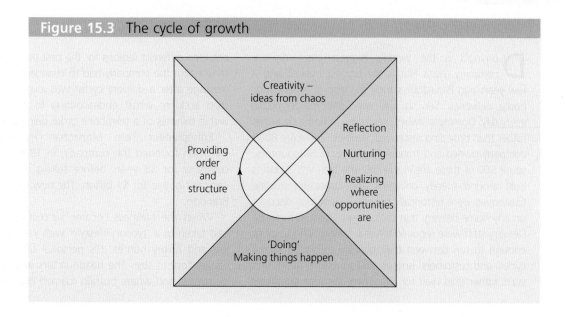

Figure 15.3   The cycle of growth

As individuals, we are likely to feel comfortable in one or two of these four roles and less comfortable in the others. Hence entrepreneurs and strategic leaders must build management teams to make sure they secure the help they need to overcome their naturally weaker areas.

Leading strategic change

We looked at different styles of strategic leadership, at strategic issues in leadership and at intrapreneurial organizations in Chapter 9. We used the term 'meta strategy' for the leader's vision of how strategies should be created, implemented and changed. The leadership contribution of Steve Jobs to Apple over nearly 30 years, and his temporary replacement by others, before he was called back to Apple, highlights wonderfully the tension between entrepreneurial vision and bureaucratic discipline. Both are required to some degree, and over time their relative significance waxes and wanes as both strategies and structures change. See Case 15.1.

Kotter (1990) argues it is the leader's job to 'create and manage change' and from this he delineated four important differences between managers and leaders:

- Leaders work with the future in mind and do not always have to be bound by timescales (although sometimes time pressures to deliver are paramount), whilst managers are more concerned with planning and budgeting within defined time frames.

- Leaders champion organizational communications whilst managers work with the form of the organization.

- Managers concentrate on problem solving whilst leaders aim to inspire and motivate others.

- Managers work to targets and can be expected to behave predictably; leaders must at times be unpredictable if they are to effectively champion change.

See the online "Blackpool Pleasure Beach" case for an example of this section's theory in practice

Kotter acknowledges that managers can be leaders – and leaders managers – at one and the same time. It follows from these points that we might expect changes of strategy and/or structure when the strategic leader changes – as we can see in Case 15.2 on Domino's Pizza and Online Case 15.1, Blackpool Pleasure Beach.

Case 15.2

Domino's Pizza   US Int

Domino's is the world's biggest pizza delivery company. Pizza Hut is the biggest overall; and a few years ago Papa John's took the lead in America for home deliveries. Serving well over one million pizzas every day, Domino's always specialized in home deliveries rather than providing restaurant facilities. There are 8000 company-owned and franchised outlets in 50 countries; some 500 of these are in the UK. The business model is built around speedy deliveries and consistent quality. Customers were historically offered a generous discount on any home delivery that took longer than 30 minutes. Delivery staff were required to wear trainers and to be fit enough to run between their delivery trucks (or motor cycles) and customers' houses, and to run up apartment stairs rather than wait for lifts. There were competitions between different regions for the best pizzas and fastest service. But the company had to change its promotional message after a delivery cyclist was involved in a nasty road accident whilst endeavouring to deliver a pizza within minutes of a telephone order being placed.

Entrepreneur Tom Monaghan in Ann Arbor, Michigan founded the company, in 1960. He ran the company for 38 years before selling it to a venture capitalist buy-in for $1 billion. The new CEO was David Brandon.

When the business became successful, Monaghan had taken to a 'tycoon lifestyle' with yachts, corporate jets and luxury homes. His personal office was 3000 square foot in size. The headquarters was in farmland he owned and where buffalo roamed quite freely. Yet, paradoxically perhaps, he was a committed Catholic. Later he concluded that he had allowed his personal pride to dominate his actions and he set out to change the culture and style. During the 1990s a new dress code was enforced. Men must wear dark suits and white shirts; women must wear skirts. By the time he sold the business he had divested many of the corporate 'possessions' he had bought. Since 1998 he has devoted his energies – and some of his fortune – to helping social causes. During the 1990s sales increased but Domino's market share declined. Brandon introduced a series of changes – and in five years managed to increase net profits by 50 per cent. Market share also recovered. He:

- Abandoned the formal dress code
- Set out to lower (the high) staff turnover and improve service
- Freshened up the stores, refitting many of them
- Added new senior managers to the existing team
- Extended the bonus scheme
- Strengthened top-down communications linked to a personal visible presence and availability
- Became more discerning about overseas locations
- Extended the local-market toppings the company offered.

Domino's has always been an innovative business:

- It was the first pizza outlet to use fibreglass trays for dough – which simplify handling and ensure better preservation
- It introduced the sturdy corrugated box for take-aways – the moisture and any fat from the pizzas doesn't make the box soggy and the cheese doesn't stick to the top

- Later it introduced the 'HeatWave' delivery bags – each bag contains a heater disc to substantially reduce heat loss during delivery
- It also developed the 'Pizza Screen' – a mesh tray which allows the base to be cooked more evenly
- In 1999 Domino's was the first to offer on-line ordering.
- It pioneered 'commissaries' to provide and deliver dough to every store so staff there can focus of finishing, cooking and delivering pizzas
- Finally Domino's has created a number of distinctive pizzas.

Prior to the credit crunch (2008) and economic recession the popularity of take-away food was predicted to continue expanding at a healthy rate.

Questions

1 Had you been Brandon would you have stuck with the 'delivery only' business model or introduced complementary restaurant facilities?
2 From your own experiences, what might give a pizza delivery company a competitive edge?

02-25-09 © NAOMI BASSITT

Heifetz and Linsky (2002) caution that strategic leadership can be 'dangerous' [to a leader's mental health] because it involves asking people to adapt. Real leadership – linked to the change agenda – involves confronting people with adaptive challenges that they would often rather ignore. And that they may well rebel against. One problem for some leaders is that they assume the relevant change pressures can be dealt with in a 'technical' (or managerial) way, using existing tools and capabilities – but if this happens any change benefits will only be short-lived. Adaptive change is quite likely to involve restructuring and job losses … hardly popular! Sometimes certainty must be abandoned for uncertainty. Leadership frequently involves giving people news that they would rather not hear.

Meanwhile Buchanan *et al.* (1999) put forward the thesis that leaders are courting trouble if they encourage or permit what they term 'initiative overload'. This occurs when individual managers are unable to deal effectively with the uncertainty facing them and it causes them to become cynical about any new change demands. They lose motivation; they become less coherent and less productive; they may even get burnt out. Change is not managed effectively in the organization. When there is any real likelihood of this happening it is the leader's role to clarify priorities and help people to stay focused on what matters.

The increasing number and popularity of 'my story' books by prominent strategic leaders highlights the potential rewards from organizational success. But, at the same time, strategic leaders may have to pay the price for failure. Shareholders and other stakeholders demand that the leader is held accountable when expectations are not met. That said, they rarely leave empty handed – golden handshakes can be very generous!

Institutional pressures, then, can ensure that the strategic leader is seen to be responsible for his or her strategic decisions and the performance of the company. Three years after the stock market crash of 1987, for example, only one chief executive from the ten worst performing companies (measured by their share price movements) was still in the post. Visible 'losers' included Sir Ralph Halpern of Burton (Halpern had earlier been responsible for turning Burton around after a poor performance during the 1970s) and George Davies, the creator of Next. Halpern largely disappeared from the corporate scene – but Davies reinvented himself as the entrepreneurial designer he really is. He first introduced the hugely successful George clothing range to ASDA before creating the Per Una range for Marks and Spencer. Although almost all of Britain's largest companies are quoted on the stock exchange, in large part due to their need for equity funding at certain stages of their development, some of the country's most dynamic entrepreneurs find this to be an uncomfortable state. They perceive the price of being a public company too high. Richard Branson (Virgin) and Jim McColl (Clyde Blowers) both bought back and re-privatized the successful companies that they had developed. Havelock Europa, the shopfitting group, and its chief executive of 20 years Hew Balfour must wonder about this very same thing. The shares of Havelock Europa in 2009 have fallen to just under 40 pence from a peak of 376p in 1996 yet the business continues to post healthy profits of £6.3 million and a dividend payout of 4.6p which represents £12 in dividends for every £100 invested in shares at current levels.

Although sometimes described as losers, many such chief executives resign and receive generous golden handshakes. Interestingly, after Robert Ayling resigned as chief executive of British Airways in 2000, institutional shareholders demanded that the board review the generous payout that was being proposed. This was only the start of this kind of controversy; and very much the same continues to happen elsewhere. In 2004 Sir Peter Davis at Sainsbury was set to receive a final pay package of at least £3.2m – and yet he had not been regarded as a success in his relatively short spell as CEO and then Chairman. To many shareholders there was an element of being rewarded for failure – not unlike the reaction to the bonuses being paid to UK bankers in 2009. Often the real losers, of course, are the employees who also lose their jobs in the contraction, and at times the shareholders.

Change then can be a risky business. But change remains essential. Would it be unreasonable to argue that for many strategic leaders in dynamic industries with intense competition that they are 'damned if they do' – and yet they would certainly be 'damned if they didn't'?

We look in greater detail at some of these issues in the next sections of this chapter.

15.2 Issues in the management of change

It was mentioned earlier that organizations face change pressures from the environment, and the significance, regularity and impact of these pressures will be determined by the complexity and volatility of the environment (see Chapter 2).

There comes a time in the life of most businesses when their fundamental *raison d'être* is about to change. This is quite likely to be the result of outside forces at work. New technological developments may be occurring. A competitor may have come up with something that will change the rules of competition; maybe this competitor is a 'breaker-in'. Something could be happening elsewhere in the supply chain, with components or distribution possibilities. Maybe something is changing in a parallel business which could switch demand away from you and others like you; maybe customers are simply changing their preferences for some reason or another.

Whatever the reason might be, the business in question has grown to a particular level and is now approaching a metaphorical fork in the road. Continuing straight on, continuing with existing products, processes and services, is not a realistic option. The business must change direction. If it makes the appropriate decision, it can continue uphill and enjoy renewed growth, albeit with something different. If it makes an inappropriate decision, the route is downhill.

The problem is, the business often reaches this fork relatively suddenly and unexpectedly. What Grove (1996) calls **strategic inflection points** are characterized by uncertainty, but for the ready and flexible organization, they can be a real new opportunity. Dealing with these change pressures is always going to be hardest for the successful, entrenched business.

Grove (1996) believes it is important to be a first mover at the strategic inflection point. The secret of the way forward is to find new and appropriate ways of adding value that matter to customers – not simply alternatives that are different from rival organizations – and to price at a level the customer will accept quickly. Somehow costs then have to be driven down to a level where a margin is possible. This was, of course, always the strategy of Ryanair. The budget airline priced its product low to attract business and then looked for cost reduction opportunities, without sacrificing safety!

Because the timing of strategic inflection points will always be characterized by uncertainty it is vital to recognize just who in the organization is in the best position to be spotting trends and signals and engage them in discussion. People who seem to be 'off-the-wall' should not be dismissed because they are 'off-line'. Cassandra foretold danger for the Trojans, but they ignored her. Complacent, they never spotted the horse in their midst! Remember the time to worry is when you are doing well. Organizations must somehow recognize when it is essential to give up on analysis (of largely historical data) and rely more on someone's intuition. After all, we can never predict the future with certainty. But we can unlock the secrets of the present if we ask the right questions, think about the answers we are being given, look at signals and triggers in the environment, think about new resource-based possibilities, properly identify problems and look for creative opportunities to make things more as we feel they should be.

At any time managers may see opportunities and wish to adapt existing strategies. There are therefore several forces which encourage change, and a variety of different change situations. Change, though, affects people, their jobs and responsibilities and their existing behavioural patterns. It can also lead to changes in the underlying culture of the organization. For these reasons people may be wary or even hostile. This is increasingly likely if they fail to understand the reasoning behind the proposed changes and if they personally feel that they are losing rather than gaining from the changes. The various forces for change, the reasons why people resist change, and an outline framework for the effective management of change are considered in this section.

Forces for change

Five major forces for change are as follows.

1 *Technical obsolescence and technical improvements* – Technical change pressures can stem from outside the organization in the form of new developments by competitors and the availability of new technologies which the organization might wish to harness. Internal research and development and innovatory ideas from managers can generate technical change internally. In high-technology companies and industries, and particularly where product life cycles are becoming shorter, this can be a very significant issue. Some organizations follow product strategies built around short life cycles, product obsolescence (both physical and design) and persuading customers to replace the product regularly. In the last decade this scenario has really kicked in with the massive use of mobile telephones.

Handsets that seemed state of the art look like something from the stone age a year or two on. Design, screen size, camera mega pixels, MP3 capacity are all features that have changed dramatically.

2 *Political and social events* – Many of these change pressures will be outside the control of the firm, but companies will be forced to respond. In the mid-to-late 1980s there was considerable pressure on companies not to trade with South Africa, and in the late 1980s increased public awareness of environmental issues began to place pressure on certain firms. Government encouragement for the use of lead-free petrol, in the form of both media coverage and price advantages from lower taxation, forced car manufacturers to respond. In the 1990s, oil companies such as BP and Shell were forced to respond to the concerns of the public on environmental pollution issues. In the first decade of the 21st century one of the key pressure areas from the public on supermarkets is over the concept of 'Fairtrade' in terms of paying growers a fair price for the produce they cultivate. Also under scrutiny are the payment policies of major companies when using Third World labour in the goods produced for them. Recently one of the major names in the high street, Primark, has been exposed for breaking its own pledge to pay overseas workers a decent wage rate.

3 *The tendency for large organizations and markets to become increasingly global* – While this again has provided opportunities and new directions of growth for many organizations, others have been forced to respond to changing competitive conditions. The growing incidence of joint ventures and strategic alliances, discussed in Chapter 11, is a feature of this.

4 *Increases in the size, complexity and specialization of organizations* – The growth of organizations, linked to internal changes of structure, creates pressure for further changes. Large complex specialist organizations have made increasing use of information technology (IT) in their operations, introducing automation and just in time (JIT) systems. These create a need for greater specialist expertise from both managers and other employees, possibly necessitating training and changes in their jobs. Effective use of these technological opportunities also requires greater co-operation and co-ordination between functions and managers. It has also led to the massive growth in out-sourcing where IT based product help desks serving the UK are located in places like Bangalore in India.

5 *The greater strategic awareness and skills of managers and employees* – Able and ambitious managers, and employees who want job satisfaction and personal challenges, need opportunities for growth within the organization. These can be promotion opportunities or changes in the scope of jobs. Such changes require both strategic development and growth by the company, and appropriate styles of non-autocratic leadership. However, how many companies really only pay lip service to the slogan 'our staff are our greatest asset' and all that this should mean?

The current dynamics of change

The strategic environment, especially competitive forces, determines how proactive and change orientated an organization must be if it is to be effective. While the forces and their relative intensity vary between industries and organizations, Peters (1989) suggests that several factors require that most organizations must be receptive to the need for change. Specifically, he highlights the following:

● the general dynamics and uncertainty of world economies
● time horizons, which he argues can be a strategic weapon in the face of uncertainty. It was discussed earlier (in Chapter 3) how successful retailers now use IT to monitor demand

changes very quickly and to build distribution systems which allow them to respond to changes. As product life cycles shorten, the development time for new products must also be cut

- organization structures must be designed to enable decisions to be made quickly
- quality, design and service – which must be responsive to customer perceptions and competitor activities – are essential for competitive advantage.

Levels of change

Change decisions can be categorized in terms of their significance to the organization and the appropriate level of intervention (Table 15.1). The six levels form a vertical hierarchy, and it is crucial to clarify and tackle needs and problems appropriately. If the problem is one of operating efficiencies, then the intervention should be at functional strategy level, but this alone would be inadequate for dealing with higher order needs. As one ascends the hierarchy the challenges and difficulties increase – as shown in Chapter 5, changing the culture of the organization can be slow and problematical. Structural changes can sometimes be difficult to implement as well, particularly where individuals perceive themselves to be losing rather than benefiting.

In recent years the recession-hit high street banks have introduced major changes in an attempt to protect and consolidate their profits, and these have systematically moved up to the highest level. A variety of approaches has been used to improve productivity and reduce costs, but this alone was inadequate. The services provided to customers have been reviewed, resulting, for example, in new branch interiors and the introduction of personal bankers and specialist advisers. These changes have been linked to restructuring, the closure of some small branches, job losses and increased market segmentation of business clients. More recently the banks have re-thought their corporate strategies, having pursued growth through diversification and overseas expansion during the early 1980s. Concentration on core activities is now preferred. During the 1990s the cultural focus saw a reduced emphasis on image and marketing and a return to the more productive utilization of assets, harnessing IT, in order to improve margins.

Case 15.3 examines change in the UK National Health Service and picks up on a number of these issues.

Table 15.1 Levels of change

Need	Level of change	Approaches/tactics
New mission; different ways of doing things	Values; culture, styles of management	Organizational development
New corporate perspective/strategy	Objectives; corporate strategy	Strategic planning
	Organization structure	New organization design
Improved competitive effectiveness (existing products and service)	Competitive strategies; strategic positioning; systems and management roles	Empowerment; management by objectives; performance management; job descriptions; policies
	Business processes	Business process re-engineering
Improved efficiencies	Functional strategies; activities; organization of tasks	Method study; job enrichment

Case 15.3

The UK National Health Service – III   UK

Implementing change

In 2006 retired corporate CEO and television presenter (Sir) Gerry Robinson spent a period of time with the NHS Trust hospital in Rotherham. The engagement was filmed for the BBC and Robinson's self-imposed task was to reduce waiting lists and waiting times.

In his endeavours he engaged with the Chief Executive and consultants and anaesthetists, hospital managers, theatre sisters and ward nurses in different parts of the hospital. Some individuals were 'up for change' whilst others were clearly feeling threatened by the thought of change. There was no real culture of change, and supporters and opponents could be found in any staff group, and were, in fact, actually found in all of them.

Essentially Robinson was trying to enable the entrepreneurs within the hospital to be given a chance.

It was clear to Robinson that he was not looking for a 'one-size-fits-all' answer – what might work was going to be different in different sections. It was, therefore, all about empowerment and local initiatives – and then about sharing the outcomes so others could learn. Interestingly, the CEO was an NHS-outsider but needed to be encouraged by Robinson to 'walk the floors', to *lead* and to speak routinely with the staff. His interventions, when they happened, clearly affected staff confidence to try out changes in their own areas.

The following is a list of different initiatives (suggested and championed by staff in various roles) that were tried, many of which, but not all, worked favourably:

- One additional patient on every consultant list for every (half-day) clinic – this improved waiting lists for children quite markedly
- Switching from two (half-day but specified target hours) lists a day to one all-day list
- Parallel theatre lists where two consultants and their teams could work adjacently and use capacity more effectively – moving from one procedure to another when and where it made sense
- Using theatres routinely on a Friday afternoon rather than only exceptionally

- Pooling patients amongst a qualified team – which was tried in endoscopy, but wouldn't be appropriate everywhere
- Anaesthetists providing recovery services so that surgeons were able to move on more quickly.

The follow-up in 2007

Gerry Robinson returned to Rotherham General Hospital roughly a year after his first visit. He confirmed there had been changes, largely driven by the CEO taking more ownership.

But that did not mean everything was working effectively. He commented that it seemed to take staff forever to reach a point where they are doing what had been staring them in the face when they started talking and deliberating. The structure and systems continued to inhibit.

The following points came out of the programme:

- The NHS remains driven by government policy and initiatives and some of these are questionable. The Rotherham Primary Care Trust was investing huge amounts to build a convenient new drop-in centre in the town centre (a Polyclinic) where people could turn up for quick-and-easy treatments – but the impact would be lower utilization of some hospital resources.
- Governments appear to understand policy better than they do front-line (local) management. The issue is not so much changing policy but making existing policies work on the ground.
- There need to be *champions* of change and also a *willingness to make it happen.* There is a need for 'enablers' to influence the culture.
- Small successes 'every day' can be more influential than occasional big impacts. Linked to this, it is perhaps better to focus on making things work within existing structures rather than changing the structure.
- There will continue to be tensions and clashes between staff groups. Who runs the hospital, for example – managers, consultants or the CEO? But these can be resolved – sometimes using humour. In the first programme one frustrated manager had

asked of the consultants – *How old are they behaving today?* In response the consultants had acquired T-shirts with 'Delinquent' printed on the front and 'I am acting ? years old today' on the back. In this context it is worth remembering that creativity and innovation prosper in a culture of fun and irreverence, even though the work is serious and taken seriously.

The situation in 2009

Robinson wrote an article for the *Daily Telegraph* in March 2009, where he suggested that crises in patient care (continue to) stem from 'excessive bureaucracy and poor quality leadership'. In recent years, he said, the number of people in management positions had soared and exceeded the number of consultants tending to the sick. Their salaries had also risen substantially. The outcome: more managers but not better management. Robinson argued for better 'checks and balances' and monitoring procedures. Lines of responsibility were ineffective. The complexity was slowing down decision-making and hiding accountability.

He cited an abundance of paper checks (box ticking to document everything) but questioned whether this was ever followed up. One telling comment was that Chief Executives are apparently so tied up managing their managers they don't manage the medical staff, who then go their own way. One conclusion is that the whole system of what is centralized and what is decentralized needs revisiting.

'Until we learn to manage the NHS more effectively we will never have the health service we pay for – and deserve.'

Reference for last section

Robinson, G (2009) Cure the NHS with far fewer managers, *Daily Telegraph*, 28 March.

Questions

1 What do you think are the main lessons to be learned from this case?
2 Will it ever be easy to engineer change in an institution like the NHS?
3 Does the saying 'two steps forward, one step back' explain the very best that could be hoped for?

Types of change

Summarizing these points, Daft (1983) specifies four basic types of change which affect organizations:

- technology – production processes
- the product or service – the output of the business
- administrative changes – structure; policies; budgets; reward systems
- people attitudes – expectations; behaviour.

Invariably, a change in one of these factors will place demands for change on one or more of the others.

When an organization decides to launch a new product it may also need to invest in new technology, modify its existing production plant and either acquire people with, or train existing employees in, the new skills required.

Major changes in the strategic perspective, say the acquisition of a similar sized firm, will force changes in the organization structure, which in turn necessitates changes in jobs and behaviour patterns.

However necessary the changes may be, and however ready the organization might be to implement them, the outcomes will not necessarily be positive for everyone affected.

The change process

Change frequently disrupts normality. Job security seems threatened; existing behaviour patterns and values are questioned; people are required to be more flexible and to take more risks. While the organization may be facing strong external pressures it is unrealistic to expect managers and other employees not to query or resist the need to change. This is particularly true if individuals feel threatened, or perceive themselves to be losing out rather than benefiting or not being rewarded in some way for co-operating.

It is important to encourage people to recognize the need for change, the benefits, and the external threats from not changing. This can involve the engineered crisis. Managed change should be planned and evolutionary, although some organizations have attempted to become more flexible such that people not only accept change, but constantly seek new opportunities for change and improvement. Although change can be speedy and dynamic – normally when it is forced by powerful external influences – managing change positively in a growth situation, taking advantage of opportunities rather than responding to threats, requires that the process begins gradually and on a limited scale, and then spreads. Advancement needs consolidation and learning. The innovation stage, which can easily go wrong, requires that the change agents (who will not always be the strategic leader) find powerful and influential allies and supporters. Time and effort must be invested in explaining, justifying and persuading. Trial and error leads to incremental learning. Early supporters should be visibly rewarded for their commitment, and this will encourage others and begin to consolidate the changes. Conservative people are inevitably going to be late joiners; and some older people, together with those who are very set in their ways, are likely to be laggards. Because changes can be slow to take off they often appear to be failing once the process is well under way. This will renew opposition and resistance. During the process it is important to continue to monitor the environment. The programme may need amendment if circumstances alter.

> *Remember, it is not always the man on the shop floor who opposes change. It can be the second or third tier of management who are the most reactionary.*
>
> SIR PETER GIBBINGS, EX-CHAIRMAN, ANGLIA TELEVISION

> *No positive changes will occur within a company unless the chief executive realizes that people are basically opposed to change. A climate for change must be created in people's minds.*
>
> *Changes need to be planned and everyone must be reassured that these changes will be for the betterment of the company, its employees, customers and shareholders. Changes have therefore to be managed against a set of objectives and to a timetable.*
>
> JACQUES G. MARGRY, WHEN GROUP CHIEF EXECUTIVE, PARKER PEN LTD

Resistance to change

> *People do not resist change per se … they resist loss.*
>
> HEIFETZ AND LINSKY, 2002

There are several reasons why change pressures might be resisted, and certain circumstances where the implementation of change will have to be planned carefully and the needs of people considered.

- Some resistance can be expected where people have worked out ways of doing things which are beneficial to them in terms of *their* objectives and preferences. They may see change as a threat. Similarly, when people have mastered tasks and feel in control of their jobs and responsibilities, they are likely to feel relatively safe and secure personally. Again, change may be perceived as a threat to their security, although the aim might be to ensure the security of the organization as a whole. The university sector is a particularly difficult sector in which to achieve change. Academics are mainly rewarded for being selfish in terms of pursuing their research and getting it published. This means that most if not all their energy goes into this process. As a result they often just do not support change or anything else that would detract from their main aim – their research output – as this output often leads to increased status and financial rewards in a new institution.

- Resistance to 'sideways change' (expanding certain activities while contracting elsewhere) is likely unless the people affected are fully aware of the reasons and implications.

- Where particular policies, behaviour patterns and ways of doing things have been established and accepted for a long time and in effect have become part of the culture of the organization, change will require careful implementation. The need for change may not be accepted readily.

- It is not unusual for people to have some fear of the unknown and to feel comfortable with situations, policies and procedures that they know. Awareness and understanding is therefore an important aspect of change.

- The organization itself, or particular managers, may resist external pressures if the change involves considerable expense, investment in new equipment and the associated risks. This issue can be exacerbated where there has previously been substantial investment in plant and equipment which technically is still satisfactory. Although demand may be falling there may be a reluctance to sell or close.

- Resistance is likely to be forthcoming where there are perceived flaws or weaknesses in the proposal. Change decisions may be made by the strategic leader and then delegated for implementation. Managers who are closer to the market may have some justified reservations if they have not been consulted during the formulation process.

The opposition may be to the change itself, or to the proposed means of implementation. Both can and must be overcome if changes are to be implemented successfully.

Casualties are, however, possible and sometimes inevitable. Some people will leave because they are uncomfortable with the changes.

Kotter and Schlesinger (1979) have identified six ways of overcoming resistance to change, and these are described in Critical reflection 15.1. They suggest that each method has both advantages and disadvantages and can be appropriate in particular circumstances. Issues raised by some of these alternatives are developed further in this chapter. Organizational development is considered as an approach to gaining support through active participation by managers on a continuous basis; manipulative approaches are discussed as a Machiavellian use of power and influence. The next section considers a number of general aspects in the management of change before specific strategies are discussed in more detail.

Argyris and Schön (1978) concluded that it is the most knowledgeable and experienced employees who are most likely to feel inhibited and frustrated by change demands. Their sense of inhibition causes disbelief and distrust; employees lose their sense of commitment and they develop defensive routines in an attempt to either impede or prevent change. This resistance becomes so embedded it is hard to overcome – and it cannot be defeated by force under any normal circumstances. Instead, the culture must be transformed until it reaches a state where change is welcomed. Argyris and Schön developed 'action science' in an attempt to achieve this.

Fundamentally this requires the generation of powerful, shared knowledge that is relevant to the needs of both the business and its employees. Communications, understanding and trust are at the core.

Implementing change: a general overview

Effective change occurs when managers and employees modify their behaviour in a desired or desirable way, and when the important changes are lasting rather than temporary.

Critical reflection 15.1

Six Ways of Overcoming Resistance to Change

1   Education and communication
Education and communication should help people to understand the logic and the need for change. A major drawback can be the inherent time delays and logistics when a lot of people are involved. It also requires mutual trust.

2   Participation and involvement
The contention is that people will be more supportive of the changes if they are involved in the formulation and design. Again, it can be time-consuming; and if groups are asked to deliberate and make decisions there is a risk that some decisions will be compromises leading to sub-optimization.

3   Facilitation and support
This can involve either training or counselling but there is no guarantee that any resistance will be overcome.

4   Negotiation and agreement
Negotiation and agreement are normally linked to incentives and rewards. Where the resistance stems from a perceived loss as a result of the proposed change, this can be useful, particularly where the resisting force is powerful. However, offering rewards every time changes in behaviour are desired is likely to prove impractical.

5   Manipulation and co-optation
This encompasses covert attempts to influence people, for example by the selective use of information and conscious structuring of events. Co-optation involves 'buying off' informal leaders by personal reward or status. These methods are ethically questionable, and they may well cause grievances to be stored for the future.

6   Explicit and implicit coercion
The use of threats can work in the short run but is unlikely to result in long-term commitment.

Source

Kotter, JP and Schlesinger, LA (1979) Choosing strategies for change, *Harvard Business Review*, March–April.

Lewin (1947) contends that permanent changes in behaviour involve three aspects: unfreezing previous behaviour, changing, and then refreezing the new patterns. These three stages are crucial if changes in culture are required.

Unfreezing is the readiness to acquire or learn new behaviour. People are willing to accept that existing strategies and ways of doing things could be improved and made more effective. Normally this needs a trigger such as declining sales or profits, or the threat of closure or acquisition.

Change occurs when people who perceive the need for change try out new ideas. The changes could be introduced gradually or they may be more dramatic. Choosing the appropriate change strategy once the need is clarified may involve the selection of one from a number of alternatives, and consequently there are opportunities for involving the people who are most likely to be affected. Power structures are likely to be altered and consequently resistance might be evident from certain people.

Particularly where the pressures for change are significant, and the likely impact of the changes will be dramatic and felt widely throughout the organization, the change strategy will need a champion. Organizations in difficulty quite often appoint a new strategic leader to introduce fresh ideas and implement the changes. Newcomers are unlikely to be associated with the strategies which now need changing. Similarly, general managers might be moved to different business units when strategic changes are necessary.

Refreezing takes place when the new behaviour patterns are accepted and followed willingly. People are supportive and convinced of the wisdom of the changes; ideally the new approaches become established within the culture. Rewards are often influential in ensuring that refreezing does in fact take place.

Whilst this simple model provides an excellent outline of the basic stages in a managed change process, if we want to foster a culture which embraces perpetual change we need to be careful about refreezing new behaviours.

Throughout the change process it is important that people are aware of why changes are being proposed and are taking place, and that they understand the reasons. The key issues are participation, involvement and commitment.

Margerison and Smith (1989) suggest that the management of change exhibits four key features:

1 *dissatisfaction* with the present strategies and styles

2 *vision* of the better alternative – a clear picture of the desired state which can be communicated and explained to others (this again emphasizes the need for a champion of the change)

3 a *strategy* for implementing the change and attaining the desired state

4 *resistance* to the proposals at some stage.

Force-field analysis

Lewin (1951) has proposed that changes result from the impact of a set of driving forces upon restraining forces. Figure 15.4 illustrates Lewin's theme of a state of equilibrium which is always under some pressure to change. The extent to which it does change will depend upon whether the driving forces or the restraining forces prove to be stronger. The driving forces, which may be external or internal in origin, are likely to have economic aspects. There may be a need to increase sales, to improve profitability, to improve production efficiencies or to generate new forms of competitive advantage. Corporate, competitive and functional strategies may appear in need of change, but existing strategies may have people who are loyal and committed to them. People will be affected and may feel concerned. Any resistance will constitute a restraining force, seeking to abandon or modify the change proposals.

A nursing team in a geriatric hospital wanted the seats of the toilets raised for the comfort of their patients. Hospital management was silent to their pleas. The team re-presented their request and argued that the change would reduce the amount of laundry and in turn the laundry bills. The proposal was approved and implemented.

ANECDOTE TOLD BY CHRISTINE HANCOCK, EX-GENERAL SECRETARY, ROYAL COLLEGE OF NURSING

Figure 15.4   Force-field analysis

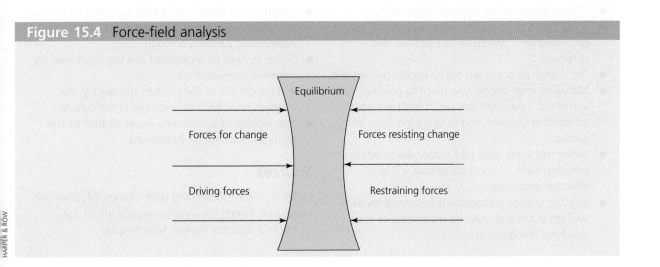

Although the driving forces will be concerned with improving organizational efficiency and effectiveness, the opposition is more likely to stem from personal concerns than from disagreement that improved efficiency and effectiveness are desirable. Lewin suggests that the driving forces are based more on logic and the restraining forces on emotion. However, people who are aware of the situation may seek to argue their opposing case in relation to the relative ability of the change proposal to achieve the required improvements. As a result, the ensuing debate concentrates on these issues. The opponents may choose not to be honest and open about their personal fears, feeling that their arguments must concentrate on the economic issues. When this happens the decision, whatever it might be, has not encompassed important underlying behavioural issues.

Effective managers of change situations will be clearly aware of both the driving forces and the real restraining forces. They will seek to strengthen the justifications by communication and explanation and diffuse opposition by exploring the likely impact with the people affected. Critical reflection 15.2 summarizes a number of important issues for the effective management of change.

This section has looked generally at the issues which affect and underpin the management of change. Lewin's force-field analysis is particularly helpful for establishing a holistic view of the change situation in terms of cause and likely effect. From this a clearer strategy for implementing the change can emerge. A number of strategies is explored in the following section. Where the extent of the change is substantial, and changes in culture are involved, it is important to ensure that the new behaviour patterns are permanent rather than temporary.

To many, uncertainty is a shadow of the unknown, to be avoided; far better, as we are stuck with an uncertain world, is to look upon it as the spice of life.

SIR PETER HOLMES, WHEN CHAIRMAN, SHELL UK

Teach people that change is inevitable and, if embraced, can be fun.

LESLIE HILL, WHEN CHAIRMAN AND CHIEF EXECUTIVE, CENTRAL INDEPENDENT TELEVISION PLC

Critical reflection 15.2

Issues in Effective Change Management

- Change programmes must be championed.
- There needs to be a clear purpose to which people can subscribe … which can be justified and defended.
- The change proposals will not be backed by everyone.
- Managers must decide how much to communicate and when – there are dangers in both inadequate information provision and in being too open and candid.
- Senior managers must take responsibility; while empowerment is important, people still need effective leadership.
- Effective change management frequently involves well-led teams and may require process or even structural change.

- Creating and broadcasting early successes speeds up the process, especially as programmes often lose momentum part-way through.
- Setbacks must be anticipated and managed, and the momentum maintained.
- It is dangerous to claim victory too quickly; the changes must become anchored in the culture.
- The feelings of people who might be hurt by the changes must not be overlooked.

Sources

Eccles, T. (1994) *Succeeding With Change*, McGraw-Hill.
Kotter, J.P. (1995) Why transformation efforts fail, *Harvard Business Review*, March–April.

15.3 Strategies for implementation and change

It is possible to view implementation as an activity which follows strategy formulation – structures and systems are changed to accommodate proposed changes in strategy. However, implementation, instead of following formulation, may be considered in depth at the same time as the proposed strategy is thought through and before final decisions are made. This is more likely to happen where several managers, especially those who will be involved in implementation, are consulted when the strategy is evaluated. Strategies may evolve from the operation of the organization structure. Where managers are encouraged to be innovatory and make incremental changes, elements of trial and error and small change decisions are often found. Implementation and formulation operate simultaneously; the changes are contained rather than dramatic and resistance may similarly be contained. Innovatory organizations can develop change orientation as part of the culture. People expect things to change regularly and accept changes.

Bourgeois and Brodwin (1984) have identified five distinct basic approaches to strategy implementation and strategic change.

- The strategic leader, possibly using expert planners or enlisting planning techniques, defines changes of strategy and then hands over to senior managers for implementation. The strategic leader is primarily a thinker/planner rather than a doer.

- The strategic leader again decides major changes of strategy and then considers the appropriate changes in structure, personnel, and information and reward systems if the strategy is to be implemented effectively. Quinn (1988) contends that the strategic leader may reveal the strategy gradually and incrementally as he or she seeks to gather support during implementation. This theme is developed later in this section.

- In both these cases the strategic leader needs to be powerful as both involve top-down strategic change.

- The strategic leader and his or her senior managers (divisional heads, business unit general managers or senior functional managers) meet for lengthy discussions with a view to formulating proposed strategic changes. All of the managers are briefed and knowledgeable, and the aim is to reach decisions to which they will all be committed. Strategies agreed at the meetings are then implemented by the managers who have been instrumental in their formulation. While this approach involves several managers it is still primarily centralized.

- The strategic leader concentrates on establishing and communicating a clear mission and purpose for the organization. He or she seeks to pursue this through a decentralized structure by developing an appropriate organization culture and establishing an organization-wide unity of purpose. While the strategic leader will retain responsibility for changes in the strategic perspective, decisions concerning competitive and functional strategy changes are decentralized to general and functional managers who are constrained by the mission, culture, policies and financial resources established by the strategic leader.

- Managers throughout the organization are widely encouraged to be innovative and come up with new ideas for change. The strategic leader establishes a framework for evaluating these proposals – recognizing that those which are accepted and resourced result in increased status for the managers concerned.

Ghoshal and Caulkin (1998) express a concern that major and dramatic change is often associated with charismatic and tough strategic leaders who attract and reward ambitious high-flying managers who, like them, are willing to subscribe to a dehumanizing style of management to drive through the changes. There is 'a lot of change, a lot of stress and a lot of fear'. Instead, they argue, organizations need either people who can exercise power robustly but with wisdom, passion and constraint or checks to ensure that people are not forgotten in the drive for change.

Ideas for change, of course, can start at the bottom of the organization rather than always at the top; and change can be seen as both a clearly managed process and the incremental outcome of the decisions taken in an innovative, change-orientated organization where managers are empowered.

These basic approaches highlight a number of general themes and ideas, which are considered below.

Top-down strategic change

A number of approaches can be involved in drawing up the strategic plans for the organization, but here changes in strategy are ultimately centralized decisions. This approach can be both popular and viable as long as the strategies that are selected can be implemented effectively. It was mentioned earlier that resistance can be expected if managers who are charged with carrying out changes in strategy feel that there are flaws in the proposals. It is important to ensure that the appropriate level of consultation takes place during formulation.

Capable managers are needed throughout the organization to deal with operational issues, and the quality of the information systems which underpin the planning is a crucial issue. The approach is attractive to strategic leaders who are inclined more towards the analytical aspects of strategy than they are towards behavioural issues.

Quinn's incremental model

While Quinn's model is another primarily top-down approach it suggests a high degree of political skill on the part of the strategic leader, who appreciates the difficulties involved in implementing change. These skills are discussed in detail towards the end of the chapter.

Quinn (1988) argues that the hardest part of strategic management is implementation as transition and change impact structures and systems, organization culture and power relationships. The strategic leader is critical in the process because he or she is either personally or ultimately responsible for the proposed changes in strategy, and for establishing the structure and processes within the organization.

Quinn's approach is as follows:

- The strategic leader will develop his or her own informal information and communication channels, both within and external to the organization, and will draw on this as much as using the formal systems.

- The strategic leader must generate *awareness* of the desired change with the appropriate managers within the organization. This involves communication and cultural issues.

- The strategic leader will seek to legitimize the new approach or strategy, lending it authority, if not, at this stage, credibility.

- He or she will then seek to gather key supporters for the approach or strategy.

- The new strategy may be floated as a minor tactical change to minimize resistance, and possibly keep the ultimate aim unclear. Alternatively, the strategy may be floated as a trial or experiment.

- Opposition will be removed by, for example, ensuring that supporters chair key committees, and that stubborn opponents are moved to other parts of the organization.

- The strategy will be flexible so that incremental changes can be made in the light of the trials. There will be a strong element of learning by doing, so that any unexpected resource limitations, such as a shortage of key skills, will be highlighted.

- Support for the change will harden.

- The proposals will be crystallized and focused.

- Finally, the proposed changes will be formalized and ideally accepted within the organization. This should involve honest evaluation and attempts to improve upon the original ideas. It is particularly important to look ahead and consider how the new strategy might be developed further in the future.

Quinn's approach incorporates an appreciation of the likely impact upon people and the culture, and pragmatically searches for a better way of doing things once the decision to change has been made.

Empowerment and change

To sustain a culture of change employees must be empowered, but not everyone is comfortable with added responsibilities and accountability. They are risk averse, and again, resistance can be expected. It would seem inevitable that change-focused organizations will be happy to see such people leave, for while they stay they constitute barriers to change. They actively seek to prevent changes which may be essential for the future of the business. Unfortunately, many of these people are likely to be very experienced and knowledgeable, and their underlying expertise is valuable. Their expertise might also be useful – at least temporarily – to a competitor, and for this reason there may be a reluctance to release them.

Empowerment cannot succeed without an appropriate reward system to support it. Financial rewards will remain important, but they are not the complete answer. People must not be rewarded simply because they are holding down a particular job or position; part of their pay must be based on their measured contribution. Outstanding performers must be rewarded for their continuing efforts, and as organizations are increasingly flattened, with fewer layers in the hierarchy, a series of promotions no longer provides the answer.

Empowered middle managers are critically important for the effective management of strategic change, but all too often they are hostile because of fear and uncertainty in a culture of blame. Mistakes are not tolerated, and people are reluctant to take risks. Such managers are portrayed as villains, when really it is the organizational climate which is making them victims. Change and empowerment will only happen when managers are not afraid to 'unfreeze and learn'.

Organizations can benefit from developing people, building their abilities and self-confidence and then providing them with greater stimulation and challenge. Success will yield the opportunity to take on more responsibility. Initially the organization motivates them but they become increasingly self-motivated. Part of their reward package is their enhanced reputation in a successful business, together with increased informal power and influence. They develop the ability to foster and champion innovation and change – strategic changes which they *own*.

A culture of innovation and gradual but continuous change will impact mainly on competitive and functional strategies – the lowest two levels of the hierarchy featured in Table 15.1 earlier. Clearly, they also support corporate strategic changes which may themselves be emergent in nature or the outcome of either a visionary or a planning mode of strategy creation.

Organizational development and innovation

The basic underlying theme of organizational development (OD) is that developing an appropriate organizational culture will generate desirable changes in strategy.

Beckhard (1969) defined OD as effort which is 'planned, organization-wide, and managed from the top, designed to increase organizational effectiveness and health through planned interventions in the organization's processes, using behavioural science knowledge'.

OD is, in essence, planned cultural change. The model which has been used to provide the structure for this book shows strategic leadership and culture as being central to both strategic awareness and decision-making. The appreciation by managers of the effectiveness of the current match between resources and the environment, their ability and willingness to make adaptive changes to capitalize on environmental changes, and the formulation and implementation of major changes in corporate strategy are all influenced by the culture of the organization and the style of strategic leadership. Hence, it is crucial for the strategic leader to develop the appropriate culture for the mission and purpose that he or she wishes to pursue. OD helps to develop a co-operative and innovative culture.

The aim of OD is to establish mechanisms that encourage managers to be more open, participative and co-operative when dealing with problems and making decisions. Specifically, the objectives are:

- improved organizational effectiveness and, as a result
- higher profits and better customer service (in its widest context)
- more effective decision-making
- the ability to make and manage changes more smoothly
- increased innovation
- reduced conflict and destructive political activity
- greater trust and collaboration between managers and business units.

Organized OD programmes involve activities such as team building and collaborative decision-making, bringing managers together and encouraging them to share and discuss problems and issues. The thinking is that when managers learn more about the problems facing the organization as a whole, and about other managers who may have different technical or functional perspectives, they become more aware of the impact of the decisions that they make. In addition, if they collaborate and share responsibilities, they are more likely to feel committed to joint decisions.

While one aim is to change the attitudes and behaviour of people in organizations, OD can also allow and encourage the same people to initiate and implement changes through their discussions. Establishing the programmes is likely to involve outside experts who can be seen as objective. OD programmes are not normally a response to specific problems but rather a general approach to the management of change in the longer term.

Given that one idea behind OD is collaboration and collective responsibility, a key theme is the reduction of conflict between managers, functions, business units or divisions within the organization. A reduction in the use of manipulative styles of management, or dysfunctional political activity, whereby managers pursue personal goals in preference to the wider needs of the organization, is also implied. Functional and dysfunctional political activity is explored in the last section of this chapter, which looks at the bases and uses of power by managers.

15.4 Transformational change and strategic regeneration

Powerful environmental issues such as deregulation, globalization, the in-balance of the factors of production, and economic recessions have presently combined to place enormous pressures on companies to survive and adapt. The individual significance of these issues will vary from year to year but, in aggregate terms, the outcome is an increasingly turbulent and uncertain business environment for most organizations, private and public sector, manufacturing and service, large and small, profit-seeking and not-for-profit.

Companies have responded. Many have sought to manage their assets and strategic resources more efficiently and effectively – again the lowest two levels of the change hierarchy. Some have restructured; others have radically changed their processes through business process re-engineering.

However, continuous improvement to an organization's *competitive* capabilities, essential as it is, will not always be sufficient to meet these pressures.

Tom Peters (1992) argues that for some companies the challenge is 'not just about a *programme* of change ... strategies and structures need to change perpetually'. Peter Drucker (1993) agrees and contends that 'every organization must prepare to abandon everything it does'. Both authors are implying wholesale corporate renewal or reinvention, which we call transformational change. The terms 'strategic regeneration' and 'discontinuous change' are synonymous.

Successful transformation requires both an external and an internal focus. Externally, organizations must search for new product, new service and new market opportunities, working with suppliers, distributors and customers to redefine markets and industries. Internally, structures, management styles and cultures must be capable of creating and delivering these products and services. Innovation is dependent on processes and people. Strategic awareness, information management and change are critically important if the organization is to outperform its competitors.

Achieving this position may require *simultaneous* changes to corporate strategies and perspectives, organization structures and styles of management. In order to implement **transformational change**, Goss *et al.* (1993) insist that companies must be able to change their *context* – 'the underlying assumptions and invisible premises on which their decisions and actions are based'. Their 'inner nature or being' must be altered. Managers must learn how to think strategically, and be open to new paradigms and perspectives. The requirement is that they change what the company is and not simply the things that it does. Companies are being challenged with changing all the levels of the change hierarchy simultaneously, a huge and complex task for any organization.

Incremental change at the competitive and functional level, trying harder and searching for improvements, must appear to offer an easier, less painful route. The fundamental question is: alone, is it enough to meet the strategic demands of the contemporary business environment?

Some of the international companies featured in this book have clearly attempted to tackle these important challenges. British Airways (BA) realized in the 1980s that, contrary to much popular opinion at the time, airline customers are willing to pay extra for service. The challenge lies in defining that service and differentiating successfully. BA consequently changed its strategies, structure and culture and became one of the most profitable airlines in the world. The changes at BA have proved successful, but this success has been diminished somewhat by external events post September 11. The move to a more business-orientated clientele has also come under threat from rival airlines such as EasyJet. General Electric (GE) of the USA is another example. The transformation philosophy and programme at GE is described in Case 15.4. Although this case recounts events that took place a number of years ago it remains a useful, insightful, story.

Pascale *et al.* (1997) argue that for effective transformation it is critically important that people understand the organization and its businesses – the big picture. Robust straight-talking should be encouraged to tease out the existing weaknesses in the organization as well as ideas for new opportunities. Transformation then involves 'managing from the future'. A shared purpose and direction sets the agenda. Setbacks must be harnessed in true entrepreneurial fashion. People must accept accountability but, linked to proper rewards, this should be done in an inventive way that ensures that people are engaged in the process. 'There has to be a relentless discomfort with the status quo.'

Hamel (1994) contends transformational change needs vision and perseverance. Companies must invest resources in an attempt to set the new competitive high ground first by changing the key success factors. This inevitably implies time and risk, and it must be a managed and understood process. Speculative investment in the long term must be risky because *spending precedes understanding*; companies are heading into unknown territory. However, companies which choose to avoid the risk, and rely instead on monitoring and copying competitors (such that *understanding precedes spending*) may be caught out.

Hamel cites three important barriers to effective transformational change. First, too many senior managers in an industry have related, often industry-specific, backgrounds, and this inhibits

Case 15.4

Transformational Change at General Electric (GE)   US

John F (Jack) Welch became Chief Executive Officer at General Electric in 1981. His personal vision, style and approach are explored in a later case in Chapter 16. This case describes 'one of the most far-reaching programmes of innovation in business history'.

The programme involved three stages:

● *Awakening* – the realization of the need for change
● *Envisioning* – establishing a new vision and harnessing resources
● *Re-architecting* – the design and construction of a new organization.

Although Welch was the identified strategic leader, several committed senior managers worked together to drive through the cultural changes.

GE has been restructured, and clear progress has been made, but the process of change continues.

GE in the early 1980s – the need for change

The company had sound assets, reflected in a strong balance sheet, but it was seen as bureaucratic and heavily focused on the US. It was not technologically advanced and it clearly needed a more international perspective.

Specific problems were diagnosed:

● Revenue growth was slow. GE's core business (electrical equipment) was particularly slow.
● As a result, expensive investments were creating cash-flow problems.
● Poor productivity was causing low profit margins.
● Innovation was limited.
● Decision-making was slow.
● Negative internal politics was rife.

The transformation process

Awakening

Welch realized that his first challenge was to determine which managers offered the greatest potential as transformational leaders, agents of discontinuous change.

He then sought to clarify and articulate the extent of the need for change, focusing on the above weaknesses. Resistance took three forms:

● Technical – A reliance on existing bureaucratic systems and a fear of the unknown; a distrust of international expansion.
● Political – A desire to protect existing power bases, especially where the strategic value of the particular business was declining.
● Cultural – an unwillingness to accept competitive weaknesses – overconfidence from past successes.

Changes

● Welch forced people to benchmark competitors' performance standards and achievements, rather than rely only on internal measures and budgets.
● He also took control of external corporate communications, and
● Radically changed GE's approach to management training and development. Rigid rules and procedures about how things should be done were abolished.

Envisioning

A new vision was developed gradually during the mid- to late 1980s, and it finally became encapsulated in a matrix. Highlights of the new vision are featured in Table 15.2.

Welch saw the technical, political and cultural systems as three strands of a rope which must be changed and realigned together.

Re-architecting

At the heart of the vision is an 'organization without boundaries' and with an emphasis on internal and external linkages and architecture. Information must flow freely. People must be in a position – and willing – to act quickly. 'A large organization with the speed, flexibility and self-confidence of a small one.'

A number of boundaries had to be removed as part of the implementation process:

● vertical/hierarchical – management layers were removed. Welch introduced performance incentives for many more managers and employees; in the past GE had focused on only senior executives
● horizontal/internal walls – cross-functional project teams were created

	Strategy	Structure	Management style
Technical	Focus on market (segments) where the company can be no. 1 or no. 2	Decentralized	Different reward systems for different businesses, dependent on needs
		Foster the sharing of best practices and pull down internal boundaries	Continuous training and development
	Prioritize high-growth industries		
Political	Foster internal and external alliances to harness synergy potential	Flatter, open structure to remove power bases	Flexible reward systems
		Cross-function and cross-business development teams. Empowerment to lowest levels of management	'360 degree evaluations' from superiors, peers and subordinates
Cultural	Speedy change to strategies	Corporate values but individual business cultures and styles	Track attitudes and values – commitment to customers and quality – and to outperforming competitors Intrapreneurial, innovative, incremental and adaptive change – as a result of – learning from upward, downward and lateral communications

Table 15.2 Highlights of GE's corporate vision

- external – there was a new emphasis on the whole supply or added value chain; alliances were forged with suppliers; customer satisfaction levels were tracked.

Removing these boundaries clearly required radical changes to the ways in which people worked together, made decisions and carried out tasks. Welch believed that the changes must be inspired from the top and that any senior managers who resisted the new style 'would have to go'.

Reference

Adapted from Tichy, NM (1993) Revolutionize your company, *Fortune*, 13 December.

Questions

1. This case has described a major programme of change and transformation, championed by an exceptional strategic leader, Jack Welch. While it has been reported extensively, and 'the world' knows what Welch has set out to do and what he has achieved, few organizations have been able to replicate his achievement. So how valuable might our insight really be?
2. Why would a programme of this scale and ambition be difficult to replicate?

GENERAL ELECTRIC **http://www.ge.com**

their creative thinking. Second, there are political pressures to maintain the status quo from managers who feel threatened personally, an issue that is looked at next. Third there is the sheer difficulty of creating new competitive strategies in industries that are changing dynamically, continuously and chaotically.

The essential prerequisite for an effective change of direction is to create a climate throughout the organization where change is regarded positively.

Professor Hague, when he was at Manchester Business School, made the following remark which I have always remembered: 'The successful manager will expect and understand change; the outstanding manager will anticipate and create it.'

Once the right climate exists, change must be preceded and accompanied by effective and honest communication, meaningful consultation and sound decision-making. It is not easy and requires genuine top management commitment.

TOM W CAIN, ONCE DIRECTOR, HUMAN RESOURCES, THE CHANNEL TUNNEL GROUP LTD

US President Barack Obama is presently trying to signal a major change in the policies of the United States towards its postwar traditional enemies such as Iran, North Korea and much of the Muslim world. He has embarked on a round of diplomacy and public speaking trying to put across the message of change. President Obama seems to be playing the role of the outstanding manager. However, will the Senate and Congress embrace his message of change?

Abrahamson (2000) implies that major change could be going out of fashion, unless, of course, it becomes essential. Companies that periodically reinvent themselves often face resistance, distress, disaffection and upheaval. All too often the desired or planned changes are not implemented effectively, prompting another programme of change. Abrahamson therefore recommends *'dynamic stability'* – continuous tinkering with existing businesses, alternating occasional major changes with several incremental ones. His research suggests that:

- First, copying can prove very rewarding – there is no need always to be first. This point, though, needs careful interpretation. It is true that major leaps forward can be uncomfortable and disruptive for both customers and employees, and the competitors who follow when the situation has settled down again can enjoy the benefits without incurring the risk of the pioneer. However, sustained competitive advantage often comes from staying just ahead of rivals with constant innovation and leadership. It is a matter of degree.

- Second, home-grown processes are invariably more acceptable culturally than those imported from another country with an 'alien' culture.

Clearly, organizations need to ensure that they change in accordance with real external pressures and to recognize that good ideas can always be found by monitoring the world's best performers. They need to acquire and use this knowledge to craft something that can work for them.

Critical reflection 15.3 provides a summary framework for managing transformational change.

Critical reflection 15.3

Twelve Steps in Transformational Change

1 Recognize the scale of the challenge and don't ignore it.
2 Consider where the barriers to change might be strongest.
3 Build a guiding team and establish any necessary partnerships.
4 Establish a sense of urgency and bring the challenge and the issues to the attention of others.

5 Clarify a clear strategic direction or 'vision' for the transformation. This would include a defined business model, key values and drivers and recognition of the relevant strategic competencies required.
6 Communicate this vision, taking ownership and responsibility for it.

7   Seize the initiative as far as barriers to change are concerned.

8   Empower others to act on the vision. Emphasize the need for innovation, emergence and intrapreneurship. The idea is to involve people as widely as possible so the drive to change becomes systemic.

9   Seek to generate short-term wins – which can be publicized and used as a vehicle to reward the change-drivers.

10 Consolidate these short-term wins to increase and maintain the momentum.

11 Monitor and evaluate performance and achievements on an ongoing basis.

12 'Institutionalize' the changes.

References

This list of 12 steps has been developed from a number of separate sources, including:

Francis, D, Bessant, J and Hobday, M (2003) Managing radical organizational transformation, *Management Decision*, 41 (1).

Kotter, JP (1995) Why transformation efforts fail, *Harvard Business Review*, March–April.

15.5 Power and politics

The greatest leader is the one who enables people to say: 'We did it ourselves'.

CHINESE PROVERB ATTRIBUTED TO LAO-TSU

A leader can stop an organization in its tracks but he can't turn it around on his own. In a year you can change things at a superficial level, using the charismatic model, but you need five to change the culture.

MORPETH HEADMASTER, ALASDAIR MACDONALD, DISCUSSING CHANGE IN SECONDARY SCHOOLS

The management of change requires that managers have the requisite power to implement decisions and that they are able to exert influence. There are several bases of power, both organizational and individual, which constitute resources for managers. The processes that they adopt for utilizing these power bases, their styles of management, determine their success in influencing others. The ability of managers to exert power and influence is manifested in a number of ways, including:

- budgets
- rewards
- organization structure and positions
- promotions and management development
- information systems
- symbols of power and status.

Managers who regularly attempt to get things done, both with and through other people, and introduce changes, have the problem of generating agreement, consent or at least compliance with what should be done, how and when. Typically, opinions and perspectives will differ. Disagreements may or may not be significant, and can range from the polite and friendly to those involving threats and coercion. Each side, quite simply, is attempting to influence the conduct of the other. In this section we consider the power resources that managers are able to use and how they might use them.

Checkland (1986) defines **organizational politics** as the process by which differing interests reach *accommodation* – a word that he chooses deliberately and in preference to consensus. These accommodations relate to the dispositions and use of power and influence, and behaviour which is not prescribed by the policies established within the organization. It will be shown later that political activity by managers in order to influence others, and ensure that their decisions and strategies are carried out, is essential. Politics can be legitimate and positive, although it can also be more negative and illegitimate. In the latter case managers are seeking to influence others in order to achieve their personal goals. This is often described as Machiavellianism and is discussed at the end of this section.

The relative power of the organization

The need for change is affected by the relative power and influence of external stakeholders in relation to the organization. Powerful customers, powerful suppliers and changes in government legislation would all represent potential threats and demands for change. In turn, the management and implementation of change is affected by the relative power of the organization. Some proposed strategies can be implemented because the organization possesses the appropriate power to acquire the resources which are needed and to generate consumer demand. Others may not be feasible.

At the same time the decisions taken within organizations concerning changes of corporate, competitive and functional strategies are influenced by the disposition of relative power between functions, business units or divisions, and the ways in which managers seek to use power and influence.

Internal and external sources of power are discussed further in Critical reflection 15.4, based on the work of Mintzberg (1983).

Critical reflection 15.4

Internal and External Sources of Power

Mintzberg (1983) contends that it is essential to consider both internal and external sources of power, and their relative significance, when assessing the demands for, and feasibility of, certain strategic changes.

The organization's stakeholders will vary in terms of their relative power and the ways in which they exert influence. The interests of the owners of the firm, for example, are legally represented by the board of directors. While large institutional shareholders may exert considerable influence over certain decisions, many private shareholders will take no active part. Employees may be represented by external trade unions, who again may or may not exert influence.

The power relationships between the firm and its stakeholders are determined by the importance and scarcity of the resource in question. The more essential and limited the supply of the resource, the greater the power the resource provider has over the firm. According to Mintzberg these external power groups may be focused and their interests pulled together by a dominant power, or they may be fragmented.

Where there are very strong external influences, the organization may seek to establish close co-operation or mutual dependence, or attempt to reduce its dependence on the power source. The historic relationship between Marks and Spencer and many of its suppliers is a good example of mutual dependence of this nature. Marks and Spencer encouraged many of their clothing suppliers to invest in the latest technology for design and manufacturing in order that they can both succeed against international competition. Marks and Spencer have typically been the largest customer of their suppliers, buying substantial quantities as long as both demand and quality are maintained. However, it is important that their suppliers are aware of fashion changes because they bear the risk of over-production and changes in taste.

Internal power is linked to the structure of the organization. It is manifested in four ways:

- the personal control system of the strategic leadership
- rules, policies and procedures
- political activities external to these two factors
- cultural ideologies that influence decision-makers.

External and internal power sources combine to determine a dominant source of power at any time, and Mintzberg suggests six possibilities:

- *a key external source*, such as a bank or supplier, or possibly the government as, say, a key buyer of defence equipment – the objectives of the source would normally be clearly stated and understood
- *the operation of the organization structure*, and the strategies and activities of general and functional managers who are allocated the scarce resources: the relative power of business units is influenced by the market demand for their products and services, but generally external sources exert indirect rather than direct influence; functional managers can enjoy power if they are specialists and their skills are in short supply
- *strong central leadership*
- *ideologies* – certain organizations, such as charities or volunteer organizations, are often dominated by the underlying ideologies related to helping others
- *professional constraints* – accountants' and solicitors' practices, for example, have established codes of

professional practice which dictate and influence behaviour. On occasions this can raise interesting issues for decision-makers. A frequently used example is the television journalist or news editor working for the BBC or ITN and able to influence reporting strategies and policies. When assessing sensitive issues does the person see himself or herself as a BBC or ITN employee or as a professional journalist, and do the two perspectives coincide or conflict?

- *active conflict* between power sources seeking dominance: while this can involve either or both internal and external sources it is likely to be temporary, as organizations cannot normally survive prolonged conflict.

The dominant source of power becomes a key feature of the organizational culture, and a major influence on manager behaviour and decision-making.

Reference

The source of the basic arguments is Mintzberg, H (1983) *Power In and Around Organizations*, Prentice-Hall.

Political activity

Farrell and Petersen (1982) classify political activity in terms of three dimensions:

- legitimate or illegitimate
- vertical or lateral
- internal or external to the organization.

For example, a complaint or suggestion by an employee directly to a senior manager, bypassing an immediate superior, would be classified as legitimate, vertical and internal. Discussions with fellow managers from other companies within an industry would be legitimate, lateral and external, unless they involved any illegal activities such as price fixing. Informal communications and agreements between managers are again legitimate, while threats or attempts at sabotage are clearly illegitimate.

Power and politics are key aspects of strategy implementation because they can enable managers to be proactive and to influence their environment rather than being dominated and manipulated by external events. The issues affect managers at all levels of the organization and decisions concerning both internal and external changes.

The bases of power

Seven bases of manager power were introduced and described in Chapter 7: reward, coercive, legitimate, personal, expert, information and connection. The extent to which managers and other employees in organizations use each of these sources of power is a major determinant of corporate culture.

Reward and coercive power (the ability to sanction and punish) are two major determinants of employee motivation, and both can be very significant strategically. Thompson and Strickland

(1981) argue that motivation is brought about primarily by the reward and punishment systems in the organization; and Blanchard and Johnson (1982) suggest that effective management involves three key aspects: establishing clear objectives for employees, and rewarding and sanctioning performance against objectives appropriately. Strategic leaders who dominate their organizations and coerce their senior managers can be effective, particularly when the organization is experiencing decline and major changes in strategy are urgently required.

Legitimate power is determined primarily by the organization structure, and consequently changes in structure will affect the power, influence and significance of different business units, functions and individual managers.

Personal power, which can lead to the commitment of others to the power holder, can be very important in incremental changes. Managers who are supported and trusted by their colleagues and subordinates will find it easier to introduce and implement changes.

Expert power can also be useful in persuading others that proposed changes in strategy are feasible and desirable. While expert power may not be real, and instead be power gained from reputation, it is unlikely that managers who genuinely lack expertise can be successful without other power bases. Moreover, expertise is job related. An expert specialized accountant, for example, may lose expert power temporarily if he or she is promoted to general manager. Consequently, an important tactic in the management of change is to ensure that those managers who are perceived to be expert in the activity or function concerned are supportive of the proposed changes.

Information and related *connection power* are becoming increasingly significant as IT grows in importance.

These seven power bases are all visible sources. There is, in addition, *invisible power*. One source of invisible power is the way in which an issue or proposal is presented, which can influence the way it is dealt with. Managers who appreciate the objectives, perspectives and concerns of their colleagues will present their ideas in ways that are likely to generate their support rather than opposition. Membership of informal, but influential, coalitions or groups of managers can be a second source of power, particularly if the people involved feel dependent on each other. Third, information that would create opposition to a decision or change proposal might be withheld. In the same way that access to key information can be a positive power source, the ability to prevent other people obtaining information can be either a positive or a negative source of power.

Lukes (1974) has identified three further important aspects of power, namely:

- the ability to prevent a decision, or not make one
- the ability to control the issues on which decisions are to be made
- the ability to ensure that certain issues are kept off agendas.

The use of such power by individuals can inhibit changes which might in the long-term be in the best interests of the organization.

In discussing the nature of power and how it is exercised we should consider just how the exercise of power needs to be legitimate if it is to be successful over time. Rawls (1971) outlined two principles of justice. The first was with respect to the basic structure of society regarding the basic liberties of citizens based on freedom of speech, thought, assembly, conscience and the rule of law. To condense the views of Rawls we can say that any exercise of power that took away any of these rights would be unfair – it would not be just and it would be legitimate to oppose such actions.

The second principle outlined by Rawls concerned 'the distribution of income and wealth and the design of organizations that make use of the differences in authority and responsibility, or chains of command. While the distribution of wealth and income need not be equal, it must be to everyone's advantage, and at the same time, positions of authority and offices of command must be accessible to all... The distribution of wealth and income must be consistent so that everyone benefits or if an unequal distribution is to everyone's advantage. Injustice, then, is simply inequalities that are not to the benefit of all.'

In the case of many businesses facing financial difficulties it could be a concern about justice and how justice and fairness is exercised if large financial institutions are saved, and then they fail to play their part in lending some of that money to their customers so that everyone benefits in some way. It could be argued that that would be an illegitimate exercise of power by the banks, it would remove the cloak of fairness and justice from them and make them legitimate targets because they had failed to live up to their part of the social and economic bargain.

Political effectiveness

Hayes (1984) contends that effective managers appreciate clearly what support they will need from other people if proposed changes are to be carried through, and what they will have to offer in return. In such cases they reach agreements (or accommodations) which provide mutual advantages. It is important for the organization as a whole that general and functional managers are effective and politically competent if personal objectives are to be restrained and undesirable changes, championed by individual managers, prevented. Problems can occur where some managers are politically effective and able to implement change, and others are relatively ineffective and reach agreements with other managers whereby their personal interests, and the interests of the organization, are adversely affected.

Allen *et al.* (1979) and Dixon (1982) point out that certain sources of personal power are essential for managers who are effective politically and able to influence others. In addition, they suggest certain tactics for managing change. These are featured in Table 15.3. It is important that managers are perceived by others to have expertise and ability, and it is useful if they have a reputation built on past successes. Depending on the relative power of outside stakeholders, such as suppliers or customers, external credibility can also prove valuable. It is essential to have access to information and to other powerful individuals and groups of managers.

It can be a disadvantage for a manager to be perceived as a radical agent of change, as this can arouse fear and uncertainty, possibly leading to opposition, in others. As discussed earlier, it can sometimes be valuable to implement a change of strategy gradually and incrementally, allowing people to make adaptive changes as the learning experience develops. At the same time it is important to ensure that opposition is manifested and brought out into the open rather than being allowed to develop without other people being aware.

Managers who are effective and successful politically, and able to implement their decisions and proposed changes, will generally appreciate and understand organizational processes and be sensitive to the needs of others. It is extremely useful if the strategic leader is an able politician. The type and incidence of incremental changes in strategies throughout the organization will also be affected by the political ability of managers. Those with ability will be instrumental in introducing changes. Where the strategic leader wishes to encourage managers to be adaptive and innovative it is important to consider the political ability of the managers concerned. Political ability relates to the use of power and influence in the most appropriate way in particular circumstances. This is the subject of the next section.

Uses of power and influence

MacMillan (1978) argues that introducing and implementing change frequently requires the use of power and influence, which he examines in terms of the control of situations and the ability to change people's intentions. Where a person wishes to exercise control over the behaviour of other people, either within the organization or external to it, he or she has two basic options. First, they can *structure the situation* so that others comply with their wishes; second, by communicating with other people, they can seek to change their perceptions so that they see things differently and

Table 15.3 Political power bases and tactics

Bases of personal power

Expertise	Particularly significant where the skill is in scarce supply
	It is possible to use mobility, and the threat of leaving, to gain support for certain changes of strategy – again dependent upon the manager's personal importance to the firm
Assessed stature	A reputation for being a winner or a manager who can obtain results. Recent successes are most relevant
Credibility	Particularly credibility with external power sources, such as suppliers or customers
Political access	Being well known around the organization and able to influence key groups of managers
Control over information	Internal and external sources
	Information can be used openly and honestly or withheld and used selectively – consequently, it is crucial to know the reliability of the source
Group support	In managing and implementing change it is essential to have the support of colleagues and fellow managers

Political tactics to obtain results

Develop liaisons	As mentioned above, it is important to develop and maintain both formal and informal contacts with other managers, functions and divisions
	Again, it is important to include those managers who are most powerful
Present a conservative image	It can be disadvantageous to be seen as too radical an agent of change
Diffuse opposition	Conflicts need to be brought out into the open and differences of opinion aired rather than kept hidden. Divide and rule can be a useful strategy tactic.
Trade-off and compromise	In any proposal or suggestion for change it is important to consider the needs of other people whose support is required
Strike while the iron is hot	Successful managers should build on successes and reputation quickly
Research	Information is always vital to justify and support proposals
Use a neutral cover	Radical changes, or those that other people might perceive as a threat to them, can sometimes be usefully disguised and initiated as minor changes. This is linked to the next point
Limit communication	A useful tactic can be to unravel change gradually in order to contain possible opposition
Withdraw strategically	If things are going wrong, and especially if the changes are not crucial, it can be a wise tactic on occasions to withdraw, at least temporarily

- Politically successful managers understand organizational processes and they are sensitive to the needs of others.
- Effective political action brings about desirable and successful changes in organizations – it is functional.
- Negative political action is dysfunctional, and can enable manipulative managers to pursue their personal objectives against the better interests of the organization.
- The strategic leader needs to be an effective politician.

Sources: Allen, RW, Madison, DL, Porter, LW, Renwick, PA and Mayes, BT (1979) Organisational politics: tactics and characteristics of its actors. *California Management Review*, 22, Fall and Dixon, M (1982) The world of office politics, *Financial Times*, 10 November.

decide to do as the manager suggests. In other words he or she succeeds in *changing their intentions*. Both of these approaches are categorized as strategies of manipulation.

Where a manager is concentrating on structuring the situation they are using certain power bases as enabling resources; where they are attempting to change intentions they are seeking to use influence. Power, in particular personal power, is again important as a source of influence.

The outcome from both the situational and intentional approaches can be either positive or negative. When the effect is positive the other people feel that they are better off as a result of the changes; the effect is negative if they feel worse off.

MacMillan identifies four tactics in relation to these points:

- *Inducement* – this implies an ability to control the situation, and the outcome is perceived as beneficial by others involved. A large retail organization with several stores might require managers to be mobile as a condition of their employment, and reward them with improved status, salary increases and relocation expenses every time they move. The situation is controlled; ideally the managers concerned feel positive about the moves.

- *Coercion* – the situation is again controlled, but the outcome is perceived negatively. In the above situation the same managers might be threatened with no further promotions unless they agreed to certain moves within the company.

- *Persuasion* – the manager does not try to control or change the situation but argues that the other people can or will benefit by behaving in certain ways. The desired outcome is positive. People might be persuaded to agree to a change which is not immediately desirable by suggestions that future rewards will be forthcoming.

- *Obligation* – this is another intentional tactic, but the outcome is negative. People are persuaded to behave in a certain way by being made to feel that they have an obligation. It might be suggested that people
  - owe the company something for the money that has been invested in their previous training, or
  - owe particular managers a favour for something that has happened in the past, or
  - are obligated to the group of people that they have been working with for some years and should not let them down.

In particular cases, individual managers may or may not have a number of alternative tactics to select from. Tactics that have positive outcomes must normally be preferable to those that cause negative feelings if both are available and likely to yield the desired results. At times managers whose power bases are limited and who need speedy results may have little option but to coerce or obligate people. Kanter (1983) emphasizes that successful managers of change situations are able to keep their power invisible both during and after the change. Participation in the change is then perceived to stem from commitment or conviction rather than from power being exercised over people. Kanter contends that it is very important for middle managers in organizations to be skilful in managing change as they implement the detailed strategies, and that it is important for strategic leaders to ensure that they have support from their middle managers for the overall corporate strategy.

Organizational politics and culture

Culture broadly encapsulates manifest actions and behaviours and underlying beliefs, and effective cultural change must include both (see Chapter 5). Where this happens, there will be willing support for, and compliance with, the change. Without a change in beliefs, compliance will be reluctant. Strong, political managers who oppose the changes will show either covert or even overt non-compliance, their choice reflecting their style and power.

Bartlett and Ghoshal (1995) argue that the radical and forced downsizing of the early 1990s left many companies with a context of 'compliance, control, contract and constraint'. Behaviours have changed, but not beliefs; elements of the old culture remain to create confusion. The challenge for these companies is one of creativity and innovation; they must find ways of adding new values for competitive advantage, which will require a context of support, trust and liberation, and a willingness to accept stretching objectives, alongside appropriate control disciplines.

Organizational politics and ethics

It is clear that managers can use political behaviour both for and against the best interests of the organization; at the same time, they can also behave either ethically or unethically. Positive and ethical behaviour is required to satisfy all the stakeholders effectively; negative politics, while ethical, implies that internal stakeholders (maybe even individual managers and functions) receive priority over external stakeholders. Positive politicking which is unethical may well appear successful in the short term, but possibly with a long-term downside risk. Where negative politics combine with unethical behaviour, there is likely to be corruption.

Machiavellianism

Machiavellianism is the term often used to describe coercive management tactics. Marriott (1908), translating Machiavelli's book *The Prince*, written in the sixteenth century, uses the expression to cover 'the ruthless use of power, particularly coercive power, and manipulation to attain personal goals'. While coercive power can be used effectively by managers it may not always be easy to justify, especially if other alternatives are available. Coercion may not be practical on a repeat basis, and any fear of threats not carried out quickly recedes.

Jay (1967), however, contends that Machiavelli also offers much useful advice for ethical managers. Basing his arguments on Machiavelli's views on strategies and tactics for annexing and ruling nations, Jay argues that chief executive strategic leaders should concentrate their efforts outside the organization, developing and strengthening the strategic perspective. In order for them to feel able to do this, the internal structure and systems must be sound and effective, and managers must be supportive of proposals from the top. General and functional managers should be free to operate and feel able to make certain changes, but their overall power should be contained. They should exercise leadership, which is based on power. This power yields the freedom to decide how things should be done. Managers, though, should be afraid to pursue personal goals against the interest of the organization as a whole. Achieving this requires a clear awareness of what is happening throughout the organization and the appropriate punishment of offenders. Successful managers should be rewarded.

Pearce and DeNisi (1983) stress that most organizations are managed partially by informal coalitions or groupings of managers superimposed on the formal structure. It is particularly important that managers in key positions in the organization, those in charge of important resources or responsible for products upon which the profits or reputation of the organization depend, are known to be committed and loyal to the strategic leader. Moreover, any informal and powerful coalitions that develop should also be supportive. To achieve both of these it may be appropriate for the strategic leader to remove or switch senior managers occasionally as a reminder of his or her overall power. This is particularly likely to happen after an acquisition, during a restructuring exercise, or on the appointment of a new strategic leader.

Strategic coalitions can be a major force behind strategy formation, especially where the overall strategic leader is relatively weak. An effective leader will therefore seek to use coalitions that already exist, and encourage the formation of other loyal ones.

In considering the feasibility of changes and how to implement them, it is very important to examine the underlying political abilities and behaviour within the firm: who has power, how it is manifested and how it is used. Without taking these factors into account, implementation is likely to prove hazardous.

> *Machiavelli recommended that vanquished foes should be eliminated, but counselled that quite often only the King or Chief needs to be sacrificed; those spared will soon fall into line through fear. This was essentially the Roman way. When conquering a city, the Romans would often make an example of a small number of important people such as the Chief by killing him. The conquered population were to take note from this in that as long as they did what was expected of them in the way of taxes and tribute to Rome, they would often be given a degree of autonomy and freedom. To rebel against Rome would only lead to the severest of penalties.*
>
> *Research into hostile takeovers and acquisitions in the UK between 1990 and 1994 shows that within one year of the takeover 70 per cent of the chairmen of the acquired businesses had left; 57 per cent of the chief executives left within two years.*
>
> *However it could alternatively be added that in* The Godfather, *the approach of the Don would have been much more ruthless to all the male family members of the rival gang for their disrespect.*

Case 15.5 concludes this chapter. It traces the growth of the Disney Corporation and the role of its entrepreneurial founder, Walt Disney. It then concentrates on the era of Michael Eisner's leadership. Eisner made a number of key contributions – and a number of strategic errors. His style and approach were often controversial. We can see several themes from the chapter incorporated in this case.

Case 15.5

Walt Disney Corporation   US

Walt Disney's fame and initial success was based substantially upon films, books and comics featuring cartoon characters like Mickey Mouse and Donald Duck. Walt Disney himself was an entrepreneur and cartoonist who eventually found his fortune in the moving picture industry of the 1930s. His first full-length cartoon feature film was *Snow White* in 1937, which he has followed up with countless movies based on fairy tales. He was not, however an 'overnight' success. To further exploit these characters, which Disney saw as resources, and to capitalize upon increased leisure spending (a window of opportunity) the first Disneyland theme park was later opened in 1955 in Anaheim, California. Within one year Disneyland contributed 30 per cent of the company's revenue. The success of the theme park strategy must be attributed to Walt personally, as others in the corporation – including his brother, Roy – were against the development.

Although Walt Disney died in 1966 his strategies were continued. The Magic Kingdom was opened in Florida in 1971, followed eleven years later by Epcot. These have proved immensely successful, but were not seen as 'really new'. In the 1980s the environment for leisure businesses was perceived to be changing dramatically, but Disney was no longer regarded as a trend setter. Revenues, profits and stock prices all fell.

Disney Corporation appointed a new strategic leader, Michael Eisner, in 1984, and he successfully opened several new windows of opportunity for the corporation. He introduced more aggressive marketing (together with price increases) at the theme parks, and throughout the 1980s the numbers of visitors, including foreigners, grew steadily. Additional attractions, including the Disney-MGM film studio in 1989, were added, together with a support infrastructure including Disney resort hotels. Eisner found hundreds of cartoons not previously syndicated to television. New marketing and licensing opportunities for Disney characters have always been sought. Disney established a new film company, Touchstone Pictures, to enable it to make movies with more adult themes for restricted audiences without affecting the Disney name and family image. They also invested in videos and satellite television. One key theme pervades most of the developments – the hidden wealth of the Disney name and characters. Disney has been a successful, growing, profitable company, partially thanks to relatively recent films such as the three *Pirates of the Caribbean* movies and animations such as *Aladdin*, *The Lion King* and *Chicken Little*. Thanks to a joint distribution deal with Pixar, Disney has also been associated with *Finding Nemo*, *Toy Story*, *Monsters Inc.* and *The Incredibles*.

Simply Disney had developed distinctive competencies in story telling and 'set' management and continually sought – and found – new ways of exploiting these competencies. Of course, over time it also strengthened its competency in these key areas.

Six Eisner strategic developments

In 1992 Disney opened EuroDisney, its new theme park outside Paris – the concept had already been moved successfully to Japan. However the initial visitor, revenue and profit targets had to be revised downwards after the first trading year. Drastic refinancing of the project was required. Whilst attendance levels were disappointing, the key problem was that visitors, affected by the recession, were not spending liberally. The recession was also affecting Disney's ability to sell associated properties in the theme park; the projected cash flows needed this extra income. High French interest rates then compounded the difficulties. However, it was also apparent that European employees were initially unable to replicate the enthusiasm of their US counterparts, and the overall service package was not the same. EuroDisney has since established itself and become profitable, but there was a steep learning curve, which involved the need to bring in outside partners to help finance overseas developments of this magnitude. In 1999 Disney announced it would build a second park outside Paris – Disney Studios should open in 2002.

In 1993 Disney acquired Miramax Studios. Later Miramax would make blockbusters including *The English Patient*, *Gangs of New York*, *Reservoir Dogs* and *Cold Mountain*. The businesses parted twelve years later, close to the time when Eisner stepped down. There had been 'differences of opinion on where Miramax should focus'.

In 1994, environmentalist opponents forced Disney to abandon plans for a new park in Virginia (near Washington) which would have celebrated the main events in US history. Disney concluded it had 'lost the perception game'. Arguably Disney perceived itself as a 'guardian of wholesome American values' but to its opponents it came over as an 'outsize entertainment company with a penchant for sugar-coating'. Disney has not confirmed that the idea has been shelved permanently!

One year later, in 1995, and following a gradual downward trend in theme park attendances in Florida, Disney began to construct a new attraction – Disney's Wild Animal Kingdom, its biggest so far – which it billed as 'a celebration of all animals that ever or never existed'. The live animals would (unusually) be presented in 'true-life adventure stories of mystery, danger and humour' rather than in zoo or safari park settings. Mechanical, mythical animals feature alongside the live ones. Also in 1995 Disney paid the equivalent of £12 billion to acquire Capital Cities/ABC, owner of ABC Television in America, to create the world's largest entertainment company. A major *content* company, Disney, was merging with a leading *distribution* company. The deal was justified with two arguments. One, Disney's valuable intellectual property would enjoy enhanced media access – ABC owned eight television stations, ESPN cable TV and an extensive radio network. ABC also published newspapers, books and magazines. Two, Disney's existing distribution network was ideally placed to exploit and syndicate ABC's programmes. On the other hand, having mainly concentrated on content and intellectual property, Disney was now diversifying into a new area with new strategic demands. It was moving away from direct competition with focused companies like Viacom to rival communications giants such as Time Warner. The promised synergy was not immediately forthcoming. Again there were differences of opinion over priorities and some resultant conflict. ABC executives appeared to spurn Disney programmes. But they were successful with series such as *Lost* and *Desperate Housewives*. ABC also spawned the hugely successful *High School Musical*, which Disney developed after an original made-for-TV movie. In the end the benefits of collaboration seem obvious.

In 1998 Disney launched its first cruise ships – named *Disney Magic* and *Disney Wonder*. These identical ships could carry 1750 passengers and they sailed on short cruises between Florida and the Bahamas all through the year. Disney Cruises are designed for families, but adults who wish to be kept apart from children can achieve this aim. The lounges are, inevitably, Disney themed, and the shows are 'unlike any other in the cruise industry'. Disney invested in 1000 seat theatres with state-of-the-art acoustics. Naturally there are also cinemas on board its ships. Externally the ships look like other cruise liners, but internally they incorporate the latest in technology.

Interim questions

How would you evaluate these six strategic developments?

Eisner was credited with many successes but some notable failures.

In 1994, when he was recuperating from heart bypass surgery, and upon the sudden death of a key colleague, he chose not to promote Jeffrey Katzenberg to be his deputy, and instead recruited (from outside the business) his friend Michael Ovitz. Eisner and Katzenberg had worked well together for a number of years but some thought Eisner saw him as too much of a threat. Ovitz was fired by the Disney board in 2006 – but paid a $140 million settlement. Katzenberg left the corporation to co-found the more successful animation business, Dreamworks, in partnership with Steven Spielberg. *Shrek* was one of their successes.

In 2003 Eisner was part of a plot to oust Roy Disney from the corporation board; there would be repercussions. In 2004 he fell out with Steve Jobs, founder of Pixar, and also CEO of Apple Computers.

He finally left in 2006, accused by some of seeing Disney as a personal fiefdom. However when he took over in 1984 the profits of a fragmented Disney business were $100 million and the corporation was capitalized at $3 billion. When he left profits were $4.5 billion. There were five times as many employees and the business was valued at $47 billion.

Eisner was replaced by Bob Iger, an internal promotion who was seen by some critics, including Roy Disney, as a hand-picked successor. He inherited a strong empire, but one lagging behind Pixar and Dreamworks in respect of creative competency. Iger declared he would concentrate on international expansion, new technologies and content creation.

There would be greater decentralization than under Eisner. How has he fulfilled these?

In 2006 Disney acquired Pixar for $7.4 billion. Jobs was given a main board seat at Disney and he became the largest individual shareholder in the corporation. Disney also acquired a Bollywood studio and made some of its films available for iTunes downloads. In 2007 Disney acquired Club Penguin, an on-line virtual world for children and also announced plans to develop a new resort complex in Hawaii.

The next move by Disney took place in August 2008 when Disney paid $4 billion to acquire Marvel Entertainment. Under the terms of the deal Disney will acquire ownership of characters such as Iron Man, Spider-Man and X-Men. 'We believe that adding Marvel to Disney's unique portfolio of brands provides significant opportunities for long-term growth and value creation,' Iger said. Disney is a Dow 30 company with revenues of $38 billion in its latest fiscal year.

In almost an immediate response Warner Brothers announced that the DC Comics business would now be fully integrated into Warner Bros. The battle lines seem drawn.

Questions

1   How would you evaluate the contribution of Michael Eisner?
2   How strong do you think Disney is today?

© D. HURST / ALAMY

Summary

Most organizations must compete or operate in dynamic environments where change is inevitable. Some of this will always be reactive, but the most effective organizations manage, as well as manage in, their environments. Much comes down to the strategic leader and the organization culture, which realistically drive the whole change process.

Effective *change management* requires:

- a clear perception of need – dissatisfaction with the existing status quo
- a way forward – a new direction or perceived opportunity
- the capability to change – the necessary resources
- commitment – change needs managing.

A four-stage cycle of change can be identified: beginning with a creative idea, an opportunity is nurtured before an action stage grows the business. Structure follows to provide control. At this time it is important to find new ideas to maintain the cycle of growth.

There is a number of *levels* of change:

- the corporate culture
- the organizational mission
- corporate strategies
- organization structures, systems and processes
- competitive strategies
- operational tasks and activities.

As we ascend this hierarchy the complexity and the difficulty of the challenge increases.

A simple model of change *management* would have three stages:

- unfreezing existing behaviours
- changing behaviour
- refreezing the new behaviour as common practice.

However, there is an argument that organizations should have a culture that accepts and embraces constant change, and consequently we need to be careful about the implications of refreezing.

There are forces for and against change. There is always likely to be resistance to change – after all, people's jobs are affected and some will perceive themselves to be losing out.

Change can be *continuous*, *innovatory* and *improvemental* – on occasions it will be *discontinuous and transformational*, implying simultaneous changes to strategy, structure and style. Sometimes this is essential, but it can be very disruptive and unsettling for people.

Change management cannot be separated from *power*. Power and influence are required to engineer and effect change – they may also be used in an attempt to stop it. There are two key dimensions: the relative power of the organization in respect of its external environment; and the relative power of different businesses, divisions, departments and individuals within the organization itself.

There are seven key *power bases*: reward, coercive, legitimate, personal, expert, information and connection.

The way that individuals use power and influence is a manifestation of their political abilities. *Organizational politics* can be positive if it is used to carry through and implement decisions that are clearly in the interests of the organization. Negative politics is the tool of Machiavellian managers who are minded to pursue self-interest at the expense of other colleagues and maybe at the expense of the whole organization.

Online cases for this chapter

Online Case 15.1: Blackpool Pleasure Beach

Questions and research assignments

1 Describe an event where you have personally experienced forces for change, and discuss any forces that were used to resist the change. What tactics were adopted on both sides?

2 Describe a strategic leader (any level in an organization of your choice) whom you consider to be a powerful person. What types of power does he or she possess?

3 Describe a manager whom you believe is successful at using organizational politics. On what observations and experiences are you basing your decision? How might you measure political effectiveness and the elements within it?

4 As a manager, what are your personal power bases? How politically effective are you? How could you increase your overall power and improve your effectiveness?

Internet and library projects

1 Select an industry or company and ascertain the forces that have brought about changes in the last ten years. How proactive/reactive have the companies been, and with what levels of success?

2 Analyse the news broadcasts of two rival TV networks, such as the BBC and ITN, or Sky and CNN, and evaluate whether their reporting of industrial and business news is similar or dissimilar. Are they reporting to inform or to persuade about, say, the merits or demerits of government policy? To what extent are they constrained by government?

3 Research and update the Apple Computers case. How would you evaluate:

 a The contribution of Steve Jobs?

 b Jobs as a strategic leader?

 c Whether Apple is now less crisis prone than it was and more in control of the change agenda?

4 Who, do you feel, has been the bigger influence on the development of home computers - Steve Jobs or Bill Gates?

5 As well as acting as an occasional consultant to Apple, co-founder Steve Wozniak has started two new businesses, one in the 1980s and another in the last few years. How successful were these businesses? Does this picture of Wozniak affect your views on the role and contribution of Steve Jobs?

Strategy activity

Kraft   US

Measured by value, Kraft is the second largest food company in the world, behind Nestlé. It has become best known for its processed macaroni and cheese. Its leading brands include Ritz Crackers and Dairylea cheese spread; but in the US it is also famous for Oreo cookies, Jell-O and Kool-Aid.

At the end of the last century there were 175 plants, but since that time 20 have had to close with the loss of 8000 jobs. There were two main reasons for this: hostility from certain consumers worried about problems of obesity, and pressure from own-label brands.

Kraft's CEO, Roger Deromedi, was concerned to develop foods that were healthier. More whole grains were added to cereals and extra calcium was added to processed cheese, for example. Kraft declared it would no longer direct advertisements for junk foods to under-12s. He also concluded Kraft's marketing people were

'spending too much time planning … they need to be out with customers'.

He streamlined decision-making inside the organization and invited customers to suggest new product ideas. New ideas from the public – that Kraft has developed – include parmesan cheese packaged in a disposable plastic cheese grater and a microwaveable hot dog and bun.

Recently a new issue has arisen. The cost of milk, a major ingredient for Kraft, has been rising around the world.

Questions

1 Do you agree with Deromedi's approach? How much of a strategic challenge does he face?

2 How would you evaluate the strategic logic of Kraft's bid to acquire Cadbury's in late 2009?

Further reading

Abrahamson, E (2000) Dynamic stability, *Harvard Business Review*, January–February.

Bartlett, C and Ghoshal, S (1994) Beyond strategy to purpose, *Harvard Business Review*, November–December.

Bourgeois, LJ and Brodwin, DR (1984) Strategy implementation – five approaches to an elusive phenomenon, *Strategic Management Journal*, 5.

Francis, D *et al.* (2003) Managing radical organizational transformation, *Management Decision*, 41 (1).

Goss, T, Pascale, R and Athos, A (1993) The re-invention roller coaster – risking the present for a powerful future, *Harvard Business Review*, November–December.

Hamel, G (1996) Strategy as revolution, *Harvard Business Review*, July–August.

Kotter, JP (1995) Why transformation efforts fail, *Harvard Business Review*, March–April.

Pascale, R, Millemann, M and Gioja, L (1997) Changing the way we change, *Harvard Business Review*, November–December.

Quinn, J (1980) Managing strategic change, *Sloan Management Review*, Summer.

Richardson, WA (1994) Comprehensive approach to strategic management – leading across the strategic management domain, *Management Decision*, 32 (8).

Salancik, GR and Pfeffer, J (1977) Who gets power – and how they hold on to it: a strategic-contingency model of power, *Organizational Dynamics*, Winter.

Tichy, N (1996) Simultaneous transformation and CEO succession – key to global competitiveness, *Organizational Dynamics*, Summer.

References

Abrahamson, E (2000) Dynamic stability, *Harvard Business Review*, January–February.

Allen, RW, Madison, DL, Porter, LW, Renwick, PA and Mayes, BT (1979) Organizational politics: tactics and characteristics of its actors, *California Management Review*, 22, Fall.

Argyris, C and Schön, D (1978) *Organization Learning: A Theory of Action Perspective,* Addison Wesley.

Bartlett, C and Ghoshal, S (1995) Rebuilding behavioural context: turn process re-engineering into people rejuvenation, *Sloan Management Review*, Autumn.

Beckhard, R (1969) *Organization Development: Strategies and Models*, Addison-Wesley.

Blanchard, K and Johnson, S (1982) *The One Minute Manager*, Morrow.

Blanchard, K and Waghorn, T (1997) *Mission Possible*, McGraw Hill.

Bourgeois, LJ and Brodwin, DR (1984) Strategic implementation: five approaches to an elusive phenomenon, *Strategic Management Journal*, 5.

Buchanan, D, Clayton, T and Doyle, M (1999) Organization development and change – the legacy of the 90s, *Human Resource Management Journal*, 9 (2).

Checkland, PB (1986) The politics of practice. Paper presented at the IIASA International Round-table 'The Art and Science of Systems Practice', November.

Daft, RL (1983) *Organization Theory and Design*, West.

Dixon, M (1982) The world of office politics, *Financial Times*, 10 November.

Drucker, P (1993) *Managing in Turbulent Times*, Butterworth-Heinemann.

Eccles, T (1994) *Succeeding With Change*, McGraw-Hill.

Farrell, D and Petersen, JC (1982) Patterns of political behaviour in organizations, *Academy of Management Review*, 7 (3).

Ghoshal, S and Caulkin, S (1998) An escape route from ruthlessness, *Financial Times*, 18 November.

Goss, T, Pascale, R and Athos, A (1993) The reinvention roller coaster: risking the present for a powerful future, *Harvard Business Review*, November–December.

Grove, AS (1996) Only The Paranoid Survive, Harper Collins.

Hamel, G (1994) Competing for the Future, Economist Conference, London, June.

Hayes, J (1984) The politically competent manager, *Journal of General Management*, 10 (1).

Heifetz, R and Linsky, M (2002) *Leadership On The Line,* Harvard Business School Press.

Jay, A (1967) *Management and Machiavelli*, Holt, Rinehart & Winston.

Kanter, RM (1983) The middle manager as innovator. In *Strategic Management* (ed. RG Hamermesch), John Wiley.

Kotter, JP (1990) *A Force for Change: How Leadership Differs from Management,* The Free Press.

Kotter, JP (1995) Why transformation efforts fail, *Harvard Business Review*, March–April.

Kotter, JP and Schlesinger, LA (1979) Choosing strategies for change, *Harvard Business Review*, March–April.

Lewin, K (1947) Frontiers in group dynamics: concept, method and reality in social science, *Human Relations*, 1.

Lewin, K (1951) *Field Theory in Social Sciences*, Harper & Row.

Lukes, S (1974) *Power: A Radical View*, MacMillan.

MacMillan, IC (1978) *Strategy Formulation: Political Concepts*, West

Margerison, C and Smith, B (1989) Shakespeare and management: managing change, *Management Decision*, 27 (2).

Marriott, WK (1908) Translation into English of *The Prince* written by N Machiavelli in the 1500s.

Mintzberg, H (1983) *Power In and Around Organizations*, Prentice-Hall.

Pascale, R, Millemann, M and Gioja, L (1997) Changing the way we change, *Harvard Business Review*, November–December.

Pearce, JA and DeNisi, AS (1983) Attribution theory and strategic decision making: an application to coalition formation, *Academy of Management Journal*, 26, March.

Peters, T (1989) Tomorrow's companies: new products, new markets, new competition, new thinking, *The Economist*, 4 March.

Peters, T (1992) *Liberation Management – Necessary Disorganization for the Nanosecond Nineties*, Macmillan.

Quinn, JB (1988) Managing strategies incrementally. In *The Strategy Process: Concepts, Contexts and Cases* (eds JB Quinn, H Mintzberg and RM James), Prentice-Hall.

Rawls, J (1971) *A Theory of Justice*, Oxford University Press.

Thompson, AA and Strickland, AJ (1981) *Strategy and Policy: Concept and Cases*, Business Publications.

Waterman, RH Jr (1987) *The Renewal Factor*, Bantam.

Chapter 16

Managing strategy in the organization

Learning objectives

Having read to the end of this chapter you should be able to:

- describe and explain a number of alternative approaches to the management of a corporate portfolio

- distinguish between the alternative control mechanisms which large, diverse organizations might use

- define the terms 'heartland' and 'corporate parenting' and explain their significance and implications

- explain the role and contribution of corporate headquarters to large, multibusiness organizations

- discuss the role and skills of general managers in these organizations

- consider organizations at the beginning of the 21st century

- distinguish between resource allocation issues at corporate and business unit level

- define risk, identify the risks faced by organizations and discuss how they might be approached and managed

- identify the main issues in crisis avoidance and management.

Growth is often an important objective for organizations. Frequently this growth has involved diversification and acquisitions in either related or unrelated areas. In recent years the strategic logic of large, diversified conglomerates has been questioned as many organizations have instead chosen to focus on related businesses, technologies or core competencies, where they can more readily add value across the businesses and generate synergy. Whatever the strategic choice, though, it must be implemented successfully. The opening case looks at how GE has become the world's leading company (by asset value) whilst remaining extensively diversified. Conglomerate, diversified businesses cannot be dismissed automatically; they can be both successful and profitable if they can find new, suitable businesses to acquire, opportunities for growth with their subsidiary businesses and if their strategic control system is appropriate. Simply, the strategy can still be justified if it can be implemented successfully. This chapter explores alternative approaches to strategic control and applies these issues to diversified conglomerates. The relationship between the corporate centre and individual businesses is examined. Typically, in recent years, corporate head offices have been slimmed down as organizations have become more decentralized.

The implementation of intended strategies, and the ability of the organization to be responsive in a dynamic, competitive environment, require the organization's strategic resources to be deployed and managed both efficiently and effectively. It is also vital for the organization, on the one hand, to seek to be crisis averse rather than crisis prone and, on the other hand, to be able to deal with crises if and when they do occur. All of these issues are a reflection of the organization's ability to appreciate and manage risk and they are also discussed in this chapter.

This is a chapter of debates, opinions and interpretations, but few clear-cut answers. Simply, both the strategy and the structure need to change but stay complementary as the business environment changes. If accomplishing this was straightforward and clear-cut many organizations would be more successful than they actually are.

Case 16.1

General Electric (GE)

US

The Welch years

General Electric (GE) is diversified into four 'long cycle businesses' – power systems, aircraft engines, defence electronics and medical systems (such as brain and body scanners) – and four 'short cycle businesses' – plastics engineering, household consumer goods, lighting and NBC Television in the USA. GE also provides financial services (through the specialist GE Finance subsidiary) – which in terms of monetary assets is effectively the fourth largest bank in America.

The company is truly global – it sells more in Europe than British Aerospace, one of the UK's leading manufacturers and a direct competitor. GE, under Chief Executive Jack Welch, proved that a business does not have to be 'focused on one or two related activities' to be successful and profitable. Before he retired Welch:

- Changed the culture
- 'Turned people on' and
- Delivered results through carefully crafted incentives.

Welch delayed his planned retirement by a year whilst he attempted to acquire Honeywell, only to be thwarted by the European Competition Commission – which feared there was a conflict of interests between GE Finance (which has a huge aircraft leasing arm) and Honeywell Engines.

[Welch's succession is significant in the cases of Albertsons & Home Depot where it is evident that a number of those executives who were overlooked have gone on to run other large and very successful organizations. Case 15.5 on transformational change at GE explained the culture change programme in more detail.]

Unlike many other diversified conglomerates, GE sought to gain 'maximum' value from its disparate activities by investing to provide a platform for growth. GE wants to be Number One or Number Two in every market segment in which it competes. It seeks to exploit the breadth and diversity of its portfolio to find new ways for adding value and new customers.

Being a conglomerate makes no sense unless you can leverage the size and diversity of the company and spread learning and best practices across the company.

LARRY JOHNSTON, EX-GE EXECUTIVE

The company is decentralized and employees are encouraged to speak out and pursue ideas. External contacts and sources are constantly monitored for new leads and opportunities. 'We'll go anywhere for an idea.' Welch always believed 'the winners of the 1990s would be those who could develop a culture that allowed them to move faster, communicate more clearly, and involve everyone in a focused effort to serve ever more demanding customers'. GE has its own 'university' and brings managers of various levels in all the businesses together regularly to explain what they are doing and to share new ideas.

We have this incredible intellect in GE ... we are exposed to so many industries that when we [senior managers] all get together we have the opportunity to maximize our intellect. That's the advantage of a multi-business company ... we can share ideas.

WELCH

Much of this is facilitated through Management Councils – comprising people from different businesses and divisions – who meet quarterly. Every member of a council must bring to every meeting at least one idea from which other managers could learn something valuable or useful. One notable example was the idea of 'reverse mentoring' to deal with the demands of e-commerce. Older managers were encouraged to use younger and more aware managers as their mentors, even though they might be lower in the current hierarchy.

Fortune magazine declared Welch to be the 'manager of the century' for his achievement in turning a 'slumbering dinosaur' into a 'lean and dynamic company with a paradigm of a new management style'. Whereas Percy Barnevik redesigned the ABB structure (explained in the case on ABB), Welch transformed GE through management style. They both believed 'small is beautiful' and that innovation and intrapreneurship is critical. The decentralization at GE aims to 'inject down the line the attitudes of a small fast-moving entrepreneurial business and thereby improve productivity continuously.' Integration strategies promote the sharing of ideas and best practices.

There is a developed strategy of moving managers between businesses and countries to transfer ideas and create internal synergy, together with a reliance on employee training. It has been said that 'if you sit next to any GE executive on a 'plane they will all tell the same story about where the company is going'. There is a shared and understood direction and philosophy, despite the diversity. Promotion is normally given to those managers who can prove they are 'boundary-less'.

Welch regularly attended training courses to collect opinion and feedback. 'My job is to listen to, search for, think of and spread ideas, to expose people to good ideas and role models.' GE's *work out* programme involves senior managers presenting GE's vision and ideas to other managers and employees, and then later reconvening to obtain responses and feedback on perceived issues and difficulties. All employees in a unit, regardless of level, are thus provided with an opportunity to review and comment upon existing systems and procedures. The check is always based on whether they add value. External advisers (such as university academics) monitor that communications are genuinely two-way. GE also developed *Six Sigma Quality Management* which has been adopted by companies around the world.

Managers are actively encouraged to work closely with suppliers and customers, and they have '360 degree evaluations', with inputs from superiors, peers and subordinates. 'People hear things about themselves they have never heard before.' Products and businesses should be Number One or Number Two in a market, and if they are not achieving this, their managers are expected to ask for the resources required to get there.

Welch summarized his philosophy as follows:

If we are to get the reflexes and speed we need, we've got to simplify and delegate more – simply trust more. We have to undo a 100-year-old concept and convince our managers that their role is not to control people and stay on top of things, but rather to guide, energize and excite. But with all this must come the intellectual tools, which will mean continuous education of every individual at every level of the company.

Nevertheless some felt that Welch's reign spawned an emphasis on cost cutting and leaner management.

Jeffrey Immelt

It was inevitable that people would question whether GE could survive when Welch retired in 2001. His chosen successor, Jeffrey Immelt, made changes – but only limited ones to the structure and style – and the company continued to thrive and prosper. Immelt had a marketing background and was promoted from Chief Executive of GE Medical Systems. In 2003 Vivendi Universal was merged with GE's NBC. Also in 2003 GE acquired the UK healthcare group, Amersham, which had a number of important biotechnology activities. This was followed, in 2004, by a leading airport security scanning system business. Since 9/11 airport security has been a growing business around the world.

In 2004 Immelt declared 'GE was to evolve from an industrial and financial conglomerate dedicated to the relentless pursuit of profit to an innovator bent on finding long term growth opportunities'. Science – including nanotechnology – would be instrumental. Developments could and would be applied across the GE businesses. One significant innovation was satellite tracking systems. These were utilized by TIP, GE's recently acquired European trailer leasing business, to track any vehicles or loads that had been hijacked.

Healthcare and energy would be targeted markets. To contribute to the necessary changes a number of managerial competencies were to be stressed: namely external focus, clear thinking, imagination, inclusive leadership and confident expertise. Some critics of Welch felt his style had 'spread a fear of failure and stifled risk taking'. Reflecting his background in marketing, Immelt emphasized the need for organic growth, and there was to be a real focus on generating such growth. The percentages of revenues and profits generated outside the US would be increased. That said, throughout 2004 GE proceeded to acquire a series of businesses to support its existing activities and priorities. Altogether some $16.5 billion was spent.

In 2005 GE's insurance business activities were sold to Swiss Re – its recent profits had been 'disappointing'. In 2006 the nuclear power units were moved into a joint venture with Hitachi. Profits were holding up but GE's stock was under-performing the main indices.

In 2007 GE paid $4.8 billion to buy the aerospace division of Smiths Industries (see Case 16.5 on Smiths).

The business makes components including computer systems, cockpit displays and landing gear. The detection and security businesses of the two groups would also be joined together in a new joint venture, Smiths GE Detection.

In early 2008 first quarter profits fell below declared projections and analysts' expectations. Maybe Immelt's investments were not paying off…however strategically logical they might appear to be. Welch went on record and said 'Immelt had a credibility issue'. At the same time he defended his successor's strategy.

Questions

1 Do you think Welch's management style could be easily copied by other organizations?

2 Why?

3 Why not?

4 Do you agree with the changes introduced by Immelt?

5 How difficult is it to balance long term growth and investments with the need for regular profits?

GENERAL ELECTRIC **http://www.ge.com**

© PHILIP SCALIA/ALAMY

16.1 Introduction: corporate strategy and implementation

In this chapter we explore decisions concerning which corporate level strategies organizations might choose and how these might be implemented successfully. Good choices and effective implementation both matter; they are related but they are different as we can see from Table 16.1. The decisions about what to do require competency in strategic thinking; and the focus is on ideas and direction. Implementation is more operational and tactical and it demands expertises in systems and management. It is possible to argue that new strategic ideas can be seen as potential new projects and so project management competency is essential.

There are a number of key themes to a synergistic, successful and profitable portfolio of businesses:

- related competencies and capabilities, which can be transferred between businesses and between each of these businesses and the corporate headquarters, or the overall strategic leader
- the ability to create and build value, both individually and collectively, by the businesses and the corporate headquarters

Table 16.1 Managing strategy and implementation

Managing corporate strategy	Strategy implementation
Need to think strategically	Tactical and operational perspective
What we call 'strategic management'	Realistically resource management
About direction	About systems and management
Focus on new ideas and options	Focus on delivery
What the organization is doing	How the organization does things
Choices concern businesses to be in or not be in – and how to be competitive	Choices relate to the management of projects and activities – operational rather than strategic

- the ability to implement strategies and strategic ideas to achieve their potential. This contribution is again individual (in, say, the form of profit streams because of a strong competitive position) and collective, through learning, sharing and the transfer of skills and resources.

In this chapter, therefore, a number of key themes are brought together.

First, the relatedness of the actual businesses in the portfolio. Where technologies or markets are similar or even the same, there must be relatedness. However, some diversified conglomerates have shown that they can relate unlike businesses to create value – see Case 16.1 This relates to issues of style and culture, rather than basic strategic logic.

Second, the management of the portfolio of activities to ensure that strategies are implemented effectively. As a result, the overall organization should be demonstrably better off from the existence of the businesses and strategies involved. It is clearly possible for a problematical business to be a distraction which draws resources (people, money and time in particular) away from potentially more lucrative opportunities.

Figure 16.1 shows how strategy and implementation must work together harmoniously for competitive, strategic and (where relevant) financial success. Where the strategy is stretched or particularly demanding for the resources possessed by the organization, there is still likely to be under-achievement even where there is sound implementation. If the accompanying implementation is also weak, the organization is likely to seem fragmented and fragile. A basically sound strategy, poorly implemented, would typically suggest structural and stylistic flaws.

The basic dilemma for many organizations is understanding why, when something is wrong. If performance is below expectations, is it the strategy or the implementation which is mainly to blame? The reaction of many businesses to the very competitive and increasingly global business environment of the 1990s has been to work on both. Strategies have typically become more focused and structures less hierarchical.

Richter and Owen (1997) show how there has been:

- refocusing – organizations have reduced the number of industries in which they compete, and

- simpler structures – characterized by smaller head offices and fewer layers of management.

Figure 16.1 Strategy and implementation

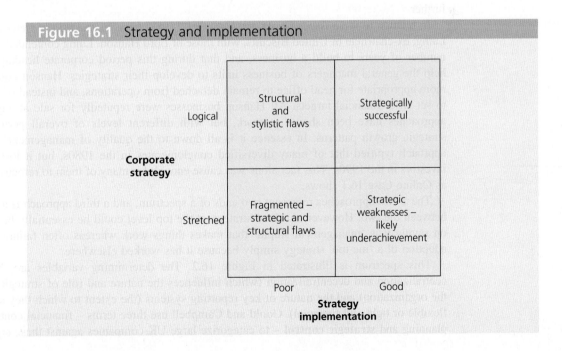

In the end we are left to question whether there has been too much reaction and an over-aggressive response, partly the result of pressure from institutional investors and the financial markets, which have tended to be intolerant of diversity. Yet one of the most valuable and respected business in the world, General Electric, remains a very diversified conglomerate. We have tended to assume that diversified conglomerates are strategically illogical, and yet it could be that many managers have simply been unable to manage them in the 1990s when a radically different approach was required from that which succeeded with diversified conglomerates in the 1980s.

Richter and Owen (at the London School of Economics and Public Science) used primary research and secondary data to track the strategic progress of large UK and German companies between 1986 and 1996. They found that over this decade 75 per cent of British companies became more focused compared with only 50 per cent in Germany. The figure for the US was even lower. Only 16 per cent of acquisitions (32 per cent for Germany) were in unrelated businesses. Germany experienced more vertical integration than the UK, where it was almost non-existent.

At the same time large UK businesses experienced:

- head-office personnel reductions, from an average of 175 to 100
- the number of business heads reporting to boards coming down from eight to six and
- the number of layers of management in the operating businesses being reduced from seven to five.

16.2 Styles of corporate management

The questions addressed in this section are the following. What is the appropriate role for corporate headquarters in divisionalized organizations? How much power should be centralized? How independent should the divisions and business units be? These relate to the difference between the divisional and the holding company structures and styles of management, and the themes of integration and behavioural processes within the structural framework are explored further.

In relation to these issues Goold and Campbell (1988) have contrasted the views of Sir Hector Laing, ex-chairman of United Biscuits, with those of Lord Hanson. Laing contended that it takes a number of years to build a business, and that during this period corporate headquarters should help the general managers of business units to develop their strategies. Hanson argued that it is more appropriate for head office to remain detached from operations, and instead of involvement, to set strict financial targets. All Hanson businesses were reputedly for sale at any time. Both approaches have been shown to work, but with different levels of overall performance and strategic growth patterns. In essence it is all down to the quality of management! The Hanson approach typified that of many diversified conglomerates in the 1980s, but it lost favour with investors in the 1990s. This fact alone was cause enough for many of them to refocus or break up, as Online Case 16.1 shows.

These two approaches represent two ends of a spectrum, and a third approach is a compromise between the two. However, much of strategy at the top level could be essentially based correctly on saying it is 'management stupid' that makes things work whereas often failure is about the adoption of a 'me too' strategy simply because it has worked elsewhere.

This spectrum is illustrated in Figure 16.2. The determining variables are the extent of centralization and decentralization (which influences the nature and role of strategic planning in the organization) and the nature of key reporting systems (the extent to which they are loose and flexible or tight and financial). Goold and Campbell use three terms – financial control, strategic planning and **strategic control** – to categorize large UK companies against these criteria.

Figure 16.2   Corporate management style

Financial control companies

See the online "Hanson" case for an example of this section's theory in practice

Financial control is seen as an ideal approach for a holding company where the businesses are independent and unrelated. Hanson, discussed in Online Case 16.1, was an excellent example and advocate of this style, which for many years under the leadership of Lord (Arnold) Weinstock was also preferred by the more focused GEC. As we can see from the case the strategy was changed when it (and the company) lost the support of shareholders.

- Strategy creation is heavily decentralized to business unit managers. Within their agreed financial targets they are free to develop and change their competitive and functional strategies.
- Budgets and targets – and their achievement – are critically important control mechanisms.
- The small head office monitors financial returns closely and regularly, intervening when targets are missed – head office is a 'controller'.
- Head office also acts as a corporate investment banker for investment capital.
- Achievement is rewarded, and units are encouraged to put forward and chase ambitious targets. Underperforming managers are likely to be removed.
- The head office adds value by acquiring and improving under-performing businesses; if additional value cannot be added it may well sell off businesses.
- There will, typically, be few interdependencies and links between the businesses.
- Growth is more likely to be by acquisition than organic investment, with many financial control companies taking a short-term view of each business and being reluctant to invest in speculative research and the development of longer-term strategies.

Owen Green, chief executive and architect of BTR, had the following philosophy:

1 Never pursue extra sales at the expense of profit margins.
2 Raise prices whenever there is an opportunity.
3 Investment should never exceed the amount written off in depreciation.

The result was high profit margins but a lack of capital investment; growth was mainly by acquisition rather than by investing in the existing businesses. Herein lay the ultimate limitations.

Strategic planning companies

Strategic planning tends to be adopted in organizations which focus on only a few, and preferably related, core businesses. Examples include Cadbury Schweppes, United Biscuits and BP. Historically it has been the favoured approach for most public-sector organizations.

- Strategic plans are developed jointly by head office and the business units, with head office retaining the final say. Strategic planning is centralized.
- Day-to-day operations only are wholly decentralized.
- Head office sets priorities and co-ordinates strategies throughout the organization, possibly initiating cross-business strategies, and thereby acts as an orchestrator.
- A long-term perspective is realistic, and the search for opportunities for linkages and sharing resources and best practice can be prioritized. This normally requires central control. Individually the businesses would tend to operate more independently; organization-wide synergies may involve sacrifices by individual businesses.
- Goold and Campbell conclude that there are co-ordination problems if this approach is used in truly diversified organizations.
- Budgets are again used for measuring performance.
- The tight central control can become bureaucratic and demotivate managers, who may not feel *ownership* of their strategies.

Other dangers are that thinking may become too focused at the centre, with the potential contributions of divisional managers under-utilized; and that the organization may be slow to change in response to competitive pressures. Value can be added successfully if corporate managers stay aware and expert in the core businesses and if the competitive environment allows this style to work.

Strategic control companies

Financial control and strategic planning are appropriate for particular types of organization, but both styles, while having very positive advantages, also feature drawbacks. The strategic control style is an attempt to obtain the major benefits of the other two styles for organizations that are clearly diversified but with linkages and interdependencies. Value is added by balancing strategic and financial controls.

- Strategy creation involves decentralization to the business units, although head office still controls the overall *corporate* strategy.
- The role of head office is to review divisional and business plans, and approve strategic objectives and financial targets, accepting that they may need to be changed in a competitive environment. Performing a coaching role, head office encourages businesses to achieve their potential by active involvement and by fostering the spreading of learning and good practice through the organization.
- Strategy creation and budgetary control can be separated, allowing for more creative performance measurement. Sometimes competitive pressures and misjudgements mean strategies have to be changed, and hoped-for financial targets may be missed. A strategic control style can recognize this and deal with the implications.
- Head office does, however, monitor and control financial performance and success against strategic milestones and objectives.

Although decentralization is a feature, head office still requires considerable detail about the various businesses if it is to ensure that the synergy potential is achieved and very short-term thinking is avoided. Political activity will be prevalent as individual businesses compete with each other for scarce corporate resources.

In Online case 13.4 it is mentioned that GEC, under Lord Weinstock – who was in charge for 32 years – adopted a financial control style. When he retired (in 1996) and was replaced by Lord George Simpson the style was quickly changed to strategic control. Simpson inherited a GEC that was diversified and financially sound, but it was risk averse and experiencing relatively low growth. It was also in possession of a legendary cash mountain of £2.5 billion. Simpson created a new agenda for growth. With divestments and acquisitions the portfolio was changed. The style also changed. There was to be more focus on customers and people and less on cost control. There was greater decentralization, accompanied by robust reporting systems. It is not unusual to see changes of strategy, structure and style accompanying a change of leadership, especially if a company is in difficulty or the predecessor has been in place for a long time.

Two leading organizations that utilized the strategic control style – ICI and Courtaulds – both concluded that they were over-diversified. This belief was strongly reinforced by institutional investor pressure. The attitude of the stock market and their shareholders meant that their share prices were underperforming against the index, the average of the UK's largest companies. There were numerous businesses in each organization, although some were clearly interlinked. At the same time these clusters had little in common and featured different strategic needs and cultures. Because of these differences, and the inevitable complexity, corporate headquarters could not add value with a single entity. Both companies split into two distinct parts to enable a stronger focus on core competencies and strategic capabilities. Courtaulds was split into Courtaulds Chemicals (subsequently acquired by Akzo Nobel of Germany) and Courtaulds Textiles (sold to Sara Lee of the US). ICI separated its chemicals and pharmaceuticals businesses. The former remained as ICI, but many of the activities were divested and replaced by more consumer-focused businesses. ICI continued to struggle. The others were renamed Zeneca, which soon merged into Astra Zeneca. This story is told in more detail in Case 16.2, where we see a classic example of the decline of UK manufacturing. It begs the unanswerable question: with a different strategy and style would the story have been different?

Case 16.2

ICI and Zeneca   UK

This case charts the recent history of one of the UK's long-established 'manufacturing giants' in the chemical industry, which is an industry that has seen more and more production exported to lower labour cost countries. Companies like ICI – which was started at the end of the World War I – have been hugely important to the UK – but many have been seriously affected by competition and have not survived. Was their decline inevitable – even with major strategic changes?

This case can usefully be read in parallel with the case on Hanson. At the beginning of the 1990s Hanson bought a small stake in ICI and it was thought by many that Hanson would make a full bid and then seek to split up ICI. ICI attacked the Hanson approach to strategy aggressively in the press and no bid ever ensued. Some years later the business was broken up – but by then was it already too late? Would there have been a benefit if the company had changed sooner than it did?

ICI's strategic and structural problems were partially a result of the range and diversity of its products. These ranged from bulk chemicals (including chlorine and petro-chemicals [plastics from oil and gas] to more sophisticated products such as pharmaceuticals and pesticides. The prospects for bulk chemicals are traditionally dependent on the world economic cycle, and consequently profits vary dramatically from year to year. Drugs are classically immune from the economic cycle, and they are also cash generative. ICI's dilemma concerned the utilization of its profits for research and development and capital investment, and whether to cross-subsidize or treat the businesses separately. During the boom years of the mid-1980s chemicals and related products were very profitable; but in the recession of 1991 they contributed just 30 per cent of ICI's profits from 70 per cent of the turnover.

Between 1980 and 1985, chaired by Sir Maurice Hodgson and later Sir John Harvey-Jones, ICI reduced its global workforce from 225,000 to 175,000 and purged its costs. The early 1980s were also recession years. ICI's competitive position strengthened. The company was also restructured into seven global product divisions co-ordinated through nine regional territories. Financial responsibilities were split amongst the divisions and the regions. UK inflation later in the 1980s meant ICI's costs started to rise again, and faster than those of its main competitors. The workforce was further reduced (to 132,000 in 1990) and productivity improved – but it was still not enough.

In 1990 ICI was restructured again in an attempt to place greater emphasis on the global nature of its businesses, increase the financial accountability of the divisional business managers, and focus greater attention on improving shareholders' wealth. The head office was slimmed down, and the number of regional chairmen was reduced to three. The regions lost any managerial responsibility over individual businesses. The product division heads became autonomous, and they could spend up to £10 million without reference to the main board. When Hanson acquired 2.8 per cent of ICI's shares in spring 1991, and raised the threat of a hostile takeover bid, the company was encouraged to evaluate again both its strategy and structure. No actual bid ever materialized, but Hanson and external analysts questioned whether ICI was effectively exploiting its assets. In the end the Hanson view that ICI would be better split up was defensible, but arguably what followed came too late.

ICI declared it would now concentrate on businesses where it could achieve a strong global position. The fibres operations were swapped for the acrylics businesses of Du Pont early in 1992, for instance.

In July 1992 ICI's board announced plans to split the company into two separate businesses in 1993 – ICI and ICI Bio, later renamed Zeneca. Shareholders in ICI would be given an equivalent shareholding in the new company. ICI would retain industrial chemicals, paints and explosives; it would have 88,000 employees world-wide and be the seventh largest chemical company in the world (relegated from fifth). These businesses were all high volume and capital intensive. Zeneca, geared more towards differentiated, high added value products, would comprise the drugs and agrochemicals businesses and be the ninth largest pharmaceutical company in the world. There would be 35,500 employees. It was assumed that most of ICI's cash reserves would remain with the bulk chemicals when it was announced that Zeneca would have an early rights issue. The opportunities for synergy really lay within the two product clusters, not between them.

Moreover, each business had different strategic needs. A successful split would enable the necessary further rationalization at ICI and foster new product investment in Zeneca. Both companies should now become better protected from hostile takeover. ICI might appear to be relatively unattractive; Zeneca would probably be very expensive whilst ever it remained successful and profitable. Immediately after the split Zeneca shares performed well when compared with those of other international drugs companies; ICI shares, by contrast, were poor performers in the international chemicals industry.

ICI reached an agreement with Union Carbide of the USA to exchange information for benchmarking purposes; ICI realized that it was overstaffed and that its costs were still relatively high and had to be reduced further. In 1995 ICI appointed a new chief executive, a recruit from Unilever, Charles Miller-Smith. He found 'a traumatized organization of survivors from one of the world's most comprehensive management delayerings'. After extensive deliberation, Miller-Smith decided ICI needed to focus on intermediate (acrylic and polyester film products) and consumer-oriented products (including Dulux paints) and not bulk chemicals. Additionally ICI's future would be more dependent on investment and development in the USA and Asia than in Europe.

In May 1997 it was formally announced that ICI was looking to sell off 60 per cent of its businesses (mainly bulk chemicals and worth approximately £3 billion) to help fund its acquisition of Unilever's speciality chemicals businesses, which would then constitute 70 per cent of a 'new' ICI, which was more focused on consumer markets. A reverse take-over in everything but name. The purchase price was £4.9 billion. Charles Miller-Smith had joined ICI from Unilever Chemicals; he knew the businesses involved. He also realized the cultures were different. ICI was currently focused more on production, Unilever on marketing. The Unilever businesses had typically enjoyed steady growth, while those of ICI had been far more cyclical, with the attached cash management difficulties. ICI's head office would now receive an infusion of 'tough American and gritty Dutch' managers.

Four Unilever businesses were included in the purchase:

National Starch Industrial adhesives as well as starches.

These products brought real opportunities for business with Procter & Gamble, previously prohibited as P & G are established Unilever rivals. The relevant adhesives are used in disposable nappies where Procter's Pampers product is the leading global brand.

Quest	Food flavours and fragrances.
Unichema	Lubricants and polymers from natural fats.
Crosfield	Detergent ingredients. A business ICI planned to divest.

One month later, and to help fund the Unilever acquisition, a majority share of ICI's business in Australia was sold for £1 billion; and in July ICI agreed to sell a number of its industrial chemicals businesses to Du Pont for £1.8 billion. This proposed sale included ICI's polyester and titanium dioxide plants which produce raw materials for paints and plastics. ICI was aiming to become less vertically integrated. Du Pont specializes in bulk chemicals and this acquisition would consolidate its position as the largest American chemicals company. For this reason it was subject to ratification by the US competition authorities. The deal was eventually stopped in January 1999 – and the delay had a severe impact on ICI's cash position.

The fertilizer business was sold to an American buyer in November 1997; a month later ICI's explosives business was sold. In 1998 ICI acquired a cluster of home improvements businesses from Williams, including Polyfilla, which could link with Dulux paints. A possible sale of Crosfield fell through. However, concurrent with these strategic changes, profits were declining as part of the inbuilt economic cycle and ICI was finding it difficult to deal with its accumulated debt burden of £4 billion. The disposals were going to have to be more dramatic than Miller-Smith had originally planned.

In 1999 ICI sold all its petrochemicals businesses, including polyester and titanium dioxide, to Huntsman of America for £12.7 billion. Acrylics (ingredients for paints and adhesives, bathtubs and sinks) were divested to a management buy-out. ICI had basically become a 'holding company for specialist assets'. Of the old – and once huge – ICI, only paints remained.

Five years later ICI still comprised paints (including the Dulux, Cuprinol and Polyfilla brands), National Starch, Uniqema and Quest together with some businesses in Pakistan, India and Argentina. Uniqema was sold in 2006 to Croda and Quest to Givaudan of Switzerland. Investors seemed pleased as (finally) it left the company debt free. It had had a debt problem since 1997. John McAdam had been appointed CEO in 2003 and given a remit to cut costs. ICI had been led by Brendan O'Neill for the previous four years.

In June 2007 Akzo Nobel (Holland) bid £7.2 billion for ICI – it was clear it was interested in the paints businesses. Some ten years earlier, Akzo Nobel had bought another long-standing UK chemicals business, Courtaulds. By August, after some opposition, the bid was increased to £8.1 billion. Once it was approved by the ICI shareholders the debate began on whether the name ICI would soon be consigned to history. Many of the businesses that ICI once owned continue to trade, albeit under new (and generally foreign) ownership.

Zeneca, meanwhile, merged with Astra of Sweden in 1999 and continued to grow successfully. In 2000 the agrochemicals side of the business was merged with the competing interests owned by Novartis to form a joint venture trading as Syngenta.

In the end the UK has lost a major bulk chemicals business, one on which many other industries depend. Arguably the necessary research and development did not take place during the 1960s – a time when the UK was not a member of the European Community and when, as a consequence, some market opportunities were unavailable to companies like ICI. In addition, costs had been allowed to escalate and the issue was not tackled as early as it needed to be. This was one issue to which Hanson drew attention. Some analysts argue that bulk chemicals is so tied in to the global oil industry that survival demands some form of strategic alliance, something ICI did not have.

Questions

1 What lessons on competitive strategy, corporate restructuring and strategic leadership can be taken from this story?
2 How important is timing in strategy?

Levels of success

Goold and Campbell (1988) studied 16 large UK companies, including those given as examples above, and concluded that each style has both advantages and disadvantages and that no one style is outstandingly the most successful.

Strategic planning companies proved to be consistently profitable during the 1980s, mainly through organic growth. Head office corporate staff tended to be a quite large group and differences of opinion with general managers sometimes caused frustration within the divisions and business units. *Financial control companies* exhibited the best financial performance. In a number of cases, particularly BTR and Hanson, this resulted from acquisition and divestment rather than organic growth. Short-term financial targets were felt to reduce the willingness of general managers to take risks. There were few trade-offs whereby short-term financial targets were sacrificed for long-term growth. A general manager, for example, might consider a programme of variety reduction and product rationalization with a view to developing a more consistent and effective portfolio. In the short term this would result in reduced revenue and profits before new orders and products improved overall profitability. This temporary fall might be unacceptable in the face of short-term financial targets. *Strategic control companies* also performed satisfactorily but experienced difficulties in establishing the appropriate mix of strategic and financial targets for general managers. Financial targets, being the more specific and measurable ones, were generally given priority.

Goold and Campbell concluded that while the style of management adopted within the structure determines the strategic changes that take place, the overall corporate strategy of the company very much influences the choice of style. Large diverse organizations, for example, will find it difficult to adopt a strategic planning approach. Equally, where the environment is turbulent and competitive, increasing the need for adaptive strategic change, the financial planning approach is less appropriate. Not unexpectedly, Hanson's main acquisitions were of companies in mature, slow-growth sectors.

While companies may appreciate that there is a mismatch between their corporate strategy and style, changing the style can be difficult. Moreover, many organizations will not be able to implement a new style as effectively as the one that they are used to.

Goold *et al.* (1993) revisited the organizations and their research five years later, partly stimulated by the change in fortunes in some of the companies involved. This review reinforced the conclusion that financial control is ideally suited to a group of autonomous businesses in a conglomerate, but it is less suitable for a portfolio of core businesses or ones seeking to compete globally. In 1988 Goold and Campbell had argued that the adoption of a hands-off, financial control style by GEC and other electronics companies in the UK had hindered their development as globally competitive businesses. Global development demands synergy between a number of national businesses. BTR and Hanson had already begun to focus more on selected core businesses, and their relative performance was deteriorating.

Strategic planning continued to add value as long as corporate managers had close knowledge and experience of their core businesses. Where their portfolio was arguably too diverse – although not so diverse that they could be classified as diversified conglomerates – strategic control companies were experiencing difficulties. The researchers poured scorn on the idea that a decentralized structure, supported by a modern budgeting and planning system, would enable a competent management team to add value to almost any new business. Strategic control can only work with an effective mix of tight financial control and devolved authority to instigate emergent strategic changes; to achieve this successfully, head offices again need to appreciate the detail of competitive strategies in the subsidiaries.

Appreciating the specific problems and opportunities faced by subsidiary businesses is particularly important for establishing fair reward systems.

Reward systems are likely to be based on specific performance targets, but these could relate to growth in revenue, absolute profits or profitability ratios. Stonich (1982) has suggested that business units might be categorized as having high, medium or low growth potential. Four factors could be used in evaluating their relative performances: return on assets; cash flow; strategic development programmes and increases in market share. The relative weighting attributed to each of these four factors would be changed to reflect their specific objectives and whether they were of high, medium or low-growth potential. Return on assets and cash flow would be critical for low growth business units, and market share and strategic development programmes most important for those with high growth potential. The factors would be weighted equally for medium growth.

This approach would be particularly relevant where general managers were changed around to reflect their particular styles of management and the current requirements of the business unit.

One question left unanswered concerns the extent to which the conclusions of Goold and Campbell are a result of British management strengths, weaknesses and preferences. Certain Japanese companies appear to grow organically at impressive rates while maintaining strict financial controls and directing corporate strategic change from the centre. This tendency, however, is affected by legislation which restricts the ability of Japanese companies to grow by acquisition and merger. Without this control Japanese firms may have followed different strategies.

The next section endeavours to pull together the lessons from this and other research and the cases quoted herein.

16.3   Diversification or focus: a key corporate dilemma

It is now appropriate to look in greater detail at corporate strategic trends in the UK. The emphasis seems to be on 'divest unrelated activities; acquire related ones'. Restructuring to take out costs has been emphasized, but many organizations have simply downsized; they have not *rightsized* to create an organization with the necessary competencies and motivation to stimulate renewal and new growth. In addition, a more recent trend has been share buy-backs, as company after company changes its gearing to make it less vulnerable to shareholder pressure. Really, this is an admission that they cannot find desirable growth opportunities where any accumulated cash might be deployed and used for long-term growth and effectiveness.

As seen in Chapter 11, acquisition and diversification strategies are frequently linked together. Acquisitions (agreed corporate purchases), takeovers (hostile buys) and mergers (the joining of two organizations) fuel organizational growth and, quite often, the necessary capital is available from the City if the organization does not have sufficient reserves. With such strategies, organizations are likely to be able to grow much more quickly than by investing in organic growth to build existing activities and businesses. While organic growth is always going to be important, there is often a dearth of inspirational ideas.

The downside of acquisitions is that often two (or even more) cultures need to be integrated. Growth in size happens, but it may not be accompanied by increased profitability and the synergy required to generate real growth. There is also a paradox of timing and opportunity. An acquisition will use up any spare cash, managerial expertise and managerial time – all scarce resources. Until the businesses have been integrated, resources are stretched and the organization would find it difficult to deal with a further acquisition. Do the best opportunities occur when the organization is ideally prepared or ill prepared?

Diversification implies new products, services and markets. The extent of the differences implies that the diversification is either related in some way, or unrelated. Where new technologies, new skills, new resources, new distribution channels and new markets are all implied, the learning challenge is considerable, together with the inherent uncertainty. However, related diversification, perhaps by the acquisition of an existing competitor, can provoke interest from the competition authorities in individual countries or the European Commission, which can result in its being stopped. Whatever the strategy, in the end its relative success or failure depends upon the ability of the managers involved to generate greater returns from the assets, possibly implying restructuring and some asset sales, and certainly requiring that any anticipated synergy is delivered. This in turn demands that too high a price is not paid for the acquisition in the first place unlike the purchase of ABN Amro by a consortium of banks including the Royal Bank of Scotland.

At different times, different strategies and approaches enjoy greater or lesser favour. Strategies that are popular today may be unfashionable next year; when this happens those pursuing unfashionable strategies are subjected to considerable scrutiny from the media and from analysts.

The systematic cross-border acquisitions of Rowntree and Perrier by Nestlé have contributed to the growth of a successful international foods business. There are some links between the products, with opportunities for sharing and learning. This strategic approach continues to be fashionable. Reed Elsevier (joint UK and Netherlands) merged with the Dutch company Wolters Kluwer to create the world's largest scientific and professional publishing business, now named Elsevier. Other similar examples are:

- Glaxo Wellcome's merger with SmithKline Beecham to create Glaxo SmithKline
- The acquisition of Mannesmann by Vodafone – unusual as it is rare for German companies to be acquired by non-German predators.

In contrast, in the mid-late 1990s, conglomerate diversification – building a corporation with unrelated acquisitions – became much less fashionable than it was a decade ago. There are strong arguments in favour of this change of popularity but, nevertheless, it can still be a successful strategy if it is supported with appropriate implementation skills, and it may well become more fashionable again sometime in the future.

As seen earlier, the outstanding example of a successful diversified conglomerate in recent years is General Electric. On the whole, however, GE is not acquisitive on a regular basis; there are frequent bolt-on acquisitions and very occasional major purchases which imply further diversification. Its success comes largely from its ability to foster sharing and learning among its disparate businesses and, most significantly, leverage its existing resources to create new forms of competitive advantage.

> Our intellectual capital is not US-based … we aim to get the best ideas from everywhere. Each team puts up its best ideas and processes – constantly. That raises the bar. Our culture is designed around making a hero out of those who translate ideas from one place to another, who help somebody else. They get an award, they get praised and promoted.

JOHN F (JACK) WELCH, RETIRED CHIEF EXECUTIVE, GE

This philosophy is in stark contrast to the finance-driven holding company style of Hanson and BTR (in the past), an approach which saw each business as a very independent activity and shunned major investment. The GE philosophy has also been seen to be successful at other diversified American conglomerates. Another example is United Technologies, which comprises Otis, Carrier and Sikorski – respectively, the world leaders for elevators, air conditioners and helicopters – Pratt and Whitney (jet engines), aerospace and automotive components. Here again, there is emphasis on segment leadership.

> If one of the companies needs some new ideas, they should go and grab them from wherever is appropriate.

GEORGE DAVID, PRESIDENT AND CEO, UNITED TECHNOLOGIES

Focus, then, is unquestionably fashionable. Caulkin (1996) argues that if you have relatively poor management, focus makes absolute sense as focused companies are easier to manage. Unfortunately focus, per se, is unlikely to create new value. The dilemma with diversification lies in establishing clearly whether it is the corporate logic of the diversification strategy itself which is in question, or the inability of many companies to add value to a disparate range of activities and sustain real growth in some way. Sadtler et al. (1997) defend the case for a clear focus, built around a defensible core of related activities, arguing that focus is now a more popular corporate strategy for a number of important reasons:

- It allows greater control. Diversified conglomerates must decentralize to allow flexibility and this can imply a trade-off with central control unless the organization can truly share information and learn.

- Divesting unrelated businesses can provide the finance necessary to strengthen the core.
- It often builds shareholder confidence, supporting the share price and making the organization less vulnerable to takeover.
- In increasingly competitive markets and industries poor performance is harder to hide. Focus can ensure that the weakest companies are divested and stronger businesses not held back because of the need to cross-subsidize.

For Sadtler the activity core is built around similar critical success factors (what the businesses have to be good at) and similar improvement opportunities (what they are going to have to do in the future). A corporate centre must be able to add value to every constituent business; every business in the portfolio should add value by contributing to the success of the whole organization.

Detailed criteria can be readily and sensibly established to justify what should and what should not be in the core. The factors embrace financial performance over a number of years, the company's stated mission, the relatedness of tasks and technologies, customer requirements and the opportunities for internal sharing and trading. These points are taken up later.

From their objective analysis based on these criteria, Sadtler *et al.* produced a list of American organizations which they believed were candidates for breaking up. All of the following featured prominently:

- Ford and General Motors have adopted different growth strategies in recent years. Ford has continued to struggle in recent years, and has acquired a number of upmarket brands to broaden its product range. GM has acquired other car businesses. See Case 11.5
- PepsiCo, which has divested its fast-food restaurants to concentrate on snack foods and soft drinks – a strategy which, with hindsight, has worked!
- Exxon, Amoco and Chevron, competitors in the global oil industry, which has been characterized by horizontal integration and consolidation
- Berkshire Hathaway, the investment company run by Warren Buffett which invests long term in other businesses. Perhaps inevitably the company's performance has deteriorated for short periods, but its shareholders have remained very loyal and supportive. This loyalty has been rewarded as the company has regained momentum.

In contrast, strategic leaders who have grown successful diversified businesses continue to disagree. Harold Geneen (1997), who died in 1997, is often credited as the founder of truly diversified conglomerates. Geneen's ITT at one time included telecommunications, hotels, baking, cosmetics and lightbulbs, book publishing and Avis Rent-a-Car. ITT has been comprehensively broken up – although Geneen's tight financial control style worked, when he retired there was no natural succession. However, Geneen continued to claim:

To succeed in business it is essential to take risks. But they must be smart risks – researched, understood, survivable. The conglomerate is a good vehicle for identifying and exploiting them ... but ... running a conglomerate requires working harder than most people want to work and taking more risks than most people want to take.

As soon as things go wrong, companies start talking about focus. Focus is the crutch of mediocre management ... if you are trained in the techniques of management ... you should be able to apply them across a range of companies. Diversified companies possess both defensive qualities in a recession and a springboard for new ventures in more expansive times.

SIR OWEN GREEN (1994), EX-BTR, HAS DEFENDED CONGLOMERATES EVEN MORE STRONGLY:

This argument is further borne out by the success of the US conglomerate, Textron, which outperformed the Wall Street stock index by 50 per cent during the 1990s. Textron remains (in 2009) a diversified manufacturer with interests in aircraft (Cessna planes and Bell helicopters), industrial products and automotive components, fastening systems and finance. Sheaffer (pens) was another known brand that Textron acquired. Founded in 1923 it is ranked 202 on the Fortune 500 list of largest companies. Given the major shakeout in the Fortune 500 list in recent years Textron has performed well. The company argues that its balanced diversity (not being overdependent on any one product) allows it consistently to improve its overall earnings through economic cycles. This case has always been used as an argument to defend diversity, while recognizing that with the wrong approach it can become dangerously short-termist. To succeed it needs a particular management style.

Summarizing this section of the chapter, most strategies can be made to work effectively and efficiently, but the ultimate success of any strategy lies in its implementation. Decisions concerning the implementation issues of structure and management style, as well as those affecting the competitiveness of each product or service in the portfolio, provide additional dilemmas which need to be investigated further.

It should not be forgotten that concentrating the debate on this manifestation of corporate strategy can draw attention away from the real strategic issue, which is creating new values. With Hanson and BTR, once businesses had been turned around and profitability restored, little new value was being added, and so there was an argument that the individual businesses might be better off on their own or with a new parent. Is this an argument for focus or for a different style of corporate management? Reinforcing earlier points, Hamel and Prahalad (1994) contend that today there is too much strategic convergence. High-performance organizations reinvent industries and regenerate core strategies. They innovate around the theme of positioning.

> *If the past couple of years have taught anything about corporate structure,*
> *it is that broad generalizations about integration versus specialization, or conglomeration*
> *versus focus, are worthless. Everything depends on the pressures affecting individual*
> *industries: and within them, the different circumstances of the companies themselves.*
>
> JACKSON (1995)

16.4 Managing the corporate portfolio

Porter (1987) argues that corporate strategy is that which makes the corporate whole add up to more than the sum of its parts, but further contends that the corporate strategies of too many companies dissipate rather than create shareholder value. He comments:

> *Moving from competitive strategy to corporate strategy is the business equivalent of passing through the Bermuda Triangle. The failure of corporate strategy reflects the fact that most diversified companies have failed to think in terms of how they really add value.*

Porter's arguments are as follows. Corporate strategy involves two key questions or issues. First, what businesses should the company choose to compete in; second, how strategically distinct businesses should be managed at the corporate level?

When the debate on issues related to strategic growth and corporate strategy opened in Part 4 of this book, synergy was held out as the justification for strategic changes, especially if they involved diversification. The ideas behind synergy are defensible, but synergy *potential* alone cannot justify change. Implementation matters and, being realistic, synergy is frequently based on intangibles and possibilities rather than definites. When we look back on acquisitions that fail to deliver the promised synergies, we can never be sure how much the problem was the strategic logic and how much was implementation. For these reasons, portfolio management, backed by the analytical techniques discussed in Chapter 8, was attractive when it was developed by management consultants.

Portfolio management

The basic premise of portfolio management is that competition occurs at the business level and this is where competitive advantages are developed. Businesses should compete for centralized corporate investment resources, and they should be divested if there are no further opportunities for developing new values. To facilitate this, a cost-effective organization structure should enable cross-fertilization between the businesses while maintaining overall control. The role of the corporate headquarters was to seek and acquire attractive (potentially highly profitable) businesses, fit them in to the organization, assess their requirements and allocate strategic resources according to their position in the relevant matrix. Of course, in reality, many low-performing businesses were retained, diluting the earnings potential and, as a consequence, shareholders sometimes became sceptical. Their belief was that they could diversify their own portfolio of investments as a hedge against risk – they did not need the businesses to do this on their behalf.

In addition:

- undervalued companies were not always easily acquired – they were simply not available
- all too often excessive premiums were paid when businesses were acquired
- professional management and capital resources alone do not build value and yield competitive advantage
- businesses are often interdependent for all sorts of reasons and therefore strategies cannot be ring-fenced and set in isolation
- some businesses (and their managers) are defeated by the complexity and diversity of the portfolio.

However, one variant of portfolio management, restructuring, does have its logic and attraction.

Restructuring

Restructuring requires the identification of industries and companies with the potential for restructuring and transformation with new technologies, new people and/or consolidation. There is no need for them to be related to the existing businesses in the portfolio. The new parent intervenes to turn around the business: first, by cost-cutting and increased efficiency, and second, by adding new values to build a stronger competitive base and position. Once there are no further opportunities to add value the business should be sold to raise money for further acquisitions. Restructuring is not about hoarding businesses to build an empire and never divesting anything which, clearly, some strategic leaders have been prone to do.

Clear elements of restructuring can be seen in the Hanson approach. Certainly, efficiencies were increased as businesses were slimmed down, and businesses were always for sale at the right price. However, Hanson did not invest substantially to build new competitive advantages.

Restructuring works well when the strategic leadership can spot and acquire undervalued companies and then turn them around with sound management skills, even though they might be in unfamiliar industries. In a sense, there is an underlying belief that good managers can manage anything, and to a degree there is some truth in this assertion. The issue is whether they manage the renewal as well as the consolidation. The appropriate structure and style of corporate management are clearly critical. Naturally, if suitable undervalued businesses cannot be found – which is typically the case when a country's economy has been tightened and weak competitors have already disappeared as closures or acquisitions – restructuring has no basis.

Sharing activities and transferring skills

Porter's three tests for a successful acquisition were explained in Chapter 11. He argues that they are most likely to be met where there is some inter-relationship between the existing and new businesses. The basis for this might be tangible or intangible, and therefore it is easy to be deluded into thinking that there are similarities when in reality there are differences. Case 16.3 looks at this issue in relation to the recent acquisitions of the UK's three leading roadside-assistance businesses: the AA, RAC and Green Flag.

Inter-relationships are defined as 'connections among distinct businesses that lead to competitive advantage from being in both'. Hanson found a connection in low-cost capital and astute tax-avoidance strategies, but it would be more typical to see them in marketing or technology. The search for these synergies begins with an analysis of the value chains and the objective is to find opportunities for lowering costs and creating or enhancing differentiation. Activities, know-how, customers, distributors and competitors can all be shared. The benefits must outweigh the costs involved, for while there are always opportunities to share they may not lead to any competitive advantage. The outcome of sharing can be clearly tangible (such as better capacity utilization) or more intangible where it comes through learning and intelligence.

There is invariably a difficult balancing act involved. A shared salesforce is often a possibility, for example. Where this happens, higher calibre people can sometimes be recruited as there are

Case 16.3

The AA, RAC and Green Flag   UK

Changes of ownership

These three organizations dominate the roadside assistance industry in the UK. They are potentially valuable as the number of motorists and cars on the road continues to grow. If and when motorists keep their cars for longer, there is a perceived need for this type of insurance. Towards the end of the 1990s – and before they were all acquired by new owners - they had the following numbers of members:

AA	9.4 million
RAC	5.5 million
Green Flag	2.3 million

When they changed hands the key strategic question was whether their new parents would be able to share resources or transfer skills in order to improve their performance.

The first to be acquired was Green Flag, once known as National Breakdown. Unlike the AA and RAC, which employ their own staff and repair fleets, Green Flag is really a central marketing agency for local, independent roadside assistance specialists. Along with Capital Logistics (an airport coach business) Green Flag was already owned by National Parking Corporation, known as NCP, which runs 500 town and city car parks in the UK. Recently, NCP had been struggling to find good new sites through which to expand. NCP was bought by the American company Cendant in 1998. Through a series

of acquisitions Cendant had grown into the world's largest provider of consumer services, embracing hotels (Ramada and Howard Johnson), car rental (Avis) and real-estate agencies. Its strategic logic was to 'provide its marketing machinery with new products to sell to its existing customers'. Green Flag has formed alliances with motor insurers such as Direct Line, which sells its own branded receovery service which is provided by Green Flag members. By 2005 Green Flag had grown to 5 million customers, but was still third largest. In 1999 Direct Line (insurance) had bought the business. Green Flag is a more focused business than either the AA or RAC and is not involved in insurance itself.

In 1998 Cendant was also believed to be a possible bidder for the RAC – the Royal Automobile Club. At the time the RAC was 'owned' by the existing members of the RAC. A bid was prevented by government intervention, on the grounds that prices would probably rise and quality and innovation reduce if the industry was dominated by just two competitors. In the end the RAC was sold to Lex Service, a group focused on vehicle distribution and contract hire. Lex was a decentralized service operation. Its business 'units' were relatively small and operated in local markets with considerable autonomy. The parent provided central services and systems. Some years previously Lex had believed that this style of management lent itself to hotels and acquired eight up-market hotels, four in the UK and four in the USA. Lex found it difficult to acquire additional suitable properties for its portfolio, failed to reach what it believed was critical mass, and systematically divested every property. Again, Lex was looking for opportunities in consumer service, businesses. Vehicle distribution (where Lex began) was divested and the name of the whole business changed to RAC (2002). The intention now was to build a business around 'motoring and vehicle solutions'. The British School of Motoring (BSM), a leading driving school franchise, is part of the group. Financial services (car financing), motor and extended warranty insurance and personal injury claims management were seen as appropriate. The company expanded into the 'under-exploited' French market, to, in-part, capitalize on the number of UK holidaymakers who take their cars to France. The RAC was acquired by Aviva, the parent company of Norwich Union insurance, in 2005. This was an opportunity for Norwich Union to grow its vehicle insurance activities through cross-selling. Its customer numbers were around 7 million.

By 1999 the AA (the Automobile Association) had divested its previous retailing and travel businesses but it still provided insurance services. Like other organizations such as Kwik Fit and Virgin, the AA was simply exploiting its brand and its customer database. The AA does not underwrite insurance, it merely sells policies. Other specialist insurers are the real providers of the actual insurance. The business was acquired by Centrica, the trading arm of British Gas. Centrica sells gas to several million customers, and installs and maintains central-heating systems. Centrica also offered a Goldfish credit card and marketed insurance. Centrica believed that it was widening its product offering for its huge customer database and could exploit shared support services, especially centralized call centres and billing systems. In 2001 Centrica also acquired Halford's

garages (from Boots) which it immediately re-branded AA Service Centres, to build on the used car check-up service the AA already provided. The business concentrates on tyre and exhaust replacement and on MOT testing. The Halfords shops were not included in the deal – they were bought by venture capitalists who have since looked to re-float the business. These garages now trade as Nationwide.

In 2004 the AA was sold to venture capitalists CVC Capital Partners and Permira. Soon after there were 15 million members. In 2007 the business was merged with Saga, the provider of a diverse range of services for the over 50s, such as holidays and insurance, and which at the time was 80 per cent owned by private equity (Charterhouse). Saga's founder, Roger de Haan, had recently retired and sold his interests. The power of venture capitalists to cut costs, grow opportunities and increase the value of a business is illustrated in the following figures. CVC & Permira paid £1.75 billion for the AA, and when it merged with Saga it was valued at £3.35 billion. Charterhouse paid £1.35 billion for Saga and its valuation had increased to £2.8 billion.

Questions

1 Which of these three new parents at the end of the 1990s – Cendant, Lex and Centrica – had the best opportunity for sharing resources and transferring skills to a roadside-assistance business?

2 Do you think the fact that all three are now directly linked to wider insurance businesses was an inevitability?

AA **http://www.theaa.com**
RAC **http://www.rac.co.uk**
GREENFLAG **http://www.greenflag.co.uk**

more promotion prospects, buyers can be more easily accessed as more products are being sold at any one time, and less time is spent travelling between calls. However, different selling skills may be required for different products – some are sold on price, others on performance differences – and the attention given to certain ones may be inadequate.

The greatest returns should normally be found where activities are actually shared, but where this is not feasible, transferring skills can also be beneficial. The thinking here begins with a clear appreciation of strategic capabilities and the search for related industries in which these skills and capabilities could be usefully applied – again for savings or differentiation. The businesses must be sufficiently similar that sharing expertise is meaningful, and the potential advantage will always be greater if the capabilities involved are fresh to the new industry.

Where activities are to be shared and/or skills transferred, the corporate structure must be one that encourages it to happen and actively encourages managers to search out for opportunities. Many are actually structured in ways that erect barriers to sharing.

Finally, one key challenge in organizations that are heavily diversified and decentralized is to ensure that there is a shared corporate identity, which goes beyond the structural framework and comes down to the style of leadership and management. Porter concludes that diversification, decentralization and sharing can be complementary, although they may appear contradictory. They simply demand a sophisticated approach to the management of diversity.

16.5 Corporate parenting

Goold *et al.* (1994) reinforce Porter's arguments when they contend that acquisitions can be justified where the corporation can add value to the business, generating either synergy or valuable emergent properties. Any business must add value to its parent corporation; in turn, the corporation must add value to the subsidiary. The company is better off with its existing parent than it would be with another parent or on its own. **Parenting** skills, therefore, relate to the ability of a head office and strategic leadership to manage a portfolio of businesses efficiently and effectively and to change the portfolio as and when it is necessary. It is quite conceivable for head offices to destroy value if a subsidiary simply does not fit with the rest of the portfolio and is consequently held back.

Parenting skills vary between countries and cultures. In Japan, for example, the most successful companies are skilled at:

- securing and sustaining access to government, power and influence
- accessing investment capital, and
- retaining skilled managers.

Much of this is facilitated by the *keiretsu*, families of companies interlinked by share ownership and characterized by intertrading, regular meetings of senior executives and sometimes geographical proximity in a single 'corporate village'. Interestingly, and significantly, these companies are interwoven but there are no corporate headquarters.

Figure 16.3 builds on the arguments of Goold *et al.* and draws these points together. On one axis is strategic logic, the link between products, services, competencies and key success factors across the corporate portfolio. On the other axis are the parenting issues, the fit between the needs of individual businesses and the corresponding capabilities of the parent organization. Where they fit together well, there is a heartland of related businesses, which is explained below. Where there is no natural synergy between the businesses, the organization can be successful to some degree if the parent company uses a *holding company* structure. This implies strong individual companies that could survive elsewhere, but which are managed in a hands-off way. In this respect it is interesting that both Lord Hanson and Lord Weinstock had a reputation for rarely visiting the subsidiary businesses in the conglomerates that they ran.

Where the parenting issues are not addressed properly evidence will be seen of either strategic or structural flaws and the consequent under-performance. Here, *strategic flaws* again implies fragmented businesses with no real synergy potential but this time linked to an inappropriate structure and style. There is a real likelihood of poor performance. *Structural flaws* reflect a potential for synergy but a potential that is not being realized because of structural and stylistic weaknesses.

The notion of a heartland

Goold *et al.* use the term *heartland* to describe a range of businesses to which a corporation can add value and not destroy it. A heartland might be constituted by:

- common key success factors
- related core competencies and/or strategic capabilities
- a common or related industry or technology.

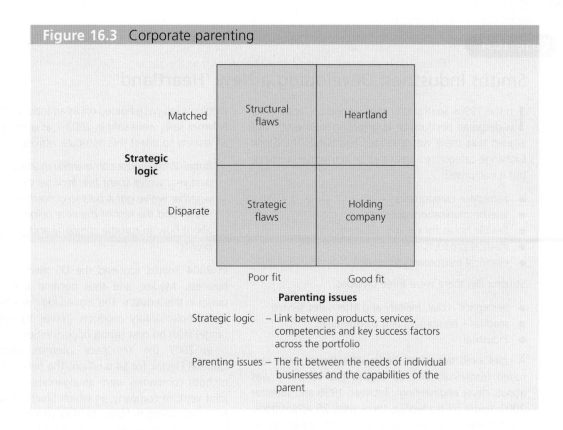

Figure 16.3   Corporate parenting

The assumption being made is that any individual business within the heartland should be able to achieve levels of success that it would not be able to achieve as an independent business or with another parent. At the same time, the parent organization should benefit both financially and strategically – in other words, other businesses in the portfolio benefit from the presence of the one under the spotlight. This implies a 'win–win' situation, whereas it can easily be a 'win–lose' or even a 'lose–lose' where the fit is so poor that there is a real resource distraction.

The relative success of conglomerate diversification is, therefore, largely an issue of strategy implementation, specifically the parenting skills of the acquirer, and the ability to add value for both the subsidiary and the parent. The basic argument is that the corporate portfolio should be based around a heartland of businesses that are in some way related. Any which are not, and especially where they are a potential or actual distraction, should be divested. As an organization divests in this way to refocus it is quite normal for this to be followed by, or concurrent with, acquisitions of related businesses to strengthen the core of the new focus. These points are illustrated in Case 16.4.

Figure 16.4 offers a framework for assessing the strategic logic of a proposed addition to the corporate portfolio. On one axis is the extent of the linkages and synergy in the existing portfolio; on the other axis is the relationship between the competencies required to run the new business effectively and the organization's existing competencies and capabilities. Logically, we are looking for a match – the top right quadrant. Where the existing match is low but the newcomer has similar competencies to certain existing businesses, there could be a logic in going ahead and divesting non-related activities at the same time – the bottom right quadrant. This could have the effect of strengthening the portfolio.

In the top left quadrant of Figure 16.4 there is the potential for an unrelated business to dilute value and synergy. An unrelated business added to a non-synergistic portfolio would merely enhance the strategic problems.

Case 16.4

Smiths Industries: Developing a New 'Heartland'   UK

In the 1990s Smiths Industries owned an 'apparently widespread portfolio of engineering businesses' but argued that there was a related heartland. The Stock Exchange categorized Smiths as an aerospace business, but it comprised:

- aerospace components
- telecommunications products
- flexible hoses for vacuum cleaners
- medical products
- electrical instruments for cars.

Structurally, there were three divisions:

- aerospace – civil, military and after-sales service
- medical – equipment and consumables
- industrial.

A chief executive, Keith Butler-Wheelhouse, was recruited from Saab and he argued the company was about 'clever engineering'. Between 1996 and summer 2000, under his leadership, there were 26 acquisitions, mainly bolt-on related businesses. The company delivered 'above average returns and profit growth from some unpromising sectors' and its share price performance was better than most engineering companies.

Butler-Wheelhouse argued that Smiths was:

- focused on niche markets and relatively small businesses
- spread across eight distinct markets such that no single business could make or break the whole organization
- able to generate a cash flow which can fund both organic growth and further acquisitions.

In 2000 Smiths acquired a 'big one'. Tube Investments, long associated with motor vehicles components, was diversified into seals (mechanical and polymer), fluid storage (cars and refrigerators) and aerospace (Dowty landing gear and general systems).

Smiths would continue to build its heartland around 'clever engineering' but the business was to be 're-invented' as an aerospace engineering business with interests in other high-growth niche opportunities – such as medical equipment and systems for detecting explosives. Various automotive businesses were put up for sale, with mixed success. In the end those that wouldn't sell were floated off as an independent group. Polymer seals were sold in 2003 – at a loss because of an anxiety to divest this non-core activity.

Butler-Wheelhouse commented in 2003 that 'in the past year we've spent five minutes wondering whether we've got a balanced portfolio of businesses and the rest of the time being concerned about how to run the company and generate profits'.

In 2004 Smiths acquired the US medical equipment business, Medex, and thus became a much bigger player in this industry. The argued logic was based more on complementary products (easier to sell a larger range) than on cost saving opportunities.

In 2007 the aerospace interests were sold to General Electric for $4.8 billion. The detection interests of both companies were amalgamated as a separate joint venture company, in which Smiths had a 64 per cent controlling holding. Neither company wanted to sell their detection interests to the other or to anyone else.

One year earlier the various contributions to revenue and profits had been:

2006	% of revenue	% of operating profits
Aerospace	36	29
Detection	12	15
Medical Equipment	21	27
Specialty Engineering	31	29

Butler-Wheelhouse retired in 2008. What exactly was his successor, Philip Bowman, inheriting? Would he split the rest of the business up or keep it intact? After all, his leading investors were arguing that 'the business was worth less than the sum of its parts'.

Bowman decided to divide the group into five parts – Medical Products (which would be based in the US), Detection (based in Watford in the UK) and three speciality engineering businesses, all to be based in America. The size of the UK headquarters was reduced substantially and more power devolved to the divisions.

Questions

1 How would you summarize the 'heartland' of Smiths Industries before and after the acquisition of Tube Investments?

2 What are your views on the 2003 quote from Keith Butler-Wheelhouse?

3 How significant (relatively) is corporate strategy and how significant is operational strategy to deliver results?

4 Do you believe that in 2009 the company has a strong heartland or is it realistically a holding company of diverse interests?

SMITHS INDUSTRIES **http://www.smiths-group.com**

Figure 16.4 Changing the corporate portfolio

Determining the heartland

The issues concern:

● first, whether the parent is able to provide – and is actually providing – the services and support the individual businesses need, and

● second, whether the businesses have the people and competencies to fulfil the expectations of the parent.

Goold *et al.* (1994) offer the following framework as a starting point for assessing the existence of, or potential for, a heartland.

1 Mental maps (or philosophies) of the parent, incorporating issues of culture and values and broad policies for dealing with events and opportunities.

2 Issues of structure, systems and processes – incorporating the style of corporate management. This would include: procedures for appointing, promoting and rewarding people; the relative significance of budgeting and financial reporting; strategic planning systems; and capital allocation procedures.

3 Central services and resources – what is provided centrally and what is devolved.

4 Key people throughout the organization; key functions; key skills and competencies.

5 The nature of any decentralization 'contracts' and expectations – linked to issues of power, responsibility and accountability; reward and sanction systems; and the expectations that subsidiaries can have for the support they receive from corporate headquarters.

The role and contribution of corporate headquarters

This section draws together many of the above issues by considering the role and contribution of company head offices. Typically, these will be larger and grander in centralized organizations; but historically powerful centres have generally been reduced in size, and their work distributed to subsidiaries, as corporations have become more decentralized and adopted flatter organization structures.

There are two fundamental purposes of corporate headquarters:

- serving the global legal and financial needs of the business, and
- supporting strategy making.

In general, this means that they:

- add and subtract businesses from the corporate portfolio
- create linkages to drive synergy throughout the organization – this can include rules or intercompany trading, opportunities for exchanging knowledge and ideas, and facilitating the sharing and transfer of assets
- design, support and maintain the organization structure – this will incorporate communications, the extent of the decentralization, the formality of systems and procedures, and systems for feedback and reward
- provide certain key services – at a minimum this will be a treasury and corporate secretarial service, but others can be added as well.

However, many head offices have historically provided a more extensive range of services to their constituent businesses, including for example:

- marketing
- management development and personnel
- property management
- centralized research and development
- corporate public relations
- industrial relations.

There is a clear need for head offices to add value to the corporation and not simply to spend the money earned by the businesses. With the recent trend for organizations to slim down the size and scope of head offices, in many cases only corporate strategy, financial reporting and control and secretarial/legal services remain centralized. Some head offices retain a responsibility for *policies* but not the activities.

Summarizing points made earlier, large, centralized head offices where all the key business heads are located in one place – Unilever has been a good example until recently – can control the corporation *efficiently*, but strategies can easily become top-down and slow to change. Decentralized organizations such as ABB in the 1990s (Case 14.5) push profit responsibility down to the businesses and empower managers. The head office provides more of a support role with few discrete functions. The new challenge is one of co-ordination.

In considering how head offices can best add value to the business as a whole, four broad issues must be addressed:

- how to control and co-ordinate the constituent businesses – issues of structure, corporate leadership and internal communications and synergy
- how to advise the strategic leader and keep him or her strategically aware
- driving performance and improvement through effective reward systems
- deciding which activities should be

  – provided from head office – for which a fee should be levied
  – devolved to the individual businesses
  – bought in from outside specialists.

The alternative approaches include the stand-alone holding company, financial control approach; centralizing specific functions and services; controlling strategic change at the corporate level; and fostering linkages, learning and sharing good practices.

Head offices can destroy value if they:

- become established as *the* perceived centre for expertise in the corporation – they cannot understand all of the important detail about competitiveness in their constituent businesses, whose managers will become demoralized if their potential contribution is not acknowledged
- assume that potential linkages and synergy will happen automatically
- duplicate effort and costs unnecessarily
- buy and sell businesses at the wrong prices
- create or perpetuate a culture where internal competition takes precedence over the need to compete with external rivals.

Here at head office, we don't go very deep into much of anything, but we have a smell of everything. Our job is capital allocation – both intellectual and financial capital. We smell, feel, touch, listen, then allocate.

JOHN F WELCH, WHEN CHIEF EXECUTIVE OFFICER, GENERAL ELECTRIC

16.6   The role of general managers

Basically, general managers co-ordinate the work of subordinate specialist managers; they are responsible for the management of strategy implementation and, in certain cases, strategy formulation. The chief executive or managing director of the company, the overall strategic leader, is a general manager. So too are the heads of divisions and business units, and the heads of operating units in a matrix structure. Their task is to match the resources they control with their particular environment effectively and to achieve E–V–R congruence.

Divisionalized organizations were examined in Chapter 14, where it was shown that the degree of decentralization and the power, authority and responsibility enjoyed by general managers will be affected by their relationship with head office and headquarters corporate staff. Whatever the extent of the decentralization from head office to business units, the business units themselves might be highly centralized. This depends on the style of management adopted by the particular general manager in charge.

Each division or business unit is part of a larger organization and corporate structure, and consequently it is not fully autonomous. While the organization as a whole has an external environment comprising customers, suppliers, competitors and shareholders among other influences, each division will have corporate headquarters as part of its environment. Business units may have both divisional headquarters and corporate head office in their environment. General managers in divisions and business units therefore do not have full responsibility for strategy creation and implementation. They can be pressurized by corporate headquarters, and they can turn to head office in their search for additional finance and other resources. The provision of finance within the organization may operate differently from the external market, but justification should still be required.

The relationship between general managers and head office will determine whether they are free to change their portfolios of business units and products or just adapt competitive and functional strategies. Performance measures and expectations will also affect this. Where specific short-term objectives and targets are set, and monitored strictly, general managers are less likely to focus on corporate changes and instead will concentrate on more immediate changes which can yield faster results. Their flexibility to make changes will increase as their targets become more vague and directional and less specific. Even though the general managers of business units may not be responsible for the formulation of changes in the corporate strategy which will affect their sphere of influence, they will invariably be responsible for the implementation of the changes.

General management skills and values

It has been established, then, that effective strategic management concerns issues of formulation and implementation. Strategic choices concern:

- the nature and orientation of the organization – the strategic perspective
- the deployment of its resources, ideally to achieve and sustain competitive advantage.

The strategic choice is implemented by the strategic leader, either the chief executive, the owner–manager in the case of a small business, or a general manager. It was pointed out in Chapter 9 that different strategic leaders (a) exhibit different patterns of behaviour and styles of management, and (b) will have different technical skills and biases as a result of their background. Arguably, alternative general managers would seek to implement basically the same strategy in different ways. The views of a number of authors concerning the relationship between general manager skills and particular strategies are discussed below.

Herbert and Deresky (1987) have examined the issue of match between the general manager and the strategy, concluding that the orientations and styles given below were important for particular strategies:

Strategy	Styles and qualities required
Development (start-up and growth)	Aggressive, competitive, innovative, creative and entrepreneurial
Stabilizing (maintaining competitive position)	Conservative, careful and analytical
Turnaround	Autonomous, risk and challenge oriented and entrepreneurial

Herbert and Deresky contend that financial skills are important for all strategies, with marketing skills being particularly important at the development stage and production and engineering skills invaluable for stabilizing strategies. This raises three issues.

1   Which specialist functional managers might be most appropriate for promotion to general management in particular circumstances? More recent research in the US confirms that the most typical background for large company chief executives is finance; the same pattern applies in the UK. Marketing, technical and manufacturing specialisms also feature but it is rare for a manager with a human resources background to become the strategic leader.

2 Is a change of general manager appropriate as products and businesses grow and decline and need changes in their strategies?

3 As strategies evolve and change should general managers adapt their styles of management accordingly?

Dixon (1989) suggests that *innovatory general management skills* are most required in the early and late stages of the life of a business or product in its present form. These skills are required to establish or recreate competitive advantage and, in the case of terminal decline, to find an alternative product, service or business. These changes are often best accomplished by outsiders with fresh ideas. Correspondingly, the constant search for efficiencies and improvements while an established product or business is maturing is normally best carried out by specialists.

A major problem with this type of innovation lies in the fact that changes in senior management, structure or values may be involved. The outlook and styles of general managers are likely to be different, and their responses to different sets of expectations and performance targets will vary. Again, this raises the issue of which managers are most appropriate for managing particular strategies.

There are similarities and differences in these various conclusions, reflecting again that there is no one best answer. The issue of match between general manager and strategy is important, and consequently one might expect that changes in one will lead to changes in the other.

Clearly, as organizations become flatter and more decentralized skills in synthesis and integration are critically important.

16.7 The modern organization

Kanter's view

Developing these arguments further, Rosabeth Moss Kanter (1989) has researched the general management skills required to run businesses effectively in the competitive environment of the late 1980s and the 1990s. We first mentioned these views in Section 9.4.1 of Chapter 9. Large companies, she contended, must be able to match corporate discipline with entrepreneurial creativity in order to become leaner and more efficient whilst being committed to both quality and innovation.

Three strategies are particularly important:

1 restructuring to improve synergy from diverse businesses

2 the development of joint ventures and strategic alliances to input new ideas

3 the encouragement of intrapreneurship within organizations.

The points are explained in greater detail in Critical reflection 16.1.

Kanter's main conclusion is that *process is more important than structure*. She suggests that:

- general managers must be able to balance maintenance and entrepreneurial skills (Chapter 9). We would argue for a balance of professional management skills and entrepreneurial skills. The combination of the professional organization with the entrepreneurial organization would be perhaps the best of both worlds.

- internal competition (typically fostered in organizations which are divided into discrete divisions and business units) can be harmful and impede synergy

- incentive and reward schemes should reflect the need for co-operation and support between business units

- the increasing incidence of joint ventures, which requires the forging of closer links with other external businesses, suggests that structures may need revision if the potential and desired synergy is to be achieved.

Critical reflection 16.1

Rosabeth Moss Kanter on Competitiveness

Future success lies in the capability to change and to accomplish key tasks by using resources more efficiently and more effectively. Organizations must be innovative and, at the same time, control their costs. Sustainable competitive advantage, however, does not come from either low costs, or differentiation, or innovation alone. It needs the whole organization to be *focused, fast, flexible and friendly*.

Being *focused* requires investment in core skills and competencies, together with a search for new opportunities for applying the skills. Intrapreneurship should be fostered to improve the skills constantly; and managers throughout the organization should be strategically aware and innovative. They should own the organization's mission, which, by necessity, must be communicated widely and understood.

Fast companies move at the right time, and are not caught out by competitors. New ideas and opportunities from the environment will be seized first. Ideally, they will be innovating constantly to open up and sustain a competitive gap, because gradual improvements are likely to be more popular with customers than are radical changes. However, instant success takes time – the organization culture must be appropriate.

Flexibility concerns the search for continual improvement. The implication is a learning organization where ideas are shared and collaboration between functions and divisions generates internal synergy. This, in turn, suggests that performance and effectiveness measures, and rewards, concentrate on outcomes.

Internal synergy can be achieved with cross-functional teams and special projects, and by moving people around the organization in order to spread the best practices. General Motors allows components and assembly workers, who work in separate plants in different locations, to contact each other by telephone to sort out problems and faults without relying on either written communications or messages which go 'up, across and down again'. These workers see each other as 'colleagues in the *whole* organization'. It is important that internal constraints (imposed by other functions and divisions) and which restrain performance are highlighted and confronted. To be effective this requires a clear and shared vision and purpose for the organization, decentralization and empowerment.

Friendly organizations are closely linked to their suppliers and customers to generate synergy through the added value chain. Such external collaboration may be in the form of strategic alliances.

Reference

The material in this box is summarized from: Kanter, RM (2000) *When Giants Learn To Dance*, Touchstone.

Handy's view

Charles Handy (first articulated in 1994, 1995) continues to contend that in order for companies to remain competitive internationally they have had to rethink their basic structures. 'Fewer key people at the heart of the organization, paid very well, producing far more value.' Handy acknowledges that it is quite feasible that corporations will continue to grow, either organically or through acquisition, but believes that either physically or behaviourally they need to be in small units, focused and closely networked to their suppliers and customers. More activities and components will be bought in from specialists than is the case at the moment; internally, they will also comprise networks characterized by subsidiarity, with the centre (as distinct from a traditional head office) doing only what the parts cannot do themselves. The real power will switch from the top of the organization to the businesses, and consequently a co-ordinating mission and purpose will be essential. Handy favours 'federalism' or reverse delegation – the centre acts on the bidding of, and on agreement with, the parts. Basically, Handy is supporting the decentralization trend, but going much further.

Supported by sophisticated information technology and systems, people will become recognized as the most important strategic resource and, because their expertise and intelligence is an intangible asset, largely unquantifiable, it will become harder to value the *real* assets of a business. Consequently, the appropriate measures of performance must be carefully evaluated, and reward systems will have to be derived which motivate and keep those managers who are potentially the most mobile. The valuable managers will not all be at the most senior levels. Disagreeing with many strategic leaders of global organizations, Handy believes that switching jobs regularly and moving people between different parts of the organization, perhaps to other countries, can be dysfunctional. Simply, they will not be in place long enough to become known and, in the future, trust will be an essential element in management, strategic change and strategy implementation.

> *We have designed organizations based on distrust. We have designed organizations so that people will not make mistakes. And, of course, we now encourage people to make mistakes because that is how they learn.*
>
> HANDY

Handy's arguments imply major changes to strategies, structures and styles of management for many organizations. Where these changes are simultaneous – amounting to *strategic regeneration* in effect – the changes are dramatic, painful and often difficult to carry through. This was discussed in Chapter 15.

> *Perhaps the most apposite definition of strategy for me is drawn from the world of chess. Strategy is knowing what to do when there is nothing to do; tactics is knowing what to do when there is something to do.*
>
> SIR TREVOR HOLDSWORTH, EX-CHAIRMAN, GKN, QUOTED IN THE
> *STRATEGIC PLANNING SOCIETY NEWS*, 1991

> *On 25 June 1876 General George Armstrong Custer was informed that a significant number of Indians were gathering at the Little Big Horn. Without further intelligence or analysis, he decided he would ride out with his 250 men to 'surround the Indians'. It is difficult for 250 soldiers to surround 3000 Indians – Custer made a serious error of judgement.*

16.8 Strategic resource management

Figure 16.5 recapitulates how the corporate mission and purpose provide the basis from which corporate and competitive strategies are derived. The corporate portfolio provides a number of ways for the organization to pursue its mission – but each business in the portfolio will require different levels of attention and resourcing. These decisions relate to priorities linked to the potential of, and desired outcomes from, each business. The achievement of competitive advantage and success comes down, in the end, to individual contributions, and to guide and manage these, objectives, targets and milestones will be set.

Once intended strategies have been determined, either in broad outline or in greater detail, the organization must plan their implementation. This means, first, that the resources required for implementation – including capital equipment, people and finance – are available where and when they are needed. Resources need to be *allocated* to different managers, functions and businesses, and then *co-ordinated* to generate synergy. Second, the managers responsible for implementation must understand what is expected of them and be empowered and motivated to take the necessary decisions and actions. In addition, *monitoring and control* systems are required.

At the corporate strategy level, organizations might establish priorities for different divisions and businesses using portfolio analysis, and evaluate the strategic and financial implications of alternative investments. Decisions may be taken within the constraints of existing capital,

Figure 16.5   Strategy implementation and resource management

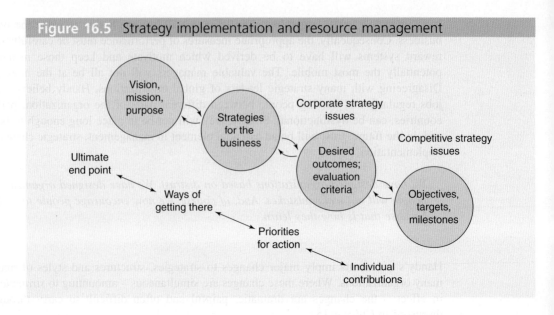

financial and human resources; if they demand new resources, then these must be obtained in an appropriate timescale. Proposed acquisitions may require an organization to raise funding externally; organic development of new products may require new skills and competencies. Resources can be switched from one part of a business to another.

At the functional level, *policies* and procedures can guide managers and other employees in the utilization of these corporate resources to add value, create competitive advantage and achieve the desired objectives. These policies can be tightly defined to maintain strong, central control, or very loose and flexible to enable people to use their initiative and be flexible. The ongoing management of the resources will then use action plans and budgets.

Action plans relate to the detailed strategies and plans for the various key functions, the activities which must be carried out if competitive and corporate strategies are to be implemented successfully; *budgets* add a crucial financial dimension to these plans. Together they attempt to integrate sales, supply potential, production activities and cash flow to ensure that resources are available to produce goods and services where and when they are required. The organization would like to avoid a situation where it has requests that it would like to take, or worse, it has booked orders, but it does not have the resources to enable production or supply. The potential danger here is one of over-trading and over-commitment. Both its bank and its customers can easily end up disappointed. It would also wish to avoid situations where it has idle capacity and no orders, or instances where it is producing for stock rather than for customers. This dilemma is one faced all the time by many small businesses, and in it we can see an endeavour to balance the resource-based perspective of strategy with the opportunity-driven approach.

This planning process then provides a useful check that the corporate and competitive strategies that have been formulated are both appropriate and feasible in the sense that they can be implemented. At the same time, this planning and budgeting must not be so rigid that the organization is unable to be responsive. Forecasts and judgements will never be completely accurate; when intended strategies are implemented there will need to be incremental changes and revisions to plans. To respond to new environmental opportunities and competitor initiatives, the organization will need to be adaptive. Emergent strategic change of this nature demands resource flexibility, at both the corporate and functional levels.

The plans should incorporate clear milestones – target levels of achievement against a timescale. By constant monitoring the organization can check whether it is booking sufficient business, whether it is producing the necessary quality on time, whether it is under-producing or over-producing, whether its costs and prices are different from those that it forecast, and whether it is managing the movement of cash in and out of the business to the budgeted targets.

A review of progress can highlight potential deficiencies to either resource requirements or likely outcomes. If orders are exceeding expectations, then additional resources may be required if the organization is to properly satisfy the new level of demand. If these cannot be found, schedules will need to be changed and maybe future supplies rationed. If orders are below expectations, then either new business opportunities will need targeting at short notice, possibly implying very competitive prices and low margins, or end-of-year targets revised downwards. Vigilance and pragmatism here can help to ensure that the organization does not face unexpected crises. Effective communications and management information systems are essential for planning, monitoring and control.

The allocation of resources at a corporate level is closely tied in to the planning system through which priorities must be established. Portfolio analyses such as the directional policy matrix may well be used to help to determine which products and business units should receive priority for investment funding; and any new developments that are proposed will require resources. An acquisition, for example, will need to be financed, but the integration of the new business after the purchase may also involve the transfer of managers and other resources.

Corporate resource planning and organization growth

Corporate resources may be allocated in different ways in line with the speed of growth of the organization and the degree of instability in the environment.

Rapid growth

Where the business overall, or selected business units within it, are growing rapidly the resource allocation process must be able to accommodate this growth and the consequent and possibly continual demand for additional resources. The process could be either centralized or decentralized, or a mixture of the two, influenced by the management style of the overall strategic leader and the interdependencies between the various parts of the organization.

If the process is centralized, priorities will be established by head office corporate staff using some formal planning system and periodic review of the potential of all business units. Business units will need to provide the necessary information. With a decentralized approach the priorities would again be decided centrally, but after allowing all divisions and business units to formulate their own preferred strategies and make their case for the corporate resources that they would require to implement their preferences. A mixed approach would involve resources for continuing activities being allocated through centralized mechanisms and incremental additions funded through a bidding process.

In all cases the decisions should balance the potential financial gains with the strategic logic implied. While divisions or business units may be making individual requests for resources to support certain programmes, the opportunities for synergy, sharing activities and transferring skills across activities should be assessed. In addition, the desirability of the implications of the various proposals for the overall strategic perspective of the organization should be considered.

Limited change and stability

Where businesses are growing more steadily and in a relatively stable environment, resource allocation for continuing programmes could be a straightforward extrapolation of previous budgets, incorporating an allowance for inflation. However, a mere continuation of present strategies without evaluation and proper review may lead to ineffectiveness.

Established policies, such as fixing advertising budgets at an agreed percentage of projected sales revenue or maintaining particular levels of stocks, are likely to be a key feature of this approach.

Decline situations

Where businesses or business units are in decline some quite tough decisions often have to be taken. Where the organization as a whole is in difficulty the strategic leader must search for new opportunities for redeploying resources. In the case of selected business units that are experiencing decline, unless there are opportunities for turnaround, resources should be transferred to activities with better growth and profit potential. In both cases the decisions are likely to be centralized, particularly as there may have to be structural changes to accommodate the rationalization, divestment or other strategic changes.

Once resources are allocated to divisions, business units and functions there will be further allocations to individual managers within each area; and this to a greater or lesser extent will be delegated to the general manager or functional manager in charge of each one. This is known as functional or operational resource planning; in the process it is important not to overlook any interdependencies between the budget holders.

Functional resource planning

When resources are allocated to functions, and to particular activities within functions, there are a number of essential considerations.

1 It is important to consider the relative importance of each function; the concept of the value chain, explained in Chapter 3, could prove helpful in establishing this.

2 Competitive advantage is established within functional activities; consequently, an appreciation of key success factors and competitive opportunities is crucial if the resource allocation is to lead to strategic effectiveness.

3 The important linkages between functions, which are the sources of potential synergy, should be considered. Any appropriate sharing of resources should be encouraged. To this end, activities should be complementary and supportive.

4 Where there are sequential dependencies, the whole resource allocation process must take account of these. For example, if activity Z is dependent upon activity X which precedes it, then it is both inefficient and ineffective to allocate resources to Z unless adequate resources are also given to X. An obvious application of this would be production activities which must be built around any bottlenecks. Similarly, the capacity of hospital operating theatres should be consistent with the number of beds available for recuperation.

Efficiency and effectiveness in resource allocation and management

It is important to consider both efficiency and effectiveness measures in relation to the allocation and deployment of resources. An examination of the way in which resources are employed and managed in the production and marketing of existing products and services can also be used to search for improvements. Savings in time and costs (without threatening quality) lead to higher productivity, higher profits and the freeing up of resources which can be deployed elsewhere. This is essentially a search for greater efficiency.

At the same time, it is also useful to consider whether resources are being allocated to those products, services and activities which are most important for the organization as a whole and for the achievement of its objectives. This analysis is applicable at organizational, divisional and business unit level – wherever there is an opportunity cost of the resources in question. If resources are finite and limited to the extent that choices have to be made concerning which products to concentrate resources on and which to give low priority to, then the opportunity cost of the resources should be considered. If growth or profitability or both are important objectives, the resources should be allocated to those products and services which can best fulfil the objectives. This is an assessment of effectiveness. However, as discussed above, it is important to ensure that sufficient resources are allocated to development programmes that will lead to growth and profits in the future.

If decisions are made to alter resource allocations and concentrate them in different areas, issues of managing change arise; these are considered in Chapter 15. It hould be appreciated that particular business units, products and services are likely to have their champions within the organization. Resource reductions in favour of alternative products may be resisted by certain managers. Their ability and willingness to resist change pressures from higher management will be related to their power bases and their ability to influence decisions. These issues also are considered in Chapter 15.

It is now appropriate to consider in more detail how resources are allocated to managers and how policies influence the way in which resources are used. Put simplistically, managers are allowed certain resources, which represent costs to the organization, and are then expected to use them to generate revenues and profits. The budgeting process determines how many of which resources managers are allocated. Their agreed objectives and targets concerning particular products and services determine how the resources are further deployed, and established policies influence the way in which they are deployed and managed.

Too many businesses spend money they have yet to earn to buy things they don't need to impress people they don't even like.

16.9 Management and control

Measurement and control systems

The need to measure and evaluate performance, and to make changes when necessary, applies at all levels of the organization. Budgets establish quantitative targets for individual managers, departments, business units and divisions. Progress against these targets can be measured through the information system; and the feedback should be both fast and accurate to enable any corrective actions to take place quickly.

The ability of all of these budget holders to achieve their targets will be useful when reviewing their futures.

When establishing budgets and performance targets it is, however, important to ensure that the attention of managers is not focused too narrowly on only their areas of responsibility. Their contributions to other managers and their commitment to the overall interests of the organization are the sources of synergy. While these measures of individual performances are crucial, the effectiveness of all functional, competitive and corporate strategies and their abilities to achieve corporate objectives are the ultimate measures.

The effectiveness of the contribution of such activities as research and development is difficult to assess, but this is no excuse for not trying.

Figure 16.6 summarizes these ideas and Figure 16.7 charts a number of possible performance measures – those on the right focus on efficiency and reflect a financial control culture; those on the left are crucial indicators of a commitment to service, quality and excellence. The culture of the organization will dictate which measures are given priority. Establishing such excellence measures requires a real attempt to reconcile the different expectations of the stakeholders. Where there is no common agreement, the objectives and measures selected will reflect the relative power of the various stakeholders. In any case, commercial pressures invariably focus attention on resource management and efficiencies, which are easier to set and monitor. There is then always

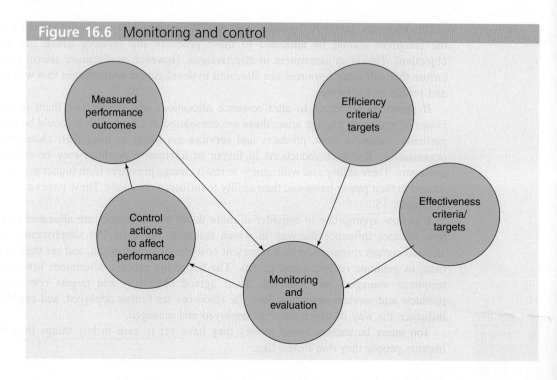

Figure 16.6 Monitoring and control

the danger that because efficiency measures are possible, and often straightforward, they may become elevated in significance and, as a result, begin to be seen as the foundation for the objectives. In other words, measurement potential rather than stakeholder satisfaction dictates objectives.

Performance expectations

Arguably the central issue in measurement and control is what is communicated to managers in terms of performance expectations, and how they are rewarded and sanctioned for their success or failure to achieve their targets. The two issues are linked, and resources should be allocated to enable managers to perform as required and, at the same time, to motivate them.

Reed and Buckley (1988) argue that when this is handled effectively then strategy implementation through action plans can be proactive, and strategies can be adapted in line with changes in the environment. Where it is poorly thought through there is likely to be more reaction to events and external threats. Research indicates that this aspect of implementation is difficult to achieve, however.

Wernham (1984) contends that managers benefit from an appreciation of 'superordinate organizational goals' and the overall strategic perspective, and that any perceived internal inconsistencies between the performances expected of different managers can be demotivating. Communication and information systems should therefore seek to make managers aware about where the organization is going strategically and how well it is doing. Wernham's argument also implies that resource allocations and strategic priorities should be seen as fair and equitable, and that political activity to acquire or retain resources for the pursuit of personal objectives, or to support ineffective strategies, must be contained.

McMahon and Perrit (1973) have demonstrated that the effectiveness of managers in achieving their objectives is enhanced when the control levers are high, but Lawrence and Lorsch (1967) indicate that these controls also need to be loose and flexible if the environment is volatile.

Figure 16.7 Some possible measures of performance

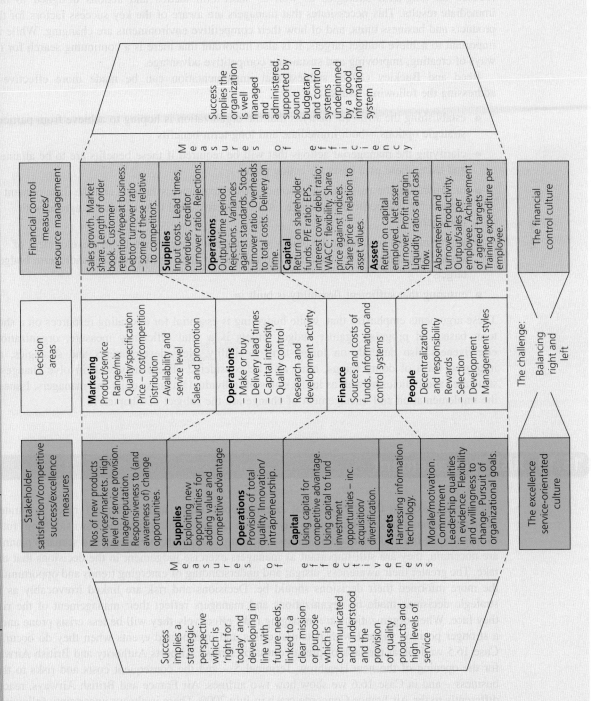

It has been argued that resources are allocated through the budgeting process and that this establishes a quantitative short-term link between expectations and resources. It has also been argued that managers need to be aware of wider strategic issues, and that their attention should be focused on long-term strategies as well as short-term tactics and actions designed to bring immediate results. This necessitates that managers are aware of the key success factors for their products and business units, and of how their competitive environments are changing. While it is important to achieve budget targets, it is also important that there is a continuing search for new ways of creating, improving and sustaining competitive advantage.

Reed and Buckley (1988) suggest that implementation can be made more effective by addressing the following issues:

- establishing the *strategic benefits* that the organization is hoping to achieve from particular strategic options – both immediate and long-term benefits
- clarifying the managerial actions that will be required if these benefits are to be attained, and using these as a basis for action plans
- incorporating the matching of resources with key success factors, and the development of sustainable competitive advantage, in the objectives and targets that are agreed with managers
- appraising and rewarding the ability of managers to contribute to the development of sustainable competitive advantage and not merely their ability to meet short-term budget targets
- ensuring that sufficient flexibility is built in.

These arguments emphasize that, while budgeting is essential for allocating resources on a short-term basis and progress against budget targets is a vital efficiency measure, organizational effectiveness also depends on longer-term flexibility. New developments and strategies, and improved ways of doing things, must also be considered. These may well involve changes in structures and policies as well as in the status of individual business units and managers. Issues in the implementation and management of change are the subject of Chapter 15.

16.10 Risk management

There are risks in the choices that organizations make and (different) risks in strategy implementation. The key elements in any risk are the potential upside and downside from future events and the likelihood of certain things happening. Although forecasting and scenario planning are uncertain, they are still important as managers exercise judgement in the decisions that they take. The greater their awareness, insight and understanding of emerging trends and opportunities, the more informed their decisions should be. Decisions and risk are linked irrevocably as the strategic decisions made by organizations and managers reflect their management of the risks they face. When organizations are managing risks effectively they will be less crisis prone and in a stronger position to deal with potential crises and unexpected events when they do occur. In Case 16.5 we look at the lack of preparedness by British Airports Authority and British Airways for the opening of the new Heathrow Terminal 5 – and the consequent costs and risks to their business – and in Case 16.6 we show how two airlines, Air France and British Airways, reacted differently to the Air France Concorde crash in July 2000. There is always uncertainty following a disaster such as this, but BA believed that its safety preparations were robust and it kept its Concordes in the air. Air France opted to ground its planes until it had more knowledge. Both airlines were fully aware of the interest of the world's media but they had different perceptions of the risk.

Case 16.5

BAA and Heathrow's Terminal 5

UK

In early 2009 the UK government approved the construction of a third runway at the UK's leading airport, London Heathrow. Anyone who travels through this airport will know how busy and congested it can be; but a new runway would be controversial as it would affect homes (that might need demolishing), transport networks and noise levels in the area. The immediate outcome was protests by people determined to voice their opposition to the development. This happened just months after problems with the opening of the newest terminal, Terminal 5, at Heathrow.

The new terminal 'belonged' to British Airways (BA) but the airport is controlled and managed by BAA, British Airports Authority. The terminal had been due to be fully functional in April 2008, and whilst it did open it wasn't ready. It had cost £4.3 billion and it would allow BA to move many flights from other terminals, especially Terminal 4, thus freeing up space there for other airlines – although considerable work was required to make Terminal 4 ready for other airlines to move in.

As soon as the terminal opened it was clear that staff were not coping. Many were finding it hard to even get to work on time because of parking problems and tight security checks once they arrived on site. This was compounded by staff shortages in key areas. Check-in queues were consequently lengthy and either flights were delayed or cancelled, or passengers missed their flights. Temporary marquees were erected outside the terminal to accommodate people who could not access the terminal building itself because of the sheer numbers of people ahead of them.

Bags were not being loaded on to planes because of systems problems in baggage handling and also because of inadequate staff training in the new procedures. This applied to both new check ins and transfers. Simply, bags were being checked in and transferred in faster than staff could take them off the belts and route them to where they should be going for their onward flight. Thousands of cases went astray for a period of time – if not permanently. The media carried stories of enterprising business people who were buying (unseen) job lots of lost bags – hoping they were buying cases with valuables and clean clothes rather than dirty washing!

Very quickly it was announced that the opening would be cancelled and postponed until the summer. More extensive training and testing would take place. Both BA and BAA were seen as accountable in different ways. The pilots' union, BALPA, claimed BA needed a 'major management and management style shake-up'. BA's response was that it had taken a 'calculated risk' opening up in April and that things had gone wrong – BA admitted it had 'compromised on the test programme'.

BA's Chief Executive, Willie Walsh, further admitted the self-imposed problems in the first five opening days cost the airline £16 million. But, he said, their analysis indicated delaying the opening would have been more expensive. The problem ... the opening was subsequently delayed! Certain management staff left BA. Shortly afterwards staff also left BAA, including the person responsible for overseeing the opening of the new terminal.

Further down the line, and prior to the real opening in August 2008, came an expensive advertising campaign designed to 'restore confidence'. Some wondered whether this would only serve to remind people of the much-publicized chaos four months earlier.

All of these problems arose at a time when BAA was under attack for quite different reasons. The UK Competition Commission had been investigating BAA and concluded it was too powerful and in control of too many airports. BAA was originally in the public sector but it was one of the companies privatized by the Thatcher government in the 1980s. Much more recently it had been bought by the Spanish company Ferrovial.

BAA ran three airports in the London area, Heathrow, Gatwick and Stansted, three in Scotland, Glasgow, Edinburgh and Aberdeen, and also Southampton. Its powerful position was adjudged to be causing 'adverse consequences for consumers' – there was some feeling that it had become too focused on exploiting its lucrative retail and catering concessions. There had to be some reason why too many passengers and flights were being delayed.

The Commission ruled – subject to further discussion and possible appeal – that BAA should sell two London and one Scottish airport. BAA responded that the ruling was 'disproportionate' and that Heathrow would not be sold under any circumstances.

It soon emerged that others were interested in Gatwick. These included a consortium involving Virgin

Atlantic and also Manchester Airport, which also owns East Midlands Airport. One sting in the tail is that these forced sales might have to go through during the economic recession when prices would be far lower than earlier valuations of the assets.

Questions

1 To what extent do you think the tough ruling might have been affected by BAA's involvement in the aborted opening of Terminal 5?
2 Is this an (other) example of good strategy and poor implementation?

© GREG BALFOUR EVANS/ALAMY

Case 16.6

Air France, British Airways and the Concorde Disaster   UK Eur

Concorde

To understand the impact of a major accident with Concorde a number of background factors must be remembered.

- Concorde became a symbol of pride for Britain and France.
- Technologically it was a triumph.
- People have always made efforts to see it, let alone wanted to fly in it.
- The project helped to cement Anglo-French relations when the UK was wanting to be seen to be European.
- It proved that two countries could work together and challenge American dominance of the aerospace industry. In this respect it was a forerunner to the Airbus consortium.
- The project ran late and was heavily over budget.
- The plane was barred from flying overland at supersonic speeds because of the noise factor.
- Only two airlines ever flew it – when it began both were nationalized. British Airways (BA) has since been privatized.
- The BA Concorde services paid their way operationally, but all of the development costs were absorbed by the British and French governments – in today's money some £9 billion was absorbed.
- The services were mainly London and Paris to New York, but there were some UK to West Indies flights and a wide range of charter opportunities.

- In 1999 BA earned £140 million in revenues and Air France £70 million from Concorde – BA's services were marginally profitable; Air France lost money.

The first crash of a Concorde plane happened on the last Tuesday of July 2000. The passengers on the Air France flight from Paris to New York were German tourists flying out to meet a cruise ship. The plane was seen to be on fire before it even left the ground at Charles de Gaulle airport, but once Concorde has reached a certain speed on the runway take-off cannot be aborted. Two minutes later it had crashed onto a hotel on the outskirts of Paris. Altogether 113 people, the bulk of them passengers and air crew, died. The whole sequence of events was filmed by two amateur video-makers and so the disaster was very high profile.

Immediate speculation blamed an engine fire. There are two engines slung under each wing and those on one side had been clearly on fire. Moreover, the flight had been delayed in Paris while one of these engines was repaired. However, the landing gear was still down: in the little time he had available the pilot had reported that the hydraulics had also failed. Why?

In the event it was to transpire that a rogue strip of metal on the runway had punctured a tyre, and then tyre debris had punctured a fuel tank incorporated in the wing. It later became apparent that the metal strip had probably been jettisoned from a Continental Airlines DC10 a few minutes earlier. The escaping fuel was ignited by the heat of the adjacent engines. The engines, and in turn the engineers who had repaired one of them, were not to blame. But, of course, the fact the fuel container could be punctured in the way it was caused huge concern.

The Air France response

- The chairman went to the crash site immediately, signalling a personal involvement.
- All five remaining Concordes were grounded immediately, communicating that safety was the first priority.
- Later, the chairman attended a number of the family funerals and was available to talk to families of the victims.
- Air France provided free flights for relatives to and from Germany.
- Interim compensation payments were offered.

British Airways

BA opted to keep its seven Concordes flying, although flights were suspended for the first 24 hours. This determination continued even when one had to make an emergency landing in Newfoundland after passengers complained that there was a smell of smoke in the cabin.

BA's pilots were happy about this – they had no fears for the aircraft's safety. Their representatives, together with retired pilots, were all happy to be interviewed by television reporters to confirm this view. Passengers were generally undeterred as well.

It transpired that in 24 years of flying there had been 70 previous incidents where tyres had burst, but never with catastrophic consequences. As a result of this BA had made certain modifications to the wheels which Air France had not copied. In addition, BA used new tyres (Air France used remoulds) which it changed regularly, after a fixed (and limited) number of take-offs or landings.

On 15 August, some three weeks after the crash, BA announced that it too was grounding its Concordes. This pre-empted the withdrawal of its Certificate of Air Worthiness by the Civil Aviation Authority (CAA) on 16 August. Air France commented that it was surprised that it had taken as long as it had.

Senior BA pilots demanded an immediate reprieve and suggested that it could be a ploy by France to end Concorde flights altogether because they were afraid of the cost of possible modifications that might be necessary.

The UK Civil Aviation Authority

The CAA duly withdrew the Certificate of Air Worthiness, in reality a very rare event. The only time this had happened before as the result of a civil accident was when McDonnell Douglas DC10s were grounded temporarily in 1979.

The CAA was asked why it had not acted earlier. The reply was that there had been speculation but no concrete evidence. Only now was the cause of the accident clear. The CAA emphasized its belief that Concorde remained a safe aircraft but that (as yet unspecified) modifications would be required. There was, however, a real concern that a tyre burst had been able to trigger the catastrophic chain of events that followed. Some commentators believed that the reluctance of Air France to restore Concorde services implied that there was an unacceptable risk with the plane.

Final outcomes

Ways to protect the fuel containers were devised – based on a kevlar protective lining – and modifications were made by British Airways. Concorde was allowed to fly again – and did. Services to New York were restored. But in the meantime 9/11 had happened, affecting demand for air transportation. And passengers had become more accustomed to (cheaper) first class travel in 'ordinary' aircraft. Transatlantic flights might take longer, but the new first class cabins had private sleeping areas and completely flat beds. One downside to Concorde was the relative lack of seating space – it was not a large aircraft. Ticket sales did not reach the levels enjoyed before the crash. BA decided that maintenance and other costs did not justify keeping Concorde in the air and its final flight was in October 2003. The remaining aircraft are grounded museum pieces.

Questions

1 Regardless of the actual facts and motives, whose reputation do you think might be most enhanced (or at least protected) by its reaction and behaviour?
2 Did BA do the right thing in the circumstances or should it have reacted differently?
3 Did this disaster merely accelerate the inevitable? Had it not happened, would Concorde still be flying today?

Strategic risks

Risk can be best understood as an uncertain prediction about future behaviour in a market or industry, with a chance that the outcome of this behaviour could be detrimental to an organization. Clearly, an organization must try to manage these risks to reduce both the likelihood of a particular event and the extent of any possible downside. In turn, this demands a clear understanding of the inherent risks in decisions and situations.

Opportunities and strategies that involve new customers, new markets, new countries and/or new competencies all imply risk – an element of chance that something can go wrong. The greater the potential impact (the downside) of what could go wrong, the greater the risk. This reinforces the value of a heartland of related businesses, which in turn should reduce the number of risk variables. When a company moves away from what it knows it increases its risk because there are more unknown factors. At the same time, not changing in a dynamic environment can also be very risky! Futures, simply, are uncertain.

Companies, then, must make strategic choices – and sometimes they get it wrong. Sometimes what appears to be a poorly judged choice can be turned around with appropriate changes during the implementation phase. It follows, therefore, that risk is best managed in an organization that has a culture of flexibility and innovation and is successful at getting its people involved and committed.

Certain business environments involve higher risks than others. High-technology industries, where there is constant innovation and technological change, involve high levels of risk. In pharmaceuticals it takes a number of years to develop and test a new drug before it can be introduced on to the market, and for much of this time there will be a real possibility that the new drug may never become a commercial success. A third example is oil exploration. Oil companies have to invest several million pounds in the hope of finding oil. While they can reduce their risk with sophisticated geological surveys before full exploration is embarked upon, there is always a risk of failure and loss of investment.

Summarizing the points so far, risk occurs whenever anyone must make a choice and the potential outcomes involve uncertainty. If a manager is faced with a decision and the alternative choices involve estimated potential gains and losses which are not certainties, the situation involves risk. The outcome of a typical decision will be dependent on a number of factors, such as customer reaction, levels of demand and competitor responses. Some managers will understand the situation better than others might, and partly for this reason be happier to accept the risk involved in a particular choice. Personality also affects the willingness to accept and take a particular risk. It is important that there is compatibility between the strategic leader's attitude towards risk and the demands of the industry. A risk-averse strategic leader in a high-risk industry may miss valuable opportunities.

Risk increases as the amount of potential loss increases. As a simple example, a person might be offered a ticket in a raffle which costs £1.00, and the chance of winning the first prize of £150 might be 1 in 200. Another person might be offered the opportunity to invest £100 with a similar 1 in 200 chance of winning £15,000. Although the odds of winning and losing are identical, the risk involved in each situation is different. The potential loss in the second case is 100 times greater than in the first, and it consequently involves greater risk. The key issues are the uncertainty (the odds of certain eventualities, and which may or may not be predictable) and the amount that could be lost.

The following four criteria are important in the decision:

- the attractiveness of each option to the decision-maker
- the extent to which he or she is prepared to accept the potential loss in each alternative
- the estimated probabilities of success and failure
- the degree to which the decision-maker is likely to affect the success or failure.

Case 16.7 examines the inherent risks and uncertainty in the decision by the UK government to bid for the 2012 Olympics.

Case 16.7

The 2012 Olympics UK

The UK was awarded the 2012 Olympic Games to great jubilation and celebration in 2005. As always there had been serious competition with the main rival appearing to be Paris. The government, led at that time by Tony Blair, had been strongly in favour. The bid team was led by Barbara Cassani (the retired CEO of Go, the low cost airline sprung out of BA and sold on to EasyJet); the ex-Olympic gold medallist and MP (Lord) Sebastian Coe was her deputy. Soon afterwards Cassani stepped down and Coe took over the leadership. Many retired Olympians and other sports personalities and celebrities lent their weight to the promotional campaign, designed to persuade the country that this was a good bid to have won.

But it soon became apparent just how much of a challenge implementing this was going to be. Beijing was investing billions in a very successful and high profile 2008 Olympics. London's initial budget was never going to be enough to come close to these standards. As the Olympic flag was ceremonially handed over when the 2008 Games concluded, it was stated that London would be different and not such a high profile event. A few months later, as the economic recession took hold, the problems were exacerbated as the private sponsorship money incorporated into the bid and the budget seemed less and less likely to come through.

Although there were critics, it was also apparent that this was a great opportunity for the UK to have a global visibility, and that London's East End would benefit enormously from the economic regeneration involved in building stadia and an Olympics village for the athletes. Transport would be improved – but arguably this would have happened anyway and so these costs should not be wholly factored into the calculations. On the other hand, as many pointed out, the recent reconstruction of Wembley Stadium had been late and over-budget. Are events like this something the UK is good at?

Money needed to be spent on:

- New stadia and facilities
- Operating the games
- The athletes' village
- Security
- Redevelopment
- Transport

- *Plus secondary investment in the relevant sports to increase the country's chances of medals at the Games.*

The money to pay for all this would come from:

- Lottery funding (a dedicated twice-weekly game, Dream Number)
- Television rights
- Sponsorship and merchandising
- Ticket sales
- Licensing deals
- London taxpayers
- The government.

In 2006 it emerged that VAT would have to be paid on many of the construction projects, thus increasing their costs. A year later it was apparent that the costs were now going to be in excess of £9 billion, some three times the amount stated when the bid document was first sent to the Olympics Committee. Some were also questioning whether the new venues would really be valuable once the event was over.

Although strong rumours started in 2008, in early 2009 it was clear that funding for certain Olympics sports would be less than they had been hoping for. In 2008 cycling, rowing and sailing had all performed well, but, in respect of medals won and also expectations, athletics was disappointing. The 'winners' and those with the best medal prospects were always more likely than the others to gain future funding. Less prominent sports were likely to have to build their teams on reduced funds. The funds for shooting, for example, appeared to be enough for a team of around 10, when over 40 had been the target number. 'Team GB may not be able to field a team in every Olympic sport.'

It was commented that the overall body, UK Sport, and the individual sports themselves, had not set about securing private sponsorship when economic circumstances were strong, and instead relied on public funds – now, in a recession, it may be too late.

Questions

1 Should the UK have bid for the 2012 Olympics?
2 Is this potentially a 'great idea' but one with serious implementation implications?

Extension question

In 2007 the Football Association confirmed it was serious about bidding for the 2018 World Cup – and it did indeed bid in 2009. The UK has only hosted the football World Cup once, in 1966, when England won – the only time that it has. The event should be more straightforward as most of the stadia will have been built regardless. Does this bid make (more) sense?

© LONDON 2012/HANDOUT/REUTERS/CORBIS

Risk, entrepreneurship and decision-making

In considering risk in an organization a number of factors are worth investigating. It may well have an effect if the strategic leader is a significant shareholder rather than a minor one. Similarly, in the case of managers throughout the organization who are involved in strategic decisions in various ways, the culture and values of the organization with regard to reward for success and sanction for failure will be important. Here we are returning to the subject of entrepreneurs and intrapreneurs.

Entrepreneurs are often described as risk takers. Indeed, they do take risks, including a personal risk – it is their business, often their money and usually their reputation that is at stake. This personal risk can increase as the business becomes more successful and visible. The rewards for entrepreneurial success can be very high; the social stigma of a major failure can be traumatic.

The issue of entrepreneurs and risk is a complex one. There is an argument that risk awareness and opportunity awareness should be separated. Risk then concerns that which can be quantified, and opportunity that which is much more judgemental. A professional manager, trained in a business school, may well seek to measure and evaluate the risk in the decisions that he or she has to take. Where there is an uncertain opportunity he may well perceive the risk to be too great. There is a potential downside that he is anxious to avoid. Entrepreneurs are aware of both but are attracted by the opportunity.

In chasing an uncertain opportunity, then, the entrepreneur is taking a risk. Sometimes entrepreneurs have a feel for, or an insight into, a situation and an opportunity. This may be the outcome of learning from previous experiences. Basically, though, they know what they are doing; and in many instances they do not see themselves taking major risks; in which case, they are really *managing* the risks, even though they may not be able to quantify them. They are accepting and retaining the inherent risk and going ahead. Other people, whose understanding of the situation, and perception of the inherent risk, is different, may be unwilling to take the same risk. They do not pursue the opportunity.

Some successful entrepreneurs also recognize when an opportunity is beginning to disappear and they time their exit carefully, and focus their endeavours on a new opportunity. This is an excellent illustration of risk management, for they are seeking to avoid future risks.

A case can also be made that entrepreneurs have a lack of risk awareness. In other words, they either elect not to quantify the risks, or they simply turn a blind eye to them. Their philosophy is one of 'take things as they come'. They accept that things will not proceed straightforwardly or go according to plan, and so they brace themselves to deal with the setbacks and challenges as they occur. They have a great faith in their courage and their ability to deal with these setbacks – and in many instances this is good judgement on their part. They are creative and innovative and they do overcome the difficulties, often turning a potential threat into a new opportunity.

Their perception of risk will change over time and with experience. Once an entrepreneur has grown one venture successfully he or she is likely to develop confidence alongside their experience. The notion here is in the concept of entrepreneurial learning. Do entrepreneurs (or some entrepreneurs) really learn from their mistakes and if so what do they learn and how does this learning manifest itself? The canny entrepreneur will accumulate a 'pot of capital' that can be reinvested in a way that does not imply bankruptcy if something goes wrong. Some entrepreneurs, however, start with a failure. Kets de Vries (1997) articulates a view that many entrepreneurs do indeed start in this way but are then determined to start all over again with a fresh risk. They are convinced that the world is against them – there is a resentment of people who succeed – and so failure can be expected. Their challenge is to have another go, but this time to succeed. 'The b*******s won't get me a second time.'

Attitudes towards risk affect the way in which all managers make decisions. Dunnette and Taylor (1975), whose research involved industrial managers, concluded:

> *High risk takers tended to make more rapid decisions, based on less information than low risk takers, but they tended to process each piece of information more slowly ... although risk-prone decision makers reach rapid decisions by the expedient of restricting their information search, they give careful attention to the information they acquire.*

Environmental factors may prove significant. The availability and cost of finance, forecasts of market opportunities and market buoyancy, and feelings about the strengths and suitability of internal resources will all be important. For other managers within the organization the overall culture and styles of leadership and the reward systems will influence their risk taking.

Managing risk

The term 'risk management' is often associated with the idea of insurance and, indeed, insurance is relevant, but it is too narrow a perspective.

Organizations will often pursue strategies that seek to manage or minimize risk. Hanson (Online Case 16.1), for example, always investigated the downside in any strategy or proposed deal. Lord Hanson said of his late partner, Lord White: 'We would actually have done a lot more deals if Gordon did not have so many worries. He is constantly looking for the potential trouble in a deal.' The whole Hanson strategy was based on spreading risk. The small corporate headquarters retained the overall financial risk for the organization; all of the market risks were delegated to the individual businesses. When Richard Branson started Virgin Atlantic Airways, clearly a high-risk venture, he was cautious and spread his risk in a different way. He began with just one Boeing plane on sale or return for one year. Stelios with EasyJet did much the same thing, leasing aircraft and effectively leasing sub-contracted staff.

The first main step in risk management is clarifying the risks involved. There are four elements:

- personal risk
- opportunity risk
- (business) environmental risks, and
- resource-based risks.

Table 16.2 provides a framework for evaluating the environmental and business risks.

The second step is deciding what to do about the various risks, selecting from a number of alternatives:

- *retain* the risk and prepare for possible eventualities – some risks have to be taken or an opportunity or a venture would have to be abandoned
- *transfer* the risk – this could be achieved by switching it to someone else (divesting a business), diluting it (through a joint venture or strategic alliance) or insuring against it
- *regulate* the risk, perhaps by investing to reduce it.

Table 16.2   Assessing business risks

Type of risk	Example
External environmental risks	
Supply risks	Over-dependency on a supplier
	Outsourcing something which is strategically critical
Market/demand risks	Customer preference changes
Stakeholder risks	Misjudged priorities
Social responsibility and ethical issues	Failure to deal effectively with a chemical spill or a major incident
Politico-economic risks	Turbulence in an overseas market
Innovation risks	Misjudging market acceptance for a new idea
Competitive risks	Existing competitors 'out-innovate' the business
	Price competition
	Powerful new rivals enter the industry
Resource-based risks	
Materials risks	Need to handle/transport dangerous materials
Process risks	Corner-cutting to save time and money
Managerial risks	People's ability to cope with the dynamics of change in the organization
People risks	Inadequate or inappropriate training
Commitment risks	Individuals do not pull their weight, especially in a crisis
Structural risks	Inappropriate balance between centralization (for control) and decentralization (for flexibility)
	Internal barriers to co-operation
Complexity	The spread of activities is too complex and leads to fragmentation and internal conflict
Financial risks	Undercapitalization
	Cash-flow problems
Technology risks	Inadequate information systems

If you make a mistake in the UK you have had it … consequently we have a low expectation of achievement and too many people try and survive by not making a screw-up. In America they don't consider you're a businessman until you've screwed something up, because by definition you are not pushing at the frontiers. Almost everything done in the UK, by banks as well as companies, is an endeavour not to make a mistake – and when this happens we are never in front.

SIR JOHN HARVEY-JONES, EX-CHAIRMAN, ICI

Silicon Valley is a graveyard … failure is Silicon Valley's greatest asset.

There is a belief that in some instances organizations do not take certain risks sufficiently seriously. They place people's lives in danger – either by not appreciating the existence of a risk, or by ignoring the dangers. With some health and safety regulations it is clearly cheaper to ignore and pay a fine if caught out rather than invest to regulate the risk in the first place. Safety demands on the railways were stepped up after the tragic crashes at Paddington and Hatfield – the downside is delays and increased costs. In 2000 UK civil servants began drafting a new bill to revise the law on corporate manslaughter. The proposal was that where a company can be shown to have been negligent, and lives have been lost, individual senior managers could be held accountable and sentenced to imprisonment. The intention is to circumvent the 'collective failure' defence. The legislation that came from this is the Corporate Manslaughter and Corporate Homicide Act 2007 which means, for the first time, companies and organizations can be found guilty of serious management failures resulting in a gross breach of duty of care.

Clarke and Varma (1999) argue that changes in the external business environment mean that satisfying stakeholders effectively is more risky and uncertain for organizations than it was in the past. Risk management has really become a strategic issue but too many organizations still treat it tactically and piecemeal. As a consequence they are more crisis prone than ideally they should be. This is the subject of the next section.

The risk-taking organization

Drawing together a number of points discussed earlier in the book, Birch and Clegg (1996) list a number of characteristics that will restrict risk taking by individual managers and employees:

- centralized and/or committee decision-making
- adherence to formal systems and budgets
- reliance on performance rewards based on preset (and inflexible) plans
- early evaluation of new ideas and proposals
- mistakes being sanctioned too readily (arguably making the same mistake more than once should be punished, of course!)
- management by fear
- a culture of caution.

Risk taking can be encouraged by:

- decentralization and informality
- initiatives and projects which cut across organizations
- rewarding managers and employees for new initiatives which have succeeded
- providing resources to develop new ideas
- limited adherence to 'badges of office' and job titles
- encouraging and respecting learning
- trusting people and encouraging them to enjoy what they do – a culture with an element of fun.

Remember chaos in time of order. Watch out for danger and chaos while they are still formless.

SUN TZU, SOME 2000 YEARS AGO

16.11   Crisis avoidance and management

Crisis management concerns the management of certain risks and future uncertainties. Organizations should be ready to deal with both opportunities and surprises, and resources should be managed to cope with unexpected and unlikely events in the organization's environment: E–V–R (environment–values–resources) congruence again. It is important strategically because failure to deal effectively with crises can lead to losses of confidence, competitiveness, profits and market share.

Crisis management involves elements of planning and management. Planning constitutes crisis prevention or avoidance – the search for potential areas of risk, and decisions about reducing the risks. Management is being able to deal with crises if and when they occur. The way in which organizations do deal with crises can either enhance or damage their reputation. After all, there is always going to be an economic cost and there is little logic in trying to avoid it. Case 16.8 looks at how Swissair and TWA reacted to two separate air crashes, with different outcomes for each airline. Swissair was judged to have coped well and received considerable praise for its behaviour. However, this did not prevent the company becoming insolvent and ceasing to trade.

Simplified, there are three decision areas in determining the crisis strategy:

Case 16.8

TWA and Swissair – Two Different Responses to a Crash   US, Eur

In 1996 a TWA jet en route from New York to Europe came down off Long Island shortly after take-off. TWA was accused of incompetence and insensitivity for the way in which it responded to queries from families of the victims. The Mayor of New York and the media were both critical of TWA. Lasting damage was done to the airline's reputation. What had happened?

- Publication of the passenger list was delayed until every victim's family had been contacted.
- A special toll-free number was set up but calls went unanswered.
- Only limited help was provided for families of the victims who wanted to travel to the crash scene.

In reality, TWA was not a wealthy airline and it had only limited resources with which to respond to an incident of this nature. Moreover, there was immediate speculation that the crash might be the work of terrorists and, consequently, government agencies intervened and banned relatives from the crash site.

Several years after the crash there was still uncertainty as to its cause. Terrorism had been officially ruled out and an electrical fault linked to an internal fuel tank was thought to be the most likely explanation. To this day some interested parties retain a real conviction that there has been a cover up and believe a Stinger missile was used by terrorists to attack the TWA flight.

Two years later, in September 1998, a Swissair flight out of New York plunged into the sea off the coast of Nova Scotia. Swissair was praised for its efficiency and compassion; public confidence in the airline remained intact. This time the Mayor of New York was full of praise.

- The passenger manifest was published within hours.
- Families were provided with quick access to crisis counsellors.
- Flights from Switzerland to the crash site were organized, and families were provided with expenses for the trip.

Swissair was provided with support from its code-share partner, Delta Airlines, which immediately seconded its full crisis team. Moreover, the response was affected by new legislation which had been enacted after the TWA crash.

The issues from the two contrasting incidents are:

1 The speed of response in the first 24 hours is critical. This is the 'make-or-break' period. If confidence is not built with the affected families in this time then conflict will follow.
2 Rehearsal really helps.
3 Money has to be found and spent to do what is necessary. This is clouded by a cultural issue in America, where there is a fear that providing financial assistance for travel and accommodation could merely provoke additional litigation as it implies an admission of guilt.

Footnote

In 2001 TWA was acquired by its larger rival, American Airlines. Also in 2001 Swissair collapsed – it could not pay its bills. It was first rescued as Swiss International Air Lines and then acquired by Lufthansa in 2005.

Source of basic material: Tomkins, R (1998) *Moments that build or destroy reputations, Financial Times*, 29 September.

Questions

1 What are the key lessons for all organizations from the alternative reactions illustrated here?
2 Are there any comparisons or contrasts with the situation described in the case on the Concorde crash?

THE FLIGHT 800 INVESTIGATION
http://www.twa800.com

1 Decisions concerning what can go wrong, the probability of it happening, and the impact it will have if it does happen.

2 Crisis planning – decisions about investing in prevention in order to reduce or minimize the risk. Invariably this implies cost increases; and for this and other reasons less is often done than it conceivably could be done.

3 Mechanisms for contingency management.

The decisions involve trade-offs between costs and risks in an attempt to find the best balance between points 2 and 3. The successful management of crisis situations involves both awareness and the ability to deal effectively with unexpected change pressures.

Fire provides a useful example of these points. Fires are caused by such events as smoking, overheating machinery and electrical faults. All of these are predictable. The likelihood of a fire happening will differ from situation to situation, and the potential damage will similarly vary. Smoking can be banned and all conceivable safety measures can be invested in, if necessary, in order to minimize the risks. However, these may not always be practical or affordable, and consequently detectors, sprinklers and fire doors to isolate areas are used as contingency measures. Nuclear power generation and airlines are examples of businesses which invest substantially in safety and prevention, often led by legislation. Situations are, however, frequently unclear. In 1991, following research after the 1985 fire on board a Boeing 737 at Manchester Airport, the Civil Aviation Authority (CAA) ruled out the use of passenger smoke hoods on aircraft. The CAA argued that they delayed the time required to evacuate an aircraft and thereby risked causing more deaths. The Consumers' Association is one group who disagreed, saying that it was 'outraged' at the decision.

Similarly, and as an outcome of 9/11, there have been demands for armed sky marshals to travel on aircraft on certain routes. This has been standard practice on El Al (Israel's national airline) for many years. The reaction of American airlines to this suggestion has been much more supportive than most European airlines.

Defining crises

The word *crisis* covers a number of different issues and events, and it includes a mixture of technical and managerial elements. Some incidents are clearly 'thinkable' and efforts can be made to avoid them or reduce their potential impact. Others remain more unthinkable. Fires, fraud and computer failure are typical crises that might affect any organization almost any time. Poisoning scares or contamination with food products, and oil or chemical spillages, are foreseeable crises for particular companies. Major transport accidents, when they happen, are crises for the railway, shipping company or airline involved. Sometimes, but not always, the accident will prove to have been preventable. In relation to these there is an obvious logic in making contingency plans and being prepared. In addition, organizations can sometimes be affected by natural disasters, events outside their control.

Shrivastava *et al.* (1988) provide us with a valuable definition for a major crisis: 'Organizationally-based disasters which cause extensive damage and social disruption, involve multiple stakeholders, and unfold through complex technological, organizational and social processes'.

Figure 16.8 provides a framework for categorizing different incidents. On one axis is the issue of 'thinkability', while the horizontal axis separates the planned from the unplanned response. Here the terms 'crisis management' and 'disaster management' are used as a convenient form of separating the planned and unplanned response to a major event. We feature four examples in the diagram. The roll-on roll-off car ferry *Herald of Free Enterprise* sank in 1987 as it was leaving Zeebrugge. It transpired the front bow doors were not closed properly; and there was a clear trail of responsibility. 193 passengers and crew lost their lives. In the crush at the Hillsborough football stadium two years later, 96 Liverpool FC fans died – over 750 others were injured. Much has been

Figure 16.8   A framework for crises and disasters

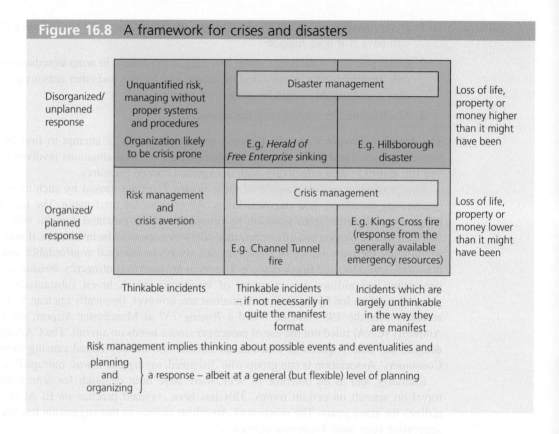

said about this incident and *The Sun* newspaper was castigated for headlines claiming Liverpool fans were intoxicated. The real problem was the police misjudged the risk involved in opening some gates to the ground which led to fans pouring through turnstiles and down a single tunnel into an already overcrowded pen. The decision was hastened by the fact that the kick-off was imminent and hundreds of restless fans were still trying to get into the ground.

The fire at Kings Cross Underground station also happened in 1987. The most likely cause was a discarded (and still lit) match thrown into an escalator shaft, presumably by a smoker. 31 people died, but it could have easily been far more. This is the type of conceivable incident that led to the banning of cigarette smoking in public places. In theory it already was banned at Kings Cross. There have been two major fires in the Channel Tunnel, the most recent in 2008. The first, in 1996, happened when a lorry caught fire just before the train that was carrying it entered the tunnel. There were no deaths but several drivers needed treatment for smoke inhalation. There was also considerable damage to the tunnel infrastructure. Fire procedures were criticized in the subsequent investigation.

Knight (2000) reports on research at Oxford University which confirms that catastrophes – defined as man-made, rather than natural, crises or disasters – invariably have an immediate negative effect on share prices. Over time, the share prices either recover or stay depressed. The long-term impact is rarely neutral.

In a quite different way, strategic changes can also lead to crises of confidence, particularly amongst employees. Rumours that a firm might be taken over often imply redundancies; falling sales and profits suggest possible cutbacks or closure. Good internal communications and openness are required to minimize the potential damage, especially as competitors might see these situations as competitive opportunities.

Understanding crises

Smith (1990) identifies three levels that help to explain why some crises happen when they might have been avoided.

The first level is a set of organizational problems which make the organization crisis prone. These relate to issues of culture and power, misguided strategies and poor control systems. There might be evidence of dangerous cost-cutting or simple neglect.

The second level is the incident itself, often provoked when particular external events clash with the organizational problems.

The third level is one of legitimation. When the incident or crisis is investigated there is a ready willingness to apportion blame and a failure to learn properly from the experiences. Organizational change does not take place and consequently the problems are merely reinforced. The same type of crisis could easily happen again.

Smith concludes that many organizations are actually frail, rather than strong, and relatively crisis prone. There is often an over-inflated view of their strengths and competencies and too much belief in their infallibility. If this is linked to arrogance – as seen many years ago with the sinking of the 'unsinkable' *Titanic* in 1912 with the loss of 1503 passengers and crew – it can be very dangerous. Smith provides us with a 7-Cs framework for investigating crises. His elements are summarized in Table 16.3.

He argues that we tend to focus our interest on the cold factors, and by ignoring the warm ones we make the organization more crisis prone.

Strategy in action 16.1 applies these points to the Millennium Dome in Greenwich. London.

Organizational difficulties and crises, then, occur in several ways and take many forms. Weak strategies (which may have been strong in the past), substandard products and services, unacceptably low prices or excessive costs can often be remedied by diagnosing the problem and acting on it. They have a hard or cold element and often an external focus. They are a relative weakness because of the relative strengths of competitors. They can be observed and measured by monitoring competitor activities, tracking sales and market shares, and simply talking to customers and distributors.

Ineffective management practices, the softer or warmer side, have internal origins and require a different approach. Moreover, they may be hidden because people divert attention away from them by blaming problems and crises on external, competitive factors and on unexpected events.

Crisis fighting in organizations

It is generally accepted that organizational environments have become increasingly dynamic and turbulent in recent years, and that as environments spring more and more shocks and surprises on them, organizations must develop new ways of dealing with the uncertainty. Some organizations actively seek to influence and even manage their environments; others rely more heavily on their ability to react and respond quickly. These latter organizations, in particular, may well make a

Table 16.3 The 7-Cs crisis management framework	
Warm factors – people related	Culture
	Communications
	Configuration – issues of power and influence
Cold factors – technocratic	Control
	Coupling and complexity – the nature of the event itself
	Costs
	Contingency planning.

Strategy in action 16.1

The Millennium Dome – an Application of the Crisis Management Framework

The intention with the Millennium Dome was to build a lasting structure in Greenwich, London, funded with a mixture of government funding, lottery money and private sponsorship. It would be opened on the evening of 31 December 1999 to celebrate the new millennium and then used for one year as a special exhibition with individual zones designed and funded by the sponsors. It was not to be a theme park, but it was to be a signal to the world that Britain could manage a major and ambitious celebratory project 'as well, if not better, than anyone else in the world'. After 2000 the Dome would be sold to a private company for a use to be determined later. The whole project was tied in to public-transport developments, notably the Jubilee Line Extension of the London Underground– for parking at the Dome was to be severely limited.

The initial outcomes

- The Dome was opened on time.
- However, many of the guests for the special opening night ceremonies had not received their tickets and had to queue for them at an underground station.
- There was hostile media criticism from the moment the Dome was opened. Many visitors commented on the lack of any 'wow' factor. Ironically, the London Eye, the viewing wheel built by British Airways, which experienced technical difficulties and a delayed start, received a better reaction and has proved very popular and lucrative.
- It quickly transpired that the sales and revenue projections were over-optimistic and were never going to be met. They have been revised downwards more than once.
- Additional money from the National Lottery has been provided on more than one occasion to prevent bankruptcy.
- The person appointed as chief executive of the New Millennium Experience Company (which managed the whole project), Jennie Page, was forced to resign, as was the non-executive chairman of the board, Robert Ayling of British Airways. Jennie Page was replaced by Pierre-Yves Gerbeau from Euro-Disney; Ayling by David Quarmby, chairman of the

British Tourist Authority. After just a few weeks in the post, Quarmby returned to his original non-executive role on the board. David James, an experienced 'company doctor', was recruited to rescue a rapidly deteriorating situation. James took over some of Gerbeau's responsibilities.

- After just one day in the post James commented publicly that he was 'appalled' at the financial systems that he had inherited. Controls were inadequate and there was no proper register of assets. Visitor projections (already reduced substantially) were still unrealistic and yet more lottery funding was required if the Dome was to remain open until the end of 2000.
- The Conservative (opposition) party called for the Dome to be closed early and for political resignations. Both demands appeared to 'fall on deaf ears', although Prime Minister Blair acknowledged that mistakes had been made. It was also commented that the Dome 'had always been a regeneration project and not a visitor attraction'.
- Nomura (the Japanese Bank) initially agreed to buy the building, to develop theme park activities in 2001, but pulled out of negotiations when it was unable to gain access to the financial information that it needed for its planning.

Applying the crisis management framework

Culture
- Arrogant assumptions about what people (paying customers) would want.
- Arrogance about British achievements – in the event France's lighting of the Eiffel Tower received more praise.
- There was a clear culture of blame.
- There was a failure to synthesize the political agenda of the government and private sector project management.

Communications
- Clearly fragmented.
- Lack of cohesion amongst the stakeholders.
- Some 'truths' were kept hidden.

- Arguably, the general public was never fully clear about the project and what it stood for.
- What was to be a 'triumph' has become an embarrassment linked to 'face saving' and damage limitation.
- The media generally became hostile towards the project.

Configuration
- There was a clear political agenda, driven by the early leadership of Peter Mandelson. The project had to be seen as a success.
- There was also a secondary agenda – it was to be linked with public-transport developments. The Jubilee Line itself was fraught with problems and was handed over to American contractors to complete.

Control
- There was a lack of clear governance and responsibility – who actually 'owned' the project?
- Financial controls were inadequate.
- The immovable completion deadline added a new dimension with extra pressures.

Coupling and complexity
- There were too many perspectives and expectations.
- This was exacerbated by the underlying desire to demonstrate creativity, innovation and 'great achievement'.

Costs
- Poor forecasting – especially concerning paying visitors –meant that the costs and break-even projections were never realistic.
- There was a very visible need to 'beg' for more subsidy which reinforced a perception of mismanagement.

Contingency planning
- An early closure was never a realistic option for the government.
- This made cost overruns more likely and sponsorship more difficult.

- Revenue shortfalls would be allowed, but only in a culture of blame.

Final outcomes

A number of potential bidders – interested in developing both homes and leisure facilities – came forward after the Dome closed, only to either withdraw or be rejected by the Government. After protracted negotiations a developer was found for the Dome site, which would become a 20,000 seat concert arena, one of the largest and most popular in Europe. An initial opening date of 2006 was put back to 2007, but since it opened as The O2 Arena, it has been very successful with a wide mix of concerts and events.

When the Dome closed some £800 million had been sunk in to the project. The proposed developments should, over time, recoup some £550 million of this. Meanwhile the interim on-going management and maintenance cost the taxpayer £10 million per year.

Activity

Given these figures it is interesting to check the current events schedule at the O2 Arena – and the ticket prices – and consider the current financial returns. It is also important to factor in the wide range of restaurants, bars, shops, snack outlets and concession stands which add to the revenues.

© ISTOCK

virtue out of their ability to crisis fight. After all, crisis situations often bring out the best in people who call on their reserves of inner strengths. However, extensive crisis fighting carries a downside risk. It is time-consuming, reducing the time and space available for wider strategic thinking, and consequently real growth opportunities may well be missed.

It is unrealistic to think that a 'perfect' organization which is successful, seen as successful, and unaffected by crises, can be created. But most organizations could manage their resources more efficiently and more effectively and, as a result, be less prone to crises. Sometimes an externally generated crisis occurs; on other occasions, the organization actually creates the crisis.

As shown above, the long-term situation is made worse when an organization, having somehow dealt with a crisis, fails to learn and make itself less crisis prone for the future.

Crisis aversion demands both single-loop and double-loop learning. Programmed responses to perceived events, the acceptance of current operating practices, norms and policies, can be speedy and efficient. They can reflect the organization's ability to share and learn and to benefit from its experiences. However, there is an important distinction between 20 years of accumulated learning and one year's experiences repeated 20 times over. The danger signals are present when 'we've seen it all before; this is the way we do it here' is utilized too readily and without checking the current circumstances. Double-loop learning demands that managers question why things are done in a particular way, paying attention to environmental changes whose impact will require more than a programmed response.

It is both significant and salutary to emphasize that managerial competency in crisis fighting will often be perceived as a strength and a virtue. People complain about stress levels but paradoxically enjoy the challenge of a crisis. Dealing with the problem quickly and pragmatically gives people satisfaction and a sense of achievement. Even laid-back people can find new motivation and strength. It is human nature. We have all seen television programmes which report how passers-by willingly help in an emergency situation, sometimes improvising on the spot, and frequently with only limited regard for their own safety, until expert help can be called in. In turn, those with expertize also have to improvise on many occasions; instructions and procedures cannot predict every eventuality. At the Hillsborough football stadium disaster in 1989, traumatized people who had just escaped the crush themselves returned to the terraces to help other victims.

People prove themselves to be naturally inventive in particular circumstances. Yet how difficult might it be to persuade many of the same people to be more innovative and intrapreneurial on a day-to-day basis, and to try and move away from the crisis-fighting paradigm?

Crisis fighting in organizations takes up time. Managers are pragmatic but often not thoughtful beyond the confines of their immediate span of responsibility. Internal rivalry may well be reinforced such that people's competitive energy is focused on beating other parts of the organization (who are perceived as rivals rather than colleagues) instead of the real external competitors.

It forces a short-term time horizon on many issues and decisions. People then become frustrated and lose confidence in their organization because they seem to be operating in an organizational darkness where, metaphorically, the right hand does not know what the left hand is doing. It was mentioned earlier that one major retailer recently ran a special promotion where people who spent a certain amount on anything could buy an extra item at a very substantial discount. Unfortunately, the supply chain let the stores down; there were insufficient stocks of the discounted item. A disillusioned staff simply gave out vouchers for use when stocks were renewed.

Ironically, though, crisis fighting can be very customer orientated as managers react to customer pressures and requests. Consequently, the long-term damage to the organization, which it is fostering through a failure to learn properly, can be hidden behind short-term successes. This is further reinforced by people using the short-term successes to hide and ignore the deeper problems.

In contrast, trying to eliminate the regular and ubiquitous crisis fighting and replace it with a more harmonious culture where people share information and trust and help each other may seem positively boring. However, success with this frees up time and can foster valuable innovation. It goes further than opening up new windows of opportunity for an organization; it can elevate it to a new level of opportunity which previously it could not access. In this respect it is like promotion from the Championship in English football to the Premier League and possibly winning a place in the Champions League. Here, promotion opens the door to millions of pounds of television and sponsorship money which hopefully will be invested sensibly to strengthen both the team and ground facilities. It is a world inhabited by only the privileged clubs who will work hard to maintain their status and position. Over time, the gap between the Premier League and the other divisions widens, and the poorest clubs inevitably become more crisis prone often as a result of investing too much to try and join the elite they feel that they deserve to be part of. One of the stock phrases in the vocabulary of a professional footballer joining a top club is about the fact they feel that club X or Y is a 'big club' and deserves to be in the Champions League due to past exploits. But past exploits are not a place to metaphorically rest the corporate head.

Organizations must invest in people if they are to prevent a competitive gap, let alone a chasm, developing between them and the industry leaders internationally. While organized programmes such as *Total Quality Management* and *Investors in People* have a relevance, the emphasis must be on cultural rather than procedural change. Scenario building, contingency planning and crisis management strategies can all help with unexpected events, which to some large extent are often foreseeable but not necessarily avoidable. Well-managed innovation and new product and service developments can strengthen an organization's competitiveness and reduce its crisis proneness. Internal crises generated by complacency with current good fortune, a reluctance to change, poor decisions and weak management demand a change in culture and style. Understanding, trust and commitment must be fostered.

Crisis proneness and crisis aversion

There are, then, several characteristics which indicate crisis proneness in an organization, and these are listed in Table 16.4. Organizations need to determine the extent to which they are manifest.

Managers often believe that they are better at knowing what needs to be changed than in actually managing and implementing the changes. However, this may well be based too much on personal opinion and judgement. Without openness, trust, sharing and learning it is highly likely that organizations will not realize what they already know; consequently, they will not be able to leverage and exploit a critical strategic resource, their knowledge.

Moreover, they will not realize what they do not know – they will not fully appreciate the opportunities available to the privileged competitors in an industry.

Figures 16.9 and 16.10 summarize the important themes of this section and highlight the demands on an organization. A fragmented organization with a focus on the short term will spend too much time and waste resources in crisis fighting. If it fails to manage the soft issues involved in establishing trust and co-operation it is likely to under-achieve as it develops longer-term strategies. If, however, it can manage the people issues more effectively it can single-loop learn

Table 16.4   The crisis-prone organization

- Specialist functions that cannot or do not think and act holistically
- A tendency to look inwards at the expense of looking outwards – internal-competition not external-competition focus
- A strong, rigid belief in present (even past) competitive paradigms
- A reluctance or inability to properly embrace the demands of a changing environment
- Inadequate communications – e.g. vertical but not horizontal; horizontal at discrete levels but only vertical downwards
- An inability correctly to interpret triggers and signals
- Willingness of individuals to break rules and procedures readily for short-term results – and hide the detail, their knowledge.

and foster innovative improvements with existing products and services. Now as it develops longer-term strategies it will be better placed to take a more holistic view and improve its overall effectiveness.

> *It's not going to be one heroic act or gesture by me that's going to make the real difference; it's going to be thousands and thousands of separate actions by people in the company, every hour of the day, that will make the difference. Add all these up and the combined power is enormous.*
>
> BEVERLEY HODSON, EX-RETAIL MANAGING DIRECTOR, WH SMITH, AFTER HER APPOINTMENT, QUOTED IN THE COMPANY'S INTERNAL MAGAZINE, *NEWSLINK*, JUNE 1997

It is essential that the thousands of actions are self-supporting to foster synergy, rather than fragmented.

Crisis avoidance

Bartha (1995) suggests that many, but certainly not all, crises occur because they evolve gradually and nobody spots their progress. These potential crises can be prevented if organizations objectively monitor their environment and assess the emerging strategic issues. Consequently, an organization can develop a relative aversion to crises – as opposed to being crisis prone – if it develops associated competencies in awareness, learning and stakeholder management. The challenge is to identify, assess and deal with potential opportunities and threats before opportunities disappear (perhaps because they have been exploited by a competitor) or threats turn into crises. Another manifestation of an emerging threat would be a gap between the performance level expected of the organization by its stakeholders, especially its shareholders, and the actual performance level.

A number of elements is involved in *scanning the environment*. Competitor activity should be monitored as far as possible; while their most recent actions and changes will be visible, the challenge is to determine future strategic changes before they are implemented. There should be constant contact with key stakeholders, such as customers, distributors and suppliers; and the organization should be aware of pending government legislation and pressure group developments. The media can be a valuable source of information.

However, the strategic challenge is not one of obtaining information, but rather discerning the important messages and separating out the key issues. Quite often it is necessary to synthesize snippets of information to create a meaningful pattern. The significance of the issue then needs determining and appropriate action plans need to be initiated. Managerial judgement will be an important element.

Opportunities will emerge where the organization can build upon its strengths or tactically outmanoeuvre a rival; the crisis might occur if the opportunity is missed by the organization but picked up by a competitor. A potential threat can be present in a number of ways: new legislative restrictions, a disappearing market, financial difficulties for an important supplier or distributor. Information and triggers can be received anywhere in the organization at any time; making sure that their significance is appreciated and that they are channelled to those people, functions and businesses who could benefit is the next critical step. Communication systems are crucial, together with the ability of individual managers to take an organization-wide, or holistic, perspective.

> *The fact you may get knocked down is not the issue – what matters is whether you get up again.*
>
> BASED ON A QUOTE FROM A US FOOTBALL COACH

> *If you think education is expensive, think what ignorance might cost you.*
>
> ORIGINAL QUOTATION BY CLAUS MOSER

Figure 16.9 Strategy implementation and crises

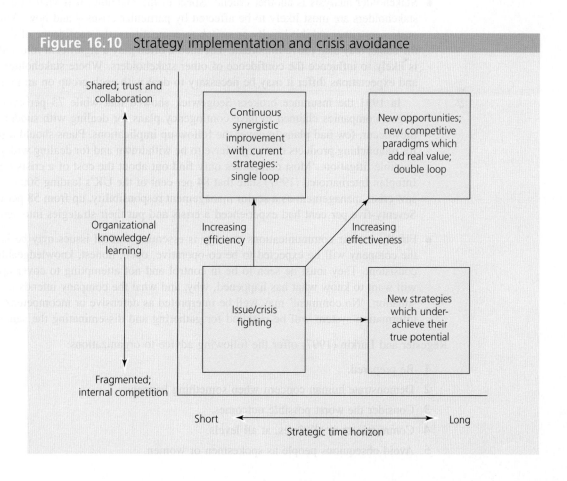

Figure 16.10 Strategy implementation and crisis avoidance

The ability of managers to act upon the information will, in turn, depend upon organizational policies and the extent of their empowerment; their willingness to act will be affected by their personality, their competencies, their motivation and the reward/sanction system practised by the organization.

Crisis management

There are a number of identifiable steps in attempting to manage crises effectively:

- Initially it is necessary to identify the most obvious areas of risk.

- Following on from this firms should establish procedures and policies for ensuring that risks do not become crises. Discussing possible scenarios, training sessions and actual rehearsals can all contribute, in addition to the investment in physical prevention.

- A crisis management team should be identified in advance, trained and prepared to step aside from all normal activities in the event of a crisis occurring. Experience suggests that the expertise required will be primarily communications and public relations, financial and legal. Clear leadership of the team by the strategic leader will be expected; and personnel, operations and marketing skills can be added as required. Secretarial support is sometimes overlooked.

- Building the team is one aspect of a planning process which should also cover how to get hold of key people over weekends and during holidays, how to restore critical facilities that might go down, and how to gain fast access to important regulatory bodies.

- Stakeholder analysis is another crucial aspect of the planning. It is vital to clarify which stakeholders are most likely to be affected by particular crises – and how. After a crisis customers either exhibit loyalty or switch to competitors; the confidence of distributors and the banks may also prove important. The media often play a significant role and their stance is likely to influence the confidence of other stakeholders. Where stakeholder perspectives and expectations differ it may be necessary to deal with each group on an individual basis.

  In 1991 the insurance brokers Sedgewick showed that while 75 per cent of Britain's largest companies claimed to have contingency plans for dealing with sudden crises when they occur, few had plans to cover the follow-up implications. Plans should also be in hand for relaunching products that might have to be withdrawn and for dealing with investors and possible litigation. 'Most companies only find out about the cost of a crisis once it's over.' Infoplan International (1997) state that 84 per cent of the UK's leading 500 companies then saw crisis management as a senior management responsibility, up from 58 per cent in 1995. Seventy-five per cent had experienced a crisis and put their strategies into action.

- Finally, a clear communications strategy is essential. Ethical issues may be involved, and the company will be expected to be co-operative, open, honest, knowledgeable and consistent. They must be seen to be in control and not attempting to cover up. The media will want to know what has happened, why, and what the company intends to do about the situation. 'No comment' may well be interpreted as defensive or incompetent. An effective information system will be required for gathering and disseminating the salient facts.

Regester and Larkin (1997) offer the following advice to organizations:

1 Be prepared.
2 Demonstrate human concern when something happens.
3 Consider the worst possible outcomes.
4 Communicate at all times, at all levels.
5 Avoid obsequious people as spokesmen or women.

6 Do not believe that procedure manuals prevent incidents.

7 Do believe 'there is a first time for everything'.

The crisis-averse organization

Figure 16.11 highlights that an organization must meet the needs and expectations of all its stakeholders if it is to survive. It is vital to retain customers; new customers then bring new business rather than merely replace others who have been lost or neglected. Employee support and commitment is essential for delivering the competitive quality and service that customers demand. To achieve this, employees must be motivated and rewarded. In addition, financial targets must be met to ensure shareholder loyalty.

Achieving these outcomes is dependent upon aspects of both strategy and structure, which in turn depend upon effective strategic leadership. A sound, appropriate, communicated and shared purpose

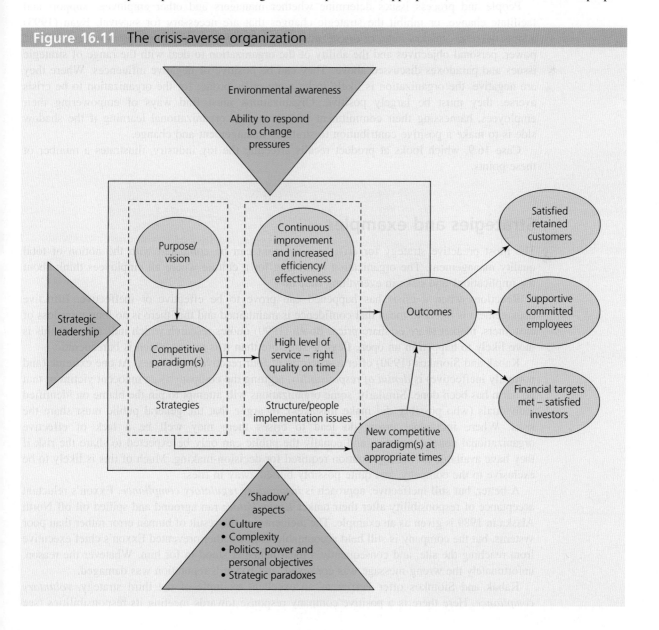

Figure 16.11   The crisis-averse organization

and vision should be manifested in appropriate, feasible and desirable corporate and competitive strategies. These must be:

- implemented with a high level of customer service
- improved continuously, and
- changed to new corporate and competitive paradigms at appropriate times and opportunities.

This demands environmental awareness and the ability of the organization to respond to change pressures and to external strategic disturbances. While we talk about an organization-wide response, the real challenge lies with individual managers and employees, who are closest to customers, suppliers and distributors. Innovative people drive functional-level improvements which can strengthen competitiveness; but they must be empowered and committed – issues of structure, style and implementation. The hard aspects of strategy – leadership, vision and ideas – must be supported by the soft people aspects.

People and process issues determine whether managers and other employees support and facilitate change, or inhibit the strategic changes that are necessary for survival. Egan (1993) adopts the term 'shadow side' of organizations to embrace issues of culture, complexity, politics, power, personal objectives and the ability of the organization to deal with the range of strategic issues and paradoxes discussed above. They can be positive or negative influences. Where they are negative, the organization is likely to be more crisis prone; for the organization to be crisis averse, they must be largely positive. Organizations must find ways of empowering their employees, harnessing their commitment and promoting organizational learning if the shadow side is to make a positive contribution to strategic management and change.

Case 16.9, which looks at product recalls affecting the toy industry, illustrates a number of these points.

Strategies and examples

The most proactive strategy for crisis management can be compared with the notion of total quality management. The organization is looking for a culture where all employees think about the implications and risks in everything they do.

Reactions when a crisis has happened can prove to be effective or ineffective. Effective management is likely to mean that confidence is maintained and that there is no long-term loss of customers, market share or share price. Booth (1990) quotes research which indicates that this is more likely to happen in an open, flexible structure than it is in one which is bureaucratic.

Kabak and Siomkos (1990) offer a spectrum of four reactive approaches. At one extreme (and normally ineffective) is *denial of responsibility*, arguing the company is an innocent victim or that no harm has been done. Similarly, some organizations will attempt to pin the blame on identified individuals (who possibly did make mistakes), or argue that the general public must share the risks. Where individual errors do lead to crises there may well be a lack of effective organizational control systems; and equally the public can only be expected to share the risk if they have available all the information required for decision-making. Much of this is likely to be exclusive to the company, and quite possibly buried away in files.

A better, but still ineffective, approach is *involuntary regulatory compliance*. Exxon's reluctant acceptance of responsibility after their tanker *Exxon Valdez* ran aground and spilled oil off North Alaska in 1989 is given as an example. The incident was the result of human error rather than poor systems, but the company is still held accountable. Bad weather prevented Exxon's chief executive from reaching the site, and consequently a local manager stood in for him. Whatever the reason, unfortunately the wrong message was conveyed, and Exxon's reputation was damaged.

Kabak and Siomkos offer Perrier as an excellent example of the third strategy, *voluntary compliance*. Here there is a positive company response towards meeting its responsibilities (see

Case 16.9

Product Recalls in the Toy Industry

US AS

When products that have been sold through retailers have to be recalled because there is some problem or danger, then costs can be substantial and corporate reputations can be damaged. For companies there are issues of public relations, supply chain management and crisis management. In recent years a number of toy products have been recalled and replaced. It is not the only industry where this problem occurs; and although there is a common theme to the instances related here – manufacturing in China – this is not the only reason recalls happen.

Mega Brands is a Montreal-based distributor of children's building sets – its Mega Blocks compete with Lego, for example – art materials and magnetic toys. Sales in 2006 amounted to some $500 million.

In November 2005 a toddler in Seattle died after swallowing some small magnets that had become detached from a Magnetix toy sourced from a New Jersey (US) company that Mega Brands had acquired six months earlier. The toys originated in China and Mega 'did everything it could' to make sure new toys coming through were safe. Products were redesigned to ensure the magnets were embedded more securely, and new production standards and inspection procedures put in place. Labelling and instructions were also made clearer. But hostile press coverage continued and eventually, in 2006, this led to a huge number of products being recalled and replaced although there did not appear to have been any further serious incidents. Continuing stories suggested, for example, that the company might have gone further. Labelling might be improved, but the basic packaging had been retained. Did it need to be changed, or not? The *perception* was that it did. In 2007 there was a second recall.

It also became apparent that in today's world of selling old toys on auction sites such as eBay, normal recall programmes may not be enough. Mega set out to buy any items it spotted being sold on in this way. Although there is still a handful of outstanding lawsuits, the number of customer complaints now seems to have died down.

In August 2007 leading toy distributor Mattel recalled 18 million Chinese-made toys after concerns over lead paint and magnets. These included Barbie dolls and die-cast cars. Mattel has contract manufacturing plants in China – but it emerged these had been sub-contracting the painting operations.

Two months earlier, in June 2007, Fisher Price recalled 1.5 million toys over lead content concerns. And just before this a New York based distributor had recalled 1.5 million Thomas the Tank Engine products – again for lead. Toys R Us had recalled vinyl baby bibs – yet again for lead.

Moreover, these problems were not confined to the US. Leading New Zealand distributor, The Warehouse, had recalled children's pyjamas containing formaldehyde – some children had been badly burned when their nightclothes accidentally caught fire.

The US Consumer Safety Commission began to argue that toys must be tested more rigorously before they left China – which would increase costs and slow down supplies. But perhaps a price worth paying .. ..

It is perhaps useful to think of these issues in the context of the Chinese baby milk contamination stories that happened in 2008. Products had been contaminated with melamine to reduce production costs – over 50,000 children, most of them in China itself, became quite seriously ill and four died. The issue was taken seriously, executives charged with murder, convicted and sentenced to death.

Questions

Although recalls and replacements can prove very costly, it will arguably always be tempting to look for cost reduction opportunities wherever they can be found – as these can lead to either (or both) lower prices and higher profits. But can we ever legislate for companies that either cut corners or seek to take what turn out to be inappropriate risks?

SOURCE: THIS CASE STUDY WAS PREPARED USING PRIMARILY PUBLICLY AVAILABLE SOURCES OF INFORMATION FOR THE PURPOSES OF CLASSROOM DISCUSSION. IT DOES NOT INTEND TO ILLUSTRATE EITHER EFFECTIVE OR INEFFECTIVE HANDLING OF A MANAGERIAL SITUATION.

Case 16.10). The incident highlights that even though companies may have crisis management strategies unforeseen difficulties are likely to be encountered.

The other extreme strategy is the *super effort*, whereby the company does everything it can, openly and honestly, and stays in constant touch with all affected stakeholders. In 1982 an

Case 16.10

Perrier

Eur US

In 1989 Perrier was the world leader in the fast-growing market for bottled water. In the UK, for example, the Perrier brand accounted for over one-third of the market for sparkling water, which represented 20 per cent of the whole market. Perrier also owns Buxton, which is second to Evian in the still water segment. The name 'Perrier' had become synonymous with bottled water.

In February 1990 minute traces of benzene were discovered in a sample during routine tests in North Carolina, America. The trace, six parts per billion, did not represent any discernible health risk. Within one week every Perrier brand world-wide had been withdrawn from sale. This amounted to 160 million bottles in 110 countries.

Even if it is madness, we decided to take Perrier off the market everywhere in the world. I don't want the least doubt, however small, to tarnish our product's image of quality and purity.

GUSTAVE LEVEN, THEN CHAIRMAN, PERRIER

Leven, 77 years old in 1990, had built Perrier from a run-down business to world leadership over 40 years. He retired later in 1990.

Perrier had created crisis management strategies some years earlier ... 'Everyone knew what they were supposed to do ... in spite of this we never, ever, imagined a worldwide withdrawal. We'd never dreamed of a problem of such magnitude.' Only Tylenol had previously been withdrawn on such a scale; and in that crisis people had died.

Actions in the UK

Local tests were arranged as soon as news spread from the US. The tests took a normal 48 hours, and benzene was again found in the sample. Unfortunately, during this period a Perrier spokesman in Paris speculated prematurely that a greasy rag might have introduced the wrong cleaning fluid onto bottling equipment. Moreover, when the worldwide withdrawal was announced to the world's press in Paris – rather than local press conferences – the room was too small for the press and television crews attending.

On the following day advertisements appeared around the world, explaining the situation, and clarifying what people, including retailers, should do. The 24-hour emergency telephone network in the UK 'received mostly friendly calls'.

A major problem in the UK concerned the disposal of all the water and the further disposal or recycling of the bottles. A large proportion of the stocks was in the distinctive Perrier green glass which, recycled, has few alternative uses.

The source of the contamination was quickly traced to a filter at the bottling plant in France, a filter used to purify carbon dioxide being added to the water. This revelation suggested that Perrier is not 100 per cent naturally carbonated, although the label on the bottles stated 'naturally carbonated natural mineral water'. It transpired that the gas used is collected underground with the water and added back after purification. Only the gas, not the water, is purified. Nevertheless the publicity caused Sainsbury's to refuse to stock Perrier for a period after it was relaunched in April 1990.

One month after the relaunch Perrier was already selling at half its previous volume; and market leadership was quickly regained. The worldwide cost was estimated to be £125 million.

Competitors had not attempted to exploit the situation, possibly believing they might spread a scare by association and affect the market for all bottled water.

It has been suggested that the very popularity of Perrier had caused the problem. Demand worldwide had put pressure on the supply side. Some years earlier, and before the increased consumer awareness and concern with health issues, the problem would probably have been contained on a smaller scale.

The balance of opinion seems to be that Perrier got the big decisions right. It adopted a worst case scenario, acted fast, and spoke out honestly.

Shortly after the crisis Perrier was bought by Nestlé, which already owned the Vittel brand and the top US bottled water, Poland Spring. It remains a popular and premium priced product all round the world.

Sources

Butler, D (1990) Perrier's painful period, *Management Today,* August.

Caulkin, S (1990) Dangerous exposure, *Best of Business International,* Autumn.

Footnote – A parallel case?

Dasani is Coca-Cola's bottled still water brand. Some 200 million cases are sold every year around the world, but principally in America, where it has been available since 1999. Dasani was launched in the UK in January 2003 – in March the same year all stocks were removed from shelves. The water had been found to contain an illegal level of bromate, which could increase the risk of cancer. However, the levels did not pose any risk to public health or safety. The company seemed to have acted quickly and positively. However it would soon emerge that instead of being natural spring water, Dasani *in the UK* is purified tap water, using a process perfected by NASA. There was something of an outcry and many remembered an episode of *Only Fools and Horses* where a scam had been run selling untouched bottled tap water as 'Peckham Spring'. Interestingly one month later, in April, Dasani was launched in France, the home of Perrier and Evian (the most popular brand of still water). The public were assured that this time it was natural spring water!

Question

1 Do you agree that Perrier 'got the big decisions right'?

PERRIER **http://www.perrier.com**

Tasks

1 Ascertain the current situation with Dasani and compare and contrast the relevant marketing and crisis strategies of Nestlé and Coca-Cola.
2 Earlier, in 1999 Coca-Cola withdrew its Coke product from shelves in Belgium. What caused the incident and how well did Coca-Cola deal with it?
3 To what extent do you think it contributed to the early retirement of chief executive Douglas Ivester at the end of that year?

COCA-COLA **http://www.coca-cola.com**

© FEFERONI | DREAMSTIME.COM

extortionist succeeded in introducing cyanide to packs of Tylenol in America. Tylenol is manufactured by Johnson and Johnson and at the time it was the country's leading painkiller with a 35 per cent market share. Six people died.

All stocks were recalled immediately 'to contain the crisis and demonstrate responsibility'. The media were provided with constant up-to-date information. The product was relaunched in tamperproof containers and the associated heavy advertising featured the new containers rather than simply claiming that the product was safe. The incident was costly, but market share was quickly regained. Some had suggested that Johnson and Johnson should drop the Tylenol brand name, but this was resisted. Interestingly, the name Townsend Thoresen was dropped by its parent company, P&O, after the ferry *Herald of Free Enterprise* capsized off Zeebrugge in 1987.

While there is little argument against the logic of planning ahead of a crisis, some organizations are cautious about the extent to which one should attempt to plan.

> *The scale of the Bhopal [Union Carbide chemical plant in India] disaster [gas leak in 1984] was unimaginable. There is simply no way anyone could have anticipated it.*
>
> UNION CARBIDE DIRECTOR OF CORPORATE COMMUNICATIONS, QUOTED IN NASH (1990)

While the extent and magnitude of a disaster may be unexpected, events such as Bhopal are predictable, often because there have been similar incidents in the past. Union Carbide argued that they tried to be as honest as they could, but they were limited by the lack of hard facts from a remote area of India. Nash comments that the organization appreciated the need to act quickly and develop effective communications but, after the event, remained sceptical about establishing rigid guidelines, arguing that one can never be certain in advance about the actual nature and detail of any crisis.

A crisis management framework

Companies succeed if they meet the needs and expectations of their stakeholders; companies which fail to meet these needs and expectations, long term, must be in trouble and they may collapse. Perception of relative success and failure is critical. Companies that are succeeding need to be recognized for this. Companies that are not succeeding will want to cover up their weaknesses if they can.

The simple matrix illustrated in Figure 16.12 is based on these premises. Companies that satisfy their stakeholders, and are seen to do so, are classified as crisis avoiders. Crisis-prone organizations fail on both counts. Companies with a strong reputation they do not wholly deserve are termed 'thin high profile' as the situation is likely to be very fragile and fluid. The fourth quadrant contains 'unsung heroes', companies whose reputation does not do justice to their real achievements.

It is worth considering in which quadrant the following two companies should be placed.

The Body Shop saw its share price and price to earnings ratio fall in the 1990s as it faced increasing competition internationally. In 1996, disillusioned with City investors, the Body Shop looked at the viability of re-privatization, but concluded that it would not be an appropriate strategy to follow. Nevertheless, its customers and employees remained loyal and supportive, and, despite some cynicism and criticism, the company's reputation as an environmentally concerned organization also remained strong. However, in recent years, the founders, Anita and Gordon Roddick, have systematically seen their power and influence wane.

In 1995 Shell, one of Europe's most successful and respected companies, was forced to change an important strategic decision following a high-profile campaign by a leading pressure group.

Figure 16.12   A crisis-management framework

Corporate reputation: the stakeholders' view of the company

Strong — Weak

Thin high profile | Crisis avoiding
Crisis prone | Unsung heroes

Low — High

Corporate competency reflected in the company's ability to satisfy the needs and expectations of its stakeholders* effectively

*The stakeholders: customers; employees; investors; suppliers; environmentalists

Shell had chosen to sink its redundant Brent Spar oil platform in deep seas some 150 miles west of Scotland. It had reached an agreement with the UK government that, scientifically, this was the most appropriate means of disposal for the platform. Greenpeace objected and protesters boarded the platform, claiming that it still contained 5000 tonnes of oil which would eventually be released to pollute the sea. The ensuing and professionally orchestrated publicity fuelled public opinion, and there were protests in a number of European countries, including attacks on petrol stations in Germany. Shell backed down and agreed to investigate other possibilities for disposal.

The UK government expressed both anger and disappointment with this decision. Independent inspectors later proved that Greenpeace's claims were gross exaggerations – the residual oil was much, much less than 5000 tonnes. The press concluded: 'Shell went wrong in spending too much time convincing government of the case for sea-bed dumping, but not attaching enough importance to consulting other stakeholder groups.' Shell had been made to appear socially irresponsible, even though the ethics of the Greenpeace campaign are questionable.

Summary

Strategies must be implemented if they are to be judged successful and effective. This is accomplished through the structural framework, as we have seen earlier. There are two key variables:

- First, the logic of the *corporate portfolio*. Is synergy a realistic possibility?
  Is the range too diverse? Is the portfolio built around activities and businesses with overlapping or similar competencies?
- Second, are the *structure and style* of management appropriate for the actual portfolio and its diversity? Does the style of managing the corporation ensure that the potential synergies are achieved?

Goold and Campbell (1988) have described three broad styles of corporate management. The *financial control style* is akin to a holding company, where the head office adopts a very decentralized approach to manage a portfolio where there is (normally) little natural interdependency between the businesses. The *strategic planning style* is based on centralization – the strategic leader believes that he or she is in the best position to dictate strategy for all the businesses in the portfolio. The *strategic control style* is a sort of half-way house that attempts to build on the strengths of the other two.

Defining corporate strategy as the overall strategy for a diversified firm, Michael Porter described four approaches to managing a corporate portfolio. *Portfolio management* is the approach whereby each business is looked at independently to assess its worth to the firm. The assessment is based on industry attractiveness and competitive strengths. Investment should be targeted at priority businesses. *Restructuring* is the attempt to make both an industry and a business more attractive by improving competitiveness – when an organization can no longer add any further value, the business should be divested. *Sharing assets* offers the best opportunity for creating and exploiting synergy across a range of businesses, but *transferring skills* can also prove valuable.

Goold *et al.* (1994) have highlighted the importance of *corporate parenting* – essentially the fit between a head office and the subsidiary businesses in an organization and the opportunities for two-way benefits. Where each business can benefit from being part of an organization, and at the same time make a positive contribution to the whole organization, we have what Goold *et al.* call a *heartland* of related businesses. Businesses should be acquired and divested to strengthen the heartland.

The *corporate headquarters* drives the strategy of the business and provides the structural framework. The range of services which remain centralized is a reflection of the adopted style of corporate management. Head offices should add value and not merely spend money earned by the subsidiaries. In recent years, head offices have been slimmed down.

In conjunction with decentralization, an appropriate role must be found for the general managers in charge of each subsidiary business.

To cope with the pressures and demands of contemporary business environments Rosabeth Moss Kanter (1989) argues that the organization must be *focused, fast, flexible and friendly*. She argues that competitive advantage comes from the way in which everything is integrated and works together.

Charles Handy (1994, 1995) puts forward a more radical thesis and argues for *federal organizations*, where head offices are merely there to serve the needs of subsidiaries.

Successful strategy implementation requires that strategic resources are allocated and controlled efficiently and effectively. In reality, the availability and suitability of resources is a determinant of the feasibility of a particular strategic option. Of course, the existence of resources does not, in itself, guarantee effective implementation – they have to be managed. In addition, resources should be flexible to allow adaptive and incremental change.

We can think of *resource allocation* at two key levels:

- The allocation of *corporate* resources to particular businesses or divisions, based on perceived needs and priorities, and often linked to the growth of the business or industry in question
- The allocation of *functional* resources to build and add value in order to create and sustain competitive advantage.

Policies are designed to guide the use of resources by managers.

Budgets are used to allocate resources for particular activities and tasks. Budgets, however, are often short term in scope and the measurement of performance against budget targets may be more an evaluation of efficiency in the use of resources than of longer-term strategic effectiveness.

Resource allocation and management – and the inherent decisions – reflect the way in which the organization and its managers are dealing with the risks that they face. The key dimensions of risk are:

- the likelihood of certain eventualities – some of which could imply a detrimental impact for the organization, and
- the extent of the downside (perhaps a loss of orders, revenues or confidence) if the particular incident in question does occur.

While there is always a personal risk for entrepreneurs and strategic leaders in corporate strategy changes, a useful framework for clarifying and analysing risks is based on external (environmental) and internal (resource-based) factors.

Risks can be retained, transferred or regulated.

The relative success or relative failure of an organization to deal with the risks that it faces determines the extent to which it is crisis prone or crisis averse.

Crises can be major or minor, 'thinkable' in advance or more realistically unforeseeable. Consequently, organizations need strategies for avoiding crises in the first place and then for dealing with those crises that do occur. Handled well, a crisis can enhance the reputation of an organization. Handled badly, the impact can be substantial and prolonged.

Crises and disasters contain a mixture of 'cold' (technocratic) and 'warm' (people-related) elements. All too often organizations focus their attention on the cold elements when it is the warm ones that hold the key. By not learning lessons and by apportioning blame too readily organizations can legitimate crises and simply increase the likelihood of them happening again.

It remains a paradox that many managers are proud of their ability to crisis fight and deal with problems as they arise. This merely reinforces a reactive attitude and a short-term perspective, and it can be short-sighted.

Online cases for this chapter

Online Case 16.1: Hanson
Online Case 16.2: Three Diversification Strategies – BTR, Tomkins and Williams

Online Case 16.3: Black Cat/Standard Fireworks

Questions and research assignments

1 For which (general) corporate strategies are the financial control, strategic planning and strategic control styles of corporate management most appropriate?
2 How do you think the need for general managers might have changed as organization structures have generally been flattened and delayered?

3 Reflect on the work of Kanter and Handy in the late 20th century – sections 16.7.1 and 16.7.2 in the text. What view if any has best profiled the nature of the modern organization?
4 Are you personally risk averse or perceived as a risk taker? On what evidence are you drawing this conclusion?

Internet and library projects

1 Update the material on any or all of the four conglomerate businesses discussed in Online Case 16.1 on Hanson and Case 16.6 on BTR, Tomkins and Williams.

Using this and details of the corporate strategies pursued by other large companies with which you are familiar, which of the following two statements do you most agree with?

'Conglomerate diversification has now given way to focus strategies – focus is here to stay.'

'Focus strategies cannot generate sufficient growth long-term to satisfy shareholders – diversification will make a comeback.'
2 Take any large organization with which you are familiar. How have its head office structure and roles changed in recent years?
3 For an organization with which you are familiar, ascertain the main stated policies for finance, production, personnel and marketing.

How are these policies used? How were they created? How do they rate in terms of the principles of good policies discussed in the text?

4 Ascertain the budgeted resources and targets allocated to one manager whom you are able to interview.

What measures of performance are utilized? What feedback is provided? What does the manager do with the feedback? What do you believe is the personal impact of the budget and measures of performance on the manager? Is he or she motivated? Rewarded or sanctioned for success or failure?

5 Either by contacting a local councillor or using the Internet, ascertain how planning and budgeting are managed in your local authority. What have been the priority areas in the past? What are the current priorities? How have the changes in priority been decided?

6 In August 2000 the Russian nuclear submarine *Kursk* sank in the Barents Sea after an internal explosion. The whole crew was lost and the Russian government was criticized for not calling on foreign help and expertise as quickly as it might have done. What are the lessons in risk and crisis management from this incident?

7 Use the Internet to assess the possible long-term damage to Ford Motors when it was discovered (in 2000) that the Bridgestone/Firestone tyres used on its Explorer four-wheel drive vehicles were potentially dangerous and had been the cause of a number of accidents over a period of time. How do you think both Ford and Bridgestone handled the crisis – effectively or ineffectively?

Strategy activity

Jollibee

Jollibee, based in the Philippines, became the most rapidly expanding fast-food chain in Asia. It was established in 1978 by five Chinese–Filipino brothers, the Tan Caktiong family, since when it has acquired well over half of the fast-food market in the Philippines. At the beginning of the 21st century, there were over 400 branches worldwide, with half of these in the Philippines – of which one-third of this 200 were in Manila. McDonald's had 84 outlets; Wendy's and Kentucky Fried are also active competitors. By the end of 2007 there were 1650 branches and total sales in excess of US$ 1 billion. 600 of these were in Indonesia. The company mascot (named Jollibee) is a large bee in a blazer, shirt and chef's hat; it obviously competes with Ronald McDonald!

Boosted by a relaxation of laws concerning the extent of foreign investment in Filipino companies, Jollibee expanded abroad. An Australian, Tony Kitchener, was appointed to spearhead international developments. The early concentration was in South-East Asia and the Arab Gulf states, targeting especially Filipinos living in Indonesia, Malaysia, Brunei, Bahrain and Dubai. The number of overseas branches soon began to expand at a rate of 30 each year, with Hong Kong, China, Los Angeles and Rome high on the list of later priorities. Vietnam would follow. Increasingly, non-Filipinos have been attracted by the chain's individual products, which have been designed for low- to middle-income families with a sweet tooth, and for children's parties. Prices are kept slightly below those of McDonald's. The main product is an Asian-style hamburger, distinctive because it is cooked *with* the spices rather than them being placed on top afterwards – McDonald's has countered this with its local McDough brand. In addition, there are Spaghetti Fiesta (a Chinese-type mixed chow), salads and mango pie (a locally popular dish). While the hamburger tends to be ubiquitous, different countries have separate menus. Chicken masala is the most popular product in Malaysia and the Gulf. The bulk of the beef is imported from Australia and Jollibee makes all its own bread.

Jollibee waited for critical mass before announcing that 'its burgers are THE Asian fast food'. The company has also diversified, beginning with the acquisition of a pizza chain in the Philippines in 1993.

Expansion is now with joint ventures and franchising such that capital for growth is not a big problem. A majority of the outlets are now franchised. It also takes some account of the fact that Jollibee's first independent overseas development in Taiwan (in 1988) was not altogether successful. The chosen location was wrong. In 1994 Jollibee acquired Greenwich Pizza, another Indonesian business which allowed it to access the local pizza-pasta market. More recently it has acquired business interests in China.

In 1997 Jollibee had to overcome one interesting setback. After the company opened a branch in Port Moresby in Papua New Guinea someone, possibly a competitor, placed the following advertisement in a newspaper: 'Wanted urgently, dogs and cats, any breed.

Will pay 40 toea (equivalent to 24 US cents) per kilo live weight. Apply to the Jollibee....' The company described this as a criminal attempt to try and sabotage their business, but failed to track down the instigator.

In 1998 and 1999 Jollibee, like many Asian businesses, had to deal with what might have been a far bigger potential crisis – the uncertainty caused by high domestic inflation and drastic falls in the value of local currencies. In the event this turned into a wonderful opportunity for Jollibee – whose growth continued unabated. Redundant, experienced executives were keen to buy franchises – in part because the demand for fast food grew. In a part of the world where eating out is normal, the lower-priced fast food outlets took business away from the more expensive restaurants.

Questions

1 Can anything sensible be done to *prevent* an incident such as the rogue advertisement, or does it always come down to effective reaction?

2 Do you think this amounts to anything more than 'bad luck'?

3 Do you think it is coincidental that McDonald's has also been targeted by activists?

Further reading

Bishop, JD (1991) The Moral Responsibility of Corporate Executives for Disasters, *Journal of Business Ethics*, 10.

Ford, JD (1981) The management of organizational crises, *Business Horizons*, May–June.

Goold, M and Campbell, A (1987) Managing diversity – strategy and control in diversified British companies, *Long Range Planning*, 20 (5).

Goold, M and Campbell, A (2002) Parenting in complex structures, *Long Range Planning*, 35.

Porter, ME (1987) From competitive advantage to corporate strategy, *Harvard Business Review*, May–June.

References

Bartha, P (1995) Preventing a high-cost crisis, *Business Quarterly*, Winter.

Birch, P and Clegg, B (1996) *Imagination Engineering*, Pitman.

Booth, S (1990) Dux at the crux, *Management Today*, May.

Caulkin, S (1996) Focus is for wimps, *Management Today*, December.

Clarke, CJ and Varma, S (1999) Strategic risk management – the new competitive edge, *Long Range Planning*, 32 (4).

Dixon, M (1989) The very model of a mythical manager, *Financial Times*, 10 May.

Dunnette, MD and Taylor, RN (1975) Influence of dogmatism, risk taking propensity and intelligence on decision making strategy for a sample of industrial managers, *Journal of Applied Psychology*, 59 (4).

Egan, G. (1993) Adding Value: A Systematic Guide to Business-driven Management and Leadership, Jossey Bass.

Friedman, M (1979) The social responsibility of business is to increase its profits. In *Business Policy and Strategy* (eds DJ McCarthy, RJ Minichiello and JR Curran), Irwin.

Geneen, H (1997) *The Synergy Myth*, St. Martin's Press.

Goold, M and Campbell, A (1988) *Strategies and Styles*, Blackwell.

Goold, M, Campbell, A and Luchs, K (1993) Strategies and styles revisited: strategic planning and financial control, *Long Range Planning*, 26 (5); Strategies and styles revisited: strategic control – is it tenable? *Long Range Planning*, 26 (6).

Goold, M, Campbell, A and Alexander, M (1994) *Corporate Level Strategy*, John Wiley.

Green, O (1994) Quoted in *Management Today*, June.

Hamel, G and Prahalad, CK (1994) *Competing for the Future*, Harvard Business School Press.

Handy, C (1994) *The Empty Raincoat*, Hutchinson.

Handy, C (1995) *Beyond Certainty: The Changing Worlds of Organizations*, Hutchinson.

Herbert, TT and Deresky, H (1987) Should general managers match their business strategies? *Organizational Dynamics*, 15 (3).

Infoplan International (1997) *Review of Crisis and Risk Management*, London.

Jackson, T (1995) Giant bows to colossal pressure, *Financial Times*, 22 September.

Kabak, IW and Siomkos, GJ (1990) How can an industrial crisis be managed effectively? *Industrial Engineering*, June.

Kanter, RM (1989) *When Giants Learn to Dance*, Simon & Schuster.

Kets de Vries, M (1997) Creative rebels with a cause, in Birley, S and Muzyka, D, *Mastering Enterprise*, Financial Times/Pitman.

Knight, RF (2000) Recovering well from tragedy, *Financial Times*, 3 August.

Lawrence, PR and Lorsch, JW (1967) *Organization and Environment*, Richard D Irwin.

McMahon, JT and Perrit, GW (1973) Toward a contingency theory of organizational control, *Academy of Management Journal*, 16.

Nash, T (1990) Tales of the unexpected, *The Director*, March.

Porter, ME (1987) From competitive advantage to corporate strategy, *Harvard Business Review*, May–June.

Reed, R and Buckley, MR (1988) Strategy and action: techniques for implementing strategy, *Long Range Planning*, 21 (3).

Regester, M and Larkin, J (1997) *Risk Issues and Crisis Management*, Institute of Public Relations.

Richter, A and Owen, G (1997) The UK cut down to size, *Financial Times*, 10 March.

Sadtler, D, Campbell, A and Koch, R (1997) *Break Up! When Large Companies are Worth More Dead Than Alive*, Capstone.

Shrivastava, P, Mitroff, I, Miller, D and Miglani, M (1988) Understanding industrial crises, *Journal of Management Studies*, 25 (4).

Smith, D (1990) Beyond contingency planning – towards a model of crisis management, *Industrial Crisis Quarterly*, 4 (4).

Stonich, PJ (1982) *Implementing Strategy*, Ballinger.

Wernham, R (1984) Bridging the awful gap between strategy and action, *Long Range Planning*, 17.

Chapter 17

Final thoughts: the purpose of strategy

PART 1
Understanding strategy

1 Introducing strategy and strategic management

STRATEGIC MANAGEMENT: AWARENESS AND CHANGE

PART 5
Strategic management

14 Strategy implementation

15 Leading change

16 Managing strategy in the organization

17 Final thoughts – the purpose of strategy

PART 2
Strategic positioning

2 Strategic thinking, environmental analysis, synergy and strategic positioning

3 Resource-led strategy

4 The dynamics of competition

5 Introducing culture and values

PART 4
Issues in strategic growth

11 Strategic growth

12 International strategy

13 Failure, consolidation and recovery strategies

PART 3
Strategic analysis and choice

6 Strategic purpose

7 Strategic success

8 An introduction to strategy creation and planning

9 Strategic leadership, entrepreneurship and intrapreneurship

10 Strategic alternatives, strategy evaluation and strategy selection

Success is never final.

WINSTON CHURCHILL

Things may come to those who wait – but only the things left by those who hustle.

ABRAHAM LINCOLN

17.1 Introduction

In these last few pages the main ideas from this book are synthesized in order to reinforce the key ideas and to address two questions: first – what is the purpose of strategy? – and second – what is strategy?

Many organizations are now operating or competing in dynamic, turbulent, uncertain, and chaotic financial and business environments. In business terms this is partly the result of industries and markets becoming ever more global; it is also driven by continual improvements in technology which, among other things, causes product, service and **strategic life cycles** to shorten. In turn this means that organizations must act, react and change more quickly. Some of these changes will be continuous and emergent, as vigilant, responsive organizations seize opportunities and innovate ahead of their rivals.

Other changes will be discontinuous and imply changes in competitive paradigms. Technology can both create and destroy industries, markets and windows of opportunity; breakpoints – or switches to new competitive rules and agendas – happen increasingly frequently. Organizations cannot ignore this reality and the pressures that they bring, however disruptive the changes might be.

17.2 The purpose of strategy

Famous, and hopefully long lasting organizations, such as Coca-Cola, Apple and Walt Disney, continue to survive these breakpoints – sometimes actually creating them – and, as a result, they thrive, grow and prosper. They are recognized around the world and they exploit their competencies and their reputation. They create E–V–R (environment–values–resources) congruency and sustain it with carefully managed change. These organizations can be many things – perhaps entrepreneurial, maybe professional. Whatever, they are exceptional. We can learn from their actions, strategies and behaviours, although it will always remain difficult to explain fully all of the reasons for their success. Simply attempting to copy their behaviour is not an adequate answer to the challenges facing organizations.

Other companies grow more steadily and uncertainly; they never seem to have the same command over their environment. Nonetheless, they do survive, partly with innovation, partly with contingent reaction. Others survive for some period of time, but then decline as they lose E–V–R congruency. Some organizations only survive with a change of leadership, style and culture. However, some businesses disappear every year, some to takeover, others to liquidation. It is, therefore, all too easy for currently successful firms to lose their edge and their competitive advantage. Miles and Snow (1994) argue that there are four main reasons for this:

- a lack of awareness and a failure to be alert to new opportunities and threats
- retaining a belief in a successful competitive paradigm for too long. Market leaders seem particularly prone to do this; they tend to rely on *continuous* change to retain their leadership

- an unwillingness to accept the need for structural or cultural change, and

- poor judgement, causing a company to make poor, inappropriate decisions.

There are important lessons to be learned from their relative demise.

In looking at strategic effectiveness and success, we can take two related, but distinct, perspectives. The first concerns success: what reasons lie behind the relative prosperity of our most successful organizations, those which continue to add value for their customers, differentiate their products and services, and control their costs? The second perspective concerns survival and environmental management: what factors distinguish a crisis averse from a crisis prone organization? The latter will typically lurch from problem to problem, difficulty to difficulty, crisis to crisis, never really managing its environment. It is fashionable, in the authors' opinion, to talk about competitiveness, competitive advantage and success; it is less fashionable, but equally important – and in many cases, more relevant – to explore the issues behind crisis aversion. Too many organizations hover on the narrow line which separates survival from failure.

Organizations are systems that comprise people who are trying to act purposefully rather than thrash around without any real purpose (Checkland 1981). However, people differ in their perspective and perceptions. They use their personal meaning systems to interpret events, actions, opportunities and threats and to decide upon responses. While their personal strengths must be captured and exploited, organizational information systems should ensure that they work within the parameters of the corporate purpose, vision and policies, and that their initiatives and contributions are shared and understood.

Remember the two key themes: opportunity and risk. Success over time requires organizations to be entrepreneurial, to find new opportunities and to manage the inherent and inevitable risks.

The new technological revolution and the increase in globalization have forced change on organizations everywhere, regardless of their type, size and sector. Few are unscathed. Some have embraced change positively and willingly; others more reluctantly. Those who have failed to change have probably been sold or liquidated. One outcome of this can be a more flexible, but slimmed-down workforce.

On the positive side, many managers and employees are better educated. They are information technology (IT) literate, knowledge workers in a knowledge-based society. Some of them possess scarce skills. In some organizations people have become less constrained and more empowered, willing to be creative and show initiative in a more open, less hierarchical firm. Finally, information often flows more horizontally and freely, enriching and speeding up decision-making.

But this, clearly, is not the case everywhere.

Many workers are now part-time and 'peripheral', as opposed to 'core'. When re-engineering their processes and changing their structures too many companies have gone too far. They have downsized but not rightsized. Important skills and competencies have been lost. Linked to this, strategies of focusing on core activities and competencies, and divesting those which are non-core, have created an increasing incidence of strategic alliances and networks. Managing these networks effectively demands new capabilities, which many organizations have yet to develop fully. People today feel under greater pressure and stress; there is more fear and insecurity. To some extent the bounty of globalization and technology is stress. Hard as distinct from soft human resource strategies are practised in too many companies, and many employees, instead of committing themselves to a single company, look to switch organizations and industries as they take more control of their working lives, and this despite the widespread managerial unemployment and insecurity.

Sadly, many large organizations, composed of very intelligent people, are still slow to respond to change pressures and, when they do, their behaviour is often ponderous. In the new world of rapid change having the 'right' strategic leader is ever more important. Individuals can, and often do, act dynamically and entrepreneurially; yet many organizations have still to work out how to capture the intelligence and learning in order to facilitate the change process. They still do not manage well their human assets. This is the paradox of the large organization – learning how to behave like the archetypal small business.

The challenge of embracing both the hard and soft elements of strategic management in order to increase strategic awareness and manage strategic change more effectively remains a major challenge for many organizations. It is a challenge that is more likely to intensify than to disappear.

This final chapter, therefore:

- identifies ten key elements of strategy
- reviews the strategic paradoxes which have been debated throughout the book
- finishes with a view on what strategy is.

17.3 Ten key elements of strategy

Figure 17.1 shows ten elements of strategy that have been discussed at various points in the book. The first six (in the central box) are interdependent and if they are interwoven effectively the organization should be more crisis averse than crisis prone. The remaining four impact upon the whole process of strategy creation and implementation.

1 **Perspectives of strategy** Strategy can be about the past (emergent patterns from previous decisions), the present (strategic positions) and the future (strategic plans). It can also be treated at the levels of broad purpose and narrow tactical ploys. All of these perspectives are relevant to the debate about what strategy is. The relevance of strategy will also vary for different people. The main perspective for the strategic leader is the overall corporate

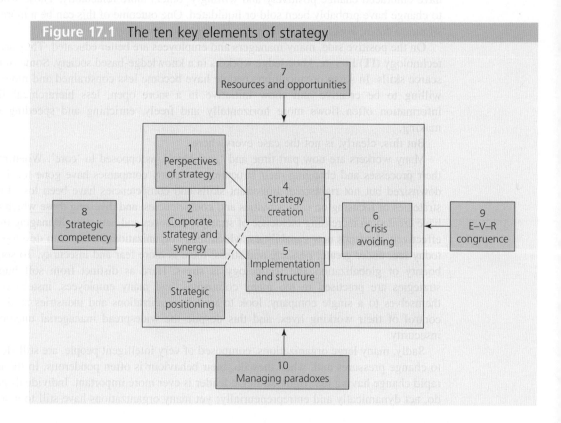

Figure 17.1   The ten key elements of strategy

strategy for the whole organization, although the other levels are clearly relevant. Other senior managers will be focused on competitive positions and the competitive strategies which determine whether or not the organization enjoys competitive advantage. The activities and functional strategies are perhaps most important to lower-level middle and junior managers but, at the same time, it is vital they understand the wider picture and the contribution that they make.

2 **Corporate strategy and synergy** The issue here, which was discussed towards the end of the book, is whether or not there is a logical and defensible heartland of related businesses comprising the corporate portfolio. Ideally, each business will be individually competitive and successful in its own right and, at the same time, contribute synergistically to the corporate parent and to other businesses in the portfolio. The parent organization should equally be able to contribute value to each business.

3 **Strategic positioning and competitive advantage** To be successful, each business or activity will need to establish – and sustain with change – a clear and strong competitive position. Where this position delivers either a cost advantage (when compared with rivals in the market) or a differentiated position which customers perceive as relevant and valuable, or both, then competitive advantage is a real possibility. The advantage does not come from the position itself, but from the activities – competencies and capabilities – which create and sustain the position of advantage.

4 **Strategy creation** Strategy creation is about change. Consequently, the approach that the organization takes to strategy creation is dictated by the strategic leader and influenced, and possibly constrained, by the culture of the organization. Three broad approaches were identified. First, visionary or entrepreneurial strategy creation, itself a reflection of strong strategic leadership. Second, planned strategy, the outcome of analysis and possibly the outcome of a planning system. Together, these reflect intended strategies. Third, emergent strategy creation, which takes two forms: incremental changes to intended strategies during the implementation phase, and adaptive strategy creation in a dynamic and turbulent environment. Organizations need to find an effective blend of the three, all of which are likely to be present to some degree.

5 **Strategy implementation and structure** Strategies must be implemented before they can be deemed successful. While organization structures are designed to ensure that intended strategies can be implemented effectively, the very operation of the structure is the foundation for emergent strategy creation. This issue is naturally tied in to the relative significance of centralization and decentralization, and the extent to which managers are empowered.

6 **Crisis avoiding** If these first five points are being dealt with effectively the organization should be relatively crisis averse in a dynamic environment. Where there are significant weaknesses, the organization is likely to be more crisis prone.

7 **Resources and opportunities** There are three approaches to the management of strategy. While they are different, it is a mistake to adopt one approach at the expense of the others. The approaches are complementary and should be pursued together. The opportunity-driven approach begins with a scan of the external business environment in a search for new opportunities that the organization might be able to exploit. The resource-based approach builds on the organization's core competencies and strategic capabilities. In essence, the successful organization will address two questions simultaneously. One, what new windows of opportunities are opening up that we might wish to follow because we possess, or can obtain, the necessary strategic resources? Two, what are our distinctive competencies and capabilities and where are there untapped possibilities for exploiting them further? The third approach is more tactical and reactive in nature and it concerns the ability and willingness to deal with competitor tactics and initiatives as and when they occur.

8 **Strategic competency** Strategic competency goes beyond the idea of core (technological) competencies and strategic (process) capabilities discussed above. It embraces everything an organization must be capable of doing effectively, or at least satisfactorily, if it is to survive, grow and prosper. This embraces strategic thinking and stakeholder satisfaction, the capability to deliver consistent quality, change competencies, social responsibility and crisis avoidance. A more extensive discussion of these competencies is found in Richardson and Thompson (1996).

9 **E–V–R congruence** Successful organizations create and sustain congruency between the external environment (the source of fresh opportunities and threats), their values and their resources (competencies, capabilities and strengths). It is these values that dictate the ability of the organization to change both continuously (incrementally) and discontinuously (occasionally to new competitive paradigms).

10 **Strategic paradoxes** This is discussed in the next section of this chapter. Simply, the organization must work out a stance for dealing with a whole series of issues and challenges for which there are no clear-cut answers.

17.4 Strategic paradoxes

Strategic issues, challenges or paradoxes concern things the organization has to make decisions about, and for which the answers are not clear-cut. The choices that the organization makes – and the relatedness of the decisions that it takes on each of the issues – will have a marked impact upon its strategic effectiveness.

This section recaps the main ones – readers will appreciate how every one of these has been debated at some stage in the book.

Paradox 1: Past and future   All organizations build on the past. Sometimes they learn from their successes; on other occasions they learn from their mistakes. Normally, developments from the past will imply continuous improvement around the same competitive paradigm. Sometimes, however, the future requires more dramatic and discontinuous change which implies that past and current competitive paradigms are abandoned. It is a mistake to persist with yesterday's and today's products if their life cycle is heading for decline but, equally, change for the sake of change can be unnecessarily disruptive and threaten control and quality. The challenge, then, is one of balance.

Paradox 2: Intended and emergent strategy   Strategic analysis and planning plays an important role in strategy, as does the contribution of a strong and charismatic entrepreneurial leader. However, plans and intentions must be seen as flexible and there is an inherent danger in being reliant on just one main source of ideas. In such a dynamic and competitive environment, learning and emergent strategy will always be vital. The challenge is again one of balance.

Paradox 3: Reactive or proactive?   Some students of this subject argue that the real challenge for organizations is one of coping in an environment that is chaotic, unpredictable and uncertain. Organizations must be able both to manage in and to manage their environments. They must respond to the unexpected events and surprises; they must at times lead the change agenda.

Paradox 4: Resource-based or opportunity driven?   This point was explained earlier in this chapter, when it was highlighted that both need adopting simultaneously. The chances are that one or the other will take priority – but which, and with what emphasis?

Paradox 5: Cost or differentiation?   Again, the answer is both! Organizations, in their search for competitive advantage, can never ignore costs. There is, however, a distinction between striving to be the cost leader (with lower costs than one's main rivals for the same product or service) and effective cost management. Organizations that look to add new values and differentiate their products and services in distinctive ways must invest (and increase their costs) to create this difference – at the same time, there is no benefit in adding costs and benefits that are of little consequence to customers. The secret lies in understanding and managing the key cost drivers.

Paradox 6: Focus or diversify?   Contemporary strategic logic says focus. The era of the diversified conglomerate is over, at least for the moment. However, a very tight focus can restrain growth, and consequently most organizations that are seeking to grow will diversify in justifiably related areas. The link might be technology or markets.

Paradox 7: How big?   The focus/diversify dilemma is related to growth ambitions. The large organization may be able to claim critical mass, perhaps important in its industry, especially where it has ambitions to be a global competitor. Some very successful organizations deliberately set out to be number one or number two in every market segment in which they compete. Their challenge is to retain the flexibility and the innovation of the small, entrepreneurial business as they grow, to ensure that they do not reach a position of stasis in the cycle of growth and maybe have to engineer a crisis to address the need for renewed creativity. Even the largest, global organizations need to be relevant locally around the world.

Paradox 8: Centralize or decentralize?   Centralization certainly retains control at the top of the organization and allows for hands-on leadership from the strategic leader. Unfortunately, it can make the organization slow to respond in a dynamic environment. Decentralization and empowerment can increase flexibility, in conjunction with a hands-off leadership style, but now control has to be achieved through a carefully crafted information system. It seems impossible to balance the two in a totally satisfactory manner and so organizations continually swing from one to the other. Sometimes the adjustments are minor; on other occasions there are major structural changes.

17.5 In conclusion – what is strategy?

To answer this we return to the 12-question strategy framework model in Chapter 1, Figure 1.8. Strategy is about being aware and being in control of the change agenda. It requires organizations to have clear answers for a number of key strategic questions.

Strategy, therefore, is:

- *Knowing where the organization is and how well it is performing* – this demands a clear understanding of strategic positioning, backed up by effective performance measures
- *Ensuring that employees know and support what the organization stands for and where it is going* – this implies that strategies are value driven and that employees appreciate the role and significance of their contribution. It is accomplished with a sound and shared mission, purpose and direction
- *Knowing how the organization intends to follow this direction* – this lies with intended strategies which build on, and exploit, key resources, competencies and capabilities – in the context of identified opportunities

- *Ensuring that strategies and strategic ideas are implemented, while recognizing that there will be a constant need for vigilance and flexibility* – specifically, an organization which can respond to environmental turbulence, competitor actions and occasional setbacks – and innovate to change its strategies; one in which people have some control over the work they contribute.

The appropriate performance measures concern efficiency (doings things right) and effectiveness (doing the right things). Effectiveness encompasses the interests of all key stakeholders – in particular employees, who contribute ideas and ensure that strategies are implemented, customers, for whom the value is created and built, and the shareholders who retain faith in the business and support it financially. Where these are in place we should have an organization which can demonstrate E–V–R congruence and which will be more crisis averse than crisis prone.

In a nutshell, strategy is about what organizations do.

It is about doing the right things right – and for the right reasons.

These activities are carried out by everyone in the organization. Managers 'everywhere' and at all levels affect the choices, decisions and tactics. It is therefore important that managers think strategically and appreciate the (holistic) impact of their decisions, choices and actions. Having read this book you may (and should) think this is not 'rocket science'. So, why is this not more evident?

References

Checkland, PB (1981) *Systems Thinking, Systems Practice*, John Wiley.

Miles, RE and Snow, CC (1994) *Fit, Failure and the Hall of Fame: How Companies Succeed or Fail*, Free Press.

Richardson, B and Thompson, JL (1996) Strategic and Competitive Success: Towards a Model of the Comprehensively Competent Organization, *Management Decision*, Vol 34, No 2.

Glossary

acquisition—the purchase of one company by another, for either cash or equity in the parent. Sometimes the word *takeover* is preferred when the acquisition is hostile, and resisted by the company being bought. Similarly, *mergers* are when two companies simply *agree* to come together as one.

activities—those things – acts and tasks – undertaken by an organization which, when aggregated, dictate the strength of a *strategic position*.

adaptive strategic change—strategies that emerge and develop on an ongoing basis as companies learn of new environmental opportunities and threats and adapt (or respond) to competitive pressures.

adding value—technically, the difference between the value of a firm's outputs and its inputs; the additional value is added through the deployment and effort of the organization's resources. Successful organizations will seek to add value to create outputs which are perceived as important by their customers. The *added value* or *supply chain* is the sequential set of activities from suppliers, through manufacturers and distributors, which is required to bring products and services to the marketplace.

alliance (strategic alliance)—an agreement, preferably formalized, with another organization. The alliance might be with an important supplier, with a major distributor, or possibly with a competitor, say for joint research and development.

appropriability—the ability of an organization to ensure that at least some of the benefits earned from the value that it creates and adds comes back to the organization, rather than only benefiting others, such as suppliers, customers or even competitors.

architecture—a relational network involving either or both external linkages (see *alliance*) or internal linkages between managers in a company or businesses in a conglomerate. The supply chain is one such network. The main benefits concern information exchanges for the mutual gain of those involved, and *synergies* (see below) from interdependencies. Sometimes linked with reputation and innovation as key strategic resources for an organization.

backward (vertical) integration—the process by which a manufacturer acquires direct control over its inputs, such that it makes what it previously bought in. See also *vertical integration.*

benchmarking—a process of comparative evaluation – of products, services and the performances of equipment and personnel. Sometimes companies attempt to benchmark their competitors; on other occasions they will benchmark those organizations which are seen as high performers.

bird approach—is an approach to strategic management resembling a bird scanning the horizon for the best tree to land on, thus experiencing almost unlimited choice. It is often viewed as an arbitrary and risky approach.

blue ocean strategy—is where organizations discover radical new opportunities for competitive advantage and thus reduce the likelihood of damage from aggressive price competition.

branding—the additional value and reassurance provided to customers through the reputation of the business, represented by the strength and visibility of its brand name.

break-even—the level of activity where the total costs incurred in producing and selling a product or service – or pursuing a particular strategy – are equal to the total revenues generated.

business environment—see *environment.*

business ethics—the principles, standards and conduct that an organization practises – and sometimes states formally – for the way in which it deals with its people, its external stakeholders and environmental issues that arise.

business model—a concise summary of the organization and its strategy which answers three questions – what, for whom and why? What products and business activities the organization will engage in – and what it will not, who the target market is for each product or business and what their compelling reason to buy is – the why element.

business process re-engineering—the analysis and redesign of workflows and processes within organizations and between them (i.e. along the supply chain).

combination strategies—term used where more than one discrete strategic alternative is pursued at the same time. Particularly relevant for a mixture of market penetration, market development and product development strategies; and invariably implies innovation.

competitive advantage—the ability of an organization to add more value for its customers than its rivals, and thus attain a position of relative advantage. The challenge is to sustain any advantage once achieved.

competitive logic— linked to Competitive Advantage, competitive logic concerns the robustness and viability of the competitive strategy for a product, service or business.

competitive platforms—the important bases of competition in an industry and for an individual competitor.

competitive strategy—the means by which organizations seek to achieve and sustain competitive advantage. Usually the result of distinctive *functional strategies.*

There should be a competitive strategy for every product and service produced by the company.

competitor gap analysis—a comparison of the organization with its leading competitors in terms of their respective ability to satisfy key success factors. Ideally, this will involve an input from relevant customers.

competitor-influenced strategy—strategies and tactics that arise from a need to compete in an industry or environment – for both markets and resources. When an organization introduces changes, competitors are likely to react, forcing further incremental changes. At the same time, competitors introduce new strategic ideas that vigilant organizations will respond to.

concentration ratios—normally the degree to which added value and/or turnover and/or assets in an industry are concentrated in the hands of a few suppliers. High concentration is reflected in monopoly and oligopoly industry structures. Sometimes measured in terms of aggregate output controlled by the largest companies in a country.

controls—means by which progress against stated objectives and targets is measured and monitored, and changed as necessary.

core competencies—distinctive skills, normally related to a product, service or technology, which can be used to create a competitive advantage. See also *strategic capability*. Together, they form key resources that assist an organization in being different from (and ideally superior to) its competitors.

corporate governance—the selection, role and responsibilities of the strategic leadership of the organization, their conduct and their relationships with internal and external stakeholders. Sometimes responsibility for overall strategy and ongoing operations will be separated.

corporate strategy—the overall strategy for a diversified or multiproduct/multiservice organization. Refers to the overall scope of the business in terms of products, services and geography.

cost leadership—the lowest cost producer in a market, after adjustments for quality differences. An important source of competitive advantage in either a market or a segment of a market. Specifically, the cost leader is the company that enjoys a cost advantage over its rivals through the management of its resources, and not simply because it produces the lowest quality.

cost of capital—the cost of capital employed to fund strategic initiatives, combining the rate of interest on debt and the cost of equity. The typical formula used is the weighted average cost of capital which encompasses the relative proportions of debt and equity. Should normally be lower than the discounted rate of return from the investment or initiative – see *discounted cash flow*.

credit crunch—a term used to explain a shortage of credit in an economy. The impact is felt by organizations which experience difficulties in borrowing money to invest and expand.

crisis management—how the organization (a) seeks to reduce the likelihood of, and (b) manages in the event of, a major disturbance which has the potential to damage the organization's assets or reputation. Some crises are the result of mismanagement or inadequate controls; others begin outside the organization and may be unavoidable.

critical mass—relates to the actual and relative size of an organization in terms of its ability to be influential and powerful in its industry or environment.

critical success factors—see *key success factors*.

culture—the values and norms of an organization, which determine its corporate behaviour and the behaviour of people within the organization.

decentralization/centralization—the extent to which authority, responsibility and accountability are devolved throughout the organization. Centralization should yield tight control; decentralization motivates managers and allows for speedier reactions to environmental change pressures.

delayering—the flattening of an organization structure by removing layers of management and administration.

demerger or divestment—term used when an organization sells or spins off (or maybe even closes) a business or activity. Usually linked to a strategy of increased focus.

differentiation—products and services are differentiated when customers perceive them to have distinctive properties that set them apart from their competitors.

directional policy matrix—a planning technique used to compare and contrast the relative competitive strengths of a portfolio of products and services produced by an organization. Used to help in evaluating their relative worth and investment potential.

discounted cash flow (DCF)—the sum of the projected cash returns or flows over a period of years from a strategic investment or initiative. Future figures are reduced (specifically, inflation is removed) to bring them into line with present values.

diversification—the extent of the differences between the various products and services in a company's portfolio (its range of activities). The products and services may be *related* through say marketing or technology, or *unrelated*, which normally implies that they require different management skills.

divestment—see *demerger*.

divisionalization—a form of organization structure whereby activities are divided and separated on the basis of different products or services, or geographical territories.

dot.com companies—organizations that have emerged as the power and potential of the Internet has been realized and exploited. Dot.com companies will normally trade over the Internet, but some are essentially service providers.

double-loop learning—an assessment of the continuing appropriateness and value of existing competitive positions and paradigms and the ability to create new competitive positions, ideally ahead of competitors. See also *single-loop learning*.

downsizing—sometimes associated with business process re-engineering, downsizing occurs when organizations rationalize their product/service ranges and streamline their processes. People, in particular layers of management, are removed. See also *rightsizing*.

e-commerce—short for electronic commerce, and meaning trading over the Internet.

e-markets—markets is the term used for when buyers and sellers come together to engineer an exchange. E-markets is the term used when this trading is via the Internet.

economies of scale—cost savings accrued with high volume production, which enables lower unit production costs.

effectiveness—the ability of an organization to meet the demands and expectations of its various stakeholders, those individuals or groups with influence over the business. Sometimes known as 'doing the right things'.

efficiency—the sound management of resources to maximize the returns from them. Known as 'doing things right'.

emergent strategy—term used to describe and explain strategies which emerge over time and often with an element of trial and error. Detailed implementation is not prescribed in advance. Some emergent strategies are *incremental changes* with learning as intended strategies are implemented. Other *adaptive strategies* are responses to new environmental opportunities and threats.

empowerment—freeing people from a rigid regime of rules, controls and directives and allowing them to take responsibility for their own decisions and actions.

entrepreneur—someone who perpetually creates and innovates to build something of recognized value around perceived opportunities.

entrepreneurial/visionary strategies—strategies created by strong, visionary strategic leaders. Their successful implementation relies on an ability to persuade others of their merit.

environment—everything and everyone outside the organization or organizational boundary – including competitors, customers, financiers, suppliers and government.

E–V–R (environment–values–resources) congruence—the effective matching of an organization's resources (R) with the demands of its environment (E). A successful and sustained match has to be managed and frequently requires change; successfully achieving this depends on the organization's culture and values (V).

experience curve—the relationship between (reducing) unit costs and the total number of units ever produced of a product. Usually plotted as a graph, and often with a straight-line relationship on logarithmic axes. The percentage unit cost reduction holds steady every time output is doubled.

financial control—term used to describe the form of control normally found in a *holding company* structure. Strategy

creation is decentralized to independent business units which are required to meet agreed financial targets.

focus strategy—concentration on one or a limited number of market segments or niches.

forward (vertical) integration—when an organization takes control of aspects of its distribution, transport or direct selling. See also *vertical integration*.

functional strategies—the strategies for the various functions carried out by an organization, including marketing, production, financial management, information management, research and development and human resource management. One or more functional strategies will typically be responsible for any distinctive competitive edge enjoyed by the company.

functional structure—a structure based around individual functions, such as production, sales and finance, all of which report to an identifiable managing director/chief executive.

generic strategies—the basic competitive strategies – based on cost leadership, differentiation and focus – which are open to any competitor in an industry, and which can be a source of competitive advantage.

global strategies—strategies for companies which manufacture and market in several countries and/or continents. Issues concern, for example, the location of manufacturing units and the extent to which control is centralized at a home base or decentralized on a local basis.

governance—the location of power and responsibility at the head of an organization. See also *corporate governance*.

heartland—term used to describe a cluster of businesses (in a multibusiness organization) which can be justifiably related and integrated to generate synergies.

holding company—a structure where the various businesses are seen as largely independent of each other and managed accordingly.

horizontal integration—the acquisition or merger of firms at the same stage in the supply chain. Such firms may be direct competitors or focus on different market segments.

implementation—see *strategy implementation*.

incremental strategic changes—changes to intended (possibly planned) strategies as they are implemented. Result from ongoing learning and from changes in the environment or to forecast assumptions.

innovation—changes to products, processes and services in an attempt to sharpen their competitiveness – through either cost reduction or improved distinctiveness. Strategically, it can apply to any part of a business.

intangible (strategic) resources—resources which have no physical presence, but which can add real value for the organization. Reputation and technical knowledge would be typical examples.

intellectual capital—the hidden value (and capital) tied up in an organization's people which can set it apart from its competitors and be a valuable source of competitive advantage and future earnings. Difficult to quantify and value for the balance sheet. Linked to *knowledge*.

intended strategies—prescribed strategies the organization intends to implement, albeit with incremental changes. Sometimes the result of (formal) strategic planning; sometimes the stated intent of the strategic leader. May be described alternatively as *prescriptive strategies*.

intrapreneurship—the process of internal entrepreneurship. Occurs when managers or other employees accept responsibility and actively champion new initiatives aimed at making a real difference.

joint venture—a form of strategic alliance where each partner takes a financial stake. This could be a shareholding in the other partner or the establishment of a separate, jointly owned, business.

just in time (JIT)—systems or processes for ensuring that stocks or components are delivered just when and where they are needed, reducing the need for inventory.

key (or critical) success factors—environmentally based factors which are crucial for competitive success. Simply, the things that an organization must be able to do well if it is to succeed.

knowledge—an amalgamation of experience, values, information, insight and strategic awareness – which goes beyond the notions of data and information. Retained, managed and exploited it can be a valuable source of competitive difference and advantage. See also *intellectual capital*.

leadership—see *strategic leader*.

learning organization—one which is capable of harnessing and spreading best practices, and where employees can learn from each other and from other organizations. The secret lies in open and effective communications networks.

leverage—the exploitation, by an organization, of its resources to their full extent. Often linked to the idea of *stretching resources*.

life cycle—see *strategic life cycle*.

liquidation—the closing down of a business, normally because it has failed. Typically a last resort, when a rescue or sale has either not been possible or not successful.

logical incrementalism—term adopted by John B. Quinn to explain strategy creation in small, logical, incremental steps.

(the) long tail—relates to an extended product life cycle, especially for products (or services) whose popularity rises and falls rapidly due to 'fashion'. Through e-commerce, products (such as CD titles and books) can remain available without normal distribution channels needing to carry expensive inventory.

Machiavellianism—where individuals use power and influence to structure situations and events, and bring about outcomes, which are more in their own personal interests than those of the organization. Linked to *organizational politics*.

market development—continuing with existing products and services but, and possibly with modifications and additions, seeking new market and new market segment opportunities.

market-driven strategy—alternative term for *opportunity-driven strategy*.

market penetration—persisting with existing products/services and existing customers and markets but accepting that continuous, incremental improvement is possible to strengthen the relevant strategic position. The assumption is that sales and revenue can be increased.

market segment(ation)—the use of particular marketing strategies to target identified and defined groups of customers.

mass marketing—where one product (or service) is sold to all types of customer.

matrix organization—a multidivisional organization which seeks to link the various functional activities across the divisions, to achieve the synergy benefits of interdependency.

merger—see *acquisition*.

milestones—interim targets which act as indicators or measures of progress in the pursuit of objectives and the implementation of strategies.

military strategy—strategy and planning in the context of warfare through the ages. Strategy has its origins in warfare and consequently a study of military strategy can provide valuable insights into corporate behaviour.

mission statement—a summary of the essential aim or purpose of the organization; its essential reason for being in business.

monopoly power—the relative power of an individual company in an industry. It does not follow that a dominant competitor will act against the best interests of customers and consumers, but it could be in a position to do so.

monopoly structure—term for an industry with a dominant and very powerful competitor. Originally based on the idea of total control, competitive authorities around the world now consider a 25 per cent market or asset share to be a basis for possible monopoly power.

multinational company—a company operating in several countries. See *global strategies*.

niche marketing—concentration on a small, identifiable market segment with the aim of achieving dominance of the segment.

not-for-profit organization—term used to describe an organization (such as a charity) that does not have profit as a fundamental objective. Such organizations will, however, have to achieve a cash surplus to survive.

objectives—short-term targets or milestones with defined measurable achievements. A desired state and hoped-for level of success.

oligopoly—(structure) an industry dominated by a small group of competitors.

opportunity-driven strategy—strategy creation and development that begins with an analysis of external environmental threats and opportunities. See also *resource-based strategy*.

organizational politics—the process by which individuals and groups utilize power and influence to obtain results. Politics can be used legitimately in the best interests of the organization, or illegitimately by people who put their own interests above those of the organization.

outsource/outsourcing—procuring products and services from independent suppliers rather than producing them within the organization. Often linked to strategies of focusing on core competencies and capabilities.

paradigm—a recipe or model for linking together the component strands of a theory and identifying the inherent relationships, a competitive paradigm explains the under-pinning logic of a competitive strategy or position.

parenting—the skills and capabilities used by a head office to manage and control a group of subsidiary businesses. The head office should be able to add value for the businesses, while the businesses should, in turn, be able to add value for the whole organization.

performance indicators or measures—quantifiable measures and subjective indicators of strategic and competitive success.

PEST analysis—An analysis of the *political, economic, social* and *technological* factors in the external environment of an organization, which can affect its activities and performance.

plan—a statement of intent, generally linked to a programme of tactics for strategy implementation.

planning—see *strategic planning.*

planning gap—a planning technique which enables organizations to evaluate the potential for, and risk involved in, seeking to attain particular growth targets.

policies—guidelines relating to decisions and approaches which support organizational efforts to achieve stated (intended) objectives. Can be at any level in the organization, and can range from mandatory regulations to recommended courses of action. They may or may not be written down formally.

portfolio analysis—techniques for evaluating the appropriate strategies for a range of (possibly diverse) business activities in a single organization. See *directional policy matrix.*

power—the potential or ability to do something or make something happen. Externally, it refers to the ability of an organization to influence and affect the actions of its external stakeholders. Internally, it concerns the relationships between people.

prescriptive strategies—see *intended strategies.*

private equity funds—venture capital funds whereby professional investors secure funds to invest in organizations, sometimes parachuting in a new management team when they take ownership. The funders are usually looking to sell or float the business in a relatively short timescale to recover their funds and at the same time make a healthy return.

product development—developing additional and normally related products and services to enhance the range available to existing customers and markets, and thereby increase sales and revenue.

profit—the difference between total revenues and total costs. Often profit is a fundamental objective of a manufacturing or service business.

profitability—financial ratios which look at profits generated in relation to the capital that has been employed to generate them. Two different ratios relate (a) trading profit (or profit before interest and tax) to total capital employed (known as the return on capital employed) and (b) profit after interest and tax to shareholders 'funds (known as the return on shareholders' funds).

public sector organizations—*(p 73–4)* organizations controlled directly or indirectly by government and/or dependent on government for a substantial proportion of their revenue. Includes local authorities, the National Health Service in the UK and the emergency services.

quality—strategically, quality is concerned with the ability of an organization to 'do things right – first time and every time' for each customer. This includes internal customers (other departments in an organization) as well as external customers. *Total quality management* is the spreading of quality consciousness throughout the whole organization.

reputation—the strategic standing of an organization in the eyes of its customers and suppliers.

resource-based strategy—strategy creation built around the further exploitation of core competencies and strategic capabilities.

revenue model—linked directly to the Business Model, the revenue model illustrates why and how a product, service or business is profitable.

retrenchment—strategy followed when an organization is experiencing difficulties and needs to cut costs and consolidate its resources before seeking new ways to create and add value. Sometimes involves asset reduction (perhaps the sale of a business) and job losses.

rightsizing—linked to downsizing, implies the reduction in staffing is to a level from which the organization can grow effectively. On occasions downsizing can mean that strategically important skills and competencies are lost; rightsizing implies this is not the case.

risk management—the understanding where and how things can and might go wrong, appreciating the extent of any downside if things do go wrong, and putting in place strategies to deal with the risks either before or after their occurrence.

scenarios—conceptual possibilities of future events and circumstances. Scenario planning involves using these to explore what might happen in order to help prepare managers for a wide range of eventualities and uncertainties in an unpredictable future environment.

single-loop learning—the ability to improve a competitive position on an ongoing and continuous basis, acknowledging there is always the possibility of improvement. Sometimes the competitive paradigm itself has to be changed – see *double-loop learning.*

small- and medium-sized enterprises (SMEs)—term used to embrace new and growing businesses, and those which (for any number of reasons) do not grow beyond a certain size.

social responsibility—strategies and actions that can be seen to be in the wide and best interests of society in general and the environment. Sometimes associated with the notion of mutual self-interest.

spheres of influence—building an arsenal of products and services that enable real influence across a wide range of critical interests. Routes to growth around a key *heartland*. Also related to protecting existing interests in the face of competition.

squirrel approach—to strategic management resembling a squirrel climbing a tree, cautiously moving upwards from the trunk. The squirrel has limited options and makes many small well informed decisions. This approach is viewed as less risky, as the squirrel is on familiar territory.

stakeholders—any individual or group capable of affecting (and being affected by) the actions and performance of an organization.

strategic alliance—see *alliance*.

strategic architecture—see *architecture*.

strategic awareness—appreciating the strategic position and relative success of the organization. Knowing how well it is doing, why and how – relative to its competitors – and appreciating the nature of the external environment and the extent of any need to change things.

strategic business unit—a discrete grouping within an organization with delegated responsibility for strategically managing a product, a service, or a particular group of products or services.

strategic capability—process skills used to add value and create competitive advantage.

strategic change—changes that take place over time to the strategies and objectives of the organization. Change can be gradual, emergent and evolutionary, or discontinuous, dramatic and revolutionary.

strategic control—a style of corporate control whereby the organization attempts to enjoy the benefits of delegation and decentralization with a portfolio of activities which, while diverse, is interdependent and capable of yielding synergies from cooperation.

strategic inflection points—introducing important changes at the right moment – related to both competition and customer expectations. Can act as a transformation point in the history of an industry.

strategic issues—current and forthcoming developments inside and outside the organization which will impact upon the ability of the organization to pursue its mission and achieve its objectives.

strategic leader—generic term used to describe a manager who is responsible for changes in the corporate strategy.

strategic life cycle—the notion that strategies (like products and services) have finite lives. After some period of time they will need improving, changing or replacing.

strategic management—the process by which an organization establishes its objectives, formulates actions (strategies) designed to meet these objectives in the desired timescale, implements the actions, and assesses progress and results.

strategic planning—*(p 16) in strategy creation:* the systematic and formal creation of strategies – to be found in many organizations, and capable of making a very significant contribution in large, multiactivity organizations. *In strategic control:* centralized control, most ideal where there is a limited range of core businesses.

strategic positioning—the chosen or realized relationship between the organization and its market. Clearly linked to competitive strategies and competitive advantage. The position itself is not a source of advantage, but the activities that underpin the position are.

strategic regeneration (or renewal)—major and simultaneous changes to strategies, structures and styles of management. See also *transformational change*.

strategic thinking—the ability of the organization (and its managers) to (a) synthesize the lessons from past experiences and to share the learning, (b) be aware of current positions, strengths and competencies and (c) clarify the way forward for the future.

strategy—the means by which organizations achieve (and seek to achieve) their objectives and purpose. There can be a strategy for each product and service, and for the organization as a whole.

strategy creation—umbrella term for the formulation and choice of new strategies. Encapsulates direction from the strategic leader (or an entrepreneur), strategic planning, and emergent strategy. See: *emergent strategy; entrepreneurial strategies; strategic planning*.

strategy implementation—the processes through which the organization's chosen and intended strategies are made to happen.

stretching resources—the creative use of resources to add extra value for customers – through innovation and improved productivity.

supply chain—the linkage between an organization, its suppliers, its distributors and its customers.

sustainable competitive advantage—a sustained edge over competitors in an industry, usually achieved by first creating a valuable difference and then sustaining it with improvement and change.

SWOT analysis—an analysis of an organization's *strengths* and *weaknesses* alongside the *opportunities* and *threats* present in the external environment.

synergy—term used for the added value or additional benefits which ideally accrue from the linkage or fusion of two businesses, or from increased co-operation either between different parts of the same organization or between a company and its suppliers, distributors and customers.

Internal co-operation may represent linkages between either different divisions or different functions.

tactics—specific actions that follow on from intended strategies but which can also form a foundation for emergent strategy.

tangible resources—the organization's physical resources, such as plant and equipment.

transfer price—associated with the transfer of products, components or services between businesses in the same organization. A particularly important issue where there are considerable interdependencies between businesses. The (corporately) imposed or agreed transfer price can be of markedly different attractiveness to the buying and selling businesses and can be a source of friction.

transformational change—major and simultaneous changes to strategies, structures and styles of management. See also *strategic regeneration*

turnaround strategy—an attempt to find a new competitive position for a company in difficulty.

values—the underpinning attitudes and manifest behaviours (perhaps desired as well as actual) that an organization wishes to have and to demonstrate.

value chain—framework for identifying (a) where value is added and (b) where costs are incurred. There is an internal value chain and one that embraces the complete supply chain. Internally, it embraces the key functions and activities.

vertical integration—where firms directly enter those parts of the added value chain served by their suppliers or distributors, the term used is vertical integration. To achieve the potential benefits of vertical integration (specifically synergy from co-operation) without acquiring a business which normally requires specialist and different skills, firms will look to establish strong alliances and networks.

vision—a statement or picture of the future standing of an organization. Linked to the mission or purpose, it embraces key values.

Index